A HARD DA

WEEK

RAILROVER TRAINSPOTTING

ON THE LONDON MIDLAND REGION

AUGUST 1965

GRANT DOWIE

An environmentally friendly book printed and bound in England by
www.printondemand-worldwide.com

Mixed Sources
Product group from well-managed
forests, and other controlled sources
www.fsc.org Cert no. TT-COC-002641
© 1996 Forest Stewardship Council
FSC

PEFC Certified
This product is
from sustainably
managed forests
and controlled
sources
www.pefc.org
PEFC
PEFC/16-33-415

This book is made entirely of chain-of-custody materials

Foreword

A Hard Day's Week Railrover Trainspotting on the London Midland Region was originally written completely in longhand over a few years after our original trip. Part One was completed in December 1966. Part Two was completed in September 1968. The final Part Three was completed on 1 October 1970.

I had thought about publishing shortly after the book was completed but for a variety of reasons dust gathered rather than publishing momentum. The hand written manuscripts survived some moves of houses and eventually from 2006 I began to word process the complete text. The big bonus was that the advance of the internet and other new information sources allowed me to rigorously examine and enhance the original data set of observations.

I hope that you will enjoy this rather lengthy tale and that the book represents a detailed camera shot of eight days of the decline of steam on British Rail three years before its ultimate demise in August 1968.

The author can be contacted at grant.dowie@hotmail.co.uk. All comments are very welcome.

Edinburgh

Cover Photo

The author looks out of the cab of ex G.W.R. No. 2268 (Collett 3MT 2251 Class 0-6-0 1930) on the dead line at 6C Croes Newydd (Wrexham) Motive Power Depot on Thursday 5th August 1965.

To the M.M.M.R.S.

The MUSSELBURGH MONKTONHALL MODEL RAILWAY SOCIETY

The Members:-

David Archibald
Grant Dowie
Ian Firth
Andrew Forsyth
Derek Newton
Alex Storie
Iain Storie
Denis Stott
Graham Strachan
Neil Woodcock (Honorary Member)

and
to all past members of Scottish Railfans
and
The Railway Society of Scotland

With special thanks to Reg Parsons for permission to print
certain of his photographs taken by him at Carlisle
on Saturday 31st July 1965.

Thanks also to James Crowe a former Secretary of The Railway Society of Scotland
who gave me every encouragement to publish this book

www.fast-print.net/store.php

A Hard Day's Week Railrover Trainspotting on the London
Midland Region August 1965
Copyright © Grant Dowie 2011

ISBN 978-178035-024-0

CONTENTS

Page

PROLOGUE   **6**

DAY 1 Saturday 31st July 1965   **57**
       Edinburgh Departure and a day at Carlisle

DAY 2 Sunday 1st August 1965   **103**
       Carlisle Departure and a Day in London

DAY 3 Monday 2nd August 1965   **163**
       Bletchley, Wellingborough, Leicester Colwick,
       Nottinghamshire, Derbyshire and Derby Arrival

DAY 4 Tuesday 3rd August 1965   **231**
       Derby, Barry Docks, Cardiff, Banbury and
       Leamington Spa Arrival

DAY 5 Wednesday 4th August 1965   **329**
       Leamington Spa, Birmingham, Wolverhampton,
       Crewe and Shrewsbury Arrival

DAY 6 Thursday 5th August 1965   **396**
       Shrewsbury, Wrexham, Chester, Crewe Works,
       Stoke, Nuneaton and Manchester Arrival

DAY 7 Friday 6th August 1965   **451**
       Manchester, Stockport, Warrington and
       Liverpool Arrival

DAY 8 Saturday 7th August 1965   **520**
       Liverpool, Lancashire, Skipton,
       Carlisle and Home

EPILOGUE   **624**

Prologue
and
Day 1

SATURDAY 31st JULY 1965

Edinburgh Departure
and
a day at Carlisle

PROLOGUE

<u>THE PLAN</u>

It was now August 1964. We had made a recent pilgrimage to Carlisle that month for the end of the Glasgow Trades and it was apparent that the steam engines days were strictly numbered. It was time that we organised one grand Railtour of England. Our previous sorties south had been restricted to Carlisle.

Neil Woodcock proposed a two week tour of England and Wales utilising the special two week "Freedom of Britain Railway ticket". He drafted up a draft tour timetable but I did not like the look of it on two counts. Firstly, there was the expense of a two week ticket when my budget was strictly limited being financed by a newspaper delivery round providing 15 shillings (75 new pence) per week. Secondly, Woody's timetable provided a return home every couple of days and that was an extremely wasteful use of valuable spotting time. It would be much more efficient and cheaper to purchase a London Midland Region Railrover for one week. The price would be £10 pounds and ten shillings (£10.50 new pence) - *later to be increased to an extortionate £11 pounds and ten shillings (£11.50)*. Under 14's travelled at half price and it might be difficult for me to masquerade as one. Woody was a lot smaller and a year younger than me and he should be able to travel as an under 14 for £5 and five shillings (£5.25 new pence).

Some available Railrovers and prices:-

RAILROVERS	One week	Two weeks
Freedom of Britain	£18.00	£27.00
LMR Railrover	£11.50	
Freedom of Wales	£8.25	
Northern Railrover	£11.50	
North Eastern Region	£6.30	

Ordinary singles
3.25 old pence per mile
over 200 miles rate is slightly lower
children under 14 half price

specimen fares		calculated
Edinburgh to Carlisle	£1.35	£1.37
York to Edinburgh	?	£2.78
York to London	£2.56	£2.55

I expressed my interest to Neil in an LMR only one week Railrover and told Denis Stott about it (he will now be mentioned only as D.S. and other "slanderous" names). He expressed his interest also.

"And then there were two of us"

LMR TOUR PERSONNEL

Although Neil Woodcock started off the idea in September 1964 he soon decided he would go on a Freedom of Wales during his 1965 Easter holidays instead.

For a variety of reasons only two of the M.M.M.R.S. would participate in the grand LMR tour (D.S. and I)

NEIL WOODCOCK   Started off the idea. Gave a little help in September 1964. By October had decided he would go on a Freedom of Wales during his Easter Holidays instead.

IAN FIRTH   Gained interest by the end of the year. Was helpful in writing for a few permits. Helped to show D.S. how to write letters for permits. Said we would discuss places to visit. Told us an amazing tale of his visit to Lancaster MPD when there were NO engines at all on shed. He had found out that I was thinking of including Lancaster in the tour. He said he would have a snooze in the station waiting room while D.S. and I explored the "emptiness" (as he put it) of Lancaster MPD. I thought that as it has an allocation the engines must be there sometimes. It was worth trying anyway. By March Ian had decided he would go to Butlins and asked me if I wanted to go. He did not ask D.S. of course. Ian is a sensible chap. I said that I would still rather go to the LMR. Ian's last words on the subject (trying to make me change my mind) were:-

1.   You'll get bored
2.   You won't want to write down another number after two days of it
3.   Your eyes will get funny

His remarks were neither words of wisdom or rubbish.

Time would tell!

Ian Firth would have been a good person to have on the tour. We had a terrific Manchester and Crewe trip together in December 1964 which fairly whetted my appetite for more LMR.

If Ian went on the tour it would make pre-timetabling a two man job (Ian and I).

GRAHAM STRACHAN   Interested, a little jealous but could not muster money. At first he had said he would not have been allowed to go. After restrictions had been lifted by his mother it was too late to raise the money. Tough!

DEREK NEWTON   Sceptical about the tour. Did not think it would be enjoyable. Never interested.

7

IA1N and ALEX STORIE	Gave me some helpful information about Kirkby (16E) and Annesley (16B) in Notts where they holidayed nearby.
ANDREW FORSYTH	Almost at the last minute to said he wanted to go. Said he could raise the money. Talked it over with his Dad. Broken hearted he told me that his Dad said he was too young. Too young to die I replied.
DENIS STOTT	Denis Stott "D.S." (date of birth 2nd July 1947) would be 18 at the start of the tour. He had left school at 16 and worked in his uncle's newspaper shop. He hosted the weekly Thursday night M.M.M.R.S. meetings at his parent's house where a good, decent sized model railway was located in his bedroom.
GRANT DOWIE	I (date of birth 1st June 1949) would be 16 at the start of the tour and was at Musselburgh Grammar School (along with everyone but D.S. who had left the school a few years ago). The "Grammar" was the local secondary school and sounded a lot grander than it actually was.

LMR TOUR PREPARATIONS

Sheds to be Visited

I had won the school geography prize for my year and with that had purchased Ian Allan's British Railways Pre-Grouping Atlas and Gazetteer. That valuable publication combined with Aidan L.F. Fuller's British Locomotive Shed Directory would enable me to make up an initial shed visit programme for the week. Although being good at geography with a knowledge of where most places in England were I was totally unaware of where for example 8G Sutton Oak, 10D Lostock Hall and 10F Rose Grove actually were located.

I print this initial timetable to allow readers to view how different the finished timetable (9 months later) turned out to be.

The sheds were to be visited in the order shown.

Pre-tour Saturday
Do 12A   Carlisle Kingmoor
Do 12B   Carlisle Upperby
Do 12D   Workington

Sunday alight in early morning at Crewe, Cheshire
Do 5A   Crewe North
Do 5B   Crewe South
Do   Crewe Diesel Depot
Do CW   Crewe Works

On way to Manchester
Do 8E   Northwich

Manchester and Stockport Area

Do 9E	Trafford Park
Do 9H	Patricroft
Do 9J	Agecroft
Do 9D	Newton Heath
Do 9C	Reddish
Do 9G	Gorton
Do 9A	Longsight
Do 9B	Stockport (Edgeley)
Do 9F	Heaton Mersey
Do 9L	Buxton

South and West Central Lancashire and West Yorkshire

Do 9M	Bury
Do 9K	Bolton
Do 10H	Lower Darwen
Do 10E	Accrington
Do 10F	Rose Grove (Burnley)
Do 10G	Skipton

Leeds Area

Do 55D	Royston
Do 55E	Normanton
Do 56A	Wakefield
Do 56B	Ardsley
Do 55A	Leeds Holbeck
Do 55B	Stourton
Do 55C	Farnley Junction
Do 55H	Leeds Neville Hill

North Lancashire and South Cumbria

Do 10J	Lancaster
Do 10A	Carnforth
Do 12C	Barrow
Do 10C	Fleetwood

Central Lancashire

Do 10B	Blackpool
Do 10D	Lostock Hall (Preston)
Do 8M	Southport
Do 8F	Spring's Branch (Wigan)
Do 8G	Sutton Oak (St.Helens)
Do 8B	Warrington

Liverpool Area

Do 8K	Bank Hall
Do 8L	Aintree
Do 8A	Edge Hill
Do 8J	Allerton
Do 8C	Speke Junction
Do 8H	Birkenhead

Chester and North Wales

Do 6A   Chester
Do 6B   Mold Junction
Do 6G   Llandudno Junction (time permitting)
Do 6H   Bangor(time permitting)
Do 6J   Holyhead (time permitting)

Welsh Borders

Do 6C   Croes Newydd
Do 6E   Oswestry
Do 6D   Shrewsbury

Staffordshire

Do 5C   Stafford
Do 5D   Stoke

Derbyshire

Do 16F   Burton-on-Trent
Do 16K   Etches Park
Do 16C   Derby
Do   Derby Works
Do 16A   Toton
Do 16G   Westhouses
Do 16H   Hasland

Sheffield and Doncaster Area

Do 36A   Doncaster
Do   Doncaster Works
Do 41A   Tinsley
Do 41B   Sheffield Darnall
Do 41C   Wath
Do 41D   Canklow (Rotherham)
Do 41E   Staveley (Barrow Hill)
Do 41H   Staveley G.C.

Nottinghamshire Area

Do 41J   Langwith
Do 41M   Shirebrook West
Do 16E   Kirby-In-Ashfield
Do 16B   Annesley
Do 16D   Nottingham
Do 40E   Colwick

Leicestershire Area

Do 15E   Coalville
Do 15A   Leicester (Midland)
Do 15C   Kettering
Do 15B   Wellingborough

Home Counties and Northants

Do 14C   Bedford
Do 1E   Bletchley
Do 1H   Northampton
Do 1G   Woodford Halse

Greater Birmingham Area

Do 1F	Rugby
Do 5E	Nuneaton
Do 2F	Bescot
Do 2G	Ryecroft (Walsall)
Do 2B	Oxley
Do 2K	Bushbury
Do 2A	Tyseley
Do 2E	Saltley
Do 2J	Aston
Do 2H	Monument Lane
Do 2C	Stourbridge
Do 2P	Kidderminster
Do 2L	Leamington Spa
Do 2D	Banbury (via Birmingham)

Greater London

Do 1C	Watford
Do 1A	Willesden
Do	Willesden Electric Depot
Do 81A	Old Oak Common
Do 14A	Cricklewood East
Do 14B	Cricklewood West
Do 1B	Camden
Do 1D	Marylebone
Do 34B	Hornsey
Do 34G	Finsbury Park
Do 30A	Stratford
Do 73C	Hither Green
Do 75C	Norwood Junction
Do 70A	Nine Elms
Do 75D	Stewart's Lane
Do 81C	Southall
Do 70B	Feltham

Journey Home to Carlisle

See 12E	Tebay

A trifle ambitious?
Perhaps.

References will be made to this first listing of sheds to be visited in due course.

I went round to D.S.'s "Cavern" (bedroom conference room, where the model railway was located, in his prefab house) that same night and proudly showed him it.

D.S. read the timetable out aloud,

> WITH ABOMINABLE PRONUNCIATION, HE ADMITTED THAT HE DID NOT KNOW MOST OF THE PLACES

D.S. then came out with the remarkable statement,

"WE'LL HAVE TO WATCH OURSELVES IN LONDON. LONDON'S GOT A POPULATION OF 200,000."

Ha-ha, ho-ho.

D.S. (a little hurt) asked what Graham Strachan and I were laughing at.

"My dear D.S., are you saying that London is only ten times greater than Musselburgh? Even Edinburgh has a population of almost 500,000."

I then informed D.S. that if he saved up £20 by next July he need not bother about permits, timetables and all arrangements. I told him a kind boy would see to that.

Two things had to get settled:-

1.   Timetable
2.   Permits

On 7th September 1964 the new timetables came out. I cycled the six miles up to Edinburgh Waverley Station in a thunderstorm to get the new LMR timetable and the Eastern Region timetable. I must have been keen!

I had promised D.S. that:

    (i)   we would spend 2 days in London; and
    (ii)   to end our tour at London

(a)   I was worried at first that we would need far more sheds to fill in the week. After weeks of consultation with the timetable I was trying to fit in sheds into the week. Obviously one day in London had to be enough.

(b)   Grant Dowie likes value for money so a logical start to the tour was: - TO START OUR RAILROVER AT 00.01 ON SUNDAY 1ST AUGUST 1965.

     Firstly I must tell you why the week 1st - 8th August was chosen (the 5th week of my school holidays).

     July - first 2 weeks - Edinburgh Trades Annual Two Weeks holiday
     (I would holiday with my family that first week at hopefully an English destination)

     July - second 2 weeks - Glasgow Trades Two Weeks holiday

     (BR decides to run trains at any time)

     therefore: 1st-8th August 1965 was decided on and this would tie in neatly with our annual visit to Carlisle on 31st July 1965 for the end of the Glasgow Trades.

Back to the story:-

There was a sleeper and non-sleeper for London at approximately 00.30 on Sunday 1st August. It would be useless getting off before London at some early hour because we would have to wait for daylight and Sunday train services are disgraceful outside London. Therefore it was essential that the minimum of travelling must be done on the Sunday. Answer to problem:-

LONDON
Underground, bus and suburban services first class on Sundays.

To get value for money our trip must end as near to 23.59 on Saturday 8th August 1965.

Answer:-

Luckily, the last train before midnight was a SATURDAYS ONLY train from Carnforth. Therefore: Last shed to be visited should be 10A Carnforth

We would catch the 20.55 Carnforth to Carlisle.

After a few months toil with the timetable an itinerary was worked out.

Saturday July 31st	Carlisle (all day) and Workington
Sunday August 1st	London
Monday August 2nd	Bletchley, Leicester, Nottingham, Derbyshire, Nottinghamshire, (Langwith also) and to Derby.
Tuesday August 3rd	Derby - Cardiff, Banbury, Part of Brum (i.e. Birmingham)
Wednesday August 4th	Bescot, Rugby, Nuneaton, Stoke, Crewe, Oxley, Shrewsbury, Wrexham to Chester
Thursday August 5th	Chester - Sheffield, Doncaster, Leeds (outwith Railrover last two)
Friday August 6th	Manchester - Warrington - Liverpool
Saturday August 7th	Liverpool - St Helens - Wigan - Bolton - Blackburn - Rose Grove - Skipton – Carnforth and tour end at Carlisle

A little footnote is required to Tuesday's itinerary.

Neil Woodcock after starting this Railtour project lost interest and dropped out. That Easter 1965 he went to Wales (and to Barry Docks). His description of Barry Docks aroused such envy in D.S. and me that an alteration to our timetable would be required. We would go outwith our LMR Railrover to Barry Docks. This meant less time to visit other sheds.

Some alterations to the original list of sheds to be visited:-

Manchester and Stockport Area

Delete 9G   Gorton   closed June 1965 as a result of closure of the Great Central line to freight

Delete 9L   Buxton   (too far out of the way)

South and West Central Lancashire and West Yorkshire

Delete 9M   Bury   closed to steam April 1965 now an electric "bucket" depot

Delete 10E   Accrington   (a diesel railcar (i.e. "bucket") depot of no interest to us!)

North Lancashire and South Cumbria

Delete 10J   Lancaster

Ian Firth remarked that when he went there, there were no engines. I did not believe that this was the usual case as it had a decent allocation of 19 steam locos. However, something had to be omitted from the final Saturday's timetable.

Delete 12C   Barrow

A decent allocation of 21 steam. I've seen all the diesel Co-Bo's and the train service is the slowest in Britain. Barrow is far too out of the way. Sorry D.S. Co-Bo less D.S. starts to cry.

Delete 10C   Fleetwood

I had scheduled for D.S. and I to visit 10C Fleetwood (25 steam locos) but at end June 1965 my family decided to holiday in nearby Blackpool for a week. I hauled my father off to Fleetwood, conducted him round the shed where my father and I were chased by a dock policeman. Luckily we escaped through the shed on to a passing tram. What do you think they would do to you (D.S.) at Fleetwood?

Central Lancashire

Delete 10B   Blackpool   closed October 1964

Delete 8M   Southport   a bit out of the way and only a small allocation (11 steam)

Chester and North Wales

Delete 6G   Llandudno Junction (far too out of the way)

Delete 6H   Bangor   closed June 1965

Delete 6J   Holyhead   (far too out of the way)

Welsh Borders

Delete 6E   Oswestry   closed January 1965

Staffordshire

Delete 5C   Stafford   closed July 1965

Derbyshire

Delete 16H   Hasland   closed September 1964

Delete 16K   Etches Park   (I am not a diesel shunter hunter)

Sheffield and Doncaster Area

Delete 41H   Staveley G.C.   closed June 1965 with the demise of the Great Central line to freight

Delete 41D   Canklow   closed June 1965

Leicestershire Area

Delete 15E	Coalville	(No passenger railway link. 17 steam locos only.)
Delete 15C	Kettering	closed June 1965

Home Counties and Northants

Delete 1G	Woodford Halse	closed June 1965 with the demise of the Great Central Line to freight
Delete 1H	Northampton	quite a good shed (26 steam) but too far out of the way and has a shocking train service with Rugby.

Greater Birmingham Area

Delete 2G	Ryecroft	(I am not a diesel shunter hunter)
Delete 2K	Bushbury	closed April 1965
Delete 2L	Leamington Spa	closed June 1965
Delete 2P	Kidderminster	closed August 1964
Delete 2M	Wellington	closed August 1964
Delete 2C	Stourbridge	(pretty good shed – 33 steam - but a bit out of the way and 30 minutes walking time from Stourbridge Junction)

Greater London

Delete 1C	Watford	closed March 1965
Delete 1D	Marylebone	(I am not a diesel shunter hunter)
Delete 75C	Norwood Junction	closed January 1965
Delete 75D	Stewart's Lane	I heard it is a difficult shed to get into. All electric sheds are. We will only go if we have time and that's very, very unlikely).

Timetable Additions:-

Cardiff Area

Add	Barry Docks
Add 88A	Cardiff East Dock
Add 88B	Cardiff Radyr
Add 86A	Cardiff Canton

I mentioned in my initial timetable that I did not know where 10D Lostock Hall and 10F Rose Grove were located. I consequently consulted my father's gigantic railway book which he used for his job when despatching paper from the Inveresk paper mill in Musselburgh. I noted that Lostock Hall was between Ormskirk and Liverpool and Rose Grove was between Burnley and Hapton. I also found out the information that Rose Grove had a crane that could lift 20 cwt. of paper. I asked him if that was good.

It was not until long after the LMR tour was over, at the January 1966 Higher Prelims that I learned from my marker of my composition "The Day the Signals Failed" that I had been spelling Camden wrongly i.e. Cambden.

PERMITS

Negotiations were started early.

A sample letter is shown below.

21, Stoneybank Crescent
MUSSELBURGH
Midlothian
Scotland
2/1/65

G B Gray Esq.
LMR - Divisional Manager
Alan House
5 Clumber Street
NOTTINGHAM
Nottinghamshire
England

Dear Sir,

I am writing on behalf of the MUSSELBURGH RAILWAY SOCIETY. We would like to visit several depots in your area. I am writing especially early in order to cause you the least possible inconvenience.

Our society caters only for genuine enthusiasts and we would find the visit very interesting, informative and educational. Our party will be of twelve in number and they will all be over sixteen years of age and in the charge of a responsible adult. We shall be travelling by London Midland Region Railrover. The Motive Power Depots we would wish to visit are:-

On Monday 2nd August

16D	Nottingham at 11 a.m.	
16B	Annesley at 1 p.m.	
16E	Kirkby at 2 p.m.	
16G	Westhouses at 3 p.m.	
16A	Toton at 4 p.m.	

On Tuesday 3rd August

16C	Derby at 9 a.m.	
16K	Etches Park at 10 a.m.	
16F	Burton at 12 noon	

If you could grant us the permits I would be very grateful. A stamped-addressed envelope is enclosed.

Yours faithfully

G Dowie
Secretary

The maximum number of permits allowed was three in the Manchester area and also three in the Birmingham area.

We wanted far more there so multiple applications would be necessary.

Ian Firth had been showing a great interest in our LMR tour and said he would write letters on behalf of the EAST EDINBURGH RAILWAY SOCIETY on the same lines as mine on behalf of the MUSSELBURGH RAILWAY SOCIETY.

We then told D.S. to try to write a letter on behalf of the MIDLOTHIAN RAILWAY SOCIETY. After using up a stack of paper he gave up as English had not been his best subject at school.

Losing patience with him we then decided to dictate the two necessary letters to him, spelling every word of every letter out, saying capital letter, new sentence, comma etc where appropriate.

He thus succeeded in completing his letters.

In this way we were to receive three batches of permits (as we required) for the Manchester area.

> 9A Longsight/9B Stockport Edgeley/9C Reddish
> 9E Trafford Park/9F Heaton Mersey/9H Patricroft
> 9J Agecroft/9K Bolton/9M Bury

> Missing out 9D Newton Heath was an oversight particularly as 9M Bury was to close to steam in April 1965

We were also to receive three batches for the Birmingham area

> 2A Tyseley/2B Oxley/2C Stourbridge Junction
> 2D Banbury/2E Saltley/2F Bescot
> 2J Aston/2L Leamington Spa

The first permits I received back were for the Stoke Division. I staggered into the house on New Year's Day. On seeing the letter I thought it was a summons for New Year activities. I then opened it and was pleased to see it was the first batch of permits.

> 5A Crewe North/5B Crewe South/5C Stafford/5D Stoke

> Not applying directly to Crewe Works for a permit was another oversight

From the London Division I received permits for: - 1A Willesden (1B Camden was said to be closed which I did not believe) and also for 1E Bletchley/1F Rugby/1G Woodford Halse and 14A Cricklewood East/14B Cricklewood West

The Liverpool and Chester Division and I broke off diplomatic relations after three angry letters to each other on two counts.

1.   No Saturday permits (8 area)
2.   Said my timing was too sharp for Chester area (6 area) and for some of Liverpool area to be visited on Friday.

The Preston area (10 area) officials have been called a lot of bastards by Scottish Railfans officials on numerous occasions. Permits are unknown. My correspondence was ignored of course.

I did not bother to write for permits from the Carlisle area (12 area) which I thought would be a pushover.

It needed two letters to the Leicester Division to part with permits for:

   15A Leicester Midland/15B Wellingborough/15C Kettering

The Nottingham Divisional Manager was a good kid and parted with eight (I repeat) eight permits without fuss. For some odd reason I received another batch of permits exactly the same as the first batch a few weeks later.

      Permits:- 16A Toton/16B Annesley/16C Derby/16D Nottingham/16E Kirkby-In-Ashfield/16F Burton/16G Westhouses/16K Etches Park

The Stratford area was fairly strict. After pleading in two letters for a Sunday permit I had to make do with a permit for early on Monday. The Divisional Managers motto must have been "no Sunday visits". We had no intention of visiting Stratford on the Monday but we would present the permit on the Sunday and hope for admittance.

      Permit 30A Stratford

Permits were not issued to anybody for Eastern Region diesel depots:

      34B   Hornsey
      34G   Finsbury Park

It took two letters to persuade the Doncaster Division to part with permits for:

      40E   Colwick
      36A   Doncaster
             Doncaster Works

It was stated on the permits in big sprawling letters that this permit was for the one date and the one time only I then thought that we could get into a little trouble if we arrived early or late at any of these depots.

After two letters to the Sheffield Division I was informed that no permits were issued for the diesel depots in their area.

      41A   Tinsley
      41B   Darnall
      41C   Wath

He arranged our visit to the steam depots.

      41D   Canklow
      41E   Staveley Barrow Hill
      41H   Staveley GC
      41J   Langwith

I did not bother to write for permits for North Eastern Region, /Southern Region and Western Region depots.

THE CHAUFFEUR DRIVEN E-TYPE JAGUAR AFFAIR

Dear Reader

Picture the quiet scene in Stoneybank Crescent. It is a sunny May morning. The inhabitants of the Crescent are mostly dozing around in the pleasant sunshine. Mrs Dowie is in her house having a look at the colourful picture of washing whizzing inside her Bendix washing machine.

At just after 11 o'clock a high-powered engine sound (like that of an aeroplane) rends the air. This climaxed in a sudden slamming of brakes as a sleek E-type Jaguar screeched to a halt outside 21 Stoneybank Crescent. A smartly dressed chauffeur in a blue uniform sprang out of the car marched round to the other side and standing at attention opened the door to what looked like a business tycoon or at least an executive. By this time the neighbours had fallen of their deck-chairs and were staring with dazed expressions at the scene.

Having ordered the chauffeur to remain in the car he rang the door bell of 21 Stoneybank Crescent.

The following conversation ensued in the house.

STRANGER   Good morning, madam. I am Mr Alexander, Scottish Regional Manager - Edinburgh Division - British Railways. Could I speak to Mr Dowie please?

The term British Railways left no doubt in Madam D's head whom he wished to see.

MADAME D   He's at school. I think it's my son Grant who you wish to see.
MR ALEXANDER   At s-c-h-o-o-l (somewhat surprised)

MADAME D   What do you want to see him about?

MR ALEXANDER   I have been told by one of the LMR Divisional Managers that he is going a tour of the London Midland Region by Railrover.

MADAME D   That will be with the club.

She was obviously thinking of Scottish Railfans and not about the Musselburgh Railway Society of which she knew nothing about.

MR ALEXANDER   Of course.

He was obviously referred to the phantom Musselburgh Railway Society of which I was the secretary.

MR ALEXANDER   I have got an application from here for party rate travel. The minimum is 12 people for such a reduction. There is a very reasonable reduction in the price of each Railrover ticket. Even 11 people would get a reduction.

19

MADAME D   I am sure the club will be able to take advantage of it.

A lengthy conversation ensued between the two about his work. Madame D was very flattered about him coming down to see me. Mr Alexander said it was all part of his job and that he was always trying to encourage rail travel and let people know of the advantages.

When I arrived home at dinner-time (some time after Mr Alexander had left) I was staggered firstly, shocked secondly, and after hearing Madame D's account of the conversation I was relieved that no serious damage to the Musselburgh Railway Society had been done. The visit could have gone a lot worse if Madame D had known about our Society and had told him it had only three or four members.

I assumed it was somebody that I had written to for permits had informed him of our visit. Probably one of the well-run London Divisions (Euston or Stratford).

I first tipped off D.S. about his visit and warned him that as he wrote to two divisions for permits (Birmingham and Manchester), he too might receive a visit. I briefed him on what to say and he in turned briefed his mother on what to say.

I was now a bit lost on what to do about Mr.Alexander's application form. On all my permits it said 12 people would visit each depot (the minimum they would give a permit to). He would expect a booking for around that number.

After much thought I wrote to Mr. Alexander with the following points in my letter.

1.   Thanking his for his visit.
2.   Regretting my absence.
3.   Telling him that the final number was not yet ascertained as some members had not made their minds up.
4.   Telling him that I would hand the form into the Waverley Station Booking Office when plans were finalised.

Luckily, D.S. did not get a visit which could have meant disaster. I concluded that the divisions he had written to had not tipped off Mr Alexander.

FINAL PREPARATIONS

I sent the first timetable round to D.S. but he found trouble in writing as usual and gave up trying to copy it out after reaching Bedford on the second day.

I had a serious talk with D.S. and said that he need not make a copy if he was incapable of making one. I told him that I would tell him the depots when we reached them and as long as he had a pen and paper with him he would not miss much. I asked him if he like Mystery Tours. He said he did. I joked to him that this Mystery Tour would be the longest he would ever be on. This one would last one week.

- - - - - - - - - - - - - - - - - -

When the new summer 1965 timetables came out in mid-June naturally I rushed up to Edinburgh Waverley Railway station to get them. Neil Woodcock had informed me that the new LMR timetable was a "monster". He assured me that it weighed the proverbial ton.

In fact the new timetable was 832 pages. I was pleased to find that the new timetable had (at long last) used the 24 hour clock. I thought that this was a great innovation. It was attractively styled and a lot easier to look up.

I also enquired at the station Enquiry Office of the times of trains between Cardiff and Radyr and Cardiff and Barry.

- - - - - - - - - - - - - - - - - - -

A friend of mine Ian Smith had told me that at a price he would give me a loan of his privilege ticket for the LMR tour. Unfortunately his father had recently left the railway so that was out.

- - - - - - - - - - - - - - - - - - -

D.S. and I went down to Bennet's Travel Agency a week before (on the Thursday) and booked our LMR Railrover tickets.

Shortly before our trip BR had nastily added 10% to their ticket prices. The price of the Railrover had therefore gone up from £10 and ten shillings (£10.50) to £11 and ten shillings (£11.50).

We also reserved our seats on the 00.33 Carlisle to London Euston. I persuaded D.S. that the fee of 2/- (10 new pence) each was not dear for the guarantee of a seat on a train which would probably be packed. A good rest would be a blessing after what would be a strenuous Saturday.

- - - - - - - - - - - - - - - - - - -

During the past few months before our LMR visit the Southern Region's railmens go-slow had been raging. It had looked on a few occasions that this would develop in to a national go slow. This would of course have ruined my timetable (the go-slow) and spoilt our trip. Luckily for us the Southern Region go-slow was settled between management and staff. So there would be no national go-slow! Thank goodness!

Went to see "It's A Mad, Mad, Mad, Mad World" in the cinema on the Monday before the trip. Very funny film! Somehow I felt that the title was a warning of things to come on the LMR tour.

On the Thursday afternoon 29th July 1965 we went to Bennet's Travel Agency in Musselburgh to collect our Railrover tickets and reserved seats. I immediately snatched the reserved seat which said Facing the Engine and told D.S. that he would have to take the one which said Back to the Engine. I told him that I would be looking forward. The assistant in Bennet's did not think I would see much at 00.33 in the morning. So it would not make any difference she said.

I had not thought of that!

One consolation was that it would be light at about 4.00 a.m.

Inwardly I thought that the girl assistant thought that "we were mad to spend a holiday on British Railways" (or British Rail should I say?) - "and for a whole week" - "and for £11.10/- (£11.50) each" - "not my cup of tea" I could imagine her saying to herself.

- - - - - - - - - - - - - - - - - -

It had been our first intention to stay each night in a hostel is possible and I had even told Madame D that D.S. and I were going on a hostelling holiday.

I even spent 5/- (25 new pence) in joining the Youth Hostels Association as a juvenile member. I craftily altered my birth date to make myself three months younger on the application form. If I had not I would have had to pay 10/- (50 new pence) as a junior member and have also to paste a passport picture of myself on to the card.

So it was good to be a juvenile.

At D.S.'s residence one March day previously Ian Firth (while he was still interested) and I discussed whether we would use the Youth Hostels at night.

D.S. of course sat on a large armchair not venturing to speak while Ian and I reasoned the advantages and disadvantages out.

The reasoning went something like this.

1.   FOR - The Youth Hostel provided an inexpensive and comfortable night's sleep.

2.   AGAINST - Every Youth Hosteller must be in his bed by 22.30 (10.30 p.m.). This was a bit early but as it would be dark by 21.00 (9.00 p.m.) approx. this would not be too bad but in the morning the trouble would arise.

        SILENCE MUST BE OBSERVED UNTIL 7A.M. was one rule in the handbook. It would only be a kind hearted warden who would let us out at 7.30 a.m. because one is not expected to leave until around 10 a.m. when one has finished hostel duties given out by the warden.

        In my timetable there would be no time to mess around until 10 a.m. My timetable starts at the crack of dawn - at the first train around 6 a.m. in fact.

3.   AGAINST - Youth Hostels were not situated very conveniently.

        Sunday - London Highgate YH was 30 mins. from St Pancras
        Monday - No YH within reach
        Tuesday - Leamington Spa YH (about 20 miles from Birmingham)
        Wednesday - Chester YH well situated
        Thursday - No YH within reach

22

Friday - No YH within reach
Saturday - Carlisle YH well situated

4.   Alternative - Spending the night at the last BR station reached. Ian Firth warned of railway police but we would have Railrover tickets I said. Ian admitted that that would be a favourable point. BR stations would also be suitable for early starts.

Therefore in March the YOUTH HOSTEL IDEA WAS OUT.

- - - - - - - - - - - - - - - - - -

It was now Friday 30th July 1965 the day before our trip and I had second thoughts. D.S. had taken this day off. I told him that in an emergency I would of course use the hostel but he (not being a member) could not stay there. I told him not to worry because he could sleep in the garden. I told him that after awakening from a restful comfortable night in the hostel I could smuggle out a roll at breakfast and that I would toss it out of the kitchen window to him.

At this D.S. was really hurt!

I must join the Hostels Association he roared and he hared off to the SYHA headquartered at 7 Bruntsfield Crescent, Edinburgh to join. I told him to buy the 1965 handbook of the England and Wales Youth Hostels Association.

I told D.S. that as he was old he would have to pay 10/- (50 new pence) for a junior membership. Even if he wore short trousers they would not believe he was a 5/- (25 new pence) a year juvenile. His haggard face would be a giveaway I assured him.

When he came back he had bought the YHA Handbook. But they had told him that he would require a passport type picture for his new membership card before he could join. They told him that a "Polyfoto" machine which gives three pictures for two shillings (10 new pence) available at the bigger railway and bus stations would do.

He informed me that he would get a "Polyfoto" on tour. That evening I had to talk with D.S. and his parents about the trip. They had been a bit worried because D.S. could not tell them very clearly where we were going. He knew that we started at Carlisle and ended at Carlisle and thought we were in London on the second day but that was about it. I reassured them and put them in the picture.

I returned home and finished off the timetable which I had copied out into a lab book which was secured from Bud Wright, Room 15, Head Geography Teacher, Musselburgh Grammar School. Little did I know that I would use it for my LMR timetable and not for geography notes. I think he suspected some skulduggery because he used to ask us if we put our fish and chips (as he put it) in our new lab books (so often did we ask for them).

Anyway it was put to good purpose and the timetable was finished around 9.00 p.m. on Friday night.

I now reproduce in full my timetable for the week. At the time I thought it was a good timetable. The week would prove how good it was. One particular aim was very much to target the steam engine which was now very much being rundown as dieselisation continued its relentless spread. This is how steam looked at end April/early May 1965.

THE FINAL TIMETABLE

DAY 1   **SATURDAY 31ST JULY 1965**

		MILES
Depart EDINBURGH PRINCES STREET	08.30	0
Arrive CARSTAIRS	09.07	27

Journey - see **64C Dalry Road**

Do 66E Carstairs

Depart CARSTAIRS	09.17	27½
Arrive CARLISLE	10.31	102½

Journey - **see 66F Beattock** (north west of station)   62¾

Do 12B Carlisle Upperby

retire to Locospotter's Haven - Upperby Bridge for return of Glasgow Trades Specials

Depart CARLISLE	16.35	0
Arrive WORKINGTON MAIN	17.25	33¼

Do 12D Workington

Depart WORKINGTON MAIN	18.35	0
Arrive CARLISLE	19.30	33¼

Do 12A Carlisle Kingmoor

retire to Carlisle Station

DAY 2   **SUNDAY AUGUST 1ST 1965**   **LMR DAY 1**

		MILES
Depart CARLISLE	00.33	0
Arrive CREWE	-	141
Depart CREWE	03.45	141
Arrive RUGBY MIDLAND	04.52	216½
Depart RUGBY MIDLAND	05.00	216½
Arrive WATFORD JUNCTION	06.23	281½

Journey:-

see 12A	**Tebay** (south west of station)		37
see 8F	**Wigan** (1 mile south east of station)		105¼
see 8B	**Warrington** (1 mile north west of station)		117
see 5A	**Crewe North** (north west of station)		141
see 5B	**Crewe South** (south west of station)		141
see 5C	**Stafford** (north west of station)		165½
see 5E	**Nuneaton** (south west of station)		202
see 1F	**Rugby Midland** (east of station)		216½
see 1E	**Bletchley** (north west of station)		252¼

Do 1C Watford (20 mins. approx)

Depart WATFORD JUNCTION	06.40 07.10 07.35 07.53 08.08	0
Arrive WILLESDEN JUNCTION	07.10 07.40 08.05 08.23 08.38	<u>11</u>

Do 81A Old Oak Common (60 mins.)

Do 1A Willesden (40 mins. approx)

Do Willesden Electric Depot (25 mins. approx)

Depart WILLESDEN JUNCTION	Frequent service	0
Arrive QUEENS PARK	(10 mins.)	1¾

TUBE -   UNDERGROUND   -   Bakerloo Lane

Depart QUEENS PARK
Arrive PADDINGTON

Do Paddington Station

TUBE   -   Metropolitan or Circle Line Train

Depart PADDINGTON
Arrive KING'S CROSS/ST PANCRAS

TUBE   -   Northern Line (Edgware Bound)

Depart KING'S CROSS/ST PANCRAS
Arrive CHALK FARM

Do 1B Camden

Depart CHALK FARM
Arrive KING'S CROSS/ST PANCRAS

TUBE   -   Piccadilly Line

Depart KING'S CROSS/ST PANCRAS
Arrive TURNPIKE LANE

<u>Do 34B Hornsey (ex-34B)</u>

Depart TURNPIKE LANE
Arrive FINSBURY PARK

<u>Do 34G Finsbury Park</u>

Depart FINSBURY PARK
Arrive KING'S CROSS/ST PANCRAS

<u>Do King's Cross Station</u>

<u>Do St Pancras Station</u>

<u>BRITISH RAIL</u>		<u>MILES</u>
Depart ST PANCRAS	.00 on the hour	0
Arrive CRICKLEWOOD	.12 past the hour	<u>5¼</u>

<u>Do 14A Cricklewood East</u>
<u>Do 14B Cricklewood West</u>

Depart CRICKLEWOOD	.04 past the hour	0
Arrive ST PANCRAS	.18 past the hour	<u>5¼</u>

<u>Do Cambridge Street Diesel Depot</u>

TUBE   -   Piccadilly Line

Depart KING'S CROSS/ST PANCRAS
Arrive HOLBORN

TUBE   -   Central Line

Depart HOLBORN
Arrive STRATFORD

<u>Do 30A Stratford</u>

TUBE   -   Central Line

Depart STRATFORD
Arrive TOTTENHAM COURT ROAD

TUBE   -   Northern Line

Depart TOTTENHAM COURT ROAD
Arrive STRAND

British Rail - Southern Region
Depart CHARING CROSS
Arrive HITHER GREEN

Do 73C Hither Green

Depart HITHER GREEN
Arrive WATERLOO

Do Waterloo Station

Depart WATERLOO
Arrive VAUXHALL STATION

Do 70A Nine Elms (walk)

British Rail - Southern Region

Depart VAUXHALL	29 and 59 minutes past the hour
Arrive HOUNSLOW	57 and 27 minutes past the hour
-	LT Bus No 110 or LTB Bus 111

Do 70B Feltham

BUS   -   LT Bus No 111

Depart POWDER MILL LANE
Arrive GREAT WEST ROAD

BUS   -   LT Bus No 120

Depart GREAT WEST ROAD
Arrive SOUTHALL STATION

Do 81C Southall

British Rail - Western Region

			Miles
Depart	SOUTHALL	21.34	0
Arrive	PADDINGTON	21.53	9

Do Paddington Station

TUBE   -   Metropolitan or Circle Line Train

Depart PADDINGTON
Arrive KING'S CROSS/ST PANCRAS

Do King's Cross Station

<u>Do St Pancras Station</u>

TUBE   -   Northern Line

Depart KING'S CROSS/ST PANCRAS
Arrive EUSTON

<u>Do Euston Station</u>

Night: -   Euston Waiting Room

<u>Comments:-</u>

This was (after doing Willesden) a do as much as possible timetable.
These sheds would be left out in an emergency:

1C   Watford (near closure)
1B   Camden (Divisional Manager informed me it was closed. I did not entirely believe him)
Cambridge Street Diesel depot
73C   Hither Green

DAY 3   **MONDAY AUGUST 2ND 1965**   LMR DAY 2

<u>MILES</u>

Depart EUSTON	05.10		0
Arrive WATFORD JUNCTION	05.53		17½

Journey:
     see 1B Camden - 1½ miles north west of Euston
     see 1A Willesden - north west
     see 1C Watford - east

Depart WATFORD JUNCTION	06.05		17½
Arrive BLETCHLEY	06.58		<u>46¾</u>

<u>Do 1E Bletchley (20 mins. approx)</u>   Recovery time
                                                           - 4

Journey:
     see 1E sub-shed Leighton Buzzard - south east   40¼

Depart BLETCHLEY	07.14	(08.08)	0
Arrive BEDFORD ST JOHN'S	07.44	(08.45)	<u>16</u>
		alternative	

<u>Do 14C Bedford (20 mins. approx)</u>

Depart BEDFORD MIDLAND ROAD	08.23	(09.15)	0
Arrive WELLINGBOROUGH MIDLAND ROAD	08.42	(09.33)	15¼

<u>Do 15B Wellingborough (35 mins. approx)</u>

Recovery time + 18

Depart WELLINGBOROUGH MIDLAND ROAD	09.35	15¼
Arrive LEICESTER LONDON ROAD	10.19	<u>49¼</u>

Journey:
  see 15C (ex) Kettering - north east   22¼
  see 15A sub Market Harborough   33¼

<u>Do 15A Leicester Midland (60 mins. approx)</u>

Recovery time - 20 or + 43

A

Depart LEICESTER CENTRAL	10.59	0
Arrive NOTTINGHAM VICTORIA	11.35	<u>23½</u>

<u>Do 16D Nottingham (50 mins. approx)</u>

Recovery time +28

If connection from Leicester Central to Nottingham Victoria is missed then:

B

Depart LEICESTER LONDON ROAD	11.52	0
Arrive TRENT	12.16	<u>20¾</u>

Change at Trent

Journey:
  see Brush Works, Loughborough   12½

Depart TRENT	12.23	0
Arrive NOTTINGHAM MIDLAND	12.37	<u>6¾</u>

Both timetables coincide now with:-

Depart Nottingham London Road High Level	12.53	0
Arrive NETHERFIELD & COLWICK	12.58	<u>2¾</u>

<u>Do 40E Colwick (40 mins. approx)</u>

Recovery time NIL

Depart NETHERFIELD & COLWICK	13.38	0
Arrive Nottingham London Road High Level	13.44	<u>2¾</u>
Depart NOTTINGHAM MIDLAND	13.53	0
Arrive ALFRETON AND SOUTH NORMANTON	14.24	<u>23</u>

<u>Do 16G Westhouses and Blackwell</u> (47 mins. approx) Recovery time
NIL

1¼ miles run there and back and time to do shed

Journey:
      see 16A Toton - west
      see 16D Nottingham - south west

Depart ALFRETON AND SOUTH NORMANTON	15.11	0
Arrive STAPLEFORD AND SANDIACRE	15.33	<u>13½</u>

<u>Do 16A Toton (60 mins. approx)</u>   Recovery time
+ 69

Depart STAPLEFORD AND SANDIACRE	17.42	0
Arrive KIRKBY-IN-ASHFIELD EAST	18.25	<u>16½</u>

<u>Do 16E Kirkby</u>

Trent Bus No 61 (Nottingham)

Depart KIRKBY NAG'S HEAD PUBLIC HOUSE
Arrive NEWSTEAD VILLAGE

<u>Do 16B Annesley</u>

Trent Bus No 61 (Mansfield)

Depart NEWSTEAD VILLAGE
Arrive MANSFIELD NOTTINGHAM ROAD

Mansfield District Bus No 1 or No 7 (Langwith)

Depart MANSFIELD WEST GATE
Arrive ELAND ROAD

<u>Do 41J Langwith</u>

WALK-   Route from Shirebrook to Langwith

Turn left outside the station and continue for about 150 yards. Turn right along the Langwith Road and continue for almost ½ mile. Turn right into Eland Road and the shed entrance is at the end of the short cul-de-sac (20 mins. approx).

<u>Do 41M Shirebrook West</u>

East Midland Bus No 72 or No 73

Depart SHIREBROOK WEST
Arrive MANSFIELD BATH STREET

Trent Bus No. 61 or No 62

Depart MANSFIELD NOTTINGHAM ROAD
Arrive NOTTINGHAM HUNTINGDON STREET

<u>British Rail</u>   <u>MILES</u>

Depart NOTTINGHAM MIDLAND	21.30 or 22.20 or 22.55	0
Arrive DERBY MIDLAND	22.05 or 22.51 or 23.25	<u>16</u>

Night: -   Derby Waiting Room

- - - - - - - - - - - - - - - - - -

<u>Comments</u>:-

First I had better put you in the picture on a few timetable points. In some instances there is a time after the shed.

       e.g.   40E Colwick (40 mins. approx)

This time is the one which I take to be ample to walk to the shed, visit the shed and walk back to the station. The walking time is ascertained from Aidan Fuller's celebrated "The British Locomotive Shed Directory". The visit time I allow in addition to the walking time to and from the shed is from 10-30 minutes depending on locomotive allocations.

The actual visiting time is the time from the arrival at the station to the departure from the station after visiting the shed. The time of walking to and from and visiting the shed (mentioned in the previous paragraph) is then subtracted from the actual visiting time and the recovery time is found.

e.g.:-

Arrive Leicester London Road	10.19	Netherfield/Colwick	12.58	Stapleford/Sandiacre	15.33
Depart Leicester Central	10.59	Netherfield/Colwick	13.38	Stapleford/Sandiacre	17.42
Actual Visiting Time	40min		40min		2hr 9min
Required Walking and Visiting Time	50+10min		40min		60 mins.

Subtract:

From this it will be seen that the recovery times with a minus number are timed a bit tightly for comfort.

Back to Monday's timetable the Leicester Recovery Time of -20 is very, very tight.

As you will notice the Westhouses and Blackwell actual visiting time is 47 minutes. Into 47 minutes would be crammed a 2½ mile run (the total mileage to and from the shed) and the visiting time required. I had told D.S. about this paced out 1¼ miles up the Mucklets Road and made him run up and down it until he could do the 2½ miles in 20 minutes. He lost 3lb. in the process.

DAY 4	**TUESDAY AUGUST 3RD 1965**	**LMR DAY 3**

Reveille 05.00

Do 16C Derby
Do Derby Works (we hope)

MILES

Depart DERBY MIDLAND	06.10	0
Arrive BURTON-ON-TRENT	06.24	11

Do 16F Burton (50 mins. approx)

Recovery time + 13

Depart BURTON-ON-TRENT	07.27	0
Arrive BIRMINGHAM NEW ST.	08.08	41
Depart BIRMINGHAM NEW ST.	08.15	41
Arrive CHELTENHAM SPA MALVERN ROAD	09.05	
Depart CHELTENHAM SPA MALVERN ROAD	-	
Arrive GLOUCESTER CENTRAL	09.18	
Depart GLOUCESTER CENTRAL	-	
Arrive CARDIFF GENERAL	10.20	

Miniature Buffet Car

Journey:-

> **see 1E Saltley - south east**
> **see 85B sub Cheltenham - west**
> **see 85B Gloucester - north**
> **see 86E Severn Tunnel Junction - east**
> **see 86B Newport Ebbw Junction - 1 mile north west**
> **see 86B sub Newport Godfrey Road - north west**

					Miles
Depart	CARDIFF GENERAL	10.38	11.04		0
Arrive	BARRY	11.07	11.25		11
	Do Barry Docks				

Journey:-

       see 86A Cardiff Canton - south west

The ex 88C Barry shed is on the south of the line, east of Barry Station.

Turn right outside Barry Station into Broad Street; turn first right into and under the railway bridge. A cinder path leads from the right hand side of this road to the shed (5 minutes).

Do ex 88C Barry

Depart	BARRY	12.03	12.33	13.03	0
Arrive	CARDIFF GENERAL	12.29	12.59	13.29	11

WALK-   **Do 86A Cardiff Canton (40 mins.)**

Cardiff Corporation Bus No 16 (Pier Head)
Depart ST MARY' S STREET
Arrive DOCK ENTRANCE

Do 88A Cardiff East Dock

Depart DOCK ENTRANCE
Arrive ST MARY'S STREET

			Miles
Depart	CARDIFF GENERAL	13.01	0
Arrive	RADYR	13.16	4¾
	Do 88B Cardiff Radyr		
Depart	RADYR	13.53	0
Arrive	CARDIFF GENERAL	14.05	4¾

Do 88B Cardiff Radyr (closed)

Depart CARDIFF GENERAL   14.20
Arrive BIRMINGHAM NEW STREET   16.30

see same sheds as southbound journey

Miniature Buffet Car

Depart BIRMINGHAM NEW STREET	16.42	0
Arrive VAUXHALL AND DUDDESTON	16.46	1¼

          (Lichfield Train)

Do 2E Saltley (45 mins. approx)   Recovery Time
                                                    - 5

Depart VAUXHALL AND DUDDESTON	17.26	1¼
Arrive ASTON	17.29	2½

Do 2J Aston (30 mins. approx)

Recovery Time
+ 7

Depart ASTON	18.06	0
Arrive BIRMINGHAM NEW STREET	18.17	2½
Depart BIRMINGHAM NEW MOOR STREET	18.40	0
Arrive TYSELEY	18.46	3¼

Do 2A Tyseley (30 mins. approx)

Recovery Time
+ 26

Depart TYSELEY	19.42	0
Arrive BIRMINGHAM SNOW HILL	19.47	3¼
Depart BIRMINGHAM SNOW HILL	20.00	0
Arrive LEAMINGTON SPA GENERAL	20.21	23¼
Depart LEAMINGTON SPA GENERAL	20.28	23¼
Arrive BANBURY	20.48	43

Journey:-

     see ex 2L Leamington Spa - south east

Do 2D Banbury (35 mins. approx)

Recovery Time
+ 3

Depart BANBURY	21.26	0
Arrive LEAMINGTON SPA GENERAL	21.45	19¾
Depart LEAMINGTON SPA GENERAL	21.49	19¾
Arrive BIRMINGHAM SNOW HILL	22.17	43

Buffet Car

Do Birmingham Snow Hill Station

WALK-   Snow Hill to New Street

Do Birmingham New Street Station

Night: -   Birmingham New Street Waiting Room

Comments

In the timetable I write Miniature Buffet Car/Buffet Car etc. whenever there is a chance of something to eat on the train. Remember that during the hours of daylight there is never much chance to get something to eat. Railway station catering rooms and buffet cars on train would be our best eating places to save time.

D.S. did not like this idea much as he wanted an hour off at midday. I put it to him MORE TIME, MORE SHEDS, BETTER VALUE FOR MONEY.

WEDNESDAY AUGUST 4TH 1965

<u>MILES</u>

Depart BIRMINGHAM NEW STREET	06.06	0
Arrive BESCOT	06.29	<u>9¼</u>

<u>Do 2F Bescot (25 mins. approx)</u> Recovery Time
+ 3

Depart BESCOT	06.57	0
Arrive BIRMINGHAM NEW STREET	07.24	<u>9¼</u>

Depart BIRMINGHAM NEW STREET	07.30	0
Arrive RUGBY MIDLAND	08.23	<u>30¼</u>

<u>Do 1F Rugby (30 mins. approx)</u> Recovery Time
+ 30

Depart RUGBY MIDLAND	09.23	0
Arrive NUNEATON TRENT VALLEY	09.40	14½

<u>Do 5E Nuneaton (35 mins. approx)</u> Recovery Time
+ 30

Depart NUNEATON TRENT VALLEY	10.45	14½
Arrive STAFFORD	11.18	<u>51</u>

<u>See 5C Stafford - North West</u>

Depart STAFFORD	11.25	0
Arrive STOKE-ON-TRENT	11.47	<u>16¼</u>

<u>Do 5D Stoke (50 mins. approx)</u>
<u>Do Cockshute Diesel Depot (40 mins. approx)</u> Recovery Time
- 2

Depart STOKE-ON-TRENT	13.15	0
Arrive CREWE	13.41	<u>14¾</u>

See ex 5E Alsager - South East 8½

<u>Do Crewe Station</u>
<u>Do ex 5A Crewe North</u>
<u>Do 5B Crewe South</u>
<u>Do 5A Crewe Diesel Depot</u>

Depart CREWE	15.17	0
Arrive WOLVERHAMPTON HIGH LEVEL	16.08	<u>39¾</u>

Journey:-
  see 5C Stafford - north west 24½
  see ex 2K Bushbury - 1½ miles north east 38½

<u>**Do 2B Oxley (80 mins. approx)**</u>   Recovery Time
+ 3

Depart WOLVERHAMPTON HIGH LEVEL	17.14	0
Arrive SHREWSBURY	18.23	<u>29¾</u>

<u>**Do 6D Shrewsbury (65 mins. approx)**</u>   Recovery Time
+ 12

Buffet Car

Depart SHREWSBURY	19.40	29¾
Arrive WREXHAM GENERAL	20.27	60

<u>**Do 6C Croes Newydd (45 mins. approx)**</u>   Recovery Time
+ 73

Buffet Car

Depart WREXHAM GENERAL	22.25	60
Arrive CHESTER GENERAL	22.52	<u>72¼</u>

Restaurant Car

Night: -   Chester Waiting Room

<u>Comments</u>:-

Only 1hr 36 minutes at Crewe. Therefore Electric Depot and Crewe Works are out. Anyway they would be hard to get round.

DAY 6   <u>**THURSDAY AUGUST 5TH 1965**</u>   **LMR DAY 5**

Reveille: - Dawn

<u>**Do 6A Chester Midland**</u>
<u>**Do 6B Mold Junction**</u>

<u>MILES</u>

Depart CHESTER NORTHGATE	06.35 or 07.21 or 07.40 or 08.25 or 08.50	0
Arrive NORTHWICH	07.06 or 07.52 or 08.11 or 08.56 or 09.22	18

<u>**Do 8E Northwich (20 mins. approx**</u>

Depart NORTHWICH   07.20 or 07.52 or 08.11 or 08.18 or 09.01 or 09.22 or 10.03   18
Arrive MANCHESTER CENTRAL 08.04 or 08.40 or 08.53 or 09.05 or 09.44 or 10.07 or 10.49   <u>38¾</u>

Depart MANCHESTER PICCADILLY   08.30 or 09.10 or 11.10 or 12.10   0
Arrive SHEFFIELD VICTORIA   09.26 or 10.10 or 12.05 or 13.04   <u>41½</u>

FROM THIS POINT ALL TRAVEL IS OUTWITH LMR RAILROVER

BUS   -   Sheffield Joint Committee No 87 (Maltby)

Depart SHEFFIELD POND STREET BUS STATION
Arrive BRINSWORTH THREE MAGPIES

<u>Do 41A Tinsley</u>

BUS (same)

Depart STAVELEY BARROW HILL
Arrive SHEFFIELD POND STREET

BUS   -   Sheffield Corporation No 71 or No 52

Depart WICKER
Arrive RIBSTON ROAD

<u>Do 41B Darnall</u>

BUS (same)

Depart RIBSTON ROAD
Arrive COMMERCIAL STREET or FITZALAN SQUARE

<u>British Rail</u>

Depending on time spent in Sheffield area Timetable A or Timetable B.

Timetable A

Depart SHEFFIELD MIDLAND   12.36
Arrive DONCASTER   13.20

<u>Do 36A Doncaster</u>
<u>Do Doncaster Works</u>

Timetable B

Depart SHEFFIELD VICTORIA	14.26
Arrive DONCASTER	15.08

Do 36A Doncaster only

Timetables A and B

Depart DONCASTER	16.00
Arrive WAKEFIELD WESTGATE	16.25

Do 56A Wakefield (80 mins. approx)

Bus or British Rail (hourly service)
Depart WAKEFIELD KIRKGATE
Arrive NORMANTON

Do 55E Normanton

Bus or British Rail (infrequent)
Depart NORMANTON
Arrive ROYSTON & NOTTON

Do 55D Royston

Bus or British Rail (infrequent)
Depart ROYSTON & NOTTON
Arrive LEEDS CITY

In Leeds to visit these sheds in this order (time permitting):

Do 55A	**Holbeck (1)**
Do 55B	**Stourton (4)**
Do 55C	**Farnley Junction (2)**
Do 55H	**Neville Hill (3)**

There is a third alternative C if at Doncaster we would rather save money and not visit the North Eastern Region (outwith our Railrover).

Timetable C

Depart DONCASTER	16.02
Arrive KILNHURST WEST	16.24
Depart KILNHURST WEST	16.51
Arrive WATH NORTH	17.02

Do 41C Wath (25 mins. approx)

Recovery Time
NIL

Depart WATH NORTH	17.27

Arrive SHEFFIELD MIDLAND   17.59

2 hours at leisure (trainspotting probably) in Sheffield

		MILES
Depart SHEFFIELD VICTORIA	19.45	0
Arrive MANCHESTER PICCADILLY	20.45	41½

Night: -   Manchester Victoria or Exchange Waiting Room

Depart LEEDS CITY	22.42
Arrive MANCHESTER EXCHANGE	00.26

Night: -   Manchester Exchange or Victoria Waiting Room

Comments:-

Many comments are needed her. Manchester Central must be reached before 09.10 as if the 09.10 from Piccadilly is missed then there is a gap until 11.10 before the next train.

In Sheffield Area:-

41D Canklow (closed)
41H Staveley (closed)

The order of visiting the Leeds sheds is important because (1) Holbeck has Jubilees and other good LMR locos. (2) Farnley Junction has Jubilees (3) Neville Hill had Q6 locos (4) Stourton (although having a sizable allocation) had only unspectacular LMR locos. As we would be pushed for time I wanted the best sheds first in case we are unable to visit one or more.

All bus services are indicated in the "British Locomotive Shed Directory".

DAY 7   **FRIDAY AUGUST 6TH 1965**   LMR DAY 6

Timetable D

		MILES
Depart MANCHESTER VICTORIA	05.50	0
Arrive DEAN LANE	05.57	2¾

Do 9D Newton Heath (35 mins. approx)   Recovery Time + 9

Depart DEAN LANE	06.41	0
Arrive MANCHESTER VICTORIA	06.48	2¾

Depart MANCHESTER EXCHANGE	07.10	0
Arrive PATRICROFT	07.21	4¾

Do 9H Patricroft

Salford Corporation Bus No 27

Depart PATRICROFT MONTON ROAD
Arrive AGECROFT BANK LANE

Do 9J Agecroft

Salford Corporate Bus No 57 or 77

Depart BANK LANE
Arrive PICCADILLY

Depart PICCADILLY   )   Manchester Corporation
Arrive KIRKMANSHULME LANE   )   92-93-94-95

Do 9A Longsight

Depart CROMWELL STREET
Arrive REDDISH NORTH STATION

Do 9C Reddish

Depart REDDISH NORTH	(10.42) 11.12	(11.42)		0
Arrive MANCHESTER PICCADILLY	(10.54) 11.23	(11.54)		4
Depart MANCHESTER PICCADILLY	(10.57) 11.27	(11.57)		0
Arrive MANCHESTER OXFORD ROAD	(10.59) 11.29	(11.59)		½
Depart MANCHESTER OXFORD ROAD	(11.10) 11.30	(12.10)		0
Arrive WARWICK ROAD	(11.15) 11.35	(12.15)		2½

Do 9E Trafford Park (45 mins. approx)   Recovery Time -7

Depart WARWICK ROAD	(11.35) 12.13	(12.53)	0
Arrive MANCHESTER OXFORD ROAD	(12.00) 12.20	(13.00)	2½
Depart MANCHESTER OXFORD ROAD	(12.05) 12.35	(13.05)	0
Arrive STOCKPORT EDGELEY	(12.19) 12.49	(13.19)	6¼

Do 9F Heaton Mersey (75 mins. approx)
Do 9B Stockport Edgeley (35 mins. approx)

Depart STOCKPORT EDGELEY	14.00	14.16	14.30	14.46	15.00	15.16	0
Arrive MANCHESTER PICCADILLY	14.08	14.27	14.39	14.57	15.08	15.27	5¾

Depart MANCHESTER CENTRAL	(14.30)	15.30	(15.33)	0
Arrive WARRINGTON CENTRAL	(14.49)	15.49	(16.13)	15¼

Do 8B Warrington (60 mins. approx)

Recovery Times	+ 8	+ 8	+ 3

Depart WARRINGTON CENTRAL	(15.57)	16.57	(17.16)	15¼
Arrive GARSTON	(16.22)	17.22	(17.44)	28

Do 8C Speke Junction (40 mins. approx)
Do 8J Allerton (35 mins. approx)

Recovery Times	- 7		- 7 or + 12	- 12		
Depart ALLERTON	17.19	17.31	17.56	18.14	19.04	0
Arrive EDGE HILL	17.31	17.46	18.07	18.25	19.15	4½

Do 8A Edge Hill (40 mins. approx)

Liverpool Corporation Bus No 4/4B/79C/79D

Depart EDGE HILL TIVERTON STREET
Arrive CITY CENTRE

Depart LIVERPOOL CENTRAL or	05.	15.	25.	35.	45.	55.	0
JAMES STREET	06.	16.	26.	36.	46.	56.	½
Arrive BIRKENHEAD CENTRAL	12.	22.	32.	42.	52.	02.	2¼

Do 8H Birkenhead (40 mins. approx)

Depart BIRKENHEAD CENTRAL	40.	50.	00.	10.	20.	30.	0
Arrive JAMES STREET	45.	55.	05.	15.	25.	35.	1¾

Night: -   Liverpool Station Waiting Room

- - - - - - - - - - - - - - - - - -

Comments:-

Alternative times in brackets. Railway recovery times ideal and lenient even the minus recovery times should not pose must problem. Bus service timings open to question. Left considerable time for bus connections. Can only hope.

Birkenhead electric trains are of a good frequency so minutes past hour are just shown.

<u>MILES</u>

Depart LIVERPOOL EXCHANGE	05.30	0
Arrive AINTREE SEFTON ARMS	05.41	<u>4¾</u>

<u>**Do 8L Aintree (45 mins. approx)**</u>   Recovery Time - 10

Depart AINTREE SEFTON ARMS	06.16	0
Arrive SANDHILLS	06.26	<u>3¼</u>
Depart SANDHILLS	06.32	0
Arrive BANK HALL	06.34	<u>½</u>

<u>**Do 8K Bank Hall (17 mins. approx)**</u>   Recovery Time + 1

Depart BANK HALL	06.52	0
Arrive LIVERPOOL EXCHANGE	07.00	<u>2</u>
Depart LIVERPOOL LIME STREET	07.28	0
Arrive ST HELEN'S SHAW STREET	07.45	10¼

<u>**Do 8G Sutton Oak (60 mins. approx)**</u>   Recovery Time - 3

Depart ST HELEN'S SHAW STREET	08.51	10¼
Arrive WIGAN NORTH WESTERN	09.11	<u>19</u>

<u>**Do 8F Spring's Branch (80 mins. approx)**</u>   Recovery Time - 23

Depart WIGAN WALLGATE	10.08	0
Arrive BOLTON	10.24	<u>9½</u>

<u>**Do 9K Bolton (45 mins. approx)**</u>   Recovery Time - 5

Depart BOLTON	11.04	0
Arrive PRESTON	11.35	<u>20</u>
Depart PRESTON	11.52	0
Arrive LOSTOCK HALL	11.59	<u>3</u>

<u>**Do 10C Lostock Hall (22 mins. approx)**</u>

BUS   -   Local service

Depart LOSTOCK HALL
Arrive PRESTON STATION

Depart PRESTON	13.34	
Arrive BLACKBURN	14.03	

Do 10H Lower Darwen (60 mins. approx)   Recovery Time + 25

Depart BLACKBURN	15.28	0
Arrive ROSE GROVE	15.53	9¾

Do 10F Rose Grove (40 mins. approx)   Recovery Time + 31

Depart ROSE GROVE	17.04	0
Arrive SKIPTON	17.37	18¼

Do 10G Skipton (45 mins. approx)   Recovery Time + 21

Depart SKIPTON	18.43	0
Arrive WENNINGTON	19.48	28¼

see Hellifield - North West (19.06)

Depart WELLINGTON	19.59	0
Arrive CARNFORTH	20.18	9¼

Do 10A Carnforth (30 mins. approx)   Recovery Time + 7

Depart CARNFORTH	20.55	0
Arrive CARLISLE	22.44	62¾

See 12A Tebay (21.45) - West

END OF LMR RAILROVER

Comments:-

Two stiff recovery times:-

1.	8F Wigan (Spring's Branch)	-23
	Remedy - get bus	

2.	8L Aintree	-10
	Remedy - hurry	

Also   8G Sutton Oak (-3) - Get bus
           9K Bolton (-5) - No dilly dallying

Note: -   The 20.55 from Carnforth is the last train to reach Carlisle before midnight. Therefore it is a must that we will be on it.

This timetable will operate if we spend too long in Leeds.

DAY 7	**FRIDAY AUGUST 6TH 1965**	LMR DAY 6

		MILES
Depart LEEDS CITY	06.20	0
Arrive MANCHESTER EXCHANGE	08.01	26
See 55G Huddersfield - North West	(06.59)	
Depart MANCHESTER EXCHANGE	08.15	0
Arrive PATRICROFT	08.26	4¾

Do 9H Patricroft (25 mins. approx)   Recovery Time - 1

Depart PATRICROFT	08.50	0
Arrive MANCHESTER EXCHANGE	09.03	4¾
Depart MANCHESTER VICTORIA	09.12	0
Arrive NEWTON HEATH	09.19	2¾

Do 9D Newton Heath (35 mins. approx)   Recovery Time + 21

Depart DEAN LANE	09.15	0
Depart MANCHESTER VICTORIA	09.22	2¾

BUS	Depart	City Centre	)	Salford Corporation
	Arrive	Agecroft Bank Lane	)	50-28-57-77

Do 9J Agecroft

BUS	Depart	Agecroft Bank Lane	)	Salford Corporation
	Arrive	City Centre	)	50-28-57-77

Depart REDDISH NORTH STATION	12.42	(13.12)	0
Arrive MANCHESTER PICCADILLY	12.54	(13.24)	4
Depart MANCHESTER PICCADILLY	12.57	(13.27)	0
Arrive MANCHESTER OXFORD ROAD	12.59	(13.29)	½
Depart MANCHESTER OXFORD ROAD	13.10	(13.30)	0
Arrive WARWICK ROAD	13.15	(13.35)	2½

Do 9E Trafford Park (45 mins. approx)   Recovery Time - 7

Depart WARWICK ROAD	13.53	(14.13)	0
Arrive MANCHESTER OXFORD ROAD	14.00	(14.20)	2½

Depart MANCHESTER OXFORD ROAD	14.05		(14.35)				0
Arrive STOCKPORT EDGELEY	14.19		(14.49)				6¼

Do 9B Stockport Edgeley (74 mins. approx)
Do 9F Heaton Mersey (35 mins. approx)

Depart STOCKPORT EDGELEY	16.10	16.16	.19	.30	.40	.46	0
Arrive MANCHESTER PICCADILLY	16.16	16.22	.27	.39	.48	.57	5¾

Depart MANCHESTER CENTRAL	16.30	17.00	(17.30)	0
Arrive WARRINGTON CENTRAL	16.49	17.34	(17.51)	15¼

Do 8B Warrington (60 mins. approx)   Recovery Time + 4

If arrive at WARRINGTON 16.49 then **Timetable E** continues

Depart WARRINGTON GENERAL	17.53	0
Arrive GARSTON	18.14	12¾

Do 8C Speke Junction (40 mins. approx)
Do 8J Allerton (35 mins. approx)

Depart ALLERTON	19.56	0
Arrive EDGE HILL	20.07	4½

Do 8A Edge Hill (65 mins. approx)

Depart EDGE HILL	21.25	0
Arrive LIVERPOOL LIME STREET	21.30	1

- - - - - - - - - - - - - - - - - -

If we arrive at Warrington at 17.34 or 17.51 then **Timetable E/F** comes into operation after doing 8B Warrington.

Depart WARRINGTON	18.52	0
Arrive LIVERPOOL CENTRAL	19.17	12¾

Depart LIVERPOOL CENTRAL LOW LEVEL	19.25	0
Arrive BIRKENHEAD CENTRAL	19.32	2¼

Do 8H Birkenhead (30 mins. approx)

Depart BIRKENHEAD CENTRAL	20.00	0
Arrive JAMES STREET	20.05	1¾

Liverpool Corporation Bus No 4B and 79C

Depart LORD STREET, CITY CENTRE
Arrive TIVERTON STREET, EDGE HILL

Do 8A Edge Hill

	British Rail	MILES
Depart EDGE HILL	21.51 or 21.25	0
Arrive LIVERPOOL LIME STREET	21.55 or 21.30	<u>1</u>

Comments:-

If timetable E applies then night is spent in LIVERPOOL EXCHANGE waiting room.
If timetable E/F applies then night is spent in LIVERPOOL CENTRAL waiting room.
Both timetables will coincide on the Saturday by this method.

DAY 8   **SATURDAY AUGUST 7TH 1965**   LMR DAY 7

TIMETABLE E

		MILES
Depart LIVERPOOL EXCHANGE	05.30	0
Arrive AINTREE SEFTON ARMS	05.41	<u>4¾</u>

### Do 8L Aintree Sefton Arms (45 mins. approx)		Recovery Time - 10
Depart AINTREE SEFTON ARMS	06.16	0
Arrive SANDHILLS	06.26	<u>3¼</u>
Depart SANDHILLS	06.32	0
Arrive BANK HALL	06.33	<u>½</u>

### Do 8K Bank Hall (18 mins. approx)		Recovery Time + 3
Depart BANK HALL	06.54	0
Arrive LIVERPOOL EXCHANGE	07.00	<u>2</u>
Depart JAMES STREET	07.16	0
Arrive BIRKENHEAD CENTRAL	07.22	<u>1¾</u>

### Do 8H Birkenhead (30 mins. approx)		Recovery Time - 2
Depart BIRKENHEAD CENTRAL	07.50	0
Arrive LIVERPOOL CENTRAL Low Level	07.58	<u>2¼</u>
Depart LIVERPOOL LIME STREET	08.25	0
Arrive ST HELEN'S SHAW STREET	08.57	10¼

<u>see 8A Edge Hill – East</u>

<u>**Do 8G Sutton Oak (50 mins. approx)**</u>   Recovery Time
                                                        NIL

Depart ST HELEN'S SHAW STREET	09.41	10¼
Arrive WIGAN NORTH WESTERN	10.01	<u>19</u>

TIMETABLE E/F

Depart LIVERPOOL CENTRAL	05.05	0
Arrive GARSTON	05.16	<u>5½</u>

<u>**Do 8C Speke Junction (40 mins. approx)**</u>
<u>**Do 8J Allerton (35 mins. approx)**</u>   Recovery Time
                                                    + 5

Depart GARSTON	06.36	0
Arrive LIVERPOOL CENTRAL	06.51	<u>5½</u>
Depart LIVERPOOL EXCHANGE	07.10	0
Arrive BANK HALL	07.14	<u>2</u>

<u>**Do 8K Bank Hall (18 mins. approx)**</u>   Recovery Time
                                                     NIL

Depart BANK HALL	07.32	0
Arrive SANDHILLS	07.34	<u>½</u>
Depart SANDHILLS	07.47	0
Arrive AINTREE SEFTON ARMS	07.56	<u>3¼</u>

<u>**Do 8L Aintree Sefton Arms (45 mins. approx)**</u>   Recovery Time
                                                               + 2

Depart AINTREE SEFTON ARMS	08.43	0
Arrive LIVERPOOL EXCHANGE	05.58	<u>4¾</u>
Depart LIVERPOOL LIME STREET	09.15	0
Arrive ST HELEN'S SHAW STREET	09.41	10¼
Depart ST HELEN'S SHAW STREET	09.41	10¼
Arrive WIGAN NORTH WESTERN	10.01	<u>19</u>

Journey:-
          see 8G Sutton Oak - east (09.41)
          see 8A Edge Hill - east

Timetables E and E/F have now coincided at Wigan North Western at 10.01.

<u>**Do 8F Wigan (Spring's Branch) (80 mins. approx)**</u>   Recovery Time
                                                                   + 4

Depart WIGAN WALLGATE	11.25	0
Arrive BOLTON	11.43	<u>9</u>

<u>**Do 9K Bolton (45 mins. approx)**</u>   Recovery Time
+ 11

Depart BOLTON	12.39	0
Arrive PRESTON	13.16	<u>20</u>

BUS   -   Local Service

Depart PRESTON STATION
Arrive LOSTOCK HALL STATION

<u>**Do 10D Lostock Hall**</u>

BUS   -   Local Service

Depart LOSTOCK HALL STATION
Arrive PRESTON STATION

Depart PRESTON	14.25	0
Arrive BLACKBURN	14.44	<u>11¼</u>

<u>**Do 10H Lower Darwen (80 mins. approx)**</u>   Recovery Time
NIL

Depart BLACKBURN	16.04	14¼
Arrive ROSE GROVE	16.24	<u>21</u>

<u>**Do 1F Rose Grove (20 mins. approx)**</u>   Recovery Time
+ 18

Depart ROSE GROVE	17.02	0
Arrive SKIPTON	17.37	<u>18¼</u>

<u>**Do 10G Skipton (35 mins. approx)**</u>   Recovery Time
+ 31

Depart SKIPTON	18.43	0
Arrive WENNINGTON	19.48 (Train split)	28¼
Depart WENNINGTON	19.59	28¼
Arrive CARNFORTH	20.18	<u>38</u>

Journey:-
    see Hellifield (north west)   (19.06)

<u>**Do 10A Carnforth (30 mins. approx)**</u>   Recovery Time
+ 7

Depart CARNFORTH	20.55	0
Arrive CARLISLE	22.44	<u>62¾</u>
See 12A Tebay - West	(21.45)	35¾

END OF RAILROVER

<u>Comments</u>: - None!

DAY 9   **<u>SUNDAY AUGUST 8TH 1965</u>**

<u>Do 12A Carlisle Kingmoor</u>

<u>Do 12B Carlisle Upperby</u>

Depart CARLISLE	13.32 or 16.37
Arrive CARSTAIRS	15.25 or 18.30

<u>Do 66E Carstairs</u>

Depart CARSTAIRS	15.35 or 18.40
Arrive EDINBURGH WAVERLEY	16.14 or 19.18

<u>Alternative</u>

Depart CARISLE RIBBLE BUS	15.30	16.18	17.18
Arrive EDINBURGH	19.35	20.25	21.25

Fare 15/3d (76p)

<u>Do 64A St Margarets</u>

<u>Do 64B Haymarket</u>

<u>LE FIN DE LA TOUR</u>

GOODBYE - GOODNIGHT

Set out below is the steam we would be aware of when we started our week's tour. The end April/early May date provided us with the last reported allocations as per the Modern Railways monthly magazine before our August trip. For comparison I set out the actual position for our week's tour which we did not, of course, know until finally reported in Modern Railways some months later.

By the time of our visit some sheds had been closed to steam – some we knew about and some we didn't!

LONDON MIDLAND REGION STEAM					
		allocation	*allocation*		
	Shed	*end April*	*early August*	*Change*	
Shed	*Code*	*1965*	*1965*		*Pre-grouping*
Willesden	1A	67	50	-17	London & North Western
Bletchley	1E	34	0	-34	London & North Western
Rugby	1F	14	0	-14	London & North Western
Woodford Halse	1G	18	0	-18	Great Central
Northampton	1H	26	25	-1	London & North Western
Tyseley	2A	39	45	6	Great Western
Wolverhampton Oxley	2B	58	49	-9	Great Western
Stourbridge	2C	34	29	-5	Great Western
Banbury	2D	23	32	9	Great Western
Saltley	2E	49	41	-8	Midland
Bescot	2F	62	63	1	London & North Western
Aston	2J	23	15	-8	London & North Western
Leamington Spa	2L	13	0	-13	Great Western
Crewe North	5A	38	0	-38	London & North Western
Crewe South	5B	60	81	21	London & North Western
Stafford	5C	9	0	-9	London & North Western
Stoke	5D	76	72	-4	North Staffordshire
Nuneaton	5E	37	36	-1	London & North Western
Chester	6A	29	32	3	London & North Western
Mold Junction	6B	28	39	11	London & North Western
Croes Newydd	6C	38	34	-4	Great Western
Shrewsbury	6D	45	33	-12	GWR/LNWR
Machynlleth	6F	13	7	-6	Cambrian
Llandudno Junction	6G	22	15	-7	London & North Western
Bangor	6H	20	0	-20	London & North Western
Holyhead	6J	15	29	14	London & North Western
Sub-Total		**890**	727	*-163*	

LONDON MIDLAND REGION STEAM (continued)

Shed	Shed Code	allocation end April 1965	allocation early August 1965	Change	Pre-grouping
Edge Hill	8A	50	50	0	London & North Western
Warrington Dallam	8B	38	38	0	London & North Western
Speke Junction	8C	57	61	4	London & North Western
Northwich	8E	16	16	0	Cheshire Lines
Springs Branch	8F	59	58	-1	London & North Western
Sutton Oak	8G	29	26	-3	London & North Western
Birkenhead	8H	75	78	3	LNWR/GWR
Bank Hall	8K	17	21	4	Lancashire & Yorkshire
Aintree	8L	44	34	-10	Lancashire & Yorkshire
Southport	8M	10	9	-1	Lancashire & Yorkshire
Stockport (Edgeley)	9B	33	29	-4	London & North Western
Newton Heath	9D	79	98	19	Lancashire & Yorkshire
Trafford Park	9E	29	42	13	Cheshire Lines
Heaton Mersey	9F	36	56	20	Cheshire Lines
Gorton	9G	48	0	-48	Great Central
Patricroft	9H	51	59	8	London & North Western
Agecroft	9J	26	24	-2	Lancashire & Yorkshire
Bolton	9K	57	53	-4	Lancashire & Yorkshire
Buxton	9L	20	17	-3	London & North Western
Carnforth	10A	41	46	5	London & North Western
Fleetwood	10C	25	26	1	Lancashire & Yorkshire
Lostock Hall	10D	33	43	10	Lancashire & Yorkshire
Rose Grove	10F	24	31	7	Lancashire & Yorkshire
Skipton	10G	22	17	-5	Midland
Lower Darwen	10H	15	15	0	Lancashire & Yorkshire
Lancaster	10J	19	19	0	Midland
Carlisle Kingmoor	12A	120	118	-2	Caledonian
Carlisle Upperby	12B	22	29	7	London & North Western
Barrow	12C	21	21	0	Furness
Workington	12D	23	26	3	London & North Western
Tebay	12E	9	9	0	London & North Western
Leicester Midland	15A	24	37	13	Midland
Wellingborough	15B	17	0	-17	Midland
Coalville	15E	17	14	-3	Midland
Toton	16A	8	6	-2	Midland
Annesley	16B	61	14	-47	Great Central
Derby	16C	42	35	-7	Midland
Kirkby-In-Ashfield	16E	43	42	-1	Midland
Burton	16F	34	33	-1	Midland
Westhouses	16G	42	36	-6	Midland
		1,436	1,386	-50	
LMR total steam		**2,326**	**2,113**	**-213**	

EASTERN REGION STEAM		Shed	allocation end April	allocation early August	Change	
Shed		Code	1965	1965		Pre-grouping
Doncaster		36A	64	67	3	Great Northern
Frodingham		36C	41	38	-3	Great Central
Retford		36E	35	0	-35	Great Northern/ Great Central
Immingham		40B	27	17	-10	Great Central
Colwick		40E	48	56	8	Great Northern
Canklow (Rotherham)		41D	27	0	-27	Midland
Staveley Midland		41E	33	34	1	Midland
Staveley G.C.		41H	22	0	-22	Great Central
Langwith Junction		41J	33	43	10	Great Central
Eastern Region total steam			**330**	**255**	**-75**	

NORTH EASTERN REGION STEAM		Shed	allocation end April	allocation early August		
Shed		Code	1965	1965		Pre-grouping
York		50A	64	55	-9	North Eastern
Hull Dairycoates		50B	35	33	-2	North Eastern
Goole		50D	13	14	1	Lancashire & Yorkshire
Darlington		51A	37	26	-11	North Eastern
West Hartlepool		51C	32	30	-2	North Eastern
Gateshead		52A	18	10	-8	North Eastern
Tweedmouth		52D	8	8	0	North Eastern
North and South Blyth		52F	48	44	-4	North Eastern
Sunderland		52G	23	22	-1	North Eastern
Tyne Dock		52H	25	23	-2	North Eastern
Consett		52K	8	0	-8	North Eastern
Leeds Holbeck		55A	41	41	0	Midland
Stourton (Leeds)		55B	25	24	-1	Midland
Farnley Junction		55C	12	12	0	London & North Western
Royston		55D	32	31	-1	London Midland Scottish
Normanton		55E	21	21	0	Lancashire & Yorkshire
Bradford Manningham		55F	11	11	0	Midland
Huddersfield		55G	12	12	0	London & North Western
Leeds Neville Hill		55H	15	13	-2	North Eastern
Wakefield		56A	84	83	-1	Lancashire & Yorkshire
Ardsley		56B	45	37	-8	Great Northern
Mirfield		56D	19	19	0	Lancashire & Yorkshire
Low Moor		56F	17	18	1	Lancashire & Yorkshire
North Eastern Reg. total steam			**645**	**587**	**-58**	

SCOTTISH REGION STEAM		allocation	allocation		
	Shed	end April	early August	Change	
Shed	Code	1965	1965		Pre-grouping
Ferryhill	61B	15	13	-2	Caledonian / North British
Thornton	62A	37	38	1	North British
Dundee Tay Bridge	62B	31	31	0	North British
Dunfermline	62C	29	28	-1	North British
Perth	63A	29	21	-8	Caledonian
St Margarets	64A	40	36	-4	North British
Dalry Road	64C	16	14	-2	Caledonian
Bathgate	64F	14	14	0	North British
Hawick	64G	5	5	0	North British
Eastfield	65A	6	7	1	North British
St Rollox	65B	13	13	0	Caledonian
Grangemouth	65F	30	27	-3	Caledonian
Stirling South	65J	9	9	0	Caledonian
Polmadie	66A	39	34	-5	Caledonian
Motherwell	66B	20	19	-1	Caledonian
Greenock Ladyburn	66D	12	10	-2	Caledonian
Carstairs	66E	16	19	3	Caledonian
Beattock	66F	6	6	0	Caledonian
Corkerhill	67A	32	27	-5	Glasgow & South Western
Hurlford	67B	28	27	-1	Glasgow & South Western
Ayr	67C	32	33	1	Glasgow & South Western
Dumfries	67E	19	14	-5	Glasgow & South Western
Stranraer	67F	3	3	0	Caledonian /GSW
Scottish Region total steam		481	448	-33	

SOUTHERN REGION STEAM		allocation	allocation		
	Shed	early May	early August	Change	
Shed	Code	1965	1965		Pre-grouping
Nine Elms	70A	39	34	-5	London & South Western
Feltham	70B	9	11	2	London & South Western
Guildford	70C	29	24	-5	London & South Western
Eastleigh	70D	103	107	4	London & South Western
Salisbury	70E	24	29	5	London & South Western
Bournemouth	70F	39	38	-1	London & South Western
Weymouth	70G	23	22	-1	Great Western
Ryde IoW	70H	16	16	0	Isle of Wight Central
Redhill	75B	18	0	-18	South Eastern & Chatham
Southern Region total steam		300	281	-19	

WESTERN REGION STEAM

Shed	Shed Code	allocation early May 1965	allocation early August 1965	Change	Pre-grouping
Southall	81C	42	18	-24	Great Western
Didcot	81E	17	0	-17	Great Western
Oxford	81F	25	41	16	Great Western
Bristol Barrow Road	82E	41	28	-13	Midland
Bath (Green Park)	82F	18	19	1	SDJR/Midland
Westbury	83C	8	6	-2	Great Western
Exmouth Junction	83D	22	0	-22	London & South Western
Yeovil Town	83E	10	0	-10	London & South Western
Templecombe	83G	13	15	2	Somerset & Dorset Joint
Worcester	85A	23	22	-1	Great Western
Gloucester Horton Road	85B	33	23	-10	Great Western
Newport Ebbw Junction	86B	26	20	-6	Great Western
Severn Tunnel Junction	86E	22	13	-9	Great Western
Pontypool Road	86G	1	0	-1	Great Western
Neath	87A	11	0	-11	Great Western
Llanelli	87F	22	10	-12	Great Western
Cardiff East Dock	88A	31	0	-31	Great Western
Cardiff Radyr	88B	31	0	-31	Great Western
Rhymney	88D	9	0	-9	
Western Region total steam		**405**	**215**	**-190**	

BR RAILWAY WORKS STEAM

Works	Shed Code	allocation end April 1965	allocation early August 1965	Change	
Crewe Works	CW	13	12	-1	
Horwich Works	HW	2	2	0	
Wolverton Works	WW	4	4	0	
Works total steam		**19**	**18**	**-1**	

OVERALL SUMMARY

STEAM BY REGION	end APRIL/early May 65		early AUGUST 65		
	Number	Per Cent.	Number	Per Cent.	
London Midland	2,326	51.6%	2,113	53.9%	
Eastern Region	330	7.3%	255	6.5%	
North Eastern	645	14.3%	587	15.0%	
Scottish	481	10.7%	448	11.4%	
Southern	300	6.7%	281	7.2%	
Western	405	9.0%	215	5.5%	
Works	19	0.4%	18	0.5%	
GRAND STEAM TOTAL	4,506	100.0%	3,917	100.0%	

Overall, the LMR provided us with approximately half of the available steam.

Back to Friday 31st July 1965

What does one need for such a tour?

Here is what went into my portmanteau (that's the wrong word) - big grip – that's correct! Some went into my anorak and some into my school bag.

1.   **Anorak** - wear it

Into Anorak

2.   My **Loco Notebook setting out all present shed allocations**
3.   **Shed Permits** (a great wad)
4.   **Locomotive Shed Directory**
5.   **Locoshed Book**
6.   **Loads of pens and pencils**
7.   **One wallet** - to contain approx £7, Railrover Ticket and Reserved Seat Ticket
8.   **One purse** - holds one £5 note and all loose change
9.   **Compass** (I must have been worried. I even stumped up 3/6d (17 new pence) for it. We get lost. Never!)
10.   **Comb**
11.   **Youth Hostel Card**
12.   **Tin Opener**

I must have had a big anorak! A valuable one too with all that cash in it!

Into Schoolbag (the type that hung at your side. Rucksack type)

12.   **Waterproof Trousers**
13.   **Waterproof Jacket**
14.   **Bicycle Lamp** (in case we visit sheds which are dark or in the dark. One never knows)
15.   **My working timetable for LMR**
16.   **Allocations Book** (a complete list of every engine allocated to every shed which we would visit)
17.   **LMR Map** (inside Allocations Book) (official LMR map given with timetable)
18.   **Food** (at the time there was a plastic container of tomatoes put in. More food would be put in the following morning)
19.   **Vacuum flask**

Into Grip

20.   **One other change of shoes**
21.   **One other change of clothes** (no change of trousers, 4 pairs of socks)
22.   **Sleeping bag** (if hostels are used)
23.   **Mug**
24.   **Soap and towels**
25.   **Toothbrush and toothpaste**
26.   **Boot polish and brush**
27.   **Ian Allan Locoshed Book**
28.   **Ian Allan Combined volume**
29.   **A few extra pens**
30.   **Knife and fork and spoon**

Miscellaneous

1. One camera and two spools would be collected from Graham Strachan at Carlisle on the Saturday.
2. Wristwatch would of course be taken.
3. A money-belt round waist as an additional precaution. My party of three had once been held up by some young thugs outside 66A Polmadie shed (probably one of the direst areas for a shed) but I had been spared losing money as they had missed my money belt round my waist!

Not taken

1. I considered the 832 page "monster" LMR timetable, too heavy and bulky to take. We would just have to make do without it. My working timetable should suffice.
2. D.S. and I were banned from taking alarm clocks with us. Unfortunate this; considering every day was an early rise. We would have to think of something else.

Incidentally D.S. and I had a tour round the banks in the afternoon changing our Scottish pound notes to English pound notes. They do not like Scottish notes in England. Some people think them foreign and do not accept them there.

This did not turn out to be a problem over the years. I only had my Scottish pound rejected once in England. Years later I was at Kempton Park races in London when I wanted £2 to win on a horse. The bookmaker accepted the English pound but rejected the Scottish pound so I said fine I'll only put on £1 to win. As the horse lost I saved £1 so it was great that the Scottish pound got rejected!

I think that before I can conjure up some more introductory remarks I had better get on with the story.

D-DAY (Day 1)

Saturday July 31st 1965

06.00   Up bright and early. Went to Masons Home Bakery at Stoneybank for ½ doz. rolls, one fruit tart, College Creams. Crammed provisions into my school bag. Checked rest of luggage.

07.00   D.S. was supposed to be at my house by now. He's normally late (at least 15 mins.). I suppose that's the cause.

07.03   D.S. breaks all known records by being only three minutes late.

07.50   Everything OK. Have bought exorbitant singles to Carlisle at 27/- (£1.35). Daylight robbery! Zoombala priced as Michael Bentine would say. We are of course in our station of departure, Edinburgh Princes Street at the opposite end from Waverley Station.

We got to the station quickly to ensure that we got a seat. Found ourselves at the node of the queue (the first six in fact) for the 08.30 train to Carlisle.

08.10   Enormous queue formed behind us. No sign of the train yet. Note that Neil Woodcock and Derek Newton are at the end of the queue.

Today was what could be called Locospotter's Day at Carlisle. This was the end of the Glasgow trades. On the returning Saturday of the Glasgow trades Musselburgh railwayists converge on Carlisle. The previous year Neil Woodcock, Derek Newton, David Archibald, Graham Strachan and I had made a day of it. A very successful one at that.

This year would bring out last year's merry band but this year Andrew Forsyth would come along too.

08.20   Andrew Forsyth had been with us for some time. D.S. and I were now waiting only for Graham and the train! At last Graham came panting up with a mournful story about the papers (his paper round).

I also noticed our old pals Mike Thurlow and Tommy Williamson in the ranks behind us.

08.25   At last our Carstairs train arrived. D.S., Andrew, Graham and I after having our tickets checked did the 50 yards dash in double quick time to overtake the half-dozen who were in front of us and made ourselves at home in the first compartment we came to. It was one of BR's re-done up carriages and was rather comfortable.

Having a look round the station I noted two "Black Fives" on empty stock workings:-

44700	of 66E Carstairs
45389	of 65J Stirling

Our comfort was short-lived however when a man and his wife came barging in with innumerable children (at least four) and after finally squeezing everybody in asked if

we didn't mind. He then proceeded to tell us that we were in the danger coach. If a train crashes into us from behind and we were in the last compartment......
Charming fellow I must say. Does he want us to move out? Trying to scare us? We will stay put.

08.35 A "Black Five" was at the head of our train. At last the driver of 45309 of 66E Carstairs decided to get a move on. He had succeeded in making our departure five minutes late. Just as well our connection at Carstairs was guaranteed.

Goodbye Edinburgh.

The train began to pick up speed at Dalry. Sadly we saw a B1:-

61245   "Murray of Elibank" of 64C Dalry Road lying withdrawn.

It was a rather overcast day and I thought that we would be lucky if the day passed without rain.

		Schedule	Actual	Miles
Depart	EDINBURGH PRINCES STREET	08.30	08.35	0
Arrive	CARSTAIRS	09.07	09.12	27½
	See 66E Carstairs			

EDINBURGH PRINCES STREET TO CARSTAIRS							
		Home shed			Built	Withdrawn	Scrap
Steam							
Stanier 5MT 4-6-0 "Black Five" 1934							
44700		66E	Carstairs		Jul-1948	Jul-1966	Oct-1966
45309	hauled	66E	Carstairs		Jan-1937	Sep-1966	Feb-1967
45389		65J	Stirling		Jul-1937	Oct-1965	Jan-1966
Total	3						
Thompson 5MT 4-6-0 B1 1942							
61245	"Murray of Elibank"	64C	Dalry Road		Oct-1947	Jul-1965	Oct-1965
Total	1						
On Journey	4	Kops	0				
Steam	4	Diesels	0				
Withdrawn	1						
		Home Area		3	Visitors	1	
Shed	66E	2	65J	1			
Distribution	64C	1					
Steam Classes	2						
Steam Origin	LMS	3	LNER	1			

The journey to Carstairs was uneventful enough but as we passed the fenced-off criminal mental asylum. One wag in our party asked D.S. to hide his head in his hands unless any of the wardens could pick him out with their binoculars and recognise him as one of their escaped patients. D.S. survived that testing moment. Our driver had not picked up any time and we arrived at Carstairs five minutes late at 09.12.

Brush Type 4 D1840 with the Glasgow section was already waiting for us. We were due to leave at 09.17 and there was time only for a quick look round 66E Carstairs shed.

Noted around Carstairs shed were:-

66E CARSTAIRS

			Home shed		Built	Withdrawn	Scrap
Diesels							
BR 0-6-0 Shunter 1953							
D3284			66C	Hamilton	Nov-1956		
Total		1					
Steam							
Stanier 5MT 4-6-0 "Black Five" 1934					**Built**	**Withdrawn**	**Scrap**
44791			66E	(ex 67A Corkerhill)	Jun-1947	Nov-1966	Apr-1967
44973			66E		May-1946	Sep-1965	Dec-1965
44991			66B	Motherwell	Dec-1946	May-1967	Sep-1967
45106			12A	Carlisle Kingmoor	May-1935	Jan-1967	May-1967
45492			66E		Jan-1944	Dec-1966	Apr-1967
Total		13					
Thomson 8P7F 4-6-2 A2 1946							
60522	"Straight Deal"		ex 66A	Polmadie	May-1947	Jun-1965	Oct-1965
Total		1					
On Shed		7	Kops	0			
Steam		6	Diesels	1			
Withdrawn		1					
Home Locos		3	Home Area		3	Visitors	1
Shed	66E		3	66A	1	66B	1
Analysis	12A		1				
Steam classes on view		2					
Steam Origin	LMS			5	LNER	1	
Shed Highlight:-	60522		"Straight Deal"		ex 66A	Polmadie	
Steam	**Sep-50**	50	**Mar-59**	41	**Apr-65**	16	
Allocation					Aug-65	19	
				Closed to Steam:-		Dec-66	
Home Steam							
On/Off Shed	On Shed	3	Off Shed	16	% On Shed	16%	
Not on Shed							
Fairburn 4MT 2-6-4T 1945			42058	42125	42169	42274	42694	5
"Black Fives"		44700	44952	44953	44954	44956	45011	
			45090	45171	45245	45309	45478	11
							total	16
	saw elsewhere on the tour					2	

Review of 66E Carstairs

Extremely sad to see the withdrawn A2 Pacific 60522 "Straight Deal." Since April three A2's had been withdrawn (including "Straight Deal") leaving only three members of this former 40 strong class left in service. The three survivors 60528 "Tudor Minstrel", 60530 "Sayajirao" and 60532 "Blue Peter" were all allocated to 62B Dundee Tay Bridge M.P.D.

On we go

At 09.20 (three minutes late) our Edinburgh section had been manoeuvred on to the Glasgow section and we were off. Black 5's 44908 and 44786 both of 66B Motherwell were noted on two Glasgow bound freights soon after Carstairs.

My first KOP of the tour came about a mile north of Beattock when to ecstatic cheers Black 5 44778 of 10A Carnforth passed us at speed with a fitted freight heading north. A stranger indeed but very welcome.

I will spell KOP - K-O-P not COP as I hate COPS. Get the picture. Right, you've been told. We picked up speed in going down Beattock Bank and I hoped the driver would pick up a few lost minutes. Two tank locos which were used as banking locos to aid trains up the formidable Beattock Bank were noted outside 66F Beattock shed, which we flew past at high speed.

66F BEATTOCK (pass)								
			Home shed			Built	Withdrawn	Scrap
Steam								
Fairburn 4MT 2-6-4T 1945 dev. of Stanier 1935								
42169			66E	Carstairs		*Sep-1948*	*Feb-1966*	*Dec-1966*
42693			66F			*Sep-1945*	*Oct-1966*	*Jan-1967*
Total	2							
On Shed	2		**Kops**	0				
Steam	2		**Diesels**	0				
Withdrawn	0							
Home Locos	1	**Home Area**		1	**Visitors**	0		
Shed	66F	1	66E	1				
Analysis								
Steam classes on view		1						
Steam Origin		**LMS**		2				
Steam	*Sep-50*	16	*Mar-59*	10	*Apr-65*	6		
Allocation					*Aug-65*	6		
				Closed to Steam:-		**May-67**		
Home Steam	excluding withdrawn locos							
On/Off Shed	On Shed	1	Off Shed	5	% On Shed	17%		
Not on Shed								
Fairburn 4MT 2-6-4T 1945						42129	42260	2
BR 4MT 2-6-0 1953							76090	1
BR 4MT 2-6-4T 1953						80005	80045	2
							total	5
		saw elsewhere on the tour				1		
		recently withdrawn not on shed or seen elsewhere				1	*scrap*	
					Fairburn 4MT 2-6-4T 1945	42688	*Jul-65*	

66F Beattock was a small shed with its allocation used for banking locos up Beattock Bank. Home Steam only amounted to six of which one was noted on shed. 9F 92012 of 12A Kingmoor had passed us on one of those endless up freights to Glasgow near the Scottish Border.

CARSTAIRS TO CARLISLE OUTSKIRTS								
			Home shed			Built	Withdrawn	Scrap
Steam								
Stanier 5MT 4-6-0 "Black Five" 1934								
44674			12A	Carlisle Kingmoor		*Mar-1950*	*Dec-1967*	*Mar-1968*
44778			10A	Carnforth		*Jun-1947*	*Nov-1967*	*Feb-1968*
44786			66B	Motherwell		*Apr-1947*	*Aug-1966*	*Dec-1966*
44908			66B	Motherwell		*Nov-1945*	*Jun-1966*	*May-1967*
Total	4							
BR Standard 2-6-4T 1951 Brighton								
80045			66F	Beattock		*Sep-1952*	*May-1967*	*Sep-1967*
Total	1							
BR Standard 9F 2-10-0 Brighton 1954								
92012			12A	Carlisle Kingmoor		*May-1954*	*Oct-1967*	*Feb-1968*
Total	1							

On Journey	6	Kops	0	
Steam	6	Diesels	0	
Withdrawn	0			
Shed	10A	1 12A	2	
Analysis	66B	2 66F	1	
Steam classes on view		3		
Steam Origin	LMS	4 BR	2	

The journey to the outskirts of Carlisle had proved to be fruitful.

We were now nearing 12A Carlisle Kingmoor shed and we all got our pens and notebooks out in anticipation.

12A CARLISLE KINGMOOR (PASS)

		Home shed		Built	Withdrawn	Scrap
Diesels						
BR 0-6-0 Shunter 1953						
D3087		12A		Oct-1954		
Total	*1*					
LMS and BR 0-6-0 Shunter 1945						
12083		12A		Nov-1950	Oct-1971	
Total	*1*					
Steam				**Built**	**Withdrawn**	**Scrap**
Ivatt 4MT 2-6-0 1947						
43139		12A		Jul-1951	Sep-1967	Feb-1968
Total	*1*					
Stanier 5MT 4-6-0 "Black Five" 1934						
44986		12A		Oct-1946	May-1967	Nov-1967
45105		12A		May-1935	Oct-1966	Feb-1967
45235		12A		Aug-1936	Jan-1966	Apr-1966
45259		12A		Oct-1936	Dec-1967	Apr-1968
Total	*4*					
Stanier 6P5F 4-6-0 "Jubilee" 1934						
45675	"Hardy"	55A	Leeds Holbeck	Dec-1935	Jun-1967	Nov-1967
Total	*1*					
BR Standard 7P6F 4-6-2 "Britannia" Derby 1951						
70002	"Geoffrey Chaucer"	12A		Mar-1951	Jan-1967	Jun-1967
70008	"Black Prince"	12A		Apr-1951	Jan-1967	Jun-1967
70016	"Ariel"	12A		Jun-1951	Aug-1967	Jan-1968
Total	*3*					
On Shed	11	Kops	1			
Steam	9	Diesels	2			
Home Locos	10 Home Area		0	Visitors	1	
Shed	12A	10				
Distribution:-	55A	1				
Steam classes on view		4				
Steam Origin	LMS	6 BR	3			
Shed Highlight:-	45675	"Hardy"				

The Britannias were lying in a particularly dirty state waiting to greet us.

Jubilee 45675 "Hardy" of 55A Holbeck was a welcome visitor from 55A Leeds Holbeck. The year before "Hardy" had been there to greet us resplendent in an ex-works coat of unlined black paint. "Hardy" did like going on holiday to Kingmoor at the end of the Glasgow Trades holidays.

Only 28 of the "Jubilees" remained in service of this magnificent and popular class. *Remarkably eight "Jubilees" (including "Hardy") would remain in service into 1967.*

Eyes west for Kingmoor Yard. Kingmoor Yard was very impressive but all that was there were the two diesel shunters noted above.

On we go

At last we drew into the station all of 5 minutes late. We had lost another 2 minutes since Carstairs. Tut-tut British Rail. With meticulous care we checked our luggage into the left luggage office. We put our luggage in the left luggage office at the station. It cost me 1/6d (7½p). 1/- (5p) for the grip and 6d (2½p) for my school bag. We then bundled ourselves on to the platform. Carlisle station proved to be rather busy.

CARLISLE STATION ARRIVAL							
			Home shed		Built	Withdrawn	Scrap
Diesels							
English Electric Type 4 1-Co-Co1 1958							
D 212	"Aureol"		1B	Camden	*May-1959*		
Total	*1*						
BR Sulzer Type 2 Bo-Bo 1958							
D5149			52A	Gateshead	*Feb-1961*		
Total	*1*						
English Electric Type 3 Co-Co 1961							
D6786			52A	Gateshead	*Dec-1962*		
Total	*1*						
Steam					Built	Withdrawn	Scrap
Stanier 5MT 4-6-0 "Black Five" 1934							
44833			5B	Crewe South (ex 1A)	*Aug-1944*	*Sep-1967*	*Mar-1968*
44977			67C	Ayr	*Jun-1946*	*Nov-1966*	*May-1967*
Total	*2*						
3F 0-6-0T 1924 "Jinty" Midland dev. of Johnson 1899							
47326			12A	Carlisle Kingmoor	*Jul-1926*	*Dec-1966*	*Sep-1967*
Total	*1*						
7P6F "Britannia" 1951 BR 4-6-2 Derby							
70003	"John Bunyan"		12A	Carlisle Kingmoor	*Mar-1951*	*Mar-1967*	*Dec-1967*
70034	"Thomas Hardy"		9D	Newton Heath	*Dec-1952*	*May-1967*	*Oct-1967*
Total	*2*						
BR Standard 4-6-0 1951 5MT Doncaster							
73072			66A	Polmadie	*Dec-1954*	*Oct-1966*	*May-1967*
73103			67A	Corkerhill	*Sep-1955*	*Dec-1966*	*Apr-1967*
73134	*Caprotti valved*		9H	Patricroft	*Oct-1956*	*Jun-1968*	*Oct-1968*
Total	*3*						
On Station	**11**		**Kops**		**2**		
Steam	**8**		**Diesels**		**3**		
			Home Area		**2**	**Visitors**	**9**
Shed	**12A**	**2**					
Distribution:-	**1B**	**1**	**5B**		**1**	**9D**	**1**
	9H	**1**					
	66A	**1**	**67A**		**1**	**67C**	**1**
Steam classes on view		**4**					
Steam Origin	**LMS**		**3 BR**			**5**	

An interesting and cosmopolitan lot with only two local engines on view.

We quickly got onto the station concourse and I bought a Conway Stewart Black Fybriter pen for 1/6d (12½p). The pen had a fibre glass point and would be ideal for the tour. We then made our way to the Locospotters Haven (namely Upperby Bridge).

It was now about 10.45 and we resolved to get the nearby 12B Carlisle Upperby shed done as quickly as possible. D.S., Graham, Andrew and I set out for the shed. We crossed the corrugated iron bridge and got into the shed. We entered the shed by a corrugated iron bridge which avoided the railway cops and officials ridden shed offices. However, we had got about half-way round the roundhouse when I think the foreman came up to us. Ivatt 2-6-2 Tank 41217 was making a tremendous noise and row steaming off and we could not hear what he was saying. Judging by his angry red face and his gesticulations it seemed that he wanted us to leave the premises. We walked away in the direction of the exit bridge and as soon as he went away we came back and continued our tour without further incident.

		12B CARLISLE UPPERBY				
		Home shed		**Built**	**Withdrawn**	**Scrap**
Diesels						
English Electric Type 4 1Co-Co1 1958						
D 292		1A	Willesden	*Sep-1960*		
Total	1					
Brush Type 4 Co-Co 1962						
D1633		5A	Crewe Diesel	*Nov-1964*		
Total	1					
BR 0-6-0 Shunter 1953						
D3566		12A	Carlisle Kingmoor	*Dec-1958*		
Total	1					
Steam				**Built**	**Withdrawn**	**Scrap**
Ivatt 2MT 2-6-2T 1946						
41217		12B		*Sep-1948*	*Dec-1966*	*Sep-1967*
41264		12B		*Jul-1950*	*Dec-1966*	*Jan-1968*
41285		12B		*Nov-1950*	*Dec-1966*	*May-1967*
Total	3					
Fairburn 4MT 2-6-4T 1945 dev. of Stanier 1935						
42225		12E	Tebay	*Apr-1946*	*Aug-1966*	*Oct-1966*
Total	1					
Midland 4F 0-6-0 1911						
43953		12D	Workington	*Dec-1921*	*Nov-1965*	*Jan-1966*
43964		12D	Workington	*Dec-1921*	*Sep-1965*	*Jul-1966*
Total	2					
Midland 4F 0-6-0 1924						
44390		12B		*Oct-1926*	*Nov-1965*	*Jan-1966*
44449		12D	Workington	*Jan-1928*	*Aug-1965*	*Dec-1965*
Total	2					
Stanier 5MT 4-6-0 "Black Five" 1934						
44913		6A	Chester Midland	*Nov-1945*	*Jul-1967*	*Mar-1968*
45025		10J	Lancaster	*Feb-1950*	*Aug-1968*	*saved*
45069		8A	Edge Hill	*Jan-1935*	*Jun-1967*	*Dec-1967*
45363		12A	Carlisle Kingmoor	*Jun-1937*	*Oct-1967*	*Mar-1968*
45371		12B		*Jun-1937*	*Apr-1967*	*Aug-1967*
45408		8F	Springs Branch (Wigan)	*Sep-1937*	*Nov-1966*	*May-1967*
45494		5B	Crewe South	*Jan-1944*	*Sep-1967*	*Feb-1968*
Total	7					
Stanier 6P5F 4-6-0 "Jubilee" 1934						
45563	"Australia"	8B	Warrington	*Aug-1934*	*Nov-1965*	*Mar-1966*
Total	1					
Ivatt 2MT 2-6-0 1946						
46432		12D	Workington	*Dec-1948*	*May-1967*	*Nov-1967*
46455		12B		*Apr-1950*	*May-1967*	*Oct-1967*
46458		12B		*May-1950*	*Dec-1966*	*May-1967*
46513		12B	(ex 9D Newton Heath)	*Dec-1952*	*Jul-1966*	*Jan-1967*
Total	4					

		Home shed		Built	Withdrawn	Scrap
BR Standard 7P6F 4-6-2 "Britannia" Derby 1951						
70005	"John Milton"	12A	Carlisle Kingmoor	*Apr-1951*	*Jul-1967*	*Jan-1968*
70011	"Hotspur"	12B		*May-1951*	*Dec-1967*	*Apr-1968*
70020	"Mercury"	12B	(ex 5A then ex 5B)	*Jul-1951*	*Jan-1967*	*Jun-1967*
70029	"Shooting Star"	12B		*Nov-1952*	*Oct-1967*	*Mar-1968*
70044	"Earl Haig"	9D	Newton Heath (ex5B)	*Jun-1953*	*Dec-1966*	*Feb-1967*
70049	"Solway Firth"	12B		*Jul-1954*	*Dec-1967*	*Mar-1968*
70052	"Firth of Tay"	5B	Crewe South (ex 5A)	*Aug-1954*	*Apr-1967*	*Nov-1967*
Total	7					

On Shed	30		**Kops**	11			
Steam	27		**Diesels**	3			
Withdrawn	0						

Home Locos		12 Home Area		8	**Visitors**	10		
Shed	12B	12	12A	3	12D	4	12E	1
Distribution:-	1A	1					5	
	5A	1	5B	2				
	6A	1						
	8A	1	8B	1	8F	1		
	9D	1	10J	1				
Steam classes on view		8		**Post Grouping:- LNWR**				
Steam Origin	LMS		20	BR		7		
Shed Highlight:-		45563	"Australia"		8B	**Warrington**		

Steam	*Sep-50*	87	*Mar-59*	103	*Apr-65*	22	*Jul-65*	29
Allocation					**Closed to Steam:-**		*Jan-68*	
Home Steam								
On/Off Shed	On Shed	12	Off Shed	17	% On Shed	41%		
Not on Shed								
Ivatt 2MT 2-6-2T					41207	41222	41229	3
Midland 4F 0-6-0 1924							44081	1
"Black Fives"				44911	44937	44939	45081	4
Ivatt 2MT 2-6-0 1946						46426	46434	2
"Britannias"		70013	70019	70022	70030	70031	70032	7
							70048	
							total	17
		saw elsewhere on the tour				11		
		saw on Dec 64 Manchester and Crewe trip				1		
		saw on July 65 Preston area trip				1		

Review of 12B Carlisle Upperby

The shed was on the east side of the main Penrith line south of Carlisle Station. Walking time was 20 minutes from Carlisle station.

I had seen "Jubilee" 45563 "Australia" for the first time during our family holiday to Blackpool three weeks previously. Blackpool was our resort and Preston Station (several times), 10C Fleetwood, 10D Lostock Hall, 8B Warrington and 8F Springs Branch (Wigan) were visited during my stay.

12B Carlisle Upperby used to be a high class shed but steam numbers had dwindled from 103 in 1959 to 22 in April 1965. Surprisingly since then steam numbers had increased to 29 thanks to steam being pushed further north by the rapid dieselisation south of and at Crewe. 12 Home Steam (41%) were on shed and 17 off shed.

BR Standard 7P6F "Britannia" 70032"Tennyson" at 12A Carlisle Kingmoor shed 31/07/1965

Copyright Reg Parsons

Rewind Carlisle Upperby Sunday 7th September 1958

Carlisle as a young nine and a quarter old was my first trip with Scottish Railfans when we visited 12A Carlisle Kingmoor, 12B Carlisle Upperby and 12C Carlisle Canal together with the engine stabling shed of Durranhill or Dung Hill as we used to call this far from salubrious depot.

12B CARLISLE UPPERBY REWIND 7th SEPTEMBER 1958		Home shed		Built	Withdrawn	Scrap
Steam						
Midland 2P 4-4-0 1928						
40628				*Dec-1929*	*Jan-1961*	*Apr-1962*
40656				*Oct-1931*	*Nov-1959*	*Nov-1960*
Total	2					
Stanier 4MT 2-6-4T 1935 dev of Fowler 1927						
42426				*Feb-1936*	*Dec-1965*	*Mar-1966*
42467				*Nov-1936*	*Oct-1961*	*Dec-1961*
42539				*Dec-1935*	*Feb-1961*	*Aug-1961*
42594				*Nov-1936*	*May-1964*	*May-1964*
Total	4					
Midland 4F 0-6-0 1911						
43896				*Dec-1919*	*Nov-1959*	*Feb-1960*
44016				*Dec-1922*	*Jul-1962*	*Aug-1962*
Total	2					
Midland 4F 0-6-0 1924						
44060				*Sep-1925*	*Mar-1964*	*Apr-1964*
44346				*Jan-1927*	*Nov-1965*	*Jan-1966*
44351		11A	Barrow	*May-1927*	*Apr-1963*	*Jun-1964*
44443		11A	Barrow	*Dec-1927*	*Aug-1965*	*Dec-1965*
44594		11A	Barrow	*Oct-1939*	*Oct-1962*	*Jan-1963*
Total	5					

12B CARLISLE UPPERBY (continued)
REWIND 7th SEPTEMBER 1958

	Home shed				Built	Withdrawn	Scrap
Stanier 5MT 4-6-0 "Black Five" 1934							
45106					May-1935	Jan-1967	May-1967
45140					Jun-1935	Sep-1966	Feb-1967
45244					Sep-1936	Aug-1963	Sep-1963
45248					Sep-1936	Feb-1966	Jul-1966
45258					Oct-1936	Mar-1968	Jun-1968
45296					Dec-1936	Feb-1968	May-1968
45317		11A	Barrow		Feb-1937	Nov-1963	Nov-1963
45348					Apr-1937	Aug-1966	Nov-1966
45371					Jun-1937	Apr-1967	Aug-1967
45394					Aug-1937	Jul-1968	Dec-1968
45402					Aug-1937	Apr-1967	Oct-1967
45412					Sep-1937	Aug-1967	Jul-1968
45414					Oct-1937	Feb-1965	Mar-1965
45494					Jan-1944	Sep-1967	Feb-1968
Total	*14*						
Fowler 6P5F 4-6-0 unrebuilt "Patriot" 1933							
45504	"Royal Signals"				Jul-1932	Mar-1962	Mar-1962
45508	*stovepipe chimney*				Aug-1932	Nov-1960	Dec-1960
45513					Sep-1932	Sep-1962	Oct-1962
45537	"Private E.Sykes V.C."				Jul-1933	Jun-1962	Sep-1962
45543	"Home Guard"				Mar-1934	Jun-1964	Nov-1964
45549					Apr-1934	Jun-1962	Aug-1962
Total	*6*						
Stanier 6P5F 4-6-0 "Jubilee" 1934							
45588	"Kashmir"				Dec-1934	May-1965	Aug-1965
45617	"Mauritius"				Sep-1934	Nov-1964	Apr-1965
45723	"Fearless"				Aug-1936	Sep-1964	Jan-1965
Total	*3*						
Stanier 7P 4-6-0 "Royal Scot" 1943 rebuild of Fowler 1927							
46126	"Royal Army Service Corps"				Aug-1927	Sep-1963	Nov-1963
46136	"The Border Regiment"				Sep-1927	Apr-1964	Apr-1964
46148	"The Manchester Regiment"				Nov-1927	Nov-1964	Jan-1965
46165	"The Ranger (12th London Regiment)"				Oct-1930	Nov-1964	Mar-1965
Total	*4*						
Stanier 8P 4-6-2 "Coronation" 1937							
46236	"City of Bradford"				Jul-1939	Mar-1964	Apr-1964
46237	"City of Bristol"				May-1939	Oct-1964	Dec-1964
Total	*2*						
2MT 2-6-0 Ivatt 1946							
46455	*on shed*	Jul-65	11B	Workington	Apr-1950	May-1967	Oct-1967
46457					May-1950	May-1967	Oct-1967
Total	*2*						
Midland 3F "Jinty" 0-6-0T 1924 dev. of Johnson 1899 design							
47288					Oct-1924	Nov-1964	Mar-1965
47292					Oct-1924	Dec-1962	Jul-1963
47295					Oct-1924	Apr-1965	Jul-1965
47326					Jul-1926	Dec-1966	Sep-1967
47340					Aug-1926	Mar-1962	May-1962
47377					Sep-1926	Oct-1966	Mar-1967
47408					Dec-1926	Nov-1965	Feb-1966
47415					Dec-1926	Apr-1966	May-1966
47475					Dec-1927	Feb-1962	Mar-1962
47492					Feb-1928	Aug-1964	Jan-1965
47602					Sep-1928	Jan-1966	Apr-1966
47614					Nov-1928	Jul-1965	Oct-1965
47618					Nov-1928	Oct-1963	Oct-1963
47664					Apr-1929	Jan-1965	Apr-1965
Total	*14*						

12B CARLISLE UPPERBY (continued)						
REWIND 7th SEPTEMBER 1958						

Steam	58					
Steam classes on view		11				
Steam Origin	LMS		56			
Shed Highlights:-		the "Patriots"				

Home Steam

On/Off Shed	On Shed	53	Off Shed	58	% On Shed	48%		
Not on Shed								
Midland 2P 4-4-0 1928							40629	1
Stanier 4MT 2-6-4T 1935				42430	42449		42664	3
Midland 4F 0-6-0 1924		44081	44121	44126	44326		44596	5
"Black Fives"	44770	44936	44939	45025	45070		45185	
	45197	45246	45259	45286	45293		45295	
	45297	45315	45316	45323	45329		45344	
	45351	45368	45397	45437	45438		45445	
							45451	25
"Patriots"	45502	45506	45507	45512	45519		45524	
			45526	45533	45541		45551	10
"Jubilees"				45593	45599		45672	3
"Royal Scots"					46141		46167	2
"Coronations"	46226	46238	46244	46250	46255		46257	6
2MT 2-6-0 Ivatt 1946							46449	1
"Jinties"							47666	1
Johnson 2F 0-6-0 1917							58217	1
								58
saw elsewhere on the tour					13			
saw on Dec 64 Manchester and Crewe trip					1			
saw on July 65 Preston area trip					3			
saw on June 67 Carlisle visit					2			

Review of 12B Carlisle Upperby Rewind September 1958`

Carlisle Upperby was the "quality" shed with 12A Carlisle Kingmoor being the artisan shed. Particularly Upperby had a host of "Coronations", unrebuilt "Patriots" and "Royal Scots". Less than seven short years on and all the "Coronations" and unrebuilt "Patriots" had been withdrawn. Only two rebuilt "Patriots" and two rebuilt "Royal Scots" remained in service all now allocated to sister shed 12A Carlisle Kingmoor". Other quality visitors were on show but through the mists of time I now only have a definitive record of home locos seen that impressive day. Can't complain about six unrebuilt "Patriots", three "Jubilees", four "Royal Scots" and two "Coronations"!

A "missing" class nowadays was the Midland 2P 4-4-0's which were extinct by the end of 1962.

Remarkably although a Sunday only 53 (48%) of the 111 strong home steam allocation was on shed that day. Also not on shed was 58218 an example of the extinct Johnson 2F 0-6-0 1917 class.

53 Home Steam (48%) on shed with 58 off shed.

Fast Forward to 12B Carlisle Upperby 3rd June 1967

Dave Archibald and I were to pay one further visit to Carlisle (by Honda 50 motorcycles at a slow speed of just over 30 m.p.h.) just over a year before the final end for steam.

			12B CARLISLE UPPERBY				
			FAST FORWARD 3RD JUNE 1967				
			Home shed		**Built**	**Withdrawn**	**Scrap**
Steam							
Ivatt 2MT 2-6-2T 1946							
41217	*on shed*	*Jul-65*	12A	Carlisle (Kingmoor)	*Sep-1948*	*Dec-1966*	*Sep-1967*
41222			12A	Carlisle (Kingmoor)	*Sep-1948*	*Dec-1966*	*Sep-1967*
41264	*on shed*	*Jul-65*	12A	Carlisle (Kingmoor)	*Jul-1950*	*Dec-1966*	*Jan-1968*
Total		3					
Stanier 5MT 4-6-0 "Black Five" 1934							
44770			12A	Carlisle (Kingmoor)	*Apr-1947*	*Oct-1967*	*Feb-1968*
44932			10F	Rose Grove	*Sep-1945*	*Aug-1968*	*saved*
45196			10F	Rose Grove	*Oct-1935*	*Dec-1967*	*Mar-1968*
45262			10F	Rose Grove	*Oct-1936*	*Aug-1968*	*Sep-1968*
45279			12A	Carlisle (Kingmoor)	*Nov-1936*	*Mar-1968*	*Dec-1968*
45447			12A	Carlisle (Kingmoor) ex 6D	*Dec-1937*	*Aug-1968*	*Dec-1968*
45493			12A	Carlisle (Kingmoor) ex 6D	*Jan-1944*	*Jan-1968*	*Apr-1968*
Total		7					
Ivatt 2MT 2-6-0 1946							
46455	*on shed*	*Jul-65*	12A	Carlisle (Kingmoor)	*Apr-1950*	*May-1967*	*Oct-1967*
46457			12A	Carlisle (Kingmoor)	*May-1950*	*May-1967*	*Oct-1967*
46470			12A	Carlisle (Kingmoor)	*Jul-1951*	*May-1967*	*Oct-1967*
46486			10A	Carnforth	*Nov-1951*	*May-1967*	*Sep-1967*
46522			10A	Carnforth	*Mar-1953*	*May-1967*	*Feb-1968*
Total		5					
Stanier 8F 2-8-0 "Big Eight" 1935							
48393			10D	Lostock Hall	*Apr-1945*	*Aug-1968*	*Dec-1968*
48400			10A	Carnforth (ex 10F)	*Jun-1943*	*Aug-1968*	*Dec-1968*
48451			10A	Carnforth (ex 10F)	*Sep-1944*	*May-1968*	*Sep-1968*
48666			10D	Lostock Hall	*Apr-1944*	*Aug-1968*	*Dec-1968*
48730			10D	Lostock Hall	*Sep-1945*	*Aug-1968*	*Jan-1969*
Total		5					
			Home shed		**Built**	**Withdrawn**	**Scrap**
BR Standard 7P6F 4-6-2 "Britannia" Derby 1951							
70012	"John of Gaunt"		12A	Carlisle (Kingmoor)	*May-1951*	*Dec-1967*	*Apr-1968*
70014	"Iron Duke"		12A	Carlisle (Kingmoor)	*Jun-1951*	*Dec-1967*	*Apr-1968*
70029	"Shooting Star"		12A	Carlisle (Kingmoor)	*Nov-1952*	*Oct-1967*	*Mar-1968*
70051	"Firth of Forth"		12A	Carlisle (Kingmoor)	*Aug-1954*	*Dec-1967*	*Mar-1968*
Total		4					
BR Standard 4MT 4-6-0 Brighton 1951							
75019			12E	Tebay (ex 10A)	*Mar-1952*	*Aug-1968*	*Nov-1968*
75027			12E	Tebay (ex 10A)	*May-1954*	*Aug-1968*	*saved*
Total		2					
On Shed		26					
Withdrawn		8					
Home Locos		0 Home Area			16 Visitors		10
Shed	12A		14 12E		2		
Distribution:-	10A		4 10D		3 10F		3
Steam classes							
on View		6					
Steam Origin		LMS	20 BR		6		
Shed Highlight		all the Britannias					
Steam	*Sep-50*	87	*Mar-59*	103	*Apr-65*	22	
Allocation					*Jun-67*	0	
					Closed to Steam:-		*Dec-66*

Review of 12B Carlisle Upperby Fast Forward 3rd June 1967

Two years later and a strictly limited number of steam classes remained. Hard working and reliable "Black Fives" and "Big Eights" combined with more modern designs including the very well respected "Britannias" which had been brilliant successes since their reallocation to the LMR in the mid 60's. Three of the steam locos had also been on shed on July 31st 1965.

On we go

After our interesting tour of 12B we returned to the Locospotter's Haven - Upperby Bridge. The bridge was in a tremendous position and we could see the Leeds line, the main line south to Preston and Crewe, and a line to Kingmoor Yard (avoiding the station) together with the Workington branch line. 12B Carlisle Upperby was a hop, skip and a jump away. This was to be our base camp until 16.35 when we were due to leave for Workington.

At the start of the day Mike Thurlow, Neil Woodcock, Derek Newton, David Archibald, Graham Strachan and Andrew Forsyth were all at the haven. Throughout the day they went out in pilgrimages to 12A Carlisle Kingmoor shed. I had already informed D.S. that we were going to Kingmoor after we returned from visiting 12D Workington.

Derek Newton and David Archibald came back with the tale that they had been stopped by a railway cop and an Alsatian. Two other twits had ran and were expertly caught by the four legged monster and as a result were "booked" by the cop. Luckily for Derek and David they had finished the shed and told the cop that the shedmaster had told them that they could not go round and were now leaving. The gullible fellow believed their story and let them go. Nothing daunted Graham and Andrew decided to have a go and left the Haven. Graham and Andrew were away for so long that we came to the conclusion that they had been caught and were now in the clink. After a snap count of the haven's finances we found that we could not afford bail for them. But, wonders after we had given up even watching for them they finally arrived back. Their simple story was that they got round the shed OK and were just plain late.

From the time that we left Upperby until about 2 p.m. we were blessed with frequent showers of rain although mostly of short duration. There was a handy disused railway bridge for shelter though. Dinner had been none too exotic for me - rolls, a flask of coffee, fruit pies and packet of College Creams. That was to do till the evening too. During the afternoon I had reason to interrogate a London trainspotter. He informed me that Nine Elms was as hard as I had heard to get round. He explained a sneak entrance to me through some timber yard. It could come into operation the next day at Nine Elms. If I didn't forget it!

Our stay at the haven (before we left for Workington) brought the following fabulous list of engines into view.

CARLISLE UPPERBY - THE BRIDGE						
		Home shed		Built	Withdrawn	Scrap
Diesels						
BR Sulzer "Peak" Type 4 1Co-Co1 1959						
D 20		55A	Leeds Holbeck	*Feb-1961*		
D 27		55A	Leeds Holbeck	*Apr-1961*		
Total	2					
English Electric Type 4 1Co-Co1 1958						
D 213	"Andania"	5A	Crewe Diesel	*Jun-1959*		
D 218	"Carmania"	9A	Longsight	*Jul-1959*		
D 221	"Ivernia"	9A	Longsight	*Jul-1959*		
D 228	"Samaria"	9A	Longsight	*Aug-1959*		
D 279		52A	Gateshead	*Jun-1960*		
D 307		1B	Camden	*Oct-1960*		
D 317		12B	Carlisle Upperby	*Feb-1961*		
D 318		5A	Crewe Diesel	*Feb-1961*		
D 323		1E	Bletchley	*May-1961*		
D 384		1B	Camden	*Mar-1962*		
Total	10					

CARLISLE UPPERBY - THE BRIDGE (continued)

		Home shed		Built	Withdrawn	Scrap
Brush Type 4 Co-Co 1962						
D1837		5A	Crewe Diesel	*May-1965*		
D1844		5A	Crewe Diesel	*May-1965*		
D1847		5A	Crewe Diesel	*Jun-1965*		
D1850		5A	Crewe Diesel	*Jun-1965*		
D1853		5A	Crewe Diesel	*Jun-1965*		
D1854		5A	Crewe Diesel	*Jul-1965*		
D1855		5A	Crewe Diesel	*Jul-1965*		
Total	7					
BR Sulzer Type 2 Bo-Bo 1958						
D5150		52A	Gateshead	*Feb-1961*		
D5179		52A	Gateshead	*Feb-1963*		
D5209		ML	Derby Division	*Jun-1962*		
D5228		ML	Derby Division	*Sep-1963*		
Total	4					
Steam						
Ivatt 2MT 2-6-2T 1946						
41207		12B	Carlisle Upperby (ex6D)	*Dec-1946*	*Nov-1966*	*Mar-1967*
41222		12B	Carlisle Upperby	*Sep-1948*	*Dec-1966*	*Sep-1967*
Total	2					
Ivatt 4MT 2-6-0 1947						
43040		12A	Carlisle Kingmoor	*Jul-1949*	*Dec-1966*	*Mar-1967*
43049		12A	Carlisle Kingmoor	*Nov-1949*	*Aug-1967*	*Dec-1967*
Total	2					
Stanier 5MT 4-6-0 "Black Five" 1934						
44658		8B	Warrington	*May-1949*	*Nov-1967*	*Mar-1968*
44662		55A	Leeds Holbeck	*Jun-1949*	*Oct-1967*	*Mar-1968*
44675		10C	Fleetwood	*Mar-1950*	*Sep-1967*	*Feb-1968*
44696		9D	Newton Heath	*Dec-1950*	*May-1967*	*Feb-1968*
44715		5B	Crewe South(ex 1F)	*Nov-1948*	*Jan-1968*	*Apr-1968*
44765		5B	Crewe South(ex 5A)	*Dec-1947*	*Sep-1967*	*Mar-1968*
44767		12A	Carlisle Kingmoor	*Dec-1947*	*Dec-1967*	*saved*
44878		12A	Carlisle Kingmoor	*May-1945*	*Jul-1968*	*Feb-1969*
44896		55C	Farnley Junction	*Sep-1945*	*Sep-1967*	*May-1968*
44898		12A	Carlisle Kingmoor	*Sep-1945*	*Aug-1967*	*Mar-1968*
44937		12B	Carlisle Upperby	*Nov-1945*	*May-1967*	*Nov-1967*
45015		8A	Edge Hill	*Apr-1935*	*Sep-1967*	*Feb-1968*
45018		12A	Carlisle Kingmoor	*May-1935*	*Dec-1966*	*Jun-1967*
45028		12A	Carlisle Kingmoor	*Sep-1934*	*Mar-1967*	*Nov-1967*
45081		12B	Carlisle Upperby	*Mar-1935*	*Nov-1965*	*Mar-1966*
45105		12A	Carlisle Kingmoor	*May-1935*	*Oct-1966*	*Feb-1967*
45212		10A	Carnforth(ex8C)	*Nov-1935*	*Aug-1968*	*saved*
45228		12A	Carlisle Kingmoor	*Aug-1936*	*Mar-1967*	*Dec-1967*
45254		12A	Carlisle Kingmoor	*Sep-1936*	*May-1968*	*Aug-1968*
45259		12A	Carlisle Kingmoor	*Oct-1936*	*Dec-1967*	*Apr-1968*
45388		8C	Speke Junction	*Jul-1937*	*Aug-1968*	*May-1969*
45399		10A	Carnforth	*Aug-1937*	*Dec-1966*	*Jun-1967*
Total	22					
Stanier 6P5F 4-6-0 "Jubilee" 1934						
45626	"Seychelles"	55A	Leeds Holbeck	*Nov-1934*	*Nov-1965*	*Jan-1966*
45660	"Rooke"	55A	Leeds Holbeck	*Dec-1934*	*Jun-1966*	*Oct-1966*
45697	"Achilles"	55A	Leeds Holbeck	*Apr-1936*	*Sep-1967*	*May-1968*
Total	3					
Stanier 7P 4-6-0 "Royal Scot" 1943 rebuild of Fowler 1927						
46115	"Scots Guardsman"	12A	Carlisle Kingmoor	*Sep-1927*	*Dec-1965*	*saved*
Total	1					
2MT 2-6-0 Ivatt 1946						
46485		12D	Workington(ex9D)	*Nov-1951*	*Aug-1967*	*May-1968*
Total	1					

7P6F "Britannia" 1951 BR 4-6-2 Derby						
70008	"Black Prince"	12A	Carlisle Kingmoor	*Apr-1951*	*Jan-1967*	*Jun-1967*
70018	"Flying Dutchman"	5B	Crewe South(ex 5A)	*Jun-1951*	*Dec-1966*	*Jun-1967*
70032	"Tennyson"	12B	Carlisle Upperby	*Nov-1952*	*Sep-1967*	*Mar-1968*
70045	"Lord Rowallan"	6J	Holyhead(ex2B)	*Jun-1954*	*Dec-1967*	*Mar-1968*
Total	4					
BR Standard 5MT 4-6-0 Doncaster 1951						
73124		67A	Corkerhill	*Feb-1956*	*Dec-1965*	*Mar-1966*
Total	1					
BR Standard 9F 2-10-0 Brighton 1954						
92009		12A	Carlisle Kingmoor	*Mar-1954*	*Mar-1968*	*Jul-1968*
92161		12A	Carlisle Kingmoor(ex9D)	*Dec-1957*	*Dec-1966*	*May-1967*
92208	*double chimney*	12A	Carlisle Kingmoor	*Jun-1959*	*Oct-1967*	*Feb-1968*
Total	3					

On View	62	**Kops**	19	
Steam	39	**Diesels**	23	
Withdrawn	0			

		Home Area			23	**Visitors**		39
Shed	12A		16	12B	6	12D		1
Distribution:-	1B		2	1E	1			
	5A		9	5B	3			
	6J		1					
	8A		1	8B	1	8C		1
	9A		3	9D	1			
	10A		2	10C	1			
	ML		2					
	52A		3	55A	6	55C		1
	67A		1					

Steam classes on view		9		
Steam Origin	LMS	31	BR	8
Highlight:-	the three 55A Holbeck "Jubilees"			
	and "Royal Scot" 46115 "Scots Guardsman"			

Stanier 6P5F Jubilee 45697 "Achilles" arrives from the Leeds area on 31/7/1965
Copyright Reg Parsons

For most of the morning Mike Thurlow had been raving to me about the fab engines that hauled for The Railway Correspondence and Travel Society (R.C.T.S) specials. Neil Woodcock begged to differ and said BR liked to shove a diesel on their specials. The argument raged all morning and began to peter out in the afternoon because nobody had seen an R.C.T.S. special to put their two theories to the test.

About two o'clock to a tumultuous reception of cheers a rather grimy but very, very welcome "Jubilee" 45660 "Rooke" emerged at the head of an R.C.T.S. special from the Leeds area.

Appropriately Neil was the only person not to kop her and I congratulated Mike on "his" R.C.T.S. special providing easily my best kop of the day. David Archibald by this time was a near hospital case of hysteria having cheered one kop too many.

Steamwise it could be argued that they day had been a little disappointing. The Trades specials are normally almost solely in the hands of steam. The previous year Coronations and Jubilees were much in evidence but this year there were no Coronations (all withdrawn) and only 3 Jubilees on specials (all on the Leeds line) - and only one had been seen on Upperby. The Black Fives" this year although numerous were nothing startling either. I only kopped four from other areas.

Things ain't what they used to be!

- - - - - - - - - - - - - - - - - - -

At about 16.15 we said tatti bye to the inhabitants of the haven and said that we hoped we would be back in time to see them off on their homeward train. Graham gave me his camera after he had taken out his spool and I put a fresh one in, ready for the exciting week ahead. David Archibald gave me some parting words of advice. The bucket to Workington will be hot, stuffy, packed and you will probably have to sit next to a fat woman (as he had to on a previous trip). He was not certain if the bucket had a loo or not. So D.S. and I left for the station.

At Carlisle station we stumped up 9/- (45p) a trifle zoombala even for a day return to Workington. This worked out at half the ordinary single rate though. Our LMR Railrover was not in operation yet. After circumnavigating the main platform looking for hidden (non-existent) locos we finally decided to get on the bucket at 16.30. Five minutes before blast off time, a horrifying sight met our eyes. People, people everywhere and not a seat to spare. David Archibald was right. Wish we had been quicker and nabbed a seat. But what's this? Someone had dumped his cases on a double seat. Look irate D.S. and sit on his luggage. That's done it here he comes to move it. Ta mister! We got the last seats on the bucket, only mugs stand!

Our bucket driver finally decided to move the bucket at 16.40 - five minutes late. As we left the station "Royal Scot" 46115 "Scots Guardsman" was waiting to enter with one of the last of the specials. Apart from that all seemed quiet. In fact after 1 p.m. the line had been pretty quiet. We then left the main line and took the Workington branch.

		Schedule	Actual	Miles
Depart	CARLISLE	16.35	16.40	0
Arrive	WORKINGTON MAIN	17.25	17.29	33¼

The journey was about as boring as it could be and I kept myself interested by having a look at some of the local industrial plants. I was promised by a boy (in the know) that I was to expect a Midland 0-6-0 in Wigton Yard. Wigton yard came but the 0-6-0 must have been having a tea break, on strike and took the day off. Nothing on four wheels could be seen anywhere. Aspatria was also passed without incident. Reaching the West Coast I half expected Workington to appear but first Maryport and then Flimby four minutes later before we finally arrived four minutes late at 17.29.

By this time it has turned into a pleasant evening which helped to cheer up the surroundings. The ticket collector grabbed our tickets and carefully inserted them in their allocated place in the pile. "The Collector" was an appropriate name for him.

D.S. and I had an hour in Workington. Plenty time to visit the shed which was located on the east side of the line south of the station. A short five minutes walk. We went across the station yard and turned right into a narrow street (the middle of three turnings) and went right again into a short cul-de-sac and continued along a cinder path. The shed entrance was a gate on the right-hand side at the end of it.

D.S. on seeing the shed could not dream of doing anything official and impetuously "broke" into the shed yard by jumping over a rickety old fence. I, although preferring legal entrances, reluctantly followed. Workington had its own special motive power that rarely ventured outside the local area. Midland 0-6-0's made up the bulk of their largely antiquated force. Workington shed was almost deserted except for the engines. About the only person we saw was steaming up the 0-6-0T "Jinty" 47612. He posed while we took a photograph of her. We also took photographs of a condemned 0-6-0 Midland 44536 which was the cleanest of them all. We also photographed "Flying Pig" Mogul 43008 (a more modern loco). Three Co-Bo's were on shed and D.S. wanted to chase after a fourth which was about half a mile down the main line. I persuaded him not to. 46424 was surprisingly seen as my shed-book said it belonged to 8C Speke Junction. A long way off! Unknown to me she had recently been transferred here. I thought that it was really 46436 of Upperby which I needed and had not seen it in Carlisle that day. The number was a bit grubby we reflected but of course when we read of the transfer later we were sure that it really was 46424.

12D WORKINGTON					
		Home shed	Built	Withdrawn	Scrap
Diesels					
BR 0-6-0 Shunter 1953					
D3580		12D	Oct-1958		
Total	1				
Metropolitan Vickers Type 2 Co-Bo 1958					
D5701		12C	Barrow	Aug-1958	Sep-1968
D5710		12C	Barrow	Feb-1959	Dec-1967
D5719		12C	Barrow	Oct-1959	Sep-1968
Total	3				
LMS and BR 0-6-0 Shunter 1945					
12086		12A	Carlisle Kingmoor	Dec-1950	Jul-1969
Total	1				
Steam			Built	Withdrawn	Scrap
Fairburn 4MT 2-6-4T 1945 dev. of Stanier 1935					
42267		12C	Barrow(ex 6H then 6A)	Jan-1947	May-1967	Apr-1968
Total	1				
Ivatt 4MT 2-6-0 1947					
43006		12D		Jan-1948	Mar-1968	May-1968
43008		12D		Jan-1948	Mar-1968	Jun-1968
43122		12D	(ex 9D Newton Heath)	Aug-1951	Mar-1967	Jan-1968
Total	3				
Midland 4F 0-6-0 1924					
44061		12D		Sep-1925	Jun-1965	Oct-1965
44157		12D		Dec-1925	Jul-1965	Nov-1965
44160		12D		Feb-1926	Dec-1965	Mar-1966
44192		12D	(ex 9E)	Jun-1925	Apr-1965	Aug-1965
44200		12C	Barrow	Oct-1925	Jul-1965	Jan-1966
44310		12D	(ex9L then 10G Skipton)	Oct-1926	Feb-1966	May-1966
44356		12D		Jun-1927	Nov-1965	Jan-1966
44451		12A	Carlisle Kingmoor	Feb-1928	Dec-1965	Mar-1966
44462		12D		May-1928	Nov-1965	Feb-1966
44489		12D		Dec-1927	Aug-1965	Nov-1965
44505		12D		Nov-1927	Sep-1965	Dec-1965
44536		12D		Sep-1928	Aug-1965	Dec-1965
44597		12D		Mar-1940	Sep-1965	Jan-1966
Total	13				

		Home shed			Built	Withdrawn	Scrap
Stanier 5MT 4-6-0 "Black Five" 1934							
44904		10A	Carnforth		*Oct-1945*	*Dec-1965*	*Apr-1966*
45027		10A	Carnforth (ex1E)		*Sep-1934*	*May-1968*	*Oct-1968*
45203		9D	Newton Heath		*Nov-1935*	*Jun-1968*	*Feb-1969*
Total	3						
Ivatt 2MT 2-6-2T 1946							
46424		12D	(ex 8C Speke Junction)		*Nov-1948*	*Dec-1966*	*May-1967*
46488		12D			*Nov-1951*	*Jun-1965*	*Oct-1965*
46491		12D			*Dec-1951*	*May-1967*	*Nov-1967*
Total	3						
Midland 3F "Jinty" 0-6-0T 1924 dev. of Johnson 1899 design							
47279		12D			*Aug-1924*	*Dec-1966*	*saved*
47612		12D			*Oct-1928*	*Dec-1966*	*Dec-1967*
47676		12D			*Aug-1931*	*Aug-1965*	*Nov-1965*
Total	3						
Stanier 8F 2-8-0 "Big Eight" 1935							
48774		8C	Speke Junction		*Aug-1940*	*Jul-1965*	*Apr-1966*
Total	1						

On Shed	32	**Kops**	21				
Steam	27	**Diesels**	5				
Withdrawn	6						

Home Locos		21	**Home Area**		7	**Visitors**	4
Shed	**12D**		21	**12A**		2 **12C**	5
Distribution:-	**8C**	1					
	9D	1					
	10A	2					
Steam classes on view		7					
Steam Origin		**LMS**		27			
Shed Highlight:-		**The Midland 4F 0-6-0's**					

Steam	*Sep-50*	27	*Mar-59*	31	*Apr-65*	23	*Jul-65*	26
Allocation					*Closed to Steam:-*		*Jan-68*	
Home Steam	*(excluding withdrawn locos)*							
On/Off Shed	*On Shed*	16	*Off Shed*	10	*% On Shed*	62%		
Not on Shed								
4MT 2-6-0 1947					43017	43025	43073	3
4F 0-6-0 1911						43953	43964	2
4F 0-6-0 1924						44346	44449	2
2MT 2-6-2T						46435	46485	2
"Jinty"							47473	1
							total	10
		saw elsewhere on the tour			5			

Review and Appraisal of 12D Workington

The shed was on the west side of the main line north of the station. Walking time was 5 minute from Workington Station.

It worked out at about 4½d (2p) a kop for us but a very worthwhile visit.

42267 of 12C Barrow (ex 6A Chester Midland) had a bit of a history for me. A few years ago she belonged to the Scottish Region. Likewise "Big Eight" 48774 also on shed used to belong to 66A Polmadie. Scotland had three "Big Eights" 48773-5 for many years. Their small number in Scotland led to their withdrawl. 48774 had been withdrawn from Polmadie, resuscitated, transferred to 8C Speke and now again sadly finally withdrawn.

13 antiquated but very welcome Midland 4F 0-6-0's were on shed. 44310 had finally arrived at Workington after being first transferred from 9L Buxton in Derbyshire to 10G Skipton in Yorkshire and then on to Workington. 44192 had been withdrawn in April at the time of her

transfer from 9E Trafford Park. She must have been withdrawn immediately on inspection at arrival at Workington.

These diabolical Co-Bo's were very unwelcome to me as at least four of them used to clutter up Polmadie every Sunday when shedded at Derby. They used to muck about on the "Condor" and other long distance freights. Naturally I soon completed the class after three years of frequent visits to 66A Polmadie in Glasgow. Co-Bo less D.S. was delighted, however, and had been upset that we would not be visiting 12C Barrow where they were all 20 of this small diesel class were now shedded. D5710 was the last one I needed at the time and I saw her again on Workington.

As expected most (16 out of 26) of 12D's steam allocation was on shed and we were to see five of the absent ten around the Carlisle area today.

On we go

While waiting for our bucket back to Carlisle I finished off the remainder of my food and drink (coffee namely)!

The bucket arrived from Whitehaven and we left Workington 4 minutes late at 18.39.

		Schedule	Actual	Miles
Depart	WORKINGTON MAIN	18.35	18.39	0
Arrive	CARLISLE	19.30	19.30	33¼
	Do 12A Carlisle Kingmoor			

Our bucket was invaded by a bunch of rockers at Maryport and we felt a bit uneasy until they finally stopped prancing around and sat down.

D.S. informed me of a quickly spreading blue mark on my anorak and I found my two blue BIC pens overflowing as a result of the sultry evening. I dumped them in an ash-tray and now I had only my fabulous Conway Stewart Black Fybriter, a green BIC in my grip and a couple of pencils. I took this timely reminder to get cleaned up in the loo and remove the blue smudges from my anorak as quickly as possible.

As I watched the fields go past I got a frightful feeling that this tour was a complete waste of money. "I wanna go home ", I said inwardly. After seeing the pleasant shed at 12D Workington I thought that I had seen enough, would see no better and wanted to get the hell out of there. To blazes with the Railrover I want to go home. With these sad thoughts I saw that we were entering Carlisle Station but D.S. seemed to be happy enough.

We had caught up some time and arrived at the station on time at 19.30. Our happy band of Scottish cavaliers (Mike, Neil, Derek, David, Andrew and Graham) were due to leave at 19.37 for Edinburgh. We were just in time to see them off. I thanked Graham again for his camera. I think they all wished to go with us (especially Neil who I think regretted not going now). I felt like going home but I did not say so.

I found out that we did not miss anything much while at Workington. Of that I was glad.
I bade our friends a goodbye at 19.40, and now D.S. and I were left for one week on the LMR all alone!!! HELP!!

We then chased around the station to about 8 p.m. noting the following.

			Home shed		Built	Withdrawn	Scrap
Diesels							
English Electric Type 4 1-Co-Co1 1958							
D 292		12A	Carlisle Kingmoor		Sep-1960		
Total	1						
Brush Type 4 Co-Co 1962							
D1631		5A	Crewe Diesel		Oct-1964		
D1635		5A	Crewe Diesel		Nov-1964		
D1841		5A	Crewe Diesel		May-1965		
D1845		5A	Crewe Diesel		May-1965		
Total	4						
Steam					Built	Withdrawn	Scrap
Stanier 5MT 4-6-0 "Black Five" 1934							
44935		8B	Warrington		Oct-1945	Oct-1966	Apr-1967
45105		12A	Carlisle Kingmoor		May-1935	Oct-1966	Feb-1967
45112		12A	Carlisle Kingmoor		Jun-1935	Oct-1966	Jun-1967
45120		12A	Carlisle Kingmoor		Jun-1935	Jun-1967	Nov-1967
Total	4						
BR Standard 7P6F 4-6-2 "Britannia" Derby 1951							
70013	"Oliver Cromwell"	12B	Carlisle Upperby		May-1951	Aug-1968	saved
70036	"Boadicea"	12A	Carlisle Kingmoor		Dec-1952	Oct-1966	Feb-1967
70039	"Sir Christopher Wren"	12A	Carlisle Kingmoor		Feb-1953	Sep-1967	Feb-1968
Total	3						

CARLISLE STATION EVENING

On Station	12		Kops	0	
Steam	7		Diesels	5	
		Home Area		7	Visitors	5
Shed	12A	6	12B	1	
Distribution:-	5A	4	8B	1	
Steam classes on view		2			
Steam Origin	LMS		4 BR	3	

I then informed D.S. that it was about time for us to visit 12A Kingmoor. We left the station by Court Square and boarded a (C4 St Ann's) bus in English Street.

The bus journey gave me a bit of a scare as I thought we had missed Etterby Road but we had not. We got off when we saw a mutilated sign bearing the name "Erby Road". From the right-hand side of the road we went down a cinder path to the shed. We were now in the twilight of the evening and hoped the shedmaster and railway cops had pooped off to sleep. We ran across the shed yard and disappeared behind the dead line. I did not wish to pass the shedmaster's office until we had finished the shed.

After noting the sad decaying sign of two Royal Scots and 1 Jubilee - all condemned -the shedmaster at the other side of the yard did in fact see us but did not bother to chuck us out. Seeing two such genuine enthusiasts I suspect he allowed us to continue. The shed was packed and it took us some considerable time to go round it.

12A CARLISLE KINGMOOR

		Home shed		Built	Withdrawn	Scrap
Diesels						
BR Sulzer "Peak" Type 4 1Co-Co1 1959						
D 28		55A	Leeds Holbeck	*May-1961*		
Total	1					
BR 0-6-0 Shunter 1953						
D3171		12A		*Sep-1955*		
D3172		12A		*Sep-1955*		
Total	2					
BR Sulzer Type 2 Bo-Bo 1958						
D5025		1A	Willesden	*Oct-1959*		
Total	1					
English Electric Type 1 Bo-Bo 1957						
D8113		66A	Polmadie	*Feb-1962*		
D8118		66A	Polmadie	*Mar-1962*		
Total	2					
Clayton Type 1 Bo-Bo 1962						
D8596	*pass shed*	52A	Gateshead	*Jul-1964*	*Dec-1968*	
D8603	*pass shed*	52A	Gateshead	*Sep-1964*	*Oct-1971*	
Total	2					
LMS and BR 0-6-0 Shunter 1945						
12079		12A		*Nov-1950*	*Sep-1971*	
12080		12A		*Nov-1950*	*Apr-1971*	
12085		12A		*Dec-1950*	*May-1971*	
Total	3					
Steam				*Built*	*Withdrawn*	*Scrap*
Fairburn 4MT 2-6-4T 1945 dev. of Stanier 1935						
42232		12E	Tebay	*Jun-1946*	*Jan-1966*	*May-1966*
Total	1					
Ivatt 4MT 2-6-0 1947						
43000		12A		*Dec-1947*	*Sep-1967*	*Nov-1967*
43004		12A		*Jan-1948*	*Sep-1967*	*Apr-1968*
43025		12D	Workington	*Jan-1949*	*Sep-1965*	*Jan-1966*
43028		12A		*Mar-1949*	*Nov-1967*	*Feb-1968*
43040		12A		*Jul-1949*	*Dec-1966*	*Mar-1967*
43049		12A		*Nov-1949*	*Aug-1967*	*Dec-1967*
43120		12A	ex 9F Heaton Mersey	*Jul-1951*	*Aug-1967*	*Dec-1967*
43139		12A		*Jul-1951*	*Sep-1967*	*Feb-1968*
Total	8					

Below: - Big Eight 2-8-0 8F 48104 and 2-10-0 9F 92114 at 12A Carlisle Kingmoor on 28/7/1965. Copyright Reg Parsons.

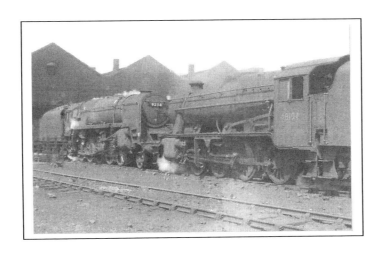

			Home shed		Built	Withdrawn	Scrap
Stanier 5MT 4-6-0 "Black Five" 1934							
44662			55A	Leeds Holbeck	Jun-1949	Oct-1967	Mar-1968
44668			12A		Dec-1949	Apr-1966	Jul-1966
44669			12A		Dec-1949	Oct-1967	Feb-1968
44670			12A		Jan-1950	Jan-1966	Apr-1966
44692			12A		Oct-1950	May-1966	Aug-1966
44724			67C	Ayr (ex 63A)	Apr-1949	Oct-1966	Jan-1967
44727			12A		May-1949	Oct-1967	Feb-1968
44802			12A		Jun-1944	Jun-1968	Oct-1968
44878			12A		May-1945	Jul-1968	Feb-1969
44883			12A		Jun-1945	Jul-1967	Dec-1967
44898			12A		Sep-1945	Sep-1967	Mar-1968
44899			12A		Sep-1945	Jul-1968	Jan-1969
44901	*to Barry Docks*		12A		Oct-1945	Aug-1965	saved
44908			66B	Motherwell	Nov-1945	Jun-1966	May-1967
44935			8B	Warrington	Oct-1945	Oct-1966	Apr-1967
44972			67B	Hurlford	Apr-1946	Nov-1966	Apr-1967
45013			12A		Apr-1935	May-1968	Sep-1968
45018			12A		May-1935	Dec-1966	Jun-1967
45061			12A		Dec-1934	Nov-1967	Mar-1968
45069			8A	Edge Hill	Jan-1935	Jun-1967	Dec-1967
45072			10A	Carnforth	Jun-1935	Sep-1967	Feb-1968
45097			12A		Apr-1935	Jun-1966	Nov-1966
45120			12A		Jun-1935	Jun-1967	Nov-1967
45135			12A		May-1935	Oct-1967	Mar-1968
45156	"Ayrshire Yeomanry"		8A	Edge Hill	Jul-1935	Aug-1968	Dec-1968
45163	*to Barry Docks*		12A		Aug-1935	May-1965	saved
45195			12A		Oct-1935	Jul-1966	Oct-1966
45202			9D	Newton Heath	Oct-1935	Jun-1968	Nov-1968
45217			12A		Nov-1935	Nov-1966	Jun-1967
45228			12A		Aug-1936	Mar-1967	Dec-1967
45235			12A		Aug-1936	Jan-1966	Apr-1966
45236			12A		Aug-1936	Dec-1967	Apr-1968
45253			12A	ex 16F Burton	Sep-1936	Apr-1968	Oct-1968
45254			12A		Sep-1936	May-1968	Aug-1968
45295			12A		Dec-1936	Dec-1967	Apr-1968
45337	*to Barry Docks*		12A		Apr-1937	Feb-1965	saved
45475			63A	Perth	Jun-1943	Sep-1966	Dec-1966
45481			12A		Sep-1943	Sep-1967	Mar-1968
Total	38						
Ivatt 7P 4-6-0 "Patriot" 1947 rebuild of Fowler 1933							
45530	"Sir Frank Ree"		12A		Apr-1933	Dec-1965	Jul-1966
45531	"Sir Frederick Harrison"		12A		Apr-1933	Nov-1965	Mar-1966
Total	2						
Stanier 6P5F 4-6-0 "Jubilee" 1934							
45588	"Kashmir"		12A		Dec-1934	May-1965	Aug-1965
45629	"Sraits Settlements"		12A		Nov-1934	May-1965	Aug-1965
45675	"Hardy"		55A	Leeds Holbeck	Dec-1935	Jun-1967	Nov-1967
45697	"Achilles"		55A	Leeds Holbeck	Apr-1936	Sep-1967	May-1968
45742	"Connaught"		12A		Dec-1936	May-1965	Aug-1965
Total	5						
Stanier 7P 4-6-0 "Royal Scot" 1943 rebuild of Fowler 1927							
46128	"The Lovat Scouts"		12A		Aug-1927	May-1965	Aug-1965
46140	"The King's Royal Rifle Corps"		12A		Oct-1927	Nov-1965	Mar-1966
46160	"Queen Victoria's Riflemen"		12A		Aug-1930	May-1965	Aug-1965
Total	3						

			Home shed		Built	Withdrawn	Scrap
Midland 3F "Jinty" 0-6-0T 1924 dev. of Johnson 1899 design							
47471			12A		*Jan-1928*	*Dec-1966*	*Sep-1967*
47641			12A		*Jan-1929*	*Dec-1966*	*Feb-1968*
47667			12A		*Apr-1931*	*Nov-1966*	*Mar-1967*
Total		3					
Stanier 8F 2-8-0 "Big Eight" 1935							
48158			55A	Leeds Holbeck	*Jan-1943*	*Sep-1967*	*Mar-1968*
Total		1					
Gresley 7P6F 2-6-2 V2 1936							
60813			64A	St. Margarets	*Sep-1937*	*Nov-1966*	*Jan-1967*
60846			64A	St. Margarets	*Feb-1939*	*Oct-1965*	*Jan-1966*
Total		2					
Thompson 5MT 4-6-0 B1 1942							
61350			64A	St. Margarets	*Jul-1949*	*Nov-1966*	*Apr-1967*
Total		1					
BR 7P6F "Britannia" 4-6-2 Derby 1951							
70002	"Geoffrey Chaucer"		12A		*Mar-1951*	*Jan-1967*	*Jun-1967*
70005	"John Milton"		12A		*Apr-1951*	*Jul-1967*	*Jan-1968*
70016	"Ariel"		12A		*Jun-1951*	*Aug-1967*	*Jan-1968*
70038	"Robin Hood"		12A		*Jan-1953*	*Aug-1967*	*Feb-1968*
Total		4					
BR 6P5F "Clan" 4-6-2 Derby 1952							
72006	"Clan Mackenzie"		12A		*Feb-1952*	*Jun-1966*	*Oct-1966*
72007	"Clan Mackintosh"		12A		*Mar-1952*	*Dec-1965*	*Mar-1966*
72009	"Clan Stewart"		12A		*Apr-1952*	*Aug-1965*	*Dec-1965*
Total		3					
BR Standard 4-6-0 1951 5MT Doncaster							
73099			66A	Polmadie	*Dec-1955*	*Oct-1966*	*Jun-1967*
73124			67A	Corkerhill	*Feb-1956*	*Dec-1965*	*Mar-1966*
73130	*Caprotti valved*		9H	Patricroft	*Sep-1956*	*Jan-1967*	*Sep-1967*
Total		3					
BR Standard 9F 2-10-0 Brighton 1954							
92010			12A		*May-1954*	*Apr-1966*	*Jun-1966*
92015			12A		*Sep-1954*	*May-1967*	*Nov-1967*
92017			12A		*Oct-1954*	*Dec-1967*	*Apr-1968*
92052			9D	Newton Heath	*Aug-1955*	*Aug-1967*	*Jan-1968*
92055			8B	Warrington	*Sep-1955*	*Dec-1967*	*Apr-1968*
92076			12A		*Mar-1956*	*Feb-1967*	*Jun-1967*
92114			12A		*Dec-1956*	*Jul-1967*	*Feb-1968*
92161			12A		*Dec-1957*	*Dec-1966*	*May-1967*
92249	*double chimney*		12A		*Dec-1958*	*May-1968*	*Sep-1968*
Total		9					

On Shed		94	**Kops**	16			
Steam		83	**Diesels**	11			
Withdrawn		7					

Home Locos		65 Home Area			2 Visitors		27
Shed	12A		65 12D		1 12E		1
Distribution:-	1A		1 10A		1		
	8A		2 8B		2		
	9D		2 9H		1		
	52A		2 55A		5		
	63A		1 64A		3		
	66A		3 66B		1		
	67A		1 67B		1 67C		1
Steam classes on view		14					
Steam Origin	LMS		61 LNER		3 BR		19
Shed Highlights:-		45156 "Ayrshire Yeomanry"		8B	Warrington		
		45675 "Hardy"		55A	Leeds Holbeck		
		45697 "Achilles"		55A	Leeds Holbeck		

Steam	Sep-50	142	Mar-59	143	Apr-65	119	
Allocation					Jul-65	118	
				Closed to Steam:-		Jan-68	
Home Steam	excluding withdrawn locos						
On/Off Shed	On Shed	53	Off Shed	65	% On Shed	45%	
Not on Shed							
4MT 2-6-0 1946					43023	43121	2
4F 0-6-0 1911						43981	1
4F 0-6-0 1924						44451	1
"Black Fives"	44671	44672	44674	44677	44689	44726	
	44767	44790	44792	44795	44809	44884	
	44886	44887	44900	44902	44903	44986	
	44989	44993	45012	45028	45082	45105	
	45106	45112	45118	45126	45138	45148	
	45185	45210	45259	45293	45363	45364	
					45442	45455	38
"Royal Scot"						46115	1
"Jinty"						47326	1
"Britannias"	70001	70003	70006	70008	70009	70010	
	70033	70035	70036	70037	70039	70040	
						70041	13
"Clan"						72008	1
BR 9F 2-10-0	92009	92012	92019	92110	92130	92208	7
						92233	
						total	65
	saw elsewhere on the tour				27		
	saw on Dec 64 Manchester and Crewe trip				4		
	saw on July 65 Preston area trip				4		
	saw on September 58 Carlisle visit				6		
	saw on June 67 Carlisle visit				10		
	recently withdrawn not on shed or seen elsewhere				2		scrap
				"Britannia"	70007		Jul-65
				"Clan"	72005		Jul-65

("Black Five" 45491 also recently withdrawn but was to be seen at Barry Docks fast forward and also seen at 12A Carlisle Kingmoor rewind September 1958).

Midland 3F 0-6-0 "Jinties" 47641 and 47667 at 12A Carlisle Kingmoor on 31/7/1965 Copyright Reg Parsons

Review and Appraisal of 12A Carlisle Kingmoor

The shed was on the east side of the main line about 1½ miles north of Carlisle Station. Walking time was 45 minutes from Carlisle Station.

When we came to the second dead line of the shed I had almost given up hope of seeing 45337 (my last "Black Five" that I needed from the Carlisle Area). I was very, very elated and happy to see her there. 45337 was transferred from 8M Southport to Carlisle and almost immediately withdrawn. I was very lucky that she had not been sent to the breakers as she had been withdrawn several months before.

Since the merciless hacking up of the Jubilees I had become rather fond of the "Black Fives" and no fewer than 38 were on shed. Of these 10 were visitors. The most interesting "Black Five" was one of the few named 45156 "Ayrshire Yeomanry" of 8A Edge Hill. Only two English based Black 5's were named and here was one of them. The rest of the enthusiasts from Musselburgh had gone home having visited Kingmoor but not having seen her this day. In my visit to Lancashire in early July I had seen her in Preston Station previously but it was nice to see her again.

Carlisle Kingmoor now had no Jubilees of her own. Three were lying condemned. Only two were in steam (both in on specials from the Leeds Area). The Patriots were still in steam but reaching the twilight of their careers and would be sadly both be withdrawn by the end of the year. Of 12A's four Royal Scots two were lying condemned, 46140 was still in service and 46115 was seen a few hours ago at Carlisle station. Sadly again the remaining two "Royal Scots" would be withdrawn by the end of the year. Carlisle had a few months ago lost all her Big Eights and a Holbeck one was the only one of the class represented. It seemed to me that Carlisle had swapped her Big Eights for Standard 9F 2-10-0's in return. There were nine on shed.

70016 "Ariel" (although not withdrawn) was lying a terrible state in the first dead line. Surprisingly she escaped from the dead line via perhaps an overhaul at Crewe Works and she lasted out until finally withdrawn in August 1967. Alongside "Ariel" were the two condemned Royal Scots and 45742 "Connaught" (also withdrawn). I was desperate to get a picture of one of the condemned Royal Scots but by now the light was a bit poor. D.S. thought out an ingenious method of obtaining a first class picture by mounting his camera on some handy bricks and he took a minute long exposure of 46128 "The Lovat Scouts" (the one in the better condition of the two). The whole operation had to be done very skilfully by him because if the camera was moved the slightest bit the proverbial "crap" picture would result. A remarkable 83 steam locos were on shed of which seven had been withdrawn. There were many visitors as only 53 (45%) of 12A Kingmoor's steam allocation was on shed.

Sadly all withdrawn: - Jubilee 4-6-0 6P5F 45742 "Connaught", Royal Scots 4-6-0 7P 46128 "The Lovat Scouts", 46160 "Queen Victoria's Riflemen" and 2-6-0 4MT 43028 on 12A Kingmoor on 31/7/65. Copyright Reg Parsons.

Black Five 4-6-0 5MT 44677 and 9F 2-10-0 92233 with in the background Jubilee 4-6-0 6P5F 45742 "Connaught", Royal Scots 4-6-0 7P 46128 "The Lovat Scouts" and 46160 "Queen Victoria's Riflemen" on 12A Kingmoor on 31/7/65. Copyright Reg Parsons.

Rewind to 12A Carlisle Kingmoor Sunday 7th September 1958

12A CARLISLE KINGMOOR						
		REWIND 7th SEPTEMBER 1958				
		Home shed		Built	Withdrawn	Scrap
Steam						
Midland 2P 4-4-0 1928						
40602		12A		Nov-1928	Oct-1961	Aug-1963
40613		12A		Oct-1929	Oct-1961	Jun-1963
40615		12A		Nov-1929	Oct-1961	Sep-1963
40651		12A		Sep-1931	Nov-1961	Jul-1963
Total	4					
Stanier 4MT 2-6-4T 1935 dev of Fowler 1927						
42440		12A		May-1936	Oct-1963	May-1964
Total	1					
Hughes/Fowler 5MT 2-6-0 "Crab" 1926						
42748		12A		May-1927	Oct-1964	Mar-1965
42757		12A		Jul-1927	Jun-1964	Oct-1964
42793		12A		Oct-1927	Dec-1964	Mar-1965
42831		12A		May-1930	Dec-1965	Mar-1966
42833		12A		May-1930	Dec-1962	Nov-1963
42836		12A		Jul-1930	Dec-1962	Nov-1963
42837		12A		Jul-1930	Dec-1962	Nov-1963
42876		12A		May-1930	Dec-1962	Nov-1963
42877		12A		May-1930	Dec-1962	Sep-1963
42881		12A		Jun-1930	Nov-1962	Dec-1962
42882		12A		Jun-1930	Dec-1962	Nov-1963
42883		12A		Jun-1930	Dec-1962	Nov-1963
42884		12A		Jun-1930	Dec-1962	Nov-1963
42905		12A		Sep-1930	Jul-1965	Feb-1966
42906		12A		Sep-1930	Dec-1962	Oct-1963
42907		12A		Sep-1930	Oct-1964	Mar-1965
Total	16					
Johnson Midland 3F 0-6-0 1885						
43241		12A		Dec-1890	Jul-1959	Jul-1960
43301		12A		Oct-1891	Nov-1958	Jun-1959
43514		12A		Jan-1897	Oct-1962	May-1963
43622		12A		Jan-1899	Dec-1959	Nov-1962
43678		12A		May-1901	Dec-1959	Feb-1960
Total	5					

12A CARLISLE KINGMOOR					
REWIND 7th SEPTEMBER 1958					
	Home shed		**Built**	**Withdrawn**	**Scrap**
Fowler Midland 4F 0-6-0 1911					
43868		12A	Dec-1918	Nov-1960	Feb-1961
43922		12A	Dec-1920	Jul-1961	Aug-1961
44008		12A	Dec-1921	Sep-1962	Nov-1962
44009		12A	Dec-1921	Jun-1964	Dec-1964
Total	*4*				
Midland 4F 0-6-0 1924					
44181		12A	Feb-1925	Aug-1965	Jan-1966
44183		12A	Mar-1925	Oct-1963	Mar-1964
44315		12A	Dec-1927	May-1964	Oct-1964
44324		12A	Jan-1928	Nov-1961	Mar-1962
Total	*4*				
Stanier 5MT 4-6-0 "Black Five" 1934					
44669		12A	Dec-1949	Oct-1967	Feb-1968
44670		12A	Jan-1950	Jan-1966	Apr-1966
44671		12A	Feb-1950	Feb-1967	Jun-1967
44672		12A	Feb-1950	Mar-1968	Jun-1968
44673		12A	Feb-1950	May-1965	Aug-1965
44676		12A	Apr-1950	Jul-1964	Jul-1964
44726		12A	May-1949	Oct-1966	May-1967
44727		12A	May-1949	Oct-1967	Feb-1968
44790		12A	Jun-1947	Mar-1967	Nov-1967
44792		12A	Jul-1947	Sep-1967	Feb-1968
44877		12A	Apr-1945	Aug-1968	Dec-1968
44878		12A	May-1945	Jul-1968	Feb-1969
44882		12A	Jun-1945	Jul-1967	Dec-1967
44886		12A	Jul-1945	Oct-1967	Mar-1968
44898		12A	Sep-1945	Oct-1967	Mar-1968
44902		12A	Oct-1945	Oct-1967	Mar-1968
44903		12A	Oct-1945	Apr-1968	Oct-1968
44958		12A	May-1946	Mar-1967	Aug-1967
44993		12A	Jan-1947	Dec-1967	Apr-1968
45012		12A	Apr-1935	Oct-1966	Mar-1967
45013		12A	Apr-1935	May-1968	Sep-1968
45082		12A	Mar-1935	Jul-1966	Oct-1966
45100		12A	May-1935	Oct-1963	Oct-1963
45112		12A	Jun-1935	Oct-1966	Jun-1967
45118		12A	Jun-1935	Oct-1966	Mar-1967
45120		12A	Jun-1935	Jun-1967	Nov-1967
45122		12A	Jun-1935	Apr-1964	Apr-1964
45126		12A	May-1935	May-1967	Nov-1967
45138		12A	Jun-1935	Sep-1966	Mar-1967
45163	*to Barry Docks*	12A	Aug-1935	May-1965	saved
45330		12A	Mar-1937	Aug-1968	Dec-1968
45363		12A	Jun-1937	Oct-1967	Mar-1968
45466		12A	Nov-1938	Feb-1967	May-1967
45481		12A	Sep-1943	Sep-1967	Mar-1968
45491	*to Barry Docks*	12A	Dec-1943	Jul-1965	saved
Total	*35*				
Stanier 6P5F 4-6-0 "Jubilee" 1934					
45640	"Frobisher"	12A	Dec-1934	Mar-1964	Jan-1965
45657	"Tyrwhitt"	12A	Dec-1934	Sep-1964	May-1965
45679	"Armada"	12A	Dec-1935	Dec-1962	Nov-1963
45696	"Arethusa"	12A	Apr-1936	Aug-1964	Jan-1965
45704	"Leviathan"	12A	May-1936	Jan-1965	Apr-1965

		Home shed		Built	Withdrawn	Scrap
Midland 3F "Jinty" 0-6-0T 1924 dev. of Johnson 1899 design						
47332		12A		Jul-1926	May-1962	Aug-1962
47354		12A		Jul-1926	Oct-1964	Jan-1965
47356		12A		Jul-1926	Sep-1962	Dec-1962
47515		12A		May-1928	Jul-1964	Jan-1965
47527		12A		Mar-1928	Mar-1960	Jun-1961
47537		12A		Apr-1928	Sep-1960	Sep-1960
47540		12A		Apr-1928	Apr-1961	May-1961
47667		12A		Apr-1931	Nov-1966	Mar-1967
Total	8					
Stanier 8F 2-8-0 "Big Eight" 1935						
48472		12A		May-1945	May-1966	Aug-1966
48536		12A		Jun-1945	Jan-1967	Jun-1967
48758		12A		Dec-1945	Dec-1967	Mar-1968
Total	3					
McIntosh Caledonian 3F 0-6-0T 1895						
56235		12A		Dec-1895	Nov-1959	Mar-1960
56316		12A		Oct-1907	Oct-1959	Apr-1960
56332		12A		Oct-1910	Oct-1959	Apr-1960
56333		12A		Oct-1910	Oct-1959	Nov-1959
56340		12A		Apr-1911	Oct-1959	Oct-1959
56373		12A		May-1922	Oct-1959	Apr-1960
56374		12A		May-1922	Oct-1959	Apr-1960
Total	7					
Pickersgill Caledonian 3F 0-6-0 1918						
57653		12A		Jul-1919	Jan-1961	May-1963
Total	1					
BR 6P5F "Clan" 4-6-2 Derby 1952						
72005	"Clan Macgregor"	12A		Feb-1952	May-1965	Jul-1965
72006	"Clan Mackenzie"	12A		Feb-1952	Jun-1966	Oct-1966
72007	"Clan Mackintosh"	12A		Mar-1952	Dec-1965	Mar-1966
72008	"Clan Macleod"	12A		Mar-1952	Apr-1966	Jun-1966
72009	"Clan Stewart"	12A		Apr-1952	Aug-1965	Dec-1965
Total	5					
WD 8F 2-8-0 "Austerity" Riddles 1943						
90464		12A		May-1944	Mar-1964	Apr-1964
Total	1					
WD 8F 2-10-0 "Austerity" Riddles 1943						
90763		12A		Jul-1945	Dec-1962	Nov-1963
WD601		12A		Aug-1945	Feb-1959	1967
Total	2					
Steam	108					
Steam classes on view		15				
Steam Origin		LMS	100 BR		5 WD	3
Shed Highlights:-		the	"Jubilees"			

12A CARLISLE KINGMOOR (continued)
REWIND 7th SEPTEMBER 1958

Home Steam	excluding withdrawn locos					
On/Off Shed	On Shed	108 Off Shed		45 % On Shed	71%	
Not on Shed						
Stanier 4MT 2-6-4T 1935					42542	1
"Crabs"	42720	42751	42752	42804	42830	
	42832	42834	42835	42875	42899	10
4F 0-6-0 1911				43902	43973	2
"Black Fives"	44668	44674	44675	44725	44795	
	44883	44884	44899	44900	44901	
	45018	45081	45083	45281	45334	17
				45364	45455	
"Jubilees"	45691	45697	45716	45718	45724	6
					45731	
"Jinties"			47342	47349	47358	3
"Big Eights"	48321	48464	48612	48708	48756	5
WD 8F 2-8-0 1943					90170	1
						45

	saw on shed Jul 65	5
	saw elsewhere on the tour	11
	saw on Dec 64 Manchester and Crewe trip	1
	saw on July 65 Preston area trip	1
	saw on June 67 Carlisle visit	1

Review of 12A Carlisle Kingmoor Sunday 7th September 1958

Despite being the "artisan" shed 12 "Jubilees" and 5 "Clans" were on display. Strangely all the "Jubilees" on shed were named after naval vessels and none after colonies.

16 "Crabs" were on display but they seemed rapidly to go out of favour with a particular purge at December 1962. Carlisle nowadays was very much "Crabless".

Midland 0-6-0's came in three batches: - 1885, 1911 and 1924. The 1885 batch had disappeared by 1965 and five of them were on shed in September 1958. Great consternation was caused at the time as 43301 was missing from the combined volume at the time. Ian Allan had obviously withdrawn this loco in error. However, 43301's lifespan was not lengthened by much as she was officially withdrawn just two months later in November 1958 and scrapped in June 1959.

Some long defunct classes were seen in addition to the 2P 4-4-0's also seen at 12B Carlisle Upperby. They were seven examples of the McIntosh Caledonian 3F 0-6-0 Tanks 1895 and one example of the Pickersgill Caledonian 3F 0-6-0 1918. 108 of the 153 steam locos (71%) allocated to 12A Kingmoor were on shed. A goodly number!

Fast Forward to 12A Carlisle Kingmoor 3rd June 1967

12A CARLISLE KINGMOOR FAST FORWARD 3RD JUNE 1967	Home shed	Built	Withdrawn	Scrap
Steam				
Ivatt 4MT 2-6-0 1947				
43106	12A	Apr-1951	Jun-1968	saved
43120	12A	Jul-1951	Aug-1967	Dec-1967
43121	12A	Aug-1951	Nov-1967	Feb-1968
43139	12A	Jul-1951	Sep-1967	Feb-1968
Total	4			

			Home shed		Built	Withdrawn	Scrap
Stanier 5MT 4-6-0 "Black Five" 1934							
44659			8L	Aintree	May-1949	Jun-1967	Dec-1967
44672			12A		Feb-1950	Mar-1968	Jun-1968
44674			12A		Mar-1950	Dec-1967	Mar-1968
44675			12A		Mar-1950	Sep-1967	Feb-1968
44691			12D	Workington	Oct-1950	Apr-1967	Dec-1967
44725			8C	Speke Junction	Apr-1949	Oct-1967	Mar-1968
44759			12D	Workington	Sep-1947	Nov-1967	Mar-1968
44767			12A		Dec-1947	Dec-1967	saved
44790			12A		Jun-1947	Mar-1967	Nov-1967
44802			12A		Jun-1944	Jun-1968	Oct-1968
44829			12D	Workington	Aug-1944	May-1968	Jul-1968
44862			12A		Jan-1945	Jul-1967	Dec-1967
44886			12A		Jul-1945	Oct-1967	Mar-1968
44887			12A		Aug-1945	Dec-1967	Feb-1968
44911			12A		Nov-1945	Oct-1967	Apr-1968
44928			12A		Mar-1946	Jun-1967	Dec-1967
44936			12A		Nov-1945	Aug-1967	Nov-1967
44937			12A		Nov-1945	May-1967	Nov-1967
44942			10D	Lostock Hall	Dec-1945	Jun-1968	Jan-1969
44989			12A		Dec-1946	Feb-1967	Sep-1967
44993			12A		Jan-1947	Dec-1967	Apr-1968
45013			12A		Apr-1935	May-1968	Sep-1968
45028			12A		Sep-1934	Mar-1967	Nov-1967
45061			12A		Dec-1934	Nov-1967	Mar-1968
45126			12A		May-1935	May-1967	Nov-1967
45228			12A		Aug-1936	Mar-1967	Dec-1967
45232			8H	Birkenhead	Aug-1936	Nov-1967	Sep-1966
45253			12A		Sep-1936	Apr-1968	Oct-1968
45274			12A		Nov-1936	May-1967	Nov-1967
45340			12A		Apr-1937	Apr-1967	Jul-1967
45383			12A		Jul-1937	Feb-1967	Sep-1967
45437			12A		Nov-1937	Oct-1967	Feb-1968
45481			12A		Sep-1943	Sep-1967	Mar-1968
Total	33						
Stanier 6P5F 4-6-0 "Jubilee" 1934							
45562	"Alberta"		55A	Leeds (Holbeck)	Aug-1934	Nov-1967	May-1968
Total	1						
Midland 3F "Jinty" 0-6-0T 1924 dev. of Johnson 1899 design							
47471			12A		Jan-1928	Dec-1966	Sep-1967
47641			12A		Jan-1929	Dec-1966	Feb-1968
Total	2						
Stanier 8F 2-8-0 "Big Eight" 1935							
48024			10F	Rose Grove	Mar-1937	Nov-1967	Mar-1968
48053			10F	Rose Grove	Oct-1936	Mar-1967	Mar-1968
48104			55A	Leeds (Holbeck)	Feb-1939	Jul-1967	Nov-1967
48115			9F	Heaton Mersey	Apr-1939	Jul-1968	Oct-1968
48163			8F	Springs Branch (Wigan)	Mar-1943	Jun-1967	Nov-1967
48220			5B	Crewe South	Sep-1942	Aug-1967	Feb-1968
48438			10D	Lostock Hall	May-1944	Nov-1967	Jun-1968
Total	7						

		Home shed		Built	Withdrawn	Scrap
BR 7P6F "Britannia" 4-6-2 Derby 1951						
70006	"Robert Burns"	12A		Apr-1951	May-1967	Nov-1967
70015	"Apollo"	12A	(ex 9B Stockport)	Jun-1951	Aug-1967	Feb-1968
70016	"Ariel"	12A		Jun-1951	Aug-1967	Jan-1968
70021	"Morning Star"	12A	(ex 9B Stockport)	Aug-1951	Dec-1967	May-1968
70027	"Rising Star"	12A		Oct-1952	Jun-1967	Nov-1967
70033	"Charles Dickens"	12A		Dec-1952	Jul-1967	Aug-1968
70034	"Thomas Hardy"	12A		Dec-1952	May-1967	Oct-1967
70037	"Hereward the Wake"	12A		Dec-1952	Oct-1966	Feb-1968
70038	"Robin Hood"	12A		Jan-1953	Aug-1967	Feb-1968
70040	"Clive of India"	12A		Mar-1953	Apr-1967	Dec-1967
70046	"Anzac"	12A		Jun-1954	Jul-1967	Jan-1968
70048	The Territorial Army 1908-1958"	12A		Jul-1954	May-1967	Oct-1967
70049	"Solway Firth"	12A		Jul-1954	Dec-1967	Mar-1968
70052	"Firth of Tay"	12A		Aug-1954	Apr-1967	Nov-1967
70053	"Moray Firth"	12A		Sep-1954	Apr-1967	Oct-1967
Total	15					
BR Standard 9F 2-10-0 Brighton 1954						
92004		12A		Jan-1954	Mar-1968	Jul-1968
92012		12A		May-1954	Oct-1967	Feb-1968
92015		12A		Sep-1954	May-1967	Nov-1967
92018		12A		Oct-1954	Apr-1967	Aug-1967
92019		12A		Oct-1954	Jun-1967	Jan-1968
92023	*Crosti boilered*	8H	Birkenhead	Mar-1955	Nov-1967	Apr-1968
92025	*Crosti boilered*	8H	Birkenhead (ex 8C)	Jun-1955	Nov-1967	Apr-1968
92026	*Crosti boilered*	8H	Birkenhead	Jun-1955	Nov-1967	Apr-1968
92079	*double chimney*	8H	Birkenhead	Mar-1956	Nov-1967	Apr-1968
92080		12A		Apr-1956	May-1967	Nov-1967
92082		8H	Birkenhead	May-1956	Nov-1967	Apr-1968
92093		12A		Jan-1957	Aug-1967	Feb-1968
92114		12A		Dec-1956	Jul-1967	Feb-1968
92125		12A		Mar-1957	Dec-1967	Apr-1968
92137		12A		Jun-1957	Sep-1967	Feb-1968
Total	15					

Steam	77					
Withdrawn	23					

Home Locos		57 Home Area			3 Visitors	17	
Shed	**12A**	57	12D	3			
Distribution:-	**5B**	1	9F	1	55A	2	
	8C	1	8F	1	8H	6	
	8L	1	10D	2	10F	2	

Steam classes on view		7				
Steam Origin	**LMS**		47 BR		30	
Shed Highlight:-		45562	"Alberta"			
Steam	Sep-50	142	Mar-59	143	Apr-65	119
Allocation					Jun-67	97
			Closed to Steam:-		Jan-68	

	12A CARLISLE KINGMOOR (continued)						
	FAST FORWARD 3RD JUNE 1967						
Home Steam	excluding withdrawn locos						
On/Off Shed	On Shed		36 Off Shed		61 % On Shed	37%	
Not on Shed							
4MT 2-6-0 1946						43049	1
"Black Fives"	44669	44677	44727	44770	44775	44792	
	44795	44817	44825	44878	44882	44883	
	44884	44898	44899	44900	44902	45120	
	45135	45212	45236	45254	45259	45279	
		45295	45363	45447	45455	45493	29
"Britannias"	70004	70005	70010	70011	70012	70013	
	70014	70022	70023	70024	70025	70028	
	70029	70031	70032	70035	70039	70045	
					70047	70051	20
BR 9F 2-10-0	92009	92017	92051	92056	92071	92110	
		92129	92208	92223	92233	92249	11
						total	61
	saw on shed July 65 Carlisle visit				11		
	saw elsewhere on the tour				30		
	saw on Dec 64 Manchester and Crewe trip				3		
	saw on July 65 Preston area trip				6		
	saw on September 58 Carlisle visit				2		
	saw on June 67 trip at 12B Carlisle Upperby				3		
	recently withdrawn not on shed or seen elsewhere				7		scrap
	"Black Fives"		44689	Mar-67	44982	44986	May-67
	"Britannias"	70003	Mar-67	70041	Apr-67	70042	May-67
	9F 2-10-0					92074	Apr-67

Review of 12B Carlisle Kingmoor Fast Forward 3rd June 1967

77 steam on shed was a huge turnout but sadly 24 were withdrawn. The last two "Jinties" withdrawn in December 1966 still remained on shed. 11 of the 33 "Black Fives" were also withdrawn and sadly seven of the 15 "Britannias" were also withdrawn. Remarkably "Jubilee" 45562 was still operational and she would not be withdrawn until November 1967. Three of the fifteen hard-working Standard 9F 2-10-0's were also withdrawn. Seven "Big Eights" were on shed but only one was withdrawn.

The clear highlight of the day was seeing Jubilee "Alberta" in splendid condition having arrived with a special from the Leeds Area. We took the opportunity to get some good photos. The author complete with carried crash helmet can be seen in the final photo!

Stanier 6P5F 4-6-0 "Jubilee" 1934 45562 "Alberta" of 55A Leeds Holbeck on 3rd June 1967

On we go

As we were about to leave after D.S. had taken his picture of "Royal Scot" 46128 "The Lovat Scouts" – *all D.S's initial batches of photos on the tour were ruined by a friend who offered a cheap which turned out to be very expensive developing service-* my ultra-sensory perception picked up a very strange continuous sound coming from the north. D.S. heard it too and for about 10 minutes we looked up the line. Then the lights changed to green and two Claytons emerged in the distance at the head of what I thought was a mineral train. "Two crummy Polmadie Claytons" I murmured to D.S. but we had better stay here and get their numbers for the records. As they passed my jaw dropped as I gaped at the numbers. I absent-mindedly scrawled down their numbers D8596 and D8603 and then exclaimed "Gateshead Claytons!" What a surprise as we did not know that they worked to Carlisle. We could not work that one out but that did not matter much.

As we left the shed yard I suddenly felt relieved at getting round 12A Kingmoor without mishap and shook D.S.'s hand to mark this achievement and hoped that these successes would continue during the week. We boarded a bus at "Erby Road" and returned to the city centre. D.S. normally by this time is gasping for something to eat when we went day visits but strangely he had not been dragging me to the nearest tuck shop. By this time (9 p.m.) even I was feeling a bit peckish. We wandered passed Carlisle Station and up Botchergate and I pointed out to D.S. the vast metal tower in the distance which I told D.S. was Carlisle Rocket Station. D.S. did not believe me. On my way to Blackpool a fellow traveller had informed me that it was a rocket tracking station. It still seemed a sensible suggestion to me but D.S. thought I was pulling his leg. "Well what was it if it isn't a rocket station D.S.?" Our know-all made no comment.

THE BEECHAM POWDER AFFAIR

As we were watching up Botchergate D.S. informed me that he was suffering from an acute loss of appetite. I told him that he was probably so excited (the tour getting too hectic for the old, decaying boy) that he had got one of his frequent cramps - this time in a new place (the stomach). I told him that some food would put some life into his degenerate self. When I tried to force him into one of several Chinese restaurants he refused point-blank. Chinese restaurants conjured up in his puzzled mind chop-sticks and rice. I told him you could get anything under the sun in them and with knives and forks. But no! He believed otherwise.

After some hunting I (ravenously hungry) smelt out a fish and chip shop up a side-street. I ordered fish and chips and looked round the busy shop packed with noisy, hungry customers, all tucking in I looked round again and saw D.S. waiting to be served. I was glad to see that he appeared to have got his appetite back. I hoped he wouldn't order a fish supper. The word "supper" means nothing in England. To avoid getting a dirty look one must ask for fish and chips. He was to get more than a dirty look!

D.S. staggered me and the servers by speaking out loudly "One Beecham Powder" after the server had asked pleasantly "What's your order luv?" Smiles were now wiped off the servers faces. The noisy customers had now stopped eating and speaking and all looked round in amazement at D.S. For a whole minute the boss and the two servers stared at D.S. while he distinctly got redder with embarrassment. At last one server broke the ice by chirping "Wot, No chips!" D.S. whispered back "No chips."

The boss then roared out "Trying to make our customers think that our chips are so lousy that you need a Beecham's Powder after taking them. Serve the skate Mabel. Double quick!" Mabel obeyed and D.S. stumped up four pence (two new pence). The boss then retorted "Don't come it loppylugs. We know your type. Scram before I stuff the powder down your throat and don't come back!"

To the angry cries of "lynch him" and "dot him" from the now hostile customers D.S. made a hasty exit with his precious Beecham Powder. I smiled and smiled and smiled and laughed again and again at the hilarious scene. Some people are touchy. Poor D.S.!

As I caught up with D.S. outside the chip shop I found him making extremely suggestive comments to a girl (about twenty yards ahead) taking her dog for a walk. The girl after giving some interesting answers to his offensive comments ran away and turned right at the foot of the road. I surmised that she was after the nearest cop and I quickly ushered D.S. to the left at the foot of the road. I just cannot leave him for just one minute! The sooner he gets to Stanlow Oil Refinery to get rid of his crude words the better. If they can refine oil at Stanlow it should not pose them too great a problem to refine D.S. That would have to wait till Friday though when I could boot him off the train at that point.

After that I had my very enjoyable fish supper. Not surprisingly D.S. could not be tempted with a chip. D.S. told me after we got back into the station that he had had his Beecham Powder and that it had relieved his bad stomach ache.

Rewind to 12C Carlisle Canal Sunday 7th September 1958 – A Ghost Story

		Home shed		Built	Withdrawn	Scrap
12C CARLISLE CANAL						
REWIND 7th SEPTEMBER 1958						
Steam						
Ivatt 4MT 2-6-0 1947						
43139		12C		*Jul-1951*	*Sep-1967*	*Feb-1968*
Total	1					
Gresley 7P6F 4-6-2 A3 1927						
60068	"Sir Visto"	12C		*Aug-1924*	*Aug-1962*	*Sep-1962*
60079	"Bayardo"	12C		*Oct-1924*	*Sep-1961*	*Oct-1961*
60093	"Coronach"	12C		*Nov-1928*	*May-1962*	*May-1962*
60095	"Flamingo"	12C		*Jan-1929*	*Apr-1961*	*Oct-1961*
Total	4					
Thompson 5MT B1 4-6-0 1942						
61064		12C		*Aug-1946*	*Nov-1962*	*Aug-1963*
61217		12C		*Aug-1947*	*Mar-1962*	*Jul-1962*
61222		12C		*Aug-1947*	*Jan-1962*	*Feb-1962*
61239		12C		*Oct-1947*	*Aug-1962*	*Jan-1963*
61290		12C		*Feb-1948*	*Mar-1962*	*Jul-1962*
61395		12C		*Feb-1952*	*Oct-1962*	*Nov-1962*
Total	6					
Gresley 5P6F 2-6-0 K3 1924						
61851		12C		*Mar-1925*	*Nov-1961*	*Aug-1962*
61882		12C		*Oct-1929*	*May-1960*	*Jun-1960*
61916		12C		*May-1931*	*Dec-1960*	*Apr-1961*
61937		12C		*Jan-1935*	*Apr-1960*	*Apr-1960*
Total	4					
Gresley 4P 4-4-0 D49 1927						
62734	"Cumberland"	12C		*May-1929*	*Mar-1961*	*Mar-1961*
Total	1					
Reid 3F 0-6-0 J35 1908						
64478		12C		*Dec-1908*	*Aug-1962*	*Dec-1962*
64499		12C		*Dec-1909*	*Nov-1962*	*Mar-1963*
Total	2					

	Home shed	Built	Withdrawn	Scrap
Gresley 4P5F 0-6-0 J39 1926				
64727	12C	May-1927	Nov-1962	Sep-1963
64733	12C	Jun-1927	Jan-1961	Aug-1962
64875	12C	Jun-1935	Nov-1962	Sep-1963
64880	12C	Jul-1935	Nov-1962	Jun-1963
64884	12C	Aug-1935	Mar-1962	Jun-1962
64888	12C	Sep-1935	Nov-1962	May-1963
64892	12C	Oct-1935	Jul-1960	Jul-1960
64895	12C	Oct-1935	Nov-1962	Jun-1963
64899	12C	Aug-1936	Nov-1962	May-1963
64932	12C	May-1937	Jul-1961	Aug-1961
64948	12C	Apr-1938	Apr-1960	May-1960
64964	12C	Jun-1938	Apr-1961	Nov-1961
Total 12				
Holmes 2F 0-6-0 J36 1888				
65293	12C	May-1897	Dec-1962	Feb-1965
65312	12C	Mar-1899	Dec-1962	May-1963
65321	12C	May-1899	Dec-1962	May-1963
Total 3				
Reid 3MT 0-6-2T N15 1910				
69155	12C	Aug-1912	Sep-1962	Jun-1963
69174	12C	Sep-1916	Nov-1958	Dec-1958
69215	12C	Dec-1913	Nov-1959	Apr-1960
Total 3				
Gresley 3P2F 0-6-2T N2 1925				
69564	12C	Nov-1925	Jun-1961	Jul-1962
Total 1				

Steam	37			
Steam classes on view	10			
Steam Origin	**LMS**	**1 LNER**	**36**	
Shed Highlight:-	**"Shire"** 62734	**"Cumberland"**		
			Pre-Grouping :- North British Railway	
Steam	Sep-50 59	Mar-59 41	Apr-65 0	
Allocation			Jul-65 0	
		Closed to Steam:-	Jun-63	
Home Steam				
On/Off Shed	On Shed 37	Off Shed 6	% On Shed 86%	
Not on Shed				
Midland 4F 0-6-0 1924			44157	1
Gresley 5P6F 2-6-0 K3 1924		61898	61936	2
Gresley 4P 4-4-0 D49 1927			62747	1
Gresley 4P5F 0-6-0 J39 1926		64877	64912	2
				6

Review of 12C Carlisle Canal Sunday 7th September 1958

The shed is on the west side of the Hawick line just north of the junction of the Silloth line. Walking time 35 minutes.

By July 1965 everyone had about forgotten about 12C Carlisle Canal but in September 1958 it was very much alive and kicking. It was the old North British railway shed whereas 12A Carlisle Kingmoor was originally the pre-grouping Caledonian Railway shed while 12B Carlisle Upperby was the London and North Western Railway shed. The locos meandered up the old Waverley route via Hawick to Edinburgh and also to Newcastle. As expected it was full of L.N.E.R. locos just the types one would see at 64A St.Margarets shed in Edinburgh. Some interesting locos in retrospect. Four A3's, six B1's, four K3's and one of the "Shire/Hunt" passenger 4P 4-4-0's. There had been two "Shires" allocated here until earlier in the year but one (62732 "Dumfries-shire") had been withdrawn and to replace her 62747

"The Percy" was on her way to 12C Carlisle Canal from 50A York.

The "Shires/Hunts" were to disappear from the scene in the early 60's but thankfully 62712 "Morayshire" was preserved as can be seen nowadays (with D.S. in regular attendance) at the Bo'ness and Kinneil Preserved Railway. I remember watching the 1958 Empire Games at Cardiff in mid-July 1958 when I was starting out on my trainspotting career having spent my first week of trainspotting during the first week in July at 67C Ayr station when I holidayed at Ayr with our family. I had been told that every weekday night 62712 "Morayshire" was rostered to haul a local passenger train at tea-time from Edinburgh to North Berwick and that if I ventured up the line to the Mucklets Bridge, Stoneybank, Musselburgh on the main Edinburgh to London mainline I would duly kop her. The first night I watched instead the Marathon at the Empire Games when Dave Power of Australia beat local hero John Merriman of Wales. The following night there was no marathon to distract me and I duly went up the line and kopped her on the usual early evening train.

Reid, Gresley and Holmes classes completed the complement on show. At the time it was not so stunning for me as the classes were all well known to me in Edinburgh albeit after only two months trainspotting but having made regular Sunday visits to 64A St. Margarets, 64B Haymarket and 64C Dalry Road.

One particular delight was going to Edinburgh on a weekday evening either by cycling the seven miles up to 64C Dalry Road or spending two pence (one new pence) on a Number 26 Edinburgh Corporation Bus from Eastfield on the Edinburgh-Musselburgh boundary. The reward for this endeavour was seeing normally a "Jubilee" from the Liverpool/Manchester area on the six five special arrival from I think Liverpool. By the time we arrived at about 7 p.m. she would be being coaled up at 64C Dalry Road shed (the former Caledonian railway shed) ready for the return journey the following morning. My first kop off that service was "Jubilee" 45596 "Bahamas". This service was the only direct one up the west coast line to Edinburgh. Normally the Edinburgh portion of the Glasgow bound expresses was hooked off at Carstairs and some local steam loco would undertake the final leg of the journey to Edinburgh.

12C Carlisle Canal was not a place for strangers or local locos to stray much out of their territory. 37 (86%) of the 43 steam locos allocated were on shed that day. Why the ghost story? Well, 12C Carlisle Canal closed on June 1963 and of the 37 steam locos seen on shed only one survived after the end of 1962. A3's, B1's etc. did not survive the purge in the run down of the shed. The only survivor would be the only LMS engine on shed namely "Flying Pig" Ivatt 4MT 2-6-0 1947 43139 which made the short survival journey to 12A Carlisle Kingmoor.

On we go

It was now 21.30 and we had to "kick our heels" in the station until 00.33 when we would get our London train. D.S. (as I have said) was greatly relieved by the Beecham Powder and we retired to the Refreshment room.

To make sure that I was getting my full share of vitamins I got a (schhh you know whose) Tomato juice bottle and some of BR's exorbitantly priced sandwiches (8d (3.5p) to 1/- (5p)). D.S. was obviously hungry now as he spent 4/- (20p) on sandwiches alone. We sat there in the refreshment room making our drinks least while discussing the trip to London. We had no alarm clocks so something would have to be worked out so that we could get off at Watford Junction and not be awakened at 07.30 by some attendant at Euston Station.

After what D.S. had been telling me before we went that he wanted a good night's sleep every night I was surprised when he was all for shifts on the way down so that one person was always awake. We decided that I would sleep until Crewe and that D.S. would sleep until Watford. Our discussions were interrupted at about 22.45 when "Britannia" 70030 "William Wordsworth" stormed in with the 18.37 from Crewe which terminated at Carlisle and that was the last train in from the south before we left. "William Wordsworth" was a very welcome kop and now the two of us were greatly sharpened up and raring to go.

After that bit of excitement things died down a bit and I got a cup of tea. Coffee would have kept me awake (so I believed). At 23.10 the station was pierced by many shouts and screams the mods, rockers and some local riff-raff (which I had complained of earlier) were (after having left the dance-halls) getting the last bucket back to Workington.

We then moved into the waiting-room and for some odd reason tried to get some sleep before the journey. Luckily our attempts were unsuccessful or we might have missed our train to London!

Around midnight things began to liven up and we got our bags out of the left luggage. I awakened the attendant there by a very loud "Thank you sir". "Peak" D28 brought in a Leeds express from Glasgow via Kilmarnock and 70010 "Owen Glendower" came in with the mail train to provide a second very welcome kop.

				CARLISLE STATION NIGHT SAT 31 JUL/ SUN 01 AUG				
			Home shed			Built	Withdrawn	Scrap
Diesels								
BR Sulzer "Peak" Type 4 1Co-Co1 1959								
D 20			55A	Leeds Holbeck		Feb-1961		
Total		1						
English Electric Type 4 1Co-Co1 1958								
D 228	"Samaria"	hauled	9A	Longsight		Aug-1959		
D 317			12B	Carlisle Upperby		Feb-1961		
Total		2						
Brush Type 4 Co-Co 1962								
D1844			5A	Crewe Diesel		May-1965		
D1847			5A	Crewe Diesel		Jun-1965		
Total		2						
BR Sulzer Type 2 Bo-Bo 1958								
D5105			52A	Gateshead		Sep-1960		
Total		1						
Steam						Built	Withdrawn	Scrap
Stanier 5MT 4-6-0 "Black Five" 1934								
45138			8B	Warrington		Jun-1935	Sep-1966	Mar-1967
Total		1						
BR Standard 7P6F 4-6-2 "Britannia" Derby 1951								
70010	"Owen Glendower"		12A	ex 5A then ex 5B		May-1951	Sep-1967	Jan-1968
70030	"William Wordsworth"		12B	ex 5A then ex 5B		Nov-1952	Jun-1966	Oct-1966
Total		2						

On Station	9		Kops	2			
Steam	3		Diesels	6			
		Home Area		3	Visitors	6	
Shed	12A		1 12B	2			
Distribution:-	5A		2 8B	1 9A	1		
	52A		1 55A	1			
Steam classes on view			2				
Steam Origin		LMS	1 BR	2			

DAY 1   **<u>SATURDAY 31ST JULY 1965</u>**

		Schedule	Actual	Miles
Depart	EDINBURGH PRINCES STREET	08.30	08.35	0
Arrive	CARSTAIRS	09.07	09.12	27½
	See 66E Carstairs			

Journey - see 64C Dalry Road

		Schedule	Actual	Miles
Depart	CARSTAIRS	09.17	09.20	27½
	See 66F Beattock			
Arrive	CARLISLE	10.31	10.31	101¼
	Do 12B Carlisle Upperby			

retire to Locospotter's Haven - Upperby Bridge for return of Glasgow Trades Specials

		Schedule	Actual	Miles
Depart	CARLISLE	16.35	16.40	0
Arrive	WORKINGTON MAIN	17.25	17.29	33¼
	Do 12D Workington			
		Schedule	Actual	Miles
Depart	WORKINGTON MAIN	18.35	18.39	0
Arrive	CARLISLE	19.30	19.30	33¼
	Do 12A Carlisle Kingmoor			

retire to Carlisle Station

A very successful day. No train more than a few minutes late and 12A Carlisle Kingmoor, 12B Carlisle Upperby and 12D Workington all visited without a hitch.

Remarkably as the analysis shows below there was still plenty of steam around Carlisle with 221 of the 280 locos seen being steam. With the demise of 12C Carlisle Canal there were very few LNER locos seen.

DAY 1 EDINBURGH, CARLISLE AND WORKINGTON

	Visits	GWR	SR	LMS	LNER	WD	BR	Steam Total	Diesel Total	Electric Total	Grand Total
	Edinburgh Caley			3				3			3
	Dalry Road (pass)				1			1			1
64C	Carstairs (pass)			5	1			6	1		7
66E	Beattock (pass)			2				2			2
66F	Edinburgh to Carlisle			4			2	6			6
12A	Carlisle Kingmoor (pass)			6			3	9	2		11
	Carlisle Station Arrival			3			5	8	3		11
12B	Carlisle Upperby			20		1	6	27	3		30
	Bridge at Carlisle Upperby			31			8	39	23		62
12D	Workington			27				27	5		32
	Carlisle Station evening			4			3	7	5		12
12A	Carlisle Kingmoor			61	3		19	83	11		94
	Carlisle Station night			1			2	3	6		9
	GRAND TOTAL	0	0	167	5	1	48	221	59	0	280

REWIND 7th September 1958

		GWR	SR	LMS	LNER	WD	BR	Steam Total
12A	Carlisle Kingmoor 070958			100		3	5	108
12B	Carlisle Upperby 070958			58				58
12C	Carlisle Canal 070958			1	36			37
		0	0	159	36	3	5	203

FAST FORWARD 3rd June 1967

		GWR	SR	LMS	LNER	WD	BR	Steam Total
12A	Carlisle Kingmoor 030667			47			30	77
12B	Carlisle Upperby 030667			20			6	26
		0	0	67	0	0	36	103

Let's keep our fingers crossed that the next week proves to be as successful as today was!

END OF DAY ONE

Some detailed steam seen analyses Appendices follow:-

STEAM ENGINE CLASSES ON SHED ACTIVE — DAY 1	total 12A — BR C Kingmoor	12A pass — not on eve	12B — C Upperby	12D — Workington	64C — Dalry Road	66E — Carstairs	66F — Beattock	On Shed — DAY 1
Ivatt 2MT 2-6-2T 1946								3
41200-41329	130			3				
Fairburn 4MT 2-6-4T 1945 dev. of Stanier 1935								5
42050-42299; 42673-42699	277	1		1			2	
Ivatt 4MT 2-6-0 1947								11
43000-43161	162	8			3			
Fowler Midland 4F 0-6-0 1911								2
43835-44026	192			2				
Midland 4F 0-6-0 1924								11
44027-44606	580			2	9			
Stanier 5MT 4-6-0 "Black Five" 1934								54
44658-45499	842	36	3	7	3	5		
Ivatt 7P 4-6-0 "Patriot" 1947 rebuild of Fowler 1933								2
45512/4/21-3/5-9/30-2/34-6/40/5	18	2						
Stanier 6P5F 4-6-0 "Jubilee" 1934								3
45552-45734/7-42	189	2		1				
Stanier 7P 4-6-0 "Royal Scot" 1943 rebuild of Fowler 1927								1
46100-70	71	1						
Ivatt 2MT 2-6-0 1946								6
46400-46527	128			4	2			
Midland 3F "Jinty" 0-6-0T 1924 dev. of Johnson 1899 design								6
47260-47681	417	3			3			
Stanier 8F 2-8-0 "Big Eight" 1935								1
48000-48775	666	1			0			
Gresley 7P6F 2-6-2 V2 1936								2
60800-60983	184	2						
Thompson 5MT 4-6-0 B1 1942								1
61000-61409	410	1				0		
BR Standard 7P6F 4-6-2 "Britannia" Derby 1951								12
70000-70054	55	4	1	7				
BR Standard 6P5F 4-6-2 "Clan" Derby 1952								3
72000-72009	10	3						
BR Standard 5MT 4-6-0 Doncaster 1951								3
73000-73171	172	3						
BR Standard 9F 2-10-0 Brighton 1954								9
92000-92250	251	9						
		76	4	27	21	5	2	135

STEAM ENGINE CLASSES / DAY 1 WITHDRAWN	total BR	Withdrawn 12A (C Kingmoor not on eve)	Withdrawn 12A pass (C Kingmoor)	Withdrawn 12B (C Upperby)	Withdrawn 12D (Workington)	Withdrawn 64C (Dalry Road)	Withdrawn 66E (Carstairs)	Withdrawn 66F (Beattock)	Total Withdrawn DAY 1
Midland 4F 0-6-0 1924 — 44027-44606	580								
Stanier 5MT 4-6-0 "Black Five" 1934 — 44658-45499	842	4							4
Stanier 6P5F 4-6-0 "Jubilee" 1934 — 45552-45734/7-42	189	2							2
Stanier 7P 4-6-0 "Royal Scot" 1943 rebuild of Fowler 1927 — 46100-70	71	1			2				3
Ivatt 2MT 2-6-0 1946 — 46400-46527	128				2				2
Stanier 8F 2-8-0 "Big Eight" 1935 — 48000-48775	666				2				2
Thompson 8P7F 4-6-2 A2 1946 — 60500-60539	40						1		1
Thompson 5MT 4-6-0 B1 1942 — 61000-61409	410					1			1
Total		7	0	0	6	1	1	0	15

STEAM ENGINE CLASSES

(OFF SHED DAY 1	total BR	Edinburgh Caley	Edin to Carlisle arrival	Carlisle Bridge at Upperby	Carlisle st evening	Carlisle st night	Carlisle	Total Off Shed
Ivatt 2MT 2-6-2T 1946								
41200-41329	130				2			2
Ivatt 4MT 2-6-0 1947								
43000-43161	162				2			2
Stanier 5MT 4-6-0 "Black Five" 1934								
44658-45499	842	3	4	2	22	4	1	36
Stanier 6P5F 4-6-0 "Jubilee" 1934								
45552-45734/7-42	189				3			3
Stanier 7P 4-6-0 "Royal Scot" 1943 rebuild of Fowler 1927								
46100-70	71				1			1
Ivatt 2MT 2-6-0 1946								
46400-46527	128				1			1
Midland 3F "Jinty" 0-6-0T 1924 dev. of Johnson 1899 design								
47260-47681	417			1				1
BR Standard 7P6F 4-6-2 "Britannia" Derby 1951								
70000-70054	55			2	4	3	2	11
BR Standard 5MT 4-6-0 Doncaster 1951								
73000-73171	172			3	1			4
BR Standard 4MT 2-6-4T Doncaster 1953								
80000-80154	155		1					1
BR Standard 9F 2-10-0 Brighton 1954								
92000-92250	251		1		3			4
		3	6	8	39	7	3	66

STEAM ENGINE CLASSES
SUMMARY TOTALS DAY 1

	total BR	Off Shed Day 1	Off Shed Grand Total	On Shed Day 1	On Shed Grand Total	Withdrawn Day 1	Withdrawn Grand Total	All Day 1	All Grand Total
Ivatt 2MT 2-6-2T 1946	130	2		3				5	
Fairburn 4MT 2-6-4T 1945 dev. of Stanier 1935	277	5						5	
Ivatt 4MT 2-6-0 1947	162	2		11				13	
Fowler Midland 4F 0-6-0 1911	192			2				2	
Midland 4F 0-6-0 1924	580			11		4		15	
Stanier 5MT 4-6-0 "Black Five" 1934	842	36		54		2		92	
Ivatt 7P 4-6-0 "Patriot" 1947 rebuild of Fowler 1933	18			2				2	
Stanier 6P5F 4-6-0 "Jubilee" 1934	189	3		3		3		9	
Stanier 7P 4-6-0 "Royal Scot" 1943 rebuild of Fowler 1927	71	1		1		2		4	
Ivatt 2MT 2-6-0 1946	128	1		6		1		8	
Midland 3F "Jinty" 0-6-0T 1924 dev. of Johnson 1899 design	417	1		6				7	
Stanier 8F 2-8-0 "Big Eight" 1935	666			1		1		2	
Thompson 8P7F 4-6-2 A2 1946	40					1		1	
Gresley 7P6F 2-6-2 V2 1936	184			2				2	
Thompson 5MT 4-6-0 B1 1942	410			1		1		2	
BR Standard 7P6F 4-6-2 "Britannia" Derby 1951	55	11		12				23	
BR Standard 6P5F 4-6-2 "Clan" Derby 1952	10			3				3	
BR Standard 5MT 4-6-0 Doncaster 1951	172	4		3				7	
BR Standard 4MT 2-6-4T Doncaster 1953	155	1						1	
BR Standard 9F 2-10-0 Brighton 1954	251	4		9				13	
		66		135		15		216	

100

STEAM ENGINE CLASSES ON SHED REWIND SEPTEMBER 1958	total BR	CARLISLE REWIND Sep-58 12A C Kingmoor	12B C Upperby	12C C Canal	Total Carlisle Rewind All
Midland 2P 4-4-0 1928					
40563-40700	136	4	2		6
Stanier 4MT 2-6-4T 1935 dev of Fowler 1927					
42425-42672	243	1	4		5
Hughes/Fowler 5MT 2-6-0 "Crab" 1926					
42700-42944	245	16			16
Ivatt 4MT 2-6-0 1947					
43000-43161	162			1	1
Johnson Midland 3F 0-6-0 1885					
43191-43763	324	5			5
Fowler Midland 4F 0-6-0 1911					
43835-44026	192	4	2		6
Midland 4F 0-6-0 1924					
44027-44606	580	4	5		9
Stanier 5MT 4-6-0 "Black Five" 1934					
44658-45499	842	35	14		49
Fowler 6P5F 4-6-0 unrebuilt "Patriot" 1933					
45500-11/3/5-9/20/4/33/37-9/41-44/46-51	34		6		6
Stanier 6P5F 4-6-0 "Jubilee" 1934					
45552-45734/7-42	189	12	3		15
Stanier 7P 4-6-0 "Royal Scot" 1943 rebuild of Fowler 1927					
46100-70	71		4		4
Stanier 8P 4-6-2 "Coronation" 1937					
46220-57	38		2		2
Ivatt 2MT 2-6-0 1946					
46400-46527	128		2		2
Midland 3F "Jinty" 0-6-0T 1924 dev. of Johnson 1899 design					
47260-47681	417	8	14		22
Stanier 8F 2-8-0 "Big Eight" 1935					
48000-48775	666	3			3
McIntosh Caledonian 3F 0-6-0T 1895					
56230-56376	147	7			7
Pickersgill Caledonian 3F 0-6-0 1918					
57650-57691	29	1			1
Gresley 7P6F 4-6-2 A3 1927					
60035-60112	78			4	4
Thompson 8P6F 4-6-2 A1 1945					
60113-60162	50			6	6
Gresley 5P6F 2-6-0 K3 1924					
61800-61992	193			4	4
Gresley 4P 4-4-0 D49 1927					
62700-62775	76			1	1
Reid 3F 0-6-0 J35 1908					
64460-64535	70			2	2
Gresley 4P5F 0-6-0 J39 1926					
64700-64988	289			12	12
Holmes 2F 0-6-0 J36 1888					
65210-65346	123			3	3
Reid 3MT 0-6-2T N15 1910					
69126-69224	99			3	3
Gresley 3P2F 0-6-2T N2 1925					
69490-69596	107			1	1
BR Standard 6P5F 4-6-2 "Clan" Derby 1952					
72000-72009	10	5			5
Riddles WD 8F 2-8-0 "Austerity" 1943					
90000-90732	733	1			1
Riddles WD MOS 8F 2-10-0 "Austerity" 1943					
90750-90774, WD601	26	2			2
		108	58	37	203

CARLISLE FAST FORWARD JUNE 1967

STEAM ENGINE CLASSES FAST FORWARD JUNE 1967 ON SHED

BR	total	12A C Kingmoor Active	12A C Kingmoor Withdrawn	12B C Upperby Active	12B C Upperby Withdrawn	Total Carlisle Fast Fwd Active	Total Carlisle Fast Fwd Withdrawn	Total Carlisle Fast Fwd All
Ivatt 2MT 2-6-2T 1946 41200-41329	130	2	1			2	1	3
Ivatt 4MT 2-6-0 1947 43000-43161	162	1			3	1	3	4
Stanier 5MT 4-6-0 "Black Five" 1934 44658-45499	842	22	11	7		29	11	40
Stanier 6P5F 4-6-0 "Jubilee" 1934 45552-45734/7-42	189	1				1		1
Ivatt 2MT 2-6-0 1946 46400-46527	128				5		5	5
Midland 3F "Jinty" 0-6-0T 1924 dev. of Johnson 1899 design 47260-47681	417	2				2		2
Stanier 8F 2-8-0 "Big Eight" 1935 48000-48775	666	6	1	5		11	1	12
BR Standard 7P6F 4-6-2 "Britannia" Derby 1951 70000-70054	55	8	7	4		12	7	19
BR Standard 4MT 4-6-0 Brighton 1951 75000-75079	80			2		2		2
BR Standard 9F 2-10-0 Brighton 1954 92000-92250 except	166	8	3	0		8	3	11
BR Standard 9F 2-10-0 Brighton 1954. 1957 double chimney 92000-1; 92006; 92079; 92165-7; 92178; 92183-92249	75		1				1	1
BR Standard 9F 2-10-0 Brighton 1954. 1955 Crosti boiler 92020-29	10	3				3		3
		53	24	18	8	71	32	103

Part Two

SUNDAY 1st AUGUST 1965

The Tour Continues

Carlisle Departure
and
a Day in London

Very Early Morning – Carlisle Station shortly after midnight

THE MISSING CARRIAGE AFFAIR

We were now expecting our train to London at any minute and by 00.20 I was wishing that it would arrive on time and we would get away. At 00.25 our train entered from the north end of the station. I pressed the reservation slip for seat tickets (carriage A4 seat No's 7and 8) into D.S.'s hot little hand and told him to guard it with his life.

English Electric Type 4 D228 "Samaria" slowly went past us at the head of our train and we looked anxiously for our carriage. The first carriage was A5, the second had no special number, and the third was A3. No other carriages at the front of the train bore any reservation number and D.S. and I belted down the platform looking vainly for carriage A4. We were stopped by the sleeping car attendant who told us that they were all sleeping cars at that end of the train. He told us that A4 would be at the front end of the train. As we passed up the train looking for carriage A4 or a seat reservation sign I saw that the train was absolutely packed. D.S. by now was seething with anger and said that the carriage in between A5 and A3 must be our carriage A4 although it did not bear that number nor had any seat reservation stickers on the windows. We entered that carriage and found every seat occupied and what should have been our seats occupied! D.S. was just not going to stand for this and if I had not restrained him he would have entered one compartment where seats 7 and 8 were and would have claimed his rights by flashing about the reservation seats and have ejected the middle-aged, sleepy couple who were there. We had no right to do it though because although it was clearly what should have been our carriage there was no indication that it was.

Obviously there had been some slip-up at the Glasgow end and our seats had not been reserved. I told D.S. that we had better get out of the corridor on to the platform and look for some authority. If the worst came to the worst we agreed that we would sit in first-class accommodation and I would show our reservation tickets to any ticket-collector and he could get the muddle sorted out. We staggered out of the carriage to find an elderly couple having a few anxious words with the Station Inspector about the whereabouts of the phantom coach A4. We told them that we were in the same plight.

The Station Inspector quickly ascertained that there was no A4 and he ushered us into a first-class carriage. He ushered the elderly couple into the first compartment (apologising all the time for any inconvenience). We thanked him for his help because now we would be travelling first-class at no extra-charge!

He told us to go into the second compartment and D.S. poked his head inside and almost cracked me on the head so quickly did he retreat back into the corridor. He garbled out something about "birds" being in there. So much the better and I fought my way past him inside and took one middle seat with my back to the engine and D.S. took the other middle seat facing the engine. We dumped our luggage and generally made ourselves comfortable. A few minutes later the Station Inspector came in with a sticky label and pasted it on the window. It proclaimed that 2nd class passengers were allowed to use this compartment. We were famous! Almost as soon as he had left our friend, the sleeping car attendant came in to the compartment in his additional role as ticket collector. British Rail was really economising!

We fumbled about and produced our precious LMR tickets. Our friend did not ask us how we ended up here in a 1st class carriage and accepted our Railrover ticket without question. I was thankful that he did not mutilate the ticket by punching a hole in it as I had visions of our ticket crumbling in to nothingness long before the end of our tour. Thankfully this did not seem to be the procedure. He disappeared again and I checked my watch. It was 00.35. This entire hullabaloo had taken place in under twelve minutes. It had seemed like an eternity.

- - - - - - - - - - - - - - - - -

A sudden jerk and we were off - two minutes late.

I now had time to look around at what D.S. had shied at. On both sides of me were two girls (about D.S.'s age). I preferred the one on the right. D.S. had another girl (rather plump) on his right-hand side and there was a boy on his left hand side.

The first-class carriage was really good and it seemed to me that it would give me a fair chance of some sleep. It was not as cramped as the 2nd class carriages. It seated eight whereas the 1st class seated six. There were non-folding arm-rests and head rests which neatly cut off each seat.

My last glimpse of Carlisle was Ivatt 2MT 2-6-0 46458 at 12B Upperby shed. Then the compartment blinds were drawn down and it was goodnight to D.S. and all. Wake me up at Crewe D.S.

I just closed my eyes and thought about getting to sleep. I guarantee anyone if you try to get to sleep you will not be particularly successful if you are excited about the week that had now begun. The minutes ticked by and after we had been travelling about an hour I heard somebody speak. I had been half asleep but now I had been awakened again. I did not want to converse with D.S. so pretended to be asleep. D.S. had just said "Thanks I haven't had one of these for some time" to the attractive girl beside me. I curiously opened one eye to see what he was talking about. He was in fact talking about Polos. Make a sweet advert that. Still pretended to be asleep but for some odd reason unable to get to sleep. At Preston I officially awoke and promised D.S. that there would be something in the old shed - which turned out to be empty and told him to expect a BR Standard 2MT 2-6-0 78XXX class at the end of the station. There she was as promised but it was too dark to get the number as the illuminations ended just before her.

I told him to wake me up at Wigan (15 minutes further on) and officially went back to sleep. I then turned my mind to the physics of sleeping on a train and I decided that one has a far better chance of getting to sleep if you are originally facing the engine than if you have your back to the engine. I looked at the problem in this way; with your back to the engine what you are leaning on (the back of the carriage) is being swept backwards with the engine away from your back. With yourselves facing the engine you are leaning backwards in the opposite direction from the engine. The back of the carriage is being pulled forward in the same direction as the engine into your back. I originally would have been in the "best" position and D.S. would have had his back to the unfavourable back to the engine position but now with all this hullabaloo the position was reversed and that lucky D.S. had the best position. I was sure that nobody else had written a thesis on that subject so I was determined to send it to Edinburgh University when I got home. If it was accepted I would get my PhD (Director of Philosophy) and be known as Dr G.D. *I had second thoughts when I arrived home a week later and did not pursue the matter.*

I was just about to have a nervous breakdown thinking about all these physics when D.S. "woke" me up again and announced that we were in Wigan. All this movement in the carriage had awakened everyone else and we all looked out at the Wigan illuminations. 8F Springs Branch was in darkness unfortunately and although it was packed we did not see anything which could be noted down.

We sped on past Warrington past the dark 8B Warrington Bank Quay shed. We would be in Crewe in 30 minutes and I was really looking forward to that.

Before Hartford the train braked violently and for ten minutes we went along very slowly. Track-relaying operations were underway under floodlights. Concrete sleepers were being laid and continuous welded rails probably too. I was rather taken aback when I saw the ghostly silhouette of English Electric Type 4 D337 on these operations. In a recent issue of Modern Railways I had read that D337 was stored as unserviceable. What a pack of lies! Now Crewe would soon be here and I leaned back ready for that. I expected to see a lot of main line Co-Co Electric locos there.

C
R
SLEEP   E   SLEEP
W
E

The last time I had looked at my watch it was 03.30. Now it was 04.20 and I had fallen asleep (when I did not want to) about six miles outside Crewe. It was now beginning to get light. Our friend D.S. should have awakened me at Crewe for me to relieve him. He had not. He must have probably thought we had not reached Crewe. "Did you not notice that the train stopped for 15 minutes." I inquired "Oh, yes." "Did you see much?", "Nothing much there." and so it went on. The twit must have been looking through dark glasses not to see anything.

D.S. inquired when we would reach Crewe because I would let him get some sleep then.

"That station we stopped at was Crewe!" I exclaimed to D.S... For fear of offending the girls in the carriage I had to restrict the language which I wished to shower upon him. Now I was on duty I told him to get some sleep as "nicely" as I could.

Judging by the way the train was whistling through the countryside now I guessed that D228 "Samaria" had been taken off at Crewe and one of the new BR Electric Mainline E3XXX Classes had been substituted. We whistled through Nuneaton Trent Valley and were able to catch a glimpse of 5E Nuneaton at a slightly lower level to the west of the line.

"Black Five" 4-6-0 45001 of 5E Nuneaton was gratefully kopped by me near 5E Nuneaton. 15 minutes later we reached Rugby Midland. Rugby shed was now closed to steam but was now a changeover point from electric to diesel traction. As a new traction changeover point Rugby had recently been allocated additional English Electric Type 4 English Electric diesels. It also had a flourishing electric depot.

We had arrived at Rugby at 05.10 (18 minutes late) and I did not venture to go out as the late train could leave at any minute. I looked out the window to see our BR Mainline electric loco moving away from our train. Doubtless another English Electric Type 4 would be substituted. While D.S. was in a somewhat dazed state (for no apparent reason) I went through several carriages until I was opposite the diesel depot. The electric depot could not be seen.

RUGBY AREA

		Home shed		Built	Withdrawn	Scrap
Diesels						
English Electric Type 4 1Co-Co1 1958						
D 229	"Saxonia"	1B	Camden	*Sep-1959*		
D 236		12B	Carlisle Upperby	*Oct-1959*		
D 372		1B	Camden	*Jan-1962*		
D 375	*hauled*	1B	Camden	*Feb-1962*		
D 378		1B	Camden	*Feb-1962*		
Total	5					
North British 0-4-0 Shunter 1958		1F	Rugby	*Dec-1959*	*Feb-1967*	
D2913						
Total	1					
BR Sulzer Type 2 Bo-Bo 1958		1A	Willesden	*Jul-1960*		
D5092						
Total	1					
Steam				**Built**	**Withdrawn**	**Scrap**
Stanier 5MT 4-6-0 "Black Five" 1934		5E	Nuneaton (ex 1F)	*Mar-1935*	*Mar-1968*	*Jun-1968*
45001						
Total	1					

			Kops		4			
On Journey	8		Diesels		7			
Steam	1							
		Home Area			5	Visitors	2	
			1B		4	1F	1	
Shed	1A	1						
Distribution	5E	1						
	12B							
Steam Classes	1	1						
Steam Origin	LMS		1					
Journey Highlight:-		45001	(Steam!)					

I returned to our compartment and we left Rugby Midland at 05.26 - 16 minutes late.

English Electric Type 4 D378 gave us a smooth ride and I spent the next half hour conversing with my pretty girl travelling companion on my right. I now came to the conclusion that it was her exotic perfume that had drugged me to sleep before Crewe. She offered me a cigarette which I was pleased to accept and twenty minutes later I returned the compliment with an offer of one of my Rothmans King Size cigarettes.

D378 whistled through what I took to be Bletchley at high speed. 1E Bletchley went past unnoticed.

I take this opportunity to record the journey timing:-

		Schedule	*Actual*	*Miles*
Depart	CARLISLE	00.33	00.35	0
Depart	CREWE	03.45	?	141
Arrive	RUGBY MIDLAND	04.52	05.10	216½
Depart	RUGBY MIDLAND	05.00	05.16	216½
Arrive	WATFORD JUNCTION	06.23	06.38	281½

The train screeched to a halt at Watford Junction and D.S. and I made a hasty exit from the compartment. After appropriate farewells to our fellow travellers we got out of the carriage just as quickly. The train drew away and we noticed that we were the only people who had got out there. The only person in sight was the Station Inspector. He told me that IC Watford was now closed. This did not surprise me much as on my last check it had an allocation of one LMS 0-6-0 Shunter. It was now 06.39 and he told us that the first electric bucket of the day was due to leave for Willesden in one minute. We took the hint and ran down the steps from the platform, along a tunnel, up some more steps to the far away platform and got on the electric bucket just before it left.

The bucket could have been aptly termed a "slow bucket to China" as it crawled along at 20 M.P.H. D5010 of 1E Bletchley fairly zipped past us on some early train from the London Area. As we crawled along the suburban line our impatience grew. It was a nice day though and there was a few Big Eights passing periodically with freight trains which were going even slower than us in the opposite direction. These two things alleviated my impatience somewhat.

After travelling eight miles with seven needless stops at suburban stations (with nobody getting on and off) we arrived at South Kenton, after 30 tedious minutes. At South Kenton I was aghast when we were politely requested to get out along with the other passengers. This was unscheduled! On enquiry I found out that these was something wrong with the conductors on the line that we were travelling on and another electric bucket would collect us on the other platform and then our journey would continue.

After another unscheduled wait of 15 minutes our journey continued. We arrived at Willesden Junction at 07.24 - 14 minutes late. I was walking out of the station when D.S. said we would get some good photographs here. I agreed, looked for Graham's camera and found it was missing. I belted back to the bucket without a word to a puzzled D.S. and took possession of Graham's camera which I had left on the seat. My absent-minded streak in me had shown itself again and for once I had something to praise D.S. about for a change (for his unknown reminder).

		Schedule	Actual	Miles
Depart	WATFORD JUNCTION	06.40	06.40	0
	7 intermediate stops			
Arrive	SOUTH KENTON	06.59	05.10	8
Depart	SOUTH KENTON	06.59	07.10	8
	4 intermediate stops			
Arrive	WILLESDEN JUNCTION	07.14	07.24	12¼

WATFORD TO WILLESDEN							
		Home shed		Built	Withdrawn		Scrap
Diesels							
BR 0-6-0 Shunter 1953							
D3016		1A	Willesden	Feb-1953			
D3849		1B	Camden	Aug-1959			
Total	2						
BR Sulzer Type 2 Bo-Bo 1958							
D5010		1E	Bletchley	Mar-1959			
Total	1						
Steam				Built	Withdrawn		Scrap
Stanier 8F 2-8-0 "Big Eight" 1935							
48073		16C	Derby	Dec-1936	Apr-1967		Sep-1967
48411		6B	Mold Junction	Sep-1943	Jul-1967		Nov-1967
48688		1H	Northampton(ex 1E)	Feb-1944	Jul-1965		Oct-1965
48739		1H	Northampton	Dec-1945	Jan-1967		Jul-1967
Total	4						
On Journey	7	Kops		7			
Steam	4	Diesels		3			
		Home Area		5	Visitors	2	
Shed	1A	1	1B	1	1E	1	
Distribution:-	1H	2					
	6B	1	16C	1			
Steam classes on view	1						
Steam Origin	LMS		4				

Two of the "Big Eights" really were strangers (one from 16C Derby and one from 6B Mold Junction). 48688 seemed to be on her last journey as later withdrawl records showed her to be very recently withdrawn.

- - - - - - - - - - - - - - - -

We turned left outside Willesden Junction Station and walked along to the electric depot.

We went along a path at the side of the yard until I thought we had better cut across the yard into the electric shed because we did not want to walk foolishly in front of the offices. That would be asking for trouble!

THE FRIED FEET AFFAIR

To get to the electric depot some rusted London Transport Board 3-rail track (one conductor rail) had to be negotiated. D.S. thought that they were live but I showing my Sherlock Holmes streak told him that they were at least 20 years old and quite harmless. We skipped over the conductor rails (without touching them) and were just about to disappear inside the electric depot when one of the guards roared out "What the hell are you doing here?" We turned round to see that he had come out off the offices. When Graham Strachan had been here a man had showered a vast array of adjectives (quite unprintable) onto him. He took the hint and left. Before the man could give us the treatment I told him that we had a permit for Willesden (meaning the electric depot). He was a bit shocked at this and ordered me to show him it. D.S. stood trying to look pretty and tried to put on his best expression while I rummaged about and found it. The boss looked over it carefully and said that is was for 1A Willesden up the road and was not valid here. I knew that perfectly well and had hoped it would fool him. He said that they did not issue permits for the Electric Depot as there were no electrics her as yet and only then would the shed be officially open. It was filled, with interesting BR Type 2's and EE Type 4's though and I hopefully asked if we could still get round! The boss said that he could not allow that because the "juice" (as he put it) was on (and) we could not go round in these circumstances. He then added that we had better watch these LTB 3-rail tracks that we had hopped over going in because they were live too - 650 volts DC.

With a last mournful look at the diesels inside the electric depot we left taking a route round the rusty but live 3-rail tracks. Why did they have to choose today of all days to test out the electric depots overhead caterny when there were no electrics there?

D.S. was still a bit white as we walked back to the path. He still could not believe that he had been hopping over live rails. He was too shocked to give me a row for letting him dice with death. Of course I would never have stood on one of the conductor rails. I even avoid the lines on a pavement!

- - - - - - - - - - - - - - - -

As we walked back to Willesden Junction I had the pleasure of kopping D217 "Carinthia" of 1A Willesden on an express passenger to London. D369 of 1B Camden was noted on a passenger train going in the other direction.

WILLESDEN JUNCTION							
			Home shed		Built	Withdrawn	Scrap
Diesels							
English Electric Type 4 1Co-Co1 1958							
D 217	"Carinthia"		1A	Willesden	*Jul-1959*		
D 369			1B	Camden	*Dec-1961*		
Total	2						
At Junction	2		**Kops**	1			
Steam	0		**Diesels**	2			
		Home Area		2	**Visitors**	0	
Shed	1A	1	1B	1			
Distribution:-							

We walked pasted the station turned left into Old Oak Lane and then right into Goodhall Street. Now after a short five minutes walk 1A Willesden steam depot was in sight. Naturally, after our rather alarming experience at the electric depot we were a little apprehensive as we entered the shed and hoped that the failure to get round Willesden Electric Depot would not be the first of many failures to get round sheds.

We kept on walking past the office and popped into the roundhouse. We had a permit but it was for twelve persons and I did not like to chance it. I would flourish it about if we were stopped though.

There were 11 diesels in the roundhouse and 1 Big Eight (funny!). D235 "Apapa" was noted with interest as it was supposed to be stored as unserviceable (according to Modern Railways correspondent). It certainly did not seem to be unserviceable or stored!

We left the diesel roundhouse and came upon the dead line: - Four LMS 2-6-4 Tanks and two other interesting condemned locos. 82032 had been transferred from 6H Bangor to 70A Nine Elms along with several of her sisters who all had passed through Willesden unharmed. Some defect was found in 82032 at Willesden and here she remained condemned. Modern Railways had given her a mentioned the previous month and she was expected and welcomed by us. "Doodle-Bug" 46509 was lying condemned also. After paying our respects we continued our tour.

We entered the largest part of 1A (the steam running depot) after D.S. had made an unsuccessful chase after a green (ex Western Region) "Doodle Bug" which (probably on seeing him) moved further up the shed yard. The running shed was packed with locos and there were plenty of railway workers about for a Sunday morning.

As we emerged at the other end of the running shed after having completed it I saw Willesden's last Jinty 47432 up by herself on a side-line quietly rusting away (in a dreadful condition) in the open-air. A sad sight as of course she too would be withdrawn this month. As I was paying my last respects D.S. saw his green "Doodle Bug" again and hared off after her. The "Doodle Bug" on seeing her old friend moved off again leaving D.S. dejected and frustrated.

I went over to console him and then the shed master appeared in the shed-yard also. He walked past us a few times (while we waited for the green Doodle-bug) but he did not bother us. At last the "Doodle Bug" took pity on us, came back, and D.S. took a photograph of her.

1A WILLESDEN

Diesels

English Electric Type 4 1Co-Co1 1958

		Home shed		Built	Withdrawn	Scrap
D 234	"Accra"	1F	Rugby	Sep-1959		
D 235	"Apapa"	1F	Rugby	Oct-1959		
D 304		1A		Dec-1960		
D 341	pass shed	5A	Crewe Diesel	Apr-1961		
Total	4					

Hudswell-Clarke 0-6-0 Shunter 1956

D2518		1A		Nov-1961	Feb-1967	
Total	1					

BR 0-6-0 Shunter 1953

D3050		1A		May-1954		
Total	1					

BR Sulzer Type 2 Bo-Bo 1958

D5087		1A		Jun-1960		
D5090		1A		Jun-1960		
D5031		1A		Jun-1959		
D5074		1A		Mar-1960		
D5088		1A		Jun-1960		
Total	5					

English Electric Type 1 Bo-Bo 1957

D8002		1A		Jul-1957		
D8035		1A		Sep-1959		
D8036		1A		Oct-1959		
Total	3					

Steam

		Home shed		Built	Withdrawn	Scrap

Fairburn 4MT 2-6-4T 1945

42106		1A		Oct-1950	May-1965	Oct-1965
42114		1A		Jun-1949	Jun-1965	Oct-1965
42222		1A		Mar-1946	May-1965	Oct-1965
42289		1A		Oct-1947	May-1965	Oct-1965
Total	4					

Ivatt 4MT 2-6-0 1947

43007		1A		Jan-1948	Sep-1967	Dec-1967
43018		1A		May-1948	Nov-1966	Apr-1967
Total	2					

Stanier 5MT 4-6-0 "Black Five" 1934

44661		1A		Jun-1949	Aug-1967	Feb-1968
44763		1A	(ex1G Woodford Halse) Oct-1947		Sep-1965	Mar-1966
44766		2F	Bescot	Dec-1947	Aug-1967	Dec-1967
44774		1A		May-1947	Aug-1967	Mar-1968
44780		1A		Jul-1947	Jun-1968	Dec-1968
44860		1A		Dec-1944	Jan-1967	Apr-1968
45292		1A		Dec-1936	Nov-1967	Mar-1968
45379	to Barry Docks	1A		Jul-1937	Jul-1965	saved
Total	8					

Ivatt 2MT 2-6-2T 1946

46507		to 6C	Croes Newydd	Nov-1952	Jun-1965	Oct-1965
46509	D.S. Photo	1A		Dec-1952	Oct-1966	Jan-1967
Total	2					

Midland 3F "Jinty" 0-6-0T 1924 dev. of Johnson 1899 design

47432		1A		Oct-1926	Aug-1965	Feb-1966
Total	1					

		Home shed		Built	Withdrawn	Scrap
Stanier 8F 2-8-0 "Big Eight" 1935						
48081		to 10F	Rose Grove	*Jan-1937*	*Mar-1968*	*Jun-1968*
48173	*to Barry Docks*	6B	Mold Junction	*Jun-1943*	*Jul-1965*	*saved*
48203		1A	(ex 1E Bletchley)	*Jul-1942*	*Apr-1966*	*Jul-1966*
48365		1H	Northampton(ex1F)	*Sep-1944*	*May-1968*	*Sep-1968*
48450		2C	Stourbridge Junction	*Aug-1944*	*Sep-1967*	*Sep-1968*
48518	*to Barry Docks*	1A		*Aug-1944*	*Jul-1965*	*saved*
48554		1A	(ex 1E Bletchley)	*Jun-1945*	*Aug-1966*	*Nov-1966*
48601	*to Barry Docks*	1A		*Feb-1943*	*Jun-1965*	*Oct-1965*
48624		1A		*Dec-1943*	*Jul-1965*	*saved*
48626		1A	(ex 1E Bletchley)	*May-1943*	*Jan-1968*	*Jul-1968*
48747		2F	Bescot	*May-1946*	*Sep-1966*	*Jan-1967*
Total	*11*					
BR Standard 4-6-0 1951 5MT Doncaster						
73031		81F	Oxford(ex85B)	*Jul-1953*	*Sep-1965*	*Dec-1965*
73165	*Caprotti valved*	9H	Patricroft	*Mar-1957*	*Sep-1965*	*Dec-1965*
Total	*2*					
BR Standard 4MT 2-6-0 Doncaster 1953						
76035		to 6A	Chester Midland	*May-1954*	*May-1966*	*Aug-1966*
76037		1A		*Jun-1954*	*May-1967*	*Nov-1967*
76041		1A		*Jul-1954*	*Apr-1967*	*Feb-1968*
Total	*3*					
BR Standard 2MT 2-6-0 Doncaster 1953				*Built*	*Withdrawn*	*Scrap*
78003		1A	(ex 6H Bangor)	*Dec-1952*	*Dec-1966*	*Sep-1967*
78018	*to Barry Docks*	1A		*Mar-1954*	*Nov-1966*	*saved*
78019	*to Barry Docks*	1A		*Mar-1954*	*Nov-1966*	*saved*
78029		1A		*Jul-1954*	*Sep-1965*	*Jan-1966*
78032		1A	(ex 6H Bangor)	*Sep-1954*	*Sep-1965*	*Jan-1966*
78033		1A		*Oct-1954*	*Sep-1965*	*Nov-1965*
78034		1A		*Oct-1954*	*Jan-1966*	*Apr-1966*
78035		1A		*Nov-1954*	*Dec-1965*	*Apr-1966*
78038		1A		*Nov-1954*	*Sep-1966*	*Dec-1966*
78039		1A		*Nov-1954*	*Sep-1966*	*Mar-1967*
78043		1A		*Dec-1954*	*Sep-1965*	*Jan-1966*
78058		1A	(ex 6H Bangor)	*Sep-1956*	*Dec-1966*	*Sep-1967*
78059	*to Barry Docks*	1A	(ex 6H Bangor)	*Sep-1956*	*Nov-1966*	*saved*
78060		1A		*Oct-1956*	*Oct-1966*	*Mar-1967*
78063		1A		*Nov-1956*	*Dec-1966*	*Dec-1967*
Total	*15*					
BR Standard 3MT 2-6-2T Swindon 1952						
82032		ex 6H	Bangor	*Jan-1955*	*May-1965*	*Nov-1965*
Total	*1*					
BR Standard 9F 2-10-0 Brighton 1954. 1957 double chimney						
92218		2D	Banbury	*Jan-1960*	*May-1968*	*Jul-1968*
Total	*1*					

On Shed	64	**Kops**		58		
Steam	50	**Diesels**		14		
Withdrawn	11					

Home Locos		51	**Home Area**		3	**Visitors**	10
Shed	1A	52	1F		2	1H	1
Distribution:-	2C	1	2D		1	2F	2
	5A	1	6B		1	ex 6H	1
	9H	1	81F		1		

Steam classes on view		11				
Steam Origin		LMS	28	BR	22	
Shed Highlights:-		82032 ex 6H	Bangor			
Steam	*Sep-50*	135	*Mar-59*	130	*Apr-65*	67
Allocation					*Aug-65*	51
		Closed to Steam:-			*Sep-65*	

1A WILLESDEN (continued)							
Home Steam	excluding withdrawn locos						
On/Off Shed	On Shed	31	Off Shed		21	% On Shed	60%
Not on Shed							
"Black Fives"	44760	44862	44865	44985	45299	45331	
						45418	7
"Jinty"						47435	1
"Big Eights"	48010	48121	48336	48517	48526	48527	
	48531	48549	48603	48628	48754	48757	12
BR 4MT 2-6-0						76039	1
						total	21
	saw elsewhere on the tour				8		
	saw on Dec 64 Manchester and Crewe trip				1		
	saw on June 67 Carlisle visit				1		

Review and Appraisal of 1A Willesden

The shed was on the west side of the line just north of Willesden Junction Station. Walking time was 5 minutes.

The reason for a "Big Eight" being in the diesel roundhouse was obvious after consideration of the weeks transfers at a later date. 48108 was due to be transferred to 10F Rose Grove in Lancashire later that week. Obviously the shed master wanted her out of the road unless she was accidentally worked or rostered on some long distance freight from the running shed.

All the 2-6-4 tanks on shed were condemned. All the rest of Willesden's allocation had been recently transferred elsewhere. Eleven withdrawn engines were on shed plus the "Jinty" to be withdrawn this month. *Remarkably three of the four withdrawn "Big Eights" on shed and the withdrawn "Black Five" would end up at Barry Docks and be eventually rescued from there.*

Interesting locos on shed consisted of three "Big Eights" and one "Big Nine" from depots ranging from Banbury, the Birmingham area and Mold Junction.

In all a great steam shed, mostly home-based, and let's have others like Willesden.

Of the 15 78XXX class on shed I had previously seen 78018 at Carlisle in September 1958 when she belonged to the then 12D Kirby Stephen. A couple of interesting Standard 4-6-0 5's on shed one from faraway 9H Patricroft and one from 81F Oxford. 46507 an Ivatt 2MT 2-6-0 had been transferred to 6C Croes Newydd but had never made the journey and was withdrawn from here in June 1965.

60% of the Home Steam locos were on shed (31/52). 10 of the missing steam locos were to be seen elsewhere on the tour and a couple more had previously been seen on recorded trips. *It was extremely sad to relate and hard to believe that this busy steam shed was to be closed to steam within two months on 27 September 1965.*

THE IVORY CASTLE AFFAIR

As we passed by the roundhouse on our way out we saw two unfortunates getting chucked out by the shedmaster. We had been luckier! We were passing near to the offices on our way out when D.S. asked for some water.

I carefully filled up his cup from my vacuum flask and expected him to quench his thirst. D.S. then put down the cup and rummaged around in his bag and brought out a toothbrush and toothpaste and then proceeded to brush his teeth in the middle of the shed entrance. What an idiotic, stupid place to clean his teeth. He was in full view of the offices too! While he cleaned his teeth I rained some unprintable adjectives on him. I doubt if anybody here had seen someone clean their teeth in the shed yard! Never have I been so ashamed and embarrassed of the company I kept.

D.S. after listening attentively to my comments with his mouth full of toothpaste saliva gave up trying to explain as I retreated out of earshot for fear of having toothpaste spat at me. D.S. finally finished and his "dazzling" ivory castles fairly blinded me as he walked away from the public eye out of the shed.

On we go

We then turned right outside Willesden and made our way along Old Oak Lane in the direction of 81A Old Oak Common. In Old Oak Common Lane we caught up with a sensible older railwayist who told us a few things about 81A. We gathered that we had to look out for the watchman.

The three of us walked in the main entrance and the very aged watchman saw us and was about to say something about "GET OUT!" when the London bloke about turned and we walked with him. Rather crestfallen I thought that the London bloke had no guts to question and argue with the old bloke. Who knows we might have got round. Now we seemed to be walking back after another unsuccessful venture.

Then about a hundred yards from the main entrance the London youth turned sharp right away from the road and started to follow the canal bank. "Oh, did I forget to tell, how forgetful of me. This is the back entrance to the shed along this path!" "Kind of tradesman's entrance for trainspotters mostly."

We followed along the path keeping a respectful distance from the canal which was a mere twenty feet deep I was told. OK for those that could swim I thought. Finally, we came to a broken down wall. The entrance! Our informant told us "No offices to pass now. We are now in the running sheds area. They must think that it lowers the tone for trainspotters to use the main entrance. They never bother about this one."

In front of me was the interesting sight of an open former steam roundhouse with one Warship, 3 Westerns and 1 Hymek in it. They were just basking in the sunshine there. I had always wanted to see examples of these classes.

A lot of demolition was going on in the roundhouse area. This (one of the old steam roundhouses) was earmarked to go I thought. When Graham Strachan had visited Old Oak it has been intact and he had told me that is was so dark that he had difficulty in making out the numbers.

While this modernisation was going on the "roundhouse" was still used. We moved cautiously through the debris and I noted Western D1062 "Western Courier", Warship D865 "Zealous" and Hymek D7056. We continued on to the shed yard looking warily for shedmaster. After disposing of the shed yard we chanced the maintenance depot. Inside I shouted a warning to D.S. about oil on the ground and to prove my point I promptly skidded on a patch and ended up on my back.

Our last place of looking was what I took to be the repair depot in there we had the pleasure to see the founder member of the Western class D1000 "Western Enterprise". Thus we completed a splendid depot - diesel - but nevertheless splendid. It must have been an incredible depot to see in steam times with majestic "Kings", "Castles" etc.

81A OLD OAK COMMON

		Home shed		Built	Withdrawn	Scrap
Diesels						
BR "Warship" Type 4 B-B 1958						
D 832	"Onslaught"	84A	Laira (Plymouth)	*Feb-1961*	*Dec-1972*	saved
Total	1					
North British "Warship" Type 4 B-B 1960						
D 837	"Ramilles"	83A	Newton Abbot	*Nov-1960*	*May-1971*	
D 865	"Zealous"	83A	Newton Abbot	*Jun-1962*	*May-1971*	
Total	2					
BR "Western" Type 4 C-C 1958						
D1000	"Western Enterprise"	81A		*Dec-1961*	*Feb-1974*	
D1006	"Western Stalwart"	82A	Bristol (Bath Road)	*Jun-1962*	*Apr-1975*	
D1010	"Western Campaigner"	84A	Laira (Plymouth)	*Oct-1962*	*Feb-1977*	saved
D1019	"Western Challenger"	84A	Laira (Plymouth)	*May-1963*	*May-1973*	
D1030	"Western Muskateer"	84A	Laira (Plymouth)	*Dec-1963*	*Apr-1976*	
D1032	"Western Marksman"	84A	Laira (Plymouth)	*Dec-1963*	*May-1973*	
D1033	"Western Trooper"	84A	Laira (Plymouth)	*Jan-1964*	*Sep-1976*	
D1039	"Western King"	84A	Laira (Plymouth)	*Sep-1962*	*Jul-1973*	
D1041	"Western Prince"	82A	Bristol (Bath Road)	*Oct-1962*	*Feb-1977*	saved
D1049	"Western Monarch"	84A	Laira (Plymouth)	*Dec-1962*	*Apr-1976*	
D1055	"Western Advocate"	87E	Landore	*Mar-1963*	*Jan-1976*	
D1056	"Western Sultan"	87E	Landore	*Mar-1963*	*Dec-1976*	
D1057	"Western Chieftain"	87E	Landore	*Apr-1963*	*May-1976*	
D1059	"Western Empire"	87E	Landore	*Apr-1963*	*Oct-1975*	
D1062	"Western Courier"	87E	Landore	*May-1963*	*Aug-1974*	saved
D1065	"Western Consort"	84A	Laira (Plymouth)	*Jun-1963*	*Nov-1976*	
D1069	"Western Vanguard"	87E	Landore	*Oct-1963*	*Oct-1975*	
D1073	"Western Bulwark"	81A		*Dec-1963*	*Aug-1974*	
Total	18					
Brush Type 4 Co-Co 1962						
D1599		82A	Bristol (Bath Rd.)ex87E	*Jul-1964*		
D1661	"North Star"	87E	Landore	*Mar-1965*		
D1690		2B	Oxley	*Nov-1963*		
D1691		86A	Cardiff Canton	*Nov-1963*		
D1708		81A		*Jan-1964*		
D1727		81A		*Apr-1964*		
D1731		86A	Cardiff Canton	*Jun-1964*		
D1732		82A	Bristol (Bath Road)	*Apr-1964*		
D1836		87E	Landore (ex D16)	*Apr-1965*		
Total	9					
BR 0-6-0 Shunter 1953						
D3030		81A		*Oct-1953*		
D3598		81A		*Oct-1958*		
D3601		81A		*Oct-1958*		
D3756		81A		*Oct-1959*		
D3804		81A		*Jan-1959*		
D3966		81A		*May-1960*		
D4000		81A		*Oct-1960*		
D4003		81A		*Nov-1960*		
Total	8					
North British Type 2 B-B 1959						
D6326		81A		*May-1960*	*Oct-1971*	
D6343		81A		*May-1962*	*Oct-1971*	
D6351		81A		*Jun-1962*	*Nov-1968*	
D6355		81A		*Aug-1962*	*Sep-1968*	
D6356		81A		*Sep-1962*	*Oct-1971*	
Total	5					
Beyer Peacock (Hymek) Type 3 B-B 1961						
D7026		81A		*Mar-1962*	*Oct-1974*	
D7049		82A	Bristol (Bath Road)	*Oct-1962*	*Jan-1972*	
D7056		81A		*Nov-1962*	*Jan-1972*	
D7057		81A		*Nov-1962*	*Jan-1972*	
D7061		81A		*Dec-1962*	*Jan-1972*	
D7073		81A		*Mar-1963*	*Jan-1972*	
D7076		81A		*May-1963*	*May-1973*	
D7080		81A	(ex 86A Cardiff Canton)	*Dec-1963*	*Nov-1972*	
Total	8					

On Shed	51	Kops	50			
Steam	0	Diesels	51			
Withdrawn	0					
Home Locos	24	Home Area		0	Visitors	28
Shed	81A	24				
Distribution:-	2B	1				
	82A	5	83A	2	84A	9
	86A	2	87E	8		
Shed Highlights:-	D1000	"Western Enterprise" of 81A Old Oak Common				
Steam	Aug-50	193	Mar-59	173	May-65	0
Allocation					Jul-65	0
		Closed to Steam:-			Mar-65	

Review and Appraisal of 81A Old Oak Common

The shed was at the north side of the junction of the Reading and High Wycombe lines two miles west of Westbourne Park. Walking time was 10 minutes from Willesden Junction Station.

Old Oak Common used to be the premier Western Region steam shed with an allocation of 193 steam engines in 1950 packed with quality mainline engines including the beloved "Kings". Sadly the shed had closed completely to steam a few months ago. How I would have loved to visit Old Oak in the late 50's or early 60's before the steam culls of the "Grim Reaper." The 1959 allocation of 173 steam included 13 "Kings", 35 "Castles", 20 "Halls" and 8 "Modified Halls". O happy days! Sadly steam had departed completely a few months ago.

All the 18 "Westerns" were in maroon livery. None were in green lively (I think). The North British Type 2's had been recently acquired from the 83A/84A area where the class had been based. They work empty carriages from Paddington to the carriage sheds at Old Oak. This hydraulic class seemed to have few troubles unlike their deplorable diesel sisters (D6100 class) in Scotland where the majority are smashed up, burnt out or are stored awaiting Paxman engines.

The D63XX class here seemed identical to me but inside the transmission was different. There were only 3 Warships on shed but the enormous number of Westerns D1XXX class probably explained that. In the first semi-demolished roundhouse (already mentioned) I was pleased to kop D1661 North Star the first of the class to be named. The only engine not kopped by me on shed was D1836 (on loan from the LMR). On Saturday 10th July I was travelling back from Warrington to Wigan with the 20.05 diesel bucket when I noted D1836 near Newton-Le-Willows passing me going south on a car train for the Western Region (from Bathgate possibly!). This was during my July 4th - 11th Blackpool stay.

On we go

We made our way out by the tradesman's entrance and our local friend asked of our tour. He found out that we planned to use the underground extensively. Get a tube-rover he said. Its only 10 shillings (50p) and you can use London Transport Buses as well. That would be a saving I thought. Fancy having tube-rovers! Who wants to muck about underground stations for day! Apart from us - who? He said that we would be able to get one at Paddington Station (our second call after Queen's Park which was out first but not certain to have tube-rovers on sale). We thanked our friendly local for all his help and he disappeared off just before we got on the local electric train (DC) for Queen's Park. Two diesels and one "Black

Five" were noted on the journey.

WILLESDEN TO QUEENS PARK						
		Home shed		Built	Withdrawn	Scrap
Diesels						
English Electric Type 4 1Co-Co1 1958						
D 308		1B	Camden	Nov-1960		
Total	1					
BR Sulzer Type 2 Bo-Bo 1958						
D5033		1A	Willesden	Aug-1959		
Total	1					
Steam				Built	Withdrawn	Scrap
Stanier 5MT 4-6-0 "Black Five" 1934						
44760		1A	Willesden	Sep-1947	Oct-1966	Jan-1967
Total	1					
On Journey	3	Kops		3		
Steam	1	Diesels		2		
		Home Area		3	Visitors	0
Shed	1A	2	1B	1		
Distribution						
Steam Classes	1					
Steam Origin	LMS	1				
Journey Highlight:-	44760	(Steam!)				

		Schedule	Actual	Miles
Depart	WILLESDEN JUNCTION	9.38	9.38	0
Arrive	QUEENS PARK	9.40	9.40	1¾
Depart	QUEENS PARK	Bakerloo Line		
Arrive	PADDINGTON			

We got off at Queens Park and changed on to the Bakerloo Line of London Underground.
We paid the ticket collector at Paddington for our short seven minute tube journey. We took the opportunity of leaving our grips in the left luggage office for the day after queuing for ten valuable minutes. D.S. was probably feeling empty after his long fast from the previous afternoon and now infuriated me by demanding that we went into the refreshment room and get some breakfast. I wanted to push on as we had a heavy schedule ahead and of course I was thinking of sheds to be visited and not thinking about some food to eat. I was not in the slightest bit hungry. We had an argument over it and in the end I gave way to D.S.'s pleas that he would die for lack of food "Did your Beecham Powder not fill you up?" I shouted after D.S. as he disappeared inside the refreshment room.

The refreshment room was packed and D.S. ordered me to keep a place for him while he went over to the self-service and got himself some grub. D.S. bought three of BR's exorbitantly priced sandwiches (ranging from 9 pence (4p) to one shilling and three pence (6p), a tiny but zoombala priced pie and a cup of tea). I reluctantly followed suit and bought a cup of coffee and one sandwich. D.S. wanted to remain seated for some time and I got up and made a tour of the station.

PADDINGTON STATION (MORNING)						
		Home shed		Built	Withdrawn	Scrap
Diesels						
Brush Type 4 Co-Co 1962						
D1668		87E	Landore	Mar-1965		
Total	1					
BR 0-6-0 Shunter 1953						
D3031		81A	Old Oak Common	Nov-1953		
Total	1					
North British Type 2 B-B 1959						
D6326	seen at 81A	81A	Old Oak Common	May-1960	Oct-1971	
Total	1					

On Station	3	Kops	2		
Steam	0	Diesels	3		
		Home Area		2 Visitors	1
Shed	81A	2 87E	1		
Distribution:-					

I heard something about the 10.30 "Cornish Rivera Express" leaving over the public address system and I flew away up the platform after the engine at the front but whatever it was had dashed good acceleration and I never even caught sight of it! D6326 (seen at Old Oak) was noted on its empty carriage workings with interest. I returned to the refreshment room and D.S. was ready to go. I glanced at my watch - twenty minutes to eleven. We might make the St Pancras - Cricklewood train on the hour if we are lucky. After making enquiries at the underground ticket office we were sent to an office back upstairs at the station and we both got a 10/- tube-rover. No need to waste time queuing for tickets now and we passed the ticket office by and hopped on to a Circle line tube.

Depart	PADDINGTON	Circle Line	
Arrive	KINGS CROSS ST.PANCRAS		

I was surprised to find Baker Street tube station out in the open air when we stopped there. Hopped off at Kings Cross/St Pancras and via a maze of interchange corridors reached St Pancras main line station with three minutes to spare before our train left. Flashed out Railrover tickets about and boarded the bucket (diesel multiple unit). We left promptly on the hour.

		Schedule	Actual	Miles
Depart	LONDON ST.PANCRAS	11.00	11.00	0
Arrive	CRICKLEWOOD	11.12	11.12	5¼

I had been warned by a Peterborough railwayist (who I had a long, interesting talk about trains when he had visited Edinburgh on the day of the Wales-Scotland rugby international in February) that St Pancras goods yard or Cambridge Street was well worth visiting on a Sunday as "Peaks", "Type 2's" etc were stabled over the weekend there. If D.S. and I had not suddenly seen it on our right we would have visited it after our return from 14A and 14B. We were so startled unexpectedly seeing a line of diesels that only three numbers were snatched down as we speeded past. At least we would have our eyes skinned on the return journey!

ST.PANCRAS TO CRICKLEWOOD							
			Home shed		Built	Withdrawn	Scrap
Diesels							
BR Sulzer "Peak" Type 4 1Co-Co1 1959							
D 17			55A	Leeds Holbeck	Dec-1960		
Total	1						
BR Sulzer Type 2 Bo-Bo 1958							
D5108			52A	Gateshead	Oct-1960		
D5241			D14	Cricklewood Division	Jan-1964		
D5280			D16	Nottingham Division	Jun-1964		
D5399			D14	Cricklewood Division	Jul-1962		
D7525			D16	Nottingham Division	Jan-1965		
D7597			ML	Midland Lines	Aug-1964		
Total		6					
Birmingham R.C. & W. Co.Type 2 Bo-Bo 1958							
D5394			D15	Leicester Division	Jun-1962		
D5406			ML	Midland Lines	Aug-1962		
Total		2					
On Journey	9		Kops		7		
Steam	0		Diesels		9		
			Home Area		2 Visitors	7	
Shed	D14		2				
Distribution:-	D15		1 D16		2 ML	2	
	52A		1 55A		1		

118

We arrived at Cricklewood Station on time and were the only two people to get off. We intended to visit 14A Cricklewood East first. It was now a nice sunny day and we dawdled along the road. This district seemed a lot better than some - a decent residential area. We turned into Midland Brent Terrace (a private road) and I noted from the shed directory that the entrance was amusingly between houses Nos. 49 and 50. D.S. did not wish to make his entry official (although we had a permit) and like Workington he climbed a fence and broke in. I reluctantly followed.

14A Cricklewood East was the Midland Lines servicing depot in the London Area (D14 as its main-line locos are coded). Cricklewood Servicing Depot was quite modern with inspection bays and with trolleys to clamber over as well. Few workers were about. We saw one boss and I asked him if the depot across the line at Cricklewood West was still open. Yes he said. He did not ask us for our permit. All very pleasant - as diesel depots go.

14A CRICKLEWOOD EAST

		Home shed		Built	Withdrawn	Scrap
Diesels						
BR Sulzer "Peak" Type 4 1Co-Co1 1959						
D 113		ML	Midland Lines	*Aug-1961*		
D 122		ML	Midland Lines	*Oct-1961*		
D 124		ML	Midland Lines	*Oct-1961*		
D 136		ML	Midland Lines	*Dec-1961*		
Total	4					
BR 0-6-0 Shunter 1953						
D3179		14B	Cricklewood West	*Oct-1955*		
D3181		14B	Cricklewood West	*Oct-1955*		
D3306		14B	Cricklewood West	*May-1956*		
D3773		14B	Cricklewood West	*Jun-1959*		
Total	4					
BR Sulzer Type 2 Bo-Bo 1958						
D5221		D14	Cricklewood Division	*Aug-1963*		
D5230		ML	Midland Lines	*Oct-1963*		
D5285		ML	Midland Lines	*Jul-1964*		
Total	3					
Birmingham R.C. & W. Co.Type 2 Bo-Bo 1958						
D5396		D14	Cricklewood Division	*Jun-1962*		
D5407		D14	Cricklewood Division	*Aug-1962*		
D5409		D14	Cricklewood Division	*Aug-1962*		
D5410		D14	Cricklewood Division	*Sep-1962*		
Total	4					
LMS and BR 0-6-0 Shunter 1945						
12069		14B	Cricklewood West	*Jun-1950*	*Mar-1971*	
Total	1					

On Shed	16	Kops	13		
Steam	0	Diesels	16		
		Home Area	10	Visitors	6
Shed	D14	5 14B	5		
Distribution:-	ML	6			

Review and Appraisal of 14A Cricklewood East

The shed was on the east side of the main line north of the station. Walking time 15 minutes from Cricklewood Station.

I expected more to be on shed. A bit disappointing. Birmingham RCW and BR Type 2's have same electrical equipment Sulzer 6 cylinder GLDA28-B of 1250 b.h.p. at 750 r.p.m. Only four "Peaks" on shed but D14 had none allocated.

On we go

After having got quickly round the shed we surveyed the other shed which was about ¼ mile away on the other side of line. To go the proper way back to the station and to 14B via Edgware Road it would take 30 minutes. We would miss the next train. Of course we chose to cross the main line and when we reached it we found an official boarded crossing. At the other side we found a deep cutting separated us from the shed and we wasted a few minutes by taking an easier route around it.

14B was the old steam shed and D158 was noted outside the roundhouse. I had seen this Peak from 14A and that was the major reason why I asked the boss of 14A if it was open. The Regional Boss in London had earlier (by letter) told me it was closed. What a liar! It looked rather quaint seeing a line of diesels in a roundhouse. Very quaint. A fantastic contrast of clean colourful diesels arranged in a circular pattern round a dirty, drab, red-bricked roundhouse. We had not got very far when the typical steam shed master came up to us. He was a bit taken aback at seeing us and rather kindly said "You can't go wandering around here". I told him that we had a permit and I showed him it without complaining. He said that was OK then and asked us to hand it in before we left. He was a good bloke generally.

We "wandered" around the shed and I sent D.S. away to give him his permit. D.S. was away for a full five minutes while I waited patiently for him. I thought that he must be getting detained for questioning. When he arrived back finally he had nothing out of the ordinary to report. It was just a case of the "late" D.S. Some mothers do have them! Five minutes to hand in a permit. Tut Tut!

14B CRICKLEWOOD WEST						
		Home shed		Built	Withdrawn	Scrap
Diesels						
BR Sulzer "Peak" Type 4 1Co-Co1 1959						
D 158		D16	Nottingham Division	Mar-1962		
Total	1					
BR 0-6-0 Shunter 1953						
D3024		14B		Jun-1953		
Total	1					
BR 0-6-0 Shunter 1955						
D4116		14B		Jan-1962		
D4117		14B		Feb-1962		
D4134		14B		Jun-1962		
Total	3					
BR Sulzer Type 2 Bo-Bo 1958						
D5213		D14	Cricklewood Division	Jul-1962		
D5231		ML	Midland Lines	Dec-1963		
D5242		ML	Midland Lines	Jan-1964		
D5288		ML	Midland Lines	Aug-1964		
D5291		D14	Cricklewood Division	Aug-1964		
D7515		D14	Cricklewood Division	Dec-1964		
D7578		D16	Nottingham Division	Nov-1963		
Total	7					
Birmingham R.C. & W. Co.Type 2 Bo-Bo 1958						
D5400		D14	Cricklewood Division	Jul-1962		
D5405		ML	Midland Lines	Jul-1962		
Total	2					
LMS and BR 0-6-0 Shunter 1945						
12065		14B		Dec-1949	May-1971	
Total	1					
On Shed	15	Kops	15			
Steam	0	Diesels	15			
Home Locos	5	Home Area		4	Visitors	6
Shed	14B	5	D14	4		
Distribution:-	D16	2	ML	4		
Steam	Sep-50	193	Mar-59	173	Apr-65	0
Allocation					Jul-65	0
		Closed to Steam:-			Dec-64	

Review and Appraisal of 14B Cricklewood West

The shed was on the west side of the main line north of the station. Walking time would have been 15 minutes from Cricklewood Station.

Unfortunately the Cricklewood Area had closed to steam in December 1964 so we had to make do with pretty much the same fare as the 14A Cricklewood East (the Diesel Depot). Everything kopped though. Good for a shed I thought was closed. Must have been some shed in 1959 with 173 steam locos!

On we go

We took the Edgware Road exit from the shed and decided to reach the station via that road. Our walking rate got very slow in the midday sunshine and suddenly I looked at my watch and found that our return train left in under ten minutes. Mass panic ensued and I issued a few shouts to D.S. to get him to run like blazes. We belted down Edgware Road. D.S. ran as fast as his two ton army surplus boots could carry him. We much have looked very odd. I suppose the passer-by's point of view was that D.S. was doing his best to catch me. After anxious squints at the roads we passed on our left-hand sides we ascertained from a passer-by what road to take for Cricklewood Station. We arrived at the foot of the station steps and ran up the steps past a very astonished ticket collector and flopped down on a station seat. While we were recovering our breath I glanced anxiously at my watch. Two minutes to spare I noted with relief. Happiness is getting to a station just in time to catch a train. If we had missed it there would have not been another train for an hour.

		Schedule	Actual	Miles
Depart	CRICKLEWOOD	12.04	12.04	0
Arrive	LONDON ST.PANCRAS	12.18	12.18	5¼

Neither our eyesight nor our pens failed us when we approached St Pancras at a crawl past Cambridge Street Diesel Stabling Point. Every diesel visible from our vantage point was noted. It was a pleasure to see a Bristol "Peak" at a place where it probably rarely works to. Inside St Pancras station a rather shiny "Peak" attracted our attention. It was at the head of an express passenger train. To my disappointment it was D103 of ML. A few weeks before I had kopped it at Millerhill on the Mossend freight for Glasgow. It was then in a "candidatus" ex-works condition. Now it was deteriorating into the abominable condition of some of its disreputable sisters. D4136 of 14B was also noted on the station.

CRICKLEWOOD TO ST.PANCRAS						
		Home shed		Built	Withdrawn	Scrap
Diesels						
BR Sulzer "Peak" Type 4 1Co-Co1 1959						
D 35	*Cambridge St. Yard*	82A	Bristol (Bath Road)	*Jul-1961*		
D 62	*Cambridge St. Yard*	ML	Midland Lines (ex D16)	*Mar-1962*		
D 103	*St.Pancras Station*	ML	Midland Lines (ex D16)	*Mar-1961*		
Total	3					
BR 0-6-0 Shunter 1953						
D4136	*St.Pancras Station*	14B	Cricklewood West	*Jun-1962*		
Total	1					
BR Sulzer Type 2 Bo-Bo 1958						
D5198	*Cambridge St. Yard*	ML	Midland Lines	*May-1963*		
D5229	*Cambridge St. Yard*	ML	Midland Lines	*Oct-1963*		
Total	2					
On Journey	6	**Kops**		5		
Steam	0	**Diesels**		6		
		Home Area		1	Visitors	5
Shed	14B	1				
Distribution:-	ML	4 82A		1		

121

To go or not to go to 1B Camden is the question. Whether tis better to go and find out if the shed is closed as the "liar" at the head of the London Division of the Midland Region had informed me and possibly find nothing there or kop a few of the elusive 1B Type 4's. Or is it better not to take the risk and continue on our tight schedule. D.S. stood gaping (speechless at my eloquence) while I meditated on the problem. We shall not go to Camden was my conclusion.

Our next shed to be visited was Hornsey. Officially closed but in my epic conversation with that Peterborough chap I learned that Hornsey was well worth visiting. It was in fact a sub-shed of 34G Finsbury Park.

In the interchange corridor to the underground a tall chap stopped us and told us that Brush Type 4 D1570 of Holbeck was in Kings Cross station. I wonder why he thought that would interest us. Anyway it interested me as I needed it. We went through a few more corridors and came up to Kings Cross Station. Sure enough D1570 was in the diesel stabling point at the far end of the station. We made a quick tour of the station.

KINGS CROSS STATION							
			Home shed		Built	Withdrawn	Scrap
Diesels							
Brush Type 4 Co-Co 1962							
D1511			34G	Finsbury Park	Feb-1963		
D1551			34G	Finsbury Park (ex41A)	Jan-1964		
D1570			55A	Leeds Holbeck	Mar-1964		
Total		3					
Brush Type 2 A1A-A1A 1957							
D5601			34G	Finsbury Park	Mar-1960		
D5615			34G	Finsbury Park	May-1960		
D5648			34G	Finsbury Park	Sep-1960		
Total		3					
English Electric "Deltic" Type 5 Co-Co 1961							
D9004	"Queen's Own Highlander"		64B	Haymarket	May-1961		
Total		1					
On Station		7	Kops		3		
Steam		0	Diesels		7		
		Home Area		5	Visitors		2
Shed	34G		5				
Distribution:-	55A		1	64B	1		

With our new accomplice still with us we went down the underground and got a Piccadilly Line tube train for Turnpike Lane.

Depart	KINGS CROSS ST.PANCRAS	Piccadilly Line	
Arrive	TURNPIKE LANE		

After a pleasant ten minute walk we arrived at Hornsey MPD. Our friend (who came from Lancaster) on hearing that permits were not given for the 34 area said we had better be careful then.

He asked me for my wad of permits so he could go into the office and flash them about and then ask hopefully round. I suggested that we could continue round until we were stopped and then we could hopefully flash the permits about. That we agreed on. We also went up three different lines so we could get as far round as possible in case we were stopped. Thus we completed the shed. Got the lines that did not go down from somebody else and they got some numbers from me and so on. Then finally we went up the lines that somebody else did and checked up. A good idea if you are about to get chucked out but we got round OK.

34G HORNSEY sub-shed

		Home shed		Built	Withdrawn	Scrap
Diesels						
BR Sulzer "Peak" Type 4 1Co-Co1 1959						
D 182		52A	Gateshead	Sep-1962		
Total	*1*					
English Electric Type 4 1Co-Co1 1958						
D 345		50A	York	May-1961		
Total	*1*					
BR 0-6-0 Shunter 1953						
D3334		34G	Finsbury Park	Jan-1957		
D3716		34G	Finsbury Park	Sep-1959		
D3718		34G	Finsbury Park	Oct-1959		
Total	*3*					
BR Sulzer Type 2 Bo-Bo 1958						
D5054		34G	Finsbury Park	Dec-1959		
D5055		34G	Finsbury Park	Dec-1959		
D5058		34G	Finsbury Park	Jan-1960		
D5061		34G	Finsbury Park	Jan-1960		
D5062		34G	Finsbury Park	Jan-1960		
D5063		34G	Finsbury Park	Jan-1960		
D5069		34G	Finsbury Park	Jan-1960		
D5071		34G	Finsbury Park	Feb-1960		
D5094		34G	Finsbury Park	Feb-1960		
Total	*9*					
Brush Type 2 A1A-A1A 1957						
D5596		34G	Finsbury Park	Mar-1960		
D5605		34G	Finsbury Park	Apr-1960		
D5608		34G	Finsbury Park	Apr-1960		
D5610		34G	Finsbury Park	Apr-1960		
D5625		34G	Finsbury Park	Jun-1960		
D5643		34G	Finsbury Park	Aug-1960		
D5654		34G	Finsbury Park	Sep-1960		
D5675		34G	Finsbury Park	Dec-1960		
D5684		41A	Tinsley	Jan-1961		
Total	*9*					
English Electric "Baby Deltic" Type 5 Bo-Bo 1959						
D5902		34G	Finsbury Park	May-1959	Nov-1969	
Total	*1*					
British Thomson Houston Type 1 Bo-Bo 1957						
D8232		34G	Finsbury Park	Aug-1960	Mar-1971	
D8233		34G	Finsbury Park	Aug-1960	Feb-1969	
D8235		34G	Finsbury Park	Sep-1960	Oct-1968	
D8236		34G	Finsbury Park	Oct-1960	Oct-1968	
Total	*4*					
LMS and BR 0-6-0 Shunter 1945						
12138		34G	Finsbury Park	Jan-1953	Nov-1968	
Total	*1*					

On Shed	29	Kops		22		
Steam	0	Diesels		29		
		Home Area	26	Visitors		3
Shed	34G	26				
Distribution:-	41A	1				
	50A	1	55A		1	
Shed Highlights:-		D5902				
Steam	Aug-50	81	Apr-59	58	May-65	0
Allocation					Aug-65	0
			Closed to Steam:-		Jul-61	

Review and appraisal of 34G sub-shed Hornsey

The shed was at the east side of the station, being separated from the main line by a goods yard. Walking time was less than 5 minutes from Hornsey Station.

Must be the greatest sub-shed in the country! I was pleased to see my first "Baby Deltic". I had seen five of the BR Type 2's the previous July when I journeyed to France and back via London. Only three engines on shed were visitors. The shed by the way was lifeless - no workers were about. I suppose somebody was in the offices though.

On we go

THE POLYFOTO AFFAIR

Another pleasant walk back and we were back at Turnpike Lane underground station. Lo and behold D.S. saw a "Polyfoto" machine where you go inside, draw the curtain, sit down, insert Two shillings (10p) and three pictures of you are taken. You wait three minutes and the three pictures come out of a slot in the machine. As D.S. was so old he had to have a passport type photograph for his Youth Hostels Association card or they would not let him join. I was a juvenile member and did not require one. D.S. got his photograph taken and we waited patiently for the results. When I saw the results I summed the three pictures up as truly awful. Our tall Lancaster friend summed them up as revolting. D.S. did his own summing up by turning red. He could not help what the pictures looked like we agreed. Anyway it was a passport type-picture.

Depart	TURNPIKE LANE	*Piccadilly Line*	
Arrive	FINSBURY PARK		

Onto another tube and we are soon at Finsbury Park.

Still a fabulous sunny day and in 10 minutes we were at the shed entrance in Tollington Road.

We decided to bypass the offices and enter via the back of the shed. Anyway we had no permit. We had not got very far when one of the foremen stopped us. We were redirected to the shedmaster in the offices.

We found the shedmaster busy watching two erring vandals filling up some forms for the railway cops. I gathered that they had broken two windows in the shed. Tut tut!

I waved my wad of permits at the shedmaster. Oh! You cannot go round until the railway police have finished with them. You can have a list of what is on the shed from the charts outside and take a glance up the lines without actually going up the maintenance lines. Sorry about this boys but I dare not disobey the railway police. He turned round again to look at the interrogation at the other side of the room.

Trust this upset to happen! Shedmasters always were scared of railway cops. We had better make the best of a bad lot.

We noted the numbers off the maintenance chart and checked them off as we looked down the four lines of the maintenance depot. I had been told that Finsbury Park was a small shed and so it was. The maintenance and servicing depot was composed of only four lines. The shed had a total capacity of 20 only. Diesel depots tend to be small nowadays. We left the shed by the main entrance and went into the park beside the shed. To the cries of an enraged London "suit" who was sitting on one of the many seats I trespassed by walking on the grass. I ran up to the railings and noted another eight engines in the shed yard.

34G FINSBURY PARK

Diesels		Home shed		Built	Withdrawn	Scrap
Brush Type 4 Co-Co 1962						
D1502		34G	Finsbury Park	Nov-1962		
D1504		34G	Finsbury Park	Jan-1963		
D1531		34G	Finsbury Park	Jul-1963		
D1539		34G	Finsbury Park	Sep-1963		
D1541		34G	Finsbury Park	Sep-1963		
D1864	brand new	41A	Tinsley	May-1965		
D1886	brand new	40B	Immingham	Aug-1965		
Total	7					
BR 0-6-0 Shunter 1953						
D3307		34G	Finsbury Park	May-1956		
D3712		34G	Finsbury Park	Aug-1959		
D3715		34G	Finsbury Park	Sep-1959		
Total	3					
BR Sulzer Type 2 Bo-Bo 1958						
D5051		34G	Finsbury Park	Dec-1959		
D5055		34G	Finsbury Park	Dec-1959		
D5066		34G	Finsbury Park	Dec-1959		
D5067		34G	Finsbury Park	Dec-1959		
D5070		34G	Finsbury Park	Jan-1960		
Total	5					
Brush Type 2 A1A-A1A 1957						
D5590		34G	Finsbury Park	Feb-1960		
D5613		34G	Finsbury Park	May-1960		
D5640		34G	Finsbury Park	Aug-1960		
D5646		34G	Finsbury Park	Sep-1960		
D5678		34G	Finsbury Park	Dec-1960		
Total	5					
English Electric "Baby Deltic" Type 5 Bo-Bo 1959						
D5907		34G	Finsbury Park	May-1959	Oct-1968	
Total	1					
English Electric Type 1 Bo-Bo 1957						
D8026		34G	Finsbury Park	Dec-1959		
Total	1					
British Thomson Houston Type 1 Bo-Bo 1957						
D8230		34G	Finsbury Park	Jul-1960	Mar-1971	
Total	1					
English Electric "Deltic" Type 5 Co-Co 1961						
D9018	"Ballymoss"	34G	Finsbury Park	Nov-1961		
Total	1					
LMS and BR 0-6-0 Shunter 1945						
12112		34G	Finsbury Park	Jul-1952	Oct-1969	
12129		34G	Finsbury Park	Nov-1952	Sep-1967	
Total	2					

On Shed	26	Kops		15	
Steam	0	Diesels		26	

Home Shed		24 Home Area	0	Visitors	2
Shed	34G	24			
Distribution:-	40B	1 41A		1	
Shed Highlights:-		D1886 (brand new)			

Review and Appraisal of 34G Finsbury Park

The shed was on the west side of the line about ½ mile south of Finsbury Park Station. Walking time was 10 minutes from Finsbury Park Station.

Hornsey was better than that! All locos belonged to Finsbury Park. Two new Brushes from Derby works on shed. Good!

Good to kop another Baby Deltic. Nothing else to rave about. I expected it to have only about 30 on shed. My Peterborough acquaintance had told me of that (amongst many other things).

On we go

Another 10 minute walk back and we were back at the underground station. Next shed on our list was that great diesel depot - need I say so? I'd better - 30A Stratford.

No you can't have anything to eat D.S. I told D.S. what a gannet he must be! I told him that he had a few sandwiches at Paddington earlier that day. D.S. got angry and demanded that we have one square meal a day. I told him that he was a square and anyway I was not hungry. No time to eat when there is plenty of sheds to do.

Our Lancaster fellow who was still with us was an interesting conversationalist and I enjoyed and appreciated what he had to say. He was a pleasant change from the pestering D.S. I looked at the Lancaster boy's notebook and saw that he had seen almost a hundred engines the previous day at Stratford. Absolutely great was how he summed up Stratford. If that's what he saw on Saturday (a weekday) today should be really stupendous. I was really looking forward to the visit.

D.S. momentarily stopped thinking about his empty stomach and said what about the sub-machine gun post at the entrance, the searchlights, the tracker dogs and the guards. All devices to keep the trainspotters out. Admittedly I had envisaged 30A Stratford to be like this at one time but not nowadays I thought differently. I asked my Peterborough acquaintance about this (on that never-to-be forgotten day the February before on the day of the Scotland-Wales Rugby match) during our epic two hour conversation. He agreed that there used to be a man on the gate who stopped anybody from going round who had not a permit in the days when it had the biggest steam allocation in Britain. He told me that this lasted until the steam engines at Stratford had gone until the shed was dieselised. They did not bother then about trainspotters mucking about with their diesels and he told me the watchman had been taken off for good a few months before. That was good news at the time. I did not pass the news on to D.S. that from being the hardest shed to get round it was now comparatively easy. I preferred to keep on telling D.S. that it was a real high security shed. Hence his frightening pictures in his mind of what 30A Stratford would be like.

Our Lancaster friend thought that the quickest way to Stratford was via Moorgate, Aldersgate (*now called Barbican*) and Bank. This involved a few changes of trains and it was a Sunday service. We decided to obey the Locomotive Shed Directory finally and take its advice (probably the best).

Depart	FINSBURY PARK	*Piccadilly Line*	
Arrive	HOLBORN		
Depart	HOLBORN	*District Line*	
Arrive	STRATFORD		

These two tube trains entailed our longest tube journey of the day. It took about half an hour.

We left the underground station and entered the tunnel entrance to the shed. This was the only entrance to the shed (under the railway). No wonder the watchman at the other end of the tunnel had an easy job to keep locospotters out. This time as promised there was no watchman to stop us.

From the tunnel it was about another 5 minutes walk to the shed. We passed by a disused goods shed, over rusty tracks, various closed sheds and what appeared to be a goods yard.

One man and three boys caught us up and asked if we had a permit. They had not got a permit. He said that he and the boys were up from Newcastle for the day. He said it was a long way to come from if they were not to get round. They had had a few awkward conversation at Finsbury Park but had finally got round. We could believe that. We explained that no Sunday visits were allowed at Stratford and that my permit was for 09.30 on Monday. We decided to ask to get round. No harm in trying. It was better to be in a party - that increased our chanced. Our good Lancaster friend went into the shedmasters office.

While he was away I took a few diesel shunter numbers down from the shunter shed where we were standing in case we were refused admittance and ordered off the premises.

Nothing to worry about because our pal came back with the splendid news that we could go round. He had said to the shedmaster that there had been an alteration to our plans and that we would be leaving London tonight. We could not make our Monday morning date at Stratford as planned. He accepted our tale of woe and said that he would explain it to the Divisional Manager.

We commenced our tour by doing the shunter depot. We next made our way down to the maintenance depot after going down a long line of assorted Type 1's between the two depots. The maintenance depot had the odd sight of Deltic D9009 "Alycidon" in it. I put this down to it being here for some specialized form of repair that 34G Finsbury Park could not do. Deltics are not normally seen in the 30/31/32 areas of course. We next went round the servicing depot and another queer stranger was noted. This time is was D186 of 52A Gateshead. Her ailment being attended to was a badly buckled chassis. How that could have happened amazed me. There were no signs of collision at either end.

I dragged the rest of the party back to a shed that they had missed. When they passed it by on the way to the servicing depot they had thought it closed as it was closed at both ends. Peering through a crack I had spotted D1562 of March. There must be more inside! After a tour around it we found a small door. On it the simple words Repair Shed was on it. We opened the door to find a watchman peering at us.

"Oh, you cannot come in here. Even if you have a permit this is off limits. This is the repair shed and it's my responsibility that the engine pieces are not moved, tampered with or stolen. If anything happened I would be in trouble."

This must be last outpost of security in what once was a top security shed. We pleaded with him with no success until one of the small Newcastle boys asked what the number of a Brush Type 2 was that he could just see. The watchman relented (after having a good look around outside) and let us in. The Newcastle man had a friendly chat with him while the rest of us carefully (without disturbing anything) noted the occupants down. D8202 in the repair shed was a unique loco because stencilled on the front (the nose) of the loco was its number in large white numerals. This corresponded with the smokebox numberplate on steam locos. Of course it had its number on the sides as well. That was the first time that I had seen a diesel with its number on the front. I wonder if any other diesel has this almost unknown feature? Why did British Rail not do that with all its diesels? It would make trainspotting easier if diesels had their numbers on their front ends as well.

We then thanked the man for allowing us round and left. I suppose it was a good idea to have repair depots guarded.

As Stratford was made up of several sheds we checked that we had done all the sheds and that we had got all the locos which were standing outside and in the yards of the various depots. We then went back to the offices.

THE SECRET SANCTUARY AFFAIR

A host of locos to be preserved were at Stratford. I had learned this from Modern Railways.

We had not seen any sign of them. Funny, peculiar?

We went into the offices and asked the shedmaster. Yes, they were still here he said but he refused to tell us where they were. They are in stored in a secret place and because they are so valuable the Divisional Manager had ordered him to tell no one (even permit holders) where they were for security reasons. Souvenir hunters would soon reduce them to worthless chunks or iron if they got their hands on them. They are locked up. I am afraid I am unable to help you.

Thanks for nothing I thought as we left. The Newcastle four immediately lost interest and left. Our Lancaster friend said that he had heard that the locos were stored in a shed beside some old boilers. We had seen none in the shed area. Therefore by elementary detection we expected the secret locos sanctuary to be somewhere between the offices and the exit tunnel. We agreed that the shed might be somewhere in the region of where the closed Stratford Works used to be.

Our Lancaster friend said cheerio for the meantime and left for the station. He would wait for us there. On our search D.S. spotted an ancient shed with some old boilers in the vicinity. This could be it I agreed to D.S. but how did they get the engines into the shed. The approach track had been lifted. Come on D.S. it cannot be in there. D.S. stupidly ran up the outside of the shed in an attempt to see inside. He started to jump up and down. Finally he succeeded in getting a handhold and levered himself up to one of the large windows and peered inside through the mucky windows. How could it be in there??? D.S. then screamed out Lord Nelson's in there! The heat must be going for the old boy. He was killed at Trafalgar. I had better go and calm him down though. D.S. now in fits of hysterical happiness forced me up on to the window. I was just about to complain to him that he had mucked me up by pushing me up there when to please him I (in the direction of his frantic gestures) looked through the dirt and saw the mythical number of 30850 "Lord Nelson" in front of my eyes. I fell off the window ledge with fright and shock. He had been right.

I apologised a thousand times to (Sherlock) D.S. (Holmes) and recovering my composure started to climb up another window sill. This time 63460 the Q7 greeted me. D.S. and I then jumped up on to the other window sills and noted what we could see. Pity we could not get inside. 30587 one of the ancient Beattie 2-4-0 Tanks built long ago in 1874 was noted. Western Region King 6000 "King George V" was also noted. At first 6000 was not going to be preserved because she had a cracked frame but the authorities changed their minds, thankfully. LNWR 0-8-0 49395 was also noted together with Bulleid 0-6-0 33001 was noted. 3300X class is what I have always thought was the ugliest class on BR. Erroneously, the Southern Region streamlined Pacifics had been given the name "Spam Cans" when more learned individuals believed that this term was originally meant for the Bulleid 33XXX Class. They were however the most modern 0-6-0 ever made nevertheless. Robinson Great Central 2-8-0 63601 was also noted.

Crafty BR taking the rails that led up to the shed away. I bet that foxed all sensible locospotters (including me) but not D.S. Oh No! Well done D.S.

30A STRATFORD SECRET SANCTUARY			Built	Withdrawn
Steam				
Collett 8P 6000 4-6-0 "King" 1927				
All engines modified since 1947 with 4-row superheater and since 1955 with double chimney.				
6000	"King George V"		Jun-1927	Dec-1962
Total	*1*			
Beattie 0P 2-4-0 Class 0298 1874.				
L.S.W.design, rebuilt by Adams (1884-92), Urie (1921-22) and Maunsell (1931-35)				
30587			Jun-1874	Dec-1962
Total	*1*			
Maunsell 7P 4-6-0 "Lord Nelson" 1926				
modified by Bulleid from 1938, with multiple-jet blastpipe, large diameter chimney, and re-design				
cylinders and tender				
30850	"Lord Nelson"		Aug-1926	Aug-1962
Total	*1*			
Bulleid 5F 0-6-0 Q1 1942				
33001			Mar-1942	May-1964
Total	*1*			
Beames L.N.W.R. 7F 0-8-0 G2 1921				
Development of Bowen-Cooke G1 superheated design of 1912				
49395			Nov-1921	Nov-1959
Total	*1*			
Raven N.E. design 8F 0-8-0 Q7 1919				
63460			Oct-1919	Dec-1962
Total	*1*			
Robinson G.C. design 7F 2-8-0 O4/1 1911				
63601			Jan-1912	Jun-1963
Total	*1*			
Total:- 7 locos stored pending preservation				
	ex GWR	*1*		
	ex SR	*3*		
	ex LMS	*1*		
	ex LNER	*2*		

30587 was particularly interesting. Beattie 2-4-0T. Original number 298.BR Class 30585 - 7
used for working Wenford Bridge Mineral line in North Cornwall. Only suitable
locos for the line. The class had originally 88 members built for suburban
passenger working. The other 85 were withdrawn by 1899. These three for the
mineral line outlived their sisters by over 60 years. Fantastic!

One unidentified NCB tank was noted. All were in a shocking unrestored condition. No
nameplates on them of course.

The seven locos seen were deemed as wonderful by me. They were the first locos of their
respective classes that I had ever seen.

To say that we were pleased was an understatement.

30A STRATFORD

		Home shed		Built	Withdrawn	Scrap
Diesels						
BR Sulzer "Peak" Type 4 1Co-Co1 1959						
D 186		52A	Gateshead	*Nov-1962*		
Total	*1*					
Brush Type 4 Co-Co 1962						
D1509		34G	Finsbury Park	*Feb-1963*		
D1559		31B	March	*Mar-1964*		
D1562		31B	March	*Mar-1964*		
D1803		41A	Tinsley	*Jan-1965*		
Total	*4*					
BR Gardner 0-6-0 Shunter 1957						
D2003		34D	Hitchin	*Dec-1957*	*May-1969*	
Total	*1*					
Drewry 0-6-0 Shunter 1952						
D2211		30A		*Sep-1954*	*Jul-1970*	
Total	*1*					
Drewry 0-6-0 Shunter 1955						
D2215		30A		*Jul-1955*	*Feb-1969*	
Total	*1*					
North British 0-4-0 Shunter 1958						
D2900		30A		*Apr-1958*	*Feb-1967*	
D2901		30A		*Apr-1958*	*Feb-1967*	
D2902		30A		*May-1958*	*Feb-1967*	
D2903		30A		*May-1958*	*Feb-1967*	
D2905		30A		*Jun-1958*	*Feb-1967*	
D2906		30A		*Jul-1958*	*Feb-1967*	
Total	*6*					
Barclay 0-4-0 Shunter 1956						
D2956		to 9D	Newton Heath (from 30A)	*Mar-1956*	*May-1966*	
Total	*1*					
Ruston & Hornsby 0-4-0 Shunter 1956						
D2957		30A		*Mar-1956*	*Apr-1967*	
D2958		30A		*May-1956*	*Jan-1968*	
Total	*2*					
Brush 0-4-0 Shunter 1960						
D2999		30A		*Sep-1960*	*Oct-1967*	
Total	*1*					
BR 0-6-0 Shunter 1953						
D3300		30A		*Apr-1956*		
D3681		30A		*Jul-1958*		
D3683		30A		*Aug-1958*		
D3724		34G	Finsbury Park	*Nov-1959*		
Total	*4*					
BR 0-6-0 Shunter 1955						
D3496		30F	Parkeston	*Jun-1958*		
D3498		30A		*Dec-1957*		
D3502		30A		*Jan-1958*		
D3631		30A		*Oct-1958*		
D3632		30A		*Oct-1958*		
D3635		30A		*Nov-1958*		
D3636		30A		*Nov-1958*		
D4191		30A		*Aug-1962*		
Total	*8*					
BR Sulzer Type 2 Bo-Bo 1958						
D5038		32B	Ipswich	*Sep-1959*		
Total	*1*					

		30A STRATFORD (continued)		Built	Withdrawn	Scrap
		Home shed				
Brush Type 2 A1A-A1A 1957						
D5506		30A		Mar-1958		
D5507		30A		Apr-1958		
D5509		30A		May-1958		
D5531		32A	Norwich	May-1959		
D5534		30A		Jun-1959		
D5550		32B	Ipswich	Sep-1959		
D5564		32A	Norwich	Nov-1959		
D5566		32A	Norwich	Nov-1959		
D5582		31B	March	Jan-1960		
D5609		34G	Finsbury Park	Apr-1960		
D5620		30A		Jun-1960		
D5632		30A		Jul-1960		
D5634		31B	March	Jul-1960		
D5645		30A		Sep-1960		
D5666		30A		Nov-1960		
D5696		30A		May-1961		
Total	16					
English Electric Type 3 Co-Co 1961						
D6704		30A		Jan-1961		
D6707	near station	30A		Feb-1961		
D6710		30A		Feb-1961		
D6716		30A		Jun-1961		
D6721		30A		Jul-1961		
Total	5					
English Electric Type 1 Bo-Bo 1957						
D8013		30A		Nov-1957		
D8014		30A		Dec-1957		
D8016		30A		Jan-1958		
D8017		30A		Jan-1958		
D8019		30A		Mar-1958		
Total	5					
British Thomson Houston Type 1 Bo-Bo 1957						
D8200		30A		Nov-1957	Mar-1971	
D8202		30A		Feb-1958	Sep-1968	
D8203		30A		Mar-1958	Mar-1969	
D8205		30A		May-1958	Sep-1968	
D8208		30A		Jul-1958	Sep-1968	
D8210		30A		Oct-1959	Mar-1971	
D8212		30A		Nov-1959	Sep-1968	
D8213		30A		Dec-1959	Dec-1968	
D8215		32B	Ipswich	Jan-1960	Dec-1970	
D8217		32B	Ipswich	Jan-1960	Mar-1968	
D8221		32B	Ipswich	Mar-1960	Mar-1971	
D8234		30A		Sep-1960	Mar-1971	
D8237		30A		Nov-1960	Mar-1969	
D8238		30A		Dec-1960	Sep-1968	
D8241		30A		Feb-1961	Apr-1968	
D8242		30A		Feb-1961	Mar-1971	
D8243		30A		Feb-1961	Feb-1969	
Total	17					
North British Type 1 Bo-Bo 1958						
D8400		30A		May-1958	Jul-1968	
D8401		30A		Jun-1958	Sep-1968	
D8402		30A		Jul-1958	Jul-1968	
D8403		30A		Jul-1958	Jul-1968	
D8404		30A		Aug-1958	Feb-1968	
D8405		30A		Sep-1958	Sep-1968	
D8409		30A		Sep-1958	Sep-1968	
Total	7					
English Electric "Deltic" Type 5 Co-Co 1961						
D9009	"Alycidon"	34G	Finsbury Park	Jul-1961		
Total	1					
LMS and BR 0-6-0 Shunter 1945						
12105		30A		Apr-1952	Jan-1971	
12106		30A		Apr-1952	Jul-1970	
12111		30A		Jul-1952	May-1971	
12127		30A		Oct-1952	Oct-1972	
12128		30A		Oct-1952	Jul-1970	
12130		30A		Nov-1952	Jul-1972	
Total	6					

			30A STRATFORD (continued)					
On Shed	88		Kops		81			
Steam	0		Diesels		88			
Home Shed		68	Home Area	1		Visitors	19	
Shed	30A	68	30F		1			
Distribution:-	31B	4						
	32A	3	32B		5			
	34D	1	34G		4			
	41A	1						
	52A	1						
Diesel classes on view:-		19						
Steam	Aug-50	383	Apr-59		197	May-65	0	
Allocation						Jul-65	0	
				Closed to Steam:-			Sep-62	

Review and Appraisal of 30A Stratford

The shed was in a maze of lines at the north-west side of the station. Walking time was 10 minutes from Stratford station.

Stratford used to be the biggest steam shed in the country. In August 1950 it had the incredible allocation of 383 steam locos. By April 1959 this was down to 197 engines followed by its regrettable closure to steam in September 1962.

I was a bit disappointed that none of her English Electric Type 4's were on shed. 10 (D200-9) belonged to Stratford. That was a mystery. I knew they were thinking of transferring them to the LMR but I did not think they had done it yet. A few could be in Crewe Works, but of the rest I could not hazard a guess where they were.

Stratford has over 30 Type 3's belonging there but only four were on shed. This was again disappointing. Where were they all?

Stratford had about 50 Type 2's but only 17 were on shed. Even that number was lower than I expected.

A high percentage of Type 1's were on shed. 29 out of 41 were on shed.

Who bothers much about shunters! However, interesting to see nine different types on shed. Of course I could not really complain as it was far better than any other diesel shed so far. 88 diesels on shed.

One interesting loco which belonged to Stratford D5835 was missing. The rest of its class were normal Brush Type 2's but this loco was unique because it was temporarily uprated to 2,000 b.h.p. This super-charged loco was hence a Type 4. Pity it was missing.

Stratford had a few sub-sheds which would have a considerable number of the missing locos on today, I supposed, Colchester, Tilbury, Temple Mills and last but not least Ripple Lane.

Ripple Lane is an important freight terminal. A good number of Type 2's and 3's were probably there. We had intended going to Ripple Lane but *"tempus fugit, thou knowest"* and we now could not afford the time. It was far too far out of the way anyway and it's the later on steam of 81C Southall and 70B Feltham which appealed to me not some distant diesel depot.

A few more comments on specific locos. Why did I not kop D8400 and D8402? Within the space of a few weeks in 1958 I had kopped both of them (D8402 first for some odd reason) on their delivery runs (light engine) from North British Works Glasgow to Stratford.

Obviously I missed the rest of them. I kopped them on the Edinburgh to London mainline at the Mucklets Bridge, Musselburgh.

One of the few BR Type 2's which belonged to the Eastern Region was on shed. D5038 of 32B Ipswich was on shed. Stratford had no BR Type 2's as part of its allocation.

The Brush Type 4's had a few months previously taken over all express work from the 750 hp inferior, far too heavy, 1 Co-Co 1 English Electric Type 4's and had made a favourable impression. Four were on shed and two were kopped.

No stream of adjectives could describe fully how fabulous the stored steam locos were. All were kopped by me and indeed I had never seen any of the classes before. I was glad to see the LNWR 0-8-0 49395. Two of this class in January '64 were on 64A St Margarets in Edinburgh en route to a Glasgow scrapyard. I had unfortunately missed them. A few were stored at (ex 24K) Preston before they too were removed a few months before I visited Preston (July '65). I had intended going to Birmingham for a weekend in December 1964 but Iain Firth had persuaded me to go with him to Manchester and Crewe instead. I had therefore missed the opportunity of seeing the last 3 active 0-8-0's of 2F Bescot. Now at last I have seen one of the elusive class. 49395 had been withdrawn in 1959. Where had she been stored all these years?

I had never been within miles of any of the other stored locos.

On we go

As we departed from the secret sanctuary D6707 of 30A was noted (light engine) in the vicinity of the station.

For a year or two she carried the name "The East Anglian Regiment". For some reason that I do not know the name had been taken off some months before. Possibly British Rail wanted only Type 4's and above to carry nameplates. My Peterborough acquaintance during those tremendous three hours had previously told me that two other Type 3's bore names for a short time. They were named the "2nd East Anglian Regiment" and the "3rd East Anglian Regiment". "Not very original" he said at the time. I agreed. They carried their names for an even shorter period. A matter of a few months in fact. British Rail must have agreed with him.

D.S. and I went down the exit from the yard into the tunnel. Almost at the tunnel exit Graham's camera fell from my shoulder to the ground with a fearful bump. D.S. examined the camera and said it was damaged badly and could not possibly be used again. I told D.S. that the only bash in the camera was at the bottom. The buckle of the camera strap had slipped and it had fallen I surmised.

We returned to Stratford main-line station. We met out cheerful Lancaster friend and told him the fabulous news of the Secret Sanctuary. We gave him an idea of where it was and he determined to find it on a later date. He was happy that we had found it.

We waited at Stratford station for several minutes and I had time to examine Graham's camera carefully. D.S. was correct. The cameras focus was completely off. Some light might have got in and ruined the pictures that I had already taken. No more pictures could be taken either and I had hoped to fill four spools with some interesting shots of locos too!

How unlucky I am. I thought. Now I would have to get copies of D.S.'s shots and his idea of good locos to photograph might not be mine.

As a mark of respect for Graham's camera I have missed a line.

Our Lancaster friend hopped on to a local electric train for Liverpool Street. D.S. had been complaining of hunger again and was demanding his "one square meal a day" (as he ineptly put it). I gave in to his pleas finally and our Lancaster friend shouted to us that he would meet us in the station buffet.

"Where's that?" we shouted.
"It's upstairs on a sort of bridge. You can't miss it." He shouted back.

D.S. and I went downstairs to the underground station.

We waited for about ten minutes and then hopped on to a Central line train for Stratford (tube).

Depart	STRATFORD	Central Line	
Arrive	LIVERPOOL STREET		

We had a look round Liverpool Street main-line station for any stray Type 2's etc. Without success!

We went up the stairs and found the promised buffet. It was a tiny buffet. It was very compact though and filled with as many tables and chairs as possible. The buffet was also packed with people but our Lancaster pal was at the far side of the buffet. We squeezed past (the word squeezed was no understatement) the other diners and battled our way to him. There were no spare chairs (except at two odd tables) and we did not want to get separated in this jungle. The two people at our pals table were about finished and we expertly ushered them away as quickly as possible and we got two precious seats. Our pal recommended the mixed grill at 5/6d (27p) as a good buy. Glancing over the menu I noted that it was the dearest. I should hope it's the best! Anyone moneys no object and D.S. and I battled our way to the serving counter. We asked for two mixed grills but they were off but we could have sausage and mash at 2/6d (12.5p). Why do they have a menu? When most of the items are non existent? I thought. Trust BR I sighed. Two sausage and mash and two coffees we decided on finally. D.S. had seen the light and did not ask for that evil beverage namely tea.

Admittedly the meal was OK and I ate it in a hungry enough fashion. We told our friend that our next shed was to be 73C Hither Green. Our friend said sorrowfully that he had to be back for 6 and it was now after four o'clock. D.S. and I gave him a rousing send off because we really like the 6 foot 3 giant. I was a small 6 foot at the time. I think he wished that he could have come with us. We would not have objected because he was a great companion.

D.S. and I finished our tea and left shortly after. I wandered away from him and I noted a D200 Class Type 4 at the far end of one of the platforms. It was light engine. I had earlier complained to D.S. that there had been none on Stratford - and ten (D200-D209) belonged there. This time I could not be bothered to get a platform ticket and chase after it. After my horrible luck with the camera I would have half expected it to move off when I got near it. Discretion is the better part of valour and I lazily decided not to go after it. I rejoined D.S. and the two of us seeing nothing interesting in the station disappeared into the underground. We got on:-

Depart	LIVERPOOL STREET	Central Line	
Arrive	TOTTENHAM COURT ROAD		

We interchanged lines here. Our next shed to be visited was diesel depot 73C Hither Green. Blissfully believing that we had still plenty of time to visit steam sheds 70A Nine Elm, 70B Feltham and 81C Southall.

Depart	TOTTENHAM COURT ROAD	Northern Line
Arrive	STRAND	

We got off at Strand tube station not Charing Cross tube station. For some reason Charing Cross station was at Strand tube station. The LMR timetable had kindly put a warning note in their timetable to alert travellers.

By an interchange corridor we arrived at Charing Cross station. I left D.S. to his own amusement at a bookstall and went off and got two day returns to Hither Green. I considered the price exorbitant (or too dear to the less informed reader). When I looked at the ticket the reasons became apparent. It said day return to some distant station and all intermediate stations. Hither Green was one of the intermediate stations and one of the first. Shame on the Southern Region. It is ridiculous to pay the same return price to every station. Especially if you are getting off pretty soon.

I returned to D.S. and found him writing out some lovely postcards to dear mum and dad and the clan with guess what on the front. Yes! You probably guessed correct dear old Big Ben. I told him to get a move on as our train leaves in three minutes. Why bother to send postcards? They will be worried if they do not hear from me, D.S. said. That was touching!

I bundled D.S. on to the electric bucket and we were soon off. We took an active interest in the scenery around us - buildings and more buildings. It was a pleasant change from dreary underground tunnels which we seemed to have been frequenting for the most part of the day. The electric train first stopped at Waterloo. We would get off there on the way back.

D6515 of 73C was noted on the journey (light engine). The line that we were on was very busy but of course only with SR electric buckets.

Depart	CHARING CROSS	Southern Region
Arrive	HITHER GREEN	22 minutes approx.

After a short journey of around 20 minutes we got off smartly at Hither Green Station. These buckets stopped only for about half a minute at each station and one had to get out quickly.

A quick glance at the shed directory and we noted that the entrance to the shed was from No. 4 platform. Handy I thought but where is No 4 platform? Hither Green was a queer station. Two lines from different directions met there. The station was in two parts to serve the two lines as a result.

D.S. and I crossed the overbridge over the line that our train had taken and reached the main part of the station which was on the other line. Still no luck! We crossed another bridge and got to the other side of the other line. No 4 platform at last!

Carefully avoiding the offices we entered from the shed yard end. Unfortunately like Hornsey and Workington at the top of the shed at the other end were glass fronted offices. We went round warily and stealthily hardly daring to make a noise. Even D.S. realised that we had better shut-up. We got round without incident luckily. We had not got a permit of course.

			Home shed		Built	Withdrawn	Scrap
73C HITHER GREEN							
Diesels							
BR Gardner 0-6-0 Shunter 1957							
D2084			73C		Mar-1959		
Total	1						
Drewry 0-6-0 Shunter 1955							
D2252			73C		May-1957	Oct-1968	
D2253			73C		May-1957	Mar-1969	
Total	2						
BR 0-6-0 Shunter 1953							
D3043			73C		Mar-1954		
D3098			73C		Jan-1955		
D3719			73C		Apr-1959		
Total	3						
Birmingham R.C. & W. Co.Type 3 Bo-Bo 1960							
D6503			73C		Mar-1960		
D6507			73C		May-1960		
D6513			73C		Jun-1960		
D6514			73C		Jul-1960		
D6515			73C		Jul-1960		
D6516			73C		Jul-1960		
D6518			73C		Aug-1960		
D6522			73C		Sep-1960		
D6551			73C		Apr-1961		
D6557			73C		Jun-1961		
D6568			73C		Sep-1961		
D6569			73C		Sep-1961		
D6575			73C		Oct-1961		
D6577			73C		Nov-1961		
D6581			73C		Dec-1961		
D6593			73D	St. Leonards	Mar-1962		
Total	16						
BR 0-6-0 Shunter 1949							
15214			73C		May-1949	Oct-1971	
15215			73C		May-1949	Mar-1968	
Total	2						
On Shed	24		**Kops**		24		
Steam	0		**Diesels**		24		
Home Shed		23	**Home Area**	1		**Visitors**	0
Shed	73C	23	73D	1			
Distribution:-							
Diesel classes on view:-		5					
Steam	Aug-50	383	May-59		197	May-65	0
Allocation						Aug-65	0
			Closed to Steam:-			Oct-61	

Review and Appraisal of 73C Hither Green

The shed was in the triangle of the Hither Green-Grove Park-Lee lines. Walking time was less than 5 minutes.

16 out of the 55 Birmingham RCW's allocated were on shed. A disappointing percentage! I expected the shed to be bigger better and have more engines on shed. The shed had not been converted to a diesel depot but still remained in the shape of an old steam depot which had closed to steam in October 1961.

The Birmingham RCW Type 3's were not a new class to me. I had seen one before allocated to 73D St Leonards on my way to France with a school pupil exchange from Musselburgh Grammar School in July 1964.

On we go

136

I had got round the shed OK but where in the blazes had D.S. gone? He was not to be seen! He must be away out. The conniving rat might have told me. Wait till I catch him. I'll give him a piece of my mind.

I went out and back to No 4 platform but he was not to be seen. He must still be in the shed! Don't tell me the stupid twit had been caught. What a clot. Well I am not going in after him. I stayed at the exit wall of the shed and dangled my feet over the live rails.

I watched a porter come out of the main station building cross over the bridge and head straight for me. Don't tell me he thinks I am going to jump on to the live rails and he's going to tell me to get back on to No 4 platform. I shouldn't have bothered as he glacidly walked past me and went up the path leading to the shed. I was now getting a bit irate at D.S.'s tardiness, where in the blazes was he?

After a long ten minutes wait he emerged from the shed vicinity. No, he told me had had not met the shedmaster. He had been looking at a diesel shunter at the far side of the shed. I told him we had no time for dillydallying particularly with three steam sheds still to visit.

D.S. now saw an E5XXX main-line electric loco about a half mile down the main line. D.S. said "I'll have a saunter down the side of the man line and kop it." "I have not got any of that class." I thought carefully over his suggestion. I supposed it was too much to hope for him to trip over a live rail and that would end my worries over him. He would not be alive to worry about! The chance was too remote to take. My answer was a short "No!" and it was final. I about turned D.S. and turned him in the direction of No 4 platform.

We spent a frustrating quarter of an hour watching SR buckets approach from the distance run over the correct overbridge, arrive on the correct platform panting for breath and then have the heartbreaking experience of seeing it whistle past us at 60 m.p.h. without stopping.

This cannot continue I told D.S. and I told him to keep calm while I flew off downstairs to search for the booking office. I then ascertained from a booking clerk when the next train for Waterloo was. I had to explain why we did not know that the trains were not at regular intervals for some odd reason.

We duly got on the advertised train and left the queer station. For a change our journey to Waterloo was pretty uneventful except for the BCW Type 3 which was unfortunately hidden behind a row of electric buckets when we reached it. Anyway this time we got off at Waterloo.

Depart	HITHER GREEN	Southern Region
Arrive	WATERLOO	20 minutes approx.

Our tickets were for Charing Cross but the collector at Waterloo did not bother to look. We had got off at Waterloo suburban station and we had a walk over a viaduct to get into the station proper.

Here we were at Waterloo at last. Where Wellington had won some battle or did he? Where Winston Churchill was hauled to Blenheim for burial by 34051 "Winston Churchill" in January earlier in the year as part of the state funeral. I looked in on the latter occasion on TV and determined to get to Waterloo Station and kop my first Southern Region Pacifics as soon as possible. I always regarded SR Pacifics with the highest esteem. In my first few years of trainspotting activities this was the class I most wanted to see them. I always preferred the unrebuilt streamlined Pacifics to the rebuilt ones. I have not quite forgiven the Southern Region from de-streamlining all the Merchant Navies (and about 60 of the 110 West Country and Battle of Britains) however more easy it was to maintain them. I will never forgive the people who had the cheek to call the unrebuilt ones "spam cans" although I suspect that this comment was originally attributable to the 33XXX Class – definitely the ugliest steam class that ever appeared in the U.K. making "flying pigs" look line swans.

Waterloo Station did not disappoint me. It was truly enormous. It had bookshops, booking and enquiry offices galore with plenty of room too. D.S. and I found a fantastic new machine which had the answers to 100 questions on train times, restaurant facilities on trains, Sunday services etc. You just pressed the correct button and out popped the answer. I had seen the machine on that gem of a programme "Blue Peter" before. Obviously the novelty had not worn off at this station. There was a great crowd around it. This was what attracted us first. We had thought that there must be a fight but no it was the machine. The people that were using the machine were just doing it out of fun. Some mothers do have them! The people who really wanted to use the machine were unable to battle through the crowd to get to it and had to resign themselves to queue at the enquiry office. It was quicker for them that way! Shame!

Obviously the machine would have to be removed and sent back to the USA because it was **too** popular!

I dragged a goggling D.S. away from the machine and told him we had better get back to business. Electric buckets predominated but seeing some black smoke at the right side of the station and we headed for there.

A certain Mr Derek Newton had told me that he had not gone to Waterloo Station when he was in London (and as a result saw no SR Pacifics) because the railway police did not allow trainspotters there because of the electrified lines. Preston and Crewe were supposed to be the same when I went I went there. The security lark was only a facade. So with Waterloo I thought.

D.S. and I reached the "steam" platforms but I did not intend getting a platform ticket. At all big stations there is a parcels platform. Waterloo did not disappoint me. We moved the barrier back and "broke-in". We were about half way up the platform when a Pacific came storming in with an express. It was one of the rebuilt ones. I smiled when I saw her name - 34021 "Dartmoor". I hoped that someone would take D.S. away earlier and now it looked as through my wish had come true. Unfortunately no prison officers got off or if they did they did not notice D.S. Poor D.S. was really sick at "Dartmoor" being his first Southern Region pacific. It was my first one too. I had to admit to D.S. though that the rebuilt class were quite impressive though. We gazed at "Dartmoor" for a minute or two (taking in her impressive measurements) and then continued on to the end of the platform.

Two standard 2-6-4 Tanks were noted on empty stock workings with 82018 being the first of this Standard Class that I had ever seen.

Another express entered the station. This time it was diesel hauled. A Warship Type 4 was at the front. This diesel class had displaced the Pacifics from the Exeter and Plymouth expresses. This changeover had been in operation for several months. This had resulted in Warship Type 4's being seen at Waterloo for the first time. For some reason the North British "Warships" were not allowed on the Waterloo run (D833-65).

On closer examination of the Warship I at last remembered to jot down the number. Seeing nothing else to interest us we made our way back to the main concourse. "Next shed is 70A Nine Elms" I informed D.S. "The top security shed." he said. D.S. had remembered that.

		Home shed		Built	Withdrawn	Scrap
Diesels						
BR "Warship" Type 4 B-B 1958						
D 831	"Monarch"	84A	Laira (Plymouth)	*Jan-1961*	*Oct-1971*	
Total	*1*					
Steam				*Built*	*Withdrawn*	*Scrap*
1957 7P6F dev. of Bulleid 7P5F 4-6-2 "West Country & Battle of Britain" 1945						
34021	"Dartmoor"	70A	Nine Elms	*Jan-1946*	*Jul-1967*	*Mar-1968*
Total	*1*					
BR Standard 4MT 2-6-4T Doncaster 1953						
80142		70E	Salisbury (ex75B)	*Aug-1956*	*Mar-1966*	*Jul-1966*
Total	*1*					
BR Standard 3MT 2-6-2T Swindon 1952						
82018		70A	Nine Elms	*Sep-1952*	*Jul-1966*	*Oct-1966*
Total	*1*					

On Station	4	Kops	4
Steam	3	Diesels	1

	Home Area			3 Visitors		1
Shed	70A		2 70E		1	
Distribution:-	84A		1			
Steam classes on view		3				
Steam Origin	SR		1 BR		2	

I got out the "Locoshed Directory" and noted that Nine Elms was on a spur off the main line between Vauxhall and Queens Road Stations. 75D Stewart's Lane was nearest to Queen's Road. Handy to have both depots on the main line I thought.

I bought two day returns to Vauxhall and asked the booking clerk when the next train was to Vauxhall. He had the cheek to answer "You'll find the service good enough." We went across to the giant timetable on the concourse and looked at the clock - 19.30. I then checked the timetable. He was not joking. There was a train approx. every five minutes for Vauxhall. We got on the 19.32 electric bucket and we were soon speeding on our way.

Depart	WATERLOO	Southern Region
Arrive	VAUXHALL	

THE NINE ELMS SHED HUNT AFFAIR

I was having a look at the skyscrapers which were quite near to the railway and was thinking that London was growing upwards at last when D.S. nastily disturbed my thoughts by asking me how long a walk we had after we reached Vauxhall. I grudgingly unearthed the timetable and looked it up. 15 minutes walk from Wandsworth Road station I said. D.S. queried and said "Wandsworth Road." That's right I said "Wandsworth Road". Did I hear myself right. I distinctly went very pale (according to D.S.) and let out a few curses. The Locoshed Directory only had directions from Wandsworth Road Station and not from Vauxhall Station. D.S. now had something to complain about for a change. He said in his "sweet" way "On the wrong line, going to the wrong station." and gave me a dirty look.

The train stopped. It was Vauxhall Station. "Better get out D.S." I said. I looked at the shed directory again. "The shed is on a spur off the main line between Vauxhall and Queen's Road." I read this aloud to D.S. This was what had made me stupidly get tickets to Vauxhall in the first place. The shed could not be too far from Vauxhall I guessed from what the shed directory said.

"Look, let's ask that porter if he knows how to get to Nine Elms". The young porter did not know where the shed was exactly but he directed us to Wandsworth Road. After a five minute walk we reached Wandsworth Road. I told D.S. that all was not over because

Wandsworth Road was a good few miles long. We could only keep walking and look for Brooklands Road which was somewhere off Wandsworth Road and Nine Elms would be finally found. We walked up the road in the pleasant sunlight of the sunset. It had been a lovely day but thankfully it had not been too warm. After about another ten minutes D.S. (getting a little anxious) persuaded me to ask a passer-by if he knew where Brooklands Road or Nine Elms was. The London know-all said that although he did not know where Brooklands Road was that is we walked back in the direction from which we came we would come to Nine Elms Road.

We walked along that road for about ten minutes when D.S. saw some wooden buildings about ½ mile to our left. He thought that they might be the sheds. I told him that I could see no smoke. He agreed. It was too far off the main road anyway. We continued on for another five minutes and agreed that we were getting nowhere and stopped two passer-by's. They told us to continue for a good bit. I told D.S. that we were probably being directed to 75D Stewart's Lane now and that would be some walk - and we did not want to go there. We should not have left Wandsworth Road either I said because the shed is somewhere off that road. We shouldn't have believed that London know-all. He was probably directing us to 75D as well. Let's cut straight across and make our way back to Wandsworth Road.

D.S. brought up the subject of the buildings that we had seen earlier. OK. I finally said we'll make for them. I only did that to please him knowing full well that the shed could not be there. Anyway it was in the right direction.

D.S. then shouted to a young London boy in front in him and wanted to know if he knew were Nine Elms sheds were. The boy ignored D.S. which caused D.S. to swear at him and the boy disappeared into the entrance to a block of flats. He had probably been taught not to speak to crude strangers or possibly he was a little b..... Probably the latter. D.S. had better leave all asking in future to me. His first attempt could be at the best termed a snub.

I enquired again and was told if we turned left at the pub we would find the sheds about two hundred yards further on. Thanks!

We had been misdirected too many times before though. It must be the hobby of the people around this blooming joint. We reached the pub as promised. Pity it was closed though. I've never felt more like a pint of heavy. Was I thirsty after all our walking around. The English beer particularly the keg stuff is pretty pale, bitter and weak though. I prefer the opposite but in these dire circumstances I would be the last to complain. After another mournful look at the pub we turned left and continued on. Brooklands Road was supposed to cut Wandsworth Road across.

D.S. was sure that Nine Elms lay at the end but I was a bit doubtful. He kept on saying that the buildings he had seen must be Nine Elms. Glory be! We did come to Brooklands Road and round another corner was Nine Elms Motive Power Depot at long last! There were no riotous celebrations by us. We had at last found it after all our misdirections. D.S. had been right about the buildings.

Nine Elms was supposed to be a top security shed with watchful shedmasters with sub-machine guns and almost impossible to get round. An English bloke had told us at Carlisle the previous day that he never stupidly used the main entrance but sneaked in via a timber yard. D.S. and I could not be bothered to look for timber yards and chanced the main entrance. If stopped we would plead that we wanted to see Nine Elms wonderful Pacifics. Nine Elms now only had a handful now but according to my February Peterborough acquaintance the last time he was there no less than 27 were on shed - 24 visitors. That would do for us!

To get to the shed we had to pass a row of offices and then walk approx 220 yards to the main shed. A sizeable task. "Best food forward" I said to D.S. We walked straight past the offices. A shedmaster was in the office busy either did not see us, did not hear us or was not bothered. What an anti-climax! We walked past the turntable and to the main shed without an incident. We'd better make the use of our luck then and get round as quickly as possible (*quam celerrime*).

When we entered the shed we were in the "twilight zone". It would be dark by the time we had finished. I had completely forgotten that in summer it gets dark earlier in London than it does in the North. The darkness seems to come down far quicker too. It appeared to be a relatively short time between sunset and dark. Virtually almost no twilight. Our wanderings had taken us a valuable hour.   It was now half past eight. Obviously Nine Elms was to be our last shed of the day. Goodbye steam sheds 70B Feltham and 81C Southall.   What a disaster.

Our first Pacific of the shed was 34090 "Sir Eustace Missenden". A rebuilt Pacific in all her ex-works splendour. I was glad that she still carried her ornate nameplate.   Some unfortunately had lost them recently - to collectors probably.

Inside the shed it was pitch black in places and my torch was required. The named Standard Black 5's 73085/6 and 73110/12 all had had their nameplates removed. In a dirty corner of the shed the mucky number of 34064 was discerned. This unrebuilt Pacific was in an absolutely shocking condition. After a moment's thought I remembered her name - "Fighter Command". This was the Pacific with the Geisl oblong ejector. A condemned mark X was scraped on the grime in her tender although she wasn't actually withdrawn until May 1966. Generally it was a case of jotting down the number of one unrecognisably clarty West Country or Battle of Britain.

I had a habit of forming speaking acquaintances going round sheds and I met up with a Hull boy domiciled in London. He directed us to the nearest and the only Merchant Navy on shed - 35004 "Cunard White Star". I had a good look at the ugly, but interesting 1942 Bulleid "Austerity" locos.   33006/9/26 were on shed.   One of the last of the S15's with smoke deflectors was also on shed - 30839.

70A NINE ELMS					
		Home shed		Built	Withdrawn
Diesels					
BR 0-6-0 Shunter 1953					
D3045		70B	Feltham	Mar-1954	
Total	1				
Steam				Built	Withdrawn
Maunsell 1936 dev. of Urie 6F S15 4-6-0 Urie 1920 (with smoke deflectors)					
30839		70B	Feltham	May-1936	Sep-1965
Total	1				
Bulleid 5F 0-6-0 Q1 1942					
33006		70A	(ex 70C Guildford)	Jun-1942	Jan-1966
33009		70A	(ex 70C Guildford)	Jul-1942	Sep-1965
33026		70A	(ex 70C Guildford)	Jul-1942	Sep-1965
Total	3				
Bulleid 7P5F "West Country & Battle of Britain Class 4-6-2 1945					
34002	"Salisbury"	70A		Jun-1945	Apr-1967
34063	"229 Squadron"	70E	Salisbury	May-1947	Aug-1965
34064	"Fighter Command"	70D	Eastleigh	Jul-1947	May-1966
Total	3				

		Home shed		Built	Withdrawn	Scrap
1957 7P6F dev. of Bulleid 7P5F 4-6-2 "West Country & Battle of Britain" 1945						
34009	"Lyme Regis"	70D	Eastleigh	Sep-1945	Oct-1966	Nov-1967
34024	"Tamar Valley"	70F	Bournemouth	Feb-1946	Jul-1967	Sep-1968
34026	"Yes Tor"	70E	Salisbury	Apr-1946	Sep-1966	Oct-1967
34036	"Westward Ho"	70D	Eastleigh	Jul-1946	Jul-1967	Mar-1968
34059	"Sir Archibald Sinclair"	70E	Salisbury	Apr-1949	May-1966	Barry save
34071	"601 Squadron"	70D	Eastleigh	Apr-1948	Apr-1967	Sep-1967
34077	"603 Squadron"	70D	Eastleigh	Jul-1948	Mar-1967	Sep-1967
34087	"145 Squadron"	70D	Eastleigh	Dec-1948	Jul-1967	Sep-1968
34090	"Sir Eustace Missenden"	70D	Eastleigh	Jan-1949	Jul-1967	Mar-1968
34095	"Westward Ho"	70D	Eastleigh	Oct-1949	Jul-1967	Apr-1968
Total	10					
1956 dev. of Bulleid 8P 4-6-2 "Merchant Navy" 1941						
35004	"Cunard White Star"	70F	Bournemouth	Dec-1941	Oct-1965	Feb-1966
Total	1					
BR Standard 5MT 4-6-0 Doncaster 1951						
73022		70C	Guildford (ex 70D)	Oct-1951	Apr-1967	Nov-1967
73065		70C	Guildford (ex 70A)	Oct-1954	Jul-1967	Apr-1968
73085	"Melisande"	70A		Aug-1955	Jul-1967	Apr-1968
73086	"The Green Knight"	70A		Sep-1955	Oct-1966	Feb-1967
73110	"The Red Knight"	70D	Eastleigh	Oct-1955	Jan-1967	Jun-1967
73112	"Morgan le Fay"	70A		Oct-1955	Jun-1965	Dec-1965
73169		70D	Eastleigh	Apr-1957	Oct-1966	Jun-1967
73170		70D	Eastleigh	May-1957	Jun-1966	Jan-1967
Total	8					
BR Standard 4MT 4-6-0 Brighton 1951						
75074		70D	Eastleigh (ex 70A)	Nov-1955	Jul-1967	Feb-1968
75075		70D	Eastleigh	Nov-1955	Jul-1967	Feb-1968
Total	2					
BR Standard 4MT 2-6-0 Doncaster 1953						
76009		70D	Eastleigh	Feb-1953	Jul-1967	Jan-1968
76068		70D	Eastleigh	Aug-1956	Oct-1965	Feb-1966
Total	2					
BR Standard 4MT 2-6-4T Doncaster 1953						
80069		70A		Sep-1953	Jan-1966	Apr-1966
80133		70A		Mar-1956	Jul-1967	Mar-1968
80143		70A		Sep-1956	Jul-1967	Jan-1968
80152		70E	Salisbury (ex 75B)	Feb-1957	Jul-1967	Mar-1968
80154		70A		Mar-1957	Apr-1967	Oct-1967
Total	5					
BR Standard 3MT 2-6-2T Swindon 1952						
82006		70A		May-1952	Sep-1966	Feb-1967
82019		70A		Sep-1952	Jul-1967	Mar-1968
82022		70A		Oct-1954	Oct-1965	May-1966
82026		70A		Nov-1954	Jun-1966	Oct-1966
82027		70A		Nov-1954	Jan-1966	Apr-1966
Total	5					

On Shed	41		Kops	41	
Steam	40		Diesels	1	
Withdrawn	1				

Home Locos		15 Home Area		26 Visitors	0
Shed	70A	15	70B	2	70C	2
Distribution:-	70D	14	70E	4		
Steam classes on view		10			
Steam Origin	SR		18 BR		22

Shed Highlights:-	the unrebuilt "West Country and Battle of Britains"	34002/63/64
(of many)	the "Merchant Navy"	35004
	the Urie S15	30839
	the pairing of "The Green Knight" and "The Red Knight"	73086/112

Steam	Aug-50	99	May-59	90	Apr-65	39
Allocation					Aug-65	34
			Closed to Steam:-		Jul-67	

70A NINE ELMS (continued)						
Home Steam	excluding withdrawn locos					
On/Off Shed	On Shed	15 Off Shed		19 % On Shed	44%	
Not on Shed						
Bulleid 5F 0-6-0 Q1 1942				33020	33027	2
Bulleid 7P5F 4-6-2 1945					34038	1
Bulleid 7P6F 4-6-2 1957				34001	34021	2
BR 5MT 4-6-0 1951			73016	73084	73088	3
BR 4MT 2-6-4T 1953				80095	80137	2
BR 3MT 2-6-2T 1952	82005	82018	82020	82021	82023	
		82024	82028	82029	82033	9
					total	19
saw elsewhere on the tour				3		
recently withdrawn not on shed or seen elsewhere				1	Bulleid 5F 0-6-0 Q1 1942	
					33018	

Review and Appraisal of 70A Nine Elms

The shed was on a spur off the main line between Vauxhall and Queens Road Stations. Walking time was said to be 15 minutes from Wandsworth Road Station.

The best shed yet! This shed certainly had not an outstanding quantity of locos on shed but for quality it was invincible. A great steam shed. Thankfully only one insignificant diesel shunter had infiltrated. Not quite up to 1959 standards when Nine Elms had five "King Arthurs", four "Schools" – both classes long gone, 25 "West Country and Battle of Britains" (down to four by April) and 10 "Merchant Navies" - none allocated now.

Every possible version of my favourites - the Bulleid Pacifics were on view. Both unrebuilt and rebuilt West Countries and Battle of Britains and one Merchant Navy to add spice to the collection. Only one of the Pacifics belonged to Nine Elms strangely but Nine Elms only had a handful shedded to it – three were off shed.

34064 "Fighter Command" easily got into the locomotive highlights. This loco and 92250 are the only locos on BR to be fitted with a Geisl oblong ejector. From our vantage point it could not be seen but if we had got up on top of the loco we would have found the chimney different. Probably it would be rectangular in shape. This ejector causes the engines coal consumption to be cut rapidly down (in theory at least) in comparison with her sisters.

30839 qualifies also as a shed highlight. There were only a few of this old smoke deflector class left at the time and it was very nice to see one before her imminent withdrawal.

By reason of some of the SR 73XXX standards being named I had acquired a new respect for them by the time I had finished the shed. This was one class I absolutely loathed in Scotland. The named ones had already had their nameplates removed but that did not make me hold them in any lower esteem. The picturesque King Arthur like names quite enchanted me! As soon as I had noted down "The Green Knight" I had chased round the shed looking for his "blood" brother the "Red Knight". It made my day to see this dynamic duo.

The 82XXX standards were a new class to me that day as well. Their better known "big brothers" the 80000 class were on shed in force.

I could go on for pages praising this shed so I had better finish off before I bore you. Back to the story.

On we go

Telling the Hull boy how relieved we were that we had got round I asked him if the strict security had been slackened somewhat. He agreed. Our Hull acquaintance caught sight of our old friend 34090 "Sir Eustace Missenden" on the turntable and said to us that he would go and ask for a ride back into the shed. As he hared off I remarked to D.S. that they must be really lax if they allow that sort of thing.

We caught up with our Hull kid standing dejectedly beside "Sir Eustace" at the turntable. He said mournfully that the driver had agreed but on second thoughts he said no because the foreman might see him from the nearby offices and then he (the driver) would be in trouble. Too bad!

THE NINE ELMS AFFAIR - EPILOGUE

We thus left.   It was now almost completely dark.   We left by Brooklands Road. Wandsworth Road was only about 100 yards from the shed via Brooklands Road. We had only walked down Wandsworth Road for about 200 yards when I noticed a familiar landmark on the other side of the road. That was the place where we had first asked for directions from the London "know-all" and where we were so terribly misdirected. If D.S. had kept his gob shut and not asked me to ask someone we would have only had to walk a further 220 yards up the road and we could not have failed to notice Brooklands Road and then there would only have been the short walk to Nine Elms.

O me miserum! Merde!

Heartbreak is walking 2 miles when 200 yards will suffice.

- - - - - - - - - - - - - - - - -

Our Hull friend said he would escort us back to Vauxhall. I did not want to get lost or misdirected again. In ten minutes we were passing Nine Elms Road (that fateful road) on our left. We continued under the railway bridge and then wandered around for another five minutes and I told our Hull friend that I thought we were lost. He turned me round and there was us facing the station entrance "Great trick that D.S.". His good deed done for the day (like the good Boy Scout he was) he bade us farewell.

Up the steps, a minute wait and we were on our way back to Waterloo.

I of course, was fascinated by the myriads of lighted windows which flanked the track and by the gleaming rails which reflected their lights. The number of tracks leading into Waterloo Station was truly unbelievable. About 40 lines served the 20 platforms.

Depart	VAUXHALL	Southern Region	
Arrive	WATERLOO		

We got off the (non-corridor of course) bucket and had our tickets collected and left the platform. I dragged D.S. up the parcels platform again and our tour was profitable.

D803 "Albion" of 84A Laira was noted on the inevitable West Country express. D6526 of 70D Eastleigh was noted at the head of probably a semi-fast and yet another 3MT 2-6-2 Standard 82024 was noted on empty stock working. Nothing else about I noted and turned D.S. around and directed him in the direction of the main concourse. I told him there that he could now give his pen a rest for a few minutes because that was us finished for the day. Next stop Paddington Station for our left luggage and then Euston.

WATERLOO STATION LATE						
		Home shed		Built	Withdrawn	Scrap
Diesels						
BR "Warship" Type 4 B-B 1958						
D 803	"Albion"	84A	Laira (Plymouth)	Mar-1959	Jan-1972	
Total	1					
Birmingham R.C. & W. Co.Type 3 Bo-Bo 1960						
D6526		70D	Eastleigh	Oct-1960		
Total	1					
Steam				Built	Withdrawn	Scrap
BR Standard 3MT 2-6-2T Swindon 1952						
82024		70A	Nine Elms	Oct-1954	Jan-1966	May-1966
Total	1					
On Station	3	Kops		3		
Steam	1	Diesels		2		
		Home Area		2 Visitors		1
Shed	70A	1	70D	1		
Distribution:-	84A	1				
Steam classes on view		1				
Steam Origin	BR		1			

Paddington was a considerable distance from Waterloo and required two tubes. Down again into the underground. I showed my tube-rover for the umpteenth time during the day. At least we had got our money's worth but best of all we had saved countless minutes by not joining endless queues for tickets. We could skip them by.

I had now plenty of time to think of nothing in particular. My mind finally asked me to think about underground stations, trains and last of all adverts. The stations always interested me - the escalators especially. I do not mean stupidly running down stairs which are moving up - I left that to D.S. but the enlightening adverts which I passed by on the walls as the stair ascended or descended. Strangely most of the adverts were for women's underwear. It was a pleasant enough subject to glance at. The underground is not the place to advertise things like detergents.

They even had communication chord things in the underground trains. It was not even a chord but some metal device where one pulled the handle and I presume it resulted in the brakes being applied. I noted that like "big brother BR" the fine for illegal use had gone up from £5 to £25. I could afford paying £5 (at the time) to find out what happened when I pulled it - but £25 - not likely.

Another queer thing is the automatically closing doors (operated by the guard I think). You arrive breathless (after running down some stairs) and see an underground train waiting to leave. You make a dive into the inside of the carriage fearing all the time the hiss of compressed air, the rapidly closing door and then you might have a hand, a foot or your body stuck in the door. You get dragged into the tunnel and then with live rails below you ....

I thought that happened when I came here but our Lancaster friend had told us before his departure that if the doors close on anything they immediately re-open again. A drunk had caught his hand in the door the previous night he had told me. The train of course did not start until it was "removed" he assured me.

There was one item that I had noticed in every underground station. It was one special advert (the adverts stretch from one end of the platform to the other). The advert was this: - a well developed, pretty bride had just left the church and her husband was looking at her with a smile of infatuation. The advert was for an insurance company. I could never bring myself to believe that the infatuated husband was thinking of insurance but of .... (I leave it to the imagination).

D.S. nastily interrupted my thoughts by saying that we were now at Baker Street. Only two more stops to Paddington I said - Marylebone then Edgware Road. The train left Baker Street and after a longer than usual interval stopped. It was St John's Wood Station. "Must be a new station." said D.S. I glanced up at the map in the carriage and exclaimed "We are on the wrong line now." I ushered D.S. out of the carriage just before the doors closed. D.S. wanted to know why we had got out at the wrong station. We want to get back to Baker Street, don't we? After reflection I remembered that we had got on a Stanmore bound train instead of a Queen's Park bound train.

We had a considerable wait for a tube train back to Baker Street.

Depart	WATERLOO		*Bakerloo Line*	
Arrive	ST.JOHNS WOOD			
Depart	ST.JOHNS WOOD		*Bakerloo Line*	
Arrive	BAKERS STREET			

D.S. was surprised that the underground were "'crying out for staff". Judging by the adverts he had seen he came to the conclusion that its starting wage of £12 per week plus bonuses was very reasonable. Why not pack up your £6 a week grocers shop "slave-labour" job and work down here. The London Underground needs you. You could start work tomorrow - never mind about the trip - tell your parents to send down your things - you'll get digs easily enough - the night life in London' is fantastic. You'll be able to get a job as a ticket seller and when you pass your driving test you'll be able to get the top job which you have always cherished that of train driver. How exciting it would be flying at 30 m.p.h. through all these tunnels all day long. Will you join the underground D.S.? What an opportunity! D.S.'s answer was short - No! How unfortunate - it would have been much better financially for D.S.

D.S. then pointed outside. We were now at Baker Street. Better get out this time. We don't want to go back to Waterloo however tempting that may seem. *Strangely enough just eight years later Baker Street would be my local tube station when I would spend two very enjoyable years at Sussex Place Regents Park studying at London Business School doing a Post Graduate M.B.A. course. Unfortunately steam had disappeared five years before then.*

D.S. and I had another considerable wait (10 minutes) before a Queen's Park bound train came. The service was getting a bit sporadic late on a Sunday night. It was only to be expected though!

Depart	BAKERS STREET		*Bakerloo Line*	
Arrive	PADDINGTON			

PADDINGTON STATION LATE							
		Home shed			**Built**	**Withdrawn**	**Scrap**
Diesels							
Brush Type 4 Co-Co 1962							
D1612		82A	Bristol Bath Road		*Aug-1964*		
Total	1						
North British Type 2 B-B 1959							
D6355		81A	Old Oak Common		*Aug-1962*	*Sep-1968*	
Total	1						
Beyer Peacock (Hymek) Type 3 B-B 1961							
D7060		81A	Old Oak Common		*Dec-1962*	*Oct-1971*	
Total	1						
On Station	3	**Kops**		3			
Steam	0	**Diesels**		3			
		Home Area			2 Visitors		1
Shed	81A	2 82A		1			
Distribution:-							

The Type 2 was on empty stock workings. The other two had arrived on passenger expresses.

D.S. spotted his favourite snack bar and was about to make a run for it when I with enviable quick thinking and comprehension of the situation caught him. I chastised him for his actions - all the time moving him further away from the tempting smells of the snack bar. I promised D.S. that he could spend the rest of the evening at the snack bar in Euston.

We repossessed our bags after the usual wait at the left luggage and went down into the underground again and boarded a tube train to Kings Cross St.Pancras

Depart	PADDINGTON	Metropolitan and	
Arrive	KINGS CROSS ST.PANCRAS	Circle Line	

Changed lines

Depart	KINGS CROSS ST.PANCRAS	Northern	
Arrive	EUSTON	Line	

When we arrived at Euston after our 30 minute journey what struck us was what on Earth had struck Euston. Euston was completely bombed up. The station was almost an open air one. It had no front and the cars could be seen zooming past us not 30 yards from us. Of course I knew that Euston was in the process of being rebuilt - but this! - I didn't think they were going to start their re-building by completely demolishing the old building. I supposed it would be ready for the first electric services from Euston to Liverpool and Manchester though.

D.S. and I searched round the station for anything which might claim to be new. D.S. was especially interested in finding a snack bar. To say that D.S. was feeling peckish could be termed a gross understatement.

On close examination we found modern toilets and a large relatively modern waiting room. At this time of the night we expected to find the waiting-room about empty. Our illusions were soon put in the correct perspective. It was absolutely packed with unfortunates.

I reminded D.S. that he wanted to stay the first night in London. D.S. pleaded with me to get on the train and spend the night somewhere else. I did not need much persuading and he did not have to ask me twice. OK, we will spend the night at Bletchley station. We were going to get a train to Bletchley tomorrow morning anyway, D.S.

That was all of the new Euston we saw. On enquiry from a porter we found out that all the old restaurants and snack bars had been demolished. As yet they had not started to build the new replacements he said. Can I get a bite to eat anywhere in the station, D.S. queried. The man pointed to a sizeable crowd milling round a small caravan type thing. That was their antiquated mobile canteen. I suggested to D.S. that it would be a good stall for a Punch and Judy show. D.S. hungrily agreed but he was more interested in getting something to eat.

I told D.S. that I wanted a cup of tea and he joined the end of the long queue. I told him that I would find out when there was a train to Bletchley. I chose tea on two counts. Firstly, after last night's one solitary hour of sleep I wanted to get considerable more to night. A renowned coffee-drinker myself I did not want the caffeine in the coffee to stimulate me into another restless sleepless night. Secondly, although I hated tea I preferred BR's tea to the foul, undrinkable beverage which was an insult for coffee that I had been served up at the Carlisle refreshment room. The coffee here would be at least as bad.

I checked up the station timetable and found that the next train which stopped at Bletchley was the 23.55 train to Crewe. It stopped at Bletchley at 01.06. Late! but it couldn't be helped.

Meanwhile D.S. had battled almost to the head of the queue and I looked around for a seat. After a detailed inspection I came to the conclusion that the station had none. Only to be expected in such a barren dump. I found a porters trolley on a platform and dumped my luggage on it. That would be our headquarters for the next hour or so. I do not care to think where the rest of the passengers waited unless they used that fearful waiting room. Pity on them if they did!

D.S. duly arrived with the phenomenal BR tea. Nothing like it on sale anywhere else. Must cost them at least 1¼d a cup and the 1d will be for the paper cup itself - the ¼d for the tea. They sell the "beverage" for 6d (2.5p). I have heard that there is arsenic in tea. If people kept taking BR tea they would have no ill effects though. BR must put in at least two leaves per cup. After all it was almost colourless.

D.S. ground into his plate of sandwiches and not to be called a miser I went and got a sandwich. At least it was not as bad as the tea. You paid through the nose for it though.

Before 23.45 we had noted an assortment of Type 1's, Type 2's and Type 4's around the platforms.

I gave D.S. a good nudge and that made him wake up sharpish and pointed in the direction of the platform as it was now 23.45 and our train left in 10 minutes. D.S. grunted and gathered his possessions together and we made our way to the barrier and scouted up and down the platform looking for a spare compartment. We finally found one and made ourselves at home in the very comfortable, newly re-upholstered compartment.

D8000 of 1B Camden was noted passing us by as we waited for our train to start. D269 was at the head of our train - also of Camden. As our train left Euston station another Bo-Bo Type 1 was noted. This time it was D8037 of Camden.

EUSTON STATION							
		Home shed			Built	Withdrawn	Scrap
Diesels							
English Electric Type 4 1Co-Co1 1958							
D 269	*hauled to Bletchley*	1B	Camden		*Apr-1960*		
D 290		1F	Rugby		*Aug-1960*		
D 297		1A	Willesden		*Oct-1960*		
D 380		1B	Camden		*Mar-1962*		
Total	4						
BR Sulzer Type 2 Bo-Bo 1958							
D5023		1B	Camden		*Sep-1959*		
D5077		1A	Willesden		*Feb-1960*		
Total	2						
English Electric Type 1 Bo-Bo 1957							
D8000		1B	Camden		*Jun-1957*		
D8004		1A	Willesden		*Aug-1957*		
D8037		1B	Camden		*Oct-1959*		
Total	3						
On Station	9	**Kops**		6			
Steam	0	**Diesels**		9			
		Home Area			9	**Visitors**	0
Shed	1A	3	1B		5	1F	1
Distribution:-							

Camden MPD was about 1½ mile north of Euston to the West of the line. The Divisional

148

Manager had written to tell me that it was closed but I believed that he was a liar and I warned D.S. to keep a sharp lookout for it.

Camden MPD was very much open and 8 well illuminated locos were noted in the open as we ambled past. Our pens went "ten to the dozen" (or something like that) to get that lot down. We then glanced at our notebooks to see what we had splashed down. One Type 4 and one Type 2 kop for me out of eight on shed.

			Home shed		Built	Withdrawn	Scrap
1B CAMDEN							
Diesels							
English Electric Type 4 1Co-Co1 1958							
D 214	"Antonia"		1B	Camden	*Jun-1959*		
D 231	"Sylvania"		1F	Rugby	*Sep-1959*		
D 255			12B	Carlisle Upperby	*Jan-1960*		
D 304			1A	Willesden	*Dec-1960*		
D 370			1B	Camden	*Dec-1961*		
D 372			1B	Camden	*Jan-1962*		
D 378			1B	Camden	*Feb-1962*		
Total	7						
BR Sulzer Type 2 Bo-Bo 1958							
D5088			1A	Willesden	*Jun-1960*		
Total	1						
On Shed	8		**Kops**		2		
Steam	0		**Diesels**		8		
			Home Area		7	**Visitors**	1
Shed	**1A**	2	**1B**		4	**1F**	1
Distribution:-	**12B**	1					

A few miles further on and we passed by our "favourite" electric cum diesel depot at Willesden on the east of the line. Only two locos could be discerned from our compartment. They were on the outer part of the shed. The rest were under cover.

About ¼ mile further on the west of the line another two locos were noted in Willesden Shed Yard (steam shed).

			Home shed			Built
EUSTON to BLETCHLEY						
Diesels						
English Electric Type 4 1Co-Co1 1958						
D 227	"Parthia"		9A	Longsight	*at Bletchley Station*	*Aug-1959*
Total	1					
BR Sulzer Type 2 Bo-Bo 1958						
D5081			1A	Willesden	*at Willesden Electric Depot*	*Mar-1960*
D5141			1B	Camden	*at Willesden Yard*	*Nov-1960*
Total	2					
English Electric Type 1 Bo-Bo 1957						
D8003			1A	Willesden	*at Willesden Electric Depot*	*Aug-1957*
D8008			1A	Willesden	*at Willesden Yard*	*Oct-1957*
Total	2					
On Journey	5		**Kops**		4	
Steam	0		**Diesels**		5	
			Home Area		4	**Visitors**	1
Shed	**1A**	3	**1B**		1		
Distribution:-	**9A**	1					

The excitement now over we took turn about to use BR's excellent (and that is not a sarcastic comment for once) and free washing up facilities to take the first and last chance of the day to get rid of the London grime and generally get a good wash.

Now I felt better and probably looked better. Goodbye London - and roll on Bletchley. By the time I got back to the compartment D.S. was asleep. I gave him the usual heavy nudge and told him that we were getting off in half an hour.

		Schedule	Actual	Miles
Depart	LONDON EUSTON	23.55	23.55	0
Arrive	BLETCHLEY	01.06	01.06	46¾

At about five to one our train stopped. It was not Bletchley though it was a station rejoicing in the name of Leighton Buzzard.

THE QUEER WAITING ROOM AFFAIR

We reached Bletchley in time and bundled ourselves out of the train. The train left and I noted D227 "Parthia" in a siding opposite our platform. I told D.S. that we had better look for our waiting-room. We looked up the one side of the station - no waiting room. Crossed the bridge and looked over the other side of the platform - no waiting room. Checked all over the station but we could still find no waiting room. A sad state of affairs - all very queer.

Finally we went to the station exit where the ticket collector was probably waiting for us. I asked him if there was a Youth Hostel at Bletchley. Of course I knew his answer would be none. Then I blethered on about our Railrover tour. Was there a waiting room where we could stay the night before moving on to Bedford the next day? We learned that like Euston the station was being rebuilt. There was a sort of waiting room though. We were led to a workman's shed type of thing. Inside it had two long benches (without arms or back). It did have an electric light and our ticket collector friend switched the heater on for us. We thanked him and he said that we would not be bothered by passing trains as none were due to pass till the morning. Goodnight!

I was remarking to D.S. about how cosy this "waiting room" of sorts was. Just the right size. With two benches only, just the right number. The word 'benches' seemed to ring some bell in the somnambulating D.S.'s head. Straining his mind to the maximum he noted that one bench was about a foot from the wall and the other right up against it. D.S. stood staring at the bench about a foot from the wall wondering if it was advantageous or disadvantageous. I then turned round to see what D.S. was doing and found him staring at it. I quickly saw the reason for his predicament and made a move for the bench a foot from the wall. Unfortunately D.S. got in the road and I only succeeded in pushing him on to it. D.S.'s predicament had been answered by me and he refused to take the other bench. So I had unluckily been accidentally beaten by D.S. to have my own way.

I was annoyed at not getting the best the bench (from the diagram it is easily seen where the two benches were in relation to the wall). Whereas D.S. could rest on his side in a comfortable space of two feet I had only the bench to lie on. Although stretched full out I was cramped on my side against the wall. It I made the slightest movement I would overbalance and fall backwards from the bench on to the floor and do myself an injury. The chance of me moving while I slept was almost 100% certain because I wake up in the morning at home in a tangle of clothes in a position unbelievably different from the one in which I fell asleep in. My mother always said that my bed looked as though a battle had been fought in it. My older brother when I was a good deal younger had the misfortune to sleep in the same bed as me and many mornings he woke up on the floor having been kicked out of the bed while I "peacefully" slept.

I contemplated on the day past.

This had been the plan for the day:-

DAY 2   **SUNDAY AUGUST 1ST 1965**   **LMR DAY 1**

<u>MILES</u>

Depart CARLISLE	00.33	0
Arrive CREWE	-	141
Depart CREWE	03.45	141
Arrive RUGBY MIDLAND	04.52	216½
Depart RUGBY MIDLAND	05.00	216½
Arrive WATFORD JUNCTION	06.23	<u>281½</u>

Journey:-

see 12A	**Tebay** (south west of station)		37
see 8F	**Wigan** (1 mile south east of station)		105¼
see 8B	**Warrington** (1 mile north west of station)		117
see 5A	**Crewe North** (north west of station)		141
see 5B	**Crewe South** (south west of station)		141
see 5C	**Stafford** (north west of station)		165½
see 5E	**Nuneaton** (south west of station)		202
see 1F	**Rugby Midland** (east of station)		216½
see 1E	**Bletchley** (north west of station)		252¼

Do 1C Watford (20 mins. approx)

Depart WATFORD JUNCTION	06.40 07.10 07.35 07.53 08.08	0
Arrive WILLESDEN JUNCTION	07.10 07.40 08.05 08.23 08.38	<u>11</u>

Do 81A Old Oak Common (60 mins.)

Do 1A Willesden (40 mins. approx)

Do Willesden Electric Depot (25 mins. approx)

Depart WILLESDEN JUNCTION	Frequent service	0
Arrive QUEENS PARK	(10 mins.)	1¾

TUBE -   UNDERGROUND   -   Bakerloo Lane

Depart QUEENS PARK
Arrive PADDINGTON

<u>Do Paddington Station</u>

TUBE   -   Metropolitan or Circle Line Train

Depart PADDINGTON
Arrive KING'S CROSS/ST PANCRAS
TUBE   -   Northern Line (Edgware Bound)

Depart KING'S CROSS/ST PANCRAS
Arrive CHALK FARM

Do 1B Camden

Depart CHALK FARM
Arrive KING'S CROSS/ST PANCRAS

TUBE   -   Piccadilly Line

Depart KING'S CROSS/ST PANCRAS
Arrive TURNPIKE LANE

Do 34B Hornsey (ex-34B)

Depart TURNPIKE LANE
Arrive FINSBURY PARK

Do 34G Finsbury Park

Depart FINSBURY PARK
Arrive KING'S CROSS/ST PANCRAS

Do King's Cross Station

Do St Pancras Station

BRITISH RAIL		MILES
Depart ST PANCRAS	.00 on the hour	0
Arrive CRICKLEWOOD	.12 past the hour	5¼

Do 14A Cricklewood East
Do 14B Cricklewood West

Depart CRICKLEWOOD	.04 past the hour	0
Arrive ST PANCRAS	.18 past the hour	5¼

Do Cambridge Street Diesel Depot

TUBE   -   Piccadilly Line

Depart KING'S CROSS/ST PANCRAS
Arrive HOLBORN

TUBE   -   Central Line

Depart HOLBORN
Arrive STRATFORD

Do 30A Stratford

TUBE   -   Central Line

Depart STRATFORD
Arrive TOTTENHAM COURT ROAD

TUBE   -   Northern Line

Depart TOTTENHAM COURT ROAD
Arrive STRAND

British Rail - Southern Region

Depart CHARING CROSS
Arrive HITHER GREEN

Do 73C Hither Green

Depart HITHER GREEN
Arrive WATERLOO

<u>Do Waterloo Station</u>

Depart WATERLOO
Arrive VAUXHALL STATION

Do 70A Nine Elms (walk)

British Rail - Southern Region

Depart VAUXHALL   29 and 59 minutes past the hour
Arrive HOUNSLOW   57 and 27 minutes past the hour

BUS   -   LT Bus No 110 or LT Bus 111

Do 70B Feltham

BUS   -   LT Bus No 111

Depart POWDER MILL LANE
Arrive GREAT WEST ROAD

BUS   -   LT Bus No 120

Depart GREAT WEST ROAD
Arrive SOUTHALL STATION

Do 81C Southall

British Rail - Western Region

			Miles
Depart	SOUTHALL	21.34	0
Arrive	PADDINGTON	21.53	9

<u>Do Paddington Station</u>

TUBE   -   Metropolitan or Circle Line Train

Depart PADDINGTON
Arrive KING'S CROSS/ST PANCRAS

<u>Do King's Cross Station</u>

<u>Do St Pancras Station</u>

TUBE   -   Northern Line

Depart KING'S CROSS/ST PANCRAS
Arrive EUSTON

<u>Do Euston Station</u>

Night: -   Euston Waiting Room

We had arrived 15 minutes late at Watford Junction but almost immediately picked up a bucket. The bucket journey was delayed a bit through some trouble with the rails and we ended up at Willesden Junction at 07.24 (only ten minutes behind timetable). We caught up on timetable almost immediately as the day's tour then began badly with the "Fried Feet Affair" at Willesden Electric Depot and we did not get round it.   However, we got round 1A Willesden and 81A Old Oak Common safely enough. The latter shed we got round courtesy of our London friend who took us in via the tradesmen's entrance after we got kicked out the main entrance. We also saved a lot of time at his suggestion by buying ten shillings (50p) Tube/Bus Rovers for the day.

We sensibly left our bags at Paddington where we lost a bit of time in D.S. needing to have some breakfast. This time lost was not particularly costly as feeding D.S. neatly tied in with making the hourly service from St.Pancras to Cricklewood and back. We had a stroke of luck at King's Cross Station when we met our tall friend from Lancaster who went with us to 34G Finsbury Park, its sub Hornsey and 30A Stratford. We were a little lucky to get round 30A Stratford as our permit was for the following day (Monday) as no Sunday permits were allowed. We temporarily added to our party size by acquiring the Newcastle four there. 30A Stratford turned out to be simply wonderful by D.S. sniffing out the "Secret Sanctuary" and all her great steam inhabitants.

Ripple Lane and Camden had been omitted by this time but they were of course diesel depots. The sardine-cans would be around for some time to come to and "steam" was what we most wanted to see. After Stratford the day went badly wrong. I could not blame D.S. for wanting to eat something in the cafeteria at Liverpool Street as it had been a long day but this took up more valuable time. We bade a sorrowful farewell to our Lancaster friend there and I made the disastrous decision to visit diesel depot 73C Hither Green rather than take the tube to Waterloo and visit in sequence the great steam sheds of 70A Nine Elms, 70B Feltham and 81C Southall.

What hopes I had of visiting the steam depots of Feltham and Southall faded abruptly as a result of the wasted time in going to 73C Hither or rather "Dither" Green and getting lost and misdirected in going from Vauxhall Station to 70A Nine Elms. To my surprise as we were a lot further south than Edinburgh it also got darker earlier in London whereas in winter it gets darker earlier in Edinburgh. Early darkness thus posed a final problem. I should, however, have done all the steam sheds first to avoid such a disastrous finale to the day.

This is what we should have done after we arrived at Paddington station having visited 1A Willesden and 81A Old Oak Common:-

					Miles
Depart	PADDINGTON	11.03			0
Arrive	SOUTHALL	11.20			9
	Do 81C Southall				
	London Transport south bound 120 bus to Great West Road				
	change to south bound				
	London Transport 111 bus to Powder Mill Lane				
	Do 70B Feltham				Miles
	London Transport northbound 110 or 111 bus to Hounslow rail station				
Depart	HOUNSLOW	13.00	13.30		0
Arrive	VAUXHALL	13.32	14.02		13¾
	Do 70A Nine Elms				

81C Southall was still a great steam shed. A lot of steam engines had been recently withdrawn but doubtless none of them would have been carted off to the scrapbreakers yet:-

81C SOUTHALL				
Steam				
1933 dev. of Collett 3F 5700 0-6-0PT 1929				
3608	3620	3763	4609	
4611	4638	9659	9726	
Total	0			
Collett dev.1938 of Churchward 8F 2-8-0 1903				
3812	3818	3820	3848	
3851	3854	3859	3866	
Total	0			
Hawksworth 4F 9400 0-6-0PT 1947				
8498	9418	9463	9477	
9495				
Total	0			
Collett 4MT 6100 2-6-2T 1931 dev. Of 5101 Class				
6106	6112	6117	6132	
6134	6135	6141	6143	
6156	6161	6163	6165	
6167				
Total	13			
Hawksworth 5MT 6959 4-6-0 "Modified Hall" 1944				
6959	6998			
Total	2			
BR Standard 9F 2-10-0 Brighton 1954				
92216	92240	92241	92246	
Total	3			
Grand Total	18			
Recently		*Surviving*	3	
Withdrawn	22	*Steam Classes*		
Saw at Barry Docks				
revisited Aug-70	1			
Steam	**Aug-50**	71	**Mar-59**	58
Allocation	**May-65**	42	**Jul-65**	18
	Closed to Steam:-		**Dec-65**	

We could well have seen around 40 steam locos (including withdrawn locos) on shed! When 81A Old Oak had been closed to steam in the spring most of the serviceable locos had been transferred to 81C Southall. Seeing the two "Modified Halls" would have been particularly welcome plus seeing loads of 5700 0-6-0 Pannier Tanks, 3800 2-8-0's, 9400 0-6-0 Pannier Tanks, 6100 2-6-2 tanks plus a few Standard 9F 2-10-0's.

70B Feltham didn't have a big steam allocation but all Southern Region steam would have been very welcome to us particularly the fast disappearing Urie S15 4-6-0's.

	70B FELTHAM				
Steam					
Maunsell 1936 dev. of Urie 6F S15 4-6-0 Urie 1920 (with smoke deflectors)					
30833	**30837**	**30838**	*30839*		
Total	3				
BR Standard 3MT 2-6-2T Swindon 1952					
80033	80034	80068	80085		
80089	80094	80140	80141		
Total	8	*Surviving*			
Grand Total	11	*Steam Classes*	2		
Recently		*Saw Elsewhere*			
Withdrawn	1	*on the Tour*	1		
Steam	*Aug-50*	77	*May-59*		60
Allocation	*Apr-65*	9	*Aug-65*		11
	Closed to Steam:-		*Jul-67*		

After D.S. was replete from his sandwiches at Paddington we should have got the train to 81C Southall rather than start an all diesel depot tour (apart from the Secret Steam sanctuary at 30A Stratford) until we finally reached the steam haven of 70A Nine Elms. We could not have gone wrong with this itinerary. We would have taken a time-check after 70A Nine Elms and would have decided which diesel depots to drop but definitely not 30A Stratford with its "Secret Sanctuary". Almost certainly 73C Hither Green would have been dropped as this depot was outside our Railrover. In all the day had gone well until the disastrous finale after 30A Stratford when we missed doing 70B Feltham and 81C Southall. This is how the day had panned out for the record:-

		Schedule	Actual	Miles
Depart	CARLISLE	00.33	00.35	0
Depart	CREWE	03.45	?	141
Arrive	RUGBY MIDLAND	04.52	05.10	216½
Depart	RUGBY MIDLAND	05.00	05.16	216½
Arrive	WATFORD JUNCTION	06.23	06.38	281½
		Schedule	Actual	Miles
Depart	WATFORD JUNCTION	06.40	06.40	0
	7 intermediate stops			
Arrive	SOUTH KENTON	06.59	05.10	8
Depart	SOUTH KENTON	06.59	07.10	8
	4 intermediate stops			
Arrive	WILLESDEN JUNCTION	07.14	07.24	12¼
	Do 81A Old Oak Common			
	Do 1A Willesden			
		Schedule	Actual	Miles
Depart	WILLESDEN JUNCTION	9.38	9.38	0
Arrive	QUEENS PARK	9.40	9.40	1¾
Depart	QUEENS PARK	Bakerloo Line		
Arrive	PADDINGTON			

			Schedule	Actual	Miles
Depart	PADDINGTON	Circle Line			
Arrive	KINGS CROSS ST.PANCRAS				
			Schedule	Actual	Miles
Depart	LONDON ST.PANCRAS		11.00	11.00	0
Arrive	CRICKLEWOOD		11.12	11.12	5¼
	Do 14A Cricklewood East				
	Do 14B Cricklewood West				
			Schedule	Actual	Miles
Depart	CRICKLEWOOD		12.04	12.04	0
Arrive	LONDON ST.PANCRAS		12.18	12.18	5¼
	See Cambridge Street diesel Depot				
Depart	KINGS CROSS ST.PANCRAS	Piccadilly Line			
Arrive	TURNPIKE LANE				
	Do 34G sub Hornsey				
Depart	TURNPIKE LANE	Piccadilly Line			
Arrive	FINSBURY PARK				
	Do 34G Finsbury Park				
Depart	FINSBURY PARK	Piccadilly Line			
Arrive	HOLBORN				
Depart	HOLBORN	District Line			
Arrive	STRATFORD				
	Do 30A Stratford				
Depart	STRATFORD	Central Line			
Arrive	LIVERPOOL STREET				
Depart	LIVERPOOL STREET	Central Line			
Arrive	TOTTENHAM COURT ROAD				
Depart	TOTTENHAM COURT ROAD	Northern Line			
Arrive	STRAND				
Depart	CHARING CROSS	Southern Region			
Arrive	HITHER GREEN	22 minutes approx.			
	Do 73C Hither Green				
Depart	HITHER GREEN	Southern Region			
Arrive	WATERLOO	20 minutes approx.			
Depart	WATERLOO	Southern Region			
Arrive	VAUXHALL				
	Do 70A Nine Elms				
Depart	VAUXHALL	Southern Region			
Arrive	WATERLOO				
Depart	WATERLOO	Bakerloo Line			
Arrive	ST.JOHNS WOOD				
Depart	ST.JOHNS WOOD	Bakerloo Line			
Arrive	BAKERS STREET				
Depart	BAKERS STREET	Bakerloo Line			
Arrive	PADDINGTON				
Depart	PADDINGTON	Metropolitan and			
Arrive	KINGS CROSS ST.PANCRAS	Circle Line			
Depart	KINGS CROSS ST.PANCRAS	Northern			
Arrive	EUSTON	Line			
			Schedule	Actual	Miles
Depart	LONDON EUSTON		23.55	23.55	0
Arrive	BLETCHLEY		01.06	01.06	46¾

DAY 2 CARLISLE, LONDON and BLETCHLEY ARRIVAL

Code	Visits	GWR	SR	LMS	LNER	WD	BR	Steam Total	Diesel Total	Electric Total	Grand Total
	Carlisle to Watford			1				1	7		8
	Watford to Willesden			4				4	3		7
	Willesden Junction								2		2
1A	Willesden			28			22	50	14		64
81A	Old Oak Common								51		51
	Willesden to Queens Park			1				1	2		3
	Paddington Station 1								3		3
	St.Pancras to Cricklewood								9		9
14A	Cricklewood East								16		16
14B	Cricklewood West								15		15
	Cricklewood to St.Pancras								6		6
	Kings Cross Station								7		7
34G sub	Hornsey sub-shed								29		29
34G	Finsbury Park								26		26
30A	Stratford	1	3	1	2			7	88		95
73C	Hither Green								24		24
70A	Waterloo Station 1		1				2	3	1		4
	Nine Elms		18				22	40	1		41
	Waterloo Station 2						1	1	2		3
	Paddington Station 2								3		3
	Euston Station								9		9
1B	Camden (pass)								8		8
	London Euston-Bletchley								5		5
	GRAND TOTAL	**1**	**22**	**35**	**2**	**0**	**47**	**107**	**331**	**0**	**438**

In terms of steam dieselisation was proceeding relentlessly. Thanks to missing 70B Feltham and 81C Southall only 107 steam locos had been seen on the day. We were a little late in our visit as 14B Cricklewood West closed to steam in December 1964 and 81A Old Oak Common in March 1965. *1A Willesden was too last just two months to the end of September 1965. 81C Southall closed to steam in December 1965 while the two Southern Region sheds 70A Nine Elms and 70B Feltham fared better finally closing to steam in July 1967.*

BACK TO THE QUEER WAITING ROOM.

You can gather from these frightening tales of moving in my sleep that I was worried that I would end up asleep and sore on the floor. I was also worried about was now about 1.30 in the morning and I contemplated and contemplated ----------------------------------

END OF DAY TWO

Some steam seen analyses follow:-

DAY 2 STEAM ENGINE CLASSES					1A	70A	On Shed
ON SHED					Willesden	Nine Elms	DAY 2
6F S15 4-6-0 Urie 1920 (with smoke deflectors) Maunsell 1936 development							
30838-30847					10	0	1
Maunsell 7P LN 4-6-0 "Lord Nelson" 1926							
33001-33040					40	0	3	3
Bulleid 7P5F "West Country & Battle of Britain Class 4-6-2 1945							
34002/6/7/11/5/9/20/3/30/3/5/8/41/3/9/51/4/5/7/61/3-70/2-6/8-81/3/4/6/					53	0	3	3
34091/2/4/6/9/34102-8/10							
1957 7P6F dev. of Bulleid 7P5F 4-6-2 "West Country & Battle of Britain" 1945							
34001/3-5/8-10/2-4/6-8/21/2/4-9/31/2/4/6/7/9/40/2/4-8/50/2/3/6/8/9/60/					57	0	10	10
71/7/82/5/7-9/90/3/5/7/8/34100/1/9							
Bulleid 8P 4-6-2 "Merchant Navy" 1941							
35001-30					30	0	1	1
Ivatt 4MT 2-6-0 1947							
43000-43161					162	2	0	2
Stanier 5MT 4-6-0 "Black Five" 1934							
44658-45499					842	7	0	7
Ivatt 2MT 2-6-0 1946							
46400-46527					128	1	0	1
Midland 3F "Jinty" 0-6-0T 1924 dev. of Johnson 1899 design							
47260-47681					417	1	0	1
Stanier 8F 2-8-0 "Big Eight" 1935							
48000-48775					666	7	0	7
BR Standard 5MT 4-6-0 Doncaster 1951							
73000-73171					172	2	7	9
BR Standard 4MT 4-6-0 Brighton 1951							
75000-75079					80	0	2	2
BR Standard 4MT 2-6-0 Doncaster 1953							
76000-76114					115	3	2	5
BR Standard 2MT 2-6-0 Doncaster 1953							
78000-78064					65	15	0	15
BR Standard 4MT 2-6-4T Doncaster 1953							
80000-80154					155	0	5	5
BR Standard 3MT 2-6-2T Swindon 1952							
82000-82044					45	0	5	5
BR Standard 9F 2-10-0 Brighton 1954							
92000-92250					251	1	0	1
						39	39	78

DAY 2 STEAM ENGINE CLASSES
WITHDRAWN LOCOS

	1A Willesden	30A Stratford	70A Nine Elms	Withdrawn DAY 2
Collett 8P 6000 4-6-0 "King" 1927				
6000-6029	30			1
Beattie 0P 2-4-0WT Class 0298 1874.				
30585-30587	3			1
Maunsell 7P LN 4-6-0 "Lord Nelson" 1926				
30850-30865	16		1	1
Bulleid "Austerity" 5F Q1 0-6-0 1942				
33001-33040	40		1	1
Fairburn 4MT 2-6-4T 1945 dev. of Stanier 1935				
42050-42299; 42673-42699	277	4		4
Stanier 5MT 4-6-0 "Black Five" 1934				
44658-45499	842	1		1
Ivatt 2MT 2-6-0 1946				
46400-46527	128	1		1
Stanier 8F 2-8-0 "Big Eight" 1935				
48000-48775	666	4		4
Beames LNWR 7F 0-8-0 G2 1921				
49395-49454	60		1	1
Raven N.E. design 8F 0-8-0 Q7 1919				
63460-63474	15		1	1
Robinson 8F 2-8-0 O4 1911				
63570-63920	271		1	1
BR Standard 5MT 4-6-0 Doncaster 1951				
73000-73171	172		1	1
BR Standard 3MT 2-6-2T Swindon 1952				
82000-82044	45	1		1
	1	11	7	19

DAY 2 STEAM ENGINE CLASSES
OFF SHED AND SUMMARY TOTALS FOR THE DAY

	carlisle to watford	watfd to willesden	willesden to queens station 1	waterloo station 1	waterloo station 2	Off Shed Day 2	On Shed Day 2	Withdrawn Day 2	"Total" Day 2
Collett 8P 6000 4-6-0 "King" 1927								1	1
Beattie 0P 2-4-0WT Class 0298 1874.								1	1
6F S15 4-6-0 Urie 1920 (with smoke deflectors) Maunsell 1936 development								1	1
Maunsell 7P LN 4-6-0 "Lord Nelson" 1926								1	1
Bulleid "Austerity" 5F Q1 0-6-0 1942							3	1	4
Bulleid 7P5F "West Country & Battle of Britain Class 4-6-2 1945							3		3
1957 7P6F dev. of Bulleid 7P5F 4-6-2 "West Country & Battle of Britain" 1945			1			1	10		11
Bulleid 8P 4-6-2 "Merchant Navy" 1941							1		1
Fairburn 4MT 2-6-4T 1945 dev. of Stanier 1935								4	4
Ivatt 4MT 2-6-0 1947								2	2
Stanier 5MT 4-6-0 "Black Five" 1934	1					1	9		10
Ivatt 2MT 2-6-0 1946							2		2
Midland 3F "Jinty" 0-6-0T 1924 dev. of Johnson 1899 design								1	1
Stanier 8F 2-8-0 "Big Eight" 1935		4				4	7	4	15
Beames LNWR 7F 0-8-0 G2 1921								1	1
Raven N.E. design 8F 0-8-0 Q7 1919								1	1
Robinson 8F 2-8-0 O4 1911								1	1
BR Standard 5MT 4-6-0 Doncaster 1951				1		1	9		10
BR Standard 4MT 4-6-0 Brighton 1951							2		2
BR Standard 4MT 2-6-0 Doncaster 1953							5		5
BR Standard 2MT 2-6-0 Doncaster 1953							15		15
BR Standard 4MT 2-6-4T Doncaster 1953					1	1	5		6
BR Standard 3MT 2-6-2T Swindon 1952				2		2	5	1	8
BR Standard 9F 2-10-0 Brighton 1954							1		1
	1	4	1	3	1	10	78	19	107

Part Three

MONDAY 2nd AUGUST 1965

The Tour Continues

**Bletchley, Wellingborough, Leicester
Colwick, Nottinghamshire, Derbyshire
and
Derby Arrival**

Reveille – A Waiting Room at Bletchley

I awoke up. Fantastic, fabulous, unbelievable I had remained in my cramped position without moving an inch. Amazing thing willpower is.

I pulled up my sleeve and noted the time 05.25. Four precious hours of sleep I had had. I looked over at where D.S. was. Still asleep, of course. I had now had five hours sleep during the past 48 hours. Not very much but it would have to do.

I staggered out of the shed (I must have looked a dreadful sight) and made my way on to the platform. I was still half asleep. A Type 4 approached from the north end of the station at high speed at the head of an express passenger. As it flew passed I vainly tried to make out its number without success. I had better be more awake for my eyes to focus on the next train that passed.

D5013 of 1F Rugby was noted waiting to leave with the 05.42 for Euston. The local D3796 of 1E Bletchley was already out and noted on station pilot duty. The next express to pass through the station was hauled by another Type 4. By this time I was awake enough to catch sight of the number as it flashed past me. D234 "Accra" of 1F Rugby was at the head of it. I found out that it was the "Irish Mail" due in at Euston at 06.20.

Another express flashed by quickly on its heels. This time it was D341 of 5A Crewe on it. It was the 21.45 from Glasgow Central due in at 06.29 at Euston.

I now though it high time to wake D.S. up. I stormed into the waiting room shed and awakened him with a playful dig in the back. He awoke from his much more comfortable position and rubbed his back. He looked lost to the world and complained of a pain in the back. I told him that he was lucky because when I woke up I was seized with cramp. He then asked what time it was, I told him it was a quarter to six and that I had seen a few interesting Type 4's in the past twenty minutes.

D.S. was jealous and demanded to know why I had been so rotten as not to wake him up. I cheekily answered that I thought he needs his beauty sleep by the look of him. Strangely D.S. was not offended. I think he might have believed me. I asked him if he had got to sleep easily. D.S. said surprisingly that he had taken a full hour (or so he thought) to get to sleep. I told him that I had slept like a top. Serves the git right I thought, that he took ages to get to sleep. He stole the best bench. He must have found his bench too comfy.

I finally got him interested in leaving the waiting room and we noted D5081 of 1A Willesden on station work. The fourth express of the morning flashed by at 90 m.p.h. This time it was D384 of 1A Willesden. It was the 22.10 from Glasgow Central due in at 06.54 at Euston.

BLETCHLEY STATION

		Home shed		Built	Withdrawn	Scrap
Diesels						
English Electric Type 4 1Co-Co1 1958						
D 234	"Accra"	1F	Rugby	*Sep-1959*		
D 324		1A	Willesden	*Jun-1961*		
D 341		5A	Crewe Diesel	*Apr-1961*		
Total	*3*					
BR 0-6-0 Shunter 1953						
D3796		1E	Bletchley	*Nov-1959*		
Total	*1*					
BR Sulzer Type 2 Bo-Bo 1958						
D5013		1F	Rugby	*Apr-1959*		
D5081		1A	Willesden	*Mar-1960*		
Total	*2*					
On Journey	6	Kops		3		
Steam	0	Diesels		6		

		Home Area		**5 Visitors**		**1**
Shed	1E	1				
Distribution:-	1A	2	1F	2		
	5A	1				

About time we visited the shed. Correct D.S. He agreed. Quite a good steam shed I said. About 25 steam belong there. We walked along and off the end of the station and turned left into the shed yard. All I could see were rows of diesel and not a wisp of steam in sight. Where had all the steam gone? Long time passing - not quite I still thought it had plenty steam.

I went up to the first railwayman I could find and asked him when the shed was dieselised. He said it had been dieselised for about a month. I also asked our information man if Bletchley was to be used as a changeover depot from electric to diesel power before the electrification was completed to Euston. Also yes!

A sad state of affairs. Dieselisation had struck again. There was a little compensation though when we made our way though the diesels up to the back of the shed we found two stored condemned Jinties and a stored and condemned Standard 84000 class 2MT Tank. One of the Jinty's was 47606. That was the number carried by Triang's model Jinty. Obviously the rest of the workable steam had been transferred elsewhere - possibly a large number to 1H Northampton. Unfortunately although 1H Northampton had a decent allocation it was too far out of the way to visit on the tour. We had already seen at Workington one of the 2-6-0 Moguls which had recently belonged to Bletchley. That did not seem to me significant to me at Workington at the time.

1E BLETCHLEY

		Home shed		Built	Withdrawn	Scrap
Diesels						
English Electric Type 4 1Co-Co1 1958						
D 227	"Parthia"	9A	Longsight	*Aug-1959*		
D 235	"Apapa"	1F	Rugby	*Oct-1959*		
D 306		1A	Willesden	*Oct-1960*		
D 309		1A	Willesden	*Nov-1960*		
D 312		1A	Willesden	*Dec-1960*		
D 331		1E	(ex 5A Crewe Diesel)	*Feb-1961*		
D 376		1B	Camden	*Feb-1962*		
Total	*7*					

			Home shed		Built	Withdrawn	Scrap
Hudswell-Clarke 0-6-0 Shunter 1956							
D2510			1E	(ex 1C Watford)	Sep-1961	Aug-1967	
Total	1						
BR 0-6-0 Shunter 1953							
D3069			1E	(ex 1C Watford)	Nov-1953		
Total	1						
BR Sulzer Type 2 Bo-Bo 1958							
D5003			1E	(ex 1F Rugby)	Dec-1958		
D5004			1A	Willesden	Dec-1958		
D5011			1E	(ex 1F Rugby)	Mar-1959		
D5024			1A	Willesden	Oct-1959		
D5031			1A	Willesden	Jun-1959		
D5032			1A	Willesden	Jul-1959		
D5047			32B	Ipswich	Nov-1959		
D5079			1A	Willesden	Feb-1960		
D5080			1A	Willesden	Mar-1960		
Total	9						
LMS and BR 0-6-0 Shunter 1945							
12073			1E		Aug-1950	Nov-1971	
12074			1E		Aug-1950	Jan-1972	
Total	2						
Steam					Built	Withdrawn	Scrap
Midland 3F "Jinty" 0-6-0T 1924 dev. of Johnson 1899 design							
47500			1E		Apr-1928	Jul-1965	Oct-1965
47606			1E		Oct-1928	Jun-1965	Nov-1965
Total	2						
BR Standard 2MT 2-6-2T Derby 1953							
84002			1E		Jul-1953	Apr-1965	Sep-1966
Total	1						

On Shed	23		**Kops**	17			
Steam	3		**Diesels**	20			
Withdrawn	11						
Home Locos		10	**Home Area**		11	**Visitors**	2
Shed	1E	10					
Distribution:-	1A	9	1B	1	1F	1	
	5A	1	9A	1			
Steam classes on view		2					
Steam Origin	LMS		2 BR		1		

Shed Highlights:-		84002	1E Bletchley			
Steam	Sep-50	59	Mar-59	54	Apr-65	34
Allocation					Aug-65	0
			Closed to Steam:-		Jul-65	

Review and Appraisal of 1E Bletchley

The shed was on the west side of the main line just north of Bletchley Station with the shed entrance a gate in the station yard.

Pity the steam had largely departed. Of the three steam 84002 was the first loco of the Standard 2MT 2-6-2T's that I had ever seen. Good, excellent! In anticipation of the shed being an important traction changeover point the LMR had given Bletchley some EE Type 4's. One of them was on shed. In fact 7 Type 4's were noted on shed. An unusually large number.

Of the other diesels D5047 of 32B Ipswich was easily the most interesting. How had it got here? Possibly by working to Cambridge on the Eastern Region it had been used on some sort of traffic over the cross-country route from Cambridge to Bletchley.

On we go

We walked back to the station and I noted a Diesel Bucket on the far platform. On closer inspection we found that it was a bucket for Bedford. I told D.S. that if we got on this early bucket we might be lucky and get at Bedford an early train to Wellingborough. D.S. agreed.

The bucket was composed of two small cars. This cross-country service must not be well patronised I thought or it might not be a popular train because it is so early.

We left Bletchley at 06.35 prompt. On the intersection where we left the main line for the Bedford line 040 an electric multiple-unit (built for the still to be opened new electric service between Euston and Rugby) was noted at the new electric multiple unit depot.

Now for the7 Midland Lines of BR.

Cross-country was the word for our journey. This line meandered from one University town (Cambridge) to Oxford. 77 miles in 180 minutes was the snail like timetable. Our stretch from Bletchley to Bedford provided us with just lots of wheat fields to greet our eyes. Our slow bucket to Bedford stopped at eight intermediate stations. All were antiquated and small. They seemed to be serving populations of 50 at the most. No wonder our friend Dr. Beeching wanted this line closed. Our pleasant and fantastically boring journey brought us through the following "old-world" stations: - Fenny Stratford, Woburn Sands, Aspley Guise, Ridgmont, Lidlington, Millbrook, Stewartby and Kempston Hardwick. A motley lot. One consolation was that we did not stop at Bow Brickhill. That must make it a semi-fast or an express! I half expected the laird of the manor to greet us at each station.

		Schedule	Actual
Depart	BLETCHLEY	06.35	06.36
Arrive	BEDFORD ST.JOHNS	07.09	07.10

Eight intermediate stops.

Bedford St Johns duly arrived and we asked the ticket collector there how to get to Bedford Midland Road. He seemed quite shocked to think that we would change from his shanty railway to the superb modern Midland main line station. After he recovered he gave us a flood of directions. The porter came over as well to see the "main attraction" and waved his arms around and jabbered out another flood of directions. I gathered from them what the general direction was and we left the wee station.

We kept following the road into the town. It was over a mile's walk to Bedford (Midland Road). As you will imagine it was now 07.15 and a flood of people were going to their work. Armadas of workers all on bicycles (mostly old) passed us. Everybody seemed to be going to work by bicycle. It was a very unusual and surprising sight. It left me gaping seeing all these cyclists and even D.S. remarked on the fact.

After getting re-directed on to the correct road we finally arrived at Bedford Midland Road Station. I rushed up and asked when the next train to Wellingborough was. It's not till 08.23. Have we just missed one? No he said the last one was the 05.26 if you can call that one missed. Our rush to Bedford had brought us no reward.

D.S. was beginning to feel the first pangs of hunger. The gannet went away to look for the snack bar so that he could get some breakfast. The gannet found it closed and on enquiry found it opened at 08.30. Too late for him. Disgruntled he went over to a bench curled up and went to sleep. He had nothing better to do. I had!

I went away and decided to visit Bedford M.P.D. It had once had a shed code but now was only a diesel stabling point if it was open at all. I got out the faithful shed directory and noted the relevant details. The shed is on the west side of the avoiding line south of the station. I left the station, went up a flight of steps and in 5 minutes I was at the shed entrance. The shed looked drab from the inside. Inside I found the departmental loco ED3 and that was all. What a dump.

I went completely through the shed and about 100 yards further on the junction with the avoiding line south of the station I noticed 3 Birmingham Sulzer Type 2's . The three locos had obviously been stabled overnight at the shed and were now departing. I gave chase to where they were standing. The first one "escaped" on to the London line but I was able to get the other two. A diesel shunter was also noted.

D5293 (recently built) looked for better in its two-tone green lining. D5073 looked drab in its BR green with unsightly gangwayed ends, ventilations on the side instead of on the roof on D5293 and no four character indicator board either.

BEDFORD DIESEL STABLING POINT(ex 14C)						
		Home shed		Built	Withdrawn	Scrap
Diesels						
BR 0-6-0 Shunter 1953 English Electric engine						
D4132		14B	Cricklewood West	Jun-1962		
Total	1					
BR Sulzer "Peak" Type 2 Bo-Bo 1958						
D5073		1A	Willesden	Mar-1960		
D5273		D16	Nottingham Division	May-1964		
Total	2					
John Fowler & Co. 0-4-0 shunter 1936						
ED3		Dept	Lenton P.W.Depot	1949		
Total	1					
On Shed	4	Kops	4			
Steam	0	Diesels	4			
Home Locos	0	Home Area		2 Visitors	2	
Shed	14B	1 D16		1 Dept.	1	
Distribution	1A	1				
Shed		ED3 - departmental diesel loco				
Highlight						

Review of ex-14C Bedford Diesel Stabling Point

The shed was on the west side of the avoiding line south of Bedford Midland Road Station. The walking time was 5 minutes.

A tiny diesel stabling point! Interesting in seeing the departmental diesel shunter.

On we go

I left the shed and was on the railway bridge when I saw a rare sight. It was one of the new Freightliner Liner trains out on trial. It must have been on one of the first trial lines. It took the avoiding line to the station and was going south. D1830 of D16 Nottingham Division was at the head.

Back at the station I found D.S. still asleep and chose not to disturb him just yet. I scouted around the station until 08.15. Only one of the Type 2's was on a freight. The other three were working about light engine.

D.S. was still asleep and I woke him up with a playful rabbit-punch to the neck. D.S. woke up and complained of a stiff neck. Must be the position I was sleeping in he said. I knew better. I aroused D.S.'s jealousy by telling him of the freightliner train that he had missed. D.S. came to the conclusion that he had better stay awake in future.

		BEDFORD STATION			**Built**	**Withdrawn**	**Scrap**
		Home shed					
Diesels							
Brush Type 4 Co-Co 1962							
D1830		D16	Nottingham Division		*Mar-1965*		
Total	1						
BR 0-6-0 Shunter 1953 English Electric engine							
D3022		14B	Cricklewood West		*May-1953*		
Total	1						
Birmingham RCW Type 2 Bo-Bo 1958							
D5403		D14	Cricklewood Division		*Jul-1962*		
D5404		ML	Midland Lines		*Jul-1962*		
D5408		D14	Cricklewood Division		*Aug-1962*		
D5413		ML	Midland Lines		*Sep-1962*		
Total	4						
On Station	6	Kops	6				
Steam	0	Diesels	6				
		Home Area	3	**Visitors**	3		
Shed	14B	1 D14	2				
Distribution	ML	2 D16	1				

At 08.20 our train arrived from London St Pancras. It was a second-class only diesel bucket. What a come down I had expected a "Peak" at least. We left Bedford Station on time at 08.23. We did not pass the shed on the way to Wellingborough I assured D.S. I told him that Bedford M.P.D. was south of the station. D.S. did not believe me and he scanned the track anxiously for Bedford Shed and ED3. D.S. especially wanted to see ED3 because I told it was a new 4000 HP Type 6 Diesel out on trial and not an insignificant works shunter.

Our journey from Bedford to Wellingborough was a bit more interesting than the Bletchley-Bedford St John's was. We did not see anything but the changing industrial scene was pleasant on the eye.

		Schedule	*Actual*	*Miles*
Depart	BEDFORD MIDLAND ROAD	08.23	08.23	0
Arrive	WELLINGBOROUGH	08.42	08.42	16¾

THE WALK TALL EPISODE

We duly arrived at Wellingborough Station on time at 08.42. When we got out the first thing that struck me about the station was a 7ft tall youth in the service of BR. I presumed he was the ticket collector. Quite a few people got out the train while D.S. and I were taking in his full height. The other passengers walked past him and out of the station without showing their tickets. Funny! D.S. walked round one side of him and I walked round the other. He did not ask us for our tickets either. After we had passed him we again turned round and observed him from the rear. Wonder what his job is I said to D.S. Must be the ticket collector. Nobody checked our tickets though. He just stands there erect and motionless. His eyes seemed to flicker about from side to side taking in and mentally noting every passenger who got off. If D.S. and I happened to bump off the shedmaster of the M.P.D. and all the police's description was two strangers I would certainly expect him to pick us out from hundreds of other in an identity parade. Possibly it was his spectacles which gave me that impression. I told D.S. that I was very impressed with him. An imposing figure. I think sincerely that if British Rail had ornaments like him in every station the railways in general would be lifted out of the red, so much would the public's esteem of the railway increase.

For some odd reason I had always had a soft spot for Wellingborough. Possibly it was the long name that appealed to me. It also used to have many BR Standard 9F 92XXX class locos. Possibly that. There was no real reason why D.S. and I should spend an hour in Wellingborough and visit a run-down depot (most of Wellingborough's allocation had been transferred to Leicester). This cut down the allocation from an impressive number to a paltry five steam locos. Why, indeed! Why spend an hour here when the hour could be put to better use when we would "battle" against the timetable later in the day in trying to fit in sheds out in the wilds in the heart of Derbyshire and Nottinghamshire. As the man in the Bertola Cream sherry advert on TV says "I cannot tell you why but I know only it is so". So with me and so with the visit to Wellingborough.

We left the station and reassured D.S. that he would not have to put any undue strain on the heart as we had about 15 minutes recovery time. Ample!

I consulted the shed directory and when D.S. saw that the cinder path we had to follow went up a steep incline he almost had heart failure. Why did I want to go to this old-fashioned, iron-mining town with the steep incline? I cannot tell you why but I only know it is so.

Up the steep incline, across and over the railway and in less than 10 minutes we were at the shed entrance. The first notice that we noticed was a big one saying "NO SPOTTERS ALLOWED". One to be ignored of course. The roundhouse was immediately in front of us and we went in there. The only locos in there were four "Big Eights". The roundhouse itself was in a terrible state and obviously it would be closed soon. I peered out of the other end of the roundhouse and I noticed a 9F 92XXX about 100 yards down the shed yard. There's something better I said to D.S.

We had not gone but 50 yards when a smallish man from the direction of the 9F came marching towards us shouting "Get out, get away, we've had enough of spotters. Didn't you see the notice? Get out, come on, get out." He went on and on without actually swearing. This needs desperate action. I shouted as he was shouting "We've got a permit" a few times. Finally it got through to him and he shouted "Lemme see it". I showed him the permit after I extracted it from the wad and he read it. It was dated for the Sunday 1st August (an error by the Leicester Divisional Manager) and was of course for twelve people. He did not notice this or was not bothered as long as we had a permit. "Sorry about this," he said, "but we have terrible trouble from spotters and vandals."

He was all very apologetic now and his attitude from one of anger had changed to a friendly one. Amazing what a permit could do. He was not the shedmaster I guessed. He was probably the worried foreman. He said that the shed was closing down in a few months and with a reminder not to miss the diesel servicing depot which was out of sight about another 100 yards up the shed yard, he departed. Good of him to tell us.

We finally arrived at the 9F which turned out to be an 8H Birkenhead one. She was quite dead and looked as though she had not been moved for some time. A stranger indeed but not to the shed which used to handle innumerable 9F's on the local iron ore trains a few years previously. 92101 might have belonged to Wellingborough not so long ago. D.S. found her an ideal subject and took a picture of her. A splendid subject I thought. My camera of course had been damaged at Stratford or I too would have taken a picture.

We found the secluded diesel servicing depot and it was really small. It had room only for four mainline locos. Four Peaks and a diesel shunter were noted there. Can't complain as one of them was named "Sherwood Forester". Further up the line a 9F 92XXX was noted in the yard and an 8F 48XXX class waiting to leave it with a freight.

15B WELLINGBOROUGH

		Home shed		Built	Withdrawn	Scrap
Diesels						
BR Sulzer "Peak" Type 4 1Co-Co1 1959						
D 51	pass shed	ML	Midland Lines	Jun-1962		
D 72		ML	Midland Lines	Nov-1960		
D 100	"Sherwood Forester"	ML	Midland Lines (ex D16)	May-1961		
D 133	pass shed	ML	Midland Lines	Dec-1961		
D 160		D15	Leicester Division	Mar-1962		
D 161		D15	Leicester Division	Mar-1962		
Total	6					
BR 0-6-0 Shunter 1953 English Electric engine						
D3776		15A	Leicester Midland	Jul-1959		
Total	1					
Birmingham R.C. & W. Co.Type 2 Bo-Bo 1958						
D5382	pass shed	ML	Midland Lines	Apr-1962		
Total	1					
Steam				Built	Withdrawn	Scrap
Stanier 8F 2-8-0 "Big Eight" 1935						
48065		15A	Leicester Midland	Nov-1936	Feb-1966	May-1966
48212		15A	Leicester Midland	Aug-1942	Jun-1968	Oct-1968
48382		15A	Leicester Midland (ex 15B)	Jan-1945	Oct-1967	Feb-1968
48530		15A	Leicester Midland (ex 15B)	Apr-1945	Mar-1966	Jun-1966
48545		15A	Leicester Midland (ex 15B)	Feb-1945	Feb-1967	Aug-1967
Total	5					
BR Standard 9F 2-10-0 Brighton 1954						
92096		16B	Annesley	Apr-1957	Feb-1967	Jun-1967
92101	D.S. photo	8H	Birkenhead	Aug-1956	Oct-1967	Aug-1968
Total	2					

On Shed	15	Kops	14		
Steam	7	Diesels	8		
Withdrawn	0				

Home Locos	0 Home Area			8 Visitors	7
Shed	15A	6	D15	2	
Distribution	8H	1	16B	1	
	ML	5			
Sream Classes	2				
Steam Origin	LMS	5	BR	2	

Shed Highlight:-

Steam 92101 of 8H Birkenhead

Steam	Sep-50	77	Mar-59	63	Apr-65	17
Allocation					Aug-65	0
		Closed to Steam:-			Jun-66	

Review and Appraisal of 15B Wellingborough

The shed was on the east side of the main line north of Wellingborough Station. Walking time was 10 minutes.

As good as could be expected of the shed. A lot of work to get here for a dozen locos though and I hoped that the time expended doesn't come back to haunt us later today. Interesting to see a named "Peak" in the shape of D100 "Sherwood Forester". 92101 of 8H Birkenhead in the Liverpool Area was an extremely interesting visitor. How did she get here? By what line? Tell me or *digame as they say in Spanish!* Certainly, 15B Wellingborough had suffered a severe rundown (17 in April only and I found out later that by the time of our visit the shed had a NIL allocation)! As the foreman had said it would be closed for good very soon but it was to stagger on to June 1966 for some reason.

On we go

On our way back from the diesel depots two Peaks were seen on main line expresses. D51 of ML on the 08.05 from St Pancras to Manchester and D133 on the 08.00 from Nottingham to

St Pancras. We passed by the roundhouse and were crossing the overbridge when I noticed a Birmingham RCW approaching with a freight. It was D5382 of ML. The strange thing was that I had seen her before. D5382 was the only Midland BRCW Type 2 I had seen before the start of the tour. I had seen her on 64A St Margarets one Sunday about three months previously. She certainly was a surprise visitor there at the time and she must have worked up to Scotland on one of the car trains.

WELLINGBOROUGH STATION AREA						
		Home shed		**Built**	**Withdrawn**	**Scrap**
Diesels						
BR Sulzer "Peak" Type 4 1Co-Co1 1959						
D 51		ML	Midland Lines	*Jun-1962*		
D 133		ML	Midland Lines	*Dec-1961*		
Total	2					
Birmingham R.C. & W. Co. Type 2 Bo-Bo 1958						
D5382		ML	Midland Lines	*Apr-1962*		
Total	1					
On Station	3	**Kops**	2			
Steam	0	**Diesels**	3			
		Home Area	0	**Visitors**	3	
Shed	ML	3				
Distribution						

We arrived back at the station and we found ourselves with 20 minutes to spare. D.S. saw a refreshment room and I for one was not going to stop him. It was not a BR catering establishment but a privately owned one. It had approximately the same range of food and drink. D.S. indulged himself in a mound of sandwiches and a cup of tea while I rejoiced in a cup of coffee and some biscuits. I was glad of the coffee to stimulate me into booting D.S. around in order to keep to our timetable for another day. That would come though.

I drank the last of my coffee to ensure that I had got all the caffeine that was going and I paid up. Their prices compared favourably with British Rail's zoombala prices. D.S. and I bought cans of their strongest drink. This turned out to be lemonade shandies about 4% proof. These would do for the train!

Modern Railways had always given wide publicity to the Midland Lines late-running and I had my toes crossed hoping that our train would be on time. It was and our train the 08.15 London St. Pancras - Nottingham came into the station on time at 09.33. With a final glance at the Wellingborough walk tall boy I climbed into the carriage.

D.S. had secured an empty carriage for us! How lucky. There were tables in between the seats. How handy. Our train left promptly at 09.35. We quickly acquired a thirst! A knife was found and with two vicious blows D.S. punctured holes in our cans. A shower of lemonade spray splattered out as the shaking of the cans caused undesired explosions. I enjoyed what was left of my drink and D.S. his. We mopped up the table for good measure.

At 09.44 we arrived at Kettering. We left at 09.46. I kept a lookout for the shed on the north-east of the station but there was nothing on shed. Kettering (ex 15C) had been closed a few months before but I still expected something to be on. Bedford had been closed for a much longer time but was still used as a diesel stabling point.

At 09.59 we arrived at Market Harborough. We left at 10.01. Market Harborough (according to the shed directory) had a shed to the north-west of the station. It was supposed to be a sub-shed of 15A Leicester Midland. I saw no shed and no engines. After what had been in Kettering shed it was only to be expected.

Our "Peak" at the head of our train had been in wonderful form and we were being given a fast journey. I almost forgot to tell you (forgive me) D88 of ML was at the head of our train. For the most part of our journey it had been four-track and plenty wagons and empty stock had been noticed by us. We had even noticed five locos on freights either going north or south.

WELLINGBOROUGH TO LEICESTER						
		Home shed		**Built**	**Withdrawn**	**Scrap**
Diesels						
BR Sulzer "Peak" Type 4 1Co-Co1 1959						
D 88	*hauled*	ML	Midland Lines	*Mar-1961*		
D 123		ML	Midland Lines	*Oct-1961*		
Total	2					
BR Sulzer "Peak" Type 2 Bo-Bo 1958						
D7597		ML	Midland Lines	*Aug-1964*		
Total	33					
Steam				**Built**	**Withdrawn**	**Scrap**
Stanier 8F 2-8-0 "Big Eight" 1935						
48085		2E	Saltley	*Jan-1937*	*Aug-1967*	*Nov-1967*
48750		16G	Westhouses	*Aug-1946*	*Jan-1968*	*Jun-1968*
Total	2					
WD 8F 2-8-0 "Austerity" Riddles 1953						
90471		41E	Staveley(Barrow Hill) ex41D	*May-1944*	*Apr-1966*	*Sep-1966*
Total	1					
On Line	6	**Kops**		6		
Steam	3	**Diesels**		3		
		Home Area		0 **Visitors**		6
Shed	**ML**	3				
Distribution	2E	1	16G	1	41E	1
Steam Classes	2					
Steam Origin	LMS	2	**WD**	1		

All three steam locos were a good distance from their home depots.

		Schedule	Actual		Miles
Depart	WELLINGBOROUGH	09.23	09.23		0
Arrive	LEICESTER LONDON ROAD	10.19	10.19		34

Our trusty Peak brought us into Leicester at 10.19. On time! Our recovery time here was -20 or +43. Our first and desired way was to visit 15A get back to Leicester and then get a bus to Leicester Central station and then get the 10.59 diesel bucket. If we missed that we had a 45 minute wait at Leicester London Road before we could get a train to Nottingham Midland. One was obviously cutting things too finely and the other one wasting 45 minutes of valuable time in waiting for a train. Well we could only try.

As soon as we got into Leicester Station we were up the steps had our tickets checked and out. I noticed that outside the station there was a bus stop from where the services to the Central (Great Central Line) station originated. We had 40 minutes to do the shed and get to Central station. The shed directory said 15 minutes walking time to the shed. That's half an hour wasted in walking. That leaves us 10 minutes in which to visit 15A and get a bus to Central. Impossible! Let's run D.S. and I mean run if we are going to get the train. We will save some of the walking time.

With the shed directory in one hand, my grip in the other and my bag slung over my shoulder. I made a spirited sprint and carefully dodged the bewildered pedestrians in the main road. After some time I looked round for D.S. Nowhere to be seen! Where had he got to? He arrived five minutes later at his own pace. No, he had not got lost. He had found it impossible to run as his boots were like lumps of lead - and the luggage was killing him. Our friend D.S. was obviously out of training judging by the red puffy face and the exhausted pants which he made continuously. He also complained of a sharp pain in his side. His usual stitch of course. "I'll never get that train, in time". "Let's take our time and get the later one". I had no option, D.S. had taken as long as the shed directory or even longer - and I had wanted to take 20 minutes of that time. Now D.S. had made it really impossible. With a few well-chosen oaths I let the matter slip and I continued at D.S.'s snail pace with reluctance. We finally arrived at the shed-entrance in Beal Street after 20 minutes. Five minutes longer than the LocoShed directory's time. That takes the biscuit!

Leicester shed looked very impressive from our entrance point and so did the glass-fronted offices which we had to pass. Of course I was not going to show them our permit unless we had to. They might not be willing to listen to two people who possessed a permit for the Sunday and for a party of 12.

We walked past the offices and quickly darted into the rather modern glass-roofed, half glass sides, round house. We dumped our bags down in a handy corner and began our visit. One of a bunch of greasy apprentices had the cheek to ask me for my permits. I refused politely. I said "Get stuffed". It seemed to me that their consensus of opinion was that I did not have a permit. D.S. meanwhile had stupidly disappeared round the other side of the roundhouse. A swearing and slanging match began with me and the apprentices. I found them resorting to throwing stones at this Scottish infiltrator and hastily continued on my way round the roundhouse. I rejoined D.S. when we completed it and then went out to explore the shed yard. The roundhouse had been great. It had been filled to capacity with steam locos.

The shed yard was great too - the mainline diesels were to be found there and some shunters also. Big 8's were mucking about there to. The shedmaster was there also but he was not interested in us. A good shedmaster. The yard was very busy indeed - one of the busiest shed yards I had ever seen. Every loco seemed to be either about to start or just running up and down for the fun of it. On our way out we found a solitary deadline up the back of the depot where 5 Big Eights out of steam were noted. All of them had recently arrived from other depots within the region.

			15A LEICESTER MIDLAND				
			Home shed		**Built**	**Withdrawn**	**Scrap**
Diesels							
Brush Type 4 Co-Co 1962							
D1831			D16	Nottingham Division	*May-1965*		
D1878			41A	Tinsley (Sheffield)	*Jun-1965*		
Total		2					
BR 0-6-0 Shunter 1953 English Electric engine							
D3058			15A		*Aug-1954*		
D3059			15A		*Aug-1954*		
Total		2					
BR 0-6-0 Shunter 1953 English Electric engine							
D3788			15A		*Oct-1959*		
Total		1					
			Home shed		**Built**	**Withdrawn**	**Scrap**
BR Sulzer Type 2 Bo-Bo 1958							
D5013			1F	Rugby	*Apr-1959*		
D5186			D16	Nottingham Div. (ex D15)	*Mar-1963*		
D5188			D16	Nottingham Div. (ex D15)	*Mar-1963*		
D5245			2E	Saltley	*Jan-1964*		
D5292			D14	Cricklewood Division	*Aug-1964*		
Total		5					
Birmingham R.C. & W. Co.Type 2 Bo-Bo 1958							
D5383			ML	Midland Lines	*Apr-1962*		
D5384			ML	Midland Lines (ex D14)	*May-1962*		
D5392			D15	Leicester Division	*Jun-1962*		
D5393			D15	Leicester Division	*Jun-1962*		
Total		4					
Brush Type 2 A1A-A1A 1957							
D5581			31B	March	*Jan-1960*		
Total		1					

Steam		Home shed		Built	Withdrawn	Scrap
Ivatt 2MT 2-6-2T 1946						
41219		15A	(ex 1H Northampton)	Sep-1948	Oct-1965	Jan-1966
Total	1					
Stanier 5MT 4-6-0 "Black Five" 1934						
44777		2E	Saltley	Jun-1947	Jun-1968	Jan-1969
Total	1					
Stanier 8F 2-8-0 "Big Eight" 1935						
48082		15A	(ex 15B Wellingborough)	Jan-1937	Apr-1967	Nov-1967
48107		15A	(ex 15E Coalville)	Feb-1939	Apr-1968	Jul-1968
48132		15A	(ex 15E Coalville)	Mar-1941	Jun-1968	Nov-1968
48180		15A	(ex 15B Wellingborough)	Mar-1942	Mar-1967	Jul-1967
48279		15A		Aug-1942	Oct-1967	Mar-1968
48285		15A	(ex 15B Wellingborough)	Sep-1942	Sep-1965	Mar-1966
48292		8C	Speke Junction (ex16E)	Aug-1941	Apr-1968	Aug-1968
48315		15E	Coalville	Dec-1943	Aug-1967	Dec-1967
48361		15A		Aug-1944	Oct-1966	Mar-1967
48394		55B	Stourton	May-1945	Jul-1967	Nov-1967
48414		15A		Oct-1943	Oct-1966	Feb-1967
48607		15A	(ex 15E Coalville)	Sep-1943	Aug-1965	Nov-1965
48637		15A		Sep-1943	Sep-1967	Aug-1968
48645		15A		Nov-1943	Jun-1967	Oct-1967
48685		15A		Feb-1944	Apr-1967	Nov-1967
48698		15A		May-1944	Apr-1966	Jul-1966
48699		15E	Coalville	May-1944	Sep-1967	Feb-1968
48759		15A	(ex 15B Wellingborough)	Dec-1945	Nov-1965	Mar-1966
Total	18					
BR Standard 2MT 2-6-0 1953 Derby						
78021		15A		May-1954	May-1967	Nov-1967
78027		15A		Jun-1954	Sep-1965	Feb-1966
78061		15A		Oct-1956	Nov-1966	Mar-1967
Total	3					
BR Standard 2MT 2-6-2T Derby 1953						
84005		15A		Aug-1953	Nov-1965	Sep-1966
84006		15A		Aug-1953	Nov-1965	May-1966
84008		15A		Sep-1953	Nov-1965	Jan-1966
Total	3					

On Shed	41	Kops		39	
Steam	26	Diesels		15	
Withdrawn	0				

Home Locos		26 Home Area			2 Visitors	13
Shed	15A		24 D15		2 15E	2
Distribution	D14		1 D16		3 ML	2
	1F		1 2E		2 8C	1
	31B		1 41A		1 55B	1

Steam Classes	5			
Steam Origin	LMS	20	BR	6
Shed Highlight:-		48394	55B Stourton	

Steam	Aug-50	80	Apr-59	63	May-65	24
Allocation					Jul-65	37
			Closed to Steam:-		Jun-66	

Home Steam	excluding withdrawn locos				
On/Off Shed	On Shed	21 Off Shed		16 % On Shed	57%
Not on Shed					
2MT 2-6-2T 1946				41212	1
"Big Eights"	48065	48165	48185	48212	48381	48382
	48492	48528	48530	48545	48609	48625
						48671	13
2MT 2-6-0 1953					78013	78028	2
						total	16

saw elsewhere on the tour				6		scrap	
recently withdrawn not on shed or seen elsewhere				1 "Big Eight"		48183 Nov-65	

The shed was on the east side of the main line north of Leicester London Road station. Walking time was 15 minutes.

An excellent shed. As good as I had hoped for. The large number of Big Eights on shed pleased me. So did the three 84XXX Class Standards - the whole allocation on shed. After 1A Willesden I wondered if there were many Standard Doodle Bug 78XXX Class left to see. We saw three here at Leicester. 78013 and 78028 were unfortunately not on shed. Only one "Black Five" on shed. The Midland Lines do not see so much of them.

A good diesel cross-section was on shed. The two major types of Type 2 were well represented. D5581 of 31B March was doubtlessly here on trial. I had read in Modern Railways of some such exchanges. Two Brush Type 4's were on shed and that pleased me. D1878 had been recently built. This of course was a weekday and to find such a high number of steam engines on a shed 21 out of 37 (57%) seemed little short of a phenomenal to me. 64A St. Margarets in Edinburgh is a right wash-out but on weekdays to draw a comparison. *A bustling shed and hard to believe that it would be closed completely to steam on June 1966.*

On we go

After D.S.'s capers earlier I was now resigned to the fact of waiting 45 minutes here in Leicester and I told D.S. that I would allow him to take his own time back to the station.

THE FREE FALL EPISODE

About half-way back when D.S. found walking a bit too energetic he stopped beside a butcher's shop to rest. For once I did not bother to shout at him to get going because he had plenty time to waste. I put my grip down on the ground and propped my bag up against a nearby window-sill. We waited there for a few minutes saying nothing. Unknown to me some external force or a moving of its contents exerted a turning moment on it. As a result the centre of gravity of the bag was altered, now in neutral equilibrium it accordingly toppled forward from the window-sill and it came to rest with a fearful bump on the ground after being subjected to a force of 32ft/sec according to the laws of gravity. The bag in fact fell only 4ft so we can work out the time of fall = 4/32 = .125 sec or 1/8 sec. Here endeth the physics lesson!

Aghast at what had happened to my bag for no apparent reason I picked it up and checked the contents to see what damage had been done. Only one thing could have been damaged - my vacuum flask.

Post-mortem of the Vacuum Flask
Symptoms   a noise of shattered glass when shaken.
Examination   on opening up the patient severe internal damage was found. The
                    silver lining and the double-walled container were found to be broken.
A "write- off"!
Advice on Disposal   Deposit in nearest waste paper basket or dustbin and leave in peace.

I was very annoyed at my broken vacuum flask. Up to now it had probably been my useful possession. It had been handy to fill it with water and take a drink at leisure or use it when the freak takes you to brush your teeth in as one ignominious person who shall remain nameless had already done in the course of the tour. I could always blame D.S. for the broken vacuum flask as he had asked me to stop and if I had not stopped I would not have put it on the window sill and it would not have fallen and it would not have got smashed and I would still have it. Shame on you D.S. I have a good mind to ask you to buy me a new one.

D.S. refused.

After the slight catastrophe we got back to the station and I deposited the vacuum flask into a handy waste-paper basket. No use crying over broken vacuum flasks so I did not.

One possible shed to visit today would have been 15E Coalville. However, the rail passenger service to Coalville had been chopped probably as a result of Dr.Beeching and we would not be undertaking a 25 mile round trip by bus to Coalville and back from Leicester Bus station.

Coalville itself was a heavy duty type of shed and this was no great surprise when the town was called Coalville. Coalville's allocation was 14 "Big Eights" three of which we would see later.

15E COALVILLE					
Steam					
Stanier 8F 2-8-0 "Big Eight" 1935					
48137	48219		48315	48376	
48380	48388		48467	48552	
48617	48619		48644	48687	
48696	48699				
Total	14				
Grand Total	14				
Recently		Surviving			
Withdrawn	0	Steam Classes	1		
Saw Elsewhere					
on the Tour	3				
Steam	Sep-50	33	Mar-59		24
Allocation	Apr-65	17	Aug-65		14
	Closed to Steam:-		Oct-65		

Originally "A Hard Day's Week on the LMR" was produced in three Parts. Part One was first released in December 1966. Part Two of the original continues.

About 11.15 at Leicester London Road Station.

"I just saw three red Brushes"

D.S. was glad to hear that I thought our next shed to be visited 40E Colwick would be a pushover. He remarked that we had not had much trouble so far in getting round sheds. D.S. did not touch wood (neither did I).

After making sure that I had drunk my cup of coffee to the last drop I interested D.S. in rising from the table and suggested having a stroll round the station. On our stroll we came across D73 of ML (Midland Lines). The Peak Type 4 was gratefully kopped by me.

At 11.49 (bang on time) another Peak Type 4 D45 of ML brought in the 10.15 from London St Pancras "The Thames Clyde Express". We would take this train as far as Trent and then change for Nottingham there. The train was very busy and after a little hunting about we found two empty seats. The train left on time at 11.52. Goodbye Leicester Station (the last resting place of my great vacuum flask).

			Home shed		Built	Withdrawn	Scrap
LEICESTER STATION							
Diesels							
BR Sulzer "Peak" Type 4 1Co-Co1 1959							
D 45	*hauled*		ML	Midland Lines	*Sep-1961*		
D 73			ML	Midland Lines	*Nov-1960*		
Total		2					
On Station		2	**Kops**		2		
Steam		0	**Diesels**		2		
		Home Area			0	**Visitors**	2
Shed	ML		2				
Distribution							

45308 of 1H Northampton was noted on freight outside Leicester Station. D.S. put down 45438 at first. I told him that that was the wrong number. D.S. scored it out and put down withdrawn stove-pipe chimney "Patriot" 45508 this time. Now I know how he saw all these fab engines, which he used to talk about. It's easy to put down the wrong number; D.S. seemed to have an exceptional talent for it. I told D.S. the correct number of the engine he had just seen - 45308. He probably would have marked into his book the wrong number and would never think of checking up on its home depot. Never mind - that might have been only the first wrong number he had written down during the past few days. It's not my worry anyway about what he writes down as long as I can concentrate on writing the correct number down myself.

Leicester Midland M.P.D. looked impressive on the east of the main line as we passed it though there were unfortunately no new engines in the shed yard which were not on shed when we visited it earlier.

After a high-speed 15 minutes we zoomed into Loughborough. D.S. was looking out westwards and I was looking out to the east of the line. Suddenly we were passing a long workshop type building beside the main line. I turned round and we saw B.R.C.W. Type 2 D5386 on the other side of the line. On the workshop side was the Brush Works at Loughborough and we saw three Brushes in workshop red waiting to go to Derby Works to be painted and numbered. We had therefore just seen three anonymous Brushes and would never know what their numbers were. How many people have seen a Brush without a number (not in a workshop) and a red one at that. Not very many I bet. This must make us one of the elite! A highlight of the tour indeed!

About a mile or two before Trent we began to pass an empty train of mineral wagons. The train was enormous and finally our express passed the engine at the head of the freight. It was D108 of D16. Our express belted over a viaduct and arrived at Trent at 12.16 (on time). I now realised that the river our train had crossed was (wait for it!) the River Trent. We got off and tried to wait patiently (with about thirty others who had got off the "Thames Clyde Express") for our connection to Nottingham.

By the way our journey timing from Leicester was:-

		Schedule	Actual	Miles
Depart	LEICESTER LONDON ROAD	11.52	11.52	0
Arrive	TRENT	12.16	12.16	20¾

LEICESTER TO TRENT

		Home shed		Built	Withdrawn	Scrap
Diesels						
BR Sulzer "Peak" Type 4 1Co-Co1 1959						
D 108		D16	Nottingham Division	*Jul-1961*		
Total	1					
Brush Type 4 Co-Co 1962						
new 1	ex works	new				
new 2	ex works	new				
new 3	ex works	new				
Total	3					
Birmingham R.C. & W. Co.Type 2 Bo-Bo 1958						
D5386		ML	Midland Lines (ex D14)	*May-1962*		
Total	1					
Steam				Built	Withdrawn	Scrap
Stanier 5MT 4-6-0 "Black Five" 1934						
45308		1H	Northampton	*Jan-1937*	*Aug-1967*	*Jan-1968*
Total	1					

On Line	6	Kops	6
Steam	1	Diesels	5

	Home Area			0 Visitors		6
Shed	ML	1	D16	1	new	3
Distribution	1H	1				
Steam Classes	1					
Steam Origin	LMS	1				

The freight train which we had passed several minutes before trundled through Trent behind D108. Judging by the length of the train the "Peak" certainly had some hard work to do.

Trent was an island station but an important junction for Nottingham nevertheless. The signals changed to green. This will be our train coming, I thought. Instead D1812 of D16 at the head of another long freight appeared but where was our train? It should have left Trent at 12.23 but here we were at 12.23 and it had not arrived yet. Another train pegged but it turned out to freight with 48096 of 16E Kirkby at the head. Good station for trainspotting D.S. murmured. Not bad seeing a "Peak", a "Brush" and a "Big Eight" I muttered approval but where in the blazes was our train. I was more worried about that for the moment. Can't have missed it because there are about thirty other people besides us waiting for it. I knew that D.S. was not worried about it. He did not have to worry about the timetable. Our train finally arrived at 12.33 - all of ten minutes late. It was a two-coach diesel bucket. Trust these buckets again for being late.

My judgement (on reflection) seemed to have been a little harsh on the bucket because British Rail's trains had been running remarkably well for us. All had been near enough on time. Even the "Midlands Accelerated Timetable" which Modern Railways used to slam seemed to be going well. Anyway I had to feel angry about something. By the time D.S. and I had gathered our bags and barged into the train I had cause to be angry once again. The blooming bucket was packed. Why did BR have only two coaches on the train? While I was ranting about British Rail my extra sensory perception guessed that D.S. was going to make a run for a seat. I bustled past him and plonked down on the last seat in the bucket. That's me got my own back after Bletchley waiting room. He'll have to stand like many others. D.S. was not to be outdone and (again using his mental powers to the full like at Bletchley) he calmly walked up the row and then made a dash into the 1st class section of the train and dived into a seat there. What a cheap skate! He's ended up better than me again in the question of accommodation. Two-nil to D.S., but I'll fight back - just wait and see. What a chancer but I don't think he's allowed to use 1st class accommodation if all the second-class seats are full. The other twits who are standing certainly did not. I'll wait and see if a ticket collector comes.

TRENT STATION

		Home shed		Built	Withdrawn	Scrap
Diesels						
Brush Type 4 Co-Co 1962						
D1812		D16	Nottingham Division	Feb-1965		
Total	1					
Steam				Built	Withdrawn	Scrap
Stanier 8F 2-8-0 "Big Eight" 1935						
48096		16E	Kirkby	Dec-1938	Nov-1965	Jan-1966
Total	1					
On Station	2	Kops	2			
Steam	1	Diesels	1			
		Home Area		2 Visitors	0	
Shed	D16	1	16E	1		
Distribution						
Steam Classes	1					
Steam Origin	LMS	1				

Our driver seemed to be content to keep the train only 10 minutes late. After two stops at Attenborough and Beeston, Nottingham was at last in sight. Nottingham M.P.D. would be to the south of the line I thought. We passed a yard to the north of the line and there was the promised M.P.D. to the south of the line. Nottingham M.P.D. had lost some of its gilt as it had been dieselised several months before we came. Nevertheless, any "sardine-can" or shunter was slapped down as we sped by the yard and the M.P.D. After the missed connection at Leicester there was no time to visit the M.P.D. It <u>was</u> a diesel depot and we now had a chance to see something on shed. I would not lose any sleep or tears over not visiting that depot.

16D NOTTINGHAM (PASS) LUNCHTIME

			Home shed		Built	Withdrawn	Scrap
Diesels							
BR Sulzer "Peak" Type 4 1Co-Co1 1959							
D 4	"Great Gable"		D16	Nottingham Division	Sep-1959		
D 75			ML	Midland Lines (ex D16)	Dec-1960		
D 146			D16	Nottingham Division	Dec-1961		
D 153			D16	Nottingham Division	Jan-1962		
D 163	"Leicestershire and Derbyshire Yeomanry"		D16	Nottingham Division	Apr-1962		
Total	5						
Brush Type 4 Co-Co 1962							
D1617			D16	Nottingham Division	Sep-1964		
Total	1						
BR 0-6-0 Shunter 1953 English Electric engine							
D3246			16D	Nottingham	May-1956		
D3290			16D	Nottingham	Dec-1956		
Total	2						
BR Sulzer "Peak" Type 2 Bo-Bo 1958							
D5212			ML	Midland Lines	Jun-1962		
D5255			D16	Nottingham Division	Mar-1964		
D7503			D16	Nottingham Division	Oct-1964		
D7545			D16	Nottingham Division	May-1965		
Total	4						
LMS and BR 0-6-0 Shunter 1945							
12096			16D	Nottingham	Dec-1951	Jan-1969	
Total	1						
On Shed	13		Kops	13			
Steam	0		Diesels	13			
Home Locos	11	Home Area		0 Visitors	2		
Shed	16D		3 D16	8			
Distribution	ML		2				
Shed							
Highlight	D 4		"Great Gable"		D16 Nottingham Division		

Mini Review and Appraisal of 16D Nottingham

At least I saw a good cross-section of Midland diesel Motive Power. I especially liked the BR Type 2. Since I had first seen them at Cricklewood I had taken to their external appearance. D7545 looked as though it was almost new. The sight of a Midland Brush appealed to me. I found it pleasant to see one on the Midland Region unlike the sickening feeling on the Scottish Region after the novelty had worn off. Doubtless it would wear off during the day on the Midland Lines. I noted D163 "The...." (whatever the name is) again. The previous September I can distinctly remember myself on a school holiday going round Glasgow singing, whistling, humming, muttering and mumbling Herman's Hermits first smash hit (as it was a smash hit at the time) "I'm in for Something Good" (or something like that). The song seemed to work for me that day and one of a fruitful days noting was D163 which "I spied" at 65B St Rollox. The pain on seeing her again was a little sharper than it should have been so I suppose I have seen her since St Rollox - possibly at 64A St Margarets. At the time of the St Rollox visit I was very eager to see a named "Peak" especially one with such a gigantic name. I remember being envious of Derek Newton seeing D163 at Durham before I saw her. There's something about diesels, which pain me a bit on seeing them a second time. I could stand seeing "Jubilee" 4-6-0's forever but perhaps not a sardine-can twice. Be seen and be scrapped would be a good motto for diesels and electrics in general. Judging by the way D1743 demolished a signal-box and itself at Shrewsbury diesels seem to heed this advice occasionally and scrap themselves.

Back to 16D Nottingham shed. I don't think I missed much that would be hidden inside the shed because it was a weekday after all and BR works its diesels a dashed sight harder than their steam engines were ever worked. Anyway I snatched down enough to make opening my eyes and frantic running from one side of the bucket to the other worthwhile. The ticket collector was obviously not on the bucket and I moved to the recently vacated seat beside D.S. I had a look over what he had jotted down. One look was enough! D.S. had noted hardly a thing since we had left Trent. He had even missed Nottingham shed.

D4 "Great Gable" was an interesting loco. D1-D10 (the first ten "Peaks" were not surprisingly named after mountains and hence the name of the class) were a little underrated at 2,300 b.h.p as against their sister engines at 2,500 b.h.p. at 750 r.p.m. I understood that because of their lower engine ratings they tended to work heavy freights between Toton and the Birmingham area. So this one was a bit off of its normal haunts.

On we go

"Your boots were not made for running, D.S."

Our bucket driver had been keeping strictly to his schedule of 10 minutes late and as we neared the station approaches it looked to me as though we would remain 10 minutes late. A quick look at the working timetable, a glance at my street map of Nottingham and I noted that Nottingham London Road Station was the nearest station to Nottingham Midland for our next train. Our next train was for Colwick and it would leave Nottingham London Road High Level at 12.53. That would give us 6 minutes approx. when we got into Midland Station. If we ran we might just make it in time.

		Schedule	*Actual*	*Miles*
Depart	TRENT	12.23	12.33	0
Arrive	NOTTINGHAM MIDLAND ROAD	12.37	12.47	6¾

We ground to a halt the expected 10 minutes late and bundled ourselves out the bucket. D.S. seemed to admire the station surroundings and muttered something about putting our grips in the left luggage. No time for that now and I redirected D.S.'s energies to be used in running up the stairs to ground level. We waved our Railrovers at the ticket collector and left the station for busy London Road. We would be stopping off at London Road Station before we reached London though! Four minutes to the train. Away we belted down London Road carrying our heavy grips and shoulder bags. After about one minute D.S. shouted to me from somewhere in the rear that he had a stitch. He complained that he was tired out and that his feet felt like lead. He could not go a step further he pleaded. Let's walk and get the next train. "I know how your feet feel tired (I shouted back) it's these blooming, enormous, ton weight, hob nailed army surplus boots that you are wearing"! I understood D.S.'s point of view because the sweat was lashing of me and I did feel tired but that train we needed to get. Obviously the dynamic D.S. needed re-charging. He was not as fit as he used to say he was by reason of his daily ten mile cycle to work and back. D.S. obviously did not feel like wandering round the LMR without a timetable if he was left behind by me and he succeeded in travelling at something approaching a reasonable rate. One minute to go and where was the station? There it was on the left at an under-bridge. I redoubled my energies and with a last sprint ran over the road, up the stairs and collapsed on to a seat. D.S. soon arrived. No sign of the train but it was 12.53 and it should be here. Don't think we could have missed it though. It must be a little late! D.S. and I remarked that for a city station London Road was really small. It was not much bigger than the likes of a suburban station.

Our train arrived in the shape of a two-coach diesel bucket at 12.56. The train was 3 minutes late. D.S. and I need not have used up all that vital energy in getting here. It did D.S. some good anyway. It was just the thing to keep him in trim for the 2½ mile run to Westhouses shed this afternoon. Forty-five minutes is not all that much when you have to visit 16G Westhouses shed and run 2½ miles back to Alfreton station. D.S. had given warning to me that he wasn't as much as a human dynamo as he thought he was. We will make this afternoon timing at 16G Westhouses though if it means dragging D.S. along behind me.

D.S. suddenly felt himself in a talkative mood and asked me where we were going! Didn't I tell you at Leicester Station - can't you remember? With a flash of genius D.S. remembered and blurted out "Is it Colickton?" Trust D.S. to get the name Colwick muddled up. I felt like a bit fun so I said "That's right." I spelt out Colickton to him and he added the name to his notebook. D.S. then asked how many locos we would see there. I replied that it once had the fifth largest loco allocation in the country but now I wouldn't complain if we saw 30 locos. It's a steam depot anyway, so you should like that. Colwick is officially an Eastern Region shed. In fact the Eastern Region starts at the station we get off at. This line from Nottingham Victoria to Grantham is an ex L.N.E.R. line. I had mentioned Colwick a few times but D.S. probably thought that it was an abbreviation, which I used for Colickton or didn't think at all!

In the first five minutes of our short journey we head seen nothing but here at last was something coming. It was a WD 2-8-0 at the head of a freight coming from Grantham Station. It was very easy to spot any approaching train from a glass fronted - and sided bucket (unlike when travelling in conventional BR carriages). A quick glance at the smoke box number plate and I splashed it down - 90471. There seemed something vaguely familiar to me about that number. A quick glance through the day's haul in my notebook and my suspicions were proved - We had seen this same WD on a freight when we were travelling from Wellingborough to Leicester earlier today. Surprising seeing her twice in the same day and a bit of a distance apart.

		Schedule	Actual	Miles
Depart	Nottingham London Road High Level	12.53	12.56	0
Arrive	Netherfield and Colwick	12.58	13.03	2¾

We arrived at Netherfield and Colwick station five minutes late at 13.03. The driver had lost two more minutes en route. Our bucket had fairly idled along the route - probably due to adverse signals or some permanent way slack that I had not noticed.

One interesting fact about the station was the enormously long station signs, which were required for such a long name as Netherfield and Colwick!

We were due to catch our return train at 13.38. Our previous recovery time was NIL. Our train arrived 5 minutes late so it was now -5. D.S. and I would now have to avoid handing in the permit into the office and fly round in 15 minutes if we were to get out return train. We might be able to cut a few minutes off our ten-minutes walking time to the shed and our ten minutes walking time back to the station. We still had our grips with us and I did not want to run anywhere for D.S.'s sake. I wanted D.S. to conserve what energy he had left for the Westhouses run later today.

THE SPYCATCHER AFFAIR
or TO TRAP TWO SPIES

The LocoShed Directory was rummaged from my anorak and I hastily consulted it, turn right down Meadow Road to cross-roads then along Victoria Road. Simple enough. It was a fair walk and it took us just under 10 minutes to reach the shed entrance on the left hand side.

I noticed something like an unlawful sneak entrance to the shed up the side of the shed. Let's go up through here I suggested to D.S. We don't want to produce our permit unless absolutely necessary. We could get asked some nasty questions over it. We were making our way up the side when ''Hoy!" a worker had shouted to us from the top of the entrance.

Back we went. I said to him that we were looking for the main entrance. "It's not up there." he said "You would have got into a lot of trouble if you had been caught doing that. We've had trouble before." I said that we had a permit. He took this statement with mild disbelief. I'll show you to the shedmaster's office then. To change the subject I said to the railwaymen "Didn't this shed have one of the biggest allocations in Britain a few years ago?" "The biggest." He replied. What a gross terminological inexactitude. I knew Stratford had this shed licked. Well, I asked a question I knew the answer of (actually the 5th biggest shed) and I get that answer. I suppose I deserved that answer. It used to be a great shed anyway. He had a high opinion of the shed. This time we followed him up the main entrance and he showed us to the glass-fronted office. The shedmaster was busy marking up some charts and did not appear to notice us at first. Wish he would hurry up or we shall miss the train I thought.

At last he caught sight of us and came across to the office "speaking hole." I pushed the permit over to him. The shedmaster was the typical British one or what I took the typical shedmaster to be, roundish, in his fifties and wearing glasses with very thick lenses. He carefully read over every word as though he had never seen anything like it before.

While D.S. and I were waiting impatiently for him to give us it back he struck a surprising unexpected blow.

HIM: - "This permit is for February 12th. Its six months old. It's well out of date."

I grabbed the permit back and then gave a smile of relief. How can anyone be so dim? I pointed to the date, which he had seen.

ME:- "That's the date when I received the permit from the Divisional Manager. There's the date at the foot of the permit when we are supposed to visit the depot."

I was relieved and I explained it patiently to the shedmaster. Now he can let us round! Unknown to me the shedmaster had a great deal more craft than I took him for. This was just the failure of his first attack. He must have been thinking (unknown to me) I'll catch these black and white anoraked bastards out yet.

That took a few minutes of explanation. This twit obviously does not handle many permits I thought. He muttered something about it being a joke. D.S. had been standing trying to look pretty all this time. I nudged him and started laughing. D.S. followed suit a little reluctantly. Lets humour him let him have his joke and let's get round the shed.

ME: - "So, it's a joke." (in an enthusiastic voice).

Thinking what a warped sense of humour the shedmaster had.

HIM: - "No, no joke." (while we had been full of joy he had been pouring over the permit. He renewed the attack). "Your permits still not even for the right day. It's for 09.30 tomorrow morning. Do you think you can get away with a permit for the wrong time? How come you're here now?"

Trust him to worry about "trivialities" like that. I'd better make the excuse good. I can feel the railway police closing in. Wonder if we could get the hell out of here and back to the station. We've still got our heavy grips with us though. I would be lucky if I got twenty yards - D.S. ten yards. I'll just have to battle it out diplomatically. We had got a permit for all that was worth!

ME: - "Well it's like this." (A lame start. Buck up. Look confident. I did). "When the Society received the permit we did intend visiting here at 09.30 tomorrow but by the demand of our members they wanted us to include a visit to Barry Docks, South Wales in our timetable. There's over a hundred withdrawn steam locos there and they especially wanted to visit it. We complied with their wishes but the only way the Welsh visit could be fitted in was to leave Burton-on-Trent at 06.00 tomorrow. Obviously we could not visit here than so we brought forward our visit to this afternoon as we still wished to visit this good steam shed."

That's right, praise his shed I thought. He'll be chuffed at that. The excuse seemed ingenious and impressive to me. By coincidence the excuse was true as well. That helps! I hoped he found it believable, above all. Danger momentarily averted.

The shedmaster must have been thinking that was an impressive pack of lies. I've got a right bloody smart Alex here. So he thinks he can clear everything up with a yarn like that.

Judging by the pause I was certain that he would say "OK then, hand the permit in when you have finished the shed." I was to be surprised again.

HIM: - "So you are here a day early Huh! I think you could have found the permit somewhere. You talk about some Welsh lark." (He spoke the words slowly, looking at the permit intently then he fired out quickly another question).

HIM: - "What's your name supposed to be?"

I was thunderstruck, astounded and shattered. What a question to ask. Surely he didn't think we were impostors? Now what is my name? The question had unsettled me somewhat.

ME: - "G Dowie."

The shedmaster must have been licking his lips now (he must be thinking: - that staggered him. It took him long enough to remember his own name or what the name on the permit was). He must now be sensing victory in sight.

HIM: - "What's your address?"

ME: - "21, Stoneybank Crescent."

HIM: - "Town?"

ME: - "Musselburgh."

HIM: - "Where's that?"

ME: - "Midlothian, Scotland."

I hope that's enough I thought. It wasn't. Shedmaster must have now been thinking that this skates learnt up this information.

The shedmaster rambled on. It was to turn into another sneak attach. His voice seemed suddenly friendlier.

SHEDMASTER: - "Musselburgh, you "say" you came from. I was stationed up that way in the war."

Now we'll get a description of how he guarded the camp garbage dump through all weathers, I thought. I was to be mistaken though.

SHEDMASTER: - "I know Musselburgh well enough. Tell me what it is like and where you live in it."

It took no special powers to guess that he was lying now. He must hope that we will break down at his question, openly confess to our sins and reveal our true identity. He's got a hope! We held the power though so I refrained from giving him a dot on the nose through the glass partition however tempting it looked. Now I must make Musselburgh seem a weird town. He knows no better! Or does he? Better not chance it.

ME: - "We live in the Stoneybank part of Musselburgh."

The shedmaster had noticed the hesitation. So marked about some of my answers, he must be thinking. Only one attack away from them breaking down.

SHEDMASTER: - "Huh! You could have guessed that from the address."

This bloke here must be Bernard Archer who starred in that BBC programme "Spycatcher" a few years ago. The scene was very like this. At one side was the Spycatcher (this time our esteemed shedmaster) and on the other side facing him was a suspicious incoming foreigner suspected of being a spy (in this case it was two unwelcome visitors - us) who had come to his sacred shed with a very suspicious permit.

The shedmaster was now scanning our faces intently looking for a sign that would tell him that our resistance was crumbling. He recognised that it wasn't forthcoming. He would see about changing this state of affairs.

SHEDMASTER: - "Tell me more about Musselburgh."

I'd better not waste any more time so I'd better give him an admirable geographical description.

ME: - "Stoneybank is an upland part of Musselburgh. The mucky River Esk (poisoned by paper mill effluent pollution) winds past our doorsteps through the town and goes into the Firth of Forth. Musselburgh is six miles from Edinburgh, the capital of Scotland. The passenger railway service was withdrawn last September."

This shedmaster was obviously a liar about his knowledge of my "'burgh" and did not ask for more. It was evident to me that if I said that there was a rocket station in Musselburgh he would believe that as well. He must be thinking I am a wise guy. My answer was a little too flowery. D.S. was scratching his head wondering what all this questioning was about. Our shedmaster was far from a spent force and played what he thought was his ace card.

SHEDMASTER: - "Dowie, you say your name is. Do you know a chap called Cowie in Musselburgh? Not Dowie, Cowie?"

To try to get us off our guard he said it in a quiet matter of fact voice as though it was a passing comment. It was no passing comment and our shedmaster friend was waiting expectantly for the answer. I was just able to refrain from laughing at this imaginary character the lying shedmaster invented. I say yes he'll immediately know that we were impostors. How could we know this Cowie chap? He would arrest us and inflict the penalty whatever that might be. He would probably take us to the line and get one of his handy WD 2-8-0's to have a run over us. He would tell the authorities that we had sneaked into the shed and got accidentally run over. I know this sadistic type. Huh! So he thinks he can catch me out with a question like that. I looked round to see what D.S. was thinking. He was open-mouthed and all agog obviously the question had shattered him and as a result something must have fused somewhere in his mind. I'd better answer him or he'll get cross-eyed staring at me.

ME: - "No, can't say we do know somebody called Cowie in Musselburgh. Musselburgh is a big place."

I was glad that D.S. had not blurted out yes or we would have been in deep trouble. Just as well the question shattered him or we might have been shattered by the consequences if his answer was not to the shedmaster's liking. The shedmaster looked disappointed at my answer. Foiled again he must be thinking. He must admit defeat now and honourably let us round. Our shedmaster was not to be outdone and staggered me (for the umpteenth time) by launching a ferocious counter-attack.

SHEDMASTER: - "It says here on your permit that it is for twelve people of the MUSSELBURGH RAILWAY SOCIETY. What's happened to your other ten members?"

Our friend had been reading the permit again. Some society with only two members he must be thinking. Now, how can I explain the loss of ten imaginary members? I'd better think of something, which sounds true, or Spycatcher will come down on top of us like a million tons of Big Eights.

ME: - "The twelve of us travelled up to London yesterday and visited some M.P.D.'s there. We had a disagreement over the timetable and the others left from Euston this morning and said they would visit the Western Lines."

That sounded good and even the shedmaster seemed to almost believe it. It was only a momentary hesitation on his part and he struck savagely again.

SHEDMASTER: - "So you say you and your party were in London then. Any proof that you were?"

Checkmate! Got you now he must be thinking. These pair of jokers cannot lie their way out of this one. No! We couldn't lie our way out of this one. I thought of somewhere we need our permit. I could think of two: - 14B Cricklewood West and 30A Stratford. These were the only two sheds where we had needed our permits. The Cricklewood shedmaster know that there were only two of us but at Stratford there were D.S. and I, our Lancaster chap and but that mob from Newcastle. It must have looked about a party of twelve to the Stratford shedmaster. That would nicely cover our party tale.

ME: - "We visited Stratford M.P.D. and the shedmaster has our permit. Our full party visited it."

At least I knew he wouldn't check up on a depot outside his own area. Unknown to me the shedmaster was thinking the writing is on the wall now; all I have to do is to phone up the shedmaster at Stratford to find out if this Dowie and party visited yesterday. Catching these two blighters will be worth the long distance call. The expense department will take kindly to it. It's so easy I could cry. So he thought he was smart.

He looked strangely pleased at my reply for no apparent reason. He looked as though he was victorious. I couldn't guess why.

SHEDMASTER: -"I'll soon find out if you and your accomplices were at Stratford yesterday. You two wait, while I phone up."

He went across to the phone in his office. I wondered if he was bluffing. It didn't seem as though he was, he seems to be phoning right enough. I was neither staggered nor shattered; nothing would surprise me now about this shedmaster. My attitude had turned fatalistic or at least pessimistic.

While he had his back turned I thought that we had better shuffle up the entrance a bit and have a look inside the shed. It would probably be our one and only look. D.S. looked ashen but I nodded blankly in the direction of the engines and he understood. We walked the few yards and peered in. There were steam engines everywhere. I looked across to the far side of the shed. I saw the number 61943. Huh! A K3? I looked on and at the other engines. Psychologically I was probably at low ebb but something made me think over that sight of a K3. It finally dawned on me - all the K3's were gone and scrapped. The last one went two or three years ago. Or did it? I wasn't seeing things. D.S. wasn't either! It was a K3. Fantastic, unbelievable but true. Why wasn't it scrapped? They must use it for some sort of work. It looks clean enough. Could be a stationary boiler. D.S. agreed.

There was a nagging pain in my head which bothered me when I looked round at the rows of engines. Now, what was worrying me? I thought. The shedmaster! That was it! The sight of the K3 had unbalances me somewhat. It was something beautiful in an ugly shed with an uglier shedmaster. D.S. and I walked quickly back down the passageway to the office.

I now felt the surge of stimulating adrenalin through my blood. The K3 had the great effect of relieving all gloom and making me ready to pulverise this painful shedmaster. It had the effect of a purple heart to a depressed nervous system (not talking from experience). Let me at the shedmaster! The old twit was still at the phone. Haggling with the Stratford shedmaster, no doubt would be what he was doing! Hope the nut has to pay for this long distance call. It'll serve him right for meddling.

Our faithful shedmaster finished shouting into the phone and slammed it back on to the receiver. Judging by the look of chagrin on his face he had been foiled again. Hope he's thinking off the cost of the phone call. Our noble Stratford shedmaster must have verified my story admirably. That Newcastle mob had come to the rescue of the Musselburgh Railway Society by a very strange method!

Our shedmaster friend did not apologise. He must know that we weren't impostors now!

SHEDMASTER: - "Why are you here early?"

I groaned inwardly. Here we were back at the start of his investigation. If he's going to go through all that again, D.S. and I are as well giving up and try and get away from this place. Let's have one last bash before he forces checkmate or stalemate should I say.

I mentioned about leaving early tomorrow morning for Barry.
The shedmaster seemed to remember and he began to think.
What was going to come out of his big trap now?
He would surely think of something vicious to say.
A gleam came into his eyes. He had thought of something.

SHEDMASTER: - "I can't let you two go round at the wrong time. I could get into some trouble if I did."

With that last remark he realised he couldn't "book" us but he could at least get rid off us. I wasn't going to waste time here for nothing. He did surprise me by actually using the words "getting round" in his impressive speech. He had never used these words before. I thought nothing could surprise me but his admission that it could be possible to visit Colwick did surprise me. A definite weakness in his invincible defence. A quick counter attack was necessary before we were thrown out.

ME: - "The Divisional Manager at Gresley House would surely let us round if he knew about the alteration to our tour."

Can't get myself reported he must have said to himself. I'll phone him up and that will shut this blighter up for good. He said nothing but ambled across to the phone. This time it did not take him so long. He was not phoning long distance and he could hardly shout and argue with the beaks of Gresley House. The "beak" would surely help BR's strained public relations by putting this insult of a shedmaster in his place.

Back he came!

SHEDMASTER: - "The Divisional Manager wants a letter from you explaining why you couldn't visit here at the proper time when you have finished your tour. He's leaving it entirely to my own discretion if you can visit the depot."

That "discretion" was probably a pack of lies. The Divisional Manager had probably snubbed him and told him to let us round. He was just trying to avoid looking a fool. Our shedmaster's last card had been played; his attack had crumbled into nothingness. He had failed!

I told him I would be pleased to write to the Divisional Manager after our tour had finished.

SHEDMASTER: - "If you want to visit the depot you will have to see the shed foreman first and see if he'll allow you; and you can give your explanation to him as well. You will find his office at the other end of the shed on the left hand side. You can come back here and tell me what he says."

It must have hurt him to say that to us. That's two notches he won't be able to carve on his desk. Well, we had better get away to the foreman before he wants some additional information. I remarked to D.S. that you couldn't help admiring his persistence. British froo and froo. I wonder if we were the first official visitors to the depot. Hardly anybody else could have survived the questioning that we went through. He didn't even apologise for all the delay, which we suffered.

I glanced at my watch. I had allotted twenty minutes to visit the shed and that had been taken up with Schhh (you know who). No chance of catching our train back. We will bus it if we got the shed finished in the next hour!

We walked up the row of engines in the furthest away line and as promised we found the shed foreman's office. After enquiring we were pointed out the appropriate office. The shedmaster wanted me to explain it all again to the foreman. He's got a hope. If we are questioned he'll get the same answers - one nut is enough. I told the foreman that the shedmaster had sent us here to see if it was all right for us to visit the depot. I showed him our permit.

The foreman asked no questions but said that he would send a guide round with us to show us the depot. Changed days! His attitude could be termed as sweet and soothing compared with another person (who shall remain anonymous). Now we were going to be shown round in style.

With our guide we went back through the shed to "Chairman Mao's" office. Surely he hadn't thought of some more other nasty questions in our absence?

ME: - "The foreman says it's OK for us to go round. Here's the permit."

SHEDMASTER: - "Hand the permit in when you've been round. You may be stopped and asked to produce it. The railwaymen have got strict orders to ask any strangers for permits. If they haven't ----......."

We surely wouldn't be stopped when we had a railwayman going round with us. He's just trying to be awkward as usual.

ME: - "Can we leave our bags in your office?"

SHEDMASTER: - "No, no, no. You can't leave them here."

That takes the biscuit - good riddance.

Our railwayman guide told us to put them up against the wall inside the shed. They'll be safe enough there, he assured me. Probably safer than with that shark in the office, I thought.

We gave a few disapproving looks in the direction of the shedmaster's office and our railwayman guide guessed what we had been through.

We went across to that fabulous ex LNER K3 61943 first and had a look at her. She was in magnificent external condition. She was a stationary boiler as I had thought. Does a good job our guide assured us.

What's this loco? I stared in amazement. It was a Brush Type 2 D5699. We have quite a few main line diesels here on loan our interesting guise assured us. This one is here on loan from March M.P.D. for a few months. Is the shed marked down for early dieselisation, I inquired? Although our shed has still got a good steam allocation they may have our shed dieselised by next summer or in the winter of 66/67 at the latest. Did he like the new diesels? A lot cleaner and quicker but they'll never have the same attraction to me as our steam locos. An opinion held by almost everybody, I thought.

You seem to have a lot of WD locos here still. Have they given good service? The "Austerity" locos you mean, he answered. They just built them to last out the war and they are still going strong today. They are grand engines and we've got plenty of them.

We now strolled over to the dead line. From the dead-line we could see the approaches to Colwick yard. The first engine we saw was 61141, neglected desolate and decaying on an incline. It was alone from all the others. Our guide seemed to look at it rather sadly. It had been his favourite engine. He said that she was always the best B1 on shed and always gave him a great ride. It was only during the last few months that she began to go downhill in condition, was refused a major overhaul and withdrawn. I reflected that it seemed harsh that she was withdrawn while some of her sister B1's were still going strong on shed. He sadly agreed.

We passed on down the line and five WD's, a Robinson 2-8-0 and three other B1's were noted. The Robinson loco interested me greatly as she was the first one I had ever seen. We had a good clamber over the withdrawn engines. The 2-8-0 was one of the earliest types built by Robinson and looked old-fashioned with its large single splasher over its wheels. The class had been another great design and Colwick had plenty of them on view.

Another saunter and we were over at the other side of the shed and we noticed a "Big Nine" 9F 2-10-0 lying out of steam. I remarked to our friendly guide that Colwick recently had a lot of 9F's but now Colwick had hardly any. I asked it they didn't like them. He said that 41J Langwith had been crying out for them and they had been transferred there. Now Langwith is getting dieselised and we're getting them back again now, he laughed. He always found them good engines but they had a hell of a lot of works inside them. We nicknamed them "Pipes and Organs" because of that, he said. D.S. and I thought the nickname really good. Quite a mine of information was our guide. We seemed to go a very roundabout way of doing the shed but finally we finished it with the diesel shunter depot.

40E COLWICK						
		Home shed		Built	Withdrawn	Scrap
Diesels						
Brush Type 4 Co-Co 1962						
D1528		34G	Finsbury Park	*Jul-1963*		
Total	1					
Drewry 0-6-0 Shunter 1955						
D2241		40E		*Jun-1956*	*Apr-1971*	
Total	1					
Drewry 0-6-0 Shunter 1959						
D2296		40E		*Sep-1960*	*Nov-1969*	
D2298		40E		*Sep-1960*	*Dec-1968*	
Total	2					
BR 0-6-0 Shunter 1955 English Electric engine						
D3626		40E		*Oct-1958*		
D3627		40E		*Oct-1958*		
D4088		40E	(ex 40B Immingham)	*Mar-1962*		
Total	3					
BR Sulzer "Peak" Type 2 Bo-Bo 1958						
D5195		40E	(ex D16 Nottingham Div.)	*May-1963*		
D5267		D16	Nottingham Division	*May-1964*		
D5285		ML	Midland Lines (ex D14)	*Jul-1964*		
D7500		D16	Nottingham Division	*Oct-1964*		
D7555		D16	Nottingham Division	*Jul-1965*		
Total	5					

40E COLWICK (continued)

			Home shed		Built	Withdrawn	Scrap
Brush Type 2 A1A-A1A 1957							
D5598	*on loan*		34G	Finsbury Park(ex 30A)	*Mar-1960*		
D5699	*on loan*		31B	March(ex 30A)	*Apr-1961*		
Total		2					
Steam							
Thompson 5MT 4-6-0 B1 1942							
61089			40E	(ex 40B immingham)	*Oct-1946*	*Apr-1966*	*Jul-1966*
61092			40E		*Oct-1946*	*Feb-1966*	*Jul-1966*
61141			40E		*Apr-1947*	*Jul-1965*	*Dec-1965*
61194			40E		*May-1947*	*Aug-1965*	*Oct-1966*
61210			40E		*Jul-1947*	*Feb-1966*	*Jun-1966*
61232			40E		*Sep-1947*	*Feb-1966*	*Jun-1966*
61264	*to Barry Docks*		40E		*Dec-1947*	*Dec-1965*	saved
61281			40E		*Jan-1948*	*Feb-1966*	*Jul-1966*
61285			40E		*Feb-1948*	*Dec-1965*	*Aug-1966*
61299			40E		*Mar-1948*	*Jul-1965*	*Dec-1965*
61302			40E		*Mar-1948*	*Apr-1966*	*Jul-1966*
61361			40E		*Mar-1950*	*Dec-1965*	*Mar-1966*
61365			40B	Immingham	*Apr-1950*	*Jul-1965*	*Oct-1965*
61390			40E		*Dec-1951*	*Feb-1966*	*Jul-1966*
61392			40E	(ex 41D Canklow)	*Dec-1951*	*Jun-1965*	*Oct-1965*
Total		15					
Gresley 5P6F 2-6-0 K3 1924							
61943			ex 40E		*Aug-1935*	*Sep-1962*	*Feb-1966*
Total		1					
Robinson 8F 2-8-0 O4 1911							
63607	*O4/1*	1911	40E	(ex 36E Retford)	*Jan-1912*	*Sep-1965*	*Mar-1966*
63639	*O4/8*	1944	40E		*Oct-1918*	*Dec-1965*	*Mar-1966*
63674	*O4/8*	1944	40E		*Oct-1917*	*Jan-1966*	*Apr-1966*
63675	*O4/8*	1944	40E		*Oct-1917*	*Jan-1966*	*Apr-1966*
63707	*O4/1*	1911	40E		*Sep-1912*	*Jul-1965*	*Apr-1966*
63770	*O4/7*	1939	40E		*Apr-1918*	*Dec-1965*	*Mar-1966*
63781	*O4/8*	1944	40E	(ex 36C Frodingham)	*May-1918*	*Apr-1966*	*Jul-1966*
63819	*O4/8*	1944	40E		*Jul-1918*	*Nov-1965*	*Mar-1966*
Total		8					
Riddles WD 8F 2-8-0 "Austerity" 1943							
90002			40E		*Mar-1943*	*Apr-1966*	*Aug-1966*
90037			40E		*Jan-1944*	*Apr-1966*	*Aug-1966*
90038			40E		*Jan-1944*	*Aug-1965*	*Nov-1965*
90103			40E		*Feb-1943*	*Nov-1965*	*Apr-1966*
90104			40E		*Feb-1943*	*Feb-1966*	*Jun-1966*
90146			ex 36E	Retford	*May-1943*	*Jun-1965*	*Aug-1965*
90187			40E	(ex 10H Lower Darwen)	*Aug-1943*	*Feb-1966*	*Jul-1966*
90241			40E	(ex 10F Rose Grove)	*Jun-1943*	*Jan-1966*	*May-1966*
90255			36A	Doncaster	*Aug-1943*	*Dec-1965*	*Mar-1966*
90259			40E		*Aug-1943*	*Oct-1965*	*Jan-1966*
90279			36A	Doncaster	*Nov-1943*	*Jun-1965*	*Oct-1965*
90393			40E	(ex 9G Gorton)	*Dec-1944*	*Aug-1965*	*Jan-1966*
90432			40E		*Dec-1943*	*Oct-1965*	*Jan-1966*
90443			40B	Immingham	*Mar-1944*	*Jun-1965*	*Oct-1965*
90466			40E		*May-1944*	*Dec-1965*	*Apr-1966*
90492			40E		*Aug-1944*	*Oct-1965*	*Feb-1966*
90510			40E		*Dec-1944*	*Jul-1965*	*Apr-1966*
90514			40E	(ex 36E Retford)	*Jan-1945*	*Jan-1966*	*May-1966*
90533			40E	(ex 36E Retford)	*Jun-1943*	*Feb-1966*	*Jun-1966*
90540			36C	Frodingham	*Jul-1943*	*Jul-1965*	*Apr-1966*
90545			40E		*Jul-1943*	*Oct-1965*	*Jan-1966*
90606			40E		*Dec-1943*	*Feb-1966*	*Jun-1966*
90629			40E		*Mar-1944*	*Sep-1965*	*Dec-1965*
90639			56A	Wakefield	*May-1944*	*Jan-1967*	*May-1967*
90669			40E	(ex 36E Retford via 36C)	*Oct-1944*	*Feb-1966*	*Jun-1966*
90689			40E	(ex 36E Retford via 36C)	*Dec-1944*	*Feb-1966*	*Jun-1966*
90703			40E		*Feb-1945*	*Jul-1965*	*Apr-1966*
Total		27					

			40E COLWICK (continued)				

			Home shed		Built	Withdrawn	Scrap
BR Standard 9F 2-10-0 Brighton 1954							
92082			8H	Birkenhead	May-1956	Nov-1967	Apr-1968
92202	double	chimney	40B	Immingham	Dec-1958	Dec-1965	Mar-1966
Total	2						

On Shed	67	Kops	63		
Steam	53	Diesels	14		
Withdrawn	12				

Home Locos	51	Home Area	3 Visitors		13	
Shed	40E	52 40B	3			
Distribution	8H	1 ML	1 D16		3	
	31B	1 34G	2			
	36A	2 36C	1 ex 36E		1	
	56A	1				
Steam Classes	5					
Steam Origin	LNER	24 BR	2 WD		27	
Shed Highlights:-						
	1 K3	61943				
	2 The Robinson 7F 2-8-0 04's					

Steam	Aug-50	167	Mar-59	154	Apr-65	48
Allocation					Aug-65	56
			Closed to Steam:-		Dec-66	
Home Steam	excluding withdrawn locos					
On/Off Shed	On Shed	37 Off Shed	19 % On Shed	66%		
Not on Shed						
Thompson 5MT 4-6-0 B1 1942		61070	61145	61188	61248	4
Robinson 8F 2-8-0 O4 1911			63644	63816	63873	3
Riddles WD 8F 2-8-0 1943	90036	90051	90080	90130	90316	
	90413	90423	90437	90438	90528	
				90665	90674	12
						19
saw elsewhere on the tour			1		scrap	
recently withdrawn not on shed or seen elsewhere			1 "B1"		61094 Nov-65	
			both ex 41D		61191 Sep-65	

Review and Appraisal of 40E Colwick "WD Ville"

The shed was in the fork of the Colwick North Junction-Colwick East junction, and Colwick North Junction-Netherfield and Colwick goods line. Walking time was 10 minutes from Netherfield and Colwick Station.

A fantastically good shed. First-class. Seeing K3 61943 was a great highlight of the tour so far, I think. I expected 30 locos on shed and we got double that. Only 5 steam classes: - B1's, Robinson 2-8-0's, the K3, 9F 2-10-0's and WD's. In effect 40E Colwick had only three classes as the K3 Class was now withdrawn and the BR Standard 9F 2-10-0's were visitors. 27 WD's were an enormous total I thought. This class was currently being purged from the London Midland region but still was a numerous and staple class for the Eastern and North Eastern Regions.

Really good to see the Robinsons. I had seen them for the first time. It was really good in seeing two 04/1's the oldest of the class left. These Birkenhead 9F's seemed to wander about the joint. I remember seeing 92101 of Birkenhead earlier in the day at Wellingborough. Pity diesels are infiltrating this steam depot though. Steam days here must be numbered. The Brush Type 2's were through for crew training. Colwick was one of the last places I expected to find a Brush Type 4 (and a Finsbury Park one at that!). I didn't find out if it was through for crew training. Could be! The BT Type 2's would soon be on the increase I thought. Great to see over 50 steam locos on shed!

"You're on the wrong side of the road"

D.S. and I thanked our railwayman guide profusely. He had really provided us with "'the works". With a final cheerio we left him. We popped the permit into sour face in his office and left. D.S. and I agreed that all the trouble had been worth it to get round a shed as good as that one.

Our return train had been missed ages ago so I told D.S. that we would have to bus it. We walked along Victoria Road back over the level crossing and came to the first bus stop in Netherfield, still in Victoria Road. I fished out the faithful Locomotive Shed Directory and found that a 67, 69 or 70 would take us back into town (Nottingham). Must be a good service, I thought, if three buses serve it.

What bus stop was ours? There were two. The train came from that direction so we go back in that direction. This is our bus-stop D.S. We waited a few minutes. Time for a thesis I thought. There was only one other person at our bus stop going into Nottingham and at the other side of the road there was about a dozen people going from Netherfield in the other direction.

THE WRONG BUS-STOP AFFAIR

Funny I thought. I would have expected it to be the other way around. My thesis was that more people would be going into Nottingham. My superb thesis cannot be wrong! Greatly daring I asked the other person at the bus stop if this was the bus stop for Nottingham. This question staggered and shocked him for some odd reason. He looked at us unbelievably for a few moments; quite speechless. Finally he blurted out, the stop for Nottingham is on the other side of the road and that we were going the wrong way. A quick word of thanks, a strategic shove in D.S.'s back and were darting across the road. D.S. didn't seem to know what was going on! We were just in time to catch a no. 69 bus at the other side - for Nottingham!

My thesis had been correct. Nothing like exercising the brain with elementary logic when I have nothing else to do but wait for a bus. The results can be most satisfying.

We duly arrived at Nottingham Huntingdon Street bus station. Our timetable was now up the ... creek (fill in blank if you feel inclined). The next train out of Nottingham was the 15.05 (we had missed the 13.54 to Alfreton) to Toton or Westhouses. That would mean us waiting more than half an hour for it - but I couldn't have such blatant time wasting as this! A quick look round the bus station and a bus going to Kirkby was noted with interested. I asked the conductor if it went through Newstead. You'll have to go to Mount Street for a Newstead bus, was his reply. Right then I told D.S., we are going to Kirkby-In-Ashfield now.

The bus was soon away and typical Nottinghamshire weather settled in after about 10 minutes. Rain started to belt down. The bus didn't do much business as it sped through the countryside and our conductor took a special interest in his two laden, colourful passengers and asked if we wanted to go to Newstead first. Was it far out of the way, I queried. You can get off at Treton Bole Hole (or something like that) and you can get a bus to Newstead there. It's not a very long journey. We took the hint, I put on my waterproof jacket and trousers, collected my grip and bag and we disappeared into the rain at Treton Bole Hole after our conductor had pointed out the bus stop.

THE WRONG BUS-STOP AFFAIR - Epilogue

Unfortunately there were two bus stops where the conductor had pointed. I checked my compass and decided that the farther stop was the Newstead one. The rain was lashing down and we had an uncomfortable time though the waterproofs kept us dry enough. Other unfortunates at the other stop were picked up by their bus after we had been waiting for almost ten minutes. In another five minutes our "red" bus appeared on the horizon. We picked up our things and stopped the bus. On the front was proudly displayed its destination - Kirkby-in-Ashfield. We were at the wrong stop again. The other stop was the Newstead one. Well I'm not waiting another half hour for a bus to Newstead in this rain. Let's get this bus to Kirkby. Once on and settled down we remembered an unfortunate but not costly wrong bus stop occurrence in Victoria Road after visiting Colwick. D.S. frankly summed it up with his candid comment

"Somebody up there doesn't like us."

We duly arrived at Kirkby - about half an hour later than if we had just stayed on our first bus. Kirkby was the summer residence of two friends of D.S. and I - the famous Storie Brothers. Sometime ago they had provisionally arranged to go round Nottingham with us but their mama had put paid to that by changing the dates of their holidays so that curtailed that. From their tales I half expected to find a little village with the old inhabitants of it to be seen sitting outside the local pub ("the Nags Head") enjoying the summer sunshine. My dream was shattered somewhat as Kirkby was a bustling town of about 20,000 population (mainly in mining, our course, and it was raining cats and dogs and judging by the severity of the storm some elephants thrown in as well). Once more we intrepid two braved the storm and hunted for the Nag's Head pub (for less sinister reasons than you'll be thinking). Seeing a level crossing we went down to it and noted the almost closed Kirkby station. It had only one passenger service a day. The man up in the signal-box seemed to be taking too much of an interest in us looking around so I stared directly up at him until he stopped gazing at colourful us. We would never find the "Nags Head" in the station so we walked back up the way we came up on this main road for about 220 yards and finally found our checkpoint. It was a far more impressive pub than I had imagined and was a massive, modern stone structure.

D.S. was about to pop into the pub for a "quick one" when I stopped him. Where do you think you are going? The "Nags Head" is where we turn off for the shed. D.S. was a little downhearted at this. He now started on his favourite subject of food. He complained that he had had no dinner. Don't worry, I said, you're getting none. We followed instructions and went along Low Moor Road North. An appetising smell was coming out of a baker's shop. It was too much for D.S. and he sneaked off to it. I hadn't the hearts to stop the old boy and followed him in. D.S. bought a couple of cakes and I bought one myself. It was a short break from the torrential rain anyway. The cakes were good.

Onwards into the rain we travelled and soon came to the shed entrance on the left hand side. The shed seemed busy enough, but after Colwick I wasn't keen on handing in our permit to our shedmaster. D.S. wanted to know what the name of the shed was! Well! Well! We are about to visit Kirkby. How do you spell that? D.S. queried. Well, well I had told D.S. for Colwick - Colickton so I would have a little more fun with him. C-I-R-C-B-I that's right. D.S. writes it down. Ha, ha! Back to the serious business of visiting sheds.

No. I asked if they had been to Annesley. I had noted that Annesley's allocation had been transferred in the past few months and that it might be closed or not worth a visit. A quick glance at his notebook and I saw that it was very much open. There were only about a dozen on shed when they visited it but one engine on shed fairly staggered me. It was 73119 "Elaine". Well, well, well! A Southern Region Standard on Annesley. I should have asked them if we could join them as we had permits a plenty. They were going next in the other direction to us if we decided to visit 16B Annesley but we could have dumped going to 16B Annesley with its small number on shed and I am sure they would have been very happy for us to join them for the rest of the day particularly with our valuable shed permits. We left the two kids and I told D.S. that now we would have to visit Annesley. I had thought if missing it out before meeting them. We just had to see "Elaine" (shades of a girl friend of our celebrated Musselburgh Monktonhall Model Railway Society member Ian Firth) and there were also some "Black Fives" on shed. I wanted to see as many as possible of them during the tour. The reason for this seems obscure but I'll put it down to the fact that there were the most numerous class on BR - all 842 of them. I had seen a lot of them and wanted to see more of them! Time was galloping on relentlessly but we just had to visit Annesley.

On with the shed! I peered out. It was still bucketing rain down. "Well, we are not staying in here". I said to D.S. Let's get going. A rather faint-hearted D.S. did not wish to brave the storm but after a scientific good old shove he was out in the elements.

Nothing but dead 9F's, Big Eights and Midland 0-6-0's could be seen. The shed had nothing in it but the yard was full of engines. I looked into my pocket for a handbook on "How to write down loco numbers in a thunderstorm without the book becoming awash and the ink running riot over the page. I found that the imaginary book had not materialised so I had to tackle the problem from first principles.

I went up to the footplate of the first Big Eight and under the safe cover of that I wrote down as many loco numbers as I could see. The operation seemed successful enough until a giant globule of water dripped from it on to the notebook. The ink of my back Fybriter was supposed to be waterproof but faced with such an attack of water as this its resistance waned and a watery trace of black ink trickled down the page. The numbers I had written were still visible though.

Most of the "Big Eights" were stored. Sacking over their chimneys was noticeable. Why they did this I couldn't guess. I suppose it was to prevent rust! That dynamic duo, the Storie Brothers had told me that they were used as brake-tenders to help the braking of BR Type 2 diesels and Brush Type 4 diesels. Seemed a sensible suggestion to me.

I had been told by the Storie Brothers to look out for the condemned and withdrawn Robinson 2-8-0 63842. She had come from 41J Langwith. The star attraction was sighted and she did not disappoint me. I had been told she had one specific peculiarity and she had one indeed – she had no chimney! It certainly looked odd. The last engine I had seen with no chimney was Jubilee 45592 "Indore" on 9D Newton Heath shed on 12 December 1964 when Iain Firth and I had made a lightning and devastating overnight visit to Manchester and Crewe. Of the two the Jubilee "Indore" was odder because unlike 63842 she had been in immaculate, shining, ex-works black livery. "Indore" looked wonderful except for that one specific peculiarity.

Diesels had infiltrated on the scene. The rain had somewhat cleaned them and brightened them up. Two BR Type 2's and a Brush Type 4 were on shed.

Surprise, surprise --- or was it? Our old friend 90471 had come to see us again. Right faithful WD this one ---eh D.S. For the forgetful we had already seen her on the journey to Leicester and also on the journey from Nottingham to Colwick. Now where will we see her next I said to D.S. Toton or Westhouses? D.S. favoured Toton but I was inclined to favour Westhouses. Maybe she would surprise us all and buzz off for good. In the crab-like fashion of bending down beneath footplates to keep our notebooks out of the rain we finished the shed.

16E KIRKBY-IN-ASHFIELD							
		Home shed			Built	Withdrawn	Scrap
Diesels							
Brush Type 4 Co-Co 1962							
D1832		D16	Nottingham Division		Apr-1965		
Total	1						
BR Sulzer Type 2 Bo-Bo 1958							
D7507		D16	Nottingham Division		Oct-1964		
D7528		D16	Nottingham Division		Feb-1965		
Total	2						
Steam					Built	Withdrawn	Scrap
Stanier 5MT 2-6-0 1933							
42977		9F	Heaton Mersey (ex 9G)		Jan-1934	Jun-1966	Sep-1966
Total	1						
Fowler 4F Midland 0-6-0 1911							
43982		16E			Dec-1922	Jul-1965	Sep-1965
Total	1						
Midland 4F 0-6-0 1924							
44043		16E			Feb-1925	Jul-1965	Oct-1965
44334		16E			Oct-1926	Jun-1965	Oct-1965
44401		16E			Jan-1927	Jun-1965	Oct-1965
Total	3						
Stanier 8F 2-8-0 "Big Eight" 1935							
48003		16E			Jun-1935	Mar-1966	Jun-1966
48063		16E	(ex 15E Coalville)		Nov-1936	Mar-1968	Jul-1968
48097		16E			Dec-1938	Jul-1965	Nov-1965
48098		16E			Jan-1939	Mar-1967	Sep-1967
48102		16E			Jan-1939	Aug-1965	Feb-1966
48105		16E	(ex 15E Coalville)		Feb-1939	Mar-1967	Jul-1967
48156		16E			Nov-1942	Aug-1965	Feb-1966
48186		16E			Apr-1942	Oct-1966	Jan-1967
48192		16E			May-1942	Apr-1968	Aug-1968
48215		16E			Aug-1942	Jul-1966	Nov-1966
48225		16E			Sep-1942	Oct-1966	Feb-1967
48267		16E			May-1942	Jun-1968	Feb-1969
48272		16E			Jun-1942	Mar-1968	Jul-1968
48282		16E			Aug-1942	Jun-1968	Jan-1969
48303		16E			Oct-1943	Jul-1966	Oct-1966
48304		16E	(ex 16B Annesley)		Oct-1943	Mar-1968	Jul-1968
48317		16E			Jan-1944	Mar-1968	Aug-1968
48334		16E			Nov-1943	Jan-1968	May-1968
48342		16E			Feb-1944	Sep-1966	Dec-1966
48346		16E			Mar-1944	Jul-1966	Nov-1966
48383		16E			Jan-1945	Jan-1966	Apr-1966
48405		16E			Aug-1943	Jul-1966	Oct-1966
48541		16E			Dec-1944	Jun-1966	Sep-1966
48614		16E			Aug-1943	May-1968	Aug-1968
48621		16E			Nov-1943	Jul-1966	Oct-1966
48643		16E			Nov-1943	Jun-1967	Dec-1967
48694		16E			Apr-1944	Mar-1966	Jul-1966
Total	27						
Robinson 7F 2-8-0 O4/3 1917							
63842		41J	Langwith		Feb-1919	Apr-1965	Aug-1965
Total	1						
WD 8F 2-8-0 "Austerity" Riddles 1943							
90471		Our friend!	41E	Staveley Barrow Hill (ex41D)	May-1944	Apr-1966	Sep-1966

		Home shed		Built	Withdrawn	Scrap
Total	1					
BR Standard 9F 2-10-0 Brighton 1954						
92072		16E	(ex 16B Annesley via 9D)	*Jan-1956*	*Nov-1967*	*Feb-1968*
92075		16E	(ex 16B Annesley)	*Mar-1956*	*Sep-1966*	*Jan-1967*
92093		16E	(ex 16B Annesley)	*Jan-1957*	*Aug-1967*	*Feb-1968*
92095		16E	(ex 16B Annesley)	*Mar-1957*	*Sep-1966*	*Apr-1967*
Total	4					
On Shed	41	Kops		38		
Steam	38	Diesels		3		
Withdrawn	6					
Home Locos	35	Home Area		3	Visitors	3
Shed	16E	36	D16	3		
Distribution	8F	1	41E	1	41J	1
Steam Classes	7					
Steam Origin	LMS	32	LNER	1	BR	4
	WD	1				
Shed Highlights:-						
		Robinson 7F 2-8-0 O4/3 1917 - 63842 (ex 41J Langwith)				
Steam	Sep-50	63	Mar-59	48	Apr-65	43
Allocation					Aug-65	42
			Closed to Steam:-			Oct-66
Home Steam	excluding withdrawn locos					
On/Off Shed	On Shed	30	Off Shed	12	% On Shed	71%
Not on Shed						
"Big Eights"		48004		48092	48096	48100
		48119	48201	48277	48364	48395
				48442	48673	48678	12
					total	12
saw elsewhere on the tour				3		
recently withdrawn not on shed or seen elsewhere				3	Midland 4F 0-6-0 1924	
				44250	44414	44429
			scrap	Aug-65	Aug-65	Aug-65

Review and Appraisal of 16E Kirkby-In-Ashfield alias the "dead shed" or "Big Eightsville."

The shed was on the east side of the line north of Kirkby-in-Ashfield east Station. Walking time was 10 minutes.

Yes! Big Eightsville was certainly very good. My list of Big Eights seen is certainly improving fast. Kirkby must be one of the first sheds to start withdrawing them. Difficult to stop diesels taking over their business in this part of the country with the recent demise and rundowns of steam at 16A Toton, 16B Annesley and 16D Nottingham and the closure of 16H Hasland. Kirkby's Standard 9F 2-10-0's had recently been ousted out of a job by being transferred to the Liverpool area and had been replaced by Big Eights and Brush Type 4's. Now Kirkby had received some more "Big Eights" from the very rundown 16B Annesley. I wonder how long they will last here. Kirkby and Annesley used to have about 50 9F's between them but now Kirkby only had a handful and Annesley none. It was very interesting finding 42977 of 8F Springs Branch (Wigan) here. She must be a very rare visitor. It was the case of the end of an era for the Midland 0-6-0's. Kirkby recently had about 30 of them. Now they were all withdrawn. I wondered why shed highlight LNER Robinson O4 63842 was lying here. I suppose there could be a scrap-breaker nearby. I*n practice, the loco departed for scrapping to Cashmore's Great Bridge near Birmingham later in the month.* In all, no complaints about Kirkby. Remarkably for a weekday 30 (70%) of Kirkby's 43 surviving steam engines were on shed.

On we go

Just as we finished the shed the rain stopped. D.S. asked where we were going next. I said that we were going to Annesley to pick up "Elaine". How do you spell it he queried? After Colickton and Circbi I spelt it for him as Annillay.

We were about 50 yards from the main road when a Newstead bus whistled past. A dramatic chase ensued. The bus stopped at the next stop so things were looking up. D.S. and I were about 10 yards from it when the rattish bus driver started it up again and it flew off. Back to the stop to wait for the next bus then. Frustration is missing a bus by a few feet. Aha, what do we see? A pork butcher's shop. What's that? A strange Derbyshire custom? Perhaps not, this is Nottinghamshire. Well, never mind what do we see in the window? An enormous pie for a bob (one shilling – later 5 new pence). I asked D.S. to keep the bus stop warm while I bought one for myself. Putting on my best Derbyshire neck accent I succeeded in buying one. D.S. of course was hungry as well (as always) and went in and bought one. Fantastic pies they were. I did not know what was in them. It certainly wasn't a Scots mince pie. Some elementary deduction was required. Wasn't this a pork butcher? Then it was pork inside it. Wonder what the pies would taste like hot perhaps better than cold but I had been rather peckish and had wolfed it down.

Hello, here comes the bus! We had only to wait ten minutes for it. Still had not completely finished our pies but paid our fares and finished them off on the bus to the probable annoyance of other passengers. After a fifteen minute journey we were dumped off at Newstead Village. The term village was rather a misnomer. I had expected to find about half a dozen decaying houses, a level crossing and a closed railway station. The village, however, was pretty sizeable. They even had TV out here in the wilds of Nottinghamshire. I saw a paper boy delivering evening newspapers and most of the houses were pretty new.

"Continue through the village, over a level crossing, pass Newstead Colliery Yard, and proceed over a further level crossing by a closed station. Bear right and the shed entrance is on the left hand side a short distance further on." the LocoShed directory stated. I couldn't even see the colliery or level crossing. The shed was located between the Great Northern Leon Valley Branch (closed to passenger traffic) and the main Great Central Nottingham to Staveley line about 2½ miles north of Hucknall. At this point it helpfully said the Nottingham to Mansfield (Midland Railway), Leon Valley (Great Northern Railway) and Nottingham to Staveley (Great Central Railway) are running parallel and close together. The LocoShed directory even gave a National Grid reference! We walked down through the village for about half a mile and walked over the level crossing. I noticed the closed station, which was tiny. The only building was about the size of a small cowshed. It must have been one of the smallest stations in the UK. It was on the Nottingham-Mansfield line, which had closed to passenger traffic in September 1964.

In contrast the colliery at Newstead was vast. We were now in the yard of the colliery. The famous Storie Brothers had recently been thrown out of this shed (rundown or not).
Two men came briskly up to us. "Are you Derby News?" one of them said. What was this about? Was it some sort of advance shed guard? I was absolutely speechless for the second time today. The first time had been at Colwick earlier today. I stared in disbelief. They wondered at our hesitation and said "Derby News" again. D.S. suddenly sprang to life and said we were not bringing in newspapers. The men said "Sorry" and walked away. Fancy being mistaken for newspaper sellers! We took the required turning right at the yard, walked along a path and were almost immediately at the shed. The shed was large but from the path it looked deserted (as I had expected it too). All I could see from the path was one "Black Five". Like all the 16 area sheds I had a permit. I was not going to take any chances and was only going to show the permit if stopped. The shed seemed quiet enough though. We

accidentally walked in front of a glass-fronted office and saw the shedmaster sitting there. He did not seem to be bothered about us and we walked on. Inside the shed we saw Iain Firth's girl friend "Elaine". She was very mucky and had lost all her nameplates. We noted one Big Eight and the rest were Black Fives.

16B ANNESLEY

		Home shed		Built	Withdrawn	Scrap
Steam						
Stanier 5MT 4-6-0 "Black Five" 1934						
44835		16B		Sep-1944	Jul-1967	Mar-1968
44847		16B		Nov-1944	Nov-1966	May-1967
44848		16B		Nov-1944	Feb-1968	Jul-1968
45299		1A	Willesden	Jan-1937	Nov-1967	Apr-1968
45301		16B		Jan-1937	Jul-1965	Dec-1965
45333		16B		Mar-1937	Jul-1966	Oct-1966
45334		16B		Mar-1937	Jul-1965	Dec-1965
45406		16B		Sep-1937	Jul-1967	Dec-1967
45416		16B		Oct-1937	Jul-1965	Dec-1965
Total	9					
Stanier 8F 2-8-0 "Big Eight" 1935						
48378		16B		Dec-1944	Aug-1965	Feb-1966
Total	1					
BR Standard 4-6-0 1951 5MT Doncaster						
73119	"Elaine"	70D	Eastleigh	Dec-1955	Mar-1967	Oct-1967
Total	1					
On Shed	11	**Kops**	10			
Steam	11	**Diesels**	0			
Withdrawn	3					
Home Locos	9 Home Area			0 Visitors	2	
Shed	16B	9				
Analysis	1A	1 70D		1		
Steam classes on view	3					
Steam Origin	LMS	10 BR		1		
Shed Highlight:-(no prizes for guessing!)						
	73112 Elaine of 70D Eastleigh					
Steam	Sep-50	77	Mar-59	70	Apr-65	61
Allocation					Aug-65	14
			Closed to Steam:-		Jan-66	
Home Steam	excluding withdrawn locos					
On/Off Shed	On Shed	6 Off Shed		8 % On Shed	46%	
Not on Shed						
"Black Fives"		44665	44932	44984	45267	4
"Big Eights"					48142	1
BR 9F 2-10-0			92043	92068	92096	3
					total	8
		saw elsewhere on the tour			2	
		saw on June 67 Carlisle visit			1	
		recently withdrawn not on shed or seen elsewhere			1 "Black Five"	45335
					scrap	Dec-65

Review and Appraisal of 16B Annesley

The shed was between the Great Northern. Leen Valley Branch and the main Great Central Nottingham-Staveley line, about 2½ miles north of Hucknall. At this point the Nottingham-Mansfield (Midland Railway), Leen Valley (G.N.) and Nottingham-Staveley (G.C.) lines were running parallel, and were close together. Walking time from the closed Newstead station was 5 minutes.

On transfer to the Midland region, the LNER/GCR types such as 04's, A3's (including "Flying Scotsman" that spent a time allocated to Leicester Central), V2's and B17's were slowly supplanted by Black 5's, Jubilees, 8F's, Scots, Britannia's and 9F's. Only the B1's hung-on to near the very end. For the Woodford-Leicester section there were still the odd "Hall", "Castle" or Bulleid working through from Banbury on inter-regional services.

Though the end of the route's life was drawing near, it could still muster that old GCR joie de vivre. The worn-out Britannia's drafted-in to Annesley in 1962 were fettled and put to good work on the expresses. Just as these were becoming good locomotives once again, they were replaced by even more dilapidated Royal Scots. 9Fs had been on the GC for some time. The GC found them far more reliable than some of the other hand-me-downs that had to be endured. The 9Fs inevitably found their way onto passenger trains. It could only be the GC crews that found that they actually made quite good express passenger locomotives! So much so that the practice drew the attention of the higher levels of management who soon put a stop to this practice.

Not that the freights were any the less impressive. The fast and frequent Annesley - Woodford fitted freight trains were known locally as "Windcutters". An inspiring name, and one that really conjures-up the image of a 9F steaming at a brisk pace, a long, uniform line of wagons clattering along behind. The "Windcutters" were as much a part of GC lore as the Master Cutler. The "Scots" finally went for scrap, leaving the GC with a diet of 9F, 8F, Black 5 and occasional B1.

Excursion trains to Wembley could produce any motive power, steam or diesel and provided the GC spotters with rare types to break the Black 5 monotony. In the main though, with the writing on the wall, the GC south of the Midlands Coalfields was the preserve of worn-out steam traction rather than the new cost-saving, fast and train crew popular diesels. With the Scots gone the passenger duties fell to Black 5s and the odd Jubilee. In the meantime the expresses had all become semi-fasts and the average length of the trains was just four coaches.

On 14th June 1965 the final through freights were withdrawn. With them the demise of 1G Woodford Halse shed and yards. Britannia's made a brief re-appearance working out of Banbury because facilities for the fuelling and maintenance of steam traction at the London end of the route had all but vanished, and the "Brits" had large tenders. The requirement being for something that could work from Nottingham to London and back as a round-trip. December 1965 saw the demise of 16B Annesley shed.

As good as could be expected from a rundown shed. The writing had been on the wall for 16B Annesley once the Great Central line had closed to freight earlier in the year. This resulted in the abrupt closures of 9G Gorton, 41H Staveley (Great Central) and 1G Woodford Halse.

Seeing 73119 "Elaine" was excellent. According to the two famous Storie Brothers (who terrorise Kirkby especially and Annesley in the summer months) Annesley plays host to many unusual visitors. I heard from them of a fleeting visit of a Western Region "Grange" 4-6-0 to Annesley. The kleptomaniac instinct is strong in Annesley as in other trainspotting centres and sordid to relate our "Grange" had her nameplates nicked during her stay. Was it coincidental that Elaine had lost her nameplates? I'll give the shed the benefit of the doubt and give my verdict that her nameplates had been swiped before she came here. In mitigation all her sisters that we had seen at 70A Nine Elms on Sunday were devoid of nameplates. Another eight "Black Fives" on shed to add to my prized collection. I have always been partial to seeing "Black Fives". The last of Annesley's Big Eights was lying withdrawn.

Condolences were offered above.

With the impending closure of the Great Central line I suppose Annesley will be completely closed with it. Pity the Great Central line was no longer in full swing. If it had been we would have seen about 30 BR standard 9F 2-10-0's on shed. It wasn't and so we didn't. Annesley now had a mini total steam allocation of 14 Home Steam engines of which six (46%) were on shed.

On we go

Now D.S. where shall we visit now? D.S. gave his normal look of blank amazement. He had no idea where we were going this week far less knowing what shed we should visit next. D.S. thought we had just visited Annillay.

To ease readers out of their suspense I will let you into a secret that we are going to Mansfield next to visit 41J Langwith (and see some of these modern Robinson 2-8-0's which had been missing from Colwick). Originally, 41M Shirebrook West, the new diesel servicing depot would also have been visited time permitting but certainly not now.

We walked back through the colliery yard and after a ten minute walk through the village duly arrived at the main road. D.S. being a good camper said, "No bus stops here, just wait and stick your hand out when the bus comes and it'll stop. Right country yokel D.S. is at heart. Can't see any bus stop though. D.S. got a point there. We'll wait here then. After our thunderstorms at Kirkby it had turned into a warmish afternoon. Changed weather for the better.

"I thought I heard a noise." (from the Pirates of Penzance)

What's that roaring noise like a diesel type 2 with a mangled transmission in the background? D.S. admitted hearing it. So I wasn't hearing things after all! The noise was coming from the direction of a vast stretch of woodland on the opposite side of the village. A quick thought and it seemed that it must be the noise of the new M1 motorway – what a horrible noise to live next to.

The bus we wanted to get was the Trent bus service 61 (Nottingham – Mansfield). No bus was forthcoming so I walked across the road and spoke to a bloke who was waiting for a bus going in the other direction. I gathered that there was one due in five minutes – and that we were not standing at the bus stop – and there was a proper bus stop round the corner! D.S. and his no bus stop rot. We walked on round the corner and duly found the bus stop. The bus arrived and we hopped on. We asked for two singles to Mansfield and I was amazed at the price – two blinking bob (two shillings – 10 new pence). No wonder the **** conductor can wear his *** Polaroid sunglasses. He must be in for a cut of our fare. No wonder they supply their staff with *** cream jackets and have *** seat covers on every seat! They can well afford to. These dear country services with exorbitant zoombala prices.

Our bus whizzed through Kirkby on the way back and after about a twenty-minute journey we arrived in Mansfield. Mansfield Town Football club had been pipped on goal average from being promoted from the English League Division Three to Division Two by Bristol City. Hope nobody here finds out that I am a Bristol City supporter or I'll get lynched. If the shedmaster at Langwith wants to throw us out I'll just shout "Bristol City" to him and make a run for it. A look at the shed directory and I found that we had to get our Langwith bus from West Gate which was off Stockwell Gate. We could see Stockwell Gate so West Gate must be up a long hill stretching in front of us.

"Saperlipoppette." *(or Crumbs to the non French amongst us)*

After an enthralling walk up this hill we found nothing and I asked a local yokel about where West Gate was. The yokel found the question to be a funny one and went into hysterics. That last day promotion pip must have made their population soft in the head I thought. Our yokel recovered his senses somewhat and said we were walking in the wrong direction for West Gate. We had just walked half a mile away from it! He gave us re-directions. Now we knew why he was killing himself with laughter. We must have looked right mugs – and we were!

We made our sorrowful journey back the half a mile towards where we started and I noticed an Alfreton bus at the terminus (not the terminus for the West Gate-Langwith bus). I checked my watch and noted alarmingly that the sands of time were running out fast. Let's stuff Langwith – we can't waste an hour (which I thought it might easily take us) doing it. D.S. did not seem to bother. There was some reasoning behind my decision though. Now we would be certain of doing 16A Toton with 16G Westhouses probably thrown in all went well (which it hadn't been doing today).

41J LANGWITH				
Steam				
Ivatt 4MT 2-6-0 1947				
43064				
Thompson 5MT B1 4-6-0 1942				
61050	**61051**	*61093*	**61313**	
61315	*61372*	**61394**		
Total	6			
Thompson 7F 2-8-0 O1 1944 rebuild of Robinson O4 1911				
63589	*63590*	*63630*	*63646*	
63650	*63768*	*63868*		
Robinson 8F 2-8-0 O4 1911				
63612	*63679*	**63691**	**63697**	
63701	**63706**	**63732**	**63739**	
63828	*63842*	**63843**	*63850*	
63893				
Total	8			
Riddles WD 8F 2-8-0 "Austerity" 1943				
90043	**90069**	*90088*	**90149**	
90153	*90271*	*90275*	**90292**	
90301	*90398*	**90401**	**90418**	
90449	**90558**	**90658**	**90697**	
90719				
Total	13			
BR Standard 9F 2-10-0 Brighton 1954				
92040	**92041**	**92042**	**92141**	
92144	**92145**	**92146**	**92148**	
92149	**92173**	**92178**	**92179**	
92182	**92186**	**92189**	**92191**	
92195	**92200**			
Total	16			
Grand Total	43			
Recently		**Surviving**		
Withdrawn	21	**Steam Classes**	4	
Saw Elsewhere		**Saw on July 65 Preston**		
on the Tour	1	**trip**	1	
Steam	*Aug-50*	61	*Apr-59*	71
Allocation	*May-65*	33	*Jul-65*	43
	Closed to Steam:-		*Feb-66*	

A dubious decision in retrospect as 41J Langwith as can be seen above was a terrific steam shed (both surviving and probably with long deadlines of withdrawn steam locomotives). 41J Langwith's allocation had recently been augmented by the closures of 41D Canklow (Rotherham) and 41H Staveley (Great Central). Langwith had an allocation of 43 steam locos plus 21 recently withdrawn ones so it was a big miss for us. The allocation included 20 original and rebuilt O4's.

In fact there were two buses going to Alfreton. A Trent one and a blue Midland and General one. I asked a yokel who was deliberating which one was best. He thought the Midland one. He said he didn't travel by Trent much. With Trent's *** exorbitant, zoombala fares that did not surprise me one bit. These Notts yokels know how to save money - unlike D.S. and I. We were learning fast though.

D.S. and I made ourselves at home in the Midland bus and I dumped Graham's useless camera in the rack and flung my grip and my other bag up beside it.

After about five minutes our local yokel came up to us again and said that the Trent bus would get there first. Apparently the Midland bus went via Kirkby, which was apparently a roundabout way. We thanked him and undaunted the magnificent two took his advice. I picked up my grip and bag and D.S. and I hurriedly made our departure.

We made ourselves at home in the Trent bus and it left soon afterwards. I handed the conductor half a crown *(two shillings and six pence – 12.5 new pence)* and asked for two singles to Alfreton. "It'll cost you more than that mate was his reply. Of course, this was these zoombala Trent bus prices again. I must apply for a directorship of this bus company when I get back home. I handed over the extra ten pence to the conductor – fizzing 1shilling and eight pence each (8 new pence) for ten measly miles *** 2 pence a *** mile.

I asked the conductor if Westhouses stopped at this bus (Einstein would be pleased) "No it doesn't". We would look up Westhouses train times when we got into Alfreton. We would get one if there is one. Note the last stipulation. If there is not one – well. Remember that two and a half mile run in 30 minutes that I promised you for today from Alfreton to Westhouses but was cancelled owing to our hot reception at Colwick, which rather gave our timetable a kick in the teeth. You do? Well, wait and wonder because that run might be taking place in ten minutes. By the way Westhouses is a pretty good shed. He would need at least that unless there were a lot of photographs of that lot in recent combined loco volumes. Then you would not need as many by your special "kopped it from a photograph rule". That last remark of mine was very cutting and meant to be. D.S. told me that the rule was now defunct and that I knew he had stopped doing that. How forgetful of me! I mustn't let him forget his iniquitous early trainspotting days.

For the second time today the rain was belting down which was a pain. My sixth sense was also nagging at me. What was the problem? I noted my grip and bag but no sign of Ragham Trashcan's damaged camera. Damn, I had left it on the Midland bus.

WE WILL MISS TWO LINES WHILE I GET ANGRY WITH MYSELF

D.S. commented on how stupid I was and how I was always leaving the camera behind. I said it was the local yokel's fault for advising us to change buses. If he had said nothing I would still have the camera!

We arrived at Alfreton beside the station. I had thought of waiting for the other Midland bus there but not while it was bucketing with rain and the camera anyway was damaged probably beyond repair. So I would have to pay Graham the ten shillings that it originally cost him for the camera.

A dash over the road through the pelting rain and we were quickly into the station. A chalked notice stated, "No spotters allowed". What a bloody cheek. It amused me no end. What nut would want to train spot at Alfreton Station, which seemed to be a pretty rundown place? It seemed to be a one horse station!

A cool look at the timetable was now required. This time the official LMR one. As that great sailor Sir Francis Chichester would say, "We were in a hell of a pickle". It was now 7.15 P.M. (19.15 on the BR twenty four hour clock). If we had been ten minutes earlier we could have hopped on the 19.03 to Westhouses, do 16G Westhouses and get the 19.47 to Nottingham. The next train to Westhouses was the 20.49 with a train back at 22.01 arriving at Stapleford & Sandiacre at 22.28 to do Toton. The question of going and getting round a shed in pitch darkness at half past ten at night is dodgy to say the least. From there we were stranded as the Long Eaton stations were closed for the night. Our only chance would be to walk or get a bus the three or four miles to Sawley Junction and get the 00.13 train to Derby. This alternative looked too risky to me so now I had to sacrifice Westhouses, after sacrificing Langwith and Shirebrook less than an hour before. Obviously a lot had gone wrong today. We would have the post mortem later in the evening.

16G WESTHOUSES				
Steam				
Fowler Midland 4F 0-6-0 1911				
	43865	43991		
Midland 4F 0-6-0 1924				
	44113	44118	44203	44218
	44243	44278	44355	44420
	44528			
Total		7		
Johnson Midland 3F 0-6-0T 1899				
	47231	47250		
Total		1		
Midland 3F "Jinty" 0-6-0T 1924 dev. of Johnson 1899 design				
	47534	47535	47543	47611
Total		4		
Stanier 8F 2-8-0 "Big Eight" 1935				
	48045	48046	48112	48127
	48143	48145	48177	48184
	48195	48196	48197	48204
	48214	48258	48286	48384
	48393	48432	48507	48538
	48600	48620	48638	48661
	48750	48763		
Total		24		
Grand Total		36		
Recently Withdrawn		7	Surviving Steam Classes	4
Saw Elsewhere on the Tour		4		
Saw Carlisle trip June 1967		1	Saw Manch Crewe trip Dec-64	1
Steam Allocation	Sep-50	61	Mar-59	33
	Apr-65	42	Aug-65	36
	Closed to Steam:-		Oct-66	

Another dubious decision in retrospect and another good steam shed gone west. There were two ways of visiting Toton (largely by rail). Firstly, by getting on the 19.47 train and getting off at Pye Bridge at 19.52. At Pye Bridge we would have to get a bus to Long Eaton. We knew nothing of bus connections. Secondly, we could get the 19.47 all the way to Nottingham Midland arriving there at 20.17. From Nottingham we could get the 20.55 to Stapleford and Sandiacre. After doing Toton we could get the 22.28 to Beeston arriving at 22.39. From Beeston we would get the 22.50 for Derby arriving at 23.17. We therefore had two alternatives.

Our problems resolved themselves when we met "The Laird" (the station porter) who I think fancied himself as station master. Our ambitious sixty something year old porter doubted us getting a bus from Pye Bridge to Long Eaton. D.S. talked on with the Laird while I decided that the second alternative seemed best and would be the course taken. Suddenly, The Laird left D.S. when he saw some "aristocracy" worth speaking to who were waiting for the same 19.47 train as us.

The train was on the other platform and we had to reach it by crossing the line by a boarded crossing. We were stopped from doing so by a Brush Type 4 diesel. Here, British Rail pedestrians do not have the right of way at crossings. The Brush which was D1796 of 41A Tinsley ambled past us at about 15 MPH at the head of a long empty mineral train. The train seemed to take ages to pass us. It was amazingly long.

We hopped over the crossing and got on the 19.47. It comprised a two coach diesel bucket. Pye Bridge (which was the only stop before Nottingham) was as desolate and uninviting as The Laird had promised.

ALFRETON STATION to NOTTINGHAM							
		Home shed		Built	Withdrawn		Scrap
Diesels							
BR Sulzer "Peak" Type 4 1Co-Co1 1959							
D 6	"Whernside"	D16	Nottingham Division	Nov-1959			
D 10	"Tryfan"	D16	Nottingham Division	Feb-1960			
Total	2						
Brush Type 4 Co-Co 1962							
D1796		41A	Tinsley	Jan-1965			
Total	1						
Steam				Built	Withdrawn		Scrap
Stanier 8F 2-8-0 "Big Eight" 1935							
48196		16G	Westhouses	Jun-1942	Oct-1966		Feb-1967
Total	1						
On Line	4	**Kops**	4				
Steam	1	**Diesels**	3				
		Home Area	3		Visitors	1	
Shed	16G	1 D16		2			
Distribution	41A	1					
Steam Classes	1						
Steam Origin	LMS	1					

We had a good bucket's eye view of the line ahead as we sped forward. Big Eight 48196 of 16G Westhouses was noted at the head of a fitted freight. A little further on we noticed a "Peak" diesel. I looked at the number. The single number seemed odd, strange, and ghostly. It was D6 "Whernside". She was at the head of a heavy freight probably on the way from Toton yard to Birmingham. The original 10 Peaks D1-D10 were of 2300 HP (200 HP less than their improved sisters). Further on Peak D10 "Tryfan" was noted at the head of a similar freight to that of her sister "Whernside".

We were now approaching the outskirts of Nottingham Station and eyes were skinned for the yard on the left and Nottingham shed on the right. In a frantic spell of looking and writing the following were noted: -

16D NOTTINGHAM AND YARD MONDAY EVENING							
		Home shed			Built	Withdrawn	Scrap
Diesels							
BR Sulzer "Peak" Type 4 1Co-Co1 1959							
D 55	"Royal Signals"	ML	Midland Lines		*Sep-1962*		
D 75		ML	Midland Lines (ex D16)		*Dec-1960*		
D 146		D16	Nottingham Division		*Dec-1961*		
D 147		D16	Nottingham Division		*Dec-1961*		
D 153		D16	Nottingham Division		*Jan-1962*		
Total	5						
Brush Type 4 Co-Co 1962							
D1617		D16	Nottingham Division		*Sep-1994*		
D1820		D16	Nottingham Division		*Feb-1965*		
Total	2						
BR 0-6-0 Shunter 1953 English Electric engine							
D3246		16D			*May-1956*		
D3290		16D			*Dec-1956*		
Total	2						
BR Sulzer Type 2 Bo-Bo 1958							
D5255		D16	Nottingham Division		*Mar-1964*		
D5257		D16	Nottingham Division		*Mar-1964*		
D5294		D16	Nottingham Division		*Sep-1964*		
D5297		D16	Nottingham Division		*Sep-1964*		
D7525		D16	Nottingham Division		*Jan-1965*		
D7547		D16	Nottingham Division		*May-1965*		
Total	6						
LMS and BR 0-6-0 Shunter 1945							
12096		16D			*Dec-1951*	*Jan-1969*	
Total	1						
On Shed/Yard	16	**Kops**		14			
Steam	NIL	**Diesels**		16			
Home Locos	14	**Home Area**			0	**Visitors**	2
Shed	16D	3	**D16**		11		
Distribution	ML	2					
Shed Highlight:-		D55 "Royal Signals" (at least she had a name!)					

Mini Review and Appraisal of 16D Nottingham

Seeing "Peak" D55 "Royal Signals" again had not exactly made my day. She was a rather common visitor to 64A St. Margarets in Edinburgh via the car train.

On we go

Inside the station D.S. went wandering away probably looking for food. D.S. had been on a diet of a pie and a cake today. I took the opportunity to change clothes in the wash and brush up joint.

BR Type 2's D5260 and D5246 were noted at the east end of the station in multiple. At 20.50 D.S. emerged from the cafeteria replete and our train (another two coach diesel bucket) left on time at 20.55. Darkness was silently catching up on us so a rummage in my bag for my torch would be necessary.

NOTTINGHAM STATION MONDAY EVENING						
		Home shed		Built	Withdrawn	Scrap
Diesels						
BR Sulzer Type 2 Bo-Bo 1958						
D5246		2E	Saltley	Jan-1964		
D5260		D16	Nottingham Division	Apr-1964		
Total	2					
On Station	2	Kops		2		
Steam	0	Diesels		2		
		Home Area		1 Visitors	1	
Shed	D16	1				
Distribution	2E	1				

On the track before Beeston the strange sight of an Eastern Region Brush Type 2 A1A-A1A on LMR metals was seen. She was D5688 of 40A Lincoln. A few of them had been on loan to the LMR for trials. This would be one of them. D5688 was at the head of a train of milk empties.

After the stops at Beeston and Attenborough there was now only one stop (Long Eaton) before our stop of Stapleford and Sandiacre. We would in fact pass the shed and yard of Toton between the two stations.

The yard was immense and the shed from the line looked enormous. The shed was a gigantic diesel maintenance depot. Very impressive. BR Type 2 D7538 was noted on a freight passing through the yard.

NOTTINGHAM TO TOTON						
		Home shed		Built	Withdrawn	Scrap
Diesels						
BR Sulzer Type 2 Bo-Bo 1958						
D7538		D16	Nottingham Division	Mar-1965		
Total	1					
Brush Type 2 A1A-A1A 1957						
D5688		40A	Lincoln	Feb-1961		
Total	1					
On Line	2	Kops		2		
Steam	0	Diesels		2		
		Home Area	1	Visitors	1	
Shed	D16	1				
Distribution	40A	1				

When we got out at the station it was now pretty dark so we would have to be pretty cautious in going round the shed.

		Schedule	Actual	Miles
Depart	NOTTINGHAM MIDLAND	20.55	20.55	0
Arrive	STAPLEFORD AND SANDIACRE	21.14	21.14	9½

According to our shed directory there was a cinder path running from the shed to the station. We duly found it. In fact the directory was a bit out of date as the cinder path was now a reasonable road. Periodically, speed crazed railwaymen would career out from the shed car park along this road and successfully try to ditch us from their road. With headlights full on they would speed by. Of course, it would not be good sport to dip their headlights as they passed people on the road.

From a distance the diesel maintenance depot looked like the carnival with its oasis of light in a sea of darkness all around it. It did look inviting.

After about a ten minute walk we reached the shed. My torch was rummaged out and we decided to do the steam lines first. Toton's steam numbers had been viciously hacked down in recent months so I was glad to see any at all.

The first two locos which were spotlighted were real strangers. I wondered if I was seeing things. They were 9F 92024 of 8H Birkenhead and even more astonishing BR Standard 75000 of 85A Worcester (ex 83E Yeovil Town). If this is a sample let me see the rest.

Unfortunately there were no more surprises in store for us. All were local stuff but were gratefully received by us: - Black Fives, Standard Doodle Bugs, 9F's, Big Eights etc.
No need for us to have a torch for the diesel shed. It could hardly be better lit. I had a permit, but of course the shedmaster would take a dim view of us going round at this time of night.

We started from the back of the shed and stealthily made our way round. The maintenance shed was the largest and most modern I had ever seen with all the usual inspection bays etc. We were making our way round when a railwayman stopped us "You had better watch out for the railway police. You don't want to get caught here." We told him we had a permit and asked him where the police and shedmaster's offices were. He pointed them out. We thanked him and he went on his way. "Now we know what to keep clear of." I said to D.S. at the same time nodding in the direction of the offices. D.S. understood.

The shed was a good one to go round. Peak Type 4's, Brush Type 4's, BR Type 2's, BRCW's etc. It was just great. A few named "Peaks" in the treasured D1-D10 range were added. D2 "Hellvellyn" was quite a sight. Her body was about twenty feet in the air held up by a crane with her bogies lying discontentedly on the ground. Worth seeing!

We finally finished the depot and I told D.S. that I had seen a dead line of steam locos away over the back of the shed when we passed it by bucket. We tramped over stumbling over rubbish and old sleepers in the dark and found nothing but some old wagons. The strain of the tour must be showing when I seem to be imagining things. D.S. had his usual sneering laugh about it.

16A TOTON						Home shed			Built
Diesels									
BR Sulzer "Peak" Type 4 1Co-Co1 1959									
D 2	"Helvellyn"					D16	Nottingham Division		Sep-1959
D 3	"Skiddaw"					D16	Nottingham Division		Sep-1959
D 4	"Great Gable"					D16	Nottingham Division		Sep-1959
D 5	"Cross Fell"					D16	Nottingham Division		Oct-1959
D 47						ML	Midland Lines		Sep-1961
D 56	"The Bedfordshire and Hertfordshire Regiment"					ML	Midland Lines		Nov-1962
D 58	"The King's Own Royal Border Regiment"					ML	Midland Lines		Feb-1962
D 65	"Grenadier Guardsman"					ML	Midland Lines		Apr-1962
D 66						ML	Midland Lines		Apr-1962
D 108						D16	Nottingham Division		Jul-1961
D 111						ML	Midland Lines		Aug-1961
D 125						ML	Midland Lines		Nov-1961
D 129						ML	Midland Lines		Nov-1961
D 133						ML	Midland Lines		Dec-1961
D 134						ML	Midland Lines (ex 2E)		Dec-1961
D 139						D16	Nottingham Division		Nov-1961

		Home shed		Built
D 140		ML	Midland Lines	Nov-1961
D 143		D16	Nottingham Division	Dec-1961
D 145		D16	Nottingham Division	Dec-1961
D 148		D16	Nottingham Division	Dec-1961
D 149		D16	Nottingham Division	Dec-1961
D 151		D16	Nottingham Division	Jan-1962
D 159		D15	Leicester Division	Mar-1962
D 162		D16	Nottingham Division	Apr-1962
D 183		52A	Gateshead	Oct-1962
D 187		52A	Gateshead	Nov-1962
Total	26			
Brush Type 4 Co-Co 1962				
D1618		D16	Nottingham Division	Sep-1964
D1623		D16	Nottingham Division	Oct-1964
D1624		D16	Nottingham Division	Oct-1964
D1626		D16	Nottingham Division	Oct-1964
D1629		D16	Nottingham Division	Oct-1964
D1630		D16	Nottingham Division	Oct-1964
D1807		D16	Nottingham Division	Jan-1965
D1818		D16	Nottingham Division	Feb-1965
D1821		D16	Nottingham Division	Mar-1965
D1823		D16	Nottingham Division	Mar-1965
D1831		D16	Nottingham Division	May-1965
D1873		41A	Tinsley	May-1965
Total	12			
BR 0-6-0 Shunter 1953 Crossley engine				
D3122		16A		Sep-1955
D3125		16A		Jun-1957
Total	2			
BR 0-6-0 Shunter 1953 English Electric engine				
D3860		16D	Nottingham	Nov-1959
D3861		16D	Nottingham	Nov-1959
Total	2			
BR Sulzer Type 2 Bo-Bo 1958				
D5189		D15	Leic. Division (ex D16)	Mar-1963
D5204		ML	Midland Lines	Jun-1962
D5206		ML	Midland Lines	Jun-1962
D5215		D14	Cricklewood Division	Jul-1963
D5235		ML	Midland Lines	Dec-1963
D5252		D15	Leicester Division	Feb-1964
D5256		D16	Nottingham Division	Mar-1964
D5259		D16	Nottingham Division	Mar-1964
D7509		D16	Nottingham Division	Nov-1964
D7510		D16	Nottingham Division	Nov-1964
D7513		D16	Nottingham Division	Nov-1964
D7521		D16	Nottingham Division	Jan-1965
D7523		D16	Nottingham Division	Jan-1965
D7530		D16	Nottingham Division	Feb-1965
D7531		D16	Nottingham Division	Feb-1965
D7547		D16	Nottingham Division	May-1965
D7552		D16	Nottingham Division	Jun-1965
D7553		D16	Nottingham Division	Jun-1965
D7583		D16	Nottingham Division	Jan-1964
D7584		ML	Midland Lines	Feb-1964
D7594		D16	Nottingham Division	Jun-1964
Total	21			
Brush Type 2 A1A-A1A 1957				
D5388		D15	Leicester Division	Jun-1962
D5394		D15	Leicester Division	Jun-1962
D5397		D15	Leicester Division	Aug-1962
D5412		ML	Midland Lines	Sep-1962
D5415		D14	Cricklewood Division	Oct-1962
Total	5			
LMS and BR 0-6-0 Shunter 1945				
12038		16A	(withdrawn Dec 69)	Dec-1945
Total	1			

Steam			Home shed		Built	Withdrawn	Scrap
Stanier 5MT 4-6-0 "Black Five" 1934							
44690			16C	Derby	*Oct-1950*	*Aug-1968*	*Dec-1968*
44811			16C	Derby	*Oct-1944*	*Oct-1966*	*Feb-1967*
44830			16C	Derby	*Aug-1944*	*Aug-1967*	*Jan-1968*
44920			16C	Derby	*Dec-1945*	*Nov-1967*	*Mar-1968*
Total	*4*						
Stanier 8F 2-8-0 "Big Eight" 1935							
48083			16C	Derby	*Jan-1937*	*Nov-1966*	*May-1967*
48198			16C	Derby	*Jun-1942*	*Sep-1965*	*Dec-1965*
48313			16C	Derby	*Dec-1943*	*Sep-1967*	*Aug-1968*
Total	*3*						
BR Standard 4MT 4-6-0 Brighton 1951							
75000			85A	Worcester (ex83E)	*May-1951*	*Dec-1965*	*Apr-1966*
Total	*1*						
BR Standard 2MT 2-6-0 1953 Derby							
78020			16C	Derby	*Apr-1954*	*May-1967*	*Nov-1967*
78042			16A		*Dec-1954*	*Sep-1965*	*Dec-1965*
78044			16A		*Dec-1954*	*May-1967*	*Oct-1967*
78055			16A		*Aug-1956*	*Feb-1967*	*Jun-1967*
78064			16C	Derby	*Nov-1956*	*Nov-1966*	*Mar-1967*
Total	*5*						
BR Standard 9F 2-10-0 Brighton 1954							
92024	*Crosti boilered*		8H	Birkenhead(ex 12A)	*Jun-1955*	*Nov-1967*	*May-1968*
92043			16B	Annesley	*Jan-1965*	*Jul-1966*	*Oct-1966*
Total	*2*						

On Shed	84		Kops		75		
Steam	15		Diesels		69		
Withdrawn	0						

Home Locos		6 Home Area			49 Visitors		29
Shed	16A	6	16B		1	16C	9
Distribution	16D	2					
	D16	37	ML		16		
	D14	2	D15		6		
	41A	1	52A		2		
	8H	1	85A		1		

Steam Classes	5					
Steam Origin	LMS	7	BR	8		
Shed Highlights:-		75000	85A Worcester (ex83E)			
		the named original "Peaks"				

Steam	*Sep-50*	155	*Mar-59*	98	*Apr-65*	8
Allocation					*Aug-65*	6
			Closed to Steam:-		*Dec-65*	
Home Steam	*excluding withdrawn locos*					
On/Off Shed	*On Shed*	3	*Off Shed*	3	*% On Shed*	*50%*
Not on Shed						
"Big Eights"			48037	48167	48193	3
					total	3

recently withdrawn not on shed or seen elsewhere			1	"Big Eight"	48116
				scrap	*Dec-65*

Review and Appraisal of 16A Toton "the big diesel shed"

The shed was on the west side of the main line between Long Eaton and Stapleford and Sandiacre Stations. Walking time from Stapleford and Sandiacre Station was 15 minutes.

A terrific shed if you particularly like diesels. Certainly easily be the best diesel shed that D.S. and I had visited so far with the bonus of fifteen good steam locos also.

Of the Type 2's D7552 and D7553 were both in "candidatus" condition. Obviously the two were put into service very recently. In a splendid state, the Type 2's looked really good, both being pleasant to the eye and attractively painted in dark green with a light green band. More BRCW's for our collection were noted and appreciated.

D1873 of 41A Tinsley was another Brush, which had only been in service a few weeks. This 16 area of the LMR was now receiving quite a collection of Brushes. They provided a contrast to the predominant "Peaks" of this area.

Of the Peaks I hadn't seen before I had probably seen them at 64A St. Margarets in Edinburgh off some car train. Why hadn't I seen Skiddaw for the first time? You'll be wanting to know. Since you insist I'll tell you. Skiddaw was up at 64B Haymarket in Edinburgh in late 1959 on a trial run one Sunday. Of course, yours truly was there to see her. For the record, about one in six of the Midland based "Peaks" were on Toton shed tonight. Impressive? Yes! "Grenadier Guardsman" is about the most common "Peak" seen in Edinburgh.

92024 was one of my old friends from Carlisle. I had seen her last year at the end of the Glasgow Trades at Carlisle. Great seeing the founder member of the 75000 class – especially at an out of the way spot for a 85A Worcester loco to be. For some strange reason Annesley had been left with one solitary 9F 92043, which was now lying in state here. Must be an oversight on Modern Railways part as she must surely have been transferred away from rundown Annesley.

A sizeable Derby allocation was on Toton for some reason. Four wonderful rare Black 5's, Three good Big Eights and two Standard "Doodle Bugs" from Derby were all seen with interest. Toton had only three steam locos representing itself: all three were Standard "Doodlebugs". Must have seen about all of the Standard Doodlebug class I said to D.S. We had seen plenty at 1A Willesden, some more at 15A Leicester and now more here.

On we go

Undaunted at not finding the mystery dead line the magnificent two went on their perilous way. We staggered on and off the winding road from the shed, which was quite impossible to be seen in the pitch darkness. Occasionally a speed-crazed driver would pass us at the wheel of a Triumph Herald. The affluent society again!

Time for a time check from my ever wrong Timex I said to D.S. It was now 10 p.m. (22.00). Half an hour to bucket time. We wandered on along our perilous road back to Stapleford and Sandiacre station. D.S. proved himself an unlawful kid for the third time on our tour. (May I remind you of his entrances to Workington and Cricklewood East)? D.S. saw that if you ran across the main line from our road to the platform that he would save five minutes of walking to the end of the road along the main road for ten yards; in the main station entrance along the subway over the line for about twenty yards and then going down a lengthy flight of steps to get to the same platform. Think of the valuable horsepower and calories that he would save. There were signs that he was failing badly (see Nottingham Station to London Road run earlier today) and if this gives him an extra five minutes of his battery life who would be silly enough to argue with him. The five minutes saved might come in handy sometime on the tour I thought. Must budget ahead of course and make D.S. last the whole week without collapsing. I followed him into the night across the main line and we made the platform without mishap.

THE KARATE AFFAIR
"That's right D.S. smash the partition down"

We sat down on a handy bench and meditated. It's good for you D.S. this transcendental meditation, The Indians favour it. Know what D.S. the cigarette adverts TV ban set by the government came into effect today. Must say I liked these Benson & Hedges adverts on TV. I liked the one when the burglar was robbing the Bank of England of its gold reserves and stopped for a Benson and Hedges packet of cigarettes and lit up. Then the cops nabbed him. I'll miss these adverts. Pity their cigs aren't as good as their advertising. D.S. blurted out a sentence about how bad smoking was. I agreed with him for once!

Know what D.S. (this meditation must be good for stimulating the mind. One comes out with some amazing deductions). One was that there was no one in the station except us. D.S. looked about, I checked, nobody else here. Know what D.S. this station might be closed – we didn't come in through the main entrance. At this thought we were on the frantic side of disturbed. We made a dash up the stairs through the subway and into what we took to be the main booking hall. After a scurry about looking for the times of the trains we at last found a notice board with train times. It's OK the station seems to be open but what's this there is a line scored through the 22.38 to Nottingham. Hell's teeth don't say that this train does not run.

D.S. knew better and the Sherlock instinct in him found a chink of light coming from the apparently closed booking booth. Yes there was a chink of light showing under the closed partition. D.S. was now the man of the moment and he gave a heavy chop at the closed wooden partition. No answer, D.S. panicked and he continued to rain vicious blows with the sides of his hands at the partition. A serial karate killer in the making I thought. D.S. did about everything to the partition other than sticking the boot or his head into it. This would eventually have been the climax of his pugilist power. However, suddenly the partition opened and a very worried, terrified booking clerk peered out and caught sight of D.S. as his assailant. D.S. seemed breathless as a result of his efforts so I enquired diplomatically if the 22.38 to Nottingham was the next train. It was. Thanks. The booking clerk hastily closed down the partition again.

"At least you got service." I said to D.S. as we wandered back to the platform. You almost wakened the dead and scared the living daylights out of the alive in getting an answer I added as an afterthought. His high pressure attack had worked without even a complaint from the clerk (too astonished to complain I suppose). At least we were not stranded at the station.

In the next twenty minutes three good freight trains ambled through. The three locos were "Peak" Type 4 D65 "Grenadier Guardsman" (our old friend again), Brush Type 4 D1623 (which had also been on shed at Toton and Type 2 D7510 (also on shed). Perhaps a good station for a day trip. By now a few more people than us (including the booking clerk) were also waiting for this last train of the day.

Right on time we left Stapleford and Sandiacre at 22.28 on the diesel bucket for Beeston. Why go to Beeston you may ask? Ok, I'll tell you. If we get this bucket to Nottingham we arrive there at 22.46 and might miss the 22.55 for Derby. Better to get this bucket to Beeston and arrive there at 22.39 with plenty time to catch the 22.55 from Nottingham for Derby.

Recovery time +23 minutes rather than +9 minutes.

		Schedule	Actual	Miles
Depart	STAPLEFORD AND SANDIACRE	22.28	22.28	0
Arrive	BEESTON	22.39	22.39	6¼

Our journey to Beeston was fantastically boring. So boring I won't tell you about it.

We arrived at Beeston on time and our wait for our bucket began. Beeston Station was rather small and was about the same size as the tiny Inveresk Station near Musselburgh. We ascertained from the one and only (I think) member of staff which of the two platforms our train was due at. Our porter – come station master cum booking clerk come ticket collector come signalman told us.

D.S. and I sat down and enjoyed the high life of Beeston Station. Generally it had been a strenuous day for us I thought as I eyed our heavy grips, which with luck we could have left at the left luggage in Nottingham station instead of having to lug them around the countryside all day.

At 22.49 D.S. and I got that peculiar sensation that we were on the wrong platform when a bucket flew in and stopped. We raced over to the other platform via the overbridge only to find out on enquiry that it was the 22.20 from Derby for Nottingham. Couple of nuts we've got here the station all jobs man must have been thinking. We slunk back to the other platform. What's it like to look like fools D.S.? Have a look at us.

In the next ten minutes two fast freights whizzed by. Brush Type 2's D7501 of D16 Nottingham Division and Type 2 D5198 of ML Derby Division were noted and kopped.

BEESTON STATION						
		Home shed		*Built*	*Withdrawn*	*Scrap*
Diesels						
BR Sulzer Type 2 Bo-Bo 1958						
D5198		ML	Midland Lines	*May-1963*		
D7501		D16	Nottingham Division	*Oct-1964*		
Total	2					
On Line	2	**Kops**		2		
Steam	0	**Diesels**		2		
		Home Area	1	**Visitors**	1	
Shed	**16D**	1				
Distribution	**ML**	1				

At 23.00 another bucket rumbled in. This time it was on our platform. We ascertained from the guard that it was indeed our train. We tumbled into the bucket and little old Beeston was left behind at 23.02. Must remember to look for Trent I thought. Trent wasn't too bad a station this morning. Trent, Trent, Trent, --------------------------

A sharp jolt and I looked out. We were at Derby Station. I had been in slumberland for the past half hour. D.S. was still asleep. A light karate chop on D.S.'s ear and he abruptly awoke too. Everybody out – it was now 23.35.

		Schedule	Actual	Miles
Depart	BEESTON	23.02	23.02	0
Arrive	DERBY MIDLAND	23.35	23.35	12¾

I don't suppose I would have seen much on the journey. 'Twas on the black side of dark.

Goodness knows what the other travellers thought of us lowering the tone by sleeping. They probably thought it was a "tramps special".

THE FLATFEET AFFAIR
or THE BLUEBOTTLE AFFAIR
or THE ALL NIGHT AFFAIR
or THE CASE OF THE PERSISTENT POLICEMEN

Tick which one you find the most apposite. That means read and vote.

It was now 23.35 and was about time for beddibyes. The first item on our agenda was to find a waiting room. Preferably a bigger one than the one at Bletchley I hoped! A tour around the Station revealed two. There was a modern moderately sized one on the island platform and an older one but bigger one on the main concourse.

D.S. and I went for the one on the main concourse. Let's dump our grips in the left luggage I said. D.S. agreed and we did that. Our small bags were ideal for pillows on the hard benches. Did I say ideal? I did? Well they were hardly ideal when a host of tin openers, combined volumes and other such junk are boring through the canvas bags into your skull but they are better than nothing and better than a wooden bench boring into your skull.

D.S. and I fancied seeing what the high life was like in the station and went for a stroll. Two Peak Type 4's D28 of 55A Holbeck (Leeds) and a welcome stranger D36 of 82A Bristol Bath Road were also out for a dander.

DERBY STATION MONDAY EVENING						
		Home shed		Built	Withdrawn	Scrap
Diesels						
BR Sulzer "Peak" Type 4 1Co-Co1 1959						
D 28		55A	Leeds Holbeck	May-1961		
D 36		82A	Bristol Bath Road	Jul-1961		
Total	2					
On Station	2	Kops		1		
Steam	0	Diesels		2		
		Home Area		0 Visitors		2
Shed	55A	1				
Distribution	82A	1				

A mobile kiosk like an ice-cream cart was noted. A small crowd had gathered around it. What was the delicacy on sale? It was BR tea at sixpence (two and a half new pence) a cup. You've only had that pie today D.S. (although I thought you sneaked something in at Nottingham this evening) so I'll let you wash it down with a cup. D.S. had been very commendably on diet today. Our "dishwater" purchased from the kiosk D.S. and I made our way back to our home for the night. I remarked to D.S. that Iain "Froth" Firth had said to us before our trip that the railway cops would give us hell about using their waiting rooms as hotels. D.S. said, "Touch wood." We've got Railrover Tickets so how can they chuck us out. D.S. thought that was a good point.

Back inside the waiting room there were a few people still waiting for trains so it would be a few minutes before we could stretch out and get a sleep. One woman said to me. "Been youth hostelling? You look sunburnt." Had I washed my face today? I thought. Yes I seem to remember that such a happening took place. Sunburnt – How? I said jokingly "It's probably the effects of being weather-beaten more than any sun. We had been caught in a terrific thunderstorm in the middle of Nottinghamshire today." It must be the badges on my anorak that made her think we were hostellers. I suppose we were in a way. We had joined the YHA anyway.

I looked at my watch – it was now 23.55 and everyone had suddenly left. No D.S. had not taken his boots off. It must have been the last train! We had enough benches this time to choose from and they were all alike so there would be no fighting over them like at Bletchley. I chose one where I could sleep on my right side and be facing the wall. I think I'll elucidate on my choices. I sleep on my right side because there is less strain on the heart than if you sleep on your left side (I recommend that you do the same). I also prefer sleeping looking at a wall about six inches from my nose rather than the agoraphobic alternative of looking across the empty waiting room.

Gid nicht D.S. Now for five hours sleep. Being an expert at the art of getting to sleep I was soon in that pleasant state. KAPOW ZAP BANG some big thing is murdering me! It must be a nightmare. I awoke to find that the big thing was a railway cop who had rudely awakened me. A barrage of questions were aimed at me "You can't sleep here", "Where are you going?", and "What age are you?" Help, it looks as though I'll need my Irish grandfather to talk myself out of this one.

ME "We are youth hostellers (pointing to the sleeping D.S.) on tour with Railrover tickets."

COP "That doesn't entitle you to sleep here."

ME "But there is no youth hostel here."

COP "That still doesn't entitle you to sleep here."

I wondered if he was any relation to the Colwick shedmaster. Must be. Our cop again took up the running, as I appeared to have nothing profound to say.

COP "Look it's 12.20, you can get beds for the night at the Salvation Army hostel. It closes at 12.40 so you two had better hurry up – and it's raining."

The cop noted that D.S. was still asleep and gave him a couple of hefty shoves. While D.S. was coming back to life the cop asked how old I was. What's the best age to say I thought. I'm sixteen but there might be something about being unable to prosecute if you are under that age.

ME "Fifteen."

COP "Anyway you will have to get out of here."

D.S. by this time got to his feet and was rubbing himself at the painful experience of being awakened. Thus time it was not me who had forcefully awakened him but the cop. He of course guessed that something not quite right was up. Disconsolately we walked out of the waiting room. The cop hands on hips watched us go. I said to D.S. that he had told us to stay the night at the Salvation Army hostel. D.S. did not fancy that one bit – neither did I. The Colwick shedmaster did not get the last laugh and neither would this joker. Of that fact we were sure. I looked around. PC 49 had disappeared into the waiting room – probably for a fly ciggie I thought.

I walked past the station exit. D.S. looked quizzically on where I was going. Look casual I said and we walked up to the overbridge, crossed it and dived into the other waiting room on the island platform. D.S. and I were chuffed. Good of BR to have two waiting rooms. Let's get some sleep then D.S. said.   A good idea!

At 12.40 another cop struck. I was awakened again. Why do they always pick on me? Why don't they wake D.S. and let me get an extra minute of two of sleep – not him. However I suppose the second man gets the rougher awakening judging by the treatment that D.S. got at the first waiting room by the other cop.

What did the cop want?

COP2 "What train are you waiting for?"

ME "We have got Railrovers."

COP2 "That does not mean that you can sleep in a waiting room at twenty to one."

The Railrovers do not pull much weight in Derby I reflected.

COP2 "Where are you going to?"

I felt like saying to market you ugly cop.

ME "Burton on Trent."

COP2 "There is a train in ten minutes and you had better be on it."

The cop went over to where D.S. was sleeping and with urbane savagery brought him from his slumbers to being fully awake and sore. The cops do not differ much here. I was glad that he had awakened me first. It could hardly have been as vicious as that. Cannot complain to him though or he will find something to book us for "polluting a public waiting room" or some other obsolete obscure law.

D.S. was awake and aware and we left the waiting room. The cop saw us cross the overbridge and guessed that we were going to get the Burton train. Two tramps had been disposed of.

Our roving microphone picked up this conversation.

D.S. "Where has he sent us now? The salvation army is closed for the night."

ME "Let's go, let's go to Burton."

D.S. "What?"

ME "We have to do a Burton."

D.S. "Stop blethering."

ME "This time I told the new cop that we were going to Burton. Unfortunately yours truly did not know there is a train to Burton in five minutes so he wants us to be on it. It is the last train as well."

D.S. "Are we going to be on it?" (Expecting a negative answer and hoping for one).

ME "No, we can always go back to that first waiting room we were in. The second cop will think that we got the Burton train. We are on the right platform for it. The same platform as the other waiting room. We will have to take pot luck. If we are caught again we will be nicked, sent out into the rain or quick marched to Burton. The last thing we want is to go to Burton. We have not done Derby shed yet so we don't wish to go to Burton and then have to come back here and do the shed. That would jigger up our timetable for tomorrow (or is it today? It is). Follow?"

I didn't think D.S. did exactly but it sounded good to him and of course he trusted my calculations implicitly as usual.

D.S. and I arrived back at our first rest home on the main concourse and looked in. Our 12.20 COP1 had disappeared so we made ourselves comfortable for the third time. Third time lucky D.S. Keep alert if you hear me talking to a cop in your slumbers. If you do hear that you had better wake up sharpish because you will be sixty seconds from being kicked awake. There is no chance of him questioning you first because they seem to like wakening me up first. I think they were frightened of you or what you looked like asleep so they put me through the mill and leave you alone for the time being. D.S. pleaded for some shuteye so I shut up.

At 02.30 I was sleeping pleasantly. At 02.31 wakey wakey, KAPOW ZAP etc. Inquisitor no.3 had arrived to question me. Another meddling cop – another different one. They must be breeding! This time it was a young cop. He looked worried and embarrassed while the other two had been plain angry.

COP3 "Are you waiting for a train?"

ME "Oh yes." (I glanced at my wristwatch. It was 02.31. Now what train could come through Derby in the middle of the night? Long distance? Good guess.

ME "We are waiting for the 03.30 to Cardiff. Here's my ticket." I showed him the Railrover.

COP3 "Railrover. Eh. He's with you. Eh."

The cop woke D.S. up. A bit more gently than the other two cops did or it might have killed the poor boy. D.S. was mad at getting awakened again and his enraged look almost turned the policeman to stone. D.S. managed to control himself though.

COP3 "Can't say I know this Cardiff train. Is it a special?"

Neither did I but here was a chance to agree with him.

ME "It's an overnight special from Sheffield."

COP3 "Oh, aye. Sorry I bothered you. Just checking up. You'd better not fall asleep again or you'll miss your train."

With that last remark COP3 disappeared into the night. "At least we don't have to move this time." I said to D.S. D.S. said "We'd better not miss our train now." And we almost laughed the place down. Hope that COP3 hadn't heard us laughing. "By the way we will be doing Derby shed at 05.00 so that we can catch the train to Burton at 06.10." *Gid nicht* for the last time or should I say good morning. *Bonne nuit, bon matin, buenas noche, buena notte* D.S. It was now 02.40.

Review of the Day

This was the original timetable:-

DAY 3   **MONDAY AUGUST 2ND 1965**   **LMR DAY 2**

<u>MILES</u>

Depart EUSTON	05.10	0
Arrive WATFORD JUNCTION	05.53	17½

Journey:
        see 1B Camden - 1½ miles north west of Euston
        see 1A Willesden - north west
        see 1C Watford - east

Depart WATFORD JUNCTION	06.05	17½
Arrive BLETCHLEY	06.58	<u>46¾</u>

<u>Do 1E Bletchley (20 mins. approx)</u>   Recovery time
- 4

Journey:
        see 1E sub-shed Leighton Buzzard - south east   40¼

Depart BLETCHLEY	07.14	(08.08)	0
Arrive BEDFORD ST JOHN'S	07.44	(08.45)	<u>16</u>
		alternative	

<u>Do 14C Bedford (20 mins. approx)</u>

Depart BEDFORD MIDLAND ROAD	08.23	(09.15)	0
Arrive WELLINGBOROUGH MIDLAND ROAD	08.42	(09.33)	15¼

<u>Do 15B Wellingborough (35 mins. approx)</u>   Recovery time
+ 18

Depart WELLINGBOROUGH MIDLAND ROAD	09.35	15¼
Arrive LEICESTER LONDON ROAD	10.19	<u>49¼</u>

Journey:
        see 15C (ex) Kettering - north east   22¼
        see 15A sub Market Harborough   33¼

<u>Do 15A Leicester Midland (60 mins. approx)</u>   Recovery time
- 20 or + 43

A

Depart LEICESTER CENTRAL	10.59	0
Arrive NOTTINGHAM VICTORIA	11.35	<u>23½</u>

Do 16D Nottingham (50 mins. approx)   Recovery time
                                                      +28

If connection from Leicester Central to Nottingham Victoria is missed then:
B

Depart LEICESTER LONDON ROAD	11.52	0
Arrive TRENT	12.16	<u>20¾</u>

     Change at Trent

Journey:
     see Brush Works, Loughborough   12½

Depart TRENT	12.23	0
Arrive NOTTINGHAM MIDLAND	12.37	<u>6¾</u>

Both timetables coincide now with:-

Depart Nottingham London Road High Level	12.53	0
Arrive NETHERFIELD & COLWICK	12.58	<u>2¾</u>

Do 40E Colwick (40 mins. approx)   Recovery time
                                                 NIL

Depart NETHERFIELD & COLWICK	13.38	0
Arrive Nottingham London Road High Level	13.44	<u>2¾</u>
Depart NOTTINGHAM MIDLAND	13.53	0
Arrive ALFRETON AND SOUTH NORMANTON	14.24	<u>23</u>

Do 16G Westhouses and Blackwell (47 mins. approx) Recovery time
                                                               NIL

1¼ miles run there and back and time to do shed

Journey:
     see 16A Toton - west
     see 16D Nottingham - south west

Depart ALFRETON AND SOUTH NORMANTON	15.11	0
Arrive STAPLEFORD AND SANDIACRE	15.33	<u>13½</u>

Do 16A Toton (60 mins. approx)   Recovery time
                                               + 69

Depart STAPLEFORD AND SANDIACRE	17.42	0
Arrive KIRKBY-IN-ASHFIELD EAST	18.25	<u>16½</u>

Do 16E Kirkby

219

Trent Bus No 61 (Nottingham)

Depart KIRKBY NAG'S HEAD PUBLIC HOUSE
Arrive NEWSTEAD VILLAGE

Do 16B Annesley

Trent Bus No 61 (Mansfield)

Depart NEWSTEAD VILLAGE
Arrive MANSFIELD NOTTINGHAM ROAD

Mansfield District Bus No 1 or No 7 (Langwith)

Depart MANSFIELD WEST GATE
Arrive ELAND ROAD

Do 41J Langwith

WALK-   Route from Shirebrook to Langwith

Turn left outside the station and continue for about 150 yards. Turn right along the Langwith Road and continue for almost ½ mile. Turn right into Eland Road and the shed entrance is at the end of the short cul-de-sac (20 mins. approx).

Do 41M Shirebrook West

East Midland Bus No 72 or No 73

Depart SHIREBROOK WEST
Arrive MANSFIELD BATH STREET

Trent Bus No. 61 or No. 62

Depart MANSFIELD NOTTINGHAM ROAD
Arrive NOTTINGHAM HUNTINGDON STREET

British Rail		MILES
Depart NOTTINGHAM MIDLAND	21.30 or 22.20 or 22.55	0
Arrive DERBY MIDLAND	22.05 or 22.51 or 23.25	<u>16</u>

Night   : -   Derby Waiting Room

- - - - - - - - - - - - - - - - - - - -

What went wrong today? A lot did!!!! It started well enough with Bletchley, Bedford and Wellingborough all being done smoothly enough. But then Leicester –20 recovery time. Impossible with a pedestrian D.S. At the next minus recovery time I'll have to boot him to the shed and back to make us get the next connection on time. That escapade at Leicester cost us Nottingham shed. That miss did not worry me unduly for two reasons. Firstly, Nottingham shed was a diesel depot and secondly we would pass the shed three times during the day.

With a hectic rush we got the vital train to Colwick and rejoined our timetable. We were unavoidably delayed by the shedmaster (as you will probably have read and heard plenty about) at Colwick (or Colickton as D.S. thinks it is called). So we arrived back at the bus station at about half past two having easily missed the 13.53 to Alfreton and South Normanton to do Westhouses. We then got on a Kirkby bus. Somehow the conductor overheard that we wanted to go to Newstead and we got off at Treton Bole Hole. Going to Newstead first would save us time, as Newstead was a few miles south of Kirkby. This time saving device only works if you stand at the correct bus stop. Goodness knows what the service is like so when we did find out we were at the wrong bus stop we just had to go on to Kirkby. We could not wait for another Newstead bus because we had just missed one (unknown to us) and it could be a half hour or even hourly service. Time lost – about half an hour. Kirkby was finished about as quickly as possible (heavy rain slowed us up). Now we had to do Newstead. We missed one bus and had to wait 15-20 minutes for another one. Newstead (16B Annesley) was OK. We bussed it to Mansfield in about half an hour. At Mansfield we got near enough to lost looking for the Langwith bus stop so we scrubbed off Langwith and Shirebrook West and bussed to Alfreton. Graham's camera was regrettably lost on the journey.

At Alfreton after a quick timetable check we found that rail connections were so bad that if we did do 16G Westhouses we would arrive at Long Eaton (Toton) at 22.28. It would be bad enough doing 16A Toton at around quarter to eleven at night (I didn't think BR would take too kindly to that) but the main thing was that we would then be stranded. The last train to Nottingham was the one we would have arrived on. How would we have got to Derby? Almost certainly the bus service would be closed for the night. We could not take the chance for the night. We could not take the chance and be waiting at Toton Station (the bus is supposed to pass it by) at around half past eleven at night for a bus, which might or might not be coming until around half past six the following morning. The nearest rail link to Toton was Sawley Junction (for Long Eaton it said on the timetable). It was too far away. Trent Station was about three miles from Toton. Yes, we could get a train to Derby from Trent, yes at 02.48 in the morning, arriving in Derby at 03.08. That was hardly on – even for the keenest (soon to be the tiredest).

It was therefore a straight choice between Toton and Westhouses at Alfreton and we chose Toton. No regrets about the shed choice but our blunderings of the day had cost us two good steam sheds (Westhouses and Langwith).

This is what actually happened:-

	Do 1E Bletchley	Schedule	Actual	Miles
Depart	BLETCHLEY	06.35	06.36	0
Arrive	BEDFORD ST.JOHNS	07.09	07.10	16
	Do 14C Bedford	Schedule	Actual	Miles
Depart	BEDFORD MIDLAND ROAD	08.23	08.23	0
Arrive	WELLINGBOROUGH	08.42	08.42	16¾
	Do 15B Wellingborough	Schedule	Actual	Miles
Depart	WELLINGBOROUGH	09.23	09.23	0
Arrive	LEICESTER LONDON ROAD	10.19	10.19	34
	Do 15A Leicester Midland	Schedule	Actual	Miles
Depart	LEICESTER LONDON ROAD	11.52	11.52	0
Arrive	TRENT	12.16	12.16	20¾
		Schedule	Actual	Miles
Depart	TRENT	12.23	12.33	0
Arrive	NOTTINGHAM MIDLAND ROAD	12.37	12.47	6¾

		Schedule	Actual	Miles
Depart	Nottingham London Road High Level	12.53	12.56	0
Arrive	Netherfield and Colwick	12.58	13.03	2¾
	Do 40E Colwick			
Depart	Netherfield and Colwick	*bus*		
Arrive	Nottingham Huntingdon Street			
Depart	Nottingham Huntingdon Street	*bus*		
Arrive	Treton Bole Hole			
Depart	Treton Bole Hole	*bus*		
Arrive	Kirkby-in-Ashfield			
	Do 16E Kirkby-in-Ashfield			
Depart	Kirkby-in-Ashfield	*bus*		
Arrive	Newstead Village			
	Do 16B Annesley			
Depart	Newstead Village	*bus*		
Arrive	Mansfield			
Depart	Mansfield	*bus*		
Arrive	Alfreton			
		Schedule	Actual	Miles
Depart	ALFRETON	19.47	19.47	0
Arrive	NOTTINGHAM MIDLAND	20.17	20.17	23
		Schedule	Actual	Miles
Depart	NOTTINGHAM MIDLAND	20.55	20.55	0
Arrive	STAPLEFORD AND SANDIACRE	21.14	21.14	9½
	Do 16A Toton			
		Schedule	Actual	Miles
Depart	STAPLEFORD AND SANDIACRE	22.28	22.28	0
Arrive	BEESTON	22.39	22.39	6¼
		Schedule	Actual	Miles
Depart	BEESTON	23.02	23.02	0
Arrive	DERBY MIDLAND	23.35	23.35	12¾

Could we have done Langwith and Westhouses even after arriving back at Nottingham at 14.30 after the Colwick debacle? I think so.

The Nottinghamshire and Derbyshire countryside had been a Bermuda Triangle for us with repeated blunders. Unbelievable that we managed only three sheds after 40E Colwick (16E Kirkby, 16B Annesley and 16A Toton). We certainly should have asked the two boys whom we met at 16E Kirkby to join them in their car tour.

We would also have had more success by sticking to the railway and also saving money from exorbitantly priced buses. Like this: -

		Schedule		Miles
Depart	NOTTINGHAM	15.05		0
Arrive	STAPLEFORD AND SANDIACRE	15.24		9½
	Do 16A Toton			

		Schedule		Miles
Depart	STAPLEFORD AND SANDIACRE	16.59		9½
Arrive	WESTHOUSES AND BLACKWELL	17.37		24¼
	Do 16G Westhouses			

At around 18.30 we would have then got on a bus to Mansfield from Alfreton. 41J Langwith could then have been done. Bus to Kirby and do 16E Kirkby, bus to Newstead (going south all the time) and do 16B Annesley. None of that double tracking that we did. After Annesley we would have a pleasant half hour bus journey back to Nottingham and finally get the 22.55 train to Derby (the same one as we got on at Beeston). Moreover, we would have left our heavy grips in the left luggage at Nottingham Station for the day.

The most annoying thing was the closure of the Nottingham to Mansfield railway line in September 1964 which resulted in no rail service to 16B Annesley, 16E Kirkby and 41J Langwith. A ridiculous decision by BR. *Years later and this service is now fully operational again.* A rail service would have saved us a lot of time rather than use sporadic and expensive bus services.

A big part of the day ruined was that we did not realise that 1E Bletchley was closed to steam and 15B Wellingborough had lost all its allocation of steam. We had thus wastefully visited two sheds which we would have dropped from our itinerary if we had known the facts. This is how the final timetable would have been recast:-

		Schedule		Miles
Depart	LONDON EUSTON	23.55		0
Arrive	NORTHAMPTON CASTLE	01.30		65¾
	Do 1H Northampton			

We would have therefore not got off the train at dieselised Bletchley but stayed on the train to Northampton and would have spent the night there in the waiting room.

Up bright and early the next morning to do 1H Northampton which would have taken about one and a half hours (30 minutes to walk there, 30 minutes to do the shed and 30 minutes to walk back).

1H NORTHAMPTON				
Steam				
Ivatt 2MT 2-6-2T 1946				
41218				
Total	*0*			
Stanier 5MT 4-6-0 "Black Five" 1934				
44869	44936	45051	45134	
45287	45302	45308	45349	
45392	45398	45426	45454	
Total	*12*			
Midland 3F "Jinty" 0-6-0T 1924 dev. of Johnson 1899 design				
47286	47499	47590		
Total	*3*			
Stanier 8F 2-8-0 "Big Eight" 1935				
48020	48349	48365	48385	
48440	48449	48550	*48688*	
48739				
Total	*8*			
BR Standard 9F 2-10-0 Brighton 1954				
92033	92087			
Total	*2*			
Grand Total	**25**			
Recently		*Surviving*		
Withdrawn	*2*	*Steam Classes*	*4*	
Saw Elsewhere		*Saw Carlisle*		
on the Tour	*7*	*June 1967*	*1*	
Steam	*Sep-50*	*37*	*Mar-59*	*37*
Allocation	*Apr-65*	*26*	*Aug-65*	*25*
	Closed to Steam:-	*Sep-65*		

Steam at 1H Northampton was on the way out and would close to steam at the same time as

1A Willesden (27 September 1965). But like 1A Willesden the shed was very much alive and kicking at the time of our tour. 1H Northampton had decent allocation of 25 (largely Black Fives (12) and "Big Eights" (8) plus two recently withdrawn locos.

1F Rugby had been closed to steam at the end of May 1965 but to get to 15A Leicester we would have needed to travel via Rugby.

				Miles
Depart	NORTHAMPTON CASTLE	06.33		0
Arrive	RUGBY	07.04		16¾
	See 1F Rugby			
Depart	RUGBY	07.20		0
Arrive	LEICESTER CENTRAL	07.54		19¾
	Do 15A Leicester Midland			

Just time for a brief glimpse of the diesel shed which was at Rugby station then off to Leicester via the Great Central line. Stacks off time to visit 15A Leicester then off to visit 40E Colwick via Nottingham.

				Miles
Depart	LEICESTER LONDON ROAD	10.00		0
Arrive	NOTTINGHAM MIDLAND	10.49		24½
Depart	Nottingham London Road High Level	BUS		0
Arrive	Netherfield and Colwick			2¾
	Do 40E Colwick			
Depart	Netherfield and Colwick	12.06		0
Arrive	Nottingham London Road High Level	12.12		2¾

Back on the train to Nottingham where we would leave our heavy grips in the left luggage then off by train to visit 16G Westhouses. Then importantly, take the train from Westhouses on to Chesterfield and take the bus to Staveley to visit the key shed of 41E Staveley (Barrow Hill).

Depart	NOTTINGHAM MIDLAND	12.23		0
Arrive	WESTHOUSES AND BLACKWELL	13.22		24¼
	Do 16G Westhouses			
Depart	ALFRETON & SOUTH NORMANTON	14.24		0
Arrive	CHESTERFIELD	14.40		8¾
Depart	CHESTERFIELD	BUS	9 or 99	East Midland
Arrive	STAVELEY BARROW HILL	30 mins approx		
	Do 41E Staveley Barrow Hill			

41E Staveley (Barrow Hill) was a shed that we very much wanted to visit as it had allocated the last remaining two Deeley Midland 0-4-0 Tanks 1907 and the oldest surviving steam locos on British Rail I think the five Johnson Midland 1F 0-6-0 Tanks 1878. Seeing some of them would have been a real highlight of the tour! Moreover there were also two Kitson 0-4-0 Saddle Tanks 1932.

41E Staveley (Barrow Hill) had a terrific steam allocation of 35 plus 18 recently withdrawn locos which would be doubtless still on display on the deadlines. The other surviving classes there were the Ivatt 4MT 2-6-0's 1947 (five surviving and five recently withdrawn), three recently withdrawn Robinson 1911 O1's and 21 (plus eight recently withdrawn) of the ubiquitous WD 2-8-0's.

41E STAVELEY BARROW HILL

Steam

Deeley Midland 0F 0-4-0T 1907

41528	41533		
Total	2		

Johnson Midland 1F 0-6-0T 1878

41708	41734	41763	41804
41835			
Total	5		

Ivatt 4MT 2-6-0 1947

43062	43080	**43082**	43089
43108	43109	43111	43143
43149	43153	43159	43161
Total	5		

Kitson 0F 0-4-0ST 1932

47001	47005		
Total	2		

Thompson 7F 2-8-0 O1 1944 rebuild of Robinson O4 1911

63725	63863	63879	
Total	0		

Riddles WD 8F 2-8-0 "Austerity" 1943

90084	90085	90121	90148
90189	90190	90220	90227
90258	90266	90295	90306
90340	90346	90367	90368
90384	90410	**90471**	90474
90491	90509	90529	90572
90573	90587	90695	90706
90730			
Total	21		

Grand Total	35			
Recently		*Surviving*		
Withdrawn	18	**Steam Classes**	5	
Saw Elsewhere				
on the Tour	3			
Steam	*Aug-50*	71	*Apr-59*	67
Allocation	*May-65*	33	*Jul-65*	35
	Closed to Steam:-		*Oct-65*	

41E Staveley (Barrow Hill) was another last chance to see steam as it would close to steam in October 1965. On by bus back to Chesterfield and another bus to do 41J Langwith. There would be no time to waste so diesel depot 41M Shirebrook West would be given the miss.

Depart	STAVELEY BARROW HILL	BUS	9 or 99	East Midland
Arrive	CHESTERFIELD	30 mins approx		
Depart	CHESTERFIELD			
Arrive	SHIREBROOK/LANGWITH	75 mins approx.		
	Do 41J Langwith Junction			

On by bus via Mansfield to do 16E Kirkby-in-Ashfield

Depart	SHIREBROOK/LANGWITH	BUS	1 or 7	
Arrive	MANSFIELD	30 minutes	Mansfield District	
Depart	MANSFIELD	BUS	61 or 84	
Arrive	KIRKBY IN ASHFIELD	30 mins approx		
	Do 16E Kirkby-in-Ashfield			

Then do 16B Annesley on the way back to Nottingham.

Depart	KIRKBY IN ASHFIELD	BUS	61	
Arrive	NEWSTEAD	20 mins approx		
	Do 16B Annesley			
Depart	NEWSTEAD	BUS	61	
Arrive	NOTTINGHAM	25 mins approx		

We would then pick up our heavy grips from the left luggage and visit 16A Toton via the same trains which we actually travelled on.

Depart	NOTTINGHAM MIDLAND	20.55	20.55	
Arrive	STAPLEFORD AND SANDIACRE	21.14	21.14	
	See 16D Nottingham			
	Do 16A Toton			
				Miles
Depart	STAPLEFORD AND SANDIACRE	22.28	22.28	0
Arrive	BEESTON	22.39	22.39	6¼
		Schedule	*Actual*	*Miles*
Depart	BEESTON	23.02	23.02	0
Arrive	DERBY MIDLAND	23.35	23.35	12¾

It was indeed unfortunate that the Nottingham–Annesley– Kirkby–Langwith line had closed down at the end of the previous year. The previous timetable from September 1964 had shown a sporadic (pre-closure last appeals?) rail timetable but something would have been better and cheaper than nothing!

		Miles						
Depart	**Nottingham Midland**	0	11.58	15.11	16.40	17.11	17.14	18.07
Depart	**Newstead**	10¾	12.18	15.39	17.10	17.40		18.34
Depart	**Kirkby in Ashfield East**	13¼	12.26	15.47	17.19	17.48	18.20	18.42
Arrive	**Langwith**	23	12.55	16.16	17.50	18.16		19.11
Depart	**Langwith**	0		16.09	17.53	20.29		
Depart	**Kirkby in Ashfield East**	9¾	13.11	16.41	18.28	21.02		
Depart	**Newstead**	12¼	13.17	16.47	18.34	21.08		
Arrive	**Nottingham Midland**	23	13.42	17.14	18.58	21.29		

Rural Nottinghamshire and Derbyshire rail services had been a "black hole" for us and even the 1965 service still intact via Toton and Westhouses to Chesterfield (for Staveley) was extremely poor.

		Miles							
Depart	**Nottingham**	0	12.23	13.54	15.05	16.40	17.15	18.09	19.55
Depart	**Stapleford & Sandiacre**	9½	12.42		15.24	16.59	17.37	18.29	20.14
Depart	**Alfreton**	23	13.19	14.24	16.01	17.34		19.03	20.49
Depart	**Westhouses**	24¼	13.22		16.04	17.37		19.06	20.52
Arrive	**Chesterfield**	33	13.36	14.40	16.18	17.51		19.20	21.05
	Kirkby						18.20		
Depart	**Chesterfield**	0	13.07	14.54	16.23	17.37	18.23	19.30	
Depart	**Westhouses**	9	13.21		16.38	17.49	18.37		
Depart	**Alfreton**	10	13.25	15.11	16.42	17.52	18.42	19.47	
Depart	**Stapleford & Sandiacre**	23½	13.54	15.33	17.15		19.15		
Arrive	**Nottingham**	33	14.16	15.52	17.39	18.27	19.36	20.17	

We were even lucky to find the last train from Alfreton to Nottingham at 19.47!

What did we actually see today?

DAY 3 BLETCHLEY, WELLINGBOROUGH, LEICESTER, COLWICK, ANNESLEY, TOTON -DERBY

	Visits	GWR	SR	LMS	LNER	WD	BR	Steam Total	Diesel Total	Electric Total	Grand Total
	Bletchley Station								6		6
1E	Bletchley			2			1	3	20		23
ex 14C	Bedford								4		4
	Bedford Station								6		6
15B	Wellingborough			5			2	7	8		15
	Wellingborough Station								3		3
	Welling to Leicester			2		1		3	3		6
15A	Leicester Midland			20			6	26	15		41
	Leicester Station								2		2
	Leicester to Trent			1				1	5		6
	Trent Station			1				1	1		2
16D	Nottingham (pass)								13		13
40E	Colwick				24	27	2	53	14		67
16E	Kirkby			32	1	1	4	38	3		41
16B	Annesley			10			1	11			11
	Alfreton to Nottingham			1				1	3		4
16D	Nottingham (pass) ev.								16		16
	Nottingham Station								2		2
	Nottingham to Toton								2		2
16A	Toton			7			8	15	69		84
	Beeston Station								2		2
	Derby Station								2		2
	GRAND TOTAL	**0**	**0**	**81**	**25**	**29**	**24**	**159**	**199**	**0**	**358**

In all, only seven sheds visited and another one 16D Nottingham Diesel seen twice. Despite carelessly missing 41J Langwith and 16G Westhouses we had still managed to see 159 steam locos. Diesels at 199 locos continued to be in the ascendancy. It was now shut eye time (again!). I had been bouncing about since 05.25 at Bletchley and it was now getting on for 02.55. Twenty one hours had passed and only twenty minutes sleep on the bucket to Derby and some winks and disturbed sleep in between COP1, COP2 and COP3. Sleep, sleep------------------------

END OF DAY THREE

Some steam seen analyses follow:-

227

STEAM ENGINE CLASSES
ACTIVE ON SHED ANALYSIS

Class	Numbers	BR total	1E Bletchley	15A Leicester	15B Wellingbro	16A Toton	16B Annesley	16E Kirby Ashf	40E Colwick	Total Active On Shed DAY 3
Ivatt 2MT 2-6-2T 1946	41200-41329	130		1						1
Stanier 5MT 2-6-0 1933	42945-84	40							1	1
Stanier 5MT 4-6-0 "Black Five" 1934	44658-45499	842		1		4	6			11
Stanier 8F 2-8-0 "Big Eight" 1935	48000-48775	666		18	5	3	1	26		53
Thompson 5MT 4-6-0 B1 1942	61000-61409	410							11	11
Robinson 8F 2-8-0 O4 1911	63570-63920	271						0	7	7
BR Standard 5MT 4-6-0 Doncaster 1951	73000-73171	172					1			1
BR Standard 4MT 4-6-0 Brighton 1951	75000-75079	80				1				1
BR Standard 2MT 2-6-0 Doncaster 1953	78000-78064	65		3		5				8
BR Standard 2MT 2-6-2T Derby 1953	84000-84029	30	0	3						3
Riddles WD 8F 2-8-0 "Austerity" 1943	90000-90732	733						1	21	22
BR Standard 9F 2-10-0 Brighton 1954	92000-92250 except	166			2	1		4	1	8
BR Standard 9F 2-10-0 Brighton 1954. 1957 double chimney	92000-1; 92006; 92079; 92165-7, 92178; 92183-9249	75						1		1
BR Standard 9F 2-10-0 Brighton 1954. 1955 Crosti boiler	92020-29	10				1				1
			0	26	7	15	8	32	41	129

STEAM ENGINE CLASSES
WITHDRAWN ANALYSIS

	BR 1E	15A	15B	16A	16B	16E	40E	Total Withdrawn	On Shed
	total Bletchley	Leicester	Wellingbro	Toton	Annesley	Kirby Ashf	Colwick		DAY 3
Fowler Midland 4F 0-6-0 1911									
43835-44026	192						1	**1**	
Midland 4F 0-6-0 1924									
44027-44606	580						3	**3**	
Stanier 5MT 4-6-0 "Black Five" 1934									
44658-45499	842					3		**3**	
Midland 3F "Jinty" 0-6-0T 1924 dev. of Johnson 1899 design									
47260-47681	417	2						**2**	
Stanier 8F 2-8-0 "Big Eight" 1935									
48000-48775	666						1	**1**	
Thompson 5MT 4-6-0 B1 1942									
61000-61409	410							**4**	4
Gresley 5P6F 2-6-0 K3 1924									
61800-61992	193							**1**	1
Robinson 8F 2-8-0 O4 1911									
63570-63920	271						1	**2**	1
BR Standard 2MT 2-6-2T Derby 1953									
84000-84029	30	1						**1**	
Riddles WD 8F 2-8-0 "Austerity" 1943									
90000-90732	733							**6**	6
		3	0	0	0	3	6	**24**	12

STEAM ENGINE CLASSES
OFF SHED AND GRAND TOTALS ANALYSIS

Class	BR Nos	wellingbro total to leicester	leicester to trent	trent station	alfreton to nottingh	Off Shed Day 3 Grand Total	On Shed Day 3 Grand Total	Withdrawn Day 3 Grand Total	All Day 3 Grand Total
Ivatt 2MT 2-6-2T 1946	41200-41329	130					1		1
Stanier 5MT 2-6-0 1933	42945-84	40				1			1
Fowler Midland 4F 0-6-0 1911	43835-44026	192						1	1
Midland 4F 0-6-0 1924	44027-44606	580					3		3
Stanier 5MT 4-6-0 "Black Five" 1934	44658-45499	842	1			1	11	3	15
Midland 3F "Jinty" 0-6-0T 1924 dev. of Johnson 1899 design	47260-47681	417						2	2
Stanier 8F 2-8-0 "Big Eight" 1935	48000-48775	666				1	53	4	58
Thompson 5MT 4-6-0 B1 1942	61000-61409	410	2	1	1		3	1	4
Gresley 5P6F 2-6-0 K3 1924	61800-61992	193					11	4	15
Robinson 8F 2-8-0 O4 1911	63570-63920	271						1	1
BR Standard 5MT 4-6-0 Doncaster 1951	73000-73171	172					7	2	9
BR Standard 4MT 4-6-0 Brighton 1951	75000-75079	80				1			1
BR Standard 2MT 2-6-0 Doncaster 1953	78000-78064	65					8		8
BR Standard 2MT 2-6-2T Derby 1953	84000-84029	30				1			1
Riddles WD 8F 2-8-0 "Austerity" 1943	90000-90732	733				1	22	6	29
BR Standard 9F 2-10-0 Brighton 1954	92000-92250	251					10		10
Total			3	1	1	6	129	24	159

Part Four

TUESDAY 3rd AUGUST 1965

The Tour continues

Derby, Barry Docks,
Cardiff, Banbury
and
Leamington Spa Arrival

Reveille – A Waiting Room at Derby Station

I awoke as I hoped at 05.00. Nice time to visit Derby shed. At least the bluebottles had not disturbed us further that night. D.S. was given the normal strong nudge awake and he awoke from his twilight zone.

We first had a tour around the station and one "Peak" was noted:-.

DERBY STATION TUESDAY MORNING							
					Home shed		*Built*
Diesels							
BR Sulzer "Peak" Type 4 1Co-Co1 1959							
D 50	"The King's Shropshire Light Infantry"				ML	Midland Lines	*May-1962*
Total	*1*						
On Station	**1**		**Kops**	**1**			
Steam	**0**		**Diesels**	**1**			
		Home Area			**0 Visitors**		**1**
Shed	**ML**	**1**					
Analysis							

Next stop Derby shed. At least we had a permit for Derby so it couldn't be so difficult. It was always supposed to be a hard shed to get round. Only Willesden Electric Depot had stopped us so far and that was no great loss.

We left the station consulted the shed directory and proceeded to the shed. After a five minute walk we reached the footbridge which crossed the line – the shed was at the end of it. It all looked O.K. but there was an office come checkpoint at the foot of the bridge. More difficult than most shed accesses. "Tread softly D.S., here's Checkpoint Charlie."

We were not more than a pace or two past the office when the expected hail came. Back to the office we went and the watchman was there to greet us.

WATCHMAN "Got a permit?"

ME "Of course."

I pulled out my wad of about 50 permits from my anorak pouch. The watchman gave a detected gasp when he saw the wad. I was pleased that it impressed him (so much the better) *tanto uberior.* I carefully fingered my way through the wad and brought out the Derby one and handed it to him.

WATCHMAN "You're a bit early." (The permit was for 08.30).

ME "We have to come here now because we want to catch the 07.10 train to Cardiff."

WATCHMAN "I'll phone across to the shed."

WATCHMAN (on phone to the shedmaster) "I've got a party of two here with a permit for 08.30." The party of two really hurt – not impressive.

WATCHMAN "They've got a permit for about every shed in Great Britain." That was more impressive!

We couldn't hear any of the shedmaster's replies but the watchman was smiling. He replaced the receiver.

WATCHMAN "Go across the bridge and report to the shedmaster's office."

A word of thanks to the watchman and we were off. D.S. and I paused on the bridge and had a look at the station from it and in the other direction the sheds – and what we took to be the shedmaster's office.

A short walk and we found the office at the top of the roundhouse without much difficulty. The shedmaster was a big round chap and he seemed to find us a curiosity worth seeing that had stopped him from telling the watchman to tell the party of two to get lost. If they've got as many permits as that they must be worth seeing was probably his line of thinking.

His first comment was a surprising one.

SHEDMASTER "You're here too early. You should have taken five minutes to get here from the bridge."

Trying to be funny I thought. Considering D.S. and I had stopped to have a look around on the bridge we were late if anything! Hope it wasn't going to be a Colwick style interrogation. He looked friendlier at least. No reply and smile quietly at his first comment. Must be a local joke.

SHEDMASTER "Where's the other eight in your party of ten?" trust him to ask that.

ME "We split up in London yesterday morning over a timetable dispute and they're away up the Western lines." The shedmaster (unlike the Colwick one seemed to believe me. I really liked that lie).

SHEDMASTER "You're here early enough. Going to Cardiff. Eh?

ME "We want to go to Barry Docks. There are about 150 steam engines there awaiting scrap".

The shedmaster seemed satisfied now that we were two accomplished globetrotters and hadn't the heart to stop our progress.

SHEDMASTER "Been round here before?"

ME "No."

SHEDMASTER "I'd better send a man round with you. It's a funny place here – especially if you've never been round before."

The shedmaster duly got a "man" and we dumped our bags at the top of the roundhouse. "A friendly change to the Colwick shedmaster that was." I said to D.S. He agreed.

We found out from our railway guide that this was Derby No.3 shed (the roundhouse). Were there at one time three sheds I asked? There was or had been apparently. No 2 shed (another roundhouse) had been recently demolished. The railwayman said that the architecture was really beautiful in the number 2 shed and wished we had seen it. D.S. and I didn't completely share his feelings for railway architecture but rather more for railway engines. His point was well made though.

Plenty of BR Type 2's and diesel shunters were on view. A soon to be condemned "Big Eight" 48429 of 9F Heaton Mersey was noted with interest. How did it get here? Brush Type 2 D5659 was also a stranger – on loan from March (31B) we found out from our guide. It was here for crew training. So was D6878 from Cardiff Canton (86A) we were told.

Surprise, surprise and we found 47000 one of the little Kitson 0-4-0ST's (saddle tanks). She was shedded here at Derby but worked solely the Cromford to High Peak line in Derbyshire along with her sister 47006. Her sister had undergone detail alterations but here was the founder member of the class. She was hardly treated as a celebrity here because she was in a filthy state in a dirty corner of the roundhouse. Familiarity breeds contempt here! What's this? It was another soon to be condemned Heaton Mersey "Big Eight". It was 48490. Now we came to the conclusion that they were passing through Derby en route to some scrap breakers yard. Our railway friend thought that as well. *Both were destined for Ward's scrapyard at Beighton, Sheffield.*

Surprises – another stranger. This time it was 42765 of 8H Birkenhead. A "Crab" in Derby? Must be a rare sight. Our friend didn't know how she got here or how she'd get back to Birkenhead. She wasn't withdrawn either. I have only remarked on the celebrities that struck our eye: - "Black Fives", "Big Eights", "Flying Pigs" (43000 Class), "Doodlebugs" (Standard ones) were also in evidence but not in as large numbers as we would have liked.

The roundhouse finished (which had been interspersed with diesels as well) we ventured out into the shed yard. I remarked to our guide that I (D.S. was sleeping at the time in Bedford station) had seen a Freightliner at Bedford on trial yesterday morning. Our guide seemed interested at that. About 08.00 he said. Yes, I said (wondering how he knew). Going south, he said. Yes, I said (still wondering how he knew). He said that we looked amazed. We were. He said that he knew all about it because he was the driver!!!!! That answered all our questions.

In the yard we noticed four familiar diesels on the scrap line. They were 10000 – the LMS Co-Co diesel built along with 10001 in 1947. In company with her sister they hauled the Royal Scot train on a number of occasions. Now she was awaiting scrap while her sister lived on at 1A Willesden mainly on freight runs (but strangely she had not been at Willesden when we visited there on Sunday).

10201, 10202 and 10203 were built between 1951 and 1954 and were slightly more powerful than their LMS predecessors and spent their short lives on the Southern region of BR – mainly at Stewart's Lane (75D) I think. Now they too were awaiting the chopper.

Our guide asked if we wanted to go round Derby Works. This was an unexpected invitation. I glanced at my watch. If we went round the works we would miss the Burton train. What is best – Burton or Derby Works? I told D.S. that it would be a straight swap. While D.S. had certainly heard of Burton's the Tailors he had never heard of the town of Burton which was the biggest beer producing centre in Britain. Burton has a Home Steam allocation of 33 (largely "Big Eights" and "Black Fives"). Moreover we would pass the shed on the way to Cardiff so Derby Works seemed the correct choice. Our guide added that Burton was a small shed – and he should know being a driver.

Talking about sheds I told our guide that we had visited a tremendous diesel depot in 16A Toton (I pronounced it "toe-tun). Last night. He said that they called it "Tout-un." He said that there was certainly nothing like Toton that he had seen elsewhere. He remarked that the worst thing about Toton was that it was so isolated. OK if you live in Long Eaton or wanted to live there but if you lived in Derby or Nottingham or anywhere else it was some journey. They just couldn't get staff for it was his conclusion and weren't likely to attract much either. Obviously he and many others didn't like signing on or off at Toton for one of the many freight rosters at the marshalling yard and be faced with a longish journey to and from Derby.

We saw the "Midland Pullman" outside the works. "Like to see inside the driving compartment?" said our driver friend. No need to ask us twice and we jumped at the chance. Inside was something similar to a diesel bucket and a main line diesel's cab but it was strangely luxurious. This must be to keep it in line with the luxury Pullman coaches behind! Apparently it had just been overhauled and would shortly be returning to service. He went over the controls and the procedures really well and explained it perfectly to us who had only a scanty knowledge of how it moved. We jumped out once he was satisfied that we were "top-link" drivers. "I think we'll have to drive the diesel bucket ourselves now from Derby to Cardiff!" We all laughed at the thought.

Next stop was the repair shop of the works. Inside I wasn't surprised to see an absence of steam because Derby Works had been closed to steam, months earlier but I was surprised to see no one about. I asked the driver about this. He said that it was easy to answer because the works staff didn't start work this early. I had forgotten that it was only going on for six o'clock.

We were told that the works undertook repairs to diesel shunters, BR Type 2's and Peak Type 4's from almost anywhere. Diesels were strewn around in various stages of collapse with engines, bogies, chassis and bodywork scattered everywhere. How they ever put them back together was beyond me but I was assured from our friend that there was method in this chaos.

One Peak Type 4, which we located at the bottom of the repair shop, could be classed as a celebrity in my book. It was "Peak" D94 resplendent in shining ex-works livery. D94 was famous or infamous for two reasons. Firstly, she was the only Peak to be allocated to 16E Kirkby-in-Ashfield. The second reason was a deadly one. I said to our guide "she's a killer." He wanted to know why. I had read an Accident Report in Modern Railways recently about an accident that D94 had about a year ago. Apparently, she was at the head of a freight train and for no reason she ran away with the freight train, plunged through red signals and finally crashed killing both the driver and second man. In the report the only possible cause given was that the driver and the second man had both fallen asleep.

How the dead man's handle had not worked was another mystery. The only answer given to that was that it must have been set to neutral. The accident was virtually unbelievable. There could not have been many odder or stranger. The railwayman (and indeed a driver) found it possible because "These Peaks are right Tatars". Anything could and did go wrong with them. Some of them spend their lives in here he said. At times less than half of them are working, the rest are waiting to get into the works or are being patched up as best as possible in their home depots.

Next stop was the paint shop for us. D1891 and D1892 were noted freshly painted outside the shop. The Brushes run from Loughborough in workshop red before being painted in BR colours and entering service. Inside the shop there were only two diesels. BR Type 2 D5037 of 32B Ipswich (a stranger) was almost completely repainted. She had been repainted to be in line with her newer sisters with a light green band above the bogies. Peak D36 of 82A Bristol Bath Road (another stranger) was awaiting the same treatment. Unlike the repair shop there was a man in here but he seemed to be a watchman. I asked if they sprayed the diesels by machine. No, they were all hand-painted said the railwayman. Apparently they had tried mechanical spraying but they had not found that to be successful and had reverted back to painting by hand – and a tremendous job they did too! I had seen plenty of cats in the repair shop and there were more scuttling about in here. I found out that nobody owned them but that the workers fed them.

The paint shop over our guide said that there were only the lines outside the works to see. I asked about the assembly shops where the BR Type 2's were made. He seemed doubtful and said as far as he knew there were only engines tested there. Possibly he hadn't the authority to go into that section of the works. It seemed possible because he had asked the chap in the paint shop if we could come in or perhaps being a driver he might not know where the BR Type 2's were made in the works. What's a row of sardine cans anyway?

We toured the perimeter of the works noting stray locos and lines awaiting entry. We arrived back at the roundhouse and collected our grips. His job for him was not finished yet and he told us he would take us back by the side of the main line to the station to save us "that long way round by the road." He led us and showed us where to get on to the platform at Derby Station. We thanked our driver friend profusely for what had been a fantastically interesting tour of the works and for him sparing his time to show us around. It had been really wonderful and I would not swap Derby Works for Burton.

16C DERBY AND DERBY WORKS							
			Home shed		Built	Withdrawn	Scrap
Diesels							
BR Sulzer "Peak" Type 4 1Co-Co1 1959							
D 18			55A	Leeds Holbeck	*Dec-1960*		
D 19			55A	Leeds Holbeck	*Dec-1960*		
D 33			82A	Bristol Bath Road	*Jun-1961*		
D 34			82A	Bristol Bath Road	*Jul-1961*		
D 36			82A	Bristol Bath Road	*Jul-1961*		
D 42			82A	Bristol Bath Road	*Aug-1961*		
D 43			ML	Midland Lines (ex 2E)	*Sep-1961*		
D 49			ML	Midland Lines	*Oct-1961*		
D 63			ML	Midland Lines	*Mar-1962*		
D 67			ML	Midland Lines (ex 2E)	*May-1962*		
D 77			D16	Nottingham Division	*Dec-1960*		
D 80			ML	Midland Lines	*Dec-1960*		
D 82			ML	Midland Lines	*Dec-1960*		
D 85			ML	Midland Lines	*Feb-1961*		
D 87			ML	Midland Lines	*Feb-1961*		
D 90			ML	Midland Lines	*Mar-1961*		
D 94			D16	Nottingham Division (ex D15)	*Apr-1961*		
D 102			D16	Nottingham Division	*May-1961*		
D 106			ML	Midland Lines	*Jun-1961*		
D 114			ML	Midland Lines	*Aug-1961*		
D 144			D16	Nottingham Division	*Dec-1961*		
D 145			D16	Nottingham Division	*Dec-1961*		
D 149			D16	Nottingham Division	*Dec-1961*		
Total	23						
Brush Type 4 Co-Co 1962							
D1529			34G	Finsbury Park	*Jul-1963*		
D1827			D16	Nottingham Division	*Mar-1965*		
D1830			D16	Nottingham Division	*Mar-1965*		
D1891	*ex works*		New	to 41A Tinsley	*Aug-1965*		
D1892	*ex works*		New	to 41A Tinsley	*Aug-1965*		
Total	5						
Drewry 0-6-0 Shunter 1952							
D2208			5B	Crewe South	*Feb-1953*	*Sep-1968*	
Total	1						
Drewry 0-6-0 Shunter 1955							
D2221			5B	Crewe South (ex 5C)	*Sep-1955*	*Jul-1968*	
D2228			9D	Newton Heath	*Nov-1955*	*Jun-1968*	
Total	2						

		Home shed		Built	Withdrawn	Scrap
BR 0-6-0 Shunter 1955 Gardner engine				Oct-1961	May-1968	
D2379		16C		Oct-1961	Jun-1972	saved
D2381		16C		Nov-1961	Jun-1972	
D2382		16C				
Total	3					
Hudswell-Clarke 0-6-0 Shunter						
D2502		8H	Birkenhead	Jan-1956	Oct-1967	
Total	1					
North British 0-4-0 Shunter 1958						
D2910		5B	Crewe South	Oct-1958	Feb-1967	
Total	1					
BR 0-6-0 Shunter 1953 English Electric engine						
D3067		1A	Willesden (ex 1G)	Oct-1953		
D3068		1H	Northampton (ex 1A)	Oct-1953		
Total	2					
BR 0-6-0 Shunter 1953 English Electric engine						
D3304		14B	Cricklewood West	May-1956		
D3587		16C		Nov-1958		
D3592		9D	Newton Heath	Jan-1959		
D3792		16C		Oct-1959		
D3832		6B	Mold Junction	Jan-1960		
D3864		16C		Dec-1959		
Total	6					
BR 0-6-0 Shunter 1955 Crossley engine						
D3118		16A	Toton	Jun-1955		
D3126		16A	Toton	Jun-1957		
Total	2					
BR 0-6-0 Shunter 1955 Blackstone engine						
D4144		1F	Rugby	Sep-1962		
Total	1					
BR Sulzer Type 2 Bo-Bo 1958						
D5006		5A	Crewe Diesel (ex 1F)	Jan-1959		
D5018		1B	Camden	Jun-1959		
D5028		1A	Willesden	Nov-1959		
D5037		32B	Ipswich	Sep-1959		
D5113		52A	Gateshead	Jan-1961		
D5144		1F	Rugby	Dec-1960		
D5172		51L	Thornaby	Feb-1962		
D5200		ML	Midland Lines	Jun-1963		
D5203		ML	Midland Lines	Jun-1962		
D5205		ML	Midland Lines	Jun-1962		
D5209		ML	Midland Lines	Jun-1962		
D5217		D14	Cricklewood Division	Aug-1963		
D5226		2E	Saltley	Aug-1963		
D5230		ML	Midland Lines	Oct-1963		
D5238		D16	Nottingham Division	Dec-1963		
D5254		ML	Midland Lines	Feb-1964		
D5260		D16	Nottingham Division	Apr-1964		
D5264		D16	Nottingham Division	Apr-1964		
D5269		D16	Nottingham Division	May-1964		
D5288		ML	Midland Lines (ex D14)	Aug-1964		
D7502		D16	Nottingham Division	Oct-1964		
D7512		D16	Nottingham Division	Nov-1964		
D7526		D16	Nottingham Division	Jan-1965		
D7527		D16	Nottingham Division	Jan-1965		
D7529		D16	Nottingham Division	Feb-1965		
D7537		D16	Nottingham Division	Mar-1965		
D7542		D16	Nottingham Division	Apr-1965		
D7549		D16	Nottingham Division	May-1965		
D7551		D16	Nottingham Division	Jun-1965		
D7560	ex works	New		Sep-1965		
D7576		ML	Midland Lines	Nov-1963		
D7579		ML	Midland Lines	Dec-1963		
D7580		ML	Midland Lines	Dec-1963		
Total	33					

16C DERBY AND DERBY WORKS(continued)

		Home shed		Built	Withdrawn	Scrap
Birmingham R.C. & W. Co.Type 2 Bo-Bo 1958						
D5380		ML	Midland Lines	Apr-1962		
D5398		D14	Cricklewood Division	Jul-1962		
Total	*2*					
Brush Type 3 A1A-A1A 1958						
D5659	*On loan*	31B	March	Oct-1960		
Total	*1*					
English Electric Type 3 Co-Co 1961						
D6878	*On loan*	D16	Nottingham Division (ex 86A)	Oct-1963		
Total	*1*					
LMS Type 3 Co-Co 1947						
10000		*none*		Nov-1947	Dec-1963	Jan-1968
10001		1A	Willesden	Jul-1948	Mar-1966	
Total	*2*					
BR Type 3 or 4 1Co-Co1 1951(type 3) 1954 (type 4)						
10201	*type 3*	*none*		Nov-1950	Dec-1963	Jan-1968
10202	*type 3*	*none*		Oct-1951	Dec-1963	Jan-1968
10203	*type 4*	*none*		Mar-1954	Dec-1963	Jan-1968
Total	*3*					
LMS 0-6-0 Shunter 1939						
12018		8C	Speke Junction	May-1940	Oct-1967	
12022		5B	Crewe South	Jul-1940	Nov-1966	
12031		8F	Spring's Branch (Wigan)	Jul-1942	Dec-1967	
Total	*3*					
LMS and BR 0-6-0 Shunter 1945						
12033		16C		Apr-1945	Jan-1969	
12035		2E	Saltley	Jun-1945	Nov-1968	
12039		2E	Saltley	Aug-1947	Oct-1968	
12051		16D	Nottingham	Feb-1949	Oct-1970	
12053		1A	Willesden	Apr-1949	Apr-1971	
Total	*5*					
Steam				**Built**	**Withdrawn**	**Scrap**
Hughes/Fowler 5MT 2-6-0 "Crab" 1926						
42765		8H	Birkenhead	Aug-1927	Dec-1966	saved
Total	*1*					
Ivatt 4MT 2-6-0 1947						
43032		40E	Colwick	Apr-1949	Jan-1965	Aug-1965
43082		41E	Staveley Barrow Hill	Nov-1950	Jun-1965	Sep-1965
Total	*2*					
Stanier 5MT 4-6-0 "Black Five" 1934						
44945		2E	Saltley	Jan-1946	Oct-1966	Mar-1967
45089		2F	Bescot	Apr-1935	Aug-1967	Dec-1967
Total	*2*					
Kitson 0F 0-4-0ST 1932						
47000		16C		Nov-1932	Oct-1966	Feb-1967
Total	*1*					
Stanier 8F 2-8-0 "Big Eight" 1935						
48124		16C		Jun-1939	May-1968	Oct-1968
48149		16C		Aug-1942	Jan-1967	Jan-1968
48194		16F	Burton	Jun-1942	Aug-1967	Dec-1967
48270		16C		Jun-1942	Dec-1966	Jun-1967
48350		16C		Apr-1944	Sep-1967	Aug-1968
48359		16C		Jul-1944	Sep-1967	Feb-1968
48370		16C		Oct-1944	Nov-1966	May-1967
48429		9F	Heaton Mersey	Jan-1944	Sep-1965	Dec-1965
48490		9F	Heaton Mersey (ex 9G)	Jun-1945	Sep-1965	Dec-1965
48604		16C		Jun-1943	May-1967	Nov-1967
48613		9F	Heaton Mersey	Jul-1943	Jul-1967	Dec-1967
48666		16C		Apr-1944	Aug-1968	Dec-1968
48671		15A	Leicester (ex 15B)	Dec-1943	Aug-1967	Dec-1967
Total	*13*					
BR Standard 2MT 2-6-0 1953 Derby						
78000		16C		Dec-1952	Jul-1965	Jan-1966
Total	*1*					

On Shed	117	Kops	105
Steam	20	Diesels	97
Withdrawn	7 (3 steam and 4 diesels)		

Home Locos		40 Home Area		4 Visitors	73
Shed	16C	17 D16	23		
Distribution	16A	2 16D	1 16F	1	
	ML	22 D14	2		
	1A	4 1B	1 1F	2	
	1H	1			
	2E	4 2F	1		
	5A	1 5B	3 6B	1	
	8C	1 8F	1 8H	2	
	9D	2 9F	3		
	14B	1 15A	1		
	31B	1 32B	1 34G	1	
	40E	1 41E	1		
	51A	1 51L	1 55A	2	
	82A	4			
	new	3 none	4		
Steam Classes	6				
Steam Origin	LMS	19	BR	1	

Shed Highlights:-

	Steam	47000 of 16C Derby
	Diesel	10000

Steam	Sep-50	138	Mar-59	113	Apr-65	42
Allocation					Aug-65	35
			Closed to Steam:-		Mar-67	

Home Steam	excluding withdrawn locos					
On/Off Shed	On Shed	9 Off Shed		26 % On Shed	26%	
Not on Shed						
"Black Fives"		44659	44690	44811	44830	44920	7
					45190	45289	
Kitson 0F 0-4-0ST						47006	1
"Big Eights"		48000	48060	48064	48073	48083	
		48103	48153	48170	48198	48284	
		48313	48362	48510	48627	48653	
						48666	16
BR 2MT 2-6-0					78020	78064	2
					total		26
		saw elsewhere on the tour		11		
		saw on Dec 64 Manchester and Crewe trip		1		
		saw on June 67 Carlisle visit		1		

Review and Appraisal of 16C Derby and Derby Works

The shed was at the south end of Derby Midland station on the east side of the London line. Walking time was 5 minutes.

13 "Big Eights" wasn't a bad haul but Derby was a haven for them. I reckoned 24 "Big Eights" were allocated here according to my allocation book. The majority seen were local but some others were of interest. Two had been transferred to 16G Westhouses from Derby very recently but did not seem to have been moved yet.

Two "Black Fives" were a miserable turnout. They were from the Birmingham Area and not from the Derby area so where were all the seven "Black Fives" allocated here? Possibly it was due to us visiting the shed on a weekday when the local "Black Fives" were out working.

Seeing two Moguls was very good and unexpected. The one from 41E Staveley Barrow Hill was not withdrawn but the 40E Colwick one was! (That swear word Colwick coming up again). The likes of Colwick would not be quickly forgotten). *Again the "Flying Pig" was destined to be despatched to Ward's at Beighton, Sheffield, later in the month.*

Another Standard "Doodle Bug" to add to our enormous collection. This time the founder 78000 as well. Depressing to report she was condemned *and would be despatched to Cashmore's at Great Bridge, Birmingham in January 1966.*

And now for the cream! Firstly, to whet the appetite 42765 - a 8H Birkenhead Crab. *Little did we know at the time that 42765 was destined to be famous. One of the Crab's regular duties at this shed was to work the Birkenhead-Paddington trains to and from Chester, together with some of the local freight, and when withdrawn at the end of 1966 it was amongst the last five Crabs to remain in service. She arrived at Barry Docks Scrapyard in June 1967 and was purchased privately and moved to the Keighley & Worth Valley Railway in April 1978 where she was restored to her original LMS maroon livery. Then LMS Crab 2765 in February 1937 was involved in an accident while working an overnight express freight from Manchester to London St. Pancras. Travelling at speed she became derailed just outside West Hampstead Station, tearing up the track for some distance with its train of box vans piled up in disarray behind it. Fortunately the engine embedded itself in the earth and remained upright ensuring there were no casualties but it still took the breakdown crane from Kentish Town a long while to clear up the mess!*

The greatest highlight at the time of our visit, however, was seeing that terrific little Kitson 0-4-0 Saddle Tank 47000.

A diesel is a diesel whatever you look at it but some are better than others. That's how I looked at it. The expected assortment of Peak Type 4's, BR Type 2's and ignominious diesel shunters were all there in numbers. A lot of them were presumably in for maintenance. But to add spice we saw new ex-works Brush Type 4's D1891 and D1892. It took at the time a few seconds to register that they were indeed new diesels.

At Derby Works we saw locos from distant depots (particularly with the Peaks and shunters). Leeds Holbeck and Bristol "Peaks" were noted under repair in addition to Drewry, North British and Hudswell Clarke shunters.

Easily the highlight of the diesel section was seeing the early LMS diesel prototype 10000 along with its sister 10001 and the Southern Region prototypes 10201, 10202 and 10203. All were withdrawn other than 10001 from 1A Willesden which strangely was not.

Only 8 (23%) Home Steam on shed with a massive 27 Home Steam off shed. A bit disappointing for a six o'clock in the morning visit when you would expect plenty of locos on shed.

On we go

The epilogue of the: -
FLATFEET AFFAIR
ALL NIGHT AFFAIR
BLUEBOTTLE AFFAIR
CASE OF THE PERSISTENT POLICEMEN

Well D.S., Derby shed was fantastic and the works fantastic plus. I have pleasure in telling you that we are now going straight to Barry Docks with the 07.10 train from here. Let's get our stuff from the left luggage.

We walked up the concourse leisurely when suddenly I saw two blue things walking towards us with a third hurrying along behind. "Do you see what I see D.S.?" I hope I'm seeing things. D.S. said "He saw what I saw". In a rather nervous voice D.S. had gone a whiter shade of pale!

Cheer up I said to D.S. as we're leaving anyway. The three musketeers advanced menacingly closer to us. D.S. and I finally came to a halt facing the firing squad. Mount Vesuvius (the 01.40 cop) was about to erupt. His face got redder and redder, his eyeballs rolled, his mouth twitched menacingly and his bushy moustache suddenly appeared jagged and bristling. He finally erupted into a fiery passion charged tirade. (He would get all the Oscars going for this out of the world acting. Got a right schizophrenic here I thought).

COP2 (the 01.40 COP) "You never intended going to Burton this morning. You deliberately missed the train." (I half expected him to start tearing his hair out). Maybe the locals obeyed the cops here and he wasn't used to the rebellious attitude taken by these two scum.

ME (I always pride myself in finding quotes to meet every situation. My retort was a bit near the bone and was short). "We decided to do a Burton."

A chain reaction like the detonation of an atom bomb went off from firstly, COP2 (01.40) then COP1 (01.20) and last of all (probably to keep up appearances) COP3 (the 02.30 cop). They were seen almost to explode.

Perhaps my answer was a little too apt; perhaps it was a chargeable offence. Luckily for us COP2 the 01.40 cop was speechless and appeared to be close to a nervous breakdown.

COP1 (the 01.20 cop) took up the running. "So you didn't go to the hostel either but went to the other waiting room. One of you is only fifteen too."

A few words from me seemed necessary to quieten them (at least the 01.20 and 01.30 cops as the 02.30 cop seemed to see the funny side of all this).

ME "We're leaving in ten minutes."

At this COP2 (the 01.40 cop) recovered to shout. "If you are in any of our waiting rooms tonight we'll get you." With that final threat he marched off with the other two cops.

Well I said to D.S. we seem to have got the last laugh and I hope that it makes up for the kickings you got from them. Glad we won't be staying here tonight. D.S. had now quite recovered from his whiter shade of pale complex and had quite enjoyed the action packed encounter. D.S. ended on a philosophical note. Probably takes a Yorkshireman to outwit a Scotsman. The Colwick shedmaster and these cops were not Yorkshiremen! How profound.

I said to D.S. that I didn't think the Midlands liked us very much after our experiences. Now at least we were leaving the Midlands, their people and their rain. Now at least we were back on timetable again with the 07.10 train to South Wales.

Our train was duly waiting for us at the main platform and after a few moments searching we found one of the through coaches for Cardiff General. We didn't want to be left at Birmingham while the rest of the train went on to Cardiff.

"D.S. goes to sleep"
"Grant gives Burton a peep"

Our train left on time at 07.10. We were lucky enough to get a compartment to ourselves. His luggage chucked up on the overhead rack D.S. curled up and promptly fell asleep. Clearly the cops had disturbed his overnight shuteye and combined with an early start he was anxious to make up lost sleep.

Goodbye Derby, good riddance cops 1, 2 and 3. 8F WD 90024 of 36C Frodingham was noted at the head of a fitted freight bound for Derby. On the approach to Burton I looked at D.S. He was out for the count and judging by the look of his tired face best not to disturb him.

A quick look at my LocoShed Directory and I noted that 16F Burton shed was on the west of the line south of the station. Somehow misinterpreting this information I decided that Burton shed was before the station. I looked and looked and was extremely disappointed to see no shed. We arrived at Burton at 07.27.

After a short stop the train continued its journey. I was more than pleased when Burton shed suddenly came into view. I made as many hieroglyphic scribbles as fast as I could of the scenery (the engines on shed). It was a great shed to see from the line. It had a roundhouse, which was semi-circular and opened on to the line. The shed yard ran parallel to the line. After the shed had whistled past it was time for a look at my notebook to decipher my scribbles and take in what had been seen on shed.

16F BURTON (pass)						
		Home shed		Built	Withdrawn	Scrap
Diesels						
Brush Type 4 Co-Co 1962						
D1622		D16	Nottingham Division	Sep-1964		
Total	1					
BR 0-6-0 Shunter 1953						
D3569		16F		Dec-1958		
D3572		16F		Jan-1959		
Total	2					
Steam				Built	Withdrawn	Scrap
Stanier 5MT 4-6-0 "Black Five" 1934						
45262		16F		Oct-1936	Aug-1968	Sep-1968
Total	1					
Johnson Midland 3F 0-6-0T 1899						
47250		16G	Westhouses	Jun-1902	Aug-1965	Dec-1965
Total	1					
Stanier 8F 2-8-0 "Big Eight" 1935						
48077		10J	Lancaster(ex 1E)	Dec-1936	Mar-1968	Jun-1968
48124		16C		Jun-1939	May-1968	Oct-1968
48271		16F		Jun-1942	Aug-1967	May-1968
48617		15E	Coalville	Nov-1943	Mar-1968	Jul-1968
48627		16C	Derby	May-1943	Mar-1966	Jun-1966
48651		16F		Nov-1943	Nov-1966	Jun-1967
48662		16F		Jul-1944	Nov-1966	May-1967
48700		16F		May-1944	Mar-1968	May-1968
Total	8					
BR 7P6F 4-6-2 "Britannia" 1951 Derby						
70022	"Tornado"	12B	Carlisle Upperby	Aug-1951	Dec-1967	Apr-1968
Total	1					

On Shed	14		Kops	13		
Steam	11		Diesels	3		
Withdrawn	0					
Home Locos	8	Home Area		3 Visitors	3	
Shed	16F	8	16C	1 16G	1	
Distribution	D16	1				
	10J	1	12B	1 15E	1	
Steam Classes	4					
Steam Origin	LMS	10	BR	1		
Shed Highlights:-						
	Steam	47250	16F Burton			
		70022	12B Carlisle Upperby			
Steam	Sep-50	108	Mar-59	89	Apr-65	34
Allocation					Aug-65	33
			Closed to Steam:-		Sep-66	
Home Steam	excluding withdrawn locos					
On/Off Shed	On Shed	5	Off Shed	28	% On Shed	18%
Not on Shed						
"Black Fives"	44825	44839	44851	44858	44941	44962
				45224	45232	45464	9
"Jinties"			47313	47464	47629	47643	4
"Big Eights"	48056	48117	48128	48194	48254	48266
	48314	48332	48367	48368	48606	48672
				48681	48690	48728	15
					total	28
			saw elsewhere on the tour		2	
			saw on Dec 64 Manchester and Crewe trip		1	
			saw on June 67 Carlisle visit		1	

Mini Review of 16F Burton

It wasn't a bad wee shed. I almost noted every engine on shed as almost every engine (or its smokebox number in the roundhouse) was completely visible. Perhaps I should have awakened D.S. to help!

Seeing 70022 "Tornado" was tremendous. I had missed seeing her at Carlisle many a time. It was amazing (in my estimation) seeing a "Brit" at Burton. Good also to see "Old Jinty" 47250 albeit very sadly en route to the scrap heap as she was to be withdrawn this month. *Strangely I don't know which scrapyard she ended up at.*

Not surprising to see only 5 Home Steam (18%) on shed with a further 28 Home Steam off shed as we passed rather than visited the shed.

On we go

D.S. was still continuing in his deep sleep so I decided against waking him up to tell him the good news of what he missed. I felt peckish so I had a look in my grip. Hello? What's this? I had found a plastic container. What's in it? I opened it to find a block of chocolate and some tomatoes. So that's what my 79 year old Grandma had put in my grip. The plastic container had acted as a miniature greenhouse and a few had swollen up and burst. That would not deter me from my vegetarian breakfast and I gobbled a few down. Rather acidic, perhaps, but rather nice.

D.S. was beginning to have contortions in his sleep so it looked as though I would have to awaken him before he did himself an injury. WD 90223 whistled past with another Derby bound fitted freight. Another 36C Frodingham loco. These WD's from Frodingham seem to have a monopoly of these freights.

I gave D.S. the necessary nudges and he awoke with his usual start. I told him of what he had missed at Burton and that I didn't like to disturb his deep sleep at the time. He was not pleased and said that I should have woken him up.

DERBY TO TAMWORTH								
			Home shed			**Built**	**Withdrawn**	**Scrap**
Steam								
Riddles WD 8F 2-8-0 "Austerity" 1943								
90024			36C	Frodingham		*Sep-1943*	*Feb-1966*	*Jun-1966*
90223			36C	Frodingham (ex 36E)		*Apr-1943*	*Aug-1965*	*Oct-1965*
Total	2							
On Line	2		Kops		2			
Steam	2		**Diesels**		0			
		Home Area			0 Visitors		2	
Shed								
Analysis	36C	2						
Steam Classes	1							
Steam Origin	WD	2						

It was now twenty to eight and we flew into Tamworth High Level to stop. Interesting story about Tamworth I said to D.S. It had banned locospotters from its platforms. I told D.S. that some old codger of about fifty had asked to see the wonderful new rebuilt station and had asked for platform tickets for himself and his companions. He had got the sneering reply from the BR official that they didn't cater for spotters and was told to remove himself and his family from the premises. "Nasty" said D.S. He wanted to know if he reported the official. Oh yes, they did I replied. The Divisional Manager at Stoke, George Dow, who was a great supporter of railway enthusiasts kicked up a fuss with the Tamworth staff and now if anybody wants to see the station a BR official (probably the same one as in the story) will graciously guide them around. Of course, the guide will probably have a sub-machine gun strapped to his side, I added. D.S. wanted to know what that would be for. He was in a querulous mood today. That question is easily answered. To shoot down any of the party who stray from the official tour and snatch down the odd loco number. Boldness and audacity would be rewarded by a round of .38 slugs.

We decided against throwing light bulbs from our compartment at the station staff in Tamworth and our train left at 07.41.

Our train made good progress through the Midlands and Castle Bromwich was reached on time at 07.56. I told D.S. to get his pen sharpened because in another five minutes we would pass 2E Saltley. D.S. and I would be visiting Saltley later in the day after we came back from Cardiff.

I checked my old companion (the LocoShed Directory) to ascertain on what side of the line Saltley was and whether we would be able to see the shed from the line! The shed according to the directory was on the east side of the line south of the station. It was only partially visible from the line. Pity! D.S. and I would have our eyes skinned nevertheless.

After Saltley Station had been passed D.S. and I had a good time scrawling down engine numbers which we saw on both sides of the line. We saw quite a few in the shed yard. Perhaps the best engine we saw was 6851 "Hurst Grange" of 2A Tyseley on the west side of the line light engine just before Saltley shed. I thought that seeing a Western region loco was terrific. Especially good was a Collett "Grange". My solitary Western region loco up to today was 6819 "Highnam Grange" which Ian "Froth" Firth and I had seen outside 5B Crewe South on our whirlwind tour of Manchester and Crewe on 12th December 1964. The Grange looked really quaint. She was shorn off her nameplates and smokebox plates. 6851 was painted on her cab where her numberplate should be. Strictly speaking 6851 was my third GWR loco as I in September 1959 travelled through to Glasgow with the purpose of seeing 3440 "City of Truro" which had travelled up for the Scottish Industries Exhibition. I spotted her outside 66A Polmadie shed on the Saturday of the exhibition to make an enjoyable day for myself. Not bad for a ten year old! 3440 was in official GWR stock at the time after being restored to working order and returned to service in 1957. She had been repainted in the old 1903 GWR livery style. Therefore I must agree on consideration that 6851 was in fact my third Western Region loco. I am straying off the track a bit with that reflection.

Our run in to Birmingham New Street was really rewarding and I could hardly wait to visit Saltley at 16.30 today.

TAMWORTH TO BIRMINGHAM NEW STREET							
		Home shed		Built	Withdrawn		Scrap
Diesels							
Brush Type 4 Co-Co 1962							
D1605		86A	Cardiff Canton	Aug-1964			
D1618		D16	Nottingham Division	Sep-1964			
D1657		87E	Landore	Feb-1965			
D1722		82A	Bristol Bath Road	Mar-1964			
Total	4						
BR 0-6-0 Shunter 1953							
D3167		2E	Saltley	Aug-1955			
D3168		2E	Saltley	Aug-1955			
Total	2						
BR Sulzer Type 2 1958							
D7518		2E	Saltley	Dec-1964			
D7571		D16	Nottingham Division	Oct-1963			
Total	2						
LMS and BR 0-6-0 Shunter 1945							
12040		2E	Saltley	Sep-1947	Oct-1968		
12059		2E	Saltley	Oct-1949	Jan-1969		
12061		2E	Saltley	Nov-1949	Oct-1971		
Total	3						
Steam							
Collett "Grange" 5MT 4-6-0 1936				Built	Withdrawn		Scrap
6851	"Hurst Grange"	2A	Tyseley	Oct-1937	Aug-1965		Jan-1966
Total	1						
Stanier 5MT 4-6-0 "Black Five" 1934							
44666		2E	Saltley	Jul-1949	Feb-1967		Sep-1967
44944		2E	Saltley	Jan-1946	Sep-1967		Feb-1968
Total	2						
Ivatt 2MT 2-6-0 "Doodle Bug" 1946							
46448		2E	Saltley	Mar-1950	May-1967		Oct-1967
46470		2A	Tyseley (ex 2L)	Jul-1951	May-1967		Oct-1967
Total	2						
Stanier 8F 2-8-0 "Big Eight" 1935							
48339		2E	Saltley	Jan-1944	Oct-1966		Jan-1967
48375		2F	Bescot	Nov-1944	Sep-1967		Apr-1968
48471		6D	Shrewsbury	Apr-1945	May-1968		Sep-1968
Total	3						
BR 9F 2-10-0 Brighton 1954							
92029	Crosti	boilered 2E	Saltley	Apr-1955	Nov-1967		Feb-1968
Total	1						

TAMWORTH TO BIRMINGHAM NEW STREET (continued)						
On Line	20		Kops	18		
Steam	9		Diesels	11		
		Home Area		14 Visitors		6
Shed Analysis	2A	2	2E	11	2F	1
	6D	1	D16	2		
	82A	1	86A	1	87E	1
Steam Classes	5					
Steam Origin	GWR	1	LMS	7	BR	1
Line Highlight	6851	"Hurst Grange"	2A		Tyseley	

Shed/ Yard review of 2E Saltley Area

You can imagine my disgust and consternation on returning home after the trip and looking at the latest list of withdrawals that 6851 "Hurst Grange" had been withdrawn. She must have been on one of her last runs when we saw her very much alive.

It was interesting to see the ex-Crosti boilered 9F 92029 at Saltley. She was quite different from her less interestingly featured sisters. A few Western Region based Brush Type 4's were also noted. We would see some more at 86A Cardiff Canton this afternoon.

		Schedule	Actual	Miles
Depart	DERBY MIDLAND	07.10	07.10	0
Arrive	BURTON ON TRENT	07.27	07.27	11
	See 16F Burton			
Arrive	TAMWORTH	07.41	07.41	24
Arrive	BIRMINGHAM NEW STREET	08.08	08.08	41

On we go

We thundered into Birmingham New Street exactly on time at 08.08. So this is where we are sleeping tonight I said to D.S. looking at the ruins of Birmingham New Street Station. They fairly like to demolish the old before starting on the "new" New Street (sorry about the pun!). What a dump! Can't say I fancy sleeping the night here! I can't even see a waiting room. They might have knocked that down too. Like another Bletchley with no waiting room pending modernisation I said to D.S.! Hope not! There's always a wooden bench over there for you to sleep on I said to D.S. pointing out one through the carriage window. Looks comfy for you, Eh!

After our Cardiff tour we'll be back here at New Street at 16.30 to start our whiz Brum district tour. Thought you might like to know where we are going D.S.! I said to D.S. that he'll be pleased to hear that he'll have to stump up something like a quid (£1) of cash on this journey. We are travelling past the outer limits of our LMR Railrover. So your Barry Docks journey is going to cost you a bit of dosh. At this D.S. was really hurt as he said that there wasn't a lot of money in his wallet but he could squeeze out the necessary dosh. We were making this valuable 8 hours and 22 minutes of precious daylight to visit only two sheds in Cardiff (Canton and East Dock). But there was also Barry Docks the *raison d'etre* of our visit.

It was soon blast off time and our through coaches had been hitched to the back of the Cardiff express. Just as well we aren't going from Birmingham Snow Hill to Cardiff. It's one of the slowest routes (inter-city) on BR. A train left Snow Hill at 08.05 but would not arrive at Cardiff general until 11.26 (fully an hour after we arrive there via this train).

We left Birmingham New Street at 08.15 (on time)! Our train sped past Selly Oak. I told D.S. that there was a useful horse racing sprinter called Selly Oak. D.S. was not too impressed. Past Bournville our train sped. I told D.S. that was another name with a story. "Another horse?" D.S. inquired. Not this time. That's where Cadbury has their chocolate factory and more to your interest their used to be a wee shed here on the west side of the line. Its shedcode was 21B Bournville whereas Saltley was 21A. Can't say we saw much evidence of the shed (which closed in 1960) as we passed.

Doodle Bug Ivatt 2MT 2-6-0 46492 of 2J Aston was noted light engine. D375 of 1B Camden was also noted at the head of a Birmingham bound passenger train.

This stretch of line to Blackwell was fruitful. "Big Eight" 48412 of 2C Stourbridge was gratefully noted particularly as we had had to cut 2C Stourbridge out of the final timetable. Standard 76038 of 2E Saltley was also noted along with D7595 of ML (Derby Division). All a bit much for D.S. who curled up and fell asleep again. 9F 2-10-0 92223 of 2A Tyseley sped past on freight. Here was another locomotive with a story. 92223 was the first BR 9F 2-10-0 to be withdrawn. She was withdrawn from some dirty depot in the Western Region. Everyone thought it was ridiculous withdrawing an engine just over five years old. The LMR would not have this Western Region wastefulness ant took over the loco, resuscitated it and allocated it to 2A Tyseley a few months ago. After 92223 a few of her sisters were also withdrawn from Western Region depots. Unfortunately they had not been so lucky and had stayed withdrawn although my Peterborough friend mentioned in Saturday's tome had said that the LMR would take over the ones withdrawn from 81C Southall.

"Grant sees his first Hall"
"D.S. isn't on the ball"

I peered out of the window and to my joy saw a mainline Western Region steam loco coming towards us at the head of a medium sized freight. A glance at the painted number on the cabside and it was 7907 as it sped past us. It was "Hart Hall!" My first "Hall!" I awoke D.S. to tell him the good news of what he had missed. He was rather annoyed at missing a "Hall" and resolved to stay awake from now on. "Hart Hall" was allocated to 82E Bristol Barrow Road. At one time Barrow Road used to have an allocation of about thirty LMR engines but no WR locos. Since Bristol Bath Road was dieselised however (made into one of the new WR diesel maintenance depots) the steam locos had to be shoved elsewhere. So Bristol Barrow Road (82E) changed from being an entirely LMS shed (housing Jubilees etc.) to a great WR steam stronghold housing Halls, Granges and a few Castles.

What was the last station that we saw I said to D.S.? Blackwell he answered. So we are at the top of the famous Lickey Incline. Stand by for action. Then I remembered that there was a strict speed limit on trains descending the Lickey. So there wouldn't be too much action at least at speed. Banking locos at the bottom of the incline were worth looking for though. First of all the WR had said that they would use Hymek Type 3 diesels (some locos of the class D7000-D7100) for all banking duties. The WR may well have changed their minds because a Modern Railways correspondent had noted only English Electric Type 3's on banking duties.

On our trip down the Lickey we indeed saw three English Electric Type 3's (D6941, D6943 and D6944 all of 86A Cardiff Canton). They were in different short sidings presumably awaiting their banking duty turns to assist trains up the incline.

This famed incline had used some big banking engines over the years. The big ones were 33 2-6-6-2 Beyer Garratts (tractive effort 45,620 lbs) which were all withdrawn by 1958. The most famous one was perhaps the 1919 Midland Region 0-10-0 58100 (tractive effort 43,315 lbs). An interesting note is that no power classification was given to these monsters. Even the LNER giant 69999 (the biggest loco ever on BR) had a luckless spell on the Lickey before she was sent packing back to the LNER in disgrace.

D.S. was beginning to look dangerously rundown so I thought he might need some sustenance. After all the timetable showed by its teacup sign that this train had a miniature buffet car.

D.S. seemed to think that this was about the best thing I had said all day and needed no persuasion to retire to the miniature buffet car.

The train was fairly belting along now and we felt quite chuffed at reaching the buffet car without serious mishap as the train lurched from side to side.

"that was my coffee that was"
"it's spilt let it be"

D.S. said that he would take a coffee for a change instead of his normal tea. He must think that he needs a stimulant to keep him awake. Perhaps he had eyed the reasonably sized coffee cups and the fact that the attendant had filled my coffee cup to the brim. D.S. and I thought that the coffee was good value with good service for 9 pence (4 new pence each).

Then the train shakes struck. Our driver up front was doing a fast speed and keeping a cup of coffee steady was impossible as we tried to move over to a table. The carriage gave another violent lurch and before I knew it half of my coffee was in the saucer. D.S. was not doing appreciably better with his cup. Another violent lurch and I was pleased to see that no more of my coffee had spilt over. However, none remained in the saucer. A little had spilt over on to the floor but the majority had splashed on to my sleeve much to my disgust.

With superhuman lunges we reached seats and what we took to be safety. No wonder BR can afford to be so generous with their coffee on this journey. No one ever gets to drink all of it and the full cups must be some sort of joke for the buffet car attendant. When the journey's over the slippery floor is probably an inch deep in coffee, which presumably they scrape up again and redistill for more soon to be unlucky customers. Oh yes there are no flies on BR. No wonder the attendant was smiling (and controlling his mirth) at our antics as we tried to reach seats safely. I'll say this, however, what coffee was actually left in our cups was really very good. It may have been pure ground coffee. But was it worth it? You weren't even safe when you were seated, as you still had to escape further lurches when you picked the cup up to drink the coffee!

Rather disconcerting that coffee escapade. D.S. and I decided against buying further cups of coffee for fear of the consequences. However, D.S. bought one of their exorbitantly priced sandwiches. I refrained on moral reasons. Who is going to pay one shilling (5 new pence) for that angrily glaring at D.S.'s measly sandwich? As D.S. ate we noted what we thought to be a "Hall" speeding by. Unfortunately we could not make out the number. Not to be outdone I saw another railwayist further up the buffet car. He had a little notebook in front of him and the Hall had passes right by his nose He must have seen it!

ME: - "Excuse me, did you get the number of the "Hall" which just passed."
RAILWAYIST: - "You mean the "Manor"."
ME: - (Stupid me can't seem to be able to tell a Manor from a Hall). "That's right."
RAILWAYIST: - "It was 7816 "Frilsham Manor"."
ME: - "Ta!"

Looking up my LocoShed book I saw that she came from 85B Gloucester. That was our first "Manor" that was! Now for my first "Castle" and my first "King"! The former should be fulfilled as we passed Gloucester shed while we would have to wait for Barry Docks hopefully for our first (and second) King so long as the scrapbreaker had not been up to his tricks.

D.S. and I retired from the buffet and went back to our compartment. We soon spotted Brush Type 4 D1583 of 86A Cardiff Canton. A Western Region Brush Type 4 was rostered to haul the Milford Haven – Thornton Yard (Esso Oil train) from South Wales-Scotland. I saw D1583 off that train on Sunday 16th May 1965 at 64A St.Margarets shed. The first recorded instance of this oil train was on 2nd April 1965 although a few other correspondents had noted the train in late March. The oil train had brought fever pitched excitement Musselburgh railwayists for a few months. Everyone had thought it was great seeing Western Region Brushes well off their beaten track. D.S. had also been with me at 64A St.Margarets that Sunday.

We noted English Electric Type D6940 of 86A Cardiff Canton. Probably another one that was used for Lickey Incline banking duties. We rolled into Cheltenham Spa Lansdown Station on time at 09.03. To greet us we noted Brush Type 4 D1613 of 82A Bristol Bath Road and two 85B Gloucester 0-6-0 Diesel Shunters D3990 and D3993.

After a quick stop at Cheltenham we were off again. We noted Brush Type 4 D1660 whistling past at the head of an express passenger train. It had recently been named "City of Truro". All the named Brushes were on the Western Region. This Brush had the same name as 3440, which I had seen in Glasgow in 1959 at the Scottish Industries Exhibition.

Now where was 85B Gloucester going to appear from? The shed directory was rather vague. Gloucester had two stations Eastgate and Central and I understood that we passed the shed before Eastgate. I thought of a solution to where 85B Gloucester was and went back to the buffet car and checked with the railwayist. I bustled back to our compartment and told D.S. the good news. He wanted to know how I found out. I thought I would pull D.S.'s leg and told him I went to the guards van and asked the guard who offered to phone up the 85B shedmaster to find out. D.S. admitted not knowing that guard's vans had phones.

BIRMINGHAM TO GLOUCESTER						
		Home shed		Built	Withdrawn	Scrap
Diesels						
English Electric Type 4 1Co-Co1 1958						
D 375		1B	Camden	Feb-1962		
Total	1					
Brush Type 4 Co-Co 1962						
D1583		86A	Cardiff Canton	May-1964		
D1613		82A	Bristol (Bath Road)	Sep-1964		
D1660	"City of Truro"	87E	Landore	Mar-1965		
Total	3					
BR 0-6-0 Shunter 1953 English Electric engine						
D3990		85B	Gloucester (Horton Rd.)	Sep-1960		
D3993		85B	Gloucester (Horton Rd.)	Sep-1960		
Total	2					
English Electric Type 3 Co-Co 1961						
D6940		86A	Cardiff Canton	Sep-1964		
D6941		86A	Cardiff Canton	Sep-1964		
D6943		86A	Cardiff Canton	Oct-1964		
D6944		86A	Cardiff Canton	Oct-1964		
Total	4					
BR Sulzer Type 2 Bo-Bo 1958						
D7595		ML	Midland Lines	Jun-1964		
Total	1					

BIRMINGHAM TO GLOUCESTER(continued)

Steam					Built	Withdrawn	Scrap
Hawksworth 5MT 4-6-0 "Modified Hall" 6959 1944							
7907	"Hart Hall"		82E	Bristol Barrow Road	Jan-1939	Nov-1965	Feb-1966
Total		1					
Collett 5MT 7800 4-6-0 "Manor" 1938							
7816	"Frilsham Manor"		85B	Gloucester Horton Rd.(e	Jan-1950	Dec-1965	Jul-1966
Total		1					
Ivatt 2MT 2-6-0 1946							
46492			2J	Aston	Dec-1951	Jun-1967	Feb-1968
Total		1					
Stanier 8F 2-8-0 "Big Eight" 1935							
48412			2C	Stourbridge Jct.	Oct-1943	Dec-1966	Jun-1967
Total		1					
BR Standard 4MT 2-6-0 Doncaster 1953							
76038			2E	Saltley	Jul-1954	Sep-1966	Dec-1966
Total		1					
BR Standard 9F 2-10-0 Brighton 1954. 1957 double chimney							
92223	double chimney		2A	Tyseley	Jun-1958	Apr-1968	Sep-1968
Total		1					
On Line		17	Kops	15			
Steam		6	Diesels	11			

		Home Area			7	Visitors		10
Shed Analysis		2A	1	2C	1	2E		1
		2J	1					
		1B	1	ML	1			
		82A	1	82E	1	85B		3
		86A	5	87E	1			
Steam Classes		6						
Steam Origin		GWR	2	LMS	2	BR		2

Pens at the ready in anticipation our train neared the outskirts of Gloucester. The shed duly appeared at the north side of the line. I scanned the yard and almost froze with excitement at seeing three Castles. I picked out a number. It looked rusty at the distance (she still had its brass numberplate). The ghostly number was 7034. The numbers of the other two Castles were also hard to discern.

85B GLOUCESTER (pass)

			Home shed		Built	Withdrawn	Scrap
Diesels							
Brush Type 4 Co-Co 1962							
D1604			86A	Cardiff Canton	Aug-1964		
D1645			87E	Landore	Jan-1965		
Total		2					
Steam					Built	Withdrawn	Scrap
Collett 3F 5700 Class 0-6-0PT 1933							
3643			85B		Oct-1939	Nov-1965	Feb-1966
Total		1					
Collett 7P 4073 Class "Castle" 4-6-0 1923							
5042	"Winchester Castle"		85B		Jul-1935	Jun-1965	Oct-1965
7022	"Hereford Castle"		85B		Jun-1949	Jun-1965	Sep-1965
7034	"Ince Castle"		85B		Aug-1950	Jun-1965	Sep-1965
Total		3					
Hawksworth 5MT 6959 Class "Modified Hall" 4-6-0 1944							
7927	"Willington Hall"		86B	Newport Ebbw Jct.	Oct-1950	Dec-1965	saved
Total		1					
BR Standard 3MT 2-6-2T Swindon 1952							
82040			85B	(ex 83D Exmouth Jct.)	May-1955	Jul-1965	Nov-1965
82042			85B	(ex 83D Exmouth Jct.)	Jun-1955	Aug-1965	Feb-1966
Total		2					
BR Standard 9F 2-10-0 Brighton 1954							
92000	double	chimney	85B		Jan-1954	Jul-1965	Nov-1965
Total		1					

85B GLOUCESTER (pass)

On Shed	10	Kops	9		
Steam	8	Diesels	2		
Withdrawn	5				

Home Locos	8 Home Area			0 Visitors	2
Shed Analysis	85B	8			
	86A	1 86B		1 87E	1
Steam Classes	5				
Steam Origin	GWR	5 BR	3		
Shed Highlight:-	7034 "Ince Castle"		85B	Gloucester	

Steam	Aug-50	99	Mar-59	84	May-65	33
Allocation					Aug-65	23
			Closed to Steam:-		Dec-65	

Home Steam	excluding withdrawn locos					
On/Off Shed	On Shed	2 Off Shed	21 % On Shed	10%		
Not on Shed						
3F 5700 0-6-0PT 1933	3616	3675	3759	3775	4689	7
				4698	8745	
4MT 5101 2-6-2T 1929					4100	1
4MT 6100 2-6-2T 1931				6113	6160	2
"Castle"					7029	1
"Manor"		7808	7814	7816	7829	4
Midland 4F 0-6-0 1924					44560	1
BR 2MT 2-6-0 1953			78001	78004	78006	3
BR 3MT 2-6-2T 1952				82030	82044	2
					total	21

saw elsewhere on the tour	2		
saw at Barry Docks revisited Aug 70	3		
recently withdrawn not on shed or seen elsewhere	7		scrap
Collett 3MT 2251 0-6-0 1930		2242	Aug-65
		2287	Sep-65
Midland 4F 0-6-0 1924		44123	to Barry
		44422	to Barry
BR 5MT 4-6-0 1951		73091	Aug-65
BR 3MT 2-6-2T 1952		82039	Nov-65

Mini Review of 85B Gloucester (Horton Road)

Great seeing the three Castles but very sad that they were all withdrawn. D1604 had earlier been seen by me on 13th June 1965 off the Milford Haven oil train at St.Margarets.

Only four "Castles" remained all allocated to 85B Gloucester. Seeing three of them was really good albeit they were withdrawn. The only "Castle" not withdrawn was 7029 "Clun Castle" and judging by recent reports was still in "good nick". She was absent or hidden inside the shed today. *7927 "Willington Hall" would eventually end up at Barry Docks. Although later saved nowadays the loco is to be used to provide parts for the project to build a new "County" and a new "Grange" – both classes which are sadly extinct.*

It was particularly good seeing 92000 the founder member of the BR 9F 2-10-0's but again she was disappointingly withdrawn. This Class designed at Brighton had been introduced in 1954.

In all what lacked in quantity certainly was compensated by quality.

On we go

Our train arrived at Gloucester Central at 09.16. After a few minutes we were off again. A glance at my map and I reckoned that there was barely anything to raise the blood pressure other than 86E Severn Tunnel Junction. Unfortunately on further inspection it seemed that we would take the avoiding line past Severn Tunnel Junction. We would look out at the appropriate time after Chepstow and hope.

D.S. disappeared up the train and guess that came to visit me – the ticket collector. Now for a bit of explaining. I first showed him my Railrover ticket and said that we would have to pay the Western region part of the journey and would need two-day returns for that part. The price turned out to be twenty three shillings and six pence each (£1.17 and a half new pence). I stumped up the money and he gave me two white queer looking break of journey tickets. They looked good enough for travel though. When D.S. came back I asked him for 23/6d. At this D.S. got very angry. "What di ye want if fir" he said. I told him and he stumped up for his little white scrap of paper.

Our journey to Newport was remarkable but not surprising. We didn't see Severn Tunnel Junction. On the journey we saw English Electric Type 3's D6881 of 86A Cardiff Canton and D6884 of 87E Landore. After seeing the Type 3's we saw another Modified Hall 7915 "Mere Hall" of 2A Tyseley on a freight. Good! Brush Type 4 D1609 of 86A Cardiff Canton was also noted speeding by. Of particular interest was seeing D1018 "Western Buccaneer" of 87E Landore on an express.   Another RED "Western".   Where had all the green ones gone? Nearing Newport we saw English Electric Type 3's D6824, D6835, D6867 and D6877 all of 86A Cardiff Canton. Yet another RED Western D1017"Western Warrior" was noted by us on another express.   On the outskirts of Newport Station 57XX 0-6-0 PT 9675 of 86B Newport Ebbw Junction was gratefully noted. D1677 of 86A Cardiff Canton flew out of Newport Station just as we entered it.

The rather surprising sight of Warship D854 "Tiger" greeted us in Newport station. I thought that they stayed on the London-Bristol-Devon runs these days. Not complaining though. We departed on time at 10.05. At Godfrey Road diesel depot outside the station we saw diesel shunter D3817 of 86B Newport, and English Electric Type 3's D6866 and D6879 of 86A Cardiff Canton.

A busy fifteen minutes ensued on the very busy line to Cardiff General. Yards lined both sides of the line from time to time. The south side of the line was generally the most interesting. Steam seems to have practically ended in South Wales but we did see 6872 "Crawley Grange" of 85A Worcester (ex 88A Cardiff East Dock) – probably en route to her new shed.

We arrived at Cardiff General a few minutes late at 10.23 rather than 10.20. "Tiger" had been there to greet us at Newport now it was "Odin's" turn to greet us. "Odin" however was a Brush Type 4 D1666 rather than a Warship. Another named Western Region Brush!

					Built	Withdrawn	Scrap
GLOUCESTER TO CARDIFF							
			Home shed				
Diesels							
BR Sulzer "Peak" Type 4 1Co-Co1 1959							
D 23	*hauled*		55A	Leeds Holbeck	*Apr-1961*		
Total	1						
North British "Warship" Type 4 B-B 1958							
D 854	"Tiger"		83A	Newton Abbot	*Sep-1961*	*Oct-1971*	
Total	1						
"Western" BR Type 4 C-C 1961							
D1017	"Western Warrior"		87E	Landore	*Mar-1963*	*Aug-1973*	
D1018	"Western Buccaneer"		87E	Landore	*Apr-1963*	*Jun-1973*	
Total	2						
Brush Type 4 Co-Co 1962							
D1609			86A	Cardiff Canton	*Aug-1964*		
D1646			87E	Landore	*Jan-1965*		
D1666	"Odin"		87E	Landore	*Mar-1965*		
D1677			86A	Cardiff Canton	*May-1965*		
D1730			82A	Bristol Bath Road (ex 8(	*Apr-1964*		
Total	5						

		Home shed		Built	Withdrawn	Scrap
BR 0-6-0 Shunter 1953 English Electric engine						
D3103		86E	Severn Tunnel Jct.	*Feb-1955*		
D3104		86E	Severn Tunnel Jct.	*Feb-1955*		
Total	*2*					
BR 0-6-0 Shunter 1953 English Electric engine						
D3190		86E	Severn Tunnel Jct.	*Nov-1955*		
D3256		86A	Cardiff Canton	*Jun-1956*		
D3260		86A	Cardiff Canton	*Jun-1956*		
D3594		86A	Cardiff Canton	*Sep-1958*		
D3607		86A	Cardiff Canton	*Nov-1958*		
D3807		86A	Cardiff Canton	*Dec-1958*		
D3817		86B	Newport Ebbw Jct.	*Mar-1959*		
Total	*7*					
English Electric Type 3 Co-Co 1961						
D6824		86A	Cardiff Canton	*May-1963*		
D6835		86A	Cardiff Canton	*Apr-1963*		
D6866		86A	Cardiff Canton	*Sep-1963*		
D6867		86A	Cardiff Canton	*Sep-1963*		
D6877		86A	Cardiff Canton	*Oct-1963*		
D6879		86A	Cardiff Canton	*Oct-1963*		
D6881		86A	Cardiff Canton	*Oct-1963*		
D6884		87E	Landore	*Nov-1963*		
D6904		86A	Cardiff Canton	*Nov-1963*		
D6911		87E	Landore	*Jan-1964*		
D6983		86A	Cardiff Canton	*May-1965*		
Total	*11*					
BR 0-6-0 Shunter 1948						
15102		86A	Cardiff Canton	*Apr-1948*	*Jul-1967*	
Total	*1*					
Steam				**Built**	**Withdrawn**	**Scrap**
Collett 3F 0-6-0PT 5700 1933						
9675		86B	Newport Ebbw (ex85B)	*Mar-1949*	*Oct-1965*	*Dec-1965*
Total	*1*					
Collett 5MT 4-6-0 6800 "Grange" 1936						
6872	"Crawley Grange"	85A	Worcester (ex 88A)	*Mar-1939*	*Dec-1965*	*May-1966*
Total	*1*					
Hawksworth 5MT 4-6-0 6959 Class 1944						
7915	"Mere Hall"	2A	Tyseley	*Mar-1950*	*Oct-1965*	*Jan-1966*
Total	*1*					

On Line	33	**Kops**		33		
Steam	3	**Diesels**		30		

	Home Area			23	**Visitors**	10
Shed	2A	1	55A	1		
Distribution	82A	1	83A	1	85A	1
	86A	18	86B	1	86E	3
	87E	6				
Steam Classes	3					
Steam Origin	GWR	3				

I went up to the head of our train after we bundled ourselves out and was surprised to find a 55A Leeds Holbeck "Peak". It was D23. She was a common sight on the St.Pancras-Edinburgh Waverley express. D.S. was so annoyed he refused to record the number. He had expected a Bristol Peak or at least a Midland Peak at the worst. Nevertheless she gave us a good run from Derby. Amazing how these Holbeck diesels wander. Changed days now that all loco boundaries appear to have been removed with the diesels.

		Schedule	Actual	Miles
Depart	BIRMINGHAM NEW STREET	08.15	08.15	0
Arrive	CHELTENHAM SPA LANSDOWN	09.03	09.03	45¼
Arrive	GLOUCESTER EASTGATE	09.16	09.17	51¾
	See 85B Gloucester			
Arrive	NEWPORT	10.03	10.05	96¼
Arrive	CARDIFF GENERAL	10.20	10.23	108

"One Welsh Nationalist has a laugh"

To get rid of our luggage was number one on our list. I asked a little porter where the left luggage was. The terrier said it was downstairs first on the right.

D.S. and I duly followed his directions and came across a door marked "police". Funny peculiar. Curiously we pushed the door open. Inside we rang the service bell. Certainly didn't look like a left luggage office. Who came through the door to greet us but a bloody railway cop. I told him that the porter had told me that this was the left luggage office. At this we promptly made a hasty exit leaving a bewildered cop wondering if he was being had. D.S. opined "If I see that porter again I'll kick his head in". That little Welsh Nationalist porter must be killing himself laughing now!

D.S. and I after a little further searching around the concourse duly found the left luggage office and deposited our luggage. Our train to Barry was at 10.38. We went to buy our tickets. On our tickets we noted that it was a day return to Barry Island (including all intermediate stops).

Back on the main concourse we found stacks of people waiting for the Barry train. Our train appeared five minutes late. It was a two coach diesel bucket. There was a scramble to get into the packed carriages and D.S. and I ended up standing up.

86A Cardiff Canton shed was on the south side of the main line west of Cardiff General Station so we would be ready for that. We would visit Canton when we got back from Barry and do 88A Cardiff East Dock as well.

Our bucket left at about 10.45. Straight away Canton shed loomed up and we had a great time pushing and shoving people around to get the best possible view.

86A CARDIFF CANTON		Home shed		Built	Withdrawn	Scrap
Diesels						
"Western" BR Type 4 C-C 1961						
D1060	"Western Dominion"	87E	Landore	Apr-1963	Nov-1973	
Total	1					
BR 0-6-0 Shunter 1953						
D3263		86A		Jul-1956		
D3265		86A		Aug-1956		
D3747		86A		Jul-1959		
D3748		86A		Jul-1959		
D3823		86A		Apr-1959		
Total	5					
English Electric Type 3 Co-Co 1961						
D6900		86A		Oct-1963		
D6919		87E	Landore	Jan-1964		
Total	2					
Hymek Type 3 B-B 1961						
D7033		86A		May-1962	Jan-1972	
D7034		86A		May-1962	Jan-1972	
Total	2					
BR 0-6-0 Diesel Shunter 1948						
15101		86A		Apr-1948	Aug-1967	
Total	1					
On Shed	11	Kops	11			
Steam	0	Diesels	11			

86A CARDIFF CANTON(Continued)							
Home Locos		9 Home Area			0 Visitors		2
Shed	86A	9					
Analysis	87E	2					
Shed Highlight:-							
	D1060	"Western Domination" of 87E Landore					
Steam	Aug-50	105	Mar-59		131	May-65	0
Allocation						Jul-65	0
				Closed to Steam:-		Sep-62	

Mini Review of 86A Cardiff Canton

Another RED "Western" noted along with seeing my first two Hymeks (a reliable class but fated to disappear relatively early when all hydraulics were given the death card).

On we go

Our journey was to be a short one of 25 minutes and the time passed quickly enough. Barry Docks station came up quicker than anticipated and we bundled ourselves out. Out the station we went and looked for the engines and looked and looked and looked. Neil Woodcock had told me that you could see the locos from the station. Who was he trying to kid? D.S. and I walked down the road to the Docks climbed up a few grassy inclines and looked and looked and saw nothing. Had they all been scrapped? Hardly. I half expected someone to shout August fool and the engines to mysteriously appear.

I saw what I took to be a dock worker coming along the road and I asked him. The engines? He said. You've got a bit to go. They're another half mile or mile along. Just keep following this road and you'll see them at the top of a grass bank.

		Schedule	Actual	Miles
Depart	CARDIFF GENERAL	10.38	10.38	0
Arrive	BARRY	11.06	11.06	11

Well at least they hadn't disappeared. How come Barry Dock's station is half a mile from the engines? This doesn't tie in with Neil Woodcock's statement. We must have got off at the wrong station! What's the station we had got off at then? No prizes for guessing – Barry.

We miss a couple of line while we felt sick.

Now the long walk to Barry Docks and the engines. Worth it though. D.S. and I made the walk in ten to fifteen minutes climbed up an incline and there indeed was the "Works" section. A look down into the "valley" and slightly further to the west at a lower level was the "Docks" section of the scrapyard. To the north was Barry station where we had come from with Barry Docks Station further west.

It was a lovely day. Just the weather for tramping around. If anything it might be a little too bright for really first class photography with an unadjustable camera. The prints of the locos might come out with the locos features showing undesirable reflections. I wouldn't worry too much about that though. What was important was that we had arrived!

The great thing about Barry is that there are no nasty shedmasters to bar the entrance or railway cops to chase you about. D.S. and I had been given a lesson from Neil Woodcock on how to get the numberplate of Western Region engines devoid of brass cab side and smokebox numberplates. Apparently, the number was stamped on the centre of the middle driving wheel. Easy when you know how!

This "Works" section of the scrapyard with its shoulder high grass surrounding the engines could only be called ALCATRAZ WITHOUT BARS. (If you haven't heard of Alcatraz you should be sent there to teach you a lesson). After battling through the grass jungle we saw hordes of decaying engines quietly rusting away. This struggle seems to have been worth it!

The first engine we actually saw was a Southern Region S15 30841 with smoke deflectors. As we weaved our way up the lines slowly we blinked down at the driving wheels to pick up the Western Region numbers. We ambled past Halls, Castles, Churchward 2-8-0's, two ex Somerset and Dorset Railway 2-8-0 7F's, 2 Jubilees, 56XX locos, 43XX locos and a host of other SR and GWR stock.

We seemed to dawdle around (just stupefied by the mass of terrific locos). It was as though the engines were in a poppy field and everyone was overcome by the smell of opium. D.S. had time or rather made time to take four photographs in the "Works" section:-

S15   30841 4-6-0 SR
51XX   5199 2-6-2T GWR
"Maindy Hall"   4942 4-6-0 GWR
"Thornbury Castle" 7027 4-6-0 GWR

Now for the "Docks" section of the scrapyard. I glanced at my watch. It was now 12.15 and regrettably we would have to push on if we were to get back and get East Dock and Canton done.

We left the "Works" section behind and climbed down the embankment and we were struck by the strange sight of an odd little man hacking away at a Pannier tank with an oxyacetylene burner. Only one man seemed to be working on scrapping. Thankfully, it would take them about fifty years to get all the locos in Barry cut up at this rate I thought.

D.S. and I enquired from the man what the loco number was. Surprisingly he knew. It was 5794 which was a 57XX Class 0-6-0 Pannier tank. Having paid our last respects we walked the short journey to the "Docks" section of the scrapyard. It now looked as though the 13.10 back to Cardiff would be the first bucket, which we would be able to catch.

The "Docks" section had its own unique different types of locos on show. We noted many interesting classes: - GWR 43XX, 45XX, 42XX, 56XX, 57XX and two more Halls. Southern Region Pacifics West Country and Battle of Britain (mostly unrebuilt) were particular highlights along with four rebuilt SR Merchant Navies. Some oddments were a SR Q class member and another S15 4-6-0. To represent the decline of modern steam power were two 9F 2-10-0's.

The complete highlight of the Docks section was when we came across the two Kings 6023 and 6024, which were almost at the end of the Docks section.

D.S. got out his little camera again and photographed a West Country SR Pacific, a Battle of Britain Pacific and one of the Kings.

I looked around for D.S. and he was gone. After a five minute search I found him contemplating a Churchward 2-8-0 3862. She was well away from the other locos. D.S. said that the light might give him some trouble for his photo but took one anyway.

30841
Maunsell 1936 development of Urie 1920
6F S15 4-6-0 (with smoke deflectors)

5199
Collett 4MT 5101 2-6-2T 1929 rebuild
of Churchward 3100 Class

7027 "Thornbury Castle"
Collett 7P 4073 4-6-0 "Castle" 1923

4929 "Maindy Hall"
Collett 5MT 4900 4-6-0 "Hall" 1928

34092 "City of Wells"
Bulleid 7P5F "West Country" Class 4-6-2 1945

34070 "Manston"
Bulleid 7P5F "Battle of Britain" Class 4-6-2 1945

6023 "King Edward II "
Collett 8P 6000 4-6-0 "King" 1927

3862
Collett dev. 1938 of Churchward 8F 2-8-0 1903

BARRY DOCKS TUESDAY 3RD AUGUST 1965

	First Built	Date Withdrawn	1959/first Shed	Last Shed at Withdraw	Arrived Barry	Left Barry	Dep No
Steam							
Churchward 8F 2800 2-8-0 1903							
2807	May-1905	Mar-1963	83A Newton Abbot	86E Severn Tun. Jct.	Nov-63	Jun-81	130
2857	Apr-1918	Apr-1963	84B Oxley	86G Pontypool Road	Sep-63	Aug-75	69
2859	May-1918	Dec-1964	84B Oxley	88A Cardiff East Dock	Mar-65	Oct-87	193
2861	May-1918	Mar-1963	86E Severn Tun. Jct.	86E Severn Tun. Jct.	Nov-63	?	194
2873	Nov-1918	Dec-1964	86E Severn Tun. Jct.	81C Southall	Feb-65	?	195
2874	Nov-1918	May-1963	86C Cardiff Canton	87A Neath	Jul-63	Aug-87	191
Total							6
Collett dev.1938 of Churchward 8F 2-8-0 2800 1903							
2885	Mar-1938	Jan-1964	84E Tyseley	86E Severn Tun. Jct.	Mar-64	Mar-81	123
3803	Jan-1939	Jul-1963	85B Gloucester	86E Severn Tun. Jct.	Nov-63	Nov-83	149
3814	Mar-1940	Dec-1964	81F Oxford	81E Didcot	Feb-65	Jul-86	176
3822	Apr-1940	Jan-1964	86G Pontypool Road	88A Cardiff East Dock	Jul-64	May-76	80
3845	Apr-1942	Jun-1964	86C Cardiff Canton	2D Banbury	Sep-64	?	196
3862	Nov-1942	Feb-1965	83D Laira(Plymouth)	6C Croes Newydd	Jul-65	?	197
Total							6
Collett 7P 4073 4-6-0 "Castle" 1923							
5029 "Nunney Castle"	May-1934	Dec-1963	85A Worcester	88A Cardiff East Dock	May-64	May-76	81
5043 "Earl of Mount Edgcumbe"	Mar-1936	Dec-1963	81A Old Oak Common	88A Cardiff East Dock	Jun-64	Aug-73	43
5051 "Earl Bathurst"	May-1936	May-1963	87E Landore	87F Llanelly	Oct-63	Feb-70	4
5080 "Defiant"	May-1939	Apr-1963	87G Carmarthen	87F Llanelly	Oct-63	Aug-74	62
7027 "Thornbury Castle"	Aug-1949	Dec-1963	81A Old Oak Common	81D Reading	May-64	Aug-72	23
Total							5
Churchward 7F 4200 2-8-0T 1910							
4247	Mar-1916	Apr-1964	86A Newport(Ebbw Jct.)	86F Tondu	Aug-64	Apr-85	161
4248	Apr-1916	May-1963	86A Newport(Ebbw Jct.)	86E Severn Tun. Jct.	Nov-63	May-86	172
4253	Mar-1917	Apr-1963	86B Newport(Pill)	86B Newport (Pill)	Aug-63	Aug-87	190
4270	Dec-1919	Sep-1962	86C Cardiff Canton	88A Cardiff Canton	Aug-63	Jul-85	167
4277	Apr-1920	Jun-1964	86H Aberbeeg	86H Aberbeeg	Aug-64	Jun-86	173
Total							5

BARRY DOCKS TUESDAY 3RD AUGUST 1965(continued)

	First Built	Date Withdrawn	1959/first Shed	Last Shed at Withdrawal	Arrived Barry	Left Barry	Dep No
Churchward 1923 5205 8F dev. of Churchward 7F 4200 2-8-0T 1910							
5224	May-1924	Apr-1963	86E Severn Tun. Jct.	88L Cardiff East Dock	Aug-63	Oct-78	96
5227	Jun-1924	Feb-1963	86A Newport(Ebbw Jct.)	86A Ebbw Junction	Nov-63	?	199
5239	Aug-1924	Apr-1963	87A Neath	87A Neath	Nov-63	Jun-73	42
Total							3
Churchward 4MT 2-6-0 4300 1911							
5322	Aug-1917	Apr-1964	81D Reading	86G Pontypool Road	Nov-64	Mar-69	3
Total							1
1932 dev. of Churchward 4MT 4300 2-6-0 1911							
9303 now 7325	Feb-1932	Apr-1964	86G Pontypool Road	86G Pontypool Road	Nov-64	Aug-75	70
Total							1
Churchward 4MT 4500 2-6-2T 1906							
4561	Oct-1924	May-1962	83A Newton Abbot	83D Plymouth Laira	Sep-62	Sep-75	71
4566	Oct-1924	Apr-1962	83G Penzance	83D Plymouth Laira	Sep-62	Aug-70	8
Total							2
1927 4575 dev. of Churchward 4MT 4500 2-6-2T 1906							
4588	Mar-1927	Jul-1962	83G Penzance	83D Plymouth Laira	Nov-62	Oct-70	11
5521	Dec-1927	Apr-1962	83B Taunton	83D Plymouth Laira	Sep-62	Sep-75	72
5526	May-1928	Jun-1962	82D Westbury	82D Westbury	Nov-62	Jul-85	166
5532	Jun-1928	Jul-1962	82C Swindon	83D Plymouth Laira	Nov-62	Mar-81	124
5538	Jul-1928	Oct-1961	85B Gloucester	89A Shrewsbury	Mar-62	Jan-87	185
5539	Jul-1928	Apr-1962	83E St.Blazey	83E St.Blazey	Sep-62	?	200
5541	Aug-1928	Jul-1962	89C Machynlleth	83D Plymouth Laira	Nov-62	Oct-72	25
5542	Jul-1928	Dec-1961	82D Westbury	82D Westbury	Mar-62	Sep-75	73
5552	Nov-1928	Oct-1960	83F Truro	83F Truro	May-61	Jun-86	174
5553	Nov-1928	Nov-1961	89C Machynlleth	83E St.Blazey	Mar-62	Jan-90	201
5557	Nov-1928	Oct-1960	83E St.Blazey	83E St.Blazey	1961	Aug-65	28S
5572	Feb-1929	Apr-1962	83D Laira(Plymouth)	83D Plymouth Laira	Sep-62	Aug-71	15
Total							12

BARRY DOCKS TUESDAY 3RD AUGUST 1965(continued)

	First	Built	Date Withdrawn	1959/first Shed	Last Shed at Withdraw	Arrived Barry	Left Barry	Dep No
Collett 5MT 4900 4-6-0 "Hall" 1928								
4930	"Hagley Hall"	May-1929	Dec-1963	83B Taunton	82C Swindon	May-64	Jan-73	29
4936	"Kinlet Hall"	Jun-1929	Jan-1964	83A Newton Abbot	88A Cardiff East Dock	Jun-64	May-81	126
4942	"Maindy Hall"	Jul-1929	Dec-1963	84C Banbury	81E Didcot	Jun-64	Apr-74	51
4953	"Pitchford Hall"	Aug-1929	Apr-1963	82C Swindon	88A Cardiff East Dock	Nov-63	Feb-84	150
4965	"Rood Ashton Hall"	Nov-1929	Dec-1963	81E Didcot	82B St.Philips Marsh	Jun-64	Oct-70	10
4979	"Wooton Hall"	Feb-1930	Dec-1963	81F Oxford	82B St.Philips Marsh	Jun-64	Oct-86	179
5900	"Hinderton Hall"	Mar-1931	Dec-1963	84A Wolverhampton	81F Oxford	Jun-64	Jul-71	14
5952	"Cogan Hall"	Dec-1935	Jun-1964	85A Worcester	82B St.Philips Marsh	Jun-64	Aug-87	187
5967	"Bickmarsh Hall"	Mar-1937	Jun-1964	83A Newton Abbot	88A Cardiff East Dock	Sep-64	Sep-81	136
5972	"Olton Hall"	Apr-1937	Dec-1963	83D Laira(Plymouth)	82D Westbury	Jul-64	May-81	125
Total								10
Hawksworth 5MT 6959 4-6-0 "Modified Hall" 1944								
6960	"Raveningham Hall"	Mar-1944	Sep-1964	81D Reading	81F Oxford	Jul-64	Oct-72	26
6989	"Wightwick Hall"	Mar-1948	Jun-1964	85C Hereford	85B Gloucester	Aug-64	Jan-78	88
7903	"Foremarke Hall"	Apr-1949	Jun-1964	81A Old Oak Common	88A Cardiff East Dock	Aug-64	Jun-81	129
Total								3
Collett 4MT 5101 2-6-2T 1929 rebuild of Churchward 3100 Class 1903								
4141		Aug-1946	Mar-1963	85B Gloucester	85B Gloucester	Nov-63	Jan-73	28
5164		Nov-1930	Apr-1963	83A Newton Abbot	86G Pontypool Road	Nov-63	Jan-73	30
5193	now 9351	Oct-1934	Oct-1962	83E St.Blazey	87H Neyland	Sep-62	Aug-79	103
5199		Nov-1934	Mar-1963	84F Stourbridge Jct.	85B Gloucester	Nov-63	Jul-85	165
Total								4
Collett 5MT 5600 0-6-2T 1924								
5619		Mar-1925	Jun-1964	88C Barry	88C Barry	Sep-64	May-73	40
5637		Sep-1925	Jun-1964	88F Treherbert	88C Barry	Sep-64	Aug-74	61
5643		Oct-1925	Jul-1963	88E Abercynon	88C Barry	Nov-63	Sep-71	16
5668		Jun-1926	Sep-1964	88F Treherbert	88C Barry	Nov-64	Aug-87	189
Total								4

BARRY DOCKS TUESDAY 3RD AUGUST 1965(continued)

	First Built	Date Withdrawn	1959/first Shed	Last Shed at Withdrawal	Arrived Barry	Left Barry	Dep No
1927 dev. of Collett 5MT 5600 0-6-2T 1924							
6619	Jan-1928	Mar-1963	88F Treherbert	88F Treherbert	Nov-63	Oct-74	64
6634	Aug-1928	Apr-1964	86G Pontypool Road	86G Pontypool Road	Aug-64	Jun-81	131
6686	Oct-1928	Apr-1964	87B Duffryn Yard	88D Merthyr	Aug-64	?	202
6695	Oct-1928	Jul-1964	87E Landore	88B Cardiff Radyr	Sep-64	May-79	99
Total							4
Collett 3F 5700 0-6-0PT 1929							
5794	Oct-1930	Dec-1959	86H Aberbeeg	86H Aberbeeg	1961	Aug-65	32S
Total							1
1933 dev. of Collett 3F 5700 0-6-0PT 1929							
3612	Mar-1939	Oct-1964	86D Llantrisant	86D Llantrisant	Mar-65	Dec-78	98
9629	Dec-1945	Oct-1964	83C Exeter	86G Pontypool Road	Mar-65	May-81	128
Total							2
Collett 8P 6000 4-6-0 "King" 1927							
6023 "King Edward II"	Jun-1930	Jun-1962	81A Old Oak Common	86C Cardiff Canton	Dec-62	Dec-84	159
6024 "King Edward 1"	Jun-1930	Jun-1962	81A Old Oak Common	86C Cardiff Canton	Dec-62	Mar-73	36
Total							2
Collett 8F 7200 2-8-2T rebuild of Churchward 4200 Class 2-8-0T							
7200	Jul-1930	Jul-1963	87E Landore	87F Llanelly	Sep-63	Sep-81	137
7202	Aug-1930	Jun-1964	88A Cardiff Cathays	88C Barry	Jul-64	Apr-74	52
7229	Mar-1926	Jul-1964	86A Newport(Ebbw Jct.)	86B Newport Ebbw Jct	Nov-64	Oct-84	156
Total							3
Hawksworth 4F 9400 0-6-0PT 1947							
9466	Feb-1952	Jul-1964	85A Worcester	88B Cardiff Radyr	Nov-64	Sep-75	74
Total							1
Urie 6F S15 4-6-0 1920 (with smoke deflectors)							
30499	May-1920	Jan-1964	70B Feltham	70B Feltham	Jun-64	Nov-83	148
30506	Oct-1920	Jan-1964	70B Feltham	70B Feltham	Oct-64	Apr-76	79
Total							2

	First Built	Withdrawn Date	1959/first Shed	Last Shed at Withdraw	Arrived Barry	Left Barry	Dep No
Maunsell 1927 dev. of Urie 6F S15 4-6-0 Urie 1920 (with smoke deflectors)							
30825	Apr-1927	Jan-1964	72B Salisbury	72B Salisbury	Jun-64	Nov-86	181
30828	Jul-1927	Jan-1964	72B Salisbury	72B Salisbury	Jun-64	Mar-81	122
30830	Aug-1927	Jul-1964	72B Salisbury	72B Salisbury	Dec-64	Sep-87	192
Total							3
Maunsell 1936 development of Urie 1920 6F S15 4-6-0 (with smoke deflectors)							
30841	Jul-1936	Jan-1964	72A Exmouth Jct.	70B Feltham	Jun-64	Sep-72	24
30847	Dec-1936	Jan-1964	72B Salisbury	70B Feltham	Jun-64	Oct-78	95
Total							2
Maunsell 4F Q 0-6-0 1938 (with multiple jet blastpipe and large diameter chimney)							
30541	Jan-1939	Nov-1964	71B Bournemouth	70C Guildford	Feb-65	May-74	54
Total							1
Maunsell 4P3F U 2-6-0 1928							
31618	Oct-1928	Jan-1964	71A Eastleigh	70C Guildford	Jan-64	Jan-69	2
31625	Mar-1929	Jan-1964	70C Guildford	70C Guildford	Jan-64	Mar-80	111
31638	May-1931	Jan-1964	70F Fratton	70C Guildford	Jun-64	Jul-80	114
Total							3
Maunsell 4P3F U1 2-6-0 1928 (rebuilt from ill-fated "River" Class 2-6-4T 1917)							
31806	Jun-1928	Jan-1964	70D Basingstoke	70C Guildford	Jun-64	Oct-76	85
Total							1
Maunsell 4P5F N 2-6-0 1917							
31874	Sep-1925	Mar-1964	73B Bricklayers Arms	83D Exmouth Junction	Jun-64	Mar-74	48
Total							1
Bulleid 7P5F "West Country & Battle of Britain Class 4-6-2 1945							
34067 "Tangmere"	Sep-1947	Nov-1963	73A Stewarts Lane	83D Exmouth Jct	Apr-65	Jan-81	118
34070 "Manston"	Oct-1947	Aug-1964	73H Dover	83D Exmouth Jct	Dec-64	Jun-83	146
34072 "257 Squadron"	Apr-1948	Oct-1964	72A Exmouth Jct.	70D Eastleigh	Mar-65	Nov-84	158
34073 "249 Squadron"	May-1948	Sep-1964	73H Dover	70D Eastleigh	Apr-65	?	205
34081 "92 Squadron"	Sep-1948	Aug-1964	72A Exmouth Jct.	70D Eastleigh	Apr-65	Nov-76	86
34092 "City of Wells"	Sep-1949	Nov-1964	73A Stewarts Lane	72B Salisbury	Mar-65	Oct-71	17
34105 "Swanage"	Mar-1950	Oct-1964	71B Bournemouth	70D Eastleigh	Feb-65	Mar-78	90
Total							7

BARRY DOCKS TUESDAY 3RD AUGUST 1965(continued)

	First Built	Date Withdrawn	1959/first Shed	Last Shed at Withdrawal	Arrived Barry	Left Barry	Dep No
1957 development of Bulleid 7P6F 4-6-2 "West Country & Battle of Britain" (air-smoothed casing removed)							
34016 "Bodmin"	Nov-1945	Jun-1964	73G Ramsgate	70D Eastleigh	Nov-64	Jul-72	22
34027 "Taw Valley"	Apr-1946	Aug-1964	73G Ramsgate	72B Salisbury	Dec-64	Apr-80	112
34028 "Eddystone"	May-1946	May-1964	71B Bournemouth	70D Eastleigh	Nov-64	Apr-86	171
34058 "Sir Frederick Pile"	Dec-1948	Oct-1964	72A Exmouth Jct.	70D Eastleigh	Apr-65	Jul-86	175
Total	4						
1956 dev. of Bulleid 8P 4-6-2 "Merchant Navy" 1941							
35006 "P&O Steam Navigation C	Jan-1942	Aug-1964	72B Salisbury	72B Salisbury	Dec-64	Mar-83	144
35009 "Shaw Savill"	Jun-1942	Sep-1964	72A Exmouth Jct.	83D Exmouth Jct	Dec-64	?	206
35018 "British India Line"	May-1945	Aug-1964	70A Nine Elms	70A Nine Elms	Dec-64	Mar-80	110
35025 "Brocklebank Line"	Nov-1948	Sep-1964	71B Bournemouth	83D Exmouth Jct	Dec-64	Feb-86	169
Total	4						
Stanier 6P5F 4-6-0 "Jubilee" 1934							
45690 "Leander"	Mar-1936	Mar-1964	82E Bristol Barrow Rd.	82E Bristol Barrow Rd.	Jul-64	May-72	18
45699 "Galatea"	Apr-1936	Nov-1964	82E Bristol Barrow Rd.	6D Shrewsbury	May-65	Apr-80	113
Total	2						
Stanier 8F 2-8-0 "Big Eight" 1935							
48431	Mar-1944	May-1964	82B St. Philip's Marsh	82F Bath Green Park	Aug-64	May-72	19
Total	1						
Fowler ex Somerset & Dorset Joint Railway 7F 2-8-0 1914							
53808	Jul-1925	Mar-1964	82F Bath Green Park	82F Bath Green Park	Jun-64	Oct-70	9
53809	Jul-1925	Jun-1964	82F Bath Green Park	82F Bath Green Park	Aug-64	Dec-75	78
Total	2						
BR Standard 9F 2-10-0 BR Brighton 1954. Double chimney development 1957							
92207	Jun-1959	Dec-1964	82B St.Philips Marsh	86B Ebbw Junction	Mar-65	Oct-86	180
92245	Nov-1958	Dec-1964	81A Old Oak Common	81C Southall	Mar-65	?	213
Total	2						
On Shed	110						
Steam	110						

BARRY DOCKS TUESDAY 3RD AUGUST 1965(continued)		1959 Shed Dates			
Barry Docks Highlights:-					
The two Kings	6023 "King Edward II"	SR - 1 May 59			
	6024 "King Edward I"	WR - 21 Mar 59	ER - 11 Apr 59		
Steam Classes	31				
Steam Origin	GWR 75	SR 28		LMR 5	BR 2

Review and Appraisal of Barry Docks

A mouth watering 110 steam engines were noted. The above listing shows their 1959 sheds (or first allocation) for comparison with their shed at withdrawl. Some interesting long closed sheds appeared on the 1959 listing. Some classes had stuck to specific areas (45XX Class – South West of England), (56XX Class – South Wales valleys) while some had roamed around the whole system.

All withdrawn (no surprise!). No adjectives could describe how terrific Barry Docks was particularly for a pair of LNER railwayists. D.S. and I were well placed with LNER and LMS stock. Even the departed "Coronation" class had been very familiar to us through visits to Carlisle and to Glasgow. Stratford Works (the secret sanctuary) and Barry Docks had provided the end to our heartaches of no Southern and Western Region engine sightings. We were now in a peaceful state of meditation brought about by seeing them for the first time. No need to drool over pictures in a combined volume of a Southern Region "Pacific" or a Western Region "Castle" or "King". They were here in Barry Docks as large as life. You could bang your head of their boilers (if you were daft enough) to make sure that it wasn't all a dream. It had been no mirage. D.S. had even taken eight photographs (all that he could spare from his film) and in future years we could thumb over our photo albums and remember the great days of steam! We had been here to see the twilight if not the end of an era. The two 9F 2-10-0's had lasted less than seven years with 92207 built as recently as June 1959.

One thing about Barry that appealed to me was that it was a M.P.D. "Sunday" every day. No engine "worked out" from here. Everything once "on shed" stayed "on shed". Unlike other steam engine sheds that are being run down Barry is getting more engines each month.

This "arrival" rate was far greater than the "scrapping rate".

The following classes noted were extinct on British Railways at the time of our visit: -

4F Q 0-6-0, ex S&DJR 7F 2-8-0, Churchward 8F 28XX, 2-6-0 43XX Class and of course the 8P "Kings"

Barry Revisited August 1970 – The BARRY MIRACLE

Little did I know at the time I was to visit Barry Docks once more during the late Bank Holiday weekend in August 1970 accompanied by Dave Archibald and another well known railwayist John Clarke. Incredibly while a Pannier Tank (5794) was in course of being cut up at the time of our 1965 visit only one further steam engines 45XX 5557 that we had seen had been cut up (later in 1965) before our 1970 visit. Apparently it was much easier to cut up wagons with steam engine cutting up confined to quiet periods and eventually hardly at all.

There had been lots of new arrivals: -

BARRY DOCKS REVISITED AUGUST BANK HOLIDAY WEEKEND 1970

Steam	First Built	Date Withdrawn	1959/first Shed	Last Shed	Arrived Barry	Left Barry	Dep No
Churchward (1903) 8F 2800 2-8-0. Collett 1938 development							
3802	Dec-1938	Aug-1965	84B Oxley	82E Bristol Barrow Rd.	Oct-65	Sep-84	154
3817	Mar-1940	Aug-1965	86C Cardiff Canton	6C Croes Newydd	1965	Mar-73	06S
3850	Jun-1942	Aug-1965	86J Aberdare	6C Croes Newydd	Oct-65	Mar-84	151
3855	Oct-1942	Aug-1965	86C Cardiff Canton	6C Croes Newydd	Oct-65	Aug-87	188
Total							4
3F 5700 0-6-0PT Collett 1929 1933 development							
3738	Sep-1937	Aug-1965	81D Reading	88A Cardiff East Dock	Oct-65	Apr-74	49
4612	Feb-1942	Aug-1965	82C Swindon	88A Cardiff East Dock	Oct-65	Jan-81	119
9681	May-1949	Aug-1965	89A Oswestry	88A Cardiff East Dock	Aug-65	Oct-75	75
9682	May-1949	Aug-1965	84E Tyseley	88B Cardiff Radyr	Oct-65	Nov-82	141
Total							4
Collett 4MT 5101 2-6-2T 1929 rebuild of Churchward 3100 Class 1903							
4110	Oct-1935	Jun-1965	84H Wellington(Salop)	86E Severn Tunnel Jct.	Aug-65	May-79	100
4115	Oct-1936	Jun-1965	85C Hereford	86E Severn Tunnel Jct.	Aug-65	?	198
4121	Dec-1937	Jun-1965	86F Tondu	88J Aberdare	Aug-65	Feb-81	120
4144	Sep-1946	Jun-1965	86F Tondu	86E Severn Tunnel Jct.	Aug-65	Apr-74	50
4150	Jun-1947	Jun-1965	83A Newton Abbot	86E Severn Tunnel Jct.	Aug-65	May-74	57
4160	Sep-1948	Jun-1965	88A Cardiff Cathays	86E Severn Tunnel Jct.	Aug-65	Aug-74	60
Total							6
5MT 4900 "Hall" 4-6-0 Collett 1928							
4920 "Dumbleton Hall"	Mar-1929	Dec-1965	83A Newton Abbot	82E Bristol Barrow Rd.	Feb-66	Jun-76	82
Total							1
Hawksworth 5MT 6959 4-6-0 "Modified Hall" 1944							
6984 "Owsden Hall"	Feb-1948	Dec-1965	85A Worcester	82E Bristol Barrow Rd.	Feb-66	Oct-86	178
6990 "Witherslack Hall"	Apr-1948	Dec-1965	81A Old Oak Common	82E Bristol Barrow Rd.	Feb-66	Nov-75	76
7927 "Willington Hall"	Oct-1950	Dec-1965	81A Old Oak Common	81F Oxford	Feb-66	?	203
Total							3

BARRY DOCKS REVISITED AUGUST BANK HOLIDAY WEEKEND 1970(continued)

	First Built	Withdrawn Date	1959/first Shed	Last Shed	Arrived Barry	Left Barry	Dep No
Collett 5MT 7800 "Manor" 1938							
7802 "Bradley Manor"	Jan-1938	Nov-1965	89C Machynlleth	6D Shrewsbury	Jul-66	Nov-79	109
7812 "Erlestoke Manor"	Jan-1939	Nov-1965	83D Laira(Plymouth)	6D Shrewsbury	May-66	May-74	56
7819 "Hinton Manor"	Feb-1939	Nov-1965	89A Oswestry	6D Shrewsbury	May-66	Jan-73	31
7820 "Dinmore Manor"	Nov-1950	Nov-1965	83D Laira(Plymouth)	6D Shrewsbury	May-66	Sep-79	104
7821 "Ditcheat Manor"	Nov-1950	Nov-1965	84E Tyseley	6D Shrewsbury	May-66	Jun-81	132
7822 "Foxcote Manor"	Dec-1950	Nov-1965	89A Oswestry	6D Shrewsbury	May-66	Jan-75	65
7828 "Odney Manor"	Dec-1950	Oct-1965	84G Shrewsbury	6D Shrewsbury	May-66	Jun-81	133
Total	7						
Bulleid 7P5F "West Country & Battle of Britain Class 4-6-2 1945							
34007 "Wadebridge"	Sep-1945	Oct-1965	70A Nine Elms	70E Salisbury	May-66	May-81	127
Total	1						
1957 development of Bulleid 7P6F 4-6-2 "West Country & Battle of Britain" (air-smoothed casing removed)							
34010 "Sidmouth"	Sep-1945	Mar-1965	70A Nine Elms	70D Eastleigh	Sep-65	Nov-82	140
34039 "Boscastle"	Sep-1946	May-1965	71B Bournemouth	70D Eastleigh	Sep-65	Jan-73	33
34046 "Braunton"	Nov-1946	Oct-1965	71B Bournemouth	70F Bournemouth	Jan-66	?	204
34053 "Sir Keith Park"	Jan-1947	Oct-1965	72B Salisbury	70F Bournemouth	Mar-66	Jun-84	153
34059 "Sir Archibald Sinclair"	Apr-1949	May-1966	72B Salisbury	70E Salisbury	Oct-66	Oct-79	108
34101 "Hartland"	Feb-1950	Jul-1966	73A Stewarts Lane	70D Eastleigh	Oct-66	Jul-78	92
Total	6						
1956 dev. of Bulleid 8P 4-6-2 "Merchant Navy" 1941							
35005 "Canadian Pacific"	Jan-1942	Oct-1965	70A Nine Elms	70G Weymouth	Jan-66	Mar-73	38
35010 "Blue Star"	Jul-1942	Sep-1966	71B Bournemouth	70G Weymouth	Mar-67	Jan-85	160
35011 "General Steam Navigation"	Dec-1944	Feb-1966	72A Exmouth Junction	70F Bournemouth	Jun-66	?	207
35022 "Holland-America Line"	Oct-1948	May-1966	71B Bournemouth	70G Weymouth	Oct-66	Mar-86	170
35027 "Port Line"	Dec-1948	Sep-1966	71B Bournemouth	70G Weymouth	Mar-67	Dec-82	142
35029 "Ellerman Lines"	Feb-1949	Sep-1966	70A Nine Elms	70G Weymouth	Mar-67	Jan-74	47
Total	6						
Ivatt 2MT 2-6-2T 1946							
41312	May-1952	Jul-1967	73E Faversham	70A Nine Elms	Jan-68	Aug-74	63
41313	May-1952	Nov-1965	73E Faversham	70D Eastleigh	Feb-66	Jul-75	68
Total	2						

BARRY DOCKS REVISITED AUGUST BANK HOLIDAY WEEKEND 1970(continued).

First	Built	Date Withdrawn	1959/first Shed	Last Shed	Arrived Barry	Left Barry	Dep No
Hughes/Fowler 5MT "Crab" 2-6-0 1926							
42765	Aug-1927	Dec-1966	24F Fleetwood	8H Birkenhead	Jun-67	Apr-78	91
42859	Mar-1930	Dec-1966	1A Willesden	8H Birkenhead	Jun-67	Dec-86	183
Total							2
Stanier 5MT 2-6-0 1933							
42968	Jan-1934	Dec-1966	5A Crewe North	8F Wigan(Springs Br.)	Jun-67	Dec-73	45
Total							1
Midland 4F 0-6-0 1924							
44123	Jul-1925	Jun-1965	85E Glouc.(Barn Wood)	85B Gloucester	Aug-65	Dec-81	138
44422	Oct-1927	Jun-1965	82F Bath (Green Park)	85B Gloucester	Aug-65	Apr-77	87
Total							2
Stanier 5MT 4-6-0 "Black Five" 1934							
44901	Oct-1945	Aug-1965	12A Carlisle Kingmoor	12A Carlisle Kingmoor	Jan-66	?	208
45163	Aug-1935	May-1965	12A Carlisle Kingmoor	12A Carlisle Kingmoor	Jan-66	Jan-87	184
45293	Dec-1936	Aug-1965	12B Carlisle Upperby	12B Carlisle Upperby	Jan-66	Dec-86	182
45337	Apr-1937	Feb-1965	26B Agecroft	12A Carlisle Kingmoor	Jan-66	May-84	152
45379	Jul-1937	Jul-1965	5A Crewe North	1A Willesden	Oct-65	May-74	55
45491	Dec-1943	Jul-1965	12A Carlisle Kingmoor	12A Carlisle Kingmoor	Jan-66	Jul-81	134
Total							6
Ivatt 2MT 2-6-0 1946							
46428	Dec-1948	Dec-1966	8F Wigan(Springs Br.)	5B Crewe South	Sep-67	Oct-79	106
46447	Mar-1950	Dec-1966	11B Workington	8F Wigan(Springs Br.)	Jun-67	Jun-72	20
46512	Dec-1952	Dec-1966	89A Oswestry	5B Crewe South	Jun-67	May-73	41
46521	Feb-1953	Oct-1966	89B Brecon	6F Machynlleth	Mar-67	Mar-71	12
Total							4
Midland 3F "Jinty" 0-6-0T 1924 dev. of Johnson 1899 design							
47279	Aug-1924	Dec-1966	14E Bedford	8G Sutton Oak	Jun-67	Oct-79	101
47298	Oct-1924	Dec-1966	8G Sutton Oak	8G Sutton Oak	Jun-67	Jul-74	58
47324	Jun-1926	Dec-1966	6C Birkenhead	8H Birkenhead	Jun-67	Feb-78	89
47406	Dec-1926	Dec-1966	24L Lancaster	8A Edge Hill	Jun-67	Jun-83	147
47493	Feb-1928	Dec-1966	8C Speke Junction	8A Edge Hill	Jun-67	Nov-72	27
Total							5

BARRY DOCKS REVISITED AUGUST BANK HOLIDAY WEEKEND 1970(continued)

	First Built	Date Withdrawn	1959/first Shed	Last Shed	Arrived Barry	Left Barry	Dep No
Stanier 8F 2-8-0 "Big Eight" 1935							
48151	Sep-1942	Jan-1968	41D Canklow	8E Northwich	Sep-68	Nov-75	77
48173	Jun-1943	Jul-1965	2A Rugby	6B Mold Junction	Oct-65	?	209
48305	Nov-1943	Jan-1968	2E Northampton	8C Speke Junction	Sep-68	Nov-85	168
48518	Aug-1944	Jul-1965	1A Willesden	1A Willesden	Oct-65	?	210
48624	Nov-1943	Jul-1965	1A Willesden	1A Willesden	Oct-65	Jul-81	135
Total		5					
Thompson 5MT B1 4-6-0 1942							
61264	Dec-1947	Dec-1965	30F Parkeston	40E Colwick	Sep-68	Jul-76	83
Total		1					
BR Standard 8P 4-6-2 Derby 1954							
71000 "Duke of Gloucester"	May-1954	Nov-1962	5A Crewe North	5A Crewe North	Oct-67	Apr-74	53
Total		1					
BR Standard 5MT 4-6-0 Doncaster 1951							
73082	Jul-1955	Jun-1966	73A Stewarts Lane	70C Guildford	Nov-66	Oct-79	107
73096	Nov-1955	Nov-1967	84G Shrewsbury	9F Patricroft	Feb-68	Jul-85	164
Total		2					
BR Standard 5MT 4-6-0 Doncaster 1951. Caprotti valve gear 1956 development.							
73129	Aug-1956	Nov-1967	26F Patricroft	9H Patricroft	Feb-68	Jan-73	32
73156	Dec-1956	Nov-1967	41B Sheff(Grimesthorpe)	9K Bolton	Feb-68	Oct-86	177
Total		2					
BR Standard 4MT 4-6-0 Brighton 1951							
75014	Dec-1951	Dec-1966	6A Chester(Midland)	6D Shrewsbury	Oct-67	Feb-81	121
75069	Sep-1955	Sep-1966	73H Dover	70D Eastleigh	May-67	Mar-73	37
75078	Jan-1956	Jul-1966	70D Basingstoke	70D Eastleigh	Nov-66	Jun-72	21
75079	Jan-1956	Nov-1966	70D Basingstoke	70D Eastleigh	Apr-67	Mar-82	139
Total		4					

	First Built	Date Withdrawn	1959/first Shed	Last Shed	Arrived Barry	Left Barry	Dep No
BR Standard 4MT 2-6-0 Doncaster 1953							
76017	Jul-1953	Jul-1965	71A Eastleigh	70E Salisbury	Jan-66	Jan-74	46
76077	Dec-1956	Nov-1967	8G Sutton Oak	8F Wigan(Springs Br.)	Sep-68	May-87	186
76079	Feb-1957	Nov-1967	8G Sutton Oak	8F Wigan(Springs Br.)	Sep-68	Jul-74	59
76080	Feb-1957	Dec-1967	24D Lower Darwen	8F Wigan(Springs Br.)	1968	Apr-72	72S
76084	Mar-1957	Nov-1967	24J Lancaster	8F Wigan(Springs Br.)	Sep-68	Jan-83	143
Total							5
BR Standard 2MT 2-6-0 Doncaster 1953							
78018	Mar-1954	Nov-1966	12D Kirkby Stephen	6D Shrewsbury	Jun-67	Oct-78	97
78019	Mar-1954	Nov-1966	12D Kirkby Stephen	5B Crewe South	Jun-67	Mar-73	35
78022	May-1954	Sep-1966	41C Millhouses	10D Lostock Hall	Mar-67	Jun-75	67
78059	Sep-1956	Nov-1966	6D Chester(Northgate)	5B Crewe South	Jun-67	May-83	145
Total							4
BR Standard 4MT 2-6-4T Doncaster 1953							
80064	Jun-1953	Sep-1965	1C Watford	82E Bristol Barrow Rd.	Oct-65	Feb-73	34
80072	Nov-1953	Jul-1965	33B Tilbury	2A Tyseley	Jan-66	?	211
80078	Feb-1954	Jul-1965	33B Tilbury	6C Croes Newydd	Jun-66	Sep-66	84
80079	Mar-1954	Jul-1965	33B Tilbury	6C Croes Newydd	May-67	May-71	13
80080	Mar-1954	Jul-1965	33B Tilbury	6C Croes Newydd	Jan-66	Nov-80	115
80097	Dec-1954	Jul-1965	33A Plaistow	6F Machynlleth	Jan-66	May-85	162
80098	Dec-1954	Jul-1965	33A Plaistow	6F Machynlleth	Jan-66	Nov-84	157
80100	Jan-1955	Jul-1965	33A Plaistow	6D Shrewsbury	Jan-66	Oct-78	94
80104	Mar-1955	Jul-1965	33A Plaistow	6F Machynlleth	Sep-66	Sep-84	155
80105	Apr-1955	Jul-1965	33A Plaistow	6F Machynlleth	Oct-66	Oct-73	44
80135	Apr-1956	Jul-1965	33A Plaistow	6D Shrewsbury	Jan-66	Apr-73	39
80136	May-1956	Jul-1965	33A Plaistow	6D Shrewsbury	Jun-66	Aug-79	102
80150	Dec-1956	Oct-1965	75A Brighton	70D Eastleigh	Jan-66	?	212
80151	Jan-1957	May-1967	75A Brighton	70D Eastleigh	Oct-67	Mar-75	66
Total							14

BARRY DOCKS REVISITED AUGUST BANK HOLIDAY WEEKEND 1970(continued)	First Built	Date Withdrawn	1959/first Shed	Last Shed	Arrived Barry	Left Barry	Dep No
9F 2-10-0 BR Brighton 1954							
92085	May-1956	Dec-1966	15A Wellingborough	8H Birkenhead	1967	1980	74S
92134	May-1957	Dec-1966	15A Wellingborough	8H Birkenhead	Jun-67	Jul-80	116
Total	2						
9F 2-10-0 BR Brighton 1954. Double chimney development 1957							
92212	Sep-1959	Jan-1968	84C Banbury	10A Carnforth	Sep-68	Sep-79	105
92214	Oct-1959	Aug-1965	86C Cardiff Canton	86E Severn Tunnel Jct.	Oct-65	Dec-80	117
92219	Jan-1960	Mar-1965	82B St.Philips Marsh	88A Cardiff East Dock	Oct-65	May-85	163
92240	Oct-1958	Aug-1965	81A Old Oak Common	81C Southall	Oct-65	Oct-78	93
Total	4						
Diesels							
B-B "Warship" Class 4 1958							
D601 "Ark Royal"	1958	Dec-1967	83D Laira(Plymouth)	?	1968	Jul-1980	77S
Total	1						
Type 2 Bo-Bo North British 1959							
D6122	1959	Dec-1967	?	?	?	Jun-1980	78S
Total	1						
Steam	105						
Diesels	2						

Steam Classes: - 27

Steam Origin: - GWR 25; SR 13; LMS 27; LNER 1; BR 38

The newcomers since our 1965 were interesting. Less Great Western and Southern Region arrivals but these included clutches of GWR "Manors" and Southern Region Bulleid Pacifics. A much enhanced LMS representation including "Black Fives", "Big Eight's" and "Jinty's". The most numerous class turned out to be BR 2-6-4 Tanks. The great majority of them had originally plied their trade from Liverpool Street on the Eastern Region and had ended up at Shrewsbury, Croes Newydd and Machynlleth.

We had missed only six engines that were at Barry Docks post 1965. One Manor, a Midland 0-6-0 and a couple of Jintys had arrived post our 1965 visit and departed for restoration and preservation before our 1970 visit. A couple of diesels including Warship D600 "Active" had also arrived post 1965 and been cut up prior to our 1970 visit:-

BARRY DOCKS ENGINES MISSED post August 1965 and pre August 1970

	Built	Date Withdrawn	First 1959 Shed	Last Shed	Arrived Barry	Left Barry	Dep No
Steam							
Collett 5MT 7800 4-6-0 "Manor" 1938							
7827 "Lydham Manor"	Dec-1950	Oct-1965	89A Oswestry	6D Shrewsbury	May-66	Jun-70	5
Total	1						
Midland 4F 0-6-0 1911							
43924	Oct-1920	Jun-1965	85E Glouc.(Barm Wood)	82E Bristol Barrow Rd.	Oct-65	Sep-68	1
Total	1						
Midland 3F "Jinty" 0-6-0T 1924 dev. of Johnson 1899 design							
47327	Jul-1926	Dec-1966	27F Brunswick(Liverpool)	8L Aintree	Jan-68	Jul-70	6
47357	Jul-1926	Dec-1966	8A Edge Hill	8A Edge Hill	Nov-67	Jul-70	7
Total	2						
Diesels							
B-B "Warship" Class 4 1958							
D600 "Active"	1958	Dec-1967	83D Laira(Plymouth)	?	1968	Mar-1970	76S
Total	1						
Type 1 British Thomson-Houston Bo-Bo							
D8206	1957	Sep-1968	1D Devons Road (Bow)	?	?	Feb-1970	79S
Total	2						

Steam	4
Diesels	2

1959 Shed Dates
LMR - 21 Mar 59
SR - 1 May 59
WR - 21 Mar 59
ER - 11 Apr 59

The incredible Barry Preservation Miracle is that 213 engines found new homes and departed Barry. Virtually everything was saved after the autumn of 1965 but 79 engines were not so lucky as we can see from the listing below.

BARRY DOCKS SCRAP LIST

	First Built	Date Withdrawn	1959 Shed	Last Shed at Withdraw	Arrived Barry	Date Scrapped
Steam						
Collett 0-6-0PT 1F 1366 Class 1934 (Class extinct)						
1367	Feb-1934	Oct-64	71G Weymouth	72F Wadebridge	1965	*Mar-1965*
1368	Feb-1934	Oct-64	71G Weymouth	72F Wadebridge	1965	*Mar-1965*
Total						2
Churchward 2-6-2T 4MT 3150 Class 1906 (Class extinct)						
3170	Jun-1907	Aug-58	86A Newport Ebbw Jct.	86A Newport Ebbw Jct.	1959	*Sep-1959*
Total						1
Collett 3F 5700 0-6-0PT 1929						
5794	Oct-1930	Dec-59	86H Aberbeeg	86H Aberbeeg	1961	*Aug-1965*
7702	Mar-1930	Sep-60	84D Leamington Spa	84D Leamington Spa	1961	*Jun-1961*
7712	Apr-1930	Jul-60	86G Pontypool Road	86G Pontypool Road	1960	*Jun-1961*
7719	Jun-1930	Sep-60	82B St. Philips Marsh	85A Worcester	1960	*Jan-1961*
7722	Jun-1930	Nov-60	81A Old Oak Common	84F Stourbridge Jct.	1960	*Aug-1965*
7723	Jun-1930	Aug-60	85B Gloucester	22B Gloucester Barnwood	1960	*Mar-1965*
7725	Dec-1929	Aug-60	86F Tondu	86F Tondu	1960	*Jun-1961*
7758	Dec-1930	Jun-60	87B Duffryn Yard	87B Duffryn Yard	1960	*Feb-1962*
Total						8
1930 dev. of Collett 3F 5700 0-6-0PT 1929						
6753	Aug-1947	Jan-1961	87K Swansea(Paxton Str.)	87K Swansea(Paxton Str.)	1961	*Jun-1961*
Total						1
1933 dev. of Collett 3F 5700 0-6-0PT 1929						
3727	Jun-1937	Apr-1964	88A Cardiff Cathays	88C Barry	1964	*Mar-1965*
3794	Oct-1938	Dec-1964	83C Exeter	81F Oxford	1965	*Aug-1965*
8749	Jul-1931	Oct-1964	87F Llanely	85B Gloucester Hort.Rd.	1964	*Mar-1965*
Total						3
Churchward (1903) 8F 2800 2-8-0. Collett 1938 development						
3817	Mar-1940	Aug-1965	86C Cardiff Canton	84J Croes Newydd	1965	*Mar-1973*
Total						1

BARRY DOCKS SCRAP LIST(continued)

	First Built	Withdrawn Date	1959 Shed	Last Shed at Withdraw	Arrived Barry	Date Scrapped
Collett 4MT 5101 2-6-2T 1929 rebuild of Churchward 3100 Class 1903						
4156	Aug-1947	Jun-1965	86E Severn Tun. Jct.	86E Severn Tun. Jct.	1965	Jul-1980
4157	Aug-1947	Jun-1965	83B Taunton	86E Severn Tun. Jct.	1965	Oct-1965
4164	Sep-1948	Jan-1960	86E Severn Tun. Jct.	86E Severn Tun. Jct.	1960	Dec-1960
5182	Mar-1931	May-1962	85B Gloucester	85B Gloucester Hort.Rd.	1962	Jul-1964
Total 4						
Collett 2-6-2T 4MT 6100 Class 1931 (Class Extinct)						
6115	Sep-1931	Nov-1964	81B Slough	86E Severn Tun. Jct.	1965	Apr-1965
Total 1						
Churchward 4MT 4500 2-6-2T 1906						
4550	Feb-1915	Oct-1960	87H Neyland	83E St.Blazey	1961	May-1961
4559	Sep-1924	Oct-1960	83E St.Blazey	83E St.Blazey	1961	May-1961
Total 2						
1927 4575 dev. of Churchward 4MT 4500 2-6-2T 1906						
4594	Apr-1927	Nov-1960	87H Neyland	87H Neyland	1961	Jun-1961
5504	May-1927	Oct-1960	83B Taunton	82D Westbury	1960	Mar-1961
5510	Nov-1927	Oct-1960	82C Swindon	83D Laira(Plymouth)	1961	Apr-1965
5514	Nov-1927	Nov-1960	85B Gloucester	83F Truro	1961	Jun-1961
5546	Oct-1928	Sep-1960	83C Exeter	83F Truro	1960	Sep-1961
5547	Oct-1928	Feb-1962	82C Swindon	82C Swindon	1962	Mar-1965
5557	Nov-1928	Oct-1960	83E St.Blazey	83E St.Blazey	1961	Aug-1965
5558	Nov-1928	Oct-1960	83A Newton Abbot	83A Newton Abbot	1961	Aug-1965
Total 8						
Churchward 4MT 2-6-0 4300 1911						
5312	Jun-1917	Oct-1958	87F Llanelly	87F Llanelly	1959	Aug-1959
5345	Mar-1918	Jun-1959	86G Pontypool Road	86G Pontypool Road	1959	Dec-1959
5355	Aug-1918	Apr-1959	85D Kidderminster	85D Kidderminster	1959	Oct-1959
5360	Jan-1919	Sep-1958	86C Cardiff Canton	86C Cardiff Canton	1959	Dec-1959
5392	Oct-1920	Aug-1958	85A Worcester	85A Worcester	1959	Dec-1959
5397	Nov-1920	Jul-1958	81E Didcot	81E Didcot	1959	Dec-1959
6331	Apr-1921	Apr-1959	84C Banbury	84C Banbury	1959	Oct-1959
6334	May-1921	Apr-1959	82C Swindon	82C Swindon	1959	Oct-1959
Total 8						

BARRY DOCKS SCRAP LIST(continued)

	First Built	Date Withdrawn	1959 Shed	Last Shed at Withdraw	Arrived Barry	Date Scrapped
Collett 5MT 5600 0-6-2T 1924						
5651	Jan-1926	Dec-1964	84K Wrexham(Rhondda)	88A Cardiff Cathays	1965	May-1965
5669	Jun-1926	Sep-1964	88A Cardiff Cathays	88A Cardiff Cathays	1964	Mar-1965
Total	2					
1927 dev. of Collett 5MT 5600 0-6-2T 1924						
6621	Jan-1928	Dec-1964	86H Aberbeeg	88A Cardiff Cathays	1965	Mar-1965
6696	Oct-1928	Dec-1963	84J Croes Newydd	88C Barry	1964	Apr-1964
Total	2					
Collett 0-6-0PT 2P 6400 Class 1932						
6406	Mar-1932	Jun-1960	83D Laira(Plymouth)	83D Laira(Plymouth)	1960	Jun-1961
Total	1					
Collett 8F 7200 2-8-2T rebuild of Churchward 4200 Class 2-8-0T						
7226	Mar-1926	Nov-1964	87D Swansea East Dock	86J Aberdare	1964	Mar-1965
Total	1					
1949 development of Hawksworth 4F 9400 0-6-0PT 1947						
8419	Apr-1950	Jan-1960	88C Barry	88C Barry	1961	Mar-1965
8473	Aug-1951	Jan-1961	83G Penzance	83G Penzance	1961	Aug-1961
8475	Nov-1951	Sep-1964	87D Swansea East Dock	88A Cardiff Cathays	1964	Jan-1965
8479	Jun-1952	Oct-1964	82B St. Philips Marsh	88A Cardiff Cathays	1964	Mar-1965
9436	Jan-1951	Jul-1960	87E Landore	87E Landore	1960	Jun-1961
9438	Feb-1951	Jun-1959	85B Gloucester	85B Gloucester	1960	Jun-1961
9439	Feb-1951	Jun-1959	83C Exeter	83C Exeter	1960	Jun-1961
9443	Mar-1951	Jun-1959	86C Cardiff Canton	86C Cardiff Canton	1960	Jun-1961
9445	Apr-1951	Jan-1960	85B Gloucester	85B Gloucester	1961	Jan-1965
9449	Jun-1951	Jun-1960	84C Banbury	84C Banbury	1961	Jan-1965
9459	Nov-1951	Sep-1959	86H Aberbeeg	86H Aberbeeg	1960	Jun-1961
9462	Dec-1951	Nov-1960	83A Newton Abbot	83A Newton Abbot	1961	May-1965
9468	Feb-1952	Aug-1960	86A Newport(Ebbw Jct.)	86A Newport(Ebbw Jct.)	1961	Aug-1965
9491	Mar-1954	Jun-1959	87D Swansea East Dock	87D Swansea East Dock	1960	Mar-1965
9492	May-1954	Jun-1959	85B Gloucester	85B Gloucester	1960	Feb-1962
9496	Oct-1954	Dec-1959	84A Wolverhampton	84A Wolverhampton	1960	Jun-1961
9499	Jul-1955	Sep-1959	82B St. Philips Marsh	86H Aberbeeg	1961	Mar-1965
Total	17					

	First Built	Date Withdrawn	1959 Shed	Last Shed at Withdrawal	Arrived Barry	Date Scrapped
Collett 0-6-0PT 1P 5400 Class 1931 (Class extinct)						
5407	Jan-1932	Jun-1960	84C Banbury	84C Banbury	1960	Aug-1961
5417	Jun-1932	Jan-1961	85B Gloucester	84C Banbury	1961	Sep-1961
5422	Nov-1935	Jun-1960	89A Oswestry	89A Oswestry	1960	Mar-1965
Total						
3						
Urie 6F S15 4-6-0 1920 (with smoke deflectors)						
30512	Feb-1921	Mar-1964	70B Feltham	70B Feltham	1964	Jan-1965
Total						
1						
6F S15 4-6-0 Urie 1920 (with smoke deflectors) Maunsell 1936 development						
30844	Oct-1936	Jun-1964	72A Exmouth Jct.	70B Feltham	1964	Jan-1965
Total						
1						
Bulleid 7P5F "West Country & Battle of Britain Class 4-6-2 1945						
34094 "Mortehoe"	Oct-1949	Aug-1964	70A Nine Elms	70A Nine Elms	1964	Nov-1964
Total						
1						
1957 7P6F dev. of Bulleid 7P5F 4-6-2 "West Country & Battle of Britain" 1945						
34045 "Ottery St. Mary"	Oct-1946	Jun-1964	71B Bournemouth	70F Bournemouth	1965	May-1965
Total						
1						
Ivatt 2MT 2-6-2T 1946						
41248	Nov-1949	Nov-1964	82G Templecombe	83F Barnstaple Junction	1965	Mar-1965
41303	Mar-1952	Oct-1964	73B Bricklayers Arms	75A Brighton	1965	Mar-1965
Total						
2						
BR Standard 4MT 2-6-0 Doncaster 1953						
76080	Feb-1957	Dec-1967	24D Lower Darwen	8F Springs Branch	1968	Apr-1972
Total						
1						
BR Standard 4MT 2-6-4T Doncaster 1953						
80067	Aug-1953	Jun-1965	1C Watford	83G Templecombe	1965	Sep-1965
Total						
1						
BR Standard 9F 2-10-0 Brighton 1954						
92085	May-1956	Dec-1966	15A Wellingborough	8H Birkenhead	1967	Jul-1980
Total						
1						
BR Standard 9F 2-10-0 Brighton 1954. Double chimney development 1957						
92232	Aug-1958	Dec-1964	86C Cardiff Canton	88A Cardiff East Dock	1965	Mar-1965
Total						
1						

BARRY DOCKS SCRAP LIST(continued)

	First Built	Date Withdrawn	1959 Shed	Last Shed at Withdrawal	Arrived Barry	Date Scrapped
Diesels						
B-B "Warship" Class 4 1958						
D600 "Active"	1958	Dec-1967	83D Laira(Plymouth)	?	1968	*Mar-1970*
D601 "Ark Royal"	1958	Dec-1967	83D Laira(Plymouth)	?	1968	*Jul-1980*
Total	2					
Type 2 Bo-Bo North British 1959 (Class extinct)						
D6122	1959	Dec-1967	not yet built	?	?	*Jun-1980*
Total	1					
Type 1 Bo-Bo British Thomson-Houston 1957						
D8206	1957	Sep-1968	1D Devons Road(Bow)	?	Feb-70	*Feb-1970*
Total	1					
Steam	75					
Diesels	4					

BARRY CUT UP ANALYSIS

Date Withdrawn		Date Arrived		Date Cut Up		Engines at Year End
1958	5	1958	0	1958	0	0
1959	13	1959	9	1959	9	0
1960	26	1960	20	1960	1	19
1961	3	1961	18	1961	21	16
1962	2	1962	2	1962	2	16
1963	1	1963	0	1963	0	16
1964	19	1964	10	1964	2	24
1965	4	1965	14	1965	36	2
1966	1	1966	0	1966	0	2
1967	4	1967	1	1967	0	3
1968	1	1968	4	1968	0	6
1970	0	1970	1	1970	2	4
1972	0	1972	0	1972	1	3
1973	0	1973	0	1973	1	3
1980	0	1980	0	1980	4	0
	79		**79**		**79**	

Of the list some had particular interest. 0-6-0 Pannier Tank's 1367 and 1368 were two of Collet's much photographed dock shunting tanks, which latterly saw service at Weymouth Docks. 2-6-2T 3170 had been the last survivor of Churchward's 3150 class (built 1907). 0-6-0 Pannier Tank's Nos. 5407, 5417 and 5422 were three of this 25 strong class of auto-fitted tanks. None of this class had been preserved. Bulleid Pacifics 34045 & 34094 were very unlucky – the only two to be cut up at Barry. Both were cut up in 1965 before the post August 65 halt in general scrapping. Warship D601 "Ark Royal" had been earmarked for purchase and restoration but the purchase eventually fell through and she was cut up in July 1980.

You may ask if you could have a complete Barry Docks listing of all the engines steam and diesel that were ever there and the fates that befell them. Here it is: -

BARRY DOCKS CONSOLIDATED LIST

	First Built	Date Withdrawn	1959 Shed	Last Shed at Withdrawal	Arrived Barry	Left Barry	Where To
Steam							
Collett 0-6-0PT 1F 1366 Class 1934							
1367	Feb-1934	Oct-1964	71G Weymouth	72F Wadebridge	1965	**Mar-1965**	Cut up at Barry
1368	Feb-1934	Oct-1964	71G Weymouth	72F Wadebridge	1965	**Mar-1965**	Cut up at Barry
Total	2						
Churchward 8F 2800 2-8-0 1903							
2807	May-1905	**Mar-1963**	83A Newton Abbot	86E Severn Tun. Jct.	Nov-63	Jun-81	Gloucestershire Warwickshire
2857	Apr-1918	**Apr-1963**	84B Oxley	86G Pontypool Road	Sep-63	Aug-75	Severn Valley Railway
2859	May-1918	**Dec-1964**	84B Oxley	88A Cardiff East Dock	Mar-65	Oct-87	Llangollen Railway
2861	May-1918	**Mar-1963**	86E Severn Tun. Jct.	86E Severn Tun. Jct.	Nov-63	?	Vale of Glamorgan Railway Centre
2873	Nov-1918	**Dec-1964**	86E Severn Tun. Jct.	81C Southall	Feb-65	?	South Devon Railway
2874	Nov-1918	**May-1963**	86C Cardiff Canton	87A Neath	Jul-63	Aug-87	West Somerset Railway
Total	6						
Collett dev.1938 of Churchward 8F 2-8-0 2800 1903							
2885	Mar-1938	**Jan-1964**	84E Tyseley	86E Severn Tun. Jct.	Mar-64	Mar-81	Birmingham Moor Street Station
3802	Dec-1938	**Aug-1965**	84B Oxley	82E Bristol Barrow Rd.	Oct-65	Sep-84	Llangollen Railway
3803	Jan-1939	**Jul-1963**	85B Gloucester	86E Severn Tun. Jct.	Nov-63	Nov-83	South Devon Railway
3814	Mar-1940	**Dec-1964**	81F Oxford	81E Didcot	Feb-65	Jul-86	North Yorkshire Moors
3817	Mar-1940	**Aug-1965**	86C Cardiff Canton	84J Croes Newydd	1965	**Mar-1973**	Cut up at Barry
3822	Apr-1940	**Jan-1964**	86G Pontypool Road	88A Cardiff East Dock	Jul-64	May-76	Didcot Railway Centre
3845	Apr-1942	**Jun-1964**	86C Cardiff Canton	2D Banbury	Sep-64	?	Goodman's Yard Wishaw
3850	Jun-1942	**Aug-1965**	86J Aberdare	6C Croes Newydd	Oct-65	Mar-84	West Somerset Railway
3855	Oct-1942	**Aug-1965**	86C Cardiff Canton	6C Croes Newydd	Oct-65	Aug-87	East Lancashire Railway
3862	Nov-1942	**Feb-1965**	83D Laira(Plymouth)	6C Croes Newydd	Jul-65	?	Northampton & Lamport Railway
Total	10						
Collett 8F 7200 2-8-2T rebuild of Churchward 4200 Class 2-8-0T							
7200	Jul-1930	**Jul-1963**	87E Landore	87F Llanelly	Sep-63	Sep-81	Buckinghamshire Railway Centre
7202	Aug-1930	**Jun-1964**	88A Cardiff Cathays	88C Barry	Jul-64	Apr-74	Didcot Railway Centre
7226	Mar-1926	**Nov-1964**	87D Swansea East Dock	86J Aberdare	1964	**Mar-1965**	Cut up at Barry
7229	Mar-1926	**Jul-1964**	86A Newport(Ebbw Jct.)	86B Newport Ebbw Jct.	Nov-64	Oct-84	East Lancashire Railway
Total	4						
Churchward 2-6-2T 4MT 3150 Class 1906 (Class extinct)							
3170	Jun-1907	**Aug-1958**	86A Newport Ebbw Jct.	86A Newport Ebbw Jct.	1959	**Sep-1959**	Cut up at Barry
Total	1						

	Name	First Built	Date Withdrawn	1959 Shed	Last Shed at Withdrawal	Arrived Barry	Left Barry	Where To
Collett 7P 4073 4-6-0 "Castle" 1923								
5029	"Nunney Castle"	May-1934	Dec-1963	85A Worcester	88A Cardiff East Dock	May-64	May-76	Tyseley Locomotive Works
5043	"Earl of Mount Edgcumbe"	Mar-1936	Dec-1963	81A Old Oak Common	88A Cardiff East Dock	Aug-64	Aug-73	Tyseley Locomotive Works
5051	"Earl Bathurst"	May-1936	May-1963	87E Landore	87F Llanelly	Oct-63	Feb-70	Didcot Railway Centre
5080	"Defiant"	May-1939	Apr-1963	87G Carmarthen	87F Llanelly	Oct-63	Aug-74	Buckingham Railway centre
7027	"Thornbury Castle"	Aug-1949	Dec-1963	81A Old Oak Common	81D Reading	May-64	Aug-72	Railway Age Crewe
Total								5
Collett 4MT 5101 2-6-2T 1929 rebuild of Churchward 3100 Class 1903								
4110		Oct-1935	Jun-1965	84H Wellington(Salop)	86E Severn Tunnel Jct.	Aug-65	May-79	Tyseley Locomotive Works
4115		Oct-1936	Jun-1965	85C Hereford	86E Severn Tunnel Jct.	Aug-65	?	Vale of Glamorgan Railway
4121		Dec-1937	Jun-1965	86F Tondu	88J Aberdare	Aug-65	Feb-81	Tyseley Locomotive Works
4141		Aug-1946	Mar-1963	85B Gloucester	85B Gloucester	Nov-63	Jan-73	Great Central Railway
4144		Sep-1946	Jun-1965	86F Tondu	86E Severn Tunnel Jct.	Aug-65	Apr-74	Didcot Railway Centre
4150		Jun-1947	Jun-1965	83A Newton Abbot	86E Severn Tunnel Jct.	Aug-65	May-74	Severn Valley Railway
4156		Aug-1947	Jun-1965	86E Severn Tun. Jct.	86E Severn Tun. Jct.	1965	Jul-1980	Cut up at Barry
4157		Aug-1947	Jun-1965	83B Taunton	86E Severn Tun. Jct.	1965	Oct-1965	Cut up at Barry
4160		Sep-1948	Jun-1965	88A Cardiff Cathays	86E Severn Tunnel Jct.	Aug-65	Aug-74	West Somerset Railway
4164		Sep-1948	Jan-1960	86E Severn Tun. Jct.	86E Severn Tun. Jct.	1960	Dec-1960	Cut up at Barry
5164		Nov-1930	Apr-1963	83A Newton Abbot	86G Pontypool Road	Nov-63	Jan-73	Severn Valley Railway
5182		Mar-1931	May-1962	85B Gloucester	85B Gloucester Hort.Rd	1962	Jul-1964	Cut up at Barry
5193	now 9351	Oct-1934	Jun-1962	83E St.Blazey	87H Neyland	Sep-62	Aug-79	West Somerset Railway
5199		Nov-1934	Mar-1963	84F Stourbridge Jct.	85B Gloucester	Nov-63	Jul-85	Llangollen Railway
Total								14
Churchward 7F 4200 2-8-0T 1910								
4247		Mar-1916	Apr-1964	86A Newport(Ebbw Jct.)	86F Tondu	Aug-64	Apr-85	Bodmin and Wenford Railway
4248		Apr-1916	May-1963	86A Newport(Ebbw Jct.)	86E Severn Tun. Jct.	Nov-63	May-86	Swindon Steam Railway Museum
4253		Mar-1917	Apr-1963	86B Newport(Pill)	86B Newport (Pill)	Aug-63	Aug-87	Pontypool and Blaenavon Railway
4270		Dec-1919	Sep-1962	86C Cardiff Canton	88A Cardiff Canton	Aug-63	Jul-85	Gloucestershire Warwickshire
4277		Apr-1920	Jun-1964	86H Aberbeeg	86H Aberbeeg	Aug-64	Jun-86	Paignton and Dartmouth
Total								5

	First Built	Date Withdrawn	1959 Shed	Last Shed at Withdraw	Arrived Barry	Left Barry	Where To
Churchward 4MT 2-6-0 4300 1911							
5312	Jun-1917	Oct-1958	87F Llanelly	87F Llanelly	1959	Aug-1959	Cut up at Barry
5322	Aug-1917	Apr-1964	81D Reading	86G Pontypool Road	Nov-64	Mar-69	Didcot Railway Centre
5345	Mar-1918	Jun-1959	86G Pontypool Road	86G Pontypool Road	1959	Dec-1959	Cut up at Barry
5355	Aug-1918	Apr-1959	85D Kidderminster	85D Kidderminster	1959	Oct-1959	Cut up at Barry
5360	Jan-1919	Sep-1958	86C Cardiff Canton	86C Cardiff Canton	1959	Dec-1959	Cut up at Barry
5392	Oct-1920	Aug-1958	85A Worcester	85A Worcester	1959	Dec-1959	Cut up at Barry
5397	Nov-1920	Jul-1958	81E Didcot	81E Didcot	1959	Dec-1959	Cut up at Barry
6331	Apr-1921	Apr-1959	84C Banbury	84C Banbury	1959	Oct-1959	Cut up at Barry
6334	May-1921	Apr-1959	82C Swindon	82C Swindon	1959	Oct-1959	Cut up at Barry
Total 9							
1932 dev. of Churchward 4MT 4300 2-6-0 1911							
9303 now 7325	Feb-1932	Apr-1964	86G Pontypool Road	86G Pontypool Road	Nov-64	Aug-75	Severn Valley Railway
Total 1							
1927 4575 dev. of Churchward 4MT 4500 2-6-2T 1906							
4588	Mar-1927	Jul-1962	83G Penzance	83D Plymouth Laira	Nov-62	Oct-70	Paignton and Dartmouth
4594	Apr-1927	Nov-1960	87H Neyland	87H Neyland	1961	Jun-1961	Cut up at Barry
5504	May-1927	Oct-1960	83B Taunton	82D Westbury	1960	Mar-1961	Cut up at Barry
5510	Nov-1927	Oct-1960	82C Swindon	83D Laira(Plymouth)	1961	Apr-1965	Cut up at Barry
5514	Nov-1927	Nov-1960	85B Gloucester	83F Truro	1961	Jun-1961	Cut up at Barry
5521	Dec-1927	Apr-1962	83B Taunton	83D Plymouth Laira	Sep-62	Sep-75	Poland
5526	May-1928	Jun-1962	82D Westbury	82D Westbury	Nov-62	Jul-85	South Devon Railway
5532	Jun-1928	Jul-1962	82C Swindon	83D Plymouth Laira	Nov-62	Mar-81	Llangollen Railway
5538	Jul-1928	Oct-1961	85B Gloucester	89A Shrewsbury	Mar-62	Jan-87	Dean Forest Railway
5539	Jul-1928	Apr-1962	83E St.Blazey	83E St.Blazey	Sep-62	?	Llangollen Railway
5541	Aug-1928	Jul-1962	89C Machynlleth	83D Plymouth Laira	Nov-62	Oct-72	Dean Forest Railway
5542	Jul-1928	Dec-1961	82D Westbury	82D Westbury	Mar-62	Sep-75	Gloucestershire Warwickshire
5546	Oct-1928	Sep-1960	83C Exeter	83F Truro	1960	Sep-1961	Cut up at Barry
5547	Oct-1928	Feb-1962	82C Swindon	82C Swindon	1962	Mar-1965	Cut up at Barry
5552	Nov-1928	Oct-1960	83F Truro	83F Truro	May-61	Jun-86	Bodmin and Wrenford
5553	Nov-1928	Nov-1961	89C Machynlleth	83E St.Blazey	Mar-62	Jan-90	West Somerset
5557	Nov-1928	Oct-1960	83E St.Blazey	83E St.Blazey	1961	Aug-1965	Cut up at Barry
5558	Nov-1928	Oct-1960	83A Newton Abbot	83A Newton Abbot	1961	Aug-1965	Cut up at Barry
5572	Feb-1929	Apr-1962	83D Laira(Plymouth)	83D Plymouth Laira	Sep-62	Aug-71	Didcot Railway Centre
Total 19							

BARRY DOCKS CONSOLIDATED LIST(continued)

	First Built	Withdrawn Date	1959 Shed	Last Shed at Withdraw	Arrived Barry	Left Barry	Where To
Churchward 4MT 4500 2-6-2T 1906							
4550	Feb-1915	Oct-1960	87H Neyland	83E St.Blazey	1961	*May-1961*	Cut up at Barry
4559	Sep-1924	Oct-1960	83E St.Blazey	83E St.Blazey	*1961*	*May-1961*	Cut up at Barry
4561	Oct-1924	May-1962	83D Plymouth Laira	83D Plymouth Laira	Sep-62	Sep-75	West Somerset
4566	Oct-1924	Apr-1962	83G Penzance	83D Plymouth Laira	Sep-62	Aug-70	Severn Valley Railway
Total							4
Collett 5MT 4900 4-6-0 "Hall" 1928							
4920 "Dumbleton Hall"	Mar-1929	Dec-1965	83A Newton Abbot	82E Bristol Barrow Rd.	Feb-66	Jun-76	South Devon Railway
4930 "Hagley Hall"	May-1929	Dec-1963	83B Taunton	82C Swindon	May-64	Jan-73	Severn Valley Railway
4936 "Kinlet Hall"	Jun-1929	Jan-1964	83A Newton Abbot	88A Cardiff East Dock	Jun-64	May-81	Tyseley Locomotive Works
4942 "Maindy Hall"	Jul-1929	Dec-1963	84C Banbury	81E Didcot	Jun-64	Apr-74	Didcot Railway Centre
4953 "Pitchford Hall"	Aug-1929	Apr-1963	82C Swindon	88A Cardiff East Dock	Nov-63	Feb-84	Tyseley Locomotive Works
4965 "Rood Ashton Hall"	Nov-1929	Dec-1963	81E Didcot	82B St.Philips Marsh	Jun-64	Oct-70	Tyseley Locomotive Works
4979 "Wootton Hall"	Feb-1930	Dec-1963	81F Oxford	81F Oxford	Jun-64	Oct-86	Lakeside and Haverthwaite railway
5900 "Hinderton Hall"	Mar-1931	Dec-1963	84A Wolverhampton	82B St.Philips Marsh	Jun-64	Jun-71	Didcot Railway Centre
5952 "Cogan Hall"	Dec-1935	Jun-1964	85A Worcester	88A Cardiff East Dock	Nov-64	Sep-81	Cambrian Railway Trust
5967 "Bickmarsh Hall"	Mar-1937	Jun-1964	83A Newton Abbot	83C Westbury	Jul-64	Aug-87	Northampton and Lamport Railway
5972 "Olton Hall"	Apr-1937	Dec-1963	83D Laira(Plymouth)	88A Cardiff East Dock	May-64	May-81	Carnforth Steamtown
Total							11
Hawksworth 5MT 6959 4-6-0 "Modified Hall" 1944							
6960 "Raveningham Hall"	Mar-1944	Sep-1964	81D Reading	81F Oxford	Jul-64	Oct-72	Gloucestershire Warwickshire
6984 "Owsden Hall"	Feb-1948	Dec-1965	85A Worcester	82E Bristol Barrow Rd.	Feb-66	Oct-86	Gloucestershire Warwickshire
6989 "Wightwick Hall"	Mar-1948	Jun-1964	85C Hereford	85B Gloucester	Aug-64	Jan-78	Buckinghamshire Railway Centre
6990 "Witherslack Hall"	Apr-1948	Dec-1965	81A Old Oak Common	82E Bristol Barrow Rd.	Feb-66	Nov-75	Great Central Railway
7903 "Foremarke Hall"	Apr-1949	Jun-1964	81A Old Oak Common	88A Cardiff East Dock	Aug-64	Jun-81	Gloucestershire Warwickshire
7927 "Willington Hall"	Oct-1950	Dec-1965	81A Old Oak Common	81F Oxford	Feb-66	?	County/ Grange project
Total							6
Churchward 1923 5205 8F dev. of Churchward 7F 4200 2-8-0T 1910							
5224	May-1924	Apr-1963	86E Severn Tun. Jct.	88L Cardiff East Dock	Aug-63	Oct-78	North Yorkshire Moors
5227	Jun-1924	Feb-1963	86A Newport(Ebbw Jct.)	86A Ebbw Junction	Nov-63	?	Vale of Glamorgan Railway Centre
5239	Aug-1924	Apr-1963	87A Neath	87A Neath	Nov-63	Jun-73	Paignton and Dartmouth
Total							3

	First Built	Date Withdrawn	1959 Shed	Last Shed at Withdrawal	Arrived Barry	Left Barry	Where To
Collett 0-6-0PT 1P 5400 Class 1931 (Class extinct)							
5407	Jan-1932	Jun-1960	84C Banbury	84C Banbury	1960	**Aug-1961**	Cut up at Barry
5417	Jun-1932	Jan-1961	85B Gloucester	84C Banbury	1961	**Sep-1961**	Cut up at Barry
5422	Nov-1935	Jun-1960	89A Oswestry	89A Oswestry	1960	**Mar-1965**	Cut up at Barry
Total						3	
Collett 5MT 5600 0-6-2T 1924							
5619	Mar-1925	Jun-1964	88C Barry	88C Barry	Sep-64	May-73	Gloucestershire Warwickshire
5637	Sep-1925	Jun-1964	88F Treherbert	88C Barry	Sep-64	Aug-74	East Somerset Railway
5643	Oct-1925	Jul-1963	88E Abercynon	88C Barry	Nov-63	Sep-71	Llangollen Railway
5651	Jan-1926	Dec-1964	84K Wrexham(Rhondda)	88A Cardiff Cathays	1965	**May-1965**	Cut up at Barry
5668	Jun-1926	Sep-1964	88F Treherbert	88C Barry	Nov-64	Aug-87	Pontypool and Blaenavon
5669	Jun-1926	Sep-1964	88A Cardiff Cathays	88A Cardiff Cathays	1964	**Mar-1965**	Cut up at Barry
Total						6	
1927 dev. of Collett 5MT 5600 0-6-2T 1924							
6619	Jan-1928	Mar-1963	88F Treherbert	88F Treherbert	Nov-63	Oct-74	Gloucestershire Warwickshire
6621	Jan-1928	Dec-1964	86H Aberbeeg	88A Cardiff Cathays	1965	**Mar-1965**	Cut up at Barry
6634	Aug-1928	Apr-1964	86G Pontypool Road	86G Pontypool Road	Aug-64	Jun-81	LNWR Locomotive Co.
6686	Oct-1928	Apr-1964	87B Duffryn Yard	88D Merthyr	Aug-64	?	Vale of Glamorgan Railway Centre
6695	Oct-1928	Jul-1964	87E Landore	88B Cardiff Radyr	Sep-64	May-79	West Somerset Railway
6696	Oct-1928	Dec-1963	84J Croes Newydd	88C Barry	1964	**Apr-1964**	Cut up at Barry
Total						6	
Collett 3F 5700 0-6-0PT 1929							
5794	Oct-1930	Dec-1959	86H Aberbeeg	86H Aberbeeg	1961	**Aug-1965**	Cut up at Barry
7702	Mar-1930	Sep-1960	84D Leamington Spa	84D Leamington Spa	1961	**Jun-1961**	Cut up at Barry
7712	Apr-1930	Jul-1960	86G Pontypool Road	86G Pontypool Road	1960	**Jun-1961**	Cut up at Barry
7719	Jun-1930	Sep-1960	82B St. Philips Marsh	85A Worcester	1960	**Jan-1961**	Cut up at Barry
7722	Jun-1930	Nov-1960	81A Old Oak Common	84F Stourbridge Jct.	1960	**Aug-1965**	Cut up at Barry
7723	Jun-1930	Aug-1960	85B Gloucester	22B Gloucester Barnwoo	1960	**Mar-1965**	Cut up at Barry
7725	Dec-1929	Aug-1960	86F Tondu	86F Tondu	1960	**Jun-1961**	Cut up at Barry
7758	Dec-1930	Jun-1960	87B Duffryn Yard	87B Duffryn Yard	1960	**Feb-1962**	Cut up at Barry
Total						8	
1930 dev. of Collett 3F 5700 0-6-0PT 1929							
6753	Aug-1947	Jan-1961	87K Swansea(Paxton Str., 87K Swansea(Paxton S		1961	**Jun-1961**	Cut up at Barry
Total						1	

BARRY DOCKS CONSOLIDATED LIST(continued)

	First	Built	Withdrawn Date	Shed 1959	Last Shed at Withdraw	Arrived Barry	Left Barry	Where To
1933 dev. of Collett 3F 5700 0-6-0PT 1929								
3612		Mar-1939	Oct-1964	86D Llantrisant	86D Llantrisant	Mar-65	Dec-78	Severn Valley Railway (spares)
3727		Jun-1937	Apr-1964	88A Cardiff Cathays	88C Barry	1964	Mar-1965	Cut up at Barry
3738		Sep-1937	Aug-1965	81D Reading	88A Cardiff East Dock	Oct-65	Apr-74	Didcot Railway Centre
3794		Oct-1938	Dec-1964	83C Exeter	81F Oxford	1965	Aug-1965	Cut up at Barry
4612		Feb-1942	Aug-1965	82C Swindon	88A Cardiff East Dock	Oct-65	Jan-81	Bodmin
8749		Jul-1931	Oct-1964	87F Llanelly	85B Gloucester Hort.Rd	1964	Mar-1965	Cut up at Barry
9629		Dec-1945	Oct-1964	83C Exeter	86G Pontypool Road	Mar-65	May-81	Pontypool
9681		May-1949	Aug-1965	89A Oswestry	88A Cardiff East Dock	Aug-65	Oct-75	Dean Forest Railway
9682		May-1949	Aug-1965	84E Tyseley	88B Cardiff Radyr	Oct-65	Nov-82	Chinner & Princes Risborough
Total								9
Collett 8P 6000 4-6-0 "King" 1927								
6023	"King Edward II"	Jun-1930	Jun-1962	81A Old Oak Common	86C Cardiff Canton	Dec-62	Dec-84	Didcot Railway Centre
6024	"King Edward 1"	Jun-1930	Jun-1962	81A Old Oak Common	86C Cardiff Canton	Dec-62	Mar-73	6024 Preservation Society
Total								2
Collett 2-6-2T 4MT 6100 Class 1931								
6115		Sep-1931	Nov-1964	81B Slough	86E Severn Tun. Jct.	1965	Apr-1965	Cut up at Barry
Total								1
Collett 0-6-0PT 2P 6400 Class 1932								
6406		Mar-1932	Jun-1960	83D Laira(Plymouth)	83D Laira(Plymouth)	1960	Jun-1961	Cut up at Barry
Total								1
Collett 5MT 7800 4-6-0 "Manor" 1938								
7802	"Bradley Manor"	Jan-1938	Nov-1965	89C Machynlleth	6D Shrewsbury	Jul-66	Nov-79	Severn Valley Railway
7812	"Erlestoke Manor"	Jan-1939	Nov-1965	83D Laira(Plymouth)	6D Shrewsbury	May-66	May-74	Severn Valley Railway
7819	"Hinton Manor"	Feb-1939	Nov-1965	89A Oswestry	6D Shrewsbury	May-66	Jan-73	Severn Valley Railway
7820	"Dinmore Manor"	Nov-1950	Nov-1965	83D Laira(Plymouth)	6D Shrewsbury	May-66	Sep-79	West Somerset Railway
7821	"Ditcheat Manor"	Nov-1950	Nov-1965	84E Tyseley	6D Shrewsbury	May-66	Jun-81	Cambrian Railways Trust
7822	"Foxcote Manor"	Dec-1950	Nov-1965	89A Oswestry	6D Shrewsbury	May-66	Jan-75	Llangollen Railway
7827	"Lydham Manor"	Dec-1950	Oct-1965	89A Oswestry	6D Shrewsbury	May-66	Jun-70	Paignton and Dartmouth
7828	"Odney Manor"	Dec-1950	Oct-1965	84G Shrewsbury	6D Shrewsbury	Jun-81	Jun-81	West Somerset Railway
Total								8

BARRY DOCKS CONSOLIDATED LIST(continued)

	First Built	Date Withdrawn	1959 Shed	Last Shed at Withdrawn	Arrived Barry	Left Barry	Where To
1949 development of Hawksworth 4F 9400 0-6-0PT 1947							
8419	Apr-1950	Jan-1960	88C Barry	88C Barry	1961	Mar-1965	Cut up at Barry
8473	Aug-1951	Jan-1961	83G Penzance	83G Penzance	1961	Aug-1961	Cut up at Barry
8475	Nov-1951	Sep-1964	87D Swansea East Dock	88A Cardiff Cathays	1964	Jan-1965	Cut up at Barry
8479	Jun-1952	Oct-1964	82B St. Philips Marsh	88A Cardiff Cathays	1964	Mar-1965	Cut up at Barry
9436	Jan-1951	Jul-1960	87E Landore	87E Landore	1960	Jun-1961	Cut up at Barry
9438	Feb-1951	Jun-1959	85B Gloucester	85B Gloucester	1960	Jun-1961	Cut up at Barry
9439	Feb-1951	Jun-1959	83C Exeter	83C Exeter	1960	Jun-1961	Cut up at Barry
9443	Mar-1951	Jun-1959	86C Cardiff Canton	86C Cardiff Canton	1960	Jun-1961	Cut up at Barry
9445	Apr-1951	Jan-1960	85B Gloucester	85B Gloucester	1961	Jan-1965	Cut up at Barry
9449	Jun-1951	Jun-1960	84C Banbury	84C Banbury	1961	Jan-1965	Cut up at Barry
9459	Nov-1951	Sep-1959	86H Aberbeeg	86H Aberbeeg	1960	Jun-1961	Cut up at Barry
9462	Dec-1951	Nov-1960	83A Newton Abbot	83A Newton Abbot	1961	May-1965	Cut up at Barry
9466	Feb-1952	Jul-1964	85A Worcester	88B Cardiff Radyr	Nov-64	Sep-75	Tyseley Locomotive Works
9468	Feb-1952	Aug-1960	86A Newport(Ebbw Jct.)	86A Newport(Ebbw Jct.)	1961	Aug-1965	Cut up at Barry
9491	Mar-1954	Jun-1959	87D Swansea East Dock	87D Swansea East Doc	1960	Mar-1965	Cut up at Barry
9492	May-1954	Jun-1959	85B Gloucester	85B Gloucester	1960	Feb-1962	Cut up at Barry
9496	Oct-1954	Dec-1959	84A Wolverhampton	84A Wolverhampton	1960	Jun-1961	Cut up at Barry
9499	Jul-1955	Sep-1959	82B St. Philips Marsh	86H Aberbeeg	1961	Mar-1965	Cut up at Barry
Total	18						
Urie 6F S15 4-6-0 1920 (with smoke deflectors)							
30499	May-1920	Jan-1964	70B Feltham	70B Feltham	Jun-64	Nov-83	East Lancashire Railway
30506	Oct-1920	Jan-1964	70B Feltham	70B Feltham	Oct-64	Apr-76	Watercress Line
30512	Feb-1921	Mar-1964	70B Feltham	70B Feltham	1964	Jan-1965	Cut up at Barry
Total	3						
Maunsell 1927 dev. of Urie 6F S15 4-6-0 1920 (with smoke deflectors)							
30825	Apr-1927	Jan-1964	72B Salisbury	72B Salisbury	Jun-64	Nov-86	North Yorkshire Moors
30828	Jul-1927	Jan-1964	72B Salisbury	72B Salisbury	Jun-64	Mar-81	Watercress Line
30830	Aug-1927	Jul-1964	72B Salisbury	72B Salisbury	Dec-64	Sep-87	North Yorkshire Moors
Total	3						
Maunsell 1936 dev. of Urie 1920 6F S15 4-6-0 (with smoke deflectors)							
30841	Jul-1936	Jan-1964	72A Exmouth Jct.	70B Feltham	Jun-64	Sep-72	North Yorkshire Moors
30844	Oct-1936	Jun-1964	72A Exmouth Jct.	70B Feltham	1964	Jan-1965	Cut up at Barry
30847	Dec-1936	Jan-1964	72B Salisbury	70B Feltham	Jun-64	Oct-78	Bluebell Railway, Sussex
Total	3						

BARRY DOCKS CONSOLIDATED LIST(continued)

		First Built	Withdrawn Date	1959 Shed	at Withdraw Last Shed	Barry Arrived	Barry Left	Where To
Maunsell 4F Q 0-6-0 1938 (with multiple jet blastpipe and large diameter chimney)								
30541		Jan-1939	Nov-1964	71B Bournemouth	70C Guildford	Feb-65	May-74	Bluebell Railway, Sussex
	Total 2							
Maunsell 4P3F U 2-6-0 1928								
31618		Oct-1928	Jan-1964	71A Eastleigh	70C Guildford	Jun-64	Jan-69	Bluebell Railway, Sussex
31625		Mar-1929	Jan-1964	70C Guildford	70C Guildford	Jan-64	Mar-80	Mid-Hants Railway
31638		May-1931	Jan-1964	70F Fratton	70C Guildford	Jun-64	Jul-80	Bluebell Railway, Sussex
	Total 3							
Maunsell 4P3F U1 2-6-0 1928 (rebuilt from ill-fated "River" Class 2-6-4T 1917)								
31806		Jun-1928	Jan-1964	70D Basingstoke	70C Guildford	Jun-64	Oct-76	Mid-Hants Railway
	Total 1							
Maunsell 4P5F N 2-6-0 1917								
31874		Sep-1925	Mar-1964	73B Bricklayers Arms	83D Exmouth Junction	Jun-64	Mar-74	Mid-Hants Railway
	Total 1							
Bulleid 7P5F "West Country & Battle of Britain Class 4-6-2 1945								
34007	"Wadebridge"	Sep-1945	Oct-1965	70A Nine Elms	70E Salisbury	May-66	May-81	Mid Hants Railway
34067	"Tangmere"	Sep-1947	Nov-1963	73A Stewarts Lane	83D Exmouth Jct	Apr-65	Jan-81	Southall
34070	"Manston"	Oct-1947	Aug-1964	73H Dover	83D Exmouth Jct	Dec-64	Jun-83	Swanage Railway
34072	"257 Squadron"	Apr-1948	Oct-1964	72A Exmouth Jct.	70D Eastleigh	Mar-65	Nov-84	Swanage Railway
34073	"249 Squadron"	May-1948	Sep-1964	73H Dover	70D Eastleigh	Apr-65	?	Bury
34081	"92 Squadron"	Sep-1948	Aug-1964	72A Exmouth Jct.	70D Eastleigh	Apr-65	Nov-76	North Norfolk Railway
34092	City of Wells	Sep-1949	Nov-1964	73A Stewarts Lane	72B Salisbury	Mar-65	Oct-71	Keighley and Worth Valley
34094	"Mortehoe"	Oct-1949	Aug-1964	70A Nine Elms	70A Nine Elms	1964	Nov-1964	Cut up at Barry
34105	"Swanage"	Mar-1950	Oct-1964	71B Bournemouth	70D Eastleigh	Feb-65	Mar-78	Mid-Hants Railway
	Total 9							

BARRY DOCKS CONSOLIDATED LIST (continued)

		First Built	Date Withdrawn	1959 Shed	Last Shed at Withdraw	Arrived Barry	Left Barry	Where To
1957 development of Bulleid 7P6F 4-6-2 "West Country & Battle of Britain" (air-smoothed casing removed)								
34010	"Sidmouth"	Sep-1945	Mar-1965	70A Nine Elms	70D Eastleigh	Sep-65	Nov-82	Herston Works, Swanage
34016	"Bodmin"	Nov-1945	Jun-1964	73G Ramsgate	70D Eastleigh	Nov-64	Jul-72	Mid-Hants Railway
34027	"Taw Valley"	Apr-1946	Aug-1964	73G Ramsgate	72B Salisbury	Dec-64	Apr-80	Severn Valley Railway
34028	"Eddystone"	May-1946	May-1964	71B Bournemouth	70D Eastleigh	Nov-64	Apr-86	Swanage Railway
34039	"Boscastle"	Sep-1946	May-1965	71B Bournemouth	70D Eastleigh	Sep-65	Jan-73	Great Central Railway
34045	"Ottery St. Mary"	Oct-1946	Jun-1964	71B Bournemouth	70F Bournemouth	1965	*May-1965*	*Cut up at Barry*
34046	"Braunton"	Nov-1946	Oct-1965	71B Bournemouth	70F Bournemouth	Jan-66	?	West Somerset Railway
34053	"Sir Keith Park"	Jan-1947	Oct-1965	72B Salisbury	70F Bournemouth	Mar-66	Jun-84	Sellindge, Southern Locos Ltd.
34058	"Sir Frederick Pile"	Dec-1948	Oct-1964	72A Exmouth Jct.	70D Eastleigh	Apr-65	Jul-86	Avon Valley Railway
34059	"Sir Archibald Sinclair"	Apr-1949	May-1966	72B Salisbury	70E Salisbury	Oct-66	Oct-79	Bluebell Railway, Sussex
34101	"Hartland"	Feb-1950	Jul-1966	73A Stewarts Lane	70D Eastleigh	Oct-66	Jul-78	North York Moors
	Total 11							
1956 dev. of Bulleid 8P 4-6-2 "Merchant Navy" 1941								
35005	"Canadian Pacific"	Jan-1942	Oct-1965	70A Nine Elms	70G Weymouth	Jan-66	Mar-73	Mid Hants Railway
35006	"P&O Steam Navigation Co."	Jan-1942	Aug-1964	72B Salisbury	72B Salisbury	Dec-64	Mar-83	Gloucestershire Warwickshire
35009	"Shaw Savill"	Jun-1942	Sep-1964	72A Exmouth Jct.	83D Exmouth Jct	Dec-64	?	East Lancashire Railway
35010	"Blue Star"	Jul-1942	Sep-1966	71B Bournemouth	70G Weymouth	Mar-67	Jan-85	Colne Valley Rrailway
35011	"General Steam Navigation"	Dec-1944	Feb-1966	72A Exmouth Junction	70F Bournemouth	Jun-66	?	West Somerset Railway
35018	"British India Line"	May-1945	Aug-1964	70A Nine Elms	70A Nine Elms	Dec-64	Mar-80	South Coast Steam, Portland
35022	"Holland-America Line"	Oct-1948	May-1966	71B Bournemouth	70G Weymouth	Oct-66	Mar-86	Southall London
35025	"Brocklebank Line"	Nov-1948	Sep-1964	71B Bournemouth	83D Exmouth Jct	Dec-64	Feb-86	Sellindge, Kent
35027	"Port Line"	Dec-1948	Sep-1966	71B Bournemouth	70G Weymouth	Mar-67	Dec-82	Southall London
35029	"Ellerman Lines"	Feb-1949	Sep-1966	70A Nine Elms	70G Weymouth	Mar-67	Jan-74	National Railway Museum
	Total 11							
Ivatt 2MT 2-6-2T 1946								
41248		Nov-1949	Nov-1964	82G Templecombe	83F Barnstaple Junction	1965	*Mar-1965*	*Cut up at Barry*
41303		Mar-1952	Oct-1964	73B Bricklayers Arms	75A Brighton	1965	*Mar-1965*	*Cut up at Barry*
41312		May-1952	Jul-1967	73E Faversham	70A Nine Elms	Jan-68	Aug-74	Mid Hants Railway
41313		May-1952	Nov-1965	73E Faversham	70D Eastleigh	Feb-66	Jul-75	Isle of Wight Steam Railway
	Total 4							
Hughes/Fowler 5MT "Crab" 2-6-0 1926								
42765		Aug-1927	Dec-1966	24F Fleetwood	8H Birkenhead	Jun-67	Apr-78	East Lancashire Railway
42859		Mar-1930	Dec-1966	1A Willesden	8H Birkenhead	Jun-67	Dec-86	RAF Binbrook, Linconshire
	Total 2							

BARRY DOCKS CONSOLIDATED LIST (continued)

	First Built	Date Withdrawn	1959 Shed	Last Shed at Withdrawn	Arrived Barry	Left Barry	Where To
Total						2	
Stanier 5MT 2-6-0 1933							
42968	Jan-1934	Dec-1966	5A Crewe North	8F Wigan(Springs Br.)	Jun-67	Dec-73	Severn Valley Railway
Total						1	
Midland 4F 0-6-0 1911							
43924	Oct-1920	Jun-1965	85E Glouc.(Barn Wood)	82E Bristol Barrow Rd.	Oct-65	Sep-68	Keighley and Worth Valley
Total						1	
Midland 4F 0-6-0 1924							
44123	Jul-1925	Jun-1965	85E Glouc.(Barn Wood)	85B Gloucester	Aug-65	Dec-81	Avon Valley Railway
44422	Oct-1927	Jun-1965	82F Bath (Green Park)	85B Gloucester	Aug-65	Apr-77	West Somerset Railway
Total						2	
Stanier 5MT 4-6-0 "Black Five" 1934							
44901	Oct-1945	Aug-1965	12A Carlisle Kingmoor	12A Carlisle Kingmoor	Jan-66	?	Vale of Glamorgan Railway
45163	Aug-1935	May-1965	12A Carlisle Kingmoor	12A Carlisle Kingmoor	Jan-66	Jan-87	Colne Valley Railway
45293	Dec-1936	Aug-1965	12B Carlisle Upperby	12B Carlisle Upperby	Jan-66	Dec-86	Colne Valley Railway
45337	Apr-1937	Feb-1965	26B Agecroft	12A Carlisle Kingmoor	Jan-66	May-84	East Lancashire Railway
45379	Jul-1937	Jul-1965	5A Crewe North	1A Willesden	Oct-65	May-74	Mid Hants Railway
45491	Dec-1943	Jul-1965	12A Carlisle Kingmoor	12A Carlisle Kingmoor	Jan-66	Jul-81	Midland Railway Butterley
Total						6	
Stanier 6P5F 4-6-0 "Jubilee" 1934							
45690 "Leander"	Mar-1936	Mar-1964	82E Bristol Barrow Rd.	82E Bristol Barrow Rd.	Jul-64	May-72	East Lancashire Railway
45699 "Galatea"	Apr-1936	Nov-1964	82E Bristol Barrow Rd.	6D Shrewsbury	May-65	Apr-80	West Coast Railway Company
Total						2	
Ivatt 2MT 2-6-0 1946							
46428	Dec-1948	Dec-1966	8F Wigan(Springs Br.)	5B Crewe South	Sep-67	Oct-79	East Lancashire Railway
46447	Mar-1950	Dec-1966	11B Workington	8F Wigan(Springs Br.)	Jun-67	Jun-72	Buckinghamshire Rail Centre
46512	Dec-1952	Dec-1966	89A Oswestry	5B Crewe South	Jun-67	May-73	Strathspey Railway
46521	Feb-1953	Oct-1966	89B Brecon	6F Machynlleth	Mar-67	Mar-71	Great Central Railway
Total						4	

BARRY DOCKS CONSOLIDATED LIST (continued)

	First Built	Date Withdrawn	1959 Shed	Last Shed at Withdrawal	Arrived Barry	Left Barry	Where To
Midland 3F "Jinty" 0-6-0T 1924 dev. of Johnson 1899 design							
47279	Aug-1924	Dec-1966	14E Bedford	8G Sutton Oak	Jun-67	Aug-79	Keighley and Worth Valley
47298	Oct-1924	Dec-1966	8G Sutton Oak	8G Sutton Oak	Jun-67	Jul-74	Llangollen Railway
47324	Jun-1926	Dec-1966	6C Birkenhead	8H Birkenhead	Jun-67	Feb-78	East Lancashire Railway
47327	Jul-1926	Dec-1966	27F Brunswick (Liverpool)	8L Aintree	Jan-68	Jul-70	Midland Railway Centre
47357	Jul-1926	Dec-1966	8A Edge Hill	8A Edge Hill	Nov-67	Jul-70	Midland Railway Centre
47406	Dec-1926	Dec-1966	24L Lancaster	8A Edge Hill	Jun-67	Jun-83	Great Central Railway
47493	Feb-1928	Dec-1966	8C Speke Junction	8A Edge Hill	Jun-67	Nov-72	Spa Valley Railway
Total			7				
Stanier 8F 2-8-0 "Big Eight" 1935							
48151	Sep-1942	Jan-1968	41D Canklow	8E Northwich	Sep-68	Nov-75	West Coast Railway Company
48173	Jun-1943	Jul-1965	2A Rugby	6B Mold Junction	Oct-65	?	Churnet Valley Railway
48305	Nov-1943	Jan-1968	2E Northampton	8C Speke Junction	Sep-68	Nov-85	Great Central Railway
48431	Mar-1944	May-1964	82B St. Philip's Marsh	82F Bath Green Park	Aug-64	May-72	Llangollen Railway
48518	Aug-1944	Jul-1965	1A Willesden	1A Willesden	Oct-65	?	County/ Patriot project
48624	Nov-1943	Jul-1965	1A Willesden	1A Willesden	Oct-65	Jul-81	Darley Dale, Peak Rail
Total			6				
Fowler ex Somerset & Dorset Joint Railway 7F 2-8-0 1914							
53808	Jul-1925	Mar-1964	82F Bath Green Park	82F Bath Green Park	Jun-64	Oct-70	West Somerset Railway
53809	Jul-1925	Jun-1964	82F Bath Green Park	82F Bath Green Park	Aug-64	Dec-75	Midland Railway Centre, Butterley
Total			2				
Thompson 5MT B1 4-6-0 1942							
61264	Dec-1947	Dec-1965	30F Parkeston	40E Colwick	Sep-68	Jul-76	Thompson B1 Loco Trust
Total			1				
BR Standard 8P 4-6-2 Derby 1954							
71000 "Duke of Gloucester"	May-1954	Nov-1962	5A Crewe North	5A Crewe North	Oct-67	Apr-74	71000 Trust
Total			1				
BR Standard 5MT 4-6-0 Doncaster 1951							
73082	Jul-1955	Jun-1966	73A Stewarts Lane	70C Guildford	Nov-66	Oct-79	Bluebell Railway
73096	Nov-1955	Nov-1967	84G Shrewsbury	9F Patricroft	Feb-68	Jul-85	Mid-Hants Railway
Total			2				
BR Standard 5MT 4-6-0 Doncaster 1951. Caprotti valve gear 1956 development.							
73129	Aug-1956	Nov-1967	26F Patricroft	9H Patricroft	Feb-68	Jan-73	Midland Railway Centre
73156	Dec-1956	Nov-1967	41B Sheff(Grimesthorpe)	9K Bolton	Feb-68	Oct-86	Great Central Railway
Total			2				

BARRY DOCKS CONSOLIDATED LIST(continued)

	First Built	Date Withdrawn	Shed 1959	Last Shed at Withdrawl	Arrived Barry	Left Barry	Where To
BR Standard 4MT 4-6-0 Brighton 1951							
75014	Dec-1951	Dec-1966	6A Chester(Midland)	6D Shrewsbury	Oct-67	Feb-81	Paignton and Dartmouth
75069	Sep-1955	Sep-1966	73H Dover	70D Eastleigh	May-67	Mar-73	Severn Valley Railway
75078	Jan-1956	Jul-1966	70D Basingstoke	70D Eastleigh	Nov-66	Jun-72	Keighley and Worth Valley
75079	Jan-1956	Nov-1966	70D Basingstoke	70D Eastleigh	Apr-67	Mar-82	Mid-Hants Railway
Total							4
BR Standard 4MT 2-6-0 Doncaster 1953							
76017	Jul-1953	Jul-1965	71A Eastleigh	70E Salisbury	Jan-66	Jan-74	Mid-Hants Railway
76077	Dec-1956	Nov-1967	8G Sutton Oak	8F Wigan(Springs Br.)	Sep-68	May-87	Gloucestershire Warwickshire
76079	Feb-1957	Nov-1967	8G Sutton Oak	8F Wigan(Springs Br.)	Sep-68	Jul-74	East Lancashire Railway
76080	Feb-1957	Dec-1967	24D Lower Darwen	8F Springs Branch	1968	Apr-1972	Cut up at Barry
76084	Mar-1957	Nov-1967	24J Lancaster	8F Wigan(Springs Br.)	Sep-68	Jan-83	Lincolnshire, private purchaser
Total							5
BR Standard 2MT 2-6-0 Doncaster 1953							
78018	Mar-1954	Nov-1966	12D Kirkby Stephen	6D Shrewsbury	Jun-67	Oct-78	Darlington Railway Centre
78019	Mar-1954	Nov-1966	12D Kirkby Stephen	5B Crewe South	Jun-67	Mar-73	Great Central Railway
78022	May-1954	Sep-1966	41C Millhouses	10D Lostock Hall	Mar-67	Jun-75	Keighley and Worth Valley
78059	Sep-1956	Nov-1966	6D Chester(Northgate)	5B Crewe South	Jun-67	May-83	Bluebell Railway
Total							4
							being converted to 84030
BR Standard 4MT 2-6-4T Doncaster 1953							
80064	Jun-1953	Sep-1965	1C Watford	82E Bristol Barrow Rd.	Oct-65	Feb-73	Bluebell Railway
80067	Aug-1953	Jun-1965	1C Watford	83G Templecombe	1965	Sep-1965	Cut up at Barry
80072	Nov-1953	Jul-1965	33B Tilbury	2A Tyseley	Jan-66	?	Llangollen Railway
80078	Feb-1954	Jul-1965	33B Tilbury	6C Croes Newydd	Jun-66	Sep-66	Swanage Railway
80079	Mar-1954	Jul-1965	33B Tilbury	6C Croes Newydd	Jan-66	May-71	Severn Valley Railway
80080	Mar-1954	Jul-1965	6C Croes Newydd	6C Croes Newydd	Jan-66	Nov-80	Midland Railway Centre
80097	Mar-1954	Jul-1965	6C Croes Newydd	6F Machynlleth	Jan-66	May-85	East Lancashire Railway
80098	Dec-1954	Jul-1965	6F Machynlleth	6F Machynlleth	Jan-66	Nov-84	Churnet Valley Railway
80100	Dec-1954	Jul-1965	6F Machynlleth	6F Machynlleth	Jan-66	Oct-78	Bluebell Railway
80104	Mar-1955	Jul-1965	6F Machynlleth	6D Shrewsbury	Jan-66	Sep-84	Swanage Railway
80105	Apr-1955	Jul-1965	6F Machynlleth	6F Machynlleth	Jan-66	Oct-73	Bo'ness & Kinneil Railway
80135	Apr-1956	Jul-1965	6F Machynlleth	6F Machynlleth	Jan-66	Apr-73	North Yorkshire Moors Railway
80136	May-1956	Jul-1965	6D Shrewsbury	6D Shrewsbury	Jun-66	Aug-79	Llangollen Railway
80150	Dec-1956	Oct-1965	75A Brighton	70D Eastleigh	Jan-66	?	Barry Island
80151	Jan-1957	May-1967	75A Brighton	70D Eastleigh	Oct-67	Mar-75	Bluebell Railway
Total							15

BARRY DOCKS CONSOLIDATED LIST(continued)

	First Built	Date Withdrawn	1959 Shed	Last Shed at Withdraw	Arrived Barry	Left Barry	Where To
BR Standard 9F 2-10-0 Brighton 1954							
92085	May-1956	Dec-1966	15A Wellingborough	8H Birkenhead	1967	**Jul-1980**	Cut up at Barry
92134	May-1957	Dec-1966	15A Wellingborough	8H Birkenhead	Jun-67	Jul-80	Railway Age Crewe
Total	2						
BR Standard 9F 2-10-0 BR Brighton 1954. Double chimney development 1957							
92207	Jun-1959	Dec-1964	82B St.Philips Marsh	86B Ebbw Junction	Mar-65	Oct-86	Shillingstone Railway Centre
92212	Sep-1959	Jan-1968	84C Banbury	10A Carnforth	Sep-68	Sep-79	Mid-Hants Railway
92214	Oct-1959	Aug-1965	86C Cardiff Canton	86E Severn Tunnel Jct.	Oct-65	Dec-80	East Lancashire Railway
92219	Jan-1960	Mar-1965	82B St.Philips Marsh	88A Cardiff East Dock	Oct-65	May-85	Midland Railway Centre
92232	Aug-1958	Dec-1964	86C Cardiff Canton	88A Cardiff East Dock	1965	**Mar-1965**	Cut up at Barry
92240	Oct-1958	Aug-1965	81A Old Oak Common	81C Southall	Oct-65	Oct-78	Bluebell Railway
92245	Nov-1958	Dec-1964	81A Old Oak Common	81C Southall	Mar-65	?	Vale of Glamorgan Railway Centre
Total	7						
Diesels							
B-B "Warship" Class 4 1958							
D600 "Active"	1958	Dec-1967	83D Laira(Plymouth)	?	1968	**Mar-1970**	Cut up at Barry
D601 "Ark Royal"	1958	Dec-1967	83D Laira(Plymouth)	?	1968	**Jul-1980**	Cut up at Barry
Total	2						
Type 2 Bo-Bo North British 1959							
D6122	1959	Dec-1967	?	?	?	Jun-1980	Cut up at Barry
Total	1						
Type 1 Bo-Bo British Thomson-Houston 1957							
D8206	1957	Sep-1968	1D Devons Road(Bow)	?	Feb-70	**Feb-1970**	Cut up at Barry
Total	1						

1959 Shed Dates

WR - 21 Mar 59
SR - 1 May 59
LMR - 21 Mar 59
ER - 11 Apr 59

Steam	290
Diesels	4

I am indebted for the post 1965 Barry Update to Alan Warren's "Barry Scrapyard – The Preservation Miracle" first published in 1988 and also for the Greatwestern.org website.

On we go

Once D.S. had paid his photographic tribute to 3862 I got him interested in kicking up some dust by heading him Barry Docks station wards. We noted the closed (formerly 88C Barry) shed with interest. Of no interest were the contents. D.S. ventured in and did his old Mother Hubbard act and found the cupboard to be bare.

We eventually reached the station and in the company of another railwayist got on to the 13.03 to Cardiff.

		Schedule	Actual	Miles
Depart	BARRY	13.03	13.03	0
Arrive	CARDIFF GENERAL	13.29	13.29	11

Our diesel bucket duly departed and we paid our last glance at the greatest collection of engines ever assembled in one place. Quantitatively I recollect seeing 177 engines at 66A Polmadie in November 1958 and 842 engines in all in an unforgettable visit to Glasgow with Scottish Railfans (now the posher named Railway Society of Scotland). That day we visited 65A Eastfield, 65B St.Rollox, 65C Parkhead, 65E Kipps, 66A Polmadie, 66B Motherwell, 66C Hamilton and 67A Corkerhill (65D Dawsholm was not visited on that occasion). 842 engines from only eight sheds makes you think. *It would have been interesting to list them for historical purposes but my notebooks disappeared around 1974-1975 when my parents temporarily moved house while their own house was being upgraded.* Quantitatively that must rank as my greatest memory but qualitatively there would never be or has ever been anything like Woodhams Scrapyard at Barry Docks.

In the Barry area we noted English Electric Type 3's D6935 and D6994. Both came from 86A Cardiff Canton. D6994 looked candidatus (brand new) and had probably been out shopped newly built from a railway works a few days before. It could be the latest English Electric Type 3 in service.

BARRY TO CARDIFF					Built	Withdrawn	Scrap
			Home shed				
Diesels							
English Electric Type 3 Co-Co 1961							
D6935		86A	Cardiff Canton		Apr-1964		
D6994		86A	Cardiff Canton		Aug-1965		
Total	2						
On Journey	2	Kops	2				
Steam	0	Diesels	2				
		Home Area		2 Visitors	0		
Shed	86A	2					
Distribution							

"Discretion says we can't visit East Dock"
"Valour says we can do it!"

Our railwayist friend whom we had met at Barry Docks station asked us if we were doing more sheds in the area. I glanced at my watch. We would be in Cardiff General by about 13.30. That left us about an hour before our 14.20 train back to Birmingham New Street. I had earlier worked out that the least time we could do 88A Cardiff East Dock was 85 minutes. That gave us a recovery time of minus 25 minutes. D.S. had already botched up Leicester where we had a recovery time of minus 20 minutes. Doubtless he would need to be only somewhere near his usual degenerate self to botch up any thoughts of doing East Dock in an hour and getting the train. No, 86A Cardiff Canton was the better bet. It was a diesel depot but nevertheless a pretty good diesel depot. Only 16A Toton resembled it in size. Cardiff Canton's recovery time was an ample +15 minutes. Even making allowances for the depreciating D.S. through his deteriorating physical condition there still seemed to be ample time to do Canton.

Then fate took a hand

Our friend showed us that there were about 20 dead GWR locos at East Dock including Modified Halls, Manors, Granges and the last BR steam engine to be built – 92220 "Evening Star." The temptation was very great. It was made even greater when our railwayist said that East Dock could easily be done in an hour. He said that you could get there in 15-20 minutes. He promised to show us part of the way for his "quick way" to East Dock.

That was that! We are going to East Dock and we were going to forget about visiting dieselised Canton. Back at the ranch (or rather at Cardiff General) we wasted no time in bustling out of the station. Our guide fairly knew the ropes and we covered the first ¾ of a mile through busy Cardiff city centre and down the quieter Herbert Street in fast time. Then opposite the Cambridge Bar our guide showed us the Docks entrance and said he would see us back at the station. So far we were beating the clock.

According to our LocoShed directory the shed was a further ¾ of a mile along the dock wharf. As we turned into the Docks we were met by an open roundhouse. No walls just a radial railway section. On "shed" were three 0-6-0 BR diesel shunters. Presumably a Canton sub-shed!

It was a lovely day by now and rather warm. Our "four minute mile run" was now reduced to mere jogging or a fast walk. The harbour looked on the deep side of deep so I kept clear of the edge. I suggested to D.S. to take a plunge after the visit if he felt hot and take a shortcut by water back to the station. He wasn't amused. I spotted a Russian cargo ship on the quayside as we marched past with East Dock shed in our sights. Now's your chance to defect to Russia I said to D.S.

On arriving at 88A Cardiff East Dock shed on the left hand side of the docks road two things stuck me. They could be summed up by two words DEATH and DEVASTATION. Nothing stirred. No sign of any life humans or engines. Something like the Barry Docks atmosphere with a Marie Celeste ghostly theme.

In the shed proper we found 92220 "Evening Star" in a dark corner of the shed in a shocking dirty condition. The number could barely be discerned in the muck. Here she was withdrawn and awaiting preservation. She had been withdrawn owing to a cracked frame and it was indeed a buckled mess and a difficult preservation restorative job.

Of course, everything on shed was withdrawn. All South Wales steam, in fact, was more or less withdrawn. At least we were lucky visiting East Dock before all the condemned engines were consigned to scrapyards (other than the lucky "Evening Star"). The actual East Dock shed was now officially closed and with it the last of South Wales steam (or at least an important part of it).

88A CARDIFF EAST DOCK

			Home shed		Built	Withdrawn	Scrap
Diesels							
BR 0-6-0 Shunter 1953							
D3364			86A	Cardiff Canton	Jun-1957		
D3405			86A	Cardiff Canton	Dec-1957		
D3603			86A	Cardiff Canton	Oct-1958		
Total		3					
Steam			Home shed		Built	Withdrawn	Scrap
Collett dev.1938 of Churchward 8F 2-8-0 1903							
3808			ex 86B	Newport	Sep-1939	Jul-1965	Oct-1965
3830			ex 86B	Newport	Nov-1940	Jun-1965	Oct-1965
3837			ex 86B	Newport	Jan-1942	Jul-1965	Oct-1965
3840			ex 86B	Newport	Jan-1942	Jul-1965	Oct-1965
3861			ex 86B	Newport	Nov-1942	Jul-1965	Oct-1965
3864			ex 86B	Newport	Nov-1942	Jul-1965	Oct-1965
Total		6					
Churchward 7F 4200 2-8-0T 1910							
5202			ex 88A		Dec-1922	Jun-1965	Jun-1966
Total		1					
Churchward 1923 5205 8F dev. of Churchward 7F 4200 2-8-0T 1910							
5208			ex 88A		Aug-1923	Jun-1965	May-1966
5241			ex 86B	Newport	Aug-1924	Jun-1965	May-1966
Total		2					
Collett 5MT 5600 0-6-2T 1924							
5621			ex 88D	Merthyr	Jun-1925	Jun-1965	Oct-1965
5665			ex 88A	ex 86G Pontypool Rd.	Jun-1926	Jun-1965	Aug-1965
5688			ex 88D	Merthyr	Jan-1927	Jun-1965	Oct-1965
5692			ex 88B	Radyr	Jan-1927	Jul-1965	Oct-1965
Total		4					
1927 dev. of Collett 5MT 5600 0-6-2T 1924							
6657			ex 88B	Radyr	Aug-1928	Jun-1965	Oct-1965
6661			ex 88B	Radyr	Sep-1928	Jun-1965	Oct-1965
6672			ex 88B	Radyr	Sep-1928	Jul-1965	Oct-1965
6689			ex 88B	Radyr	Oct-1928	Jun-1965	Oct-1965
Total		4					
1933 dev. of Collett 3F 5700 0-6-0PT 1929							
3654			ex 88A	(ex 87A Neath)	Dec-1939	Aug-1965	Feb-1967
3738	*to Barry Docks*		ex 88A		Sep-1937	Aug-1965	saved
4612	*to Barry Docks*		ex 88A	(ex 87A Neath)	Feb-1942	Aug-1965	saved
9651			ex 88A		Jun-1946	Jul-1965	Oct-1965
9676			ex 88A		Mar-1949	Jun-1965	Oct-1965
9681	*to Barry Docks*		ex 88A		May-1949	Aug-1965	saved
Total		6					
Collett 4MT 6100 2-6-2T 1931 dev. of 5101 Class							
6116			ex 88B	Radyr	Sep-1931	Jun-1965	May-1966
Total		1					
Collett 5MT 6800 4-6-0 "Grange" 1936							
6820	"Kingstone Grange"		ex 88A		Jan-1937	Jul-1965	Oct-1965
6837	"Forthampton Grange"		ex 88A		Sep-1937	Jul-1965	Oct-1965
6869	"Resolven Grange"		ex 88A		Mar-1939	Jul-1965	Oct-1965
Total		3					
Hawksworth 5MT 6959 4-6-0 "Modified Hall" 1944							
6978	"Haroldstone Hall"		ex 86B	Newport	Nov-1947	Jul-1965	Oct-1965
7923	"Speke Hall"		ex 88A		Sep-1950	Jun-1965	Oct-1965
Total		2					
Collett 5MT 7800 4-6-0 "Manor" 1938							
7811	"Dunley Manor"		ex 88A		Dec-1938	Jul-1965	Oct-1965
Total		1					

		Home shed		Built	Withdrawn	Scrap
1949 dev. of Hawksworth 4F 9400 0-6-0PT 1947						
9437		ex 88B	Radyr	*Jan-1951*	*Jun-1965*	*Oct-1965*
Total	1					
BR Standard 9F 2-10-0 Brighton 1954. Double chimney dev. 1957						
92220	"Evening Star"	ex 88A		*Mar-1960*	*Mar-1965*	*saved*
Total	1					

On Shed	35	**Kops**	32		
Steam	32	**Diesels**	3		
Withdrawn	32	**To be preserved**	1		

Home Locos	15	**Home Area**		**9 Visitors**	12	
Shed	**88A**	15	**88B**	7	**88D**	2
Distribution	**86A**	3	**86B**	8		
Steam Classes on View	12					
Steam Origin	**GWR**	31	**BR**	1		

General Pattern	5MT 5600 0-6-2T - Welsh Valleys	
	3F 5700 0-6-0PT East Dock	
	8F 2800 2-8-0 Newport	

Shed Highlight:-

	Steam		92220 "Evening Star" - of course!!!				
Steam	*Aug-50*	62	*Mar-59*	0	*May-65*	31	
Allocation					*Aug-65*	0	
			Closed to Steam:-			*Aug-65*	
Home Steam	withdrawn but not yet scrapped locos						
On/Off Shed	On Shed	15	Off Shed	6	% On Shed	71%	
Not on Shed							
0-6-0PT 1933			3790	4623	4639	4663	4
		scrap	Oct-65	Oct-65	Oct-65	Oct-65	
BR 9F 2-10-0				92219		92248	2
				to Barry	scrap	Aug-65	
						total	6
	recently withdrawn not on shed or seen elsewhere				5		
	saw at Barry Docks revisited Aug 70				1		

Review and Appraisal of 88A Cardiff (East Dock)

The shed was in the heart of Cardiff Dockland. Walking time was 30 minutes from Cardiff General Station.

Not a bad shed. Dashed good in fact. Seeing "Evening Star" was terrific plus the Modified Halls, the Manors and some interesting fast vanishing GWR steam 5205, 5700, 6100, and one 9400 0-6-0PT. 6116 was quite unique. This 6100 development was with increased boiler pressure for working on the London suburban area where all the other 68 had been based. Interesting to see all the withdrawn 86B Newport 8F's 2800 Class on shed. This class had been very evident at Barry Docks also. A terrific eleven different ex GWR classes on view.

THE ONE THAT GOT AWAY AFFAIR

After our whistle stop tour round the shed we tried to make our way back as quickly as possible. We were beating the clock nicely but made the mistake of bowing to the warm weather and decidedly slowing down our pace.

We reached the dock exit and I glanced at my watch. *Tempus fugit!* We had to get a move on. Our progress up Herbert Street was more like a fast amble than a run. It felt like running the last mile of a marathon under a temperature of 80 degrees in the shade.

We reached the end of Herbert Street and temptation took a hand. There was a nice little stop and were we thirsty! Into the shop and we emerged with a bottle of orangeade and a minute wasted.

I looked again at my watch. The clock was beating us now. Why in the blazes did we waste time on getting that pop. Hot sun creates madness. We began to run as fast as we could. I hit the City Centre of Cardiff about thirty yards in front of D.S. At least he hadn't given up the ghost yet and if he had been a racecourse the probable comment would be "running on gamely or "running on at one pace." Apart from taking a bit of a long cut to avoid some of the traffic we reached the station *"quam celerrime."* When I looked at the station clock there still was a chance. It had moved to 14.19 (one minute to go) but we still had to get our bags from the left luggage. We ran to the left luggage office and as luck would have it the attendant was at the incoming luggage porthole serving another customer. What luck! I told D.S. to shout his head off to get the luggage and I would try and get the train delayed upstairs.

I sprinted up the stairs and found our try on the point of leaving. I saw the railway inspector in charge of the departure and ran up to him and asked if he could delay a few seconds as my friend was on the way up the stairs. The railway inspector looked at his watch, shook his head and in effect said to hell with you and your friend. He blew his whistle and the train started up and began to wind slowly away from the platform. D.S. came panting up the stairs with the bags but the train was now moving too fast and we could not get. These Brush diesels and their damned quick acceleration. It was well nigh impossible to successfully board the train so we didn't try it and get arrested for our troubles. Thanks a million railway inspector.

We would not missed getting on the train by 10-15 seconds if a) we had not stopped for a bottle of orangeade or b) the delay in getting our luggage from the attendant or c) thanks to the rat of a railway inspector.

The railway inspector seemed amused at our plight and I would have gladly kicked him. However, I was conscious of the cop shop at the station that we had already seen so I had to pass kicking him on this occasion particularly as we would now have to wait for the next train to Birmingham.

We were totally dejected at missing the train, which results in a ruined timetable.

POST MORTEM ON DAMAGE TO TIMETABLE DONE BY RAILWAY INSPECTOR ETC

How annoyed can you feel? We sat down on a bench and I contemplated what to do about the vicious blow inflicted on our timetable.

I had a quick look at the timetable for trains for Birmingham: _

	Original	*Revised*
DEPART CARDIFF	14.20	15.45
ARRIVE BIRMINGHAM	16.30	19.05
Travelling time	2hrs 10 mins.	3hrs 20 mins.

We would be getting a slower train back via Hereford instead of the fast route via Cheltenham. Journey time 1 hour 10 minutes longer and we would arrive in Birmingham 2hrs

35 minutes late at 19.05. Three sheds would be lost 2E Saltley at 16.51, 2J Aston at 17.39 and 2A Tyseley at 18.51. We weren't going to visit Stourbridge (2C) originally through no time available and we certainly wouldn't be visiting it now.

All we could do would be to take up the thread of a new timetable when we arrived at Birmingham Snow Hill. So it looked as though we would be getting the 20.00 to Banbury. What about the three sheds missed? Forget about them and continue merrily on our way?

On second thoughts I found them too good to miss so we would have to visit them tomorrow. This would need a new timetable and some sheds would be definitely for the chopper in the next few days. I envisaged our costly outside LMR Railrover trips to Sheffield and Leeds extra Railrover probably being cancelled. In any event we might have run out of money visiting them. What a costly miss of a train by ten seconds!!!

What we now should have done was to visit the recently closed 88B Cardiff Radyr shed. Doubtless, like 88A Cardiff East Dock it would still have been crammed with recently withdrawn engines. This could easily have been accomplished:-

88B CARDIFF RADYR				
Steam				
Hawksworth 2F 1600 0-6-0PT 1949				
1612	*1655*			
Total	2			
1933 dev. of Collett 3F 5700 0-6-0PT 1929				
3644	*3717*	*3784*	*4650*	
4679	*9615*	*9622*	*9644*	
9667	*9682*	*9780*		
Total	11			
Collett 4MT 5101 2-6-2T 1929 rebuild of Churchward 3100 Class 1903				
4169	*4177*			
Total	2			
Collett 5MT 5600 0-6-2T 1924				
5689	*5691*	*5692*	*6654*	
6657	*6661*	*6672*	*6689*	
Total	8			
Collett 4MT 6100 2-6-2T 1931 dev. Of 5101 Class				
6116				
Total	1			
Hawksworth 4F 9400 0-6-0PT 1947				
8484	*9437*	*9464*		
Total	3			
Grand Total	27	(all withdrawn)		
Recently		**Seen at 88A**	7	
Withdrawn	27	**Cardiff East Dock**		
Saw at Barry Docks				
revisited Aug-70	1			
Steam	**Aug-50**	0	**Mar-59**	55
Allocation	**May-65**	33	**Aug-65**	0
	Closed to Steam:-		**Jul-65**	

A mouth watering collection of 27 withdrawn steam.

The timetable would have nicely accommodated the visit.

			Schedule		Miles
Depart	CARDIFF GENERAL		14.31		0
Arrive	RADYR		14.46		4¾
	Do 88B Cardiff Radyr				
Depart	RADYR		15.23		0
Arrive	CARDIFF GENERAL		15.38		4¾

I asked D.S. for his comments on what we should now do. He had none he was asleep! D.S. wasn't sleeping soundly though. He was sleep moving or at least his head was. While D.S. was snoozing his head was having a strange circular tour of its own. In his sleep D.S.'s head was slowly rotating anti-clockwise. When D.S.'s head reached a certain angle he would suddenly with a frightening start jerk his head violently forward and then the slow anti-clockwise cycle would start again.

While D.S. was in slumberland I amused myself by sitting dejectedly on the bench anxiously awaiting the 15.45 to Birmingham Snow Hill. The station was quite busy and the following engines were noted.

CARDIFF GENERAL STATION						
		Home shed		Built	Withdrawn	Scrap
Diesels						
BR "Western" Type 4 C-C 1961						
D1011	"Western Thunderer"	87E	Landore	Oct-1962	Oct-1975	
Total	1					
Brush Type 4 Co-Co 1962						
D1590		87E	Landore	May-1964		
D1602		86A	Cardiff Canton	Jul-1964		
D1639		87E	Landore	Dec-1964		
D1647		87E	Landore	Jan-1965		
D1650		87E	Landore	Jan-1965		
D1654		87E	Landore	Feb-1965		
D1678		86A	Cardiff Canton	May-1965		
D1712		82A	Bristol Bath Road	Jan-1964		
Total	8					
English Electric Type 3 Co-Co 1961						
D6830		86A	Cardiff Canton	Apr-1963		
D6908		87E	Landore	Nov-1963		
D6926		86A	Cardiff Canton	Feb-1964		
D6930		86A	Cardiff Canton	Mar-1964		
D6957		86A	Cardiff Canton	Jan-1965		
D6970		86A	Cardiff Canton	Mar-1965		
D6991		86A	Cardiff Canton	Jul-1965		
D6999	*brand new*			Aug-1965		
Total	8					
BR Paxman Type 1 0-6-0 1964						
D9532		86A	Cardiff Canton	Feb-1965	Apr-1968	
Total	1					

		Home shed		Built	Withdrawn	Scrap
Steam						
Maunsell 4F Q 0-6-0 Maunsell 1938						
30545		ex 70A	Nine Elms	*Jun-1939*	*Apr-1965*	*Sep-1965*
Total	*1*					
BR Standard 3MT 2-6-2T Swindon 1952						
82018		70A	Nine Elms	*Sep-1952*	*Jul-1966*	*Oct-1966*
Total	*1*					
At Station	20	Kops		20		
Steam	2	Diesels		18		
Withdrawn	1					

	Home Area			9 Visitors	10
Shed	86A		9		
Distribution	82A		1 87E	7	
	70A		2 new	1	
Steam Classes	2				
Steam Origin	SR		1 BR	1	
Station Highlight:-					
	Steam	30545	70A	Nine Elms	
	Diesel	D9532	86A	Cardiff Canton	

Review of Cardiff General Station

Another "Western" and another red one. Are they all red?   D9532 was the first 0-6-0 Paxman Hydraulic that I had seen. The D8500 Clayton Type 1's that are common in Edinburgh looked far superior to them. The Scottish and North Eastern Region Claytons are 900 B.H.P compared with the 650 B.H.P. Paxmans. It was also good to see the brand new or practically new English electric type 3 D6999. This class will be continued in the D6600 series. Another seven English Electric Type 3's were noted all on mixed freights. Brush Type 4's were in evidence on passenger trains.

There was one good bonus for missing our 14.20 Birmingham train when D6930 rattled through the station hauling BR Standard 82030 and Maunsell Q Class 30545. At first I thought it was a scrap special from the Southern region of the two steam locos. However, on later research I found out that whereas 30545 had been withdrawn months earlier 82018 was very much still alive and kicking.   My theory is that the 70A Nine Elms based 82018 hauled the withdrawn Maunsell 30545 from the Southern Region with the destination being a South Wales scrapyard *(unfortunately she was not destined for Barry Docks or she would have almost certainly been eventually saved. She was en route to Bird's scrapyard at Bynea, Llanelli)*. Probably D6930 gave the Standard a helping hand when it reached the busy South Wales main line.

Why didn't we go round 86A Cardiff Canton? A big diesel shed.   It was only a ten minute walk away and there would have been sufficient time before the 15.45 train to Snow Hill. However, doing 88B Cardiff Radyr would have been much more sensible if I had realised that we could have done it before our 15.45 train. It would not have been easy kicking D.S. back to life and we would have had to drag our bags around with us and the unsuccessful run to and from Cardiff East Dock had given us enough exercise for the day. After the debacle with the Station Inspector enthusiasm for going round 86A Cardiff Canton was incredibly low and it was a diesel shed after all so not a lot to be sad about missing. Better to sit dejectedly on the bench (admittedly on a good, warm day) and regroup ones energies.

At 15.30 a dirty two coach diesel bucket appeared - our train. This was in sharp contrast to the 12 coach train which we missed. Looks as though this bucket would have one speed – VERY SLOW – a slowboat to China (or rather Birmingham Snow Hill).

D.S. and I took the opportunity of taking the seats immediately behind the driving compartment. The chubby driver looked round and saw two of the world's greatest railwayists (us)! He opened the connecting door and came through for a chat. He asked if we were youth hostellers. He wouldn't have believed that we were trainspotters who slept on station waiting rooms at night so I hastily concurred that we were indeed youth hostellers. He said, "You'll be having a great time." and "I used to enjoy youth hostelling a lot when I was younger." With these friendly words he bade farewell, closed the door of the driving compartment and settled down to wait for the signal to move off.

One thing about a bucket there is nothing to beat it for seeing the line in front and at the sides. It would be good going back to Birmingham via Gloucester and Cheltenham. We would have another chance to see if anything could be seen of 86E Severn Tunnel Junction (missed earlier today). There was only one thing wrong with my thoughts. We were going a different way to Birmingham. 86G Pontypool Road, 86C Hereford and 85A Worcester would be the menu this time. Worcester was a decent shed but Pontypool Road and Hereford did not promise to be too exciting.

At 15.45 exactly (not ten seconds later) our fish-faced station inspector gave a wave, a whistle and therefore permission to the guard and our bucket driver to leave. Good riddance to him!

We noted the following engines on the line from Cardiff to Newport and at the goods yards to the south of the line at Godfrey Road diesel depot outside and around Newport Station.

CARDIFF to NEWPORT			Home shed		Built	Withdrawn	Scrap
Diesels							
Brush Type 4 Co-Co 1962							
D1742			86A	Cardiff Canton	May-1964		
Total	1						
BR English Electric 0-6-0 Shunter 1953							
D3256			86A	Cardiff Canton	Jun-1956		
D3260			86A	Cardiff Canton	Jun-1956		
D3267			86A	Cardiff Canton	Aug-1956		
D3420			86A	Cardiff Canton	Dec-1957		
D3421			86A	Cardiff Canton	Dec-1957		
D3422			86A	Cardiff Canton	Jan-1958		
D3748			86A	Cardiff Canton	Jul-1959		
D3817			86B	Newport(Ebbw Jct)	Mar-1959		
Total	8						
BR Blackstone/B.T.H. 0-6-0 Shunter 1955							
D4128			86B	Newport(Ebbw Jct)	May-1962		
D4174			86B	Newport(Ebbw Jct)	Jun-1962		
D4185			86B	Newport(Ebbw Jct)	Nov-1962		
Total	3						

		Home shed		Built	Withdrawn	Scrap
English Electric Type 3 Co-Co 1961						
D6822		86A	Cardiff Canton	*Apr-1963*		
D6828		86A	Cardiff Canton	*Jun-1963*		
D6879		86A	Cardiff Canton	*Oct-1963*		
D6902		86A	Cardiff Canton	*Oct-1963*		
D6970		86A	Cardiff Canton	*Mar-1965*		
D6973		86A	Cardiff Canton	*May-1965*		
D6994		86A	Cardiff Canton	*Aug-1965*		
Total	7					
Beyer Peacock (Hymek) Type 3 B-B 1961						
D7038		84A	Laira (ex86A)	*Jun-1962*	*Jan-1972*	
Total	1					
BR 0-6-0 Shunter 1948						
15102		86A	Cardiff Canton	*Apr-1948*	*Jul-1967*	
Total	1					
On Journey	21	**Kops**		20		
Steam	0	**Diesels**		21		
		Home Area		**20 Visitors**		1
Shed	86A	16	86B	4		
Distribution	to 84A	1				

On Wednesday 7 April 1965 I had seen D1742 on the Esso oil train normally hauled by a Western Region Brush Type 4) from Milford Haven at Millerhill Musselburgh. It was good seeing another delightful Hymek and we were unlikely to see any more as we headed north back to the LMR. Once again we missed 86B Newport Ebbw Junction perhaps because only the top of the yard is visible to the north of the line.

After our stop at Newport our bucket took a sharp left turn and we had now left the Cardiff-Gloucester main line and we were now on the quietish Cardiff-Pontypool line. Quietish it was and D.S. and I saw no engines on the line.

We were intrigued by our driver's antics at the controls in front of us. Our driver was a bit plump and our bucket was now rattling along. Rattling was the word as we were being violently shaken from side to side and I thought the walls of the bucket might cave in. Our driver was being fairly thrown about his seat through the motion of the bucket. If this journey did not make him lose a few pounds in weight I would be very surprised indeed. So this is how BR keeps their drivers in trim! Just the ticket for overweight drivers! Just send them on the back line to Birmingham from Cardiff.

Periodically an alarm bell would ring out and our driver would quickly snatch at a control to switch it off. Funny peculiar I thought. D.S. thought better and put forward a theory about the CASE OF THE ANNOYING ALARM BELL. He said (to a captivated and spellbound audience of one – me) that the alarm only went on when our train went through a signal at amber. He pointed to an electrical apparatus on the track at each signal that he said automatically triggered off the alarm bell in the driver's compartment (or braking the train if the signal was at red perhaps). The bell would keep ringing until he pressed a control to stop it continued D.S. Helps to keep the driver awake I added. D.S. agreed.

I looked out, around and about and saw absolutely no engines. Roll on Pontypool Road I thought. I yawned and contemplated and contemplated and contemplated ----------------------
----

I awoke to find that I had dropped off to sleep at my contemplation. I checked my watch and found that I had stolen an hour's sleep.

I resolved to keep awake lest I missed something of importance. Next stop on our slowboat was Hereford. It used to have a shed (86C). However, it was regretfully closed in 1964. Hereford station was a sizeable joint and the journey had produced: -

NEWPORT to HEREFORD						
		Home shed		Built	Withdrawn	Scrap
Diesels						
Brush Type 4 Co-Co 1962						
D1596		87E	Landore	Jun-1964		
D1678		86A	Cardiff Canton	May-1965		
D1741		82A	Bristol Bath Rd.(ex86A)	Jun-1964		
Total	3					
BR Gardner 0-6-0 Shunter 1957						
D2136		85A	Worcester	Mar-1960	Jan-1972	
Total	1					
BR Blackstone/B.T.H. 0-6-0 Shunter 1955						
D4180		86B	Newport(Ebbw Jct)	Sep-1962		
Total	1					
BR Paxman Type 1 0-6-0 1964						
D9513		86A	Cardiff Canton	Oct-1964	Apr-1968	
D9519		86A	Cardiff Canton	Nov-1964	Oct-1968	
Total	2					
On Journey	7	Kops		7		
Steam	0	Diesels		7		
		Home Area		4	Visitors	3
Shed	86A	3	86B	1		
Distribution	82A	1	85A	1	87E	1

After a five minute stop at Hereford we continued on the line on the Worcester leg. I expected the line to be somewhat busier than the tedious, boring Cardiff-Hereford leg. I was to be proved correct and after the dearth of South Wales steam we were delighted to see ambling by on a slow freight 4113 of 85A Worcester. She was a 4MT 2-6-2T of the 4100 Class. This class was introduced by Collett in 1929 and was a rebuild of Churchward's 3100 Class.

Further on, we saw an odd looking diesel shunter strolling along light engine. What could it be? On closer inspection we found it to be PWM650 that was one of BR's departmental locos. Shedded at Newlands it was a Ruston & Hornby 0-6-0 diesel shunter introduced in 1953. Nearing Worcester we had the exhilarating experience of a "Grange" whistling by us at the head of a freight. She looked rather disconsolate and dirty, devoid of her brass nameplates and numberplates. She was 6848 "Toddington Grange" of 85A Worcester.

		Home shed		Built	Withdrawn	Scrap
HEREFORD to WORCESTER						
Diesels						
BR Gardner 0-6-0 Shunter 1957						
D2132		85A	Worcester	*Feb-1960*	*May-1969*	
Total	*1*			*1953*	*Sep-1967*	
Ruston & Hornsby 0-6-0 Shunter 1953						
PWM650		Dept	Newland			
Total	*1*					
Steam						
Collett 4MT 5101 2-6-2T 1929 rebuild of Churchward 3100 Class 1903						
4113		85A	Worcester	*Oct-1935*	*Nov-1965*	*Jul-1966*
Total	*1*					
Collett 5MT 6800 4-6-0 "Grange" 1936						
6848	"Toddington Grange"	85A	Worcester	*Oct-1937*	*Dec-1965*	*Apr-1966*
Total	*1*					
On Journey	**4**	**Kops**		**4**		
Steam	**2**	**Diesels**		**2**		
		Home Area		**4**	**Visitors**	**0**
Shed	**85A**	**3**				
Distribution	**Dept**	**1**				
Steam Classes	**2**					
Steam Origin	**GWR**	**2**				
Journey Highlight	**6848**	**"Toddington Grange"**	**85A**		**Worcester**	

We awaited the arrival of Worcester shed on our right and we were not disappointed with it. It turned out to be a "Hall" of a shed rather than a "hell" of a shed.

		Home shed		Built	Withdrawn	Scrap
85A WORCESTER (pass)						
Diesels						
Brush Type 4 Co-Co 1962						
D1732		82A	Bristol Bath Road	*Apr-1964*		
Total	*1*					
BR 0-6-0 Diesel Shunter 1953						
D3996		2C	Stourbridge	*Oct-1960*		
Total	*1*					
Steam				*Built*	*Withdrawn*	*Scrap*
Collett 5MT 4900 4-6-0 "Hall" 1928						
6947	"Helmingham Hall"	81F	Oxford	*Dec-1942*	*Oct-1965*	*Apr-1966*
Total	*1*					
Hawksworth 5MT 6959 4-6-0 "Modified Hall" 1944						
6965	"Thirlestane Hall"	82E	Bristol Barrow Road	*Jul-1944*	*Oct-1965*	*Mar-1966*
6991	"Acton Burnell Hall"	81F	Oxford (ex 81E)	*Nov-1948*	*Dec-1965*	*May-1966*
Total	*2*					
Ivatt 2MT 2-6-0 1946						
46456		2F	Bescot	*May-1950*	*Sep-1965*	*Nov-1965*
Total	*1*					
On Shed	**6**	**Kops**		**6**		
Steam	**4**	**Diesels**		**2**		
Withdrawn	**0**					

85A WORCESTER (pass)						
Home Locos	0 Home Area			0 Visitors	6	
Shed	2C	1 2F		1		
Distribution	81F	2 82A		1 82E	1	
Steam Classes	3					
Steam Origin	GWR	3 LMS		1		
Shed Highlight:-		6947 "Helmingham Hall"		81F	Oxford	
Steam	Aug-50	85	Mar-59	64	Apr-65	33
Allocation					Aug-65	28
			Closed to Steam:-		Dec-65	
Home Steam						
On/Off Shed	On Shed	0 Off Shed		23 % On Shed	0%	
Not Seen						
3MT 2251 0-6-0 1930				2222	2244	0
3F 5700 0-6-0PT 1933	3615	3682	4664	4680	8793	4
4MT 6100 2-6-2T 1931	4113	4161	6147	6155	6159	5
5MT "Grange" 1936	6813	6816	6819	6829	6836	
		6838	6848	6856	6872	8
5MT "Modified Hall" 1944				6958	7920	0
4F 9400 0-6-0PT 1947					8415	0
BR 4MT 4-6-0 1951	75000	75003	75005	75008	75022	
					75025	6
					total	23
	saw elsewhere on the tour				7	
	recently withdrawn not on shed or seen elsewhere				7	

Mini Review and Appraisal of 85A Worcester

Pity we couldn't go round Worcester shed (not in the LMR but not far from it). What we saw in the shed yard was great but hidden in the shed there must have been much more. Seeing the "Hall" and the two "Modified Halls" was particularly good. Strangely none of the engines seen belonged to 85A Worcester. Possibly the engines in the yard were being prepared for their homeward journeys.

On we go

After a short stop at Worcester we were off on the last lap of our journey. On the final leg we passed through Droitwich, Kidderminster, and Stourbridge Junction and finally arrived at Birmingham Snow Hill on time. Like Hereford, Kidderminster used to have a shed (2P) until it was closed about a year ago. Stourbridge Junction shed (2C) was very much alive and kicking and was a good workmanlike shed. Owing to timetable pressures it had to be squeezed out in the final timetable. The major problem was that the shed was on the Stourbridge Junction-Stourbridge Town branch line. It was a 30 minutes walk from Stourbridge Junction, which would have taken a chunk out of our day walking there and back plus the time of getting a train to Stourbridge junction and back. *If breaks of journeys were allowed (not sure if they were) in our diversion ticket from Cardiff to Birmingham there could have been a case for stopping at the sheds en route 85B Gloucester, 86E Severn Tunnel Junction, 85A Worcester and 2C Stourbridge. That would have necessitated cutting out a bit of our proposed sortie to Leeds and Sheffield and might have been more cost effective.*

2C Stourbridge had a decent steam allocation of 28 locos plus two recently withdrawn.

2C STOURBRIDGE					
Steam					
1933 dev. of Collett 3F 5700 0-6-0PT 1929					
3607	**3619**	**3658**	*4665*		
4696	**8718**	**9608**	**9613**		
9614	**9641**	*9646*			
Total		*9*			
Collett 4MT 5101 2-6-2T 1929 rebuild of Churchward 3100 Class 1903					
4175					
Total		*1*			
Collett 4MT 6100 2-6-2T 1931 dev. of 5101 Class					
6129					
Total		*1*			
Collett 5MT 5600 0-6-2T 1924					
5659					
Total		*1*			
1927 dev. of Collett 5MT 5600 0-6-2T 1924					
6656	**6679**	**6683**	**6692**		
Total		*4*			
Hawksworth 4F 9400 0-6-0PT 1947					
9724	**9733**				
Total		*2*			
Stanier 8F 2-8-0 "Big Eight" 1935					
48330	**48402**	**48410**	**48412**		
48417	**48424**	**48450**	**48459**		
48460	**48468**				
Total		*10*			
Grand Total		**28**			
Recently			*Surviving*		
Withdrawn		**2**	*Steam Classes*	**7**	
Saw Elsewhere					
on the Tour		**6**			
Steam	*Aug-50*		**85**	*Mar-59*	**64**
Allocation	*Apr-65*		**33**	*Aug-65*	**28**
	Closed to Steam:-			*Jul-66*	

No ticket collector had appeared on our bucket so we would have got away with purchasing only a single from Birmingham to Cardiff. The run-in to Birmingham Snow Hill was interesting and provided three steam engines plus a clutch of diesel shunters.

On the way in to Birmingham Snow Hill it suddenly dawned on me that we were now running on LMR metals. No ticket collector had appeared on our bucket so we would have got away with purchasing only a single from Birmingham to Cardiff. The run-in to Birmingham Snow Hill was interesting and provided three steam engines plus a clutch of diesel shunters.

WORCESTER TO BIRMINGHAM SNOW HILL						
			Home shed		*Built*	*Withdrawn*	*Scrap*
Diesels						
BR 0-6-0 Shunter 1953 English Electric 350 b.h.p at 630 r.p.m.						
D3004			2C	Stourbridge	*Nov-1952*	
D3026			2C	Stourbridge	*Oct-1953*	
D3029			2C	Stourbridge	*Oct-1953*	
Total	*3*					

305

			Home shed		Built	Withdrawn	Scrap
BR 0-6-0 Shunter 1953 English Electric 350 b.h.p at 680 r.p.m.							
D3951		2A	Tyseley		Apr-1960		
D3980		2C	Stourbridge		Jul-1960		
D3981		2C	Stourbridge		Jul-1960		
D3983		2A	Tyseley		Aug-1960		
D3988		2C	Stourbridge		Aug-1960		
D3997		2C	Stourbridge		Oct-1960		
Total	6						
LMS and BR 0-6-0 Shunter 1945							
12094		2C	Stourbridge		Sep-1951	Oct-1971	
Total	1						
Steam					Built	Withdrawn	Scrap
1927 dev. of Collett 5MT 5600 0-6-2T 1924							
6656		2C	Stourbridge		Aug-1928	Sep-1965	Mar-1966
Total	1						
1933 dev. of Collett 3F 5700 0-6-0PT 1929							
9724		2C	Stourbridge		Dec-1934	Jan-1966	Apr-1966
Total	1						
BR Standard 9F 2-10-0 Brighton 1954. Double chimney dev. 1957							
92230	double chimney	86B	Newport Ebbw Junction		Aug-1958	Dec-1965	Jul-1966
Total	1						
On Journey	13		Kops		13		
Steam	3		Diesels		10		
		Home Area			12 Visitors		1
Shed	2A	2	2C		10		
Distribution	86B	1					
Steam Classes on View		3					
Steam Origin	GWR	2	BR		1		

The three steam engines were all on freights. Good! Talking about good things it had been a lovely sunny day. Let's hope we have more like them.

		Schedule	Actual	Miles
Depart	CARDIFF GENERAL	15.45	15.45	0
Arrive	HEREFORD	17.05	17.05	55¼
Arrive	WORCESTER	18.04	18.04	83¼
	See 85A Worcester			
Arrive	BIRMINGHAM SNOW HILL	19.05	19.05	118

D.S. and I bounded off the bucket on time at five past seven. If we had got the original train (i.e. the 14.20 one) we would have been in Birmingham by 16.30. I have referred earlier to the severe timetable damage this late arrival had cost us.

D.S. and I first inspected the station and were rewarded with four interesting locos: -

Brush Type 4 Co-Co D1745 of 81A Old Oak Common was noted. A little reflection and I recollected seeing D1745 three weeks ago (i.e. on Tuesday 13 July) on the British Motor Corporation lorries to Bathgate at Millerhill Yard at about 2 p.m. At the back of the station a Stanier 8F Big 8 was noted 48269. Then a couple of gems: - "Hall" 5988 "Bostock Hall" and "Modified Hall" 7929 "Wyke Hall". Sad to relate I learned afterwards that "Wyke Hall" was withdrawn later in the week and this must have been one of her last duties.

BIRMINGHAM SNOW HILL STATION TUESDAY EVENING

		Home shed		Built	Withdrawn	Scrap
Diesels						
Brush Type 4 Co-Co 1962						
D1745		81A	Old Oak Common	*Jul-1964*		
Total	*1*					
Steam				Built	Withdrawn	Scrap
Collett 5MT 4900 4-6-0 "Hall" 1936						
5988	"Bostock Hall"	2A	Tyseley	Nov-1939	Oct-1965	Dec-1965
Total	*1*					
Hawksworth 5MT 6959 4-6-0 "Modified Hall" 1944						
7929	"Wyke Hall"	2A		Nov-1950	Aug-1965	Oct-1965
Total	*1*					
Stanier 8F 2-8-0 "Big Eight" 1935						
48269		6B	Mold Junction	May-1942	Jul-1967	Dec-1967
Total	*1*					
On Station	**4**	**Kops**		**3**		
Steam	**3**	**Diesels**		**1**		
		Home Area		**2 Visitors**		**2**
Shed		**2A**	**2**			
Distribution		**6B**	**1**			
		81A	**1**			
Steam Classes	**3**					
Steam Origin	**GWR**	**2 LMS**		**1**		

We flashed our Railrover tickets, passed through the barrier, crossed the over bridge and descended a flight of stairs onto the main station concourse. D.S. was looking rather ashen, crestfallen, jaded, downhearted, dejected, out-of-sorts, melancholy, degenerate and at a low ebb. Dare I ask him why?

THE HUNGRY MAN EPISODE

I plucked up courage and asked D.S. if he was feeling the strain on his aching bones. D.S. glared angrily and began a speech full of passion, which I now repeat. "You say we can live on fresh air on the LMR so you leave no time for meals on the tour. You tell me that I can eat so long as it doesn't interfere with your golden timetable. That leaves me to have a five course meal during the hours of darkness. Where do I get something to eat at that time? He didn't expect an answer but I suggested that he try the all night Wimpy Bars. That suggestion merely added fuel to his fire. D.S. asked, "What have you allowed me to have today? D.S. then answered his own question and began to give a rundown on today's menu. "I've had a lousy cup of BR coffee and a measly BR sandwich when we were going down the Lickey Incline." At Cardiff when we were going back to catch our train for Birmingham you allowed me to have one bottle of orangeade. D.S. summed up his case for the prosecution with a plea for long regular meal breaks.

Once D.S. had cooled down to boiling point I played my trump card in the case for the defence. My case was simple. I said to D.S. "You must admit that you are one of the slowest on two legs". D.S. could not answer that one. I then asked D.S. if we got the 14.20 to Birmingham. D.S. said that we had missed it by ten seconds. Yes, I said because we wasted a minute stopping to buy the orangeade, which you so proudly mentioned. Just one little bottle of orangeade for you and me and we completely and utterly torpedo my unsinkable "Titanic" timetable for the day with knock on effects for the rest of the trip. If a bottle of orangeade can do that I just hate to think what a meal would do. Your witness!

D.S. finding that his views had been blocked again accepted defeat and disconsolately retreated to the cafeteria to console himself with some much needed food and drink. I had previously told him that we had a 46 minutes wait before our train to Banbury. Revised BR connections necessitated this long unforeseen enormous wait. D.S. could therefore thank BR for this meal break. Hopefully it would not happen again to that extent.

I am not a conscientious objector to eating if there is nothing better to do. At this time there wasn't any nice shed to visit or anything else to see on the station therefore I popped into the cafeteria also and found D.S. at the end of a short queue looking like a hungry dog before it is fed. D.S. and I bought similar items at the self-service. Gala fruit pies (like Lyons fruit pies at 8d (3.5 new pence) but probably still made by Lyons and sold with the Gala name for a penny more at nine old pence. I also took a fancy to a tomato sandwich and a jam tart. D.S. and I had boiled up for us a can of BR's exorbitantly priced small cans of Chef soup. We had cups of tea to wash down our feast.

After a twenty minute break we were back on the platform awaiting the arrival at 19.51 of our train to Banbury. It was to be a rather tiresome nail-biting wait as our train (arriving via Wolverhampton Low Level) eventually rolled in ten minutes late. At the head of our train was Brush Type 4 Co-Co D1683 of 2B Oxley.

Our train left twelve minutes late at 20.12. The train was a through train from Birkenhead (left 16.25) to London Paddington (due in at 22.10). I told D.S. that it had a buffet car on it. D.S. wasn't impressed because he explained that he had just had his breakfast come dinner cum tea cum supper at the cafeteria in Birmingham Snow Hill. I tried to cheer D.S. up by saying that we would get a cup of coffee on the train back from Banbury. However, D.S. said he needed more than that to cheer him up.

THE TIRED MAN EPISODE

D.S. pulled himself together and began his sermon to me. His lecture to me was to be on the subject of "lack of sleep." D.S. accused me of blaming him for tiredness and weariness since our tour started. I agreed and said that he was unique and that I couldn't imagine many people as tired or as weary as he seemed to be all the time. I put forward strong circumstantial evidence to prove my point. His tardiness had been very noticeable at Leicester and later that day at Nottingham where we missed connections. D.S. explained his rather inept performances on lack of sleep. He said that on the Saturday night he got very little sleep on the Carlisle to London train. On the Sunday night at Bletchley he didn't get to sleep quickly and had a very uncomfortable night on the waiting room bench. At the most he could only have had four hours sleep (01.45 to 05.45). On the Monday night at the Derby Station waiting rooms he complained that he had the harrowing experiences of being repeatedly punched awake by the persistent policemen. He had finally got to sleep at 02.45 but we had got up at 05.00 to do Derby shed. So he had about two and a half hours sleep that night. To cut a long story short he complained that he had only seven or eight hours sleep over the past few days.

I reminded him of the bonus one hour sleep this afternoon he had at Cardiff General Station. D.S. said he expected eight hours sleep a night. "What a waste of time sleeping is in an action packed week like this!" I retorted to D.S. Like eating one sleeps when there is nothing better to do I explained to D.S. slowly. I allow you to eat when we are waiting a few minutes for the next connection and I allow you to sleep when it is too dark to see anything. Of course we must be up at first light at 04.30 or 05.00 to get the most out of a day. I pointed out that he also had a long snooze on the train from Derby to Birmingham today. His answer was short "Catching up on lost sleep"

D.S. now wanted to know where we would be spending tonight. I told him that we would be spending the night or what's left of it at Birmingham New Street Station. We would get up at the crack of dawn to catch up as best we could on our timetable. D.S. thought for a minute and said that he didn't like the look of Birmingham New Street and thought that as it was being rebuilt that there would be no official waiting room (as at Bletchley) and possibly not even a temporary one. Possibly it would be only a windswept bench on a platform – possibly also being hounded by railway cops again. D.S. said "Let's get a good night's sleep at the nearest youth hostel. We would both feel the better for it." He asked why we had joined the Youth Hostels Association. For show??? In truth, we had joined to ward off questions from worried parents about where we would be staying rather than any particular intent to stay in one. Youth Hostels cost money while railway waiting rooms and benches did not. D.S. said that we could rise early from the youth hostel with little or no adverse effect on the revised timetable. D.S. was right and it had to be the best option after a few lack of sleep nights. There were no youth hostels in Birmingham or Banbury but there was one at Leamington Spa where the train would stop on the way back. D.S. had won this round!

After our summit conference it was time to relax, sit back and enjoy the journey. D.S. and I enjoyed the passing scenery as a grey dusk began to close a gloriously sunny day. I drew to D.S.'s attention the "old-fashioned" old Great Western Region signals with the signal pointing downwards in the on position, which I had thought had gone out of use last century. Apparently the reason for them going rapidly out of fashion decades ago was that one cold frosty winter's day after a heavy snowfall one railway signalman after allowing a train through his section could not get the signal to return up to the horizontal "off" position. The signal had broken down in the "on" position hanging downwards. The inevitable accident happened. In the accident report it was proposed that signals should move upwards to the "on" position and not downwards in future. This would help to avert future accidents. If the signal broke down in the up "on" position it would naturally fall down to the horizontal "off" position. Apparently, the Western Region still had not got the message and had stuck to the potentially dangerous old-fashioned signalling system. The GWR had always been a lot of crackpots and it was the GWR that had persisted in the broad gauge for several years before they finally adopted the 4'8½" standard gauge. Of interest was that the present Western Region signals seemed broader and heavier than the normal BR signal.

Leamington Spa (that hotbed of excitement) was reached at 20.31 – ten minutes late. D.S. and I had a few minutes of bitter disappointment on the east side of the line south of Leamington Spa General Station. What was the cause of our consternation? You may ask. The answer was 2L Leamington Spa shed. How can a shed disappoint somebody who is on an LMR tour visiting locosheds? You may ask. The answer was that 2L Leamington Spa shed was totally empty. It had been closed a few months ago but we had hoped that something would still be stored there or on shed as a stabling point.

Our Leamington Spa train stop was officially seven minutes. Rather long I thought. Especially long since our train was running late. Surely the station inspector would get our train away *"quam celerrime"* (as quickly as possible to those readers not initiated in Latin). It says a lot for BR efficiency that our train stayed if anything longer than our scheduled stop of seven minutes. Our train finally idled out at 20.39 (eleven minutes late).

Our twenty minute run-in to Banbury passed quickly enough and the only thing to stir the blood was a small yard north of the station.

BIRMINGHAM SNOW HILL to BANBURY						
		Home shed		**Built**	**Withdrawn**	**Scrap**
Diesels						
Brush Type 4 Co-Co 1962						
D1683	*hauled*	2B	Oxley	Oct-1963		
Total	1					
BR English Electric 0-6-0 Shunter 1953						
D3950		2A	Tyseley	Apr-1960		
D3968		2A	Tyseley	Jun-1960		
D3984		2A	Tyseley	Aug-1960		
D3985		2A	Tyseley	Aug-1960		
Total	4					
Steam		**Home shed**		**Built**	**Withdrawn**	**Scrap**
Hawksworth 5MT 6959 4-6-0 "Modified Hall" 1944						
6980	"Llanrumney Hall"	2D	Banbury	Nov-1947	Oct-1965	Dec-1965
7908	"Henshall Hall"	2A	Tyseley	Jan-1950	Oct-1965	Dec-1965
Total	2					
Stanier 5MT 4-6-0 "Black Five" 1934						
44876		2J	Aston	Apr-1945	Nov-1967	Mar-1968
Total	1					
BR Standard 5MT 4-6-0 Doncaster 1951						
73026		2A	Tyseley(ex 2L)	Dec-1951	Apr-1967	Oct-1967
Total	1					
On Journey	9	Kops		8		
Steam	4	Diesels		5		
Shed	2A	6 2B		1 2D		1
Distribution	2J	1				
	86B	1				
Steam Classes	3					
Steam Origin GWR		2 LMS		1 BR		1

A fruitful journey. A little later research and I found out when I had seen the 2J Aston "Black Five" 44876 before. In company with another of her sisters 45058 of the then 3D Aston I had seen them at Carlisle on a Scottish Railfans trip in September 1959. Great to see another couple of "Halls".

		Schedule	Actual	Miles
Depart	BIRMINGHAM SNOW HILL	20.00	20.12	0
Arrive	LEAMINGTON SPA GENERAL	20.20	20.31	23¼
Depart	LEAMINGTON SPA GENERAL	20.28	20.39	23¼
Arrive	BANBURY	20.48	21.00	43

Excluding the Leamington stop that was 43 miles in 40 minutes. A fast timing indeed but easy work (I suppose) for our Brush Type 4 at the head of our train.

Our late arrival had hacked into our recovery time. We now had just 26 minutes till we got our 21.26 return from Banbury. This train had left London Paddington at 20.10 and was due at Leamington Spa at 21.45. D.S. was fully aware that if we missed that we would be too late for Leamington Spa Youth Hostel and it would be a bench for the night at Birmingham New Street for him.

D.S. and I lost no time in getting out of the station. I didn't want another Cardiff East Dock dawdle from D.S. and another appalling narrowly missed connection. In the cool, refreshing twilight air D.S. by a superhuman D.S. effort had recharged his batteries from their flat level at Cardiff. He now could muster a sharp trot and succeeded in keeping up and even led at times as we belted out to the yards in our effort to knock 5 minutes of the 10 minutes walking time prescribed in the LocoShed directory. The directions thankfully were easy to follow and it was merely a jog down the mainline. We could see the shed in the dim distance.

I expected great things of 2D Banbury and we were not to be disappointed. The first thing that we noted were the treasured "Halls" in various stages of use and disuse. They were all shorn of their plates of course. Also on shed were "Granges", "Modified Halls", 9F 2-10-0s, "Big Eights", "Standard Black Fives", 56XX class and one of the last surviving 2251 class 0-6-0 locos on BR.

D.S. and I were enchanted by the ex GWR locos but we were soon to be disenchanted when midway through the shed we were stopped and challenged "Av you a permit to walk round here?" by a foreman like chap in blue overalls. Almost simultaneously the top pocket of my anorak was opened and a wad of permits flashed out. I think I detected (or heard?) his eyes popping. A careful sifting of the permits and the important Banbury permit was produced and flashed about. It was of course for a party of twelve and for an earlier time of the day but *"ceteris paribus"* other things being equal to the uninitiated in Latin the permit would be enough to get us round the shed. He peered at the permit in the gloom and said "From Scotland, Eh" "you're a right pair of globetrotters. I'll see you safely round".

Our new guide provided us with a mine of information. When I expressed my disappointment at their being only two BR 9F 2-10-0's being on shed he explained that by saying that they were always out on long distance heavy freights and that we would have to come on a Sunday to see them all on shed.

THE HATCHET MAN EPISODE

I also said to him that Banbury's "Halls" seemed to being rapidly withdrawn. He agreed and said that they had chopped up a good few in the last few months. "We cut up 6964 "Thornbridge Hall" the other day. *(The records of greatwestern.org however suggest that 6964 was withdrawn in September 1965 and cut up at a scrapyard in Sheffield. However, Friswell's scrap merchants did cut up locos at 2D Banbury shed so perhaps the foreman was correct and the other record was wrong. –Editor.* Enough to make anyone wince. At least anyone who liked steam locomotives. Especially "Halls"!

Once we finished the main shed we found a rather run down and decaying Fairburn 4MT 2-6-4 Tank outside. It was 42082. I asked our guide if this was a stranger to him. (being ex-1G Woodford Halse). "No" he said, "She's next for the chopper!" "She was withdrawn when the Great Central Railway and her home depot of 1G Woodford Halse closed. She couldn't be chopped up there so we said we would be glad to entertain her here and so she travelled to us from Woodford Halse to here. *Strangely again enthusiasts records show she was chopped up at Buttigiegs Newport scrapyard rather than on-site here.* A right sadist of a foreman here, I reflected. Our guide and I had a chat on the merits and demerits of the Great Central when D.S. interrupted us by pointing franticly at his watch. Apparently we had only 10 minutes till our return train blasted off at 21.26. Fancy D.S. bothering about the time and wanting me to hurry up. You could have blown me over with a feather at this surprising concern about the timetable. He must have turned over a new leaf and about time too! Might not last as I thought he is worried about losing his good night's sleep at Leamington Spa Youth Hostel. D.S. certainly had a point that the sands of time were running out very quickly so we bade au revoir to our Banbury foreman and sped off into the gathering darkness.

2D BANBURY

Diesels

		Home shed		Built	Withdrawn	Scrap
BR 0-6-0 Diesel Shunter 1953						
D3109		2D		Mar-1955		
D3112		2D		Apr-1955		
Total	2					

Steam

		Home shed		Built	Withdrawn	Scrap
Collett 3MT 2251 0-6-0 1930						
2210		2D		Sep-1939	Jun-1965	Sep-1965
Total	1					
Collett 5MT 5600 0-6-2T 1924						
5605		2A	Tyseley (ex 88D)	Jan-1925	May-1966	Dec-1966
Total	1					
1927 dev. of Collett 5MT 5600 0-6-2T 1924						
6644		2A	Tyseley	Sep-1928	Jul-1965	Jan-1966
6697		2D	(ex 2L Leamington Spa)	Oct-1928	May-1966	saved
Total	2					
Collett 5MT 4900 4-6-0 "Hall" 1928						
6903	"Belmont Hall"	2D		Jul-1940	Sep-1965	Jan-1966
6911	"Holker Hall"	2D		Jan-1941	Apr-1965	Feb-1966
6916	"Misterton Hall"	2D		May-1941	Aug-1965	Feb-1966
6922	"Burton Hall"	2A		Jul-1941	Apr-1965	Feb-1966
6926	"Holkham Hall"	2D	(ex 2A Tyseley)	Nov-1941	Jun-1965	Sep-1965
6927	"Lilford Hall"	81F	Oxford	Nov-1941	Oct-1965	Feb-1966
Total	6					
Hawksworth 5MT 6959 4-6-0 "Modified Hall" 1944						
6976	"Graythwaite Hall"	2D		Oct-1947	Oct-1965	Feb-1966
7912	"Little Linford Hall"	2D		Mar-1950	Oct-1965	Jan-1966
Total	2					
Collett 5MT 6800 4-6-0 "Grange" 1936						
6859	"Yiewsley Grange"	86E	Severn Tunnel Jct. (ex 88A)	Dec-1937	Nov-1965	Feb-1966
6876	"Kingsland Grange"	86B	Newport (ex 85B)	Apr-1939	Nov-1965	Feb-1966
Total	2					
Fairburn 4MT 2-6-4T 1945						
42082		ex 1G	Woodford Halse	Jan-1951	Jun-1965	Sep-1965
Total	1					
Stanier 8F 2-8-0 "Big Eight" 1935						
48335		2F	Bescot	Nov-1943	Apr-1968	Jul-1968
48412		2C	Stourbridge	Oct-1943	Dec-1966	Jun-1967
Total	2					
BR Standard 5MT 4-6-0 Doncaster 1951						
73013		2D	(ex 2B Oxley)	Aug-1951	May-1966	Aug-1966
73014		2D	(ex 2B Oxley)	Sep-1951	Jul-1967	Apr-1968
73021		81F	Oxford	Oct-1951	Aug-1965	Nov-1965
73048		2D	(ex 5E Nuneaton)	Dec-1953	Oct-1967	May-1968
Total	4					
BR Standard 4MT 2-6-0 Doncaster 1953						
76010		70D	Eastleigh	Feb-1953	Sep-1966	Mar-1967
Total	1					
BR Standard 9F 2-10-0 Brighton 1954						
92004		2D		Jan-1954	Mar-1968	Jul-1968
92030		2D	(ex 16B Annesley)	Nov-1954	Feb-1967	Jul-1967
92073		2D	(ex 16B Annesley)	Feb-1956	Nov-1967	Feb-1968
92203	double chimney	2D		Apr-1959	Nov-1967	saved
Total	4					

On Shed	28	Kops		28

Home Locos	17	Home Area		5	Visitors	6	
Shed	2D	17	2A	3	2C	1	
Distribution	2F	1					
	ex1G	1	70D	1			
	81F	2	86B	1	86E	1	
Steam Classes	11						
Steam Origin	GWR	14	LMS	3	BR	9	
Shed Highlights:-		2210 (first of class seen by me)					
		42082 (ex 1G Woodford Halse - from the Great Central Railway line)					
Steam	Aug-50	70	Mar-59	52	Apr-65	23	
Allocation					Aug-65	32	
			Closed to Steam:-			Oct-66	
Home Steam On/Off Shed Not on Shed	On Shed	12	Off Shed	20	% On Shed	38%	
1927 dev. of Collett 5MT 5600 0-6-2T						6671	1
"Halls"		6917		6930	6934	6951	
					6952	6964	6
"Modified Hall"						6980	1
BR 9F 2-10-0 1954		92013	92074	92128	92129	92132	
		92213	92218	92224	92227	92228	12
					92234	92247	2
							22
		saw elsewhere on the tour			5		
		saw on Dec 64 Manchester and Crewe trip			1		

Review and Appraisal of 2D Banbury aka as the "Halls" shed

The shed was on the west side of the line, south of Banbury station. Walking time was 10 minutes.

Great to see eight "Halls" on shed. Three of them were withdrawn though so the rot has begun to set in here. *Sadly the other five would all be withdrawn by the end of October 1965 just two months away.* Two "Granges" had wandered off their beaten paths in South Wales to be here tonight. One of them had been shedded at 88A Cardiff East Dock until it had been closed a few weeks ago. *Sadly both would be withdrawn in November 1965.* D.S. and I had of course found East Dock dead to the world when we had visited it earlier in the day in our ill-fated sortie. Both "Granges" on display were very welcomed.

All of the last members of the 2251 Class had recently been withdrawn. 2210 had been withdrawn in June and would be off to the scrapbreakers yard next month. Hence, here I saw the first and probably the last of the class that I would ever see. Three of the 56XX Class were on shed. The first series 5600-5699 were designed for the Welsh valleys.

The "Standard Fives" had come from a wide area to Banbury. Three of the four had recently been transferred here. The other was a visitor from Oxford. What was 76010 of 70D Eastleigh of the Southern Region doing at Banbury? Was it a regular roster from Southampton? You tell me. The "Big Eights" were two interesting visitors from the Birmingham area. The 9F's were fewer than I had hoped but the ex Great Central ex 1G Woodford Halse Fairburn tank 42082 was indeed a celebrity. A good shed!

"D.S. tries another shortcut!"

As D.S. and I darted back along the line to Banbury Station, Brush Type 4 D1747 flashed past at the head of our return train the 20.10 from London Paddington. The train was due in at Banbury station at 21.22 and would leave at 21.26 for Leamington Spa and Birmingham. It would be a close run thing as the train seemed to be a few minutes early.

We had just reached the station approaches when D.S.'s extraordinary extra sensory perception (disinclination to do the obvious) caused him to dart across the main line onto the end of No1 northbound platform and thus skipped the main entrance and the ticket collector thus saving valuable time. The Cardiff East Dock lesson had been learned. D.S. had done the same type of lawless detour at Workington, Cricklewood East and Toton sheds. A repetitive type but it worked every time without a brush with authority.

With a few minutes to spare D.S. and I got onto the train and camped down in the buffet car. Never too late for a cup of coffee so D.S. and I availed ourselves of the service. Some caffeine to keep us going on the last leg of the day to Leamington Spa Youth Hostel.

Our journey to Leamington Spa was particularly boring as it was pitch dark outside so we could see nothing of the countryside which we had recently passed through on the way to Banbury.

BANBURY TO LEAMINGTON SPA							
		Home shed			Built	Withdrawn	Scrap
Diesels							
BRUSH TYPE 4 Co-Co 1962							
D1747	hauled		81A	Old Oak Common	Jul-1964		
Total	1						
On Journey	1		Kops	1			
Steam	0		Diesels	1			
		Home Area		0	Visitors	1	
Shed	81A	1					
Distribution							

		Schedule	Actual
Depart	BANBURY	21.26	21.26
Arrive	LEAMINGTON SPA GENERAL	21.45	21.45

It was now getting on for ten and a certain warden at the Leamington Spa Youth Hostel would be closing the shutters on us if we didn't get a bit of a move on.

THERES ALWAYS AN ANNEXE IN THE GARDEN EPISODE

According to my YHA Handbook the Youth Hostel was at 69 Willes Road. That wasn't much help. According to the Handbook it was also a quarter of a mile from the Pump Rooms. An enlightening piece of information if I knew where the Pump Rooms were. Ah! Here is some more information. The relevant Ordnance survey sheet is 132 and the Grid reference is 326654. More useless information as I didn't have an Ordnance Survey map and in any event it would be pretty useless in the middle of Leamington Spa. So I read on. I at last found something, which could be followed up. It was half a mile from the station and here was a bonus "Turn off the Parade at the General Post Office. Hostel is at second crossroads. So we only had to find the Parade.

Undaunted D.S. and I left Leamington Spa General station and ventured into "downtown" Leamington. D.S. and I saw two Tardis men (cops) and asked them the way to the Youth Hostel. They kindly gave us directions. Straight down the road and sharp right some way on appeared to be the instructions. It appeared to me that we would be walking back a bit on the way we came. Obviously there was a shorter route but a route where we could easily get lost. They at least made the directions simple.

After a pleasant half a mile stroll in the cool night air D.S. and I came to the Youth Hostel entrance. The sign seemed to me to be AYH. I thought that this must stand for American Youth Hostel so I thought again. That can't be right. Then I found the perfect answer to my query. I had been looking at the sign the wrong way round! Round the other way it was indeed YHA (Youth Hostels Association). With my mind at rest D.S. and I sped into the spacious grounds of the rambling old mansion. Certainly it was an impressive building and setting. On reflection the town of Leamington Spa was well laid out, spacious residential and somewhat upper middle class. The YHA mansion was in the same tone.

D.S. and I cautiously edged our way into the hostel lobby and looked around rather nervously. A nice sign beside a service hatch said "FOR WARDEN PLEASE RING BELL." I did and we awaited with bated breath for what kind of reception we would get. I hoped that we wouldn't have another Nazi, Gestapo Colwick style interrogation. After a short pause an agreeable warden ambled up. He looked pleasant enough. I was glad that he did because friend Woodentop (Neil Woodcock) had warned me that they tended to kick up hell about late arrivals (like us) and it was now 10.15 at night.

D.S. and I asked for accommodation for the night and I produced my hostel card. D.S. unfortunately had been refused membership by the Scottish Youth Hostels Association last Friday afternoon when late as ever he decided to join. Unfortunately for him all Junior Members needed a passport type photograph to be affixed to the card. D.S. hadn't brought the necessary photograph to the SYHA so they couldn't enroll him. I was a Juvenile member being supposed to be under 16 when I recently joined. My date of birth had been stated as 1/9/1949 rather than 1/6/1949 to make me a Juvenile and not a Junior member and therefore save 5 shillings (25p) in enrollment fees and the cost of a passport type picture as this wasn't required for juveniles. In London on Sunday D.S. had finally got his passport type photo at a two shillings (10p) Polyfoto machine outside an underground station.

D.S. now slapped down a ten shillings note (50p) and his precious photo and asked if he could join here. The warden assured him he could join here but the only problem was that he had no card to give him. The warden duly made out a temporary card and said that it would do for the remainder of our holiday and that he would receive the correct card through the post from YHA headquarters. The warden then asked if we had sleeping bags. I had two sheets sown together, which would do while D.S. had his own luxurious "interior sprung" sleeping bag so we were saved the expense of hiring sleeping bags.

The warden then came up with the only potential problem. He said that the hostel was very crowded but he thought that there were two beds left in Room B. He said that he couldn't be sure because there was a lot of Germans in the hostel tonight and that they couldn't speak a word of English, were staggering about the place and that they might not know where they were supposed to be sleeping. It all sounded as if our German friends had been having a Bavarian beer festival in Leamington and in the hostel. Drinking alcohol in the hostel was against YHA rules but the warden would have had a job explaining this to the non-English speaking Germans. I hoped that there would be some booze left for D.S. and I! The warden also suggested that if we found upstairs full up we could come back down here because there was always the annex in the garden. I did not fancy a cold shivery night between the water lilies because that's how I visualized the annex. I hoped that there were two beds left upstairs!

We asked one last favour from the warden. We explained that we had a long day ahead of us tomorrow and could we please be allowed to leave very early before the advertised reveille time of 07.00 if we were quiet. Our good warden agreed and said he would give us our cards back now. We could easily be excused hostel duties because there were many other people available to do them.

D.S. and I noted that our cards were stamped with a "Royal" Leamington Spa motif on our bed nights page. As we climbed the stairs I noted that the hostel had accommodation for 50 men and women. The hostel must be busy indeed! I had heard that normally the warden kept YHA cards as security and were not returned until after breakfast and hostel duties had been done. This could be around the back of nine – far too late for us. Hence my anxiety to get out of the hostel early in the morning.

D.S. and I duly found our dormitory and there were indeed two bunks left – one at either end of the room. The dormitory was certainly a United Nations one. I could make out Irish and English voices, the American drawl and some persistent foreign interference. I decided that this coarse language which I was hearing must be German.

Normal hostel rules are that the windows should be slightly open during the night but the hostellers did not seem to like that rule. The curtains were also tightly drawn. I hoped that the sun would pierce them early in the morning to wake me up at the back of five.

It was now 10.30 p.m. and lights went officially out at 11 p.m. Time for beddi-byes. The bunks were very comfortable and better than I had expected. I took no chances and took my money belt to bed. It is disconcerting to wake up and find your wallet empty.

THE D.S. IS TRAVELLING LIGHT EPISODE

At the other end of the dorm D.S. had engaged in conversation with some Yanks and some English blokes. There was an amusing incident when one of the Yanks asked how much they were all carrying. They all answered as follows: - Hosteller 1 – 43 lbs; Hosteller 2 – 37 lbs; Hosteller 3 – 41 lbs and the Yank finished by stating that he was travelling really light with 32 lbs. The other kids asked how he could get by with so little. Then they turned to D.S. and asked him how much he was carrying. D.S. looked a little bewildered at this talk and wondered if they were thinking of bumping him off. D.S. thought better of saying "No comment" or "None of your business" and said "Just over £9". They all gasped with amazement and were flabbergasted. Then they all simultaneously peered down from their bunks and looked at D.S.'s holdall. They said that he must be joking because there's far more than 9lbs in that. D.S. retorted by saying that there is nothing at all in the holdall and that it was all in his ski jacket. D.S. thought that they were wanting to rob him while their consensus of opinion was that D.S. was bammy, round the twist, crackers, mad, insane, a lunatic and other graver things. D.S. couldn't understand why they thought him bonkers but for good measure D.S. added that it was all in his wallet in his ski jacket zip pocket.

At last it dawned on the other four about what D.S. was raving about. I had been in a fit of controlled laughter for the last minute while the episode had raged on. Now they saw the misunderstanding and almost laughed the roof down. D.S. still hadn't seen the light and was now more bewildered than ever. D.S. had thought that they had had been asking how much MONEY they had all been carrying while the first boy had asked everyone how much WEIGHT they were all carrying. The boys were all cyclists and thought that D.S. was a cyclist too. It was a fantastic Harry Worth type of misunderstanding between £ and lbs. D.S. had played and was still playing a splendid bewildered Harry Worth. He deserved an Oscar for his performance. His performance was certainly as good as the one of the flatfeet policemen in the Epilogue of the Bluebottle Affair much earlier in the day at Derby Station.

I lay writhing in my bunk in ecstasies of laughter at the episode. A stage couldn't have produced a funnier scene. All was now understood and after the laughter had subsided their conversations continued. They now considered D.S. to be a bit of a nutcase rather than a raving lunatic.

HERE ENDETH THE D.S. IS TRAVELLING LIGHT EPISODE

Their conversation raged on from a sad story of one of the boys who was broke having to go to the police to get money to go home to predictably (as we had two Yanks here) to the Vietnam War. D.S. asked a dirty question when he asked if they had received their call up papers and draft cards yet. The Yanks went a whiter shade of pale at the thought of going to Vietnam.

After those pleasurable distracting conversations I lay back and turned my mind back to business. The time had come to painfully dissect the day. It was enough to give anyone grey hairs.

Review of the Day

This was the original timetable:-

DAY 4   **TUESDAY AUGUST 3RD 1965**   LMR DAY 3

Reveille 05.00

Do 16C Derby
Do Derby Works (we hope)

		MILES
Depart DERBY MIDLAND	06.10	0
Arrive BURTON-ON-TRENT	06.24	11

Do 16F Burton (50 mins. approx)

Recovery time + 13

Depart BURTON-ON-TRENT	07.27	11
Arrive BIRMINGHAM NEW ST.	08.08	41
Depart BIRMINGHAM NEW ST.	08.15	<u>41</u>
Arrive CHELTENHAM SPA MALVERN ROAD	09.05	
Depart CHELTENHAM SPA MALVERN ROAD	-	
Arrive GLOUCESTER CENTRAL	09.18	
Depart GLOUCESTER CENTRAL	-	
Arrive CARDIFF GENERAL	10.20	

Miniature Buffet Car

Journey:-
       see 2E Saltley - south each
       see 85B sub Cheltenham - west
       see 85B Gloucester - north
       see 86E Severn Tunnel Junction - east

see 86B Newport Ebbw Junction - 1 mile north west
see 86B sub Newport Godfrey Road - north west

British Rail

Depart CARDIFF GENERAL	10.11 or 10.41 or 11.11 or 11.41
Arrive BARRY	10.36 or 11.06 or 11.36 or 12.06

Do Barry Docks

Journey: -
     see 86A Cardiff Canton - south west

88C Barry (ex)

The shed is on the south of the line, east of Barry Station.

Turn right outside Barry Station into Broad Street; turn first right into and under the railway bridge. A cinder path leads from the right hand side of this road to the shed (5 minutes).

Do ex 88C Barry

Depart BARRY	11.33) and at frequent
Arrive CARDIFF GENERAL	11.59) intervals

WALK-   **Do 86A Cardiff Canton (40 mins.)**

Cardiff Corporation Bus No 16 (Pier Head)
Depart ST MARY' S STREET
Arrive DOCK ENTRANCE

Do 88A Cardiff East Dock

Depart DOCK ENTRANCE
Arrive ST MARY'S STREET

Note: - 88B Cardiff Radyr (closed)

Depart CARDIFF GENERAL	14.20
Arrive BIRMINGHAM NEW STREET	16.30

See same sheds as southbound journey

Miniature Buffet Car

Depart BIRMINGHAM NEW STREET	16.42	0
Arrive VAUXHALL AND DUDDESTON	16.46	1¼
(Lichfield Train)		

Do 2E Saltley (45 mins. approx)   Recovery Time
                                        - 5

Depart VAUXHALL AND DUDDESTON	17.26	1¼
Arrive ASTON	17.29	2½

Do 2J Aston (30 mins. approx)

		Recovery Time +7
Depart ASTON	18.06	0
Arrive BIRMINGHAM NEW STREET	18.17	2½
Depart BIRMINGHAM NEW MOOR STREET	18.40	0
Arrive TYSELEY	18.46	3¼

Do 2A Tyseley (30 mins. approx)

		Recovery Time +26
Depart TYSELEY	19.42	0
Arrive BIRMINGHAM SNOW HILL	19.47	3¼
Depart BIRMINGHAM SNOW HILL	20.00	0
Arrive LEAMINGTON SPA GENERAL	20.21	23¼
Depart LEAMINGTON SPA GENERAL	20.28	23¼
Arrive BANBURY	20.48	43

Journey: -
     See ex 2L Leamington Spa - south east

Do 2D Banbury (35 mins. approx)

		Recovery Time +3
Depart BANBURY	21.26	0
Arrive LEAMINGTON SPA GENERAL	21.45	19¾
Depart LEAMINGTON SPA GENERAL	21.49	19¾
Arrive BIRMINGHAM SNOW HILL	22.17	43

Buffet Car

Do Birmingham Snow Hill Station

WALK-   Snow Hill to New Street

Do Birmingham New Street Station

Night: -   Birmingham New Street Waiting Room

- - - - - - - - - - - - - - - - - - -

Comments

In the timetable I wrote Miniature Buffet Car/Buffet Car etc. whenever there is a chance of something to eat on the train. Remember that during the hours of daylight there is never much chance to get something to eat. Railway station catering rooms and buffet cars on train would be our best eating places to save time.

D.S. did not like this idea much as he wanted an hour off at midday. I put it to him MORE TIME, MORE SHEDS, BETTER VALUE FOR MONEY.

We got off to a flying start on schedule at 05.00 and were back on line with our working timetable. 16C Derby was successfully done and our first decision was Derby Works or 16F Burton. We probably chose correctly and had a most interesting Derby Works tour. Any regrets? Our guide did not seem to know where the assembly line was and that would have been interesting. We therefore missed unavoidably some new BR Type 2's and a few Brush Type 4's on trial from Loughborough. I (but not D.S. who was asleep) at least saw Burton shed when we later on passed it by on the way to Cardiff. If we had visited Burton we would have seen clutches of "Jinty's", "Big Eights" and "Black Fives" but nothing special.

On to Barry and on time and no regrets i.e. until we reached Barry. Trust us to get off at Barry Station rather than Barry Docks. We wasted about 20 minutes in walking to the engines. We crawled round Barry Docks looking at all the engines but perhaps that was no bad thing. Purists would say that you should spend a full day in visiting the inhabitants of such a revered place as Barry. The result of our Barry meanderings eventually resulted in us missing a certain 14.20 train from Cardiff General. However, in truth it was our fault for not hurrying back from 88A Cardiff East Dock and wasting time buying some orangeade knowing that we would still have to pick up our luggage at the left luggage office. I have had enough to say about a certain railway inspector so I won't say anymore now but the effect on my timetable was catastrophic. 2A Tyseley, 2E Saltley, 2F Bescot and 2J Aston all should have and would have been done with ease today if we could have got the 14.20 train to Birmingham. They would have to be done very early tomorrow morning in order to catch up on my original timetable. 1F Rugby was definitely for the chop now from the timetable. I was almost sure that Rugby was now closed to steam as indeed had been 1E Bletchley. That's one shed that I won't mind missing. D.S. wouldn't care. He's probably never heard of Rugby!

Another big mistake was I did not realize until we picked up our Railrover that 81F Oxford was accessible by Railrover at no extra charge via Banbury. 81F Oxford was a jewel in the crown and we certainly missed a trick in not taking advantage of this connection. Oxford was only 22 miles and about half an hour away by train.

81F Oxford had a great allocation of 42 steam plus seven recently withdrawn. A fabulous list:-
including three "Granges" plus one recently withdrawn, 14 "Halls", 11 "Modified Halls" plus two recently withdrawn. Sadly 81F Oxford would be closed to steam by January 1966.

Certainly I had slipped up in on two counts in not finding out before the tour (a) the LMR Railrover bonus routes and (b) purchasing a Western Region summer timetable. This timetable would also have provided us with the opportunity of finding out about some more overnight routes where we would have a comfortable carriage rather than a troubled stay in a waiting room somewhere.

81F OXFORD					
Steam					
1933 dev. of Collett 3F 5700 0-6-0PT 1929					
3751	*9653*	9773	9789		
Total	3				
Collett 4MT 6100 2-6-2T 1931 dev. of 5101 Class					
6108	*6110*	6111	6126		
6136	6145	*6154*			
Total	5				
Collett 5MT 6800 4-6-0 "Grange" 1936					
6841	6849	6868	6874		
Total	3				
Collett 5MT 4900 4-6-0 "Hall" 1928					
4962	5933	6910	6921		
6923	6924	6927	6931		
6932	6937	6947	6953		
6956	6957				
Total	14				
Hawksworth 5MT 6959 4-6-0 "Modified Hall" 1944					
6960	6961	*6963*	6967		
6974	6983	6991	6993		
6999	7909	7917	7919		
7922					
Total	11				
BR Standard 5MT 4-6-0 Doncaster 1951					
73003	73021	73023	73030		
73031	*73162*	73166			
Total	6				
		Surviving			
Grand Total	43	*Steam Classes*	6		
Recently		*Saw Elsewhere*			
Withdrawn	7	*on the tour*	9		
Steam	*Aug-50*	54	*Mar-59*		62
Allocation	*Apr-65*	26	*Aug-65*		42
	Closed to Steam:-		*Jan-66*		

An example of an overnight train which we could have got from Oxford was:-

		Schedule		Miles
Depart	OXFORD	02.00		0
Arrive	BANBURY	02.45		22¾
Depart	BIRMINGHAM NEW STREET	04.00		56½
Arrive	SHREWSBURY	05.16		108
Arrive	WREXHAM	06.26		138¼
Arrive	CHESTER GENERAL	06.58		150½
Arrive	BIRKENHEAD WOODSIDE	07.57		165½

What did we actually see today? Despite the Cardiff General missed train disaster we saw 245 steam and 240 diesels. About half of the steam seen was not surprisingly at Barry Docks. *By the time of my August 1970 re-visit to Barry Dock steam numbers had incredibly doubled from 110 to 212. Very few of the engines we had seen today at Barry would have disappeared by the end of 1970. Did we need to do Barry then today? Yes! Of course we did not know that from this month scrapping at Barry would virtually cease.*

Code	Visits	GWR	SR	LMS	LNER	WD	BR	Steam Total	Diesel Total	Electric Total	Grand Total
	Derby Station								1		1
16C	Derby and Derby Works			19			1	20	97		117
16F	Burton (pass)			10			1	11	3		14
	Derby to Tamworth					2		2	0		2
	Tamworth to Birmingham	1		7			1	9	11		20
	Birmingham to Gloucester	2		2			2	6	11		17
85B	Gloucester (pass)	5					3	8	2		10
	Gloucester to Cardiff	3						3	30		33
88A	Barry Docks	75	28	5			2	110			110
	Cardiff Canton (pass)								11		11
	Barry to Cardiff								2		2
86A	Cardiff East Dock	31					1	32	3		35
	Cardiff General		1				1	2	18		20
	Cardiff to Newport								21		21
	Newport to Hereford								7		7
	Hereford to Worcester	2						2	2		4
85A	Worcester (pass)	3		1				4	2		6
	Worcester to Snow Hill	2					1	3	10		13
	Birmingham Snow Hill	2		1				3	1		4
	Snow Hill to Banbury	2		1			1	4	5		9
2D	Banbury	14		3			9	26	2		28
	Banbury to Leamington								1		1
	GRAND TOTAL	**142**	**29**	**49**	**0**	**2**	**23**	**245**	**240**	**0**	**485**

Fast Forward August 1970

Code	Visits	GWR	SR	LMS	LNER	WD	BR	Steam Total	Diesel Total	Electric Total	Grand Total
BD	Barry Docks 0870	98	41	32	1	0	40	212	2	0	214

It was now 11.30 p.m. (an exceptional early time for some shut-eye, shut-eye, shut-eye)------
END OF DAY FOUR *Some steam statistical analyses follow:-*

STEAM ENGINE CLASSES — ACTIVE ON SHED DAY 4	BR total	2D Banbury	16C Derby	16F Burton	85A Worcester	85B Gloucester	88A Car E Dock	Total Active On Shed DAY 4
Collett 5MT 4900 4-6-0 "Hall" 1928 *4900-4999, 5900-5999, 6900-6958*	258		3			1		4
Hawksworth 5MT 6959 4-6-0 "Modified Hall" 1944 *6959-6999, 7900-7929*	71		2			2	1	5
Collett 5MT 5600 0-6-2T 1924 *5600-5699*	100		1					1
1927 dev. of Collett 5MT 5600 0-6-2T 1924 *6600-6699*	100		1					1
1933 dev. of Collett 3F 5700 0-6-0PT 1929 *3600-3799, 4600-4699, 8700, 8750-8799, 9600-9682, 9711-9799*	523						1	1
Collett 5MT 6800 4-6-0 "Grange" 1936 *6800-6879*	80		2					2
Hughes/Fowler 5MT 2-6-0 "Crab" 1926 *42700-42944*	245			1				1
Stanier 5MT 4-6-0 "Black Five" 1934 *44658-45499*	842			2	1			3
Ivatt 2MT 2-6-0 1946 *46400-46527*	128					1		1
Kitson 0F 0-4-0ST 1932 *47000-47009*	10			1				1
Johnson Midland 3F 0-6-0T 1899 *47200-47259*	60				1			1
Stanier 8F 2-8-0 "Big Eight" 1935 *48000-48775*	666		2	13	8			23
BR Standard 7P6F 4-6-2 "Britannia" Derby 1951 *70000-70054*	55				1			1
BR Standard 5MT 4-6-0 Doncaster 1951 *73000-73171*	172		4					4
BR Standard 4MT 2-6-0 Doncaster 1953 *76000-76114*	115		1					1
BR Standard 3MT 2-6-2T Swindon 1952 *82000-82044*	45						1	1
BR Standard 9F 2-10-0 Brighton 1954 *92000-92250 except*	166		3					3
BR Standard 9F 2-10-0 Brighton 1954. 1957 double chimney *92000-1; 92006; 92079; 92165-7, 92178; 92183-92249*	75		1					1
			20	17	11	4	3	55

323

Class / Number ranges	BR total	2D Banbury	16C Derby	16F Burton	85A Worcester	85B Gloucester	88A Car E Dock	Total DAY 4
Collett 3MT 2251 0-6-0 1930 — 2200-2299; 3200-3219	120	1						1
Collett dev.1938 of Churchward 8F 2-8-0 1903 — 2884-2899; 3800-66	83							
Collett 7P 4073 4-6-0 "Castle" 1923 — 4000,4016,4032,4037,4073-4099, 5000-5099, 7000-7037	169						6	6
Churchward 7F 4200 2-8-0T 1910 — 4200-99; 5200-04	91						3	3
Churchward 1923 5205 8F dev. of Churchward 7F 4200 2-8-0T 1910 — 5205-5264	60						2	2
Collett 5MT 4900 4-6-0 "Hall" 1928 — 4900-4999, 5900-5999, 6900-6958	258	3			0			3
Hawksworth 5MT 6959 4-6-0 "Modified Hall" 1944 — 6959-6999, 7900-7929	71				0		2	2
Collett 5MT 5600 0-6-2T 1924 — 5600-5699	100						4	4
1927 dev. of Collett 5MT 5600 0-6-2T 1924 — 6600-6699	100	1					3	4
1933 dev. of Collett 3F 5700 0-6-0PT 1929 — 3600-3799, 4600-4699, 8700, 8750-8799, 9600-9682,9711-9799	523						6	6
Collett 4MT 6100 2-6-2T 1931 dev. of 5101 Class — 6100-6169	70						1	1
Collett 5MT 6800 4-6-0 "Grange" 1936 — 6800-6879	80						3	3
Collett 5MT 7800 4-6-0 "Manor" 1938 — 7800-7829	30						1	1
Hawksworth 4F 9400 0-6-0PT 1947 — 3400-3409; 8400-8499 ; 9400-9499	210						1	1
Fairburn 4MT 2-6-4T 1945 dev. of Stanier 1935 — 42050-42299; 42673-42699	277	1						1
Ivatt 4MT 2-6-0 1947 — 43000-43161	162		2	3				5
BR Standard 2MT 2-6-0 Doncaster 1953 — 78000-78064	65		1					1
BR Standard 3MT 2-6-2T Swindon 1952 — 82000-82044	45					1		1
BR Standard 9F 2-10-0 Brighton 1954, 1957 double chimney — 92000-1; 92006; 92079; 92165-7, 92178; 92183-92249	75	0				1		1
Total		6	3	3	0	2	32	46

STEAM ENGINE CLASSES — ACTIVE OFF SHED DAY 4

STEAM ENGINE CLASSES (ACTIVE OFF SHED DAY 4)	BR total	derby to tamwth	tamwth to birmingh	birmingham to gloucest	gloucester to cardiff	cardiff station	hereford to worcest	worcester to snow h	birmingham snow hill	snow hill to banbury	Grand Total
Collett 5MT 4900 4-6-0 "Hall" 1928 *4900-4999, 5900-5999, 6900-6958*	258			1	1				2	2	6
Collett 4MT 5101 2-6-2T 1929 rebuild of Churchward 3100 Class 1903 *4100-4179; 5101-5110; 5150-99*	140							1			1
1927 dev. of Collett 5MT 5600 0-6-2T 1924 *6600-6699*	100							1			1
1933 dev. of Collett 3F 5700 0-6-0PT 1929 *3600-3799, 4600-4699, 8700, 8750-8799, 9600-9682,97.*	523				1	1					2
Collett 5MT 6800 4-6-0 "Grange" 1936 *6800-6879*	80		1		1	1					3
Collett 5MT 7800 4-6-0 "Manor" 1938 *7800-7829*	30			1							1
Maunsell 4F Q 0-6-0 Maunsell 1938 *30530-30549*	20						1				1
Stanier 5MT 4-6-0 "Black Five" 1934 *44658-45499*	842		2								2
Ivatt 2MT 2-6-0 1946 *46400-46527*	128		2	1							3
Stanier 8F 2-8-0 "Big Eight" 1935 *48000-48775*	666		3	1					1	1	6
BR Standard 5MT 4-6-0 Doncaster 1951 *73000-73171*	172									1	1
BR Standard 4MT 2-6-0 Doncaster 1953 *76000-76114*	115			1							1
BR Standard 3MT 2-6-2T Swindon 1952 *82000-82044*	45						1				1
Riddles WD 8F 2-8-0 "Austerity" 1943 *90000-90732*	733	2									2
BR Standard 9F 2-10-0 Brighton 1954. 1957 double chimney *92000-1; 92006; 92079; 92165-7, 92178; 92183-92249*	75		1	1				1			2
BR Standard 9F 2-10-0 Brighton 1954. 1955 Crosti boiler *92020-29*	10		1								1
		2	9	6	3	2	2	3	3	4	34

STEAM ENGINE CLASSES DAY 4 SUMMARY TOTALS	BR total	Total Active On Shed DAY 4	exc Barry Total Withdrawn On Shed DAY 4	Total Withdrawn Barry DAY 4	Active Off Shed DAY 4 Grand Total	DA.. Gra.. To..
Collett 3MT 2251 0-6-0 1930	120		1			
Churchward 8F 2800 2-8-0 1903	84			6		
Collett dev.1938 of Churchward 8F 2-8-0 1903	83		6	6		
Collett 7P 4073 4-6-0 "Castle" 1923	169		3	5		
Churchward 7F 4200 2-8-0T 1910	91		1	5		
Churchward 1923 5205 8F dev. of Churchward 7F 4200 2-8-0T 1910	60		2	3		
Churchward 4MT 2-6-0 4300 1911	195			1		
1932 dev. of Churchward 4MT 4300 2-6-0 1911	20			1		
Churchward 4MT 4500 2-6-2T 1906	75			2		
1927 4575 dev. of Churchward 4MT 4500 2-6-2T 1906	100			12		
Collett 5MT 4900 4-6-0 "Hall" 1928	258	4	3	10	6	
Hawksworth 5MT 6959 4-6-0 "Modified Hall" 1944	71	5	2	3		
Collett 4MT 5101 2-6-2T 1929 rebuild of Churchward 3100 Class 1903	140			4	1	
Collett 5MT 5600 0-6-2T 1924	100	1	4	4		
1927 dev. of Collett 5MT 5600 0-6-2T 1924	100	1	5	4	1	
Collett 3F 5700 0-6-0PT 1929	250			1		
1933 dev. of Collett 3F 5700 0-6-0PT 1929	523	1	6	2	2	
Collett 8P 6000 4-6-0 "King" 1927	30			2		
Collett 4MT 6100 2-6-2T 1931 dev. of 5101 Class	70		1			
Collett 5MT 6800 4-6-0 "Grange" 1936	80	2	3		3	
Collett 8F 7200 2-8-2T 1934 rebuild of Churchward 4200 Class 2-8-0T	54			3		
Collett 5MT 7800 4-6-0 "Manor" 1938	30		1		1	
Hawksworth 4F 9400 0-6-0PT 1947	210		1	1		
Urie 6F S15 4-6-0 1920 (with smoke deflectors)	20			2		
Maunsell 1927 dev. of Urie 6F S15 4-6-0 1920 (with smoke deflectors)	15			3		
6F S15 4-6-0 Urie 1920 (with smoke deflectors) Maunsell 1936 development	10			2		
Maunsell 4F Q 0-6-0 Maunsell 1938	20			1	1	
Maunsell 4P3F U 2-6-0 1928	30			3		
Maunsell 4P3F U 2-6-0 1928 rebuild of 2-6-4T 1917 "River" K class	20			1		
Maunsell 4P5F N 2-6-0 1917	80			1		
Bulleid 7P5F "West Country & Battle of Britain Class 4-6-2 1945	53			7		
1957 7P6F dev. of Bulleid 7P5F 4-6-2 "West Country & Battle of Britain" 1945	57			4		
1956 dev. of Bulleid 8P 4-6-2 "Merchant Navy" 1941	30			4		
Fairburn 4MT 2-6-4T 1945 dev. of Stanier 1935	277		1			
Hughes/Fowler 5MT 2-6-0 "Crab" 1926	245	1				
Ivatt 4MT 2-6-0 1947	162		2			
Stanier 5MT 4-6-0 "Black Five" 1934	842	3			2	
Stanier 6P5F 4-6-0 "Jubilee" 1934	191			2		
Ivatt 2MT 2-6-0 1946	128	1			3	
Kitson 0F 0-4-0ST 1932	10	1				
Johnson Midland 3F 0-6-0T 1899	60	1				
Stanier 8F 2-8-0 "Big Eight" 1935	666	23		1	6	
Fowler ex Somerset & Dorset Joint Railway 7F 2-8-0 1914	11			2		
BR Standard 7P6F 4-6-2 "Britannia" Derby 1951	55	1				
BR Standard 5MT 4-6-0 Doncaster 1951	172	4			1	
BR Standard 4MT 2-6-0 Doncaster 1953	115	1			1	
BR Standard 2MT 2-6-0 Doncaster 1953	65		1			
BR Standard 3MT 2-6-2T Swindon 1952	45	1	1		1	
Riddles WD 8F 2-8-0 "Austerity" 1943	733				2	
BR Standard 9F 2-10-0 Brighton 1954	166	3				
BR Standard 9F 2-10-0 Brighton 1954. 1957 double chimney	75	1	2	2	2	
BR Standard 9F 2-10-0 Brighton 1954. 1955 Crosti boiler	10				1	
		55	46	110	34	2.

STEAM ENGINE CLASSES
BARRY DOCKS AUGUST 1965 and AUGUST 1970

Class	BR total	saw Barry Docks Aug-65	scrap before Aug-70	new Barry Docks Aug-70	saw Barry Docks Aug-70
Churchward 8F 2800 2-8-0 1903 2800-83	84	6			6
Collett dev.1938 of Churchward 8F 2-8-0 1903 2884-2899; 3800-66	83	6		4	10
Collett 7P 4073 4-6-0 "Castle" 1923 4000,4016,4032,4037, 4073-4099, 5000-5099, 7000-7037	169	5			5
Churchward 7F 4200 2-8-0T 1910 4200-99; 5200-04	91	5			5
Churchward 1923 5205 8F dev. of Churchward 7F 4200 2-8-0T 1910 5205-5264	60	3			3
Churchward 4MT 2-6-0 4300 1911 4303-4386(12); 5300-5399; 6300-6399; 7305-7321	195	1			1
1932 dev. of Churchward 4MT 4300 2-6-0 1911 7322-7341	20	1			1
Churchward 4MT 4500 2-6-2T 1906 4500-4574	75	2			2
1927 4575 dev. of Churchward 4MT 4500 2-6-2T 1906 4575-4599, 5500-5574	100	12	-1		11
Collett 5MT 4900 4-6-0 "Hall" 1928 4900-4999, 5900-5999, 6900-6958	258	10		4	14
Hawksworth 5MT 6959 4-6-0 "Modified Hall" 1944 6959-6999, 7900-7929	71	3			3
Collett 4MT 5101 2-6-2T 1929 rebuild of Churchward 3100 Class 1903 4100-4179; 5101-5110; 5150-99	140	4		6	10
Collett 5MT 5600 0-6-2T 1924 5600-5699	100	4			4
1927 dev. of Collett 5MT 5600 0-6-2T 1924 6600-6699	100	4			4
Collett 3F 5700 0-6-0PT 1929 5700-5799, 7700-7799, 8701-8749	250	1	-1		0
1933 dev. of Collett 3F 5700 0-6-0PT 1929 3600-3799, 4600-4699, 8700, 8750-8799, 9600-9682, 9711-9799	523	2		4	6
Collett 8P 6000 4-6-0 "King" 1927 6000-6029	30	2			2
Collett 8F 7200 2-8-2T 1934 rebuild of Churchward 4200 Class 2-8-0T 7200-7253	54	3			3
Collett 5MT 7800 4-6-0 "Manor" 1938 7800-7829	30			7	7
Hawksworth 4F 9400 0-6-0PT 1947 3400-3409; 8400-8499 ; 9400-9499	210	1			1
Urie 6F S15 4-6-0 1920 (with smoke deflectors) 30496-30515	20	2			2
Maunsell 1927 dev. of Urie 6F S15 4-6-0 1920 (with smoke deflectors) 30823-30837	15	3			3
6F S15 4-6-0 Urie 1920 (with smoke deflectors) Maunsell 1936 development 30838-30847	10	2			2
Maunsell 4F Q 0-6-0 Maunsell 1938 30530-30549	20	1			1
Maunsell 4P3F U 2-6-0 1928 31610-31639	30	3			3
Maunsell 4P3F U 2-6-0 1928 rebuild of 2-6-4T 1917 "River" K class 31790-31809	20	1			1
Maunsell 4P5F N 2-6-0 1917 31400-31414, 31810-31821, 31823-31875	80	1			1
Bulleid 7P5F "West Country & Battle of Britain Class 4-6-2 1945 34002/6/7/11/5/9/20/3/30/3/5/8/41/3/9/51/4/5/7/61/3-70/2-6/8-81/3/4/6/ 34091/2/4/6/9/34102-8/10	53	7		1	8
1957 7P6F dev. of Bulleid 7P5F 4-6-2 "West Country & Battle of Britain" 1945 34001/3-5/8-10/2-4/6-8/21/2/4-9/31/2/4/6/7/9/40/2/4-8/50/2/3/6/8/9/60/2/ 71/7/82/5/7-9/90/3/5/7/8/34100/1/9	57	4		6	10
1956 dev. of Bulleid 8P 4-6-2 "Merchant Navy" 1941 35001-30	30	4		6	10

STEAM ENGINE CLASSES BARRY DOCKS AUGUST 1965 and AUGUST 1970(continued)		saw Barry Docks Aug-65	scrap before Aug-70	new Barry Docks Aug-70	saw Barry Docks Aug-70
Ivatt 2MT 2-6-2T 1946					
41200–41329	130			2	2
Hughes/Fowler 5MT 2-6-0 "Crab" 1926					
42700–42944	245			2	2
Stanier 5MT 2-6-0 1933					
42945-84	40			1	1
Midland 4F 0-6-0 1924					
44027–44606	580			2	2
Stanier 5MT 4-6-0 "Black Five" 1934					
44658–45499	842			6	6
Stanier 6P5F 4-6-0 "Jubilee" 1934					
45552-45734/7–42	189	2			2
Ivatt 2MT 2-6-0 1946					
46400–46527	128			4	4
Midland 3F "Jinty" 0-6-0T 1924 dev. of Johnson 1899 design					
47260–47681	417			5	5
Stanier 8F 2-8-0 "Big Eight" 1935					
48000–48775	666	1		5	6
Fowler ex Somerset & Dorset Joint Railway 7F 2-8-0 1914					
53800-10	11	2			2
Thompson 5MT 4-6-0 B1 1942					
61000–61409	410			1	1
BR Standard 8P 4-6-2 Derby 1954					
71000	1			1	1
BR Standard 5MT 4-6-0 Doncaster 1951					
73000-73171	172			4	4
BR Standard 4MT 4-6-0 Brighton 1951					
75000-75079	80			4	4
BR Standard 4MT 2-6-0 Doncaster 1953					
76000-76114	115			5	5
BR Standard 2MT 2-6-0 Doncaster 1953					
78000-78064	65			4	4
BR Standard 4MT 2-6-4T Doncaster 1953					
80000-80154	155			14	14
BR Standard 9F 2-10-0 Brighton 1954					
92000-92250 except	176			2	2
BR Standard 9F 2-10-0 Brighton 1954. 1957 double chimney					
92000-1; 92006; 92079; 92165-7, 92178; 92183-92249	75	2		4	6
		110	-2	104	212

Part Five

WEDNESDAY 4th AUGUST 1965

The Tour continues

Leamington Spa, Birmingham, Wolverhampton, Crewe
and
Shrewsbury Arrival

Reveille – Leamington Spa Youth Hostel

I awoke feeling rather sleepy after an unusually comfortable sleep. After all a bed for the night was a luxury! D.S. had wanted it to be a necessity and had got his way for one night at least. I looked across at the drawn curtains and all appeared a little too bright for 5 o'clock in the morning. I also noted activity at almost every dormitory bed although noticeably (but hardly surprising) D.S. was still in the middle of his "ugly" sleep. Strange seeing so many people awake at about 5 a.m. I thought that there was supposed to be strict silence until 7 a.m. D.S. and I had received special permission to get up at the back of five but had they all got permission too? It was a mystery indeed. I then thought how wonderful it was that every morning so far I had woken up when I wanted to. Some brilliant people can do that! This morning would be no exception. I glanced at my watch (my faithful ever-wrong Timex watch) to check to see if it was 05.15 yet.

A chain reaction took place. I froze for a few seconds with my eyes fixed alarmingly on the dial of my watch. I felt my hair begin slowly to stand on its end (I think) and then there was a cry of anguish and pain. Then there was a time announced from a faint voice inside me – IT WAS HALF PAST EIGHT - 08.30 not 05.15. Then a few wondrously expressive swear words, which I shall censor.

After I had calmed down somewhat I dived out of bed, stormed over the dormitory and shook D.S. awake. A purple faced gurgling D.S. awoke and complained that every time I woke him up he felt sore somewhere. This was no time for a medical report and I asked D.S. to look at his watch. Eight thirty was his bleary reply and he said he would get up soon and turned over. Another hefty shake brought D.S. to his senses and I told him that I was leaving the hostel in five minutes even if he wasn't.

A quick wash and dress and we were out of the hostel by 08.40. D.S. on the way along to the station made the very unfunny remark that we were only three hours late in getting started. D.S. was lucky not to get punched. The original timetable had sunk even more without trace after this disastrous start. D.S. seemed to be a ten-ton weight dragging the timetable down to the bottom of the sea albeit both of us had slept in today.

After a brisk walk through a dozy Leamington spa we galloped into the station and were very lucky to find a D.M.U. about to leave. The bucket would stop at 2A Tyseley so at least we had made a "fast" but belated start. The train we should have got was the 06.30 arriving in Tyseley at 07.12. Now we were on the 09.00 arriving in Tyseley at 09.38. Two hours and twenty-six minutes lost. We had just missed the 08.43 to Tyseley but this would have saved us only twelve minutes which was next to nothing when we were hours behind schedule.

Our local bucket idled out of the station at 09.00 and made a slow dawdle to Tyseley with eight intermediate stops. Our return to Tyseley could be termed Conservative (note the capital c). We passed through a residential section of Birmingham where the Tories held a virtual unshakeable stranglehold. Solihull, a large borough, was one of our stops and probably the most Conservative town in Britain. Just like Ebbw Vale for Labour folklore says that they just weigh the votes and don't bother to count them.

Loco wise nearing Tyseley a Brush Type 4 and a LMS/BR Diesel Shunter were noted.

		Schedule	Actual	Miles
Depart	LEAMINGTON SPA GENERAL	09.00	09.00	0
Arrive	TYSELEY	09.38	09.38	20

Average speed just over 30 m.p.h. Ugh!

D.S. and I baled out at Tyseley and my first port of call was at the departures board to see when we would get a train to Birmingham Snow Hill, New Street or Moor Street after we did the shed. The only departure of interest was the 10.11 to Moor Street arriving at 10.16. Moor Street was next door to New Street. A reasonable train to get given that we can't hope for miracles when our original timetable is washed up.

Talking of all washed up D.S. seemed a bit like that. He was walking as though he was pulling the municipal dustcart behind him and was thus making tortoise progress. I told him so and we had a hell of an argument on the bridge over the mainline. We were ready to part our ways for good when unluckily or luckily depending on how you see it) a train came to our rescue. A Standard "Black Five" was fast approaching and we darted across to the side of the bridge to snatch the smokebox numberplate before it t disappeared with a great cloud of smoke underneath the bridge. She was BR Standard 5MT 73026 of 2A Tyseley (ex-2L Leamington Spa). We had seen her on the way to Banbury last night. That stopped our spat for the time being and D.S. trailed behind me on the way to Tyseley shed.

LEAMINGTON SPA TO TYSELEY

		Home shed		Built	Withdrawn	Scrap
Diesels						
Brush Type 4 Co-Co 1962						
D1717		81A	Old Oak Common	Feb-1964		
Total	1					
LMS and BR 0-6-0 Shunter 1945						
12062		2A	Tyseley	Dec-1949	Apr-1970	
Total	1					
Steam				Built	Withdrawn	Scrap
BR Standard 5MT 4-6-0 Doncaster 1951						
73026		2A	Tyseley(ex 2L)	Dec-1951	Apr-1967	Oct-1967
Total	1					

On Journey	3	Kops		2		
Steam	1	Diesels		2		
		Home Area		2	Visitors	1
Shed						
Distribution	2A	1	81A	1		
Steam Classes	1					
Steam Origin	BR	1				

The British Locomotive Shed Directory said five minutes walking time. This turned into 15 minutes D.S. walking time. At this rate D.S. is a deadly form of spreading rot. It was now 09.55. Tyseley was in the process of being converted to the chief diesel servicing depot for the Birmingham area. Steam engines were, however, stacked thickly around the diesel shed. This was a very soothing sight! We even had a permit for Tyseley but as usual we would wander round and produce it if need be if stopped. I didn't fancy explaining away a party of two instead of a party of twelve.

It was a terrific shed to go around as it was packed with GWR stock. Halls, Granges and also BR 9F 2-10-0's stood out. All GWR classes being new to me were worth a second look. D.S. had already put beyond any doubt the impossibility of getting the 10.11 train for our next destination. Anyone else would have made it with ten minutes to spare but with D.S. – never a chance! The next time I would just leave him behind. We now could afford to take our time (with the train missed we were left with the bus). All went well in our tour round until we reached the diesel depot then lo and behold a familiar figure came across to us. The familiar figure (no prizes for guessing) – the shedmaster. He appeared to be a cheerful type and was surprised to find that we in fact had a permit. I told him that we were on tour and that we were sorry for being a day late. Our permit was for yesterday but he took our scanty explanation in good faith, told us to be careful in going round and wished us luck. A good chap!

The diesel servicing depot was very disappointing in that it was crammed mostly with diesel multiple units (buckets). The only occupants of note were a motor parcels van, a Brush Type 4 and a BR Type 2. Several other diesels were standing outside the servicing depot.

2A TYSELEY			Home shed		Built	Withdrawn	Scrap
Diesels							
BR Sulzer "Peak" Type 4 1Co-Co1 1959							
D 110			D16	Nottingham Division	*Jul-1961*		
Total		*1*					
Brush Type 4 Co-Co 1962							
D1716			81A	Old Oak Common	*Feb-1964*		
D1814			2E	Saltley (ex D16)	*Feb-1965*		
Total		*2*					
BR 0-6-0 Shunter 1955							
D3248			2E	Saltley	*May-1956*		
D3957			2A		*May-1960*		
D3984			2A		*Aug-1960*		
Total		*3*					
BR Sulzer Type 2 Bo-Bo 1958							
D5008			5A	Crewe Diesel	*Feb-1959*		
D5021			1B	Camden	*Aug-1959*		
D5284			2E	Saltley	*Jul-1964*		
Total		*3*					
LMS and BR 0-6-0 Shunter 1945							
12066			2A		*Dec-1949*	*Mar-1969*	
Total		*1*					
Steam					Built	Withdrawn	Scrap
Collett 4MT 5101 2-6-2T 1929 rebuild of Churchward 3100 Class 1903							
4111			2A		*Oct-1935*	*Sep-1965*	*Feb-1966*
4125			2A		*May-1938*	*Jun-1965*	*Nov-1965*
4158			2A		*Aug-1947*	*Jun-1965*	*Feb-1966*
Total		*3*					
Collett 5MT 5600 0-6-2T 1924							
5658			2A		*Feb-1926*	*Nov-1965*	*Apr-1966*
5684			2A		*Oct-1926*	*Jul-1965*	*Oct-1965*
Total		*2*					
1927 dev. of Collett 5MT 5600 0-6-2T 1924							
6625			2A	(ex 6C Croes Newydd)	*Jan-1928*	*Nov-1965*	*Apr-1966*
6665			2A	(ex 6C Croes Newydd)	*Sep-1928*	*Oct-1965*	*Dec-1965*
6667			2A		*Sep-1928*	*Nov-1965*	*May-1966*
6681			2A		*Oct-1928*	*Oct-1965*	*Dec-1965*
Total		*4*					
1933 dev. of Collett 3F 5700 0-6-0PT 1929							
8767			2B	Oxley	*Dec-1933*	*Jul-1966*	*Nov-1966*
Total		*1*					
Collett 5MT 6800 4-6-0 "Grange" 1936							
6851	"Hurst Grange"		2A	(ex 2B Oxley)	*Oct-1937*	*Aug-1965*	*Jan-1966*
6854	"Roundhill Grange"		2A	(ex 2B Oxley)	*Nov-1937*	*Sep-1965*	*Feb-1966*
6861	"Crynant Grange"		2A		*Feb-1939*	*Oct-1965*	*Mar-1966*
6862	"Derwent Grange"		2A	(ex 2B Oxley)	*Feb-1939*	*Jun-1965*	*Nov-1965*
6864	"Dymock Grange"		2A	(ex 2B Oxley)	*Feb-1939*	*Oct-1965*	*Jan-1966*
6866	"Morfa Grange"		2A		*Mar-1939*	*May-1965*	*Aug-1965*
6879	"Overton Grange"		2A		*May-1939*	*Oct-1965*	*Mar-1966*
Total		*7*					

		Home shed			Built	Withdrawn	Scrap
Collett 5MT 4900 4-6-0 "Hall" 1936							
5988	"Bostock Hall"	2A			*Nov-1939*	*Oct-1965*	*Dec-1965*
6957	"Westol Hall"	81F	Oxford		*Mar-1943*	*Oct-1965*	*Feb-1966*
Total	2						
Hawksworth 5MT 6959 4-6-0 "Modified Hall" 1944							
7908	"Henshall Hall""	2A			*Jan-1950*	*Oct-1965*	*Dec-1965*
7925	"Westol Hall"	86B	Newport Ebbw Jct. (ex 88A)		*Oct-1950*	*Dec-1965*	*Mar-1966*
7929	"Wyke Hall"	2A			*Nov-1950*	*Aug-1965*	*Oct-1965*
Total	3						
Collett 4MT 8100 2-6-2T 1938							
8109		2A			*Feb-1905*	*Jun-1965*	*Dec-1965*
Total	1						
Stanier 5MT 4-6-0 "Black Five" 1934							
44691		2B	Oxley		*Oct-1950*	*Apr-1967*	*Dec-1967*
Total	1						
Ivatt 2MT 2-6-2T 1946							
46428	*to Barry Docks*	2A	(ex 2L Leamington Spa)		*Dec-1948*	*Dec-1966*	*saved*
Total	1						
BR Standard 5MT 4-6-0 Doncaster 1951							
73019		2B	Oxley		*Oct-1951*	*Jan-1967*	*May-1967*
Total	1						
BR Standard 4MT 2-6-0 Doncaster 1953							
75006		2A	(ex 5D Stoke)		*Sep-1951*	*Aug-1967*	*Feb-1968*
Total	1						
BR 4MT 2-6-0 Doncaster 1953							
76087		2F	Bescot		*May-1957*	*Jan-1967*	*Sep-1967*
Total	1						
BR Standard 9F 2-10-0 Brighton 1954							
92087		1H	Northampton(ex 16B via 9D)		*Aug-1956*	*Feb-1967*	*May-1967*
92204	*double*	*chimney*	2A		*Apr-1959*	*Dec-1967*	*Mar-1968*
92215	*double*	*chimney*	2A		*Nov-1959*	*Jun-1967*	*Mar-1968*
92244	*double*	*chimney*	86B	Newport Ebbw Jct. (ex 88A)	*Oct-1958*	*Dec-1965*	*Jul-1966*
Total	4						

On Shed	42	**Kops**	40		
Steam	32	**Diesels**	10		
Withdrawn	6				

Home Locos	27	**Home Area**	7	**Visitors**	8		
Shed	2A	27	2B	3	2E	3	
Distribution:-	2F	1					
	1B	1	1H	1			
	5A	1	D16	1			
	81A	1	81F	1	86B	2	
Steam Classes	14						
Steam Origin	GWR	23	LMS	2	BR	7	

Shed Highlight 4MT 1938 8100 Collett GWR 2-6-2T

	8109		2A Tyseley			
Steam	**Aug-50**	118	**Mar-59**	70	**Apr-65**	39
Allocation					Aug-65	45
			Closed to Steam:-		Nov-66	

Home Steam	excluding recently withdrawn locos					
On/Off Shed	On Shed	17	Off Shed	28	% On Shed	38%
Not on Shed						
3F 5700 0-6-0PT 1933			3625	4635	9774	3
4MT 5101 2-6-2T 1929			4147	4155	4168	3
5MT 5600 0-6-2T 1924				5605	5606	2
5MT 5600 0-6-2T 1927					6668	1
"Granges"	6853	6855	6857	6858	6879	5
"Modified Halls"					7915	1
2MT 2-6-2T 1946			46442	46457	46470	3
BR 5MT 4-6-0 1951		73026	73066	73069	73156	4
BR 9F 2-10-0 1954	92001	92002	92118	92212	92217	
					92223	6
					total	28

saw elsewhere on the tour		14			
saw at Barry Docks revisited Aug 70		1		scrap	Aug-65
recently withdrawn not on shed or seen elsewhere		1	5MT 5600 0-6-2T 1924		6633

Review and Appraisal of 2A Tyseley

The shed was on the west side of the line north of the station. Walking time was 5 minutes.

Interesting seeing three members of the 41XX class. They were a modified design of Churchward's 3100 Class (introduced 1903). In turn 8109 was one of the 8100 Class which was a later Collett rebuild with higher pressure and smaller wheels of the Churchward 5100 Class. 8109 was unique in that sadly she was the last sole surviving member of her class, which was originally numbered ten. That honour would soon die in the breaker's yard because she was condemned.

The 5600 Class locos were designed for service in the Welsh valleys. Now they were scattered over the whole system and here were six of them at Tyseley. Two of them were recent arrivals from 6C Croes Newydd (which I pronounced crows nude but Neil Woodcock knew the correct Welsh pronunciation). 6C Croes Newydd is at Wrexham and we hopefully we would be visiting that shed later in the trip. In fact only 6C Croes Newydd, 87F Llanelly and 2D Banbury had examples of the class. South Wales from this week was apparently closed for steam so the beloved Welsh valleys had seen this class and all working steam locos for the last time.

We had already seen "Bostock Hall" and "Wyke Hall" last night at Birmingham Snow Hill and as sadly mentioned that seemed to be "Wyke Hall's" last run as she was condemned later this very week. She now had to wait for the humiliating haul away to the scrap breaker's yard. *(She ended up being scrapped at Bird's Bridgend – Editor).* "Bostock Hall" was one of the oldest of the original "Halls" still running. *(Sadly her sands of time were running out and she was withdrawn in October 1965 and scrapped at Cashmore's Great Bridge).* Good to see the "Modified Halls" also.

Seven "Granges" were a terrific haul to see in these rundown days. Two were condemned. Standards were also to the fore and 75006 was a recent acquisition from 5D Stoke. One ex 88A Cardiff East Dock (now 86B Newport) 9F 2-10-0 was on shed. Main line diesels on shed came from the London, Crewe, Nottingham, Birmingham wedge. In all it was a great shed with 13 different steam classes on view. Seemed a busy shed and this was borne out by only 17(38%) of the steam allocation being on shed this weekday morning. A bit disappointing that only 17 home Steam (38%) were on shed. However, 14 different steam classes on show was magnificent.

On we go

Next stop Birmingham New Street and D.S. and I consulted the timetable at Tyseley Station and noted that the next train was at 10.44 (too long to wait) rather than the 10.11, which I had hoped for, and D.S. had scuppered. We would have to bus it. I had a good mind to ask D.S. for my bus fare. D.S. didn't look as though he was going to oblige and I decided against the expense of suing him in court. I consulted the LocoShed Directory and it recommended a No 44 (Acock's Green) or a 44J (Warwick Road) bus. We obeyed and got the first one to the city centre. After a twenty minute journey we evacuated at Birmingham New Street. Birmingham City Centre (like New Street) was undergoing major reconstruction *(start of the infamous Bull Ring road?).* Birmingham New Street was below street level and by a devious route we got to the main concourse via a metal overbridge.

I looked in my back pocket for a publication on "How to make up the best timetable at short notice" and I found it to be missing. I wondered if I had imagined it there or was the sun getting me down? I looked at the clock and told D.S. to synchronise his chronometer with it. D.S. was mystified and I clarified the comment with "Check your watch time". I suspected my Timex of going two or three minutes fast each day. However, a watch is less dangerous on the LMR tour if it runs fast than if it runs slow. *(You should be able to work that one out – Editor)*. Only two or three minutes wrong for a Timex was probably a record for Scotland's and Dundee's pride and joy.

I noted that it was getting on for eleven o'clock and remembered that Bescot had an hourly service only while Saltley and Aston had fairly regular services. The Bescot service left New Street at five minutes past the hour so I thought we had better go there first because there was a train in a few minutes and take the short waiting time now rather than have a long waiting time later on.

Our short stay at New Street provided us with two English Electric Type 4's. They were D221 "Ivernia" and D227 "Parthia". We had already seen "Parthia" at Bletchley.

BIRMINGHAM NEW STREET WEDNESDAY MORNING							
			Home shed		Built	Withdrawn	Scrap
Diesels							
English Electric Type 4 1-Co-Co-1 1958							
D 221	Ivernia		9A	Longsight	Jul-1959		
D 227	Parthia		9A	Longsight	Aug-1959		
Total	2						
On Station	2		Kops		0		
Steam	0		Diesels		2		
		Home Area			0	Visitors	2
Shed							
Distribution	9A	2					

Our bucket caused us a little worry because come 11.05 – no bucket. We were reassured when we noted several other worried people waiting on the platform. Presumably they were all waiting for the same bucket as us. At 11.12 our tardy two-coach bucket arrived. D.S. and I plonked ourselves on the front seats behind the driver. D.S. took one side and I took the other. We prepared ourselves for a profitable run through busy Birmingham to Bescot. We were not to be disappointed. At one of the intermediate stops an intriguing old fogey came up and sat down beside me.

"The bloody young vandals episode"

I thought funny peculiar. There were plenty of empty seats on the bucket without settling down beside me. I suddenly felt claustrophobic. The old bloke was leaning hard forward and his eyes were trained on the line. Was he a trainspotter? A "Big Eight" thundered past at the head of a fast fitted freight and D.S. and I didn't waste time in snatching the number down. Our old chap didn't bat an eyelid. No, he couldn't be an active trainspotter. What was he doing? Counting the sleepers? Hardly. Suddenly further up the line I noted a great bellow of grey smoke. The banking was ablaze and burning fiercely. The old chap gazed at it (eyes ablaze) and muttered angrily "Bloody young vandals!" He then looked accusingly at D.S. and I as though we were to blame and were in league with the real culprits. He then got up and stormed off at the next station.

I wondered if he was away to get the railway police to investigate the fire or to phone a complaint to his local Member of Parliament at Westminster about those bloody young vandals. At first I felt the same feeling of disgust as him and was annoyed to think that this could conceivably be the work of vandals. I reflected back to tragic incidents earlier in the year in England caused by certain young people putting heavy objects on the track and thus causing several derailments with some fatalities. I had also heard of the troubles on Britain's electrified lines with the overhead cables. People liked to throw old bicycles and other assorted junk from overbridges on to the overhead electrified cables. After a few more minutes contemplation I came to the conclusion that the embankment grass fire probably wasn't the work of bloody young vandals after all but more likely caused by a stray spark from a "Big Eight" galloping past. The grass at our local locospotters haven at Monktonhall had been set on fire by passing steam engines scores of times I reflected.

Be sure lad 'twas a beautiful line. No fewer than four Big Eights and a Black Five zipped past us on freights in our relatively short journey. That's what I call a busy line! Trains literally falling on each other's heels. All (obviously) were going in the opposite direction to us. Bescot yard was a large one and was due to be electrified later on in the year with a main line link to Birmingham New Street. A fruitful and very varied journey!

		Schedule	Actual
Depart	BIRMINGHAM NEW STREET	11.05	11.14
Arrive	BESCOT	11.28	11.35
	Do 2F Bescot		

5 intermediate stops. We arrived at Bescot seven minutes late. I could see the shed straight across the line from us and my first impression was that the shed was pretty full. This time D.S. and I had plenty time. A bucket left Bescot at 38 minutes past every hour for Birmingham New Street so we had almost an hour in which to do the shed, which was just across the line. I think even the snail-like D.S. will find this recovery time easy going. I noticed that the entrance to the shed was after a concrete over bridge. This would be a new bridge necessitated by extra clearances for the new electrified overhead line to Birmingham.

BIRMINGHAM NEW STREET to BESCOT					
	Home shed		Built	Withdrawn	Scrap
Diesels					
English Electric Type 4 1Co-Co1 1958					
D311	5A	Crewe Diesel	Dec-1960		
Total 1					
BR 0-6-0 Shunter 1953					
D3838	2J	Aston	Jan-1960		
Total 1					
LMS 0-6-0 Shunter 1939					
12012	2F	Bescot	Dec-1939	Dec-1967	
Total 1					
LMS and BR 0-6-0 Shunter 1945					
12077	2A	Tyseley	Oct-1950	Oct-1971	
12087	2F	Bescot	Dec-1950	Jul-1971	
Total 3					
Steam	Home shed		Built	Withdrawn	Scrap
Ivatt 4MT 2-6-0 1947					
43005	2F	Bescot	Jan-1948	Nov-1965	Feb-1966
Total 1					
Stanier 5MT 4-6-0 "Black Five" 1934					
45067	2F	Bescot	Jan-1935	Oct-1967	Dec-1967
45231	6A	Chester Midland	Aug-1936	Aug-1968	saved
Total 2					
Ivatt 2MT 2-6-0 1946					
46492	2J	Aston	Dec-1951	Jun-1967	Feb-1968
Total 1					
Stanier 8F 2-8-0 "Big Eight" 1935					
48061	2F	Bescot (ex 1G)	Nov-1936	Sep-1967	Oct-1968
48366	2F	Bescot	Sep-1944	Nov-1965	Jan-1966
48529	2F	Bescot	Apr-1945	Jun-1968	Nov-1968
48680	2F	Bescot	Dec-1943	Sep-1966	Feb-1967
Total 4					
BR Standard 4MT 2-6-0 Doncaster 1953					
76047	2F	Bescot	Mar-1955	Nov-1966	Feb-1968
Total 1					

BIRMINGHAM NEW STREET to BESCOT(Continued)						
On Line	14	Kops		11		
Steam	9	Diesels		5		
		Home Area		12	Visitors	2
Shed	2A	1	2F	9	2J	2
Distribution	5A	1	6A	1		
Steam Classes	5					
Steam Origin	LMS		8 BR	1		

"And now there were four"

I noticed two boys (about fourteen years old) scurrying across the bridge. When they saw us they came scurrying back and asked if we had a permit. Obviously they didn't. Four will make our party seem a little larger and mollify shedmasters about permits for twelve and a party of two in front of them. As they say two's company, four's a crowd. "And now there were four". We agreed to take them round with us.

We crossed over the bridge and I spied out the land and looked for the usual unauthorized entrance frequented by trainspotters. This shed was a bit of a problem with a five-foot wall almost completely sealing it off from the outside world. The only entrance was at the glass fronted partition of the ------ shedmaster.

My three companions played prize fools and before I could stop them they walked straight on to the office entrance at the break in the wall. But we could have walked up the side of the wall and climbed it at the back of the shed, I wailed to myself. We would be on the shedmaster's blind side there. No use wasting words now because D.S. and the two others had passed the point of no return. More than one face was peering at them from inside the glass-fronted office. Too late now, I thought, and I quickly caught up with them before any more damage was done.

One of the shedmaster's underlings motioned me to come into the office and taking D.S. with me we edged inside. Our two companions were better outside than inside as they were under age. All members of the party were supposed to be sixteen years of age. I was sixteen years and two months old and just beat the deadline while D.S. does not like to count the candles anymore. Anyway he was over sixteen as he would like to put it.

First things first and I slapped the permit for Bescot down on his desk after fishing it out of the wad. The shedmaster inspected it and noted that it was for yesterday. (In fact all my permits for the Birmingham area were for 3/8/1965 – yesterday). Barry yesterday put paid to doing the Birmingham area yesterday. A certain railway inspector at a certain Cardiff General Station yesterday did at any rate.

I explained to the shedmaster of a missed connection on our London Midland tour. He asked us where and I told him Cardiff station. He said trust the Western Region and asked how many of us there were. I said "four". He told us that it didn't matter for us being a day late as long as we did have a permit. He added that he would get someone to show us round. I thanked him. With a nod to one of his underlings a railwayman was rounded up and assigned to take us round. I remembered our terrific guides at Colwick and Derby respectively and I reflected that this was the best way to go round an engine shed. We looked forward to another informative guide with first-hand knowledge of the traits of the shed. We would have an interesting unhurried visit. What more could you ask for?

One thing about talking to a guide is that I have a distressing habit of asking the guides questions that I already know the answer of. It is even more distressing when the guide gives me an answer other than the one I had been expecting!

My opening question was one of those questions. I asked him if this was the shed from which the last of the beloved G2 0-8-0's had left a few months ago. He as expected agreed. The 0-8-0's were the last ex LNWR locos to be left in service with BR. We had missed seeing them here but earlier in the tour we had seen a stored member of the class 49395 in the secret sanctuary at Stratford. That one would be preserved but the rest of the class was all presumably chopped up. In early 1964 the stir of all stirs was caused in 64A St.Margarets MPD in Edinburgh when two of the class were noted en route to some Scottish scrap breakers. Unfortunately I missed them.

I also said to him that steam would not last much longer in this area. He agreed and said that by next summer there wouldn't be a steam engine left in this area once the electrification was completed. Bescot was a staunch LMS shed and on view were surviving examples of "Jinties", "Big Eights", "Doodle Bugs", Midland 0-6-0's and some BR 9F 2-10,0's with a few BR Standard 5's. It was nothing like the class of GWR based Tyseley but a good workmanlike shed. It was something like what I imagined 2C Stourbridge Junction to be; - nothing classy but good common steam locos.

D.S. pointed out one 9F 2-10-0 standing over in a line on its own and said that the railwayman at Colwick who had taken us round there had nicknamed them "pipes and organs" because of their complicated interior. He's right there said the fireman (he was that by profession). I said that they were popular at Colwick. Our fireman was in two minds about this and looked reflectively at them and said philosophically "They're a smooth ride but need a hell of a lot of coal to get them going". It sounded like helluvalotuv" to me. He seemed a trifle bitter about the continuous hard job to keep their fireboxes amply filled with coal. I thought to myself that it was their high coal consumption that had caused a few locos experimentally to be fitted with a mechanical stoker (92165-92167). That would certainly lessen the fireman's burden I thought. To cut down coal consumption 92250 had been experimentally fitted with a Geisl oblong ejector. This rectangular shaped contraption had apparently done wonders in Austria and tests had been successful here also. Why were more locos not subsequently fitted? Possibly the BR authorities thought that steam was officially on the way out and that therefore it might not be economic to foster a project with short term benefits but with no long term future whatsoever.

When we came up to Black 5 45222 our fireman announced that this was nicknamed the "lollipop" engine because it was involved in a derailment carrying a special children's train to Stafford. I said to him that I had read the Accident Report in Modern Railways recently. I said that there had been a few fatalities and I recollected that it was believed that the accident was caused through confusion about a speed limit at a bridge. Our fireman was surprised at me from Scotland having read about the accident to one of their locos.

On arrival home I delved into my collection of Modern Railway magazines and found the relevant Accident Report in the April 1965 issue. The report said that "the driver of a special train carrying school children from Ginsall on the Wellington to Stafford line to York via Stoke and Macclesfield on May 28 1964 is held responsible for the derailment as it passed through Cheadle Hulme station. Sadly two children and one of the railway organisers of the party were killed and a further 27 children and adults were injured in the accident.

At the time of the accident, a 10 M.P.H. temporary speed restriction was in force because of the renewal of an underbridge on the 16 chain curve at the stoke end of the station. From the evidence it was clear that the train hauled by 45222 had run over the temporary bridge at a speed of at least 45 M.P.H. and a terrible derailment ensued.

A little further down the line and we came to Stanier Black 5 4-6-0 45288. He said that this engine would mean nothing to us but he thought it to be easily the best in the shed and his favourite engine. I asked him if each railwayman was assigned a specific engine(s) resulting in the emergence of favourites. However, here at Bescot no such schemes were in operation and any driver could be assigned any engine. Our driver cum guide at Colwick had had a soft spot for B1 4-6-0 61141. Sadly 61141 was condemned and on the deadline at the time.

A little further on and our fireman's driver mate came scurrying up and told him to hurry up and get their engine ready to leave. The fireman explained "I'm taking *these* round". My ears pricked at his grammar. I did not like us being referred to as these (the plural of this). I felt like a box of kippers. Being referred to as *"these"* indeed rankled. D.S. may even have noticed the strange word **"these"** in his comment to the driver.

However, the driver wasn't going to wait 15 minutes while the fireman finished our tour round and said in so many words that he had better be finished in a couple of minutes.

I told our fireman guide that we could finish the last line of engines ourselves and thanked him for his invaluable help and comments showing us round. Thankful that we understood that he had to hurry off he said cheerio and sped off after his grumpy driver.

After finishing the shed one of the shedmaster's subordinates came out and asked if the shedmaster could have our permit for a minute. I wondered at this but the shedmaster seemed to only want to note our official time of arrival on the permit. It was handed back to us once we confirmed that we had still to visit 2E Saltley and 2J Aston. I suppose that the shedmaster would have retained the permit if we had already visited all the sheds on the permit. I thought it highly unusual when the permit arrived that all the Birmingham sheds and our visit times were listed on the one permit rather than as normal receiving a separate permit for each shed. Was the Birmingham Division economizing on paper?

Review and Appraisal of 2F Bescot

The shed was at the north end of the Bescot Station the west side of the line. Walking time was less than 5 minutes.

As I have said earlier Bescot was a good workmanlike shed with nothing spectacular to offer. This shed with only two withdrawn locos had only a trace of death around it.

One of the withdrawn locos was a real surprise. What was a withdrawn 41E Staveley (Barrow Hill) WD 2-8-0 doing at Bescot? My tentative answer was that she was en route to some scrap breaker in the Birmingham area. She might be going to Tipton where a large batch of Stanier "Coronations" were broken up in their requiem in December 1964. A highlight indeed was 90368.

The Midland 0-6-0 "Jinties" would soon be extinct and it was no surprise that the one on shed was withdrawn. Sad to relate the Birmingham Area was beginning to gnaw at the "Big Eights" and one of them on shed was withdrawn. 92213 was a local visitor from nearby 2D Banbury. Bescot had none herself allocated but 2A Tyseley, 2E Saltley and 2D Banbury had sizeable allocations therefore they would be no rarity here. Our fireman guide said that he had plenty experience of them. 76039 was a surprising visitor from 1A Willesden in the London Area. The others on shed were all good LMS locos.

2F Bescot had a big allocation of 62 Home Steam but only 19 (43%) were on shed. *Sadly electrification was coming and this fine shed would be closed to steam in March 1966*

2F BESCOT

		Home shed		Built	Withdrawn	Scrap
Diesels						
BR 0-6-0 Shunter 1953						
D3867		2F		Jan-1960		
Total	1					
Steam				Built	Withdrawn	Scrap
Midland 4F 0-6-0 1924						
44139		2F		Oct-1925	Aug-1965	Nov-1965
44188		2F		Apr-1925	Nov-1965	Feb-1966
Total	2					
Stanier 5MT 4-6-0 "Black Five" 1934						
44858		16F	Burton	Dec-1944	Dec-1967	Mar-1968
45222		2F		Dec-1935	Feb-1967	Jul-1967
45288		2F		Dec-1936	Nov-1967	Apr-1968
45410		2F	(ex 2E Saltley)	Sep-1937	Sep-1966	Feb-1967
45430		2J	Aston	Nov-1937	Sep-1966	Mar-1967
Total	5					
Ivatt 2MT 2-6-2T 1946						
46421		2F		Nov-1948	Oct-1966	Feb-1967
46445		2F		Feb-1950	Jul-1966	Oct-1966
46456		2F		May-1950	Sep-1965	Nov-1965
Total	3					
Midland 3F "Jinty" 0-6-0T 1924 dev. of Johnson 1899 design						
47437		2F		Apr-1927	Aug-1966	Apr-1967
Total	1					
Stanier 8F 2-8-0 "Big Eight" 1935						
48010		1A	Willesden (ex 1G)	Oct-1935	Jan-1968	May-1968
48101		2F		Jan-1939	Sep-1966	Oct-1966
48256		2F		Sep-1941	May-1967	Nov-1967
48392		9B	Stockport	Apr-1945	Jun-1968	Sep-1968
48522		2F		Nov-1944	Aug-1967	Feb-1968
48659		2F		Nov-1943	May-1966	Oct-1966
48705		2F		Jun-1944	Mar-1967	Aug-1967
48713		2F		Jul-1944	Mar-1966	Jul-1966
48733		2F		Oct-1945	Jun-1965	Aug-1965
48738		5D	Stoke (ex 2B Oxley)	Dec-1945	Dec-1966	Aug-1967
48767		2F		Mar-1946	Sep-1967	Jan-1968
48769		2F		Apr-1946	Aug-1965	Jan-1966
Total	12					
BR Standard 4MT 2-6-0 Doncaster 1953						
76036		2F		Jun-1954	Jan-1967	Jul-1967
76039		1A	Willesden	Jul-1954	Jun-1967	Dec-1967
76042		2F		Aug-1954	Jul-1966	Nov-1966
Total	3					
Riddles WD 8F 2-8-0 "Austerity" 1943						
90368		ex 41E	Staveley Hill	Oct-1944	Jun-1965	Sep-1965
Total	1					
BR Standard 9F 2-10-0 Brighton 1954. 1957 double chimney						
92213	double chimney	2D	Banbury	Oct-1959	Oct-1966	Feb-1967
Total	1					

On Shed	29		**Kops**		26		
Steam	28		**Diesels**		1		
Withdrawn	2						
Home Locos	21	**Home Area**			2	**Visitors**	6
Shed	2F	21	2D		1	2J	1
Distribution	1A	2	5D		1	9B	1
	16F	1	ex41E		1		
Steam Classes	8						
Steam Origin	LMS	23	**WD**		1	**BR**	4
Shed Highlight	90368	ex41E Staveley (Barrow Hill)					

Steam	Aug-50	67	Mar-59		81	Apr-65	62	
Allocation						Aug-65	62	
				Closed to Steam:-			Mar-66	
Home Steam								
On/Off Shed	On Shed	19	Off Shed		43	% On Shed	31%	
Not on Shed								
Ivatt 4MT 2-6-0 1947						43002	43005	2
4F 0-6-0 1924 Midland					44155	44210	44377	3
"Black Fives"		44766	44840		44875	44914	45048	
		45064	45067		45089	45324	45493	10
Ivatt 2MT 2-6-0 1946		46425	46429		46490	46522	46527	5
"Big Eights"		48035	48061		48335	48366	48375	
		48477	48514		48529	48556	48674	
		48680	48719		48724	48725	48726	
			48729		48747	48752	48766	19
BR 4MT 2-6-0 1953			76047		76086	76087	76088	4
							total	43
		saw elsewhere on the tour					24	
		saw on June 67 Carlisle visit					2	

On we go

"The seatless station episode"

D.S., the two English boys and I now retired to Bescot Station to wait for over half an hour for the 12.38 to Aston. I felt like a good sit down in BR's brand new or rather modernized station here at Bescot. I looked for the waiting room and found nothing. I walked around the solitary station building again and found nothing but the ticket office. I then looked for a BR bench. They are renowned the world over and I could not envisage a BR station without a bench. I looked and looked and ascertained finally that the station was seatless. Why? That's what I wanted to know. Was this the new BR image – a stand up station – or did BR expect you to squat legs crossed Japanese style on the ground? Possibly the BR Supply Depot had gone on strike and the new seats to replace the old seats now chopped up would come along later. Disconsolately we sat ourselves down on the steps of the station stairs and waited. The two boys said that if it was OK with us they would like to go around the other sheds that we would be visiting in the area. It was OK with us. It would help to give us the look of a party of twelve, which we were supposed to be. The more the merrier. It turned out that the boys were from Burton. The beer heart of England I said. They were on a local Railrover of limited extent. D.S. decided to give his camera an airing and a suitable candidate trundled along. It was a 2F Bescot "Big Eight" 48766. Like the expert cameraman he is D.S. snapped her.

48766 of 2F Bescot Stanier 8F 2-8-0 "Big Eight"1935 at Bescot Station on 4th Aug 1965

English Electric Type 4 D343 of 1F Rugby flashed past us from Birmingham with an express passenger train. The remainder of our sojourn brought us four more locos. Trundling past at its usual slow speed was an LMS/BR 0-6-0 Diesel Shunter 12056. Two more Stanier 8F 2-8-0 "Big Eights" were noted on freights. They were 48747 and 48061. The last loco we saw was a 2MT Ivatt 2-6-0 46425. Like "Wyke Hall" yesterday she was to be condemned late in the same week. This was certainly a busy line!

BESCOT STATION							
			Home shed		Built	Withdrawn	Scrap
Diesels							
English Electric Type 4 1Co-Co1 1958							
D343			1F	Rugby	May-1961		
Total	1						
LMS and BR 0-6-0 Shunter 1945							
12056			2F	Bescot	Jul-1949	Oct-1970	
Total	1						
Steam					Built	Withdrawn	Scrap
Ivatt 2MT 2-6-0 1946							
46425			2F	Bescot	Nov-1948	Sep-1965	Jan-1966
Total	1						
Stanier 8F 2-8-0 1935							
48061			2F	Bescot (ex 1G)	Nov-1936	Sep-1967	Oct-1968
48747			2F	Bescot	May-1946	Sep-1966	Jan-1967
48766	D.S. photo		2F	Bescot	Mar-1946	Feb-1967	May-1967
Total	3						
On Line	6		Kops		5		
Steam	4		Diesels		2		
		Home Area			5	Visitors	1
Shed	2F		5				
Distribution	1F		1				
Steam Classes	2						
Steam Origin	LMS		4				

Our bucket duly arrived on time at 12.38. We clambered in. Our short trip to Aston was fruitful.

BESCOT to ASTON							
			Home shed		Built	Withdrawn	Scrap
Diesels							
Brush Type 4 Co-Co 1962							
D1837			5A	Crewe Diesel	May-1965		
Total	1						
Steam					Built	Withdrawn	Scrap
Stanier 5MT 4-6-0 "Black Five" 1934							
45324			2F	Bescot	Feb-1937	Aug-1967	Dec-1967
Total	1						
Stanier 8F 2-8-0 "Big Eight" 1935							
48366			2F	Bescot	Sep-1944	Nov-1965	Jan-1966
48680			2F	Bescot	Dec-1943	Sep-1966	Feb-1967
48724			2F	Bescot	Sep-1944	Oct-1967	Aug-1968
48726			2F	Bescot	Sep-1944	Sep-1966	Jan-1967
Total	4						
On Line	6		Kops		4		
Steam	5		Diesels		1		
		Home Area			5	Visitors	1
Shed	2F		5				
Distribution	5A		1				
Steam Classes	2						
Steam Origin	LMS		5				

The Brush was noted passing Aston.

			Schedule	Actual	Miles
Depart	BESCOT		12.38	12.38	0
Arrive	ASTON		12.54	12.54	6¾

3 intermediate stops

Aston was a small shed and I was not expecting great things from it. Our return train to Vauxhall and Duddeston left at 13.34 therefore we had 40 minutes to do the shed. Even with twenty minutes walking time we should have a recovery time of ten minutes.

The Locomotive Shed Directory said 10 minutes walking time but even at our leisurely pace we did it in less than that. We popped down into the shed and who would we see leaning against the wall at the actual door to the shed but the shedmaster and one of his subordinates. He was a good old chap who still had his original teeth (about half a dozen of them!) He had a broad Midland accent and seemed intrigued at us having a permit and wanting to go round his shed. After a few inquiries at how we were getting on he waved us to go on and visit his little depot. A great chap! He seemed to be getting his kill at travellers like us.

Aston was a big shed in size but looked very empty with only a handful of engines on shed. However, it was well worth the visit. Three English Electric Type 4's were noted including D227 "Parthia" which was becoming very common to us. We had noted and kopped her at Bletchley, saw her at New Street at 11 a.m. today and now we saw her again. Two condemned Fairburn tanks were also noted. In fact Aston was a strictly Midland shed with no surprises.

			2J ASTON				
			Home shed		**Built**	**Withdrawn**	**Scrap**
Diesels							
BR English Electric Type 4 1Co-Co1 1958							
D 227			9A	Longsight	Aug-1959		
D 308			1B	Camden	Nov-1960		
D 320			1E	Bletchley (ex 5A)	Mar-1961		
Total	3						
BR 0-6-0 Shunter 1953							
D3020			2J		Apr-1953		
D3774			2J		Jul-1959		
Total	2						
Steam					**Built**	**Withdrawn**	**Scrap**
Fairburn 4MT 2-6-4T 1945							
42062			2J		Dec-1950	May-1965	Sep-1965
42075			2J	(ex 6H Bangor)	Nov-1950	May-1965	Sep-1965
Total	2						
Stanier 5MT 4-6-0 "Black Five" 1934							
44859			2J		Dec-1944	Nov-1967	Mar-1968
44914			2F	Bescot	Dec-1945	Aug-1967	Jan-1968
45038			2J		Sep-1934	Feb-1968	Jun-1968
45046			5B	Crewe South	Oct-1934	Jun-1968	Dec-1968
45114			2J		Jun-1935	Jan-1968	May-1968
45439			2J		Nov-1937	Nov-1965	Jan-1966
Total	6						
Ivatt 2MT 2-6-0 1946							
46427			2J		Dec-1948	Oct-1966	Feb-1967
Total	1						

-

		2J ASTON (continued)					
			Home shed		Built	Withdrawn	Scrap
Stanier 8F 2-8-0 "Big Eight" 1935							
48349			1H	Northampton	Apr-1944	Oct-1966	Feb-1967
Total		1					
BR Standard 4MT 2-6-0 Doncaster 1953							
76040			2J		Jul-1954	Apr-1967	Sep-1967
Total		1					
On Shed	16		Kops	13			
Steam	11		Diesels	5			
Withdrawn	2						
Home Locos	10	Home Area		1	Visitors	5	
Shed	2J	10	2F	1			
Distribution	1B	1	1E	1	1H	1	
	5B	1	9A	1			
Steam Classes	5						
Steam Origin	LMS	10	BR	1			
Shed Highlights:-		The withdrawn Fairburn tanks					
Steam	Aug-50	52	Mar-59	43	Apr-65	22	
Allocation					Aug-65	15	
			Closed to Steam:-			Oct-65	
Home Steam							
On/Off Shed	On Shed	6	Off Shed	9	% On Shed	40%	
Not on Shed							
"Black Fives"		44710	44872	44876	44942	45052	
		45058	45322	45430			8
Ivatt 2MT 2-6-0 1946				46492			1
						total	9
		saw elsewhere on the tour			3		
		saw on June 67 Carlisle visit			1		

Review and Appraisal of 2J Aston

The shed was in the fork of the Aston-Coventry and Aston-New Street lines south of Aston station. Walking time was 10 minutes.

A reasonable shed! Six (40%) of 2J Aston's allocation was on shed with 9 off shed. 2J Aston was to close to steam just two months later. I noted that one of the English Electric Type 4's was from Bletchley. Bletchley had received a whack of them because at present the electrification ended there and therefore Bletchley would now be used as a changeover point instead of Rugby, which was the changeover point until this week. Soon the electrification would be completed to London Euston Station and Bletchley would then probably lose its allocation of English Electric Type 4's as it would no longer be required as a changeover point.

The Fairburn 2-6-4 Tanks were officially condemned and would probably be soon hauled off to the scrap breaker's yard. The rest were largely Midland locos with a "Big Eight" from Northampton probably the other most interesting occupant.

On we go

We arrived back at Aston station with about ten minutes to spare for the 13.34 train for Vauxhall and Duddeston – and importantly 2E Saltley. Our bucket arrived on time and we got off at the next stop Vauxhall and Duddeston.

		Schedule	Actual	Miles
Depart	ASTON	13.34	13.34	0
Arrive	VAUXHALL AND DUDDESTON	13.40	13.40	1¼

In 1958 Saltley had 163 steam engines allocated to it. It had the largest collection of any LMR shed then and at that time carried the shedcode 2A. Last year it took part in the re-coding, which was necessitated by the transfer of Tyseley, Oxley, Stourbridge, Banbury, Leamington and Kidderminster from the WR to the LMR. Saltley was rather pulled down a peg or two by being given the new code 2E. Tyseley was made the parent depot as the new 2A in the larger Birmingham area. In BR's longer-term plans Tyseley was to be the big Birmingham diesel depot – not Saltley. However, Saltley still had a sizeable allocation shedded and I had high hopes of seeing sixty locos on shed.

The Locomotive shed directory promised a 5 minute walking time to the shed. We turned into Duddeston Mill Road and began our march to Saltley M.P.D. A short stop was called by D.S. when we passed a local baker's shop half way down the road. He went in for some cakes. We did the same and soon polished them off.

We found the shed entrance on the right hand side just past the railway overbridge so we decided to enter!

THE ONE SHEDMASTER TOO MANY AFFAIR
"Five shedmasters wish us dead
D.S. begins to lose his head"

This time there would be no Bescot boldness I resolved. I immediately checked D.S. and the two Burton boys from obeying the large sign to immediately go to the shedmaster's office inside the roundhouse. Its madness I thought to hand the permit in and possibly be sent packing for being too small a party. (Certainly we did not have the party of 15 detailed on the permit!). The LMS did not issue permits for les than parties of twelve.

This point settled we avoided the "fools" entrance to the roundhouse and the shedmaster's office. We decided to enter the shed from the back of the roundhouse on the shedmaster's blind side. We walked up the outside of the shed beside the main line and decided to enter by the south side (i.e. the top, open end of the shed).

However, our clever, cunning plan was quickly dashed. We had hardly gone twenty yards when out of nowhere an officious looking BR gentleman appeared. His interest was in us and he promptly ordered us out and shouted phrases about "it's illegal to trespass on BR property". He was like a football referee ordering someone off and pointing to the pavilion. The only difference here was that he was pointing to the way out. The railway official looked like a high powered shed master or an overlord over all shedmasters and M.P.D's in the Birmingham area. Anyway he was impressive enough. He was not going to get away with his Hitler type action though. He obviously liked ordering people out with great gusto and shouting at them from afar so I made the long ten yard journey up to him.

I quietly explained that we had a permit and were looking for the shedmaster's office. He wanted to see it so I magically produced it. He gave it a cursory glance. He then raised his voice again and said "The office certainly isn't this way. How did you miss the sign to the office? It's big enough."

As big as your bloody mouth I felt like saying. However, discretion and careful treading is our best option. I explained again "We have not been here before. Could you please show us where the office is?" We had asked something from him. He didn't like having to show this dirt the way to the office so he shouted at a worker and ordered him to take us to the shedmaster's office. He gave a huff and a puff and disappeared into the dust.

I felt like being led to a wall to be shot at by a firing squad. The worker just led the way silently and I suspected something like Colwick awaited us. I hoped to be proved wrong. The roundhouse with the office was certainly dark enough and shrouded in mystery???

We were led to the office window where the shedmaster was found (perhaps luckily) to be not at home. However, his second in command (probably the shed foreman) was ready to receive us. I handed over our permit (for the second time at this shed). Thankfully there were no hitches. An explanation was given about our late arrival at the shed and accepted. Explanation – bad connections on our rail tour.

That's us officially on our way round the shed now. I was glad that we had plenty of time in which to visit the shed. Those little encounters had been a waste of over five minutes.

Our first job was to deposit our heavy grips. To do that we left the roundhouse and for the second time walked up the side of the shed. Back to square one where we were stopped by the overlord. We saw some large oil drums lying around the diesel stores shed and we carefully "hid" our luggage behind them.

At last we could now get going. So far all I had written down in my notebook was 2E Saltley. However, when we reached the top of the shed we found a large glass fronted office at the corner of it. The way our luck was running I was expecting to be "attacked" from it. The "lookout" on duty saw us and immediately came to the door and shouted at us. He waved us over and demanded to see our permit if we had one. They say everything comes in threes and this was official three in a short space of time and I had hoped our chronic attack of shedmasteritis here was over. Grudgingly I unearthed my permit from my pocket and he grabbed it. My permit was now showing signs of fatigue and was now all oil-stained and frayed with all this extra handling. He looked at us and asked if we had seen the shedmaster. I said we had (although strictly speaking we had only seen the shed foreman in his office – not the actual shedmaster). He gave us back the permit and warned us to be careful and duly let us through.

Now at last we were free. Free from the clutches of three BR officials. On with the job! Like 40E Colwick, once all the barriers to entry had been lifted it was certainly worth visiting. The diesel sector of the shed was the first portion that we noted. They were stacked in the shed yard outside the roundhouse. Down one line we went and I exclaimed "Here's a rusty Brush type 2 down this line". We rushed down and found that the Type 2 wasn't rusty at all but decorated in the most disgusting and filthy livery I had ever seen. I put down the colour as rusty maroon but D.S. showed his knowledge of BR by stating that it was in the experimental desert sand livery. I remembered reading about a "Western" Type 4 having the same treatment. "Looks as though the experiment is a failure if this is the crap result". I said to D.S. D.S. agreed and got out his camera and snapped the odd diesel. The Burton boys just looked open-mouthed at this odd diesel.

We went into the roundhouse and received a few surprises. One nice, the other not so nice. Firstly, I was surprised to see a few Western locos interspersed with the Midland and BR locos. This could never have happened eighteen months ago when Birmingham was in divided control by the LMR and WR. Saltley was in the LMR sector and then handled strictly LMR locos.

We were admiring the unnamed Britannia 70047 when trouble reared its ugly head again.

The previously missing shedmaster was making a sneak entrance from the rear and he crossed the turntable in the middle of the roundhouse and walked straight up to us. By this time I had quietly warned D.S. and the other two to expect company. They all turned round to meet our new adversary.

This time BR official No 4 was a little less loquacious and loudmouthed than the other three. He was quiet spoken and asked if we had a permit. I was getting rather sick of that line which was getting too familiar for my liking. The shedmaster glanced over the permit and before he read it too closely I added that I had already handed it in to the office. That seemed to work and he said "Right then" handed it back to me and continued his shed inspection.

We duly finished our tour and were on our way back to collect our bags when we passed by the glass fronted office in the shed yard again. Wonders never cease. I thought we were safe of being checked there again because we were stopped on the way in. But no! As we passed, a loud rap at the window was followed by a shout. This must be BR official No 5. Somebody in there doesn't like us. Somebody wants to see our permit again.

"We've got a blasted permit". Who roared that out? I looked round. It had been D.S. There he was trembling and shaking with rage at this fifth official. It must be a case of one official too many for the old boy. He's flipped, off his rocker, gone round the bend. I half expected D.S. to start frothing at the mouth. I watched him carefully in case he made a lunge at the poor unfortunate whom D.S. had decided to assail with his unfriendly language.

And what of the victim of D.S.'s attack? The poor chap was looking a little white and taken aback. No, it wasn't the other foreman lookout who had been in here earlier. He must have popped out for lunch and this lookout must have just taken over from him. Not the thing (D.S.'s tirade), which I would like to have launched at me just after my lunch.

I felt sorry for the lookout and apologized for D.S.'s behaviour. I explained that D.S. was a little tired of officials here. Of course we had a permit (D.S. had already told him that!) The lookout was finally able to blurt out something "Just worried about your safety." That's all he seemed to be able to say. I hoped D.S. hadn't unbalanced him as well; as himself. It certainly looked as though the lookout was in a bad way. Naughty D.S.!

We beat a hasty retreat from the disaster area before D.S. could attack someone else with his views. I looked at my left hand and counted – one, two, three, four, five. Five officials too many. Reminiscent of 40E Colwick security!

Now where were our bags? We looked behind the oil drums and found nothing. They had been swiped, nicked. This would be a fitting climax to our officialdom visit here if they had decided to steal our bags. A frantic search ensued. D.S. and I went into the diesel stores shed to see if any worker could help us. Pity anyone that had pinched our grips. They weighed a ton! He wouldn't be able to get very far carrying them. Surprise, surprise in a corner of the diesel stores shed there was our luggage all neatly laid out. Before we could comment we heard a voice from behind us "So there you are. That was a silly place that you left your bags. Anyone could pinch them out there. I brought them in here for safety".

We looked round and it was our old friend shedmaster/overlord No. 1 who now seemed to be in a better humour. Some cheek to put them in here. For safety huh! How did we know that he would bring them in here (or rather arrange for them to be brought in here). Lucky that we looked for them in here. With grudging thanks to the "overlord" for saving our gear from being stolen (by putting them in here) we picked up our gear and with the two Burton boys we beat a hasty retreat from this officialdom-ridden shed before any more ill luck befell us. At least the final incident seemed to have rest D.S.'s mind after his earlier mental relapse at official 5. The sad shock of having his cherished possessions possibly stolen must have brought him back to his senses.

2E SALTLEY		Home shed		Built	Withdrawn	Scrap
Diesels						
BR Sulzer "Peak" Type 4 1Co-Co1 1959						
D 64	"Coldstream Guardsman"	ML	Derby Division	Apr-1962		
Total	1					
Brush Type 4 Co-Co 1962						
D1738		82A	Bristol Bath Rd. (ex86A)	May-1964		
D1741		82A	Bristol Bath Rd. (ex86A)	Jun-1964		
D1815		2E	(ex 5A Crewe)	Feb-1965		
Total	3					
BR 0-6-0 Shunter 1953						
D3973		2E		Jun-1960		
Total	1					
BR Sulzer Type 2 Bo-Bo 1958						
D5183		2E		Apr-1963		
D5184		D15	Leicester Div. (ex ML)	May-1963		
D5223		2E	(ex D16 Nottingham Div.)	Jul-1963		
D5228		ML	Midland Lines	Sep-1963		
D5234		2E		Dec-1963		
D5239		2E		Dec-1963		
D5246		2E		Jan-1964		
D5281		2E	(ex ML Derby Division)	Jun-1964		
D5298		2E		Oct-1964		
D7522		D16	Nottingham Division	Jan-1965		
D7584		ML	Midland Lines	Feb-1964		
D7590		ML	Midland Lines	Apr-1964		
Total	12					
Brush Type 2 A1A-A1A 1957						
D5579		31B	March	Jan-1960		
D5843		2E	Saltley (ex 41A loan)	May-1962		
Total	2					
LMS and BR 0-6-0 Shunter 1945						
12059		2E		Oct-1949	Jan-1969	
Total	1					
Steam				Built	Withdrawn	Scrap
Collett 4MT 5101 2-6-2T 1929 rebuild of Churchward 3100 Class 1903						
4154		2B	Oxley (via 2C/2D)	Jul-1947	Oct-1965	Jan-1966
Total	1					
1933 dev. of Collett 3F 5700 0-6-0PT 1929						
3619		2C	Stourbridge	Apr-1939	Sep-1966	Nov-1966
Total	1					
Collett 5MT 7800 4-6-0 "Manor" 1938						
7819	"Hinton Manor"	6D		Feb-1939	Nov-1965	saved
Total	1					
Stanier 5MT 4-6-0 "Black Five" 1934						
44666		2E		Jul-1949	Feb-1967	Sep-1967
44776		2E		Jun-1947	Oct-1967	Apr-1968
44808		2B	Oxley	Sep-1944	Dec-1966	Dec-1967
45048		2F	Bescot	Oct-1934	Nov-1967	Feb-1968
Total	4					
Stanier 8F 2-8-0 "Big Eight" 1935						
48016		2E	(ex 2B Oxley)	Jan-1937	Nov-1965	Feb-1966
48027		ex 1G	Woodford Halse	Jul-1938	Mar-1965	Oct-1965
48133		2E		Apr-1941	Nov-1966	Jul-1967
48220		2E		Sep-1942	Aug-1967	Feb-1968
48397		9J	Agecroft	Jun-1945	Oct-1966	Feb-1967
48412		2C	Stourbridge	Oct-1943	Dec-1966	Jun-1967
48646		2E		Nov-1943	Jun-1968	Dec-1968
48762		2E	(ex 2C Stourbridge)	Jan-1946	Feb-1966	Jun-1966
Total	8					

		Home shed		Built	Withdrawn	Scrap
BR 7P6F 4-6-2 "Britannia" Derby 1951						
70026	"Polar Star"	6J	Holyhead (ex 9B)	*Oct-1952*	*Jan-1967*	*May-1967*
70047		6J	Holyhead (ex 2B)	*Jun-1954*	*Jul-1967*	*Dec-1967*
Total	2					
BR Standard 5MT 4-6-0 Doncaster 1951						
73014		2D	Banbury (ex2B)	*Sep-1951*	*Jul-1967*	*Apr-1968*
73034		6D	Shrewsbury	*Aug-1953*	*Mar-1968*	*Jun-1968*
73140	*Caprotti valved*	9H	Patricroft	*Dec-1956*	*Oct-1967*	*Feb-1968*
Total	3					
BR Standard 4MT 2-6-0 Doncaster 1953						
76038		2E		*Jul-1954*	*Sep-1966*	*Dec-1966*
Total	1					
BR Standard 9F 2-10-0 Brighton 1954						
92022	*Crosti boilered*	9D	Newton Heath	*Mar-1955*	*Nov-1967*	*Apr-1968*
92129		2D	Banbury	*Apr-1957*	*Jun-1967*	*Nov-1967*
92135		2E		*Jun-1957*	*Jun-1967*	*Mar-1968*
92136		2E		*Jun-1957*	*Oct-1966*	*Feb-1967*
92138		2E		*Jun-1957*	*Jul-1967*	*Feb-1968*
92150		2E		*Oct-1957*	*Apr-1967*	*Nov-1967*
92155		2E		*Nov-1957*	*Nov-1966*	*Apr-1967*
92223	*double chimney*	2A	Tyseley	*Jun-1958*	*Apr-1968*	*Sep-1968*
Total	8					

On Shed	49		**Kops**	45			
Steam	29		**Diesels**	20			
Withdrawn	1						
Home Locos	24	**Home Area**		8	**Visitors**	17	
Shed	2E	24					
Distribution	2A	1	2B	2	2C	2	
	2D	2	2F	1			
	ex 1G	1	6D	2	6J	2	
	9D	1	9H	1	9J	1	
	D15	1	D16	1	ML	4	
	31B	1					
	82A	2					
Steam Classes		9					
Steam Origin	GWR	3	LMS	12	BR	14	

Shed Highlights:-

	Steam	92022	**of 9D Newton Heath (Crosti boilered)**
		73140	**of 9H Patricroft (Caprotti valve gear)**
	Diesel	D 5579	**of 31B March (desert sand livery)**

Steam	**Aug-50**	180	**Mar-59**	174	**Apr-65**	49
Allocation					**Aug-65**	41
			Closed to Steam:-		**Mar-67**	

Home Steam	excluding withdrawn locos					
On/Off Shed	On Shed	13	Off Shed	28	% On Shed	32%
Not on Shed						
Midland 4F 0-6-0 1924					44057	1
"Black Fives"	44663	44777	44944	44945	44965	5
Ivatt 2MT 2-6-0 1946	46443	46448	46454	46505	46526	5
"Big Eights"	48085	48109	48339	48351	48629	
				48669	48755	7
BR 4MT 2-6-0 1953				76043	76048	2
BR 9F 2-10-0 1954	92028	92029	92125	92137	92139	
			92151	92152	92164	8
					total	28
	saw elsewhere on the tour			11		
	saw on June 67 Carlisle visit			2		

Review and Appraisal of 2E Saltley

The yard was on the east side of the line south of Saltley Station. Walking time was 5 minutes from Vauxhall and Duddeston Station.

349

An interesting cross section was on view. Not as good as Tyseley but that is hardly surprising considering Tyseley was crammed with ex GWR stock. Three ex GWR locos were noted here from the Birmingham area. The "Manor" was particularly welcome. I was shocked to see that it had one of its brass numberplates still on the cab side. BR must have slipped up here! Perhaps that explains all the security in the Birmingham area when people can try to gain access to sheds to steal brass numberplates! Almost all the ex GWR locos now were shorn off both nameplates and numberplates. BR kindly painted a number on the sides where their brass numberplates used to be. It normally looked the work of a stencil so uniform were the new painted numbers.

I was pleased to note two engines from 2C Stourbridge on shed as we are unable to fit the shed into our timetable. One of the Stourbridge locos was one of the many 0-6-0 Pannier Tanks, which the Western Region used to own in hundreds. There had been surprisingly few of this class on Tyseley – only one. Possibly 2B Oxley might prove more fruitful.

Black Five's and Big Eights were mostly Birmingham area stock. Exceptions included a condemned Big Eight (the only condemned loco on shed) from the former 1G Woodford Halse. She had been condemned with the closure of 1G Woodford Halse following the demise of freight on the former Great Central Railway. We had noted another ex 1G Woodford Halse condemned Fairburn tank 42085 at Banbury last night. Presumably both were en route to Birmingham Area scrap breakers.

The Manchester area provided us with three unusual visitors. Firstly a 9J Agecroft Big Eight, secondly a 9H Patricroft "Standard 5" and thirdly a 9D Newton Heath BR 9F 2-10-0. The Patricroft Standard was one of the minority of the class who were fitted with Caprotti valve gear. The 9F was a real highlight. It was one of the ten members of the class, which were fitted with a Crosti boiler, and interestingly no smoke deflectors. As a small boy of nine years old in the summer of 1958 I was struck with awe and amazement at one of these engines which were fitted with a dummy chimney (for appearances sake) and the smoke billowed out of the boiler through a vent in the side of the locomotive. I need hardly add it was a photograph of one of these locos which I had seen then. At the time all were shedded at 15B Wellingborough and worked main line freight trains. However, the smaller "economizer" sections of the boiler had now been removed, leaving a single main boiler barrel' smaller in diameter than those fitted to the standard class. They now conventionally even had the smoke coming out of a real chimney!

Two Britannia's were on shed. I had previously seen 70026 "Polar Star" on 5B Crewe South on the 12th December 1964 when Ian "Froth" Firth and I made our lightning visit to Manchester and Crewe. At the time "Polar Star" belonged to 6J Holyhead presumably on boat train duties to get passengers to and from the Irish crossing. Since then "Polar Star" had been reallocated to 2B Oxley along with a few other Britannia's including 70047. This engine was famous because it was the only unnamed "Britannia". A few years ago there was a rumour that it would be named "Winston Churchill". It was not to be however perhaps because the Southern Region already had Southern Region Pacific 34051 named "Winston Churchill". It didn't make much difference now as all the Britannias' were now shorn of their nameplates. Standard BR policy these days. In all there were almost 30 steam on shed.

Of the diesels two of the Brushes were Western Region based. Not really surprising seeing them here. I had hoped to see a few more Peaks off Derby to Birmingham turns but "Grenadier Guardsman" was the only one on view. I had seen this Peak recently on the 15th July on the British Motor Corporation Bathgate car train.

The Brush Type 2's were interesting. Our desert sand livery D5579 was from 31B March in the Fenlands of East Anglia. D5843 was from 41A Tinsley in Sheffield. I was ninety nine per cent certain that they were here for crew training. They seemed to be allocated here for a week or two at a time before being reallocated to their home depots. The stock transfers section in Modern Railways had recently been full of funny little transfers from the Eastern Region to Saltley on loan and subsequently back to the Eastern Region again.

Judging by the number of Derby Area Type 2's on shed they must now be dominating the Derby to Birmingham freight turns perhaps to the possible exclusion of Peak Type 4's.

Saltley had an enormous steam allocation of 174 in 1959 but was now down to a much reduced 41 of which only 13 Home Steam (32%) were on shed.

On we go

We turned our backs on the rather unhappy memories of Saltley's officialdom and left the premises. Something they had wanted to do as soon as we arrived.

We turned into Duddeston Mill Road and began our walk back. A thunder of steam in the distance and we turned round in time to see 44944 (a Saltley Black Five) storm over the over bridge just north of the shed.

It again took us over 5 minutes to reach Vauxhall and Duddeston station. I concluded that the LocoShed Directory's advertised walking time of five minutes was a bit tight. Certainly it allowed for no dawdling which a certain member of our party (who shall remain nameless) was susceptible to. At least this time we had ten minutes to spare before our train back to Birmingham New Street. That shows how generous our recovery time was here. I had thought our recovery time for Saltley was about thirty minutes but our hi-jinks over the various Saltley officials and dawdling to and from the shed had reduced it to ten minutes.

On a day when time was so vital I was pleased when our bucket came into the station on time at journey to Birmingham New Street provided little of note. Black Five 44859 was noted again. We had seen her on Aston shed earlier in the day. Two station pilot 0-6-0 diesel shunters D3775 and D3838 were noted and we arrived on time at New Street.

SALTLEY TO BIRMINGHAM NEW STREET						
		Home shed		Built	Withdrawn	Scrap
Diesels						
BR 0-6-0 Shunter 1955						
D3775		2J	Aston	Jul-1959		
D3838		2J	Aston	Jan-1960		
Total	2					
Steam						
Stanier 5MT 4-6-0 "Black Five" 1934				Built	Withdrawn	Scrap
44859	on 2J today	2J	Aston	Dec-1944	Nov-1967	Mar-1968
44944		2E	Saltley	Jan-1946	Sep-1967	Feb-1968
Total	2					
On Line	4	Kops		2		
Steam	2	Diesels		2		
		Home Area		4	Visitors	0
Shed	2E	1	2J	3		
Distribution:-						
Steam Classes	1					
Steam Origin	LMS	2				

		Schedule	Actual	Miles
Depart	VAUXHALL AND DUDDESTON	14.40	14.40	0
Arrive	BIRMINGHAM NEW STREET	14.47	14.47	1¼

At New Street we first went to the timetable and looked up when the next train to Wolverhampton was. A glance at the timetable and I noted that the first train from New Street was at 15.40. Rather late! I looked up the Snow Hill departures and I noted that the situation was rather better. There was a train leaving at 15.22 arriving at Wolverhampton Low Level at 15.40.

Our two Burton boys found a visit to Wolverhampton to their liking. The Burton boys saved me from consulting the street plan of Birmingham at the back of the LocoShed Directory. It looked like a half hour walk to me through busy Birmingham. However, the Burton boys knew their stuff and in ten minutes we were at Birmingham Snow Hill Station. Surprisingly quickly I thought. They were good quick guides – it had looked over half a mile between the stations. One thing that struck me about Birmingham was the crowded nature of its streets. Quite another London. I wonder how many people D.S. thought Birmingham had. He had thought London had 200,000 people rather than the actual 8 million. He seemed to underestimate by forty fold. I didn't want to embarrass D.S. in front of the Burton boys so I decided against asking D.S. how big he thought Birmingham was.

The rot which the station inspector at Cardiff General had so successfully spread into my timetable was now repaired. We had now done all the sheds we should have done yesterday. Time wasted because of the station inspector (and our tardiness) approximately nine and three quarter hours. That is assuming a start at five in the morning. Amazing how costly missing the Cardiff to Birmingham train by a few seconds turned out to be. 88A Cardiff East Dock although quite brilliant with 92220 Evening Star and all had certainly turned out to be a fantastically expensive shed in terms of time lost.

We now had twenty minutes to spare before our train to Wolverhampton therefore I told D.S. that he could avail himself of the refreshment facilities in the cafeteria. D.S. needed no further prompting and he immediately stormed into it. D.S.'s loves were eating, sleeping and waking slowly. Feeling tired was probably his fourth love. He was now going to exhibit his first love of eating to the best of his ability. The Burton boys and I followed D.S. into the cafeteria.

THE DEADLY DECISION EPISODE
"Temptation is the root of all evil"

We ordered the usual fare. The "usual" amounted to a 9 pence (3.5 new pence) Gala fruit pie ,a cup of kidney soup from one of BR's ten pence (4 new pence) micro-sized tins of Chef soup. Although the quantity of soup was small at least it was hot. For afters there was one of BR's ten pence (4 new pence) cheese sandwiches and a six pence (2.5 new pence) cup of tea. This seemed to be our normal LMR diet. I longed for a fish supper from a fish and chip shop.

Our Burton boys suddenly turned loquacious. They asked if we were going to Crewe tomorrow for the "open day". I queried "You mean they actually let you into the place without any questions?" The Burton boys assured me that you could do anything you liked. Then I remembered that I had pointed out a poster to D.S. at Willesden Station on Sunday. BR was running tomorrow a special excursion train to Crewe with a visit thrown in of Crewe Works. There would be plenty of people at the Works tomorrow. D.S. and I could easily slip our way in with the crowd. Our Railrover tickets were valid for any excursion so what's the hell stopping us from going to Crewe Works tomorrow? The timetable? We were already ten hours behind schedule and this put our visit tomorrow to Sheffield, Doncaster and Leeds in jeopardy. Something would have to give anyway. Why not cancel this extra Railrover (and therefore expensive trip) to the Eastern and North Eastern Region? We had bought an LMR Railrover so why not save money and stick to the LMR?

What had our sally to the Eastern Region to offer in terms of rare steam locomotives? I had a hard, cool think. 36A Doncaster had 42 WD 2-8-0's. But WD's were ten a penny. We had a permit to go round Doncaster Works but it was unlikely to provide any surprises. 41A Sheffield Tinsley, 41B Sheffield Darnall and 41C Wath were in the land where steam fears to tread. 41E Staveley (Barrow Hill) was a different story. It had the last two Deeley Midland (1907) 0-4-0 0F Tanks on BR. It also had the last five Johnson Midland (1878) 0-6-0 1F Tanks on BR. The latter were the oldest locomotives still running on BR. It certainly would hurt to miss them. The Leeds area had to offer about six Jubilees, three A1 Pacifics and a few Q6 0-8-0's. Apart from those mentioned Leeds, Sheffield and Doncaster had little new blood to offer. The rest of their stock had examples on the LMR or had been previously seen by us on LNER metals.

What had Crewe Works to offer? Hordes of Brush Type 4 are being built by BR under permit from Brush Works. It was also the only works on the LMR still overhauling steam locomotives. It also had a few interesting preserved locomotives of its own. In late 1964 a party from Wakefield had made an illegal visit and came away with 253 locomotives. My resistance to Crewe Works was now growing very weak. Temptation was getting the better of me. I asked D.S. for his opinion. I told him it was more or less a straight choice between Crewe Works on the LMR costing nothing and our whole tour (or as much as we could do) of Leeds, Doncaster and Sheffield. I told him that the Eastern tour after we had arrived for nothing at Sheffield would be outside the Railrover and would cost us quite a bit. D.S. weighed up every fact in his mind and came to his conclusion. He said "We've come here on the LMR Railrover and Crewe Works is the focus of the LMR. We can't miss a chance of visiting it. It's Open Day so there is no chance of us being kicked out. Also think of the money we will save. We could get lost on the Eastern and North Eastern Region and spend a lot of money for nothing. What's these sheds got that we can't see on the LMR?"

D.S. had made a lot of good points. The ER and NER sheds had very little new classes to offer as I had already concluded. Crewe Works would be fantastic. Can't miss the chance of visiting Crewe Works. Ian Firth and I in December 1964 had got only to the Works doors before being turned away. This would make up for that. We therefore succumbed to temptation and put Crewe Works down to be fitted into tomorrow's timetable. Sheffield, Leeds, Staveley and Doncaster were now to be given the miss. We couldn't have done them all anyway as we were now ten hours behind schedule at this point. Crewe Works had better be good though. Then I would have no qualms about missing out the Eastern and North Eastern region sheds.

HERE ENDETH THE DEADLY DECISION

Our Burton boys would be going round Crewe Works at 2.30 p.m. tomorrow. I told them that D.S. and I would try to meet them outside the Works then. That was all settled, sealed and arranged then. It would probably take us two hours to go round the Works with or without the BR excursion party. We would need the rest of the day to catch up on lost sheds.

I glanced at my watch and noted that it was time that we weren't here. We left the cafeteria and made our way to the relevant platform for the 15.22 to Wolverhampton, which was due in at 15.17.

A snap inspection of the station inhabitants was rewarding :-.

353

		Home shed		Built	Withdrawn	Scrap
Diesels						
Brush Type 4 Co-Co 1962						
D1683		2B	Oxley	Oct-1963		
D1701	hauled	81A	Old Oak Common	Jan-1964		
D1746		81A	Old Oak Common	Jul-1964		
D1811		D16	Nottingham Division	Feb-1965		
Total	4					
Steam				**Built**	**Withdrawn**	**Scrap**
Collett 5MT 4900 4-6-0 "Hall" 1928						
5988	"Bostock Hall"	2A	Tyseley	Nov-1939	Oct-1965	Dec-1965
Total	1					
Collett 5MT 7800 4-6-0 "Manor" 1938						
7821	"Ditcheat Manor"	2B	Oxley	Nov-1950	Nov-1965	saved
Total	1					
BR Standard 5MT 4-6-0 Doncaster 1951						
73156		2A	Tyseley (ex 2L)	Dec-1956	Nov-1967	saved
Total	1					
On Station	7	**Kops**		6		
Steam	3	**Diesels**		4		

	Home Area			4	**Visitors**	3
Shed	2A	2	2B	2		
Distribution	D16	1	81A	2		
Steam Classes	3					
Steam Origin	GWR	2	BR	1		

An excellent station. Good to see the "Manor" and our old friend of last night at Snow Hill "Bostock Hall". Quite a few Brushes – we could rename Snow Hill as Brush Hill. Another Motor Parcels Van to add to my collection.

D1701 was at the head of our train. It was the 13.10 from Paddington. We were lucky to find an empty compartment in a rather busy train. We left a few minutes after our advertised time of 15.22.

Our journey was a short one of about twenty minutes. What struck me about it was the vast urban sprawl. The Birmingham conurbation merged "beautifully" into Wolverhampton without even a field or a patch of open countryside to signify the end of Birmingham and the start of Wolverhampton. I was trying to remember what a patch of grass looked like.

A sterling journey indeed. The "Grange" was very welcome together with the three ex GWR 5101 2-6-2 Tanks. We had seen 4111 earlier in the day at 2A Tyseley. A Bescot "Big 8" encroaches on a Western Region line. Integration rears its head!

		Schedule	Actual	Miles
Depart	BIRMINGHAM SNOW HILL	15.22	15.25	0
Arrive	WOLVERHAMPTON LOW LEVEL	15.40	15.44	12½

Average journey speed was approximately 45 m.p.h. The Brush at the head of the train was able to "play" with the load. A very easy timing for it.

BIRMINGHAM SNOW HILL to WOLVERHAMPTON

		Home shed		Built	Withdrawn	Scrap
Diesels						
BR 0-6-0 Shunter 1953						
D3752		2B	Oxley	*Aug-1959*		
D3757		2B	Oxley	*Oct-1959*		
D3951		2A	Tyseley	*Apr-1960*		
D3978		2B	Oxley	*Jul-1960*		
D3983		2A	Tyseley	*Aug-1960*		
Total	*5*					
Steam				**Built**	**Withdrawn**	**Scrap**
Collett 4MT 5101 2-6-2T 1929 rebuild of Churchward 3100 Class 1903						
4111	*on 2A today*	2A	Tyseley	*Oct-1935*	*Sep-1965*	*Feb-1966*
4155		2A	Tyseley	*Aug-1947*	*Sep-1965*	*Feb-1966*
4168		2A	Tyseley (ex 2C)	*Nov-1948*	*Sep-1965*	*Feb-1966*
Total	*3*					
Collett 5MT 6800 4-6-0 "Grange" 1936						
6855	"Saighton Grange"	2A	Tyseley (ex 2B)	*Nov-1937*	*Oct-1965*	*Mar-1966*
Total	*1*					
Stanier 8F 2-8-0 "Big Eight" 1935						
48477		2F	Bescot	*Jun-1945*	*Sep-1966*	*Jan-1967*
Total	*1*					
On Line	10	Kops		9		
Steam	5	Diesels		5		
		Home Area		10	Visitors	0
Shed	2A	6	2B	3	2F	1
Distribution						
Steam Classes	3					
Steam Origin	GWR	4	LMS	1		
Line Highlight	6855 "Saighton Grange"		2A	Tyseley		

We baled out at Wolverhampton Low Level. Our train to Crewe would not leave Wolverhampton High Level until 17.23. A rather bad connection! A connection that I would never have stood for in the original timetable. A makeshift timetable like today's (which had to be made up as we went along) certainly brought a barrowload of troubles.

Wolverhampton used to have the greatest railway road in Britain. Stafford Road and roads leading off it used to have three sheds and a railway works. They were ex 84A Stafford Road, ex 84B Oxley, 2C Bushbury and Stafford Road Works. The first to be closed several years ago was Stafford Road Works (a Western Region works). About two years ago the then 84A Stafford Road (Wolverhampton) was closed. It used to be a great shed. It handled only the classy GWR main line locomotives. "Kings", "Castles" and "Halls" were the most illustrious inhabitants. While it was open it had only a few freight and general purpose locos which all tended to be shedded at Oxley. Oxley had the quantity, Stafford road the quality. When BR took an economics lesson (finally) they closed 84A Stafford Road and transferred its allocation to 84B Oxley. Thus they made do with one Western Region depot rather than two. Oxley was promoted from a second rank to a first rank shed overnight. The ex LMS shed at 2K Bushbury was only closed a few months ago. The move of Oxley to the London Midland Region resulted in the decision that Wolverhampton should only have one shed – Oxley. Bushbury's allocation being transferred to Oxley on its closure. Thus the famous Stafford Road now had only one shed.

The Locoshed Directory offered us respite from the 35 minute walk. Trolley bus service No3 operated from Wilfruna Road past the end of Jones Road. This helped us to cut down the advertised walking time of 35 minutes down to 20 minutes. On our right was Oxley M.P.D. at the top of a steep hill. While on our left was Wolverhampton Racecourse. I noted the hurdles and steeplechase fences with interest. I remembered winning about two pence (one new pence) when Red Dove had finished second in a two-mile hurdle race here in late 1964. After a hard climb up the path up the slopes we reached the shed entrance. As usual I would not hand my permit into the office. It would be a case of using it if it was demanded by any wandering official. Just like at Saltley!

We entered the roundhouse and scanned the inhabitants. We had seen "Ditcheat Manor" at Snow Hill Station about three quarters of an hour ago. She had beaten us here. Former LMS stock was well to the fore in the shape of Black Fives mostly. BR and GWR locos were also well to the fore. The shed was truly cosmopolitan with a few Brush Type 4's interspersed with diesel shunters. To our delight we found the oldest surviving "Hall" on shed. She was 4920 "Dumbleton Hall". However, it was too dark inside the roundhouse to take photos. Outside the roundhouse we found the deadline to be spectacular. Lying deserted parallel to the main line was "Oakley Grange". I opened my eyes wide, gave my head a shake and tried to take in all her distinctive GWR detail. It would be one of our last sheds with GWR locos so I wanted to spend plenty of time browsing. To help my memory of the "Grange" D.S. kindly snapped her. A withdrawn 8G Sutton Oak "Jinty" and a condemned Aston 2-6-4 Tank were other unusual locos on shed. An express passenger train headed by Brush Type 4 D1685 whistled past on the main line. The Burton boys amused themselves by throwing bricks, stones and other junk at the train in a contest to see who could smash the most windows or injure the most passengers (some of whom were daringly looking out of open windows). BR can be thankful that their aim was poor and the contest ended in a 0-0 draw.

2B OXLEY		Home shed		Built	Withdrawn	Scrap
Diesels						
Brush Type 4 Co-Co 1962						
D1685	*pass shed*	2B		Nov-1963		
D1688		2B		Nov-1963		
Total	2					
BR 0-6-0 Shunter 1957						
D2396		2B		Aug-1961	May-1968	
Total	1					
BR 0-6-0 Shunter 1953						
D3037		2B		Dec-1953		
D3191		2B		Nov-1955		
D3757		2B		Oct-1959		
D3979		2B		Jul-1960		
Total	4					
Steam				Built	Withdrawn	Scrap
Collett 5MT 4900 4-6-0 "Hall" 1928						
4920	"Dumbleton Hall"	82E	Bristol Barrow Road	Mar-1929	Dec-1965	saved
5961	"Toynbee Hall"	86B	Newport (Ebbw Jct.)	Jul-1936	Aug-1965	Oct-1965
Total	2					
Collett 4MT 5101 2-6-2T 1929 rebuild of Churchward 3100 Class 1903						
4148		2B		Oct-1946	Sep-1965	Feb-1966
4165		2B		Oct-1948	Oct-1965	Jan-1966
4176		2B		Nov-1949	Oct-1965	Apr-1967
4178		2B	(ex 2A Tyseley)	Nov-1949	Oct-1965	Apr-1966
Total	4					
1933 dev. of Collett 3F 5700 0-6-0PT 1929						
3605		2B		Jan-1939	Oct-1966	Apr-1967
3631		2B		Jul-1939	Jul-1965	Nov-1965
3744		2B		Oct-1937	Aug-1966	Dec-1966
3776		2B		Jul-1938	Apr-1966	Aug-1966
3782		2B		Aug-1938	Oct-1966	Apr-1967
3788		2B		Sep-1938	Nov-1965	Mar-1966
3792		2B		Oct-1938	Nov-1965	Feb-1966
9640		2B		Mar-1946	Jul-1966	Nov-1966
9658		2B		Nov-1946	Oct-1966	Apr-1967
9776		2B		Mar-1936	Apr-1966	Jun-1966
Total	10					

		Home shed		Built	Withdrawn	Scrap
Collett 5MT 6800 4-6-0 "Grange" 1936						
6823	"Oakley Grange"	2B		*Jan-1937*	*Jun-1965*	*Nov-1965*
6827	"Llanfrechfa Grange"	2B		*Feb-1937*	*Sep-1965*	*May-1966*
6830	"Buckenhill Grange"	2B		*Aug-1937*	*Oct-1965*	*Jan-1966*
6838	"Goodmoor Grange"	85A	Worcester (ex 88A)	*Sep-1937*	*Nov-1965*	*Feb-1966*
6857	"Tudor Grange"	2A	Tyseley (ex 2B)	*Nov-1937*	*Oct-1965*	*Feb-1966*
6870	"Bodicote Grange"	2B		*Mar-1939*	*Sep-1965*	*Jan-1966*
Total	6					
Hawksworth 5MT 6959 4-6-0 "Modified Hall" 1944						
6984	"Owsden Hall"	82E	Bristol Barrow Road	*Feb-1948*	*Dec-1965*	*saved*
Total	1					
Collett 5MT 7800 4-6-0 "Manor" 1938						
7821	"Ditcheat Manor"	2B	*to Barry Docks*	*Nov-1950*	*Nov-1965*	*saved*
Total	1					
Stanier 4MT 2-6-4T 1935						
42604		2J	Aston	*Dec-1936*	*May-1965*	*Sep-1965*
Total	1					
Stanier 5MT 2-6-0 1933						
42946		2B		*Nov-1933*	*Nov-1965*	*Feb-1966*
42957		2B		*Dec-1933*	*Jan-1966*	*Apr-1966*
Total	2					
Stanier 5MT 4-6-0 "Black Five" 1934						
44841		2B		*Oct-1944*	*Oct-1966*	*Feb-1967*
44843		2B	(ex 2E)	*Oct-1944*	*Sep-1967*	*Mar-1968*
44919		2B		*Dec-1945*	*Dec-1966*	*Aug-1967*
45186		2B		*Sep-1935*	*Sep-1967*	*Dec-1967*
Total	4					
Midland 3F "Jinty" 0-6-0T 1924 dev. of Johnson 1899 design						
47452		ex 8G	Sutton Oak	*Oct-1926*	*Mar-1965*	*Jul-1965*
Total	1					
8F 1935 Stanier "Big Eight" 2-8-0						
48122		6B	Mold Junction (ex 6D)	*May-1939*	*Feb-1967*	*May-1967*
Total	1					
BR 7P6F 4-6-2 "Britannia" Derby 1951						
70045	"Lord Rowallen"	6J	Holyhead (ex 2B)	*Jun-1954*	*Dec-1967*	*Mar-1968*
Total	1					
BR Standard 5MT 4-6-0 Doncaster 1951						
73066		2A	Tyseley (ex 2L)	*Oct-1954*	*Apr-1967*	*Aug-1967*
73070		6D	Shrewsbury	*Nov-1954*	*May-1967*	*Nov-1967*
73133	*Caprotti* valved	9H	Patricroft	*Oct-1956*	*Jun-1968*	*Dec-1968*
Total	3					
BR Standard 4MT 2-6-0 Doncaster 1953						
76048		2E	Saltley	*Mar-1955*	*Feb-1967*	*Jul-1967*
Total	1					
BR Standard 2MT 2-6-0 Doncaster 1953						
78008		2B		*Mar-1953*	*Oct-1966*	*Jan-1967*
Total	1					

On Shed	46	**Kops**		42		
Steam	39	**Diesels**		7		
Withdrawn	4					

Home Locos	33	**Home Area**			4	**Visitors**	9
Distribution:-	2B	33	2A		2	2E	1
	2J	1					
	6B	1	6D		1	6J	1
	ex 8G	1	9H		1		
	82E	2	85A		1	86B	1
Steam Classes	15						
Steam Origin	GWR	24	LMS		9	BR	6

Shed Highlights:-

	4920 "Dumbleton Hall"	82E	Bristol Barrow Road
	47452	ex 8G	Sutton Oak

		2B OXLEY (Continued)						
Steam	**Aug-50**	**67**	**Mar-59**		**51**	**Apr-65**	**58**	
Allocation						**Aug-65**	**49**	
				Closed to Steam:-			**Mar-67**	
Home Steam								
On/Off Shed	On Shed	24	Off Shed		25	% On Shed	49%	
Not on Shed								
Collett 4MT 5101 2-6-2T 1929							4154	1
Collett 3F 5700 0-6-0PT 1933							8767	1
"Grange"			6803		6831	6833	6871	4
"Manor"							7820	1
Stanier 5MT 2-6-0 1933							42983	1
"Black Five"		44691	44805		44808	44812	44856	
		45006	45040		45263	45264	45272	
					45283			11
"Big Eight"					48415	48474	48475	3
BR 5MT 4-6-0 1951						73019	73028	2
BR 4MT 2-6-0 1953							76022	1
							total	25
			saw elsewhere on the tour					10
			saw at Barry Docks revisited Aug 70					1

Review and Appraisal of 2B Oxley

The shed was on the west side of the line north of Oxley Station and ex 84A Stafford Road MPD. Walking time would have been about 30 minutes.

A cracking good shed. Certainly as good as Tyseley. Fifteen different steam classes on view was an excellent haul. I have already remarked on the scarcity of that numerous class (the 0-6-0 Pannier tanks) in the Birmingham area. However, Oxley made up for these previous scarcities as no fewer than ten were on shed.

We had seen three of the Collett 4MT 2-6-2 Tanks on the journey and here there were another three on shed. They certainly were common around here.

All the "Halls" were visitors to Oxley. Two were from Bristol and one from Newport. One of them (4920 "Dumbleton Hall") was the oldest surviving "Hall"! Oxley was a stronghold of the "Granges" (like Tyseley). One of them was an interesting visitor from 85A Worcester.

The two "funny Crabs" as I had heard them called i.e. the two 429XX locos can only be seen at a few sheds on the LMR although they seem to wander about quite a bit. Oxley had three allocated (42983 was absent). Heaton Mersey (Stockport) had no fewer than nineteen while Springs Branch (Wigan) had the other four.

Of the other LMS stock there was a wandering 8F from 6B Mold Junction. Much more interesting were the two condemned locos: - a 2J Aston 2-6-4 Tank and an ex 8G Sutton Oak "Jinty". The Jinty had been withdrawn for over four months and it was a mystery why she was lying here over a hundred miles from her former depot. Probably she was awaiting delivery to a scrap breaker in the Birmingham area. Most of the other sheds we had visited in the Birmingham area had also had some condemned locos from outside their own area so this gave credence to local scrap breakers in the area.

Of the standards I noted that the Caprotti-valved 73133 was the second 9H Patricroft 5MT 73XXX that we had seen today. 73140 had been at 2E Saltley. I had already noted 73133 on my lightning visit to Crewe with Ian Firth on 12th December 1964. "Lord Rowallan" was no stranger to me and used to be a frequent visitor to Glasgow when shedded at 55A Leeds Holbeck. The Standard Doodle Bug (78008) was the umpteenth one that we had seen on this tour. Remarkably ten of Oxley's GWR 0-6-0 57XX Class Pannier Tanks were on shed.

24 (49%) of Oxley's Home Steam allocation of 49 were on shed. 15 steam classes on view was terrific. Four Oxley "Granges" were missing but six were on shed. *Sadly all the "Granges" seen would be withdrawn by the end of the year.*

As a suitable memento to the "Granges" D.S. expertly snapped 6823 "Oakley Grange" at rest sadly withdrawn in the shed yard.

6823"Oakley Grange" of 2B Oxley Collett 5MT 6800"Grange" 1936 on 4th August 1965

Epilogue

Oddly enough for the first time in the whole Birmingham area we had gone round the shed without a brush with officialdom. However, we were not to be disappointed! We made our way slowly back to the shed exit when a loud voice behind us hailed us. It was the shedmaster. He seemed rather disturbed by our presence. He shouted "Away and get out with you". Odd language. I didn't like to make an ignominious exit in front of a leering shedmaster. There was nothing to stop us walking straight out as he was behind us not in front of us. However, D.S. and I didn't like the shedmaster shouting at us from his big high horse and we decided to try to take him down a peg or two. We did have a permit. That at least entitled us to some respect.

D.S. snarled back "We've got a permit!" (For the second time today but with less passion than he said it at Saltley to the unfortunate Official 5). We walked up to him and handed it to him. "Why didn't you hand it in before you went round?" he queried. "Couldn't see your office" was our reply. (Of course that was a lie. We always noted where the office was when we entered a M.P.D. Then we knew where to avoid!!!) The shedmaster was angry at that and with a huff and a puff he about turned and stormed away to his office. He had kept our permit but we didn't need it now. Nasty bloke was our consensus of opinion. D.S. and I had previously heard of an exceptionally grumpy shedmaster at Oxley when the Railway Society of Scotland had visited there in September 1964. Must have been the same twit here in August 1965 was our conclusion.

On we go

We walked back to the bus stop and allowed a 3A bus to trundle past us. Ten yards behind it was a 3 bus. The Loco shed directory said a 3 bus only would do for Princes Square so we waved it down. There was a terrific jam of brakes as the bus stopped from 25 MPH to 0 MPH. Evidently the bus driver was surprised at us wanting his bus. Inside the bus a riot ensued. A perplexed conductor asked why we didn't get on to the bus in front. It went the same route as his bus he assured us. "We didn't know that" we said. Neither apparently did the Loco Shed Directory. We explained our ignorance and were saved from a lynching. We got off at Princes Square and D.S. (using his Boys Brigade training to the full) triumphantly led the way to Wolverhampton High Level station (the ex LMS station). We had arrived at the ex GWR station at Wolverhampton Low Level. D.S. however, had read the directions from Wolverhampton High Level as well as Low Level so this piece of navigation presented him with little difficulty.

D.S. noted that Wolverhampton High Level was all bombed up. Like Birmingham New Street it was in the process of reconstruction before electrification. We had plenty of time before our 17.23 train to Crewe so we sat down and meditated. I reflected that we had now finished Birmingham Division. We had a few late connections here and true to form our bucket rolled in ten minutes late at 17.33. It was the 16.00 from Coventry and it amazed us how many previous stops the train had made before our Wolverhampton High Level stop (the twelfth stop).

We rolled out eleven minutes late at 17.34. Our journey to Stafford was very uneventful. All that was noted were three Bescot diesel shunters outside Wolverhampton High Level station. The closed shed 2K Bushbury was noted on the east side of the line 1½ miles north of High Level station. Not surprisingly it was totally empty. There had been only one intermediate stop and Stafford was reached at 17.51 (nine minutes late). It was here that the two Burton boys left thanking us for our hospitality and the permits to visit. We had arranged, of course, to see them outside Crewe Works at 2.30 p.m. tomorrow. Here we were again on the main Carlisle to London main line. We were on BR's wonderful, fantastic (if you believe the adverts) new railway i.e. the electrified main line section from Manchester – Liverpool to Crewe to the end of electrification. Stafford itself I admit was a terrific example of futuristic BR architecture. Glass was the most startling feature of the modernized station. Remarkable long glass panels and immense glass windows stared down at us. The concrete and glass over bridge was perhaps the most striking feature. If Euston, Birmingham New Street, Wolverhampton High Level and even Bletchley would look like this after structural reconstruction then Britain's new railway will really be something. With bated breath we awaited our bucket restarting. What excited us was the prospect of seeing 5C Stafford MPD on the north west of the station. And what did we see? One measly "Black Five"! A rather meager reward. The run in to Crewe was more useful. Two electric locos whistled by on fast freights. Various diesel stock were also noted. Of more importance was that our bucket had really got moving on the stretch to Crewe. Businessmen returning home from Birmingham and Wolverhampton had stopped looking ominously at their watches and now bore more contented looks as our bucket caught up on lost time. In fact our bucket pulled up at Crewe at 18.21 (only four minutes late). It had caught up seven minutes since leaving Wolverhampton High Level.

		Schedule	Actual
Depart	WOLVERHAMPTON HIGH LEVEL	17.23	17.34
Arrive	STAFFORD	17.42	17.51
Arrive	CREWE	18.17	18.21

WOLVERHAMPTON HIGH LEVEL TO CREWE						
		Home shed		Built	Withdrawn	Scrap
Diesels						
English Electric Type 4 1-Co-Co-1 1958						
D 308		1B	Camden	Nov-1960		
Total	1					
BR 0-6-0 Shunter 1957						
D2385		5B	Crewe South (ex 5C)	Mar-1961	Feb-1970	
Total	1					
BR 0-6-0 Shunter 1953						
D3292		5B	Crewe South	Dec-1956		
D3867		2F	Bescot	Jan-1960		
Total	2					
BR Sulzer Type 2 Bo-Bo 1958						
D5133		5A	Crewe Diesel	Sep-1960		
Total	1					
LMS 0-6-0 shunter 1939						
12004		2F	Bescot	May-1939	Dec-1967	
Total	1					
LMS and BR 0-6-0 shunter 1945						
12093		2F	Bescot	Aug-1951	May-1971	
Total	1					

		Home shed		Built	Withdrawn	Scrap
Electrics						
English Electric AL3 Bo-Bo 1960						
E3034		LMW	London Mid. West Lines	*Feb-1961*		
Total	*1*					
BR A.E.I.(B.T.H.) motors AL5 Bo-Bo 1960						
E3056		LMW	London Mid. West Lines	*Aug-1961*		
Total	*1*					
Steam						
Stanier 5MT 4-6-0 "Black Five" 1934						
45231		6A	Chester Midland	*Aug-1936*	*Aug-1968*	*saved*
Total	*1*					

On Line	10	**Kops**		10		
Steam	1	**Diesels**		7	**Electrics**	2
		Home Area		8	**Visitors**	4
Shed	5B	2	2F	3	5A	1
Distribution	1B	1	6A	1	LMW	2
Steam Classes	1					
Steam Origin	LMS	1				

CREWE ARRIVAL

Here we were at the most important railway junction in Britain – Crewe. Even as a younger boy of nine I understood the significance of Crewe. I was disappointed not to make a Scottish Railfans visit in April 1959. The visit then was to Manchester and Crewe. By financial restrictions perhaps laziness etc. I did not make Crewe (and Manchester) till December 1964. I was only five and a half years late in getting to Crewe in December 1964! In that time I had never ventured south of Carlisle on the LMR. Better late than never, however.

Even since last December Crewe had changed. Crewe North (one time great of British M.P.D.'s) was now closed. Its allocation had been transferred to 5B Crewe South – the previous artisan shed like 84B Oxley. The Crewe Diesel Repair Depot previously unshedded had taken over the revered 5A shed code and named 5A Crewe Diesel.

We dumped our bags in the left luggage and began our Crewe tour. We had just under two hours in Crewe and our time would have to be strictly rationed everywhere. Our order of visiting would be firstly Crewe Diesel, secondly Crewe South, thirdly Crewe North and fourthly and lastly (but not least) Humphrey's. More about Humphrey's later but it would be well worth a visit although probably nothing to kop!

Crewe Station could be termed an electric loco dump. Mainline electric locos were stacked up convenient lines in ones or twos. We even walked off the end of one platform and a few dangerous yards down the mainline to get the number of a derelict electric loco. Must have been a bit enthusiastic doing that. A at the last time in Crewe in December 1964 the station pilot duties were done by "Jinties". Gratifyingly the BR 0-6-0 Diesel Shunters were not yet allowed to do these duties. D.S. snapped "Jinty" 47565 in a delightful picture of her about to leave the station in one of her station pilot duties.

A rather busy station. I had seen before most of the steam engines on my visit with Ian Firth on the 12th December 1964. Doubtless I would see some more old friends going round the Crewe sheds. However, English Electric Type 4 "Carmania" was new to me. We also noted examples of electric multiple units. i.e. electric buckets. D.S. delighted himself by putting their numbers into his notebook. He had resolved (unlike me) to collect electric bucket numbers. When it gets to collecting bucket numbers I always felt that this was close to collecting wagon or even house numbers. D.S. was certainly going for a low-grade form of trainspotting with electric bucket numbers.

CREWE STATION on ARRIVAL WEDNESDAY						
		Home shed		Built	Withdrawn	Scrap
Diesels						
English Electric Type 4 1-Co-Co-1 1958						
D 218	"Carmania"	9A	Longsight	Jul-1959		
Total	1					
Brush Type 4 Co-Co 1962						
D1598		82A	Bristol Bath Road (ex 87E	Jun-1964		
D1854		5A	Crewe Diesel	Jul-1965		
Total	2					
Electrics						
A.E.I. (British Thomson-Houston) AL1 Bo-Bo 1959						
E3017		LMW	London Midl. West Lines	May-1961		
E3019		LMW	London Midl. West Lines	May-1961		
E3022		LMW	London Midl. West Lines	May-1961		
Total	3					
English Electric AL3 Bo-Bo 1960						
E3034		LMW	London Midl. West Lines	Feb-1961		
Total	1					
A.E.I. (Metropolitan-Vickers) AL2 Bo-Bo 1960						
E3055		LMW	London Midl. West Lines	Apr-1962		
Total	1					
BR A.E.I.(B.T.H.) motors AL5 Bo-Bo 1960						
E3061		LMW	London Midl. West Lines	Dec-1961		
E3066		LMW	London Midl. West Lines	Apr-1962		
E3070		LMW	London Midl. West Lines	Oct-1962		
E3071		LMW	London Midl. West Lines	May-1962		
E3078		LMW	London Midl. West Lines	Mar-1963		
E3080		LMW	London Midl. West Lines	Mar-1963		
Total	6					
Steam		Home shed		Built	Withdrawn	Scrap
Stanier 5MT 4-6-0 "Black Five" 1934						
44761	Timken bearings	5B	Crewe South	Oct-1947	Apr-1968	Sep-1968
45253		12A	Carlisle Kingmoor (ex16F)	Sep-1936	Apr-1968	Oct-1968
45297		5B	Crewe South	Dec-1936	Sep-1967	Jan-1968
45446		5B	Crewe South	Dec-1937	Feb-1967	Sep-1967
45448		5E	Nuneaton (ex 1F)	Dec-1937	Aug-1967	Jan-1968
Total	5					
Midland 3F "Jinty" 0-6-0T 1924 dev. of Johnson 1899 design						
47325		5B	Crewe South	Jun-1926	Sep-1965	May-1966
47391		5B	Crewe South	Nov-1926	Oct-1966	May-1967
47530		5B	Crewe South	Mar-1928	Oct-1966	Feb-1967
47565	D.S. photo	5B	Crewe South	May-1928	Apr-1966	Sep-1966
Total	4					
On Station	23	Kops		11		
Steam	9	Diesels		3	Electrics	11
		Home Area		9	Visitors	14
Shed	5A	1	5B	7	5E	1
Distribution	9A	1	12A	1		
	82A	1	LMW	11		
Steam Classes	2					
Steam Origin	LMS	9				

It was hard for D.S. and I to drag ourselves away from the busy station because there was always something rattling in, out or by. However, time was precious and there was little chance of much great steam by staying here. Electrics and diesels were supreme on passenger trains while Black 5's and Jinties seemed to be about the only steam locos frequenting the station. D.S. managed to snap one 47565 which was one of the "Jinties" on station pilot/ empty stock duties.

47565 of 5B Crewe South Midland 3F "Jinty" 0-6-0T Johnson 1924 on 4ᵗʰ August 1965.

We turned left outside the station and left again into BR's private road which was between the station and the goods avoiding line. We waltzed past the parcels office and cautiously past the railway cop shop and approached the former diesel repair depot. I had drawn my own conclusion that the new 5A Crewe Diesel was the former diesel repair depot. If it wasn't there then we would have been wondering where the new elusive Crewe Diesel was.

Luckily we found the "diesel repair depot" choc a block with guess what? You have--- diesels!!! On our tour round I noticed one of the officials and I determined to find out that this was indeed the new 5A Crewe Diesel. D.S. tried to stop me because he thought that the official would chuck us out of the shed before we completed it. We hadn't a permit for it. The Stoke Division didn't issue permits for the new diesel depot. Brushing aside D.S.'s protests I went up to the official and asked if this was the new diesel depot. It was, and he didn't chuck us out. We thus completed the depot safely. Possibly the reason why they didn't issue permits was because the depot was so small. This appeared to be BR's new deal though: - relatively small two line servicing depots combined with a few large scattered maintenance depots. Of course, diesels did not have to lie idle in shed for as long as steam locos did after each run while ashes from their fireboxes were cleaned out. Therefore they could make do with relatively small servicing sheds.

5A CREWE DIESEL					Built	Withdrawn	Scrap
			Home shed				
Diesels							
English Electric Type 4 1Co-Co1 1958							
D 215	"Aquitania"		1F	Rugby	*Jun-1959*		
D 217	"Corinthia"		1A	Willesden	*Jul-1959*		
D 255			12B	Carlisle Upperby	*Jan-1960*		
D 291			12B	Carlisle Upperby	*Sep-1960*		
D 292			1A	Willesden	*Sep-1960*		
D 300			5A		*Nov-1960*		
D 325	*on shed*	*Dec-64*	1B	Camden	*Dec-1960*		
D 331			1E	Bletchley (ex 5A)	*Feb-1961*		
D 332			5A		*Feb-1961*		
D 342			5A		*May-1961*		
D 379	*on shed*	*Dec-64*	1B	Camden	*Feb-1962*		
Total	*11*						

5A CREWE DIESEL (Continued)

		Home shed		Built	Withdrawn	Scrap
Brush Type 4 Co-Co 1962						
D1631		5A		*Oct-1964*		
D1677		86A	Cardiff Canton	*May-1965*		
D1690		2B	Oxley	*Nov-1963*		
D1837		5A		*May-1965*		
D1841		5A		*May-1965*		
D1843		5A		*May-1965*		
D1845		5A		*May-1965*		
Total	7					
Drewry 0-6-0 Shunter 1955						
D2236		5B	Crewe South (ex 5C)	*Mar-1956*	*Feb-1968*	
Total	1					
North British 0-4-0 Shunter 1958						
D2909	*on shed*	*Dec-64* 5B	Crewe South	*Oct-1958*	*Feb-1967*	
Total	1					
BR Sulzer Type 2 Bo-Bo 1958						
D5083		5A		*Apr-1960*		
D5143		5A	(ex 1A Willesden)	*Nov-1960*		
Total	2					
English Electric Type 3 Co-Co 1961						
D6892		86A	Cardiff Canton	*Feb-1964*		
Total	1					

On Shed	23	**Kops**	7			
Steam	0	**Diesels**	23			
On Shed	*Dec-64*	3				
Home Locos	10	**Home Area**		2	**Visitors**	11
Shed	**5A**	10	**5B**	2		
Distribution	**1A**	2	**1B**	2	**1E**	1
	1F	1				
	2B	1		**12B**	2	
	86A	2				
Shed Highlight:-		D6892 of 86A Cardiff Canton (some highlight!)				

5A CREWE DIESEL REWIND 12th DECEMBER 1964

		Home shed		Built	Withdrawn	Scrap
Diesels						
English Electric Type 4 1Co-Co1 1958						
D 213	"Andania"	5A	Crewe North	*Jun-1959*		
D 222	"Laconia"	9A	Longsight	*Aug-1959*		
D 325	*on shed*	*Aug-65* 1B	Camden	*Dec-1960*		
D 379	*on shed*	*Aug-65* 1B	Camden	*Feb-1962*		
Total	4					
Drewry 0-6-0 Shunter 1955						
D2221		5C	Stafford	*Sep-1955*	*Jul-1968*	
Total	1					
North British 0-4-0 Shunter 1958						
D2909	*on shed*	*Aug-65* 5B	Crewe South	*Oct-1958*	*Feb-1967*	
D2911		5B	Crewe South	*Dec-1959*	*Feb-1967*	
Total	2					

On Shed	7	**Kops**	3			
Steam	0	**Diesels**	7			
On Shed	*Aug-65*	3				
Home Locos	0	**Home Area**		4	**Visitors**	3
Shed	**5A**	1	**5B**	2	**5C**	1
Distribution	**1B**	2	**9A**	1		
Shed	*The North British 0-4-0 diesel shunters*					
Highlight						

Had D2909 moved since last December? It was still here. I wondered very much indeed. It was a North British built loco. North British locos have a problem. The Type 4 "Warships" are unreliable. The D84XX Type 1's were stopped as a class after an initial delivery of only ten. The D63XX Class Bo-Bo Type 2's are troublesome while Scotland's D6100 Bo-Bo Type 2's are undoubtedly the worst diesel class ever made. The majority of the class are out of service awaiting possible scrapping. Only new Paxman Ventura engines could save them from the scrap heap. This North British shunter D2909 looked as though it had not moved since last December and it was perhaps stored as unserviceable.

Last time this small shed was only moderately filled with probably all occupants in for repair. This time the shed was crammed and obviously not all in for repair. D325 had been under repair in December 1964 here and was also on shed now in August 1965. Perhaps this was just a coincidence – difficult to believe that an English Electric Type 4 could be out of service for that length of time.

On we go
Rewind to the soft shedmaster episode

5B Crewe South was to be our next stop. Some railwayists I knew considered Crewe South to be the hardest shed in Britain to get round. One railwayist had warned Ian Firth and me of four lookout offices positioned strategically around each corner of the shed. I was promised that there was a foreman or shedmaster in each lookout tower and furthermore no one got past them. Was all this exaggerated or were they just trying to scare us? Rewind to last December. Ian Firth and I approached Crewe South open-minded believing that the lookout towers were just fairy tales. However, we soon faltered in our tracks when we saw exactly what we had been warned against. There was an office strategically placed at each corner of the shed. The railwayist had suggested dodging about in the shed yard thus avoiding office eyes. However, that December day had been one of continuous heavy rain and we were in no mood to play around the shed yard playing cat and mouse with any shedmaster.

Nothing ventured, nothing made and we walked cautiously past the "blind side" of one of the "lookout" offices. However, through our bad luck, the shedmaster happened to glance out of the side window and unfortunately for us he saw us. We continued to walk slowly on expecting to receive a warning hail at any second followed by an ignominious throwing out of the shed. The warning hail never came. Had the shedmaster taken pity on Ian Firth and me as we hunched figures trudged mournfully onwards through the muck in the driving rain? Was he frightened of getting wet if he went out to halt us? Had Crewe South and its shedmasters quit their hard line with trainspotters and gone soft? We would never know. We cared little at the time why we were allowed round but we made full use of our escape from officialdom by going round a terrific shed.

Back to now

D.S. and I were in a stronger position than last December. We had a permit for Crewe South! It was even for the correct day. That was unusual now! We were also only an hour late for our visit. Even more unusual! It should be a piece of cake, just as I had forecasted for 40E Colwick I reflected darkly.

D.S. and I continued on past Crewe diesel depot and down the lineside. This wasn't the official entrance to 5B Crewe South but was the shortest way and the best unofficial entrance. We passed the turntable and noted the shed offices in the distance. I was pleased also to see a GWR loco on shed in the distance.

This time there was to be no discretion and we walked boldly past one of the lookout office (the same office as we walked past last December). As last time an official saw us. This time there was no such need to slink away and hope that he didn't shout after us. I went up to the office to hand him the permit. However, he said to hand it into the shedmaster inside the shed. So the lookouts weren't so permit happy after all. Wait till I tell them when we get home.

Going round Crewe South was a delight. The shed was definitely the busiest one we had been round on our LMR tour. There were stem locos galore and a pretty diverse lot. We first went down the lines at the western end of the shed which turned out to be the "dead" lines. We finished them and went back into the main building and who would we meet but the shedmaster. I went over to him and handed over the permit. To keep his mind off the details I asked him if there were any Britannia's on shed, which we could photograph. This put us in his eyes a rank above mere "number-snatchers" i.e. we were photographers and enthusiasts. That had the required effect and he handed us the permit quickly back and told us that there were several "Britannias" on shed. Crewe had so many "Britannias" it was like asking if there was any coal that we could photograph at Newcastle. It was marvellous going round the shed. Just one steam engine after another and I began to think that the golden days of steam and the days when you could see 177 locos on shed (as at 66A Polmadie (Glasgow) on late 1958) were back with us again.

Nearing the end of our tour round the shed I stopped at a WD. It was a very special WD it came from the shed of all sheds – 40E Colwick. It was 90051 and had not been on Colwick when we visited there on Monday. D.S. thought it would be a fitting reminder of Colwick and he promptly snapped her. At Colwick I had asked him to take a picture or two but he had refused on the grounds of incorrect lighting. He blamed too much sun at the time. This time he did indeed snap her!

90051 of 40E Colwick Riddles WD 2-8-0 "Austerity" 1943 on 4th August 1965

5B CREWE SOUTH

		Home shed		Built	Withdrawn	Scrap
Diesels						
Brush Type 4 Co-Co 1962						
D1846		5A	Crewe Diesel	*May-1965*		
Total	*1*					
BR 0-4-0 Shunter North British 1958						
D2911		5B		*Dec-1959*	*Feb-1967*	
Total	*1*					
BR English Electric Type 1 Bo-Bo 1957						
D8022	*ex works*	40B	Immingham (ex 41A)	*Oct-1959*		
Total	*1*					
Steam				**Built**	**Withdrawn**	**Scrap**
Collett 5MT 6800 4-6-0 "Grange" 1936						
6848	"Toddington Grange"	85A	Worcester	*Oct-1937*	*Dec-1965*	*Apr-1966*
Total	*1*					
Collett 5MT 7800 4-6-0 "Manor" 1938						
7802	"Bradley Manor"	6D	Shrewsbury	*Jan-1938*	*Nov-1965*	*saved*
7814	"Fringford Manor"	85B	Gloucester (ex 81E)	*Jan-1939*	*Sep-1965*	*Dec-1965*
Total	*2*					
Ivatt 4MT 2-6-0 1947						
43001		5B		*Dec-1947*	*Sep-1967*	*Dec-1967*
43024		5B		*Jan-1949*	*Jun-1967*	*Oct-1967*
43034		5B		*May-1949*	*Jun-1967*	*Nov-1967*
43052		5B		*Aug-1950*	*Oct-1966*	*Feb-1967*
43151		5B		*Nov-1951*	*Feb-1967*	*Aug-1967*
Total	*5*					
Stanier 5MT 4-6-0 "Black Five" 1934						
44684	*Skefko bearings*	5B		*Jul-1950*	*Sep-1967*	*Jan-1968*
44716		5B	(ex 1F Rugby)	*Nov-1948*	*Jul-1965*	*Apr-1966*
44832		5B		*Aug-1944*	*Sep-1967*	*Dec-1967*
44834		5B		*Aug-1944*	*Dec-1967*	*Aug-1968*
44844		5B	(ex 1A Willesden)	*Oct-1944*	*Nov-1967*	*Mar-1968*
44963		8B	Warrington (ex 5C)	*Jun-1946*	*Jul-1968*	*Dec-1968*
45002	*on shed Dec-64*	5B		*Mar-1935*	*Jul-1965*	*Jun-1966*
45021		5B		*Mar-1949*	*Sep-1967*	*Dec-1967*
45033		5B		*Sep-1934*	*Dec-1966*	*Sep-1967*
45056		5B		*Nov-1934*	*Aug-1967*	*Mar-1968*
45067		2F	Bescot	*Jan-1935*	*Oct-1967*	*Dec-1967*
45102		16C	Derby	*May-1935*	*Jan-1965*	*Feb-1966*
45126		12A	Carlisle Kingmoor	*May-1935*	*May-1967*	*Nov-1967*
45142		5B		*Jun-1935*	*Apr-1965*	*Jun-1966*
45146		5D	Stoke	*Jun-1935*	*Jun-1965*	*Dec-1965*
45198		6A	Chester Midland	*Oct-1935*	*Sep-1967*	*Jul-1968*
45249		8A	Edge Hill	*Sep-1936*	*Dec-1966*	*Jun-1967*
45283		2B	Oxley	*Nov-1936*	*Jan-1967*	*May-1967*
45305		6A	Chester Midland	*Jan-1937*	*Aug-1968*	*saved*
45393		5B	(ex 1A Willesden)	*Aug-1937*	*Sep-1966*	*Feb-1967*
45446	*on shed Dec-64*	5B		*Dec-1937*	*Feb-1967*	*Sep-1967*
45448		5E	Nuneaton (ex 1F)	*Dec-1937*	*Aug-1967*	*Jan-1968*
Total	*22*					
Ivatt 2MT 2-6-0 1946						
46430		5E	Nuneaton	*Dec-1948*	*Oct-1965*	*Dec-1965*
46505		2E	Saltley (ex 2L)	*Nov-1952*	*Jun-1967*	*Nov-1967*
Total	*2*					
Midland 3F "Jinty" 0-6-0T 1924 dev. of Johnson 1899 design						
47397	*on shed Dec-64*	5B		*Nov-1926*	*Sep-1966*	*Feb-1967*
47399		5B		*Nov-1926*	*Aug-1965*	*Jan-1966*
47445	*on shed Dec-64*	5B		*May-1927*	*Apr-1966*	*saved*
47450	*on shed Dec-64*	5B		*Jul-1927*	*Apr-1966*	*Sep-1966*
47482		5B		*Jan-1928*	*Oct-1966*	*Feb-1967*
47530		5B		*Mar-1928*	*Oct-1966*	*Feb-1967*
47677		5B		*Aug-1931*	*Nov-1965*	*May-1966*
47680	*on shed Dec-64*	5B		*Oct-1931*	*Jul-1965*	*Oct-1965*
Total	*8*					

			Home shed		Built	Withdrawn	Scrap
Stanier 8F 2-8-0 "Big Eight" 1935							
48001	*on shed*	*Dec-64*	16E	Kirkby	*Jun-1935*	*Jan-1965*	*Oct-1965*
48252			5B		*Dec-1941*	*May-1968*	*Sep-1968*
48255			5B		*Aug-1941*	*Nov-1966*	*Aug-1967*
48353			5D	Stoke (ex 2C)	*Jun-1944*	*Sep-1966*	*Jan-1967*
48360			ex 1E	Bletchley	*Jul-1944*	*Jul-1965*	*Jan-1966*
48385			1H	Northampton (ex 1G)	*Feb-1945*	*Nov-1966*	*Jun-1967*
48395			16E	Kirkby	*May-1945*	*Jul-1967*	*Nov-1967*
48415			2B	Oxley (ex 2A)	*Oct-1943*	*Aug-1966*	*Dec-1966*
48416			5B		*Nov-1943*	*Jul-1965*	*Dec-1965*
48423			10H	Lower Darwen (ex 8H)	*Dec-1943*	*Aug-1968*	*Dec-1968*
48445			5E	Nuneaton (ex 1F)	*Jul-1944*	*May-1968*	*Sep-1968*
48471			6D	Shrewsbury	*Apr-1945*	*May-1968*	*Sep-1968*
48478			2F	Bescot	*Jun-1945*	*Jun-1965*	*Oct-1965*
48505			5B		*Sep-1944*	*Oct-1967*	*May-1968*
48544			5B	(ex 1A Willesden)	*Jan-1945*	*Mar-1968*	*May-1968*
48551	*on shed*	*Dec-64*	5B		*Apr-1945*	*May-1968*	*Sep-1968*
48556			2F	Bescot	*Jul-1945*	*Aug-1967*	*Nov-1968*
48630	*on shed*	*Dec-64*	5B		*Jun-1943*	*Jul-1965*	*Nov-1965*
48633			5B		*Jul-1943*	*Mar-1966*	*Nov-1966*
48658			5B	(ex 1A Willesden)	*Nov-1943*	*Jul-1965*	*Dec-1965*
48727			8G	Sutton Oak	*Sep-1944*	*Aug-1968*	*Jan-1969*
48739			1H	Northampton	*Dec-1945*	*Jan-1967*	*Jul-1967*
48765			9D	Newton Heath	*Mar-1946*	*Aug-1968*	*Dec-1968*
Total	*23*						
BR Standard 7P6F 4-6-2 "Britannia" Derby 1951							
70012	"John of Gaunt"		5B	(ex 5A Crewe North)	*May-1951*	*Dec-1967*	*Apr-1968*
70014	"Iron Duke"		5B	(ex 5A Crewe North)	*Jun-1951*	*Dec-1967*	*Apr-1968*
70018	"Flying Dutchman"		5B	(ex 5A Crewe North)	*Jun-1951*	*Dec-1966*	*Jun-1967*
70019	"Lightning"		12B	Carlisle Upperby (ex 5B)	*Jun-1951*	*Mar-1966*	*Aug-1967*
70020	"Mercury"		12B	Carlisle Upperby (ex 5B)	*Jul-1951*	*Jun-1967*	*Jun-1967*
70043	"Lord Kitchener"		5B	(ex 5A Crewe North)	*Jun-1953*	*Aug-1965*	*Nov-1965*
70048	"The Territorial Army 1908		12B	Carlisle Upperby	*Jul-1954*	*May-1967*	*Oct-1967*
70051	"Firth of Forth"		5B	(ex 5A Crewe North)	*Aug-1954*	*Dec-1967*	*Mar-1968*
70052	"Firth of Tay"		5B	(ex 5A Crewe North)	*Aug-1954*	*Apr-1967*	*Nov-1967*
Total	*9*						
BR Standard 5MT 4-6-0 Doncaster 1951							
73035			9H	Patricroft (ex 6D)	*Aug-1953*	*Jan-1968*	*May-1968*
73069			2A	Tyseley (ex 2L)	*Nov-1954*	*Aug-1968*	*Mar-1969*
73127	*Caprotti valved*		9H	Patricroft	*Aug-1956*	*Oct-1967*	*Jul-1968*
73128	*Caprotti valved*		9H	Patricroft	*Aug-1956*	*May-1968*	*Aug-1968*
Total	*4*						
BR Standard 4MT 4-6-0 Brighton 1951							
75040			5D	Stoke	*Sep-1953*	*Oct-1967*	*Mar-1968*
Total	*1*						
BR Standard 4MT 2-6-0 Doncaster 1953							
76088			2F	Bescot	*May-1957*	*Jun-1967*	*Dec-1967*
Total	*1*						
BR Standard 2MT 2-6-0 Doncaster 1953							
78025			ex 9G	Gorton	*May-1954*	*Feb-1965*	*Nov-1965*
78031	*on shed*	*Dec-64*	5B		*Sep-1954*	*Oct-1966*	*Mar-1967*
78036			5B		*Nov-1954*	*Nov-1966*	*Aug-1967*
Total	*3*						
Riddles WD 8F 2-8-0 "Austerity" 1943							
90051	*D.S.*	*photo*	40E	Colwick	*May-1944*	*Oct-1965*	*Jan-1966*
Total	*1*						
BR Standard 9F 2-10-0 Brighton 1954							
92006	*double chimney*		50A	York	*Feb-1954*	*Apr-1967*	*Nov-1967*
92011			8H	Birkenhead (ex 16B)	*May-1954*	*Nov-1967*	*Jan-1968*
92111			8H	Birkenhead	*Nov-1956*	*Oct-1967*	*Feb-1968*
92124			8B	Warrington	*Mar-1957*	*Dec-1966*	*Apr-1967*
92152			2E	Saltley	*Oct-1957*	*Nov-1967*	*Mar-1968*
Total	*5*						

On Shed	90	Kops	55
Steam	87	Diesels	3
Withdrawn	13		
On Shed	Dec-64	10	

Home Locos	43	Home Area		7	Visitors	40
Shed	5B	43	5A	1	5D	3
Distribution	5E	3				
	ex 1E	1	1H	2		
	2A	1	2B	2	2E	2
	2F	5				
	6A	2	6D	2		
	8A	1	8B	2	8G	1
	8H	2				
	9D	1	ex 9G	1	9H	3
	10H	1	12A	1	12B	3
	16C	1	16E	1		
	40B	1	40E	1	50A	1
	85A	1	85B	1		
Steam Classes	14					
Steam Origin	LMS	60	GWR	3	WD	1
	BR	23				

Shed Highlights:-

	Steam	7802 "Bradley Manor"		6D	Shrewsbury
	(of many)	7814 "Fringford Manor"		85B	Gloucester

Steam	Aug-50	103	Mar-59	117	Apr-65	60
Allocation					Aug-65	81
			Closed to Steam:-			Nov-67

Home Steam	excluding withdrawn locos					
On/Off Shed	On Shed	35	Off Shed	46	% On Shed	43%

Not on Shed

Ivatt 4MT 2-6-0 1947		43020	43026	43088	43113	4
"Black Fives"	44678	44679	44680	44681	44683	
	44685	44715	44759	44761	44765	
	44829	44833	44836	44910	45046	
		45180	45243	45248	45297	
			45391	45434	45494	23
"Jinty"	47325	47338	47391	47494	47565	5
"Big Eights"		48036	48347	48559	48736	4
"Britannias"	70000	70023	70024	70025	70027	
			70028	70050	70054	8
BR 2MT 2-6-0 1953				78010	78030	2
					total	46
	saw elsewhere on the tour					25
	saw elsewhere on Dec 64 Manchester and Crewe trip					1
	saw on July 65 Preston area trip					2
	saw on June 67 Carlisle visit					2

Review and Appraisal of 5B Crewe South a.k.a. the visitors shed

The shed was on the fork of the Stafford and Shrewsbury lines south of the station. Walking time was 20 minutes.

One of the great steam sheds of BR and it didn't let us down. Crewe South was a unique shed by the enormous number of visitors – 34 from other Divisions were on shed. Home Steam on shed was only one more at 35 (43% of total Home Steam) with 46 Home Steam off shed.

Numerous (22) Black Fives were on shed. Five of them were withdrawn. One of them was from Derby. What was it doing here? Unknown to us 5C Stafford had been closed very recently. The two ex Stafford Black Fives on shed were probably on the way to their new depot of 8B Warrington. Two of Crewe South's sizeable "Jinty" allocation had also been recently withdrawn. 23 "Big Eights" on shed (from many different sheds) of which five were withdrawn. Interestingly three of the condemned locos were from afar: - ex 1E Bletchley, 2F Bescot and 16E Kirkby.

The highlights for me were the "Grange" and the two "Manors". "Manors" had been very rare so far on our tour. This helped to make up for it. One of the "Manors" was from 6D Shrewsbury. I hoped that we would see a few more there when we visited the shed later. "Britannias" were on shed in number (nine). Three were from Carlisle and one was withdrawn. The "Standard Fives" were visitors. One of them we had missed at 2A Tyseley earlier in the day while the three others were from 9H Patricroft in the Manchester Division. We had also seen some other wandering Patricroft Standard 5's in the Birmingham area earlier today.

We also saw three more of the ubiquitous BR 78XXX class. Two of them I had seen at Crewe last December. The third was formerly from 9G Gorton. Gorton was recently closed and with its closure 78025 was withdrawn. There were quite a few withdrawn locos from distant depots on shed. They could hardly all have run hot on their way to the breakers and been dumped here. Therefore there must be a scrap breaker in the Crewe Area. They certainly would not be cut up at Crewe Works. That stopped last year. D8022 was ex Crewe Works and would soon be returned to her home depot of 40B Immingham. The 9F 2-10-0's and the WD 2-8-0 were all visitors. The WD was the most interesting from 40E Colwick in fact. More has been said earlier about her. 87 steam engines on shed was truly magnificent. This great crossroads of Crewe was a haven for visiting steam. Only 35 (43%) of her 81 strong steam allocation was on shed. Remarkably we would see 25 of the missing 46 elsewhere during the week's tour.

To draw another parallel lets rewind back to the 12 December 1964 visit of Ian Firth and me.

5B CREWE SOUTH REWIND 12th DECEMBER 1964							
			Home shed		Built	Withdrawn	Scrap
Diesels							
BR English Electric Type 1 Bo-Bo 1957							
D8005	ex-works		1A	Willesden	Sep-1957		
D8036	ex-works		1A	Willesden	Oct-1959		
D8060	ex-works		41A	Tinsley	May-1961		
Total	3						
Steam							
Collett 5MT 6800 4-6-0 "Grange" 1936					Built	Withdrawn	Scrap
6819	"Highnam Grange"		85A	Worcester	Dec-1936	Nov-1965	Feb-1966
Total	1						
Stanier 4MT 2-6-4T 1935 dev of Fowler 1927							
42468			9H	Patricroft	Nov-1936	Sep-1965	Feb-1966
42573			1A	Willesden	Sep-1936	Nov-1964	Jan-1965
Total	2						
Stanier 5MT 2-6-0 1933							
42954			8F	Spring's Branch (Wigan)	Dec-1933	Feb-1967	Aug-1967
42958			1F	Rugby	Jan-1934	Nov-1965	Jun-1966
42979			2F	Bescot	Feb-1934	Dec-1964	May-1965
Total	3						
Ivatt 4MT 2-6-0 1947							
43113			5B		Apr-1951	Sep-1966	Dec-1966
Total	1						
4F 0-6-0 Midland 1924							
44192			12D	Workington (ex 9E)	Jun-1925	Apr-1965	Aug-1965
44218			5B	(ex 5D Stoke)	Jan-1926	Mar-1966	Jun-1966
44500			5B		Nov-1927	Jul-1966	Nov-1966
44571			5B	(ex 5D Stoke)	Aug-1937	Dec-1964	Aug-1965
Total	4						

			Home shed		Built	Withdrawn	Scrap
Stanier 5MT 4-6-0 "Black Five" 1934							
44735			9E	Trafford Park (ex 9D)	*Feb-1949*	*Aug-1968*	*Nov-1968*
44766	Timken	dbl chim	2F	Bescot	*Dec-1947*	*Aug-1967*	*Dec-1967*
44772			8A	Edge Hill	*May-1947*	*Oct-1967*	*May-1968*
44804			16C	Derby	*Jun-1944*	*Mar-1968*	*Jun-1968*
44808			2F	Bescot (ex 6J Holyhead)	*Sep-1944*	*Dec-1966*	*Dec-1967*
44928			9J	Agecroft	*Mar-1946*	*Jun-1967*	*Dec-1967*
45002	on shed	Aug-65	5B		*Mar-1935*	*Jul-1965*	*Jun-1966*
45046			5B		*Oct-1934*	*Jun-1968*	*Dec-1968*
45093			5B		*Apr-1935*	*Nov-1965*	*Feb-1966*
45094			8A	Edge Hill	*Apr-1935*	*Feb-1967*	*Sep-1967*
45275			6B	Mold Junction	*Nov-1936*	*Oct-1967*	*Feb-1968*
45399			10A	Carnforth	*Aug-1937*	*Dec-1966*	*Jun-1967*
45414			8A	Edge Hill	*Oct-1937*	*Feb-1965*	*Mar-1965*
45446	on shed	Aug-65	5B		*Dec-1937*	*Feb-1967*	*Sep-1967*
Total	14						
Stanier 6P5F 4-6-0 "Jubilee" 1934							
45553	"Canada"		5A	Crewe North	*Jun-1934*	*Nov-1964*	*Apr-1965*
45586	"Mysore"		5B		*Dec-1934*	*Jan-1965*	*Apr-1965*
Total	2						
Ivatt 2MT 2-6-0 1946							
46402			8F	Springs Branch (Wigan)	*Dec-1946*	*Jun-1967*	*Jan-1968*
Total	1						
Midland 3F "Jinty" 0-6-0T 1924 dev. of Johnson 1899 design							
47325			5B		*Jun-1926*	*Sep-1965*	*May-1966*
47354			5B		*Jul-1926*	*Oct-1964*	*Jan-1965*
47391			5B		*Nov-1926*	*Oct-1966*	*May-1967*
47397	on shed	Aug-65	5B		*Nov-1926*	*Sep-1966*	*Feb-1967*
47445	on shed	Aug-65	5B		*May-1927*	*Apr-1966*	*saved*
47450	on shed	Aug-65	5B		*Jul-1927*	*Apr-1966*	*Sep-1966*
47494			5B		*Feb-1928*	*Oct-1966*	*Feb-1967*
47680	on shed	Aug-65	5B		*Oct-1931*	*Jul-1965*	*Oct-1965*
Total	8						
Stanier 8F 2-8-0 "Big Eight" 1935							
48001	on shed	Aug-65	16E	Kirkby	*Jun-1935*	*Jan-1965*	*Oct-1965*
48056			16A	Toton	*Oct-1936*	*May-1968*	*Aug-1968*
48060			16C	Derby	*Oct-1936*	*Apr-1968*	*Aug-1968*
48166			16B	Annesley	*Apr-1943*	*Oct-1967*	*Apr-1968*
48310			9B	Stockport Edgeley	*Dec-1943*	*Dec-1967*	*May-1968*
48374			15B	Wellingborough	*Nov-1944*	*Jun-1968*	*Jan-1969*
48379			8F	Springs Branch (ex 16E)	*Dec-1944*	*Mar-1967*	*Sep-1967*
48532			9D	Newton Heath	*Apr-1945*	*Mar-1968*	*Jul-1968*
48551	on shed	Aug-65	5B		*Apr-1945*	*May-1968*	*Sep-1968*
48630	on shed	Aug-65	5B		*Jun-1943*	*Jul-1965*	*Nov-1965*
48692			8C	Speke Junction	*Mar-1944*	*Jun-1968*	*Oct-1968*
48743			5B		*Mar-1946*	*Mar-1967*	*Sep-1967*
Total	12						
BR Standard 7P6F 4-6-2 "Britannia" Derby 1951							
70046	"A.N.Z.A.C."	pass	6J	Holyhead	*Jun-1954*	*Jul-1967*	*Jan-1968*
Total	1						
BR Standard 2MT 2-6-0 Doncaster 1953							
78007			5B		*Mar-1953*	*May-1967*	*Dec-1967*
78010			5B		*Dec-1953*	*Sep-1966*	*Dec-1966*
78030			5B	(ex 5A Crewe North)	*Sep-1954*	*Oct-1965*	*Dec-1965*
78031	on shed	Aug-65	5B		*Sep-1954*	*Oct-1966*	*Mar-1967*
Total	4						
BR Standard 4MT 2-6-4T Doncaster 1953							
80044			6H	Bangor	*Aug-1952*	*Nov-1964*	*Jan-1965*
80125			10D	Lostock Hall	*Oct-1955*	*Oct-1964*	*Jun-1965*
Total	2						
BR Standard 9F 2-10-0 Brighton 1954							
92132			16B	Annesley	*May-1957*	*Oct-1967*	*Feb-1968*
92161			9D	Newton Heath	*Dec-1957*	*Dec-1966*	*May-1967*
92211	double chimney		50A	York	*Sep-1959*	*May-1967*	*Dec-1967*
Total	3						

5B CREWE SOUTH REWIND 12th DECEMBER 1964 (continued)							
On Shed	61		Kops		55		
Steam	58		Diesels		3		
Withdrawn	5						
On Shed	Aug-65	10					
Home Locos		24 Home Area		1	Visitors	36	
Shed	5B	24	5A	1			
Distribution	1A	3	1F	1			
	2F	3					
	6B	1	6H	1	6J	1	
	8A	3	8C	1	8F	3	
	9B	1	9D	2	9E	1	
	9H	1	9J	1			
	10A	1	10D	1			
	12D	1	15B	1			
	16A	1	16B	2	16C	2	
	16E	1					
	41A	1	50A	1	85A	1	
Steam Classes		14					
Steam Origin		LMS	47	GWR	1	BR	10

Shed Highlights:-

		45553	"Canada"	5A		Crewe North	
	(of many)	45586	"Mysore"	5B		Crewe South	

Home Steam	excluding withdrawn locos						
On/Off Shed	On Shed	23 Off Shed		40 % On Shed		37%	
Not on Shed							
Stanier 5MT 2-6-0 1933						42969	1
Ivatt 4MT 2-6-0 1947	43001	43020		43024	43026	43034	
				43052	43088	43151	8
"Black Fives"	44684	44714		44759	44832	44834	
	45021	45033		45128	45142	45248	
	45297	45321		45391	45434	45494	15
"Jinty"	47338	47399		47482	47530	47677	5
"Big Eights"	48251	48255		48292	48305	48398	
	48502	48505		48633	48736	48757	10
BR 2MT 2-6-0 1953						78036	1
						total	40
	saw on shed on August 65 tour				18		
	saw elsewhere on the Aug 65 tour				9		
	saw on July 65 Preston area trip				3		
	Barry Docks revisited Aug 70				1		

Review and Appraisal of 5B Crewe South Rewind 12th December 1964

As our August visit we found a "United Nations" shed with visitors from all points of the compass. Remarkably in these days of dwindling steam there were 87 steam engines on shed in August 1965 compared with 58 steam engines in December 1964. Partly this would be due to the closure of 5A Crewe North since our December visit. Remarkably again of the 58 steam engines we saw on shed at Crewe South in December 1964 only 10 were again on shed in August 1965. 23 Home Steam (37%) of total Home Steam on shed. This number was dwarfed by the 30 engines from other Divisions on shed.

The make-up of the steam classes had also changed. 4F Midland 0-6-0's, the 4MT Stanier 2-6-4 tanks and the 5MT Stanier 2-6-0's and the beloved "Jubilee" 6P5F 4-6-0's were not around in August 1965 and had probably left Crewe forever. Most had been scrapped while some had been pushed north into the final steam stronghold of Lancashire. 48001 of 16E Kirkby had been on the dead line in December 1964 and had still been there in August 1965. Probably the "United Nations" effect was partly caused by an influx of engines awaiting entry to Crewe Works for overhaul and repair. Some appeared to be definitely ex-works. Others, of course, had arrived off cross-country freights and would soon be returning to their home depots. The English Electric Bo-Bo Type 1's were obviously repaired and overhauled at Crewe Works. We saw ex-works examples in December 1964 and August 1965.

Last December there were no Britannias on Crewe South although one had passed by the shed during our visit. This was not surprising as Crewe South had none allocated. She had picked up "Britannias" when 5A Crewe North had been closed and others from 1A Willesden and 6J Holyhead. Strangely enough even little 2J Aston had 5 "Britannias" allocated in December 1964 but had subsequently lost the lot to 12A Carlisle Kingmoor and 12B Carlisle Upperby. The balance away from Birmingham had been partly redressed when 2B Oxley had gained a couple of "Britannias" from 6J Holyhead.

The highlight of our first visit had certainly been seeing the increasingly rare "Jubilees".

On we go

Both the December 1964 and the August 1965 visits had proved what a splendid shed was 5B Crewe South. It had the largest number of steam on shed since Carlisle Kingmoor last Saturday. D.S. also appreciated its quality.

We walked back from Crewe South back the way we came. As the station was on the way we decided to give it a call.

CREWE STATION WEDNESDAY after crewe south before crewe north						
		Home shed		Built	Withdrawn	Scrap
Diesels						
English Electric Type 4 1-Co-Co-1 1958						
D 215	"Aquitania"	1F	Rugby	*Jun-1959*		
D 291		12B	Carlisle Upperby	*Sep-1960*		
Total	2					
Electrics						
A.E.I. (British Thomson-Houston) AL1 Bo-Bo 1959						
E3017		LMW	London Midl. West Lines	*May-1961*		
Total	1					
Steam						
Stanier 5MT 4-6-0 "Black Five" 1934			*Built*	*Withdrawn*	*Scrap*	
44734		9D	Newton Heath	*Feb-1949*	*Dec-1967*	*Apr-1968*
45243		5B	Crewe South (ex 5A)	*Sep-1936*	*Sep-1967*	*Dec-1967*
Total	2					
On Station	5	Kops		0		
Steam	2	Diesels		2	Electrics	1
	Home Area			1	Visitors	4
Shed	5B	1	1F	1		
Distribution	9D	1	12B	1	LMW	1
Steam Classes	1					
Steam Origin	LMS	2				

Not much on the station!

D.S. and I were now going to visit an officially closed shed. However, that wouldn't deter us from visiting it. 1B Camden and 14B Cricklewood West were officially closed too. However, they weren't dead and closed but very much alive. We visited 14B Cricklewood West but unfortunately believed the London Divisional Manager and had omitted Camden. Not that we missed much as it was a diesel depot with a small allocation. This time we would take no chances and visit Crewe North and we expected to find it very much alive.

In our great visit of December 64 we were rather nervous of doing 5A Crewe North even more than we were of doing 5B Crewe South. It all started with a Stockport stutter. This young cleaner with a stutter whom we met when we were doing 9B Stockport Edgeley earlier in the day got us really worried. He told Ian Firth and me that anyone caught at 5A Crewe

North was promptly chucked into the cop shop and then slightly later – fined for trespassing. Charming!

Ian Firth and I took no chances. We walked carefully round the shed buildings and found the north end of the shed yard adjacent to an enormous patch of waste ground. We were separated from the shed by an impressive twelve foot high boundary fence of iron railings. Somebody didn't want us to sneak in! We walked along the edge of this fence. If there was no lucky gap I noted that we would have to do a Hilary and Tensing act and scale the fence. We provisionally had marked out a likely looking spot on the fence (with some support on our side to help us over). However, like at 66A Polmadie (Glasgow) some nice chap had pulled out a railing further along the fence. Here was the tradesman's entrance. By this devious entrance we "broke in" and cautiously made our way around.

This time D.S. and I should have no admission problems. This time we **did** have a permit. However, perhaps it was a worthless piece of paper not needed this time. We walked past an empty row of offices and began to wonder if the shed was indeed dead and closed. We were released from our perplexion by the sight of a gleaming Brush Type 4 basking in the evening sunshine. Then things began to happen. We paused at the top of the yard and looked right and saw nothing but if we looked left there was indeed something. We noted stored steam locomotives in the roundhouse and a few diesels lying in the yard and around the old running shed.

The diesels were all Type 4's. D1756 showed some signs of life and looked as though she would soon be moving out. The roundhouse was a good place for industrial archaeology. A Birkenhead 9F 2-10-0 first met our eyes. Moving on around we noted some local stuff: - a Mogul, a Standard Doodle Bug, a couple of Black Fives and a Big Eight. Then we came to the Britannias. Lastly and best of all we came to the mysterious number 70000. It was no mirage. This was the founder member of the class "Britannia". If we were to believe her smoke deflectors she had entirely different names. She was of course shorn of her nameplates. BR must have them under lock and key because she was scheduled for preservation. They had not been flogged for £30 each to some rich private enthusiast as was the normal destination for steam nameplates.

To get back to the point, merrily chalked on one of "Britannia's" nameplates (or rather where it used to be) was "Lester Piggott". On the other one was chalked "Uncle Bimbo". D.S. looked quizzically at the two names and seemed to be weighing up in his mechanical mind which was the correct one. He seemed to plump for and write down "Uncle Bimbo" in the end although the name "Lester Piggott" must have seemed vaguely familiar to him. One thing about "Britannia" was that she was in the most shocking, dirty, downtrodden, degrading condition imaginable. I would not be surprised if she was awaiting Crewe Works for restoration to her best condition. It was a possibility that she had run for the last time before preservation.

ex 5A CREWE NORTH						
		Home shed		Built	Withdrawn	Scrap
Diesels						
English Electric Type 4 1-Co-Co-1 1958						
D 291		12B	Carlisle Upperby	Sep-1960		
D 292		1A	Willesden	Sep-1960		
D 305		1A	Willesden	Oct-1960		
D 318		5A	Crewe Diesel	Feb-1961		
Total	4					
Brush Type 4 Co-Co 1962						
D1678		86A	Cardiff Canton	May-1965		
D1756		86A	Cardiff Canton	Aug-1964		
D1854		5A	Crewe Diesel	Jul-1965		
Total	3					

		Home shed		Built	Withdrawn	Scrap
Steam						
Ivatt 4MT 2-6-0 1947						
43026		5B	Crewe South	*Feb-1949*	*Sep-1966*	*Jan-1967*
Total	*1*					
Stanier 5MT 4-6-0 "Black Five" 1934						
45248		5B	Crewe South	*Sep-1936*	*Feb-1966*	*Jul-1966*
45418		1A	Willesden	*Oct-1937*	*Feb-1966*	*Oct-1966*
Total	*2*					
Stanier 8F 2-8-0 "Big Eight" 1935						
48291		5D	Stoke	*Jul-1941*	*Jul-1966*	*Oct-1966*
Total	*1*					
BR Standard 7P6F 4-6-2 "Britannia" Derby 1951						
70000	"Britannia"	5B	Crewe South (ex 5A)	*Jan-1951*	*Jun-1966*	*saved*
70021	"Morning Star"	9D	Newton Heath (ex 5A/5B)	*Aug-1951*	*Dec-1967*	*May-1968*
70050	"Firth of Clyde"	5B	Crewe South (ex 5A)	*Aug-1954*	*Aug-1966*	*Dec-1966*
Total	*3*					
BR Standard 2MT 2-6-0 Doncaster 1953						
78010		5B	Crewe South	*Dec-1953*	*Sep-1966*	*Dec-1966*
Total	*1*					
BR Standard 9F 2-10-0 Brighton 1954						
92109		8H	Birkenhead	*Oct-1956*	*Nov-1967*	*Mar-1968*
Total	*1*					

On Shed	16	**Kops**		10		
Steam	9	**Diesels**		7		
Withdrawn	0					
On Shed	Dec-64	0				

Home Locos	0	Home Area		8	Visitors	8
Shed	5A	2	5B	5	5D	1
Distribution	1A	3	8H	1	9D	1
	12B	1				
	86A	2				
Steam Classes		6				
Steam Origin	LMS		4 BR		5	
Shed Highlight:-						
(no prize for guessing)	70000		"Britannia"		5B	Crewe South

Steam	Aug-50	85	*Mar-59*	125	*Apr-65*	38
Allocation					*Aug-65*	0
			Closed to Steam:-		*May-65*	

Review and Appraisal of 5A Crewe North

The shed was on the west side of the line at the north end of Crewe Station. Walking time was 5 minutes.

Can only say it was good. After all the shed is closed with no allocation. Therefore we saw 16 more locos than we could rightfully expect.

Western Region based Brush Type 4's are quite common on the LMR. In the old steam days ex GWR steam locos rarely strayed from WR lines. Now in diesel days there did not seem to be any barriers. "Firth of Clyde" used to be one of the five "Britannia's" (70050-54) allocated to 66A Polmadie (Glasgow). Seeing 70000 "Britannia" – the founder member was utterly fantabulous. A really great highlight of the tour and certainly made the visit to this "closed" shed really worthwhile.

To draw a parallel with our December visit is a little unenlightening as a comparison. This is because 5A Crewe North was open then. However, it is interesting to note how good Crewe North used to be.

5A CREWE NORTH REWIND 12th DECEMBER 1964

		Home shed		Built	Withdrawn	Scrap
Diesels						
English Electric Type 4 1-Co-Co-1 1958						
D 303		5A		Nov-1960		
D 316		5A		Jan-1961		
D 328		5A		Jan-1961		
D 374		1B	Camden	Jan-1962		
Total	4					
Brush Type 4 Co-Co 1962						
D1631		5A		Oct-1964		
D1635		5A		Nov-1964		
Total	2					
Steam				Built	Withdrawn	Scrap
Stanier 4MT 2-6-4T 1935 dev of Fowler 1927						
42581		1A	Willesden	Oct-1936	Mar-1966	Jun-1966
Total	1					
Hughes/Fowler 5MT 2-6-0 "Crab" 1926						
42799		9G	Gorton (ex 9K)	Dec-1927	Jan-1965	May-1965
Total	1					
Stanier 5MT 4-6-0 "Black Five" 1934						
44679		5A		May-1950	Sep-1967	Jun-1968
44683		5A		Jul-1950	Apr-1968	Sep-1968
44763		5A		Oct-1947	Sep-1965	Mar-1966
44764		5A		Nov-1947	Sep-1965	Apr-1966
44765		5A		Dec-1947	Sep-1967	Mar-1968
44926		9K	Bolton	Feb-1946	Apr-1968	Oct-1968
44963		5C	Stafford	Jun-1946	Jul-1968	Dec-1968
44985		6G	Llandudno Junction	Oct-1946	Oct-1967	Feb-1968
45130		6A	Chester Midland	May-1935	Jan-1967	Mar-1968
45230		10A	Carnforth	Aug-1936	Aug-1965	Nov-1965
45243		5A		Sep-1936	Sep-1967	Dec-1967
45297		5B	Crewe South	Dec-1936	Sep-1967	Jan-1968
Total	12					
Stanier 6P5F 4-6-0 "Jubilee" 1934						
45554	"Ontario"	5A		May-1934	Nov-1964	Jun-1965
45556	"Nova Scotia"	5A		Jun-1934	Sep-1964	Jan-1965
45617	"Mauritius"	5A		Sep-1934	Nov-1964	Apr-1965
45672	"Anson"	5A		Dec-1935	Nov-1964	Apr-1965
45704	"Leviathan"	5A		May-1936	Jan-1965	Apr-1965
Total	5					
Stanier 8P 4-6-2 "Coronation" 1937						
46235	"City of Birmingham"	5A		Jul-1939	Oct-1964	saved
46240	"City of Coventry"	5A		Mar-1940	Oct-1964	Dec-1964
Total	2					
Midland 3F "Jinty" 0-6-0T 1924 dev. of Johnson 1899 design						
47437		2K	Bushbury (ex 6A)	Apr-1927	Aug-1966	Apr-1967
Total	1					
Stanier 8F 2-8-0 "Big Eight" 1935						
48320		5E	Nuneaton	Feb-1944	Mar-1967	Oct-1967
Total	1					
BR Standard 7P6F 4-6-2 "Britannia" Derby 1951						
70026	"Polar Star"	6J	Holyhead	Oct-1952	Jan-1967	May-1967
70033	"Charles Dickens"	5A		Dec-1952	Jul-1967	Jun-1968
Total	2					
BR Standard 9F 2-10-0 Brighton 1954						
92082		8H	Birkenhead	May-1956	Nov-1967	Apr-1968
Total	1					

On Shed	32	**Kops**	15	
Steam	26	**Diesels**	6	
Withdrawn	6	to be preserved	1	
On Shed	Aug-65	0		

376

5A CREWE NORTH REWIND 12th DECEMBER 1964 (continued)							
Home Locos	19	**Home Area**	3	**Visitors**	10		
Shed	5A	19	5B	1	5C	1	
Distribution	5E	1					
	1A	1	1B	1	2K	1	
	6A	1	6G	1	6J	1	
	9G	1	9K	1			
	8H	1	10A	1			
Steam Classes		9					
Steam Origin	LMS	23 BR			3		
Shed Highlights:-	46235	"City of Birmingham"					
(again no prizes	46240	"City of Coventry"					
for guessing)							
Steam	**Aug-50**	85	**Mar-59**	125	**Apr-65**	38	
Allocation					**Aug-65**	0	
			Closed to Steam:-		**May-65**		
Home Steam	excluding withdrawn locos						
On/Off Shed	On Shed	8	Off Shed	24	% On Shed	25%	
Not on Shed							
"Black Fives"	44678	44680	44681	44685	44761	44762	6
"Jubilee"					45553	45674	2
"Britannias"	70000	70015	70017	70018	70019	70025	
	70028	70030	70034	70042	70043	70044	
			70050	70051	70052	70054	16
						total	24
		saw on August 65 tour				13	
		saw elsewhere on Dec 64 Manchester and Crewe trip				1	
		saw on July 65 Preston area trip				2	
		saw on June 67 Carlisle visit				1	

Review and Appraisal of 5A Crewe North

As I have already noted it is impossible to draw any parallel between the two visits. Last December I was lucky to see the tail end of LMR mainline steam at Crewe North in the shape of the two withdrawn "Coronations" and five "Jubilees" (sadly four withdrawn). All had now left the Crewe area – the "Coronations" completely withdrawn during 1964. Unfortunately it was a day of torrential rain that December day (unlike today) and I was thus unable to pay them a well deserved photographic tribute. However, Jubilee 45595 "Southern Rhodesia" kindly posed for me at the north end of Crewe Station and I had at least one memento (cherished at that) of a wonderful but wet visit to Crewe. One interesting parallel was that the rain had stopped by now (August). At least it doesn't rain at Crewe all the time!!! It was noticeable in the December visit that Crewe North didn't draw its visitors from as wide an area as 5B Crewe South did.

Home Steam on shed at 8 (25%) was a little disappointing for a Saturday with 24 Home Steam off shed.

"Jubilee" 45595 "Southern Rhodesia" at Crewe Station on Saturday 12th December 1964

"A good one and four penneth worth"
THE FAST SHED EPISODE

We escaped out of Crewe North without incident. Three sheds done and one stop to go I remarked to D.S. He asked if we were going to Crewe Electric Depot. That's not our last stop I answered. D.S. was now running a bit hot with worry as he tried to work out where we were going. I told D.S. that we were getting the 20.25 to Shrewsbury. He looked at his watch. It was 20.05. he then overheated again as he tried to think how we could do a shed and get back to the station in time for our train. D.S. queried the timing. I told him it could take us as little as 30 seconds or as long as 5 minutes depending on how crowded it was or how long we have to wait. D.S. looked even more puzzled.

When I darted up one street and then up another D.S. began to get disturbed. He told me where the railway was. He thought I was lost. So I was! I could have sworn our last stop was down here. However, it wasn't. All these dreary, drab red-bricked, back to back "Coronation Street" houses looked the same. That was the trouble. Every street looked like every other one. I asked D.S. to make use of his large nasal capacity and see what he could sniff out.

After a Sherlock Holmes hunt we found what Ian Firth and I had found last December. It had been very welcome then. No shedmaster to bar the way this time. D.S. was strangely eager to visit this "shed" and he fairly bustled his way in. I whispered to him that he could put "Humphreys" down under what he had put down for 5A Crewe North. D.S. had been well trained by me and he did not stupidly ask for a "fish supper" and invite puzzled looks from the staff. Instead he correctly said our English brethren way and asked for "fish and chips". The dish was shoveled into a greaseproof paper bag and laid in an ungentlemanly way onto an old newspaper! This was our carryout. None of your nicely wrapped up fish suppers like we get back home in grand old Scotland.

We did not approve of the unhygienic habits down here! We could accept this as we walked out with our fish and chips both one and four pence (seven new pence) the poorer. This was a lot cheaper than the normal two and threepence (eleven new pence) charged in "dear" old Scotland. (Sorry about the pun)! D.S. admitted not surprisingly that he thought that our last stop at Crewe had been the best. D.S. put stomach first, kip second and rail-roving around sheds a poor third. One thing was certain "Humphreys" fish and chips had not deteriorated since last December. They were still as good as ever. In Scotland all the chip shops seemed to be Italian owned so we found "Humphreys" to be a curious name.

I told D.S. that it had been about time that we had fish and chips. Don't want you catching scurvy or showing signs of vitamin deficiency now, I warned. D.S. thought for a minute and said "You may laugh but it's not good doing a hard day's work on an empty stomach." D.S. gave a snort and delved into the remains of his fish supper. It was safe to use the term fish supper now as we were out of English earshot.

We successfully dawdled along the road when I noticed that we had only ten minutes to blast off for Shrewsbury time. I told D.S. to get a move on. No dice he said his feet were killing him. These blasted army surplus boots again. I "ordered" him to be on the correct platform for Shrewsbury in ten minutes or else he would be left behind. I ran ahead to the station to get our bags from the left luggage.

After a hard run I secured the bags and heavy lifted them to the platform, jumped on to the train and secured a seat. With three minutes to spare old faithful D.S. came rolling along and dawdled up. At least he wasn't late as usual and we would thus have no repetition of the

Cardiff General fiasco where we narrowly missed our train with catastrophic consequences. We had made it! Not that missing it this time would have been too much of a problem as shed visiting had finished for the day as it was getting dark and we could always have got a later train to Shrewsbury.

Our train was the 20.25 for Hereford. It was a semi-fast. We would, of course, be getting off at Shrewsbury. A Brush Type 4 was at the head of our train. We would pick up the number on arrival at Shrewsbury.

We found ourselves a cosy compartment and made ourselves at home. I glanced absentmindedly at a sixpence (2.5 new pence) which I had secured out of my change. I hadn't been getting my usual pint of milk a day on this tour. Come to think of it I hadn't had a glass of milk since early on Saturday morning. Can't go on like this or I'll run down like D.S. I remembered something good about the platform. I glanced at my watch. There was half a minute to blast off. Plenty time. I bade farewell to a flabbergasted D.S., sped out of the platform and jumped out of the train.

A stout BR bench stood in front of my objective. Nothing daunted, I showed off by leaping over it in 3000 metres steeplechase style. Must be fitter than I thought I was. I ascertained that the machine was working and inserted my sixpence. I was duly rewarded for my troubles when I picked up the carton of milk that had dropped to the bottom of the machine. With another leap over the bench I made my way back to our train. D.S. thought he would get one too but the engine driver kindly started up the diesel engine and he was stopped in his tracks. I assured D.S. that I would enjoy my milk but that if he was a good boy I might leave him a few dregs.

On our way out of Crewe Station we passed by 5B Crewe South and took the Shrewsbury line. We noted:-

CREWE STATION late WEDNESDAY EVENING						
		Home shed		Built	Withdrawn	Scrap
Diesels						
LMS 0-6-0 Shunter 1939						
12009		5B	Crewe South	Nov-1939	Sep-1967	
Total	1					
Electrics						
A.E.I. (British Thomson-Houston) AL1 Bo-Bo 1959						
E3013		LMW	London Midl. West. Lines	Dec-1960		
Total	1					
English Electric AL3 Bo-Bo 1960						
E3033		LMW	London Midl. West. Lines	Dec-1960		
Total	1					
BR A.E.I.(B.T.H.) motors AL5 Bo-Bo 1960						
E3060		LMW	London Midl. West. Lines	Jul-1961		
Total	1					
Steam				Built	Withdrawn	Scrap
BR Standard 2MT 2-6-0 Doncaster 1953						
78030		5B	Crewe South	Sep-1954	Oct-1965	Dec-1965
Total	1					
On Station/Line	5	Kops	3			
Steam	1	Diesels	1 Electrics		3	
		Home Area		2	Visitors	3
Shed	5B	2	LMW	3		
Distribution						
Steam Classes	1					
Steam Origin	BR	1				

E3033 and E3060 were on the station. On Crewe South yard we saw 78030 and 12009 while E3013 darted by on the main line. Goodbye Crewe till tomorrow. Time for a wash and brush up before a night on a platform bench or waiting room I thought. I spent an enterprising quarter of an hour trying to have a bath in a BR wash hand basin a foot square! You should try it sometime. I guarantee you'll never forget it. I peered out of the "keek" hole in the toilet as the train stopped and feared that this was Shrewsbury. However, thankfully it was only Whitchurch. We were still about twenty minutes away from Shrewsbury.

The last ten minutes of our journey was spent in the compartment watching the fields go by in the gathering darkness. This line, like the Bletchley-Bedford line and the Workington – Carlisle line provided a nadir of interest. It was a dead line. We saw nothing. Nothing saw us.

I was glad that our tedious journey was brought to a welcome halt when we barged into Shrewsbury on time at 21.04. We hopped out to note the Brush Type 4 at the head of our train. It was D1756 of Cardiff Canton. We had seen her at 5A Crewe North earlier today warming up and getting ready to leave the shed.

			Schedule	Actual		Miles
Depart	CREWE		20.25	20.25		0
Arrive	SHREWSBURY		21.04	21.04		32½

Reasonably fast timing with one intermediate stop. I never realised that Shrewsbury was so near to Crewe. I had imagined Shrewsbury as being in the middle of the Welsh mountains, although in fact this traditional "Welsh" town is in Shropshire, England. Shrewsbury turned out to be a delightful station. The station was so busy our tour lasted ten minutes.

SHREWSBURY STATION WEDNESDAY EVENING							
			Home shed		Built	Withdrawn	Scrap
Diesels							
Brush Type 4 Co-Co 1962							
D1652			87E	Landore	Feb-1965		
D1717			81A	Old Oak Common	Feb-1964		
D1756	hauled	on Crewe N	86A	Cardiff Canton	Aug-1964		
Total	3						
Steam					Built	Withdrawn	Scrap
Collett 5MT 4900 4-6-0 "Hall" 1928							
6930	"Aldersley Hall"		2D	Banbury	Nov-41	Oct-65	Feb-66
Total	1						
Collett 5MT 7800 4-6-0 "Manor" 1938							
7812	"Erlestoke Manor"		6D	Shrewsbury	Jan-1939	Nov-1965	saved
7828	"Odney Manor"		6D	Shrewsbury	Dec-1950	Oct-1965	saved
Total	2						
Stanier 5MT 4-6-0 "Black Five" 1934							
45184			6A	Chester Midland	Sep-1935	Sep-1965	Jan-1966
Total	1						
BR Standard 5MT 4-6-0 Doncaster 1951							
73038			6D	Shrewsbury (ex 5E)	Sep-1953	Sep-1965	May-1966
Total	1						
On Station	8		Kops		6		
Steam	5		Diesels		3		
		Home Area			4	Visitors	4
Shed	6D	3	6A		1	2D	1
Distribution:-	81A	1	86A		1	87E	1
Steam Classes	3						
Steam Origin	GWR	3	LMS		1	BR	1
Station Highlight:-							
(missing number!)	7828	2A	"Odney Manor"		6D	Shrewsbury	

Steamwise the station was superb with one "Hall" and two "Manors" on show together with a Black 5 and a Standard 5. How we saw "Odney Manor" was an odd story. D.S. and I had already noted 7812"Erlestoke Manor" and we found another of the class scuttling around. However, this curious "Manor" provided us with a perplexing problem. There was one alarming problem about it. She had no number!!! The brass numberplates and nameplates were, of course, removed. However, there was no stenciled painted number on the cabside. D.S. had a brainstorm and ran up to the cab and asked the driver what the loco's number was. D.S. was shocked at the driver's reply "Sorry son, I don't know. My job's to drive the loco." I was in hysterical laughter at the driver's reply. We were no nearer to solving our mystery though.

And how did we solve the same problem at Barry? Answer: - we looked at the center of the wheels. However, it was getting a bit too dark for peering at centerpieces and how do you tell the driver to move his engine for us so we could get down onto the line to read the center wheel. Just not on.

Our last chance was to give the engine one last look over. Lo and behold! We found the number chalked on the tender in the tiniest of recognisable numbers. The scrawled number was 7828! All's well that ends well as a playwright called William Shakespeare wrote (or I think he did)! *6930 "Aldersley Hall" was to suffer an ignominious death in October 1965 being cut up at 2D Banbury by Friswells.*

The time was now 21.15 and over an hour since D.S. had had his fish supper. D.S. suggested having his second supper in the BR cafeteria. Our friend D.S. was always interested in his stomach. No point in arguing with him now as shed visits were over for the day as it was now dark. Inside the cafeteria I had a light supper. That was composed of a standard BR tea and a sandwich. Naturally D.S. had more to eat than me. Over our meal I outlined to D.S. two possible revised plans, which could be enacted tomorrow.

	PLAN A				
	Do 6D Shrewsbury				
Depart	SHREWSBURY	05.31			
Arrive	WREXHAM	06.26			
	Do 6C Croes Newydd				
Depart	WREXHAM	07.28			
Arrive	CHESTER GENERAL	07.55			
	Do 6A Chester Midland				
	Do 6B Mold Junction				

After that we have to meet our Burton boys at 14.30 to do our additional visit of the tour i.e. Crewe Works. Other sheds which we would do later or earlier in the day would be 8E Northwich, 5E Nuneaton and 5D Stoke. We should have plenty of time to do them now that we have kissed goodbye to Sheffield, Staveley, Doncaster and the Leeds area. D.S. asked why and I asked him if he didn't remember that we swapped them for Crewe Works. A minute's thought and D.S. vaguely remembered us discussing the possibilities in the cafeteria at Birmingham Snow Hill station earlier in the day.

I then told D.S. that Plan A would necessitate a night in the station here at Shrewsbury. I reckoned that we would have to be up at 4.30 to do the shed then catch the 05.31 to Wrexham. At this D.S. was really hurt. I thought you said that we would be in no great hurry tomorrow D.S. said. Why get up at 04.30? Let's have something later.

I then set out Plan B

	PLAN B				
	Do 6D Shrewsbury				
Depart	SHREWSBURY	07.40			
Arrive	WREXHAM	08.28			
	Do 6C Croes Newydd				
Depart	WREXHAM	10.40			
Arrive	CHESTER GENERAL	11.08			
	Do 6A Chester Midland				
	Do 6B Mold Junction				

This would necessitate a 6.30 reveille but we would arrive more than a couple of hours later than in Plan A at Chester Midland but as the Wrexham to Chester connection was so poor we might get the bus to save a bit of time. D.S. was all ears at the "long lie" to 06.30 and he said that he much preferred that to the 04.30 reveille. I reluctantly agreed much preferring Plan A and an early start at first light. We, however, should be able to recover from the later 06.30 start as we should have bags of time for the day after our revised plan for tomorrow. In the original timetable tomorrow was our tightest timings. Not now!

6F Machynlleth was far too remote a shed to consider visiting. Machynlleth was somewhere on the way from Shrewsbury to the University town of Aberystwyth on the west Wales coast. Surprisingly, the line had a good service and a very early morning option would have been as follows!

				Miles
Depart	SHREWSBURY	04.10		0
Arrive	MACHYNLLETH	06.19		61
	Do 6f Machynlleth			
Depart	MACHYNLLETH	06.30		0
Arrive	SHREWSBURY	08.26		61

	6F MACHYNLLETH			
Steam				
Collett 3MT 2251 0-6-0 1930				
2236	*2268*	*3208*		
Total	0			
Ivatt 2MT 2-6-0 1946				
46446	**46521**			
Total	2			
BR Standard 4MT 4-6-0 Brighton 1951				
75002	**75004**	**75013**	**75028**	
75055				
Total	5			
BR Standard 4MT 2-6-4T Doncaster 1953				
80097	*80098*	*80099*	*80101*	
80104	*80105*			
Total	0			
Grand Total	7			
Recently		*Surviving*		
Withdrawn	9	*Steam Classes*	2	
Saw at Barry Docks				
revisited Aug-70	5			
Steam	*Aug-50*	53	*Mar-59*	47
Allocation	*Apr-65*	13	*Aug-65*	7
	Closed to Steam:-		*Dec-66*	
	Saw elsewhere on tour(4)			

Eleven minutes at 6F Machynlleth would not have been a long time but achievable as the shed was at the station. However, 6F Machynlleth now had a very small allocation and hence the four plus hours round trip was never seriously entertained.

D.S. was in a talkative mood and he suggested spending the night at Shrewsbury Youth Hostel in a comfy bed and not in a hard bench in a waiting room here. He had a point. There was a Youth Hostel here in Shrewsbury. We could sneak out early in the morning at 06.30 just as we **had** intended to do at Leamington Spa Youth Hostel. The obliging warden at Leamington gave us permission to do that. Of course we slept in and we couldn't afford the luxury of sleeping in again. The warden here will probably be as obliging as he was. OK, I decided, we spend the night at Shrewsbury Youth Hostel and leave it at 06.30 tomorrow morning. We had better get a move on as it is now 21.40 and we don't want to get locked out now. With these hastening words we quickly vacated the cafeteria and Shrewsbury station.

Now where was the hostel? As usual we didn't know. Did our YHA Handbook provide us with any illuminating information on its position? It said that the hostel was 30 minutes walk from the station – very unilluminating. It also said "Opposite Lord Hill's Column. 10 minutes walk from English Bridge. (Do not confuse with Welsh Bridge it said!). OK we won't. At junction of London Road and Warwick Road – where were they? O.S. Map 118 (do not confuse with a D.S. map which will get you nowhere). A footnote said Midland red S4 and S5 to The Column every 20 minutes. That was more helpful!

Outside the station D.S. and I were left with a puzzle. What was the road to The Column? Quick thinking D.S. with kip beckoning saw a pub and said he would ask in there. He ordered me to wait outside as I was under age at 16. Old D.S. was certainly of age. He duly hauled a Shrewsburyian out of the pub who kindly directed us on our way.

I noted on our walk how old world and medieval was Shrewsbury. The main street was tortuous with steep gradients and wasn't what the Ministry of Transport would have approved of. After a short ten minute walk we arrived at the local bus stop and waited on a S4 or S5 bus to The Column. It was now 21.50 and our handbook said that the frequency of the bus service was every twenty minutes. I hoped there was one due soon or we might find the shutters up when we arrived at the Youth Hostel.

I noted a GPO across the road and got a 3d (1 new pence) stamp from the machine. I had better send at least one postcard home or the "Flying Squad" might be sent out to look for two missing persons,

We were out of luck with the bus times and did not get one until 22.10. Apparently we had just missed a bus when we had arrived at the stop. We asked our conductor to let us off at the Youth Hostel at The Column. He asked if they would let us in at this time of night. I told him they had better as the doors closed at 22.30.

THE WICKED WARDEN AFFAIR
Or how D.S. and I got trapped until 09.30

We arrived at The Column and had no difficulty in finding our way to Woodlands Youth Hostel. We walked boldly into reception and D.S. enjoyed himself greatly by giving the warden's bell a vicious thump with his fist.

The warden came waddling through. I put him down in my notebook as a chap of about fifty-five. Retired sergeant major forces type I thought and he was soon to prove it. "Rather late aren't you." was his opening charge, D.S. was anxious to get into his good books (after having attacked his bell) and gave a broad cheesy smile and he said in his best Scottish slang "We've had a busy and terrible day."

The warden wasn't impressed at this Scottish upstart and asked for our cards. He immediately took offence to D.S.'s temporary membership card and D.S. spent a few anxious minutes explaining how he came by it.

He asked if we had sleeping bags. We said yes. He asked to inspect them. Mine failed as it was not up to the (or his) stringent YHA regulations. It cost me one shilling and six pence (7.5 new pence) to hire a YHA one for the night. D.S.'s sleeping bag all quilted and fly-fronted almost passed his inspection but the warden made him hire a pillow slip for the night to go with it. This cost D.S. the princely sum of six pence (2.5 new pence). Right extortionist we've got here I thought. To add fuel to the fire he even had the audacity to charge us for staying the night at his "wonderful" hostel. D.S. as a junior member paid four shillings (20 new pence) and I as a juvenile paid half a crown – two shillings and six pence (12.5 new pence).

That seemed to be everything now but the warden wasn't finished yet. "Are you walkers?" he queried. Well we weren't cyclists and youth hostellers traveling by motorized equipment e.g. cars were frowned upon to put it mildly by the YHA. My answer was longer than no – "Yes".

"I see you were at Leamington last night" (he had looked at the stamp on our hostel cards). "Quite a travel for you today." Then he added quickly "How did you get here. Did you fly in?"

No comment! Wardens little joke (perhaps not).

I had almost forgotten to ask the warden about one matter.
ME "Can we leave early in the morning before 7.30 as we have a busy day ahead of us tomorrow." Perhaps I should have said long as walkers could never be busy.

WARDEN "You can leave when your duties are done. Breakfast is at 8.30. You will be assigned your duties **after** (with emphasis) breakfast. Goodnight your dormitory is Room 2." and swiftly left reception.

No *** comment. You and your wonderful hostels D.S. How do we get out now at 06.30? Break our way out of this Parkhurst type prison? D.S. was not to be outdone and he quickly produced a master plan. "Easy" he said "Leave the hostel as planned at 06.30". "The warden's hardly likely to be guarding over the door at that hour. We'll be away from the hostel before he knows we've gone. It's an enormous hostel it says men and women 100 in the handbook. He might never miss us."

A remarkably good plan from D.S. However, there was one problem. The warden had our YHA cards so if we broke out we couldn't stay in another youth hostel this trip and we would certainly be chucked out of the YHA for our early exit (as our officious warden would certainly report us). D.S. was hopeful of another YHA stay with a better result and I was a little wary of a life ban from the YHA. So rather regretfully we decided not to chance it particularly as tomorrow would be a relatively quiet day.

What a wonderful, thoughtful, considerate, welcoming warden we came across here. Just the kind to drive hostellers to the top of Ben Nevis up the path and take a short cut down the non recommended way over the sheer precipice. One could then meditate on the futility of youth hostelling with wicked warden's to welcome them on the short journey down until you hit the ground. For the interested the short journey down the 4406 feet should take the square root of 2203 divided by 8 if my mathematics are correct. From the answer to this equation you can find out how long your meditation will last. After you have hit the ground you'll have forgotten about wicked wardens forever. Try it!

And I thought wardens were there to help us. Ideas can suddenly change. We were now trapped, imprisoned in this cage of misery until 09.00 tomorrow morning at least.

We went upstairs to the dormitory and nabbed two bunks (D.S. on the top bunk and me on the bottom bunk). Across from us a chap was fondly turning over the pages of his Ian Allan Locomotives Combined Volume. D.S. got talking to this railwayist. We gathered that he had been to the Birmingham area looking for the unnamed "Britannia" 70047. He had been unsuccessful. We told him that we had seen her earlier today at 2E Saltley. We advised him that she had looked pretty dead at the time and that she might therefore be there for a few days. D.S. also told him of Crewe Works Open Day tomorrow. That was news to him.

There was little chance of us sleeping in tomorrow as we would be getting up for 08.30 with the rest of the "incarcerated inmates". We would now have the luxury of another long lie. This would certainly **not** happen again to us. This would certainly be the last Youth Hostel, which we would stay in on this tour. There would be no repetition of tonight's fiasco.

Review of the Day

This was the original timetable:-

DAY 5	**WEDNESDAY AUGUST 4TH 1965**	LMR DAY 4
		MILES
Depart BIRMINGHAM NEW STREET	06.06	0
Arrive BESCOT	06.29	9¼
Do 2F Bescot (25 mins. approx)		Recovery Time + 3
Depart BESCOT	06.57	0
Arrive BIRMINGHAM NEW STREET	07.24	9¼
Depart BIRMINGHAM NEW STREET	07.30	0
Arrive RUGBY MIDLAND	08.23	30¼
Do 1F Rugby (30 mins. approx)		Recovery Time + 30
Depart RUGBY MIDLAND	09.23	0
Arrive NUNEATON TRENT VALLEY	09.40	14½
Do 5E Nuneaton (35 mins. approx)		Recovery Time + 30

Depart NUNEATON TRENT VALLEY	10.45	14½
Arrive STAFFORD	11.18	<u>51</u>

See 5C Stafford - North West

Depart STAFFORD	11.25	0
Arrive STOKE-ON-TRENT	11.47	<u>16¼</u>

Do 5D Stoke (50 mins. approx)
Do Cockshute Diesel Depot (40 mins. approx)   Recovery Time
- 2

Depart STOKE-ON-TRENT	13.15	0
Arrive CREWE	13.41	<u>14¾</u>

See ex 5E Alsager - South East   8½

Do Crewe Station
Do ex 5A Crewe North
Do 5B Crewe South
Do 5A Crewe Diesel Depot

Depart CREWE	15.17	0
Arrive WOLVERHAMPTON HIGH LEVEL	16.08	<u>39¾</u>

Journey: -
See 5C Stafford - north west	24½
See ex 2K Bushbury - 1½ miles north east	38½

Do 2B Oxley (80 mins. approx)   Recovery Time
+ 3

Depart WOLVERHAMPTON HIGH LEVEL	17.14	0
Arrive SHREWSBURY	18.23	29¾

Do 6D Shrewsbury (65 mins. approx)   Recovery Time
+ 12

Buffet Car

Depart SHREWSBURY	19.40	29¾
Arrive WREXHAM GENERAL	20.27	60

Do 6C Croes Newydd (45 mins. approx)   Recovery Time
+ 73

Buffet Car

Depart WREXHAM GENERAL	22.25	60
Arrive CHESTER GENERAL	22.52	<u>72¼</u>

Restaurant Car

Night: -   Chester Waiting Room

Comments:-

Only 1 hour 36 minutes at Crewe. Therefore Electric Depot and Crewe Works are out.
Anyway they would be hard to get round.

During one of our journeys today I read with interest the small print on my Railrover ticket.
The small print told us of a few lines outside the LMR which we could travel on free of
charge. I was aware that we could travel from Nottingham, Manchester and Chesterfield to
Sheffield (Eastern region) free of charge. This had been instrumental in including Sheffield in
our original timetable. Sadly we no longer had time to visit it with tomorrow's reschedule,
which had resulted in Sheffield being scrapped from the tour.

Of very much interest was the free line from Bicester to Oxford (Western Region). Oxford
was easily the best steam shed left on the Western Region and had "Halls" especially and
"Granges" galore. Certainly the prospect of free access to Oxford would have put it down on
our tour timetable. We could have fitted it in somewhere just like we should have included
85A Worcester and 85B Gloucester. Pity I hadn't this information about Oxford's free
access a few weeks ago and then I could have done something about its inclusion. I
definitely regretted missing it now. It was and is a terrific **steam** shed. This is how our day
panned out:-

		Schedule	Actual
Depart	LEAMINGTON SPA GENERAL	09.00	09.00
Arrive	TYSELEY	09.38	09.38
	Do 2A Tyseley		
Depart	TYSELEY	Bus	
Arrive	BIRMINGHAM		
		Schedule	Actual
Depart	BIRMINGHAM NEW STREET	11.05	11.14
Arrive	BESCOT	11.28	11.35
	Do 2F Bescot		
		Schedule	Actual
Depart	BESCOT	12.38	12.38
Arrive	ASTON	12.54	12.54
	Do 2J Aston		
		Schedule	Actual
Depart	ASTON	13.34	13.34
Arrive	VAUXHALL AND DUDDESTON	13.40	13.40
	Do 2E Saltley		
		Schedule	Actual
Depart	VAUXHALL AND DUDDESTON	14.40	14.40
Arrive	BIRMINGHAM NEW STREET	14.47	14.47
		Schedule	Actual
Depart	BIRMINGHAM SNOW HILL	15.22	15.25
Arrive	WOLVERHAMPTON LOW LEVEL	15.40	15.44
	Do 2B Oxley		
		Schedule	Actual
Depart	WOLVERHAMPTON HIGH LEVEL	17.23	17.34
Arrive	STAFFORD	17.42	17.51
Arrive	CREWE	18.17	18.21
	Do 5B Crewe South		
	Do Crewe North		
	Do Crewe Diesel		
		Schedule	Actual
Depart	CREWE	20.25	20.25
Arrive	SHREWSBURY	21.04	21.04

Our day started badly (through our unplanned sleep-in at the youth hostel) and the first M.P.D. was not visited until 09.30. Once we did get started we made the most of what we could. The revised timetable had some wasted time in waiting for connections but overall it was certainly the best available. We did 2A Tyseley, 2J Aston, 2F Bescot and 2E Saltley smoothly enough and then connected comfortably enough for Wolverhampton (2B Oxley) and finally an efficient visit to Crewe and its three sheds (ex-5A Crewe North, 5B Crewe South and the new 5A Crewe Diesel).

One thing that struck me about the Birmingham Area was the number of times that we were asked for our permits:-

2A Tyseley – met the SHEDMASTER
2B Oxley   - met the SHEDMASTER (on way out luckily!)
2D Banbury – met a foreman
2E Saltley - met FIVE railway officials (including shedmasters)
2F Bescot – ushered into the shedmaster's office
2J Aston - met the shedmaster

Rather a security conscious area. Wouldn't like to visit any of them without a permit!

Of the original timetable for today we had failed to visit 1F Rugby (probably now closed to steam and easy to miss out in the revised timetable), 5D Stoke, 5E Nuneaton, 6C Croes Newydd and 6D Shrewsbury so overall it had been a pretty good recovery particularly after the late start.

Here we were now at Shrewsbury Youth Hostel. It had been too late and too dark for us to visit 6D Shrewsbury when we arrived. We would do it first thing in the morning. That is assuming we could escape from this youth hostel "prison".

In all today started and ended disastrously. It had started badly with an unscheduled late start and now our wicked warden had inflicted the sentence of imprisonment here until 09.00 at least. He had made sure that tomorrow would be another late start. He had thus effectively cut short our visits for tomorrow.

A dissertation on opportunity cost

One thing was certain we would start on time back on the original timetable on Friday morning in Manchester. Therefore tomorrow would have to be a dusting up day doing all the available sheds outside Liverpool and Manchester (including Crewe Works). After a good five minutes thought on tomorrow's timetable I worked it out roughly. Our order of visits would be 6D Shrewsbury followed by 6C Croes Newydd (Wrexham), 6B Mold Junction, 6A Chester Midland, Crewe Works (a highlight indeed), 5D Stoke and finally 5E Nuneaton. Omitted by necessity would be the steam shed of 8E Northwich. According to my allocations book Northwich had two 3MT BR 2-6-0's and 14 "Big Eights". Not a bad small shed but unfortunately it could no longer be fitted into the revised timetable with tomorrow's enforced late start.

We had in effect swapped Sheffield, Staveley, Leeds area and Doncaster for Crewe Works. On paper it seemed a lot to forego and on the face of it Crewe Works had an enormous opportunity cost. See Lipsey "An Introduction to Positive Economics" for a definition of opportunity cost. However, in my own words it is simply not what you did do in the time but what you could have done but didn't do. Understand it? Then you understand my point and the dissertation was worthwhile. However, the opportunity cost is not as high as it seems because on the original timetable we would already have done 5E Nuneaton, 5D Stoke, 6C Croes Newydd, 6D Shrewsbury. This was not the case and if we reverted to the original timetable tomorrow these sheds would have to be missed out.

Alternatively, if we did the "missing sheds" first omitting Crewe Works we would have very little time to do much of Sheffield, Staveley, Doncaster and Leeds. Tomorrow's enforced late start would have made matters even worse. In all, Crewe Works now was a possible straight swap with Sheffield and Staveley. Only Staveley was steam so an easy decision to make. In cost terms the swap didn't amount to much because we could travel on the Manchester Piccadilly-Sheffield Victoria and the Sheffield to Chesterfield line for free.

What did we actually see today?

Despite all the hiccups of the late start we still managed a productive day seeing importantly 282 steam, 115 diesels and 17 electrics. Eight sheds were visited one of which (Crewe Diesel) was diesel only.

DAY 5 LEAMINGTON SPA, BIRMINGHAM, WOLVERHAMPTON, CREWE to SHREWSBURY ARRIVAL

Code	Visits	GWR	SR	LMS	LNER	WD	BR	Steam Total	Diesel Total	Electric Total	Grand Total
	Leamington to Tyseley						1	1	2		3
2A	Tyseley	23		2			7	32	10		42
	Birmingham New Street							0	2		2
	New Street to Bescot			8			1	9	5		14
2F	Bescot			23		1	4	28	1		29
	Bescot Station			4				4	2		6
	Bescot to Aston			5				5	1		6
2J	Aston			10			1	11	5		16
2E	Saltley	3		12			14	29	20		49
	Saltley to New Street			2				2	2		4
	Birmingham Snow Hill	2					1	3	4		7
	Snow Hill to Wolverhampton	4		1				5	5		10
2B	Oxley	24		9			6	39	7		46
	Wolverhampton to Crewe			1				1	7	2	10
	Crewe Station Arrival			9				9	3	11	23
5A	Crewe Diesel							0	23		23
5B	Crewe South	3		60		1	23	87	3		90
5A	Crewe Station II			2				2	2	1	5
5A	Crewe North			4			5	9	7		16
	Crewe Station Depart						1	1	1	3	5
	Shrewsbury Station	3		1			1	5	3		8
		62		**153**		**2**	**65**	**282**	**115**	**17**	**414**
	REWIND 12th Dec 1964										
5A	Crewe Diesel 121264								7		7
5B	Crewe South 121264	1		47			10	58	3		61
5A	Crewe North 121264			23			3	26	6		32
		1		**70**			**13**	**84**	**16**	**0**	**100**

Tomorrow would be another day and I had better take advantage of a good long sleep in a comfortable YHA bed. I had better make the most of it, as the next two nights would be spent in cold BR waiting rooms at Manchester Victoria and Liverpool Central respectively. It was now 23.30 and I had better get some shut-eye, shut-eye, shut-eye--

END OF DAY FIVE

Some steam analyses follow:-

390

ENGINE CLASSES STEAM ACTIVE ON SHED DAY 5	BR total	2A Tyseley	2B Oxley	2E Saltley	2F Bescot	2J Aston	5A Crewe N	5B Crewe S	Total DAY 5
Collett 5MT 4900 4-6-0 "Hall" 1928									
4900-4999, 5900-5999, 6900-6958	258	2	3						5
Hawksworth 5MT 6959 4-6-0 "Modified Hall" 1944									
6959-6999, 7900-7929	71	3							3
Collett 4MT 5101 2-6-2T 1929 rebuild of Churchward 3100 Class 1903									
4100-4179; 5101-5110; 5150-99	140	1	4	1					6
Collett 5MT 5600 0-6-2T 1924									
5600-5699	100	1							1
1927 dev. of Collett 5MT 5600 0-6-2T 1924									
6600-6699	100	4							4
1933 dev. of Collett 3F 5700 0-6-0PT 1929									
3600-3799, 4600-4699, 8700, 8750-8799, 9	523	1	9	1					11
Collett 5MT 6800 4-6-0 "Grange" 1936									
6800-6879	80	5	5					1	11
Collett 5MT 7800 4-6-0 "Manor" 1938									
7800-7829	30		1	1				2	4
Stanier 5MT 2-6-0 1933									
42945-84	40		2						2
Ivatt 4MT 2-6-0 1947									
43000-43161	162						1	5	6
Midland 4F 0-6-0 1924									
44027-44606	580				2				2
Stanier 5MT 4-6-0 "Black Five" 1934									
44658-45499	842	1	4	4	5	6	2	17	39
Ivatt 2MT 2-6-0 1946									
46400-46527	128	1			3	1		2	7
Midland 3F "Jinty" 0-6-0T 1924 dev. of Johnson 1899 design									
47260-47681	417		0		1			7	8
Stanier 8F 2-8-0 "Big Eight" 1935									
48000-48775	666		1	7	11	1	1	17	38
BR Standard 7P6F 4-6-2 "Britannia" Derby 1951									
70000-70054	55		1	2			3	9	15
BR Standard 5MT 4-6-0 Doncaster 1951									
73000-73171	172	1	3	3				4	11
BR Standard 4MT 4-6-0 Brighton 1951									
75000-75079	80	1						1	2
BR Standard 4MT 2-6-0 Doncaster 1953									
76000-76114	115	1	1	1	3	1		1	8
BR Standard 2MT 2-6-0 Doncaster 1953									
78000-78064	65		1				1	2	4
Riddles WD 8F 2-8-0 "Austerity" 1943									
90000-90732	733				0			1	1
BR Standard 9F 2-10-0 Brighton 1954									
92000-92250	251	4		8	1		1	5	19
		26	**35**	**28**	**26**	**9**	**9**	**74**	**207**

ENGINE CLASSES
STEAM WITHDRAWN DAY 5

ENGINE CLASSES	BR total	2A Tyseley	2B Oxley	2E Saltley	2F Bescot	2J Aston	5A Crewe Nth	5B Crewe Sth	Total DAY 5
Collett 4MT 5101 2-6-2T 1929 rebuild of Churchward 3100 Class 1903									
4100-4179; 5101-5110; 5150-99	140	2							2
Collett 5MT 5600 0-6-2T 1924									
5600-5699	100	1							1
1933 dev. of Collett 3F 5700 0-6-0PT 1929									
3600-3799, 4600-4699, 8700, 8750-8799, 9600-9682, 9711-9799	523		1						1
Collett 5MT 6800 4-6-0 "Grange" 1936									
6800-6879	80	2	1						3
Collett 4MT 8100 2-6-2T 1938									
8100-8109	10	1							1
Fairburn 4MT 2-6-4T 1945 dev. of Stanier 1935									
42050-42299, 42673-42699	277					2			2
Stanier 4MT 2-6-4T 1935 dev of Fowler 1927									
42425-42672	243		1						1
Stanier 5MT 4-6-0 "Black Five" 1934									
44658-45499	842							5	5
Midland 3F "Jinty" 0-6-0T 1924 dev. of Johnson 1899 design									
47260-47681	417		1					1	2
Stanier 8F 2-8-0 "Big Eight" 1935									
48000-48775	666			1	1			6	8
BR Standard 2MT 2-6-0 Doncaster 1953									
78000-78064	65							1	1
Riddles WD 8F 2-8-0 "Austerity" 1943									
90000-90732	733				1				1
		6	4	1	2	2	0	13	28

ENGINE CLASSES — STEAM OFF SHED DAY 5

Class	Serial nos.	BR total	leamingt to tyseley	new street to bescot	bescot station	bescot to aston	saltley to new str	birmingh snow hill to new str	snow hill to wolv	wolverh to crewe arrival	crewe to crewe arrival	crewe station 2	crewe departure station	shrewsb departure station	Grand Total
Collett 5MT 4900 4-6-0 "Hall" 1928	4900-4999, 5900-5999, 6900-6958	258							1		1				2
Collett 4MT 5101 2-6-2T 1929 rebuild of Churchward 3100 Class 1903	4100-4179; 5101-5110; 5150-99	140						3							3
Collett 5MT 6800 4-6-0 "Grange" 1936	6800-6879	80							1						1
Collett 5MT 7800 4-6-0 "Manor" 1938	7800-7829	30							1					2	3
Ivatt 4MT 2-6-0 1947	43000-43161	162			1										1
Stanier 5MT 4-6-0 "Black Five" 1934	44658-45499	842		5	1	1	2			1		2	1	1	14
Ivatt 2MT 2-6-0 1946	46400-46527	128			1	1									2
Midland 3F "Jinty" 0-6-0T 1924 dev. of Johnson 1899 design	47260-47681	417									4				4
Stanier 8F 2-8-0 "Big Eight" 1935	48000-48775	666		4		3			1		4				12
BR Standard 5MT 4-6-0 Doncaster 1951	73000-73171	172	1						1					1	3
BR Standard 4MT 2-6-0 Doncaster 1953	76000-76114	115			1										1
BR Standard 2MT 2-6-0 Doncaster 1953	78000-78064	65												1	1
Total			1	9	4	5	2	3	5	1	9	2	1	5	47

DAY 5 STEAM SUMMARY TOTALS

Engine Class	Off Shed DAY 5	On Shed DAY 5	Withdrawn DAY 5	Grand Totals
Collett 5MT 4900 4-6-0 "Hall" 1928	2	5		7
Hawksworth 5MT 6959 4-6-0 "Modified Hall" 1944		3		3
Collett 4MT 5101 2-6-2T 1929 rebuild of Churchward 3100 Class 1903	3	6	2	11
Collett 5MT 5600 0-6-2T 1924		1	1	2
1927 dev. of Collett 5MT 5600 0-6-2T 1924		4		4
1933 dev. of Collett 3F 5700 0-6-0PT 1929		11	1	12
Collett 5MT 6800 4-6-0 "Grange" 1936	1	11	3	15
Collett 5MT 7800 4-6-0 "Manor" 1938	3	4		7
Collett 4MT 8100 2-6-2T 1938			1	1
Fairburn 4MT 2-6-4T 1945 dev. of Stanier 1935			2	2
Stanier 4MT 2-6-4T 1935 dev of Fowler 1927			1	1
Stanier 5MT 2-6-0 1933		2		2
Ivatt 4MT 2-6-0 1947		6	1	7
Midland 4F 0-6-0 1924		2		2
Stanier 5MT 4-6-0 "Black Five" 1934	14	39	5	58
Ivatt 2MT 2-6-0 1946	2	7		9
Midland 3F "Jinty" 0-6-0T 1924 dev. of Johnson 1899 design	4	8	2	14
Stanier 8F 2-8-0 "Big Eight" 1935	12	38	8	58
BR Standard 7P6F 4-6-2 "Britannia" Derby 1951		15		15
BR Standard 5MT 4-6-0 Doncaster 1951	3	11		14
BR Standard 4MT 4-6-0 Brighton 1951		2		2
BR Standard 4MT 2-6-0 Doncaster 1953	1	8		9
BR Standard 2MT 2-6-0 Doncaster 1953	1	4	1	6
Riddles WD 8F 2-8-0 "Austerity" 1943	1	1		2
BR Standard 9F 2-10-0 Brighton 1954		12		12
BR Standard 9F 2-10-0 Brighton 1954. 1957 double chimney		6		6
BR Standard 9F 2-10-0 Brighton 1954. 1955 Crosti boiler		1		1
	47	207	28	282

STEAM CREWE REWIND DECEMBER 1964

ENGINE CLASSES	BR total	5A Crewe Nth	5A Crewe Nth	5B Crewe Sth	5B Crewe Sth	Total Active Crewe Dec-64	Total Withdrawn Crewe Dec-64	Crewe station and approaches Dec-64	Grand Total Crewe Dec-64
Collett 5MT 6800 4-6-0 "Grange" 1936									
6800-6879	80			1		1			1
Ivatt 2MT 2-6-2T 1946									
41200-41329	130							1	1
Stanier 4MT 2-6-4T 1935 dev of Fowler 1927									
42425-42672	243	1	1	1		2	1	2	5
Hughes/Fowler 5MT 2-6-0 "Crab" 1926									
42700-42944	245	1				1			1
Stanier 5MT 2-6-0 1933									
42945-84	40			3		3			3
Ivatt 4MT 2-6-0 1947									
43000-43161	162			1		1			1
Midland 4F 0-6-0 1924									
44027-44606	580			4		4			4
Stanier 5MT 4-6-0 "Black Five" 1934									
44658-45499	842	12		14		26		4	30
Stanier 6P5F 4-6-0 "Jubilee" 1934									
45552-45734/7-42	189	1	4	1	1	2	5	1	8
Stanier 8P 4-6-2 "Coronation" 1937									
46220-57	38				2		2		2
Ivatt 2MT 2-6-0 1946									
46400-46527	128			1		1			1
Midland 3F "Jinty" 0-6-0T 1924 dev. of Johnson 1899 design									
47260-47681	417	1	1	7		8	1	1	10
Stanier 8F 2-8-0 "Big Eight" 1935									
48000-48775	666	1		12		13			13
BR Standard 7P6F 4-6-2 "Britannia" Derby 1951									
70000-70054	55	2		1		3			3
BR Standard 2MT 2-6-0 Doncaster 1953									
78000-78064	65			4		4			4
BR Standard 4MT 2-6-4T Doncaster 1953									
80000-80154	155				2	0	2		2
BR Standard 9F 2-10-0 Brighton 1954									
92000-92250 except	176	1		2		3			3
BR Standard 9F 2-10-0 Brighton 1954. 1957 double chimney									
92000-1; 92006; 92079; 92165-7; 92178; 92183-9249	75			1		1			1
		20	6	53	5	73	11	9	93

Part Six

THURSDAY 5th AUGUST 1965

The Tour continues

Shrewsbury, Wrexham, Chester, Crewe Works, Stoke, Nuneaton and Manchester Arrival

Or the day we caught up on the timetable

Or the day of the enforced long lie

Reveille: Shrewsbury Youth Hostel

THE D.S. MEETS THE THING EPISODE

I awoke at around ten to eight. I noted a few other hostellers stirring in their bunks. Doubtless, one lazy hosteller (D.S.) above me would be still asleep. It's about time he was up. I hope that he will be vibrant, keen and eager for today's shed hunt. I decided that it was time that I would wake him up with a grab.

D.S., however, was far from asleep and our roving camera picked him up lying in his bunk with sleep filled eyes gazing blankly ahead. He was just about half awake and probably contemplating on what he could have for breakfast. D.S. watched fascinated and intrigued as he saw the head of one forefinger appeared at the edge of his bunk. He got slightly worried when four other fingers quickly joined the scouting forefinger. D.S. looked frantically around and noted that none of the other hostellers were yet awake. Only a few were stirring in their bunks. He was alone with this "thing" from the supernatural, from the outer limits, from the twilight zone. A palm slowly emerged behind the fingers. What was this bare hand which was groping at the covers of his bed? By now D.S. was a near hospital case as the hand moved slowly but surely over to him at the centre of the bed. Trapped in his bed like a straightjacket he felt vulnerable and unable to protect himself from this evil hand. D.S. felt a cold sweat break out over him and began to feel his hair bristle at their roots. Any second now, the hand would pounce and grab him. Must get help, must get help ---- the words spun round in his tormented mind.

The air was filled by a sudden, long, heart-rending scream like that of some beast in pain. Horrified at the noise I instantly recoiled my arm. D.S. amazed saw the thing disappear and breathed a deep sigh of relief. I must have imagined it he thought and turned over to go back to sleep. The other hostellers had all been awakened by D.S.'s scream, a strange reveille. With me they all looked in the direction of the panic stricken call from D.S.'s bed. D.S. was oblivious to the commotion he had caused and was trying to sleep off his "nightmare". The other hostellers shook their heads in disbelief and wondered if they had imagined the scream. Others were sure that it had come from D.S. and put it down to him having a bad dream.

I waited for another ten minutes for the air to clear and then got out of bed, dressed and woke D.S. up with a good shake. After D.S. got dressed I asked him if he remembered screaming the place down. D.S. looked shocked and related to me of a horrific dream he had of a hand crawling all over him. I told him that it was fact not fiction. I had tried to waken him up from the bottom bunk!!!

Downstairs the warden asked if we wanted breakfast. More time wasted I thought and before D.S. could hungrily say yes I said no. "Cooking your own then" the warden said and he disappeared.

That'll be right I murmured wanting to get the hell out of this hostel as soon as possible. I asked the second in hand when we could get our duties. He said that we'd have to wait until the warden had finished his breakfast. Thanks a million. We would be waiting for the warden as usual.

We visited the hostel store to rustle up some breakfast and found the hostel second in command again in charge. Breakfast was oblong and cost 7 pence (3 new pence). We each had a Mars bar. I told D.S. to take heed of the wrapper. It said a Mars a day helps you work, rest and play. As long as you can work, work, work at walking fast the 7 pence will have been well worth it. I noted the primitive English habit of outside toilets with disgust. We are more civilised back home in Scotland.

Breakfast was disposed off quite quickly and the warden lined us up in true army fashion and assigned us our duties. I was ordered to sweep out our dormitory and fold up the sheets. D.S. was ordered to peel the spuds for tonight's supper.

Up in the dormitory I had an enthralling time complying with the warden's instructions. D.S. would be busy with the knife elsewhere. After about five minutes the warden came upstairs and inspected the dorm. He took offence to my style of sweeping up and asked if I played cricket. He thought that I would be put to better use as an opening batsman rather than as a sweeper-up. With these comments he quickly departed from the scene. Trust the Tatar to mention England's unmentionable game of cricket. I never was much good at it. Shows how poor a judge the warden was of a cricketer.

After another few minutes scratching the brush about the floor and tossing sheets about I made my way back downstairs to reception and reported mission accomplished. I was surprised to find that D.S. already had finished his spuds peeling. He must be a bit of an expert! D.S. pointed out an LMR timetable in the rack and we scoffed that a manual of motorised transport in a youth hostel must be a blue book like "Fanny Hill". D.S. said that they probably have it here because the warden knows that you'll be so sick of hostelling after staying here and that you'll want the first train home. I availed myself of the LMR timetable and quickly made up a revised timetable for today. This was done without undue difficulty.

In a moving and touching ceremony we queued up outside the warden's office. When we reached our turn the warden asked if he could have his property back. He did not want D.S. walking off with his pillow-slip or me marching off with an YHA sleeping bag. The handover ceremonial over I got myself one of his fancy coloured postcards of Shrewsbury for five pence (two new pence). D.S. had seen the chaps in front paying one shilling and sixpence (7.5 new pence) each and walking off with a lunch packet. D.S. put out his hand for one of the bags and said "I'll have one of these". The warden was quick to stop him and told him that you had to order your lunch packet the previous evening if you wanted one. Naughty D.S. had had his knuckles rapped. Finally, we got our YHA cards back and we were out of this wretched Shrewsbury jail. It was now 09.30. We were three hours late thanks to the wicked warden.

Luckily for us Shrewsbury Motive Power Depot (on the east side of the Hereford line south of Shrewsbury station) was close to the hostel. In less than ten minutes we were at the shed entrance. This time we had no trouble with shedmasters. The shed seemed pretty lifeless as we made our way round.

Shrewsbury shed was a rather cosmopolitan shed with ex GWR, ex LMS and BR locos. D.S. and I finished the shed without mishap and we were on our way out when we noticed two Brush Type 4's up the outside of the shed facing the main line. I went back to them to note them down while D.S. sat down and had one of his usual rests.

6D SHREWSBURY						
		Home shed		Built	Withdrawn	Scrap
Diesels						
Brush Type 4 Co-Co 1962						
D1650		87E	Landore	Jan-1965		
D1672	"Collossus"	86A	Cardiff Canton	Apr-1965		
D1677		86A	Cardiff Canton	May-1965		
Total	3					

Steam				Built	Withdrawn	Scrap
Collett 5MT 7800 4-6-0 "Manor" 1938						
7801	"Anthony Manor"	6D		*Jan-1938*	*Jul-1965*	*Jan-1966*
7802	"Bradley Manor"	6D	*to Barry Docks*	*Jan-1938*	*Nov-1965*	*saved*
7822	"Foxcote Manor"	6D	*to Barry Docks*	*Dec-1950*	*Nov-1965*	*saved*
Total	3					
1933 dev. of Collett 3F 5700 0-6-0PT 1929						
9657		6D		*Nov-1946*	*Apr-1966*	*Jul-1966*
Total	1					
Ivatt 2MT 2-6-2T 1946						
41209		6D		*Dec-1946*	*Jul-1965*	*Oct-1965*
Total	1					
Stanier 5MT 4-6-0 "Black Five" 1934						
44779		8B	Warrington (ex 8F)	*Jul-1947*	*Dec-1966*	*Jul-1967*
Total	1					
Ivatt 2MT 2-6-0 1946						
46508		6C	Croes Newydd (ex 1A)	*Dec-1952*	*Dec-1966*	*Dec-1967*
Total	1					
Stanier 8F 2-8-0 "Big Eight" 1935						
48335		2F	Bescot	*Nov-1943*	*Apr-1968*	*Jul-1968*
48418		6D		*Nov-1943*	*Sep-1966*	*Feb-1967*
48436		6D		*Apr-1944*	*Feb-1967*	*Mar-1968*
Total	3					
BR Standard 5MT 4-6-0 Doncaster 1951						
73036		6D		*Sep-1953*	*Sep-1965*	*Dec-1965*
73067		6D		*Oct-1954*	*Apr-1968*	*Jun-1968*
73095		6D		*Nov-1955*	*Sep-1966*	*Jan-1967*
73167		6D		*Apr-1957*	*Aug-1965*	*Oct-1965*
Total	4					
BR Standard 4MT 4-6-0 Brighton 1951						
75004		6F	Machynlleth	*Aug-1951*	*Mar-1967*	*Aug-1967*
Total	1					
BR Standard 4MT 2-6-4T Doncaster 1953						
80048		6D		*Oct-1952*	*Jul-1965*	*Apr-1966*
80072	*to Barry Docks*	6D	ex 2L Leamington	*Nov-1953*	*Jul-1965*	*saved*
80078	*to Barry Docks*	6C	Croes Newydd	*Feb-1954*	*Jul-1965*	*saved*
80079	*to Barry Docks*	6C	Croes Newydd	*Mar-1954*	*Jul-1965*	*saved*
80080	*to Barry Docks*	6C	Croes Newydd	*Mar-1954*	*Jul-1965*	*saved*
80100	*to Barry Docks*	6D		*Jan-1955*	*Jul-1965*	*saved*
80135	*to Barry Docks*	6D		*Apr-1956*	*Jul-1965*	*saved*
80136	*to Barry Docks*	6D		*May-1956*	*Jul-1965*	*saved*
Total	8					
BR Standard 2MT 2-6-2T Derby 1953						
84000		6C	Croes Newydd	*Jul-1953*	*Nov-1965*	*Apr-1966*
84004		6C	Croes Newydd	*Aug-1953*	*Nov-1965*	*Jun-1966*
Total	2					

On Shed	28	Kops	25	
Steam	25	Diesels	3	
Withdrawn	10			

Home Locos		16	Home Area		7	Visitors	5
Shed	6D		16	6C	6	6F	1
Distribution	2F		1	8B	1		
	86A		2	87E	1		

Steam classes on view		10					
Steam Origin		LMS	6	GWR	4	BR	15

Shed Highlights:-

	Steam	7801	"Anthony Manor"		6D	Shrewsbury
		84000	6C	Croes Newydd		

Steam	**Aug-50**	120	**Mar-59**	105	**Apr-65**	45
Allocation					**Aug-65**	33
			Closed to Steam:-		**Mar-67**	

6D SHREWSBURY (continued)							
Home Steam	excluding recently withdrawn locos						
On/Off Shed	On Shed	9	Off Shed	24	% On Shed	27%	
Not on Shed							
3F 5700 0-6-0PT 1933					3709	3754	2
"Manors"		7812		7819	7827	7828	4
Ivatt 2MT 2-6-0 1946		46510		46511	46512	46519	4
"Big Eights"					48404	48471	2
BR 5MT 4-6-0 1951	73000	73025		73034	73038	73050	
					73070	73090	7
BR 4MT 4-6-0 1951	75014	75016		75038	75053	75063	5
						total	24
		saw elsewhere on tour				7	
		saw at Barry Docks revisited Aug 70				2	

Review and Appraisal of 6D Shrewsbury

The shed was on the east side of the Shrewsbury-Hereford line south of the station. Walking time was 25 minutes.

No wonder I thought that the shed was deadish when there were ten withdrawn locos on shed. Seeing the "Manors" was excellent. We had already seen 7802 "Bradley Manor" on 5B Crewe South last night. The "Manors" days at Shrewsbury would be numbered as they had lost their long time roster on the Cambrian coast Express to Aberystwyth. Standard 4's 75XXX were one of the main sources of power on the Shrewsbury – Aberystwyth line and one was on shed. Not surprisingly, she belonged to 6F Machynlleth. 7801 "Anthony Manor" was the oldest surviving "Manor" and here she lay withdrawn. A Pannier Tank was the only other example of ex-GWR motive power.

The BR Standard 4MT 8XXXX 2-6-4 Tanks had recently been withdrawn from the Wrexham and Shrewsbury area. Strange seeing such a large batch of withdrawn locos from the one class. Their smaller sisters of the 2MT 2-6-2T 84XXX class were more fortunate. They still were in running order and definitely not withdrawn. Seeing the founder member of the class: - 84000 was quite something. Both engines of the class belonged to nearby 6C Croes Newydd (Wrexham).

The Ivatt 2-6-2 Tanks were fast disappearing from the Chester Division. 41207 was one of the few remaining. Whereas the Ivatt 2-6-2 Tanks were fading from the scene the Ivatt 2-6-0 "Doodle Bugs" were strangely increasing in number in the area. 46508 had been a recent acquisition from 1A Willesden.

Shrewsbury had a sizeable whack of "Standard 5's" 4-6-0's and four were on shed (one withdrawn). A 2F Bescot "Big Eight" was the only real visitor on shed and that hardly raised our eyebrows. Of interest was a Standard 4MT 2-6-4 Tank (80072) which had been withdrawn at the closure of her shed 2L Leamington Spa. Strange seeing her lying here.

No surprise seeing Brush Type 4's on Shrewsbury. Several of them must pass through Shrewsbury station each day. One of them rather staggered us. D1672 was carrying the name "Colossus". We had heard of a few from D1660 onwards being named but did not know that the Western Region had been galloping on (unknown to us) with its Brush Type 4 naming. We could see it was official metal nameplates and not just another mock chalked on name which adorned some of the other steam locomotives.

What did we miss? The shed had been good enough but with all those withdrawn 8XXXX Tanks the balance had been somewhat upset. It had been strange that none of Shrewsbury's Standard Class 4 4-6-0's had been on shed. We had seen a 6F Machynlleth one. Nine Home Steam (27%) on shed and 24 off shed. A poor percentage. However, it was a weekday morning and a much later visit than originally envisaged. Three of the four missing "Manors" would be seen elsewhere on the tour.

On we go

After having noted the Brushes next to the main line we heard a thunderous roar and a "Hall" and a "Doodle Bug" clattered past double heading a semi-fast passenger.

SHREWSBURY SHED PASS						
		Home shed		Built	Withdrawn	Scrap
Steam						
Collett 5MT 4900 4-6-0 "Hall" 1928						
5992	"Horton Hall"	86B	Newport Ebbw Jct. (ex85B)	Dec-1939	Aug-1965	Oct-1965
Total	1					
Ivatt 2MT 2-6-0 1946						
46446		6F	Machynlleth	Mar-1950	Dec-1966	Sep-1967
Total	1					
On Line	2	Kops		2		
Steam	2	Diesels		0		
		Home Area	1	Visitors	1	
Shed	6F	1				
Distribution	86B	1				
Steam Classes	2					
Steam Origin	LMS	1	GWR	1		

A think back to the LMR timetable I had been looking at and this appeared to be the 09.25 from Crewe which left Shrewsbury at 10.10 and would arrive at Hereford at 11.02. It was now 10.12 and I said to D.S. "I believe that we had better hurry up as our train for Wrexham leaves Shrewsbury Station in eighteen minutes".

We did hurry. It's amazing what a Mars bar can do for poor old depreciating D.S. Certainly a good advert for Mars Limited of Slough. We did reach the station with a few minutes to spare. We had cut down the advertised walking time of 25 minutes down to 15 minutes. A remarkable achievement with D.S. Shows what he can do after some sustenance. On the way I popped my postcard into the G.P.O. and hopefully my parents would receive the following morning the perhaps surprising news that we were alive and well and going strongly on our tour.

Our means of transport to Wrexham turned out to be another diesel multiple unit or in our less illustrious terms another "bucket". Oddly enough our bucket left Shrewsbury on time. In and around the station we noted two BR diesel shunters.

SHREWSBURY STATION THURSDAY						
		Home shed		Built	Withdrawn	Scrap
Diesels						
BR 0-6-0 Shunter 1953						
D3193		6D	Shrewsbury	Nov-1955		
D3970		6D	Shrewsbury	Jun-1960		
Total	2					
On Station	2	Kops		2		
Steam	0	Diesels		2		
		Home Area	2	Visitors	0	
Shed Distribution	6D	2				

D.S. felt rather tired and promptly went to sleep. His exertions in getting to the station on time had taken a severe toll on his very limited resources of stamina.

On our thirty mile journey to Wrexham three southbound freights zipped past us (or rather me!). The sleeping D.S. was oblivious to all of this.

SHREWSBURY TO WREXHAM							
			Home shed		Built	Withdrawn	Scrap
Steam							
Stanier 5MT 4-6-0 "Black Five" 1934							
45031			6A	Chester Midland	Sep-1934	Jun-1967	Nov-1967
45231			6A	Chester Midland	Aug-1936	Aug-1968	saved
Total	2						
Stanier 8F 2-8-0 "Big Eight" 1935							
48122			6B	Mold Junction (ex 6D)	May-1939	Feb-1967	Aug-1967
Total	1						
On Journey	3		Kops		3		
Steam	3		Diesels		0		
		Home Area	1		Visitors	1	
Shed	6A	2	6B		1		
Distribution							
Steam Classes	2						
Steam Origin	LMS	3					

The stations we passed had queer names (possibly of Welsh origin?) like Oswestry, Chirk and Ruabon. Unexciting stops nevertheless. We rolled into Wrexham on time at 11.14.

		Schedule	Actual	Miles
Depart	SHREWSBURY	10.30	10.30	0
Arrive	WREXHAM GENERAL	11.14	11.14	30¼

Three intermediate stops with an average speed of around 40 miles per hour.

D.S. was rousted awake and we left the bucket. We obeyed the Loco Shed Directory and cut five minutes from the advertised walking time of fifteen minutes. We decided that the LSD's walking time must be a little generous particularly when its times seemed a bare minimum when D.S. was involved.

We succeeded, however, in taking the wrong road at a level crossing outside the shed. After a few paces we recognised that we were getting nowhere and decided to re read the LSD instructions. This time we went through the gate after (and not before) the level crossing and soon reached the shed.

6C Croes Newydd shed was in the triangle formed by the Ruabon-Wrexham-Brymbo line with the shed not visible from the main line with no passenger services on the other lines. This shed could therefore be termed "in the wilds." *A later inspection of the "Pre-Grouping Atlas and Gazetteer" showed Wrexham District to be riddled with little branch lines. I guessed that they must serve colliery branch lines. If you know any other use for the Wrexham branch lines please write it on a postcard and send it to this address.*

6C Croes Newydd shed seemed dead to us. D.S. and I noted all the workers sitting around a small fire in the open outside the roundhouse. Not a locomotive stirred. It might all be explained by the fact that the workers could have been taking a tea break or it could have been a local holiday or something.

Apart from a few glances the workers took little interest in us and allowed us to continue our business without mishap. We found the roundhouse to be rather empty but the dead line was more to our liking.

The Collett 3MT 0-6-0's had been withdrawn as a Class. The example here would probably be soon broken up so I jumped up into the cab of 2268 and posed for a photograph which D.S. kindly snapped.

After our sojourn over at the dead line we walked back over to the main shed. Surprise, surprise a Collett 5MT 0-6-2 Tank had started up and was about to take on water. At least there was now something moving in the shed and yard apart from us. The Collett Tank still had her brass numberplates on the cabside and also on the smokebox. Unusual that they hadn't been swiped or officially removed. For good measure she also had a 6C Croes Newydd shed plate. D.S. thought that she looked good and decided to snap her as well. The driver kindly hung on to the boiler railing at the side of the loco and posed for us. Another good photo to add to our collection!

6C CROES NEWYDD

		Home shed		Built	Withdrawn	Scrap
Steam						
Hawksworth 2F 1600 0-6-0PT 1949						
1628		6C		*Aug-1950*	*Sep-1966*	*Jan-1967*
1660		6C		*Feb-1955*	*Feb-1966*	*Jun-1966*
Total	2					
Collett 3MT 2251 0-6-0 1930						
2268	*D.S. photo*	6F	Machynlleth	*Jun-1930*	*May-1965*	*Feb-1966*
Total	1					
Collett dev.1938 of Churchward 8F 2800 2-8-0 1903						
3813		6C		*Sep-1939*	*Jul-1965*	*Dec-1965*
3855	*to Barry Docks*	6C		*Oct-1942*	*Aug-1965*	*saved*
Total	2					
Collett 5MT 5600 0-6-2T 1924						
5667		6C		*Jun-1926*	*Jul-1965*	*Oct-1965*
5676		6C		*Sep-1926*	*Nov-1965*	*May-1966*
Total	2					
1927 dev. of Collett 5MT 5600 0-6-2T 1924						
6604	*D.S. Photo*	6C		*Sep-1927*	*Oct-1965*	*Jan-1966*
6611		6C		*Sep-1927*	*Nov-1965*	*May-1966*
Total	2					
1933 dev. of Collett 3F 5700 0-6-0PT 1929						
3749		6C		*Oct-1937*	*Nov-1965*	*May-1966*
4645		6C		*Feb-1943*	*Nov-1965*	*May-1966*
9639		6C		*Feb-1946*	*Sep-1965*	*Nov-1965*
Total	3					
Hawksworth 5MT 6959 4-6-0 "Modified Hall" 1944						
6967	"Willesley Hall""	81F	Oxford	*Aug-1944*	*Dec-1965*	*May-1966*
Total	1					
BR Standard 5MT 4-6-0 Doncaster 1951						
73032		6C	(ex 5E Nuneaton)	*Jul-1953*	*Aug-1965*	*Nov-1965*
Total	1					
BR Standard 4MT 4-6-0 Brighton 1951						
75071		6C		*Oct-1955*	*Aug-1967*	*Feb-1968*
Total	1					
On Shed	15	Kops		15		
Steam	15	Diesels		0		
Withdrawn	3					
Home Locos	13	Home Area		1	Visitors	1
Shed Highlights:-		6C	13	6F	1	
Distribution:-		81F	1			
Steam Classes on View		9				
Steam Origination:-		LMS	0	GWR	13	BR	2
Shed Highlights:-						
	1628	6C		2F 1949 Hawksworth 1600 GWR 0-6-0PT		
	1660	6C		2F 1949 Hawksworth 1600 GWR 0-6-0PT		
	2268	6C		3MT 1930 Collett 2251 GWR 0-6-0		
Steam	**Aug-50**	54	**Mar-59**	41	**Apr-65**	38	**Aug-65**
Allocation					**Closed to Steam:-**		**Jun-67**

Home Steam	*excluding recently withdrawn locos*					
On/Off Shed	On Shed	11	Off Shed	23	% On Shed	32%
Not on Shed						
2F 1600 0-6-0PT 1949					1638	1
3F 5700 0-6-0PT 1933	3789	4683	9610	9630	9669	5
8F 2800 2-8-0 1938				3817	3850	2
5MT 5600 0-6-2T 1924					5677	1
5MT 5600 0-6-2T 1927				6626	6651	2
Ivatt 2MT 2-6-2T 1946					41241	1
Ivatt 2MT 2-6-0 1946					46508	1
"Big Eights"			48124	48325	48665	3
BR 5MT 4-6-0 1951				73004	73040	2
BR 4MT 4-6-0 1951			75009	75021	75029	3
BR 2MT 2-6-2T 1953				84000	84004	2
					total	23
	saw elsewhere on the tour			5		
	saw at Barry Docks revisited Aug 70			2		
	recently withdrawn not on shed nor seen			1		
	Collett 1938 8F 2800 2-8-0		3849	scrap	Aug-65	

A railwayman kindly poses for D.S. on 6604 a 1927 dev. of Collett 5MT 5600 0-6-2T 1924 sadly to be withdrawn just two months later.

The author poses for D.S. on 2268 a Collett 3MT 0-6-0 1930 withdrawn May 1965.

Review and Appraisal of 6C Croes Newydd

The shed was on the triangle formed by the Ruabon-Wrexham-Brymbo lines. Walking time was 15 minutes.

Rather disappointing to find so few on shed. However, all were good steam locos. The Hawksworth 0-6-0 Pannier Tanks were one of the last of the GWR designs before nationalisation. These interesting little 2F's were new to me although Scotland had two of them belonging to 60C Helmsdale up in the north for several years. They were 1646 and 1649.

The Churchward 2-8-0's could be termed as the GWR "Big Eights". Both examples on shed were withdrawn. The withdrawn Collett 0-6-0 was not a new class to us. We had seen one of her withdrawn sisters at 2D Banbury. Our example had arrived from isolated 6F Machynlleth. The shedmaster here was probably holding her while he awaited disposal instructions. We had met the Collett 0-6-2 tanks and the 0-6-0 Pannier tanks at a few other locations on our tour. Good to see them in such numbers.

It was wonderful seeing such a travelled visitor as the Modified Hall from 81F Oxford. Helps slightly from unfortunately omitting 81F Oxford from our tour. The two BR locos were 6C Croes Newydd based. Like Shrewsbury a disappointing 11 (32%) Home Steam on shed with 23 off shed. In all a bit disappointing on numbers on shed but a rather good shed of largely ex-GWR stock.

On we go

We wasted no time in getting back to Wrexham station. I glanced at my watch. It was 11.53. Twenty five minutes to go before blast off time. At 12.18 D.S. looked as though he had used up all the energy that his Mars bar could give him. D.S. now complained of malnutrition and of having had no breakfast. He pointed longingly to the BR cafeteria. We had got twenty five minutes he pleaded. He had a point there. I had always told him he could eat if there was nothing better to do.

Inside the cafeteria I noted that it was rather empty. A staff of two seemed to be one too many for Wrexham. I concluded that the cafeteria probably didn't do a roaring trade. The food was good but standard BR fare. We had the usual tiny tin of Chef soup in BR individual bowls – delightful. A sandwich or two, a jam tart and a cup of standard BR tea and our meal was complete. We gave the Gala fruit pies a miss this time. Refreshing and revitalised by our snack we were back on the platform in time for our train to Chester. This time we were not to travel in the usual bucket. A Brush Type 4 D1650 of 87E Landore rolled in at the head of our train. The reason for a Type 4 was that this was the first train of the day from London. It had left London Paddington station at 08.20.

The train was fairly busy and we snatched two empty seats in a compartment. Our journey proved fruitful enough. D.S. did remarkably well by staying awake for most of the journey. Most of the engines we saw were around Chester.

WREXHAM TO CHESTER				Built	Withdrawn	Scrap
	Home shed					
Diesels						
Brush Type 4 Co-Co 1962						
D1650	*hauled*	87E	Landore	*Jan-1965*		
Total	*1*					
LMS and BR 0-6-0 Shunter 1945						
12037		6A	Chester Midland	*Oct-1945*	*Oct-1968*	
12048		6A	Chester Midland	*Dec-1948*	*Jan-1969*	
12054		6A	Chester Midland	*May-1949*	*Jul-1970*	
Total	*3*					

Steam					Built	Withdrawn	Scrap
1933 dev. of Collett 3F 5700 0-6-0PT 1929							
3789			6C	Croes Newydd	Oct-1938	Oct-1965	Jan-1966
Total	1						
Ivatt 2MT 2-6-0 1946							
46457			2A	Tyseley (ex 2L)	May-1950	May-1967	Oct-1967
Total	1						
Stanier 8F 2-8-0 "Big Eight" 1935							
48090			6B	Mold Junction	Jan-1937	Apr-1968	Jul-1968
48741			9E	Trafford Park	Feb-1946	Oct-1967	Feb-1968
Total	2						
On Journey	8		Kops		6		
Steam	4		Diesels		4		
		Home Area		5	Visitors		3
Shed	6A	3	6B		1	6C	1
Distribution	2A	1					
	9E	1					
	87E	1					
Steam Classes		3					
Steam Origin	LMS	3	GWR		1		

Nearing Chester we got out into the corridor. An English woman asked us if we came from Scotland. Yes, we replied. She remarked that she thought that the sky was higher (or did she say lower?) in Scotland. I agreed to humour her and looked out of the window and up at the sky and wondered if it was any different in Scotland. Looked the same to me! After her remark about our Scottish traits I remarked on Chester's unique, circular horse racing track which we were now passing by. Nothing like it in Scotland. Chester racetrack was often called the "Circus Ring." Any horse running on it has to race round a continuous never ending bend1

We arrived at Chester Station on time at 12.46

		Schedule	Actual	Miles
Depart	WREXHAM GENERAL	12.18	12.18	0
Arrive	CHESTER	12.46	12.46	12¼

Average Speed: - rather slow – less than 30 m.p.h.

We dumped our bags in the left luggage and broke out into the open air. Chester had two sheds: - 6A Chester Midland and 6B Mold Junction. Mold Junction was out in the wilds three and a half miles west of Chester. It required a bus and then a sizeable walk to get there. 6A Chester Midland was 25 minutes walking time away according to the LSD. We had to be back for the 14.35 train to Crewe. There was no train before then so our proposed meeting with the Burton boys outside Crewe Works at 14.30 was definitely out. Two sheds in 1hr 55 minutes would be a bit steep (probably pretty impossible) in the time available. 6A Chester Midland would take us about an hour to do. 6B Mold Junction required a couple of buses and a half mile walk and would probably take a bit more than that. Therefore we had a straight choice. One would have to be missed. A consultation with my allocation notebook and I concluded that 6B Mold Junction was easily the best of the two. Besides we would pass by 6A Chester Midland on the way to Crewe. Yes, we would definitely visit 6B Mold Junction, however difficult it was to get there.

We boarded a No.1 (Saughall) bus outside the station and found our journey to be a short one. It took only a few minutes to get down City Road to Foregate Street. We were not yet at Mold Junction, however. Merely Stage 1 had been completed. Stage 2 entailed getting a

No.5 or a No.6 (Saltney-Ring Road) bus at Foregate Street. We were now confronted by the familiar problem of guessing which side of the road was the correct direction. So far our guesses had been somewhat uninspired. We had guessed wrongly at Netherfield after doing 40E Colwick on Monday. However, there a local yokel had sent us across to the correct side of the road and we thus avoided getting on the wrong bus. Then later that day we were not so lucky when there was the disaster at Treton Bole Hole as set out in the Epilogue of the Wrong Bus affair. That disaster cost us dearly and at least one shed was missed later on the day through the valuable lost minutes. So far we had guessed wrongly twice out of two decisions. This would not be a third. You've heard of third time lucky. This time there would be no need for any luck. I'll get my compass out. I didn't buy it for show. Mold Junction is west of Chester. We'll stand at the bus stop going westwards.

I unearthed my compass and released the safety catch. The needle swung round to deadlock position. Foregate Street ran approximately north to south. Our compass wasn't as helpful as we had hoped. After a little deliberation we chose the side of the street nearest to City Road. After waiting five minutes (and noting that a No.5 bus had passed us not going to the Ring Road we began to get a little uneasy. I asked the person next to us in the queue if this was the stop for Saltney and he delighted in re-directing us across the road to the other stop. Wrong again! Third time same as first and second time – unlucky!

After some minutes wait a Saltney-Ring Road bus duly arrived and we decided that we might as well get on it. Our three mile journey took about a quarter of an hour. As requested we were dumped off at Ring Road. We continued along the A55 main road to Mold for half a mile and then turned right along the Saltney to Queensferry Road B5129. After a ¼ mile walk we found the shed entrance on the left hand side just before the railway bridge. That little ¾ mile walk took us about twenty minutes.

We noted what we took to be the shedmaster playing about with some scrap outside the shed so I thought I had better ask him if we could go and visit his wonderful shed. After several angry and nasty letters about my timings being "too sharp or impossible" I had broken off diplomatic relations with the Liverpool (8 area) and Chester (6 area) divisions. Need I add that we were now permitless for both areas. The permit requests for both had been handled by the Liverpool Divisional Manager. To get back to our story "the shedmaster" chased us away as he was not in fact the shedmaster. Funny peculiar, he certainly looked like one although if I remember the foremen in the lookout offices at 5B Crewe South looked like shedmasters too. We gathered that the shedmaster was in the shed.

Inside the shed we began our tour. If we saw the shedmaster we would be expecting him. Sure enough, we reached the top of the first line and our friendly shedmaster was wandering about. I asked him if we could take a few photographs. That sounds better than asking to go round the shed. Makes us a rank above the normal number snatchers. Our shedmaster seemed interested in our photographic intentions and asked us what we wanted to snap. I told him that we would like to photo "Big Eights" and "Black 5's" especially. I didn't want to annoy the shedmaster by asking to photo classes which he didn't possess or would not be on shed. The shedmaster glanced round and was pleased to see good examples of "Big Eights" and "Black Fives" that we could photo. We thanked him and he went off and left us in his "studio". D.S. was in an ill-tempered mood after his walking exertions and didn't like to be told what to photograph. Just to be different D.S. walked up to the top of the shed yard and snapped an early LMS 0-6-0 Diesel Shunter on marshalling yard duty. D.S. had been intrigued by its motion and in particular its extra "floating" wheel. Certainly, its motion looked quaint and old fashioned (like the more modern but old fashioned wheel arrangement of the 1 Co-Co 1 English Electric Type 4's).

Back inside the shed a sentimental re-meeting took place when I came across my old friend 6819 "Highnam Grange" again. Apart from seeing in 1959 outside 66A Polmadie shed 3440

"City of Truro" (which had come up came up for the Scottish Industries Exhibition in Glasgow in 1959) she was the first ex GWR engine which I had seen. In our epic visit to Crewe last December Ian Firth and I noted her from 5B Crewe South shed standing in the distance where the ex GWR shed of Crewe Gresty Lane used to be. We asked a fellow enthusiast what the "Hall" was and we were informed that it was not a "Hall" but a "Grange" – 6819 "Highnam Grange" in fact. How ignorant we felt! We were to see no other ex GWR engine that day.

Fellow railwayists Neil Woodcock and Derek Newton had always told me rather high and mightily and full of pride that they had "Halls" named after their family names. I had told Neil Woodcock that he was only a "Modified" and that he was only a Hawksworth afterthought. Friend Newton in the "Hall" 5900 series had stronger claims to fame. He had an old country surname. I remember telling friends Woodcock and Newton that they had overlooked my surname "Dowie" in the list of "Halls". They retorted that I was having them on but they were wrong. The last "Modified Hall" built was certainly the best one. Hawksworth always left the best for last when it had such an imposing name as "Capel Dewi Hall". Friends Woodcock and Newton said it was spelt differently from my family name and only vaguely looked like it. However, "Dewi" as a Welsh name is pronounced as "Dowie". Some of you will remember the BBC's pronunciation by Cliff Morgan of Dewi Bebb the Welsh rugby player. Of course, he pronounced his name as "Dowie". In all, Dewi is merely the welsh name for "Dowie" I told them. Friends Woodcock and Newton reluctantly climbed down from their high horses and welcomed a fellow (but greater) nobleman as me!

Here endeth a question of birthright

To get back to the point of my dissertation you can gather that I was especially pleased to see my family "Hall" on shed – namely 6999 "Capel Dewi Hall." She had come all the way from 81F Oxford to come to see me and surprise me at the out of the way 6B Mold Junction of all places! Doubtless she had sprinted on the first Chester bound freight at Oxford when she had heard the sad and harrowing news that we had stupidly left out her home depot of Oxford on our travels. Her presence here certainly showed a fantastic sense of family loyalty. Come to think of it friends Woodcock and Newton had never seen their "Halls". By the end of 1963 both "Newton" and "Woodcock Halls" had been withdrawn and broken up. My other MMRS friends Iain and Alex Storie and David Archibald had not been graced with "Hall" names. After this great diatribe by me D.S. started to look anxiously around for "Simpson Hall" but no such "Hall" had ever existed. After some mild persuasion he agreed that "Capel Dewi Hall" was certainly the Dowie family "Hall".

12020 a LMS 0-6-0 Diesel Shunter 1939 on marshalling yard duties at 6B Mold Junction

6B MOLD JUNCTION

		Home shed		Built	Withdrawn	Scrap
Diesels						
LMS 0-6-0 Shunter 1939						
12020	*D.S. Photo*	6B		*Jun-1940*	*Nov-1967*	
Total	*1*					
Steam				**Built**	**Withdrawn**	**Scrap**
1933 dev. of Collett 3F 5700 0-6-0PT 1929						
9630		6C	Croes Newydd	*Dec-1945*	*Sep-1966*	*Dec-1966*
Total	*1*					
Collett 5MT 6800 4-6-0 "Grange" 1936						
6819	"Highnam Grange"	85A	Worcester	*Dec-1936*	*Nov-1965*	*Feb-1966*
Total	*1*					
Hawksworth 5MT 6959 4-6-0 "Modified Hall" 1944						
6999	"Capel Dewi Hall"	81F	Oxford	*Feb-1949*	*Dec-1965*	*May-1966*
Total	*1*					
Hughes/Fowler 5MT 2-6-0 "Crab" 1926						
42782		8H	Birkenhead	*Sep-1927*	*Dec-1966*	*Apr-1967*
Total	*1*					
Stanier 5MT 4-6-0 "Black Five" 1934						
44775		6B	(ex 2E Saltley)	*Jun-1947*	*Oct-1967*	*Mar-1968*
44779		8B	Warrington (ex 8F)	*Jul-1947*	*Dec-1966*	*Jul-1967*
44790		12A	Carlisle Kingmoor	*Jun-1947*	*Mar-1967*	*Nov-1967*
44800		6B		*May-1944*	*Mar-1968*	*Jun-1968*
45116		6B	(ex 6G Llandudno)	*May-1935*	*Jul-1967*	*Dec-1967*
45277		6B	(ex 6G Llandudno)	*Nov-1936*	*Feb-1967*	*May-1967*
Total	*6*					
Midland 3F "Jinty" 0-6-0T 1924 dev. of Johnson 1899 design						
47350		6B		*Jul-1926*	*Dec-1965*	*Feb-1966*
47598		6B	(ex 6G Llandudno)	*Nov-1928*	*Jul-1966*	*Oct-1967*
Total	*2*					
Stanier 8F 2-8-0 "Big Eight" 1935						
48120		6B	(ex 2B Oxley)	*May-1939*	*Jan-1966*	*Sep-1966*
48175		6B		*Aug-1943*	*Feb-1966*	*Jun-1966*
48259		6B		*Oct-1941*	*Jul-1965*	*Oct-1965*
48269		6B		*May-1942*	*Jul-1967*	*Dec-1967*
48287		6B		*Jul-1940*	*Jun-1967*	*May-1968*
48345		6B	(ex 6D Shrewsbury)	*Mar-1944*	*Mar-1968*	*Jul-1968*
48519		10A	Carnforth	*Sep-1944*	*Aug-1968*	*Jan-1969*
48697		6B	(ex 5D Stoke)	*Apr-1944*	*Dec-1967*	*Mar-1968*
48741		9E	Trafford Park	*Feb-1946*	*Oct-1967*	*Feb-1968*
48749		6B		*Aug-1946*	*Apr-1968*	*Jul-1968*
Total	*10*					
BR Standard 5MT 4-6-0 Doncaster 1951						
73127	*Caprotti valved*	9H	Patricroft	*Aug-1956*	*Oct-1967*	*Jul-1968*
Total	*1*					

On Shed	24	**Kops**	20		
Steam	23	**Diesels**	1		
Withdrawn	1				

Home Locos	15	Home Area		1	Visitors	8
Shed	6B	15	6C	1		
Distribution	8B	1	8H	1		
	9E	1	9F	1		
	10A	1	12A	1		
	81F	1	85A	1		
Steam classes on view		8				
Steam Origin	GWR		3 LMS		19 BR	1
Shed Highlights:-	6999		"Capel Dewi Hall"	81F	Oxford	

Steam	*Aug-50*	39	*Mar-59*	44	*Apr-65*	28
Allocation					*Aug-65*	39
			Closed to Steam:-		*Apr-66*	

6B MOLD JUNCTION (Continued)							
Home Steam	excluding withdrawn locos						
On/Off Shed	On Shed	13	Off Shed		26	% On Shed	33%
Not on Shed							
"Black Fives"	44762	44764	44842	44897	44917	44971	
	45042	45043	45237	45275	45325	45369	
						45395	13
"Jinty"						47673	1
"Big Eights"	48090	48094	48122	48253	48411	48427	
	48458	48632	48655	48656	48667	48723	12
						total	26
		saw elsewhere on the tour			4		
		saw on Dec 64 Manchester and Crewe trip			2		

Review and Appraisal of 6B Mold Junction

The shed was on the south side of the Chester-North Wales line by the closed Saltney Ferry Station.

A terrific little shed. Mold Junction was in sharp contrast to Shrewsbury and Croes Newydd by reason that there was only one withdrawn loco on shed. Croes Newydd and Shrewsbury gave me the impression of death while here there was a live, vibrant shed. We certainly made a very wise choice in going here and forgoing 6A Chester Midland.

Naturally seeing 6999"Capel Dewi Hall" was a tour highlight for me if not for D.S.! Renewing acquaintance with old friend "Highnam Grange" was good too. This time we saw her at close range and not from afar as was our lot at Crewe South last December. These two Collett examples certainly surprised us and made out visit really worthwhile. They were the only two Western Region engines on shed.

Another surprise (although only a minor one) was seeing a Croes Newydd 0-6-0 Pannier tank on shed. Seeing a "Crab" is pleasant enough and we noted a Birkenhead one on shed. We had previously noted one of her sisters 42765 of Birkenhead at 16C Derby of all places.

Of the Black Fives it was remarkable seeing a Carlisle one on shed and more remarkable that I had not seen her before. The Warrington Black 5 had been noted by me on my mini-Lancashire tour of July 1965. Of the Big Eights three raised the eyebrows. The first was a withdrawn Mold Junction one and the other two were visitors from Carnforth and Trafford Park respectively. These Patricroft Standard Class 5's fairly get around. We had noted examples on 2B Oxley and 2E Saltley yesterday and here was another example on shed. All three had Caprotti valve gear. The fast disappearing "Jinties" are a pleasant sight and D.S. would not forget his "floating wheeled" LMS 0-6-0 diesel shunter for a while.

What did we miss? I thought that there had been something lacking on Shrewsbury and Croes Newydd but this shed gave me that very satisfactory feeling of a well balanced shed with a few interesting visitors. However, I checked up my allocations book to see if the shed was really as full or as good as I thought it had been.

Very similar to 6C Croes Newydd and 6D Shrewsbury with 13(33%) Home Steam on shed and a further 26 off shed.

After all, this was a weekday and it is only to be expected that the Mold Junction "Big Eights" and "Black Fives" would be out on freight workings. One must always remember that engines are allocated to a shed not for show on shed but to dome some useful workings in their locality. I tend to forget that important fact when visiting a shed on a weekday and rather optimistically hope for a full allocation on shed and complain if most of the engines are working out. "Maximums" are exceedingly rare on Sundays and unknown on weekdays.

The larger the percentage of locos working out on a weekday shows the shed to be more efficient in using their locos to the full.

A few months back I had always imagined Mold Junction to be near the town of Mold. A consultation with the LSD and I found out that 6B Mold Junction is nearer Chester in fact. Several hundred yards after Mold Junction to the west the line did in fact diverge with one arm going along the North Wales main line while the other arm reached Mold and ultimately Denbigh. Hence the name Mold Junction.

6J Holyhead and 6G Llandudno Junction were never seriously entertained as sheds that we would visit on our Railrover.

Even utilising the "Irish Mail" it was a long way from Chester to Holyhead:-

				Miles
Depart	CHESTER GENERAL	12.02		0
Arrive	HOLYHEAD	13.42		84½

6J Holyhead had some good stuff:-

6J HOLYHEAD				
Steam				
Stanier 5MT 4-6-0 "Black Five" 1934				
	44711	44712	44770	44807
	44814	44821	44966	44981
	45132	45145	45223	45247
	45280	45298	45300	45345
	45447			
Total		17		
Midland 3F "Jinty" 0-6-0T 1924 dev. of Johnson 1899 design				
	47266	47321	47410	47439
Total		4		
BR Standard 7P6F 4-6-2 "Britannia" Derby 1951				
	70026	70042	70045	70046
	70047	70053		
Total		6		
BR Standard 4MT 4-6-0 Brighton 1951				
	75024	75052		
Total		2	*Surviving*	
Grand Total		29	**Steam Classes**	4
Saw Elsewhere			**Saw Manch Crewe trip**	
on the Tour		6	***Dec-64***	1
Saw Carlisle trip				
June 1967		3		
Steam	*Sep-50*		*Mar-59*	19
Allocation	*Apr-65*	15	*Aug-65*	29
	Closed to Steam:-		*Dec-66*	

29 steam was a good allocation swollen by the recent closure of 6H Bangor and had 17 "Black Fives" and 5 "Britannias."

The fast mail trains did not stop at Llandudno Junction so picking up 6G Llandudno Junction would have been a slow process:-

						Miles
Depart	HOLYHEAD		14.50			0
Arrive	LLANDUDNO JUNCTION		16.14			37¼
	Do 6G Llandudno Junction					
Depart	LLANDUDNO JUNCTION		17.10			37¼
Arrive	CHESTER GENERAL		18.31			84½

	6G LLANDUDNO JUNCTION				
Steam					
Ivatt 2MT 2-6-2T 1946					
41200	*41201*	**41232**	**41233**		
41272					
Total	3				
Stanier 5MT 4-6-0 "Black Five" 1934					
45004	**45045**	**45143**	**45149**		
45279	**45282**	**45285**	**45311**		
45348					
Total	9				
Midland 3F "Jinty" 0-6-0T 1924 dev. of Johnson 1899 design					
47361	**47507**				
Total	1				
BR Standard 2MT 2-6-2T Derby 1953					
84003	**84009**				
Total	2	*Surviving*			
Grand Total	15	*Steam Classes*	4		
Recently		**Saw Elsewhere**			
Withdrawn	3	**on the Tour**	1		
Saw Carlisle					
June 1967	1				
Steam	*Sep-50*	31	*Mar-59*	38	
Allocation	*Apr-65*	22	*Aug-65*	15	
	Closed to Steam:-		*Oct-66*		

6G Llandudno Junction now had a small allocation of 15 steam plus three recently withdrawn locos. Nine "Black Fives" were allocated and at the end of last year still had three "Jubilees" allocated namely 45567 "Southern Australia", 45595 "Southern Rhodesia" and 45689 "Ajax".

Ian "Froth" Firth and I had seen 45595 "Southern Rhodesia" in fine fettle at Crewe Station on 12th December 1964. Sadly all three "Jubilees" had been withdrawn some months ago.

So if we had chosen to visit 6J Holyhead and 6G Llandudno Junction it would have been a round trip from Chester of six and a half hours. Not surprisingly we didn't!

On we go

We left the shed and made out way slowly back along the B5129 road to the junction with the A55. "Another half mile to our bus at Ring Road" I remarked to D.S. He had suddenly changed from an unusually active self on arrival at the MPD to his usual tired self. The sun was beginning to roast his heavy army surplus boots and he was in low spirits. As luck would have it we didn't have to walk the half mile back to the bus stop. We found a bus stop at the junction of the B5189 and A55 roads. A notice of the bus times there showed a regular service to Chester. Good enough for us I thought. The quicker we get a bus the better for my timetable as D.S. was beginning to labour in his walk.

After a few minutes wait a bus breezed up. Inside the bus I found that I had used up all my small change and didn't want to inconvenience the conductor with a £1 note for a cheap journey. I asked D.S. to pay mine. He refused at first (the sun really must have got him down) and almost created a scene in the bus. At last he ill-tempered relented and reluctantly paid for my ticket as well as his. You'd think I had asked a total stranger to pay my fare by D.S.'s antics. D.S. must have imagined he wouldn't see his money again. D.S. had better get more sleep on the tour or he'll be having hallucinations next. The strain really was telling on him. Ian Firth's words of "Your eyes will get funny" would come true soon enough on D.S. if he wasn't careful. In fact D.S. was beginning to act as many a mad dog does on a hot summer's day. The dog's first symptoms are listlessness, and then they get testy and irritable. The third stage is that they start biting at everything in sight. The fourth stage is when they go mad and fifthly and lastly they are kindly shot by some policeman or humanely destroyed by an RSPCA official. D.S. certainly was close to or had reached the third stage and he would need careful watching to ensure that he didn't deteriorate further.

Here endeth the diagnosis on D.S.

The conductor informed us that the bus did not go anywhere near Chester Station. However, he said that he would drop us off in the main street and we could get a bus to the railway station from there. Our bus fairly rattled along the A55 and it certainly travelled the fastest of any bus that we had been on since our tour had started on Sunday.

True to his word the conductor let us off in the main street and we quickly found the bus stop for Chester station. However, there was an enormous queue in front of us and I doubted us getting on the next bus. It duly arrived and a stampede to get on it ensued. No holds were barred in the struggle to get on. Unfortunately for me I almost caused a riot by almost bumping a small old lady to the floor. She took offence at being pushed about and the crowd were not too happy either. I apologised and told her that I hadn't noticed here because she was so small. It was a cunning lie of course and she probably didn't believe my explanation but these quick words had prevented my possible arrest for breach of the peace. The result of this incident was that I had to smile through gritted teeth and let everybody else onto the bus before me. Luckily my fears about the bus being full up were groundless as there was still standing room inside. D.S. of course had managed to snatch a seat.

Inside the bus a grudging D.S. again paid my fare. I still had to break that £1 note. The reason for my over enthusiastic sally into the bus in the first place was that the clock was beginning to beat us. We had arrived at Chester at 12.46. It was now 14.20. Launching time for Crewe was 14.35. You can gather that I was a little uneasy about the chances of us catching the 14.35 train.

Our bus made reasonable time up busy Foregate Street and City road. We jumped off outside the station at 14.27 and bashed our way into it. Our only stop was at the left luggage where we collected our grips. With a few minutes to spare we reached the relevant platform and noted that we would be travelling in style again. A Brush Type 4 D1844 of 5A Crewe Diesel was at the head of our train. Our train was a through one from the North Wales coast.

When D.S. and I jumped on we were staggered to find it was packed. We walked up the train through every corridor and looked into every compartment. We came to the sad conclusion that there wasn't a seat left. In line with certain other unfortunates we put our grips down in the corridor and sat on them. It's as well that our journey is a short one. I didn't fancy this lark for one minute. More to the point why was the train packed? On a weekday too! It was unbelievable. The driver started up the Brush Type 4 and I ended my dissertation on this packed train.

I warned D.S. to stay awake as 6A Chester Midland came into view on the north side of the line. The shed duly arrived and it pleased me no end that apart from engines in the yard which we could see the interior of the shed looked rather empty. I didn't think that I would lose any sleep worrying about having to ditch 6A Chester Midland from our tour.

6A CHESTER MIDLAND (PASS)						
		Home shed		**Built**	**Withdrawn**	**Scrap**
Steam						
Collett 5MT 6800 4-6-0 "Grange" 1936						
6833	"Calcot Grange"	2B	Oxley	**Aug-1937**	**Oct-1965**	**Apr-1966**
Total	*1*					
Ivatt 2MT 2-6-2T 1946						
41220		6G	Llandudno Jct.(to 9B)	**Sep-1946**	**Nov-1966**	**Jun-1967**
Total	*1*					
Hughes/Fowler 5MT 2-6-0 "Crab" 1926						
42940		9B	Stockport Edgeley	**Dec-1932**	**Sep-1965**	**Dec-1965**
Total	*1*					
Stanier 5MT 4-6-0 "Black Five" 1934						
45044		6A		**Oct-1934**	**Oct-1966**	**Aug-1967**
45130		6A		**May-1935**	**Jan-1967**	**Mar-1968**
45300		6J	Holyhead	**Jan-1937**	**Dec-1965**	**Mar-1966**
Total	*3*					

On Shed	6	**Kops**	3		
Steam	6	**Diesels**	0		
Withdrawn	0				
Home Locos	2	**Home Area**	2	**Visitors**	2
Shed	6A	2 6G	1	6J	1
Distribution	2B	1			
	9B	1			
Steam Classes on View	4				
Steam Origin	GWR	1 LMS	5		
Shed Highlight:-	6833	"Calcot Grange"	2B Oxley		

Steam	**Aug-50**	38	**Mar-59**	46	**Apr-65**	29
Allocation					**Aug-65**	32
			Closed to Steam:-		**Jun-67**	
Home Steam	*excluding withdrawn locos*					
On/Off Shed	On Shed	2	Off Shed	30	% On Shed	6%
Not on Shed						
Fairbum 4MT 2-6-4T 1945	42224	42233	42236	42251	42252	
					42283	6
"Black Fives"	44913	45000	45031	45111	45184	
	45198	45231	45250	45305	45344	
	45353	45403	45419	45427	45429	
					45438	16
"Jinty"				47371	47389	2
BR 4MT 4-6-0 1951				75010	75012	2
BR 4MT 2-6-0 1953		76020	76035	76052	76095	4
					total	30
	saw elsewhere on the tour				7	
	recently withdrawn not on shed nor seen elsewhere				3	*scrap*
		Fairbum 4MT 2-6-4T 1945			42109	*Sep-65*
					42202	*Jul-65*
		Stanier 4MT 2-6-4T 1935			42477	*Jul-65*

Mini Review and Appraisal of 6A Chester Midland

The shed was on the north side of the Chester-Crewe line, east of Chester General Station. Walking time would have been 25 minutes.

Seeing the "Grange" was another unexpected and welcome surprise. She had evaded us at her home depot of 2B Oxley but we had caught up with her. The third "Black Five" was from 6J Holyhead. That was something good. The Ivatt 2-6-2 Tank from 6G Llandudno Junction was another surprise and explained by her recent transfer to 9B Stockport Edgeley and she was obviously stopping off en route to her new home at 9B Stockport Edgeley. A

Stockport Edgeley "Crab" completed the complement which we saw in the shed yard. In all, certainly was worth keeping the eyes open. Chester Midland although small in quantity was varied and interesting.

Like the other Chester Division sheds most of the allocation seemed to be off shed as the inside of the shed looked to be a bit deserted. We saw only 2 (6%) of the Home Steam on shed with no fewer than 30 off shed.

On we go

Our Brush Type 4 ambled through the Cheshire countryside playing with the easy schedule. The only landmark of interest was Christleton Tunnel before we passed by Waverton. Our journey to Crewe was otherwise unremarkable.

Nearing Crewe our eyes were glued on the north side of the line while we awaited the appearance of Crewe Works. It had a little shed of its own and had a sizeable allocation of locos in service there.

It was hardly worth writing the locos down as we would be visiting the Works as soon as we arrived but we did just the same. No harm in it, apart from wasting black ink from my Fybriter pen and a few lines of paper. It wasn't the best of views we had of the Works as it was hindered by several fixtures in the yard. However, we succeed in noting a few engines.

CW CREWE WORKS							
		Home shed			Built	Withdrawn	Scrap
Diesels							
BR North British 0-4-0 Shunter 1957							
D2711		CW			Apr-1961	Feb-1967	
D2743		CW			Mar-1959	Feb-1967	
Total	*2*						
Steam					Built	Withdrawn	Scrap
Midland 4F 0-6-0 1924							
44137		CW			Oct-1925	Feb-1965	Nov-1965
Total	*1*						
Midland 3F "Jinty" 0-6-0T 1924 dev. of 1899 design							
47494		5B	Crewe South		Feb-1928	Oct-1966	Feb-1967
47592		CW			Aug-1928	Mar-1966	Nov-1966
47646		CW			Feb-1929	Aug-1965	Dec-1965
Total	*3*						
On Yard	6	Kops		5			
Steam	4	Diesels		2			
Withdrawn	2						
Home Locos	5 Home Area			1	Visitors	0	
Shed							
Distribution	CW	5	5B	1			
Steam Classes	2						
Steam Origin	LMS	4					
Shed Highlight	44137	CW					
Steam	Aug-50	15	Mar-59	17	Apr-65	13	
Allocation					Aug-65	12	
			Closed to Steam:-		?		

415

		CW CREWE WORKS (Continued)					
Home Steam	excluding withdrawn locos						
On/Off Shed	On Shed	2	Off Shed		10	% On Shed	17%	
Not on Shed							
Midland 4F 0-6-0 1924					44405	44525	2
"Jinty"		47330	47384	47400	47505	47597	
				47615	47658	47661	8
						total	10
	recently withdrawn not seen on shed or seen elsewhere				1	scrap	
			Midland 4F 0-6-0 1924		44450	Sep-65	

Mini Review and Appraisal of CW Crewe Works

The Midland 0-6-0 had been withdrawn several months ago. They don't seem to send engines to the scrapbreakers as soon as they once did. One of the "Jinties" would also be withdrawn this month. The 5B Crewe South "Jinty" had somehow infiltrated the Works and would probably be sent back to Crewe South very soon. The North British 0-4-0 diesel shunters used to be all shedded in Scotland. Crewe Works had seven in all. Six of which I had noted previously in Scotland. The seventh was D2711 (formerly of 62B Dundee Tay Bridge). I had caught up with her here.

What did we miss? We had seen 2 (17%) of Home Steam from the train and had missed a further 10 of Home Steam. Hardly worth asking that as in ten minutes we would be going round Crewe Works and we should see all the engines allocated to the Works then. Frankly as none work out of the Works we should see all of them weekday or not!

		Schedule	Actual	Miles
Depart	CHESTER	14.35	14.35	0
Arrive	CREWE	15.06	15.06	21¼

On we go

We quickly hurried out of Crewe station and on to the road to the Works.

THE DECEMBER 1964 ATTEMPT

Ian Firth and I had a particularly poor time of things when we tried to visit Crewe Works last December. We first tried the Mill Street entrance and found it closed with a high iron gate barring entrance. Undaunted we tried the deviation entrance. Barring our way here was no closed gate instead there was a watchman about to brew himself some tea. He came out kettle in hand and refused us admittance. They didn't seem to take kindly to visitors at Crewe Works. The all the way from Scotland lark didn't cut much ice either. He said you can go all the way back then.

Rather daunted this time Ian Firth and I wandered round the perimeter and found what we took to be a third highly unofficial entrance to Crewe Works. We cautiously opened the door (chuffed at finding it unlocked) and peered inside. So far, all clear. We calmly closed the door and walked boldly on. Things happened quickly after that. We heard a muffled growl, a bark and an enormous Alsatian dog came bounding round the corner ready to give us a souvenir bite as a memento of our visit to Crewe Works. Ian Firth and I had never moved as quickly as we did then. There was a phenomenal burst of speed from us as we sharply turned back, a ghastly instant while we re-opened the door and another ghastly instant while we scrambled through to safety and just in time slammed the door shut in the face of the hungry animal. By the noise of the animal barking and scratching furiously at the door we decided that we were better here safe outside in the street rather than having to fight it in the Works. We reluctantly concluded that the third unofficial entrance was not for us.

On reflection we should have scaled the high iron gates outside the closed Mill Street entrance. However, it was raining elephants and hippos (rather than cats and dogs) so we were in no mood for climbing that day. Disconsolately we gave up and wandered back to Crewe Station.

BACK TO AUGUST 1965

"Meet the world's No.1 Idiot and it's neither D.S. nor me."

This time there should be no heroics necessary to get into Crewe Works. It was apparently Crewe Works Open Day and our Railrover had printed on it as plain as could be "VALID FOR ADVERTISED EXCURSION TRAINS". An excursion train run by BR from London to Crewe (with a visit to Crewe works thrown in) had arrived at Crewe a few hours before. We would say we were with them if anything awkward happened.

We reached the main Mill Street entrance after a brisk ten minute walk. I enquired at the office. "The BR party went in the deviation entrance. You had better go in there was the reply.

After another five minutes walk we were at the deviation entrance. I told D.S. that we would just walk in. However, we did not get very far because some little idiot who wore worker's overall and a worker's bonnet came out of the office to stop us.

LITTLE IDIOT (bespectacled) "You're not allowed in the Works."

ME "It's the open day at the Works."

LITTLE IDIOT "It's nothing of the sort." he squeaked.

D.S. and I sensed that somewhere in "its" phenomenally tiny mind it had stored an instant dislike for us. With good reason I felt annoyed. I knew it was the works open day whatever this "fly" would have us believe.

ME "We are with the British rail excursion from London to visit the Works."

If that doesn't cut much ice I don't know what will with this thing. I was in two minds whether to brush this "fly aside and find somebody more responsible inside the office to give us the all clear. That would mean more time wasted so I thought it would be best to stick it out here outside the office. I can try and humour this idiot.

LITTLE IDIOT "Lemme see your tickets." he growled.

The idiot took one glance at our Railrover tickets and said "Invalid, you have not got excursion tickets. You can't go round the Works".

Blind bugger he is. I'd better show him the lovely little print in black and white inside the Railrover which states valid on "ALL ADVERTISED EXCURSIONS." That will show the bum.

ME:- "See that (pointing to the relevant print on the Railrover). It's valid all right."

LITTLE IDIOT (looking disapprovingly at the Railrover). "No it's invalid. Put it away." he yelped.

If there's one thing I can't stand it's a bloody idiot who can't read bloody English. That was indeed the last straw. I'd sort him out.

I raised my arm to push him away and walk in but someone stopped me. It was not the railway cops but D.S. who grabbed my arm and held my wrist in a vice like grip. Doubtless, D.S. was visualising a night in Crewe jail if I struck him and also perforce caused the end of the tour.

D.S. "Come on, let's get away from here. It's not worth the effort."

LITTLE IDIOT "That's right. Go away before I lose my temper."

Ha Ha! The little idiot might lose HIS temper.

HERE ENDETH THE LITTLE IDIOT EPISODE
or
THE CATASTROPHE AT CREWE WORKS AFFAIR

We walked silently back down the road while I tried to cool down. Stopped from going round Crewe Works with a valid ticket by an ignorant, stupid, idiotic bastard.

We were about back at the other Mill Street entrance when we met a few boys going to do the Works. They had been on the excursion train but had done 5B Crewe South first and were now going to join the official BR train party inside the Works. Let's go back with them I said to D.S. If necessary we'll see some other official and not that stupid little idiot again. However, D.S. would have none of it. He said that he had had enough of Crewe Works for all time. D.S. didn't want to go back there again. He probably preferred hell to that. One thing about me is I hate to lose. Why I hadn't the willpower to leave D.S. behind and join the other boys in their Works visit was about the biggest mystery since the disappearance of the crew of the "Marie Celeste" or the appearance of 4,000 holes in Blackburn Lancashire as per the Beatles song. We thus trudged disconsolately back to Crewe Station.

Perchance dear reader you may find our flop at Crewe Works a rather comical failure when we had the correct entry pass (the Railrover ticket with excursion inclusions). We failed to show it to the right person and thus disastrously failed to get admittance.

We took our minds of the happenings of a few minutes ago by popping into a railway bookshop. D.S. bought a late 1963 combined volume (the one with the yellow cover) and said that he would re-sell it to Graham Strachan back home. I was pleased to see that I could buy for two shillings and sixpence (12.5 new pence) a copy of the July 1964 edition of "Modern Railways". When I was on my way to France on a school outing in late June 1964 I had stupidly left my copy on the boat train to Dover. Now my set of Modern Railways was complete from February 1964.

Back at Crewe Station I inquired about when we would get a train for Manchester after 22.43. The charming reply from the dishy girl on the enquiries counter was that the next train after that would be the 00.42 arriving at Manchester Piccadilly at 01.29. I informed D.S. that he'll be lucky if he gets a sleep in Manchester Victoria waiting room before 02.00 tomorrow morning. D.S. was not impressed and resolved to get some much needed sleep before then. I told him he would be lucky if he did.

Today had been a very light day (due to the Crewe Works detour) and now all we had time to do would be two more sheds:- 5D Stoke and 5E Nuneaton. I told D.S. that tomorrow and Saturday we would really need to keep moving. No more youth hostels for sure! D.S. warned that he would have to leave for home at about midday on Saturday. His miserly uncle boss gave him around £5 a week for working in his shop. On no account was D.S. allowed to take

Sunday off. He was expecting D.S. to be up at his shop early on Sunday morning for the Sunday papers. Poor D.S. was treated and paid as a slave by his uncle. Hopefully, D.S. would come to realise this, pull himself out of this dead-end job consigning in it to the "dark ages" in his formative years. D.S. is a good sort and deserves far better. It would be good if he could go and join a company who could offer him a well paid job commensurate with his electrical, mechanical and DIY talents. One could envisage him driving a British Relay van on his way to repair a TV set or something similar to that.

What did we miss at Crewe Works? We will never possibly know but after the event I saw the "Railway Observer" issue for September 1965 which reported the following engines on Crewe Works on Sunday 25th July 1965 (eleven days before our visit).

CW CREWE WORKS SUNDAY 25th JULY 1965

Steam				Electrics			
Stanier 5MT 4-6-0 "Black Five" 1934				EMI Bo-Bo 1950			
44673	44678	44679	44683	26026	26040	26046	
44853	44877	44910	44933	Total	3		
44963	45004	45065	45133	Main Line Electrics			
45190	45227	45242	45260	E3038	E3063	E3072	E3080
45282	45327	45395	45417	E3081	E3083	E3085	E3087
45435	45493			E3088	E3091	E3166	
Total	22			Total	11		
Stanier 6P5F 4-6-0 "Jubilee" 1934				Diesels			
45589	"Gwalior"			English Electric Type 4 1Co-Co1 1958			
Total	1			D 211	D 220	D 232	D 234
Stanier 8F 2-8-0 "Big Eight" 1935				D 245	D 251	D 270	D 284
48111	48116	48167	48322	D 290	D 294	D 295	D 312
48445	48474	48709	48727	D 319	D 330	D 333	D 346
48768				D 350	D 352	D 396	
Total	9			Total	19		
BR 7P6F "Britannia" 4-6-2 Derby 1951				Brush Type 4 Co-Co 1962			
70006	70007	70035		D1500	D1503	D1505	D1508
Total	3			D1512	D1516	D1518	D1530
BR 8P 4-6-2 Derby 1954				D1534	D1537	D1543	D1554
71000	"Duke of Gloucester".			D1569	D1577	D1581	D1590
Total	3			D1591	D1734	D1749	D1773
BR Standard 2-6-0 1954 3MT Swindon				D1794	D1804	D1842	D1855
77000				D1856	D1857	D1858	D1859
Total	1			D1860	D1861	D1886	
BR Standard 9F 2-10-0 Brighton 1954				Total	31		
92011	92021	92049	92050	Metropolitan Vickers Type 2 Co-Bo 1958			
92094	92137	92165	92212	D5705	D5709	D5715	
Total	8			Total	3		
Diesels	46	Electrics	12	English Electric Type 1 Bo-Bo 1957			
Steam	47			D8011	D8015	D8024	
Grand Total	105			Total	3		

Recently Withdrawn	4	Surviving Steam Classes	7
Saw Elsewhere on the Tour	16	Saw Carlisle June 1967	3
Saw Carlisle Sept 1958	2	Saw Barry Docks Aug 1970	2
Saw Mcester Crewe Dec 1964	6		

While very depressing at not getting round it seems that we would have missed no more than 50 steam engines with the best being the withdrawn "Jubilee" 45589 "Gwalior" which was dismantled at the Works a few months later. 71000 "Duke of Gloucester" was also there awaiting preservation but in the end only the valve gear was preserved and thankfully the engine was eventually saved from Barry Docks

It was now about 15.50 and we had an hour and a quarter to wait before our 17.05 train to Stoke. Enough time for meditation of the transcendental type. What could we do? We had visited all the other Crewe depots yesterday so we decided to stay at the station (although another quick visit to 5B Crewe South could probably have been accomplished) and allow D.S.'s batteries to recharge somewhat.

D.S., of course, by this time was feeling hungry and we popped into the cafeteria. Here was a chance to break that £1 note which had caused D.S. a lot of distress earlier in the day when he had to pay a couple of my bus fares. I noted that the speciality on the menu was "Angus" steaks at around three shillings (15 new pence) each. I decided that I had gone vegetarian on the tour for long enough and must have some meat. D.S. stayed vegetarian while I went up to the counter and ordered the Angus steak. I was alarmed when I saw the size of the steak which was tossed on to the griddle. I'll admit that it was bigger than a table tennis ball but only just. BR certainly weren't giving much away for their money. I'll admit that what there was tasted good although it cost me about one shilling (5 new pence) a bite.

Back at the station we sat down and electrics came and departed. A Britannia provided us with a bit of steam excitement. By chance we started to talk about the blue Brush Type 4 D1733 and we remembered that several months before we expected it to haul the new blue coached Talisman train. However, it was not to be - blue coaches but no new blue Brush. There was a Type 4 at the head of the train. Originally the Brush had been painted in blue livery for the XP64 train. As if by some call from D.S. and I magically D1733 rolled in at the head of an express passenger. It certainly was one of the most remarkable coincidences that we had ever experienced. Was it Extra Sensory Perception (ESP)? I would be the last to rule that out. We think wistfully that it would be good to see the blue Brush D1733 and hey presto she appears. Not a bad conjuring trick.

A young enthusiast views D1733 Brush Type 4 Co-Co 1962 resplendent in experimental blue livery

We walked up the platform to appreciate this unique Brush. Indeed I understood all main line locos were scheduled to be repainted in blue livery and to have the British rail motif emblazoned on their sides. It would make spotting numbers that bit more difficult from a distance as the number was smaller than even the standard sized diesel numbers. Changed days from the old days of "enormous" numbers on the cabsides of steam engines. The modern trend seems to be miniaturisation of numbers and hence more difficult to see for either distant or short-sighted trainspotters. D.S. sensibly snapped the Brush Type 4. He then examined all the carriage numbers to see if they were the original XP64 set. A fascinating hobby taking carriage numbers. You should try it!

CREWE STATION on THURSDAY AFTERNOON						
		Home shed		Built	Withdrawn	Scrap
Diesels						
English Electric Type 4 1-Co-Co-1 1958						
D 317		12B	Carlisle Upperby	Feb-1961		
Total	1					
Brush Type 4 Co-Co 1962						
D1589		87E	Landore	May-1964		
D1598		82A	Bristol Bath Road	Jun-1964		
D1733	D.S. photo	81A	Old Oak Common	Jun-1964		
D1851		5A	Crewe Diesel	Jun-1965		
Total	4					
Electrics						
A.E.I. (British Thomson-Houston) AL1 Bo-Bo 1959						
E3005		LMW	London Midland Western Lines	May-1960		
E3009		LMW	London Midland Western Lines	Oct-1960	Aug-1968	
E3017		LMW	London Midland Western Lines	May-1961		
E3019		LMW	London Midland Western Lines	May-1961		
Total	4					
English Electric AL3 Bo-Bo 1960						
E3026		LMW	London Midland Western Lines	Aug-1960		
E3032		LMW	London Midland Western Lines	Nov-1960		
Total	2					
A.E.I. (Metropolitan-Vickers) AL2 Bo-Bo 1960						
E3053		LMW	London Midland Western Lines	Jan-1962		
Total	1					
BR A.E.I.(B.T.H.) motors AL5 Bo-Bo 1960						
E3057		LMW	London Midland Western Lines	Jun-1961		
E3065		LMW	London Midland Western Lines	Dec-1961		
E3071		LMW	London Midland Western Lines	May-1962		
E3075		LMW	London Midland Western Lines	Jan-1962		
E3078		LMW	London Midland Western Lines	Mar-1963		
Total	5					
BR B.T.H. AL5/1 Bo-Bo 1962						
E3089		LMW	London Midland Western Lines	Jun-1963		
E3093		LMW	London Midland Western Lines	Nov-1963		
Total	2					
BR Vulcan Foundry AEI motors AL6 Bo-Bo 1965						
E3161		LMW	London Midland Western Lines	Aug-1965		
Total	1					
Steam				Built	Withdrawn	Scrap
Stanier 5MT 4-6-0 "Black Five" 1934						
44761	Timken bearings	5B	Crewe South	Oct-1947	Apr-1968	Sep-1968
Total	1					
7P6F "Britannia" 1951 BR 4-6-2 Derby						
70032	"Tennyson"	12B	Carlisle Upperby	Nov-1952	Sep-1967	Mar-1968
Total	1					

On Station	22		Kops	13		
Steam	2		Diesels	5 Electrics		15
Shed	LMW	15	5A	2	5B	1
Distribution	12B	1				
	81A	1	82A	1	87E	1
Steam Classes		2				
Steam Origin	LMS	1	BR	1		
Station Highlight	D1733	of 81A	Old Oak Common (Blue Brush!)			

Mini Review and Appraisal of Crewe Station

Crewe Station wasn't what it used to be. Electric Co-Co's and Brush Type 4's had taken complete command of all the passenger trains. The English Electric Type 4's were gradually being pushed out of mainline express passenger trains by Brush Type 4's on the non electrified lines and also by the electrics. This push out would be complete when the electrification reached Euston in not too many months hence. These antiquated 1 Co-Co 1 English Electric Type 4's would probably be shoved onto freight trains then.

Since Ian Firth and I visited Crewe last December there had been remarkable changes in the composition of its motive power but also livery changes. The electric Bo-Bo's now were receiving yellow warning panels to add to their distinctive white coat of paint around the windows at the top of the cab. BR officials were getting worried about line side safety for their permanent way men. Only a few had received the new yellow warning panels as yet but the new electric Bo-Bo E3161 had been delivered fresh from the workshop with them.

Steam was obviously on the wane. The "Jinty" station pilots were still here but in less numbers while other steam power had dwindled almost to nothing. Gone were the heady days of last December when we noted Jubilee 45595 "Southern Rhodesia" ex-works (and also resplendent in her banned South of Crewe stripe) at the north end of the station. It was all the more remarkable that this "Jubilee" was withdrawn only a month or two after she came out of the works. 45595 "Southern Rhodesia" also had her nameplates on last December something you would not see anywhere nowadays. Crewe was still easily the busiest junction on the LMR but if it is steam transport that you want to see rattling by then don't come here but go to Preston instead. Preston is in the middle of one of the last strongholds of steam in Britain i.e. Lancashire. Preston gives you the feeling that the steam engine will be with us for a few years to come. Crewe Station gives the impression that steam engines will be out of here in a few months not years.

Rewind Crewe Station and Approaches 12th December 1964

CREWE STATION AND APPROACHES REWIND 12TH DECEMBER 1964						
		Home shed		**Built**	**Withdrawn**	**Scrap**
Diesels						
English Electric Type 4 1Co-Co1 1958						
D 292		1B	Camden (ex 5A)	Sep-1960		
D 306		1A	Willesden (ex 5A)	Oct-1960		
D 343		1B	Camden	May-1961		
Total	*3*					
Brush Type 4 Co-Co 1962						
D1721		87E	Landore	Mar-1964		
D1739		86A	Cardiff Canton	Jun-1964		
D1752		87E	Landore	Aug-1964		
Total	*3*					
English Electric Type 1 Bo-Bo 1957						
D8059		41A	Tinsley	May-1961		
Total	*1*					
Electrics						
A.E.I. (British Thomson-Houston) AL1 Bo-Bo 1959						
E3015		LMW	London Midl. West. Lines	May-1960		
Total	*1*					
BR A.E.I.(B.T.H.) motors AL5 Bo-Bo 1960						
E3069		LMW	London Midl. West. Lines	May-1962		
E3084		LMW	London Midl. West. Lines	May-1964		
E3085		LMW	London Midl. West. Lines	Jul-1964		
Total	*3*					
BR B.T.H. AL5/1 Bo-Bo 1962						
E3088		LMW	London Midl. West. Lines	Feb-1963		
Total	*1*					
Steam						
Ivatt 2MT 2-6-2T 1946						
41229		5A	Crewe North	Oct-1948	Nov-1966	Apr-1967
Total	*1*					
Stanier 4MT 2-6-4T 1935 dev of Fowler 1927						
42581		1A	Willesden	Oct-1936	Mar-1966	Jun-1966
42663		5D	Stoke	Jun-1942	Mar-1967	Oct-1967
Total	*2*					
Stanier 5MT 4-6-0 "Black Five" 1934						
44900		12A	Carlisle Kingmoor	Oct-1945	May-1967	Nov-1967
44913		6H	Bangor	Nov-1945	Jul-1967	Mar-1968
45002		5B	Crewe South	Mar-1935	Jul-1965	Jun-1966
45248		5B	Crewe South	Sep-1936	Feb-1966	Jul-1966
Total	*4*					
Stanier 6P5F 4-6-0 "Jubilee" 1934						
45595	"Southern Rhodesia"	6G	Llandudno Junction	Nov-1935	Apr-1965	Aug-1965
Total	*1*					

			Home shed	Built	Withdrawn	Scrap
Midland 3F "Jinty" 0-6-0T 1924 dev. of Johnson 1899 design						
47482		5B	Crewe South	Jan-1928	Oct-1966	Feb-1967
Total	1					
On Area	21					
Steam		9 Diesels	7 Electrics		5	
		Home Area	5		Visitors	
Shed						
Distribution:-	5A	1	5B	3	5D	1
	LMW	5				
	1A	2	1B	2		
	6G	1	6H	1		
	12A	1	41A	1		
	86A	1	87E	2		
Steam classes on view		5				
Steam Origin	LMS		9			
Station Highlight:-	45595		"Southern Rhodesia"			

Mini Review and Appraisal of Rewind Crewe Station and Approaches 12th December 1964

As August 1965 mainline electrics were well to the fore. However, an example of a "Jubilee" like 45595 "Southern Rhodesia" seemed scarcer than a hens tooth now. Steam seemed now to be very scarce during the working day and in August 1965 the clutch of "Black Fives" and the Stanier Tanks (one ex-works) were noticeably missing.

On we go

At a few minutes to 17.00 D.S. and I were still admiring the scenery at Crewe Station when it dawned on me that our train left for Stoke at 17.05. There was no time to waste; we were leaving time tight as usual. I raced to the left luggage and repossessed our bags. A dash over the overbridge and down to the relevant platform. We dived into the bucket two minutes before the official starting time of 17.05.

Fancy almost missing a train when you've been waiting on the station for about an hour and a half for it. D.S. had forgotten that we were ever supposed to leave Crewe Station and he demanded to know why the sudden rush and where we were going!

Our train left on time at 17.05. I was disappointed to note that the Stoke line diverged to the east before we passed 5B Crewe South. I would have liked to have seen what was in the shed yard. I was intrigued to find that we had a ticket inspector on board. He succeeded in catching out one middle aged lady. She had no ticket. Surprisingly, he seemed to take pity on her and the only penalty appeared to be for her to stump up the full fare.

Our first stop was Alsager. It used to have a shed and was coded 5E. I looked for the shed at the east end of the station as I suspiciously wondered whether BR still used the shed. The shed being closed might mean nothing. This time my hopes were dashed as I noticed some foundations. The shed had been raised to the ground.

Regrettably 8E Northwich had to be deleted from our visits thanks to our late start today.

8E NORTHWICH						
Steam						
Stanier 8F 2-8-0 "Big Eight" 1935						
48118	48135	48155	48305			
48374	48462	48615	48631			
48639	48640	48683	48693			
48717	48735					
Total		14				
BR Standard 3MT 2-6-0 Swindon 1953						
77011	77014					
Total		2	*Surviving*			
Grand Total		16	**Steam Classes**		2	
Saw Elsewhere			**Saw on July 65 Preston**			
on the Tour		1	**trip**		1	
Saw at Barry Docks						
revisited Aug-70		1				
Steam	**Aug-50**		42	**Mar-59**		29
Allocation	**Apr-65**		16	**Aug-65**		16
	Closed to Steam:-			**Mar-68**		

8E Northwich had only 16 steam allocated but we would have liked to have visited it. The shed's allocation included two of the BR Standard 77XXX Class 3MT 2-6-0 Swindon 1953. Only 20 of this class were built and it was the last surviving intact steam class. The Scottish Region had 10 the North Eastern Region 8 with the final two at 8E Northwich. The other 14 of 8E Northwich's allocation were all "Big Eights".

Nearing Stoke we seemed to miss Cockshute Diesel Depot at the fork of the Etruria and Newcastle lines about ¾ mile of Stoke Station. However, all that we missed was probably the odd diesel shunter. Overall, the journey proved fruitful to us:-

Strange seeing the withdrawn Patricroft "Jinty" near Stoke Station. She must be en route to a scrap-breaker *(which turned out later to be Cashmore's at Great Bridge)*. We drew into Stoke station on time at 17.31.

			Schedule	Actual	Miles
Depart	CREWE		17.05	17.05	0
Arrive	STOKE		17.31	17.31	14¾

4 intermediate stops.

CREWE STATION TO STOKE STATION						
			Home shed	Built	Withdrawn	Scrap
Diesels						
BR English Electric 0-6-0 Shunter 1953						
D3798			5B	Crewe South	Dec-1959	
Total	1					
BR Blackstone/B.T.H. 0-6-0 Shunter 1955						
D4110			5D	Stoke	Dec-1961	
D4111			5D	Stoke (ex 1F)	Dec-1961	
Total	2					
Steam				Built	Withdrawn	Scrap
Ivatt 4MT 2-6-0 1947						
43034			5B	Crewe South	May-1949	Jun-1967	Nov-1967
Total	1					
Stanier 5MT 4-6-0 "Black Five" 1934						
44682			5D	Stoke	Jun-1950	Nov-1967	Apr-1968
45293			12A	Carlisle Kingmoor	Dec-1936	Aug-1965	saved
Total	2					

		Home shed		Built	Withdrawn	Scrap
Midland 3F "Jinty" 0-6-0T 1924 dev. of Johnson 1899 design						
47647		9H	Patricroft	Feb-1929	May-1965	Sep-1965
Total	1					
Stanier 8F 2-8-0 "Big Eight" 1935						
48628		5D	Stoke	May-1943	Sep-1966	Feb-1967
Total	1					
On Journey	8	Kops		7		
Steam	5	Diesels		3		
Withdrawn	1					
		Home Area		6	Visitors	2
Shed	5B	2	5D	4		
Distribution	9H	1				
	12A	1				
Steam Classes		4				
Steam Origin	LMS	5				

We lost no time in consulting the LocoShed Directory and beginning our hunt for 5D Stoke. We noted a dirty canal near Wharf Street. It was appropriately named. After a leisurely 25 minutes walk we found ourselves outside the M.P.D. Stoke shed was remarkable in the number of railway buildings around the shed. I began to wonder if George Dow, the famous author and Divisional Manager had his headquarters here. The shed certainly had a strange layout. We had to climb up a little slope to it as it was at a higher level than the street outside. The shed was also remarkable in that there were two sheds. There was what was left of a roundhouse on the side of the line where we came in and across the line there was the running shed. If I remember correctly the former Scottish 65E Kipps (Coatbridge) shed had two sheds as well.

"D.S. mistakes a "Jinty" for ex-GWR stock"

The roundhouse was a weird one as it had no roof. Just bits of the walls remained. We toured round there firstly. One of the first engines we came across was a "Jinty". She had lost part of her number and instead of "47649" was "7649". I remarked to D.S. that some silly bugger would happily slap down 7649 thinking that they had seen an ex-GWR loco.

D.S. must have been oblivious to this comment as after the tour ended I had the opportunity to check over his notebook. Checking over Stoke I noted with some merriment that he indeed had marked down "7649" rather than "47649". He must have thought I was joking or had not heard me when I had said the correct number was 47649. I hardly need add that in 1965 no ex-GWR loco carried the number 7649. D.S. had not managed to put his usual mark of an X beside the number as a kop as he hadn't been able to find it in his combined volume.

We finished the roundhouse and carefully crossed the Stone line over to the running shed. Like the roundhouse it was packed. Locomotives here were spilling out on to the shed yard. Halfway through the tour of the running shed D.S. looked up at the sky commented on the light and wandered over to where a withdrawn Fairburn 2-6-4 Tank was standing in the shed yard. He promptly took his camera out and, after a minute of shuffling about; he found the right spot and promptly snapped her. D.S. had now commendably filled three spools with photographs on the tour (8 to a spool) and was now on the second shot of the fourth spool. He assured me in his professional opinion that the photos would all develop perfectly. We finished the crowded shed without incident.

5D STOKE

		Home shed		Built	Withdrawn	Scrap
Steam						
Fairburn 4MT 2-6-4T 1945 dev. of Stanier 1935						
42070		5D		Nov-1950	Jul-1965	Sep-1965
42160	D.S. photo	5D		Jul-1948	May-1965	Aug-1965
Total	2					
Fowler 4MT 2-6-4T 1927						
42381		ex 5C	Stafford	Jun-1932	May-1965	Oct-1965
Total	1					
Stanier 4MT 2-6-4T 1935 dev of Fowler 1927						
42564		5D		Aug-1936	May-1965	Oct-1965
Total	1					
Ivatt 4MT 2-6-0 1947						
43003		5D		Jan-1948	Sep-1967	Dec-1967
43021		5D		Dec-1948	Sep-1967	Dec-1967
43112		5D		Mar-1951	Sep-1967	Nov-1967
43113		5B	Crewe South	Apr-1951	Sep-1966	Dec-1966
43115		5D		May-1951	Jun-1967	Oct-1967
Total	5					
Stanier 5MT 4-6-0 "Black Five" 1934						
44713		5D		Nov-1948	Aug-1968	Mar-1969
44810		5D		Oct-1944	Aug-1966	Nov-1966
44813		5D	(ex 5C Stafford)	Oct-1944	Sep-1966	Dec-1966
45006		2B	Oxley	Mar-1935	Sep-1967	Dec-1967
45020		5D		Aug-1934	Dec-1965	Mar-1966
45074		5D		Jun-1935	Sep-1965	Mar-1966
45241		5D		Sep-1936	Sep-1967	Mar-1968
45257		5D		Oct-1936	Nov-1965	Feb-1966
45268		5D		Oct-1936	Aug-1968	Dec-1968
45276		5D		Nov-1936	Jan-1967	Nov-1967
45292		1A	Willesden	Dec-1936	Nov-1967	Mar-1968
45440		8A	Edge Hill	Nov-1937	Sep-1967	Mar-1968
Total	12					
Midland 3F "Jinty" 0-6-0T 1924 dev. of Johnson 1899 design						
47273		5D		Aug-1924	Dec-1966	May-1967
47280		5D		Aug-1924	Apr-1966	Jul-1966
47307		5D	(ex 1E Bletchley)	Mar-1925	Sep-1966	Dec-1966
47359		ex 5C	Stafford	Jul-1926	Jul-1965	Oct-1965
47521		5D	(ex 1E Bletchley)	Feb-1928	Oct-1966	Feb-1967
47596		5D		Sep-1928	Jul-1965	Oct-1965
47649		5D		Feb-1929	Oct-1966	Feb-1967
47665		ex 5C	Stafford	Apr-1929	Jul-1965	Oct-1965
Total	8					
Stanier 8F 2-8-0 "Big Eight" 1935						
48012		5D		Dec-1936	Apr-1968	Jul-1968
48018		5D		Feb-1937	Oct-1967	Feb-1968
48054		5E	Nuneaton	Oct-1936	Sep-1967	Mar-1968
48110		5D		Feb-1939	Aug-1967	Oct-1967
48131		5D		Mar-1941	Jun-1967	Oct-1967
48207		5D	(ex 1E Bletchley)	Jul-1942	Jan-1966	Apr-1966
48248		5D		Jul-1940	Dec-1965	Apr-1966
48353		5D	(ex 2C Stourbridge Jn)	Mar-1944	Sep-1966	Jan-1967
48354		5D		Jun-1944	Nov-1966	May-1967
48359		16C	Derby	Jul-1944	Sep-1967	Feb-1968
48401		9F	Heaton Mersey (ex 9G)	Jul-1943	Sep-1965	Jan-1966
48453		5D		Sep-1944	Apr-1968	Jul-1968
48516		5D		Jul-1944	Dec-1966	Aug-1967
48517		1A	Willesden (ex 1G)	Jul-1944	Nov-1967	Feb-1968
48548		5D		Mar-1945	Apr-1967	Dec-1967
48736		5B	Crewe South	Nov-1945	Aug-1966	Nov-1966
Total	16					

		Home shed		Built	Withdrawn	Scrap
BR Standard 4MT 4-6-0 Brighton 1951						
75018		5D		*Mar-1952*	*Jun-1967*	*Nov-1967*
75023		5D		*Dec-1953*	*Jan-1966*	*Apr-1966*
75031		5D		*Jun-1953*	*Feb-1966*	*May-1966*
75036		5D		*Aug-1953*	*Jun-1966*	*Aug-1966*
75037		5D		*Aug-1953*	*Dec-1967*	*Jul-1968*
75056		5D		*Mar-1957*	*Jun-1966*	*Aug-1966*
75062		5D		*May-1957*	*Feb-1968*	*Jun-1968*
Total	7					
BR Standard 4MT 2-6-0 Doncaster 1953						
76023		5D		*Dec-1952*	*Oct-1965*	*Jan-1966*
76044		5D		*Aug-1954*	*Oct-1966*	*Mar-1967*
76051		5D		*Aug-1956*	*May-1967*	*Dec-1967*
76075		5D		*Dec-1956*	*Oct-1967*	*Apr-1968*
76085		5D		*Apr-1957*	*Aug-1966*	*Nov-1966*
76089		5D		*May-1957*	*Sep-1966*	*Dec-1966*
Total	6					
BR Standard 2MT 2-6-0 Doncaster 1953						
78056		5D		*Aug-1956*	*Jul-1966*	*Nov-1966*
Total	1					
BR Standard 9F 2-10-0 Brighton 1954						
92088		8H	Birkenhead (ex 16B via 16A)	*Oct-1956*	*May-1968*	*Oct-1968*
Total	1					

On Shed	60	**Kops**		52	
Steam	60	**Diesels**		0	
Withdrawn	7				

Home Locos	47	**Home Area**			6	**Visitors**	7
Shed	**5D**	47	**5B**		2	**ex 5C**	3	5E
Distribution	**1A**	2					
	2B	1					
	8A	1	**8H**		1		
	9F	1					
	16C	1					
Steam Classes		11					
Steam Origin	**LMS**	45		**BR**	15		
Shed Highlights:-							
	Steam	92088	8H	Birkenhead			
		5D STOKE(continued)					

Steam	*Aug-50*	100	*Mar-59*		71	*Apr-65*	76
Allocation						*Aug-65*	72
			Closed to Steam:-			*Aug-67*	
Home Steam	excluding recently withdrawn locos						
On/Off Shed	On Shed		43	Off Shed		29	% On Shed	60%
Not on Shed							
Stanier 4MT 2-6-4T 1935						42665	1
Ivatt 4MT 2-6-0 1947						43022	1
"Black Fives"		44682	44714		45003	45037	45050
		45060	45191		45240	45270	45350
							45422	11
"Big Eight"		48147	48171		48246	48291	48369
			48452		48555	48738	48768	9
BR 4MT 4-6-0 1951		75020	75030		75034	75040	75054	5
BR 4MT 2-6-0 1953							76099	1
BR 2MT 2-6-0 1953							78017	1
								29

saw elsewhere on the tour	9	
saw on Dec 64 Manchester and Crewe trip	1	
saw on July 65 Preston area trip	1	
recently withdrawn not on shed nor seen on tour	1	scrap
Midland 4F 0-6-0 1924	44571	Aug-65

Review and Appraisal of 5D Stoke

The shed was situated at the junction of the Stoke-Stone, and Stoke-Uttoxeter lines south of

Stoke station. Walking time was 15 minutes.

What a fantastic number of steam locos on shed! This was the busiest steam shed since 5B Crewe South (87 steam locos) and ahead of the 53 steam locos at 40E Colwick.

All the 2-6-4 tanks were withdrawn. It was good to see the three types of tank viz. Fowler, Fairburn and Stanier. The Fairburn tank that D.S. had snapped had been shorn of its smokebox numberplate. Sixteen "Big Eights" was a large number – close to the 23 on 5B Crewe South. The withdrawn 9F Heaton Mersey one was interesting. She had been transferred there when 9G Gorton had closed. Two of Stoke's "Big Eights" were recent acquisitions from 2C Stourbridge and the closed steam shed of 1E Bletchley.

The respective closures of 5C Stafford and 1E Bletchley (to steam) had brought four "Jinties" to Stoke. Three of Stoke's eight "Jinties" on shed were withdrawn. Good seeing the "Black Fives" and the Ivatt 2-6-0 "Moguls" on shed in number. There was one of the Standard counterparts to the Ivatt Moguls on shed. They, unlike the "Moguls" were common in Scotland. Seven Standard 4MT 75XXX 4-6-0's were on shed. They had no Scottish allocations but I can recall the strange sight of 75012 of 6A Chester Midland at 65B St.Rollox shed awaiting attention at St.Rollox Works.

Perhaps the highlight was the ex-Annesley 16B 9F 2-10-0 92088 of 8H Birkenhead. It had always appealed to me seeing one of them. None were allocated to the Scottish depots but visits by them were not uncommon especially after Carlisle received a number of them last year. As early as 1958 a Tyne Dock 9F 92060 caused a minor riot among railwayists by working up to 64B Haymarket shed in Edinburgh. It looked very peculiar to me then as it had no name on its smoke deflectors. All LNER locomotives with smoke deflectors (the A1's, A2's) were named. In 1958 the A3's did not have their shorter German type smoke deflectors but those became a common occurrence in later years. Nowadays I am accustomed to seeing a locomotive with smoke deflectors and no name as BR had shorn off all the nameplates of their named steam locomotives.

In all, Stoke was an excellent, workmanlike shed but with little in the way of spectacular highlights. However, this was made up in top-rank quantity when we had seen sixty steam locomotives on shed. Remarkably, 43 (60%) of the Home Steam were on shed on this weekday early evening. 29 were off shed. The missing locos were largely the hard working "Black Fives" (11) and "Big Eights" (9). Five Standard 4MT 4-6-0's were also off shed.

On we go

A brisk walk back and we were back at Stoke station in less than 15 minutes. D.S. tends to gather strength and vitality in the cooler evening air and he increases his pace to walking rather slowly. During the day when the temperature is hotter, his army surplus boots get roasted, his feet ache and he crawls along. Walking rather slowly now was therefore a good pace for D.S.

By the way I said to D.S. "We'll miss the "Man from U.N.C.L.E." tonight at 20.00 on the BBC. D.S. admitted that was a tragedy. *The Man from U.N.C.L.E. was considered good by us then and it certainly was novel. It took me till late '65 when it finally dawned on me that it was the same every week – boring and predictable.*

Another glance at my allocations book and I noted that we had missed four diesel shunters at 5D Stoke. Incredibly, there had been no diesels on shed. The diesels presumably would be at the nearby Cockshute Diesel Depot to the north of Stoke station at the fork of the Etruria and Newcastle lines. I doubt as if we will lose much sleep over missing Cockshute Diesel depot.

The half hour's wait at Crewe Station for our train to Stafford gave us time for meditation and recuperation. A few minutes from blast off time the rested D.S. decided to pop into the station bar and get us a couple of bottles of Guinness for the journey.

D.S. buzzed off into the bar and I heard a great clatter and smash of a bottle bursting on the floor. A minute later D.S. came out. I expected him to come out with the remains of two bottles of Guinness. I asked him about the sound of breaking glass. He explained that the woman bartender had dropped one of the bottles – not him. She, of course, gave him another bottle. D.S. must have bowled her over with his dashingness, his charm and his eloquence thus causing her to be overcome with emotion and drop one of the bottles. That certainly seemed to be the answer.

We left Stoke on time at 18.52 in another bucket. I wondered if there is a BR rule about consuming intoxicating liquor on a non-bar BR diesel bucket. Never mind though, we are on the LMR to break rules.

D.S. quickly opened the Guinness bottles with his handy screw top opener and we gulped the first draughts of the dark brown beverage down. I had looked forward to the drink immensely. Ugh! I had never tasted anything so foul or as disgusting in my life. It must be the most horrible, evil, beverage ever invented. The next thirty minutes were about the most terrible I had ever experienced as I sipped this poison down as slowly as I could. We had about reached the main London-Crewe main line at Norton Bridge before I had drunk down all this rubbish. I didn't tell D.S. about how revolting it was as he seemed to be fairly happy with his bottle of Guinness which he was savouring. His stomach must be lined with asbestos I thought. This was certainly to be my first and last taste of Guinness. Give me a can of McEwan's Export or Skol Lager anytime but never Guinness. Guinness is good for you the advert states. Pull the other leg they must be joking. *In later life after University I did briefly acquire a taste for Guinness particularly in Ireland where it seems to taste much better brewed there.*

Even in the grim Guinness sojourn I managed to bravely note down two locos on the Stoke-Norton Bridge section. We had seen Type 2 D5083 at 5A Crewe Diesel yesterday and here she was again. We also saw travelling light engine our old friend 75000. We had noted her at 16A Toton of all places and now this class founder member was making a bold bid to fight her way back to her home shed of 85A Worcester. Best of luck to her as she still had a long way to go.

STOKE TO STAFFORD						
		Home shed		Built	Withdrawn	Scrap
Diesels						
BR Sulzer Type 2 Bo-Bo 1958						
D5083		5A	Crewe Diesel	Apr-1960		
Total	1					
Steam				Built	Withdrawn	Scrap
BR Standard 4MT 4-6-0 Brighton 1951						
75000		85A	Worcester (ex 83E)	May-1951	Dec-1965	Apr-1966
Total	1					
On Journey	2	Kops		0		
Steam	1	Diesels		1		
		Home Area		1	Visitors	1
Shed	5A	1				
Distribution	85A	1				
Steam Classes		1				
Steam Origin	BR	1				

We rolled into Stafford station on time at 19.30.

		Schedule	Actual		Miles
Depart	STOKE	18.52	18.52		0
Arrive	STAFFORD	19.30	19.30		16¼

Four intermediate stops. Average speed – slow! One place that we stopped on our journey stuck in my mind. It was the town of Stone. What a crazy name for a town!

We jumped off at Stafford station and had a roam around. Our train for Nuneaton was due in at 20.00. We had half an hour to trawl the station. Stafford was one of the LMR's new showpieces. All nice, lovely and impressive in its concrete and glass. This was BR's image for the future and I couldn't help but admiring this modernised station.

Unknown to D.S. and I 5C Stafford shed had been closed very recently. We noted the shed at the north end of the station on the west side of the line. Not surprisingly it was empty. Type 4 "Ivernia" was standing outside the shed but that was all.

We went up to the glass-sided over-bridge and sat down. Our half hour was hardly uneventful. A diesel bucket rattled in. D.S. noted a headboard on it. Funny peculiar thought D.S. and showing unbelievable acceleration he hared down to the platform. A minute later an excited D.S. came back with the dramatic news that he had just seen the thousandth diesel bucket turned out by Derby Works. That's what it had said on the headboard at the side of the bucket at any rate. For the interested it was M51952. A bucket highlight of the tour, indeed! Our haven proved to be a busy spot.

STAFFORD STATION							
		Home shed			Built	Withdrawn	Scrap
Diesels							
English Electric Type 4 1-Co-Co-1 1958							
D 221	"Ivernia"	9A	Longsight		Jul-1959		
Total	1						
BR TYPE 2 Bo-Bo 1958							
D5017		5A	Crewe Diesel		Jun-1959		
Total	1						
Electrics							
A.E.I. (British Thomson-Houston) AL1 Bo-Bo 1959							
E3009		LMW	London Midl. West. Lines	Oct-1960	Aug-1968		
Total	1						
A.E.I. (Metropolitan-Vickers) AL2 Bo-Bo 1960							
E3054		LMW	London Midl. West. Lines	Nov-1961			
Total	1						
BR A.E.I.(B.T.H.) motors AL5 Bo-Bo 1960							
E3057		LMW	London Midl. West. Lines	Jun-1961			
E3080		LMW	London Midl. West. Lines	Mar-1963			
E3082		LMW	London Midl. West. Lines	Jun-1963			
Total	3						
English Electric AL3/1 Bo-Bo 1962							
E3100		LMW	London Midl. West. Lines	Jun-1962			
Total	1						
Steam					Built	Withdrawn	Scrap
Stanier 5MT 4-6-0 "Black Five" 1934							
45249		8A	Edge Hill		Sep-1936	Dec-1966	Jun-1967
Total	1						
On Station	9	Kops		7			
Steam	1	Diesels		2		Electrics	6
		Home Area	1	Visitors	8		
Shed	5A	1					
Distribution	LMW	6	8A	1	9A	1	
Steam Classes	1						
Steam Origin	LMS	1					

Electric main line locos were now appearing two a penny at the main line stations from Crewe to the South. Our train for Nuneaton rolled in on time a minute or two after 20.00. Electric Bo-Bo E3057 was at the head. The train was rather empty and we found two seats in a "tabled" corridor up the middle compartment. It was old stock but I hear that this kind of compartment is again coming into fashion with the new BR's idea of the best type of carriages.

Our train left Stafford on time at 20.05. The powerful acceleration of the Bo-Bo electric was certainly impressive. The LMR in this new era had certainly a challenger to the "Deltics" of the east coast main line. The respective Divisional General Managers were battling with the civil engineers to get more stretches of track passed for 100 m.p.h. running. As our Bo-Bo flashed through the towns and countryside at high speed D.S. and I became apparent of an excellent smoothness at high speed. Occasionally on the east coast main line a "Deltic" could give one an uncomfortable, somewhat unruly journey at high speed but not here. I balanced a threepenny (one new pence) bit on its side on our table to prove my point. Remarkably the coin was to reach our destination of Nuneaton without falling over.

I noticed the mileposts at the side of the track and timed certain sections. I stared in disbelief when I recorded instances of 105 m.p.h. on our journey. An electric ambled past the other way on a slow freight and vanished before our eyes almost before we could record her number down. Zipping through stations at 90 m.p.h. plus gave us an unmistakeable feel of high speed as the almost blurred station buildings vanished before our eyes into the twilight. Past Rugeley, past Lichfield and flying through the lower level of the controversial Tamworth station we sped. I glanced up at Tamworth High Level station which we had passed on Tuesday morning on the way to Barry. Finally, our journey came to an end at Nuneaton.

		Schedule	Actual	Miles
Depart	STAFFORD	20.05	20.05	0
Arrive	NUNEATON TRENT VALLEY	20.40	20.32	36½

An impressive average speed of 80 m.p.h. plus. A good journey. Certainly the fastest run so far on our tour. BR's new electrification from Liverpool and Manchester to London Euston should certainly be successful and a badly needed boost to BR's waning morale. Our Bo-Bo Electric had made mincemeat of her easy schedule and certainly BR would hope to tighten up timings once the electrification to London was complete. On the journey we recorded:-

STAFFORD TO NUNEATON						
		Home shed		Built	Withdrawn	Scrap
Diesels						
BR 0-6-0 Shunter 1953						
D3291		5B	Crewe South	*Dec-1956*		
D3801		5D	Stoke	*Dec-1959*		
Total	2					
LMS 0-6-0 shunter 1945						
12045		1F	Rugby	*Apr-1948*	*Jan-1969*	
Total	1					
Electrics						
A.E.I. (British Thomson-Houston) AL1 Bo-Bo 1959						
E3023		LMW	London Midl. West. Lines	*May-1961*		
Total	1					
English Electric AL3 Bo-Bo 1960						
E3031		LMW	London Midl. West. Lines	*Nov-1960*		
Total	1					
BR B.T.H. AL5/1 Bo-Bo 1962						
E3092		LMW	London Midl. West. Lines	*Feb-1964*		
Total	1					
On Journey	6	**Kops**		5		
Steam	0	**Diesels**		3	**Electrics**	3

		Home Area	2	Visitors	4
Shed	5B	1	5D	1	
Distribution	LMW	3	1F	1	

Originally "A Hard Day's Week on the London Midland Region" was produced in three parts. Part Two was released in September 1968 between years 1 and 2 of my Economics degree at Edinburgh University.

David Archibald of the Musselburgh Monktonhall Model Railway Society kindly prepared a review of Part Two at the time when it was released:-

"What are the less sinister reasons for visiting "The Nag's Head" in Kirkby? Why does one carry a compass when touring by rail? What is the thing which haunts Shrewsbury Youth Hostel? What is a cartographic and is it legal? For the answers to these intriguing questions, we turn to this large volume, the second of three, which make up Grant Dowie's finest work, which holds a unique place in railway literature. I know of at least one advance order for the as yet unwritten third volume.

The book is comic, tragic and at times academic. This volume sets a high standard in layout. In dealing with his fellow, or should I say lesser beings, Grant Dowie gives the impression that he can at times unfairly mock most of them, notably his companion D.S., and is somewhat amused at the futile efforts of British Railways employees to block his path. Often he is reminiscent of a certain well known heavyweight boxer who shall of course remain nameless. This reviewer seems remarkably well treated in the books and the author acknowledges my knowledge of Einstein's theory of relativity.

Visits to sheds and the locos seen are dealt with in great detail as are the author's opinions on them. The incidents are sometimes scarcely credible and the reader is assured of 292,620,000 micro seconds of non stop excitement during which the dynamic duo progressed from Leicester to Nuneaton – the staggering distance of 15 miles!

"A good one and seventh pence (8 new pence) worth"

On our ten minute walk to the shed which was located on the fork of the main and Coventry line south of the station I noted a fish and chip shop on the right. We would frequent it on the way back.

The electrification scourge although efficient enough was sadly sweeping steam out of the Euston-Crewe main line. 1E Bletchley and 1F Rugby had been the latest sheds to be closed to steam. Doubtless, 5E Nuneaton would soon follow. I was therefore relieved to see on approaching the shed outskirts the familiar glimpses of Stanier outlines. Steam at least still held out here.

We received one extremely pleasant surprise as we journeyed round the shed. 46235 "City of Birmingham" shorn of nameplates and numberplates was lying dead. This as far as I knew was the only Coronation scheduled for preservation. She and the last survivors had been withdrawn months ago and Ian Firth and I had seen her lying dead at 5A Crewe North in December 1964. D.S. and I clambered into the cab and commented on the disgusting condition of the engine. Her original green livery was barely discernible through the dirt and grime.

We noted with interest the office at the bottom of the shed. Luckily, all was dead there also. Our permit was for yesterday morning when we had originally intended to visit the shed. However, after we missed our train from Cardiff General our timetable was hastily recast hence our belated visit now. As we went round another Bo-Bo Electric flashed by on the mainline going south.

5E NUNEATON

		Home shed		Built	Withdrawn	Scrap
Diesels						
BR 0-6-0 Shunter 1953						
D3053		5E	Nuneaton	*Jun-1954*		
Total	*1*					
LMS and BR 0-6-0 Shunter 1945						
12046		1F	Rugby	*May-1948*	*Jan-1969*	
Total	*1*					
Electrics						
A.E.I. (British Thomson-Houston) AL1 Bo-Bo 1959						
E3005	*pass shed*	LMW	London Mid. West. Lines	*May-1960*		
Total	*1*					
Steam				**Built**	**Withdrawn**	**Scrap**
Stanier 5MT 4-6-0 "Black Five" 1934						
44866		5E	(ex 1F Rugby)	*Feb-1945*	*Sep-1967*	*Feb-1968*
45001		5E	(ex 1F Rugby)	*Mar-1935*	*Mar-1968*	*Jun-1968*
45113		5E	(ex 1F Rugby)	*Jun-1935*	*Jul-1965*	*Apr-1966*
45310		5E	(ex 2J Aston)	*Jan-1937*	*Aug-1968*	*Dec-1968*
45371		12B	Carlisle Upperby	*Jun-1937*	*Apr-1967*	*Aug-1967*
45405		5E	(ex 2J Aston)	*Sep-1937*	*Aug-1967*	*Dec-1967*
45448		5E	(ex 1F Rugby)	*Dec-1937*	*Aug-1967*	*Jan-1968*
Total	*7*					
Stanier 8P 4-6-2 "Coronation" 1937						
46235	"City of Birmingham"	ex 5A	Crewe North	*Jul-1939*	*Oct-1964*	*saved*
Total	*1*					
Ivatt 2MT 2-6-0 1946						
46520		5E		*Feb-1953*	*May-1967*	*Nov-1967*
Total	*1*					
Stanier 8F 2-8-0 "Big Eight" 1935						
48074		5E		*Dec-1936*	*Nov-1967*	*Apr-1968*
48206		5E		*Jul-1942*	*May-1968*	*Aug-1968*
48264		5E		*May-1942*	*Jul-1966*	*Nov-1966*
48289		5E		*Oct-1940*	*Oct-1966*	*Feb-1967*
48320		5E		*Feb-1944*	*Mar-1967*	*Oct-1967*
48456		5E		*Oct-1944*	*Aug-1967*	*Feb-1968*
48534		5E	(ex 1E Bletchley)	*May-1945*	*Oct-1967*	*Apr-1968*
48559		5B	Crewe South(ex 1A/1F)	*Aug-1945*	*Jan-1968*	*Apr-1968*
48610		5E	(ex 1E Bletchley)	*Apr-1943*	*Aug-1965*	*Sep-1965*
48686		5E		*Feb-1944*	*Nov-1966*	*Jun-1967*
48718		5E		*Aug-1944*	*Apr-1966*	*Feb-1967*
48751		5E		*Sep-1946*	*Feb-1967*	*Jul-1967*
Total	*12*					
BR Standard 4MT 4-6-0 Brighton 1951						
75045		5E		*Sep-1953*	*Apr-1966*	*Aug-1966*
Total	*1*					
Riddles WD 8F 2-8-0 "Austerity" 1943						
90372		36A	Doncaster	*Sep-1944*	*Dec-1965*	*Jul-1966*
Total	*1*					

On Shed	26	Kops		22		
Steam	23	Diesels		2	Electrics	1
Withdrawn	2	to be preserved		1		
Home Locos	21	Home Area		1	Visitors	4
Shed	5E	21	ex 5A	1		
Distribution	1F	1	LMW	1	12B	1
	36A	1				
Steam Classes		6				
Steam Origin	LMS	21	WD	1	BR	1
Shed Highlight		46235	"City of Birmingham" - of course!			
Steam	**Aug-50**	73	**Mar-59**	62	**Apr-65**	37
Allocation					**Aug-65**	36
			Closed to Steam:-		**Jun-66**	

433

5E NUNEATON (Continued)							
Home Steam	excluding withdrawn locos						
On/Off Shed	On Shed	18	Off Shed		18	% On Shed	50%	
Not on Shed							
"Black Fives"				44771	44831	45065	3
Ivatt 2MT 2-6-0 1946				46430	46459	46459	3
"Big Eights"		48054	48111	48154	48247	48263	
		48343	48386	48445	48504	48650	
						48753	11
BR 4MT 4-6-0 1951						75035	1
						total	18
			saw elsewhere on the tour			4	

Review and Appraisal (or Ra – after the Egyptian sun god) of 5E Nuneaton

The shed was in the fork of the main and Coventry lines south of Nuneaton station. Walking time was 10 minutes.

Naturally the highlight was seeing the last Coronation on BR metals – "City of Birmingham". I first saw her I think on September 7th 1958 at Carlisle on my then first Scottish Railfans (now the Railway Society of Scotland) outing. I was 9¼ years old at the time. A year or two later I was amused to find that its minimum age for membership was 12! It was great that she was going to be preserved. A fine old time the works boys would have in getting all this muck off her before they could repaint her in her former magnificent green livery. A green Coronation this one - being a Hearts (rather than a Hibs) supporter I, of course, much preferred maroon rather than green Coronations. Sad to see a member of this once supreme class being reduced to this ignoble, squalid state. Still, she's better off dirty and "alive" rather than scrapped and dead like all or almost all (if any others are to be preserved) of her sisters. Doubtless, she will soon be restored to her former splendour.

An industrial place, Nuneaton, and the right type of "worker" locos to go with it. A nice visitor was the WD 2-8-0 90372 from 36A Doncaster. No doubt off a cross-country freight. The electrification south of Rugby had helped to boost Nuneaton's allocation. We noted the two ex 1E Bletchley locos - one of which was withdrawn) and the ex 1A Willesden Big Eights.

In all, essentially a "Big Eight", "Black Five" type of shed. What did we miss? 18 Home Steam on shed (50%) and 18 off shed so pretty good for a weekday.

On we go

After a pleasant shedmasterless shed it was time for some chow. Today had been a very good day food-wise as D.S. would surely remember. Our diet had been somewhat copious. There was that Mars Bar for breakfast at Shrewsbury, the nice meal at Wrexham Station and an Angus steak at Crewe (admittedly BR miniaturised) and not to be forgotten was our bottles of Guinness on the journey from stoke to Nuneaton. Yes, a day of real indulgence. This would never have happened with the original timetable as one could never afford valuable railwayist time in eating! Plenty of time before the 21.47 back to Crewe so we went into our handy fish and chip shop which we had spied earlier and we got our fish suppers. Fish suppers er no. Of course, we asked for fish and chips and not fish suppers. Fish suppers are only known in Scotland. A good one and seven pence worth (eight new pence). Three pence (one new pence) dearer than Crewe but still very enjoyable and cheaper than in Scotland where a fish supper cost about two bob (ten new pence).

At Nuneaton station the light of day was rapidly fading and we sat down, subconsciously watching the onset of darkness. Our half hour wait was slightly fruitful. 46459 trundled northwards with a parcels van and a few wagons while E3100 zipped through the station with a southbound fast freight.

"D.S. is a tired fellow"

D.S. had been oblivious to all this. He saw 46459 amble past and made a motion to get his notebook out but it was not to be. He scratched at his ski-jacket pocket and attempted to get it out but fatigue had an iron grip on him. His hand made a last despairing effort but failed and it fell dead in his lap. His eyes rolled then shut and he gave out a heart rending sigh. He was out for the count and he lay there sprawled over the seat in a tangled heap of tired humanity. Perhaps the poor chap was dying from lack of food as he had often complained or from lack of sleep. Well, there was one consolation it should get harder still on Friday and Saturday when the battle against the timetable would become really fierce.

Here indeed was a good chance to get rid of D.S. and leave him to sleep here until his Railrover expires at the stroke of midnight on Saturday night. The tired, drawn, pale like shell of this former "athlete" looked as though he would gladly sleep it out until then. I decided that he would gain more from his holiday week awake so I roused him awake as our train trundled into the station. D.S. made a superhuman effort, got up and picked up his baggage and I directed him to the miniature buffet car on the train. At the smell of coffee D.S. visibly brightened and sprinted on telling me to hurry up or I would miss the train! The depreciating D.S. had evidently stopped depreciating for the meantime.

On the front of our train was another main-line electric E3109.

NUNEATON STATION						
		Home shed		Built	Withdrawn	Scrap
Electrics						
English Electric AL3/1 Bo-Bo 1962						
E3100		LMW	London Mid. West. Lines	*Jun-1962*		
Total	1					
BR Vulcan Foundry AEI motors AL6 Bo-Bo 1965						
E3109	*hauled*	LMW	London Mid. West. Lines	*Jun-1965*		
Total	1					
Steam				Built	Withdrawn	Scrap
Ivatt 2MT 2-6-0 1946						
46459		5E	Nuneaton	*May-1950*	*Sep-1965*	*Dec-1965*
Total	1					

At station	3	Kops		2		
Steam	1	Diesels		0	Electrics	2
		Home Area		1	Visitors	2
Shed	5E	1				
Distribution	LMW	2				
Steam Classes	1					
Steam Origin	LMS	1				

The miniature buffet car had an unoccupied table so we took it over and immediately took advantage of the car's facilities and bought some coffees. They were nice, or rather we thought so as we were so thirsty and dry that anything would be nice. We quickly drank our coffees and ordered second cups.

Our train was the "Northern Irishman" which had left London Euston at 19.30, picked us up on time at 21.47 and would reach Carlisle at 02.00. Thereafter they would connect with the boat at Stranraer at 07.00 eventually reaching Larne, Northern Ireland, at 09.15. The train was advertised as teacups (the BR squiggle of a teacup on the timetable) until Crewe with sleeping cars and through carriages to Stranraer.

It was on the black side of dark outside and with the coffee beginning to have an effect on D.S. he no longer felt like not staying awake (work out the double negative). We discussed the successes and failures of the day and our hopes for tomorrow which would be a very busy day.

Our interesting chat was cut short when the buffet car attendant ordered us out of the car as it was being taken off at Crewe. He had more trouble in trying to get rid of one Scots lad who was stretched out on one table asleep. No, it's not as you thought it wasn't D.S.! The attendant would wake him up and the chap would say yes and as soon as the attendant's back was turned would curl up and promptly go back to sleep. This pantomime went on for a good five minutes. The attendant would wake him up, clear something up and come back rather agitated on finding him asleep. At the fifth attempt he stayed with the lad, got him up and escorted him and us out of the buffet car finally locking the door behind us to ensure that no one came back in.

		Schedule	Actual	Miles
Depart	NUNEATON TRENT VALLEY	21.47	20.05	0
Arrive	CREWE	22.42	20.32	61

61 miles in 55 minutes so smart timing for a sleeper train!

Our train trundled into Crewe on time at 22.43. We had a two hour wait for the 00.42 to Manchester. Certainly I was looking forward to a further two hours on one of the premier BR junctions. A station like Crewe is supposedly busy 24 hours a day. I would soon find that out. With the effect of the caffeine rapidly wearing off D.S. fell off the train, scouted around the station for a resting place for his weary bones and finally found an empty parcels trailer and collapsed on to it. I threw my luggage beside him and went off for my two hour tour of the inhabitants of the station.

The two hours passed very quickly as I was kept fully occupied by passing engines first running down to the south end and then back up to the north end. The railway cops did not seem too worried by my antics. They must be used to that sort of behaviour here. However, Ian "Froth" Firth had told me that a few years ago the railway cops had chucked him and a few friends out when they had come down for the day. Last December at Crewe station had passed without incidents with the railway cops and all our visits to the station over the past couple of days. So changed days for the better here. The railway cops at Preston station in contrast were right bastards. The Preston 10 area was hopeless for getting shed permits as well. Perhaps the bad railway cops had moved from Crewe to Preston.

Naturally, the highlights were steam. None of which was on passenger trains, of course. Two Britannias were quickly noted but the biggest highlight was when I went to the north end of the station and I noted a stationary freight behind a row of carriages. The front of the engine was just discernible. I muttered "Is this a Hall?"

"No, it's a Grange. You can tell from the front."

Who said that?

I turned round and saw a grey haired, well dressed chap of about 65 years old. He was peering over my shoulder through the carriages at the "Grange" too. I always seem to anticipate a "Hall".

When I saw my first Great Western Region loco at Crewe in December last year (1964) I shouted it was a "Hall". It was about a mile away and before we could fight our way down to see it a nearby railwayist informed me that it was in fact a "Grange". That comment put me in my place. She in fact was 6819 "Highnam Grange."

Back to the present, we waited patiently for five minutes and finally the "Grange" started up and ambled forwards. Finally the cabside number appeared, she was 6856 "Stowe Grange." Certainly a marvellous highlight.

About 00.10 a "Brit" thundered in from the North and I chased her to the south end of the station. The "Brit" turned out to be a 9F 2-10-0 in the shape of 92133. Certainly, a couple of hours for mistaken guesses! Nevertheless, good to see another steam class on station. Three good "Black Fives" were also noted.

37 locos in about two hours. That is one engine every three minutes. Yes, Crewe still reigns as the supreme junction. And at hardly the rush hour as it was from 22.42-00.42. Good to see seven different steam classes.

I came back to D.S. and found him alive and kicking. He was talking to a little naff from Ashton (a sizeable town on the outskirts of Manchester). Apparently, the little naff did a bit of trainspotting and D.S. was impressing on him the magnitude of our exploits. He did not seem too impressed and appeared to be rather an obstreperous youth. Over to our platform we moved and out train arrived a few minutes late. It was the 21.00 from London Euston. The buffet car was teacups to Crewe only again so D.S. would miss his coffee nightcap. The Ashton naff ran off to the far end of the train as fast as his 14 year old legs would carry him.

CREWE STATION on THURSDAY NIGHT 22.42-00.42						
		Home shed		Built	Withdrawn	Scrap
Diesels						
English Electric Type 4 1-Co-Co-1 1958						
D 221	"Ivernia"	9A	Longsight	Jul-1959		
D 231	"Sylvania"	1F	Rugby	Sep-1959		
D 236		12B	Carlisle Upperby	Oct-1959		
D 255		12B	Carlisle Upperby	Jan-1960		
D 300		5A	Crewe Diesel	Nov-1960		
D 307		1B	Camden	Oct-1960		
D 344		5A	Crewe Diesel	May-1961		
Total	7					
Brush Type 4 Co-Co 1962						
D1611		82A	Bristol Bath Road	Aug-1964		
D1635		5A	Crewe Diesel	Nov-1964		
D1645		87E	Landore	Jan-1965		
D1678		86A	Cardiff Canton	May-1965		
D1849		5A	Crewe Diesel	Jun-1965		
D1850		5A	Crewe Diesel	Jun-1965		
Total	6					
BR Sulzer Type 2 Bo-Bo 1958						
D5135		9A	Longsight	Oct-1960		
D5241		D14	Cricklewood Div.(ex D16)	Jan-1964		
Total	2					
Electrics						
A.E.I. (British Thomson-Houston) AL1 Bo-Bo 1959						
E3017		LMW	London Midl. West. Lines	May-1961		
Total	1					
English Electric AL3 Bo-Bo 1960						
E3027		LMW	London Midl. West. Lines	Sep-1960		
E3031		LMW	London Midl. West. Lines	Nov-1960		
E3033		LMW	London Midl. West. Lines	Dec-1960		
E3035		LMW	London Midl. West. Lines	Jul-1961		
Total	4					
A.E.I. (Metropolitan-Vickers) AL2 Bo-Bo 1960						
E3054		LMW	London Midl. West. Lines	Nov-1961		
Total	1					
BR A.E.I. Type A Bo-Bo 1960						
E3056		LMW	London Midl. West. Lines	Aug-1961		
E3057		LMW	London Midl. West. Lines	Jun-1961		
E3059	hauled	LMW	London Midl. West. Lines	Jul-1961		
E3062		LMW	London Midl. West. Lines	Dec-1961		
E3077		LMW	London Midl. West. Lines	Mar-1963		
Total	5					

		Home shed		Built	Withdrawn	Scrap
BR B.T.H. Type A Bo-Bo 1962						
E3093		LMW	London Midl. West. Lines	Nov-1963		
Total	1					
Steam				Built	Withdrawn	Scrap
Collett 5MT 6800 4-6-0 "Grange" 1936						
6856	"Stowe Grange"	85A	Worcester	Nov-1937	Nov-1965	Jan-1967
Total	1					
Ivatt 4MT 2-6-0 1947						
43001		5B	Crewe South	Dec-1947	Sep-1967	Dec-1967
Total	1					
Stanier 5MT 4-6-0 "Black Five" 1934						
44679		5B	Crewe South (ex 5A)	May-1950	Sep-1967	Jun-1968
45064		2F	Bescot	Dec-1934	Mar-1967	Oct-1967
45350		5D	Stoke	May-1937	Aug-1968	Dec-1968
Total	3					
BR Standard 7P6F 4-6-2 "Britannia" Derby 1951						
70048	"Territorial Army 1908-1958"	12B	Carlisle Upperby	Jul-1954	May-1967	Oct-1967
70054	"Dornoch Firth"	5B	Crewe South (ex 5A)	Sep-1954	Nov-1966	Jun-1967
Total	2					
BR Standard 5MT 4-6-0 Doncaster 1951						
73038		6D	Shrewsbury (ex 5E)	Sep-1953	Sep-1965	May-1966
Total	1					
BR Standard 2MT 2-6-0 Doncaster 1953						
78031		5B	Crewe South	Sep-1954	Oct-1966	Mar-1967
Total	1					
BR Standard 9F 2-10-0 Brighton 1954						
92133		8H	Birkenhead	May-1957	Jul-1967	Jan-1968
Total	1					
On Station	37	Kops	22			
Steam	10	Diesels	15		Electrics	12

	Home Area		10	Visitors	27		
Shed	5A	5	5B	4	5D	1	
Distribution	LMW	12	D14	1			
	1B	1	1F	1	2F	1	
	6D	1	8H	1	9A	2	
	12B	3					
	82A	1	85A	1	86A	1	
	87E	1					
Steam Classes		7					
Steam Origin	GWR	1	LMS	4	BR	5	
Station							
Highlight	6856 "Stowe Grange"		85A		Worcester		

The train was on the full side of half full and D.S. and I found a half full compartment with three people in it. A British couple started talking. They were very friendly and said that they were going to Sheffield to find work. Where had they come from? Barry Docks! Barry Docks was apparently a dying place and it wasn't just steam locos that died there. The third occupant of the compartment was an Asian girl dressed in a sari. They noted that she had fallen asleep. Seemed a good thing to do and the next thing I remembered was being woken up by the couple at Manchester Piccadilly Station. Wishing them god luck at Sheffield we left them and the train. It was now 01.42. At least the illuminated station clock said so. Our train was late; thirteen minutes late in fact.

		Schedule	Actual	Miles
Depart	CREWE	00.42	00.47	0
Arrive	MANCHESTER PICCADILLY	01.29	01.42	30¾

A 30 m.p.h. dawdle. So much for a mainline electric at the head of our train.

At the head of our train had been E3059. We met up with the Ashton naff again but he quickly left us to chat up the cabbies to try to get a cheap taxi ride to Ashton.

We soon reached our "hotel" for the night which was Manchester Victoria station. We looked for a left luggage office but it was closed for the night. Where do we put our stuff? A left luggage locker was the answer. We put in two shillings (ten new pence) got all our stuff in the one locker, locked it and pulled out the key. Overall, a saving on depositing it with the left luggage attendant. Now for somewhere to sleep. The station not unexpectedly at this tome of the early morning was rather quiet. The waiting room, however, was full up with unfortunates so we decided to give the connecting Manchester Exchange station a try.

We thus had the formidable task of walking along the second longest railway platform in the world. This connected Victoria to exchange stations. It is 2194 feet long (D.S. attempted to measure it out as he walked)! The longest platform in the world is at Khargpar, south eastern India. So our platform had to grow another 540 feet before it became the longest in the world. D.S. said not surprisingly said that it felt like the second longest in the world and was rather relieved when we finally reached Manchester Exchange.

We were in luck and found a newish waiting room, all in the dark. Seats were upturned on tables, the lights were out and we stumbled in and found benches at the back of the room.

We were disturbed just as we were getting down to sleep by a railway porter. He said that the cops would throw us out if they found us here.

ME: "We have a Railrover, giving us unlimited usage of all BR trains for one week and that must include waiting rooms while we are waiting for our trains." (An interesting thesis which did not cut too much ice with the railway cops at Derby station but, nevertheless, we still managed to outwit, outthink and outmanoeuvre them there. I doubted whether any authority could reverse the tables here).

PORTER: "Railrover, what's that? I don't know but you had better watch out for the cops."

With that warning he sloped off and left us. So the cops put the screw on in this station as well? Seemed unlikely, from what we had seen of the other waiting room at Manchester Victoria which had been full of unfortunates.

Goodnight D.S. sweet dreams! He had already fallen asleep. Well tomorrow (or rather later today) would be a hard day and I was glad that he would have less insomnia to moan about now that he had fallen asleep. It suddenly dawned on me that our Railrovers were running out. We had only Friday and Saturday left but they would be action packed enough days. Now back on our original timetable we would bash our way around Manchester, Liverpool and all Lancashire in fact. This last stronghold of LMR steam would certainly be worth visiting.

The timetable should work particularly well after 12.00 on Saturday as D.S. has to go home then to do the Sunday newspapers in the shop in Edinburgh. However, it's better going round the LMR with somebody to speak and shout at and mess up your timetables than go round alone all nicely to timetable. As Nixon said to the US press (after earlier losing to Kennedy in the Presidential election) after losing the contest to be Governor of California "You won't have me to kick about now!" Nixon subsequently restored his fortunes by being elected USA President so perhaps there is hope for D.S. yet. One thing for sure. I'll have to indulge in soliloquies after 12.00 on Saturday I suppose but that is all in the future.

Review of the Day

This was the original timetable:-

DAY 6 <u>**THURSDAY AUGUST 5TH 1965**</u> **LMR DAY 5**

STREET PLAN OF CHESTER

Reveille: - Dawn

<u>**Do 6A Chester Midland**</u>
<u>**Do 6B Mold Junction**</u>

		<u>MILES</u>
Depart CHESTER NORTHGATE	06.35 or 07.21 or 07.40 or 08.25 or 08.50	0
Arrive NORTHWICH	07.06 or 07.52 or 08.11 or 08.56 or 09.22	18

<u>Do 8E Northwich (20 mins. approx)</u>

Depart NORTHWICH	07.20 or 07.52 or 08.11 or 08.18 or 09.01 or 09.22 or 10.03	18
Arrive MANCHESTER CENTRAL	08.04 or 08.40 or 08.53 or 09.05 or 09.44 or 10.07 or 10.49	<u>38¾</u>
Depart MANCHESTER PICCADILLY	08.30 or 09.10 or 11.10 or 12.10	0
Arrive SHEFFIELD VICTORIA	09.26 or 10.10 or 12.05 or 13.04	<u>41½</u>

FROM THIS POINT ALL TRAVEL IS OUTWITH LMR RAILROVER

STREET PLAN OF SHEFFIELD

BUS   -   Sheffield Joint Committee No 87 (Maltby)

Depart SHEFFIELD POND STREET BUS STATION
Arrive BRINSWORTH THREE MAGPIES

<u>**Do 41E Tinsley**</u>

BUS (same)

Depart STAVELEY BARROW HILL
Arrive SHEFFIELD POND STREET

BUS   -   Sheffield Corporation No 71 or No 52

Depart WICKER
Arrive RIBSTON ROAD

<u>**Do 41B Darnall**</u>

BUS (same)

Depart RIBSTON ROAD
Arrive COMMERCIAL STREET or FITZALAN SQUARE

British Rail

Depending on time spent in Sheffield area.

A or B

A

Depart SHEFFIELD MIDLAND	12.36
Arrive DONCASTER	13.20

Do 36A Doncaster
Do Doncaster Works

B

Depart SHEFFIELD VICTORIA	14.26
Arrive DONCASTER	15.08

Do 36A Doncaster only

A and B

Depart DONCASTER	16.00
Arrive WAKEFIELD WESTGATE	16.25

Do 56A Wakefield (80 mins. approx)

Bus or British Rail (hourly service)
Depart WAKEFIELD KIRKGATE
Arrive NORMANTON

Do 55E Normanton

Bus or British Rail (infrequent)
Depart NORMANTON
Arrive ROYSTON & NOTTON

Do 55D Royston

Bus or British Rail (infrequent)
Depart ROYSTON & NOTTON
Arrive LEEDS CITY

In Leeds to these sheds in this order (time permitting):

Do 55A	Holbeck (1)
Do 55B	Stourton (4)
Do 55C	Farnley Junction (2)
Do 55H	Neville Hill (3)

There is a third alternative C if at Doncaster we would rather save money and not visit the

North Eastern Region (outwith our railrover).

C

Depart DONCASTER	16.02
Arrive KILNHURST WEST	16.24

Depart KILNHURST WEST	16.51
Arrive WATH NORTH	17.02

Do 41C Wath (25 mins. approx)   Recovery Time
                                                       NIL

Depart WATH NORTH	17.27
Arrive SHEFFIELD MIDLAND	17.59

2 hours at leisure (trainspotting probably) in Sheffield

                                                                    MILES

Depart SHEFFIELD VICTORIA	19.45	0
Arrive MANCHESTER PICCADILLY	20.45	41½

Night: -   Manchester Victoria or Exchange Waiting Room
Or

Depart LEEDS CITY	22.42
Arrive MANCHESTER EXCHANGE	00.26

Night: -   Manchester Exchange or Victoria Waiting Room

- - - - - - - - - - - - - - - - - - -

Comments:-

Many comments are needed her. Manchester Central must be reached before 09.10 as if the 09.10 from Piccadilly is missed then there is a gap until 11.10 before the next train.

In Sheffield Area :-

41D Canklow (closed)
41H Staveley (closed)

In North Eastern Region :-

The order of visiting the Leeds sheds is important because (1) Holbeck has Jubilees and other good LMR locos. (2) Farnley Junction has Jubilees (3) Neville Hill had Q6 (4) Stourton (although having a sizable allocation) had only unspectacular LMR locos. As we would be pushed for time I wanted the best sheds first in case we are unable to visit one or more.

All bus services are indicated in the "British Locomotive Shed Directory.

Economists, linear programming specialists and critical path analysts would not have liked our day. We had travelled in total 223 miles, the highest since Sunday, but in fact had not achieved a great deal. It had been a day of clearing up loose ends centred on an ill-fated effort to visit Crewe Works.

The miss of the Eastern Region/ North Eastern region was regrettable but not disastrous. The

Eastern Region had been fairly decimated of steam but we had managed to visit 40 E Colwick on Monday and also should have managed to visit 41E Staveley Barrow Hill and 41J Langwith Junction that day. We had obtained permits for to visit 36A Doncaster and Doncaster Works today and they, of course, would no longer be required. 36A Doncaster was a shadow of its former great self with its large steam passenger allocations having disappeared leaving now only four surviving steam classes:-

	36A DONCASTER			
Steam				
Thompson 8P6F 4-6-2 A1 1945				
61039	**61055**	**61058**	**61087**	
61107	**61121**	**61157**	**61158**	
61196	**61208**	*61225*	**61326**	
61329	**61360**	**61367**	**61384**	
Total	*14*			
Robinson 8F 2-8-0 O4 1911				
63593	*63613*	**63688**	**63730**	
63734	**63738**	**63764**	**63785**	
63818	**63858**			
Total	*9*			
Riddles WD 8F 2-8-0 "Austerity" 1943				
90001	**90018**	**90063**	**90073**	
90096	**90154**	**90156**	**90158**	
90169	**90195**	**90203**	*90211*	
90235	**90252**	**90255**	**90277**	
90279	**90293**	**90296**	**90305**	
90330	**90364**	*90365*	**90369**	
90372	**90421**	**90428**	**90448**	
90476	**90477**	**90480**	**90484**	
90498	**90506**	**90538**	**90557**	
90580	**90636**	**90675**	**90683**	
90687	**90709**	**90718**		
Total	*39*			
BR Standard 9F 2-10-0 Brighton 1954				
92168	**92172**	**92174**	**92183**	
92190	**92201**			
Total	*5*			
Grand Total	*67*			
Recently		*Surviving*		
Withdrawn	*8*	*Steam Classes*	*4*	
Saw Elsewhere				
on the Tour	*2*			
Steam	*Aug-50*	*180*	*Mar-59*	*191*
Allocation	*Apr-65*	*64*	*Aug-65*	*67*
	Closed to Steam:-		*Apr-66*	

This is how our day actually panned out:-

		Schedule	*Actual*	*Miles*
Depart	SHREWSBURY	10.30	10.30	0
Arrive	WREXHAM GENERAL	11.14	11.14	30¼
	Do 6C Croes Newydd			
		Schedule	*Actual*	*Miles*
Depart	WREXHAM GENERAL	12.18	12.18	0
Arrive	CHESTER	12.46	12.46	12¼
		Schedule	*Actual*	*Miles*
Depart	CHESTER	14.35	14.35	0
Arrive	CREWE	15.06	15.06	21¼
	See 6A Chester Midland			
	See CW Crewe Works			

		Schedule	Actual	Miles
Depart	CREWE	17.05	17.05	0
Arrive	STOKE	17.31	17.31	14¾
	Do 5D Stoke			
		Schedule	Actual	Miles
Depart	STOKE	18.52	18.52	0
Arrive	STAFFORD	19.30	19.30	16¼
		Schedule	Actual	Miles
Depart	STAFFORD	20.05	20.05	0
Arrive	NUNEATON TRENT VALLEY	20.40	20.32	36½
	Do 5E Nuneaton			
		Schedule	Actual	Miles
Depart	NUNEATON TRENT VALLEY	21.47	20.05	0
Arrive	CREWE	22.42	20.32	61
		Schedule	Actual	Miles
Depart	CREWE	00.42	00.47	0
Arrive	MANCHESTER PICCADILLY	01.29	01.42	30¾

One shed which never was on the day's itinerary was 6F Machynlleth. The shed had suffered nine recent withdrawals and was now down to an allocation of only seven steam locos.

6F MACHYNLLETH				
Steam				
Collett 3MT 2251 0-6-0 1930				
2236	2268	3208		
Total	0			
Ivatt 2MT 2-6-0 1946				
46446	**46521**			
Total	2			
BR Standard 4MT 4-6-0 Brighton 1951				
75002	**75004**	75013	75028	
75055				
Total	5			
BR Standard 4MT 2-6-4T Doncaster 1953				
80097	80098	80099	80101	
80104	80105			
Total	0			
Grand Total	7			
Recently Withdrawn	9	**Surviving Steam Classes**	2	
Saw at Barry Docks revisited Aug-70	5			
Steam Allocation	**Aug-50**	53	**Mar-59**	47
	Apr-65	13	**Aug-65**	7
	Closed to Steam:-		**Dec-66**	
	Saw elsewhere on tour(4)			

Due to not going round Crewe Works it had been a relatively poor day for steam numbers and overall engine numbers. Of the original timetable little could be discerned in today's debacle. In fact, all that could be discerned was 6B Mold Junction. Doncaster, Sheffield and Leeds were nowhere to be seen. The Cardiff General station missed connection, extended hostel stays and the ill-fated attempt to visit Crewe Works had put them about a day beyond reach. At least we had gained some extra sleep (whether wanted or not), comfort and much needed rest from the hostel mishaps. Who knows we may have collapsed from our exertions or fallen asleep on a train (or rather both of us doing so as D.S. could hardly be said to be a great awakeist) without these extra hostel sleep-ins.

The day itself had started slowly and late thanks to the wicked warden at Shrewsbury youth Hostel. At least there was a railway timetable at the Youth Hostel and a makeshift timetable was quickly prepared and fulfilled our objectives for the day. The enforced late start enabled us to do 6D Shrewsbury and catch our train for Wrexham neatly enough. However, we arrived at Chester later than originally planned due to the wicked warden and 6A Chester Midland had to be omitted. 6B Mold Junction proved to be excellent and we at least passed 6A Chester Midland by – and it appeared to be a quiet enough shed with nothing much missed as a result.

We arrived at Crewe Station with two hours to do Crewe Works. Let's get this straight if you have got the authority or implied authority to go round Crewe Works you damned well go round and not let any officious, stupid fool stop you. Our Railrover tickets gave us access as they were valid for advertised excursions which we said we were on. That being the case if someone says that our tickets are not valid then you jolly well ignore him and walk straight in (as we could have done) or better still call for some higher authority at the Works who could swat the fly and straighten out matters in our favour. We should certainly have done this as there were other people around. There is in fact probably only one way not to go round and that was to get angry at the idiot watchman and be virtually dragged out by D.S. before I attacked him. We were there to go round the Works and not to react to an ignoramus. My actions at that the time were so silly I can hardly believe it.

Perhaps it was the surprise nature of his rejection of our request for entry knocked me off balance. By the surprise nature I mean that when we are stopped making an unauthorized entry into a shed we try to talk our way in and wave around wads of permits. 99 per cent. of the time we seem to get round by one means or another In fact, I would go as far to say that it is well nigh impossible to stop a determined person from making an unauthorized visit to a shed. And here, in the greatest paradox of the tour our credentials were impeccable. Our authorization to go round Crewe Works was higher than for any other shed on our tour. With our other authorizations they were for parties of 10-15 people. Here we were on an advertised excursion to Crewe Works with a BR party and were refused admittance. Hence, I was surprised and ready to lash out at some insignificant little idiot who tried to stop you. It is true that we were not at the time with the main BR party but on our retreat we met some boys who were with the official party but had detoured to visit 5B Crewe South first. D.S. said that he had enough of trying to get into Crewe Works at the time we met them but I should have overruled him and joined the other boys and visited Crewe Works with them. In retrospect it was a big mistake not applying for a permit for Crewe Works. I did not realize at the time of making my applications at the end of last year that Crewe Works would be choc a bloc with steam locomotives under repair. Strangely, and inexplicably our master timetable for the week had not provided for any visiting time for Crewe Works. In retrospect I should have applied for a permit.

We then went back to the station for about an hour and a half. We could have more profitably visited 5B Crewe South again or possibly had enough time to get a train to 8E Northwich and get back in time for our train to 5D Stoke. It had been something like the drained feeling at Cardiff General station when we had missed our connection and had sad disconsolately around rather than try to visit 88B Radyr or 86A Canton in the new time available.

Let's get away from Crewe and the ghost of Cardiff. 5D Stoke and 5E Nuneaton were well worth visiting and completed the visiting day. The makeshift timetable for the day had worked perfectly well once we had got out of Shrewsbury Youth Hostel and the loose sheds were picked up nicely. "Loose" in that they had slipped out of the previous day's timetable. Now we are back on the original master timetable at Manchester Exchange. Let's hope for a smooth final two days.

At the end of the day we had managed to visit only five sheds today (6D Shrewsbury, 6C Croes Newydd, 6B Mold Junction, 5D Stoke and 5E Nuneaton). All good steam sheds though. We had also travelled by 6A Chester Midland and CW Crewe Works. In all we had seen 185 steam, 43 diesels and 39 electrics today.

DAY 6 SHREWSBURY, WREXHAM, CHESTER, CREWE, STOKE, NUNEATON TO MANCHESTER

	Visits	GWR	SR	LMS	LNER	WD	BR	Steam Total	Diesel Total	Electric Total	Grand Total
6D	Shrewsbury	4		6			15	25	3		28
	pass 6D	1		1				2			2
	Shrewsbury station							0	2		2
	Shrewsbury to Wrexham			3				3			3
6C	Croes Newydd	13					2	15			15
	Wrexham to Chester	1		3				4	4		8
6B	Mold Junction	3		19			1	23	1		24
6A	Chester Midland (pass)	1		5				6			6
CW	Crewe Works (pass)			4				4	2		6
	Crewe station (afternoon)			1			1	2	5	15	22
	Crewe to Stoke			5				5	3		8
5D	Stoke			45			15	60			60
	Stoke to Stafford			1				1	1		2
	Stafford Station			1				1	2	6	9
	Stafford to Nuneaton							0	3	3	6
5E	Nuneaton			21		1	1	23	2		25
	pass 5E							0	1		1
	Nuneaton station						1	1		2	3
	Crewe station (night)	1		4			5	10	15	12	37
		24		119		1	41	185	43	39	267
REWIND 12th Dec 1964											
	Crewe Station 121264			9				9	7	5	21

It is now 02.28. I'll set myself to wake up at 04.45. That gives me about two and a quarter hours shut eye, shut eye, shut eye, ----------

----

END OF DAY SIX

Some steam classes seen today analyses follow:-

446

ENGINE CLASSES ACTIVE ON SHED DAY 6		BR total	CW Crewe Wks	5D Stoke	5E Nuneaton	6A Chester	6B Mold Jct.	6C Croes Nwd	6D Shewsbury	Total DAY 6
Hawksworth 2F 1600 0-6-0PT 1949	1600-1669	70						2		2
Collett dev.1938 of Churchward 8F 2-8-0 1903	2884-2899; 3800-66	83						1		1
Hawksworth 5MT 6959 4-6-0 "Modified Hall" 1944	6959-6999, 7900-7929	71					1	1		2
Collett 5MT 5600 0-6-2T 1924	5600-5699	100						1		1
1927 dev. of Collett 5MT 5600 0-6-2T 1924	6600-6699	100						2		2
1933 dev. of Collett 3F 5700 0-6-0PT 1929	3600-3799, 4600-4699, 8700, 8750-8799, 9600-9682,9711-9799	523					1	3	1	5
Collett 5MT 6800 4-6-0 "Grange" 1936	7800-7829	30							2	2
Ivatt 2MT 2-6-2T 1946	42700-42944	245				1	1			2
Ivatt 4MT 2-6-0 1947	44027-44606	580	0							0
Stanier 5MT 4-6-0 "Black Five" 1934	46220-57	38			0					0
Ivatt 2MT 2-6-0 1946	46400-46527	128			1				1	2
Midland 3F "Jinty" 0-6-0T 1924 dev. of Johnson 1899 design	47260-47681	417	3	5			2			10
Stanier 8F 2-8-0 "Big Eight" 1935	48000-48775	666		16	12		9		3	40
BR Standard 5MT 4-6-0 Doncaster 1951	73000-73171	172					1	1	4	6
BR Standard 4MT 4-6-0 Brighton 1951	76000-76114	115		6						6
BR Standard 2MT 2-6-0 Doncaster 1953	90000-90732	733			1					1
BR Standard 9F 2-10-0 Brighton 1954	92000-92250	251		1						1
			3	53	21	6	22	12	15	132

ENGINE CLASSES WITHDRAWN ON SHED DAY 6

Class	Numbers	BR total	CW Crewe Wk	5D Stoke	5E Nuneaton	6B Mold Jct.	6C Croes Nwd	6D Shewsbury	Withdrawn DAY 6
Collett 3MT 2251 0-6-0 1930	2200-2299; 3200-3219	120				1			1
Collett dev.1938 of Churchward 8F 2-8-0 1903	2884-2899; 3800-66	83					1		1
Collett 5MT 5600 0-6-2T 1924	5600-5699	100					1		1
Collett 5MT 7800 4-6-0 "Manor" 1938	7800-7829	30						1	1
Ivatt 2MT 2-6-2T 1946	41200-41329	130						1	1
Midland 4F 0-6-0 1924	42425-42672	243			1				1
Stanier 4MT 2-6-4T 1935 dev of Fowler 1927	42300-42424	125		1					1
Fowler 4MT 2-6-4T 1927	42050-42299; 42673-42699	277		2					2
Fairburn 4MT 2-6-4T 1945 dev. of Stanier 1935	44027-44606	580	1						1
Stanier 5MT 4-6-0 "Black Five" 1934	44658-45499	842		1					1
Stanier 8P 4-6-2 "Coronation" 1937	46220-57	38			1				1
Midland 3F "Jinty" 0-6-0T 1924 dev. of Johnson 1899 design	47260-47681	417		3					3
Stanier 8F 2-8-0 "Big Eight" 1935	48000-48775	666					1		1
BR Standard 4MT 2-6-4T Doncaster 1953	80000-80154	155						8	8
			1	7	2	1	3	10	24

ENGINE CLASSES
ACTIVE OFF SHED DAY 6

Engine class / numbers	BR total	pass shrewsb to shrewsby	shrewsby to wrexham	wrexham to chester	crewe station	crewe to stoke	stoke to stafford	stafford station	nuneaton station	crewe st night	Grand Total
Collett 5MT 4900 4-6-0 "Hall" 1928											
4900-4999, 5900-5999, 6900-6958	258	1									1
1933 dev. of Collett 3F 5700 0-6-0PT 1929											
3600-3799, 4600-4699, 8700, 8750-8799, 9600-9682, 97.	523			1							1
Collett 5MT 6800 4-6-0 "Grange" 1936											
6800-6879	80									1	1
Ivatt 4MT 2-6-0 1947											
43000-43161	162					1				1	2
Stanier 5MT 4-6-0 "Black Five" 1934											
44658-45499	842		1	1		2		1		3	8
Ivatt 2MT 2-6-0 1946											
46400-46527	128	1		1					1		3
Midland 3F "Jinty" 0-6-0T 1924 dev. of Johnson 1899 design											
47260-47681	417					1					1
Stanier 8F 2-8-0 "Big Eight" 1935											
48000-48775	666		2		2	1					5
BR Standard 7P6F 4-6-2 "Britannia" Derby 1951											
70000-70054	55									3	3
BR Standard 5MT 4-6-0 Doncaster 1951											
73000-73171	172			1							1
BR Standard 4MT 4-6-0 Brighton 1951											
75000-75079	80						1				1
BR Standard 2MT 2-6-0 Doncaster 1953											
78000-78064	65									1	1
BR Standard 9F 2-10-0 Brighton 1954											
92000-92250	251									1	1
Total		2	3	4	2	5	1	1	1	10	29

449

| ENGINE CLASSES | | | Off Shed | On Shed | Withdrawn | Grand |
DAY 6 SUMMARY TOTALS			DAY 6	DAY 6	DAY 6	Totals
Hawksworth 2F 1600 0-6-0PT 1949				2		2
Collett 3MT 2251 0-6-0 1930					1	
Collett dev.1938 of Churchward 8F 2-8-0 1903				1	1	2
Collett 5MT 4900 4-6-0 "Hall" 1928			1			
Hawksworth 5MT 6959 4-6-0 "Modified Hall" 1944				2		2
Collett 5MT 5600 0-6-2T 1924				1	1	2
1927 dev. of Collett 5MT 5600 0-6-2T 1924				2		2
1933 dev. of Collett 3F 5700 0-6-0PT 1929			1	5		6
Collett 5MT 6800 4-6-0 "Grange" 1936			1	2		3
Collett 5MT 7800 4-6-0 "Manor" 1938				2	1	3
Ivatt 2MT 2-6-2T 1946				1	1	2
Fairburn 4MT 2-6-4T 1945 dev. of Stanier 1935					2	2
Fowler 4MT 2-6-4T 1927					1	
Stanier 4MT 2-6-4T 1935 dev of Fowler 1927					1	
Hughes/Fowler 5MT 2-6-0 "Crab" 1926				2		2
Ivatt 4MT 2-6-0 1947			2	5		7
Midland 4F 0-6-0 1924					1	
Stanier 5MT 4-6-0 "Black Five" 1934			8	28	1	37
Stanier 8P 4-6-2 "Coronation" 1937					1	
Ivatt 2MT 2-6-0 1946			3	2		5
Midland 3F "Jinty" 0-6-0T 1924 dev. of Johnson 1899 design			1	10	3	14
Stanier 8F 2-8-0 "Big Eight" 1935			5	40	1	46
BR Standard 7P6F 4-6-2 "Britannia" Derby 1951			3			3
BR Standard 5MT 4-6-0 Doncaster 1951			1	6		7
BR Standard 4MT 4-6-0 Brighton 1951			1	10		11
BR Standard 4MT 2-6-0 Doncaster 1953				6		6
BR Standard 2MT 2-6-0 Doncaster 1953			1	1		2
BR Standard 4MT 2-6-4T Doncaster 1953						6
BR Standard 2MT 2-6-2T Derby 1953				2		2
Riddles WD 8F 2-8-0 "Austerity" 1943				1		
BR Standard 9F 2-10-0 Brighton 1954			1	1		2
			29	132	24	185

Part Seven

FRIDAY 6th AUGUST 1965

The Tour continues

Manchester, Stockport, Warrington
and
Liverpool Arrival

or the day of many blunders

or the day of the unscheduled mystery tour

or "BLACK FRIDAY"

Reveille: Manchester Exchange station Waiting Room

I awoke at 04.50 (five minutes later than planned) after two and a half hours shuteye. Certainly the eyes haven't been shut much this week. However, there had been a slight mistake as our train was not till 05.50 so there was little need to get up yet. I took advantage of another 30 minutes sleep and finally thought of getting up at 05.20. D.S. was still snoring and snorting away so I put one hand over his mouth and squeezed his nostrils with the other. After a few seconds D.S.'s brain began to get worried about the supply of oxygen and he made a great heave, shook my hands off and awoke spluttering for breath. Oh, that's wonderful, said D.S., to be out of that nightmare I felt I was being strangled.

It would be a busy but hopefully very fruitful day:-

		MILES
Depart MANCHESTER VICTORIA	05.50	0
Arrive DEAN LANE	05.57	2¾

Do 9D Newton Heath (35 mins. approx)   Recovery Time + 9

Depart DEAN LANE	06.41	0
Arrive MANCHESTER VICTORIA	06.48	2¾
Depart MANCHESTER EXCHANGE	07.10	0
Arrive PATRICROFT	07.21	4¾

Do 9H Patricroft (30 minutes approx.)

Salford Corporation Bus No 27

Depart PATRICROFT MONTON ROAD
Arrive AGECROFT BANK LANE

Do 9J Agecroft

Salford Corporate Bus No 57 or 77

Depart BANK LANE
Arrive PICCADILLY

Depart PICCADILLY   )   Manchester Corporation
Arrive KIRKMANSHULME LANE   )   92-93-94-95

Do 9A Longsight

Depart CROMWELL STREET
Arrive REDDISH NORTH STATION 109 Reddish North Bus

Do 9C Reddish

British Rail

Depart REDDISH NORTH	11.42	(12.12)	0
Arrive MANCHESTER PICCADILLY	11.50	(12.23)	4
Depart MANCHESTER PICCADILLY	11.57	(12.27)	0
Arrive MANCHESTER OXFORD ROAD	11.59	(12.29)	½
Depart MANCHESTER OXFORD ROAD	12.10	(12.30)	0
Arrive WARWICK ROAD	12.15	(12.35)	2½

Do 9E Trafford Park (45 mins. approx)   Recovery Time -7

Depart WARWICK ROAD	12.53	(13.13)	0
Arrive MANCHESTER OXFORD ROAD	13.00	(13.20)	2½
Depart MANCHESTER OXFORD ROAD	13.05	(13.35)	0
Arrive STOCKPORT EDGELEY	13.19	(13.49)	6¼

Do 9F Heaton Mersey (75 mins. approx)
Do 9B Stockport Edgeley (35 mins. approx)

Depart STOCKPORT EDGELEY	15.30	regular service	0
Arrive MANCHESTER PICCADILLY	15.38		5¾
Depart MANCHESTER CENTRAL	16.30 (17.00) (17.30)		0
Arrive WARRINGTON CENTRAL	16.49 (17.34) (17.51)		15¼

Do 8B Warrington (60 mins. approx)

Depart WARRINGTON CENTRAL	17.53	(18.53)	15¼
Arrive GARSTON	18.14	(19.14)	28

Do 8C Speke Junction (40 mins. approx)
Do 8J Allerton (35 mins. approx)

Depart ALLERTON	19.56	0
Arrive EDGE HILL	20.07	4½

Do 8A Edge Hill (65 mins. approx)

Depart EDGE HILL	21.25	(21.51)	0
Arrive LIVERPOOL LIME STREET	21.30	(21.55)	1

Night: -   Liverpool Station Waiting Room

Comments:-

Should be a good day with 12 motive power depots to be visited.

Alternative times in brackets. Railway recovery times ideal and lenient even the minus recovery times should not pose must problem. Bus service timings open to question. Left considerable time for bus connections. Can only hope. An outside chance that 8H Birkenhead might be fitted into the day if we gain ground in the early part of the timetable.

D.S.'s touch of asphyxia over for the moment we left the waiting room and walked down D.S.'s favourite platform (the second longest in the world) from Exchange back to Manchester Victoria station. On the way to and at Victoria we saw five good steam locos. D.S. was too tired to get his notebook out and write their numbers down. D.S. these days only seemed to note locos which were actually on shed!

MANCHESTER VICTORIA STATION EARLY FRIDAY MORNING						
		Home shed				
Steam				*Built*	*Withdrawn*	*Scrap*
Stanier 4MT 2-6-4T 1935 dev of Fowler 1927						
42656		9D	Newton Heath	*Feb-1941*	*May-1967*	*Nov-1967*
Total	*1*					
Stanier 5MT 4-6-0 "Black Five" 1934						
44943		55C	Farnley Junction	*Dec-1945*	*Oct-1967*	*Feb-1968*
45316		9E	Trafford Park	*Feb-1937*	*Mar-1968*	*Jun-1968*
Total	*2*					
BR Standard 7P6F 4-6-2 "Britannia" Derby 1951						
70051	"Firth of Forth"	5B	Crewe South (ex 5A)	*Aug-1954*	*Dec-1967*	*Mar-1968*
Total	*1*					
BR Standard 5MT 4-6-0 Doncaster 1951						
73129	*Caprotti valved*	9H	Patricroft	*Aug-1956*	*Nov-1967*	*saved*
Total	*1*					
On Station	**5**	**Kops**		**2**		
Steam	**5**	**Diesels**		**0**		
		Home Area	**3**	**Visitors**	**2**	
Shed	**9D**	**1**	**9E**	**1**	**9H**	**1**
Distribution	**5B**	**1**	**55C**	**1**		
Steam Classes	**4**					
Steam Origin	**LMS**	**3**	**BR**	**2**		

Due to an administrative slip up on my part we had omitted to request a permit for 9D Newton Heath in one of the batches. One of the ones we had was for 9M Bury – which was now closed to steam and an electric multiple unit depot so we would definitely not be visiting it! Strange having permits for all the sheds in the Manchester Area apart from the best one! Ian Firth and I had visited 9D Newton Heath along with 9B Stockport Edgeley on 12th December 1964 – both sheds being completed without incident.

Our bucket left Manchester Victoria on time for the short train trip to Dean Lane station, Newton Heath. The journey proved fruitful:-

MANCHESTER VICTORIA TO NEWTON HEATH						
		Home shed		*Built*	*Withdrawn*	*Scrap*
Diesels						
BR 0-6-0 Shunter 1953						
D3373		9D	Newton Heath	*Aug-1957*		
Total	*1*					
BR Sulzer Type 2 Bo-Bo 1958						
D5183		2E	Saltley	*Apr-1963*		
Total	*1*					

Steam				Built	Withdrawn	Scrap
Stanier 5MT 4-6-0 "Black Five" 1934						
45076		9D	Newton Heath	*Mar-1935*	*Jun-1968*	*Jan-1969*
Total	1					
Stanier 8F 2-8-0 "Big Eight" 1935						
48136		9D	Newton Heath	*Aug-1941*	*Mar-1967*	*Jul-1967*
48224		9J	Agecroft	*Sep-1942*	*Mar-1968*	*Sep-1968*
48426		9D	Newton Heath	*Dec-1943*	*Jun-1966*	*Sep-1966*
48612		9D	Newton Heath	*Jul-1943*	*Jun-1968*	*Nov-1968*
Total	4					
BR 9F 2-10-0 Brighton 1954						
92051		9D	Newton Heath	*Aug-1955*	*Oct-1967*	*Feb-1968*
Total	1					

On Journey	8	Kops		5		
Steam	6	Diesels		2		
		Home Area		7	Visitors	1
Shed	9D	6	9J	1		
Distribution	2E	1				
Steam Classes	3					
Steam Origin	LMS	5	BR	1		

Our train forked on to the Oldham line at the junction of the Oldham-Rochdale lines. Newton Heath shed was on the left and it looked nice and full as we passed. 9D Newton Heath is easily the best Manchester area steam shed and probably one of the top ten steam sheds on the LMR.

D.S. joked that he should pull the communication cord as he didn't fancy the ten minute walk back from Dean Lane station. I reassured him that the Loco Shed Directory said that the walking time was less than five minutes.

		Schedule	Actual	Miles
Depart	MANCHESTER VICTORIA	05.50	05.50	0
Arrive	DEAN LANE	05.57	05.57	2¾

14 minutes recovery time before we get the 06.41 back to Manchester Victoria. 30 minutes to do the shed and ten minutes to walk there and back.

Dean Lane was a funny old station. It had hardly changed since Victorian times when it was built. When Ian "Froth" Firth had arrived here last December we saw the old station bod who probably did all the duties turning off the gas mantle lights! However, he had already done that as it had been quite light since the back of four this morning.

We attacked the shed by a roundabout route. The long line of offices was not for us. Froth and I had walked along by the Rochdale (Newton Heath) station side to be as far away from the offices as possible. This had worked well for us then and would work for us now. We thus entered the shed by this "back door" route on the blind side of the offices. D.S. and I progressed round the shed without incident until we came to the repair and diesel shop ----

THE TIRED SHEDDIE INTERLUDE or THE WAD AFFAIR

Who would we bump into here but the shedmaster. We ignored him and continued round until he shouted and waved for us to come across to him. Trust our luck when this is our only depot without a permit for the Manchester Area. We walked across to him.

SHEDMASTER: "Have you a permit?"

ME: "Of course."

SHEDMASTER: "Why didn't you hand it in at the office?"

ME: "It's so early we didn't wish to trouble anybody."

Shedmaster heaves a sigh.

SHEDMASTER: "You had better give it to me."

Ah! So he wants the permit. But we haven't a permit for here. Thought quickly and referred mentally to my as yet unpublished book entitled "How to Fool Shedmasters". I decided to try a new ruse – the wad trick. I hoped that it would be 100 per cent. lethal. All one needs for it is a wad of permits. Yes, I had a wad of permits. Well take the wad out – all sixty of them. Proceed to flip through them one by one. While doing this fan the sheddie and irritate him by flipping through them close to his face. As you get halfway down the pile the effect becomes mesmeric. You believe yourself that the permit is in the pile and the shedmaster believes it also. His eyes are fixed on the pile almost watering in the draught created. He becomes frustrated as the wad is apparently never ending. Most sheddies crack before the halfway mark is reached but this really tough Lancashire hotpot had reached the two-thirds mark and I was almost visualising him lasting the course. What happens if he lasts the course? Do we go through the wad again? The book did not cover this possibility but the probability of this happening was hopefully nil.

I glanced up at the sheddie and he broke instantaneously. He waved his arms in frustration and ended our confrontation with these words:-

SHEDMASTER: "Acht. Never mind."

The poor very frustrated chap went away shaking his head suffering from this early morning attack of waditis. By this evening he'll believe that the incident never happened and that it had been a daydream. Perhaps during the night he'll wake up in bed screaming from a nightmare of being suffocated by permits. Secondary waditis the doctors call it. Primary waditis was the original encounter. The following day he feels completely drained – tertiary waditis.

I myself was so taken in by the wad trick that I believed that the permit was in the pile. I was disappointed when the shedmaster said "Never mind". That must be the sign of a 100% shedmaster fooler trick. It fools everyone even you as D.S. said afterwards to me.

9D NEWTON HEATH						
		Home shed		Built	Withdrawn	Scrap
Diesels						
Yorkshire Engine Co. 0-4-0 Shunter 1960						
D2859		9D		Dec-1960	Mar-1970	
Total	1					
Barclay 0-4-0 Shunter 1956						
D2954		9D		Feb-1956	Sep-1979	
Total	1					
BR 0-6-0 Shunter 1953						
D3784		9D		Sep-1959		
Total	1					
Steam				Built	Withdrawn	Scrap
Fairburn 4MT 2-6-4T 1945 dev. of Stanier 1935						
42115		9D		Jul-1949	Nov-1966	May-1967
Total	1					
Fowler 4MT 2-6-4T 1927						
42343		8F	Wigan(ex 9B)	Apr-1929	Oct-1965	Jan-1966
Total	1					

			Home shed		Built	Withdrawn	Scrap
Stanier 4MT 2-6-4T 1935 dev of Fowler 1927							
42492			9D		May-1937	Jun-1965	Oct-1965
42542			9D	(ex 5D Stoke)	Dec-1935	Jul-1965	Oct-1965
42548	on shed	Dec-64	9D		Jul-1936	Feb-1967	May-1967
42656			9D		Feb-1941	May-1967	Nov-1967
Total		4					
Hughes/Fowler 5MT 2-6-0 "Crab" 1926							
42715			9D	(ex 9G Gorton)	Apr-1927	Feb-1966	Jun-1966
42831			9D	(ex 9G Gorton)	May-1930	Dec-1965	Mar-1966
42844			9D	(ex 9G via 10H)	Oct-1930	Aug-1965	Oct-1965
42905			9D	(ex 9G Gorton)	Sep-1930	Jul-1965	Feb-1966
Total		4					
Midland 4F 0-6-0 1924							
44247	on shed	Dec-64	9D		May-1926	Dec-1965	Feb-1966
Total		1					
Stanier 5MT 4-6-0 "Black Five" 1934							
44696			9D	(ex 9B Stockport)	Dec-1950	May-1967	Feb-1968
44697	on shed	Dec-64	9D	(ex 9B Stockport)	Dec-1950	Nov-1967	Apr-1968
44795			12A	Carlisle Kingmoor	Aug-1947	Jul-1967	Dec-1967
44803			9D		Jun-1944	Jun-1968	Sep-1968
44845	on shed	Dec-64	9D		Oct-1944	Jun-1968	Dec-1968
44846			9D	(ex 16B Annesley)	Nov-1944	Jan-1968	Apr-1968
44861			9D	(ex 16C Derby)	Jan-1945	Nov-1967	Apr-1968
44890			9D		Aug-1945	Jun-1968	Jan-1969
44934			9D		Oct-1945	Sep-1967	Mar-1968
45077			9D	(ex 9H Patricroft)	Mar-1935	Aug-1965	Mar-1966
45203			9D		Nov-1935	Jun-1968	Feb-1969
45246			9D		Sep-1936	Dec-1967	Mar-1968
45291			9D	(ex 9B Stockport)	Dec-1936	Nov-1965	Jan-1966
45310			5E	Nuneaton (ex 2J)	Jan-1937	Aug-1968	Dec-1968
45336	on shed	Dec-64	9D		Mar-1937	Jan-1967	Jan-1968
45339			9D		Apr-1937	Jun-1967	Jan-1968
45341			9D		Apr-1937	Jan-1967	May-1967
45382			9D	(ex 9B Stockport)	Jul-1937	Jun-1968	Dec-1968
Total		18					
Stanier 6P5F 4-6-0 "Jubilee" 1934							
45604	"Ceylon"		9D		Mar-1935	Jul-1965	Oct-1965
Total		1					
Ivatt 2MT 2-6-0 1946							
46404			8L	Aintree	Dec-1946	May-1965	Oct-1965
46406			9D		Dec-1946	Jan-1967	Sep-1967
46412			9D		Jan-1947	Aug-1966	Nov-1966
46417			9K	Bolton	Mar-1947	Feb-1967	Jun-1967
46418	on shed	Dec-64	9D		Mar-1947	Jan-1967	Sep-1967
46437	on shed	Dec-64	9D		Jan-1950	May-1967	Oct-1967
46449			9D		Mar-1950	May-1967	Oct-1967
46501			9D		Mar-1952	May-1967	Nov-1967
46506			9K	Bolton	Nov-1952	May-1967	Nov-1967
Total		9					
Midland 3F "Jinty" 0-6-0T 1924 dev. of Johnson 1899 design							
47408	on shed	Dec-64	9D		Dec-1926	Nov-1965	Feb-1966
47480	on shed	Dec-64	9D		Jan-1928	Sep-1965	Jan-1966
47656			9D		Mar-1929	Dec-1965	Apr-1966
47681			9D	(8L via 9J Agecroft)	Oct-1931	Aug-1965	Dec-1965
Total		4					
Stanier 8F 2-8-0 "Big Eight" 1935							
48318			9D		Jan-1944	Oct-1966	Feb-1967
48321			9D		Feb-1944	Jun-1968	Nov-1968
48369			5D	Stoke	Oct-1944	Jun-1968	Jan-1969
48372	on shed	Dec-64	9D		Oct-1944	Dec-1966	Apr-1967
48391			9D		Apr-1945	Dec-1965	Mar-1966
48412			2C	Stourbridge	Oct-1943	Dec-1966	Jun-1967
48540			55D	Royston	Dec-1944	Oct-1967	May-1968

		Home shed			Built	Withdrawn	Scrap
Stanier 8F 2-8-0 "Big Eight" 1935(continued)							
48543		9D	(ex 9G Gorton)		*Jan-1945*	*Feb-1966*	*May-1966*
48557		9D	(ex 9G Gorton)		*Jul-1945*	*Jul-1967*	*Nov-1967*
48602		9D	(ex 5C Stafford)		*Apr-1943*	*Jul-1967*	*Dec-1967*
48744		9D	(ex 9B Stockport)		*May-1946*	*Mar-1968*	*Jul-1968*
48756		9D			*Nov-1945*	*Jan-1967*	*May-1967*
Total	12						
BR Standard 7P6F 4-6-2 "Britannia" Derby 1951							
70017	"Arrow"	9D	(ex 5A via 5B Crewe South)	*Jun-1951*	*Sep-1966*	*Jan-1967*
70024	"Vulcan"	5B	(ex 5A Crewe North)		*Aug-1951*	*Dec-1967*	*Apr-1968*
Total	2						
BR Standard 5MT 4-6-0 Doncaster 1951							
73126		9H	Patricroft		*Jun-1956*	*Jun-1968*	*Oct-1968*
Total	1						
BR Standard 9F 2-10-0 Brighton 1954							
92016		9D			*Oct-1954*	*Oct-1967*	*Apr-1968*
92056		9D			*Oct-1955*	*Nov-1967*	*Feb-1968*
92077		9D			*Mar-1956*	*Jul-1968*	*Oct-1968*
92080	*on shed*	*Dec-64* 9D			*Apr-1956*	*May-1967*	*Nov-1967*
Total	4						

On Shed	65	**Kops**		29			
Steam	62	**Diesels**		3			
Withdrawn	5						
on shed	*Dec-64*	11					
Home Locos	54	Home Area		3	Visitors	8	
Shed	9D	54	9H	1	9K	2	
Distribution:-	2C	1					
	5B	1	5D	1	5E	1	
	8F	1	8L	1			
	12A	1					
	55D	1					
Steam classes on view	13						
Steam Origin	LMS		55 BR		7		
Shed Highlight:-							
		45604	"Ceylon"				
Steam	*Aug-50*	167	*Mar-59*	154	*Apr-65*	79	
Allocation					*Aug-65*	98	
			Closed to Steam:-			*Oct-66*	
Home Steam	*excluding withdrawn locos*						
On/Off Shed	On Shed	47	Off Shed	51	% On Shed	48%	
Not on Shed							
Fairbum 4MT 2-6-4T 1945					42079	42087	2
Stanier 4MT 2-6-4T 1935						42464	1
"Crab"					42700	42938	2
"Black Fives"		44734	44818	44822	44891	44926	
		44933	44938	44949	45026	45076	
		45083	45101	45133	45202	45255	
			45271	45343	45420	45435	19
"Jubilee"					45600	45705	2
Ivatt 2MT 2-6-0 1946					46411	46452	2
"Jinty"						47660	1
"Big Eights"		48136	48174	48331	48426	48532	
		48533	48612	48758	48765	48775	10
"Britannias"				70021	70034	70044	3
BR 9F 2-10-0 1954		92018	92022	92031	92050	92051	
			92052	92067	92071	92081	9
							51
		saw elsewhere on the tour				21	
		saw on shed on Dec 64 Manchester and Crewe trip				5	
		saw elsewhere on Dec 64 Manchester and Crewe trip				3	
		saw on July 65 Preston trip				3	

458

Review and Appraisal of 9D Newton Heath

The shed was in the fork of the Miles Platting-Dean Lane, and Miles Platting-Newton Heath lines. Walking time was less than 5 minutes from Dean Lane Station.

A brilliant steam shed. 62 steam locos on shed on a weekday morning is good going. We helped matters by coming early before some of the engines could escape for their daily turns.

Seeing the two 0-4-0 diesel shunters was interesting. They seemed like toys. The dead line contained quite a mixture. Sad to see "Jubilee" 45604 "Ceylon" lying withdrawn here. She had known better days and was looking rather sorry for herself. It was curious seeing the Fowler 2-6-4 Tank on shed. She had just been transferred from 9B Stockport Edgeley to 8F Wigan Spring's Branch. Evidently, she was on her way and had stopped here for a rest. I think I saw her at 9B Stockport Edgeley last December. I quite like "Crabs", two of the four here were withdrawn. What is so pleasing to the eye is their ungainly massive smokeboxes (as all Fowler locos seem to have).

Newton Heath's allocation had recently been swollen by the closure of 9G Gorton. There were a few of those transferred locos on shed. The locos on shed were mostly home stock with only three of the visitors worth comment. The 55D Royston "Big Eight" had come off some cross-country freight no doubt. I was pleased at seeing the 2C Stourbridge "Big Eight" particularly as we had missed visiting the shed. We had seen a few more 2C "Big Eights" this week. They certainly get around.

I was really surprised at finding an 8L Aintree condemned "Doodle Bug" on shed. Perhaps she was going to be broken up in the Manchester area – *eventually she went for scrap in October 1965 to Cashmore's Great Bridge.* A remarkable number of "Doodle Bugs" on shed two of them from nearby 9K Bolton.

47 (48%) Home Steam on shed with 51 off shed including two "Jubilees". 32 of the missing 51 were seen by me at other places.

REWIND to Saturday 12th December 1964

9D NEWTON HEATH REWIND 12th DECEMBER 1964						
		Home shed		Built	Withdrawn	Scrap
Diesels						
BR 0-4-0 Shunter 1953						
D3372		9D		*Aug-1957*		
Total	1					
BR Sulzer Type 2 Bo-Bo 1958						
D5193		2E	2E Saltley (ex 16D)	*May-1963*		
Total	1					
Steam				Built	Withdrawn	Scrap
Fairburn 4MT 2-6-4T 1945						
42079		9D		*Jan-1951*	*May-1967*	*Oct-1967*
42087		9D		*Mar-1951*	*Oct-1966*	*Jan-1967*
Total	2					
Stanier 4MT 2-6-4T 1935 dev of Fowler 1927						
42464		9D		*Oct-1936*	*Aug-1965*	*Nov-1965*
42548	on shed	Aug-65 9D		*Jul-1936*	*Feb-1967*	*May-1967*
42640		9D		*Nov-1938*	*Sep-1964*	*May-1965*
42660		9D		*Apr-1941*	*Apr-1965*	*Aug-1965*
Total	4					
Fowler Midland 4F 0-6-0 1911						
43979		9D		*Dec-1922*	*Nov-1964*	*Feb-1965*
Total	1					

			Home shed		Built	Withdrawn	Scrap
Midland 4F 0-6-0 1924							
44247	on shed	Aug-65	9D	(ex 9L Buxton)	May-1926	Dec-1965	Feb-1966
44431			9D		Nov-1927	Sep-1964	Feb-1965
44460			9D		May-1928	Oct-1964	Feb-1965
44481			9D		May-1928	Nov-1964	Feb-1965
Total		4					
Stanier 5MT 4-6-0 "Black Five" 1934							
44697	on shed	Aug-65	9D		Dec-1950	Nov-1967	Apr-1968
44838			8A	Edge Hill	Sep-1944	Mar-1968	Jun-1968
44845	on shed	Aug-65	9D		Oct-1944	Jun-1968	Dec-1968
44933			9D		Oct-1945	Oct-1967	May-1968
45015			8A	Edge Hill	Apr-1935	Sep-1967	Feb-1968
45076			9D		Mar-1935	Jun-1968	Jan-1969
45202			9D		Oct-1935	Jun-1968	Nov-1968
45336	on shed	Aug-65	9D		Mar-1937	Jan-1967	Jan-1968
45343			9D		Apr-1937	Jun-1967	Dec-1967
Total		9					
Stanier 6P5F 4-6-0 "Jubilee" 1934							
45580	"Burma"		9D		Oct-1934	Dec-1964	Apr-1965
45592	"Indore"		9D		Dec-1934	Sep-1964	Jun-1965
45601	"British Guiana"		9D		Apr-1935	Sep-1964	Jun-1965
45653	"Barham"		9D		Jan-1935	Apr-1965	Aug-1965
Total		4					
Ivatt 2MT 2-6-0 1946							
46418	on shed	Aug-65	9D		Mar-1947	Jan-1967	Sep-1967
46437	on shed	Aug-65	9D		Jan-1950	May-1967	Oct-1967
46452			9D		Apr-1950	May-1967	Nov-1967
46472			9D		Jul-1951	Jan-1965	Apr-1965
46523			9D		Mar-1953	May-1967	Nov-1967
Total		5					
Midland 3F "Jinty" 0-6-0T 1924 dev. of Johnson 1899 design							
47408	on shed	Aug-65	9D		Dec-1926	Nov-1965	Feb-1966
47480	on shed	Aug-65	9D		Jan-1928	Sep-1965	Jan-1966
47584			9D		Dec-1928	Aug-1964	May-1965
47640			9D		Dec-1928	Sep-1964	Jan-1965
47660			9D		Mar-1929	Dec-1965	Apr-1966
Total		5					
Stanier 8F 2-8-0 "Big Eight" 1935							
48303			16F	Burton	Oct-1943	Jul-1966	Oct-1966
48331			9D		Sep-1943	Feb-1966	Sep-1966
48372	on shed	Aug-65	9D		Oct-1944	Dec-1966	Apr-1967
Total		3					
BR Standard 7P6F 4-6-2 "Britannia" Derby 1951							
70003	"John Bunyan"		12A	Carlisle Kingmoor	Mar-1951	Mar-1967	Dec-1967
Total		1					
BR Standard 5MT 4-6-0 Doncaster 1951							
73133			9H	Patricroft	Oct-1956	Jun-1968	Dec-1968
73144			9H	Patricroft	Dec-1956	Aug-1967	Feb-1968
Total		2					
BR Standard 9F 2-10-0 Brighton 1954							
92018			9D		Oct-1954	Apr-1967	Aug-1967
92076			9D	(ex 16E Kirkby)	Mar-1956	Feb-1967	Jun-1967
92080	on shed	Aug-65	9D		Apr-1956	May-1967	Nov-1967
92114			9D		Dec-1956	Jul-1967	Feb-1968
Total		4					

On Shed	46		**Kops**	43	
Steam	44		**Diesels**	2	
Withdrawn	9				
on shed	Aug-65	11			
Home Locos		39 Home Area		2	**Visitors** 5
Shed	9D	39	9H	2	
Distribution:-	2E	1	8A	2	
	12A	1	16F	1	

Steam classes on view		12					
Steam Origin	LMS		37 BR		7		
Shed Highlight:-							
	45592	"Indore"					
Steam	Aug-50	167	Mar-59	154	Apr-65	79	
Allocation					Aug-65	98	
			Closed to Steam:-			Oct-66	
Home Steam	excluding withdrawn locos						
On/Off Shed	On Shed	29	Off Shed	52	% On Shed	36%	
Not on Shed							
Fairbum 4MT 2-6-4T 1945						42115	1
Stanier 4MT 2-6-4T 1935				42492		42656	2
Midland 4F 0-6-0 1924						44544	1
"Black Fives"	44734	44803	44818		44890	44891	
	44934	45083	45101		45203	45246	
	45255	45271	45339		45341	45435	15
"Jubilee"					45642	45705	2
Ivatt 2MT 2-6-0 1946			46411		46449	46485	3
"Jinty"						47656	1
"Big Eights"	48136	48318	48321		48391	48426	
	48464	48532	48533		48612	48756	
			48758		48765	48775	13
BR 9F 2-10-0 1954	92016	92022	92026		92050	92051	
	92052	92056	92073		92077	92081	
		92110	92159		92161	92162	14
						total	52
	saw elsewhere on the tour					14	
	saw on shed on Aug 65 tour					18	
	saw elsewhere on Dec 64 Manchester and Crewe trip					1	
	saw on July 65 Preston trip					3	
	saw on September 58 Carlisle visit					1	
	saw on June 67 Carlisle visit					1	

Review and Appraisal of 9D Newton Heath rewind 12th December 1964

Very strange that there were 18 more steam engines (62 to 44) now than when Froth and I visited the shed last December. Probably this was due a bit to the closure of 9G Gorton and also our particularly early visit this morning.

Only in terms of the fast disappearing "Jubilees" was Newton Heath better last December. All the four "Jubilees" we saw then were now withdrawn and probably scrapped. What really was remarkable though was the withdrawn "Jubilee" 45592 "Indore".

"The strange withdrawl of "Indore"

"Indore" was in ex-works condition and was absolutely shining in an immaculate black unlined livery. Nothing could have looked healthier than "Indore". There was, however, something ghostly about "Indore". That was it, she had no chimney! I checked my Locoshed Directory. "Indore" had been withdrawn in September 1964. A curious case of withdrawal. The best looking steam engine on shed and she was withdrawn. What a paradox! Perhaps she had been spruced up for her funeral. Some time ago I understand engines used to be painted black on their withdrawl. I think that the practice fell into disuse when scrapings began to get out of hand. Sad, all the same and I'll never see a stranger sight. Indore was inside the shed building too, not on the deadline. Was she going to be preserved? A case similar to 61943 at 40E Colwick which had been withdrawn ages before but was in immaculate condition there. There was an easy explanation at Colwick though as 61943 was used as a stationary boiler there. That was not the case here. Here endeth the "Indore" puzzle.

Home steam on shed at 29(36%) was a bit disappointing with 52 off shed. Remarkably I was able to see 38 of the missing 52 at other places. We completed the shed last December cautiously, permitless and without sheddie trouble.

On we go

We arrived back at Dean Lane Station a good ten minutes before our bucket was due to arrive. It duly arrived on time and we had a pleasant ten minute trip back to Victoria through industrial Manchester. The last time I was here Froth and I were blessed with typical, horrible Manchester weather. It rained continually that day while we were in England. I had never seen rain like it. However, it evidently stops occasionally and I was surprised to find that it was dry today and in fact quite a good day. On the run in a couple of "Black Fives" were noted.

NEWTON HEATH TO MANCHESTER VICTORIA						
		Home shed		Built	Withdrawn	Scrap
Steam						
Stanier 5MT 4-6-0 "Black Five" 1934						
45026		9D	Newton Heath (ex 9H)	Sep-1934	Oct-1965	Apr-1966
45083		9D	Newton Heath	Mar-1935	Dec-1967	May-1968
Total	2					
On Journey	2 Kops	0				
Steam	2 Diesels	0				
	Home Area			2	Visitors	0
Shed	9D	2				
Distribution						
Steam Classes	1					
Steam Origin	LMS	2				

		Schedule	Actual		Miles
Depart	DEAN LANE	06.41	06.41		0
Arrive	MANCHESTER VICTORIA	06.48	06.48		2¾

One intermediate stop.

Now wait for it! Back we had to go down the second longest platform in the world (D.S. was visibly weakening). This was becoming a regular event and D.S. was accusing me of internationally manipulating the timetable to give him as many walks as possible. He said that if this continued he would go on strike and to hell with my timetable. Certainly, by his efforts during the week he had at times charred the timetable.

We arrived at our platform at Manchester Exchange at 07.00. Our train was due at 07.10. At that time no train. 07.15 no train. What had happened? At least there were many other people waiting too. Finally our train trundled in at 07.30 (twenty minutes late). Our worst train so far on the LMR in terms of lateness so we had been pretty lucky so far. A bit ridiculous that a train starting here could be twenty minutes late. Had the driver slept in? Nevertheless that was twenty minutes of the timetable lost. An inauspicious start but we did see some good steam :-

MANCHESTER VICTORIA-EXCHANGE FRIDAY MORNING						
		Home shed		Built	Withdrawn	Scrap
Steam						
Stanier 5MT 4-6-0 "Black Five" 1934						
44897		6B	Mold Junction	Sep-1945	Aug-1968	Dec-1968
45291		9D	Newton Heath (ex 9B)	Dec-1936	Nov-1965	Jan-1966
Total	2					

		Home shed		Built	Withdrawn	Scrap
Ivatt 2MT 2-6-0 1946						
46452		9D	Newton Heath	*Apr-1950*	*May-1967*	*Nov-1967*
Total	*1*					
Stanier 8F 2-8-0 "Big Eight" 1935						
48174		9D	Newton Heath(ex 5E)	*Jul-1943*	*May-1967*	*Nov-1967*
Total	*1*					
BR Standard 5MT 4-6-0 Doncaster 1951						
73011		9H	Patricroft	*Aug-1951*	*Nov-1967*	*Mar-1968*
Total	*1*					
BR Standard 3MT 2-6-2T Swindon 1952						
82003		9H	Patricroft	*May-1952*	*Dec-1966*	*Oct-1968*
Total	*1*					

On Station	6	**Kops**	3
Steam	6	**Diesels**	0

	Home Area			5	**Visitors**	1
Shed	9D	3	9H	2		
Distribution	6B	1				
Steam Classes	5					
Steam Origin	LMS	4	BR	2		

Our bucket finally trundled out at 07.32 (22 minutes late). It made up no time on the journey. However, the journey proved to be fruitful enough.

MANCHESTER EXCHANGE to PATRICROFT

		Home shed		Built	Withdrawn	Scrap
BR 0-4-0 Shunter 1953						
D3842		9D	Newton Heath	*Jun-1959*		
Total	*1*					
Steam				**Built**	**Withdrawn**	**Scrap**
Stanier 4MT 2-6-4T 1935						
42577		8F	Springs Branch(ex 1A)	*Sep-1936*	*Jan-1967*	*Jun-1967*
Total	*1*					
Stanier 5MT 4-6-0 "Black Five" 1934						
44863		8A	Edge Hill (ex 1E)	*Jan-1945*	*May-1967*	*Jan-1968*
45187		8A	Edge Hill	*Sep-1935*	*Jun-1968*	*Mar-1969*
45280		6J	Holyhead (ex 2E)	*Nov-1936*	*Nov-1967*	*Mar-1968*
Total	*3*					
Stanier 8F 2-8-0 "Big Eight" 1935						
48612		9D	Newton Heath	*Jul-1943*	*Jun-1968*	*Nov-1968*
Total	*1*					
BR Standard 4-6-0 1951 5MT Doncaster						
73159		9H	Patricroft	*Jan-1957*	*Oct-1967*	*Mar-1968*
Total	*1*					
BR Standard 3MT 2-6-2T 1952 5MT Swindon Doncaster						
82009		9H	Patricroft	*Jun-1952*	*Oct-1966*	*Mar-1967*
82034		9H	Patricroft	*Jan-1955*	*Dec-1966*	*Oct-1968*
Total	*2*					

On Journey	9	**Kops**	6
Steam	8	**Diesels**	1

	Home Area			5	**Visitors**	4
Shed	9D	2	9H	3		
Distribution	6J	1				
	8A	2	8F	1		
Steam Classes	5					
Steam Origin	LMS	5	BR	3		

		Schedule	Actual	Miles
Depart	MANCHESTER EXCHANGE	'07.10	'07.32	0
Arrive	PATRICROFT	'07.21	'07.43	4¾

One intermediate stop (Eccles) – shades of the Telegoons. Let's hope that this will be the last experience of late trains.

I consulted the LocoShed Directory and prepared for a short five minutes walk to the shed. However, several minutes later I began to get a little worried as we seemed to be getting further away from the railway. I rechecked the LSD. We or rather I had taken the wrong turning outside Patricroft Station. We quickly galloped back to the station and got on the right track. Another five or ten minutes wasted.

I told D.S. to be prepared for a host of Standard 5's. Patricroft had stacks of them and we had seen them all over the place during the week. What else, enquired D.S.? I told him not to worry as there should be enough to keep him amused although the shed would not be quite as good as 9D Newton Heath.

Patricroft is a unique shed in that it has two running sheds in the shape of a letter L. Probably the only formation of this kind on BR. The shed was on the fork of the Eccles-Patricroft and the Eccles-Monton Green lines. Although we had a permit we went round the shed carefully without incident. No sign of a shedmaster about the place. Obviously, this was not like the high security Birmingham Area where we met shedmasters or other authority at every shed we visited there.

9H PATRICROFT							
			Home shed		Built	Withdrawn	Scrap
Diesels							
BR 0-6-0 Shunter 1953							
D3699		1	9D	Newton Heath (ex 9G)	May-1959		
Total	1						
Steam					Built	Withdrawn	Scrap
Fowler 4MT 2-6-4T 1927							
42334			9E	Trafford Park (ex9Gvia9K)	Mar-1929	Dec-1965	Apr-1966
Total	1						
Stanier 5MT 4-6-0 "Black Five" 1934							
44856			2B	Oxley	Dec-1944	Feb-1967	Jun-1967
45046			5B	Crewe South	Oct-1934	Jun-1968	Dec-1968
Total	2						
Ivatt 7P 4-6-0 "Patriot" 1947 rebuild of Fowler 1933							
45531	"Sir Frederick Harrison"	12A	Carlisle Kingmoor	Apr-1933	Nov-1965	Mar-1966
Total	1						
Midland 3F "Jinty" 0-6-0T 1924 dev. of Johnson 1899 design							
47378			9H		Oct-1926	Nov-1965	Feb-1966
47662			9H	(ex 10A Carnforth)	Mar-1929	Jan-1966	Apr-1966
Total	2						
Stanier 8F 2-8-0 "Big Eight" 1935							
48213			9H		Aug-1942	Sep-1966	Feb-1967
48502			9H	(ex 5B Crewe South)	Aug-1944	Nov-1966	Aug-1967
48636			9H		Aug-1943	Aug-1967	Mar-1968
48714			9H		Jul-1944	Oct-1967	May-1968
48720			9H		Aug-1944	Jun-1968	Oct-1968
48745			9H		Apr-1946	May-1968	Sep-1968
48748			9F	Heaton Mersey (ex 9G)	Jun-1946	May-1966	Aug-1966
48770			9H		May-1946	Apr-1967	Oct-1967
Total	8						

		Home shed		Built	Withdrawn	Scrap
BR Standard 5MT 4-6-0 Doncaster 1951						
73006		9H		*Jun-1951*	*Mar-1967*	*Sep-1967*
73010		9H		*Aug-1951*	*Jun-1968*	*Sep-1968*
73071		9H	(ex 6D Shrewsbury)	*Nov-1954*	*Sep-1967*	*Oct-1968*
73097		9H	(ex 6D Shrewsbury)	*Dec-1955*	*May-1967*	*Oct-1967*
73127	*Caprotti valved*	9H		*Aug-1956*	*Oct-1967*	*Jul-1968*
73129	*Caprotti valved*	9H	**to Barry Docks**	*Aug-1956*	*Nov-1967*	*saved*
73130	*Caprotti valved*	9H		*Sep-1956*	*Jan-1967*	*Sep-1967*
73131	*Caprotti valved*	9H		*Sep-1956*	*Jan-1968*	*May-1968*
73138	*Caprotti valved*	9H		*Nov-1956*	*May-1968*	*Sep-1968*
73139	*Caprotti valved*	9H		*Nov-1956*	*May-1967*	*Jan-1968*
73142	*Caprotti valved*	9H		*Dec-1956*	*May-1968*	*Dec-1968*
73143	*Caprotti valved*	9H		*Dec-1956*	*Jun-1968*	*Nov-1968*
73144	*Caprotti valved*	9H		*Dec-1956*	*Aug-1967*	*Feb-1968*
73158		9H		*Dec-1956*	*Oct-1967*	*Feb-1968*
73163		9H		*Feb-1957*	*Nov-1965*	*Feb-1966*
Total	15					
BR Standard 3MT 2-6-2T Swindon 1952						
82000		9H		*Apr-1952*	*Dec-1966*	*May-1967*
82031		9H		*Dec-1954*	*Dec-1966*	*Oct-1968*
Total	2					
Riddles WD 8F 2-8-0 "Austerity" 1943						
90417		56A	Wakefield	*Mar-1945*	*Sep-1967*	*Oct-1967*
Total	1					
BR Standard 9F 2-10-0 Brighton 1954						
92117		8C	Speke Junction	*Dec-1956*	*Dec-1967*	*Apr-1968*
Total	1					

On Shed	34	**Kops**		26		
Steam	33	**Diesels**		1		

Home Locos	26	**Home Area**		3	**Visitors**	5
Shed	9H		26			
Distribution:- 9D		1	9E	1	9F	1
	2B	1	5B	1		
	8C	1	12A	1	56A	1
Steam classes on view		9				
Steam Origin	**LMS**		14	**BR**	18	
	WD		1			
Shed Highlight:-	82000	(founder member)				

Steam	*Aug-50*	73	*Mar-59*	78	*Apr-65*	51
Allocation					*Aug-65*	59
			Closed to Steam:-		*Jul-68*	
Home Steam						
On/Off Shed	On Shed	26	Off Shed	33	% On Shed	44%
Not on Shed						
"Big Eights"	48168	48181	48324	48491	48553	
					48663	6
BR 5MT 4-6-0 1951	73011	73033	73035	73039	73045	
	73053	73073	73094	73096	73125	
	73126	73128	73132	73133	73134	
	73135	73136	73137	73140	73141	
		73157	73159	73160	73165	24
BR 3MT 2-6-2T 1952		82003	82009	82034		3
					total	33
	saw elsewhere on the tour			13		
	saw on Dec 64 Manchester and Crewe trip			1		
	saw on July 65 Preston area trip			1		
	saw at Barry Docks revisited Aug 70			1		

.

Review and Appraisal of 9H Patricroft aka Standard 5'sville

The shed was in the fork of the Eccles-Patricroft and Eccles-Monton Green lines. Walking time was 5 minutes from Patricroft Station.

Certainly Standard 5 Ville was up to expectations with 15 Standard 5's on shed. I was also pleased to see 82000 the founder member of the 3MT 2-6-2 Tank BR Standard class. 90417 the WD from Wakefield was also a distinct surprise. The 9F 2-10-0 from 8C Speke Junction was a bit less surprising. Very good to see one of the two remaining "Patriots" 45531 "Sir Frederick Harrison" in action on shed. I had first seen her on a Scottish Railfans trip to Carlisle at 12B Carlisle Upperby on Sunday 7th September 1958. 45530 "Sir Frank Ree" was the other remaining "Patriot". A nice collection of "Big Eights" and a couple of visiting "Black Fives" and that was Patricroft that was.

26 (44%) of Home Steam on shed with 33 off shed so not too bad for a weekday morning.

On we go

We left the shed by the exit into Lansdowne Road and turned right along this road. We were looking for a Salford Corporation No.27 bus stop and we did not want to go in the wrong direction. My compass had proved little help so far and had caused us to go to the wrong side of the road for Newstead to do 16B Annesley on Monday and in Chester to do 6B Mold Junction yesterday. This time we would take no chances and we popped into the usual neighbourhood baker's shop bought some goodies and asked where we could catch the No.27 bus for Agecroft. The baker told us and warned us about the service which is only every 20 minutes. We wandered up to find a No.27 bus ambling off and we failed to catch it and that was a further 20 minutes lost on the timetable although we spent this interlude scoffing down our goodies from the baker's shop.

We asked the conductress to let us off at Bank Lane which was off Bolton Road. Apparently, Bolton Road is a long road and she wasn't sure where Bank Lane was but she had a good idea where it was and would let us off at her good idea! This seemed a little bit of a hit or a miss for us so D.S. would look out on the left for it and I would look out on the right for it. To be sure when we reached Bolton Road it turned out to be a long road. No call from the conductress and I was beginning to wonder if we had missed it when D.S. shouted that he had just seen Bank Lane. We jumped up, rang the bell and ran to the door. Good for D.S. The conductress said that she thought it was further on!

We walked to the bottom of Bank Lane, passed under the railway and turned right along a rough track. To our disconcertion we found that the shed was about half a mile away over a large patch of waste ground. Predictably, D.S. was particularly dischuffed at the distance to be covered. I did not help his temper when I informed him that we would have to walk all the way back again from the shed to catch a bus back for the city centre. Soon we reached the cinder path to the shed but predictably had failed to break the half mile world record over the waste ground. The shed was located on the fork of the Pendleton Broad Street to Clifton Junction and the Pendleton Broad Street to Swinton lines.

The running shed at 9J Agecroft proved to be pretty deserted. We had a permit for here but didn't need to use it. We saw the shedmaster and nodded to him but he didn't ask if we had a permit and actually he seemed quite happy to see us! A nice friendly shed what a pleasant change.

The highlight of the trip round the shed was seeing "Royal Scot" 46140 "The King's Royal Rifle Corps". She was one of the last two remaining "Royal Scots" 46115 "Scots Guardsman" being the other one. It was quite striking to see her in obviously fine fettle. She still looked magnificent as she hissed and puffed, despite her dirty condition, her missing nameplates and that ignominious banned South of Crewe yellow diagonal stripe on her cabside almost through the engine number. D.S. paid his respects by snapping her with the coaling tower in the background.

9J AGECROFT							
		Home shed		Built	Withdrawn	Scrap	
Diesels							
BR 0-6-0 Shunter 1953							
D3591		9D	Newton Heath	Dec-1958			
Total	1						
Steam				Built	Withdrawn	Scrap	
Stanier 5MT 4-6-0 "Black Five" 1934							
44781		9J		Aug-1947	Aug-1968	Dec-1968	
44817		9J		Nov-1944	Aug-1967	Dec-1967	
44929		9J		Mar-1946	Jun-1968	Dec-1968	
45368		9J		Jun-1937	Nov-1967	May-1968	
45437		9J		Nov-1937	Oct-1967	Feb-1968	
Total	5						
Stanier 7P 4-6-0 "Royal Scot" 1943 rebuild of Fowler 1927							
46140	"The King's Royal Rifle Corps"	12A	Carlisle Kingmoor	Oct-1927	Nov-1965	Mar-1966	
Total	1 DS photo						
Midland 3F "Jinty" 0-6-0T 1924 dev. of Johnson 1899 design							
47428		9J		Oct-1926	Oct-1965	Jan-1966	
Total	1						
Stanier 8F 2-8-0 "Big Eight" 1935							
48026		9J		Apr-1937	Jun-1968	Sep-1968	
48164		9J		Mar-1943	Oct-1967	Feb-1968	
48224		9J		Sep-1942	Mar-1968	Sep-1968	
48535		9J		Jun-1945	Aug-1967	Dec-1967	
48634		9J		Aug-1943	Aug-1965	Nov-1965	
48682		9J		Jan-1944	Sep-1965	Dec-1965	
Total	6						
On Shed	14	Kops		9			
Steam	13	Diesels		1			
Withdrawn	0						
Home Locos	12 Home Area		1	Visitors	1		
Shed	9J		12 9D		1		
Distribution:-	12A		1				
Steam classes on view		4					
Steam Origin	LMS		13				
Shed Highlight:-	46140		"The King's Royal Rifle Corps"				
Steam	Aug-50	56	Mar-59		53	Apr-65	26
Allocation						Aug-65	24
			Closed to Steam:-			Oct-66	
Home Steam							
On/Off Shed	On Shed	12	Off Shed		12 % On Shed	50%	
Not on Shed							
"Black Fives"		44782	44928	44987	45062	45096	6
						45424	
"Big Eights"		48250	48397	48521	48536	48539	6
						48708	
						total	12
	saw elsewhere on the tour				3		
	saw on Dec 64 Manchester and Crewe trip				1		
	saw on July 65 Preston area trip				1		
	saw on September 58 Carlisle visit				1		

Review and Appraisal of 9J Agecroft

The shed was in the fork of the Pendleton Broad –Swinton, and Pendleton Broad Street-Clifton Junction lines. Walking time would have been 30 minutes from either of the Pendleton stations.

A very alive shed. Like 9H Patricroft there were no condemned locos on view. 46140 "The King's Royal Rifle Corps" was easily the shed highlight. Certainly, not many locos on shed but 9J Agecroft only had a small allocation and I was pleased at what we did see. In all 9J Agecroft was well up to expectations although one might have hoped for more than one visitor.

12 Home Steam (50%) on shed with 12 off shed so again a pretty good haul for a weekday.

46140 "The King's Royal Rifle Corps" of 12A Carlisle Kingmoor on 9J Agecroft
Stanier 7P 4-6-0 "Royal Scot" 1943 rebuild of Fowler 1927

On we go

The shed finished we made the longish walk back over the waste ground back to Bank Lane. We had a choice of four Salford Corporation buses to take us back to the City Centre and one duly arrived very quickly. We alighted at Piccadilly after the 20 minutes journey and had again a four bus choice for 9A Longsight and again one came almost immediately after we found the bus stop after a hectic rush around.

We asked the conductor to throw us off at Kirkmanshulme Lane which he promised to do. He seemed to know this street. After a shortish journey we were duly deposited at the correct place. We forked left into Olwen Avenue, turned left into Redgate Lane and we quickly noted the shed yards with some electric locos lying around.

"Daring D.S. gatecrashes again"

I wanted to go in the official entrance because after all we did have a permit. D.S. would have none of this and bounded straight over a fence in the yard area. No one could ever accuse D.S. of being a coward. Rules or authority never worried him if he could find a shortcut. Note his past escapades this week at Cricklewood West on Sunday, Toton on Monday and other instances which escaped my memory for the moment. I did not fancy following him in breaking in and running riot in an electric depot as this was hardly likely to put us top of the popularity poll. I decided to go in the main entrance as we did have a precious permit.

Inside I waited for D.S. with a couple of local kids who I had picked up at the entrance. This handily increased our party size. A party of four looked better than a party of two. Finally, D.S. trundled up having surprisingly had not caused a major incident by running under the electric wires. We went into the office and showed our permit to the sheddie who seemed unconcerned, said OK and we were off. The other two kids ran off to run riot and we went round the shed ourselves.

That famous railwayist and honorary M.M.M.R.S member Neil "Woody", Woodcock had been to Manchester with the Railway Society of Scotland (formerly Scottish Railfans) and surprisingly they had been refused admission because of the "frequency". I never did gather from Woody how he and the others on his trip would have disturbed Longsight's frequency. We were given no warnings so we gaily trouped through every shed. Electric depots could be funny places and at the very start of our tour on Sunday morning D.S. and I had been refused admittance to Willesden Electric Depot for various reasons including that the "juice" was on.

Longsight had rapidly getting rid of its steam allocation by February 1965 and we were lucky to see two steam locos on shed.

"The Typhoid Episode"

As we finished the former LMS running shed a thirsty D.S. saw a tap and ran to it for a much need drink. D.S. was just about to drink when I saw and asked a nearby chap if the water was safe for drinking. Horrified, he turned round and saw D.S. who had washed his face in the water and was about to drink it. "Stop" he shouted "You can't drink that. It's canal water. You'll get typhoid". D.S. jerked up his head immediately almost hitting the tap and immediately his face went very pale. That was a close shave from death he thought. Nothing was more certain to quench D.S.'s thirst than the thought of catching typhoid. He mopped up the excess water from his face with his handkerchief and looked disapprovingly at it. He would need to dump it. D.S. seemed a bit crestfallen by the incident so I decided that it was best to let matters slip or we would be wasting time going to a doctor surgery for D.S. to be certified free from typhoid.

9A LONGSIGHT				Built	Withdrawn	Scrap
		Home shed		Built	Withdrawn	Scrap
Diesels						
BR 0-6-0 Shunter 1953						
D3335		9A	(ex 9G Gorton)	Jan-1957		
D3766		9A		May-1959		
D4145		9A	(ex 9B Stockport Edgeley)	Sep-1962		
Total	3					
BR Sulzer Type 2 Bo-Bo 1958						
D5145		1F	Rugby	Dec-1960		
D5146		9A		Dec-1960		
Total	2					
LMS 0-6-0 Shunter 1939						
12010		8C	Speke Junction (ex 9B)	Nov-1939	Sep-1967	
12024		9B	Stockport Edgeley	Jan-1942	Dec-1967	
Total	2					
Electrics						
English Electric AL3 Bo-Bo 1960						
E3024		LMW	London Midl. West Lines	Jul-1960		
E3034		LMW	London Midl. West Lines	Feb-1961		
Total	2					
General Electric AL4 Bo-Bo 1960						
E3039		LMW	London Midl. West Lines	Jul-1960		
E3040		LMW	London Midl. West Lines	Aug-1960		
E3041		LMW	London Midl. West Lines	Sep-1960		
E3042		LMW	London Midl. West Lines	Oct-1960		
E3044		LMW	London Midl. West Lines	Dec-1960		
Total	5					
BR A.E.I.(B.T.H.) motors AL5 Bo-Bo 1960						
E3065		LMW	London Midl. West Lines	Dec-1961		
E3084		LMW	London Midl. West Lines	May-1964		
Total	2					
BR B.T.H. AL5/1 Bo-Bo 1962						
E3093		LMW	London Midl. West Lines	Nov-1963		
Total	1					

		Home shed		Built	Withdrawn	Scrap
BR Vulcan Foundry AEI motors AL6 Bo-Bo 1965						
E3101		LMW	London Midl. West Lines	Aug-1965		
E3103		LMW	London Midl. West Lines	Aug-1965		
E3114		LMW	London Midl. West Lines	Oct-1965		
E3163		LMW	London Midl. West Lines	Aug-1965		
E3173		LMW	London Midl. West Lines	Aug-1965		
Total	5					
Steam				Built	Withdrawn	Scrap
Stanier 8F 2-8-0 "Big Eight" 1935						
48178		9E	Trafford Park (ex 9G)	Mar-1942	Nov-1966	Jun-1967
48501		9F	Heaton Mersey	Jun-1944	Jul-1967	Nov-1967
Total	2					
On Shed	24	Kops		19		
Steam	2	Diesels		7	Electrics	15
Home Locos	19	Home Area		3	Visitors	2
Shed	LMW	15	9A	4		
Distribution	9B	1	9E	1	9F	1
	1F	1	8C	1		
Steam classes on view	1					
Steam Origin	LMS	2				
Shed						
Highlight	The two "Big Eights"!			48178	48501	
Steam	Aug-50	129	Mar-59	105	Apr-65	0
Allocation					Aug-65	0
		Closed to Steam:-			Feb-65	

Review and Appraisal of 9A Longsight

The shed was on the east side of the Stockport Edgeley line about 1½ miles south of Manchester Piccadilly station. Walking time would have been 45 minutes from Manchester Piccadilly Station.

The shed used to be Manchester's greatest main line steam depot. Now steam had all but disappeared. Now with the electrification south from Piccadilly it now housed Manchester's mainline electric depot.

Good seeing the two "Big Eights" on shed when it was officially closed to steam. The old LMS diesel shunter (hard to believe that diesel shunters existed in 1949) was ex 9B Stockport Edgeley and was due to be moved to 8C Speke Junction in the Liverpool area. Five different electric classes were on shed including five of a new series.

On we go

The Rat Episode

Next stop would be 9C Reddish to see the Electrics 26000-26057 and 27000-27006 which worked on the Manchester-Sheffield line. We crossed Hyde Road into Cromwell Street and saw our 109 (Reddish) bus at the stop. We belted like mad and just got on the bus just as it was leaving. Our first stroke of luck today! We sat down on the first available seats gasping for breath. We asked the conductor to let us off at Reddish North station. The conductor seemed to disapprove of us for no apparent reason but true to his word he shouted to us to get off when we came to a bridge. He pointed up to the bridge and said "There's the station" and the bus sped away. The station looked ramshackle. We walked up to it, noting the broken windows and deserted aspect and found it to be HYDE ROAD STATION!!! It seemed to have been closed long ago. The dirty rotten scoundrel of a conductor – it seemed that he had intentionally dumped us off at this long closed station. Somehow in his feeble chemical mind he had stored an instant dislike for us.

While we stomped up and down angrily at the bus stop awaiting the next 109 bus I glanced at my watch. Tempus was fairly *fugiting* away. Thanks to our late train to Patricroft (twenty minutes lost), our lost way at Patricroft (10 minutes lost), the narrowly missed bus to Agecroft (twenty minutes lost) and now another 20 minutes lost waiting for the next bus we had lost over an hour in time. I had marked down the 11.42 train from Reddish North as the last train which we could catch to keep to our original timetable. This would result in arriving at Edge Hill at 20.30 as darkness approached to do the last shed of the day. In fact I thought that we would get either the 10.42 or 11.12 to Piccadilly from Reddish North but our earlier misfortunes had put that beyond reach. Predictably we had to wait 20 minutes for the next 109. To add to our bitterness when we reached Reddish North Station ten minutes later at 11.25 we saw its enormous white letters on maroon. Quite impossible to miss it. We asked the conductor on the second bus to let us off at Reddish North station and we would not have left the bus until we were happy that we were at our destination! Clearly the first bus conductor had intentionally dumped us at the wrong station. We now had a decision to make. If we visited 9C Reddish we would probably be on the 12.42 back to Piccadilly rather than the 11.42. There was a chance that we could manage the 12.12 but debatable whether we could manage it with D.S. It was possible but that would mean arriving at Edge Hill in darkness at 21.00. The key decider was that there was no steam at 9C Reddish. Decision made Reddish would now be thrown out to keep us on schedule for this busy day.

It is a little ridiculous going to visit 9C Reddish and leave Reddish without visiting it. We can thank King Rat (our esteemed first conductor) for that. So our first victim of the day was 9C Reddish. This upset us at the time but we reflected afterwards that 9C Reddish was only an electric shed and the electrics would be with us for years to come. So if one shed had to be chosen for us to miss then one should choose 9C Reddish. Thus there was the paradox. We visited Reddish without visiting Reddish.

We spent an "enjoyable" ten minutes at the station waiting for our train. Our train the 11.12 from Hayfield left on time at 11.42. 9G Gorton had been recently closed but we didn't jump off at Ashburys Station to see if it really was closed with time now a scarce commodity.

REDDISH TO MANCHESTER PICCADILLY

			Home shed		Built	Withdrawn	Scrap
Diesels							
BR 0-6-0 Shunter 1953							
D3686			9A	Longsight (ex 9G)	Sep-1958		
D3767			9A	Longsight	May-1959		
D3770			9B	Stockport Edgeley	May-1959		
Total		3					
Steam					Built	Withdrawn	Scrap
Hughes/Fowler 5MT 2-6-0 "Crab" 1926							
42844	on 9D	earlier	9D		Oct-1930	Aug-1965	Oct-1965
Total		1					
Stanier 5MT 4-6-0 "Black Five" 1934							
45083			9D	Newton Heath	Mar-1935	Dec-1967	May-1968
Total		1					
Stanier 8F 2-8-0 "Big Eight" 1935							
48758			9D	Newton Heath	Dec-1945	Dec-1967	Mar-1968
Total		1					
On Journey		6	Kops		3		
Steam		3	Diesels		3		
		Home Area			6	Visitors	0
Shed	9A	2	9B		1	9D	3
Distribution							
Steam Classes	3						
Steam Origin	LMS	3					

Quite a fruitful journey. The "Crab" 42844 which we had seen at 9D Newton Heath earlier today was to be withdrawn in the next few weeks so she was obviously on her swansong.

		Schedule	Actual	Miles
Depart	REDDISH NORTH	11.42	11.42	0
Arrive	MANCHESTER PICCADILLY	11.54	11.53	4

Three intermediate stops.

We received a little compensation for missing 9C Reddish by noting two of her allocation on Piccadilly at the head of a Manchester to Sheffield passenger train.

MANCHESTER PICCADILLY STATION LUNCHTIME							
		Home shed			Built	Withdrawn	Scrap
Electrics							
BR EM2 Metropolitan-Vickers Co-Co 1954							
27002	"Aurora"	9C	Reddish		*May-1954*	*Oct-1968*	
27004	"Juno"	9C	Reddish		*Sep-1954*	*Oct-1968*	
Total	2						
On Station	2	Kops	2				
Steam	0	**Diesels**	0	**Electrics**	2		
		Home Area	2	**Visitors**	0		
Shed Distribution	9C	2					

The two electrics were both of the seven member class. Froth and I had seen 27001 "Ariadne" last December at the station here and I thought it would be safe to surmise that the 27000-27006 class handled the passenger trains while their sister class 26000-26057 handled the freight turns. A pity because as none of the earlier series would be likely to enter Piccadilly terminus with a freight we were unlikely to see any of them on our travels today having just missed visiting 9C Reddish.

D.S. pointed out an electric multiple unit "bucket". Why? It was multiple unit numbered 007. The James Bond Electric bucket. Ha, ha!

However, there was little time for merriment because our train left for Manchester Oxford Road in four minutes. Luckily our bucket had arrived a minute early. We ran up to check the station timetable and found out what was the through platform for Oxford Road Station (Piccadilly has only one through platform) and raced up to it. We were just in time to catch the 11.57. It did matter as we wanted to connect with the 12.10 train to Altrincham there. The 11.57 was a through train from Crewe (left there at 11.00).

		Schedule	Actual	Miles
Depart	MANCHESTER PICCADILLY	11.57	11.57	0
Arrive	MANCHESTER OXFORD ROAD	11.59	11.59	½

No intermediate stops.

At Oxford Road we jumped out of our electric bucket as though we were jumping out of a car in a James Cagney gangster movie. We rushed up to the station inspector and asked if the bucket across the platform was the Altrincham train. Amused at our antics he scoffed with laughter "Yes! It's a beautiful train ain't it". The train for the record was ramshackle, filthy, non-corridor stock. Nevertheless the stock was serviceable and would do for us. It left on time at 12.10. I warned D.S. that the recovery time for our next shed (9E Trafford Park) was minus 7 minutes. That meant we had only 38 minutes available against a budgeted 45 minutes (15 minutes there, 15 minutes to do the shed and 15 minutes to get back). I told D.S. that we would have to move to catch our next train at 12.53. D.S. muttered back that he would take his own sweet time and I wasn't going to push him. We shall see.

It was a short five minute trip to Warwick Road Station and we noted a BR Type 2.

		Schedule	Actual	Miles
Depart	MANCHESTER OXFORD ROAD	12.10	12.10	0
Arrive	WARWICK ROAD	12.15	12.15	2½

Two intermediate stops.

MANCHESTER OXFORD ROAD TO WARWICK ROAD						
		Home shed				
Diesel						
BR Sulzer Type 2 Bo-Bo 1958						
D5277		9E	Trafford Park			
On Journey	1	Kops		1		
Steam	0	Diesels		1		
	Home Area			1	Visitors	0
Shed Distribution		9E	1			

THE HOBNAILED ARMY SURPLUS BOOTS AFFAIR

We turned right outside the west exit of the station and went along Warwick Road. I began to walk briskly ahead while D.S. disinclined to hurry up and appeared to be in an unsympathetic mood. I shouted at him to hurry up but he shouted back that he would take his own time. Okay I said I'll see you back at the station for the 12.53 and you had better be there. I crossed the main Chester Road and continued along into Warwick Road North. D.S. was soon yards behind and in horse racing terms was tailed off last. I rechecked the LSD and turned left into Railway Road and after a quarter of a mile found the cinder path which led to the shed. I glanced up at the top of the road and saw D.S. I saw him laboriously raise one hobnailed army surplus boot put it down carefully and raise the other hobnailed army surplus boot and put it also down carefully. It was painful to watch D.S. Believe it or not this is how D.S. walks. A centenarian could probably walk faster. Ah, but D.S. has missed the Railway Road turning and is continuing his slow walk along Warwick Road North.

Well, good riddance to him I hoped that he wouldn't come back. I had had enough of him and his hobnailed army surplus boots. I watched with relish as I saw him in the distance disappearing out of my view like some trundling, runaway, rundown robot. I glanced at my watch. It was now 12.23 only 30 minutes in which to get D.S. back to the station. It will be tough. Especially as that was a fair walk from the station and the LSD walking time of 15 minutes was not overgenerous.

On the brighter side the shed was absolutely full and I took the full allocated time of 15 minutes in going round it. On my way out of the shed I met an exhausted D.S. at the shed entrance. D.S. had found a railway bridge on his solitary journey down Warwick Road North and saw the shed from it. Realising his mistake he retraced his steps and found Railway Road at the second attempt. I told him that we had better run back or we shall miss the train as we have less than 15 minutes.

D.S., however, was having none of this. He said that he couldn't make the train as he had a horrible stitch in his side from all his exertions in walking. His feet were also hurting and he was dog tired. That's it D.S. had gone on strike. This is the last straw. I couldn't drag him to the station in 15 minutes so the train would be missed. We would have to get the following train, 20 minutes later at 13.13. Another 20 minutes down the drain. I told D.S. that he had better hurry up on going round as we were not going to miss the 13.13 train. D.S. duly increased his pace to a crawl and went round the shed in an impressive ten minutes. I went round again with him to ensure that he didn't flag.

		Home shed		Built	Withdrawn	Scrap
Diesels						
BR Sulzer "Peak" Type 4 1Co-Co1 1959						
D 72		ML	Midland Lines	*Nov-1960*		
D 95		ML	Midland Lines	*Apr-1961*		
D 119		ML	Midland Lines	*Sep-1961*		
D 121		ML	Midland Lines	*Oct-1961*		
Total	*4*					
BR Sulzer Type 2 Bo-Bo 1958						
D5269		D16	Nottingham Division	*May-1964*		
D5275		9E		*Jun-1964*		
D7586		9E		*Feb-1964*		
D7624		41A	Tinsley	*Jul-1965*		
Total	*4*					
Brush Type 2 A1A-A1A 1957						
D5861		9E	(ex 41A Tinsley)	*Oct-1962*		
Total	*1*					
Steam				*Built*	*Withdrawn*	*Scrap*
Fairburn 4MT 2-6-4T 1945 dev. of Stanier 1935						
42050		9E		*Sep-1950*	*Apr-1965*	*Sep-1965*
42051		9E		*Sep-1950*	*Jul-1965*	*Dec-1965*
42053		9E		*Sep-1950*	*Jun-1965*	*Oct-1965*
42064		9E		*Dec-1950*	*Jun-1965*	*Oct-1965*
42065		9E		*Dec-1950*	*Jul-1965*	*Jan-1966*
42066		9E	(ex 2J Aston)	*Oct-1950*	*Sep-1967*	*Feb-1968*
42069		9E	(ex 2J via 2B)	*Oct-1950*	*Nov-1966*	*Jun-1967*
42071		9E	(ex 1A via 2B)	*Nov-1950*	*Mar-1967*	*Sep-1967*
42076		9E		*Dec-1950*	*Mar-1967*	*Nov-1967*
42112		9E		*Jun-1949*	*Jul-1965*	*Dec-1965*
42113		9E		*Jun-1949*	*Jul-1965*	*Dec-1965*
42212		9E	(ex 6A Chester)	*Dec-1945*	*Aug-1965*	*Dec-1965*
42230		9E		*Jun-1946*	*Aug-1965*	*Apr-1966*
Total	*13*					
Fowler 4MT 2-6-4T 1927						
42327		9E	(ex 9G Gorton)	*Feb-1929*	*Aug-1965*	*Nov-1965*
Total	*1*					
Stanier 4MT 2-6-4T 1935 dev of Fowler 1927						
42455		9E		*Aug-1936*	*Apr-1966*	*Jul-1966*
42583		9E	(ex 1A via 5D Stoke)	*Oct-1936*	*Oct-1966*	*Feb-1967*
Total	*2*					
Stanier 5MT 2-6-0 1933						
42945		9F	Heaton Mersey	*Oct-1933*	*Mar-1966*	*Jun-1966*
42980		9F	Heaton Mersey(ex 9G)	*Feb-1934*	*Jan-1966*	*Apr-1966*
Total	*2*					
Stanier 5MT 4-6-0 "Black Five" 1935						
44708		9E		*Oct-1948*	*Jan-1968*	*Jan-1969*
44804		9E	(ex 16C Derby)	*Jun-1944*	*Mar-1968*	*Jun-1968*
44855		9E	(ex 9B Stockport)	*Dec-1944*	*May-1968*	*Sep-1968*
44856		2B	Oxley	*Dec-1944*	*Feb-1967*	*Jun-1967*
44888		9E	(ex 9H Patricroft)	*Aug-1945*	*Aug-1968*	*May-1969*
44895		9E		*Sep-1945*	*Dec-1967*	*Jun-1968*
45017		9E		*May-1935*	*Aug-1968*	*May-1969*
45073		9E		*Jun-1935*	*Aug-1968*	*Mar-1969*
45131		8C	Speke Junction	*May-1935*	*Apr-1968*	*Aug-1968*
45139		9E		*Jun-1935*	*Aug-1967*	*Nov-1968*
45188		8C	Speke Junction	*Sep-1935*	*Jul-1967*	*Apr-1968*
45233		9E		*Aug-1936*	*May-1966*	*Sep-1966*
45269		9E		*Nov-1936*	*Aug-1968*	*Mar-1969*
45316		9E		*Feb-1937*	*Mar-1968*	*Jun-1968*
45332		8C	Speke Junction	*Mar-1937*	*Nov-1966*	*Apr-1967*
45380		ex 9A	Longsight	*Jul-1937*	*Mar-1965*	*Dec-1965*
45446		5B	Crewe South	*Dec-1937*	*Feb-1967*	*Sep-1967*
Total	*17*					

Home shed

Stanier 6P5F 4-6-0 "Jubilee" 1934

45705	"Seahorse"	9D	Newton Heath	*May-1936*	*Nov-1965*	*Feb-1966*
Total	1					

Stanier 8F 2-8-0 "Big Eight" 1935

48273		9E		*Jun-1942*	*Aug-1965*	*Nov-1965*
48288		9E		*Aug-1940*	*Feb-1967*	*Jul-1967*
48374		8E	Northwich(via15B/15A)	*Nov-1944*	*Jun-1968*	*Jan-1969*
Total	3					

BR Standard 2MT 2-6-0 Doncaster 1953

78011		9E	(ex 9G Gorton)	*Dec-1953*	*Sep-1965*	*Dec-1965*
78012		9E	(ex 9G Gorton)	*Jan-1954*	*May-1967*	*Oct-1967*
78014		9E	(ex 9G Gorton)	*Feb-1954*	*Sep-1965*	*Dec-1965*
78023		9E	(ex 9G Gorton)	*May-1954*	*May-1967*	*Oct-1967*
78062		9E	(ex 9G Gorton)	*Oct-1956*	*May-1967*	*Oct-1967*
Total	5					

On Shed	53	**Kops**	41
Steam	44	**Diesels**	9
Withdrawn	8		

Home Locos	38	Home Area	3	Visitors	12
Shed	9E	37			
Distribution:-	ex 9A	1	9D	1	9F	2
	2B	1	5B	1	
	8C	3	8E	1	
	ML	4	D16	1	
	41A	1			
Steam classes on view		8			
Steam Origin	LMS		39	BR	5
Shed Highlights:-					
	Steam	42050	**9E**	**Trafford Park**	
	Diesel	D7624	*new*		

Steam	*Aug-50*	73	*Mar-59*	53	*Apr-65*	29
Allocation					*Aug-65*	42
			Closed to Steam:-		*Mar-68*	

Home Steam	excluding withdrawn locos				
On/Off Shed	On Shed	27	Off Shed	15	% On Shed	64%

Not on Shed

Fowler 4MT 2-6-4T 1927					42334	1
Stanier 4MT 2-6-4T 1935					42644	1
"Black Fives"	44735	44815		44871	45150	45220
					45352	45404	7
"Big Eights"	48178	48344		48356	48741	48743	5
BR 2MT 2-6-0 1953					78007	1
					total	0

saw elsewhere on the tour	6	
saw on Dec 64 Manchester and Crewe trip	2	
saw on July 65 Preston area trip	1	
saw on September 58 Carlisle visit	1	
recently withdrawn not on shed or seen elsewhere	1	"Black Five"	44673

Review and Appraisal of 9E Trafford Park

The shed was on the north side of the line about one mile east of Trafford Park and Stretford Station. Walking time was 15 minutes from Warwick Road Station.

A very good shed. I did not expect that Trafford Park would be so sensationally good. Trafford Park is the shed for the scheduled for closure Manchester Central station. Manchester Central is the connecting station for London St.Pancras. Hence the Midland lines flavour of the shed and the assortment of BR "Peaks" and "Type 2's".

The Fairburn tanks were a sad sight. Nine of the thirteen were condemned. They appeared to have gone out of favour in recent months. It was particularly good to see 42050 the founder member of the class. She had been withdrawn months ago so we were lucky to see her. Strangely Trafford Park had recently received four more of the class recently (three from the Birmingham area and one from 6A Chester Midland (now withdrawn). Perhaps Trafford Park just drives them until they need repairing and then ask for replacements.

Two "Funny Crabs" 42945 and 42980. Hardly an exact definition but an amusing one. I remember one railwayist calling a member of the class this at Carlisle a year ago. Like the "Crabs" they were 2-6-0's. There the similarity ended as they are graceful Stanier locos quite unlike the ungainly but likeable Fowler "Crabs". I had even heard them called "Lobsters" which are certainly "Funny crabs" – lots of laughs.

Seventeen "Black 5's" on shed was quite a collection and very welcome too. Seeing the five 78XXX "Standard Doodle Bugs" must about complete the class for us. We had seen all the class this week or at least it seemed like that to me although I do recall missing one at 5D Stoke last (Thursday) night. Welcome to see a non withdrawn "Jubilee" in the shape of 45705 "Seahorse" which we had missed at her home shed of 9D Newton Heath earlier today.

27 (64%) of Home Steam on shed and 15 off shed so a goodly percentage on shed for a weekday.

Another interesting fact about 9E Trafford Park is that there was no turntable. Engines turn around on a triangular piece of line. Must be one of the few triangles in the UK although this practice is common in North America.

On we go

EPILOGUE OF THE HOBNAILED ARMY SURPLUS BOOTS AFFAIR

D.S. was marched back to the station and we caught the 13.13 to Manchester Oxford Road Station with five minutes to spare. On the train I accused D.S. of throwing twenty valuable minutes away by him crawling along the road to 9E Trafford Park. I also said that we had been lucky that we had not lost more time and sheds on his account so far on the tour and that there had be no more of his time wasting or he could continue on the tour on his own. At all this D.S. was really hurt and roared "I walk at normal speed!" I retorted "It may be normal pace to you but everyone else's normal pace is twice as fast as yours!" D.S. looked out as we drew into a station. "Oxford Road" he said and added "I've had enough" stormed off the train and walked away. That silly donkey it was not Oxford Road Station but Knott Mill Station and I jumped out after him. I yelled after him that he had got off at the wrong station. D.S. came running back but it was too late and our train sped off on the final ½ mile journey to Oxford Road without us.

		Schedule	Actual	Miles
Depart	WARWICK ROAD	13.13	13.13	0
Arrive	KNOTT MILL	13.18	13.18	2

This was completely and utterly the last straw for me. He had cost us yet another 20 minutes because there would not be another train to Oxford Road until then. That's 40 minutes he had now cost us including the 20 minutes he had cost us in going to 9E Trafford Park. It's about time he was sent off. Sent off home. I told D.S. that he could continue the tour himself, and my timetable would now be safe from him. A furious argument ensued on the station platform for a full 10 minutes. Probably the leaves on the trees began to tremble at all our noise. We didn't come quite to blows because D.S. was too tired and I couldn't be bothered with making an effort to fight him. Yes, that was the argument that was.

The argument ended with D.S. agreeing to leave and suggesting that we now went to Manchester Victoria Station to get his luggage out of the left luggage locker. I would have to pay another two shillings (ten pence) to relock the locker once he got his luggage out. Suddenly, for no apparent reason I felt sorry for D.S. and his holiday week on the LMR. After all, he only gets two weeks holiday a year from his slave labour £5 a week newsagent's shop job and this would be a very sorry end to his week's holiday. I also couldn't take the responsibility of allowing him to wander on in his very tired state without me not knowing where he was going. More to the point it would be another 45 minutes wasted in going to the left luggage locker at Manchester Victoria for the split-up making a full 1½ hours to be lost because of D.S. If I kept him going now no more time might be lost.

"OK" I said "It will be silly to split up." "Let's forget about all this and get on with the tour. Next visit will be Stockport". We made up and waited for the next train to Oxford Road. We perhaps could have walked the short ½ mile to Oxford Road but we didn't attempt the walk for D.S.'s sake. Perhaps D.S. is doing his best and can't help himself.

		Schedule	Actual	Miles
Depart	KNOTT MILL	13.38	13.38	0
Arrive	MANCHESTER OXFORD ROAD	13.40	13.40	½

Next stop for us would be Stockport where we would visit 9B Stockport Edgeley and 9F Heaton Mersey. With a little luck we could just about make the 16.30 train from Manchester Exchange which arrives at Warrington Bank Quay Station at 17.00. Better still we could leave from Manchester Central Station at 16.30 arriving at Warrington Central at 16.49 and be 15 minutes nearer to 8B Warrington than Warrington Bank Quay is. Failing that we could get the 17.00 from Manchester Central. With luck we would then be able to do 8B Warrington, and get the 18.10 to Garston to do 8C Speke Junction, skip doing 8L Allerton which is only a diesel and electric depot and be back on schedule. In fact, in my original timetable there was unusually a hidden recovery time after Stockport, so that we could get something to eat at Manchester Central Station. So all was not yet lost!

THE TRAIN TO NOWHERE AFFAIR
or
THE ALDERLEY EDGE AFFAIR

D.S. seemed to be feeling a little guilty at us losing 40 minutes and was definitely now making a greater effort. We rushed off the bucket at Manchester Oxford Road station and noted another bucket waiting to go out in the Stockport direction. Yes, all trains go through Stockport from Manchester Oxford Road and Manchester Piccadilly. Of course they do so we just jumped on the bucket. No need to check.

We sat there in the bucket. The bucket was very sultry. It was a lovely afternoon and I felt quite drained. Why? Perhaps my little argument with D.S. at Knott Mill had over excited and tired me somewhat. While I was reflecting I thought I heard in the background "No madam, this train doesn't go to Stockport". It must have been someone in the station talking to a woman. What was that the man had said? That this train didn't go through Stockport? I turned to D.S. who predictably had fallen asleep. Obviously he had heard nothing. Surely, all trains go through Stockport. No, I must have been mistaken at what I had heard. Perhaps I had dreamt it. However, I was a bit below par and neither bothered to check the working timetable or go to the window to ask the station inspector. Must have been in a daze. The bucket started off. Must have been imagining things. There is only one Stockport line out of here.

Clackety, clackety clack the bucket sped on. We would soon be in Stockport. Yes this looked like the Stockport line that Ian "Froth" Firth and I had travelled on from Manchester to Crewe last December. I looked at D.S. He is a menace he'll fall asleep on his feet yet. For all he knows he could wake up at Timbuktu. He relies on me to stay awake and to boot him awake at every station. Realizing the importance of staying awake and not taking a half hour nap I thought how selfish D.S. was. It was now 13.53 and we would be in Stockport in 5 minutes. Clackety, clack, bumpety, bump -- ----------------

Time passes, time passes--- -- --

-- Clackety clack, bumpety bump, Stockport, Stockport.

My inner alarm went off subconsciously and I shouted out Stockport and awoke with a start. I looked out. This was not bloody Stockport. We were somewhere unknown on an island platform. The train was deserted but for the two of us. I looked at my watch. It was 14.35. I had fallen asleep for forty minutes. Damn.

Where in hell were we? We had evidently slept through the Stockport stop. I looked round at D.S. who was snoring gently and rousted him awake. D.S. gasped as he awoke and said "So we are at Stockport". He got his things together and we got out of the train. D.S. peered hopefully for the shed willing it to be nearby and not much of a walk.

I had no idea where we were. D.S. shouted out "Alderley Edge. This isn't Stockport." I told him "No!" and asked him to look at his watch. He said 2.36 it must be going fast and was about to rewind his watch when I told him that we had slept through Stockport about half an hour ago while we were both asleep. We were lucky that the bucket had terminated here or we could have been at Crewe by now.

Nothing else to do but to get back to Stockport. Luckily I knew where Alderley Edge was. Froth and I had stopped here or at least our bucket did on the way to Crewe last December. We didn't get off then need I add. What struck me at the time were the funny quaint names of the stations on the line viz. Goostrey, Alderley Edge, Holmes Chapel and Wilmslow. Quite a place Wilmslow. On the day that Froth and I passed it by a horse named Wilmslow Boy was running in a race at Cheltenham. We wanted to back it as a good coincidence but we were too late as the race was at 12.50. Luckily for us the horse fell. However, seeing the horse run the following Saturday at Uttoxeter we took a chance (needing funds badly) and good, old Wilmslow Boy duly obliged at the excellent odds of 100-8 (12½-1). That was a jolly good win!

This time there was nothing funny to relate about Alderley Edge. D.S. and I ran frantically to see when there was a train back to Manchester (which would pass Stockport on the way). We bumped into a ticket collector who told us that the next train was the one lying in the station. The one we had just got off! I asked him when it had arrived. He asked us why. I explained that we had fallen asleep and had missed our stop (omitting to mention that our stop had been Stockport). Laughing at our misfortune (which didn't amuse us he said that we had been on the 13.50 from Manchester Oxford Road which had arrived at Alderley Edge at 14.20. So we had slept for 25 minutes on the journey and another 15 minutes at the station I reflected. What gross negligence and what a mess of the timetable.

Back we went to the bucket. It was the 14.45 so we should be at Stockport by about 15.05. So our little escapade to Alderley Edge had cost us an hour of valuable time. Our bucket left on time for Stockport at 14.45. I got out my working timetable and glanced at the times of the trains from Oxford road to Stockport. They were half hourly at five and thirty five minutes past the hour. Funny that we had got the 13.50 and the ticket collector at Alderley Edge had confirmed it. The mystery of the 13.50 was soon to be solved. The first station we came to was Wilmslow so far so good. Then, trouble. Instead of continuing on to Cheadle Hulme and Stockport our bucket took a branch line. First Styal came up, then Heald Green, Gatley, East Didsbury, Burnage and Mauldeth Road. Stockport had been by-passed and our train terminated at Manchester Piccadilly. We shook our heads in disbelief.

What had happened to Stockport? A moment's thought then everything fitted in. We had accidentally got on a train which we thought went to Stockport. In fact, our train was the half hourly suburban service to Alderley Edge which went via the Styal branch line and bypassed Stockport. If I had not sleepily disregarded the information that the station inspector gave to a woman that our train was not stopping at Stockport we would have got off and the Alderley Edge Affair would never have happened. Also, if we had stayed awake on the wrong train that we did get we would have quickly noticed our error and would have got off the train and might have got back to Piccadilly for the 14.05 which reached Stockport at 14.19.

		Schedule	Actual	Miles
Depart	MANCHESTER OXFORD ROAD	13.50	13.50	0
Arrive	ALDERLEY EDGE	14.20	14.20	13¼
		Schedule	Actual	Miles
Depart	ALDERLEY EDGE	14.45	14.45	0
Arrive	MANCHESTER PICCADILLY	15.12	15.12	12¾

HERE ENDETH THE ALDERLEY EDGE AFFAIR

We quickly made our way on to the main concourse at Manchester Piccadilly. I noted a Buxton bucket about to depart. All Buxton trains go through Stockport and we checked the timetable on the concourse and found that it would leave in five minutes.

On station we noted 27000 "Electra" at the head of another Manchester to Sheffield express passenger train. Three main line electrics were also noted.

MANCHESTER PICCADILLY STATION FRIDAY AFTERNOON							
		Home shed			Built	Withdrawn	Scrap
Electrics							
English Electric AL3 Bo-Bo 1960							
E3026		LMW	London Midl. West Lines		Aug-1960		
Total	1						
A.E.I. (Metropolitan-Vickers) AL2 Bo-Bo 1960							
E3052		LMW	London Midl. West Lines		Dec-1960		
Total	1						
A.E.I. (British Thomson-Houston) AL1 Bo-Bo 1963							
E3096		LMW	London Midl. West Lines		Oct-1963		
Total	1						
BR EM2 Metropolitan-Vickers Co-Co 1954							
27000	"Electra"	9C	Reddish		Dec-1953	Oct-1968	
Total	1						
On Station	4	Kops		2			
Steam	0	Diesels		0	Electrics	4	
		Home Area	1		Visitors	1	
Shed Distribution		9C	1		LMW	3	

This time we managed to stay awake and arrived at Stockport Edgeley Station at 15.32

		Schedule	Actual	Miles
Depart	MANCHESTER PICCADILLY	15.20	15.20	0
Arrive	STOCKPORT EDGELEY	15.32	15.32	12¾

Two intermediate stops.

So instead of arriving here at 14.19 it was now 15.32 and a further 73 minutes had been lost. I had not got the times of our train to Warrington past 16.30 but it looked as though there would be one at 17.30. I checked the timetable at the station and it appeared that our only chance was to get the 16.46 to Manchester Piccadilly. The next train after this was the 17.10 and that would be too late. The annoying thing was that the "Pines Express" from Bournemouth came into Stockport at 16.53 but it was only allowed to set passengers down but not pick them up! This resulted in a freak 25 minute gap for trains from Stockport to Manchester Piccadilly.

I impressed upon D.S. the gravity of the situation and that we had only 75 minutes in which to do both Stockport sheds. The scheduled time to do both sheds was 110 minutes. So the recovery time was -35 minutes. Impossible you might think particularly with D.S. in tow. However, it is quite possible because one hour of the schedule was walking to 9F Heaton Mersey and back. It was indeed possible to get a bus to the shed and back so we might be able to save 30-40 minutes with luck if there were no waiting times for buses. So let's keep our toes crossed.

I had never seriously entertained visiting 9L Buxton on the tour. It seemed to be in the middle of nowhere and this feeling was summed up by its two sub sheds which were respectively sheep pasture and Middleton Top on the Cromford to High Peak line. Both of these sub sheds were so remote that they were identified by Ordnance Survey grid positions.

9L Buxton is on the Stockport line and 19½ miles from Stockport. The bucket service was not particularly fast and we would have needed to pick up one of the hourly trains at say 15.28 arriving at Buxton at 16.15. 15 minutes walk to the shed, 10 minutes to go round and 15 minutes back and we would have got the 17.25 back arriving at Stockport at 18.06. We could not allocate two and a half hours to one shed so 9L Buxton was always going to be given the miss.

9L BUXTON				
Steam				
Fowler Midland 4F 0-6-0 1911				
43967				
Total	1			
Midland 4F 0-6-0 1924				
44063	44076	44169	44271	
44399	44587	44599		
Total	4			
Ivatt 2MT 2-6-0 1946				
46401	46465	46480		
Total	3			
Stanier 8F 2-8-0 "Big Eight" 1935				
48088	48389	48428	48464	
48472	48495			
Total	6			
Riddles MOS 4F 0-6-0ST J94 1943				
68006	68012	68068	68079	
Total	3			
Grand Total	17			
Recently		Surviving		
Withdrawn	4	Steam Classes	5	
Saw Elsewhere		Saw Carlisle		
on the Tour	0	Sept 1958	1	
Steam	Sep-50	55	Mar-59	35
Allocation	Apr-65	20	Aug-65	13
	Closed to Steam:-		Mar-68	

480

9L Buxton had quite an interesting allocation of workmanlike engines including Midland 0-6-0's and four (one recently withdrawn) Riddles Ministry of Supply 0-6-0 Saddle Tanks.

The Stutter Incident

We bustled along station road turned left into Wellington Road, descended a flight of steps into Mersey Square where we hoped to catch a bus. With a stroke of luck we found one waiting in the shape of a No.39 Cheadle bound bus which would drop us off at Gorsey Bank Road which appeared to be a stone's throw from the shed. We boarded the bus, went upstairs and sat down in front of the back seat. The bus was pretty busy and started off in a couple of minutes. As the bus conductor was busy giving out tickets downstairs I began to get a bit worried that we would miss our stop. I turned round and asked the old chap sitting on the back seat if he knew where Gorsey Bank Road was. Suddenly, he started up like an organ grinder and began stuttering away. He wheezed out at the top of his voice G-g-g-g-o-o-r-r-r-s-s-s-e-e-e-y-y-y-B-b-b-b-a-a-a-n-n-n-k-k-k-R-r-r-o-o-o-a-a-a-d-d-d. T-t-t-h-h-h-i-i-i-s-s-s-i-i-i-s-s-s-t-t-t-h-h-h-e-e-e-b-b-b-u-u-u-s-s-s-f-f-f-oi-o-o-r-r-r-ch-ch-ch-ee-ee-ee-h-h-h-oo-oo-oo-l-l-l. He seemed to pronounce Cheadle as Cheehool. This went on for a good minute.

Soon everyone upstairs knew that we wanted to go to Gorsey Bank Road by his wheezing, stuttering efforts. Some laughing kids up the front began shouting out "So you want to go to Gorsey Bank Road." A minor riot was about to break out and we began to despair. Our saviour came to our rescue in the shape of a railwayman who had been sitting further up the bus. He came up to us and whispered under the din from the old chap and the kids that he was getting off there. When we turned round our stuttering old friend now quietened down and we followed the railwayman off the bus.

We followed him on to a cinder path which led across a big river. As the shed was 9F Heaton Mersey I think that we can safely conclude that it was the river Mersey. What a stench came from the river. I had never smelt anything quite as foul. We thanked our railwayman who went off to sign on for his shift.

We wanted to bustle round as quickly as possible as we had no time to waste. However, we were just about to gallop round the shed when an officious worker challenged us. He asked if we had a permit. I said we had (strangely this time we did have one) and he escorted us to the shedmaster's office.

The shedmaster was chatting with a young apprentice and seemed to be a pleasant chap. This turned out to be the case. I dropped our pile of permits down on the counter. They immediately stopped talking and gasped open-mouthed at the pile. I leafed through looking for the correct permit. Luckily, the permit was near the top of the wad so the shedmaster's health was safeguarded and in any event no need for the successful wad trick perpetrated at 9D Newton Heath early this morning. The shedmaster said he had never seen so many permits and asked if we had been all the way around Britain yet. I said we had started from Edinburgh in Scotland last Saturday and our stops during the week had included London, Nottingham, Derby, Cardiff, Birmingham, Wolverhampton, Shrewsbury, Chester, Crewe, Stoke and Manchester. The apprentice listened to all this in awe and said what we were doing was just great and how were we lasting the pace? Both of them thought that it was great that we had come all the way from Scotland to visit their shed. They were happy to receive us and wished us well.

Flattered at our treatment we proceeded around the shed without incident. Strange, being escorted by the railway worker to the shedmaster's office. At the time this worried us that we could be facing another 40E Colwick or 2E Saltley ordeal. Nothing could have been better than our treatment here.

The shed was at the south side of the fork of the Cheadle and Didsbury lines west of Tiviot Dale station. Walking time would have been 30 minutes from Stockport Edgeley Station.

9F HEATON MERSEY						
		Home shed		**Built**	**Withdrawn**	**Scrap**
Diesels						
BR Sulzer Type 2 Bo-Bo 1958						
D7592		ML	Midland Lines	*May-1964*		
Total	*1*					
Steam				**Built**	**Withdrawn**	**Scrap**
Stanier 5MT 2-6-0 1933						
42945		9F	(ex 9G Gorton)	*Oct-1933*	*Mar-1966*	*Jun-1966*
42947		9F	(ex 9G Gorton)	*Nov-1933*	*Dec-1965*	*Feb-1966*
42968	*to Barry Docks*	9F	(ex 9G via 8F Wigan)	*Jan-1934*	*Dec-1966*	*saved*
42974		9F	(ex 9G Gorton)	*Jan-1934*	*Sep-1965*	*Dec-1965*
42975		9F	(ex 9G Gorton)	*Jan-1934*	*Mar-1966*	*Jun-1966*
42980		9F	(ex 9G Gorton)	*Feb-1934*	*Jan-1966*	*Apr-1966*
Total	*6*					
Ivatt 4MT 2-6-0 1947						
43010		9F		*Mar-1948*	*Dec-1967*	*Apr-1968*
43013		9F		*Apr-1948*	*Nov-1965*	*Jan-1966*
43033		9F		*May-1949*	*Mar-1968*	*May-1968*
43048		9F		*Nov-1949*	*May-1967*	*Nov-1967*
Total	*4*					
Stanier 5MT 4-6-0 "Black Five" 1935						
45071		8C	Speke Junction	*May-1935*	*Jul-1967*	*Feb-1969*
Total	*1*					
Stanier 8F 2-8-0 "Big Eight" 1935						
48075		55D	Royston	*Dec-1936*	*May-1967*	*Sep-1967*
48176		9F	(ex 9G Gorton)	*Mar-1942*	*Aug-1967*	*Nov-1967*
48316		9F		*Dec-1943*	*Apr-1967*	*Nov-1967*
48322		9F	(ex 9G Gorton)	*Feb-1944*	*May-1968*	*Sep-1968*
48329		9F		*Apr-1944*	*May-1968*	*Sep-1968*
48390		9F		*Mar-1945*	*May-1968*	*Aug-1968*
48546		9F		*Feb-1945*	*Jul-1968*	*Nov-1968*
48613		9F		*Jul-1943*	*Jul-1967*	*Dec-1967*
48701		9F	(ex 9G Gorton)	*May-1944*	*Mar-1967*	*Sep-1967*
48731		9F		*Sep-1945*	*Aug-1967*	*Jul-1968*
Total	*10*					
BR Standard 9F 2-10-0 Brighton 1954						
92115		8C	Speke Junction	*Dec-1956*	*Feb-1966*	*Jun-1966*
92162		8H	Birkenhead (ex 9D)	*Dec-1957*	*Nov-1967*	*May-1968*
Total	*2*					
On Shed	**24**	**Kops**		**23**		
Steam	**23**	**Diesels**		**1**		
Withdrawn	**0**					
Home Locos	**19 Home Area**			**0**	**Visitors**	**5**
Shed	9F	**19**				
Distribution:-	8C	**2 8H**		**1**		
	55D	**1**				
	ML	**1**				
Steam classes on view		**5**				
Steam Origin	**LMS**		**21 BR**		**2**	
Shed Highlights:-						
	Steam	**42945**	9F	**Heaton Mersey**		
Steam	**Aug-50**	**64**	**Mar-59**	**55**	**Apr-65**	**36**
Allocation					**Aug-65**	**56**
			Closed to Steam:-		**May-68**	
Home Steam	*excluding withdrawn locos*					
On/Off Shed	On Shed	19 Off Shed		37 % On Shed	34%	

9F HEATON MERSEY (Continued)							
Not on Shed							
Stanier 5MT 2-6-0 1933	42948	42950		42951	42955	42958	
	42960	42961		42964	42967	42977	
				42978	42981	42982	13
Ivatt 4MT 2-6-0 1947	43012	43031		43042	43047	43063	6
						43106	
"Big Eights"	48089	48115		48161	48190	48208	
	48191	48327		48355	48401	48406	
	48429	48490		48501	48503	48515	
				48677	48695	48748	18
							37
saw elsewhere on the tour			9				
saw on Dec 64 Manchester and Crewe trip			1			scrap	
recently withdrawn not on shed or seen elsewhere			1	"Big Eight"		48403	Oct-65

Review and Appraisal of 9F Heaton Mersey aka the smelly shed

In sharp contrast to 9E Trafford Park the total of home steam on shed was a little disappointing. 19 Home Steam (34%) was on shed with 37 off shed. Probably the low total is accounted by a late afternoon visit and because 9F Heaton Mersey handles a lot of heavy freight engines which tend to be particularly well used.

Another strange fact was that 9F Heaton Mersey had only three steam classes allocated to it: - "Funny Crabs, "Moguls" and "Big Eights". All in strong numbers. The steam highlight was seeing 42945 the founder member of Stanier's "Funny Crab" 2-6-0 class.

The visitors were quite predictable all presumably off heavy freights. The 55D Royston was perhaps the least predictable. Seeing the Sulzer Bo-Bo Type 2 was a little surprising. Overall, although a bit disappointing in terms of numbers and steam variety a decent steam shed.

On we go

We rushed back to the bus stop and we had only a few minutes wait before the bus came. We soon reached the terminus and we made our way back to the station. I checked my watch. It was now 16.15. We had saved 35 minutes by getting the bus to and from 9F Heaton Mersey and had 30 minutes to do 9B Stockport Edgeley. It should be just about possible to get the 16.46 to Manchester Piccadilly given the advertised 10 minutes walking time to the shed.

To be sure lad 'twas a lovely afternoon, quite different from the Manchester visit of Froth and I last December. That time we took advantage of the waiting room at Stockport Edgeley Station to wring out our drenched socks much to the consternation of the other people there although one woman sympathetically showed concern saying that we might catch chilblains.

After a fair ten minutes walk we reached the shed and progressed round without encountering any shedmaster or officialdom. I was hoping to see "Jubilee" 45632 "Tonga" as she had not been on shed last December. The shed was terrific. The first "Jubilee" we came across was 45654 "Hood". She was standing outside the main shed bathed in sunshine and D.S. said that this would be the best opportunity for photographing a "Jubilee" on the tour. I agreed, certainly we could not afford to miss photographing her even if it cost us a minute or two. Inside the shed we indeed did see 45632 "Tonga" which pleased me immensely. Also inside was the double chimneyed "Jubilee" 45596 "Bahamas". I had seen "Bahamas" several times over the years. In fact, "Bahamas" was the second "Jubilee" I ever saw. The first one I saw was 45713 "Courageous" at Ayr on 9th July 1958. That was the first week that I started trainspotting. On 20th July 1958 I had seen "Bahamas" then with single chimney at 64C Dalry Road off the Birmingham – Edinburgh Caledonian Station express. We called this train the six–five special train as it arrived at Edinburgh Caledonian Station at 18.05 each weekday evening normally hauled by a "Jubilee". By 1965 the "Six five special" was summer only leaving Birmingham New Street at 11.30 and arriving at Edinburgh Caledonian (Princes Street) at 18.00 and certainly not steam hauled.

Further on we saw Britannia 70004 "William Shakespeare" one of three recently acquired Britannias (the other two being 70015"Apollo" and "70026 "Polar Star"). Once round the shed we dashed back for D.S. to photo "Hood". D.S. viewed "Hood" critically, looked up at the sun, walked round three times like some Druid ritual and finally decided on his photo position. He looked through the viewfinder but said "No!" – he was still not happy. He then climbed over a fence onto a sort of embankment. He looked to see if the sun was ideal, checked the viewfinder, gasped "Yes!" and promptly snapped her. Very impressive, D.S.'s photo shoots this week had turned him into a right professional.

Still our extended stop to photo "Hood" had come at a cost. The sands of time were running out. It was now 16.37 and we now had only 9 minutes before our train left at 16.46.

9B STOCKPORT EDGELEY							
			Home shed		Built	Withdrawn	Scrap
Steam							
Ivatt 2MT 2-6-2T 1945							
41202			9B	(ex 6G Llandudno Jct.)	Dec-1946	Nov-1966	Apr-1967
41204			9B	(ex 6G Llandudno Jct.)	Dec-1946	Nov-1966	Apr-1967
41220			9B	(ex 6G Llandudno Jct.)	Sep-1946	Nov-1966	Jun-1967
Total	3						
Hughes/Fowler 5MT 2-6-0 "Crab" 1926							
42712			9B		Mar-1927	Feb-1966	Jun-1966
42730			9B		Dec-1926	Jul-1965	Oct-1965
42734			9B		Dec-1926	Mar-1966	Jun-1966
42819			9B	(ex 9G Gorton)	Aug-1929	Sep-1965	Dec-1965
42849			9B		Dec-1930	Jul-1965	Mar-1966
42900			9B		Aug-1930	Oct-1965	Feb-1966
42940	on shed	Dec-64	9B	(ex 9G Gorton)	Dec-1932	Sep-1965	Dec-1965
Total	7						
Midland 4F 0-6-0 1924							
44394	on shed	Dec-64	9B		Oct-1926	Jul-1966	Oct-1966
Total	1						
Stanier 5MT 4-6-0 "Black Five" 1934							
44867			9B		Feb-1945	Jun-1967	Dec-1967
45225			9B		Aug-1936	Oct-1967	Jul-1968
45292			1A	Willesden	Dec-1936	Nov-1967	Mar-1968
Total	3						
Stanier 6P5F 4-6-0 "Jubilee" 1934							
45596	"Bahamas"		9B		Jan-1935	Jul-1966	saved
45632	"Tonga"		9B		Nov-1934	Oct-1965	May-1966
45654	"Hood"	DS photo	9B		Feb-1935	Jun-1966	Oct-1966
Total	3						
Stanier 8F 2-8-0 "Big Eight" 1935							
48182			9B		Apr-1942	May-1968	Oct-1968
48269			6B	Mold Junction	May-1942	Jul-1967	Dec-1967
48302			9B		Oct-1943	Jan-1966	Apr-1966
48437			9B		May-1944	Apr-1968	Jul-1968
Total	4						
BR Standard 7P6F 4-6-2 "Britannia" Derby 1951							
70004	"William Shakespeare"		9B	(ex 5A Crewe North)	Mar-1951	Dec-1967	Apr-1968
Total	1						

		Home shed		Built	Withdrawn	Scrap
BR Standard 2-6-2T 1953 2MT Derby						
84013		9B		Sep-1953	Dec-1965	Mar-1966
84014		9B		Sep-1953	Dec-1965	May-1966
84017		9B	(ex 9K Bolton)	Oct-1953	Dec-1965	Mar-1966
84026		9B		Apr-1957	Dec-1965	Mar-1966
Total	4					
BR Standard 9F 2-10-0 Brighton 1954						
92086		8H	Birkenhead (ex 8B)	Jun-1956	Nov-1967	Apr-1968
Total	1					

On Shed	27		Kops	20				
Steam	27		Diesels	0				
Withdrawn	2							
on shed	Dec-64	2						
Home Locos		21	Home Area		0	Visitors	6	
Shed	9B	21						
Distribution	1A	1						
	6B	1	6G	3				
	8H	1						
Steam classes on view		9						
Steam Origin	LMS		21	BR		6		
Shed Highlight:-	45654		"Hood"	9B		Stockport Edgeley		
Steam	Aug-50	27	Mar-59		26	Apr-65	33	
Allocation						Aug-65	29	
				Closed to Steam:-			May-68	
Home Steam	excluding withdrawn locos							
On/Off Shed	On Shed		22	Off Shed		7	% On Shed	76%
Not on Shed								
"Crab"					42710	42812	42942	3
"Black Fives"						44868	44916	2
"Big Eights"							48392	1
"Britannias"							70015	1
							total	7
		saw elsewhere on the tour						2
		saw on shed Dec 64						2
		saw elsewhere on Dec 64 Manchester and Crewe trip						1
		saw on June 67 Carlisle visit						1

Review and Appraisal of 9B Stockport Edgeley

The shed was on the west side of the line south of Stockport Edgeley station. Walking time was 10 minutes from the station.

A very useful shed. Well up to expectations. Seeing the three active "Jubilees" was sensational and very satisfying. What a marvellous snap D.S. took of "Hood". I can't wait for the photo to be developed.

The surprise of the shed was seeing the three 6G Llandudno Junction 2-6-2 Tanks. More than coincidence seeing all three. They must have been transferred here very recently. 41220 used to be push and pull working as indeed 60 of the original 130 were.

The clutch of "Crabs" and the solitary Midland 0-6-0 (also on shed last December) were very welcome. The 1A Willesden "Black Five" was a welcome surprise as indeed was the 8H Birkenhead 9F 2-10-0.

The four 84XXX BR 2-6-2 tanks were virtually identical to the later members of the Ivatt Class 41290-41329 of which three earlier examples were on shed.

22 Home Steam on shed and only 7 Home Steam off shed. A remarkable 76% for a weekday afternoon. Perhaps weekends start early here. I would finally catch up with 70015 "Apollo" in my next nostalgic visit to Carlisle on 3rd June 1967. I would see six of the missing seven elsewhere. Incredible to miss so little on shed but partly explained by my earlier visit of last December.

**45654 "Hood" of 9B Stockport Edgeley - Stanier 6P5F 4-6-0 "Jubilee" 1934.
In steam on shed Friday 6th August 1965.**

9B STOCKPORT EDGELEY REWIND SATURDAY 12th DECEMBER 1964.

The most interesting part of the visit of Ian "Froth" Firth and I was meeting a railway engine cleaner with an unfortunate stutter. Judging by our experience on the bus to 9F Heaton Mersey today Stockport seems to have a high incidence of stutterers. Perhaps it is the fortunes of the local football team which had given them the stutters. Our railway cleaner friend pointed out Stockport County Football stadium in the distance and said "See there, the greatest team in Britain plays there". Froth and I had almost collapsed with laughter at this. At the time Stockport County were 92nd of the 92 teams in the English football League. They had finished the season in the same position – stone cold last. They had had to apply for re-election to the league and luckily had been successful. Yes perhaps we can blame the bad Stockport County football team for both the old boy's and the cleaner's stutter.

Our cleaner friend gave us some good information though. Froth had come hoping to see 45596 "Bahamas" and I had hoped to see 45632 "Tonga". Both of us were to be disappointed and our cleaner friend told us that we had been unlucky as they had both worked out earlier in the morning.

That December Saturday Froth and I only visited the Crewe sheds and 9D Newton Heath and 9B Stockport Edgeley. We had also planned to visit 9G Gorton but our Edinburgh train had arrived late and it had been an easy choice to decide in favour of 9D Newton Heath rather than workmanlike 9G Gorton. I suspect at the time that we didn't know where 9F Heaton Mersey was as it could easily have been added to our Stockport stop on the way to Crewe. Our tickets did not allow us to break our journey at Stockport and the wise ticket collector stopped us and made us pay for two extra singles from Manchester to Stockport.

REWIND 9B STOCKPORT EDGELEY 12th DECEMBER 1964

		Home shed		Built	Withdrawn	Scrap
Diesels						
BR 0-6-0 Shunter 1953						
D3699		9G	Gorton	May-1959		
D3770		9B	(ex 9A Longsight)	May-1959		
Total	2					
Steam				Built	Withdrawn	Scrap
Fowler 4MT 2-6-4T 1927						
42424		9B		Jan-1934	Sep-1964	Apr-1965
Total	1					
Hughes/Fowler 5MT 2-6-0 "Crab" 1926						
42788		9B		Oct-1927	Sep-1964	Nov-1964
42793		9B		Oct-1927	Dec-1964	Mar-1965
42814		8H	Birkenhead	Jun-1929	Aug-1965	Jan-1966
42817		9B		Jul-1929	Apr-1965	Oct-1965
42826		9B		Nov-1929	Sep-1964	Jan-1965
42932		9B		Jun-1931	May-1965	Oct-1965
42940	on shed Aug-65	9G	Gorton	Dec-1932	Sep-1965	Dec-1965
42942		9B		Dec-1932	Jan-1967	Oct-1967
Total	8					
Midland 4F 0-6-0 1924						
44394	on shed Aug-65	9B		Oct-1926	Jul-1966	Oct-1966
Total	1					
Stanier 5MT 4-6-0 "Black Five" 1934						
44868		9B		Feb-1945	May-1968	Sep-1968
44916		9A	Longsight	Dec-1945	Dec-1967	Feb-1968
Total	2					
Stanier 6P5F 4-6-0 "Jubilee" 1934						
45563	"Australia" pass shed	8B	Warrington	Aug-1934	Nov-1965	Mar-1966
45670	"Howard of Effingham"	9B		Dec-1935	Oct-1964	Feb-1965
Total	2					
Stanier 8F 2-8-0 "Big Eight" 1935						
48188		8A	Edge Hill	Apr-1942	May-1966	Aug-1966
48727		8H	Birkenhead (ex 5B)	Sep-1944	Aug-1968	Jan-1969
48744		9B		May-1946	Mar-1968	Jul-1968
Total	3					
BR Standard 5MT 4-6-0 Doncaster 1951						
73125	Caprotti valve gear	9H	Patricroft	Jun-1956	Jun-1968	Oct-1968
Total	1					

On Shed	20	Kops	17		
Steam	18	Diesels	2		
Withdrawn	4				
on shed	Aug-65	2			
Home Locos	12 Home Area		4	Visitors	4
Shed	9B	12			
Distribution	9A	1 9G	2 9H	1	
	8A	1 8B	1	8H	2
Steam classes on view		7			
Steam Origin	LMS	17 BR	1		
Shed Highlight:-	45670	"Howard of Effingham"			

Steam	Aug-50	27	Mar-59		26	Apr-65	33
Allocation						Aug-65	29
			Closed to Steam:-			May-68	

Home Steam	excluding withdrawn locos					
On/Off Shed	On Shed	7 Off Shed		19 % On Shed	27%	
Not on Shed						
Fairbum 4MT 2-6-4T 1945				42121	42343	2
"Crab"	42710	42734	42772	42849	42941	5
"Black Fives"	44696	44855	44867	45225	45291	
					45382	6
"Jubilee"			45596	45632	45654	3
"Big Eights"			48302	48392	48437	3
					total	19

	saw on shed Aug 65	9	
	saw elsewhere on the tour	10	

Surprising that there were only 17 steam locos on shed last December while there were 27 steam locos on shed now in August 1965. Perhaps this is partly due to steam engines losing some of their regular turns to diesels and therefore being on shed more often.

The "Crabs" seemed to have been dealt the death card here with three condemned last December and a further two noted in our August visit. Only two engines 42940 and 44394 were on shed on both visits. It was sad to see "Jubilee" Howard of Effingham" on shed and withdrawn.

Amazing how the shed had been a bit disappointing last December but good now in August. Luck can play a part on numbers on shed other than on a Sunday when one can always expect engines in number. To crown our August visit we saw "Jubilee" 45563 "Australia" amble past the shed on a freight. "Australia" had been a very common sight recently. I had seen her at Preston a month ago, and she had been seen at Carlisle last Sunday. Doubtless, she will be on her home shed of 8B Warrington when we visit there.

Overall, last December there had been only 7 (27%) Home Steam on shed and 19 Home Steam off shed. Amazingly all 19 of the missing Home Steam were to be seen this week on the LMR tour.

JOURNEY TO MANCHESTER AND STOCKPORT 12th DECEMBER 1964

The famed trip with "Ian Froth" Firth had been dreamed up by Ian. At first we were going to Leeds and Wakefield but shortly before the visit he announced that we would be going to Manchester and Crewe so no complaints on my part! We would visit 9G Gorton and 9D Newton Heath before proceeding on to Crewe.

Our train arrived late and Ian suggested that we cut out 9D Newton Heath. I reminded him where the "Jubilees" were and 9G Gorton was cut out in favour of 9D Newton Heath a decision not to be regretted. Our schedule was as follows:-

		Schedule
Depart	Edinburgh Princes Street	23.30
Arrive	Carstairs	00.08
Depart	Carstairs	00.40
Arrive	Carlisle	02.12
Arrive	Manchester Victoria	06.14
	Do 9D Newton Heath	
Depart	Manchester Piccadilly	09.50
Arrive	Stockport Edgeley	09.58
	Do 9B Stockport Edgeley	
Depart	Stockport Edgeley	10.45
Arrive	Crewe	11.21
	Do 5A Crewe North	
	Do 5B Crewe South	
	Do Crewe Diesel	
	Do Crewe Works	
Depart	Crewe	16.41
Arrive	Carlisle	20.27
Arrive	Carstairs	22.13
Depart	Carstairs	22.30
Arrive	Edinburgh Princes Street	23.03

A busy 24 hours!

		Home shed		Built	Withdrawn	Scrap
Diesels						
English Electric Type 4 1Co-Co1 1958						
D 219	*Carstairs*	12B	Carlisle Upperby	*Jul-1959*		
D 337	*Victoria to Newton Heath*	5A	Crewe North	*Mar-1961*		
Total	2					
BR English Electric 0-6-0 Shunter 1953						
D3591	*Victoria to Newton Heath*	9D	Newton Heath	*Dec-1958*		
D3772	*at 9A Longsight*	9B	Stockport Edgeley	*Jun-1959*		
Total	2					
BR Sulzer Type 2 Bo-Bo 1958						
D5083	*Carlisle*	5A	Crewe North	*Apr-1960*		
Total	1					
English Electric Type 1 Bo-Bo 1957						
D8115	*Carstairs*	66A	Polmadie	*Feb-1962*		
Total	1					
Electrics						
English Electric AL3 Bo-Bo 1960						
E3026	*Manchester Piccadilly*	LMW	London Midl. West. Lines	*Aug-1960*		
E3030	*at 9A Longsight*	LMW	London Midl. West. Lines	*Oct-1960*		
Total	2					
General Electric AL4 Bo-Bo 1960						
E3038	*Piccadilly - Stockport*	LMW	London Midl. West. Lines	*Jun-1960*		
E3044	*Piccadilly - Stockport*	LMW	London Midl. West. Lines	*Dec-1960*		
Total	2					
A.E.I. (Metropolitan-Vickers) AL2 Bo-Bo 1960						
E3052	*Piccadilly - Stockport*	LMW	London Midl. West. Lines	*Dec-1960*		
Total	1					
BR A.E.I.(B.T.H.) motors AL5 Bo-Bo 1960						
E3071	*Manchester Piccadilly*	LMW	London Midl. West. Lines	*May-1962*		
E3077	*at 9A Longsight*	LMW	London Midl. West. Lines	*Mar-1963*		
Total	2					
English Electric AL3 Bo-Bo 1961						
E3099	*at 9A Longsight*	LMW	London Midl. West. Lines	*May-1961*		
Total	1					
BR EM2 Metropolitan-Vickers Co-Co 1954						
27001	"Ariadne" *at Piccadilly*	9C	Reddish	*Mar-1954*	*Oct-1968*	
Total	1					
Steam				**Built**	**Withdrawn**	**Scrap**
Fairburn 4MT 2-6-4T 1945						
42121	*Manchester Exch.*	9B	Stockport Edgeley	*Sep-1949*	*Jul-1966*	*Oct-1966*
Total	1					
Fowler 4MT 2-6-4T 1927						
42334	*Manchester Piccadilly*	9G	Gorton	*Mar-1929*	*Dec-1965*	*Apr-1966*
Total	1					
Stanier 4MT 2-6-4T 1935 dev of Fowler 1927						
42435	*Manchester Exchange*	9H	Patricroft (ex 8M)	*Mar-1936*	*Apr-1965*	*Aug-1965*
Total	1					
Hughes/Fowler 5MT 2-6-0 "Crab" 1926						
42878	*Manchester Victoria*	9G	Gorton (ex 8F)	*Jun-1930*	*Sep-1965*	*Dec-1965*
Total	1					
Stanier 5MT 2-6-0 1933						
42960	*Manchester Exchange*	8F	Springs Branch (Wigan)	*Dec-1933*	*Jan-1966*	*Apr-1966*
Total	2					
Ivatt 4MT 2-6-0 1947						
43023	*Carlisle*	12A	Carlisle Kingmoor	*Jan-1949*	*Dec-1967*	*Apr-1968*
Total	1					
Stanier 5MT 4-6-0 "Black Five" 1934						
44818	*Victoria to Newton Heath*	9D	Newton Heath	*Nov-1944*	*Jun-1968*	*Dec-1968*
45078	*Wigan North Western*	8B	Warrington	*Mar-1935*	*Oct-1965*	*Dec-1965*
45083	*Carlisle*	9D	Newton Heath	*Mar-1935*	*Dec-1967*	*May-1968*
45217	*Carlisle*	12A	Carlisle Kingmoor	*Nov-1935*	*Nov-1966*	*Jun-1967*
45278	*Carlisle*	8F	Springs Branch (Wigan)	*Nov-1936*	*Jun-1967*	*Jan-1968*
45363	*Carlisle*	12A	Carlisle Kingmoor	*Jun-1937*	*Oct-1967*	*Mar-1968*
45380	*Piccadilly-Stockport*	9A	Longsight	*Jul-1937*	*Mar-1965*	*Dec-1965*
Total	7					
Stanier 6P5F 4-6-0 "Jubilee" 1934						
45666	"Cornwallis" *at Wigan*	8B	Warrington	*Nov-1935*	*Apr-1965*	*Aug-1965*
Total	1					

		Home shed		Built	Withdrawn	Scrap
Midland 3F "Jinty" 0-6-0T 1924 dev. of Johnson 1899 design						
47293	Preston	10D	Lostock Hall	Oct-1924	Dec-1966	Feb-1968
47485	Victoria to Newton Heath	8A	Edge Hill	Jan-1928	Jan-1965	May-1965
Total	2					
Stanier 8F 2-8-0 "Big Eight" 1935						
48675	Carlisle	8F	Springs Branch (ex 16E)	Mar-1944	Sep-1967	Jul-1968
Total	1					
BR Standard 7P6F 4-6-2 "Britannia" Derby 1951						
70013	"Oliver Cromwell" at 66E	12A	Carlisle Kingmoor	May-1951	Aug-1968	saved
Total	1					
BR Standard 5MT 4-6-0 Doncaster 1951						
73006	Wigan	9H	Patricroft	Jun-1951	Mar-1967	Sep-1967
73128	Manchester Exchange	9H	Patricroft	Aug-1956	May-1968	Aug-1968
73158	Manchester Exchange	9H	Patricroft	Dec-1956	Oct-1967	Feb-1968
Total	3					
BR Standard 4MT 4-6-0 Brighton 1951						
75059	hauled Preston-Manch	8F	Springs Branch (Wigan)	Apr-1957	Jul-1967	Dec-1967
Total	1					
BR Standard 2MT 2-6-0 Doncaster 1953						
78002	Preston	10D	Lostock Hall	Dec-1952	Jun-1966	Oct-1966
78041	Preston	10D	Lostock Hall	Dec-1954	May-1967	Nov-1967
Total	2					
BR Standard 4MT 2-6-4T Doncaster 1953						
80075	Carstairs	66E	Carstairs	Dec-1953	Jul-1964	Mar-1965
Total	1					
BR Standard 9F 2-10-0 Brighton 1954						
92233	Preston	12A	Carlisle Kingmoor	Aug-1958	Feb-1968	Aug-1968
Total	1					

On Journies	42					
Steam	27	Diesel	6 Electrics		9	
Withdrawn	1					
		Home Area		3	Visitors	8
Shed	5A		2 LMW	8		
Distribution:-	8A		1 8B	2	8F	4
	9A		1 9B	2	9C	1
	9D		4 9G	2	9H	4
	10D		3 12A	5	12B	1
	66A		1 66E	1		
Steam classes on view		16				
Steam Origin		LMS	18 BR		9	
Highlight:-		45666	"Cornwallis"			

On the way to Manchester our coaches were hitched off at Preston and we progressed to Manchester behind Standard 4MT 4-6-0 75059 of 8F Springs Branch (Wigan).

An interesting assortment of steam engines had been seen on the way with the highlight easily being "Jubilee" 45666 "Cornwallis" which we saw at Wigan. Sadly she was to be withdrawn in April 1965. "Jubilees" were always my favourite class. 191 were built including two upgraded to 7P. The class began to be decimated in 1962 with 145 surviving at the end of that year (end 1963 - 114, end 1964 - 48 and 15 would survive until the end of 1965. Remarkably eight would still survive at the end of 1966.

On we go

Back to the present and we now had to get the 16.46 to Manchester Piccadilly, then across to Manchester Exchange to get our bags and back to Manchester Central to get the 17.30 to Warrington. A nice tour of Manchester stations in prospect.

We now had only nine minutes left as it was 16.37. We had lost a few minutes by our stop to photo "Hood" but that had been well worth it. Operating at about 50% efficiency, because of the tiring day we made the best of our way back to the station. We ran up the cinder path from the shed, turned left into Booth Street and right into Shaw Heath. We pushed relentlessly on, turned left into Greek Street and left again into Wellington Road. As we turned left into Station Road I rechecked my watch. It was 16.45. One minute left. We rushed into the station, ascertained the platform from the ticket collector, rushed up a flight of stairs on to the platform only to see our bucket speeding out of the east end of the station. We had missed catching it by about twenty seconds. Not quite as bad a miss as that at Cardiff General where we missed our connection by about five seconds. However, our bucket was gone and there was nothing we could do about it. I checked my watch. It was still 16.46. The bucket had probably left a little early which made us all the angrier as we would have caught it if it had left at the correct time. What bad luck!

We checked downstairs with the ticket collector and ascertained that the next train to Manchester Piccadilly was the 17.10 arriving at 17.19 although we might have jumped on to the "Pines Express" in a few minutes as it stopped on a set down basis only at Stockport Station but we were unaware of that fact and certainly if we had known we would have jumped on it when it stopped to let off passengers. So we had no chance at all with only eleven minutes to play with of getting our bags from Victoria and catching the 17.30 from Central. It was worth clutching at straws and there was but one straw left and that was to catch a bus. We decided to try it as there was nothing to lose but the one shilling (five new pence) fare. We made our way to Mersey Square. If we got a bus that left immediately we might just make the 17.30 to Central.

However, we were snookered again when we saw a long queue at the bus stop. It was now the start of the 17.00 rush hour. We did succeed in getting on the second bus which came along but in the rush-hour traffic the bus crawled along and it was soon clear that all hope of the 17.30 to Central was lost. Need I add, but the world's champion sleeper D.S. had fallen asleep again and he was still asleep when we reached Manchester City Centre. I felt like leaving him on the bus as I was getting sick and tired of him falling asleep. However, he had the key to the left luggage locker so I thought no more about this. I gave him a playful chop to the neck and he awoke rubbing his neck, complaining of a stiff neck

We made our way to nearby Victoria Station from where the bus dropped us off and collected our holdalls from the left luggage locker. We then went out and found out what bus took us to Manchester Central Station. The bus journey only took a few minutes and we were sure that if we had got the 16.46 from Stockport we would have easily made the 17.30 train from Central. We reached Manchester Central at just after 17.45 and found out that the next train to Warrington was at 18.30 so we had 45 minutes to burn and by the look of D.S. he badly needed some sustenance. All we had had to eat today was some goodies from the baker's shop near Patricroft early in the morning. Moreover, D.S. had missed his glass of water at 9A Longsight owing to the typhoid scare and the buckets we had been travelling on had been mainly suburban so he had missed drinking the trains dry of water.

Inside the station buffet we found that it was the rush hour too but managed to secure the last vacant table with our holdalls and queued at the self-service along with our pin-striped bowler hated businessmen with their rolled up umbrellas. They were probably returning to their suburban semi-detached paradises after a day's wizardry in the commercial and financial heart of Manchester.

We had the usual "full meal". A nine pence (3.5 new pence) Gala fruit pie (i.e. a rebadged eight pence Lyon's fruit pie to allow a monopoly profit of one pence per pie). We had our usual mortar of kidney soup from one of BR's micro cans of Chef Soup. Some more goodies and a cup of tea and that was dinner. I assured D.S. that he could eat all he wanted in the 40 minutes available but D.S. did not fancy spending any more and had the same fare as me. When it came to the pinch D.S. economised very well. All that D.S. would never economise was sleep and I doubt whether I need to convince any reader of that!

Our revised timetable for the evening would be as follows:-

		Schedule		Miles
Depart	MANCHESTER CENTRAL	18.30		0
Arrive	WARRINGTON CENTRAL	18.57		18¼
	Do 8B Warrington	50	*minutes*	
Depart	WARRINGTON CENTRAL	19.57		18¼
Arrive	GARSTON	20.22		32½
	Do 8C Speke Junction	45	*minutes*	
	Do 8J Allerton	30	*minutes*	
Depart	ALLERTON	22.06		0
Arrive	LIVERPOOL LIME STREET	22.22		5½

So the net loss of the day would still only be 9C Reddish (nothing to worry about missing a diesel and electric depot) and 8A Edge Hill which we could visit tomorrow morning. The small St.Helen's shed 8G Sutton Oak might need to be chopped tomorrow but I'll worry about that later. Will be getting a bit dark going round 8C Speke Junction and 8J Allerton but if we do 8C Speke Junction (the steam shed) first we should be OK to go round a brightly lit modern electric depot in 8J Allerton. In all, it was quite amazing that after so many catastrophes today that we had got off so lightly.

There had so far been little for us to laugh about today, far more to cry about. Certainly the Wad Affair at 9D Newton Heath had given us our greatest cause for merriment today. As we sat in the buffet at Manchester Central one could not help feeling a little sad that our tour was gradually coming to an end. I wished that we could tour forever but lack of funds unfortunately precluded this. It was all the sadder for D.S. He admitted that he dreaded tomorrow at noon when he must get the train from Preston back home without doing any of the 10 Area (Preston division) sheds. He would miss 10A Carnforth, 10D Lostock Hall, 10F Rose Grove, 10G Skipton, 10H Lower Darwen and 9K Bolton. All because his slave-driving uncle could not allow him to miss the Sunday papers. Talking about papers I did a Sunday paper round too and I largely financed this tour from the proceeds from it (ten shillings (50 new pence) per week). Luckily, I had got someone to do the paper round last Sunday and this Sunday coming. Yes 'twas very sad that we were approaching the tour's end.

Central was the Midland Railway terminus in Manchester and handled all the London St.Pancras trains. Having made sure that every last dreg of tea and crumb of sustenance had been polished off we left the buffet and made a quick tour of the station. To frank the Midland comment, three main line diesels (two "Peaks" and a Type 2) allocated to Midland Lines, Derby were noted. The Type 2's two tone green livery looked really smart and certainly as attractive as a diesel could be.

MANCHESTER CENTRAL STATION							
		Home shed		Built	Withdrawn	Scrap	
Diesels							
BR Sulzer "Peak" Type 4 1Co-Co1 1959							
D 61		ML	Midland Lines	*Mar-1962*			
D 117		ML	Midland Lines	*Sep-1961*		KOP	
Total	2						
BR Sulzer Type 2 Bo-Bo 1958							
D7591		ML	Midland Lines	*May-1964*		KOP	
Total	1						
On Station	3	Kops		2			
Steam	0	Diesels		3			
		Home Area		0	Visitors	3	
Shed Distribution		ML	3				

THE IRLAM AFFAIR

We went to catch the 18.30 to Warrington Central. We ascertained the platform from the timetable in the main concourse and went to the ticket barrier. We had the following conversation with the ticket collector at the gate for our platform.

We flashed our Railrover tickets as we always did. Normally, this produced an OK from the ticket collector but this time it was different – quite different.

TICKET COLLECTOR: - "Where are you going to?"
Nobody had wanted to know that before on our tour. Was he inquisitive, nosey or merely curious? Certainly a puzzle to me. Why did he want to know?
ME:- "Warrington."
TICKET COLLECTOR: - "Take one of the first three coaches then."

Funny, being segregated. And I thought no more about it. Nevertheless, undaunted D.S. and I got into the third coach we came to i.e. the top of the first three coaches and we sat down at the front of the coach right behind the driver. Our train was a three coach set and there was another three coach set in front of us on the same platform.

At 18.30, the three coach set in front of us started up and darted out of the station. We left the station five minutes late at 18.35. Quite disgraceful time-keeping I said to D.S. The station inspector at Cardiff General would have had a fit at this late start.

Going out of the station we saw two Standard "Doodle-Bugs" (as D.S. likes to call them) on station work. They were 78007 and 78023. Both had been transferred to 9G Gorton which was then quickly closed and they were transferred on to 9E Trafford Park .78007 had previously been allocated to 5B Crewe South and Froth and I had noted her there last December. 78023 had come from 16D Nottingham and we had noted her on 9E Trafford Park earlier in the day. In the neighbourhood of 9E Trafford Park we noted a "Black Five", a Fairburn tank and a Brush Type 2 diesel (we had seen the last two also earlier in the day on 9E Trafford Park).

MANCHESTER CENTRAL DEPARTURE AND TRAFFORD PARK AREA							
			Home shed		Built	Withdrawn	Scrap
Diesels							
BR Sulzer Type 2 Bo-Bo 1958							
D5275	*on 9E*	*earlier*	9E	Trafford Park	*Jun-1964*		
Total		*1*					
Steam					Built	Withdrawn	Scrap
Fairburn 4MT 2-6-4T 1945 dev. of Stanier 1935							
42076	*on 9E*	*earlier*	9E	Trafford Park	*Dec-1950*	*Mar-1967*	*Nov-1967*
Total		*1*					
Stanier 5MT 4-6-0 "Black Five" 1934							
44871			9E	Trafford Park	*Mar-1945*	*Aug-1968*	*saved*
Total		*1*					
BR Standard 2MT 2-6-0 Doncaster 1953							
78007			9E	(ex 9G Gorton)	*Mar-1953*	*May-1967*	*Dec-1967*
78023	*on 9E*	*earlier*	9E	(ex 9G Gorton)	*May-1954*	*May-1967*	*Oct-1967*
Total		*2*					
On Route		5	Kops		1		
Steam		4	Diesels		1		
		Home Area			5	Visitors	0
Shed							
Distribution	9E	5					
Steam Classes	3						
Steam Origin	LMS	2	BR		2		

There was something odd about our train. According to the timetable in the main concourse our train only made one intermediate stop at Padgate just before Warrington. However, our bucket first stopped at Trafford Park and then at Stretford, Urmston, Chassen Road and Flixton. Things were getting out of hand. Perhaps they had forgotten to put all the stops on the timetable in the main concourse suggested D.S. hopefully. Could be a possibility but I doubted it. There was something very odd going on but I couldn't guess what. At least we were on the Warrington line and would soon reach there. That was one consolation we did not appear to be sidetracked on to a "Style" type branch line like our ill-fated journey to Stockport this afternoon.

"Everybody Out"!

The last straw of our journey came when we reached a little station named Irlam for Cadishead. At this point everyone left on the train suddenly got up and went out. Funny, peculiar. I would have thought some passengers would be going on to Warrington. Strange how quickly a busy bucket can be reduced to emptiness.

We waited patiently for the bucket to start up again and leave Irlam behind. No go, it appeared that some sort of strike was going on. The driver started to collect his possessions together, looked round and appeared to be surprised to see D.S. and me sitting behind him still on the train. He unlocked the connecting door between the driving compartment and the first coach where we sat.

DRIVER: - "What are you doing still on the train?"

What a strange question. This is the Warrington train???.

ME:- This is the 18.30 to Warrington isn't it?"

DRIVER: - "No, this is the 18.35 train to Irlam which finishes here."

Oh, no! How could we have got on the wrong train again? This is unbelievable. Pause while we gasp, splutter and look extremely annoyed at this news.

ME:- "I'm sure the ticket collector said that this was the Warrington train."

DRIVER: - "Yes, the Warrington train left from the same platform as us. It was directly in front. You must have seen it leave at 18.30. That was the train the ticket collector must have said was yours – not the Irlam train."

D.S. and I (In unison):- "Damn!"

Nothing to do now but wait for the next train to Warrington so we got our things together and the driver escorted us off the train before we thought of possibly wrecking it in retaliation at the bad luck that BR had dealt us. This was about the umpteenth catastrophe of the day and truly remarkable all the bad luck we had had. It seemed as though the catastrophes were now getting bigger in terms of time lost.

I asked the ticket collector at the station when the next train was and he said 19.56. Another hour to wait what a bloody service. I asked about the bus service to Warrington but like the good railwayman he was (like the laird on Alfreton station on Monday night) he did not recommend it. I did not feel like bussing it especially when they probably crawled along. We sat disconsolately down on a bench to wait in tedium for an hour before the 19.56 eventually arrives. You will know about that drained feeling by now. We were used to that dejected feeling following every disaster. D.S. was different from me in that he tended to sleep them off so perhaps he looked forward to them one might stay! Yes, it was that Cardiff General Station missed train feeling again.

POST MORTEM OF THE IRLAM AFFAIR

How did it happen? The ticket collector distinctly said that we were to get into one of the first three coaches. He had obviously to us now meant the first three coaches on the platform and we had thought he had meant the first three coaches that we came to! If he had said the last three coaches was the Warrington train we would have got on the correct train by our reasoning!

Instead of this:-

		Schedule		Miles
Depart	MANCHESTER CENTRAL	18.30		0
Arrive	WARRINGTON CENTRAL	18.57		18¼

We got this:-

		Schedule	Actual	Miles
Depart	MANCHESTER CENTRAL	18.35	18.35	0
Arrive	IRLAM	18.57	18.57	8¼
Depart	IRLAM	19.56	19.56	8¼
Arrive	WARRINGTON CENTRAL	20.10	20.10	15¼

Another 90 minutes lost!!! What a catastrophe. In terms of sheds it would cost us 8C Speke junction and 8J Allerton tonight. 8C Speke Junction was too good to miss so we would have to visit it tomorrow morning necessitating another shed to be chopped tomorrow. The cumulative effects of the other catastrophes had already caused us to postpone our visit to 8A Edge Hill until tomorrow morning so tomorrow's timetable would need to be radically revised. Only one particular problem with that. I did not have the 842 LMR timetable with me in order to work out the necessary revisions. It had been too heavy and bulky for me to take with us this week. I had thought my working timetable summary would suffice. It indeed was very comprehensive but naturally assumed that we would be keeping pretty much to our scheduled timetable. Now we were adding two or three more sheds to tomorrow so major surgery had to be performed and the master 842 page timetable would need to be consulted.

I asked the ticket collector if he had an LMR timetable that I could borrow for a few minutes and he crossed the boarded platform crossing to the Manchester bound platform and disappeared into the office. He emerged without it and I wondered whether he had lost it. Instead he returned with a little booklet which he took out of his pocket and handed it to me. It was titled "Irlam, Glazebrook and some other place (which I forget)" and was one of these very local handy, pocket BR timetables. However, that was no use to us. I thanked him but I said what we really needed was the full, big LMR master timetable for the whole region. He said OK, went back and duly returned with the LMR master timetable. Great, just what we wanted and I immediately got down to work. The ticket collector was quite amused as D.S. shouted out the page numbers for the relevant services while I looked up the actual services and began to prepare a working timetable for tomorrow.

Soon, we had a really good revised timetable for tomorrow. 8A Edge Hill, 8C Speke Junction and 8L Allerton were added while 8G Sutton Oak and 10D Lostock Hall were given the chop. I had visited 10D Lostock Hall three weeks ago while our family was holidaying in Blackpool so that was no great loss. 8G Sutton Oak was also a relatively small shed and importantly necessitated a 40 minutes walk and 40 minutes back unless we managed to get one of the local buses managed in the Locoshed Directory.   It is sad to chop out sheds but these two at the time seemed the best candidates although dropping the small 10H Lower Darwen could have been considered of which more later.

Once compiled, I packed my new working timetable neatly away and took the LMR monster timetable back to the ticket collector in his office thanking him for the loan of it.   You can guess how "exciting" it was on the platform at Irlam while we waited for the 19.56.   We actually did manage to see a "Black Five" and a diesel shunter in between buckets whistling by.

IRLAM STATION						
		Home shed		Built	Withdrawn	Scrap
Diesels						
BR Shunter 0-6-0 1953						
D3870		8C	Speke Junction	Feb-1960		
Total	1					
Steam				Built	Withdrawn	Scrap
Stanier 5MT 4-6-0 "Black Five" 1934						
45329		8C	Speke Junction	Mar-1937	Nov-1966	Apr-1967
Total	1					
On Station	2	Kops		1		
Steam	1	Diesels		1		
		Home Area		2	Visitors	0
Shed	8C	2				
Distribution						
Steam Classes	1					
Steam Origin	LMS	1				

You can imagine the great excitement when our bucket arrived and we left infamous Irlam behind.   It was 19.56.   The seven mile run into Warrington Central was pretty uneventful.   We did see a diesel shunter and one of our old friends a Stanier 2-6-4 tank which had been on shed at 9E Trafford Park earlier in the day.

IRLAM to WARRINGTON CENTRAL						
		Home shed		Built	Withdrawn	Scrap
Diesels						
BR Shunter 0-6-0 1953						
D4146		8C	Speke Junction	Sep-1962		
Total	1					
Steam				Built	Withdrawn	Scrap
Stanier 4MT 2-6-4T 1935 dev of Fowler 1927						
42455	on 9E	earlier	9E	Trafford Park	Aug-1936	Apr-1966	Jul-1966
Total	1					
On Station	2	Kops		1		
Steam	1	Diesels		1		
Home Locos		Home Area		1	Visitors	1
Shed	8C	1				
Distribution	9E	1				
Steam Classes	1					

We arrived at Warrington Central on time at 20.10.   I had visited Warrington a few weeks before when I visited 8F Wigan and 8B Warrington on Saturday 10th July 1965 on the last day of my week in Blackpool.

I had visited 8B Warrington from Warrington Bank Quay station (the Crewe line) but it was a lot shorter tonight from Warrington Central Station. A fifteen minute walk compared with a 30 minute walk.   The LSD said that there was a bus service which would drop us off at the shed. D.S. naturally was keen to make use of this shortcut and we jumped onto a waiting bus. The bus conductor thought that we were dead lazy getting a bus because Kerfoot Street where we wanted off was just up the road and you could actually see it from the bus stop. We explained that if he had done as much walking today as we had today he would be happy to take the bus. So we paid over our three pence (one new pence) happily enough.

We got off the bus and turned left into Kerfoot Street bore right over the railway bridge into Folly Lane and found the shed entrance on the left hand side. It would be interesting to see if the sheds locos had changed much since my visit last month.

8B WARRINGTON

			Home shed		Built	Withdrawn	Scrap
Steam							
Stanier 5MT 2-6-0 1933							
42960			9F	Heaton Mersey (8F via 9G)	Dec-1933	Jan-1966	Apr-1966
Total		1					
Midland 4F 0-6-0 1924							
44115	*on shed*	*Jul-65*	8B		May-1925	Jul-1965	Oct-1965
44294			8B		Feb-1927	Nov-1965	Jul-1966
44349	*on shed*	*Jul-65*	8B		Apr-1927	Jul-1965	Oct-1965
44522	*on shed*	*Jul-65*	8B		Jul-1928	Oct-1965	Jun-1966
Total		4					
Stanier 5MT 4-6-0 "Black Five" 1934							
44730			8B		Jan-1949	Nov-1967	Mar-1968
44778			10A	Carnforth	Jun-1947	Nov-1967	Feb-1968
44807			6J	Holyhead	Sep-1944	Mar-1968	Jun-1968
44930	*on shed*	*Jul-65*	8B		Mar-1946	May-1967	May-1968
44935	*on shed*	*Jul-65*	8B		Oct-1945	Oct-1966	Apr-1967
45041	*on shed*	*Jul-65*	8B		Oct-1934	Dec-1967	Apr-1968
45068	*on shed*	*Jul-65*	8B	(ex 8L Aintree)	Jan-1935	Dec-1965	Apr-1966
45070	*on shed*	*Jul-65*	8B	(ex 8F Wigan)	May-1935	May-1967	Dec-1967
45078			8B		Mar-1935	Oct-1965	Dec-1965
45109	*on shed*	*Jul-65*	8B		May-1935	Apr-1967	Sep-1967
45238			8B		Aug-1936	Dec-1966	Jul-1967
45372			8F	Wigan (Spring's Branch)	Jun-1937	Nov-1966	May-1967
45375	*on shed*	*Jul-65*	8B	(ex 8F Wigan)	Jun-1937	Jan-1968	Jul-1968
45436			8B		Nov-1937	Apr-1968	Sep-1968
Total		14					
Stanier 6P5F 4-6-0 "Jubilee" 1934							
45563	"Australia"	*Jul-65*	8B		Aug-1934	Nov-1965	Mar-1966
45590	"Travancore"		8B		Dec-1934	Dec-1965	Jun-1966
45655	"Keith"	*Jul-65*	8B		Dec-1934	Apr-1965	Jun-1966
Total		3					
Stanier 8F 2-8-0 "Big Eight" 1935							
48246			5D	Stoke	May-1940	Jan-1966	Apr-1966
48276			56D	Mirfield	Jul-1942	Nov-1967	Apr-1968
48529			2F	Bescot	Apr-1945	Jun-1968	Nov-1968
48745			9H	Patricroft	Apr-1946	May-1968	Sep-1968
Total		4					
BR Standard 2-6-0 1953 4MT Doncaster							
76077			8G	Sutton Oak	Dec-1956	Nov-1967	saved
Total		1					
BR 9F 2-10-0 Brighton 1954							
92023	*Crosti*	*boilered*	8H	Birkenhead (ex 12A)	Mar-1955	Nov-1967	Apr-1968
92049			8B		Mar-1955	Nov-1967	Jun-1968
92053			8B		Sep-1955	Feb-1966	Dec-1966
92055			8B		Sep-1955	Dec-1967	Apr-1968
92058	*on shed*	*Jul-65*	8B		Oct-1955	Oct-1967	Feb-1968
92078			8B		Mar-1956	May-1967	Jan-1968
92117			8C	Speke Junction	Dec-1956	Dec-1967	Apr-1968
92123			8H	Birkenhead	Mar-1957	Oct-1967	Feb-1968
92156			8B		Nov-1957	Jul-1967	Mar-1968
Total		9					

8B WARRINGTON (Continued)							

On Shed	36	Kops	15				
Steam	36	Diesels	0				
Withdrawn	3						
on shed	Jul-65	13					
Home Locos	24	Home Area		5	Visitors	7	
Shed	8B	24					
Distribution	8C	1	8F	1	8G	1	
	8H	2					
	2F	1	5D	1	6J	1	
	9F	1	9H	1	10A	1	
	56D	1					
Steam classes on view		7					
Steam Origin	LMS		26	BR		10	
Shed Highlight:-	45590	"Travancore"					
Steam	Aug-50	59	Mar-59	53	Apr-65	38	
Allocation					Aug-65	38	
			Closed to Steam:-			Oct-67	
Home Steam	excluding withdrawn locos						
On/Off Shed	On Shed	21	Off Shed	17	% On Shed	55%	
Not on Shed							
Midland 4F 0-6-0 1924						44181	1
"Black Fives"		44658	44731	44779	44819	44963	
		45129	45221	45256	45303	45323	10
"Jubilee"						45633	1
BR 9F 2-10-0 1954		92116	92119	92124	92126	92160	5
						total	17
		saw elsewhere on the tour				9	
		saw on shed July 65				4	

Review and Appraisal of 8B Warrington

The shed was on the west side of the main line about one mile north of Warrington Bank Quay Station. Walking time was 15 minutes from Warrington Central Station.

Another excellent shed. Seeing the three "Jubilees" was the highlight. Our old friend 45563 "Australia" and also 45655 "Keith" had been on shed on July 10th on my last visit. "Australia" must be a fine loco as I had seen her all over the place. I saw her first on the Froth visit to 9B Stockport Edgeley on 12th December 1964 and also at 12B Carlisle Upperby last Saturday. As well as on shed here on 10th July I had also seen her passing through Preston station on 7th July. In contrast, "Keith" had been withdrawn several months ago, had been on the dead line last month and was still on the dead line. I had missed home based 45590 "Travancore" on 10th July but pleasingly she was on shed now.

It was nice to see the 4 Midland 0-6-0's on shed. There had been a rapid rundown of the class recently and they appeared to have been dealt the death card. Two of the four here were withdrawn.

14 "Black Fives" was quite a haul - remarkably seven had been on shed on July 10th. It was pleasing to see one from 6J Holyhead on Anglesey. The 10A Carnforth based 44778 had been seen by us on the way to Carlisle last Saturday. She gets around.

It was particularly pleasing to see 4 Big Eights as surprisingly Warrington had none allocated. 48745 had been on 9H Patricroft early this morning but we had missed the 5D Stoke and the 2F Bescot "Big Eights" at their home depots. The other Big Eight was an interesting one from 56D Mirfield – another Yorkshire Big Eight which keep cropping up off cross-country freights.

The Standard 4MT 2-6-0 from 8G Sutton Oak was pleasing to see as we had had to chop out

Sutton Oak from tomorrow's timetable. I like 9F 2-10-0's (Big Nines as Alex Storie calls them) and there were nine on shed. The most interesting one was the Crosti boilered 92023. 21 Home Steam (55%) on shed and 17 off shed so overall a good percentage on shed. 13 of the missing 17 were to be seen on the tour or had been seen on my July visit.

REWIND to visit to 8B Warrington on Saturday 10th July 1965

When I visited Warrington that evening the shed tour had been put in jeopardy because I had missed the train that I intended to get from Wigan North Western Station. This was a strange case of a missed train. The timetable in the main concourse said it would leave from Platform 1. I waited patiently there for half an hour and found out that the train had left from platform 5! Efficiency at Wigan was not what it should be. This caused me to wonder if I could still do the shed because if I did I would arrive back at Blackpool rather late at 22.28. So I got on the next train to Warrington which would pass the shed before reaching the station. The sight of a full steam shed was too much for temptation so I jolly well visited the shed rather than return to Blackpool without visiting it.

REWIND 8B WARRINGTON 10th JULY 1965							
			Home shed		Built	Withdrawn	Scrap
Diesels							
BR 0-6-0 shunter 1957							
D2372			8C	Speke Junction	Jul-1961	Nov-1970	
D2373			8A	Edge Hill	Aug-1961	May-1968	
Total	2						
LMS and BR 0-6-0 shunter 1945							
12070			8B		Jul-1950	Oct-1969	
12100			8F	Springs Branch(Wigan)	Mar-1952	Feb-1969	
Total	2						
Steam					Built	Withdrawn	Scrap
Midland 4F 0-6-0 1924							
44115	on shed	Aug-65	8B		May-1925	Jul-1965	Oct-1965
44181			8B		Feb-1925	Aug-1965	Jan-1966
44349	on shed	Aug-65	8B		Apr-1927	Jul-1965	Oct-1965
44522	on shed	Aug-65	8B		Jul-1928	Oct-1965	Jun-1966
Total	4						
Stanier 5MT 4-6-0 "Black Five" 1934							
44715			5B	Crewe South (ex 1F)	Nov-1948	Jan-1968	Apr-1968
44779			8B		Jul-1947	Dec-1966	Jul-1967
44819			8B		Nov-1944	Nov-1967	Mar-1968
44930	on shed	Aug-65	8B		Mar-1946	May-1967	May-1968
44935	on shed	Aug-65	8B		Oct-1945	Oct-1966	Apr-1967
45041	on shed	Aug-65	8B		Oct-1934	Dec-1967	Apr-1968
45068	on shed	Aug-65	8B	(ex 8L Aintree)	Jan-1935	Dec-1965	Apr-1966
45070	on shed	Aug-65	8B	(ex 8F Springs Branch)	May-1935	May-1967	Dec-1967
45109	on shed	Aug-65	8B		May-1935	Apr-1967	Sep-1967
45215			10F	Rose Grove (ex 16B)	Nov-1935	Oct-1967	Jan-1968
45230			10A	Carnforth	Aug-1936	Aug-1965	Nov-1965
45256			8B		Oct-1936	Aug-1967	Jun-1968
45321			8F	Springs Branch (ex5B)	Feb-1937	Oct-1967	Feb-1968
45323			8B	(ex 8L Aintree)	Feb-1937	Sep-1967	Mar-1968
45375	on shed	Aug-65	8B		Jun-1937	Jan-1968	Jul-1968
Total	15						
Stanier 6P5F 4-6-0 "Jubilee" 1934							
45563	"Australia"	Aug-65	8B		Aug-1934	Nov-1965	Mar-1966
45655	"Keith"	Aug-65	8B		Dec-1934	Apr-1965	Jun-1966
Total	2						
Midland 3F 0-6-0 "Jinty" 1924							
47493			8F	Springs Branch(Wigan)	Feb-1928	Dec-1966	saved
Total	1						

			Home shed		**Built**	**Withdrawn**	**Scrap**
Stanier 8F 2-8-0 "Big Eight" 1935							
48129		8A	Edge Hill		*Jan-1941*	*Mar-1966*	*Jun-1966*
48301		8L	Aintree (ex15B via15A)		*Sep-1943*	*Mar-1967*	*Sep-1967*
48331		9D	Newton Heath		*Sep-1943*	*Feb-1966*	*Sep-1966*
Total	*3*						
Thompson 5MT 4-6-0 B1 1942							
61050		41J	Langwith(ex36E via 36A)	*Jun-1946*	*Feb-1966*	*Oct-1968*	
Total	*1*						
BR Standard 9F 2-10-0 Brighton 1954							
92058	*on shed*	*Aug-65*	8B		*Oct-1955*	*Oct-1967*	*Feb-1968*
92112		8H	Birkenhead		*Nov-1956*	*Nov-1967*	*Mar-1968*
92124		8B			*Mar-1957*	*Dec-1966*	*Apr-1967*
92160		8B			*Nov-1957*	*Jul-1968*	*Oct-1968*
Total	*4*						

On Shed	34	**Kops**	22			
Steam	30	**Diesels**	4			
Withdrawn	3					
on shed	*Aug-65*	13				

Home Locos		21	**Home Area**	8	**Visitors**	5	
Shed	8B	21	8A	2	8C	1	
Distribution	8F	3	8H	1	8L	1	
	5B	1	9D	1			
	10A	1	10F	1			
	41J	1					
Steam classes on view		7					
Steam Origin	LMS		25	BR		4	LNER	1
Shed Highlight:-	61050	41J	Langwith				

Steam	*Aug-50*	167	*Mar-59*	154	*Apr-65*	79
Allocation					*Aug-65*	98
			Closed to Steam:-		Oct-67	

Home Steam	*excluding withdrawn locos*						
On/Off Shed	On Shed		17	Off Shed	21	% On Shed	45%
Not on Shed							
Midland 4F 0-6-0 1924						44294	1
"Black Fives"		44658	44730	44731	44963	45078	
		45129	45221	45238	45303	45436	10
"Jubilee"					45590	45633	2
BR 9F 2-10-0 1954		92049	92053	92055	92078	92116	
				92119	92126	92156	8
						total	21
		saw elsewhere on the tour			7		
		saw on shed August 65			11		

Review and Appraisal of rewind 8B Warrington 10th July 1965

13 engines of the 30 steam locos I saw (43 %) were also on shed today. The highlight of my earlier visit was seeing LNER BI 61050 from 41J Langwith on shed. 41J Langwith was a shed which D.S. and I would have visited but for unforeseen disasters on Monday afternoon. The smooth Thompson boiler looked quite out of place amidst the shed's largely Stanier tapered boiler occupants. Our loco in question had been allocated previously to 36E Retford until that shed's closure. How she had got here from Langwith was a total surprise. Certainly a stunning highlight. At the time I had gone round the shed with a fellow young railwayist and he was quite speechless at the sight of her.

44181 had been lying on the deadline during my July visit but now appeared to have been towed away to the scrapbreakers before our August visit. Withdrawn "Jubilee" 45655 "Keith" had not yet received the same fate although withdrawn months ago. It takes a hard heart to send a "Jubilee" to the breaker's though.

"Black Fives" had been in number on both visits (15 in July and 14 now). As in August there had been a visiting one from 10A Carnforth. It must be a regular turn. Good to see a "Jinty" from Wigan.

Only four of the hard working 9F 2-10-0's on shed in July against an impressive nine in August. Three visiting Big Eight's in July (all from nearby sheds) against four in August (all from more distant sheds). Strange to see four visiting diesel shunters on shed in July as they normally stick quite closely to their home depots. Must have been a shunter party that night as none on shed in August!

17 Home Steam (45%) on shed as against 21 off shed. The exact opposite of my July visit. 18 of the missing 21 were either seen on shed on my August visit or elsewhere on the week's LMR tour.

On we go – back to the present

That had been a good shed and wasting no time we made our way back to the bus stop. Warrington had been a particularly fine shed for shedmasters. I had seen none on both visits. This is rather good when one was permitless on both occasions.

Our bus duly arrived and we each again paid the threepenny (one new pence) fare and the bus advanced a quarter of a mile along the road to our get off point.

We were back in the station at 20.50. Our train was due to leave at 20.57 but left nine minutes late at 21.06. Just as well that these minutes no longer mattered. On the outskirts of the station we saw a couple of 9E Trafford Park engines (a Black Five and a Fairburn tank). 42076 was still alive and kicking but most of her sisters had been lying condemned at 9E Trafford Park. We had the pleasure of watching darkness fall. By the time we passed Garston Station at about 21.25 it was pitch dark outside and I decided that it would be far too risky and difficult to visit 8C Speke Junction and 8J Allerton Electric Depot. As expected it would have to be the 05.00 train from Liverpool to Garston tomorrow morning. Perhaps we should have scheduled our tour a few weeks earlier as we would have had some more daylight in the evenings.

We arrived at Liverpool Central station at 21.40 (three minutes late). The ticket collector on looking at our Railrover tickets said philosophically "Only one day to go". He was so right the sands of time were running out on us. One was beginning to dread the end of the tour. Wouldn't it have been wonderful if we could have afforded a two week "Freedom of Britain" ticket and had seen even more fast disappearing steam!

WARRINGTON CENTRAL TO LIVERPOOL CENTRAL						
		Home shed		Built	Withdrawn	Scrap
Steam						
Fairburn 4MT 2-6-4T 1945 dev. of Stanier 1935						
42076		9E	Trafford Park	Dec-1950	Mar-1967	Nov-1967
Total	1					
Stanier 5MT 4-6-0 "Black Five" 1935						
44815		9E	Trafford Park (ex 16C)	Nov-1944	Feb-1968	Jun-1968
Total	1					
On journey	2	Kops		0		
Steam	2	Diesels		0		
		Home Area		2	Visitors	0
Shed	9E	2				
Distribution						
Steam Classes	2					
Steam Origin	LMS	2				

		Schedule	Actual	Miles
Depart	WARRINGTON CENTRAL	20.57	21.06	0
Arrive	LIVERPOOL CENTRAL	21.37	21.40	18¾

Eight intermediate stops.

First things first and I noted a left luggage office nearby. I asked the young chap in charge if the office was open at five o'clock in the morning. He laughed and said "You'll never be here at five. Too early by far." We assured him that we would and he said "That'll be the day". We could not make him believe that we intended to get the 05.00 to Garston. However, on being pressed he admitted that the left luggage office would be open then so we at last deposited our luggage.

HERE ENDETH THE CASE OF THE DISBELIEVING LEFT LUGGAGE ATTENDANT

Second things, second, and I thought that D.S. deserved another bite to eat. I hoped that this would last out until he exited the tour at Wigan tomorrow lunchtime. I could not have him collapsing before then through lack of food on to the cinders (after a heart attack) at some anonymous M.P.D. as this would cost more valuable time. Overall, D.S. seemed to have about had it. Today, had seen him weaken much further. He appeared to have slept through most of it and he had become so fatigued that he would only bother to open up his notebook at actual engine sheds. D.S.'s spelling had improved little. Instead of 9A Longsight we had Longside which was a near miss by D.S.'s standards. Instead of 9E Trafford Park we had Stafford Park. D.S. however, staged a lightning recovery from his present decrepit state when I mentioned food and he quickly smelt out the station buffet at the other end of the station.

"D.S. pays through the nose"

We queued at the self service and we each got a cup of coffee and a BR pork pie. At the cash desk the lady asked for three shillings and ten pence (19 new pence) from D.S. and I gasped. I knew the tea was six pence (2.5 new pence) but three shillings and four pence (16.5 new pence) for a pork pie! That takes the biscuit. We all know about BR's zoombala prices but three shillings and four pence was just not on for a pork pie. D.S., however, appeared to be in a rather sad mental state (as well as physical state) of exhaustion and somehow by distant memory he managed to extricate three shillings and ten pence out of his pocket. He could still add up. He then hobbled away and collapsed down at a table near to some longhaired Beatle look-alikes.

Back to the scene of the swindle. I shoved my tray down on the counter and this time it was the lady's turn to gasp. "I thought he was with you" she said "I charged him for yours as well as his"! That explained a lot and cut down the price of a pork pie to a more reasonable (by BR standards) one shilling and five pence (7 new pence). I said "Thanks, I was with him but we did not expect you to charge the two meals together. I'll sort it out with him".

Back at the table I slapped down one shilling and eleven pence (9.5 new pence) and D.S. said "What's this for"? I asked him if he thought his pork pie and cup of tea was a bit dear. D.S. thought hard "Was a bit pricey". I said "You were charged for my meal too". D.S. said briefly "Uh"! and picked up the money. D.S. certainly was in a bad way. Indifference wasn't the word for it.

After a pleasant light meal and a bit of meditation and reflection we left the buffet at 22.30. We went to find a haven for the night (a waiting room). We were rather alarmed when we found it locked up for the night which was the normal anti-vagrant or anti-vandal protection. Liverpool was quite a place these days with Beatlemania and probably didn't want their waiting-rooms used as music halls.

Nothing daunted, two benches were found near the entrance to Liverpool Central Low Level (the Birkenhead line) and attempts were made to get to sleep but with absolutely no success due to the bustle of people around.

"You two can be saved"

We saw a married couple (or so I thought they didn't look the types to be living in sin). They were eyeing everyone up as though they might be candidates for their unknown purpose. Ever so often they would pick someone out and try to give them a leaflet (without much success). Suddenly, they spotted D.S. with his eyes closed lying on one of the benches, came across and said "You too can be saved" and forced a leaflet into one of his hands. D.S. awoke with a start, glared angrily at them, and they made a hasty retreat, not forgetting to hand me a leaflet on the way. I put it in my pocket to dispose of it later. D.S. had already torn his up and he threw the bits in the air after them. Quite a comical scene. D.S. was obviously more interested in sleep than being saved by any Mormons or Jehovah's Witnesses or whatever sect they were. D.S. certainly knew his priorities.

The main trouble about getting to sleep was that every few minutes as a train arrived a horde of people would emerge noisily out of the underground line from Birkenhead and in the other direction there was a steady trickle of people entering it to get a train for Birkenhead.

THE NIGHT OF THE NOMADS AFFAIR

At 23.30 the underground line closed for the night and it now appeared that we would get some peace and quiet for a sleep at last. However, at 23.45 my meditations were disturbed by a railwayman. He advised me that the station closed at midnight for the night and that the railway police would not allow us to stay here overnight. He suggested that we could try Liverpool Lime Street which was a busier and more important station and the start of the electrified main line to Crewe and then London. The closure of the station appeared to be a good point so I thanked him and said that we would take his advice. I awoke D.S. who was rather cross and irate at this interruption to his slumbers and even angrier when I told him that we had to move on.

I opened my bag and ascertained from the LSD that Lime Street station was nearby.

"The Lime Street sojourn"

In ten minutes we had reached Liverpool Lime Street and found two benches. No need to guess the waiting room was locked up for the night! They take no chances here in Liverpuddle.

There were a few other inhabitants besides us in the station namely three mainline Bo-Bo Electrics still lying at the head of their respective trains which had arrived. Much changed since steam days when immediately a train entered the engine would be uncoupled. The station pilot would then haul away the train and the engine would amble away light engine to the engine shed for a much needed clean out. So much easier with diesels and electrics which more or less can be left anywhere with minimum maintenance required.

LIVERPOOL LIME STREET STATION						
		Home shed		Built	Withdrawn	Scrap
Electrics						
A.E.I. (British Thomson-Houston) AL1 Bo-Bo 1959						
E3021		LMW	London Midl. West.Lines	May-1961		
Total	1					
English Electric AL3 Bo-Bo 1960						
E3034		LMW	London Midl. West.Lines	Feb-1961		
Total	2					
A.E.I. (Metropolitan-Vickers) AL2 Bo-Bo 1960						
E3047		LMW	London Midl. West.Lines	Jul-1960		
Total	1					
On Station	3	Kops		3		
Steam	0	Diesels		0	Electrics	3
		Home Area		0	Visitors	3
Shed						
Distribution	LMW	3				

Back to the necessity of sleep and our two benches. It was about 12.35 when our roving microphone picked up the following conversation. I had almost drifted off into sleep when I was interrupted by something in dark blue.

WARPED COP: - "You will have to go now as the station closes for the night in ten minutes at a quarter to one."

Another of these devilish closing stations!

ME:- "I've got a railrover ticket it's valid for any train."
WARPED COP: - "Sorry, Railrover or no Railrover, you are not entitled to stay here when the station is closed. That's the rules. Same for everybody."

As before in Derby our Railrover didn't cut much ice.

ME: "But we've a train to catch at five in the morning."

WARPED COP:-"Sorry, but you'll have to wait outside until the station opens again. There's always the Salvation Army." (Same suggestion as one of the Derby cops).

ME:- "That's no use. We would have to get up at 4.30 in the morning to get our train and that wouldn't be very popular then."

WARPED COP: - "Tell you what; you could wait at the Pier Head. There's a hot dog stand there too." A cop being helpful – very suspicious!

It was Hobson's Choice. The Pier Head or nothing. So it had to be the Pier Head. Here we were being given the push again. He gave me directions and ascertained that I would be taking my friend with me. D.S., need I add was asleep, curled up on a nearby bench. I was beginning to feel like one of those unfortunate gypsies who keep getting moved on by town councils. Now I know what it feels like. Liverpool Central, station closed – moved on. Liverpool Lime Street station closed – moved on. Doubtless if we went on to Liverpool Exchange Station it would be the same old story so we would give that station the miss.

I rousted D.S. awake and he awoke very angry and said, or I had better not tell you what he said although I can safely say that he was a little displeased. When I told him that the station was closing and that the cop had told us to move on to the Pier Head he almost blew his top. D.S. roared "So we are being given the push into the bloody sea"! It certainly seemed that way and I could hardly be optimistic about the Pier Head. A night on a windswept pier rocked to sleep by lashing waves and showered by drenching surf did not seem particularly enticing to me. At least that is how I visualised the Pier Head. Still it was better than nothing and a few hours sleep was badly needed even if we had had a short sleep in the afternoon via the Alderley Edge affair.

On the way to the Pier Head D.S. perked up in the cool, refreshing night air and said that if the worst came to the worst we could walk round the city until 4.30 then go to Central Station for our train. It was encouraging to hear D.S. bubbling with enthusiasm again. Although, I would hate to think of us walking for 3½ hours. By 5 o'clock we would have covered about ten miles and we would be absolutely exhausted and finished for the day ahead before it had even started. Here's hoping the Pier Head is reasonable.

One bad blunder was made on the way to the Pier Head. In the dark I stumbled on to a road which led down an incline into an illuminated tunnel. After almost being mown down by a hooting ten ton truck I happened to see a notice which said "The Mersey Tunnel – no pedestrians allowed". Yes, that lorry driver had given us the feeling that we were not wanted. Yes definitely not to be recommended for pedestrians. So I had found the famous Mersey Tunnel which goes under the Mersey estuary from Liverpool to Burke and Hare (as I like to call Birkenhead). Yes, it had been quite a day of visiting unexpected places.

Retracing our steps we avoided further arguments with lorries and were able to get back on to the proper road. We reached the Pier Head at five past one. There was no hot dog stand as promised by the cop and perhaps it had been a ploy to move us on more easily although quite possibly the hot dog vendor had driven away his van for the night. And what was the Pier Head like? Hold on to your seats while I tell you. It seemed to be the main bus terminus and was all bright and cheery. Though by now anything would look cheery. The ferry across the Mersey (of Gerry and the Pacemakers fame) was near to us.

Inside the terminus was nice and modern although I was apprehensive on seeing a cop with two sets of teeth (one perhaps false and the other set not for arguing with). He had an Alsatian with him – charming! Looking around we found no waiting room but after ascending a flight of steps we found a nice, cosy, smallish, warm modern waiting room. Just what was required.

One was nicely settling down for some much needed shuteye when five local Beatle boys burst into the waiting room. I had some fleeting visions of them pinching my wallet, my carry bag or even more importantly my LMR loco numbers book. So the waiting room had become distinctly unhealthy. I quickly got up. D.S. read my mind and decided that he did not fancy the look of that lot either and we went back downstairs.

Downstairs we met or rather passed another cop with another vicious Alsatian. He ignored us and walked by as though we weren't there. At the other end of the bus station we found some benches. A homeless man was already sitting down on one of them, awake and staring blankly in front of him. We made ourselves at home and sat down on the end of the benches thinking that the cops would probably not let us sleep full out on them. Talking about cops I wondered why there were so many about. Probably to stop vandalism I thought.

I found out several months later on a TV programme about the new Chief Constable of Liverpool that the first problem he had and the biggest was to tackle the Pier Head problem. This was where the gangs at night met and tried to smash themselves and other people up. I thought at the time that the cop at Liverpool Lime Street had been unnaturally helpful in suggesting a place where we could spend the night (quite uncoplike in being helpful). He obviously sent us to the Pier Head hoping that we would be beaten up. Yes, the usual warped cop. We were lucky that the cops were out in numbers that night on the Pier Head with their

Alsatians. Amazing at the time that I did not guess that the Pier Head was the prime trouble spot in Liverpool.

Yes the bus station was better than the windswept pier that I had envisaged earlier and I was dozing off to sleep when I heard someone moaning out "Oh, GOD please have mercy on pitiful me." Who, said that? No, it wasn't D.S. He was already asleep and that statement would have been so unD.S. like. In fact it had come from the poor homeless man on the bench beside us. He pleaded on and on and prayed out aloud for a full two minutes.

Review of the Day

This is how our timetable should have panned out:-

DAY 7   FRIDAY 6TH AUGUST 1965   LMR DAY 6

<u>MILES</u>

Depart MANCHESTER VICTORIA	05.50	0
Arrive DEAN LANE	05.57	2¾

<u>Do 9D Newton Heath (35 mins. approx)</u>   Recovery Time + 9

Depart DEAN LANE	06.41	0
Arrive MANCHESTER VICTORIA	06.48	2¾
Depart MANCHESTER EXCHANGE	07.10	0
Arrive PATRICROFT	07.21	4¾

<u>Do 9H Patricroft (30 minutes approx.)</u>

Salford Corporation Bus No 27

Depart PATRICROFT MONTON ROAD
Arrive AGECROFT BANK LANE

<u>Do 9J Agecroft</u>

Salford Corporate Bus No 57 or 77

Depart BANK LANE
Arrive PICCADILLY
Depart PICCADILLY   )   Manchester Corporation
Arrive KIRKMANSHULME LANE   )   92-93-94-95

<u>Do 9A Longsight</u>

Depart CROMWELL STREET
Arrive REDDISH NORTH STATION   109 Reddish North Bus

<u>Do 9C Reddish</u>

<u>British Rail</u>

Depart REDDISH NORTH	11.42	(12.12)	0
Arrive MANCHESTER PICCADILLY	11.50	(12.23)	4
Depart MANCHESTER PICCADILLY	11.57	(12.27)	0

Arrive MANCHESTER OXFORD ROAD	11.59	(12.29)	½

Depart MANCHESTER OXFORD ROAD	12.10	(12.30)	0
Arrive WARWICK ROAD	12.15	(12.35)	2½

Do 9E Trafford Park (45 mins. approx)   Recovery Time -7

Depart WARWICK ROAD	12.53	(13.13)	0
Arrive MANCHESTER OXFORD ROAD	13.00	(13.20)	2½

Depart MANCHESTER OXFORD ROAD	13.05	(13.35)	0
Arrive STOCKPORT EDGELEY	13.19	(13.49)	6¼

Do 9F Heaton Mersey (75 mins. approx)
Do 9B Stockport Edgeley (35 mins. approx)

Depart STOCKPORT EDGELEY	15.30	regular service	0
Arrive MANCHESTER PICCADILLY	15.38		5¾

Depart MANCHESTER CENTRAL	16.30	(17.30)	0
Arrive WARRINGTON CENTRAL	16.49	(17.49)	15¼

Do 8B Warrington (60 mins. approx)

Depart WARRINGTON CENTRAL	17.53	(18.53)	15¼
Arrive GARSTON	18.14	(19.14)	28

Do 8C Speke Junction (40 mins. approx)
Do 8J Allerton (35 mins. approx)

Depart ALLERTON	19.56	(20.56)	
Arrive EDGE HILL	20.07	(21.07)	

Do 8A Edge Hill (60 mins. approx)

Night: -   Liverpool Station Waiting Room

And this is what actually happened:-

		Schedule	Actual	Miles
Depart	MANCHESTER VICTORIA	05.50	05.50	0
Arrive	DEAN LANE	05.57	05.57	2¾
	Do 9D Newton Heath			
		Schedule	Actual	Miles
Depart	DEAN LANE	06.41	06.41	0
Arrive	MANCHESTER VICTORIA	06.48	06.48	2¾

		Schedule	Actual	Miles
Depart	MANCHESTER EXCHANGE	07.10	07.32	0
Arrive	PATRICROFT	'07.21	'07.43	4¾
	Do 9H Particroft			
Depart	PATRICROFT	Bus		
Arrive	AGECROFT			
	Do 9J Agecroft			
Depart	AGECROFT	Two		
Arrive	LONGSIGHT	Buses		
	Do 9A Longsight			
Depart	LONGSIGHT	Bus		
Arrive	REDDISH NORTH			
		Schedule	Actual	Miles
Depart	REDDISH NORTH	11.42	11.42	0
Arrive	MANCHESTER PICCADILLY	11.54	11.53	4
		Schedule	Actual	Miles
Depart	MANCHESTER PICCADILLY	11.57	11.57	0
Arrive	MANCHESTER OXFORD ROAD	11.59	11.59	½
		Schedule	Actual	Miles
Depart	MANCHESTER OXFORD ROAD	12.10	12.10	0
Arrive	WARWICK ROAD	12.15	12.15	2½
	Do 9E Trafford Park			
		Schedule	Actual	Miles
Depart	WARWICK ROAD	13.13	13.13	0
Arrive	KNOTT MILL	13.18	13.18	2
		Schedule	Actual	Miles
Depart	KNOTT MILL	13.38	13.38	0
Arrive	MANCHESTER OXFORD ROAD	13.40	13.40	½
		Schedule	Actual	Miles
Depart	MANCHESTER OXFORD ROAD	13.50	13.50	0
Arrive	ALDERLEY EDGE	14.20	14.20	13¼
		Schedule	Actual	Miles
Depart	ALDERLEY EDGE	14.45	14.45	0
Arrive	MANCHESTER PICCADILLY	15.12	15.12	12¾
		Schedule	Actual	Miles
Depart	MANCHESTER PICCADILLY	15.20	15.20	0
Arrive	STOCKPORT EDGELEY	15.32	15.32	12¾
	Do 9F Heaton Mersey			
	Do 9B Stockport Edgeley			
		Schedule	Actual	Miles
Depart	MANCHESTER CENTRAL	18.35	18.35	0
Arrive	IRLAM	18.57	18.57	8¼
Depart	IRLAM	19.56	19.56	8¼
Arrive	WARRINGTON CENTRAL	20.10	20.10	15¼
	Do 8B Warrington			
		Schedule	Actual	Miles
Depart	WARRINGTON CENTRAL	20.57	21.06	0
Arrive	LIVERPOOL CENTRAL	21.37	21.40	18¾

Four sheds were lost out of the original timetable: - 9C Reddish, 8C Speke Junction, 8J Allerton and 8A Edge Hill.

Despite the four lost sheds eight sheds were visited and a commendable 278 steam were seen out of 337 locos.

DAY 7 MANCHESTER, STOCKPORT, WARRINGTON and LIVERPOOL ARRIVAL

	Visits	GWR	SR	LMS	LNER	WD	BR	Steam Total	Diesel Total	Electric Total	Grand Total
	Manchester Victoria			3			2	5			5
	Victoria to Dean Lane			5			1	6	2		8
9D	Newton Heath			55			7	62	3		65
	Dean Lane to Victoria			2				2			2
	Victoria/ Exchange			4			2	6			6
	Exchange to Patricroft			5			3	8	1		9
9H	Patricroft			14		1	18	33	1		34
9J	Agecroft			13				13	1		14
9A	Longsight			2				2	7	15	24
	Reddish to Piccadilly			3				3	3		6
	Oxford Rd to Warwick Rd.								1		1
	Manchester Piccadilly 1									2	2
9E	Trafford Park			39			5	44	9		53
	Manchester Piccadilly 2									4	4
9F	Heaton Mersey			21			2	23	1		24
9B	Stockport Edgeley			21			6	27			27
	Manchester Central								3		3
	Central to Irlam			2			2	4	1		5
	Irlam Station			1				1	1		2
	Irlam to Warrington			1				1	1		2
8B	Warrington			26			10	36			36
	Warrington to Liverpool			2				2			2
	Liverpool Lime Street									3	3
		0	0	219	0	1	58	278	35	24	337

		GWR	SR LMS	LNER	WD	BR	Steam Total	Diesel Total	Electric Total	Grand Total
	REWIND 12th Dec 1964									
9D	Newton Heath 121264		37			7	44	2		46
9B	Stockport Edgeley 121264		17			1	18	2		20
	to Manchester and Stockpt		18			9	27	6	9	42
	REWIND 10th July 1965									
8B	Warrington 100765		25	1		4	30	4		34
			97	1		21	119	14	9	142

To lose over 5½ hours to our timetable was truly incredible. In a day's travel that lasted from 05.50 to 21.40 (almost 16 hours) over a third of this time was wasted!

		Time Lost (minutes)
1	BR decides that our train should arrive minutes late in Patricroft.	22
2	Take wrong way to Patricroft shed	10
3	Narrowly miss bus to Agecroft	20
4	Rat of conductor drops us off at the wrong station for 9C Reddish	20
5	D.S. does a go slow at 9E Trafford Park and we miss our connection	20
6	D.S. stomps off at Knott Mill - the wrong station	20
7	Take wrong train to Stockport and wake up at Alderley Edge	73
8	Miss our Stockport connection for the 17.30 train to Warrington Central	60
9	The infamous Irlam Affair where we take the wrong train and end up at Irlam	90
		335

Post Mortem on Time Lost

When one notes that over 4 hours were wasted after the Rat Affair 9C Reddish was rather unfortunate to be thrown out particularly as we were at Reddish North station at the time. Could we have accommodated every shed with a bit of luck?

		Schedule
REDDISH NORTH		12.12
MANCHESTER PICCADILLY		12.24
MANCHESTER PICCADILLY		12.27
MANCHESTER OXFORD ROAD		12.29

		Schedule
Depart	MANCHESTER OXFORD ROAD	12.30
Arrive	WARWICK ROAD	12.35
	Do 9E Trafford Park	
Depart	WARWICK ROAD	13.13
Arrive	MANCHESTER OXFORD ROAD	13.20
Depart	MANCHESTER OXFORD ROAD	13.35
Arrive	STOCKPORT EDGELEY	13.49
	Do 9F Heaton Mersey	
	Do 9B Stockport Edgeley	
Depart	STOCKPORT EDGELEY	15.30
Arrive	MANCHESTER PICCADILLY	15.38
Depart	MANCHESTER CENTRAL	16.30
Arrive	WARRINGTON CENTRAL	16.49
	Do 8B Warrington	
Depart	WARRINGTON CENTRAL	17.53
Arrive	GARSTON	18.14
	Do 8C Speke Junction	
	Do 8J Allerton	
Depart	ALLERTON	19.56
Arrive	EDGE HILL	20.07
	Do 8A Edge Hill	

So, in fact, there was enough recovery time in the original timetable for us to have done 9C Reddish Electric Depot and indeed all the scheduled sheds today. So we should have jolly well have visited the shed when we arrived at Reddish North station.

You may point out that D.S. may well have still gone on strike on the walk to and from 9E Trafford Park. This would have been a distinct possibility but we could have recovered from it.

		Schedule
Arrive	WARWICK ROAD	12.35
	Do 9E Trafford Park	
Depart	WARWICK ROAD	13.33
Arrive	MANCHESTER OXFORD ROAD	13.40
Depart	MANCHESTER OXFORD ROAD	13.50
Arrive	STOCKPORT EDGELEY	14.13
	Do 9F Heaton Mersey	
	Do 9B Stockport Edgeley	
Depart	STOCKPORT EDGELEY	15.46
Arrive	MANCHESTER PICCADILLY	15.57
Depart	MANCHESTER CENTRAL	16.30

In fact, taking the bus to and from 9F Heaton Mersey we almost certainly would have caught the 15.30 from Stockport to Manchester Piccadilly rather than the 15.46. In all, the original timetable could have accommodated the Rat Affair and the Hobnailed Army Surplus Boots Affair (D.S.'s strike at 9E Trafford Park). The Epilogue of the Hobnailed Army Surplus Boots Affair caused us a further 20 minutes loss when D.S. stomped off at Knott Mill station but there would have been a good chance that we could have connected with the 15.46 from Stockport Edgeley set out above (given the hidden recovery time of a bus to and from 9F Heaton Mersey to save time).

Now for the post mortem on the Alderley Edge affair. It transpired that we got on the wrong train for Stockport as well as falling asleep on it. Let's see what would have happened if I hadn't fallen asleep on it. Presumably we would find ourselves at an unknown station, check with the guard and get off at the next station down the line and then get a train back to Manchester Piccadilly and the timings would work out like this.

Depart	MANCHESTER OXFORD ROAD	13.50	
Arrive	BURNAGE	14.01	
Depart	BURNAGE	14.03	
Arrive	MANCHESTER PICCADILLY	14.12	
Depart	MANCHESTER PICCADILLY	14.20	
Arrive	STOCKPORT EDGELEY	14.32	
	Do 9F Heaton Mersey		
	Do 9B Stockport Edgeley		
			Alternative
Depart	STOCKPORT EDGELEY	15.46	16.00
Arrive	MANCHESTER PICCADILLY	15.57	16.08
Depart	MANCHESTER CENTRAL	16.30	16.30

Incredibly, we could still make the 16.30 to Manchester Central so disasters 1-7 could have been accommodated (provided we didn't fall asleep as the wrong train itself would have cost us only 19 minutes). After the sleep disaster we were firmly on the 17.30 to Manchester

Central if we managed to catch the 16.46 to Manchester Piccadilly which we didn't!

Unknown to us we had arrived asleep at Alderley Edge via the Styal line and had never passed Stockport on the way there. If we had bothered to check at the station when the next train to Stockport was (rather than Manchester) we would have found out that it was:-

Depart	ALDERLEY EDGE	15.00
Arrive	STOCKPORT EDGELEY	15.16
	Do 9F Heaton Mersey	
	Do 9B Stockport Edgeley	

We ourselves left Alderley Edge at 14.45 but unknown to us we would travel on the infamous Styal branch line and eventually arrive in Stockport at 15.32 (via Manchester Piccadilly). Staying where we were at Alderley Edge and catching the 15.00 would have resulted in us arriving at Stockport at 15.16 rather than 15.32 and therefore we would have easily caught the 16.46 to Manchester Piccadilly (or even the 16.40) and would connect without problem with the 17.30 from Manchester Central to Warrington Central.

So even after all our disasters 1-7 above and falling asleep the rest of the evening would have looked like this:-

Depart	MANCHESTER CENTRAL	17.30
Arrive	WARRINGTON CENTRAL	17.49
	Do 8B Warrington	
Depart	WARRINGTON CENTRAL	18.53
Arrive	GARSTON	19.14
	Do 8C Speke Junction	
	Do 8J Allerton	
Depart	GARSTON	*Two*
Arrive	EDGE HILL	*Buses*
	Do 8A Edge Hill	

8A Edge Hill would have needed to be accommodated in pitch darkness which could have been problem. There was a bus connection via Penny Lane (of Beatles fame) from Allerton to Edge Hill and this could have been a better scenario particularly if we had omitted 8J Allerton Electric Depot from our tour. If we had missed the final disaster of the day the Irlam Affair it is quite possible that we would have managed both 8C Speke Junction and also the well lit 8J Allerton Electric Depot.

		Schedule	
Depart	MANCHESTER CENTRAL	18.30	
Arrive	WARRINGTON CENTRAL	18.57	
	Do 8B Warrington	50	*minutes*
Depart	WARRINGTON CENTRAL	19.57	
Arrive	GARSTON	20.22	
	Do 8C Speke Junction	45	*minutes*
	Do 8J Allerton	30	*minutes*
Depart	ALLERTON	22.06	
Arrive	LIVERPOOL LIME STREET	22.22	

Incredibly, the loss of the day if we had managed to avoid the Irlam affair would have been restricted to only one shed - 8A Edge Hill (other than 9C Reddish) which we had already lost. That being the case 10D Lostock Hall (which I had visited the previous month) would have been chopped out of tomorrow's timetable although in theory if we could visit 8A Edge Hill at first light we might be able to get the 05.30 to Aintree and regain Saturday's timetable including 10D Lostock Hall.

I think that we can count ourselves a little unlucky with disasters today. I have counted nine (some relatively minor) but perhaps there were in fact eleven as the Alderley Edge affair concealed three disasters. Firstly (unknown to us) we were on the wrong train on the wrong line, secondly we fell asleep and thirdly (unknown to us) we were still on the wrong train on the wrong line and would have to return to Manchester to board a correct train for Stockport.

The day at least had been incident packed and incidents make interesting reading. We had only got about three hours sleep last night in the waiting room at Manchester Exchange (coupled with an hours sleep from Crewe to Manchester Piccadilly) so about four hours in total. Our week had been marked by a lack of sleep but sleep was a waste of time when there were sheds to be visited.

Our lack of sleep had made us increasingly short tempered over the week and I was ready to bawl out D.S. for the slightest slackening. I was especially annoyed because D.S. tended to sleep through every train journey relying on me to wake him up at each destination. This backfired on him when I fell asleep today and we ended up at Alderley Edge. D.S. was responsible for two disasters totalling 40 minutes which seemed at the time to be real crimes to me. 40 minutes, however, was relatively insignificant compared with total disasters amounting to 5½ hours for the day. I don't know how I fell asleep on the train today. I must have blacked out from lack of sleep or exhaustion. I had never felt the slightest bit tired with the excitement of a diet of new sheds to be visited. One thing though the fierce argument that D.S. and I had on Knott Mill Station seemed to buck him up and I had had no further trouble over his pace for the rest of the day. He made a particularly spirited attempt at Stockport to catch out train to Manchester when in obvious discomfort at the fast pace.

We had been lucky with shedmasters today and, in fact, had trouble at only two sheds of a very minor nature. We had completed the shed at 9D Newton Heath when we met the sheddie and rewarded him for his audacity in stopping us by "wadding" him. At 9F Heaton Mersey we were escorted to the shedmaster's office but found him really pleased that we had come all the way from Scotland to visit his little shed.

Tomorrow might be troublesome. I hadn't a permit for any of the sheds to be visited apart from 9K Bolton. The 10 area did not issue permits to anyone while I stupidly broke off negotiations with the 8 area when they said that my visit timings were too tight. I now knew that normally it didn't matter what day or for what time you had a permit as long as you had one particularly if you can offer a good excuse for the early or late arrival. So far we had got round every shed with the exception of Willesden Electric Depot and Crewe Works. Certainly, tomorrow's permitless day would be an exciting challenge.

It had been a day that had everything. We started with a shedmaster being "wadded" at Newton Heath, a late train to Patricroft, a wrong turning going to the shed there, a narrowly missed bus to Agecroft, a rat of a conductor putting us off at the wrong stop before Reddish North, D.S.'s go-slow at 9E Trafford Park, D.S. getting off at the wrong station and our fierce argument there with us almost going our separate ways, taking the wrong train, the wrong line and falling asleep on the way to Stockport, missing our connection back to Manchester by seconds and finally our ill-fated unscheduled journey to Irlam.

We had arrived in Liverpool to find waiting rooms locked up, two "missionaries" tried to save D.S. at Liverpool Central station where D.S. paid double for his meal without blinking, got kicked out of stations by the cops and we almost walked into the strictly vehicles only Mersey Tunnel to find our final resting place for the night at the Pier Head (where gang fights were commonplace).

What a day we had had. Tomorrow would be a busy day with 12 M.P.D.'s to be visited (four postponed from today). By necessity 10D Lostock Hall and 8G Sutton Oak would be ditched from the original timetable. D.S. would only be with me until lunchtime so the timetable might work out for once. I must surely stop now. It was now 01.15 and definitely time for some sleep, sleep, sleep, sleep, sleep --- --- --- --------------------------

END OF DAY SEVEN

Some steam analyses of the day follow:-

ENGINE CLASSES DAY 7 ACTIVE ON SHED	BR total	8B Warrington	9A Longsight	9B Stockport	9D Newton Hth	9E Tr'ford Pk	9F Heaton M	9H Patricroft	9J Agecroft	Grand Total
Ivatt 2MT 2-6-2T 1946										
41200-41329	130			3						3
Fairburn 4MT 2-6-4T 1945 dev. of Stanier 1935										
42050-42299; 42673-42699	277				1	6				7
Fowler 4MT 2-6-4T 1927										
42300-42424	125				1	1		1		3
Stanier 4MT 2-6-4T 1935 dev of Fowler 1927										
42425-42672	243				2	2				4
Hughes/Fowler 5MT 2-6-0 "Crab" 1926										
42700-42944	245			5	3					8
Stanier 5MT 2-6-0 1933										
42945-84	40	1				2	6			9
Ivatt 4MT 2-6-0 1947										
43000-43161	162						4			4
Midland 4F 0-6-0 1924										
44027-44606	580	2		1	1					4
Stanier 5MT 4-6-0 "Black Five" 1934										
44658-45499	842	14		3	18	16	1	2	5	59
Ivatt 7P 4-6-0 "Patriot" 1947 rebuild of Fowler 1933										
45512/4/21-3/5-9/30-2/34-6/40	18							1		1
Stanier 6P5F 4-6-0 "Jubilee" 1934										
45552-45734/7-42	189	2		3	0	1				6
Stanier 7P 4-6-0 "Royal Scot" 1943 rebuild of Fowler 1927										
46100-70	71								1	1
Ivatt 2MT 2-6-0 1946										
46400-46527	128				8					8
Midland 3F "Jinty" 0-6-0T 1924 dev. of Johnson 1899 design										
47260-47681	417				4			2	1	7
Stanier 8F 2-8-0 "Big Eight" 1935										
48000-48775	666	4	2	4	12	3	10	8	6	49
BR Standard 7P6F 4-6-2 "Britannia" Derby 1951										
70000-70054	55		1		2					3
BR Standard 5MT 4-6-0 Doncaster 1951										
73000-73171	172				1			15		16
BR Standard 4MT 2-6-0 Doncaster 1953										
76000-76114	115	1								1
BR Standard 2MT 2-6-0 Doncaster 1953										
78000-78064	65					5				5
BR Standard 3MT 2-6-2T Swindon 1952										
82000-82044	45							2		2
BR Standard 2MT 2-6-2T Derby 1953										
84000-84029	30			4						4
Riddles WD 8F 2-8-0 "Austerity" 1943										
90000-90732	733							1		1
BR Standard 9F 2-10-0 Brighton 1954										
92000-92250 except	166	8		1	4		2	1		16
BR Standard 9F 2-10-0 Brighton 1954. 1955 Crosti boiler										
92020-29	10	1								1
BR EM2 Metropolitan-Vickers Co-Co 1954										
27000-27006		33	2	25	57	36	23	33	13	222

ENGINE CLASSES

DAY 7 WITHDRAWN

Class / BR numbers	BR total	8B Warrington	9A Longsight	9B Stockport	9D Newton Hth	9E Tr'ford Pk	9F Heaton M	9H Patricroft	9J Agecroft	Grand Total
Fairburn 4MT 2-6-4T 1945 dev. of Stanier 1935 / 42050-42299; 42673-42699	277					7				7
Stanier 4MT 2-6-4T 1935 dev of Fowler 1927 / 42425-42672	243				2					2
Hughes/Fowler 5MT 2-6-0 "Crab" 1926 / 42700-42944	245			2	1					3
Midland 4F 0-6-0 1924 / 44027-44606	580	2								2
Stanier 5MT 4-6-0 "Black Five" 1934 / 44658-45499	842					1				1
Stanier 6P5F 4-6-0 "Jubilee" 1934 / 45552-45734/7-42	189	1			1					2
Ivatt 2MT 2-6-0 1946 / 46400-46527	128				1					1
Midland 3F "Jinty" 0-6-0T 1924 dev. of Johnson 1899 design										
Total		3	0	2	5	8	0	0	0	18

ENGINE CLASSES / DAY 7 OFF SHED	BR manch / total victoria	victoria / to dean ln	dean lane / to victoria	victoria / and excha	exch / to patricrft	reddish / to piccadilly	central / to irlam	irlam / station	irlam / to warringt	warrington day 7 / to liverp	off shed
Fairburn 4MT 2-6-4T 1945 dev. of Stanier 1935											
42050-42299; 42673-42699	277						1			1	2
Stanier 4MT 2-6-4T 1935 dev of Fowler 1927											
42425-42672	243	1			1				1		3
Hughes/Fowler 5MT 2-6-0 "Crab" 1926											
42700-42944	245					1					1
Stanier 5MT 4-6-0 "Black Five" 1934											
44658-45499	842	2	1	2	3	1		1			13
Ivatt 2MT 2-6-0 1946											
46400-46527	128			1							1
Stanier 8F 2-8-0 "Big Eight" 1935											
48000-48775	666		4	1	1	1					8
BR Standard 7P6F 4-6-2 "Britannia" Derby 1951											
70000-70054	55	1									1
BR Standard 5MT 4-6-0 Doncaster 1951											
73000-73171	172	1			1						3
BR Standard 2MT 2-6-0 Doncaster 1953											
78000-78064	65						2				2
BR Standard 3MT 2-6-2T Swindon 1952											
82000-82044	45			1	2						3
BR Standard 9F 2-10-0 Brighton 1954											
92000-92250	251		1								1
		5	6	2	8	3	4	1	1	2	38

ENGINE CLASSES
DAY 7 SUMMARY TOTALS

ENGINE CLASSES / DAY 7 SUMMARY TOTALS	Day7 On Shed	Day 7 Withdrawn	day 7 off shed	day 7 totals
Ivatt 2MT 2-6-2T 1946	3			3
Fairburn 4MT 2-6-4T 1945 dev. of Stanier 1935	7	7	2	16
Fowler 4MT 2-6-4T 1927	3			3
Stanier 4MT 2-6-4T 1935 dev of Fowler 1927	4	2	3	9
Hughes/Fowler 5MT 2-6-0 "Crab" 1926	8	3	1	12
Stanier 5MT 2-6-0 1933	9			9
Ivatt 4MT 2-6-0 1947	4			4
Midland 4F 0-6-0 1924	4	2		6
Stanier 5MT 4-6-0 "Black Five" 1934	59	1	13	73
Ivatt 7P 4-6-0 "Patriot" 1947 rebuild of Fowler 1933	1			1
Stanier 6P5F 4-6-0 "Jubilee" 1934	6	2		8
Stanier 7P 4-6-0 "Royal Scot" 1943 rebuild of Fowler 1927	1			1
Ivatt 2MT 2-6-0 1946	8	1	1	10
Midland 3F "Jinty" 0-6-0T 1924 dev. of Johnson 1899 design	7			7
Stanier 8F 2-8-0 "Big Eight" 1935	49		8	57
BR Standard 7P6F 4-6-2 "Britannia" Derby 1951	3		1	4
BR Standard 5MT 4-6-0 Doncaster 1951	16		3	19
BR Standard 4MT 2-6-0 Doncaster 1953	1			1
BR Standard 2MT 2-6-0 Doncaster 1953	5		2	7
BR Standard 3MT 2-6-2T Swindon 1952	2		3	5
BR Standard 2MT 2-6-2T Derby 1953	4			4
Riddles WD 8F 2-8-0 "Austerity" 1943	1			1
BR Standard 9F 2-10-0 Brighton 1954	16		1	17
BR Standard 9F 2-10-0 Brighton 1954, 1955 Crosti boiler	1			1
	222	18	38	278

	MANCHESTER VISIT DECEMBER 1964	to				
ENGINE CLASSES	BR	9B	9B	9D	9D	manch	**Mchster**
MANCHESTER VISIT DEC 1964	total	Stockpt	Stockpt	Newton Hth	Newton Hth	area	Total

Engine class / numbers	BR total	9B Stockpt	9B Stockpt	9D Newton Hth	9D Newton Hth	manch area	Mchster Total
Fairburn 4MT 2-6-4T 1945 dev. of Stanier 1935							
42050-42299; 42673-42699	277			2		1	3
Fowler 4MT 2-6-4T 1927							
42300-42424	125		1			1	2
Stanier 4MT 2-6-4T 1935 dev of Fowler 1927							
42425-42672	243			3	1	1	5
Hughes/Fowler 5MT 2-6-0 "Crab" 1926							
42700-42944	245	6	2			1	9
Stanier 5MT 2-6-0 1933							
42945-84	40					1	1
Ivatt 4MT 2-6-0 1947							
43000-43161	162					1	1
Fowler Midland 4F 0-6-0 1911							
43835-44026	192				1		1
Midland 4F 0-6-0 1924							
44027-44606	580	1		1	3		5
Stanier 5MT 4-6-0 "Black Five" 1934							
44658-45499	842	2		9		7	18
Stanier 6P5F 4-6-0 "Jubilee" 1934							
45552-45734/7-42	189	1	1	2	2	1	7
Ivatt 2MT 2-6-0 1946							
46400-46527	128			5		1	6
Midland 3F "Jinty" 0-6-0T 1924 dev. of Johnson 1899 design							
47260-47681	417			3	2	2	7
Stanier 8F 2-8-0 "Big Eight" 1935							
48000-48775	666	3		3		1	7
Thompson 5MT 4-6-0 B1 1942							
61000-61409	410						
BR Standard 7P6F 4-6-2 "Britannia" Derby 1951							
70000-70054	55			1		1	2
BR Standard 5MT 4-6-0 Doncaster 1951							
73000-73171	172	1		2		3	6
BR Standard 4MT 4-6-0 Brighton 1951							
75000-75079	80					1	1
BR Standard 2MT 2-6-0 Doncaster 1953							
78000-78064	65					2	2
BR Standard 4MT 2-6-4T Doncaster 1953							
80000-80154	155					1	1
BR Standard 9F 2-10-0 Brighton 1954							
92000-92250	251			4		1	5
		14	**4**	**35**	**9**	**27**	**89**

Part Eight

The Last Day of the Tour

SATURDAY 7th AUGUST 1965

**Liverpool, Lancashire, Skipton,
Carlisle
and
Home**

The day the timetable went to plan
or
the day D.S. left for home at lunchtime (perhaps the former automatically followed from the latter)

Early Morning – on a bench at Liverpool's Pier Head Bus Station

THE SOMNAMBULIST AFFAIR

My eyes opened and I glassily looked around me. What was this illuminated place I was in? It certainly wasn't a modern, illuminated diesel shed. What reason could there be for me being in this place? I pulled myself to my feet and wearily glanced around. There was nobody around but D.S. and a homeless man. We must have accidentally fallen asleep (just like we did on the way to Stockport and ended up at Alderley Edge). Twice in one day, ridiculous! I doubt if we will get much done now. We should be visiting sheds not snoring our heads off.

I gave D.S. a few digs in the ribs and he blearily awoke. I said anxiously "We should be going round the sheds. Let's hurry". D.S. gave a spluttered acknowledgement and he slowly got up and got his possessions together. "Right." D.S. said "We had better push on before any disasters befall us like we had yesterday." The word "yesterday" echoed around my mind. Today had been a disastrous day but why was D.S. talking about yesterday? Was he going mad? Yesterday had been an incident free day apart from The Wicked Warden Affair at Shrewsbury Youth Hostel and the Little Idiot Affair at Crewe Works. Yes, poor D.S. was definitely cracking up.

We shuffled up to the bus station exit and I noticed that it was pitch dark outside. On the black side of very dark. I thought nothing of it as I was totally engrossed in thinking that we should be going round sheds. However, D.S. was now realising that there was something definitely peculiar about his beloved leader's plans. "What's this?" D.S. said "Are we leaving to do sheds in pitch darkness?" D.S. checked his watch. It was 03.45 (quarter to four in the morning). An early start, again he mused again and we exited into the cool early morning air.

This rush of cool air felt pleasant to me but it rapidly brought D.S. to his senses and he again snatched a glance at his watch. His face turned ashen, his jaw dropped, disbelieving he snatched another glance at his watch. There was no doubt. The blood rushed back, his face turned bright red and he roared out "It's quarter to four in the morning!" Most of Liverpool would probably have been awakened by him but I was not. I merely said "So, what." and walked on. D.S. stood there thunderstruck, what in the blazes was happening? Surely his leader wasn't off to visit sheds. He remembered that last night we would start the day off with the 05.00 train for Garston.

Yes, Big Brother had gone mad and he galvanised himself into unD.S. like fiery action. D.S. caught up with me, grabbed my arm and started yelling "It's quarter to four in the morning. You don't do sheds in pitch darkness at that time". I peered inquisitively at D.S. for quite some time as his face went into violent contortions. What was D.S. on about? What was he trying to tell me?

Suddenly the effect of the cool night air and D.S.'s jostling took their effect and my subconscious was tapped on the shoulder by my conscious state. My conscious on hearing all D.S.'s noise decided that it was time to take over from that arch bungler the subconscious which takes over on night shifts. Luckily, nothing much happens on night shifts so the subconscious gets on relatively well but this week it had been getting out of hand. Travelling to Stockport my conscious had been knocked out for 40 minutes and now something strange was happening.

I now looked more clearly at the situation. What in the blazes was going on? D.S. was shouting that it was quarter to four in the morning and that we should not be visiting sheds. I was not sleeping on a bench getting some much needed hours off from travelling but we were standing outside the Pier Head in totals darkness getting our death of cold. Funny peculiar. I vaguely remember waking up D.S. and telling him that we should be doing sheds. I glanced at my watch, D.S. was correct. Did I wake him up and tell him that? I can hardly put the blame on poor old D.S. for this one.

At last, now fully aware of the situation I now saw that D.S. was a near hospital case from his frustrated attempts to make me see sense. He needed to be calmed quickly. I slowly said "Yes, you're dead right we shouldn't be doing sheds at quarter to four in the morning. I must have had a touch of that old somnambulating lark or possibly my automatic alarm system had awakened me about an hour early." With that terse statement I started back walking slowly into the bus station and to our bench inside. D.S. followed almost tearing his hair out from the events of the past few minutes. No I can't admit to D.S. that I had been somnambulating. Big Brother doesn't do these things; need to make sure that the morning papers don't cover this story.

How did all this happen? Was I a latent somnambulist with a malicious trait which made me play practical jokes at quarter to four in the morning? Hardly. Perhaps after all the disasters of Friday my conscious was pricking me while I slept about all the sheds which we had missed and that I was guiltily sleeping away valuable shed visiting time (hours, in fact). My subconscious had thus acquiesced with the demands of my conscious and had made me get up and start the tour a little earlier than advertised. Could be. Must have a word with my psychiatrist when I get home!

After all the excitement of the past five minutes sleep was hardly on my agenda for the rest of the night in case we slept in. At half past four D.S. and I unanimously agreed that we were awake and that we had better start making tracks for Liverpool Central Station to catch the 05.05 to Garston to visit 8C Speke Junction and 8J Allerton.

It would be a busy day. Our original timetable looked like this:-

DAY 8	SATURDAY AUGUST 7TH 1965	LMR DAY 7
	ORIGINAL TIMETABLE	

		MILES
Depart LIVERPOOL EXCHANGE	05.30	0
Arrive AINTREE SEFTON ARMS	05.41	4¾

Do 8L Aintree Sefton Arms (45 mins. approx)		Recovery Time − 10

| Depart AINTREE SEFTON ARMS | 06.16 | 0 |
| Arrive SANDHILLS | 06.26 | 3¼ |

| Depart SANDHILLS | 06.32 | 0 |
| Arrive BANK HALL | 06.33 | ½ |

Do 8K Bank Hall (18 mins. approx)		Recovery Time + 3

Depart BANK HALL	06.54	0
Arrive LIVERPOOL EXCHANGE	07.00	<u>2</u>
Depart JAMES STREET	07.16	0
Arrive BIRKENHEAD CENTRAL	07.22	<u>1¾</u>

Do 8H Birkenhead (30 mins. approx)

Recovery Time
- 2

Depart BIRKENHEAD CENTRAL	07.50	0
Arrive LIVERPOOL CENTRAL Low Level	07.58	<u>2¼</u>
Depart LIVERPOOL LIME STREET	08.25	0
Arrive ST HELEN'S SHAW STREET	08.57	10¼

see 8A Edge Hill - East

Do 8G Sutton Oak (50 mins. approx)

Recovery Time
NIL

Depart ST HELEN'S SHAW STREET	09.41	10¼
Arrive WIGAN NORTH WESTERN	10.01	<u>19</u>

Do 8F Wigan (Spring's Branch) (80 mins. approx)

Recovery Time
+4

Depart WIGAN WALLGATE	11.25	0
Arrive BOLTON	11.43	<u>9½</u>

Do 9K Bolton (45 mins. approx)

Recovery Time
+ 11

Depart BOLTON	12.39	0
Arrive PRESTON	13.16	<u>20</u>

BUS   -   Local Service

Depart PRESTON STATION
Arrive LOSTOCK HALL STATION

Do 10D Lostock Hall

BUS   -   Local Service

Depart LOSTOCK HALL STATION
Arrive PRESTON STATION

Depart PRESTON	14.25	0
Arrive BLACKBURN	14.44	11¼

Do 10H Lower Darwen (80 mins. approx)

Recovery Time
NIL

Depart BLACKBURN	16.04	11¼

Arrive ROSE GROVE	16.24	21

Do 10F Rose Grove (20 mins. approx) — Recovery Time + 18

Depart ROSE GROVE	17.02	0
Arrive SKIPTON	17.37	18¼

Do 10G Skipton (35 mins. approx) — Recovery Time + 31

Depart SKIPTON	18.43	0
Arrive WENNINGTON	19.48 (Train split)	28¼
Depart WENNINGTON	19.59	28¼
Arrive CARNFORTH	20.18	38

Journey:-
    see Hellifield (north west)   (19.06)

Do 10A Carnforth (30 mins. approx) — Recovery Time + 7

Depart CARNFORTH	20.55	0
Arrive CARLISLE	22.44	62¾
See 12A Tebay - West	(21.45)	35¾

END OF RAILROVER

Our revised timetable looked like this:-

		Schedule
Depart	LIVERPOOL CENTRAL	05.05
Arrive	GARSTON	05.16
	Do 8C Speke Junction	
	Do 8J Allerton	
		Schedule
Depart	GARSTON	06.36
Arrive	LIVERPOOL CENTRAL	06.51
		Schedule
Depart	LIVERPOOL EXCHANGE	07.10
Arrive	BANK HALL	07.14
	Do 8K Bank Hall	
		Schedule
Depart	BANK HALL	07.32
Arrive	SANDHILLS	07.34
		Schedule
Depart	SANDHILLS	07.47
Arrive	AINTREE SEFTON ARMS	07.56
	Do 8L Aintree	
		Schedule
Depart	AINTREE SEFTON ARMS	08.43
Arrive	LIVERPOOL EXCHANGE	08.58

		Schedule
Depart	JAMES STREET	09.16
Arrive	BIRKENHEAD CENTRAL	09.22
	Do 8H Birkenhead	
		Schedule
Depart	BIRKENHEAD CENTRAL	09.50
Arrive	JAMES STREET	09.55
	Bus to EDGE HILL	
	Do 8A Edge Hill	
		Schedule
Depart	EDGE HILL	11.13
Arrive	ST.HELENS SHAW STREET	11.36
Depart	ST.HELENS SHAW STREET	11.36
Arrive	WIGAN NORTH WESTERN	11.59
	DS ITINERARY	
Depart	WIGAN NORTH WESTERN	12.06
Arrive	PRESTON	12.35
Depart	PRESTON	13.57
Arrive	EDINBURGH CALEDONIAN	18.00
	GD ITINERARY	
	Do 8F Springs Branch (Wigan)	
		Schedule
Depart	WIGAN WALLGATE	13.13
Arrive	BOLTON	13.37
	Do 9K Bolton	
		Schedule
Depart	BOLTON TRINITY STREET	14.27
Arrive	BLACKBURN	14.55
	Do 10H Lower Darwen	
		Schedule
Depart	BLACKBURN	16.04
Arrive	ACCRINGTON	16.13
Depart	ACCRINGTON	16.14
Arrive	ROSE GROVE	16.24
	Do 10F Rose Grove	
		Schedule
Depart	ROSE GROVE	17.02
Arrive	SKIPTON	17.37
	DO 10G Skipton	
		Schedule
Depart	SKIPTON	18.43
Arrive	WENNINGTON	19.48
Depart	WENNINGTON	19.59
Arrive	CARNFORTH	20.18
	Do 10A Carnforth	
Depart	CARNFORTH	20.55
Arrive	CARLISLE	22.44
	Le Fin de la Tour	

Essentially we had dropped 8G Sutton Oak and 10D Lostock Hall to accommodate the sheds missed from yesterday:- 8A Edge Hill, 8C Speke Junction and 8J Allerton.

On we go

D.S. and I duly arrived at Manchester Central station at 04.45. To avoid any rush later in the day we withdrew our holdalls from the left luggage. Our young railwayman left luggage attendant who had doubted our ability to return at this early hour was unfortunately not on duty so we were unable to score a point off him.

Our bucket was an express one i.e. non-stop to Garston. It left on time at 05.05 and we were naturally on it. Talking about buckets we had not been steam hauled all week which was quite a disappointment. However, we must have an excellent chance of being steam hauled today as the North West was the last steam stronghold. Three weeks ago my Preston to Wigan train had been hauled by a Fairburn 2-6-4 Tank. After a steady 30 M.P.H. journey our bucket ambled into Garston Station on time at 05.16. Nearing the station we noted a "Big Eight" and a diesel shunter.

LIVERPOOL CENTRAL TO GARSTON							
			Home shed		Built	Withdrawn	Scrap
Diesels							
BR Shunter 0-6-0 1953							
D3855			8C	Speke Junction	Oct-1959		
Total	1						
Steam					Built	Withdrawn	Scrap
Stanier 8F 2-8-0 "Big Eight" 1935							
48692			8C	Speke Junction	Mar-1944	Jun-1968	Oct-1968
Total	1						
On Journey	2		Kops		1		
Steam	1		Diesels		1		
		Home Area			2	Visitors	0
Shed	8C	2					
Distribution							
Steam Classes	1						
Steam Origin	LMS	1					

		Schedule	Actual	Miles
Depart	LIVERPOOL CENTRAL	05.05	05.05	0
Arrive	GARSTON	05.16	05.16	5½

Our return train was at 06.36. We had a comfortable 5 minutes recovery time with 40 minutes allocated for Speke Junction and 35 minutes for 8J Allerton. Before the tour began I was a bit worried as there were two stations: - Garston and Allerton (for Garston and Woolton). The directions for both sheds were from Allerton station. However, I need not have worried as Allerton station was just along the road, on the other side of the road.

We decided to do 8C Speke (the steam depot) first just in case there were any time constraints. We moved along to Allerton station and picked up the ten minutes LocoShed Directory route. We crossed one railway bridge and went under another one. The shed was situated in the triangle of the Allerton-Garston Docks-Ditton junction lines. Speke therefore turned out to be a Parkhurst type shed, being surrounded by rails on three sides, a triangular prison!

Luck was on our side going round and the shedmaster was nowhere to be seen doubtless aided by the early 05.30 visit. The shed was very quiet. The only active inhabitant being a "Big Eight". She was in real trouble trying to get started, continually slipping on the moist rails.

		Home shed		Built	Withdrawn	Scrap
Diesels						
BR Gardner 0-6-0 Shunter 1957						
D2199		8C		Jul-1961	Jun-1972	
D2389		8C		Apr-1961	Feb-1983	
D2394		8C		Jul-1961	Nov-1968	
Total	3					
BR 0-6-0 Shunter 1953						
D3856		8C		Oct-1959		
D4148		8C		Oct-1962		
Total	2					
LMS 0-6-0 Shunter 1939						
12006		8C		Jun-1939	Sep-1967	
12015		8C		Mar-1940	Oct-1967	
12017		8C		Apr-1940	Oct-1967	
12026		8C		Feb-1942	Oct-1967	
12027		8C		Feb-1942	Oct-1967	
12028		8C		Mar-1942	Jun-1967	
12029		8C		Mar-1942	May-1966	
Total	7					
Steam				**Built**	**Withdrawn**	**Scrap**
Fairburn 4MT 2-6-4T 1945 dev. of Stanier 1935						
42076		9E	Trafford Park	Dec-1950	Mar-1967	Nov-1967
Total	1					
Stanier 5MT 4-6-0 "Black Five" 1934						
44732		8C		Feb-1949	Jul-1967	Jan-1968
44741	Caprotti valved	8C		Jun-1948	Mar-1965	Oct-1965
44743	Caprotti valved	8C		Jun-1948	Jan-1968	May-1968
44753	Caprotti valved	8C		Mar-1948	Jul-1965	Jan-1966
44779		8B	Warrington (ex 8F)	Jul-1947	Dec-1966	Jul-1967
45034		8C		Sep-1934	Feb-1968	May-1968
45057		8C		Dec-1934	Aug-1967	Jul-1968
45071		8C		May-1935	Jul-1967	Feb-1969
45137		8C		Jun-1935	Dec-1966	Jul-1967
45181		8C		Sep-1935	Jan-1966	May-1966
45188		8C		Sep-1935	Jul-1967	Apr-1968
45201		8C		Oct-1935	May-1968	Aug-1968
45329		8C		Mar-1937	Nov-1966	Apr-1967
45370		8C		Jun-1937	Aug-1966	Nov-1966
45386		8C		Jul-1937	Aug-1968	Apr-1969
45441		8C		Dec-1937	Feb-1967	Sep-1967
45466		8C		Nov-1938	Feb-1967	May-1967
Total	17					
Ivatt 2MT 2-6-0 1946						
46410		8C		Jan-1947	Mar-1966	Jun-1966
46440		8C		Feb-1950	Mar-1967	Sep-1967
46515		8C		Jan-1953	May-1967	Dec-1967
46516		8C		Jan-1953	May-1967	Nov-1967
46518		8C		Jan-1953	Mar-1966	Jun-1966
Total	5					
Stanier 8F 2-8-0 "Big Eight" 1935						
48029		8C	(ex 8A Edge Hill)	Aug-1936	Feb-1967	Aug-1967
48108		8L	Aintree	Feb-1939	Aug-1967	Feb-1968
48189		8C		May-1942	Jul-1965	Mar-1966
48191		9F	Heaton Mersey	May-1942	Aug-1968	Dec-1968
48292		8C	(ex 5B via 16E)	Aug-1941	Apr-1968	Aug-1968
48296		8C	(ex 8A Edge Hill)	Dec-1941	Sep-1966	Apr-1967
48509		8C		Nov-1944	May-1967	Mar-1968
48520		8C		Oct-1944	Sep-1966	Feb-1967
48722		8C		Aug-1944	May-1968	Jan-1969
Total	9					

			Home shed			Built	Withdrawn	Scrap
BR Standard 9F 2-10-0 Brighton 1954								
92024	*Crosti*	*boilered*	8H	Birkenhead (ex12A)		*Jun-1955*	*Nov-1967*	*May-1968*
92025	*Crosti*	*boilered*	8C			*Jun-1955*	*Nov-1967*	*Apr-1968*
92114			12A	Carlisle Kingmoor (ex 9D)		*Dec-1956*	*Jul-1967*	*Feb-1968*
92158			8C			*Nov-1957*	*Jul-1966*	*Nov-1966*
Total	*4*							
On Shed	**48**		**Kops**		**31**			
Steam	**36**		**Diesels**		**12**			
Withdrawn	**3**							
Home Locos	**42**	**Home Area**			**3**	**Visitors**	**3**	
Shed	8C	42	8B		1	8H	1	
	8L	1						
Distribution	9E	1	9F		1			
	12A	1						
Steam classes on view		**5**						
Steam Origin	LMS		32	BR		4		
Shed Highlight:-		44741	the three Caprotti valved Black 5's					
		44743						
		44753						
Steam	**Aug-50**	**43**	**Mar-59**		**33**	**Apr-65**	**57**	
Allocation						**Aug-65**	**61**	
				Closed to Steam:-			**May-68**	
Home Steam	excluding withdrawn locos							
On/Off Shed	On Shed		27	Off Shed		34	% On Shed	44%
Not on Shed								
"Black Fives"		44725	44806		44877	44950	45059	
		45131	45154		45332	45338	45388	
					45407	45412	45417	13
Ivatt 2MT 2-6-0 1946							46503	1
"Big Eights"		48163	48251		48294	48398	48408	
		48425	48457		48476	48493	48692	
					48709	48711		12
BR 9F 2-10-0 1954		92008	92027		92054	92091	92115	
					92117	92153	92154	8
								34
		saw elsewhere on the tour				9		
		saw on July 65 Preston area trip				1		
		saw on September 58 Carlisle visit				2		
		saw on June 67 Carlisle visit				2		

Review and Appraisal of 8C Speke Junction

The shed was in the triangle of the Atherton-Garston Docks-Ditton Junction lines. Walking time was 10 minutes from Allerton (for Garston and Woolton) Station.

Without any doubt the highlight of the shed was seeing the three Caprotti valved "Black Fives". Originally there were 22 "Black Fives" Caprotti fitted, 8 with Timken roller bearings. 3 with Timken roller bearings and double chimney, 2 Skefko roller bearings and double chimney. The Caprotti fitted engines had proved the most troublesome of all the "Black Fives" and had been steadily withdrawn over the last few years. In fact of the original 22 only four were left. Yes they had certainly been dealt the death card. Two of the three Caprotti valved engines here were withdrawn. The two Skefko double chimneyed members were at 8M Southport along with the surviving Timken double chimneyed member. Unfortunately 8M Southport was too out of the way to be accommodated on the tour.

The shed was very much comprised of home talent (42 of the 48 locos) on show and no visitors from any distance. We had seen our old friend Fairburn 2-6-4 tank 42076 of 9E Trafford Park twice recently. The visiting 9F Heaton Mersey "Big Eight" had not been on shed there yesterday. The two Crosti boilered 9F 2-10-0's were of course a welcome sight.

8C Speke Junction surprisingly had only five steam classes allocated to it. It perhaps could be called Shuntersville. I cannot remember seeing so many shunters at one shed this week. Perhaps our early visit increased their numbers on view. Seven of them were from the original LMS 1939 batch which D.S. loved because of their pairs of antiquated looking floating wheels.

27 Home Steam (44%) was on shed and 34 off shed. Perhaps a little disappointing for a Saturday morning. However, 8C Speke was a heavy duty shed like 9F Heaton Mersey and it was therefore not surprising that its steam engines are well used.

On we go

Whenever I think of Garston I think of ferro-concrete and booze. A strange mixture you might think but you will soon see why. Now for Allerton. We made our way back to Allerton station and got out the LocoShed Directory for the route to 8J Allerton. The shed was off Woolton Road which turned out to be a very long road but we found the entrance on the right-hand side after almost a ten minutes walk between the Ferro-Concrete Works and the Allerton Arms hotel. D.S. was disappointed that one of them wasn't open. Guess which bit I know that he doesn't like concrete particularly walking on it with his hobnailed army surplus boots.

On finding five Bo-Bo Electrics outside the depot we thought how considerate and wondered whether it was worth going in. We decided that discretion was the better part of valour and did not. I had always been wary of electric depots. My wariness had been increased by the Fried Feet Affair last Sunday and also at Willesden Electric Depot the same day when a head bod refused us entry on safety grounds. There was also Woody's dangerous frequency at 9A Longsight. However, we had got round there OK yesterday. Nevertheless, time was getting on and probably BR would take a dim view of us running around inside without a permit. Quite possibly, there were no electrics inside but we shall never know and we were not particularly disturbed if there were.

Steam is the thing and as the week had progressed we had taken very little interest in diesels and diesel depots in general. I now smile that I had originally scheduled a visit to Cockshute diesel depot at Stoke in the original timetable. Increasingly, this week diesel and electric depots had been given the push when required. 16D Nottingham, 86A Cardiff Canton, Crewe Electric Depot, Cockshute Diesel Depot had been dumped. If we had got over to Sheffield doubtless we would have dumped 41A Tinsley, 41B Darnall and 41C Wath out of the tour in favour of Sheffield, Doncaster and Leeds Areas steam sheds.

8J ALLERTON				
		Home shed		Built
Electrics				
A.E.I. (British Thomson-Houston) AL1 Bo-Bo 1959				
E3023		LMW	London Midland Western Lines	May-1961
Total	1			
BR B.T.H. AL5/1 Bo-Bo 1962				
E3086		LMW	London Midland Western Lines	Mar-1962
Total	1			
BR Vulcan Foundry AEI motors AL6 Bo-Bo 1965				
E3102		LMW	London Midland Western Lines	Aug-1965
E3161		LMW	London Midland Western Lines	Oct-1965
E3162		LMW	London Midland Western Lines	Aug-1965
Total	1			

8J ALLERTON(continued)					
On Shed	5	Kops	4		
Steam	0	Diesels	0	Electrics	5
Home Locos	5	Home Area	0	Visitors	0
Shed	LMW	5			
Distribution					

Review and Appraisal of 8J Allerton

The shed was on the east side of the main line about ¼ mile of Allerton (for Garston and Woolton) Station. Walking time was 10 minutes from the station.

The shed was located on the east side of the line about ¼ mile south of Allerton (for Garston and Woolton) station. We had seen E3161 a new series Bo-Bo Electric at Crewe on Thursday afternoon. Electrics have all the same shedcode (LMW – London Midland Western lines). How boring!

On we go

Having decided not to swing from the overhead live wires we zipped back to Garston station. D.S. was in good walking form – perhaps this last day had given him a second wind. I need not have worried though as the timings were easy and we reached the station with 20 minutes to spare.

Our return trip was relatively uneventful but we did see three good steam locos working. All were seen just after we left Garston Station. Two 9E Trafford Park locos were noted: - Stanier "Black Five" 44815 and our old friend Stanier 2-6-4 tank 42455. We had seen her on 9E Trafford Park yesterday and also on our way from Irlam to Warrington last night. The last engine which we saw was Caprotti valved Stanier Black Five 44743 which we had noted half an hour earlier warming up at 8C Speke Junction. She had had better fortune than her two withdrawn sisters there 44741 and 44753.

GARSTON TO LIVERPOOL CENTRAL						
		Home shed		Built	Withdrawn	Scrap
Steam						
Stanier 4MT 2-6-4T 1935 dev of Fowler 1927						
42455	*on 9E yesterday*	9E	Trafford Park	*Aug-1936*	*Apr-1966*	*Jul-1966*
Total	*1*					
Stanier 5MT 4-6-0 "Black Five" 1934						
44743	*Caprotti valved*	8C	Speke Junction	*Jun-1948*	*Jan-1968*	*May-1968*
44815		9E	Trafford Park (ex16C)	*Nov-1944*	*Feb-1968*	*Jun-1968*
Total	*2*					
On Journey	3	Kops		0		
Steam	3	Diesels		0		
		Home Area		1	Visitors	2
Shed	8C	1				
Distribution	9E	2				
Steam Classes	2					
Steam Origin	LMS	3				

			Schedule	Actual	Miles
Depart	GARSTON		06.36	06.36	0
Arrive	LIVERPOOL CENTRAL		06.51	06.51	5½

Three intermediate stops.

Our next port of call was Liverpool Exchange station to get the 07.10 to 8K Bank Hall. This gave us only 19 minutes to cross the not inconsiderable distance from Central to Exchange stations. We wasted no time and walked briskly through the City Centre to Exchange Station and arrived there with several minutes to spare. Another disaster averted!

We boarded the Southport bound bucket and patiently waited for it to speed off. The journey was about a good sneeze in distance. Bank Hall was only 2 miles up the road with one intermediate stop (Sandhills). Journey time was only four minutes so the timing was quite good.

THE BANK HAUL MAUL AFFAIR.

Our next M.P.D. was 8K Bank Hall. Bank Hall seemed to be the toughest timing of the day. We had to be back to get the 07.32 to Sandhills. That gave us exactly 18 minutes in which to play with. Cut off a minute at either end for late arrival or early departure and we would have just over 15 minutes to play with. Trouble was 5 minutes to the shed, 5 minutes back and 15 minutes to visit it added up to 25 minutes and we thus had a recovery time of not more than minus 7 minutes. This was on the tight side of tight and I informed D.S. of the gravity of the situation. He was suitably impressed and said that he would push it. I did not want a repeat of the Trafford Park debacle yesterday.

Our only chance of catching our train appeared to be 3 minutes there, 9 minutes to do it and 3 minutes back. This would give us a recovery time of 1-3 minutes. The timings looked paper thin but we would go down fighting if we have to lose.

I had heard some weird tales of 8K Bank Hall. Quite a few people had been thrown out even before they were into the shed as one had to down a flight of stairs past the offices to get into the shed. Folklore had it as a Stratford, Nine Elms (or even Crewe Works) degree of security. We had got round Stratford via a permit but had found 70A Nine Elms easy enough late on a Sunday evening but we had failed at Crewe Works even with some sort of authorisation and had had great difficulty at 40E Colwick and 2E Saltley (even with permits). The funny thing was that 8K Bank Hall didn't have much to hide. It had a smallish allocation, the stars being easily her four "Jubilees". I had seen one of her "Jubilees" this summer on a Saturday afternoon Glasgow – Liverpool run. This steam working had delighted all Scottish railwayists. I had heard one amusing story of a poor railwayist who had tried to get into 8K Bank Hall by an unofficial route.

This is one of my favourite shed visiting stories. He had leapt up onto the wall beside the main entrance and was about to quickly jump down the other side when he about collapsed with fright and shock. Yes, it would have been a shortcut to the shed but it was about 70 feet below him. Certainly, it was a shortcut but to oblivion. Moral of the story: - there is no shortcut into Bank Hall shed and one must use the official entrance.

		Schedule	Actual	Miles
Depart	LIVERPOOL EXCHANGE	07.10	07.10	0
Arrive	BANK HALL	07.14	07.15	2

My watch was advancing to 07.15 (about a minute late) when we rushed off the bucket and out of the station before any ticket collector could stop us. We emerged from the station into Stanley Road and what would be at the other side but the entrance to 8K Bank Hall M.P.D. Certainly less than 5 minutes walking time as the Locoshed Directory had promised. I noted with amusement the wall at the side of the entrance building, making a note to avoid the temptation to vault over the wall and meet with a sorry end on BR metals many feet below. We rushed into the entrance and found a flight of stairs going down to the shed in front of us with offices on the left. We made our way down the stairs as quickly but a silently we could. We didn't stop to hand our permit into the office as we didn't have one. Even if we had had one we had no time to waste handing one in. We dashed out of the door at the bottom of the stairs and we were out in the daylight again.

In front of us we found two shed buildings like 9H Patricroft. D.S. was bang in form today and suggested that we take one shed building each then quickly look up the lines that the other one of us had taken. We threw our holdalls down at and sped off in our respective directions at speed and moving quickly and madly around. If ever there was a case of "number snatching" at a BR shed this was it. A visit solely for locomotive spotting BR would say and not for the informative, educational, interesting and need I add – slow visit which I had promised to the respective Divisional Managers.

The great snatch went on at a rampant pace and I quickly completed my assigned shed and flew out to find D.S. bounding up having completed his shed. I then dived into D.S.'s shed and ran down it, quickly mentally noting the contents. We would exchange our lists later on. Meanwhile he had done the same with my shed.

I glanced at my watch the sands of time were moving favourably. We went crashing back over the lines when an alarm bell suddenly went off from the office area above us. We distinctly felt our blood chill. "We've been spotted" yelled D.S. to me. That was certainly the pun of the century. Apparently, our shouting, yelling and flying antics around and in the sheds and the yard had awakened the occupants of the offices from their early morning slumbers. They had been none too pleased at their impregnable castle being invaded in such a loud and defiant manner. An Englishman's home is his castle and this was a Scottish invasion. The alarm had been duly sounded and battle had to commence. We had been spotted, red-handed and to escape we must go right through the enemy's headquarters, namely up the stairs past the offices, out into Stanley Road, into Bank Hall station and away safely by means of a local bucket content with our scribbled haul of the contents of 8K Bank Hall shed.

We picked up our holdalls and were making our way up the stairs when I glanced up and groaned. The enemy had struck. The shedmaster was standing at the top of the stairs awaiting our arrival. I arrived first at the danger spot. I pretended he wasn't there and attempted to bulldoze my way through the space between the stair rail and his body. I ran into his arm which he quickly put out to cut off that escape route. I immediately tried for the new space which he had created between his body and the office wall but again he showed his marvelous reflexes by moving quickly against the wall. However, while this was going on D.S. (who was directly behind me) saw his chance and quickly pushed his way through the new gap between the stair rail and the shedmaster (which had opened when he had moved across to cut me off at the other side). So, D.S. had skillfully escaped.

The perpetual cha-cha was getting me nowhere and I resorted to the ultimate weapon – the wad! I had, of course, used the wad trick with staggering effect at 9D Newton heath early yesterday morning. I stopped dancing from side to side, unzipped my anorak and brought out the enormous wad of permits. At the sight of this the shedmaster's angry face at our antics turned to astonishment and his jaw was seen to drop. At the sight of this the shedmaster's guard had dropped and I skipped past him. I had escaped but one must complete a "wad" trick once started. I said "We have a permit and began flipping through the pile of them. I stopped suddenly and said "It's in here somewhere. Can't look for it now. Sorry, but we are in a terrible hurry to catch our train back. That's what all our rush was about". The shedmaster looked despairingly as the wad disappeared back into my anorak pocket. And queried "What train do you have to catch"? No time for chit chat I thought, time to go. I screamed "It's the 07.32 to Liverpool. Sorry must go now or we'll miss it". With that and before he could stop us or have second thoughts I belted out of the office, joined D.S. and we ran across the road to the station leaving the bemused shedmaster and Bank Hall shed behind us.

It had all been very traumatic. The wad had served its purpose. I was worried that the shedmaster would get some of his underlings together and come chasing after us. I did not know quite in what state I had left him. The "wadding" had been incomplete so he might well be in a position to retaliate. I thought we had better hide at the far end of Bank Hall Station so that anyone entering the station (the shedmaster and associates) would not see us. D.S., however, would have none of this, and tired out by his exertions had collapsed down on a bench in full view of anyone entering the station. We had arrived back at 07.26. Six minutes to spare! We had gone to the shed, did it, dallied with the shedmaster and got back in just eleven minutes. Certainly, one of the fastest visits to Bank Hall M.P.D. BR and the Bank Hall shedmaster would never see anything quite like it again. The shedmaster had certainly been given a day to remember.

I checked with the ticket collector about our train. "Yes" he said "the next train to Liverpool is the 07.32. Normally, it leaves here at 07.30". Which would have been very disconcerting if we had arrived at 07.30 (thinking we were two minutes early) to see the bucket disappearing out of the station. Yes, I don't like trains that leave early unless we are on them. I would have been furious if we had missed our train because it left an unofficial two minutes early.

The shedmaster and his underlings did not come after us, although I glanced up at the station entrance every minute. I suspect that the shedmaster was glad to see the back of us and he had certainly been reassured when he had seen the big wad of permits. Our train came in as promised at 07.30. We hopped on and had escaped from Bank Hall. It had been a troublesome shed as expected but as always honesty, bravery, virtuosity and craft (our qualities) had triumphed over an interfering shedmaster.

8K BANK HALL					
	Home shed		*Built*	*Withdrawn*	*Scrap*
Diesels					
English Electric Type 4 1-Co-Co-1 1958					
D 267	12B	Carlisle Upperby	*Mar-1960*		
Total	1				
BR 0-4-0 Shunter Yorkshire Engine Co. 1960					
D2858	8K		*Dec-1960*	*Feb-1970*	
Total	1				
Steam			*Built*	*Withdrawn*	*Scrap*
Ivatt 2MT 2-6-2T 1946					
41211	8K		*Aug-1948*	*Sep-1966*	*Feb-1967*
41244	8K		*Oct-1949*	*Nov-1966*	*Mar-1967*
41304	8K	(ex 6D Shrewsbury)	*Mar-1952*	*Nov-1966*	*Mar-1967*
Total	3				
Stanier 5MT 4-6-0 "Black Five" 1934					
44987	9J	Agecroft	*Nov-1946*	*Oct-1966*	*Feb-1967*
Total	1				
Stanier 6P5F 4-6-0 "Jubilee" 1934					
45627	"Sierra Leone"	8K	*Nov-1934*	*Sep-1966*	*Feb-1967*
45698	"Mars"	8K	*Apr-1936*	*Nov-1965*	*Feb-1966*
45721	"Impregnable"	8K	*Aug-1936*	*Sep-1965*	*Mar-1966*
Total	3				
Ivatt 2MT 2-6-0 1946					
46402	8K	(ex 8F Wigan)	*Dec-1946*	*Jun-1967*	*Jan-1968*
46405	8K	(ex 9K Bolton)	*Dec-1946*	*Dec-1966*	*Apr-1967*
46414	8K	(ex 9K Bolton)	*Feb-1947*	*Jun-1966*	*Dec-1966*
46444	8K		*Feb-1950*	*Jul-1965*	*Oct-1965*
46484	8K	(ex 8F Wigan)	*Oct-1951*	*Jun-1967*	*Feb-1968*
46497	8K		*Feb-1952*	*Apr-1965*	*Sep-1965*
Total	6				
Stanier 8F 2-8-0 "Big Eight" 1935					
48605	8L	Aintree	*Jul-1943*	*Aug-1966*	*Nov-1966*
Total	1				

8K BANK HALL(continued)				Built	Withdrawn	Scrap
	Home shed			Built	Withdrawn	Scrap
BR Standard 4MT 4-6-0 Brighton 1951						
75032	8K			Jun-1953	Feb-1968	May-1968
75046	8K			Oct-1953	Aug-1967	Feb-1968
75048	8K			Oct-1953	Aug-1968	Nov-1968
75049	8K			Oct-1953	Oct-1966	Mar-1967
75050	8K			Nov-1956	Nov-1966	Jun-1967
75060	8A	Edge Hill (ex 8L)		May-1957	Apr-1967	Oct-1967
Total	6					
On Shed	22	Kops	10			
Steam	20	Diesels	2			
Withdrawn	2					
Home Locos	18 Home Area		2	Visitors	2	
Shed	8K	18	8A	1	8L	1
Distribution	9J	1	12B	1		
Steam Classes	6					
Steam Origin	LMS	14	BR	6		
Shed Highlight:-		45627	"Sierra Leone"	8K		
		45721	"Impregnable"	8K		
		45698	"Mars"	8K		
Steam	Aug-50	46	Mar-59	41	Apr-65	17
Allocation					Aug-65	21
			Closed to Steam:-		Oct-66	
Home Steam	excluding withdrawn locos					
On/Off Shed	On Shed	15 Off Shed		6 % On Shed	71%	
Not on Shed						
"Jubilee"					45684	1
Ivatt 2MT 2-6-0 1946					46496	1
BR 4MT 4-6-0 1951		75026		75027	75033	75047	4
					total	6
		saw on July 65 Preston area trip			3	
		saw on June 67 Carlisle visit			1	

Review and Appraisal of 8K Bank Hall a.k.a the Impregnable Shed

The shed was on the west side of the line between Sandhills and Kirkdale stations. Walking time was less than 5 minutes from Bank Hall Station.

The shed was on the west side of the line between Sandhills and Kirkdale on the line on to Aintree and Ormskirk. The shed was not visible from the Liverpool to Southport line (the Bank Hall Station line).

Security conscious Bank Hall in fact held little that they needed to protect. Nevertheless twenty steam locos on shed was quite good. Terrific seeing three "Jubilees" including the aptly named 45721 "Impregnable" as a tribute to Bank Hall's defences against trainspotters! Doubtless the missing "Jubilee" 45684 "Jutland" could be in Scotland in Glasgow awaiting to take the 14.00 (Fridays and Saturdays only) to Liverpool Exchange arriving in Liverpool at 19.36. Doubtless, "Jutland" would be given a fine reception and sendoff from our Scottish railwayist acquaintances.

Seeing the 9J Agecroft Black Five was good particularly as we had missed her on shed yesterday. Two diesels were on shed. I did not expect to find an English Electric Type 4 here. The little 0-4-0 Yorkshire Engine Company shunter was interesting.

15 Home Steam on shed (71%) with only 6 off shed. An excellent percentage! 8K Bank Hall engines were popular on the Ormskirk to Preston line and a further three had been seen by me last month.

A couple of years ago Bank Hall was the proud bearer of the parent type shed code 27A. This perhaps explains the feelings of shed security. Also in her five shed 27 Area were 27B Aintree (now 8L) and 27C Southport (now 8M), 27D Wigan (Central) which became 8P but had been closed in April 1964 and finally 27E Walton on the Hill which had closed in December 1963 before renumbering took place.

On we go

Our bucket from Bank Hall bucket stopped almost immediately at Sandhills.

		Schedule	Actual	Miles
Depart	BANK HALL	07.32	07.30	0
Arrive	SANDHILLS	07.34	07.32	½

A stone's throw was the word for it. Only a half mile journey so if we had missed this bucket there was a good chance that we could have walked the half mile and got the 07.47 to Aintree. We could also have continued on this bucket to Exchange Station and caught our Aintree train from there. However, getting off at Sandhills gave us a short respite.

The respite was well needed because I had to make a note of the contents of D.S.'s shed at Bank Hall and he had to make a note of the contents of my shed there. This was done and I went down the station steps and found the staff discussing the imminent start to the football season. I interrupted them and found out what platform our Aintree train would be leaving from. Sandhills had more than one platform as it was at the junction for the Southport (Bank Hall Station) line and the Ormskirk (8L Aintree) line.

After a pleasant wait watching some black clouds ominously appear we got on our bucket on time at 07.47. Sure enough, rain began to belt down to prove that it always rains in Lancashire.

"We must have killed that sheddie at Bank Hall." I said to D.S. "That's a sure sign that it will rain just like killing a spider."

Our journey was of little interest apart from trying to locate (without success) the Aintree Grand National Racecourse.

		Schedule	Actual	Miles
Depart	SANDHILLS	07.47	07.47	0
Arrive	AINTREE SEFTON ARMS	07.56	07.56	3¼

Three intermediate stops.

Our return train was the 08.43 to Liverpool Exchange. We had 47 minutes to do the shed which gave us a tightish recovery time of 2 minutes (30 minutes there and back and 15 minutes to do the shed). D.S. was informed that there could be no slacking. The advertised walking time of 15 minutes turned out to be very generous as we made it in ten minutes. The rain was belting down even heavier now and I put my waterproof trousers and jacket on.

THE PARCHED D.S. EPISODE
Or THE SAHARA EPISODE
Or THE THIRSTY MAN EPISODE

I was still a bit worried about our traumatic exit from Bank Hall. I imagined that the Bank Hall shedmaster might have struggled to the telephone and alerted the railway police and in particular the shedmasters of the other Liverpool sheds about us. I wasn't joking either, our

Al Capone like visit to 8K Bank Hall was troubling me.

I decided that we would ask if we could go round. Certainly, this could lead to an incident free visit and would be better for our and shedmasters health in general. If we happened to be refused we would go round in any case.

We saw the shedmaster in his little office and our roving microphone picked up the following conversation which took place outside his office window as we did not want to go in and drown him with our wet clothes. As we stood outside in the torrential rain (the skies had indeed opened) the shedmaster looked up from his papers and opened the window to find out what we wanted or wished to sell.

ME:- Hello, could we please take a few photos of the engines and the shed. (The railway photographer request carried more weight than a trainspotting request).

D.S.: - Incredulously commented "In this weather!"

D.S. apparently thought that I must be nuts to ask permission to take photos in all this rain. The rain was so heavy we could hardly see more than 20 yards! I promptly stood on D.S.'s foot and he belatedly got the message and guessed my strategy.

The shedmaster smiled and felt sorry for us coming all the way in the pouring rain to photograph his engines.

SHEDMASTER: - "Sure, come and see me when you've finished." He then closed the window to escape a drenching and went back to his desk and his papers.

Apparently, the Bank Hall shedmaster had not phoned him. A little piece of civility had worked wonders.

We made our way round what turned out to be a fine shed and were quickly back at the shedmaster's window with the rain even heavier than ever if anything. I thanked the shedmaster. D.S. quickly took command.

D.S. "Could I have a glass of water please?"

That was the most incredible statement of the week. D.S. had been almost drowned by water for the last fifteen minutes and here he was with rain battering down on all sides: - thirsty! I started laughing. The shedmaster thought that D.S. was having him on but then he saw D.S. was serious, went over to the sink and filled a plastic tumbler up with water.

D.S. quickly drank it down and then came out with another cracker.

D.S. "Could I have another cup, please?"

A right Oliver Twist we have here, I thought. Fancy him wanting another cup as well. I couldn't help bursting out in fits of laughter again. The sheddie looked dumbfounded at D.S. and without speaking a word went over and filled his tumbler up again and D.S. had his "seconds" of water. It was hilarious seeing the sheddie wait on D.S. I almost turned away in embarrassment in case D.S. would ask for "thirds" but luckily he did not. The shedmaster would probably have phoned up the asylum or directed D.S. to the nearest big dub of water which had quickly formed during the thunderstorm.

D.S. gasped out gratefully as though saved from a death due to lack of water. "Thanks a lot. That was great."

Yes D.S. dying from thirst in the midst of a terrible cloudburst had to be seen to be believed. D.S.'s thirst satiated we were off again, the shedmaster musing that taking photographs must be thirsty work. Need I add, we of course didn't take any in these absolutely dreadful conditions with a simple box camera.

8L AINTREE						
		Home shed		Built	Withdrawn	Scrap
Diesels						
BR 0-6-0 Shunter 1953						
D4147		8C	Speke Junction	*Sep-1962*		
Total	*1*					
Steam				Built	Withdrawn	Scrap
Stanier 5MT 4-6-0 "Black Five" 1934						
45147		8L	(ex 5C Stafford)	*Jun-1935*	*May-1967*	*Oct-1967*
45229		8L		*Aug-1936*	*Sep-1965*	*Dec-1965*
45330		8L		*Mar-1937*	*Aug-1968*	*Dec-1968*
Total	*3*					
Ivatt 2MT 2-6-0 1946						
46439		8L	(ex 9K Bolton)	*Jan-1950*	*Mar-1967*	*Sep-1967*
46500		8L		*Mar-1952*	*Jan-1967*	*Jun-1967*
46502		8L		*Mar-1952*	*Feb-1967*	*Jun-1967*
46523		8L	(ex 9D Newton Heath)	*Mar-1953*	*May-1967*	*Nov-1967*
Total	*4*					
Midland 3F "Jinty" 0-6-0T 1924 dev. of Johnson 1899 design						
47327		8L	*to Barry Docks*	*Jul-1926*	*Dec-1966*	*saved*
47367		8L	(ex 8G Sutton Oak)	*Aug-1926*	*Dec-1966*	*Apr-1967*
47453		8L	(ex 8G Sutton Oak)	*Oct-1926*	*Apr-1966*	*Aug-1966*
47566		8L		*May-1928*	*Oct-1966*	*Mar-1967*
47655		8L		*Mar-1929*	*Nov-1965*	*Mar-1966*
Total	*5*					
Stanier 8F 2-8-0 "Big Eight" 1935						
48017		8L		*Jan-1937*	*Oct-1967*	*Jul-1968*
48268		8L		*May-1942*	*Oct-1967*	*Jun-1968*
48301		8L	(ex 15B via 15A)	*Sep-1943*	*Mar-1967*	*Sep-1967*
48363		8L	(ex 16B via 16E)	*Aug-1944*	*Nov-1967*	*Jul-1968*
48406		9F	Heaton Mersey	*Aug-1943*	*Sep-1965*	*Dec-1965*
48648		8L		*Dec-1943*	*Jul-1967*	*Nov-1967*
48676		8L		*Apr-1944*	*Oct-1967*	*Aug-1968*
Total	*7*					
BR Standard 4-6-0 1951 4MT Brighton						
75061		8L		*May-1957*	*Apr-1967*	*Oct-1967*
Total	*1*					
WD 8F 2-8-0 "Austerity" Riddles 1943						
90563		8L		*Sep-1943*	*Aug-1965*	*Jun-1966*
90632		8L		*Mar-1944*	*May-1965*	*Aug-1965*
90641		8L		*May-1944*	*Aug-1965*	*Jun-1966*
90724		8L		*Apr-1945*	*Jun-1965*	*Oct-1965*
Total	*4*					
BR Standard 9F 2-10-0 Brighton 1954						
92045		8H	Birkenhead	*Feb-1955*	*Sep-1967*	*Feb-1968*
Total	*1*					

On Shed	26	Kops	23			
Steam	25	Diesels	1			
Withdrawn	2					

Home Locos	23	Home Area		2	Visitors	1
Shed	8L	23	8C	1	8H	1
Distribution	9F	1				
Steam classes on view		7				
Steam Origin	LMS		19 BR		2 WD	4
Shed Highlight:-		48406	9F Heaton Mersey			

8L AINTREE(continued)								
Steam	Aug-50	55	Mar-59		42	Apr-65	44	
Allocation						Aug-65	34	
				Closed to Steam:-			Aug-67	
Home Steam	excluding withdrawn locos							
On/Off Shed	On Shed	21	Off Shed		13	% On Shed	62%	
Not on Shed								
"Jinty"							47289	1
"Big Eights"		48050	48108		48139	48340	48421	
			48465		48500	48605	48704	9
BR 4-6-0 1951 4MT						75043	75064	2
WD 8F 2-8-0 1943							90222	1
							total	13
saw elsewhere on the tour					3			scrap
recently withdrawn not on shed nor seen elsewhere					1	"Jinty"	47512	Sep-65

Review and Appraisal of 8L Aintree

The shed was on the fork of the Ford-Aintree and Ford-Kirkby goods lines. Walking time was 15 minutes from Aintree Sefton Arms Station.

Another decent shed. Nothing spectacular but good solid steam. I was especially pleased to see five "Jinties" on shed. They were fast disappearing and it was pleasing to see them in number. The LMR appeared to have given the death card to all its remaining WD 2-8-0's. Two were withdrawn with the other two being withdrawn this month.

The 46XXX Class was popular again with four on shed. 8K Bank Hall had six on shed. These "Doodle Bugs" as named by D.S. were his favourite class. 9F 2-10-0's had always been my favourite BR Standard class and there was one on shed from nearby 8H Birkenhead. Not much in the way of a highlight but the withdrawn Big Eight 48406 from 9F Heaton Mersey was a surprise lying here. *Perhaps she was destined for some scrapbreaker in the Liverpool area but surprisingly she ended up at Beighton's Sheffield scrapyard.*

21 Home Steam (62%) on shed with 13 off shed so another good percentage. The number of "Big Eights" off shed (nine as against six on shed) was not surprising as they tend to be incredibly well used.

On we go

We arrived back at Aintree Station with about ten minutes to spare which was particularly good given the heavy rain and the scanty two minutes of recovery time. As noted earlier the walk had been nearer ten minutes than the advertised 15 minutes walk. The newsagents stand was open. D.S. got the Daily Express in order to find out if the rest of the world still existed. I asked for a Daily Mail. They had none so I made do with sharing D.S.'s Daily Express. *At the time the Daily Express readily outsold the Daily Mail in copies by about two to one but nowadays the reverse is the case. Quite a turnaround.* While D.S. read the world news I pored over the Racing Section and the day's entries. This Northern Edition appeared to be almost as good as the Scottish edition and very much better than the London edition.

		Schedule	Actual	Miles
Depart	AINTREE SEFTON ARMS	08.43	08.43	0
Arrive	LIVERPOOL EXCHANGE	08.58	08.58	4¾

Four intermediate stops.

Our train left on time at 08.43. Our next visit would be to 8H Birkenhead which we would get from James Street station. I asked D.S. if he liked "Big Nines" (as we called 9F 2-10-0's). "Sure." he said. "Well" I replied "I'll be surprised if you don't see a good whack of them at 8H Birkenhead. Fifty five of them are allocated there." Quite a collection of steam of one class by any standards.

Our train arrived on time at Exchange at 08.58 after an uneventful journey. Thankfully, the heavy rain had stopped and we might have seen the last of it as the skies now began to brighten up. The next two hours would be critical. We had to visit 8H Birkenhead, 8A Edge Hill and be at Edge Hill Station for the 11.13 to Wigan North Western. An exceptionally tight timing. 8H Birkenhead would take about 45 minutes, we then had to get a bus to 8A Edge Hill, do the shed and then there was a 15 minute walk back to Edge Hill Station.

We quickly made our way through the City Centre to James Street station hoping to make the 09.06 train but this proved impossible as at James Street station you had to wait for the lift to take you down to this underground station. I was not too surprised that we missed the 09.06 although another 10 minutes would have been welcomed. At least it was an every ten minutes service to Birkenhead so we didn't have to wait too long for the next train.

		Schedule	Actual	Miles
Depart	JAMES STREET	09.16	09.16	0
Arrive	BIRKENHEAD CENTRAL	09.22	09.22	1¾

One intermediate stop.

Our Rock Ferry bound train left at 09.16 from the underground station. We had the eerie feeling of traveling under the River Mersey's wide estuary as we speeded from Liverpool in Lancashire to Birkenhead in Cheshire across the river in Cheshire.

We had to be back in time for the 09.50 underground bucket to James Street. Assuming 15 minutes to do the shed and 5 minutes there and 5 minutes back we had a recovery time of a scanty three minutes.

The directions from the LocoShed Directory were from Birkenhead Woodside Station and we were at Birkenhead Central Station. The directions from Woodside passed Central Station but they did not say whether we turned left or right into Argyle Street South. Quite an omission.

I checked with the ticket collector on where the shed was. He appeared very interested in us all laden with holdalls and we started up a nice chat. He asked me to guess how old he was. I said after reflection – 60? 82 was his reply. Certainly he was very sprightly for his age. So he had worked on for 17 years after the official retirement age of 65. Our chat continued when D.S. began to shuffle about uncomfortably and he tugged my arm "Come on" he said "Or we will miss our train back".

That was quite staggering. A golden moment to be treasured. D.S. for the first time and probably for the last time on the tour was here actually worrying about time and my precious timetable. D.S. couldn't have been feeling well. Certainly, he had been dying of thirst at 8L Aintree so I had better comply with his wishes or he may resort to violence to drag me away from my interesting conversation. I wished the ticket collector many more years of service for BR (he must have retired in pre-BR days at the time of nationalization in 1948) and we were off.

We were quickly at the shed entrance after a 5 minutes walk. Outside we noted a sign stating BEWARE, DOGS PATROL THESE GROUNDS. I did not fancy having a biting contest with Alsatians and neither did D.S. This looked like having to be an ASK shed like Aintree. I was still a little easy about Bank Hall and wondered if Birkenhead had been tipped off. All in all asking to go round would be better. We hadn't a permit as was the case for all the 8 Area sheds.

Inside we called at the office and asked for the shedmaster but we were told he was out around the shed. I said that we would go and look for him (and we would make sure that we avoided him).

We proceeded around the shed noting one 9F 2-10-0 after another and pleasingly did not see the shedmaster which was a blessing. Thus the shed was completed without incident and we quickly made our way back to Birkenhead Central to catch the 09.50 back to Liverpool.

8H BIRKENHEAD			Home shed		Built	Withdrawn	Scrap
Diesels							
BR 0-6-0 Shunter 1957							
D2375			8H		*Aug-1961*	*May-1968*	
Total		*1*					
Hudswell-Clarke 0-6-0 Shunter 1956							
D2505			8H		*Mar-1956*	*Aug-1967*	
D2507			8H		*May-1956*	*Mar-1967*	
D2509			8H		*Jun-1956*	*Aug-1967*	
Total		*3*					
Steam					*Built*	*Withdrawn*	*Scrap*
Fairburn 4MT 2-6-4T 1945 dev. of Stanier 1935							
42104			8H		*Sep-1950*	*Sep-1965*	*Jan-1966*
42121			8H		*Sep-1949*	*Jul-1966*	*Oct-1966*
42156			8H	(ex 16C Derby)	*Jun-1948*	*Feb-1966*	*May-1966*
Total		*3*					
Stanier 4MT 2-6-4T 1935 dev of Fowler 1927							
42566			8H		*Aug-1936*	*May-1965*	*Oct-1965*
42597			8H		*Nov-1936*	*Oct-1965*	*Jan-1966*
42606			8H	(ex 6H via 6A Chester)	*Dec-1936*	*Oct-1966*	*Apr-1967*
Total		*3*					
Hughes/Fowler 5MT 2-6-0 "Crab" 1926							
42753			8H		*Jun-1927*	*Aug-1965*	*Dec-1965*
42777			8H		*Aug-1927*	*Aug-1965*	*Mar-1966*
42814			8H		*Jun-1929*	*Aug-1965*	*Jan-1966*
42859	*to Barry Docks*		8H		*Mar-1930*	*Dec-1966*	*saved*
42936			8H		*Dec-1932*	*Jul-1965*	*Nov-1965*
Total		*5*					
Midland 3F "Jinty" 0-6-0T 1924 dev. of Johnson 1899 design							
47423			8H		*Dec-1926*	*Jul-1965*	*Nov-1965*
47447			8H		*Jun-1927*	*Dec-1966*	*May-1967*
47533			8H		*Apr-1928*	*Nov-1966*	*Apr-1967*
47659			8H		*Mar-1929*	*Nov-1966*	*Apr-1967*
Total		*4*					
Stanier 8F 2-8-0 "Big Eight" 1935							
48351			2E	Saltley	*May-1944*	*Jan-1968*	*Jun-1968*
48549			1A	Willesden (ex 1E)	*Mar-1945*	*Jun-1968*	*Feb-1969*
48611			8H		*May-1943*	*Dec-1964*	*Oct-1965*
Total		*3*					
BR Standard 9F 2-10-0 Brighton 1954							
92020	*Crosti boilered*		8H		*Mar-1955*	*Oct-1967*	*Aug-1968*
92023	*Crosti boilered*		8H	(ex 12A Carlisle Kingm.)	*Mar-1955*	*Nov-1967*	*Apr-1968*
92032			8H	(ex 16B via 16E Kirkby)	*Nov-1954*	*Apr-1967*	*Oct-1967*
92046			8H		*Feb-1955*	*Oct-1967*	*Aug-1968*
92047			8H		*Feb-1955*	*Nov-1967*	*Apr-1968*
92059			8H	(ex 8B Warrington)	*Oct-1955*	*Sep-1966*	*Jan-1967*
92083			8H	(ex 16B Annesley)	*May-1956*	*Feb-1967*	*Jul-1967*
92084			8H		*May-1956*	*Nov-1967*	*Mar-1968*
92086			8H	(ex 8B Warrington)	*Jun-1956*	*Nov-1967*	*Apr-1968*
92088			8H	(ex 16B via 16A Toton)	*Oct-1956*	*May-1968*	*Oct-1968*
92089			8H		*Sep-1956*	*Feb-1967*	*Jul-1967*

		Home shed		Built	Withdrawn	Scrap
BR Standard 9F 2-10-0 Brighton 1954 (continued)						
92102		8H		Aug-1956	Nov-1967	Mar-1968
92103		8H		Aug-1956	Jun-1967	Jun-1968
92107		8H		Sep-1956	Feb-1967	Jul-1967
92111		8H		Nov-1956	Oct-1967	Feb-1968
92112		8H		Nov-1956	Nov-1967	Mar-1968
92123		8H		Mar-1957	Oct-1967	Feb-1968
92131		8H	(ex 8C Speke Junction)	May-1957	Sep-1967	Feb-1968
92134	to Barry Docks	8H		May-1957	Dec-1966	saved
92157		8H		Nov-1957	Sep-1967	Jan-1968
92159		8H	(ex 9D Newton Heath)	Nov-1957	Jul-1967	Jan-1968
92162		8H	(ex 9D Newton Heath)	Dec-1957	Nov-1967	May-1968
92163		8H	(ex 8B Warrington)	Mar-1958	Nov-1967	May-1968
Total	23					

On Shed	45	Kops		40			
Steam	41	Diesels		4			
Withdrawn	4						
Home Locos	43	Home Area		0	Visitors	2	
Shed Distribution		8H	43				
		1A	1				
		2E	1				
Steam classes on view		6					
Steam Origin		LMS	18	BR		23	
Shed Highlights:-		Seeing	23	9F 2-10-0's			

Steam	Aug-50	93	Mar-59		56	Apr-65	75
Allocation						Aug-65	78
				Closed to Steam:-		Nov-67	

Home Steam	excluding withdrawn locos						
On/Off Shed	On Shed		35	Off Shed	43	% On Shed	45%
Not on Shed							
Fairbum 4MT 2-6-4T 1945						42086	1
"Crab"		42765	42782	42783	42827	42924	5
"Jinty"		47272	47324	47495	47627	47674	5
BR 9F 2-10-0 1954		92011	92014	92021	92024	92026	
		92045	92048	92057	92069	92070	
		92079	92082	92085	92090	92092	
		92094	92100	92101	92104	92105	
		92106	92108	92109	92113	92120	
		92121	92122	92127	92133	92165	
					92166	92167	32
						total	43
		saw elsewhere on the tour			16		
		saw on July 65 Preston area trip			2		
		saw on June 67 Carlisle visit			2		
		saw at Barry Docks revisited Aug 70			1		

Review and Appraisal of 8H Birkenhead

The shed was at the end of a short spur on the west side of the Chester line about ¾ mile south of Birkenhead Woodside Station. Walking time was 5 minutes from Birkenhead Central Station.

A tremendous shed for 9F 2-10-0's. Seeing 23 of them was marvellous. I was disappointed that the three members of the class which were fitted with mechanical stokers (92165-7) were not on shed. I would have loved to have clambered into the cab to have a look at the mechanical stoker. The fact that they were not on shed shows how popular the mechanical stoker must be with firemen. Our 2F Bescot guide had remarked to us on Wednesday "A smooth ride but they need a hell of a lot of coal to get them going". It appeared that the 9F

2-10-0 firemen had to work hard for their money. For one depot to have 55 of them was truly incredible. Birkenhead had received quite a few recently from the Nottingham (16 area) and the Leicester (15 area) as diesels began to push them out of these areas.

92162 was an engine with a story behind her. Four years ago a trainspotter appeared on the BBC nightly magazine programme "Tonight". In the interview with Cliff Michelmore a photograph of 92162 flashed up on the screen. This trainspotter had recently seen 92162 for the first time. One minute before seeing her he had seen every locomotive on BR apart from her. Cliff had asked him if it was not possible that he had missed an engine that he had not seen in some remote siding. "No" he replied "I know from the Ian Allan loco stock books that I have now seen them all".

The 9F 2-10-0's were very similar. All but two were of the original Brighton 1954 single chimneyed version. The two exceptions were 92020 and 92023 which were both Crosti boilered. I would have loved to see one of them in the days when their pre-heaters were working and smoke billowed out of the sides of the engines.

As I had guessed earlier in the tour the "Crab" class appeared to have been dealt the death card. Four out of the five on shed were withdrawn. I had taken quite a liking to the "Crabs" in the last year or two.

The visitors were all "Big Eights". Birkenhead had none allocated. As at 8L Aintree there was a withdrawn "Big Eight".

What did we miss? 35 Home Steam (45%) were on shed and 43 off shed including 32 9F 2-10-0's. Considering that the 9F's are extremely well utilised we can be well pleased with seeing 23 on shed. In all, Birkenhead had been well up to expectations and we left the shed well satisfied. In fact, every shed that we had visited today had been well up to expectations.

On we go

We arrived back at the station with a few minutes to spare and got the 09.50 back to Liverpool.

		Schedule	Actual	Miles
Depart	BIRKENHEAD CENTRAL	09.50	09.50	0
Arrive	JAMES STREET	09.55	09.55	1¾

One intermediate stop.

THE RAT AFFAIR EPILOGUE

We had a fast journey back and disappeared into the large lift with 15 other people and reappeared at street level. A 4B (Penny Lane) or 79C (Lee Park) bus operated from the Pier Head via Lord Street, Church Street and eventually past Tiverton Street, Edge Hill. So the buses pass James Street as well. Wonder why the LocoShed Directory didn't mention this? We soon found out as there were no bus stops in James Street. A logical explanation!

We quickly moved along to Lord Street and found our bus stop. We were in luck and only had to wait a few minutes when a 4B (Penny Lane) bus came along which we did not allow to go past us without stopping.

D.S. remarked what a quaint name was Penny Lane. *The Beatles obviously agreed too and a year later their famous ballad "Penny Lane" appeared to a rapturous reception in a double A side record with "Strawberry Fields Forever".*

We asked the conductor to drop us off at Tiverton Street. Conscious of yesterday's debacle when we were dropped off at the wrong station on the way back to 9C Reddish to make doubly sure I kept watching to the right and D.S. to the left.

We had travelled about ten minutes when D.S. shouted that we were passing Tiverton Street on the left. We got up to get off at the next stop when the conductor stopped us and said "I'm sure your stop is further on".

D.S. replied "I'm certain that we have just passed it". The conductor said "No, it's further on".

Remembering THE RAT AFFAIR yesterday and how fallible bus conductors were and that whatever D.S. lacked it was not good eyesight. The conductor was overruled and to cries of "You're wrong" from him we got off.

We walked back some yard and there was Tiverton Street on the right hand sight. Sure enough, D.S. had been right. We had avoided another RAT AFFAIR. Thankfully!

It was now 10.20 so we had more than 50 minutes before we had to get our 11.13 train to Wigan. We should do it easily. The quick bus journey had helped out our tight timing immensely.

We walked down Tiverton Street and crossed on to a cinder path which led though a tunnel to the shed. This, unfortunately, ended up at the shed office so whether we liked it or not this would be another "ask" shed.

We stopped at the office window and when we indicated that we would like a word with the shedmaster we were beckoned to come into the office. Putting our holdalls down was impressive and we hoped that it would look that way. I asked if we could take a few photographs of the engines and the shed (the new standard asking formula). The shedmaster thought that was a reasonable request and asked if we had been round before. We said we hadn't. He added that we had better be careful as it was a funny type of shed. Thanking him, we left our holdalls outside the office and we proceeded around.

The rather dispersed nature of the shed backed up the shedmaster's comments that it was a peculiar type of shed but D.S. and I proceeded round without incident.

			Home shed		Built	Withdrawn		Scrap
8A EDGE HILL								
Diesels								
BR 0-6-0 Shunter 1957								
D2373			8A		*Aug-1961*	*May-1968*		
Total		*1*						
BR 0-6-0 Shunter 1953								
D3019			8A		*Jun-1957*			
Total		*1*						
BR 0-6-0 Shunter 1953								
D3370			8A		*Aug-1957*			
D3578			8A		*Sep-1958*			
Total		*2*						
BR 0-6-0 Shunter 1955								
D4155			8A		*Dec-1962*			
Total		*1*						

			Home shed		Built	Withdrawn	Scrap
Steam							
Stanier 5MT 4-6-0 "Black Five" 1934							
44658			8B	Warrington	*May-1949*	*Nov-1967*	*Mar-1968*
44688			8A	(ex 16F Burton)	*Aug-1950*	*Sep-1966*	*Dec-1966*
44714			5D	Stoke	*Nov-1948*	*Nov-1966*	*May-1967*
44777			2E	Saltley	*Jun-1947*	*Jun-1968*	*Jan-1969*
44827			8A		*Jul-1944*	*Jul-1965*	*Dec-1965*
44837			8A	(ex 1E Bletchley)	*Sep-1944*	*Sep-1967*	*Feb-1968*
44892			10A	Carnforth	*Sep-1945*	*Apr-1967*	*Dec-1967*
44906			8A		*Oct-1945*	*Mar-1968*	*Aug-1968*
44964			8A		*Jul-1946*	*Oct-1967*	*Mar-1968*
45005			8A		*Mar-1935*	*Jan-1968*	*Aug-1968*
45015			8A		*Apr-1935*	*Sep-1967*	*Feb-1968*
45249			8A		*Sep-1936*	*Dec-1966*	*Jun-1967*
45284			8A		*Dec-1936*	*May-1968*	*Aug-1968*
45312			8A		*Feb-1937*	*Jun-1968*	*Feb-1969*
Total	*14*						
Stanier 6P5F 4-6-0 "Jubilee" 1934							
45633	"Aden"		8B	Warrington	*Nov-1934*	*Nov-1965*	*Mar-1966*
Total	*1*						
Ivatt 2MT 2-6-0 1946							
46503			8C	Speke Junction	*Nov-1952*	*May-1967*	*Nov-1967*
Total	*1*						
Midland 3F "Jinty" 0-6-0T 1924 dev. of Johnson 1899 design							
47285			8A		*Sep-1924*	*Aug-1965*	*Dec-1965*
47406			8A		*Dec-1926*	*Dec-1966*	*saved*
47415			8A		*Nov-1926*	*Apr-1966*	*May-1966*
47416			8A		*Dec-1926*	*Jul-1966*	*Oct-1966*
Total	*4*						
Stanier 8F 2-8-0 "Big Eight" 1935							
48078			8A		*Dec-1936*	*Aug-1965*	*Dec-1965*
48119			16E	Kirkby	*May-1939*	*Nov-1967*	*Apr-1968*
48129			8A		*Jan-1941*	*Mar-1966*	*Jun-1966*
48151			8A		*Sep-1942*	*Jan-1968*	*saved*
48188			8A		*Apr-1942*	*May-1966*	*Aug-1966*
48200			8A		*Jun-1942*	*Jan-1968*	*Apr-1968*
48512			8A		*Apr-1944*	*Sep-1966*	*Feb-1967*
Total	*7*						
BR Standard 5MT 4-6-0 Doncaster 1951							
73073			9H	Patricroft (ex5E)	*Dec-1954*	*Oct-1967*	*Feb-1968*
Total	*1*						
BR Standard 9F 2-10-0 Brighton 1954							
92069			8H	Birkenhead	*Dec-1955*	*May-1968*	*Oct-1968*
92070			8H	Birkenhead (ex 16B)	*Jan-1956*	*Nov-1967*	*Feb-1968*
92092			8H	Birkenhead (ex 8B)	*Dec-1956*	*Oct-1966*	*Apr-1967*
92105			8H	Birkenhead (ex 16B)	*Sep-1956*	*Jan-1967*	*May-1967*
92119			8B	Warrington	*Jan-1957*	*Sep-1967*	*Feb-1968*
92126			8B	Warrington	*Mar-1957*	*Aug-1967*	*Jan-1968*
Total	*6*						
On Shed	**39**		**Kops**		**25**		
Steam	**34**		**Diesels**		**5**		
Withdrawn	**1**						
Home Locos	**25**	**Home Area**			**9**	**Visitors**	**5**
Shed		**8A**		**25**	**8B**	**4**	**8C**	**1**
Distribution		**8H**		**4**			

8A EDGE HILL(continued)						
Not on Shed						
"Black Fives"	44717	44768	44772	44773	44838	
	44863	44864	44907	45039	45069	
	45094	45156	45187	45242	45261	
			45307	45376	45440	18
"Jinty"			47357	47487	47519	3
"Big Eights"	48152	48249	48280	48293	48308	
		48433	48513	48742	48746	9
BR 4MT 4-6-0 1951					75060	1
					total	**31**
saw elsewhere on the tour				7		
saw on Dec 64 Manchester and Crewe trip				2		
saw on July 65 Preston area trip				3		
recently withdrawn not on shed or seen elsewhere				1	"Black Five"	44769
					scrap	Jan-66

Review and Appraisal of 8A Edge Hill

The shed was in a maze of lines east of the junction of the Edge Hill-Mossley Hill and Edge Hill-Broad Green lines. Walking time was 20 minutes from Edge Hill Station.

8A Edge Hill was, at one time, one of the great LMR sheds and the flagship of the Liverpool area. As recently as 1962 Edge Hill proudly possessed 8 "Patriots", 5 "Royal Scots" 1 "Princess" and 3 "Coronations". Changed days with the withdrawal of the great passenger hauling LMR classes. However, it still remained an excellent shed.

Overall, a good shed particularly if you like "Black Fives" as I do. The shed could well be called "Blackfivesville" as 14 of the 34 steam engines on shed were "Black Fives". Three of them had come from a fair distance including one from 2E Saltley and one from 10A Carnforth.

Seeing another "Jubilee" in the shape of 45633 "Aden" was the highlight. She had not been on her home depot of 8B Warrington when we visited there last night or indeed when I visited 8B Warrington three weeks ago.

The clutch of six visiting 9F 2-10-0's was a surprise. All were from the Liverpool Area (4 from 8H Birkenhead and 2 from 8B Warrington). As with "Aden" the two 9F's had been absent on both my visits to 8B Warrington. Two other classes on shed were a surprise. The lone "Doodlebug" 46503 was allocated to 8C Speke Junction but not on shed earlier this morning. There was also a "Standard Five" 73073 from 9H Patricroft which had not been on shed there yesterday.

During my Blackpool stay last month I had noted quite a few of the engines, in particular, 48119 of 16E Kirkby in the Nottingham Area which had been strangely on the dead line at 10D Lostock Hall when I had visited there.

A little clutch of welcome "Jinties" and "Big Eights" and that was a useful shed that was.

What did we miss? 19 Home Steam (38%) were on shed with 31 off shed. A bit disappointing for a Saturday morning. This was partly explained by 27 of the missing steam being the well utilised "Black Fives" (18 locos) and "Big Eights" (9 locos).

On we go

It was now 10.50. I got out the LocoShed Directory and we made the short fifteen minute walk to Edge Hill Station and arrived there with ten minutes to spare before our 11.13 train to

Wigan. Another tight timing had been successfully made. We got on our bucket which left a few minutes later than advertised at 11.16 rather than 11.13.

Was this the most joyous journey of the week? When we reached Wigan D.S. would disappear off back to Scotland. With D.S. out of the way nothing could go wrong with my timetable or could it? Could today be the day of the perfect timetable? However, I would certainly miss D.S. (it had been good to have someone to moan at) and I certainly could not blame him for any timetable calamities once he had gone.

Our train stopped at Huyton at 11.23. This would have been a little known Lancashire town but for the fact that this was the constituency of the Labour Prime Minster, Harold Wilson who had never been one of my favourite persons.

Our 45 minutes journey was fruitful as the line was rather busy. We had hoped to pass by 8G Sutton Oak on the way which by necessity had been chopped from the timetable today. We duly looked out as directed by the Locoshed directory for it on the east side of the line at St. Helens. *This proved less than successful as it turned out later that the shed was indeed on the east side of the line but on a different line. The shed was located on a branch line between the two closed stations (Sutton Oak and Peasley Cross).*

10G Sutton Oak and D.S. tour extension versus 10H Lower Darwen

Should I have swapped 8G Sutton Oak for 10H Lower Darwen last night? The recast revised timetable was put together in haste at Irlam station last night to accommodate a lunchtime departure for D.S. and to allow as many sheds as possible to be visited on the last day.

One possibility that would have been looked into with more time would have been substituting 8G Sutton Oak for 10H Lower Darwen.

Not much difference in numbers. 8G Sutton Oak had 26 Home Steam plus one recently withdrawn. 10H Lower Darwen had 15 Home Steam plus six recently withdrawn. Advantage 8G Sutton Oak. Both involved long walking times: - 8G Sutton Oak 40 minutes and 10H Lower Darwen 45 minutes but in both cases buses were available.

D.S. would have been able to visit an extra shed – advantage 8G Sutton Oak or would D.S. fail and the next connection be lost? Let us have a look at the possibilities.

Arrive	ST.HELENS SHAW STREET	11.36
	Do 8G Sutton Oak (-35)	
Depart	ST.HELENS SHAW STREET	12.36
Arrive	WIGAN NORTH WESTERN	12.56
	Do 8F Springs Branch (Wigan)	
Depart	WIGAN WALLGATE	14.38
Arrive	BOLTON	14.55
	Do 9K Bolton (-3)	
Depart	BOLTON TRINITY STREET	15.37
Arrive	BLACKBURN	16.02
Depart	BLACKBURN	16.04
	POSSIBLE DS ITINERARY	
Depart	BLACKBURN	16.35
Arrive	PRESTON	17.00
Depart	PRESTON	17.31
Arrive	EDINBURGH CALEDONIAN	22.01

Yes swapping 8G Sutton Oak for 10H Lower Darwen could have been done and if I had persuaded D.S. to take a later train from Preston which would have necessitated a late evening arrival in Edinburgh D.S. could have added 8G Sutton Oak, 8F Springs Branch and 9K Bolton and still be available for his slave driving uncle's Sunday papers. The 8G Sutton Oak timing would not be achievable at -35 impossible with D.S. and impossible with me too. However, the Locoshed Directory mentioned four bus services (5,5A,5B and 6) from St.Helens close to the station to Baxters Lane near the shed so that could have made the timing achievable.

The original Wigan timing would not have been possible for D.S. to achieve and would prove difficult for me later today. However, this revised timetable provided for twenty five minutes extra at Wigan so 8F Wigan would have been achieved easily. The timing at 9K Bolton was a little tight but a reinvigorated D.S, might have managed it for his last shed to be visited on the LMR tour. Moreover, as discussed 8G Sutton Oak with 26 Home Steam plus one recently withdrawn would have been far more attractive to us:-.

8G SUTTON OAK				
Steam				
Ivatt 2MT 2-6-2T 1946				
	41234	41286		
Total		2		
Midland 4F 0-6-0 1924				
	44075	44086	44350	
Total		3		
Midland 3F "Jinty" 0-6-0T 1924 dev. of Johnson 1899 design				
	47298	47377	47393	47452
	47668			
Total		4		
Stanier 8F 2-8-0 "Big Eight" 1935				
	48033	48290	48326	48422
	48479	48623	48647	48727
Total		8		
BR Standard 4MT 2-6-0 Doncaster 1953				
	76076	76077	76078	76079
	76080	76081	76082	76083
	76084			
Total		9		
Grand Total		26		
Recently			*Surviving*	
Withdrawn		1	*Steam Classes*	5
Saw Elsewhere			*Saw at Barry Docks*	
on the Tour		6	*revisited Aug-70*	1
Saw Preston			*Carlisle*	
Trip July 65		1	*Sept 1958 trip*	1
Steam	*Sep-50*	39	*Mar-59*	31
Allocation	*Apr-65*	29	*Aug-65*	26
	Closed to Steam:-		*Jul-67*	

8M Southport with its small allocation was never contemplated as an option for the last day. The passenger rail connection with Preston had been closed during the past year and that left a connection to Wigan. It could have been visited as follows:-

Depart	WIGAN WALLGATE	14.25
Arrive	SOUTHPORT CHAPEL STREET	14.47
	Do 8M Southport	
Depart	SOUTHPORT CHAPEL STREET	16.00
Arrive	WIGAN WALLGATE	16.21
Depart	WIGAN WALLGATE	16.29
Arrive	BOLTON	16.46

However, ten Home Steam plus one recent withdrawn would never be enough to tempt us to take more than two hours to visit the shed.

8M SOUTHPORT					
Steam					
Fairburn 4MT 2-6-4T 1945					
	42061	**42078**	**42132**	**42675**	
Total		4			
Stanier 4MT 2-6-4T 1935 dev of Fowler 1927					
	42435	**42645**			
Total		1			
Stanier 5MT 4-6-0 "Black Five" 1934					
	44686	**44687**	**44757**	**45055**	
Total		4			
Grand Total		9			
Recently			*Surviving*		
Withdrawn		1	*Steam Classes*	3	
Saw on Manchester, Crewe					
Trip December 64		1			
Steam	*Sep-50*		30	*Mar-59*	29
Allocation	*Apr-65*		11	*Aug-65*	10
	Closed to Steam:-			*Jun-66*	

Our journey to Wigan proved to be fruitful!

EDGE HILL TO WIGAN							
			Home shed		*Built*	*Withdrawn*	*Scrap*
Steam							
Stanier 4MT 2-6-4T 1935 dev of Fowler 1927							
42462			8F	Spring's Branch	*Oct-1936*	*May-1966*	*Aug-1966*
42574			9K	Bolton	*Sep-1936*	*Oct-1967*	*May-1968*
Total	2						
Stanier 5MT 4-6-0 "Black Five" 1934							
45095			10A	Carnforth	*Apr-1935*	*Aug-1968*	*Dec-1968*
45108			8F	Spring's Branch	*May-1935*	*Dec-1965*	*Apr-1966*
45314			8F	Spring's Branch	*Feb-1937*	*Nov-1965*	*Apr-1966*
Total	3						
Ivatt 2MT 2-6-0 1946							
46419			8F	Spring's Branch	*Mar-1947*	*Sep-1966*	*Dec-1966*
Total	1						
Midland 3F "Jinty" 0-6-0T 1924 dev. of Johnson 1899 design							
47393			8G	Sutton Oak	*Nov-1926*	*Feb-1966*	*May-1966*
Total	1						
Stanier 8F 2-8-0 "Big Eight" 1935							
48108			8L	Aintree	*Feb-1939*	*Aug-1967*	*Feb-1968*
48261			8F	Springs Branch	*Feb-1942*	*Aug-1967*	*Dec-1967*
48278			8F	Springs Branch	*Jul-1942*	*Aug-1968*	*Jan-1969*
Total	3						
BR Standard 4MT 2-6-0 Doncaster 1953							
76080			8G	Sutton Oak	*Feb-1957*	*Dec-1967*	*Apr-1972*
76082			8G	Sutton Oak	*Mar-1957*	*Oct-1966*	*Apr-1967*
Total	2						
BR Standard 9F 2-10-0 Brighton 1954							
92114			12A	Carlisle Kingmoor (ex9D)	*Dec-1956*	*Jul-1967*	*Feb-1968*
Total	1						
On Journey	13		**Kops**		6		
Steam	13		**Diesels**		0		
		Home Area			10	**Visitors**	3
Shed	8F	6	8G		3	8L	1
Distribution	9K	1	10A		1	12A	1
Steam Classes	7						
Steam Origin	LMS	10	BR		3		

Review of the Journey

A very fine journey. 13 locos all steam in 43 minutes. One every three minutes or so. I was especially pleased to see three 8G Sutton Oak engines as, of course, we were no longer had time available to visit the shed. Remarkably I had seen all six of the 8F Springs Branch (Wigan) locos during my visit to the area last month.

		Schedule	Actual	Miles
Depart	EDGE HILL	11.13	11.16	0
Arrive	ST.HELENS SHAW STREET	11.36	11.36	9¼
Depart	ST.HELENS SHAW STREET	11.36	11.36	9¼
Arrive	WIGAN NORTH WESTERN	11.59	11.59	18

Nine intermediate stops.

THE HELLO GOODBYE D.S. AFFAIR

Operation goodbye D.S. was about to begin as he had to be back at his slave driving Draconian uncle's shop to sell tomorrow morning's Sunday papers.

D.S.'s timetable was as follows:-

	DS ITINERARY		
Depart	WIGAN NORTH WESTERN	12.06	
Arrive	PRESTON	12.35	
Depart	PRESTON	13.57	
Arrive	EDINBURGH CALEDONIAN	18.00	

Only a few minutes before D.S. got his first train at 12.06 which was the 09.35 Birmingham to Blackpool (a summer seaside special)! We now set about finding it. It had been due in at the same time as us (11.59). We found it already standing in the station probably having arrived a few minutes earlier.

Could D.S. have got a later train home? In fact, there was no need for D.S. to make as hasty a departure as this. He could have continued with me and visited 8F Springs Branch, 9K Bolton and 10H Lower Darwen before departing for home:-

	POSSIBLE DS ITINERARY	
Depart	BLACKBURN	16.35
Arrive	PRESTON	17.00
Depart	PRESTON	17.31
Arrive	EDINBURGH CALEDONIAN	22.01

And he would still be back home at Stoneybank, Musselburgh by 23.00 and in time for a good night's sleep and the following morning's Sunday paper sales. This would have been a risky scenario as the recovery time for 8F Wigan was minus ten minutes – probably completely impossible for D.S. 9K Bolton and 10H Lower Darwen were also tight timings particularly Lower Darwen.

However, all this was a little academic as I did not know until our tour stated that D.S. would be leaving early for home. So when I was looking for a train home for him at Irlam last night I immediately thought of the Birmingham to Edinburgh via Preston and had not thought of the 17.31 from Liverpool to Glasgow via Preston with through carriages to Edinburgh when the train split up at Carstairs in Scotland.

D.S. had performed well today and all of yesterday after his failure at 9E Trafford Park yesterday afternoon. Yes, we shall never know if we would have got round together 8F

Wigan, 9K Bolton and 10H Lower Darwen in time for D.S. to get the 16.35 from Blackburn to Preston to pick up the 17.31 Glasgow train with the Edinburgh connection. In all, it possibly would have been a bridge too far for D.S. but who knows?

D.S. was safely escorted onto the train and I reminded him to make sure that he did not get on to the Birmingham to Glasgow train at Preston which left six minutes before the Birmingham to Edinburgh train. He said that he intended to take advantage of BR's "Meals on Wheels" on the train and buy afternoon tea. He would be too late for lunch when he got on the train at Preston and too early for dinner. He expected value for money and I thought that he would get it. He would be very hungry from having had nothing to eat today and all he had had to drink was the two glasses of water to drink at Aintree! He would probably eat the tea table as well.

In fact, D.S. adorned in his army surplus, hobnailed boots took up the steward's invitation to have afternoon tea and proceeded to the dining car where he ate mounds of sandwiches, biscuits and endless cups of tea. The steward would time and time again come back with more food and sarcastically ask D.S. if he would like more sustenance and non-alcoholic beverages. Each time D.S. would stagger and astonish him by accepting his offer. I heard that the dining room staff ran out of food for D.S. that day. We know who he can blame. After a week of rigorous enforced dieting by me (we had no time to eat or drink) he was certainly trying to make up for all those lost calories. When he told me his story about his afternoon tea a few days later he added that he would make a point of having afternoon tea in future on BR as it was such great value! Looks as though BR catering is in for reduced profits if they accommodate any more people with DSian appetites.

PRESTON AREA REWIND JULY 1965

Sunday 4th July 1965

D.S. was on his way to Preston and our original schedule for the day would have had us arriving on schedule there at 13.16. By necessity D.S. would have had to remain in the station to get the 13.57 to Edinburgh while I would have done nearby 10D Lostock Hall and then got the 14.25 to Blackburn to do 10H Lower Darwen. Due to yesterday's disasters 8G Sutton Oak and 10D Lostock Hall had been chopped out of the timetable and I would not be visiting Preston Station today.

However, last month I had plenty experience of the area. On Sunday 4th July 1965 (almost five weeks ago) our family comprised of grandmother, aunt, Mum and Dad and me left Edinburgh for a week's holiday to Blackpool (that windswept west coast Lancastrian holiday resort). I had always been hoping that we would holiday in England each year but money for holidays was always a scarce commodity and rather than Scarborough (North Eastern Region) or Newquay (Western Region) we had ended up at a succession of Scottish holidays at towns starting with A:- Ayr (1958 when I started trainspotting), Aberdeen, Anstruther and Arbroath. This holiday was confirmed very much at the last minute and I had done no advance planning on the railway aspects of it. However, at last we had got to the B's and we were off early on the Sunday morning to Blackpool in England to stay on dinner, bed and breakfast terms at the Gainsborough Private Hotel on Blackpool's South Shore organized by the local SMT bus group.

The West Coast main line between Carlisle and Carnforth was closed that day with trains being diverted via Appleby. Continuous welding of rails was in operation replacing the old method of gaps between each length of rail to allow expansion. On the way down on the bus I saw near Penrith station 9F 2-10-0 92017 and just south of Penrith on the mainline at Clifton I saw Crosti boilered 92025 stationery with a trailer of rails for the continuous welding operations.

PENRITH AREA

			Home shed		Built	Withdrawn	Scrap
BR Standard 9F 2-10-0 Brighton 1954							
92017			12A	Carlisle Kingmoor	Oct-1954	Dec-1967	Apr-1968
92025	Crosti	boilered	8C	Speke Junction	Jun-1955	Nov-1967	Apr-1968
Total		4					

On Journey	2		Kops		1		
Steam	2		Diesels		0		
		Home Area			1	Visitors	1
Shed Distribution	12A	1	8C		1		
Steam Classes	1						
Steam Origin	LMS	0	BR		2		

We arrived in Blackpool in the late afternoon and after unpacking and having our evening meal I persuaded everyone that they must visit Fleetwood. While Grandmother, aunt and mum visited Fleetwood Harbour and smell the fish landing and processing operations my Dad and I would attend to more important matters namely visiting 10C Fleetwood M.P.D.. This shed was located too remotely to be considered for the main LMR tour in August but it was handily close to Blackpool as indeed were 10D Lostock Hall (near Preston) and 8M Southport.

Back to the "fish" saga. We all got onto the Fleetwood tram (Blackpool being the only place in Britain still with trams – Edinburgh's had gone around 1954) and we purchased our one shilling and seven pence (8 new pence) singles. "Going to visit, Fish Town" said the conductor as though Fleetwood was some lower form of life. The trams ran from Blackpool south shore to Fleetwood so we would be going all the way.

The shed was located one mile south of Fleetwood station at apparently beside a tram stop according to the LocoShed directory. Keeping my eyes open during the journey, after Cleveleys the shed came into view on the right. My father and I got off at the next tram stop leaving the others to get off at the terminus and enjoy Fleetwood harbour. On walking up the short distance to the shed entrance we found that we had got off one top earlier than we need have as there was a tram stop beside the entrance at Heathfield Road. We found the shed to be dead as good be on this pleasant summer Sunday evening and proceeded around it without incident the highlight for me being seeing my first BR light 2-6-2 Tanks.

10C FLEETWOOD REWIND 4th JULY 1965

			Home shed		Built	Withdrawn	Scrap
Diesels							
BR 0-4-0 Shunter Yorkshire Engine Co. 1960							
D2860			10C		Sep-1961	Dec-1970	
D2863			10C		Oct-1961	Dec-1969	
Total		2					
Steam					Built	Withdrawn	Scrap
Stanier 4MT 2-6-4T 1935 dev of Fowler 1927							
42431			10C	(ex 1A Willesden)	Mar-1936	May-1966	Aug-1966
42460			10C		Sep-1936	Aug-1965	Nov-1965
42494			10C		May-1937	May-1965	Aug-1965
Total		3					
Stanier 5MT 4-6-0 "Black Five" 1934							
44675			10C		Mar-1950	Sep-1967	Feb-1968
44729			10C		Jan-1949	Oct-1966	Feb-1967
44792			12A	Carlisle Kingmoor	Jul-1947	Sep-1967	Feb-1968
44982			10C		Sep-1946	May-1967	Nov-1967
44988			10C		Dec-1946	Dec-1967	Mar-1968
45069			8A	Edge Hill	Jan-1935	Jun-1967	Dec-1967

10C FLEETWOOD REWIND 4th JULY 1965(continued)							
			Home shed		**Built**	**Withdrawn**	**Scrap**
Stanier 5MT 4-6-0 "Black Five" 1934 (continued)							
45187			8A	Edge Hill	*Sep-1935*	*Jun-1968*	*Mar-1969*
45200			10C		*Oct-1935*	*Jul-1968*	*Dec-1968*
45206			10C		*Nov-1935*	*Aug-1968*	*Dec-1968*
45218			10C	(ex 10F Rose Grove)	*Nov-1935*	*Apr-1966*	*Jul-1966*
45274			10C		*Nov-1936*	*May-1967*	*Nov-1967*
45347			10C		*Apr-1937*	*Nov-1967*	*Feb-1968*
Total	12						
Ivatt 2MT 2-6-0 1946							
46505			2E	Saltley (ex 2L)	*Nov-1952*	*Jun-1967*	*Nov-1967*
Total	1						
Midland 3F "Jinty" 0-6-0T 1924 dev. of Johnson 1899 design							
47317			10C		*Jun-1926*	*Apr-1966*	*Jul-1966*
47577			10C		*Oct-1928*	*Mar-1965*	*Aug-1965*
47666			10C		*Apr-1929*	*Sep-1965*	*Jan-1966*
Total	3						
Stanier 8F 2-8-0 "Big Eight" 1935							
48099			10C		*Jan-1939*	*Jul-1965*	*Dec-1965*
48199			10C		*Jun-1942*	*Feb-1967*	*Jul-1967*
48319			10C		*Jan-1944*	*Jun-1968*	*Oct-1968*
48377			10C		*Dec-1944*	*Oct-1967*	*Jan-1968*
48413			10C		*Oct-1943*	*Nov-1965*	*Jan-1966*
48771			10D	Lostock Hall	*May-1946*	*Dec-1965*	*Apr-1966*
Total	6						
BR Standard 2MT 2-6-2T Derby 1953							
84010			10C		*Sep-1953*	*Dec-1965*	*Apr-1966*
84011			10C		*Sep-1953*	*Apr-1965*	*Dec-1965*
84016			10C		*Oct-1953*	*Dec-1965*	*Apr-1966*
84018			10C		*Oct-1953*	*Apr-1965*	*Jan-1966*
Total	4						
WD 8F 2-8-0 "Austerity" Riddles 1943							
90329			56A	Wakefield	*Jul-1944*	*Oct-1965*	*Dec-1965*
Total	1						
On Shed	32		**Kops**		29		
Steam	30		**Diesels**		2		
Withdrawn	5						
Home Locos	26	**Home Area**			1	**Visitors**	5
Shed		10C	26	10D		1	
Distribution:-		2E	1	8A		2	
		12A	1	56A		1	
Steam classes on view			7				
Steam Origin		LMS	25	BR		4	WD	1
Shed Highlights:-		46505	2E	**Saltley**			
		90329	56A	**Wakefield**			
Steam	**Aug-50**	33	**Mar-59**		23	**Apr-65**	25
Allocation						**Aug-65**	26
			Closed to Steam:-			**Feb-66**	
Home Steam	excluding withdrawn locos						
On/Off Shed	On Shed	19	Off Shed		7	% On Shed	73%
Not on Shed							
"Black Fives"			44940	45107	45421	45444	4
"Big Eights"			48005	48310	48338		3
						total	7
	saw on July 65 Preston area trip				3		

Review and Appraisal of 10C Fleetwood

The shed was on the west side of the line about one mile south of Fleetwood station. Walking time would have been 25 minutes from the station.

A nice shed. Plenty to interest me. The highlight for me at the time was doubtless seeing the four BR 2MT 2-6-2 Tanks which are identical to the later members of Ivatt's LMS 412XX Class. Two of them had been withdrawn several months ago so I was very lucky to see them.

Seeing the Ivatt 2-6-0 46505 on shed was very surprising. She was miles from her home depot of 2E Saltley in the Birmingham Area. A long way for a small engine utilised normally on local turns. 90329 the WD 2-8-0 from 56A Wakefield was also a surprise. There might be an explanation for her presence. She was probably here from the Pennines to haul back on Monday some fish from Fleetwood for the Yorkshire market.

The two 0-4-0 Yorkshire engine company diesel shunters were probably utilised for the tight work involved at the docks. The rest of the locos on shed were good steam particularly "Black Fives" (two from 8A Edge Hill and one from 12A Carlisle Kingmoor) together with six Big eights (one from nearby 10D Lostock Hall) and three of our beloved "Jinties" (sadly one withdrawn).

What did I miss? 19 Home Steam (62%) on shed with only 7 off shed so an excellent percentage on shed. Perhaps not too surprising as 10C Fleetwood is at the terminus of the Preston to Blackpool to Fleetwood line.

On I went

THE KOPPED A COP EPISODE

My father and I decided to walk down the main line to Fleetwood and soon we ended up at Wyre Dock Station with Fleetwood another half way down the line. Deciding that it wasn't worth the exercise to visit "Fish Town" we walked back up the line and crossed over the main line again at Fleetwood shed when who would pop up on the other side of the line but an officious railway cop who was waving and whistling at us and obviously wanted to give us a lecture on trespassing on BR metals and crossing railway lines. However, seeing a tram approaching our stop from Fleetwood we whistled back and waved goodbye and boarded the tram leaving the railway cop cursing as we made our escape. So much for these interfering bastard railway cops. At least we had given him some much needed exercise in his vain attempt to catch us before we boarded the tram.

Monday 5th July 1965

My first visit to Preston Station was on Monday 5th July 1965. It was quite a lucky visit. We had a pre-booked bus tour that day to Llangollen in North Wales. Fortunately for me the bus company had forgotten to book our seats so the trip was off. What better way to spend the day than in Preston Station which would be my main resting place during the week.

Preston had taken over from Crewe as the premier steam junction in Britain. Our friend, James H. Crowe, the Secretary of the Railway Society of Scotland used to spend the last day of the Glasgow Trades at Preston station while the less affluent (us) would spend it at the bridge at Upperby at Carlisle. At the end of the Glasgow Trades in 1964 he said that he had seen a vast number of Black Fives there on the final Saturday. This statistic showed what an excellent place for steam Preston Station promised to be.

Taking my packed lunch from the hotel I quickly dashed to Blackpool South Station and caught the next train to Preston with a few seconds to spare. I would be back for dinner at the hotel.

THE PRERECORDED SHEDMASTER AFFAIR

My day at Preston Station would be interrupted by an abortive (or almost abortive) visit to 10D Lostock Hall M.P.D. I bought a day return to Lostock Hall Station from Preston. Only one train fitted the timings otherwise there was a long wait for a return train. I left on the 16.34 train.

		Schedule	Actual	Miles
Depart	PRESTON	16.34	16.34	0
Arrive	LOSTOCK HALL	16.40	16.40	3

I had to get the 16.55 back so it would need to be a lightning visit even although the shed was practically next to the station. I got off the train at Lostock Hall Station and quickly left the station and found the shed entrance a few yards along the road to the south. I then made a very silly mistake because I was in a hurry to do the shed. I walked up the space between the running shed and the station fence and passed what I thought was a very dirty looking shedmaster's office. Normally, I would ascertain from a safe distance where the shedmaster's office was and find a route to avoid being seen from it.

I wandered about noting some engines outside the running shed in the yard and wandered up to the coaling tower to see the spectacular sight of "Britannia" 70009 "Alfred the Great" being coaled and mused what a surprise seeing her at Lostock Hall was. One of these tumultuous Lancashire rainstorms then quickly started. I thought I had better hurry up before I get completely soaked. The plan would be to quickly do the running shed sheltered from the rain and get back to the station for the 16.55.

Before I could execute my disappearing act into the shed who would hail me but a meddlesome shedmaster who looked rather unfriendly. I could tell a rat a mile away. I was up at the coaling tower at the time and made the long walk back down to his office while he was standing outside getting completely drenched and obviously in ill humour. He looked British through and through and obviously pulls the toilet flush every day for king and country still living in the days of good king George VI.

My fears were to be justified and our roving microphone picked up the following conversation.

SHEDMASTER: - "If you haven't got a permit you are trespassing."

An interesting opening but I could see some flaw in his statement. As he looked to be clearly the unsympathetic type I thought that this seemed a little late to make it an "ask" shed. I thought that I had better get some fun out of the situation and come back later in the week to do the shed.

Certainly, after a chat with the shedmaster there would now be no time to complete my shed visit as my train left in just over five minutes.

ME:- "No, you know as well as I do that the Preston Division are the only Division on BR that doesn't issue permits. Bet you've never seen a permit for Lostock Hall. How am I supposed to have a permit when they don't exist?"

The shedmaster wasn't used to such lip by railwayists here at Lostock Hall and he couldn't believe his ears. He completely ignored what I said and went on as follows.

SHEDMASTER: - "When you came in you completely ignored my office and went on as though you owned the place."

ME:- "So I do, and you do too and everyone else in Great Britain. The railways were nationalized in 1948."

He again ignored what I said and continued on with his diatribe. Perhaps he was stone deaf. That could be a logical explanation.

SHEDMASTER: - "Why didn't you call into my office when you came in?"

ME:- (I looked at the dirty door with the paint peeling off the shedmaster sign). "How did you expect me to see a dirty sign like that? Needs a good coat of paint doesn't it?"

SHEDMASTER: - "You're trespassing you must leave. You're trespassing you must leave."

ME:- Struggling to get a word in "Is this a pre-recorded message?"

SHEDMASTER: - "You're trespassing you must leave. You're trespassing you must leave."

ME:- "Are you an answering service."

SHEDMASTER: - "You're trespassing you must leave. You're trespassing you must leave."

Nothing could get through to him. Only violence might and it was extremely inadvisable to beat shedmaster's up. Psychological warfare is far better and leaves no marks. One last try.

ME:- "Can I speak to the shedmaster, please."

The answer was predictable.

SHEDMASTER: - "You're trespassing you must leave. You're trespassing you must leave."

One had to hand it to him. Nothing could disturb him. No one could accuse him of changing his tune. Or was he fused? Had my salvos attached him subconsciously leaving his numbed mind with only one statement "You're trespassing you must leave. You're trespassing you must leave."

I was about to rummage in my pocket for a two bob (10 pence) piece and drop it on the ground in front of him and say "That's for being a dutiful shedmaster" and smirk that after I had gone he would bend down and pick it up from the mud. A pleasing thought! However, I thought that was going a bit too far as the economist in me did not like parting with two bob even for a most satisfactory reason.

After another round of "You're trespassing you must leave. You're trespassing you must leave."

Suddenly out of the blue and totally unexpectedly he shouted "Get out." and after a pause "Yes, get out!"

He had finally changed his tune and he stood there all trembling and shivering as the rain lashed around him. Nothing more could be done now. I smiled, laughed and walked away to the shed exit and to the nearby Lostock Hall exit and arrived at the platform with a couple of minutes to spare. Perhaps if I had been nice and apologetic rather than aggressive to him he would have let me round the shed. I shall never know but he did appear to be one of the minority of "Hitler" I shall be obeyed shedmasters who hated all trainspotters. It was hardly important as I had run out of time to visit the shed and my aggressive stance (perhaps uncalled for) had produced some fun. Certainly I couldn't remember the last time that I had failed to get round a shed. I could easily have got round here but I didn't have the time available to wait a couple of minutes while he disappeared into his office and then enter the running shed with a less obtrusive approach. So I would have to come back later in the week to complete the job.

The journey back to Preston Station was eventful. Firstly, my train back to Preston which had arrived from Ormskirk was steam hauled back by Standard 75047 and this proved to be a steam double as my train to Lostock Hall had been hauled by "Black Five" 45094. Local Preston Area passenger services (apart from the bucket service on the Blackpool line) appeared to be still in the hands of steam. That was indeed a blessing.

		Schedule	Actual		Miles
Depart	LOSTOCK HALL	16.55	16.55		0
Arrive	PRESTON	17.03	17.03		3

The World's Woes Episode

I had met a retired railwayman waiting for my train on the station platform and we got into the same compartment. He gave me quite a lecture about the world during our eight minute journey back to Preston Station. Lecture was the word for it and I nodded agreement to everything he said in case he turned his wrath on me. Two of his way out views inflicted on me stuck in my memory.

Firstly, he blamed the change in all Britain's weather on the megaton hydrogen bombs that the U.S.A. and Russia were testing and exploding all over the place and also on the artificial fertilisers which farmers were using in their fields. He pointed out to the torrential rain outside as an example. Perhaps he was now complaining that it didn't rain all the time as I thought that Lancashire had always been famous for rain. It had certainly belted down last December when Ian "Froth" Firth and I had visited Manchester and Crewe.

Secondly, he told me what was at the root of the UK's difficulties. Wait for it! He said it was changing the clocks. He said that Britain had never been the same since the government started fiddling with the clocks to move from Greenwich Mean Time to British Summer Time at the end of March and back again at the end of October. He said that you couldn't fool the birds which didn't alter their roosting habits by an hour when the clocks changed. You can bamboozle the British people but you can't bamboozle the birds. The birds know the time. That was certainly an original diagnosis for Britain's troubles. Next time I meet a bird I'll ask it the time. I've heard of Tim the Speaking Clock but a speaking bird was plainly ridiculous.

Strangely enough his odd views had some sense. Erupting volcanoes and the smoke and spume emitted had been known to affect world weather. Certain countries consider it wrong to tamper with Greenwich Mean Time. You have the strange position in summer that you can get the ferry from Tarifa in Southern Spain thirteen miles due south to Tangier in Morocco and find that there is a two hour time difference – no meddling with Greenwich Mean Time in Morocco to Western European Summer Time! If you arrive in Morocco at what you think is 11 a.m. it's actually 9 a.m. and you see the kids going to school. It's very popular with Moroccan restaurateurs who can have two lunch sittings – one for European visitors and one for native Moroccans two hours later.

Although an odd eight minute journey with my companion it had passed pleasantly enough. I arrived back at Preston Station without being arrested on arrival by the railway cops for trespassing at 10D Lostock Hall! Hopefully the Lostock Hall shedmaster there had been completely broken by my verbal attack and would be a pussycat on my return later in the week.

		Home shed		Built	Withdrawn	Scrap
Diesels						
English Electric Type 4 1Co-Co1 1958						
D 213	"Andania"	5A	Crewe Diesel	*Jun-1959*		
D 269		1B	Camden	*Apr-1960*		
D 291		12B	Carlisle Upperby	*Sep-1960*		
D 301		1A	Willesden	*Nov-1960*		
D 336		5A	Crewe Diesel	*Mar-1961*		
D 337		1E	Bletchley (ex 5A)	*Mar-1961*		
D 339		5A	Crewe Diesel	*Apr-1961*		
Total	7					
Brush Type 4 Co-Co 1962						
D1716		81A	Old Oak Common	*Feb-1964*		
D1841		5A	Crewe Diesel	*May-1965*		
D1843		5A	Crewe Diesel	*May-1965*		
Total	3					
BR 0-4-0 Shunter Yorkshire Engine Co. 1960						
D2862		10D	Lostock Hall	*Oct-1961*	*Dec-1969*	
Total	1					
BR 0-6-0 Shunter 1953						
D3369		10D	Lostock Hall	*Jul-1957*		
Total	1					
BR 0-6-0 Shunter 1955						
D4114		10D	Lostock Hall	*Jan-1962*		
Total	1					
Metropolitan Vickers Type 2 Co-Bo 1958						
D5703		12C	Barrow	*Oct-1958*	*Dec-1967*	
D5711		12C	Barrow	*Feb-1959*	*Sep-1968*	
Total	2					
Steam				**Built**	**Withdrawn**	**Scrap**
Fairburn 4MT 2-6-4T 1945 dev. of Stanier 1935						
42287		10D	Lostock Hall (ex 1A)	*Oct-1947*	*Jul-1967*	*Jan-1968*
Total	1					
Stanier 4MT 2-6-4T 1935 dev of Fowler 1927						
42442		10D	Lostock Hall	*May-1936*	*Aug-1965*	*Nov-1965*
42460		10C	Fleetwood	*Sep-1936*	*Aug-1965*	*Nov-1965*
42611		8F	Wigan (ex 1A)	*Jan-1937*	*May-1967*	*Sep-1967*
42625		10D	Lostock Hall	*Aug-1938*	*May-1966*	*Aug-1966*
42644		9E	Trafford Park	*Nov-1938*	*Mar-1967*	*Oct-1967*
Total	5					
Stanier 5MT 4-6-0 "Black Five" 1934						
44729		10C	Fleetwood	*Jan-1949*	*Oct-1966*	*Feb-1967*
44734		9D	Newton Heath	*Feb-1949*	*Dec-1967*	*Apr-1968*
44759		5B	Crewe South	*Sep-1947*	*Nov-1967*	*Mar-1968*
44803		9D	Newton Heath	*Jun-1944*	*Jun-1968*	*Sep-1968*
44819		8B	Warrington	*Nov-1944*	*Nov-1967*	*Mar-1968*
44878		12A	Carlisle Kingmoor	*May-1945*	*Jul-1968*	*Feb-1969*
44884		12A	Carlisle Kingmoor	*Jun-1945*	*Jun-1968*	*Oct-1968*
44918		10D	Lostock Hall (ex 8F)	*Dec-1945*	*Jan-1967*	*Jul-1967*
44934		9D	Newton Heath	*Oct-1945*	*Sep-1967*	*Mar-1968*
44958		10F	Rose Grove (ex 8L)	*May-1946*	*Mar-1967*	*Aug-1967*
45062		9J	Agecroft (ex 16F)	*Dec-1934*	*Apr-1967*	*Sep-1967*
45094	*Hauled Lostock*	8A	Edge Hill	*Apr-1935*	*Feb-1967*	*Sep-1967*
45221		8B	Warrington (ex 8F)	*Nov-1935*	*Dec-1967*	*Mar-1968*
45246		9D	Newton Heath	*Sep-1936*	*Dec-1967*	*Mar-1968*
45448		5E	Nuneaton (ex 1F)	*Dec-1937*	*Aug-1967*	*Jan-1968*
Total	15					
Stanier 6P5F 4-6-0 "Jubilee" 1934						
45698	"Mars"	8K	Bank Hall	*Apr-1936*	*Nov-1965*	*Feb-1966*
Total	1					
Stanier 8F 2-8-0 "Big Eight" 1935						
48307		10D	Lostock Hall	*Nov-1943*	*Mar-1968*	*May-1968*
48373		10F	Rose Grove (ex 8H)	*Nov-1944*	*Jun-1968*	*Dec-1968*
48462		8E	Northwich	*Dec-1944*	*Dec-1966*	*Apr-1967*
48558		10F	Rose Grove (ex 8L)	*Aug-1945*	*Oct-1965*	*Mar-1966*
Total	4					

			Home shed		Built	Withdrawn	Scrap
BR Standard 7P6F 4-6-2 "Britannia" Derby 1951							
70005	"John Milton"		12A	Carlisle Kingmoor	*Apr-1951*	*Jul-1967*	*Jan-1968*
70024	"Vulcan"		5B	Crewe South (ex 5B)	*Aug-1951*	*Dec-1967*	*Apr-1968*
70048	"The Territorial Army 1908		12B	Carlisle Upperby	*Jul-1954*	*May-1967*	*Oct-1967*
Total	3						
BR Standard 4MT 4-6-0 Brighton 1951							
75033			8K	Bank Hall	*Jul-1953*	*Dec-1967*	*Jun-1968*
75047	*Hauled*	*Lostock*	8K	Bank Hall	*Oct-1953*	*Aug-1967*	*Feb-1968*
75050			8K	Bank Hall	*Nov-1956*	*Nov-1966*	*Jun-1967*
Total	3						
BR Standard 2MT 2-6-0 Doncaster 1953							
78037			10D	Lostock Hall	*Nov-1954*	*May-1967*	*Nov-1967*
78057			10D	Lostock Hall	*Sep-1956*	*May-1966*	*Aug-1966*
Total	2						
BR Standard 9F 2-10-0 Brighton 1954							
92015			12A	Carlisle Kingmoor	*Sep-1954*	*May-1967*	*Nov-1967*
92081			9D	Newton Heath	*Apr-1956*	*Feb-1966*	*Jun-1966*
92153			8C	Speke Jct. (ex16G)	*Oct-1957*	*Jan-1968*	*Jun-1968*
Total	3						

On Station	52		Kops		32		
Steam	37		Diesels		15		
		Home Area			15	Visitors	37
Shed	1A	1	1B	1		1E	1
Distribution	5A	5	5B	2		5E	1
	8A	1	8B	2		8C	1
	8E	1	8F	1		8K	4
	9D	5	9E	1		9J	1
	10D	10	10C	2		10F	3
	12A	4	12B	2		12C	2
	81A	1					
Steam Classes	9						
Steam Origin	LMS	26	BR	11			
Station Highlight:-		45698	"Mars"				

Review of Afternoon and Early Evening at Preston Station Monday 5th July 1965

Steam still reigned supreme at Preston station with 37 steam against only 15 diesels. The mainline English Electric Type 4's were on the long distance passenger expresses. Once the West Coast electrification was fully complete they too would be stripped of their express passenger services on the London and ultimately to Glasgow electrified main line. One of the English Electric Type 4's was allocated to Bletchley the present southern limit of the electrification. The Metropolitan Vickers Type 2's worked the passenger trains to Barrow. Three Brush Type 4's were also noted. 81A Old Oak Common shedded D1716 was noted at the head of the Milford Haven to Scotland oil train.

In all, nine steam classes on view with the stars being the three "Britannias" and one solitary "Jubilee" - 45698 "Mars". Good to see the clutch of 2-6-4 Tanks both Stanier and the newer Fairburn version. As expected plenty of "Black Fives" on view – no fewer than 15. The heavier freights were represented by 4 "Big Eights" and 3 9F 2-10-0's. The two 10D Lostock Hall Standard 2-6-0 2MT's (78037 and 78057) were involved on station pilot duties.

The Blackpool Sojourn continues

Tuesday and Wednesday were passed enjoying activities in the Blackpool area and it was Thursday before I next visited Preston Station again. One could hardly call it an actual visit because that day my Dad and I ventured to Southport to watch the second day of the British Open Golf Championship. We thought it would be a battle between Jack Nicklaus and

Arnold Palmer but eventually Australian Peter Thomson won. I should have allocated some time to visit 8M Southport while I was there but I for some unknown reason did not. This was an oversight as there would not be sufficient time on the main LMR Tour in August to visit out of the way 8M Southport. It did not have much of an allocation but when in Southport I should certainly have visited the engine shed. Interestingly, 8M Southport had three of the fast disappearing Caprotti valved type Black 5's and also six LMS tank engines.

The connection between Blackpool and Southport was by bus as the passenger railway service had been closed some months ago by BR. The day therefore comprised a bucket trip from Blackpool to Preston Station and then a return bus trip to Southport. Lightning visits around Preston Station were thus made by me during the morning and during the evening return.

PRESTON STATION REWIND THURSDAY 8TH JULY 1965							
			Home shed		Built	Withdrawn	Scrap
Diesels							
English Electric Type 4 1Co-Co1 1958							
D 291	*on station*	*Monday*	12B	Carlisle Upperby	*Sep-1960*		
Total	1						
BR 0-6-0 Shunter 1953							
D3369	*on station*	*Monday*	10D	Lostock Hall	*Jul-1957*		
Total	1						
Metropolitan Vickers Type 2 Co-Bo 1958							
D5714			12C	Barrow	*Mar-1959*	*Sep-1968*	
Total	1						
Steam					Built	Withdrawn	Scrap
Fairburn 4MT 2-6-4T 1945 dev. of Stanier 1935							
42287	*on station*	*Monday*	10D	Lostock Hall (ex1A)	*Oct-1947*	*Jul-1967*	*Jan-1968*
Total	1						
Stanier 4MT 2-6-4T 1935 dev of Fowler 1927							
42611	*on station*	*Monday*	8F	Wigan (ex1A)	*Jan-1937*	*May-1967*	*Sep-1967*
42625	*on station*	*Monday*	10D	Lostock Hall	*Aug-1938*	*May-1966*	*Aug-1966*
Total	2						
Stanier 5MT 4-6-0 "Black Five" 1934							
45107			10C	Fleetwood	*May-1935*	*Sep-1967*	*Oct-1968*
45209			10A	Carnforth	*Nov-1935*	*Jun-1968*	*Oct-1968*
45347	*on shed*	*Sunday*	10C	Fleetwood	*Apr-1937*	*Nov-1967*	*Feb-1968*
45390			10A	Carnforth	*Aug-1937*	*Aug-1968*	*Oct-1968*
Total	4						
Midland 3F "Jinty" 0-6-0T 1924 dev. of Johnson 1899 design							
47472			10D	Lostock Hall	*Dec-1927*	*Nov-1966*	*Apr-1967*
Total	1						
BR Standard 7P6F 4-6-2 "Britannia" Derby 1951							
70028	"Royal Star"		5B	Crewe South (ex 5A)	*Oct-1952*	*Sep-1967*	*Feb-1968*
70031	"Byron"		12B	Carlisle Upperby(ex5B)	*Nov-1952*	*Nov-1967*	*Mar-1968*
Total	2						
BR Standard 4MT 4-6-0 Brighton 1951							
75047	*hauled*	*Monday*	8K	Bank Hall	*Oct-1953*	*Aug-1967*	*Feb-1968*
75049			8K	Bank Hall	*Oct-1953*	*Oct-1966*	*Mar-1967*
Total	2						

On Station	15	Kops	7
Steam	12	Diesels	3
on Monday	6		

		Home Area			8	Visitors	7
Shed	10A	2	10C		2	10D	4
Distribution	5B	1					
	8F	1	8K		2		
	12B	2	12C		1		
Steam Classes	6						
Steam Origin	LMS	8	BR		4		
Station Highlight:-		47472	10D	Lostock Hall			

Of the 15 engines noted, six had been on the station on Monday (and I had been hauled by one of them – Standard 4MT 75047 back from Lostock Hall). One of the Black Fives (45347) had been on shed at 10C Fleetwood on Sunday evening. Two further "Britannias" were very welcome but the highlight was probably seeing 47472 from 10D Lostock Hall (one of the fast disappearing "Jinties") on station pilot duties.

Friday 9th July 1965

It was now Friday and the stars were in the correct position (Jupiter was in line with Mars) for a return visit to 10D Lostock Hall M.P.D. The rest of the day would be spent at Preston Station. I arrived at Preston station in mid-morning and would be back at our Blackpool hotel in time for dinner.

RETURN TO 10D LOSTOCK HALL
or
THE EPILOGUE OF THE PRERECORDED SHEDMASTER AFFAIR

I decided to visit the shed between 11.00 and 12.15 because Preston Station was at its quietest time of the day. After the Manchester to Barrow passenger train departed behind the usual Metropolitan Vickers Type 2 at 11.10 there would be no main-line passenger train until the 12.21 Tamworth to Windermere. However, there were no trains to and from Lostock Hall at that time so I ascertained what bus services were available and duly boarded one.

I noted on getting off the bus at the shed entrance that it had stopped raining since Monday so it doesn't rain at 10D Lostock Hall all the time! After Monday's debacle and traumatic encounter with the shedmaster I was looking forward to a more successful visit particularly as I had no time constraints. It would certainly not be an "ASK" shed and I had no intention of asking the little bugger of a shedmaster permission to go round as he had suggested then.

I noted a little bubble car flying around outside the running shed. Was this our now recovered shedmaster on patrol? No, apparently not. Although I was almost run over by it I found to my surprise that our faithful shedmaster was not at the wheel. I decided to take the long way round starting off with the dead line and then venturing into the running shed at the end furthest away from the shedmaster's office. I completed the dead line noting a dead 16E Kirkby "Big Eight" with interest. I went back to where the bubble car was still flying around (why I don't know) and safely entered the running shed.

I first went up the two lines furthest away from the office. Some cleaners had stopped work and had a cool look at this anorak clad intruder with green pen, notebook and small Tartan holdall type bag. They guessed by my furtive progress that I had not been to see the shedmaster. Probably 10D Lostock Hall is little visited, certainly not officially as Preston Division do not issue any permits to visit its sheds. Even James Crowe, the secretary of The Railway Society of Scotland had not been able to secure permits for an official society visit. I had made at least a couple of applications for permits but my letters had been ignored. I understand on very good authority that they even steam the stamps off the stamped address envelopes included with applications to visit the sheds.

After a deathly silence of a few seconds when I couldn't think of anything to say to the cleaners came an ice breaking "Hello" from one of them. This was quickly followed by some kindly words of advice "Watch out for the last line. It's beside the office." They were warning me of my old friend the prerecorded shedmaster. Doubtless, they knew that he did not take kindly to visits by railwayists or indeed any non railway worker "owner". I said "Thanks very much. I'll keep away from the office." I continued on my round of the running shed.

The running shed was about half full. Quite a number of the shed's allocation would be out working as Friday was a weekday and also it was around midday when engines had ventured out for the day but not returned for the night. I was in the middle of the running shed when my sixth sense detected my old friend the shedmaster walking up the last line locos between the last line and the shed wall. He appeared to be back to his normal stone-faced self and quite recovered from his sad, shaking, drenched state when I left him on Monday. I stood there from my vantage point in the middle of the shed watching him through the gaps in the locos. I wondered if he would be touring all the lines and come across to where I was and what I should say or do. No, it was not to be and he disappeared (probably back into his office) from my view at the top of the shed. I completed the rest of the shed without incident and in particular not seeing the shedmaster again.

10D LOSTOCK HALL REWIND FRIDAY 9th JULY 1965

			Home shed		Built	Withdrawn	Scrap
Diesels							
BR 0-4-0 Shunter Yorkshire Engine Co. 1960							
D2867			10D		*Nov-1961*	*Sep-1970*	
Total		*1*					
BR 0-6-0 Shunter 1953							
D3368			10D		*Aug-1957*		
D3581			10D		*Oct-1958*		
Total		*2*					
BR 0-6-0 Shunter 1955							
D4115			10D		*Jan-1962*		
Total		*1*					
Steam					*Built*	*Withdrawn*	*Scrap*
Fairburn 4MT 2-6-4T 1945 dev. of Stanier 1935							
42158			10D		*Jul-1948*	*Apr-1965*	*Aug-1965*
42286			10D		*Sep-1947*	*Dec-1964*	*Aug-1965*
42287			10D	(ex 1A Willesden)	*Oct-1947*	*Jul-1967*	*Jan-1968*
42296			10D		*Nov-1947*	*Jul-1965*	*Nov-1965*
42297			10D		*Dec-1947*	*May-1967*	*Sep-1967*
Total		*5*					
Stanier 4MT 2-6-4T 1935 dev of Fowler 1927							
42442			9D	Newton Heath	*May-1936*	*Aug-1965*	*Nov-1965*
42611			8F	Springs Branch(ex1A)	*Jan-1937*	*May-1967*	*Sep-1967*
Total		*2*					
Stanier 5MT 4-6-0 "Black Five" 1934							
44658			8B	Warrington	*May-1949*	*Nov-1967*	*Mar-1968*
45005			8A	Edge Hill	*Mar-1935*	*Jan-1968*	*Aug-1968*
45046			5B	Crewe South	*Oct-1934*	*Jun-1968*	*Dec-1968*
45197			10D		*Oct-1935*	*Jan-1967*	*Jul-1967*
45421			10C	Fleetwood	*Oct-1937*	*Feb-1968*	*Jun-1968*
45440			8A	Edge Hill	*Nov-1937*	*Sep-1967*	*Mar-1968*
Total		*6*					
Midland 3F "Jinty" 0-6-0T 1924 dev. of Johnson 1899 design							
47293			10D		*Oct-1924*	*Dec-1966*	*Feb-1968*
47336			10D		*Jul-1926*	*Jun-1966*	*Aug-1966*
47362			10A	Carnforth	*Aug-1926*	*Nov-1965*	*Jan-1966*
47454			10D		*Oct-1926*	*Jul-1965*	*Dec-1965*
47472	*on Preston*	*Thurs*	10D		*Dec-1927*	*Nov-1966*	*Apr-1967*
Total		*5*					
Stanier 8F 2-8-0 "Big Eight" 1935							
48119			16E	Kirkby	*May-1939*	*Nov-1967*	*Apr-1968*
48438			10D		*May-1944*	*Nov-1967*	*Jun-1968*
48470			10D		*Apr-1945*	*Nov-1967*	*Mar-1968*
48618			10D	(ex 10C Fleetwood)	*Sep-1943*	*Sep-1967*	*Mar-1968*
48668			10F	Rose Grove (ex 8H)	*May-1944*	*Dec-1966*	*Jun-1967*
48707			10D		*Jun-1944*	*Apr-1967*	*Sep-1967*
Total		*6*					

		Home shed			Built	Withdrawn	Scrap
BR Standard 7P6F 4-6-2 "Britannia" Derby 1951							
70009	"Alfred the Great"	12A	Carlisle Kingmoor		**May-1951**	**Jan-1967**	**Jun-1967**
Total	1						
BR Standard 4MT 4-6-0 Brighton 1951							
75060		8A	Edge Hill (ex8L)		**May-1957**	**Apr-1967**	**Oct-1967**
Total	1						
Riddles WD 8F 2-8-0 "Austerity" 1943							
90125		10D			**Mar-1943**	**Jul-1965**	**Nov-1965**
Total	1						

On Shed	31	**Kops**		24			
Steam	27	**Diesels**		4			
Withdrawn	5						
Home Locos	20	**Home Area**		3	**Visitors**	8	
Shed		10D	20				
Distribution:-		10A	1	10C	1	10F	1
		5B	1				
		8A	3	8B	1	8F	1
		9D	1	16E	1		
Steam classes on view	8						
Steam Origin		LMS	24	BR	2	WD	1
Shed Highlight:-		44658	8B	Warrington			

Steam	**Aug-50**	44	**Mar-59**	31	**Apr-65**	33	
Allocation					**Aug-65**	43	
				Closed to Steam:-		**Aug-68**	

Home Steam	excluding withdrawn locos						
On/Off Shed	On Shed	11	Off Shed	32	% On Shed	26%	
Not on Shed							
Fairburn 4MT 2-6-4T 1945				42081	42096	42187	3
Stanier 4MT 2-6-4T 1935		42436		42468	42546	42625	4
"Black Fives"	44816	44915		44918	45226	45346	
				45351	45402	45450	8
"Big Eights"	48002	48079		48141	48211	48307	
	48434	48328		48400	48716	48730	11
						48771	
BR 2MT 2-6-0 1953		78002	78022	78037	78040	78041	6
						78057	
						total	32

saw elsewhere on the tour				1			
saw on Dec 64 Manchester and Crewe trip				2			
saw on July 65 Preston area trip				11			
saw on June 67 Carlisle visit				2			
recently withdrawn not on shed or seen elsewhere				2	"Big Eights"	48039	48419
					scrap	Dec-65	Nov-65

Review and Appraisal of 10D Lostock Hall

The shed was at the south side of Lostock Hall Station. Walking time was less than 5 minutes from the station.

An unusual visit in that it took me almost four days to complete the visit. Both visits have been consolidated into one for convenience. Despite it being a weekday 31 engines on shed (27 steam) was a remarkable number.

Three of the five withdrawn locos were 2-6-4 Tanks. It looks as though their numbers are now in the decline. These little tanks handled quite a few of the remaining local passenger trains in the area, particularly the Preston to Wigan service.

The Carnforth "Jinty" on shed was puzzling. Admittedly Carnforth wasn't too far away but

"Jinties" didn't stray far from home so perhaps she had been loaned to 10D Lostock Hall. Six "Black Fives" were on shed and notably 44658 of 8B Warrington which was the last "Black Five" to be built. The original batch of "Black Fives" was from 45000-45499 when the LMS ran out of numbers as the 45500 series were already built Fowler 1933 "Patriots". They therefore began allocating "Black Five" numbers backwards from 45000 until finally 45658 in 1950 (sixteen years after the founder member 45000 in 1934) was the last to be built and numbered.

Another interesting loco on shed was a dead but not withdrawn "Big Eight" 48119 of 16E Kirkby which was lying on the dead line along with four 10D Lostock Hall 2-6-4 tanks and a "Jinty".

What had I missed? 11 Home Steam (26%) were on shed but 32 were off shed. 16 of the missing 32 were to be seen on the present tour etc.

PRESTON STATION REWIND FRIDAY 9TH JULY 1965						
		Home shed		Built	Withdrawn	Scrap
Diesels						
English Electric Type 4 1Co-Co1 1958						
D 255		12B	Carlisle Upperby	Jan-1960		
D 267		12B	Carlisle Upperby	Mar-1960		
D 296		5A	Crewe Diesel	Oct-1960		
D 309		1A	Willesden	Nov-1960		
D 315		1F	Rugby (ex 5A)	Jan-1961		
D 316		5A	Crewe Diesel	Jan-1961		
D 317		12B	Carlisle Upperby	Feb-1961		
D 326		1B	Camden	Dec-1960		
D 331		1E	Bletchley (ex 5A)	Feb-1961		
Total	9					
Brush Type 4 Co-Co 1962						
D1843		5A	Crewe Diesel	May-1965		
D1844		5A	Crewe Diesel	May-1965		
D1847		5A	Crewe Diesel	Jun-1965		
D1848		5A	Crewe Diesel	Jun-1965		
D1850		5A	Crewe Diesel	Jun-1965		
D1854		5A	Crewe Diesel	Jul-1965		
Total	6					
BR 0-6-0 Shunter 1953						
D3565		10D	Lostock Hall	Dec-1958		
Total	1					
Metropolitan Vickers Type 2 Co-Bo 1958						
D5710		12C	Barrow	Feb-1959	Dec-1967	
D5719		12C	Barrow	Oct-1959	Sep-1968	
Total	2					
Steam				Built	Withdrawn	Scrap
Stanier 4MT 2-6-4T 1935 dev of Fowler 1927						
42436		10D	Lostock Hall	Apr-1936	Jun-1966	Jul-1967
42468		10D	Lostock Hall (ex 9H)	Nov-1936	Sep-1965	Feb-1966
42546		10D	Lostock Hall	Jun-1936	Apr-1967	Dec-1967
Total	3					
Stanier 5MT 4-6-0 "Black Five" 1934						
44696		9D	Newton Heath (ex 9B)	Dec-1950	May-1967	Feb-1968
44715		5B	Crewe South (ex 1F)	Nov-1948	Jan-1968	Apr-1968
44733		10A	Carnforth	Feb-1949	Jun-1967	Nov-1967
44768		8A	Edge Hill	Apr-1947	Jun-1967	May-1968
44782		9J	Agecroft	Aug-1947	Dec-1966	Jul-1967
44792		12A	Carlisle Kingmoor	Jul-1947	Sep-1967	Feb-1968
44818		9D	Newton Heath	Nov-1944	Jun-1968	Dec-1968
44864		8A	Edge Hill	Jan-1945	May-1968	Jul-1968
44890		9D	Newton Heath	Aug-1945	Jun-1968	Jan-1969
44911		12A	Carlisle Kingmoor	Nov-1945	Oct-1967	Apr-1968
44958		10F	Rose Grove (ex 8L)	May-1946	Mar-1967	Aug-1967
45107	on station Thurs	10C	Fleetwood	May-1935	Sep-1967	Oct-1968
45156	"Ayrshire Yeomanry"	8A	Edge Hill	Jul-1935	Aug-1968	Dec-1968

			Home shed		Built	Withdrawn	Scrap
Stanier 5MT 4-6-0 "Black Five" 1934(continued)							
45196			10F	Rose Grove	Oct-1935	Dec-1967	Mar-1968
45221			8B	Warrington (ex 8F)	Nov-1935	Mar-1967	Mar-1968
45291			9D	Newton Heath (ex 9B)	Dec-1936	Nov-1965	Jan-1966
45342			10A	Carnforth (ex 16B)	Apr-1937	Aug-1968	Oct-1968
45390			10A	Carnforth	Aug-1937	Aug-1968	Oct-1968
45402			10D	Lostock Hall (ex 8A)	Aug-1937	Apr-1967	Oct-1967
45445			10J	Lancaster (ex 12C)	Dec-1937	Jun-1968	Oct-1968
45495			10A	Carnforth	Feb-1944	Mar-1967	Feb-1968
Total	21						
Stanier 6P5F 4-6-0 "Jubilee" 1934							
45627	"Sierra Leone"		8K	Bank Hall	Nov-1934	Sep-1966	Feb-1967
45684	"Jutland"		8K	Bank Hall	Feb-1936	Dec-1965	Mar-1966
Total	2						
Stanier 8F 2-8-0 "Big Eight" 1935							
48310			10C	Fleetwood (ex 9B)	Dec-1943	Dec-1967	May-1968
Total	1						
BR Standard 7P6F 4-6-2 "Britannia" Derby 1951							
70001	"Lord Hurcomb"		12A	Carlisle Kingmoor	Feb-1951	Aug-1966	Jan-1967
Total	1						
BR Standard 4-6-0 1951 5MT Doncaster							
73033			9H	Patricroft (ex 5E)	Aug-1953	Jan-1968	May-1968
Total	1						
BR Standard 2-6-0 1953 2MT Derby							
78022			10D	Lostock Hall	May-1954	Sep-1966	saved
Total	1						
WD 8F 2-8-0 "Austerity" Riddles 1943							
90430			56A	Wakefield	Nov-1943	Sep-1967	Apr-1968
90720			10D	Lostock Hall	Mar-1945	Jul-1965	Nov-1965
Total	2						

On Station	50		Kops		23		
Steam	32		Diesels		18		

		Home Area			16	Visitors	34	
Shed	10A	4	10C		2	10D	7	
Distribution	10F	2	10J		1			
	1A	1	1B		1	1E	1	1F
	5A	8	5B		1			
	8A	3	8B		1	8K	2	
	9D	4	9H		1	9J	1	
	12A	4	12B		2	12C	2	
	56A	1						
Steam Classes	8							
Steam Origin		LMS	27		BR	3	WD	2
Station Highlight:-		45156	"Ayrshire Yeomanry"					

Review of Preston Station Friday 9th July 1965

Like Monday another excellent day at Preston Station. Number of engines noted at 50 broadly similar to Monday's total of 52. However, diesels were up today at 18 against 15 on Monday while steam was down slightly at 32 as against 37 on Monday.

The composition of engines was again broadly similar. 2-6-4 Tank engines were down at three as against six on Monday. "Black Fives" at 21 were up on Monday's 15 and the highlight of the day was seeing one of the few named "Black Fives" 45156 "Ayrshire Yeomanry" of 8B Warrington. Sadly, her nameplate had been removed some railway worker wag had chalked as a replacement the name "Ena Sharples" of Coronation Street fame.

Over the two days I saw all 8K Bank Hall's three "Jubilees". Following 45698 "Mars" on Monday pleasingly I saw 45684 "Jutland" and 45627 "Sierra Leone" today. No other

"Jubilees" were seen. Whereas I saw four "Big Eights" on Monday I only saw one today. Britannias are becoming a great force in the North West following their transfer from other areas. On Monday I saw 70009 "Alfred the Great" at 10D Lostock Hall and also three further "Britannias" at Preston station: - 70005 "John Milton", 70024 "Vulcan" and 70048 "The Territorial Army". Yesterday I saw 70028 "Royal Star" and 70031 "Byron". They had been scarcer today with none on 10D Lostock Hall and only one 70001 "Lord Hurcomb" passing through Preston station.

Strangely no 9F 2-10-0's were seen today as against four on Monday but this was counterbalanced by seeing two 2-8-0 WD's. I had seen 90329 of 56A Wakefield on 10C Fleetwood last Sunday and here was 90430 of 56A Wakefield on probably a regular fish turn from Fleetwood.

There was one particularly busy 30 minutes:-

Time	Loco		Train
13.42	D 326		"The Royal Scot" (northbound)
13.45	D 331		"The Royal Scot" (southbound)
13.52	D 309		Birmingham to Glasgow
13.53	45627	"Sierra Leone"	
13.54	44768		
13.56	D1848		Birmingham to Edinburgh
13.57	D1854		Edinburgh to Birmingham
14.01	44696		
14.10	D 296		London to Blackpool
14.11	D 317		London to Perth
14.12	D1847		Glasgow to Birmingham

Saturday 10th July 1965 – the last day of my Blackpool sojourn

The plan for the day

Fortunately I had the whole day available for railway purposes leaving the family to do their holiday present purchases.

Visit as many M.P.D.'s in the day as possible?

I had been rather loathe to visit sheds this week for two reasons. Firstly, I would be visiting the great majority of the sheds in the area on our LMR tour in a few weeks time and secondly and most importantly there was a finance problem. It had taken me all my time to save up the necessary £20 or so for the LMR tour next month and hence spare cash was scarce. At the time I was in fourth year at school and my income comprised 10 shillings (50 new pence) per week from doing a Sunday paper round.

Visit M.P.D's that I wouldn't be doing next month?

This seemed to be a sensible idea.

Do 10C Fleetwood?

10C Fleetwood was easily the best shed that we would be missing on the LMR Tour proper as it was too remote to be included in the final timetable for Saturday next month. I had successfully visited 10C Fleetwood last Sunday evening and a further visit was not necessary.

Do 8M Southport?

A case could certainly be made for visiting 8M Southport. I slipped up by not making time to visit it when my Dad and I were in Southport on Thursday for the Open Golf championship. Moreover, 8M Southport had a relatively small allocation and my needs list there comprised (5 Fairburn Tanks, 1 Stanier Tank, and 3 Caprotti valved Black Fives). It would have needed a bus journey to Southport and back as the passenger railway service had recently closed. It could have been done by rail if I had first travelled to Wigan but that was probably slower than getting the bus from Preston alternative.

Depart	WIGAN WALLGATE	12.10
Arrive	SOUTHPORT CHAPEL STREET	12.52
	Do 8M Southport	
Depart	SOUTHPORT CHAPEL STREET	13.25
Arrive	WIGAN WALLGATE	13.46

No I had missed my chance of visiting Southport on Thursday and would not be visiting it today although I could have done it by rail from Wigan.

Do 10J Lancaster?

This visit could be undertaken by rail quite neatly. Either of the following connections would have worked fine with a total time commitment of 1½ -2 hours.

Depart	PRESTON	11.10	15.18
Arrive	LANCASTER	11.35	15.40
	Do 10J Lancaster		
Depart	LANCASTER	12.15	16.48
Arrive	PRESTON	12.45	17.15

Lancaster again had a relatively small allocation and my needs list there comprised 12 engines (two Ivatt 2-6-2 Tanks, two Black 5's, 5 Ivatt 464XX 2-6-0's and 3 "Big Eights"). The morning possibility looked enticing but I distinctly remember Ian "Froth" Firth warning me that when he went to 10J Lancaster he had found NO engines on shed. Certainly, on a Sunday there would be a good representation but it would be a total waste of time and money to go to Lancaster and see next to no engines on shed. I would be laughed at by my Musselburgh Monktonhall Model Railway Society chums when I got home. No, discretion is the better part of valour.

Do a Couple of Big Sheds?

This scenario looked interesting. Both 8F Wigan and 8B Warrington were directly south of Preston on the main line. Big sheds are always worth a couple of visits and the shed compositions would have changed by next month I'm sure. Yes that's what I'll do I'll get a day return to Wigan and from there I would get a day return to Warrington. This would be combined by my usual visit to Preston station until the Wigan train left in the afternoon.

Diary of the last day Saturday 10th July 1965

I had spent my previous visits to Preston Station on and around the overbridge at the south end of the station and also on the island platform at the south end. Monday, my brief sorties on Thursday and Friday (yesterday) had all passed almost without incident. There had been one incident on the Monday when I made a brief sortie to the north end of the station when a meddlesome cop shouted down from the overbridge.

COP: "Where do you think you're going?" He was obviously doing a "spotter" purge of the north end of the station.

ME: "I'm looking for the exit." I shouted back (I wasn't but that would do for an answer).

COP: - "Well, it's not down there it's up here then down the exit steps."

I did as he suggested and the cop watched me leave through the exit barrier – one spotter less he thought. I immediately went back to the ticket barrier and re-entered the platform area with the return half of my Blackpool to Preston rail ticket and escaped to the sanctuary of the south end of the station without further incident.

THE COPESS EPISODE

However, today Saturday was different. The railway cops were doing a trainspotting purge and were merrily throwing them off the platforms back behind the barriers. It surprised me that they could do this. Presumably, if they had a valid platform ticket they couldn't be moved. True, they expired after a period of time. If, however, they had a return half of a journey ticket then as far as I could see the cops couldn't move them off the platform. However, at the same time it was probably wise that I had chosen to go to Wigan today.

In, fact a pretty little non-male copess (pretty as female cops go) had the temerity to come up to me and have a few words with me.

COPESS: - "Trainspotting is not allowed on the platforms today."

ME:- "So. Are you a trainspotter then?"

COPESS: - "You can't stay here."

ME:- "Why?"

COPESS: - "Because trainspotters are not allowed!"(She was getting rather agitated at my answers).

ME:- "You can't stop me staying on this platform."

COPESS: "Yes, I can." (almost in a screech).

ME:-"How?"

COPESS: "Because I say you can't stay here."

ME:- "You have no right to".

COPESS: "I have every right. I could arrest you".

ME:-"What for?"

COPESS: "For trespassing."

ME: "For trespassing." I laughed out aloud. "If I'm trespassing then everyone else who is using the station is trespassing also."

COPESS: "Those other people using the station are either waiting for trains or have just got off trains."

ME: "So am I as well so I'm not trespassing."

COPESS: "Where are you going to then?"

ME: "Wigan."
COPESS: "What platform does it leave from?" (Clutching at straws).

ME: "This one!" Game, set and match, checkmate, goodbye Vienna.

At this reply the Copess made no comment but stormed off away. Bluebottle, flatfeet power and filth had been smashed again. Certainly, the cops in the Preston Area and indeed the local 10D Lostock Hall shedmaster are all right bastards. Coupled with Preston Division not issuing shed permits the area is a total disgrace. Quite a contrast with trainspotting friendly Crewe and quite shocking given that Preston Station is now the steam Mecca.

I sat down again on the parcels trailer at the south end of the station (there always seems to be a handy one at busy stations) and watched sadly as the cops continued their trainspotting clearances just like the "Highland Clearances" of last century and with about the same lack of grace. The kids here must be very obedient to obey the cops here. I received no further cop molestation or infection much to their annoyance I'm sure. Eventually some hours later I boarded my train to Wigan.

PRESTON STATION REWIND SATURDAY 10TH JULY 1965						
and on Journey to WIGAN/WARRINGTON and return						
			Home shed	Built	Withdrawn	Scrap
Diesels						
English Electric Type 4 1Co-Co1 1958						
D 292			1A	Willesden	*Sep-1960*	
D 337			1E	Bletchley (ex 5A)	*Mar-1961*	
D 373			1B	Camden	*Jan-1962*	
Total	*3*					
Brush Type 4 Co-Co 1962						
D1836			87E	Landore (ex D16)	*Apr-1965*	
D1842			5A	Crewe Diesel	*May-1965*	
D1850			5A	Crewe Diesel	*Jun-1965*	
D1854			5A	Crewe Diesel	*Jul-1965*	
Total	*4*					
BR 0-6-0 Shunter 1953						
D3374			10D	Lostock Hall	*Aug-1957*	
Total	*1*					
BR Sulzer Type 2 Bo-Bo 1958						
D5013			1F	Rugby	*Apr-1959*	
Total	*1*					
Stanier 5MT 4-6-0 "Black Five" 1934						
44684			5B	Crewe South	*Jul-1950*	*Sep-1967*	*Jan-1968*
44734			9D	Newton Heath	*Feb-1949*	*Dec-1967*	*Apr-1968*
44743	*Caprotti*	*valved*	8C	Speke Junction	*Jun-1948*	*Jan-1968*	*May-1968*
44761			5B	Crewe South	*Oct-1947*	*Apr-1968*	*Sep-1968*
44833			5B	Crewe South (ex 1A)	*Aug-1944*	*Sep-1967*	*Mar-1968*
45005			8A	Edge Hill	*Mar-1935*	*Jan-1968*	*Aug-1968*
45046			5B	Crewe South	*Oct-1934*	*Jun-1968*	*Dec-1968*
45056			5B	Crewe South	*Nov-1934*	*Aug-1967*	*Mar-1968*
45216			10F	Rose Grove	*Nov-1935*	*Feb-1966*	*Jun-1966*
45261			8A	Edge Hill	*Oct-1936*	*Oct-1967*	*Feb-1968*
45270			5D	Stoke	*Nov-1936*	*Sep-1967*	*Jan-1968*
45274	*on shed*	*Sunday*	10C	Fleetwood	*Nov-1936*	*May-1967*	*Nov-1967*
45291			9D	Newton Heath (ex 9B)	*Dec-1936*	*Nov-1965*	*Jan-1966*
45342			10A	Carnforth (ex 16B)	*Apr-1937*	*Aug-1968*	*Oct-1968*
45415			9K	Bolton	*Oct-1937*	*Oct-1967*	*Aug-1968*
45434			5B	Crewe South	*Nov-1937*	*Sep-1966*	*Dec-1966*
Total	*16*					
Ivatt 7P 4-6-0 "Patriot" rebuild of Fowler 1933						
45531	"Sir Frederick Harrison"		12A	Carlisle Kingmoor	*Apr-1933*	*Nov-1965*	*Mar-1966*
Total	*1*					
Ivatt 2MT 2-6-0 1946						
46414			8K	Bank Hall (ex 9K)	*Feb-1947*	*Jun-1966*	*Dec-1966*

Steam					Built	Withdrawn	Scrap
Total	1						
Stanier 8F 2-8-0 "Big Eight" 1935							
48618	on shed	Monday	10D	Lostock Hall (ex 10C)	Sep-1943	Sep-1967	Mar-1968
Total	1						
BR Standard 7P6F 4-6-2 "Britannia" Derby 1951							
70002	"Geoffrey Chaucer"		12A	Carlisle Kingmoor	Mar-1951	Jan-1967	Jun-1967
70018	"Flying Dutchman"		5B	Crewe South (ex 5A)	Jun-1951	Dec-1966	Jun-1967
70050	"Firth of Clyde"		5B	Crewe South (ex 5A)	Aug-1954	Aug-1966	Dec-1966
Total	3						
BR Standard 4MT 4-6-0 Brighton 1951							
75046			8K	Bank Hall	Oct-1953	Aug-1967	Feb-1968
75050	station	Monday	8K	Bank Hall	Nov-1956	Nov-1966	Jun-1967
Total	2						

On Station	33		Kops		15		
Steam	24		Diesels		9		

		Home Area			5	Visitors		28
Shed	10A	1	10C		1	10D		2
Analysis	10F	1						
	1A	1	1B		1	1E		1
	1F	1						
	5A	3	5B		8	5D		1
	8A	2	8C		1	8K		3
	9D	2	9K		1			
	12A	2						
	87E	1						
Steam Classes	6							
Steam Origin	LMS	19	BR		5			
Station Highlight:-	45531		"Sir Frederick Harrison"					

Review and Appraisal of Preston Station Saturday 10th July 1965

So the last day of my Blackpool week and my fourth sortie to Preston Station. Numbers down on the extended Monday and Friday stays but this was only a result of disappearing off to Wigan and Warrington in the afternoon.

Clearly the highlight of the day and perhaps of the week was seeing one of the few remaining "Patriots" 45531 "Sir Frederick Harrison" in fine fettle. Black 5's were particularly in evidence on this final day.

Over the four days I saw 14 steam classes (8 LMS, 5 BR and 1 WD). Seeing nine "Britannias", three "Jubilees" (all from 8K Bank Hall) and one "Patriot" was particularly pleasing. Steam totalled 105 over the four days with 56 "Black Fives" providing more than half of the total. An analysis of the four Preston station visits is interesting.

PRESTON STATION ANALYSIS
REWIND JULY 1965

	Mon 5th	Thurs 6th	Fri 9th	Sat 10th	GRAND TOTAL
Diesels					
English Electric Type 4 1Co-Co1 1958	7	1	9	3	20
Brush Type 4 Co-Co 1962	3	0	6	4	13
BR 0-4-0 Shunter Yorkshire Engine Co. 1960	1	0	0	0	1
BR Shunter 0-6-0 1953	1	1	1	1	4
BR 0-6-0 Shunter 1955	1	0	0	0	1
BR Sulzer Type 2 Bo-Bo 1958	0	0	0	1	1
Metropolitan Vickers Type 2 Co-Bo 1958	2	1	2	0	5
Total Diesels	15	3	18	9	45

| PRESTON STATION ANALYSIS | Mon | Thurs | Fri | Sat | GRAND |
REWIND JULY 1965 (continued)	5th	6th	9th	10th	TOTAL
Steam					
LMS					
Fairburn 4MT 2-6-4T 1945	1	1	0	0	2
Stanier 4MT 2-6-4T 1935	5	2	3	0	10
Stanier 5MT 4-6-0 "Black Five" 1934	15	4	21	16	56
Stanier 6P5F 4-6-0 "Jubilee" 1934	1	0	2	0	3
Ivatt 7P 4-6-0 "Patriot" rebuild of Fowler 1933	0	0	0	1	1
3F 0-6-0T 1924 "Jinty"	0	1	0	0	1
Ivatt 2MT 2-6-0 1946	0	0	0	1	1
Stanier 8F 2-8-0 "Big Eight" 1935	4	0	1	1	6
Total LMS	**26**	**8**	**27**	**19**	**80**
BR					
7P6F "Britannia" 1951 BR 4-6-2 Derby	3	2	1	3	9
BR Standard 4-6-0 1951 5MT Doncaster	0	0	1	0	1
BR Standard 4-6-0 1951 4MT Brighton	3	2	0	2	7
BR Standard 2-6-0 1953 2MT Derby	2	0	1	0	3
BR 9F 2-10-0 Brighton 1954	3	0	0	0	3
Total BR	**11**	**4**	**3**	**5**	**23**
WD					
WD 8F 2-8-0 "Austerity" Riddles 1943	0	0	2	0	2
Total Steam	**37**	**12**	**32**	**24**	**105**
GRAND TOTAL LOCOMOTIVES	**52**	**15**	**50**	**33**	**150**

Visit to 8F Springs Branch (Wigan) Saturday 10th July 1965

I arrived at Wigan North Western Station in mid afternoon and came out to find Wigan as everyone else found it - a bit dreary, grimy and unlovely. I was unimpressed with the properties I passed on my 30 minute walk to the shed. All seemed to have outside toilets. Quite a place was Wigan though it had a great Rugby League team and also a great shed in 8F Springs Branch. The Locoshed Directory advertised walking time of 30 minutes seemed unusually to be a bit stiff and it appeared to be a good one and a half miles walk.

Some local boys were having a sing song. I caught a few lines:-

"Want a sun-tan? Then come to Wigan"
"Dive into the river Douglas and come up mucky brown"

I made a silly mistake at 10D Lostock Hall on Monday when I walked straight past the shedmaster's office. I was not going to make the same mistake here and decided to make the usual attack via the shedmaster's blind side.

When Ian "Froth" Firth and I came back from Crewe by train last December we had been much impressed by 8F Springs Branch when we passed it by. It was too dark to make anything out but we could see that it was a hell of a shed. I went round apprehensively keeping an eye out for trouble but nothing terrible was forthcoming and I found the shed to be virtually choc a bloc, choked with steam like a shed of a few years ago on a Sunday. The shed was completely packed with steam engines and I doubted whether there would be much more on shed tomorrow (Sunday). In some parts of the country Saturday also is virtually a dead day for railway work when factories are closed and it appeared that the majority of Wigan's steam engines had at least Saturday afternoon and Sunday off at the weekend.

Wigan was an odd shed in that it had two dead lines. One beside the main line outside the running shed and the other one on the other side of the running shed far away from the main line.

		Home shed		Built	Withdrawn	Scrap
Diesels						
LMS 0-6-0 shunter 1939						
12014		8C	Speke Junction	*Mar-1940*	*Oct-1967*	
Total	*1*					
Steam						
Fairburn 4MT 2-6-4T 1945 dev. of Stanier 1935				*Built*	*Withdrawn*	*Scrap*
42102	*on shed*	*Aug-65* 8F		*Sep-1950*	*Dec-1966*	*Jun-1967*
42174		8F		*Oct-1948*	*Aug-1965*	*Jul-1966*
42235	*on shed*	*Aug-65* 8F		*Jul-1946*	*Jul-1967*	*Mar-1968*
42295	*on shed*	*Aug-65* 8F		*Nov-1947*	*Oct-1965*	*Jan-1966*
Total	*4*					
Fowler 4MT 2-6-4T 1927						
42343		8F	(ex 9B Stockport)	*Apr-1929*	*Oct-1965*	*Jan-1966*
42369		8F	(ex 9G Gorton)	*Sep-1929*	*May-1965*	*Aug-1965*
Total	*2*					
Stanier 4MT 2-6-4T 1935 dev of Fowler 1927						
42456	*on shed*	*Aug-65* 8F		*Aug-1936*	*Apr-1965*	*Oct-1965*
42462		8F		*Oct-1936*	*May-1966*	*Aug-1966*
42558	*on shed*	*Aug-65* 8F		*Aug-1936*	*Apr-1965*	*Sep-1965*
42565	*on shed*	*Aug-65* 8F		*Aug-1936*	*Nov-1964*	*Oct-1965*
42587	*on shed*	*Aug-65* 8F		*Oct-1936*	*Jun-1967*	*Jan-1968*
42601		8F		*Nov-1936*	*Apr-1965*	*Sep-1965*
42626		9K	Bolton	*Aug-1938*	*Jul-1965*	*Jul-1966*
42670	*on shed*	*Aug-65* 8F		*Dec-1942*	*Dec-1964*	*Nov-1965*
Total	*8*					
Stanier 5MT 2-6-0 1933						
42953	*on shed*	*Aug-65* 8F		*Dec-1933*	*Jan-1966*	*Jun-1966*
42959	*on shed*	*Aug-65* 8F		*Jan-1934*	*Dec-1965*	*Jun-1966*
42963	*on shed*	*Aug-65* 8F		*Dec-1933*	*Jul-1966*	*Jan-1967*
Total	*3*					
Midland 4F 0-6-0 1924						
44490	*on shed*	*Aug-65* 8F		*Dec-1927*	*Aug-1965*	*Dec-1965*
44500	*on shed*	*Aug-65* 8F		*Nov-1927*	*Jul-1966*	*Nov-1966*
Total	*2*					
Stanier 5MT 4-6-0 "Black Five" 1934						
44658		8B	Warrington	*May-1949*	*Nov-1967*	*Mar-1968*
44730		8B	Warrington	*Jan-1949*	*Nov-1967*	*Mar-1968*
44823	*on shed*	*Aug-65* 8F		*Dec-1944*	*Nov-1965*	*Mar-1966*
44864		8A	Edge Hill	*Jan-1945*	*May-1968*	*Jul-1968*
45005		8A	Edge Hill	*Mar-1935*	*Jan-1968*	*Aug-1968*
45024	*on shed*	*Aug-65* 8F		*Aug-1934*	*May-1967*	*Feb-1968*
45108	*on shed*	*Aug-65* 8F		*May-1935*	*Dec-1965*	*Apr-1966*
45278		8F		*Nov-1936*	*Jun-1967*	*Jan-1968*
45281	*on shed*	*Aug-65* 8F		*Nov-1936*	*Nov-1967*	*Jun-1968*
45296	*on shed*	*Aug-65* 8F		*Dec-1936*	*Feb-1968*	*May-1968*
45304		9K	Bolton	*Jan-1937*	*Aug-1967*	*Nov-1968*
45314	*on shed*	*Aug-65* 8F		*Feb-1937*	*Nov-1965*	*Apr-1966*
45385	*on shed*	*Aug-65* 8F		*Jul-1937*	*Oct-1966*	*May-1967*
45408		8F		*Sep-1937*	*Nov-1966*	*May-1967*
45425		8F		*Oct-1937*	*Oct-1967*	*Feb-1968*
45431	*on shed*	*Aug-65* 8F		*Nov-1937*	*Nov-1967*	*May-1968*
Total	*16*					
Ivatt 2MT 2-6-0 1946						
46419	*on shed*	*Aug-65* 8F		*Mar-1947*	*Sep-1966*	*Dec-1966*
46447	*on shed*	*Aug-65* 8F	*to Barry Docks*	*Mar-1950*	*Dec-1966*	*saved*
46517	*on shed*	*Aug-65* 8F		*Jan-1953*	*Dec-1966*	*Apr-1967*
Total	*3*					
Midland 3F "Jinty" 0-6-0T 1924 dev. of Johnson 1899 design						
47314	*on shed*	*Aug-65* 8F		*Jan-1929*	*Dec-1966*	*Apr-1967*
47395	*on shed*	*Aug-65* 8F		*Nov-1926*	*Apr-1965*	*Sep-1965*
47444	*on shed*	*Aug-65* 8F		*May-1927*	*Nov-1966*	*Apr-1967*
47603	*on shed*	*Aug-65* 8F		*Sep-1928*	*Nov-1966*	*Apr-1967*
47671	*on shed*	*Aug-65* 8F		*Jun-1931*	*Nov-1966*	*Apr-1967*
Total	*5*					

			Home shed		Built	Withdrawn	Scrap
Stanier 8F 2-8-0 "Big Eight" 1935							
48125			8F		Jun-1939	Oct-1967	Aug-1968
48187			8F		Apr-1942	Jan-1967	May-1967
48221			8F		Sep-1942	Feb-1967	Aug-1967
48261	on shed	Aug-65	8F	(ex 8E Northwich)	Feb-1942	Aug-1967	Dec-1967
48275	on shed	Aug-65	8F		Jun-1942	Jun-1967	Dec-1967
48278			8F		Jul-1942	Aug-1968	Jan-1969
48319	on 10C	Sunday	10C	Fleetwod	Jan-1944	Jun-1968	Oct-1968
48379			8F		Dec-1944	Mar-1967	Sep-1967
48605			8L	Aintree	Jul-1943	Aug-1966	Nov-1966
48675	on shed	Aug-65	8F		Mar-1944	Sep-1967	Jul-1968
48715	on shed	Aug-65	8F	(ex 8L Aintree)	Jul-1944	Aug-1968	Dec-1968
48716			10D	Lostock Hall (ex 8H)	Jul-1944	Aug-1965	Jan-1966
48764			8F		Feb-1946	Dec-1967	Apr-1968
Total	13						
BR Standard 4MT 2-6-0 Doncaster 1953							
76076			8G	Sutton Oak	Dec-1956	Nov-1966	Apr-1967
Total	1						
WD 8F 2-8-0 "Austerity" Riddles 1943							
90399			8F		Dec-1944	Mar-1965	Aug-1965
90561			8F		Sep-1943	Mar-1965	Aug-1965
90585			8F		Nov-1943	Apr-1965	Jul-1965
90686			8F		Nov-1944	Apr-1965	Jul-1965
Total	4						
BR Standard 9F 2-10-0 Brighton 1954							
92014			8H	Birkenhead (ex16B)	May-1954	Oct-1967	Aug-1968
92053			8B	Warrington	Sep-1955	Feb-1966	Dec-1966
92106			8H	Birkenhead	Sep-1956	Jul-1967	Dec-1967
92116	on shed	Aug-65	8B	Warrington	Dec-1956	Nov-1966	Jun-1967
Total	4						

On Shed	66		Kops		56		
Steam	65		Diesels		1		
Withdrawn	11						
on shed	Aug-65	34					
Home Locos	51	Home Area			11	Visitors	4
Shed	8F	51	8A		2	8B	5
Distribution	8C	1					
	8G	1	8H		1	8L	1
	9K	2					
	10C	1	10D		1		
Steam classes on view	14						
Steam Origin	LMS		56	BR		5 WD	4
Shed Highlight:-							
	47314	8F	Wigan	(ex Somerset and Dorset Joint Railway)			
Steam	Aug-50	57	Mar-59	67	Apr-65	60	
Allocation					Aug-65	58	
			Closed to Steam:-			Dec-67	
Home Steam	excluding withdrawn locos						
On/Off Shed	On Shed	40	Off Shed	18	% On Shed	69%	
Not on Shed							
Fowler 4MT 2-6-4T 1927						42374	1
Stanier 4MT 2-6-4T 1935				42577	42611	42647	3
Stanier 5MT 2-6-0 1933						42954	1
"Black Fives"		44873	45019	45091	45128	45140	
				45321	45372	45449	8
Ivatt 2MT 2-6-0 1946					46486	46487	2
"Jinty"						47493	1
"Big Eights"					48114	48494	2
						total	18
saw elsewhere on the tour				2			
saw on shed Aug 65				11			
saw on June 67 Carlisle visit				1			
recently withdrawn not on shed or seen elsewhere			1				scrap
			Stanier 4MT 2-6-4T 1935			42555	Aug-65

Review and Appraisal of 8F Springs Branch (Wigan) - Rewind Saturday 10th July 1965

The shed was on the east side of the mainline about one mile south of Wigan North Western Station. Walking time would have been 30 minutes from the station.

The shed was located on the east side of the main line about one mile south of Wigan North Western Station.

A hell of a good shed as I had anticipated and probably the premier steam shed south of Carlisle. Diesels at 8F Springs Branch seemed to be as rare as a Conservative Club in Wigan. There was only one token LMS 0-6-0 Diesel Shunter on shed although 8F has an allocation of about six of these 12XXX diesel shunters. It seems that either they are just left lying somewhere or do not get weekends off like their illustrious steam superiors.

There were eleven withdrawn engines on shed. (All of them had been withdrawn some months ago so I was quite lucky to see them). The downfall of the WD 2-8-0's at Wigan had been very sudden. About nine months ago Wigan had an allocation of 22 but in the next six months all of them had been withdrawn. Here the four last of those withdrawn sadly lay on the dead line. When "Froth" and I passed the shed last December we noticed what appeared to be a long line of presumably condemned WD 2-8-0's. The 2-6-4 tanks were also being severely mauled and seven lay withdrawn (one Fairburn, one Fowler, and four Stanier).

The highlight for me was seeing the little "Jinty" 47314. Seven "Jinties" were built for the Somerset and Dorset Joint Railway in 1929 and were subsequently taken back into the LMS. Of this batch (47310-47316) only two now survived 47313 at 16F Burton and our "friend" 47314 here at Wigan.

The shed was remarkably devoid of visitors. Of the 66 locos on shed 51 were 8F Wigan coded a further 11 from the 8 Liverpool area and only four other engines from nearby sheds (9K, 10C and 10D). The soon to be withdrawn 10D Lostock Hall "Big Eight" was a surprise. Perhaps she was en route to a local scrapbreaker Wigan is in the urban district of Ince in Makerfield so perhaps she is going to be cut up at the well known scrapbreakers at Ince. I had already seen "Big Eight" 48319 at her home depot of 10C Fleetwood last Sunday evening and it was good of her to come and say goodbye to me before we left for our Musselburgh home tomorrow.

A goodly number of "Black Fives" (16) and "Big Eights" (13) comprised almost half of the engines on shed. There were clutches of welcome "Jinties" and "Doodle-bugs" also. The Standard was from 8G Sutton Oak and perhaps the first engine that I had seen from there. A couple of Midland 0-6-0's (one sadly condemned) and that was the shed that was. A thundering good shed! A nice friendly shed too with no shedmaster seen so I completed my visit in comfort without incident.

Remarkably 40 (69%) of Home Steam on shed and only 18 off shed. Of the missing 18 no fewer than 13 were to be seen on my August LMR tour. Certainly the "double dip" for 8F Springs branch certainly worked.

Back to the Present – Wigan North Western Station – 12.05 Saturday 7th August 1965

Move on four weeks and I am back at Wigan again. Operation hello goodbye D.S. is in full swing. It was now 12.05 and D.S.'s train would be leaving in one minute. More to the point, 30 minutes to 8F Springs Branch (Wigan) shed, 20 minutes to do the shed and 30 minutes back to Wigan (Wallgate) station where I had to get the 13.13 to Bolton. That left me with 68 minutes against a scheduled time of 80 minutes. This amounted to a very searching recovery time of minus 12 minutes particularly when I now needed to carry my holdall everywhere. Just as well D.S. was departing the tour as I suspect that this timing would have proved impossible for him.

I paid my last respects to D.S. and he paid his. I wished him good Sunday newspapers, he wished me luck and I said that I would come round to see him tomorrow night to tell him what he had missed. With that I was off and out into unlovely Wigan. Still as big a dump as it was four weeks ago.

I moved quite quickly at first but soon the weight of my holdall began to have a telling effect and I was reduced from sort of jogging to as fast a walking pace as I could manage. To make matters worse it had now turned into a lovely, sunny day and my exertions were making me uncomfortably hot. I reached Warrington Road probably a bit quicker than I did a month ago when I had plenty of time to do the shed. However, the shed entrance was a good mile along Warrington Road at Morris Street. It felt a very long mile and I was conscious of time ticking by and had difficulty in keeping up a reasonable pace.

It was going on for 12.30 when I reached a bridge just before the shed and I looked down at a line below (not the main line) and to my surprise I saw four dead "Crabs" a short distance up the line. The sands of time said no but I had to say yes and dumped my holdall and had some heavy exercise in climbing over the embankment fence and then in slithering and scrambling down on to the line and I made my way up the thirty yards to them. The "Crabs" were obviously condemned and they must be lying here prior to being dispatched to the scrapbreakers at Ince as it in fact turned out to be the case. I made my way slowly back up the embankment rather breathless with my efforts. My little detour had been worthwhile but had unfortunately cost me a few more minutes. It was now about 12.35 and I now had only 48 minutes left before my train. Just past the overbridge was Morris Street and I entered the shed from this short cul-de-sac.

The shed itself proved to be as good if not a little better than it was four weeks ago. On going round the shed I was startled by the sight of a GWR 57XX Class Pannier Tank on the dead line beside the main line. Further research was later to show that she was withdrawn. Her home depot was 2A Tyseley in Birmingham and here she was presumably on the way to the scrapbreakers at Ince as it later turned out to be the case. As I was examining the little Pannier Tank "Britannia" 70020 "Mercury" thundered by at the head of a passenger train bound for Wigan station to the north.

The shed was completed much the same way as a month ago by going up the blind-side of the office first and I thus completed the shed without incident. This time I did notice the shedmaster in the distance at one point but thankfully he seemed unconcerned by my presence.

8F SPRINGS BRANCH (WIGAN)						
			Home shed	Built	Withdrawn	Scrap
Steam						
1933 dev. of Collett 3F 5700 0-6-0PT 1929						
9753	to Ince scrapyard		2A	Tyseley	May-1935	May-1965	Oct-1965
Total	1						
Ivatt 2MT 4MT 2-6-2T 1946						
41286			8G	Sutton Oak	Nov-1950	Nov-1966	Apr-1967
Total	1						
Fairburn 4MT 2-6-4T 1945 dev. of Stanier 1935						
42102	on shed	Jul-65	8F	(ex 1A Willesden)	Sep-1950	Dec-1966	Jun-1967
42235	on shed	Jul-65	8F		Jul-1946	Jul-1967	Mar-1968
42295	on shed	Jul-65	8F		Nov-1947	Oct-1965	Jan-1966
42297			10D	Lostock Hall	Dec-1947	May-1967	Sep-1967
Total	4						
Fowler 4MT 2-6-4T 1927						
42374			8F	(ex 9B Stockport)	Oct-1929	Sep-1965	Jan-1966
Total	1						

			Home shed		Built	Withdrawn	Scrap
Stanier 4MT 2-6-4T 1935 dev of Fowler 1927							
42456	on shed	Jul-65	8F		Aug-1936	Apr-1965	Oct-1965
42558	on shed	Jul-65	8F		Aug-1936	Apr-1965	Sep-1965
42565	on shed	Jul-65	8F		Aug-1936	Nov-1964	Oct-1965
42587	on shed	Jul-65	8F		Oct-1936	Jun-1967	Jan-1968
42611			8F	(ex1A Willesden)	Jan-1937	May-1967	Sep-1967
42647			8F		Dec-1938	May-1967	Nov-1967
42665			5D	Stoke	Aug-1942	Jun-1967	Jan-1968
42670	on shed	Jul-65	8F		Dec-1942	Dec-1964	Nov-1965
Total		8					
Hughes/Fowler 5MT 2-6-0 "Crab" 1926							
42772	to Ince scrapyard		9B	Stockport	Aug-1927	May-1965	Oct-1965
42817	to Ince scrapyard		9B	Stockport	Jul-1929	Apr-1965	Oct-1965
42932	to Ince scrapyard		9B	Stockport	Jun-1931	May-1965	Oct-1965
42941	to Ince scrapyard		9B	Stockport	Dec-1932	May-1965	Oct-1965
Total		4					
Stanier 5MT 2-6-0 1933							
42953	on shed	Jul-65	8F		Dec-1933	Jan-1966	Jun-1966
42954			8F		Dec-1933	Feb-1967	Aug-1967
42959	on shed	Jul-65	8F		Jan-1934	Dec-1965	Jun-1966
42963	on shed	Jul-65	8F		Dec-1933	Jul-1966	Jan-1967
Total		4					
Midland 4F 0-6-0 1924							
44086			8G	Sutton Oak	Nov-1925	Nov-1965	Apr-1966
44490	on shed	Jul-65	8F		Dec-1927	Aug-1965	Dec-1965
44500	on shed	Jul-65	8F		Nov-1927	Jul-1966	Nov-1966
Total		3					
Stanier 5MT 4-6-0 "Black Five" 1934							
44726			12A	Carlisle Kingmoor	May-1949	Oct-1966	May-1967
44823	on shed	Jul-65	8F		Dec-1944	Nov-1965	Mar-1966
44873			8F	(ex 2E via 5B)	Mar-1945	Nov-1967	Mar-1968
45004			6G	Llandudno Junction	Mar-1935	Sep-1966	Mar-1967
45019			8F		May-1935	May-1967	Dec-1967
45024	on shed	Jul-65	8F		Aug-1934	May-1967	Feb-1968
45108	on shed	Jul-65	8F		May-1935	Dec-1965	Apr-1966
45128			8F	(ex 5B Crewe South)	May-1935	Sep-1966	Mar-1967
45140			8F		Jun-1935	Sep-1966	Feb-1967
45202			9D	Newton Heath	Oct-1935	Jun-1968	Nov-1968
45221			8B	Warrington (ex 8F)	Nov-1935	Jun-1966	Mar-1968
45235			12A	Carlisle Kingmoor	Aug-1936	Jan-1966	Apr-1966
45281	on shed	Jul-65	8F		Nov-1936	Nov-1967	Jun-1968
45296	on shed	Jul-65	8F		Dec-1936	Feb-1968	May-1968
45314	on shed	Jul-65	8F		Feb-1937	Nov-1965	Apr-1966
45372			8F		Jun-1937	Nov-1966	May-1967
45385	on shed	Jul-65	8F		Jul-1937	Oct-1966	May-1967
45431	on shed	Jul-65	8F		Nov-1937	Nov-1967	May-1968
Total		18					
Ivatt 2MT 2-6-0 1946							
46419	on shed	Jul-65	8F		Mar-1947	Sep-1966	Dec-1966
46447	on shed	Jul-65	8F	to Barry Docks	Mar-1950	Dec-1966	saved
46517	on shed	Jul-65	8F		Jan-1953	Dec-1966	Apr-1967
Total		3					
Midland 3F "Jinty" 0-6-0T 1924 dev. of Johnson 1899 design							
47314	on shed	Jul-65	8F		Jan-1929	Dec-1966	Apr-1967
47395	on shed	Jul-65	8F		Nov-1926	Apr-1965	Sep-1965
47444	on shed	Jul-65	8F		May-1927	Nov-1966	Apr-1967
47493			8F	to Barry Docks	Feb-1928	Dec-1966	saved
47603	on shed	Jul-65	8F		Sep-1928	Nov-1966	Apr-1967
47671	on shed	Jul-65	8F		Jun-1931	Nov-1966	Apr-1967
Total		6					
Stanier 8F 2-8-0 "Big Eight" 1935							
48108			8L	Aintree	Feb-1939	Aug-1967	Feb-1968
48114			8F		Mar-1939	Apr-1967	Sep-1967
48261	on shed	Jul-65	8F		Feb-1942	Aug-1967	Dec-1967
48275	on shed	Jul-65	8F		Jun-1942	Jun-1967	Dec-1967

			Home shed		Built	Withdrawn	Scrap
Stanier 8F 2-8-0 "Big Eight" 1935 (continued)							
48410			2C	Stourbridge	Sep-1943	Aug-1968	Jan-1969
48422			8G	Sutton Oak (ex 8L)	Dec-1943	Mar-1966	Jun-1966
48494			8F		Aug-1945	Apr-1967	Sep-1967
48675	on shed	Jul-65	8F		Mar-1944	Sep-1967	Jul-1968
48715	on shed	Jul-65	8F	(ex 8L Aintree)	Jul-1944	Aug-1968	Dec-1968
Total	9						
BR Standard 7P6F 4-6-2 "Britannia" Derby 1951							
70020	"Mercury"	pass	12B	Carlisle Upp.(ex 5B)	Jul-1951	Jan-1967	Jun-1967
Total	1						
BR Standard 9F 2-10-0 Brighton 1954							
92015			12A	Carlisle Kingmoor	Sep-1954	May-1967	Nov-1967
92018			9D	Newton Heath	Oct-1954	Apr-1967	Aug-1967
92045			8H	Birkenhead	Feb-1955	Sep-1967	Feb-1968
92048			8H	Birkenhead (ex 8B)	Feb-1955	Sep-1967	Feb-1968
92071			9D	Newton Heath(ex16B)	Jan-1956	Nov-1967	Feb-1968
92116	on shed	Jul-65	8B	Warrington	Dec-1956	Nov-1966	Jun-1967
Total	6						

On Shed	69		**Kops**	22			
Steam	69		**Diesels**	0			
Withdrawn	10						
on shed	Jul-65	34					
Home Locos		45	Home Area		8	Visitors	16
Shed	8F	46	8B	2	8G		3
Analysis	8H	2	8L	1			
	2A	1	2C	1			
	5D	1	6G	1			
	9B	4	9D	3			
	10D	1	12A	3	12B	1	
Steam classes on view		14					
Steam Origin	LMS		61	BR		7 GWR	1
Shed Highlight:-	9753	2A	Tyseley	Collett 3F 5700 0-6-0PT 1933			
Steam	Aug-50	57	Mar-59	67	Apr-65	60	
Allocation					Aug-65	58	
			Closed to Steam:-		Dec-67		
Home Steam	excluding withdrawn locos						
On/Off Shed	On Shed	40	Off Shed	18	% On Shed	69%	
Not on Shed							
Fairburn 4MT 2-6-4T 1945						42174	1
Fowler 4MT 2-6-4T 1927						42343	1
Stanier 4MT 2-6-4T 1935					42462	42577	2
"Black Fives"	45091	45278		45321	45408	45425	
						45449	6
Ivatt 2MT 2-6-0 1946					46486	46487	2
"Big Eights"	48125	48187		48221	48278	48379	
						48764	6
						total	18
saw elsewhere on the tour				7			
saw on shed July 65				7			
saw on June 67 Carlisle visit				1			
recently withdrawn not on shed nor seen elsewhere				1	Stanier 4MT 2-6-4T 1935		42555
						scrap	Aug-65

Review and Appraisal of 8F Wigan

Certainly as brilliant a shed as it was four weeks ago. In fact there were 69 engines on shed (all steam compared with 66 last month (which included one diesel shunter). Remarkably there were no diesels on shed with Wigan's clutch of LMS 0-6-0 diesel shunters nowhere to be seen. 34 of the 66 steam engines were on shed four weeks ago.

The four dead "Crabs" which I saw on a line on their own before I entered the shed were most interesting. Wigan had no Crab allocation and these four presumably en route to the scrapbreakers at Ince and were all from 9B Stockport. "Froth" and I had seen two of them on 9B Stockport last December.

Fairburn 2-6-4 tank 42297 had been on 10D Lostock Hall when I visited there last month while the 5D Stoke Stanier 2-6-4 tank 42665 was a nice surprise. It was particularly good seeing the Ivatt 2-6-2 Tank 41286 and the Midland 0-6-0 44086. Both were from 8G Sutton Oak which sadly had to be chopped from today's timetable (along with 10D Lostock Hall) last night due ultimately to the Irlam Affair.

Easily the most interesting "Black Five" was 45004 of 6G Llandudno Junction. This was a particularly welcome visitor from afar. 6G Llandudno had been far too remote to consider for the LMR Tour. Another interesting visitor was "Big Eight" 48410 from 2C Stourbridge another shed which had been chopped out of the final timetable for the tour for logistical reasons introduced by the necessary visit to Barry Docks.

Quite the shed highlight and perhaps the biggest surprise of the week was seeing the condemned GWR 0-6-0 Pannier tank 9724 of 2A Tyseley – *another engine booked for the short, sad final journey to the scrapbreakers at Ince.* As last time there had been a small clutch of visiting 9F 2-10-0's and surprisingly 92116 from 8B Warrington had been on shed here on both occasions.

Changes in the withdrawn locos had been marked. Eight of the 14 condemned locos last time (the four WD 2-8-0's, the Lostock Hall "Big Eight" and three 2-6-4 tanks – one Fowler, one Stanier and one Fairburn) had disappeared presumably to the scrapbreakers. I had been particularly lucky in seeing the last four of Wigan's formerly numerous WD 2-8-0's last month. Now, not a trace of the class remained.

This time the number of visitors from outside the home area was sharply up (15 as against 4). Home Locos had dropped from 51 to 46, Home Area locos from 11 to 7, withdrawn locos from 14 to 11, "Big Eights" from 13 to 9. In contrast "Black Fives" had increased from 16 to 18.

What did I miss? As last month 40 Home Steam (69%) were on shed with 18 off shed.
Of the missing 18 seven had been seen last month and other seven would be seen on this week's tour. Remarkably little had therefore been missed and this showed the wisdom of visiting 8F twice – four weeks ago and now.

On I go (now being D.S. less)

THE IMPOSSIBLE TIMING EPISODE

Coming out of the shed I checked my watch. It was now 12.55. Disaster. I had only 18 minutes in which to catch the 13.13 train from Wigan Wallgate to Bolton. The LocoShed Directory and also my walk to the shed suggested 30 minutes I could possibly have made the timing without my heavy holdall but now with it.

There was another train for Bolton at 13.30 getting in at 13.54. That's not too bad you might think but after doing Bolton shed I had to catch the 14.27 train to Blackburn. Bolton shed required 45 minutes and only 33 minutes would be available thus giving a recovery time of minus 12 minutes. With a 30 minutes walk there and back I would have 3 minutes in which to do the shed! My only chance would be to take 10 minutes there and 10 minutes back leaving 13 minutes to do 9K Bolton or 10H Lower Darwen would also need to be given the chop.

However, was there a Plan B so I could still get the 13.13 from Wigan Wallgate and have none of these troubles? My only chance appeared to be to get a bus back and that wasn't mentioned in the LocoShed Directory. However, on the long mile walk up Warrington Road I had noted maroon and bright red buses scuttling by at regular intervals. Yes I would bus it. There wasn't anything to lose. I was in luck because some railwaymen were waiting at the nearest bus stop. I asked if any of the buses could take me near to Wallgate station. They said that the maroon buses wouldn't be much good but the bright red local buses would take me pretty close to the station.

To my annoyance a maroon bus came first but a local bright red bus came along a minute later and the railwaymen and I got on. We went upstairs. It turned out to be a cheap ride. The conductor asked if I was still at school. "Yes" I said and he said "Half fare then". Very good indeed as in the Edinburgh Area you paid full fare from 14. So good for Wigan Corporation and good for me.

I anxiously looked out of the window as the bus moved along. Finally our bus reached the Town Centre and I asked the railwaymen again if we were close to Wallgate station yet. They told me to get off at the next stop, cross the road and that I'd find the station on the left. Thanking them, I dashed off at the next stop noting that it was now 13.09 and I had only four minutes in which to get my train. My run along the street was a bit chaotic as I tried to avoid knocking over people with my heavy holdall on the busy town streets. Finally, I entered the station. It was now 13.12 and the train would be due off any second. I could see a bucket standing at the island platform. That must be it. I flashed my Railrover Ticket and asked the ticket collector if that was the train to "Bolton" which I pronounced "Bowltun".

"Where?" he queried

"Bolton." I said

"Where?" He queried again.

"Bolton." I yelled. This time the reaction was swifter. Either he had been stone deaf or my yelling had made my Scottish pronunciation sound like the Lancashire pronunciation of Bolton.

"Oh, Bolton (pronounced Bawlton) yu mean. That's the train standing there. You'd better hurry up or you'll miss it. It's due off now."

I needed no advice on the sands of time and ran down the steps to the platform and almost pulled the door of its hinges in my frantic attempts to get on to the bucket. I succeeded ad collapsed on to a seat and though what a close shave that had been.

Surprisingly, the bucket did not start up immediately as soon as I was on it. Considering that it was now fully 13.13 that was indeed a surprise. The bucket left two minutes late at 13.15 or was my watch going fast? One can never trust these Timex watches!

Another surprise was that the bucket started up and flew out in the opposite direction from what I had been expecting so rather than being at the front of the train behind the driving compartment I was at the back of the train.

A nine and a half mile journey to Bolton. You may think that this bucket journey would be a dull way to spend this afternoon with little of interest on the journey. Nothing could be further from the truth. Our little bucket would be passing the famous Ince Scrapyard where steam engines were regularly meeting their fate.

The scrapyard was just before Ince Station and I anxiously awaited it. I was to be in luck again today as our bucket passed the scrapyard at funereal pace. I thought that perhaps that this was for the still alive and kicking bucket to pay its appropriate respects but more likely due to signals or line working that day.

The sight of the forlorn and dejected unloved steam engines in the scrapyard was extremely sad and moving. Some tenders were missing and some engines were in various stages of dismemberment. What gems I saw including a "Coronation", a "Jubilee" and remarkably a "Hall".

INCE SCRAPYARD

			Last shed		Built	Withdrawn	Scrap
Steam							
Collett 3MT 2251 0-6-0 1930							
3208			ex 6F	Machynlleth	*Oct-1946*	*May-1965*	*Aug-1965*
Total		*1*					
Collett 5MT "Hall" 4900 4-6-0 1928							
4976	"Warfield Hall"		ex 81F	Oxford	*Jan-1930*	*May-1964*	*Aug-1965*
Total		*1*					
Fairburn 4MT 2-6-4T 1945 dev. of Stanier 1935							
42155			ex 9K	Bolton	*Jun-1948*	*May-1965*	*Aug-1965*
Total		*1*					
Fowler 4MT 2-6-4T 1927							
42369			ex 8F	Springs Branch (Wigan)	*Sep-1929*	*May-1965*	*Aug-1965*
Total		*1*					
Hughes/Fowler 5MT 2-6-0 "Crab" 1926							
42751			ex 9G	Gorton	*Jun-1927*	*Apr-1965*	*Aug-1965*
42778			ex 9G	Gorton	*Sep-1927*	*Apr-1965*	*Oct-1965*
42901			ex 9G	Gorton	*Aug-1930*	*May-1965*	*Aug-1965*
42904			ex 9G	Gorton	*Sep-1930*	*May-1965*	*Aug-1965*
42937			ex 8H	Birkenhead	*Dec-1932*	*May-1965*	*Aug-1965*
Total		*5*					
Stanier 5MT 2-6-0 1933							
42952			ex 8F	Springs Branch (Wigan)	*Dec-1933*	*Sep-1964*	*Oct-1965*
Total		*1*					
Stanier 6P5F 4-6-0 "Jubilee" 1934							
45623	"Palestine"		ex 9D	Newton Heath	*Oct-1934*	*Aug-1964*	*Sep-1965*
Total		*1*					
Stanier 8P 4-6-2 "Coronation" 1937							
46243	"City of Lancaster"		ex 8A	Edge Hill	*Jun-1940*	*Oct-1964*	*Aug-1965*
Total		*1*					
Thompson 5MT 4-6-0 B1 1942							
61144			ex 40B	Immingham	*Apr-1947*	*Apr-1964*	*Oct-1965*
Total		*1*					
WD 8F 2-8-0 "Austerity" Riddles 1953							
90245			ex 8L	Aintree	*Jun-1943*	*May-1964*	*Aug-1965*
90667			ex 8F	Springs Branch (Wigan)	*Oct-1944*	*May-1964*	*Sep-1965*
Total		*2*					

On Yard		15	Kops		12		
Steam		15	Diesels		0		
withdrawn		15					
Shed	ex 6F		1 ex 81F		1		
Analysis	ex 8A		1 ex 8F		3 ex 8H		1
	ex 8L		1				
	ex 9D		1 ex 9G		4 ex 9K		1
	ex 40B		1				
Steam classes on view		10					
Steam Origin	GWR	2	LMS		10	LNER	1
	WD	2					
Yard		1 Collett 5MT "Hall" 4900 4-6-0 1928			4976	"Warfield Hall"	
Highlights		2 Stanier 8P 4-6-2 "Coronation" 1937			46243	"City of Lancaster"	
		3 Collett 3MT 2251 0-6-0 1930			3208		
		4 Stanier 6P5F 4-6-0 "Jubilee" 1934			45623	"Palestine"	
		5 Thompson 5MT 4-6-0 B1 1942			61144		

Review and Appraisal of Ince Scrapyard

A terrific catalogue of engines. A remarkable 15 steam engines were seen including "Coronation" 46243 "City of Lancaster" minus tender and "Jubilee" 45623 "Palestine". Surprisingly there were two ex GWR locos in the yard – a long way to go to the scrapbreakers. They was a Collett 2251 0-6-0 3208 and perhaps the highlight of the whole yard a Collett first series "Hall" – 4976 "Warfield Hall". I had seen Fowler Tank 42369 withdrawn at Wigan shed four weeks ago and since then she had made her final sad journey here to be cut up. A big surprise also was seeing a Thompson LNER B1 – 61144.

The other 10 engines in the yard were less stunning but most welcome (1 Fairburn Tank, 1 Stanier Tank, 5 "Crabs", 1 Stanier so called "Funny Crab" and 2 WD 2-8-0's). Over 300 steam engines met their end at Ince over the years.

What completely surprised me was that eight of the engines had been withdrawn months ago. This led me to believe that the cut up rate here must be very slow and that obviously there must be a few other scrapyards in Lancashire to accommodate the rate of withdrawals. All in all Ince scrapyard was a stunning sight on this last day of the tour.

On to Bolton

		Schedule	Actual	Miles
Depart	WIGAN WALLGATE	13.13	13.15	0
Arrive	BOLTON	13.37	13.41	9½

Four intermediate stops (including Ince).

Other than Ince Scrapyard the journey was completely uneventful, no other locos were seen and the bucket eventually arrived four minute late at Bolton station. Bolton as stations go was larger than expected and perhaps bigger than it needs to be nowadays. Another tight timing was ahead. I needed to be back for the 14.27 to Blackburn and that left me now 46 minutes against a scheduled visit time of 45 minutes so I had a recovery time of only one minute and therefore there could be no slacking.

I climbed up the steps from the platform, went along the overbridge and left the station. It was still an excellent sunny afternoon. Bolton was quite different in this light that one gets of a cotton town or rather a declining cotton town the industry having collapsed since World War 1. The normal view of west coast Lancashire and Bolton is probably a wet one. A friend of mine lived in nearby Bury for several years. He lived in a street named Sunny Bank. The misnomer of the century he told me. Rained all the time, he wailed, hardly ever saw the sun. Well, it appears that I can consider myself lucky to be in a sunbathed Bolton today.

As I made the 15 minutes journey to the shed I remembered that Bolton was good for something else other than its rain, its engine shed and its decent football club. Then I remembered. An English girl called Kathleen Sims had been in my class at Campie Primary School and eventually she had relocated back to England – to Bolton. She had been probably the best looker in the class and I was sure that she would have developed out nicely in the meantime. I was savouring the thought of looking out for here in Bolton when my thoughts were interrupted by a crashing noise as my holdall collapsed to the ground. One of the straps had suddenly broken. Carrying a holdall by two straps is heavy enough but carrying it by one strap would be even harder. Just as well it was the last day of the tour. It would have been a lot worse if it had broken early in the tour. Better if it hadn't broken at all though. I solved the problem somewhat by looping the loose broken strap through the good strap and this method was certainly better than carrying it by one strap alone which would probably cause the other strap to snap with the strain.

All this thinking about Kathleen Sims and the collapse of one strap of the holdall slowed me up somewhat and I took the full advertised LocoShed Directory walking time of 15 minutes to get to the shed entrance. I had a permit for here as 9K Bolton was part of Manchester division but I had no time to visit the office. I hurried round as best I could completely without incident. Bolton was another very full depot and nothing much stirred in the afternoon sunlight.

		Home shed		Built	Withdrawn	Scrap
9K BOLTON						
BR 0-6-0 Shunter 1953						
D3589		9D	Newton Heath	Dec-1958		
Total	1					
Steam				**Built**	**Withdrawn**	**Scrap**
Fairburn 4MT 2-6-4T 1945 dev. of Stanier 1935						
42133		9K	(ex 9F Heaton Mersey)	Jan-1950	Apr-1967	Oct-1967
42159		9K	(ex 9F Heaton Mersey)	Jul-1948	Jul-1966	Oct-1966
42183		9K		Jan-1949	Sep-1966	Feb-1967
42240		9K		Sep-1946	Apr-1966	Jul-1966
42249		9K		Oct-1946	Jul-1966	Nov-1966
42676		9K		Apr-1945	Jun-1966	Aug-1966
Total	6					
Fowler 4MT 2-6-4T 1927						
42368		9K		Sep-1929	Jun-1965	Nov-1965
Total	1					
Stanier 4MT 2-6-4T 1935						
42426		9K		Feb-1936	Dec-1965	Mar-1966
42484		9K		Mar-1937	Jan-1966	May-1966
42626		9K		Aug-1938	Jul-1965	Jul-1966
Total	3					
Hughes/Fowler 5MT 2-6-0 "Crab" 1926						
42710		9B	Stockport	Feb-1927	Aug-1965	Dec-1965
Total	1					
Midland 4F 0-6-0 1924						
44311		9K		Oct-1926	Jul-1966	Oct-1966
Total	1					
Stanier 5MT 4-6-0 "Black Five" 1934						
44664		9K		Jun-1949	May-1968	Sep-1968
44737		9K		Mar-1949	Jan-1967	Jul-1967
44806		8C	Speke Junction	Jul-1944	Aug-1968	saved
44927		9K	.	Feb-1946	Sep-1967	Feb-1968
45059		8C	Speke Junction	Dec-1934	Jul-1967	Jan-1968
45104		9K		May-1935	Jun-1968	Feb-1969
45110		9K	(ex 5C Stafford)	Jun-1935	Aug-1968	saved
45252		9K		Sep-1936	Mar-1966	Jun-1966
45304		9K		Jan-1937	Aug-1967	Nov-1968
45377		9K		Jun-1937	Dec-1967	Apr-1968
45378		9K		Jul-1937	Mar-1965	Dec-1965
45381		9K		Jul-1937	May-1968	Aug-1968
45409		9K		Sep-1937	Aug-1967	Dec-1967
45411		9K		Sep-1937	Jun-1968	Sep-1968
45415		9K		Oct-1937	Oct-1967	Aug-1968
Total	15					
Ivatt 4MT 2-6-0 1947						
46416		9K		Feb-1947	Apr-1966	Jul-1966
46436		9K		Jan-1950	May-1967	Oct-1967
46504		9K		Nov-1952	Oct-1966	Feb-1967
Total	3					
Johnson Midland 3F 0-6-0T 1899						
47202		ex HW	Horwich Works	Dec-1899	Dec-1966	Apr-1967
Total	1					

		Home shed		Built	Withdrawn	Scrap
Stanier 8F 2-8-0 "Big Eight" 1935						
48011		9K	(via 1G/ 1A/ 9L Buxton)	*Oct-1935*	*Jun-1967*	*Nov-1967*
48026		9J	Agecroft	*Apr-1937*	*Jun-1968*	*Sep-1968*
48145		16G	Westhouses	*Apr-1942*	*Jun-1965*	*Sep-1965*
48295		9K		*Dec-1941*	*Sep-1965*	*Dec-1965*
48333		9K		*Nov-1943*	*Jul-1965*	*Dec-1965*
48371		9K		*Oct-1944*	*Oct-1967*	*Jun-1968*
48469		9K		*Mar-1945*	*Dec-1967*	*Mar-1968*
48547		9K		*Mar-1945*	*Mar-1967*	*Sep-1967*
48652		9K		*Nov-1943*	*Jun-1968*	*Oct-1968*
48702		9K		*May-1944*	*May-1968*	*Aug-1968*
48740		9K		*Jan-1946*	*Mar-1968*	*May-1968*
48773		9K		*Jun-1940*	*Aug-1968*	*saved*
Total	*12*					
BR Standard 2MT 2-6-2T Derby 1953						
84019		9K		*Oct-1953*	*Dec-1965*	*Mar-1966*
84025		9K		*Apr-1957*	*Dec-1965*	*Mar-1966*
Total	*2*					

On Shed	**46**		**Kops**	**35**		
Steam	**45**		**Diesels**	**1**		
Withdrawn	**5**					

Home Locos		**39**	**Home Area**		**3**	**Visitors**	**4**
Shed	**9K**		**40**	**9B**	**1**	**9D**	**1**
Distribution	**9J**		**1**				
	8C		**2**	**16G**	**1**	**exHW**	**1**
Steam classes on view		**10**					
Steam Origin		**LMS**		**43**	**BR**	**2**	
Shed Highlight:-		**47202**		**exHW**	**Horwich Works**		

Steam	**Aug-50**	**47**	**Mar-59**		**36**	**Apr-65**	**57**
Allocation						**Aug-65**	**54**
			Closed to Steam:-			**Jul-68**	

Home Steam	excluding withdrawn locos						
On/Off Shed	On Shed		**35**	Off Shed		19 % On Shed	65%
Not on Shed							
Stanier 4MT 2-6-4T 1935						42555	42574	2
"Black Fives"		44728	44736		44893	44947	45239	
					45260	45290	45318	8
Ivatt 2MT 2-6-0 1946						46417	46506	2
"Jinty"						47388	47520	2
"Big Eights"		48106	48166		48205	48511	48523	5
							total	19
		saw elsewhere on the tour				4		

Review and Appraisal of 9K Bolton

The shed was on the west side of the Bolton Trinity Street-Clifton Junction line. Walking time was 15 minutes from the station.

Another very fine steam shed. A very high proportion of locos (39/46) were home locos. However, there were two surprises in the six visitors. The highlight was 47202 the little original 1899 "Jinty". According to my LocoShed book she was still allocated to nearby Horwich Works but that could hardly be correct as the works closed a year or two ago. Probably she had been transferred to 9K Bolton and I had missed the transfer information in "Modern Railways" or the transfer information had not been reported in or to "Modern Railways". The other notable visitor was "Big Eight" 48145 from 16G Westhouses near Alfreton, Derbyshire. As she was withdrawn she was probably en route to some scrapbreaker in the area – *strangely she ended up being consigned for scrap the following month to Beighton's of Sheffield – hardly nearby.*

There was also a soon to be withdrawn or withdrawn 9B Stockport "Crab" on shed in the shape of 42710. I had seen four more condemned 9B Stockport "Crabs" outside 8F Springs Branch (Wigan) earlier today all to be destined for nearby Ince scrapyard. *However, 42710 ended up being cut up after a long journey to the scrapyard at Birds Morriston, Swansea in South Wales.*

The rest of the shed was fairly predictable with the solitary Fowler 2-6-4 tank (unfortunately withdrawn), the solitary Midland 0-6-0 and the two Standard BR 2MT 2-6-2 tanks being particularly pleasing. Fifteen "Black Fives" were on shed. One of them 45378 had been withdrawn some time ago in March 1965.

"Big Eight" 48773 along with 48774 and 48775 used to be allocated to 66A Polmadie in Glasgow and I had often seen here there. The Scottish Region caused a few years ago in December 1962 by withdrawing all three locos reinstating them in February 1963 during the severe winter, before withdrawing them again in June 1963. At the time they were the first "Big Eights" to be withdrawn and this caused some annoyance at the time. The London Midland Region decided to take over all three locos and resuscitated them in November 1963 and allocating them to Lancashire depots. Her two sisters were at 8C Speke Junction and 9D Newton Heath respectively.

The Scottish Region was never slow in withdrawing engines. Apart from the Caprotti valved "Black Fives" the English complement of "Black Fives" was largely intact. However, the Scottish Region had taken quite a liking to withdrawing many of them. Stanier 2-6-4 Tank 42626 had been on 8F Springs Branch when I visited that shed a month ago.

What did I miss? 35 Home steam (64%) on shed with 19 off shed so a good percentage on shed. Yes, Bolton had been a good shed, just like every shed visited today.

On I go

After completing the shed I glanced at my watch. It was 14.05. This left me with a revised recovery time of seven minutes given the 15 minute scheduled walk back. Plenty of time, but I found it to be a laborious walk with my broken holdall.

On the way back I didn't see Kathleen Sims either. As Bolton had a population of around 180,000 I suppose that I would have been very lucky to bump into her but you never know your luck and I had had plenty of good luck today unlike yesterday. Having missed seeing her I returned sadly to the station and got on to the Blackburn bucket at 14.26 on its arrival. The train had left Manchester Victoria at 14.03 and was a through train to Colne. My train left on time at 14.27. The trip was again singularly unexciting apart from going through Sough tunnel between Entwistle and Darwen. I noted 10H Lower Darwen shed my next visit to the west of the line between Darwen and Blackburn.

10H Lower Darwen would be another tight timing. My next train I had to catch was the 16.04 to Rose Grove (Burnley). That leaves me with 69 minutes. The LocoShed Directory provided 45 minutes to walk there, 45 minutes back and with 15 minutes to do the shed I needed 105 minutes. This left a recover time of minus 36 minutes. Quite an impossible timing? I agree an impossible walk. However, the shed entrance is opposite the Fernhurst Hotel which is on the main Blackburn to Darwen A666 road which carries a frequent bus service so the LocoShed Directory tells me. So all was not yet lost.

		Schedule	Actual	Miles
Depart	BOLTON TRINITY STREET	14.27	14.27	0
Arrive	BLACKBURN	14.55	14.55	13¾

Three intermediate stops.

THE COMMANDO COURSE EPISODE

At Blackburn Station my first port of call was the left luggage office to deposit my holdall with the broken handle or I would struggle to meet even a revised timetable involving buses. The left luggage attendant told me that the left luggage office closed at five o'clock but I assured him that I would be back for my holdall well before 17.00. He helpfully, on my enquiry, told me that I would get a bus for Darwen across the other side of the square from the station.

Luck continued to be with me when I boarded a Darwen bound bus just about to leave and asked the conductress if I could be dropped off at the Fernhurst Hotel. My bus soon left and in a short time I was being told that the next stop would be the Fernhurst Hotel. The 1½ mile journey had passed remarkably quickly.

I turned left along a footpath opposite the Fernhurst Hotel and groaned when I saw the shed which seemed miles away up a steep bank. I had never seen anything quite as daunting as this in all my times visiting sheds. It seemed to be a proverbial commando course to do this shed. I followed the footpath across some fields and then came to the bottom of the steep bank. An interesting sign stated "Private Road – No trespassing". I couldn't imagine anybody would want to trespass up this steep hill other than railwayists, of course. The hill felt as though it had a gradient of about 1 in 2. At least it felt like that as I crawled up it and would have been quite impossible with a heavy holdall. After a long struggle I finally reached the top and I had arrived at the shed. I felt like planting the Scottish flag having conquered the almost unconquerable steep bank to 10D Lower Darwen Motive Power depot. How it could be called "Lower" Darwen I'll never know. It felt like I had arrived at "Upper" Darwen!

The shed itself proved to be rather empty but that was not particularly surprising as it had a small allocation. I went round the shed without incident and in particular did not meet any shedmaster.

10H LOWER DARWEN						
		Home shed		Built	Withdrawn	Scrap
Diesels						
BR 0-6-0 Shunter 1953						
D3368		10D	Lostock Hall	Aug-1957		
D3782		10D	Lostock Hall	Sep-1959		
Total	2					
Steam						
Hughes/Fowler 5MT 2-6-0 "Crab" 1926				Built	Withdrawn	Scrap
42727		10H		Nov-1927	Jan-1967	Jun-1967
42732		10H		Dec-1926	Jun-1965	Oct-1965
42828		10H		Nov-1929	Nov-1965	Feb-1966
42869		10H		May-1930	Jul-1965	Nov-1965
42878		10H	(ex 9G Gorton)	Jun-1930	Sep-1965	Dec-1965
42898		10H		Aug-1930	Sep-1965	Jan-1966
Total	6					
Ivatt 4MT 2-6-0 1947						
43046		10H	(ex 9F Heaton Mersey)	Oct-1949	Nov-1967	Feb-1968
43118		10H		Jun-1951	Nov-1967	Mar-1968
43119		10H		Jun-1951	Aug-1967	Jan-1968
Total	3					
Stanier 8F 2-8-0 "Big Eight" 1935						
48062		10H	(ex 8H Birkenhead)	Nov-1936	Aug-1968	Dec-1968
48221		8F	Springs Branch(ex8E)	Sep-1942	Feb-1967	Aug-1967
48684		10H	(ex 8H Birkenhead)	Jan-1944	May-1968	Sep-1968
48691		10H	(ex 8H Birkenhead)	Mar-1944	Mar-1966	Jun-1966
Total	4					

		Home shed		Built	Withdrawn	Scrap
Riddles WD 8F 2-8-0 "Austerity" 1943						
90204		10H		*Oct-1943*	*Jun-1965*	*Oct-1965*
90261		10H		*Sep-1943*	*Jul-1965*	*Dec-1965*
Total	*2*					
On Shed	**17**	**Kops**	**14**			
Steam	**15**	**Diesels**	**2**			
Withdrawn	**4**					
Home Locos	**14**	**Home Area**		**2 Visitors**		**1**
Shed	**10H**	**14**	**10D**	**2**		
Analysis	**8F**	**1**				
Steam classes on view		**4**				
Steam Origin		**LMS**	**13 WD**		**2**	
Shed Highlight:-		**Not much perhaps the three Ivatt 4MT "Moguls"**				
Steam	*Aug-50*	*167*	*Mar-59*	*154*	*Apr-65*	*79*
Allocation					*Aug-65*	*98*
				Closed to Steam:-	*Oct-66*	
Home Steam	*excluding withdrawn locos*					
On/Off Shed	*On Shed*	*10*	*Off Shed*	*5*	*% On Shed*	*67%*
Not on Shed						
Ivatt 4MT 2-6-0 1947				*43019*	*43041*	*2*
"Black Fives"					*44958*	*1*
"Big Eights"				*48423*	*48441*	*2*
					total	*5*
saw elsewhere on the tour			*1*			
saw on July 65 Preston area trip			*1*			*scrap*
recently withdrawn not on shed or seen elsewhere			*2*	*"Crab"*	*42892*	*Aug-65*
				WD 2-8-0	*90152*	*Aug-65*

Review and Appraisal of 10H Lower Darwen

The shed was on the west side of Darwen line 1½ miles south of Blackburn Station. Walking time would have been 45 minutes from Blackburn Station.

A reasonable shed lacking in numbers but four steam classes totalling 15 steam were on view. The six "Crabs" were a fine number to have on shed. Unfortunately, the "Crabs" appear to be fast disappearing as a class and two of them here were withdrawn.

The Ivatt 4MT 2-6-0's were the first ones I had come across for some time although there are quite a few allocated to the LMR. Certain of my friends namely Dave Archibald and John Clark assure me their correct names are "Flying Pigs" rather than a light or heavy "Mogul" due to their ugly features. 10H Lower Darwen had recently received her "Big Eights" from 8H Birkenhead which had been made possible by that shed receiving a goodly number of 9F 2-10-0's largely from the Leicester (15 area) and Nottingham (16 area) Divisions.

The two WD's on shed were predictably withdrawn just as I had seen the last condemned 8F Wigan WD 2-8-0's last month. This WD Class was very much alive and kicking on the Eastern and North Eastern regions.

The two diesel shunters came from 10D Lostock Hall at Preston. Apparently, Lostock Hall farms out some diesel shunters for work in the Blackburn Area. That perhaps explains why I saw so few of 10D Lostock Hall's diesel shunter allocation when I visited 10D Lostock Hall and also around or at Preston Station.

I could hardly complain about the relatively small numbers on 10H Lower Darwen shed when 10 Home Steam (67%) were on shed and only five Home Steam off shed.

On I go

It was with great joy that I cantered back down the steep bank. I would rather run down than crawl up a steep bank! I made my way back across the fields and was soon back at the bus stop at the Fernhurst Hotel for the return journey. The service was impeccable and within a minute a bus came along and I was soon being speeded back to Blackburn.

THE VERY CLOSE SHAVE EPISODE

Getting off at the station I returned to the left luggage office where the attendant was most impressed that I had got the bus to the Fernhurst Hotel visited 10H Lower Darwen and had returned back here all within 50 minutes. "That was very quick" he said. I replied "It was well worth the left luggage charge not to have my "sick" holdall with me. Particularly when it was a commando course up to the engine shed". I had made my impossible timing of minus 36 minutes by a remarkable 19 minutes thanks to the excellent bus service and also thanks to surviving the commando course!

It was now 15.45 and had nineteen minutes to burn before the 16.04 to Rose Grove. I suddenly began to feel a little hungry and thirsty now that I had for the first time today a few minutes to spare. In fact, I couldn't remember having anything to eat or drink all day – a day that had begun at 04.30 early this morning! I had been living on adrenalin and air all day. I noted with glee a BR cafeteria on the station and made my way there. On the way there I noted LNER B1 61131 hurtle forward at the head of a passenger train possibly bound for Leeds as she was allocated to 56A Wakefield. Certainly, I was not aware that B1's handled cross-country services between Lancashire and Yorkshire. Perhaps she was at the head of a "special".

BLACKBURN STATION						
			Home shed	Built	Withdrawn	Scrap
Steam						
Thompson 5MT 4-6-0 B1 1942						
61131		56A	Wakefield	*Feb-1947*	*Dec-1966*	*Apr-1967*
Total	*1*					
On Station		1 Kops		1		
Steam		1 Diesels		0		
		Home Area			0 Visitors	1
Shed	**56A**	1				
Analysis						
Steam Classes on view		1				
Steam Origin	**LNER**	1				

Inside the cafeteria I had my usual fare of soup, cheese sandwich, cake and a cup of tea. I enjoyed it immensely as I had been so famished. I had rarely been hungry on tour and mostly ate to keep D.S. company. During the week I had been too bothered about the shed visiting and train catching timetable and the general excitement of the tour than to think much about eating although I particularly enjoyed the fish suppers on Wednesday and Thursday evenings.

At 16.00 I got up, picked my holdall up and went on to the platform. My bucket had just arrived from Bolton. It was another through train to Colne having left Manchester Victoria at 15.20 called at Bolton at 15.37 and having arrived a couple of minutes early would leave here in four minutes at 16.04.

I had been on the bucket for about a minute when I looked for my working timetable in my little school rucksack. I couldn't find it. Damn, I must have left it in the cafeteria. If I went back for it the train might start and my timetable would be up the creek again. I would need to chance that as I could hardly leave my rucksack behind. I glanced at my watch I might have a couple of minutes. I flew off the train at scarcely slower than the speed of light and ran to the cafeteria. I almost knocked over a person trying to leave it, ran up to my table and almost broke my kneecap as I crashed into it. Luck was with me. It was still on the floor where I left it. I immediately snatched it up, almost severed the door on exiting the cafeteria and ran the tantalizingly few yards to where the bucket was standing. Thankfully, I reached it safely, drew open the door and collapsed back on to my seat on the bucket with exhaustion but also with elation on having made it. Luck was with me once again today! What a close shave with disaster. To make my point more poignantly I heard the engines of the bucket start up almost immediately after I had sat down and the bucket left shortly thereafter on time at 16.04.

The bucket could easily have started off early and departed with my sick holdall but without me! How careless can you get? I had been a bit careless earlier on the tour when I dropped and broke Graham Strachan's camera and then lost it when we had changed buses at Mansfield on Monday. It would have been ironic if the first timetable disaster of the day would have been caused by carelessness when for the first time in the day I had time to spare!

Next shed of the day would be 10F Rose Grove. Whereas 10H Lower Darwen was Blackburn's shed 10F Rose Grove was Burnley's shed. There was one difference. Rose Grove still had a station while Lower Darwen station had been closed ages ago.

On the way to Rose Grove I mused that D.S. would be having his afternoon tea in the dining car of the Birmingham to Edinburgh express by now. He would be devouring mounds of sandwiches and cakes and eating them out of house and home I mused, laughing out aloud. The other passengers were looking at me strangely wondering what I could be laughing at! I must admit that life on the LMR Tour had not been quite the same since D.S. had departed for home earlier today. All had been very quiet since then. The silence in fact was driving me a bit mad. My slow pace at Wigan had been brought partly on by me not having D.S. to act as a guideline for what a standard slow pace should be. Yes, I certainly missed having D.S. to continually moan at. We certainly had had a few arguments during the week and I had wished him gone on several occasions. However, now that he was actually away for good I now missed him. However, on the debit side we would almost certainly have missed our Wigan connection for Bolton and I hate to think what would have happened to him on the Lower Darwen commando course. We shall, of course, never know what would have happened to timings at and after Wigan with him still with me.

Our bucket stopped at Accrington Station for a minute. Accrington used to sport a Football League fourth division football club which was named Accrington Stanley. My cousin Bobby Wilson had been the last captain of the club when it had run out of money and folded during the football season in March 1962 to the benefit of Oxford who were elected to the league in their place. *Remarkably Accrington fought their way back from oblivion and were promoted back to the English Fourth Division for the 2006-2007 season.*

At Accrington station "Big Eight" 48451 passed us by at speed on a freight. Doubtless, the driver was late for his tea and we would see the engine at 10F Rose Grove having got rid of its freight. Weather-wise, the sun had now disappeared and it had become very overcast with low cloud engulfing the skies. Fortunately, it did not look as though rain was imminent.

I had met a Burnley trainspotter at Preston Station on the Monday of my week at Blackpool. He had managed to lose his return ticket but said he would get off the return journey at Rose Grove (rather than Burnley) as there would be no ticket collector there.

			Schedule	Actual	Miles
Depart	BLACKBURN		16.04	16.04	0
Arrive	ACCRINGTON		16.13	16.13	5¼
Depart	ACCRINGTON		16.14	16.14	5¼
Arrive	ROSE GROVE		16.24	16.24	9¾

Our bucket arrived at Rose Grove Station on time at 16.24. Contrary to what the local trainspotter had said Rose Grove station had a ticket collector on duty although there seemed to be a bit of a party atmosphere. The ticket collector was sitting having a little *tete a tete* with a couple of non railway friends on the platform enjoying what was left of the afternoon sun. They had probably taken some chairs out of the waiting room. He did get up from his conversation to have a look at my Railrover but barely glanced at it and was quickly back to his chair to continue his conversation.

Now for 10F Rose Grove shed which would have been a D.S. special as the shed was adjacent to the station. The next train I had to catch was the 17.02 to Skipton in order to visit 10G Skipton. This left me with 38 minutes which was bags of time given the shed's location.

I made the short walk to the shed and was soon proceeding round. I noted my old friend "Big Eight" 48451 who had been speeding through Accrington Station ten minutes ago. Sure enough the driver had got rid of his freight and had signed his engine off at the shed and would be on his way home by now. Once again the shed was completed without incident. Given that we had no permits for either the 8 (Liverpool) or 10 (Preston) Areas we had been very lucky and had had no trouble at all apart from at security conscious 8K Bank Hall.

10F ROSE GROVE							
			Home shed		**Built**	**Withdrawn**	**Scrap**
Diesels							
BR 0-6-0 Shunter 1953							
D3374			10D	Lostock Hall	Aug-1957		
D3581			10D	Lostock Hall	Oct-1958		
Total	2						
Steam					**Built**	**Withdrawn**	**Scrap**
Stanier 5MT 4-6-0 "Black Five" 1934							
44909			10F	(ex 1E Bletchley)	Nov-1945	Sep-1967	Feb-1968
45196			10F		Oct-1935	Dec-1967	Mar-1968
45205			10F		Nov-1935	Oct-1966	Mar-1967
45215			10F	(ex 16B Annesley)	Nov-1935	Oct-1967	Jan-1968
45216			10F		Nov-1935	Feb-1966	Jun-1966
Total	5						
Midland 3F "Jinty" 0-6-0T 1924 dev. of Johnson 1899 design							
47383			10F		Oct-1926	Oct-1967	saved
47631			10F		Dec-1928	Jun-1966	Feb-1967
Total	2						
Stanier 8F 2-8-0 "Big Eight" 1935							
48024			10F	(via 15A/16B/16E)	Mar-1937	Nov-1967	Mar-1968
48053			10F	(via 15A/16B/16E)	Oct-1936	Mar-1967	Mar-1968
48057			10F	(ex 16B Annesley)	Oct-1936	May-1967	Nov-1967
48079			10D	Lostock (ex 16B/16A)	Dec-1938	Dec-1966	Jun-1967
48223			10F	(ex 10C Fleetwood)	Sep-1942	Nov-1966	Jun-1967
48319	on 10C	Jul-65	10C	Fleetwood	Jan-1944	Jun-1968	Oct-1968
48323			10F	(ex 8H Birkenhead)	Feb-1944	Jun-1968	Dec-1968
48348			10F	(ex 8H Birkenhead)	Apr-1944	Aug-1968	Jan-1969
48373			10F	(ex 8H Birkenhead)	Nov-1944	Jun-1968	Dec-1968
48413	on 10C	Jul-65	10C	Fleetwood	Oct-1943	Nov-1965	Jan-1966
48435			10F	(ex 8H Birkenhead)	Apr-1944	May-1967	Sep-1967

		Home shed		Built	Withdrawn	Scrap
Stanier 8F 2-8-0 "Big Eight" 1935 (continued)						
48446		10F	(ex 8H Birkenhead)	*Jul-1944*	*Jul-1965*	*Nov-1965*
48447		10F	(ex 8H Birkenhead)	*Jul-1944*	*Jan-1966*	*May-1966*
48451		10F	(ex 8L Aintree)	*Sep-1944*	*May-1968*	*Sep-1968*
48506		10F	(ex 1H Northampton)	*Oct-1944*	*Sep-1967*	*Feb-1968*
48558		10F	(ex 8L Aintree)	*Aug-1945*	*Oct-1965*	*Mar-1966*
Total	16					
WD 8F 2-8-0 "Austerity" Riddles 1943						
90040		10F		*Feb-1944*	*Jul-1965*	*Dec-1965*
90171		10F		*Jul-1943*	*Jul-1965*	*Oct-1965*
90181		10F		*Aug-1943*	*May-1965*	*Aug-1965*
90222		8L	Aintree	*Apr-1943*	*Aug-1965*	*Jun-1966*
90314		10F		*Apr-1944*	*Apr-1965*	*Aug-1965*
90420		10F		*Mar-1945*	*Aug-1965*	*Feb-1966*
90541		10F		*Jul-1943*	*May-1965*	*Aug-1965*
90681		10F		*Nov-1944*	*Jul-1965*	*Oct-1965*
90725		10F		*Apr-1945*	*Aug-1965*	*Jan-1966*
Total	9					

On Shed	34	**Kops**		24			
Steam	32	**Diesels**		2			
Withdrawn	7						
Home Locos	28	**Home Area**		5	**Visitors**	1	
Shed	10F	28	10C	2	10D	3	
Analysis	8F	1					
Steam classes on view		4					
Steam Origin	LMS		23	WD		9	
Shed Highlight:-	90222	8L	Aintree				
Steam	*Aug-50*	49	*Mar-59*		46	*Apr-65*	24
Allocation						*Aug-65*	31
			Closed to Steam:-			*Aug-68*	
Home Steam	excluding withdrawn locos						
On/Off Shed	On Shed	21	Off Shed		10	% On Shed	68%
Not on Shed							
"Black Fives"				44870	45234	45397	3
"Big Eights"	48081	48218		48257	48260	48262	
					48448	48668	7
						total	10
saw elsewhere on the tour				4			
recently withdrawn not on shed or seen elsewhere				1	WD 8F 2-8-0 Riddles 1943		90207
						scrap	Aug-65

Review and Appraisal of 10F Rose Grove

The shed was on the north side of the line west of Rose Grove Station. Walking time was less than 5 minutes from the station.

A very interesting shed. Although 32 steam locos were on shed only four Classes were represented ("Black Fives", "Jinties", "Big Eights" and WD "Austerity" locos).

Nine months ago 10F Rose Grove had no "Big Eights". However, the rundown of steam in the 1 (London) Area, the 15 (Leicester) area and the 16 (Nottingham) Area had caused a large deployment of steam engines to the 8 (Liverpool) and 10 (Preston) Areas. In particular an influx of "Big Eights" and 9F 2-10-0's and also some "Black Fives". 8H Birkenhead had received a vast influx of 9F 2-10-0's which had largely replaced its own "Big Eights". 10F Rose Grove had been a big beneficiary (particularly of ex 8H Birkenhead ones and now had an allocation of 20 "Big Eights" (including seven not on shed today). As a consequence the

WD "Austerity" Class seemed to have been condemned as a class in Lancashire being largely replaced by "Big Eights". Nine WD "Austerity" locos lay dead here condemned here – six withdrawn with the remaining three to be withdrawn this month. 90222 from 8L Aintree was an interesting visitor either already withdrawn or to be withdrawn this month.

Of the sixteen "Big Eights" on shed two were from 10C Fleetwood which I had seen on my early July Sunday visit to the shed there. There was also a 10D Lostock Hall one which it had recently received from the very rundown 16B Annesley. Three of the 10F Rose Grove "Big Eights" on shed had recently been allocated to 16B Annesley.

The general trend was for steam on the LMR being pushed up to the North West which had no Diesel Type1's, 2's, 3's and only a handful of Type 4's for passenger traffic. This had resulted in steam strongholds now being located in the 6 (Chester), 8 (Liverpool), 9 (Manchester), 10 (Preston) and 12 (Carlisle) Areas with some encroachment into the former steam stronghold of the 5(Crewe) Area. Recently 1E Bletchley and 1F Rugby had been dieselised while 1A Willesden's steam allocation was being whittled down prior to closure to steam along with 1H Northampton at the end of next month. This had resulted in transfers northwards coupled with transfers westwards due to the advancing dieselisation in the 15 (Leicester) and 16 (Nottingham Areas). The 14 (Cricklewood) area had already fallen to dieselisation at the end of last year.

Yes, the North West was the only place where steam still reigned supreme at least on non passenger traffic. In fact, I had not been steam hauled all week so here's hoping but I was running short of journeys still to be made.

The other steam on shed was comprised of five "Black Fives" (two of which were recently acquired from 1E Bletchley and 16B Annesley respectively) and a couple of beloved little "Jinties".

There were two roving 10D Lostock Hall diesel shunters on shed. I checked my notebook to make sure that they weren't the two 10D Lostock Hall shunters which I had seen on 10H Lower Darwen about an hour ago! I had seen both of the 10D Lostock Hall shunters around Preston last month so it seems that the farmed out nomads regularly change and return to their home depot of 10D Lostock Hall for scheduled servicing and maintenance.

What did I miss? Very little indeed. 21 Home Steam (68%) was on shed with 10 off shed. Certainly Saturdays are a great day to go steam hunting in the North West. I had hardly seen a freight train all day and this confirms the Monday to Friday general time span for movements of steam engines in this area.

On I go

I made my way back to Rose Grove Station and had 15 minutes to wait for my bucket to Skipton. The ticket collector's private party had broken up and probably they had all retired to the pub leaving Rose Grove station once again with no ticket collector as the Burnley trainspotter had promised.

The bucket was yet another through train which had left Manchester Victoria at 15.55 and arrived at Rose Grove at 17.01. Surprisingly the bucket was pretty full and I was lucky to get a seat. This was probably explained by the fact that it was the second last train of the day to Skipton with the last leaving at 19.45 from Rose Grove. Just as well I had caught this train or I would be well and truly stranded like at Irlam yesterday but rather worse as I needed to be back at Carlisle before my Railrover ran out at midnight!

My bucket left on time at 17.02 and first stop was Burnley. Burnley looked a bit like Wigan with row upon row of back to back houses. These seemed to have a mesmeric effect on me as I promptly fell asleep but awoke up just as we reached the bucket's destination (and mine) of Skipton. I am pretty confident in the early Saturday evening that I had missed no steam en route just as practically all the other journeys today had been steamless.

		Schedule	Actual	Miles
Depart	ROSE GROVE	17.02	17.02	0
Arrive	SKIPTON	17.37	17.37	18¼

My bucket arrived in Skipton at 17.37 on time and I was quite impressed by the station as its platforms were severely curved making it almost semi-circular in appearance. Much to my delight Skipton seemed to be a steam paradise for passenger trains. I noted "Black Five" 45445 coming dashing into the station on the 16.55 from Leeds City. This train seemed to be "a spade and pail" one as its final destination was Morecambe Promenade!

I had to be back to catch the 18.43 to Carnforth. That gave me 63 minutes as against a scheduled 35 minutes visit (10 there and 10 back and 15 minutes for the visit) which gave me a generous recovery time of 23 minutes. Hence, a rather nice amble there and back would suffice.

I turned left outside the station proceed up a slope on the right hand side of the main road and turned left over the railway bridge. Almost immediately after crossing the railway I turned right into a lane running parallel with the line. The shed entrance was on the right hand side. Before I reached the shed I noted a row of apparently dead Midland 4F 0-6-0's. I made my way down to them and then slung my heavy holdall under one of them. I would collect it upon my return. The holdall with the broken strap had proved to be a nuisance.

I continued on to the shed and as usual today made my way round without incident. Before I reached the main shed building I noted 45258 whistle pass the shed heading northwards for the station. It must be on the 16.20 from Morecambe Promenade due in to Skipton at 17.56 ultimately arriving at Leeds City at 18.48. It was clearly the return of the "spade and pail" hauling passengers back after a day (or indeed a week) at Morecambe Beach!

Going round the shed the highlight was finding another condemned Midland 0-6-0. Attached to her boiler was a label stating that she had to be delivered to a certain scrap breaker in Hull! *All seven of the withdrawn Midland 0-6-0's would meet their ultimate end at Drapers Scrapbreakers at Hull.*

10G SKIPTON						
		Home shed		**Built**	**Withdrawn**	**Scrap**
Steam						
Fowler 4F 0-6-0 Midland 1911 design						
43893		10G		Dec-1919	May-1965	Oct-1965
43913		10G		Dec-1920	Apr-1965	Sep-1965
43999		10G		Dec-1921	May-1965	Sep-1965
Total	3					
Midland 4F 0-6-0 1924						
44276		10G		Dec-1926	May-1965	Sep-1965
44277		10G		Dec-1926	May-1965	Sep-1965
44389		10G	(ex 9L Buxton)	Oct-1926	Jul-1965	Nov-1965
44527		10G		Aug-1928	Mar-1965	Aug-1965
Total	4					
Stanier 5MT 4-6-0 "Black Five" 1934						
44668		12A	Carlisle Kingmoor	Dec-1949	Apr-1966	Jul-1966
44911		12A	Carlisle Kingmoor	Nov-1945	Oct-1967	Apr-1968
45291		9D	Newton Heath (ex 9B)	Dec-1936	Nov-1965	Jan-1966
Total	11					

		Home shed		Built	Withdrawn	Scrap
Midland 3F "Jinty" 0-6-0T 1924 dev. of Johnson 1899 design						
47427		10G		Oct-1926	Sep-1966	Feb-1967
47602		10G		Sep-1928	Jan-1966	Apr-1966
Total	2					
Stanier 8F 2-8-0 "Big Eight" 1935						
48077		10J	Lancaster (ex1E)	Dec-1936	Mar-1968	Jun-1968
48218		10F	Rose Grove (ex10J)	Sep-1942	Sep-1967	Feb-1968
Total	2					
BR Standard 4MT 4-6-0 Brighton 1951						
75011		10G		Nov-1951	Oct-1966	Feb-1967
75017		10G		Jan-1952	Jan-1967	May-1967
75039		10G		Aug-1953	Sep-1967	Feb-1968
75042		10G		Sep-1953	Oct-1967	Mar-1968
75044		10G		Sep-1953	Mar-1966	Jun-1966
75057		10G		Mar-1957	Feb-1966	Jun-1966
75058		10G		Apr-1957	Dec-1967	Apr-1968
Total	7					
BR Standard 2MT 2-6-2T Derby 1953						
84015		10G		Oct-1953	Dec-1965	Apr-1966
84028		10G		May-1957	Dec-1965	Apr-1966
Total	2					

On Shed	23	**Kops**		18		
Steam	23	**Diesels**		0		
Withdrawn	7					
Home Locos	18	**Home Area**		2	**Visitors**	3
Shed	10G	18	10F	1	10J	1
Analysis	9D	1	12A	2		
Steam classes on view		7				
Steam Origin	LMS		14	BR	9	
Shed Highlight:-		The three Midland 1911 0-6-0's				
Steam	Aug-50	36	Mar-59	24	Apr-65	22
Allocation					Aug-65	16
				Closed to Steam:-		Apr-67
Home Steam	excluding withdrawn locos					
On/Off Shed	On Shed	11	Off Shed	6	% On Shed	65%
Not on Shed						
Johnson Midland 3F 0-6-0T 1899					47201	1
BR Standard 4MT 4-6-0 Brighton 1951		75015	75019	75041	75051	5
					75059	
					total	6
	saw elsewhere on the tour			2		
	saw on Dec 64 Manchester and Crewe trip			1		
	saw on June 67 Carlisle visit			1		

Review and Appraisal of 10G Skipton

The shed was on the south side of the main line west of Skipton Station. Walking time was 10 minutes from the station.

The shed was located on the south side of the main line west of the station. A good steam shed. Remarkably all steam on shed. The highlights of the visit were seeing the two clutches of Midland 0-6-0's (three of the 1911 series and four from the 1924 series). Last Saturday D.S. and I had seen the oldest survivor 43953 at 12D Workington.

These hard working uncomplaining looking locos had once been very numerous but all here were withdrawn and very few remained active on the LMR. As more modern steam locos are transferred northwards this allows the older engine classes to be withdrawn.

Skipton had no allocation of "Black Fives" (three on shed) or "Big Eights" (two on shed) and these comprised the five visitors on shed none particularly surprising. It was good seeing another two of the long serving "Jinties" and still active.

The Standard 4MT 75XXX Class was popular here with seven on shed and four off shed. 8K Bank Hall and 8L Aintree were the other Lancashire sheds where we had seen them. Two Standard 2MT Tanks were also on shed.

What did I miss? Eleven Home Steam (65%) were on shed and six were off shed so the usual good Saturday percentage on shed.

On I go

I went back to the dead Midland 0-6-0's and picked up my holdall and made my way back to the station and had time to spare before my 18.43 train to Carnforth. What better way to spend it by having another snack at the cafeteria.

This time the cafeteria was not run by BR and prices were decidedly cheaper. I had a sandwich, cake and a cup of tea. While I was enjoying this I kept my eyes trained through the open door to the platforms. This proved to be very rewarding and I was especially pleased to note "Jubilee" 45697 "Achilles" of 55A Leeds (Holbeck) storm past obviously full of herself. She was soon followed in the shape of "Black Five" 44828 also of 55A Leeds (Holbeck). I had been a little disappointed at not finding any Leeds locos on 10G Skipton but this made up for it. Incredibly, everything appeared to be steam hauled. Diesels were nowhere to be seen.

By now it was 18.30 and I was awaiting expectantly for a steam engine to haul in my train – the 17.47 from Leeds City. I heard the roar of the loco in the distance and the tell tale white smoke which was rapidly becoming a scarce commodity for passenger trains and I knew my hope for the week was about to be fulfilled. I would be steam hauled at last! Stanier "Black Five" 44889 of 10J Lancaster thundered into the station at the head of the train. How I wished that I had a camera still with me! D.S. would have been in his element taking a photo of her.

My train would split into two at Wennington with one half going on to Morecambe and the other half with me to Carnforth. Fortunately, each coach was clearly labelled just as they had been on Tuesday earlier in the week at Birmingham New Street when there had been certain through coaches to Cardiff General.

Surprisingly, it was all non-corridor Hannah stock as Neil Woodcock used to call it for reasons that I can't go into here. Seemed rather ridiculous as it had been a one hour journey from Leeds and another hour and a half to Carnforth. This left possible toilet stops for passengers of three minutes (not to be recommended) at Hellifield and eleven minutes at Wennington (two hours after leaving Leeds). The Leeds passengers probably called this train the endurance special and not recommended after a boozy afternoon in the pub!

SKIPTON TO CARNFORTH					
	Home shed		Built	Withdrawn	Scrap
Diesels					
BR Sulzer "Peak" Type 4 1Co-Co1 1959					
D 120	ML	Midland Lines	Sep-1961		
Total	1				
Steam					
Stanier 4MT 2-6-4T 1935 dev of Fowler 1927			Built	Withdrawn	Scrap
42616	*hauled!* 10A	Carnforth(ex 1A/via 5D)	Feb-1937	Oct-1967	Mar-1968
Total	1				
BR Standard 6P5F 4-6-2 "Clan" 1952 Derby					
72008	"Clan Macleod" 12A	Carlisle Kingmoor	Apr-1952	Aug-1965	Dec-1965
Total	1				

On Journey	3	Kops	2		
Steam	2	Diesels	1		
		Home Area		1 Visitors	1
Shed	10A	1	12A	1 ML	1
Distribution					
Steam Classes	2				
Steam Origin	LMS	1	BR	1	
Station Highlight:-	72008	"Clan Macleod"		12A	Carlisle Kingmoor

A STEAM HAULED JOURNEY AT LAST

The timetable for this breathtaking journey over the Pennines would be as follows:-

		Schedule		Miles
Depart	SKIPTON	18.43		0
Depart	CARGRAVE	18.51		3¾
Arrive	HELLIFIELD	19.06		10
Depart	HELLIFIELD	19.09		10
Depart	LONG PRESTON	19.12		11¼
Depart	GIGGLESWICK	19.20		15
Depart	CLAPHAM	19.33		20¾
Depart	BENTHAM	19.41		25
Arrive	WENNINGTON	19.48		28¼
Depart	WENNINGTON	19.59		28¼
Arrive	CARNFORTH	20.18		37¾

My train left on time at 18.43. This journey at 1½ hours would be one of my longer journeys of the week and steam hauled as well.

A DISSERTATION ON THE PERILS OF SMOKING DURING MY FORMATIVE YEARS

How should I celebrate? And then I remembered. I had a 20 packet of Rothman's King Size in my anorak pocket. They had barely been touched this week. I had had three cigarettes while we had a successful day at the Bridge at Carlisle Upperby last Saturday. On the way to Workington later that day I had one and last one on the way back.

On the way down to London from Carlisle early on Sunday morning the gorgeous girl sitting next to me in our luxurious first class compartment had offered me and everyone else in the platform a cigarette. Peter Stuyvesant if I remember correctly another favourite of mine and also a King sized filter. I was pleased to accept. Surprisingly, no one else in the compartment smoked, least of all D.S., who was wisely worried about catching lung cancer. Smoking certainly would have been extremely bad for D.S.'s health as this would have reduced his lung capacity and his walking speed even further.

Hours later, somewhere after Nuneaton, after daylight had struck I offered the girl one of my Rothmans and she gladly accepted. Smoking brings friendships and the girl and I had a pleasant chat until D.S. and I left the train at Watford Junction to smash up London.

LSD had also been invaluable on our tour but our LSD which helped us along so much was my LocoShed Directory "LSD"! Back to smoking. Since our journey to London I had had no more ciggies. I counted them, yes I had 13 left. Perhaps that had brought us some bad luck on the tour although we had certainly been lucky today. Why had I stopped smoking? Probably because I had been too worried about the timetable to relax and have a cigarette. Some people smoke when they are worried or nervous about something but not me. I tended to smoke when I was happy, elated and excited about something. Yes, now was the time to celebrate and I lit up a Rothmans leaving a "lucky" twelve in the packet.

I had been introduced to smoking at the Mucklets Railway Bridge (now adjacent to the new Musselburgh main line station) in the summer of 1958 at the ripe old age of nine by some older friends just after I took up trainspotting. However, sensibly I had chucked smoking by the following year.

Before this tour I had been to England very rarely. There had been Scottish Railfans (now The Railway Society of Scotland) visits to Carlisle on Sunday 7th September 1958 (when I was only 9¼ years old) and a follow up a visit a year later on Sunday 12th September 1959. Wisely by then perhaps for shed safety reasons The Society had upped the minimum age for membership to 12 years – lots of laughs. My trainspotting seemed to wane a bit for some obscure reason after spending an enjoyable week in Glasgow in July 1960. I got back on track in July 1963 when Graham Strachan wanted to visit the Glasgow M.P.D.'s and doubtless had a few cigs to celebrate our day out.

After the long gap since 1959 I was to be in England three times in 1964. First, I went with Musselburgh Grammar School on a month's visit to France in late June 1964. This involved a Sleeper Train to London King's Cross and then the boat train to Dover on fully dieselised Southern Region metals. Smoking in France on our holiday was very popular for all pupils as we picked up cigarettes on the boat duty free at two shillings and sixpence (12½ new pence) for 20 as against a UK shop price of four shillings and sixpence (22½ new pence).

I had paid my money to join a Railway Society of Scotland weekend tour of the 15 (Leicester), 16(Nottingham) and then 17 (Derby) Areas in August 1964. This would have been wonderful as this was just before steam began to be sharply run down there. Unfortunately, the trip was postponed and I did not manage to go on the rescheduled dates as my parents had opened my mail and said it was too expensive. I should have continued a strop until they relented.

My second trip to England in 1964 was to go to Carlisle at the last Saturday of the Glasgow Trades fortnight at the end of July 1964. On that trip I was accompanied by Dave Archibald, Derek Newton, Graham Strachan and Neil Woodcock of the M.M.M.R.S. Cigarettes celebrated the day's events at the Bridge at Carlisle Upperby and visits to 12A Carlisle Kingmoor and 12B Carlisle Upperby. Neil Woodcock not normally a smoker accepted one of my Rothmans. I warned him that they were quite strong but he puffed away and quickly finished it. He seemed to prove my point by falling asleep soon afterwards only to be forcibly awakened when the highlight of the day "Coronation" 46252 "City of Stoke-on-Trent" stormed past on a passenger train. That was sadly to be the "Coronation" swansong for us as the remaining ones were all withdrawn by December 1964.

A cigarette or two celebrated a great weekend visit in December 1964 to Manchester and Crewe with Ian "Froth" Firth.

On I go

However, I thought on the train to Wennington that this would be my last cigarette as I celebrated a wonderful week. Cigarettes under the Labour Government had gone up another five pence in price to four shillings eleven pence (25 new pence) for 20 cigarettes. It was an expensive way to potentially injure ones health.   It was fitting to mark the end of this great week's tour with the end of my smoking. *I didn't want to stun my growth with smoking and hence it was a good decision as I eventually ended up a couple of years later at six foot three and a half inches tall!*

I was looking forward to seeing ex24H Hellifield shed where the following historic locos were stored awaiting preservation:-

STORED AT EX 24H HELLIFIELD							
Midland Railway 2-4-0 Class 1 1866							
158A							
Total	*1*						
Midland Railway 4-2-2 Class 115 1899							
118							
Total	*1*						
London,Tilbury and Southend Railway 4-4-2T Class 79 1909							
80							
Total	*1*						
London and North Eastern Railway 2-6-2 Class V2 1936							
4771	"Green Arrow"						
Total	*1*						

My train pulled into Hellifield Station dead on time at 19.06. Already on station was a train headed south. It was the 16.37 local from Carlisle which would arrive at Bradford at 20.20 (a proverbial slowboat to China)! At the head of the train was "Clan" Pacific 72008 "Clan Macleod" of 12A Carlisle Kingmoor. Good to see a "Clan" in action as only three of the original ten survived. 72000-72004 had been allocated to Scottish depots but had been withdrawn some years ago. 72005-72009 had been allocated to 12A Carlisle Kingmoor where they had been revered more than their luckless Scottish counterparts. Recently 72005 and 72009 had been withdrawn leaving 72006-72008 as the three survivors. The "Clans" had not been a successful design very much inferior to the "Britannias". Originally, 25 had been scheduled to be built and an old 1954 Ian Allan locomotives ABC listed 72000-72024 along with names for all 25! However, construction ceased after ten were built. Here endeth the strange tale of the "Clans" but "Clan Macleod" here on station was in lively enough form and was due to leave at 19.10. Sadly she was on one of her last journeys as she was withdrawn later in the month.

My train left Hellifield Station at 19.09 and I was looking forward to seeing the four locomotives to be preserved at the ex 24H Hellifield shed to the north east of the station. However, I was to be disappointed as I found to my consternation that the shed was completely boarded up as a security measure. At 30A Stratford last Sunday I had seen a secret unpublicized sanctuary of locomotives to be preserved. At least at 30A Stratford the windows had not all been boarded up!

It was a beautiful scenic trip. Certainly an unhurried trip with the 28¼ mile trip to Wennington scheduled for 65 minutes with six intermediate stops. At Giggleswick a father and his five year old kid entered my compartment. However, we did not strike up a conversation and I contented myself listening to the welcome sounds of the "Black Five" at the head of my train.

Finally, our train reached Wennington on time at 19.48. The "Black Five" had effortlessly kept to the timetable. On Wennington Station I was surprised to see my first diesel on the line although, of course, we had left the Skipton to Settle to Carlisle line at Settle Junction. She was "Peak" Type 4 D120. She must have come in at 19.43 with the 19.17 from Morecambe Promenade departing Wennington at 19.50 and which would eventually end up at Leeds City at 21.47.

At Wennington the Carnforth coaches were unhitched and the "Black Five" departed on for Morecambe at 19.53 for Lancaster and Morecambe. With luck I would continue to be steam hauled. I was in luck and looking out of the window I noted a then unidentified LMS 2-6-4

Tank backing on to the front of our train. At 19.59 we were off to Carnforth. Nineteen minutes were allowed for the 9½ mile journey. A very pleasant steam journey and much preferable to the usual diesel, electric and bucket journeys.

At 20.18 we arrived in Carnforth and I quickly sprinted up the platform to find out what had been at the head of our train. She was Stanier 2-6-4 Tank 42616 of 10A Carnforth and had recently been transferred from 1A Willesden like quite a number of engines which I had recently seen in the North West.

SKIPTON TO CARNFORTH							
		Home shed		Built	Withdrawn	Scrap	
Diesels							
BR Sulzer "Peak" Type 4 1Co-Co1 1959							
D 120		ML	Midland Lines	Sep-1961			
Total	1						
Steam							
Stanier 4MT 2-6-4T 1935 dev of Fowler 1927				Built	Withdrawn	Scrap	
42616	hauled!	10A	Carnforth(ex 1A/via 5D)	Feb-1937	Oct-1967	Mar-1968	
Total	1						
BR Standard 6P5F 4-6-2 "Clan" 1952 Derby							
72008	"Clan Macleod"	12A	Carlisle Kingmoor	Apr-1952	Aug-1965	Dec-1965	
Total	1						
On Journey	3	Kops		2			
Steam	2	Diesels		1			
		Home Area		1 Visitors		1	
Shed	10A	1	12A	1	ML	1	
Distribution							
Steam Classes	2						
Steam Origin	LMS	1	BR	1			
Station Highlight:-		72008	"Clan Macleod"		12A	Carlisle Kingmoor	

		Schedule	Actual	Miles
Depart	SKIPTON	18.43	18.43	0
Arrive	WENNINGTON	19.48	19.48	28¼
Depart	WENNINGTON	19.59	19.59	28¼
Arrive	CARNFORTH	20.18	20.18	37¾

THE LAST SHED VISIT

10A Carnforth would be the last shed visited with my LMR Railrover Ticket. A sobering thought but it had been a terrific week. Carnforth had fairly come up in the LMR world in recent years. It used to be coded 24L and surprise after a shed allocations reshuffle a year or two ago it had ended up as parent shed 10A. Nowadays, however, there was no doubt that 10A Carnforth was the premier shed in its area. I had to do the shed and be back for the 20.55 to Carlisle. This gave me 37 minutes. However, it was only five minutes from the station and with 15 minutes to visit the shed and 5 minutes back this gave me a comfortable recovery time of 12 minutes. So as long as I did not fall asleep with fatigue this should be quite enough!

The shed was on the west side of the Barrow line to the north west of the station. I quickly turned left outside the station into Warton Road and after about 150 yards left again over a footbridge which led to the offices and behind them to the shed.

I carefully avoided the offices and went round without incident for the umpteenth time today. There had not been a hint of trouble since the traumatic Bank Haul Maul early this morning. The shed itself was another 8F Springs Branch literally choked with engines from far and wide and like 5B Crewe South had been it was a rather cosmopolitan shed.

10A CARNFORTH

		Home shed		Built	Withdrawn	Scrap
Diesels						
Brush Type 4 Co-Co 1962						
D1838		5A	Crewe Diesel	May-1965		
D1840		5A	Crewe Diesel	May-1965		
Total	2					
BR 0-6-0 Shunter 1955						
D4140		10A		Aug-1962		
D4157		10A		Dec-1962		
Total	2					
Metropolitan Vickers Type 2 Co-Bo 1958						
D5700		12C	Barrow	Jul-1958	Dec-1967	
D5701		12C	Barrow	Aug-1958	Sep-1968	
D5710		12C	Barrow	Feb-1959	Dec-1967	
Total	3					
Steam				Built	Withdrawn	Scrap
Fairburn 4MT 2-6-4T 1945 dev. of Stanier 1935						
42105		10A	(ex 1A Willesden)	Sep-1950	Dec-1966	Apr-1967
42118		10A	(ex 1A Willesden)	Aug-1949	Sep-1965	Dec-1965
42154		10A		Jun-1948	Jan-1967	Jun-1967
42247		10A	(ex 6A Chester)	Oct-1946	Aug-1965	Jul-1966
Total	4					
Fowler 4MT 2-6-4T 1927						
42322		10A		May-1928	Jul-1965	Dec-1965
Total	1					
Stanier 4MT 2-6-4T 1935 dev of Fowler 1927						
42613		10A		Jan-1937	Apr-1967	Oct-1967
42663		10A	(ex 5D Stoke)	Jun-1942	Mar-1967	Oct-1967
Total	2					
Ivatt 4MT 2-6-0 1947						
43011		10A		Mar-1948	Feb-1967	Aug-1967
43027		10A		Feb-1949	May-1968	Sep-1968
43041		10H	Lower Darwen	Aug-1949	Aug-1967	Dec-1967
43045		10A		Oct-1949	Sep-1966	Jan-1967
43066		10A		Dec-1950	Jan-1967	May-1967
43095		10A		Dec-1950	Dec-1966	Apr-1967
43103		10A		Mar-1951	Dec-1966	Mar-1967
43105		10A		Mar-1951	Jun-1967	Nov-1967
Total	8					
Midland 4F 0-6-0 1924						
44300		10A		Feb-1927	Dec-1965	Feb-1966
Total	1					
Stanier 5MT 4-6-0 "Black Five" 1934						
44709		10A		Oct-1948	Aug-1968	Nov-1968
44905		10A		Oct-1945	Nov-1967	Feb-1968
45013		12A	Carlisle Kingmoor	Apr-1935	May-1968	Sep-1968
45091		8F	Springs Branch(ex6G/5B)	Apr-1935	Sep-1966	Mar-1967
45092		10A		Apr-1935	Dec-1967	Mar-1968
45097		12A	Carlisle Kingmoor	Apr-1935	Jun-1966	Nov-1966
45200		10C	Fleetwood	Oct-1935	Jul-1968	Dec-1968
45227		10A		Aug-1936	Jan-1968	Apr-1968
45230		10A		Aug-1936	Aug-1965	Nov-1965
45261		8A	Edge Hill	Oct-1936	Oct-1967	Feb-1968
45328		10A		Mar-1937	Sep-1967	Nov-1967
45373		10J	Lancaster	Jun-1937	Sep-1967	Oct-1968
45495		10A		Feb-1944	Mar-1967	Feb-1968
Total	13					
Johnson Midland 3F 0-6-0T 1899						
47201		10G	Skipton	Dec-1899	Dec-1966	Jun-1967
Total	1					
Midland 3F "Jinty" 0-6-0T 1924 dev. of Johnson 1899 design						
47531		10A		Mar-1928	Feb-1967	Mar-1967
47599		10A		Nov-1928	Dec-1966	Sep-1967
Total	2					

		Home shed			Built	Withdrawn	Scrap
Stanier 8F 2-8-0 "Big Eight" 1935							
48166		9K	Bolton(ex16B/16E/9L)		Apr-1943	Oct-1967	Apr-1968
48213		9H	Patricroft		Aug-1942	Sep-1966	Feb-1967
48262		10F	Rose Grove(ex 8H/10H)		Jun-1941	Nov-1965	Feb-1966
48540		55D	Royston		Dec-1944	Oct-1967	May-1968
48668		10F	Rose Grove(ex 8H)		May-1944	Dec-1966	Jun-1967
48712		10A			Jul-1944	Jun-1967	Nov-1967
48727		8G	Sutton Oak (ex 5B)		Sep-1944	Aug-1968	Jan-1969
48739		1H	Northampton (to 10A)		Dec-1945	Jan-1967	Jul-1967
Total	8						
BR Standard 7P6F 4-6-2 "Britannia" Derby 1951							
70013	"Oliver Cromwell"	12B	Carlisle Upperby		May-1951	Aug-1968	saved
70030	"William Wordsworth"	12B	Carlisle Upperby(ex5A/5B)	Nov-1952		Jun-1966	Oct-1966
70051	"Firth of Forth"	5B	Crewe South (ex 5A)		Aug-1954	Dec-1967	Mar-1968
Total	3						
BR Standard 4MT 4-6-0 Brighton 1951							
75015		10G	Skipton		Dec-1951	Dec-1967	Jun-1968
Total	1						
WD 8F 2-8-0 "Austerity" Riddles 1943							
90362		55G	Huddersfield		Sep-1944	Jun-1967	Nov-1967
Total	1						
BR Standard 9F 2-10-0 Brighton 1954							
92085		8H	Birkenhead		May-1956	Dec-1966	Jul-1980
Total	1						

On Shed	53	**Kops**		31			
Steam	46	**Diesels**		7			
Withdrawn	1						

Home Locos		27 Home Area			7	Visitors	19
Shed	10A	27	10C		1	10F	2
Analysis	10G	2	10H		1	10J	1
	1H	1					
	5A	2	5B		1		
	8A	1	8F		1	8G	1
	8H	1					
	9H	1	9K		1		
	12A	2	12B		2	12C	3
	55D	1	55G		1		
Steam classes on view		13					
Steam Origin	LMS		40	BR		5 WD	1
Shed Highlight:-	47201	10G	Skipton				

Steam	Aug-50	42	Mar-59		42	Apr-65	41
Allocation						Aug-65	46
			Closed to Steam:-			Aug-68	
Home Steam	excluding withdrawn locos						
On/Off Shed	On Shed	24	Off Shed		22	% On Shed	52%
Not on Shed							
Stanier 4MT 2-6-4T 1935						42616	1
Ivatt 4MT 2-6-0 1947						43036	1
"Black Fives"		44733	44778		44874	44892	44894
		44904	44948		45027	45054	45072
		45095	45209		45212	45326	45342
					45374	45390	45399	18
"Jinty"						47362	1
"Big Eights"						48519	1
						total	22

saw elsewhere on the tour				10		
saw on July 65 Preston area trip				5		
recently withdrawn not on shed or seen elsewhere			3		
			Fairburn 4MT 2-6-4T 1945		42147	42198
				scrap	Aug-65	Jul-65
			Midland 4F 0-6-0 1924		44386	
				scrap	Oct-65	

Review and Appraisal of 10A Carnforth

The shed was on the west side of the Barrow line north-west of Carnforth Station. Walking time was 5 minutes from the station.

A remarkably fine shed. A shed remarkable for two things in particular. Firstly, the large number of different steam classes (13) on view and secondly, the high proportion of visitors including home area (at around 50%). This is probably the first time that this has occurred during the whole week's tour.

All three varieties of 2-6-4 Tanks were on shed although 42322 the sole member of the oldest tank class (the Fowler 1927 one) was withdrawn. In fact, only three of this class are still active on the LMR (two at 8F Wigan and one at 9E Trafford Park). The most interesting Tank was 42663 quite some way from her home shed of 5D Stoke. Oddly enough I saw another wandering Stanier Tank (42665) at 8F Wigan earlier today. When we had visited 5D Stoke on Thursday evening all the Stanier tanks on shed were withdrawn and 42663 had recently been transferred to Carnforth from Stoke.

Just like 10H Lower Darwen a host of Ivatt 4MT 2-6-0's on shed. The beloved "Flying Pigs" as called by some of my friends. The solitary Midland 0-6-0 was very welcome as it was a fast disappearing class.

Thirteen "Black Fives" were on shed with the six visitors from relatively nearby sheds. It was particularly good to see two from 10J Lancaster as I had not been able to fit that relatively small shed into the final timetable. Strangely my 1965 edition Locoshed Directory had 10 J Lancaster with no code of its own but marked as a stabling point for 10A Carnforth.

The biggest highlight of the shed was seeing 47201 – a member of the earlier 1899 class of "Jinties" and one of the oldest engines still active on the LMR. I thought I had missed her when I had visited her home depot of 10G Skipton but here she was having strayed the 38 miles to 10A Carnforth here. In fact, only four of this class were still active on the LMR. I had seen earlier today 47202 (the ex Horwich Works) one at 9K Bolton. The original 1899 series ran from 47200 to 47259. A much smaller series than the 1924 development which was a very large class running from 47260-47681. Two of this later "Jinty" class were also on shed.

Eight "Big Eights" were on shed with only one belonging to 10A Carnforth. It was particularly pleasing seeing 48727 of 8G Sutton Oak (formerly of 5B Crewe South) as this shed had to be cut out of today's timetable due to yesterday's disasters. A couple of the "Big Eights" were of interest. 48540 was from 55D Royston in the Leeds Area probably off some cross country freight while 48739 was from far away 1H Northampton and perhaps she had recently been reallocated with the rundown of steam in the 1 Area. *This was later confirmed perhaps there had been a delay in reporting the transfer in "Modern Railways".* 48213 had been on 9H Patricroft when we visited there on Friday morning and here she was again to wish me an LMR sendoff.

Seeing the three "Britannias" was very pleasing. With a little luck I might be "Britannia" hauled on the final leg of the Railrover from Carnforth to Carlisle. Of the other visitors there was Standard 4MT 75015 from 10G Skipton and 92085 one of 8H Birkenhead's very many 9F 2-10-0's. The WD "Austerity" Class appears to have been dealt the death card in Lancashire depots but here was 90362 from 55G Huddersfield one of the many still active on the North Eastern Region and probably off some cross country freight.

Overall, Carnforth had been a very interesting shed with hosts of visitors and pleasingly only one withdrawn locomotive of the 46 steam on shed. What did I miss? 24 Home Steam

(52%) were on shed and 22 Home Steam were off shed still a pretty good percentage for a busy shed. Ten of the missing 22 were seen elsewhere on the week's tour and a further five on last month's Preston tour. At this time on a Saturday evening it was highly unlikely that the Sunday shed occupants would differ much if at all. 12A Carlisle Kingmoor had been completely packed when we visited there last Saturday evening.

10A Carnforth is destined to be one of the last remaining great steam sheds over the next year or two as dieselisation sweeps the remaining steam from the south to the North West. Yes, Carnforth had been a very fitting end to our week's Railrover travel.

On I go

I now had to say goodbye to 10A Carnforth and all its steam and ensure that I get the 20.55 – the last train of the day to arrive in Carlisle by midnight when my Railrover ticket would run out and be no longer such a valuable ticket to ride all over the LMR. A moot point was if you got on a LMR train before midnight whether it was valid until you got off it at a LMR Station the following day. Strangely, I had heard that (not from a BR official I should add) this was indeed the case but I would not be trying the matter out. There was a final train for Carlisle which left Wigan at 23.25 but that was never really on the agenda.

There were a couple of smallish sheds in the area 10J Lancaster and 12C Barrow that I could not fit into the final day's timetable or so I thought.

However, they could have been accommodated in this manner:-

				Miles
Depart	CARNFORTH	20.52		0
Arrive	LANCASTER CASTLE	21.00		6¼

	10J LANCASTER			
Steam				
Ivatt 2MT 2-6-2T 1946				
41221	41251			
Total	*1*			
Stanier 5MT 4-6-0 "Black Five" 1934				
44667	44758	**44889**	45014	
45025	45193	**45258**	45354	
45373	45394	**45445**		
Total	*11*			
Ivatt 2MT 2-6-0 1946				
46422	46431	46433	46441	
46514				
Total	*5*			
Stanier 8F 2-8-0 "Big Eight" 1935				
48077	*48148*	48297	48679	
Total	*2*			
Grand Total	**19**			
Recently		*Surviving*		
Withdrawn	3	*Steam Classes*	*4*	
Saw Elsewhere		**Saw Carlisle**		
on the Tour	*6*	*Sept 1958*	*1*	
Steam	*Sep-50*	*40*	*Mar-59*	*35*
Allocation	*Apr-65*	*19*	*Aug-65*	*19*
	Closed to Steam:-		*Apr-66*	

10 J Lancaster had a decent 19 steam allocation plus three recently withdrawn. Certainly, the shed was not what "Froth" had predicted or merely a sub shed of 10A Carnforth as the

Locoshed Directory had indicated.

				Miles
Depart	LANCASTER CASTLE	22.50		0
Arrive	BARROW	00.01		28½
	Overnight Barrow waiting room			
	Do 12C Barrow			
Depart	BARROW	08.45		0
Arrive	CARNFORTH	09.44		34¾
	Do 10A Carnforth again			
Depart	CARNFORTH	11.29		0
Arrive	CARLISLE	13.22		62¾

I would have been able to get a late train to Barrow arriving there just after midnight. After a comfortable or uncomfortable night at Barrow waiting room I would have been able to visit 12C Barrow in the early morning before getting the 08.45 to Carnforth. Following a revisit of 10A Carnforth I could have caught the 11.29 train to Carlisle arriving there at 13.22.

There would have been time to visit 12A Carlisle Upperby and 12B Carlisle Kingmoor prior to catching the 16.37 to Edinburgh.

12C BARROW					
Steam					
Fairburn 4MT 2-6-4T 1945					
	42080	42119	42134	42267	
	42673	42697			
Total		6			
Stanier 4MT 2-6-4T 1935 dev of Fowler 1927					
	42432	42581	42610		
Total		3			
Midland 4F 0-6-0 1924					
	44200	44443	44601		
Total		2			
Stanier 5MT 4-6-0 "Black Five" 1934					
	44882	45141	45182	45294	
	45340	45383	45451		
Total		7			
Ivatt 2MT 2-6-0 1946					
	46400	46499			
Total		2			
Midland 3F "Jinty" 0-6-0T 1924 dev. of Johnson 1899 design					
	47614	47675			
Total		1			
Grand Total		21			
Recently			**Surviving**		
Withdrawn (italics)		2	**Steam Classes**	6	
Saw Elsewhere			**Saw Manchester, Crewe**		
on the Tour		2	**trip Dec 64**	1	
Saw Carlisle			**Saw Carlisle**		
Sept 1958		3	**June 1967**	2	
Steam	*Sep-50*	40	*Mar-59*		35
Allocation	*Apr-65*	19	*Aug-65*		19
	Closed to Steam:-		*Apr-66*		

As can be seen above 12C Barrow had 21 Home Steam plus two recently withdrawn. Extra expenses for the Sunday trains outside the Railrover would have been about 26 shillings

(£1.32 new pence) plus the strain and the doubt of being able to stay overnight at Barrow waiting room.

While the above scenario would have been attractive for a reasonable cost not having my monster 832 page LMR timetable and the North Eastern Region timetable made me overlook how easily it would have been to add a Day 9 of the tour. We had missed the opportunity of visiting the Leeds Area on Thursday due to timetable problems on the Tuesday and Wednesday but it could easily have been accommodated tomorrow (Sunday) as follows:-

					Miles
Depart	CARNFORTH	20.52			0
Arrive	LANCASTER CASTLE	21.00			6¼
	Do 10J Lancaster				
Depart	LANCASTER GREEN AYRE	22.59			0
Arrive	SKIPTON	00.18			38¾
Depart	SKIPTON	00.22			0
Arrive	BRADFORD FORSTER SQUARE	00.50			18¼

Plenty time to visit 10J Lancaster and then a direct train from Lancaster to Bradford. Skipton to Bradford was outwith the Railrover but a fair chance that I would not meet a ticket collector on that stretch.

There are a couple of sheds in the Bradford area 55F Bradford Manningham and 56F Low Moor but no rail services to them so I would have quickly moved on to Leeds after the Bradford arrival:-

					Miles
Depart	BRADFORD FORSTER SQUARE	01.27			0
Arrive	LEEDS CITY	01.47			13½

55F Bradford Manningham moreover had a relatively small allocation of 11 steam – all LMS and BR in origin with only three relatively unexciting classes represented:-

55F BRADFORD MANNINGHAM					
Steam					
Fairburn 4MT 2-6-4T 1945					
	42072	42093	42138	42189	
Total	4				
Ivatt 4MT 2-6-0 1947					
	43014	43016	43030	43051	
	43074				
Total	5				
BR Standard 3MT 2-6-0 Swindon 1953					
	77001	77012			
Total	2				
		Surviving			
Grand Total	11	**Steam Classes**	3		
Recently		**Saw Elsewhere**			
Withdrawn	0	**on the Tour**	0		
Steam	*Sep-50*	45	*Mar-59*		25
Allocation	*Apr-65*	11	*Aug-65*		11
	Closed to Steam:-		*Apr-67*		

56F Low Moor was a more interesting shed and I hopefully would have seen the sole remaining "Jubilee" 45565 "Victoria" shedded there. In total, 18 steam remain shedded there Including six B1's.

		56F LOW MOOR			
Steam					
Fairburn 4MT 2-6-4T 1945					
	42055	42073	42074	42107	
	42116	42177	42142	42285	
Total		8			
Stanier 4MT 2-6-4T 1935 dev of Fowler 1927					
	42664				
Total		1			
Stanier 6P5F 4-6-0 "Jubilee" 1934					
	45565				
Total		1			
Thompson 5MT 4-6-0 B1 1942					
	61023	61115	61189	*61214*	
	61309	61386			
Total		5			
Riddles WD 8F 2-8-0 "Austerity" 1943					
	90711	90723	90731		
Total		3			
		Surviving			
Grand Total		18	*Steam Classes*	5	
Recently			*Saw Elsewhere*		
Withdrawn		1	*on the Tour*	0	
Steam	*Sep-50*		37	*Mar-59*	70
Allocation	*Apr-65*		17	*Aug-65*	18
	Closed to Steam:-			*Oct-67*	

Once in Leeds I would have spent the night in the waiting room there. At first light I would have deposited my heavy hold all in the left luggage and then made my way to 55H Leeds Neville Hill. 55H Leeds Neville Hill was the old LNER shed. Its allocation had been decimated to 13 steam locos plus one recently withdrawn. The five remaining steam classes included three interesting LNER classes (Thompson A1 Pacifics (three engines), Peppercorn 2-6-0 K1 (one) and Raven Q6 0-8-0's (four)).

		55H LEEDS NEVILLE HILL			
Steam					
Fairburn 4MT 2-6-4T 1945					
	42184	42196	42699		
Total		3			
Ivatt 4MT 2-6-0 1947					
	43054	*43075*			
Total		1			
Thompson 8P6F 4-6-2 A1 1945					
	60118	60131	60134	60154	
Total		4			
Peppercorn 5P6F 2-6-0 K1 1949					
	62007				
Total		1			
Raven 6F 0-8-0 Q6 1913					
	63344	63417	63420	63426	
Total		4			
		Surviving			
Grand Total		13	*Steam Classes*	5	
Recently			*Saw Elsewhere*		
Withdrawn		1	*on the Tour*	0	
Steam	*Sep-50*		81	*Mar-59*	84
Allocation	*Apr-65*		15	*Aug-65*	13
	Closed to Steam:-			*Jun-66*	

Next stops would have been 55A Leeds Holbeck followed by 55C Farnley Junction.

55A LEEDS HOLBECK

Steam

Fairburn 4MT 2-6-4T 1945

42052	42139	42145	42271
42622			

Total 5

Fowler 4MT 2-6-4T 1927

42394			

Total 1

Ivatt 4MT 2-6-0 1947

43039	43069	43117	43124
43130			

Total 5

Stanier 5MT 4-6-0 "Black Five" 1934

44662	44824	44828	44852
44853	44854	44857	44983
45063	45075	45079	45204
45211	45273		

Total 14

Stanier 6P5F 4-6-0 "Jubilee" 1934

45573	45574	45593	45608
45626	45658	45675	45660
45661	45664	45697	

Total 9

Stanier 8F 2-8-0 "Big Eight" 1935

48104	48157	48158	48283
48399	48454	48542	

Total 7

Grand Total 41

Recently Withdrawn	2	Surviving Steam Classes	6
Saw Elsewhere on the Tour	8	Saw Carlisle June 1967	1
Steam	Sep-50	95	Mar-59	81
Allocation	Apr-65	40	Aug-65	41
	Closed to Steam:-		Oct-67	

55C FARNLEY JUNCTION

Steam

Stanier 5MT 4-6-0 "Black Five" 1934

44826	44896	44943	45080
45428			

Total 5

Stanier 6P5F 4-6-0 "Jubilee" 1934

45562	45581	45643	45647

Total 4

Stanier 8F 2-8-0 "Big Eight" 1935

48076	48080	48664

Total 3

Grand Total 12

Recently Withdrawn	0	Surviving Steam Classe.	3
Saw Elsewhere on the Tour	2	Saw Carlisle June 1967	1
Steam	Sep-50	50	Mar-59	47
Allocation	Apr-65	12	Aug-65	12
	Closed to Steam:-		Nov-66	

55A Leeds Holbeck remained a classy shed with a steam allocation of 41 all ex LMS locos. Nine "Jubilees" remained plus a couple more recently withdrawn one of which had already departed to the scrapbreakers. 55C Farnley Junction's allocation had been decimated to 12 but the twelve included four "Jubilees".

Next stop would have been 55B Stourton. 55B Stourton was another LMS shed and had a decent allocation of 24 steam locos plus three recently withdrawn. Four surviving steam classes remained. "Big Eights" would have been to the fore with 14 allocated. An interesting class to see would have been the Standard 3MT 2-6-0 77XXX Class (four locos).

	55B STOURTON				
Steam					
Ivatt 4MT 2-6-0 1947					
43044	43084		43135	43140	
Total	*4*				
Midland 4F 0-6-0 1924					
44003	**44028**		*44044*	**44570**	
Total	*2*				
Stanier 8F 2-8-0 "Big Eight" 1935					
48084	48093		48126	48130	
48146	48160		48274	48311	
48394	48473		48622	48641	
48689	48703		48721		
Total	*14*				
BR Standard 3MT 2-6-0 Swindon 1953					
77000	77003		77010	77013	
Total	*4*				
		Surviving			
Grand Total	24	*Steam Classes*	*4*		
Recently		*Saw Elsewhere*			
Withdrawn	3	*on the Tour*	*1*		
Steam	*Sep-50*	48	*Mar-59*		36
Allocation	*Apr-65*	25	*Aug-65*		24
	Closed to Steam:-		*Jan-67*		

Once the four Leeds sheds had been safely negotiated I would have picked up my heavy grip from the left luggage then on to Wakefield by train or bus.

					Miles
Depart	LEEDS CITY	10.40	13.15	13.33	0
Arrive	WAKEFIELD KIRKGATE	11.03	13.38	13.57	14

As can be seen above the train service to Wakefield on Sundays was very sporadic

56A Wakefield itself was a big shed and 56B Ardsley would hopefully have been visited and returned by a 75 bus (Woodlesford) from Wakefield bus station. My heavy holdall would have been deposited at the left luggage at Wakefield Kirkgate station while I visited both sheds. 56A Wakefield was only a 20 minutes walk from Kirkgate station.

56A Wakefield had a big allocation of 83 steam plus two recently withdrawn. Great shed if you like WD "Austerity" 2-8-0's. Remarkably 60 were allocated plus a couple recently withdrawn. The shed did also have 12 B1's and importantly two "Jubilees".

56A WAKEFIELD				
Steam				
Fairburn 4MT 2-6-4T 1945				
	42108	42150	42152	42161
	42181	42204	42269	
Total	7			
Fowler 4MT 2-6-4T 1927				
	42406			
Total	1			
Stanier 4MT 2-6-4T 1935 dev of Fowler 1927				
	42650			
Total	1			
Stanier 6P5F 4-6-0 "Jubilee" 1934				
	45694	45739		
Total	2			
Thompson 5MT 4-6-0 B1 1942				
	61022	61024	61040	61123
	61129	61131	61161	61173
	61224	61320	61353	61387
Total	12			
Riddles WD 8F 2-8-0 "Austerity" 1943				
	90054	90061	90068	90074
	90076	90089	90112	90113
	90116	90122	*90124*	90135
	90155	90160	90200	90210
	90233	90281	90300	90321
	90329	90333	90336	90339
	90341	90342	90348	90360
	90363	90370	90373	90379
	90380	90382	90385	90396
	90404	90407	90409	90415
	90417	90429	**90430**	90457
	90470	90482	90610	90611
	90615	90620	90622	90631
	90633	90639	90651	90654
	90678	90679	90684	90698
	90707	90721		
Total	60			
		Surviving		
Grand Total	83	**Steam Classes**	6	
Recently		**Saw Elsewhere**		
Withdrawn	2	**on the Tour**	3	
Saw Preston				
Trip July 65	2			
Steam	**Sep-50**	122	**Mar-59**	87
Allocation	**Apr-65**	84	**Aug-65**	83
	Closed to Steam:-		**Jun-67**	

56B Ardsley was an old L.N.E.R. shed and had four Thompson A1 Pacifics (three recently withdrawn), 15 B1 4-6-0's and 2 V2 2-6-2's. WD's were also popular with a further 13.

After 56B Ardsley the plan would have been to get a bus or a train from Wakefield to nearby Normanton.

	56B ARDSLEY			
Steam				
Ivatt 4MT 2-6-0 1947				
	43070	43096	43101	43132
	43137	43141		
Total		6		
Thompson 8P6F 4-6-2 A1 1945				
	60117	60130	*60133*	*60148*
Total		1		
Gresley 7P6F 2-6-2 V2 1936				
	60843	60923		
Total		2		
Thompson 5MT 4-6-0 B1 1942				
	61013	61014	61016	61017
	61030	61061	61110	*61218*
	61237	61238	61240	61259
	61291	61304	61322	61385
	61388			
Total		15		
Riddles WD 8F 2-8-0 "Austerity" 1943				
	90047	90056	90126	90230
	90236	90240	90361	90405
	90465	90481	90625	90642
	90644			
Total		13		
		Surviving		
Grand Total		37	**Steam Classes**	5
Recently			**Saw Elsewhere**	
Withdrawn		5	**on the Tour**	0
Steam	*Sep-50*		88	*Mar-59*	63
Allocation	*Apr-65*		45	*Aug-65*	37
	Closed to Steam:-			*Nov-65*	

	55E NORMANTON			
Steam				
Fairburn 4MT 2-6-4T 1945				
	42083	42149		
Total		2		
Ivatt 4MT 2-6-0 1947				
	43043	43116		
Total		2		
Midland 4F 0-6-0 1924				
	44170	44400	44408	44458
Total		4		
Riddles WD 8F 2-8-0 "Austerity" 1943				
	90243	90254	90318	90337
	90345	90357	90395	90617
	90652	90664	90682	90699
	90722			
Total		13		
		Surviving		
Grand Total		21	**Steam Classes**	4
Recently			**Saw Elsewhere**	
Withdrawn		0	**on the Tour**	0
Steam	*Sep-50*		49	*Mar-59*	41
Allocation	*Apr-65*		21	*Aug-65*	21
	Closed to Steam:-			*Jan-68*	

There was the odd Sunday train to Normanton and this one might have sufficed.

				Miles
Depart	WAKEFIELD KIRKGATE		18.58	0
Arrive	NORMANTON		19.05	3

Time permitting a bus trip and back to 55D Royston might have been a possibility but I suspect the Sunday service would not have been too good. There was no Sunday rail service. 55D Royston with a steam allocation of 31 plus one recently withdrawn was a far more interesting shed than 55E Normanton but would have been difficult to reach by bus on the Sunday.

55D ROYSTON				
Steam				
Fowler Midland 4F 0-6-0 1911				
	43906	43968	43983	
Total		2		
Midland 4F 0-6-0 1924				
	44056	44446		
Total		2		
Stanier 5MT 4-6-0 "Black Five" 1934				
	44912	45207	45219	
Total		3		
Stanier 8F 2-8-0 "Big Eight" 1935				
	48067	48070	48075	48113
	48123	48159	48162	48169
	48222	48281	48337	48352
	48439	48443	48466	48537
	48540	48670	48710	
Total		19		
Riddles WD 8F 2-8-0 "Austerity" 1943				
	90377	90503	90605	90645
	90650			
Total		5	*Surviving*	
Grand Total		31	*Steam Classes*	5
Recently			*Saw Elsewhere*	
Withdrawn		1	*on the Tour*	2
Steam	*Sep-50*	60	*Mar-59*	55
Allocation	*Apr-65*	32	*Aug-65*	31
	Closed to Steam:-		*Nov-67*	

There would have been a must make connection from Normanton to York.

				Miles
Depart	NORMANTON	20.40		0
Arrive	YORK	21.34		24½

50A York could have been visited in the dark if I had indeed arrived from Normanton at 21.34. This would have been problematic but perhaps not impossible.

50A York with an allocation of 55 steam plus 10 recently withdrawn would have been perhaps too good to miss. A former L.N.E.R. flagship it was still a fine shed with nine surviving steam classes including Thompson 4-6-2 A1's (seven plus two withdrawn), Worsdell 0-6-0 (3) and Raven 0-6-0 (1).

	50A YORK				
Steam					
Ivatt 4MT 2-6-0 1947					
	43055	**43071**	**43097**	**43126**	
	43133	**43138**			
Total		*6*			
Thompson 8P6F 4-6-2 A1 1945					
	60121	**60129**	**60138**	**60145**	
	60146	**60151**	*60152*	**60155**	
	60156				
Total		*7*			
Gresley 7P6F 2-6-2 V2 1936					
	60810	**60828**	**60831**	**60837**	
	60847	**60876**	**60877**	**60886**	
	60895	*60929*	*60963*		
Total		*8*			
Thompson 5MT 4-6-0 B1 1942					
	61018	**61021**	**61049**	**61176**	
	61256	**61275**	*61276*	**61303**	
	61319	**61337**			
Total		*9*			
Peppercorn 5P6F 2-6-0 K1 1949					
	62005	**62010**	**62012**	**62028**	
	62042	**62046**	*62049*	*62056*	
	62057	**62060**	**62062**	**62065**	
Total		*10*			
Worsdell 5F 0-6-0 J27 1906					
	65823	**65844**	**65846**		
Total		*3*			
Raven 1921 dev. of Worsdell 5F 0-6-0 J27 1906					
	65894				
Total		*1*			
Riddles WD 8F 2-8-0 "Austerity" 1943					
	90045	**90078**	*90217*	**90517**	
	90518				
Total		*4*			
BR Standard 9F 2-10-0 Brighton 1954					
	92005	**92006**	**92205**	**92206**	
	92211	*92221*	**92231**	**92239**	
Total		*7*			
		Surviving			
Grand Total		**55**	*Steam Classes*	*9*	
Recently			*Saw Elsewhere*		
Withdrawn		**10**	*on the Tour*	*1*	
Saw Manchester					
Crewe trip Dec 64		**1**			
Steam	*Sep-50*	**174**	*Mar-59*		*150*
Allocation	*Apr-65*	**64**	*Aug-65*		*55*
	Closed to Steam:-		*Jun-67*		

Plan B would be judging on the time reached at 56B Ardsley to dump 55E Normanton and return by bus to Leeds and then get a train to York.

					Miles
Depart	LEEDS CITY		17.20	20.15	0
Arrive	YORK		17.52	20.50	25½

Trains to Edinburgh were plentiful from York and I would hope to get a half fare on the train as money would have been running out fast. There was always Plan C which would be hitching a lift from a lorry driver up to Edinburgh from the nearby A1 trunk road. That would have pretty certain have worked. The Ordinary Single from Leeds to Edinburgh would have been a weighty £3 and two shillings odds (£3.12 new pence) so I definitely would have needed to go for half fare or a hitch on a lorry or a bus beckoned!

This was the desired train back from York:-

			Miles
Depart	YORK	02.14	0
Arrive	NEWCASTLE	03.51	80½
Arrive	EDINBURGH	06.30	205

So a late evening arrival at York would have presented no problem.

Back to the Present

I arrived back at Carnforth station at 20.40 giving me fifteen minutes to spare. Steam was still going strong and I noted "Black Five" 44681 come into the station at 20.49 on the 19.11 local train from Carlisle which would eventually terminate at Warrington Bank Quay at 22.42.

Three minutes later a marvelous event took place. I had the pleasure of seeing "Britannia" 70012 "John of Gaunt" storm into Carnforth station at the head of my train. This would be an incredibly fine finale to my tour. The train was the Saturdays only 18.37 from Crewe which would arrive at Carlisle at 22.44. It was to be expected that a Crewe shedded loco would be on the train and doubtless she would be on 12A Carlisle Kingmoor or 12B Carlisle Upperby tomorrow before returning south. I noted down 70012 "John of Gaunt" in my notebook and added the comment (jealousy will get you nowhere)!

The journey schedule would be as follows:-

		Schedule	Miles
Depart	CARNFORTH	20.55	0
Arrive	OXENHOLME	21.17	12¾
Depart	OXENHOLME	21.20	12¾
Arrive	TEBAY	21.45	25¾
Pass	SHAP		33¼
Arrive	PENRITH FOR ULLSWATER	22.17	45
Arrive	CARLISLE	22.44	62¾

You can gather that I was rather pleased at being "Britannia" hauled for the first time. However, the journey timings for a small local train would be incredibly easy for an engine with "John of Gaunt's" capabilities. If it had been a horse race "John of Gaunt" would have won the race in a common canter hard held.

The train was rather busy and I found a compartment with a window seat after some hunting up and down the train. A railwayman had taken up the other window seat. He noted that I was a railway enthusiast and soon we were involved in an interesting conversation. I found out that he was a driver from 10J Lancaster M.P.D. which I had not been able to visit this week. He said that his rosters took him generally from Carlisle in the north to Preston in the south. When he was at Carlisle he stayed in the railwaymens' hostel near 12A Carlisle Kingmoor shed.

I asked him what he thought of continuous welded rails. The main line between Carlisle and Euston would eventually be all continuous welded track. I had noted continuous welding work going on near Penrith the Sunday I went to Blackpool last month. That day trains had to be diverted over the famed Settle to Carlisle line. The driver thought that he was much in favour of continuous welded track as engines didn't roll on it. Certainly from the passengers point of view it got rid of the interminable "clackety – clack" of the trains going over the expansion joints in the rails. These new continuous welded rails should be much safer and allow higher speeds the driver added.

The driver was particularly interested in my LocoShed Book and looked up to see the listings for 10J Lancaster, 12A Carlisle Kingmoor and 12B Carlisle Upperby. He noted Ivatt tank 41221 with interest. "She's withdrawn now and I hauled her over to the dead-line today. You'd better take a note of that", he said. Good to get a piece of inside information!

Meanwhile "John of Gaunt" was making mincemeat of her schedule. She was being driven flat out by evidently a steam loving driver. It was a sensational feeling. Oxenholme was reached ten minutes early at 21.07. She had taken twelve minutes rather than the scheduled twenty two. She, of course, had to wait there until the scheduled departure time of 21.20 so a three minute stop became a fifteen minute stop.

We were so engrossed in our conversation that I completely forgot to look out for 12E Tebay shed to the north west of the station. 12E Tebay had a few banking locos allocated to aid trains up to Shap summit. The allocation comprised six 2-6-4 tanks and three Ivatt "Flying Pig" 2-6-0's. Tebay station was predictably reached ten minutes early. "John of Gaunt" stood there blowing off steam for so long that I didn't notice her moving off and the small 12E Tebay shed was missed. I wouldn't be losing too much sleep over that.

	12E TEBAY				
Steam					
Fairburn 4MT 2-6-4T 1945					
	42095	**42110**	**42210**	**42225**	
	42232				
Total	*5*				
Stanier 4MT 2-6-4T 1935 dev of Fowler 1927					
	42439				
Total	*1*				
Ivatt 4MT 2-6-0 1947					
	43009	**43029**	**43035**		
Total	*3*				
Grand Total	*9*				
Recently		*Surviving*			
Withdrawn	*0*	*Steam Classes*	*3*		
Saw Elsewhere					
on the Tour	*2*				
Steam	*Sep-50*	*10*	*Mar-59*		*11*
Allocation	*Apr-65*	*9*	*Aug-65*		*9*
	Closed to Steam:-		*Jan-68*		

"John of Gaunt" impressively took the hard climb to Shap Summit in her stride. Penrith was reached almost 15 minutes early at 22.03 and waited again until the official departure time (22.17). My driver was very annoyed at this. He could understand the train had to wait at Oxenholme and Tebay as if these connections were missed passengers would not reach Carlisle before midnight. However, he reasoned that Penrith had a good regular bus service to Carlisle so our train should have been allowed to leave early. "John of Gaunt" made one last charge and we reached Carlisle Station nine minutes early at 22.35.

At Carlisle my conversation with the Lancaster driver regretfully had to come to an end. It had been about the two most interesting hours on the tour listening fascinated as he related some of his accumulated railway experience and knowledge. The one and three quarter hours on the train had flashed by so engrossed had I been in listening and asking him questions. We said "Cheerio" and "Good luck" and I was sorry that our conversation could not be extended further.

"John of Gaunt's performance had been impressive:-

		Schedule	Actual	Miles
Depart	CARNFORTH	20.55	20.55	0
Arrive	OXENHOLME	21.17	20.06	12¾
Depart	OXENHOLME	21.20	21.20	12¾
Arrive	TEBAY	21.45	21.35	25¾
Pass	SHAP			33¼
Arrive	PENRITH FOR ULLSWATER	22.17	22.03	45
Arrive	CARLISLE	22.44	22.35	62¾

11 minutes gained to Oxenholme, 10 to Tebay, 14 to Penrith and a further 9 to Carlisle making total timetable savings of 44 minutes. "John of Gaunt" had been quite wasted on such a lax timetable and clearly the driver wanted to point that out by all his early arrivals! In all a most fitting last steam Railrover journey.

CARNFORTH TO CARLISLE						
		Home shed		Built	Withdrawn	Scrap
Steam						
Stanier 5MT 4-6-0 "Black Five" 1934						
44681		5B	Crewe South (ex 5A)	Jun-1950	Sep-1967	Mar-1968
Total	1					
BR Standard 7P6F 4-6-2 "Britannia" Derby 1951						
70012	"John of Gaunt"	5B	Crewe South (ex 5A)	May-1951	Dec-1967	Apr-1968
Total	1					
On Journey	2	Kops	1			
Steam	2	Diesels	0			
	Home Area		0	Visitors	2	
Shed Distribution	5B	2				
Steam classes on view	2					
Steam Origin	LMS	1 BR		1		
Journey						
Highlight:-	70012	"John of Gaunt"	5B	Crewe South		

It was a most sobering thought being back at Carlisle Station. This time last week D.S. and I had been waiting impatiently for the start of our tour with the 00.33 train to take us to London. Here I was back at initial departure point. It would have been good to do it all again next week having learnt from a number of mistakes. There had only been one thing stopping me going for two weeks and that had been money. It had cost me £11 pounds and ten shillings (£11.50 in new pence) for my LMR Railrover ticket and I had spent about another £10 during the week. Total outlays of about £22. The trouble was that it had taken me a year to save up the required money at a rate of about ten shillings (50 new pence) per week. I was now very much stony broke.

This week had certainly been worth it in terms of money but ideally with more cash available I would have bought a two week "Freedom of Britain" ticket for £27 and throw in say another £15 for expenses and the two weeks could have been comfortably done for just over £40. This would have been ideal and I would have been pleased to have organised a slightly more leisurely timetable and pick up all the steam pockets that I had missed e.g. Leeds, Sheffield, Doncaster, Gloucester, Worcester, Oxford, Eastleigh, Bournemouth, the old GWR line out of Paddington etc. I was sure that 1965 would be the last year to see steam over most of the railway system. Unfortunately £40 plus was outside my strictly limited budget although perhaps I should have asked my Aunt Frances if I could have dipped into a savings account which she had kindly opened for me many years ago and had made regular monthly contributions to it.

Talking about money my ticket ran out at midnight and was not valid for the Scottish Region so I need to purchase a single ticket for my return home tomorrow. Ordinary singles were a complete rip-off and I would need to fork out a further twenty seven shillings (£1.35 new pence). An ordinary single almost cost as much as a cheap day return. An option would be to get the bus back at 15 shillings and three pence (seventy six new pence). However, the bus took four hours and a bus journey would be a very ignominious end to a rail week. Yes, I would certainly take the train. Tomorrow's schedule was as follows:-

				Miles
	Do 12A Carlisle Kingmoor			
	Do 12B Carlisle Upperby			Miles
Depart	CARLISLE	16.37		0
Arrive	CARSTAIRS	18.30		73½
Depart	CARSTAIRS	18.40		73½
Arrive	EDINBURGH WAVERLEY	19.18		101

If I purchased my ticket tomorrow morning I might have to surrender my LMR Railrover ticket and I wanted to keep that as a souvenir. Therefore, I left the island platform, crossed the over bridge and showed my LMR ticket at the barrier which was still valid. I went to the booking office and paid the twenty seven shillings for an ordinary single to Edinburgh. Now I could use this ticket to go in and out of the station without surrendering my Railrover and I would show it if any cop tried to stop me from sleeping in the waiting room.

Today had not been one for eating and drinking. I had light meals at Blackburn in the middle of the afternoon and at Skipton in the early evening but that was all I had to eat all day. A bit tired and hungry now that the Railrover had ended I went into the BR cafeteria for the usual fare and had a can of soup. fruit pie, cake and a cup of tea. BR's station prices although steep are not as extortionate as those on their trains. On the trains they sell beer at half the quantity but at the same price as a full can costs elsewhere.

I sat in the cafeteria making my meal spin out until a quarter to one in the morning and reflected on the day's events. This was interrupted by dashing out from time to time when I heard the whine of a diesel or a roar of a stem loco.

Review of the Day

DAY 8   **SATURDAY AUGUST 7TH 1965**   **LMR DAY 7**

ORIGINAL TIMETABLE

MILES

Depart LIVERPOOL EXCHANGE	05.30	0
Arrive AINTREE SEFTON ARMS	05.41	4¾

Do 8L Aintree Sefton Arms (45 mins. approx)   Recovery Time - 10

Depart AINTREE SEFTON ARMS	06.16	0
Arrive SANDHILLS	06.26	3¼
Depart SANDHILLS	06.32	0

Arrive BANK HALL	06.33	½

Do 8K Bank Hall (18 mins. approx)

Recovery Time
+ 3

Depart BANK HALL	06.54	0
Arrive LIVERPOOL EXCHANGE	07.00	2
Depart JAMES STREET	07.16	0
Arrive BIRKENHEAD CENTRAL	07.22	1¾

Do 8H Birkenhead (30 mins. approx)

Recovery Time
- 2

Depart BIRKENHEAD CENTRAL	07.50	0
Arrive LIVERPOOL CENTRAL Low Level	07.58	2¼
Depart LIVERPOOL LIME STREET	08.25	0
Arrive ST HELEN'S SHAW STREET	08.57	10¼

see 8A Edge Hill - East

Do 8G Sutton Oak (50 mins. approx)

Recovery Time
NIL

Depart ST HELEN'S SHAW STREET	09.41	10¼
Arrive WIGAN NORTH WESTERN	10.01	19

Do 8F Wigan (Spring's Branch) (80 mins. approx)

Recovery Time
+4

Depart WIGAN WALLGATE	11.25	0
Arrive BOLTON	11.43	9½

Do 9K Bolton (45 mins. approx)

Recovery Time
+ 11

Depart BOLTON	12.39	0
Arrive PRESTON	13.16	20

BUS - Local Service

Depart PRESTON STATION
Arrive LOSTOCK HALL STATION

Do 10D Lostock Hall

BUS - Local Service

Depart LOSTOCK HALL STATION
Arrive PRESTON STATION

Depart PRESTON	14.25	0
Arrive BLACKBURN	14.44	11¼

Do 10H Lower Darwen (80 mins. approx)		Recovery Time NIL
Depart BLACKBURN	16.04	11¼
Arrive ROSE GROVE	16.24	<u>21</u>
Do 10F Rose Grove (20 mins. approx)		Recovery Time + 18
Depart ROSE GROVE	17.02	0
Arrive SKIPTON	17.37	<u>18¼</u>
Do 10G Skipton (35 mins. approx)		Recovery Time + 31
Depart SKIPTON	18.43	0
Arrive WENNINGTON	19.48 (Train split)	28¼
Depart WENNINGTON	19.59	28¼
Arrive CARNFORTH	20.18	<u>38</u>

Journey:-
    see Hellifield (north west)   (19.06)

Do 10A Carnforth (30 mins. approx)		Recovery Time + 7
Depart CARNFORTH	20.55	0
Arrive CARLISLE	22.44	<u>62¾</u>
See 12A Tebay - West	(21.45)	35¾

This is how the revised timetable worked out:-

Depart LIVERPOOL CENTRAL	05.05	0
Arrive GARSTON	05.16	<u>5½</u>
Do 8C Speke Junction (40 mins. approx)		
Do 8J Allerton (35 mins. approx)		Recovery Time + 5
Depart GARSTON	06.36	0
Arrive LIVERPOOL CENTRAL	06.51	<u>5½</u>
Depart LIVERPOOL EXCHANGE	07.10	0
Arrive BANK HALL	07.14	<u>2</u>
Do 8K Bank Hall (18 mins. approx)		Recovery Time NIL
Depart BANK HALL	07.32	0
Arrive SANDHILLS	07.34	<u>½</u>

Depart SANDHILLS	07.47	0
Arrive AINTREE SEFTON ARMS	07.56	<u>3¼</u>

Do 8L Aintree Sefton Arms (45 mins. approx)

Recovery Time
+ 2

Depart AINTREE SEFTON ARMS	08.43	0
Arrive LIVERPOOL EXCHANGE	08.58	<u>4¾</u>
Depart JAMES STREET	09.16	0
Arrive BIRKENHEAD CENTRAL	09.22	<u>1¾</u>

Do 8H Birkenhead (30 mins. approx)

Recovery Time
- 2

Depart BIRKENHEAD CENTRAL	09.50	0
Arrive JAMES STREET	09.55	<u>2¼</u>

Liverpool Corporation Bus No 4B and 79C
Depart LORD STREET, CITY CENTRE
Arrive TIVERTON STREET, EDGE HILL

Do 8A Edge Hill

Depart EDGE HILL	11.13	0
Arrive WIGAN NORTH WESTERN	11.59	<u>18</u>

Do 8F Wigan (Springs Branch) (80 mins. approx)

Recovery Time
-10

Depart WIGAN WALLGATE	13.13	0
Arrive BOLTON	13.37	<u>9½</u>

Do 9K Bolton (45 mins. approx)

Recovery Time
+ 11

Depart BOLTON	14.27	0
Arrive BLACKBURN	14.55	<u>13¾</u>

Do 10H Lower Darwen (105 mins. approx)

Recovery Time
-36

Depart BLACKBURN	16.04	0
Arrive ROSE GROVE	16.24	<u>9¾</u>

Do 1F Rose Grove (20 mins. approx)

Recovery Time
+ 18

Depart ROSE GROVE	17.02	0

Arrive SKIPTON	17.37	<u>18¼</u>

Do 10G Skipton (35 mins. approx)		Recovery Time + 31

Depart SKIPTON	18.43	0
Arrive WENNINGTON	19.48 (Train split)	28¼
Depart WENNINGTON	19.59	28¼
Arrive CARNFORTH	20.18	<u>38</u>

Journey:-
    See Hellifield (North West)   (19.06)

Do 10A Carnforth (30 mins. approx)		Recovery Time + 7

Depart CARNFORTH	20.55	0
Arrive CARLISLE	22.44	<u>62¾</u>
See 12A Tebay - West	(21.45)	35¾

END OF RAILROVER

Quite incredibly everything went to plan for the first time since last Saturday when all we had was an undemanding trip to Carlisle and a return trip to Workington.

The day itself had started strangely with my Somnambulist Affair at the Pier Head. That at least helped us not to sleep in. The 05.05 to Garston was our earliest start of the week as we tried to recover from the effects of the disasters of the previous day "Black Friday". Surprisingly it had not been Friday 13th but Friday 6th perhaps it had come a week early this month.

8C Speke Junction and 8J Allerton passed off without incident. Then came 8K Bank Hall. A tight timing and our antics in running around the sheds there set off an alarm and caused us problems. In that fateful encounter with the shedmaster we almost bowled him over and knocked him down the stairs. Luckily, that didn't happen but I was still concerned that our hasty exit would result in the railway police and other shedmasters being alerted. Incredibly, 8K Bank Hall turned out to be our only brush with officialdom all day.

8L Aintree turned out to be a comfortable "ask to go around shed" without problem and we had the amusing sight of D.S. dying of thirst while a thunderstorm was raging. 8H Birkenhead went well despite the notice about guard dogs which turned out to be non existent. 8A Edge Hill was another "ask to go around" shed which went well. If you ask nicely I have now concluded that you'll probably get round the vast majority of sheds in the U.K. particularly if you cite an interest in taking a few photographs which puts you a cut above the usual trainspotters. If one has to go past the shedmaster's office it is best to ask as they tend to take exception if you walk blithely past ignoring the office. We had no time to ask at 8K Bank Hall and that seemed to cause quite a stir and we got past the office on the return from the shed with the greatest of difficulty! We had no permits at all for the 8 (Liverpool) and 10 (Preston) area. As was a Saturday when most sheds were pretty dead it was easier for us to get round without problems.

Then there was Wigan and goodbye to D.S. If D.S. had remained with me it is extremely doubtful whether we would have made all our connections today. Nevertheless, there was the downside that it was all very dull and quiet without him. I don't know yet how I managed to make the Wigan Wallgate train to Bolton and I had certainly dodged a bullet. 9K Bolton also passed smoothly enough but for one of the two carrying straps for my holdall breaking. That was to be a nuisance for the rest of the day. An excellent bus service solved the impossible recovery time at 10H Lower Darwen. It is highly unlikely that D.S. would have got to the shed due to the nature of the commando course. On the way to 10F Rose Grove my train passed 10E Accrington shed which was now unfortunately only a bucket depot. 10F Rose Grove, 10G Skipton and 10A Carnforth all passed completely without incident.

The tour ended brilliantly. I arrived at Skipton never having been steam hauled all week. However, the last three journeys Skipton to Wennington, Wennington to Carnforth and Carnforth to Carlisle were all steam hauled. Firstly by a "Black Five", secondly by a Stanier 2-6-4 Tank and then finally and fittingly by "Britannia" 70012 "John of Gaunt".

Yesterday's review of the day was all about disasters and what should have gone better. Today, incredibly everything had gone to timetable. There had been a near disaster at Bank Hall and tight timings at Wigan and Lower Darwen where I stupidly almost lost one of my bags. Was it a coincidence that the day the timetable worked D.S. went home early? Overall, today had been rather incident less because the timetable had gone to plan. Deviations from the plan tend to bring incidents.

Today had been a magnificent steam day. Diesels had hardly had a look-in. The North West was a steam stronghold. How long would this last for I did not know. A record twelve M.P.D's were visited today with high proportions of home steam allocations being on shed. The revised "Irlam" timetable had been a great success. By necessity 8G Sutton Oak and 10D Lostock Hall were lost in favour of adding back 8A Edge Hill, 8C Speke Junction, 8H Birkenhead and 8L Allerton all missed yesterday. It would have been good also to visit 10J Lancaster, 12C Barrow and 12E Tebay but there had never been space to include them in the original timetable. The tour had ended on the crest of a wave rather than yesterday's troughs of despair.

At midnight I gave a cheer, much to the surprise of the other people in the cafeteria. My LMR Railrover had run its course and was now officially expired. I certainly had got good value out of it!

I checked my wallet. I found to my dismay that after buying my ticket home that I only had one pound and a few shillings left. Where had all the money gone? We had hardly been lashing the money about during the week as we had ate and drunk virtually nothing. However, the rail trips outside the Railrover (e.g. Birmingham to Barry), the many bus journeys, two youth hostel fees and London Transport expenses must have all added up. It was perhaps a blessing that we did not venture to the Doncaster and Leeds Areas as we would probably have run out of cash! At the start of the tour I believed that I would be taking home a few pounds at the end of it.

I took special note of the 00.33 train to Euston. This was the train that D.S. and I got on to begin our LMR Tour seven days ago last Sunday morning. It would have been good to get on it again and start another week's tour but it was not to be. Last week D228 "Samaria" had hauled us and this time she was replaced by D1852 a new Brush Type 4.

At about 00.45 I left the cafeteria and moved into the waiting room which was quite busy. The occupants were waiting for overnight trains with the last leaving at 02.29. There was little chance of getting any sleep while the waiting room was bust with people. To pass the time I leafed through my notebook and looked at the week's work. Periodically, I would go out to see what was on the frequent overnight trains. One of the people waiting in the waiting room was a fellow railway enthusiast. He was impressed at my week's work and he left on the 02.29 to Manchester. That was the last of the overnight trains going south and the one on which Ian "Froth" Firth and I had traveled on last December. We had left Edinburgh then at 22.30 connecting with the main Glasgow portion at Carstairs.

I leafed over my "needs" book for Carlisle in the waiting room and was surprised that after last week's visit and the tour that it amounted to just three engines. Firstly, from 12A Carlisle Kingmoor there was Fowler 1911 0-6-0 4F Midland 43981 which was now withdrawn and probably en route to some scrapbreaker somewhere. Secondly, there was 92130 a 9F 2-10-0. Finally, there was 46434 an Ivatt 2MT 2-6-0 from 12B Carlisle Upperby. So perhaps it wasn't worth staying on to visit 12A Carlisle Kingmoor and 12B Carlisle Upperby tomorrow morning before returning to Edinburgh with a lunchtime train.

It was now 02.00 and the waiting room was getting empty – there was only the railway enthusiast and another couple of people waiting for the 02.29 to Manchester. The next thing I remember was that it was now 02.45 as I had dozed off for 45 minutes. Something must have awakened me. It was no one in the waiting room which was completely empty so it must have been something else in the station. Half asleep, I staggered out of the waiting room and what would be near to me standing light engine in the station was "Jubilee" 45593 "Kholapur". Was I dreaming? No, I was not. What an engine to see at the end of my tour. Finally, after a five minute pause she ambled out of the southern exit of the station probably bound for 12B Carlisle Upperby shed.

I went back to the waiting room and soon fell asleep again. I awoke again at 03.30. I remembered that there was a train due to leave for Edinburgh in a few minutes time and would be on the platform now having got in at 03.26. I decided that "Kholapur" had been an appropriate end to the week and that I would get the train on the platform home and not stay for probably strictly limited results to visit 12A Carlisle Kingmoor and 12B Carlisle Upperby later in the morning.

I quickly got my luggage together and checked with the station inspector if the train in front of me was indeed the Edinburgh train. "Yes" he said "but you can't get on to it. It's leaving now". That was all I needed to know, if a train wasn't moving you got on to it whatever any station inspector says just as we would have done at Cardiff General Station on Tuesday afternoon if our train had not been moving off. I hurried down to the end of the train and found the coaches for Edinburgh, most of them – the ones at the front had been for Glasgow.

The Edinburgh section turned out to be full but I was able to get a seat in a six seat compartment once some luggage had been moved to the overhead rack to make room for me. Three of the five occupants appeared to be together and sounded like Glaswegians. This was funny peculiar as this was the Edinburgh section. This puzzle was cleared up when one of them asked me "Heh, Jim (as some Glaswegians tend to call everyone) do you know when this train gets into Glasgow"? He naturally pronounced Glasgow as Glesgi.

"This is the Edinburgh section of the train." I answered.

"Is that true, Jim?" He queried

"Yes." I replied "There's an Edinburgh sticker on the outside of the compartment window."

"That so. We had better get oot o' here. C'mon boys. We wir lucky ta see yi or we wid hav ended up in Enbra. Thanks a lot Jim."

With that the Glaswegians made a hasty exit and departed for the "Glesgi" section as they would say.

CARLISLE STATION SATURDAY NIGHT 7AUG and SUNDAY MORNING 8AUG

		Home shed		Built		
Diesels						
BR Sulzer "Peak" Type 4 1Co-Co1 1959						
D 129		ML	Midland Lines	*Nov-1961*	01.05 Glasgow to Marylebone	
Total	*1*					
English Electric Type 4 1Co-Co1 1958						
D 233	"Empress of England"	1A	Willesden	*Sep-1959*	00.59 perth-euston	
D 382		1B	Camden	*Mar-1962*	01.43 perth-euston	
Total	*2*					
Brush Type 4 Co-Co 1962						
D1837		5A	Crewe Diesel	*May-1965*	00.45 glasgow-euston	
D1848		5A	Crewe Diesel	*Jun-1965*	01.58 glasgow-b'ham	
D1852		5A	Crewe Diesel	*Jun-1965*	00.33 glasgow-euston	
Total	*3*					
Steam				Built	Withdrawn	Scrap
Ivatt 2MT 2-6-2T 1946						
41229		12B	Carlisle Upp.(ex5A/5B/5D)	Oct-1948	Nov-1966	Apr-1967
Total	*1*					
Stanier 5MT 4-6-0 "Black Five" 1934						
45371		12B	Carlisle Upperby	*Jun-1937*	*Apr-1967*	*Aug-1967*
Total	*1*					
Stanier 6P5F 4-6-0 "Jubilee" 1934						
45593	"Kholapur"	55A	Leeds Holbeck	*Dec-1934*	*Oct-1967*	*saved*
Total	*1*					

On Station	9	**Kops**		4	
Steam	3	**Diesels**		6	
	Home Area			2 Visitors		7
Shed	12B	2			
Distribution	1A	1 1B		1 ML	1
	5A	3			
	55A	1			
Steam Classes on view	3				
Steam Origin	LMS	3 BR		0	
Station Highlight:-	45596	"Kholapur"		55A	Leeds Holbeck

		Schedule		*Miles*
Depart	BIRMINGHAM	22.46		
Arrive	CARLISLE	03.26		0
Depart	CARLISLE	03.34		0
Arrive	CARSTAIRS	05.12		73¾
Depart	CARSTAIRS	06.55		73¾
Arrive	EDINBURGH HAYMARKET	07.29		99¾
Arrive	EDINBURGH WAVERLEY	07.33		101

The reason for the almost 1¾ hours wait at Carstairs was that the 06.55 provided an Edinburgh connection for two later trains which called at Carstairs. One train arrived at Carstairs at 06.10 (the 21.10) from London Euston and finally the 0045 from Liverpool gets to Carstairs at 06.41 and through carriages from Edinburgh are detached from it. Finally, all these through carriages are added to our train for Edinburgh and my train coupled with carriages from two others leaves at 06.55.

A very impressive steam haul today with 431 steam in all, and only 44 diesels and 5 electrics. Steam reigns supreme in this area still! 8F Springs Branch (Wigan) led the way with 69 steam on shed followed by Carnforth 46, Bolton 45, Birkenhead 41, Speke Junction 36 and Edge Hill 34.

DAY 8 LIVERPOOL, WIGAN, BOLTON, NORTH LANCASHIRE, SKIPTON AND CARLISLE ARRIVAL

Code	Visits	GWR	SR	LMS	LNER	WD	BR	Steam Total	Diesel Total	Electric Total	Grand Total
	Livpool Central to Garston	1						1	1		2
8C	Speke Junction			32			4	36	12		48
	Garston to Liverpool Ctral.			3				3			3
8J	Allerton									5	5
8K	Bank Hall			14			6	20	2		22
8L	Aintree			19		4	2	25	1		26
8H	Birkenhead			18			23	41	4		45
8A	Edge Hill			27			7	34	5		39
	Edge Hill to Wigan			10			3	13			13
8F	Springs Branch	1		61			7	69			69
	Ince Scrapyard	2		10	1	2		15			15
9K	Bolton			43			2	45	1		46
10H	Lower Darwen			13		2		15	2		17
	Blackburn Station				1			1			1
10F	Rose Grove			23		9		32	2		34
10G	Skipton			14			9	23			23
	Skipton Station			5				5			5
	Skipton to Carnforth			1			1	2	1		3
10A	Carnforth			40		1	5	46	7		53
	Carnforth to Carlisle			1			1	2			2
	Carlisle Station			3				3	6		9
		3	0	338	2	18	70	431	44	5	480

	REWIND July 1965	GWR	SR	LMS	LNER	WD	BR	Steam Total	Diesel Total	Electric Total	Grand Total
	Penrith Area 040765						2	2			2
10C	Fleetwood 040765			25		1	4	30	2		32
	Preston Station 050765			26			11	37	15		52
	Preston Station 080765			8			4	12	3		15
10D	Lostock Hall 090765			24		1	2	27	4		31
	Preston Station 090765			27		2	3	32	18		50
	Preston Station 100766			19			5	24	9		33
8F	Springs Branch 100765			56		4	5	65	1		66
8B	Warrington 100765			25	1		4	30	4		34
		0	0	210	1	8	40	259	56	0	315

622

However, all these train movements at Carstairs was unknown to me because as soon as the train left Carlisle I promptly fell asleep. The next thing I remembered was that we were at Edinburgh Haymarket station. One of the other passengers had probably awakened me in case I wanted off there. Edinburgh Waverley station was finally reached at 07.33 and I was home in Edinburgh after an eight days absence.

I was leaving the Waverley station by the eastern exit when a mischievous thought crossed my wind. I got out my 20 pack of Rothman's (there were 12 left) and got out the leaflet which one of the two religious fanatics had given me at Liverpool Central station ("the you too can be saved D.S. incident"). I put the leaflet inside the packet (just where you would find the gift certificate in certain brands) and put the packet on the ledge of the footbridge where it could easily be seen. So when someone picket up the packet he would find the religious leaflet as well and wonder if he was being watched or whether the cigarettes had been doctored. I would have loved to have seen this scene but I would never know what happened.

The green Scottish Motor Traction (S.M.T.) buses didn't run this early on a Saturday morning so I had to get an Edinburgh Corporation bus to the Edinburgh City boundary at Eastfield, Joppa.

After a half hour wait I duly boarded one at Princes Street and in another twenty minutes I was at the terminus at Eastfield. After another twenty minutes walk on a fine August day I was home at 21 Stoneybank Crescent, Musselburgh. By now D.S. would be sorting out the Sunday papers for his slave driving uncle in his uncle's shop. Luckily, I had arranged for someone to do my Sunday paper round for the second week in a row. I certainly felt like a few more hours sleep rather than delivering papers!

To conclude, it had been a hell of a fine week. This week I had seen "Castles", "Kings", "Halls", "Granges", "Manors", "Southern Region Pacifics", not forgetting "Lord Nelson" together with "Coronations", "Royal Scots", "Patriots and "Jubilees". Now I had seen a representative of about every class remaining on BR save perhaps for the small 0F 0-4-4 Tanks and 1F 0-6-0 tanks allocated to 41E Staveley. I had hoped to visit that shed but that proved not to be possible when Thursday's visit to Sheffield had to be cancelled.

One thing that had sunk home to me was the rapidity with which the steam engine was being withdrawn. An air of sadness had to accompany the week's tour on account of this. I would now hang up my notebook and Fybriter pen and retire from visiting sheds. Steam was disappearing so fast that it was good to quit on a high when steam was still in command in some areas (the north west) and surviving in other areas. I had little love for dieselisation and/or electrification apart from admiring the efficiency of it. Doubtless, I would return again to Barry Docks *(which I did in August 1970)* and perhaps the odd sortie with Dave Archibald to the North West before steam is finally gone for good but that would be all. This week had been the greatest week that I had ever spent and I wanted nothing to detract from that.

ONE THING WAS CERTAIN IT HAD BEEN A HARD DAY'S WEEK RAILROVER TRAINSPOTTING ON THE LONDON MIDLAND REGION!

This is not the beginning. *C'est le fin de la tour. Vraiment. Es la gran finale.*

EPILOGUE

A few days after the visit's conclusion BR caught up with me in the shape of 36 Area (Doncaster Division) which controlled 36A Doncaster, Doncaster Works and 40E Colwick amongst other depots. They wanted to know why we had not visited 36A Doncaster and Doncaster Works as arranged.

I wrote back blaming our non-arrival on missing our train from Cardiff General on the Tuesday afternoon. This must have sounded a very strange and amused them that this was the reason that we couldn't visit 36A Doncaster and Doncaster Works as planned on the Thursday. Oddly enough my strange explanation was the reason for the cancellation.

In the same letter back to the Division I added that our society had particularly enjoyed our visit to 40E Colwick (The Colwick Affair) on the Monday of our tour. This was where I had my battle royal with the Colwick shedmaster. If the Divisional Manager sent on my letter to the Colwick shedmaster I am sure it would have extremely infuriated him! Given that we eventually got round the shed we had no lasting grudge against the Colwick shedmaster and would not minded him being commended although on reflection we did miss our return train back to Nottingham because of him.

The Railrover ticket used:-

BRITISH RAILWAYS BOARD

SECOND CLASS　　Nᵒ 1186

RATE £ *11 : 10 : 0*

FROM ...... | **0 1 AUG 1965**

TO ...... | **0 7 AUG 1965**

AVAILABLE BY TIMETABLE AND ADVERTISED EXCURSION TRAINS
BETWEEN

ALL STATIONS on

LONDON MIDLAND REGION of BRITISH RAILWAYS

and between

Marylebone and Amersham via Harrow-on-the-Hill, South Acton and Richmond (S.R.), Clay Cross and Sheffield (Mid.) (E.R.), Grindleford and Dore & Totley (E.R.), Nottingham (Vic.) and Sheffield (Vic.) (E.R.), Sheffield (Vic.) and Woodhead Launton, Bicester and Oxford (W.R.) and on Lake Windermere (British Railways) Vessels, also **for through journeys only** between Sheffield (Mid.) and Skipton and between Paddington, Bicester and Banbury via Denham.

Issued subject to the Conditions and Regulations in the Board's Publications and Notices.

The usual supplements are payable on Pullman and Observation Cars.

Name of Holder ...... *Mr. G. Dowik* ......

NOT TRANSFERABLE

Whatever happened to the Musselburgh Monktonhall Modern Railway Society?

Regular Thursday evening meetings continued at D.S's house where we ran his model railway according to a working timetable and had various rail quizzes etc. until we left school.

David Archibald *– Graduated in Computer Science at university and worked for Hewlett Packard at South Queensferry. Now retired and lives near Edinburgh. Ran Grant's horse racing system on computer while at university which was great fun but provided us with very limited financial returns! We have always kept in touch and played bridge for some years. Dave became (and still is) a very serious railway photographer.*

Grant Dowie – *Graduated in economics at Edinburgh University. Worked for a couple of years in brand management for Procter and Gamble in Newcastle before doing a M.B.A. course at London Business School. Subsequently worked for Bank of Scotland taking early retirement in 2004. Now spends six months of the year in Marbella, Spain with the remainder in Edinburgh.*

Ian Firth – *Sadly we have lost touch with Ian who was always a great hit with the fairer sex! When last we heard he was working for the Civil Service in Edinburgh.*

Andrew Forsyth – *Sadly we have lost touch with Andrew.*

Derek Newton – *Derek got in touch again via Friends Reunited. Still works in the aerospace industry in Edinburgh. He lives in Central Scotland.*

Denis Stott – *"D.S." became a television engineer and then set up his own painting and decorating business. Now retired he continues to run his model railway and became one of the stalwart members of the Bo'ness and Kinneil Preserved Steam Railway. He continues to live near Edinburgh.*

Alex Storie – *Older brother of Iain. Alex joined Royal Bank of Scotland and retired several years ago. He continues to be a keen student of railway history subscribing to historical Scottish railway magazines and lives in the Scottish Borders.*

Iain Storie – *Graduated in Chemistry at university and then successfully completed a PhD. Taught chemistry at The Edinburgh Academy. Now retired he builds model railway engines as a hobby and lives in the Scottish Borders.*

Graham Strachan – *Graham got in touch a few years ago via Friends Reunited. He had emigrated to New Zealand many years ago where he is a primary school teacher.*

Neil Woodcock – *Neil qualified as a Chartered Accountant after leaving school and had a successful career. We remain in touch.*

David Archibald, Grant Dowie, Derek Newton, Denis Stott, Alex and Iain Storie got together for a 40 year celebration dinner of "A Hard Day's Week Railrover Trainspotting on the London Midland Region" in August 2005 and since then we have met up on at least an annual basis as the revived M.M.M.R.S. *with the normal format being a railway digital image show hosted by Dave Archibald.*

THE END

Some steam analyses and a total summary for the week follows:-

STEAM ENGINE CLASSES
DAY 8 ON SHED

Class / Numbers	BR total	8A Edge Hill	8C Speke Jct.	8F Wigan SB	8H Birkenh'd.	8K Bank Hall	8L Aintree	9K Bolton	10A Carnforth	10F Rose Grove	10G Skipton	10H Lwr Darwen	On Shed DAY 8
Ivatt 2MT 2-6-2T 1946 41200-41329	130				1		3						4
Fairburn 4MT 2-6-4T 1945 dev. of Stanier 1935 42050-42299; 42673-42699	277		1		4	3		6	4				18
Fowler 4MT 2-6-4T 1927 42300-42424	125				1								1
Stanier 4MT 2-6-4T 1935 dev of Fowler 1927 42425-42672	243				4	2		2	2				10
Hughes/Fowler 5MT 2-6-0 "Crab" 1926 42700-42944	245					4		1				4	9
Stanier 5MT 2-6-0 1933 42945-84	40				4								4
Ivatt 4MT 2-6-0 1947 43000-43161	162								8			3	11
Midland 4F 0-6-0 1924 44027-44606	580				3			1	1		0		5
Stanier 5MT 4-6-0 "Black Five" 1934 44658-45499	842	13		15	18		1	3	14	13	5	3	85
Stanier 6P5F 4-6-0 "Jubilee" 1934 45552-45734/7-42	189	1					3						4

STEAM ENGINE CLASSES		BR	8A	8C	8F	8H	8K	8L	9K	10A	10F	10G	10H	On Shed
DAY 8 ON SHED (continued)		total	Edge Hill	Speke Jct.	Wigan SB	Birkenh'd.	Bank Hall	Aintree	Bolton	Carnforth	Rose Grove	Skipton	Lwr Darwen	DAY 8
Ivatt 2MT 2-6-0 1946	46400-46527	128	1	5	3	4	4	3						20
Johnson Midland 3F 0-6-0T 1899	47200-47259	60				1				1				2
Midland 3F "Jinty" 0-6-0T 1924 dev. of Johnson 1899 design	47260-47681	417	4		5	3	5		2	2	2			23
Stanier 8F 2-8-0 "Big Eight" 1935	48000-48775	666	7	8	9	2	1	7	10	8	15	2	4	73
BR Standard 7P6F 4-6-2 "Britannia" Derby 1951	70000-70054	55					1			3				4
BR Standard 5MT 4-6-0 Doncaster 1951	73000-73171	172	1											1
BR Standard 4MT 4-6-0 Brighton 1951	75000-75079	80					6	1	1			7		15
BR Standard 2MT 2-6-2T Derby 1953	84000-84029	30							2			2		4
Riddles WD 8F 2-8-0 "Austerity" 1943	90000-90732	733						2		1	3			6
BR Standard 9F 2-10-0 Brighton 1954	92000-92250 except	241	6	2	6	21		1		1				37
BR Standard 9F 2-10-0 Brighton 1954. 1955 Crosti boiler	92020-29	10		2		2								4
			33	33	59	37	18	23	40	45	25	16	11	340

DAY 8 WITHDRAWN

STEAM ENGINE CLASSES	BR total	8A Edge Hill	8C Speke Jct	8F Wigan SB	8H Birkenh'd	8K Bank Hall	8L Aintree	9K Bolton	Ince Scrapyd	10A Carnforth	10F Rose Grove	10G Skipton	10H Lwr Darwen DAY 8	Total DAY 8
Collett 3MT 2251 0-6-0 1930														
2200-2299; 3200-3219	120									1				1
Collett 5MT 4900 4-6-0 "Hall" 1928														
4900-4999, 5900-5999, 6900-6958	258									1				1
1933 dev. of Collett 3F 5700 0-6-0PT 1929														
3600-3799, 4600-4699, 8700, 8750-8799, 9600-9682,9711	523				1									1
Fairburn 4MT 2-6-4T 1945 dev. of Stanier 1935														
42050-42299; 42673-42699	277									1				1
Fowler 4MT 2-6-4T 1927														
42300-42424	125							1	1		1			3
Stanier 4MT 2-6-4T 1935 dev of Fowler 1927														
42425-42672	243				4	1		1						6
Hughes/Fowler 5MT 2-6-0 "Crab" 1926														
42700-42944	245				4	1			5				2	12
Stanier 5MT 2-6-0 1933														
42945-84	40								1					1
Fowler Midland 4F 0-6-0 1911														
43835-44026	192											3		3
Midland 4F 0-6-0 1924														
44027-44606	580											4		4
Stanier 5MT 4-6-0 "Black Five" 1934														
44658-45499	842	1		2				1						4
Stanier 6P5F 4-6-0 "Jubilee" 1934														
45552-45734/7-42	189								1					1
Stanier 8P 4-6-2 "Coronation" 1937														
46220-57	38									1				1
Ivatt 2MT 2-6-0 1946														
46400-46527	128						2							2
Midland 3F "Jinty" 0-6-0T 1924 dev. of Johnson 1899 design														
47260-47681	417				1	1								2
Stanier 8F 2-8-0 "Big Eight" 1935														
48000-48775	666			1				2			1			5
Thompson 5MT 4-6-0 B1 1942														
61000-61409	410								1					1
Riddles WD 8F 2-8-0 "Austerity" 1943														
90000-90732	733							2	2	6			2	12
		1	1	3	10	4	2	2	5	13	1	7	2	61

Class	BR total	liv central to garston	garston to liv cent	edge hill to wigan	blackburn station	skipton station	skipton to carnfth	carnforth to carlisle	carlisle station	Off Shed Total	On Shed DAY 8	Withdrawn DAY 8	Grand Total
Collett 3MT 2251 0-6-0 1930 2200-2299; 3200-3219	120										1		1
Collett 5MT 4900 4-6-0 "Hall" 1928 4900-4999, 5900-5999, 6900-6958	258										1		1
1933 dev. of Collett 3F 5700 0-6-0PT 1929 3600-3799, 4600-4699, 8700, 8750-8799, 9600-9682, 9711-9799	523											1	1
Ivatt 2MT 2-6-2T 1946 41200-41329	130							1		1	4		5
Fairburn 4MT 2-6-4T 1945 dev. of Stanier 1935 42050-42299; 42673-42699	277							1		1	18		19
Fowler 4MT 2-6-4T 1927 42300-42424	125							1		1	3		4
Stanier 4MT 2-6-4T 1935 dev of Fowler 1927 42425-42672	243	1	2			1				4	16		20
Hughes/Fowler 5MT 2-6-0 "Crab" 1926 42700-42944	245									12	9		21
Stanier 5MT 2-6-0 1933 42945-84	40							1		1	4		5
Ivatt 4MT 2-6-0 1947 43000-43161	162										11		11
Fowler Midland 4F 0-6-0 1911 43835-44026	192										3		3
Midland 4F 0-6-0 1924 44027-44606	580	2	3			4				9			9
Stanier 5MT 4-6-0 "Black Five" 1934 44658-45499	842	2	3			4		1	1	11	85	4	100
Ivatt 7P 4-6-0 "Patriot" 1947 rebuild of Fowler 1933 45552-45734/7-42	189					1		1		2	4	1	7

STEAM ENGINE CLASSES
DAY 8 OFF SHED AND OVERALL SUMMARIES(continued)

	BR liv central total	liv central to garston	garston to liv cent	edge hill to wigan	blackburn station	skipton station	skipton to carnfth	carnforth to carlisle	carlisle station	Off Shed DAY 8	On Shed DAY 8	Withdrawn DAY 8	Grand Total
Stanier 8P 4-6-2 "Coronation" 1937													
46220-57	38											1	1
Ivatt 2MT 2-6-0 1946													
46400-46527	128			1						1	20	2	23
Johnson Midland 3F 0-6-0T 1899													
47200-47259	60										2		2
Midland 3F "Jinty" 0-6-0T 1924 dev. of Johnson 1899 design													
47260-47681	417			1						1	23	2	26
Stanier 8F 2-8-0 "Big Eight" 1935													
48000-48775	666			3						4	73	5	82
Thompson 5MT 4-6-0 B1 1942													
61000-61409	410					1				1		1	2
BR Standard 7P6F 4-6-2 "Britannia" Derby 1951													
70000-70054	55							1		1	4		5
BR Standard 6P5F 4-6-2 "Clan" Derby 1952													
72000-72009	10						1			1			1
BR Standard 5MT 4-6-0 Doncaster 1951													
73000-73171	172										1		1
BR Standard 4MT 4-6-0 Brighton 1951													
75000-75079	80										15		15
BR Standard 4MT 2-6-0 Doncaster 1953													
76000-76114	115			2						2	0		2
BR Standard 2MT 2-6-2T Derby 1953													
84000-84029	30										4		4
Riddles WD 8F 2-8-0 "Austerity" 1943													
90000-90732	733										6	12	18
BR Standard 9F 2-10-0 Brighton 1954													
92000-92250 except	241			1						1	37		38
BR Standard 9F 2-10-0 Brighton 1954. 1955 Crosti boiler													
92020-29	10										4		4
		1	3	13	1	5	2	2	3	30	340	61	431

STEAM ENGINE CLASSES
DAY 8 SUMMARY

STEAM ENGINE CLASSES / DAY 8 SUMMARY	Off Shed DAY 8	On Shed DAY 8	Withdrawn DAY 8	Grand Totals
Collett 3MT 2251 0-6-0 1930			1	1
Collett 5MT 4900 4-6-0 "Hall" 1928		1		1
1933 dev. of Collett 3F 5700 0-6-0PT 1929		1		1
Ivatt 2MT 2-6-2T 1946	1	4		5
Fairburn 4MT 2-6-4T 1945 dev. of Stanier 1935		18	1	19
Fowler 4MT 2-6-4T 1927		1	3	4
Stanier 4MT 2-6-4T 1935 dev of Fowler 1927	4	10	6	20
Hughes/Fowler 5MT 2-6-0 "Crab" 1926		9	12	21
Stanier 5MT 2-6-0 1933		4	1	5
Ivatt 4MT 2-6-0 1947		11		11
Fowler Midland 4F 0-6-0 1911			3	3
Midland 4F 0-6-0 1924		5	4	9
Stanier 5MT 4-6-0 "Black Five" 1934	11	85	4	100
Stanier 6P5F 4-6-0 "Jubilee" 1934	2	4	1	7
Stanier 8P 4-6-2 "Coronation" 1937			1	1
Ivatt 2MT 2-6-0 1946	1	20	2	23
Midland 3F "Jinty" 0-6-0T 1924 dev. of Johnson 1899 design	1	23	2	26
Johnson Midland 3F 0-6-0T 1899		2		2
Stanier 8F 2-8-0 "Big Eight" 1935	4	73	5	82
Thompson 5MT 4-6-0 B1 1942	1		1	2
BR Standard 7P6F 4-6-2 "Britannia" Derby 1951	1	4		5
BR Standard 6P5F 4-6-2 "Clan" Derby 1952	1			1
BR Standard 5MT 4-6-0 Doncaster 1951		1		1
BR Standard 4MT 4-6-0 Brighton 1951		15		15
BR Standard 4MT 2-6-0 Doncaster 1953	2			2
BR Standard 2MT 2-6-2T Derby 1953		4		4
Riddles WD 8F 2-8-0 "Austerity" 1943		6	12	18
BR Standard 9F 2-10-0 Brighton 1954	1	37	1	38
BR Standard 9F 2-10-0 Brighton 1954, 1955 Crosti boiler		4		4
	30	340	61	431

PRESTON VISIT JUL 1965

STEAM ENGINE CLASSES / PRESTON VISIT JULY 1965 ON SHED	BR total	8B Warrington active	8B Warrington withdrawn	8F Wigan SB active	8F Wigan SB withdrawn	10C Fleetwood active	10C Fleetwood withdrawn	10D Lostock Hl active	10D Lostock Hl withdrawn	Total Preston Week active on shed	Total Preston Week withdrawn on shed	Total Preston Week on shed
Fairburn 4MT 2-6-4T 1945 dev. of Stanier 1935												
42050-42299; 42673-42699	277		3	4				2		6	3	9
Fowler 4MT 2-6-4T 1927												
42300-42424	125			1	1					1	1	2
Stanier 4MT 2-6-4T 1935 dev of Fowler 1927												
42425-42672	243			5	6			2		7	6	13
Stanier 5MT 2-6-0 1933												
42945-84	40			3						3		3
Midland 4F 0-6-0 1924												
44027-44606	580	2		2					2	4	2	6
Stanier 5MT 4-6-0 "Black Five" 1934												
44658-45499	842	15		16		12		6		49		49
Stanier 6P5F 4-6-0 "Jubilee" 1934												
45552-45734/7-42	189	1			1					1	1	2
Ivatt 2MT 2-6-0 1946												
46400-46527	128			3		1				4		4
Midland 3F "Jinty" 0-6-0T 1924 dev. of Johnson 1899 design												
47260-47681	417	1		4	3			6		11	3	14
Stanier 8F 2-8-0 "Big Eight" 1935												
48000-48775	666	3		13		5	1	6		27	1	28
Thompson 5MT 4-6-0 B1 1942												
61000-61409	410	1								1		1
BR Standard 7P6F 4-6-2 "Britannia" Derby 1951												
70000-70054	55					1				1		1
BR Standard 4MT 4-6-0 Brighton 1951												
75000-75079	80					1				1		1
BR Standard 4MT 2-6-0 Doncaster 1953												
76000-76114	115			1						1		1
BR Standard 2MT 2-6-2T Derby 1953												
84000-84029	30			2		2			2	2	2	4
Riddles WD 8F 2-8-0 "Austerity" 1943												
90000-90732	733					1	4		1	1	5	6
BR Standard 9F 2-10-0 Brighton 1954												
92000-92250	251	4				4				8		8
		27	3	54	11	25	5	22	5	128	24	152

PRESTON TRIP JULY 1965

STEAM ENGINE CLASSES / PRESTON VISIT JULY 1965 OFF SHED	BR total	Penrith preston st Sunday 040765	preston st Monday 050765	preston st Thursday 080765	preston st and travel Friday 090765	preston Saturday 100765	total preston off shed Jul-65	preston on shed active Jul-65	total preston on shed withdrawn Jul-65	total preston grand total Jul-65
Fairburn 4MT 2-6-4T 1945 dev. of Stanier 1935										
42050-42299; 42673-42699	277	1		1			2	6	3	11
Fowler 4MT 2-6-4T 1927										
42300-42424	125							1	1	2
Stanier 4MT 2-6-4T 1935 dev of Fowler 1927										
42425-42672	243	5		2	3		10	7	6	23
Stanier 5MT 2-6-0 1933										
42945-84	40							3		3
Midland 4F 0-6-0 1924										
44027-44606	580							4	2	6
Stanier 5MT 4-6-0 "Black Five" 1934										
44658-45499	842	15		4	21	16	56	49		105
Ivatt 7P 4-6-0 "Patriot" 1947 rebuild of Fowler 1933										
45512/4/21-3/5-9/30-2/34-6/40/5	18				1		1			1
Stanier 6P5F 4-6-0 "Jubilee" 1934										
45552-45734/7-42	189		1		2		3	1	1	5
Ivatt 2MT 2-6-0 1946										
46400-46527	128					1	1	4		5
Johnson Midland 3F 0-6-0T 1899										
47200-47259	60			1			1			1
Midland 3F "Jinty" 0-6-0T 1924 dev. of Johnson 1899 design										
47260-47681	417							11	3	14

PRESTON TRIP JULY 1965

STEAM ENGINE CLASSES PRESTON VISIT JULY 1965 OFF SHED (Continued)	Penrith BR total Sunday 040765	preston st Monday 050765	preston st Thursday 080765	preston st Friday 090765	preston st and travel Saturday 100765	total preston off shed Jul-65	total preston on shed active Jul-65	total preston on shed withdrawn Jul-65	grand total preston Jul-65
Stanier 8F 2-8-0 "Big Eight" 1935									
48000-48775	666	4			1	6	27	1	34
Thompson 5MT 4-6-0 B1 1942									
61000-61409	410						1		1
BR Standard 7P6F 4-6-2 "Britannia" Derby 1951									
70000-70054	55	3		2	3	9	1		10
BR Standard 5MT 4-6-0 Doncaster 1951									
73000-73171	172			1	1	1			1
BR Standard 4MT 4-6-0 Brighton 1951									
75000-75079	80	3		2	2	7	1		8
BR Standard 4MT 2-6-0 Doncaster 1953									
76000-76114	115						1		1
BR Standard 2MT 2-6-0 Doncaster 1953									
78000-78064	65	2		1	1	3			3
BR Standard 2MT 2-6-2T Derby 1953									
84000-84029	30						2	2	4
Riddles WD 8F 2-8-0 "Austerity" 1943									
90000-90732	733			2		2	1	5	8
BR Standard 9F 2-10-0 Brighton 1954									
92000-92250	251	3	2			6	8		14
	2	37	12	32	24	107	128	24	259

STEAM SEEN ON SHED

LMR	DAY	LOCATION	GWR	SR	LMS	LNER	WD	BR	Stea
Fast Fwd	BD	Barry Docks 0870	98	41	32	1		40	21
4	BD	Barry Docks	75	28	5		2		11
Rewind	12A	Carlisle Kingmoor 070958			100		3	5	1
5	5B	Crewe South	3		60		1	23	8
1	12A	Carlisle Kingmoor			61	3		19	8
Fast Fwd	12A	Carlisle Kingmoor 030667			47			30	7
8	8F	Springs Branch	1		61			7	6
Rewind	8F	Springs Branch 100765			56		4	5	6
7	9D	Newton Heath			55			7	6
6	5D	Stoke			45			15	6
Rewind	5B	Crewe South 121264	1		47			10	5
Rewind	12B	Carlisle Upperby 070958			58				5
3	40E	Colwick				24	27	2	5
2	1A	Willesden			28			22	5
8	10A	Carnforth			40		1	5	4
8	9K	Bolton			43			2	4
Rewind	9D	Newton Heath 121264			37			7	4
7	9E	Trafford Park			39			5	4
8	8H	Birkenhead			18			23	4
2	70A	Nine Elms		18				22	4
5	2B	Oxley	24		9			6	3
3	16E	Kirkby			32	1	1	4	3
Rewind	12C	Carlisle Canal 070958			1	36			3
7	8B	Warrington			26			10	3
8	8C	Speke Junction			32			4	3
8	8A	Edge Hill			27			7	3
7	9H	Patricroft			14		1	18	3
5	2A	Tyseley	23		2			7	3
8	10F	Rose Grove			23		9		3
4	88A	Cardiff East Dock	31					1	3
Rewind	8B	Warrington 100765			25	1		4	3
Rewind	8B	Warrington 100765			25	1		4	3
Rewind	10C	Fleetwood 040765			25		1	4	3
5	2E	Saltley	3		12			14	2
5	2F	Bescot			23		1	4	2
7	9B	Stockport Edgeley			21			6	2

STEAM SEEN ON SHED (Continued)

LMR DAY		LOCATION	GWR	SR	LMS	LNER	WD	BR	Steam
Rewind	10D	Lostock Hall 090765			24		1	2	27
1	12B	Carlisle Upperby			20		1	6	27
1	12D	Workington			27				27
4	2D	Banbury	14		3			9	26
Rewind	5A	Crewe North 121264			23			3	26
Fast Fwd	12B	Carlisle Upperby 030667			20			6	26
3	15A	Leicester Midland			20			6	26
6	6D	Shrewsbury	4		6			15	25
8	8L	Aintree			19		4	2	25
6	5E	Nuneaton			21		1	1	23
6	6B	Mold Junction	3		19			1	23
7	9F	Heaton Mersey			21			2	23
8	10G	Skipton			14			9	23
8	8K	Bank Hall			14			6	20
4	16C	Derby and Derby Works			19			1	20
Rewind	9B	Stockport Edgeley 121264			17			1	18
6	6C	Croes Newydd	13					2	15
8	Ince	Ince Scrapyard	2		10	1		2	15
8	10H	Lower Darwen			13		2		15
3	16A	Toton			7			8	15
7	9J	Agecroft			13				13
5	2J	Aston			10			1	11
3	16B	Annesley			10			1	11
4	16F	Burton (pass)			10			1	11
5	5A	Crewe North			4			5	9
1	12A	Carlisle Kingmoor (pass)			6			3	9
4	85B	Gloucester (pass)	5					3	8
3	15B	Wellingborough			5			2	7
2	30A	Stratford	1	3	1	2			7
6	6A	Chester Midland (pass)	1		5				6
1	66E	Carstairs (pass)			5	1			6
4	85A	Worcester (pass)	3		1				4
6	CW	Crewe Works (pass)			4				4
3	1E	Bletchley			2			1	3
7	9A	Longsight			2				2
1	66F	Beattock (pass)			2				2
1	64C	Dalry Road (pass)				1			1

HOME STEAM ANALYSES

LMR	Day	Visits	Steam Total (Seen)	Home Steam	On Shed	Off Shed	% on Shed	seen on tour	Home Area	Visitors	% Visitors	Withdrawn	% Withdrawn	Steam Classes
	RW 12A	Carlisle Kingmoor 070958	108	153	108	45	71%	16	21	27	25%	0	0%	15
	1 12A	Carlisle Kingmoor	83	118	53	65	45%	27	2	21	25%	7	8%	14
	RW 12B	Carlisle Upperby 070958	58	111	53	58	48%	13	5	0	0%	0	0%	11
	7 9D	Newton Heath	62	98	47	51	48%	21	3	7	11%	5	8%	13
Fast Fwd	12A	Carlisle Kingmoor 030667	77	97	36	61	37%	41	3	17	22%	24	31%	7
	5 5B	Crewe South	87	81	35	46	43%	25	5	34	39%	13	15%	14
	RW 9D	Newton Heath 121264	44	81	29	52	36%	32	2	4	9%	9	20%	12
	8 8H	Birkenhead	41	78	35	43	45%	16	0	2	5%	4	10%	6
	6 5D	Stoke	60	72	43	29	60%	9	3	7	12%	7	12%	11
	RW 5B	Crewe South 121264	58	63	23	40	37%	27	30	30	52%	5	9%	14
	5 2F	Bescot	28	62	19	43	31%	24	5	5	18%	2	7%	8
	8 8C	Speke Junction	36	61	27	34	44%	9	3	3	8%	3	8%	5
	7 9H	Patricroft	33	59	26	33	44%	13	2	5	15%	0	0%	9
	8 8F	Springs Branch	69	58	40	18	69%	7	8	11	16%	10	14%	14
	RW 8F	Springs Branch 100765	65	58	40	18	69%	13	4	4	6%	11	17%	14
	3 40E	Colwick	53	56	37	19	66%	1	2	2	4%	12	23%	13
	8 10A	Carnforth	46	46	24	22	52%	10	7	14	30%	1	2%	14
	5 2B	Oxley	39	49	24	25	49%	10	3	8	21%	4	10%	15
	8 8A	Edge Hill	34	50	19	31	38%	7	9	5	15%	1	3%	7
	2 1A	Willesden	50	52	31	21	60%	8	1	7	14%	11	22%	11
	8 9K	Bolton	45	54	35	19	65%	4	3	2	4%	5	11%	10
	7 9F	Heaton Mersey	23	56	19	37	34%	9	0	4	17%	0	0%	5
Rewind	12C	Carlisle Canal 070958	37	43	37	6	86%		4	0	0%	0	0%	10
	5 2A	Tyseley	32	45	17	28	38%	14	4	4	13%	6	19%	14
Rewind	16E	Kirkby	38	43	30	13	70%		18	2	5%	0	0%	7
Rewind	10D	Lostock Hall 090765	27	43	11	32	26%	1	3	8	30%	6	16%	8
	7 9E	Trafford Park	44	42	27	15	64%	6	3	6	14%	8	18%	8
	5 2E	Saltley	29	41	13	28	32%	11	8	7	24%	1	3%	9
	6 6B	Mold Junction	24	39	13	26	33%	4	1	8	33%	1	4%	8
	7 8B	Warrington	36	38	21	17	55%	9	5	7	19%	3	8%	7
Rewind	8B	Warrington 100765	30	38	17	21	45%	18	5	5	17%	3	10%	7
	3 15A	Leicester Midland	26	37	21	16	57%	6	2	3	12%	0	0%	5
	6 5E	Nuneaton	23	36	18	18	50%	4	1	2	9%	2	9%	6
	4 16C	Derby and Derby Works	20	35	9	26	26%	11	1	7	35%	3	15%	6
	2 70A	Nine Elms	40	34	15	19	44%	3	24	0	0%	1	3%	7
	8 8L	Aintree	25	34	21	13	62%	3	1	1	4%	2	8%	7

HOME STEAM ANALYSES (continued)

LMR	Day	Visits	Seen Steam Total	Home Steam	On Shed	Off Shed	% on Shed	seen on tour	Home Area	Visitors	% Visitors	Withdrawn	% Withdrawn	Steam Classes
6	6C	Croes Newydd	15	34	11	23	32%	5	0	1	7%	3	20%	9
6	6D	Shrewsbury	25	33	9	24	27%	7	4	2	8%	10	40%	10
4	16F	Burton (pass)	11	33	5	28	15%	2	3	3	27%	0	0%	4
4	2D	Banbury	26	32	12	20	38%	5	3	5	19%	6	23%	11
Rewind	5A	Crewe North 121264	26	32	8	24	25%	13	3	9	35%	6	23%	9
6	6A	Chester Midland (pass)	6	32	2	30	6%	7	2	2	33%	0	0%	4
8	10F	Rose Grove	32	31	21	10	68%	4	3	1	3%	7	22%	4
1	12B	Carlisle Upperby	27	29	12	17	41%	11	7	8	30%	0	0%	8
7	9B	Stockport Edgeley	27	29	22	7	76%	2	0	3	11%	2	7%	9
Rewind	10C	Fleetwood 040765	30	26	19	7	73%	0	1	5	17%	5	17%	7
1	12D	Workington	27	26	16	10	62%	5	2	3	11%	6	22%	7
Rewind	9B	Stockport Edgeley 121264	18	26	7	19	27%	19	3	4	22%	4	22%	7
7	9J	Agecroft	13	24	12	12	50%	3	0	1	8%	1	8%	4
4	85B	Gloucester (pass)	8	24	2	22	8%	2	0	1	13%	5	63%	5
4	85A	Worcester (pass)	4	23	0	23	0%	7	0	4	100%	0	0%	3
8	8K	Bank Hall	20	21	15	6	71%	0	2	1	5%	2	10%	6
1	66E	Carstairs (pass)	6	19	3	16	16%	2	1	1	17%	1	17%	2
8	10G	Skipton	23	17	11	6	65%	2	2	3	13%	7	30%	7
8	10H	Lower Darwen	15	15	10	5	67%	1	0	1	7%	4	27%	4
5	2J	Aston	11	15	6	9	40%	3	1	2	18%	2	18%	5
3	16B	Annesley	11	14	6	8	43%	2	0	2	18%	3	27%	3
6	CW	Crewe Works (pass)	4	12	2	10	17%	0	1	0	0%	1	25%	2
3	16A	Toton	15	6	3	3	50%	0	10	2	13%	0	0%	5
1	66F	Beattock (pass)	2	6	1	5	17%	1	1	0	0%	0	0%	1
Fast Fwd	BD	Barry Docks 0870	212	N/A								212	100%	49
	BD	Barry Docks	110	N/A								110	100%	31
4	88A	Cardiff East Dock	32	N/A								32	100%	12
Fast Fwd	12B	Carlisle Upperby 030667	25	N/A								8	32%	6
	Ince	Ince Scrapyard	15	N/A								15	100%	10
1	12A	Carlisle Kingmoor (pass)	9	N/A										4
5	5A	Crewe North	9	N/A					6	2	22%	0	0%	6
2	30A	Stratford	7	N/A										7
3	15B	Wellingborough	7	N/A					5	2	29%	0	0%	2
3	1E	Bletchley	3	N/A					3	0	0%	3	100%	2
7	9A	Longsight	2	N/A					2	0	0%	0	0%	1
1	64C	Dalry Road (pass)	1	N/A					1	0	0%	1	100%	1

ENGINE CLASSES	BR	LMR	LMR	LMR	LMR
LONDON MIDLAND TRIP DAY 1- DAY 8 INCLUSIVE	total	off shed	on shed	withdrawn	total
Diesels					
BR Sulzer "Peak" Type 4 1Co-Co1 1959					
D1-D193	193	24	79	0	103
English Electric Type 4 1Co-Co1 1958					
D200-D399	200	50	39	0	89
BR "Warship" Type 4 B-B 1958					
D800-D832	33	2	1	0	3
North British "Warship" Type 4 B-B 1960					
D833-D865	33	1	2	0	3
BR "Western" Type 4 C-C 1961					
D1000-D1073	74	3	19	0	22
Brush Type 4 Co-Co 1962					
D1500-D1899	400	76	72	0	148
BR Gardner 0-6-0 Shunter 1957					
D2000-D2199 ; D2372-99	228	3	11	0	14
Drewry 0-6-0 Shunter 1952					
D2200-14	15	0	2	0	2
Drewry 0-6-0 Shunter 1955					
D2215-73	59	0	7	0	7
Drewry 0-6-0 Shunter 1959					
D2274-D2340	67	0	2	0	2
Hudswell-Clarke 0-6-0 Shunter 1956					
D2500-19	20	0	6	0	6
North British 0-4-0 Shunter 1957					
D2708-80	73	0	2	0	2
Yorkshire Engine Co. 0-4-0 Shunter 1960					
D2850-69	20	0	2	0	2
North British 0-4-0 Shunter 1958					
D2900-13	14	1	9	0	10
Barclay 0-4-0 Shunter 1956					
D2953-56	4	0	2	0	2
Ruston & Hornsby 0-4-0 Shunter 1956					
D2957-58	2	0	2	0	2
Brush 0-4-0 Shunter 1960					
D2999	1	0	1	0	1
BR English Electric 0-6-0 Shunter 1953					
D3000-D3116	117	8	18	0	26
BR Crossley 0-6-0 Shunter 1955					
D3117-D3126	10	0	6	0	6
BR English Electric 0-6-0 Shunter 1953					
D3127-36 ; D3167-D3438 ; D3454-73 ; D3503-D3611 ; D3652-D4048	808	53	72	0	125
BR Blackstone/G.E.C. 0-6-0 Shunter 1955					
D3137-D3151; D3439-D3453 ; D3473-D3502; D3612-D3651 ;	146	0	10	0	10
D4094-D4094					
BR Blackstone/B.T.H. 0-6-0 Shunter 1955					
D3152-D3166; D4095-D4192	113	9	11	0	20
BR Sulzer Type 2 Bo-Bo 1958					
D5000-D5299; D7500-D7677	478	43	141	0	184
Birmingham R.C. & W. Co.Type 2 Bo-Bo 1958					
D5300-D5415	116	8	18	0	26
Brush Type 2 A1A-A1A 1957					
D5500-D5699; D5800-D5862	263	4	37	0	41
Metropolitan Vickers Type 2 Co-Bo 1958					
D5700-D5719	20	0	6	0	6
English Electric "Baby Deltic" Type 5 Bo-Bo 1959					
D5900-D5909	10	0	2	0	2
North British Type 2 B-B 1959					
D6300-D6357	58	2	5	0	7
Birmingham R.C. & W. Co.Type 3 Bo-Bo 1960					
D6500-D6597	98	1	16	0	17
English Electric Type 3 Co-Co 1961					
D6700-D6999	300	33	9	0	42
Beyer Peacock (Hymek) Type 3 B-B 1961					
D7000-D7100	101	2	10	0	12
English Electric Type 1 Bo-Bo 1957					
D8000-D8127	128	5	12	0	17
British Thomson Houston Type 1 Bo-Bo 1957					
D8200-D8243	44	0	22	0	22

| ENGINE CLASSES | BR | LMR | LMR | LMR | LMR |
LONDON MIDLAND TRIP DAY 1- DAY 8 INCLUSIVE	total	off shed	on shed	withdrawn	total
Diesels (continued)					
North British Type 1 Bo-Bo 1958					
D8400-D8409	10	0	7	0	7
Clayton Type 1 Bo-Bo 1962					
D8500-D8615	116	0	2	0	2
English Electric "Deltic" Type 5 Co-Co 1961					
D9000-D9021	22	1	2	0	3
BR Paxman Type 1 0-6-0 1964					
D9500-D9555	56	3	0	0	3
LMS English Electric Type 3 Co-Co 1947					
10000-10001	2	0	2	0	2
BR English Electric Type 3/4 1Co-Co1 1951/4					
10201-10203	3	0	3	0	3
LMS 0-6-0 Shunter 1939					
12003-32	30	3	13	0	16
LMS and BR 0-6-0 Shunter 1945					
12033-12138	106	13	29	0	42
BR 0-6-0 Shunter 1948					
15101-15106	6	2	1	0	3
BR 0-6-0 Shunter 1949					
15211-15236	26	0	2	0	2
Ruston & Hornsby 0-4-0 Shunter 1953					
PWM650-PWM654	5	2	0	0	2
TOTAL DIESELS		352	714	0	1066
Steam					
Hawksworth 2F 1600 0-6-0PT 1949					
1600-1669	70	0	2	0	2
Collett 3MT 2251 0-6-0 1930					
2200-2299; 3200-3219	120	0	0	3	3
Churchward 8F 2800 2-8-0 1903					
2800-83	84	0	0	6	6
Collett dev.1938 of Churchward 8F 2-8-0 1903					
2884-2899; 3800-66	83	0	1	13	14
Collett 7P 4073 4-6-0 "Castle" 1923					
4000,4016,4032,4037, 4073-4099, 5000-5099, 7000-7037	169	0	0	8	8
Churchward 7F 4200 2-8-0T 1910					
4200-99; 5200-04	91	0	0	6	6
Churchward 1923 5205 8F dev. of Churchward 7F 4200 2-8-0T 1910					
5205-5264	60	0	0	5	5
Churchward 4MT 2-6-0 4300 1911					
4303-4386(12); 5300-5399; 6300-6399; 7305-7321	195	0	0	1	1
1932 dev. of Churchward 4MT 4300 2-6-0 1911					
7322-7341	20	0	0	1	1
Churchward 4MT 4500 2-6-2T 1906					
4500-4574	75	0	0	2	2
1927 4575 dev. of Churchward 4MT 4500 2-6-2T 1906					
4575-4599, 5500-5574	100	0	0	12	12
Collett 5MT 4900 4-6-0 "Hall" 1928					
4900-4999, 5900-5999, 6900-6958	258	9	9	14	32
Hawksworth 5MT 6959 4-6-0 "Modified Hall" 1944					
6959-6999, 7900-7929	71	0	10	5	15
Collett 4MT 5101 2-6-2T 1929 rebuild of Churchward 3100 Class 1903					
4100-4179; 5101-5110; 5150-99	140	4	6	6	16
Collett 5MT 5600 0-6-2T 1924					
5600-5699	100	0	3	10	13
1927 dev. of Collett 5MT 5600 0-6-2T 1924					
6600-6699	100	1	7	9	17
Collett 3F 5700 0-6-0PT 1929					
5700-5799, 7700-7799, 8701-8749	250	0	0	1	1
1933 dev. of Collett 3F 5700 0-6-0PT 1929					
3600-3799, 4600-4699, 8700, 8750-8799, 9600-9682,9711-9799	523	3	17	10	30
Collett 8P 6000 4-6-0 "King" 1927					
6000-6029	30	0	0	3	3
Collett 4MT 6100 2-6-2T 1931 dev. of 5101 Class					
6100-6169	70	0	0	1	1
Collett 5MT 6800 4-6-0 "Grange" 1936					
6800-6879	80	5	15	6	26

ENGINE CLASSES	BR	LMR	LMR	LMR	LMR
LONDON MIDLAND TRIP DAY 1- DAY 8 INCLUSIVE	total	off shed	on shed	withdrawn	total
Steam (continued)					
Collett 8F 7200 2-8-2T 1934 rebuild of Churchward 4200 Class 2-8-0T					
7200-7253	*54*	0	0	3	3
Collett 5MT 7800 4-6-0 "Manor" 1938					
7800-7829	*30*	4	6	2	12
Collett 4MT 8100 2-6-2T 1938					
8100-8109	*10*	0	0	1	1
Hawksworth 4F 9400 0-6-0PT 1947					
3400-3409; 8400-8499 ; 9400-9499	*210*	0	0	2	2
Urie 6F S15 4-6-0 1920 (with smoke deflectors)					
30496-30515	*20*	0	0	2	2
Maunsell 1927 dev. of Urie 6F S15 4-6-0 1920 (with smoke deflectors)					
30823-30837	*15*	0	0	3	3
Beattie 0P 2-4-0WT Class 0298 1874.					
30585-30587	*3*	0	0	1	1
6F S15 4-6-0 Urie 1920 (with smoke deflectors) Maunsell 1936 development					
30838-30847	*10*	0	1	2	3
Maunsell 7P LN 4-6-0 "Lord Nelson" 1926					
30850-30865	*16*	0	0	1	1
Maunsell 4F Q 0-6-0 Maunsell 1938					
30530-30549	*20*	1	0	1	2
Maunsell 4P3F U 2-6-0 1928					
31610-31639	*30*	0	0	3	3
Maunsell 4P3F U 2-6-0 1928 rebuild of 2-6-4T 1917 "River" K class					
31790-31809	*20*	0	0	1	1
Maunsell 4P5F N 2-6-0 1917					
31400-31414, 31810-31821, 31823-31875	*80*	0	0	1	1
Bulleid "Austerity" 5F Q1 0-6-0 1942					
33001-33040	*40*	0	3	1	4
Bulleid 7P5F "West Country & Battle of Britain Class 4-6-2 1945					
34002/6/7/11/5/9/20/3/30/3/5/8/41/3/9/51/4/5/7/61/3-70/2-6/8-81/3/4/6/	*53*	0	3	7	10
34091/2/4/6/9/34102-8/10					
1957 7P6F dev. of Bulleid 7P5F 4-6-2 "West Country & Battle of Britain" 1945					
34001/3-5/8-10/2-4/6-8/21/2/4-9/31/2/4/6/7/9/40/2/4-8/50/2/3/6/8/9/60/2/	*57*	1	10	4	15
71/7/82/5/7-9/90/3/5/7/8/34100/1/9					
1956 dev. of Bulleid 8P 4-6-2 "Merchant Navy" 1941					
35001-30	*30*	0	1	4	5
Ivatt 2MT 2-6-2T 1946					
41200-41329	*130*	2	12	1	15
Fairburn 4MT 2-6-4T 1945 dev. of Stanier 1935					
42050-42299; 42673-42699	*277*	2	30	17	49
Fowler 4MT 2-6-4T 1927					
42300-42424	*125*	0	4	4	8
Stanier 4MT 2-6-4T 1935 dev of Fowler 1927					
42425-42672	*243*	6	14	10	30
Hughes/Fowler 5MT 2-6-0 "Crab" 1926					
42700-42944	*245*	1	20	15	36
Stanier 5MT 2-6-0 1933					
42945-84	*40*	0	16	1	17
Ivatt 4MT 2-6-0 1947					
43000-43161	*162*	5	39	2	46
Fowler Midland 4F 0-6-0 1911					
43835-44026	*192*	0	2	4	6
Midland 4F 0-6-0 1924					
44027-44606	*580*	0	22	14	36
Stanier 5MT 4-6-0 "Black Five" 1934					
44658-45499	*842*	81	289	14	384
Ivatt 7P 4-6-0 "Patriot" 1947 rebuild of Fowler 1933					
45512/4/21-3/5-9/30-2/34-6/40/5	*18*	0	3	0	3
Stanier 6P5F 4-6-0 "Jubilee" 1934					
45552-45734/7-42	*189*	3	13	8	24
Stanier 7P 4-6-0 "Royal Scot" 1943 rebuild of Fowler 1927					
46100-70	*71*	1	2	2	5
Stanier 8P 4-6-2 "Coronation" 1937					
46220-57	*38*	0	0	2	2
Ivatt 2MT 2-6-0 1946					
46400-46527	*128*	11	45	5	61
Kitson 0F 0-4-0ST 1932					
47000-47009	*10*	0	1	0	1

| ENGINE CLASSES | BR | LMR | LMR | LMR | LMR |
LONDON MIDLAND TRIP DAY 1- DAY 8 INCLUSIVE	total	off shed	on shed	withdrawn	total
Steam (continued)					
Johnson Midland 3F 0-6-0T 1899					
47200-47259	60	0	3	0	3
Midland 3F "Jinty" 0-6-0T 1924 dev. of Johnson 1899 design					
47260-47681	417	7	55	9	71
Stanier 8F 2-8-0 "Big Eight" 1935					
48000-48775	666	43	284	21	348
Beames LNWR 7F 0-8-0 G2 1921					
49395-49454	60	0	0	1	1
Fowler ex Somerset & Dorset Joint Railway 7F 2-8-0 1914					
53800-10	11	0	0	2	2
Thompson 8P6F 4-6-2 A1 1945					
60113-60162	50	0	0	1	1
Thompson 8P7F 4-6-2 A2 1946					
60500-60539	40	0	0	1	1
Gresley 7P6F 2-6-2 V2 1936					
60800-60983	184	0	2	0	2
Thompson 5MT 4-6-0 B1 1942					
61000-61409	410	0	12	5	17
Gresley 5P6F 2-6-0 K3 1924					
61800-61992	193	0	0	1	1
Raven N.E. design 8F 0-8-0 Q7 1919					
63460-63474	15	0	0	1	1
Robinson 8F 2-8-0 O4 1911					
63570-63920	271	0	7	3	10
BR Standard 7P6F 4-6-2 "Britannia" Derby 1951					
70000-70054	55	15	35	0	50
BR Standard 6P5F 4-6-2 "Clan" Derby 1952					
72000-72009	10	0	3	0	3
BR Standard 5MT 4-6-0 Doncaster 1951					
73000-73171	172	12	51	1	64
BR Standard 4MT 4-6-0 Brighton 1951					
75000-75079	80	1	30	0	31
BR Standard 4MT 2-6-0 Doncaster 1953					
76000-76114	115	4	21	0	25
BR Standard 2MT 2-6-0 Doncaster 1953					
78000-78064	65	4	33	2	39
BR Standard 4MT 2-6-4T Doncaster 1953					
80000-80154	155	2	5	8	15
BR Standard 3MT 2-6-2T Swindon 1952					
82000-82044	45	6	8	2	16
BR Standard 2MT 2-6-2T Derby 1953					
84000-84029	30	0	13	1	14
Riddles WD 8F 2-8-0 "Austerity" 1943					
90000-90732	733	1	31	19	51
Riddles WD MOS 8F 2-10-0 "Austerity" 1943					
90750-90774, WD601	26	2	0	0	2
BR Standard 9F 2-10-0 Brighton 1954					
92000-92250 except	166	6	85	0	91
BR Standard 9F 2-10-0 Brighton 1954. 1957 double chimney					
92000-1; 92006; 92079; 92165-7, 92178; 92183-92249	75	3	10	4	17
BR Standard 9F 2-10-0 Brighton 1954. 1955 Crosti boiler					
92020-29	10	11	7	0	18
TOTAL STEAM		257	1301	342	1900

ENGINE CLASSES					BR	LMR	LMR	LMR	LM
LONDON MIDLAND TRIP DAY 1- DAY 8 INCLUSIVE					total	off shed	on shed	withdrawn	tota
Electrics									
A.E.I. (British Thomson-Houston) AL1 Bo-Bo 1959									
E3001-23					23	14	1	0	1
English Electric AL3 Bo-Bo 1960									
E3024-35					12	11	2	0	1
General Electric AL4 Bo-Bo 1960									
E3036-E3045					10	0	5	0	
A.E.I. (Metropolitan-Vickers) AL2 Bo-Bo 1960									
E3046-E3055					10	5	0	0	
BR A.E.I.(B.T.H.) motors AL5 Bo-Bo 1960									
E3056-E3085					30	20	2	0	2
BR B.T.H. AL5/1 Bo-Bo 1962									
E3086-E3095					10	4	2	0	
A.E.I. (British Thomson-Houston) AL1 Bo-Bo 1963									
E3096-E3097					2	1	0	0	
English Electric AL3/1 Bo-Bo 1962									
E3100					1	2	0	0	
BR Vulcan Foundry AEI motors AL6 Bo-Bo 1965									
E3101-3200					100	2	8	0	1
BR EM2 Metropolitan-Vickers Co-Co 1954									
27000-27006					7	3	0	0	
TOTAL ELECTRICS						62	20	0	8
OVERALL GRAND TOTALS						671	2035	342	304

STEAM ENGINE CLASSES at EARLY AUGUST 1965

OVERALL SUMMARIES — BR AUGUST 1965 TOTALS (excluding recently withdrawn highlighted)

ex Great Western Railway Classes

Class / Numbers	total BR	BR	LMR	LMR	ER	ER	NER	NER	ScR	ScR	SR	SR	WR	WR	Wks	Wks
Hawksworth 2F 1600 0-6-0PT 1949 — 1600-1669	70	8	3	3									5	3		
Collett 3MT 2251 0-6-0 1930 — 2200-2299; 3200-3219	120	11	4										7			
Collett dev.1938 of Churchward 8F 2-8-0 1903 — 2884-2899; 3800-66	83	7	19	3	2								4	17		
Collett 7P 4073 4-6-0 "Castle" 1923 — 4000,4016,4032,4037, 4073-4099, 5000-5099, 7000-7037	169	1	3										1	3		
Churchward 7F 4200 2-8-0T 1910 — 4200-99; 5200-04	91	1	1										1	1		
Churchward 1923 5205 8F dev. of Churchward 7F 4200 2-8-0T 1910 — 5205-5264	60	1	3										1	3		
Collett 5MT 4900 4-6-0 "Hall" 1928 — 4900-4999, 5900-5999, 6900-6958	258	29	5	8	2								21	3		
Hawksworth 5MT 6959 4-6-0 "Modified Hall" 1944 — 6959-6999; 7900-7929	71	29	5	7									22	5		
Collett 4MT 5101 2-6-2T 1929 rebuild of Churchward 3100 Class 1903 — 4100-4179; 5101-5110; 5150-99	140	13	13	10	2								3	11		
Collett 5MT 5600 0-6-2T 1924 — 5600-5699	100	6	11	6	2								9			
1927 dev. of Collett 5MT 5600 0-6-2T 1924 — 6600-6699	100	17	11	15	2								2	9		
Collett 3F 5700 0-6-0PT 1929 — 5700-5799, 7700-7799, 8701-8749	250	2	1										1			
1933 dev. of Collett 3F 5700 0-6-0PT 1929 — 3600-3799, 4600-4699, 8700, 8750-8799, 9600-9682, 9711-9799	523	75	68	35	4								40	64		
Collett 4MT 6100 2-6-2T 1931 dev. of 5101 Class — 6100-6169	70	24	4	1									23	4		
Collett 5MT 6800 4-6-0 "Grange" 1936 — 6800-6879	80	31	8	16	3								15	5		
Collett 8F 7200 2-8-2T 1934 rebuild of Churchward 4200 Class 2-8-0T — 7200-7253	54	5											5			
Collett 5MT 7800 4-6-0 "Manor" 1938 — 7800-7829	30	13	2	8	1								5	1		

STEAM ENGINE CLASSES at EARLY AUGUST 1965

OVERALL SUMMARIES (Continued)

BR AUGUST 1965 TOTALS (excluding recently withdrawn highlighted)

Class / Number	total	BR	BR	LMR	LMR	ER	ER	NER	NER	ScR	ScR	SR	SR	WR	WR	Wks	Wks
ex GWR Classes (continued)																	
Collett 4MT 8100 2-6-2T 1938																	
8100-8109	10	1		1													
Hawksworth 4F 9400 0-6-0PT 1947																	
3400-3409; 8400-8499; 9400-9499	210	15												15			
ex Southern Railway Classes																	
U.S.A. 3F 0-6-0T 1942																	
30061-30074	15	6										6					
Maunsell 1927 dev. of Urie 6F S15 4-6-0 1920 (with smoke deflectors)																	
30823-30837	15	2	1									2	1				
6F S15 4-6-0 Urie 1920 (with smoke deflectors) Maunsell 1936 development																	
30838-30847	10	3										3					
Maunsell 4P3F U 2-6-0 1928																	
31610-31639	30	3										3					
Maunsell 4P3F U 2-6-0 1928 rebuild of 2-6-4T 1917 "River" K class																	
31790-31809	20	1	1									1	1				
Maunsell 4P5F N 2-6-0 1917																	
31400-31414, 31810-31821, 31823-31875	80	11	2					11	2								
Bulleid "Austerity" 5F Q1 0-6-0 1942																	
33001-33040	40	5	1									5	1				
Bulleid 7P5F "West Country & Battle of Britain Class 4-6-2 1945																	
34002/6/7/11/15/9/20/3/30/3/5/8/41/3/9/51/4/5/7/61/3-70/2-6/8	53	13										13					
1957 7P6F dev. of Bulleid 7P5F 4-6-2 "West Country & Battle of Britain" 1945																	
34001/3-5/8-10/2-4/6-8/21/2/4-9/31/2/4/6/7/9/40/2/4-8/50/2/3	57	52	1									52	1				
1956 dev. of Bulleid 8P 4-6-2 "Merchant Navy" 1941																	
35001-30	30	21										21					
Isle of Wight Steam Adams O2 0-4-4T 1889																	
30177-30236, W14-W36	48	16										16					
ex London Midland Scottish Classes																	
Ivatt 2MT 2-6-2T 1946																	
41200-41329	130	46	13	21	5							16	4	9	4		

STEAM ENGINE CLASSES at EARLY AUGUST 1965

BR AUGUST 1965 TOTALS (excluding recently withdrawn highlighted)

OVERALL SUMMARIES (Continued)

ex London Midland Scottish Classes(continued0)

	total BR	BR	LMR	LMR	ER	ER	NER	NER	ScR	ScR	SR	SR	WR	WR	Wks	Wks
Deeley Midland 0F 0-4-0T 1907																
41528-41537	10	2														
Johnson Midland 1F 0-6-0T 1878																
41661-41879	95	5														
Fairburn 4MT 2-6-4T 1945 dev. of Stanier 1935																
42050-42299; 42673-42699	277	112	23	53	22		33		26		1					
Fowler 4MT 2-6-4T 1927																
42300-42424	125	8	4	4	4											
Stanier 4MT 2-6-4T 1935 dev of Fowler 1927																
42425-42672	243	35	10	32	9		3	1								
Hughes/Fowler 5MT 2-6-0 "Crab" 1926																
42700-42944	245	46	15	26	13				20		2					
Stanier 5MT 2-6-0 1933																
42945-84	40	26		26												
Ivatt 4MT 2-6-0 1947																
43000-43161	162	108	11	59	5	9	44	2								
Fowler Midland 4F 0-6-0 1911																
43835-44026	192	6	8	4	5		2	2					1			
Midland 4F 0-6-0 1924																
44027-44606	580	57	24	44	20		8	1					3	2	2	1
Stanier 5MT 4-6-0 "Black Five" 1934																
44658-45499	842	683	25	551	15		29		103		10					
Ivatt 7P 4-6-0 "Patriot" 1947 rebuild of Fowler 1933																
45512/4/21-3/5-9/30-2/34-6/40/5	18	2	2	2	2											
Stanier 6P5F 4-6-0 "Jubilee" 1934																
45552-45734/7-42	189	28	6	12	4		16	2								
Stanier 7P 4-6-0 "Royal Scot" 1943 rebuild of Fowler 1927																
46100-70	71	2	2	2												
Ivatt 2MT 2-6-0 1946																
46400-46527	128	93	5	83	4				10		1					
Kitson 0F 0-4-0ST 1932																
47000-47009	10	4	2		2											

STEAM ENGINE CLASSES at EARLY AUGUST 1965

OVERALL SUMMARIES (Continued)

BR AUGUST 1965 TOTALS (excluding recently withdrawn highlighted)

ex London Midland Scottish Classes (continued)

	total	BR	BR	LMR	LMR	ER	ER	NER	NER	ScR	ScR	SR	SR	WR	WR	Wks	Wks
Johnson Midland 3F 0-6-0T 1899																	
47200-47259	60	3	1	2	1											1	
Midland 3F "Jinty" 0-6-0T 1924 dev. of Johnson 1899 design																	
47260-47681	417	120	12	102	12					3						15	
Stanier 8F 2-8-0 "Big Eight" 1935																	
48000-48775	666	595	30	538	27			51	1					6	2		

ex London and North Eastern Classes

	total	BR	BR	LMR	LMR	ER	ER	NER	NER	ScR	ScR	SR	SR	WR	WR	Wks	Wks
Gresley 8P6F 4-6-2 A4 1935																	
60001-60034	35	10	1							10	1						
Gresley 7P6F 4-6-2 A3 1927																	
60035-60112	78	2	1							2	1						
Thompson 8P6F 4-6-2 A1 1945																	
60113-60162	50	13	9					13	9								
Thompson 8P7F 4-6-2 A2 1946																	
60500-60539	40	3	3							3	3						
Gresley 7P6F 2-6-2 V2 1936																	
60800-60983	184	34	5					21	5	13							
Thompson 5MT 4-6-0 B1 1942																	
61000-61409	410	141	19			45	12	54	4	42	3						
Peppercorn 5P6F 2-6-0 K1 1949																	
62001-62070	70	34	7			2	3	32	4								
Raven 6F 0-8-0 Q6 1913																	
63340-63459	120	47	12					47	12								
Robinson 8F 2-8-0 O4 1911 *in range 63570-63920*	271	33	12			33	12										
Thompson 7F 2-8-0 O1 1944 rebuild of Robinson O4 1911 *in range 63570-63920*	58	10				10											
Reid 5F 0-6-0 J37 1914																	
64536-64639	104	23	2							23	2						
Holmes 2F 0-6-0 J36 1888																	
65210-65346	123	9								9							

OVERALL SUMMARIES (Continued) — BR AUGUST 1965 TOTALS (excluding recently withdrawn highlighted)

	total BR	BR	LMR	LMR	ER	ER	NER	NER	ScR	ScR	SR	SR	WR	WR	Wks	Wks
ex London and North Eastern Classes (continued)																
Worsdell 5F 0-6-0 J27 1906																
65780-65859	80						50	2								
Gresley 6F 0-6-0 J38 1926																
65900-65934	35								23							
Riddles MOS 4F 0-6-0ST J94 1943																
68006-68080	75	3	10	3	1		9									
British Railways Classes																
BR Standard 7P6F 4-6-2 "Britannia" Derby 1951																
70000-70054	55		54		1											
BR Standard 6P5F 4-6-2 "Clan" Derby 1952																
72000-72009	10		4		1				4	1						
BR Standard 5MT 4-6-0 Doncaster 1951																
73000-73171	172	146	62	8					38	4	35	2	11	2		
BR Standard 4MT 4-6-0 Brighton 1951																
75000-75079	80	77	58								11		8			
BR Standard 4MT 2-6-0 Doncaster 1953																
76000-76114	115	106	34				37		35	1						
BR Standard 3MT 2-6-0 Swindon 1953																
77000-77019	20	20	2				8		10							
BR Standard 2MT 2-6-0 Doncaster 1953																
78000-78064	65	57	44	1	1				10				3			
BR Standard 4MT 2-6-4T Doncaster 1953																
80000-80154	155	88	27	15					45	5	37	6	6	1		
BR Standard 3MT 2-6-2T Swindon 1952																
82000-82044	45	27	5		1						14		8	4		
BR Standard 2MT 2-6-2T Derby 1953																
84000-84029	30	17	17													
Riddles WD 8F 2-8-0 "Austerity" 1943																
90000-90732	733	320	57	5	13	135	40	156	4	24						
BR Standard 9F 2-10-0 Brighton 1954																
92000-92250 *except*	241	195	139		26	6	16						14	6		
BR Standard 9F 2-10-0 Brighton 1954. 1955 Crosti boiler																
92020-29	10		10													
TOTAL STEAM	3917	589	2113	199	255	92	587	58	448	33	281	19	215	187	18	1